OCÉANO ATLÁNTICO
La Habana
CUBA
Santiago
REPÚBLICA
DOMINICANA
HAITÍ
Santo Domingo
San Juan
Ponce
PUERTO RICO
JAMAICA
MAR CARIBE
Lago de
Nicaragua
COSTA RICA
San José
Canal de Panamá
Panamá
PANAMÁ
Caracas
Río Orinoco
VENEZUELA
Río Magdalena
Bogotá
COLOMBIA
BRASIL

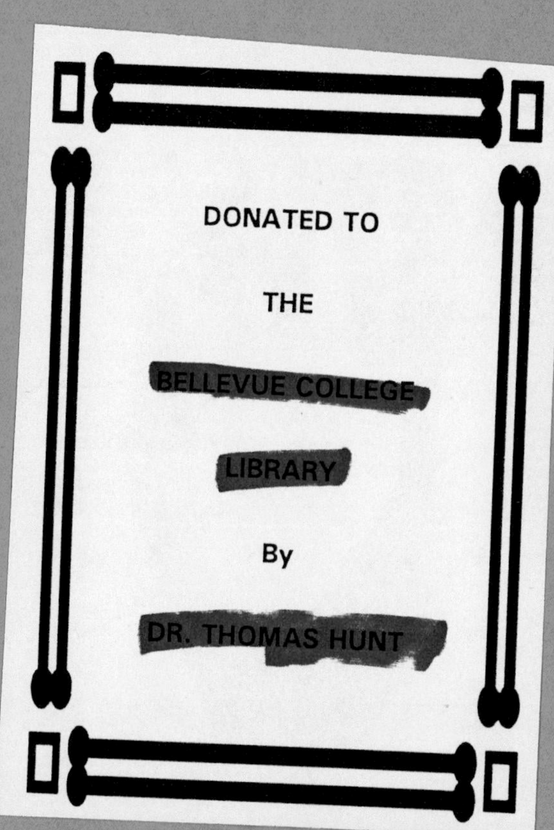
DONATED TO
THE
BELLEVUE COLLEGE
LIBRARY
By
DR. THOMAS HUNT

PUNTOS DE PARTIDA

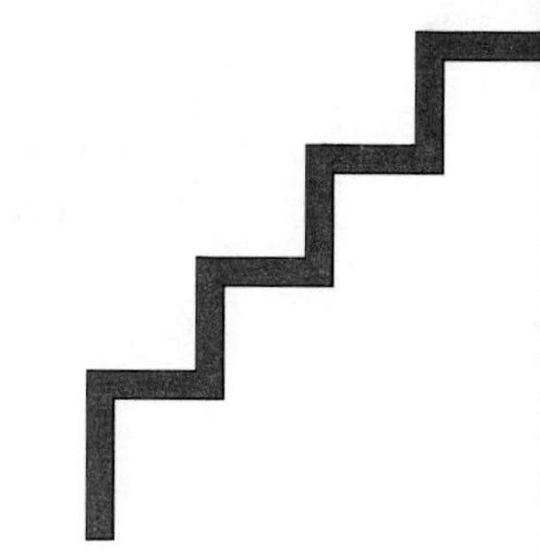

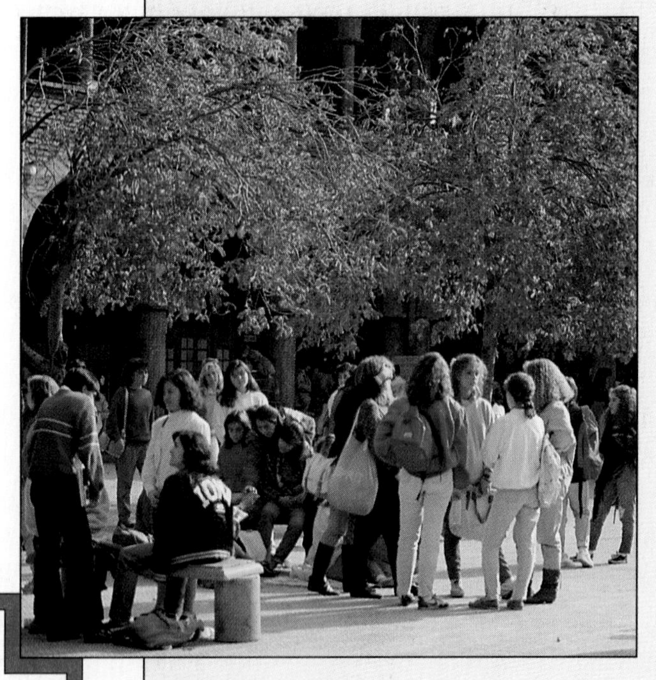

Marty Knorre

Thalia Dorwick

Bill VanPatten
University of Illinois at Urbana–Champaign

Hildebrando Villarreal
California State University, Los Angeles

Martha Alford Marks, Consultant

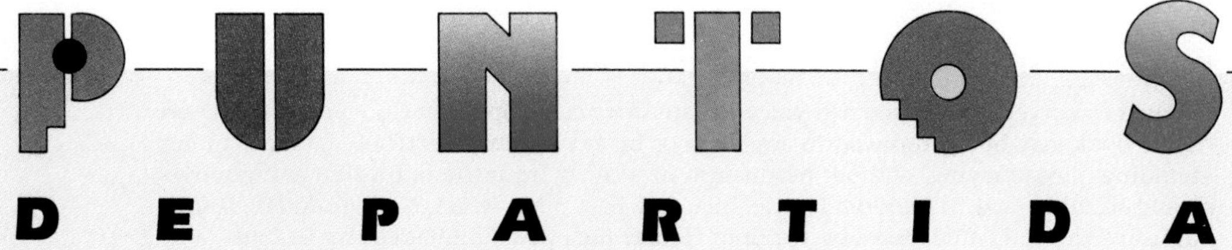

PUNTOS DE PARTIDA

AN INVITATION TO SPANISH

THIRD EDITION

RANDOM HOUSE NEW YORK
This is an EBI book.

INSTRUCTOR'S EDITION

Supplementary Materials for *Vocabulario: Preparación* sections appear at end of book.

Third Edition
9 8 7 6 5 4 3 2 1

Library of Congress Cataloging-in-Publication Data:

Puntos de partida : an invitation to Spanish / Marty Knorre ... [et al.]. — 3rd ed., Instructor's ed.
p. cm.
"This is an EBI book."
Includes index.
ISBN 0-394-37779-6
1. Spanish language—Textbooks for foreign speakers—English.
I. Knorre, Marty.
PC4129.E5P86 1989b
468.2′421—dc19 88-30754
CIP

Manufactured in the United States of America

Copyeditor: Victoria Nelson
Project editor: Jan deProsse
Art director: Jamie Sue Brooks
Text and cover designer: Juan Vargas, Vargas/Williams/Design
Art editor: Edie Williams, Vargas/Williams/Design
Illustrators: Judith Macdonald, Axelle Fortier
Photo researcher: Judy Mason
Cover artist: Pauline Phung
Production supervisor: Pattie Myers
Compositor: Graphic Typesetting Service
Color separator: Color Masters
Printer and binder: R.R. Donnelley and Sons Company

Text and art credits
Grateful acknowledgment is made for use of the following:

Photographs *page ii* (*title page*) © Peter Menzel: University of Chile, Santiago; *1* © Stuart Cohen / Comstock; *10* © Stuart Cohen / Comstock; *18 (counterclockwise from left)* © Jorge Gracia; © Elliott Varner Smith; © Hugh Rogers / Monkmeyer; © Margot Granitsas / The Image Works; © Charles Gatewood / The Image Works; *19 (top left)* © *AP / Wide World Photos; 19 (bottom left)* © Bill Nation / Sygma; *19 (center)* © G. Rancinan / Sygma; *19 (right)* © Alan D. Levenson; *26 (from top)* © José Carrillo / Click, Chicago; © Peter Menzel; © S. Salgado Jr. / Magnum; *28* © Bob Daemmrich / The Image Works; *30 (counterclockwise from left)* © Martin Bell / Archive Pictures, Inc.; © Robert Frerck / Click, Chicago; © Gilles Peress / Magnum; © Chip and Rosa Maria de la Cueva Peterson; *31* © Stuart Cohen / Stock, Boston; *51* © Chip & Rosa Maria de la Cueva Peterson; *56* © Peter Menzel; *60* © Peter Menzel, *72* © Donald Smetzer / Click, Chicago; *77* © Chip & Rosa Maria de la Cueva Peterson;

(Credits continue on page 606.)

CONTENTS

APPENDICES

VOCABULARIES

PREFACE

The coauthors of ***Puntos de partida: An Invitation to Spanish*** approached the writing of the third edition with appreciation for the many instructors who have continued to give our work a vote of confidence. We are enthusiastic about this third opportunity to present to our colleagues a text that we care deeply about and that has, we hope, had a positive impact on the teaching of foreign languages.

The first edition of ***Puntos*** (as the book is often called) was published in 1981, after a long and careful period of development that involved a dialogue between the authors and publishers of the text and a large number of Spanish instructors across the country. That edition was very well received. The second edition was even more widely accepted, coinciding with the national prominence of movements advocating teaching for communicative competence and proficiency.

Throughout the preparation of this third edition, the authors and publishers consulted a large number of users of ***Puntos de partida***, soliciting feedback on their experiences in the classroom. Much of what is new to the third edition is the direct result of that review process, as well as of the authors' response to current trends and thinking. It has been our goal to help ***Puntos*** evolve gracefully.

We believe that the text continues to provide a flexible framework that can be adapted to individual teaching situations and goals—among them, a proficiency orientation and teaching for communicative competence. The overall goals of the third edition are identical to those cited in 1981: *to help students develop proficiency in the four language skills essential to truly communicative language learning.* Each chapter has a contemporary cultural or everyday theme, and grammar is introduced and practiced within that real-world context. The text was prepared with students in mind—to help them learn *how* to learn Spanish and to give them the opportunity to use and enjoy it.

Organization of the Third Edition: Student Text

The chapter organization of ***Puntos de partida*** has not been radically altered in this edition. The text consists of an opening chapter, called **Ante todo**, and twenty main chapters.

Ante todo: This chapter provides a functional introduction to Spanish language and culture that enables students to express themselves on a wide variety of topics before the formal presentation of grammar begins. An introduction to the structure of the text itself is also included.

Cápitulos 1–19 are organized as follows:

- **Opening page** New to this edition, this brief introduction to the chapter's theme consists of a photograph plus a brief, functional dialogue: a real-life exchange about a practical aspect of the cultural theme.
- **Vocabulario: Preparación** This section presents and practices the thematic vocabulary and other simple structures that students will need for self-expression and to cope

with situations and activities that they will encounter in the rest of the chapter.

- **Pronunciación** This section, a feature of the first five chapters, focuses on individual sounds that are particularly difficult for native speakers of English.
- **Minidiálogos y gramática** This section presents one to four grammar points, each introduced by a minidialogue, cartoon, or brief reading, and followed by a series of contextualized exercises and activities that progress from more controlled (**Práctica**) to open-ended (**Conversación**). Practice materials, carefully ordered to lead students from guided to free responses, include story sequences, paraphrase, interview, partner, role-playing, and self-expression activities.
- **Situaciones** New to this edition, these dialogues illustrate functional language and practical situations related to the chapter theme. In most chapters, they are followed by **Notas comunicativas sobre el diálogo**, which highlight aspects of language and culture of particular interest in the dialogues.
- **Un poco de todo** The exercises and activities in this follow-up section combine and review all grammar presented in the chapter and important grammar from previous chapters.
- **Vocabulario** This end-of-chapter vocabulary list includes all important words and expressions considered active.

At the end of each chapter, a supplementary section called **Un paso más** presents more activities that emphasize the use of realia, conversational strategies, and creative language use in a cultural, and often humorous, context. **A propósito...** boxes in each **Un paso más** section present additional survival vocabulary, followed by realistic role-playing situations that students might encounter when traveling in a Hispanic country. The **Un paso más** sections conclude with a cultural reading with reading strategies in the first ten chapters and guided writing exercises throughout that help students to compose short paragraphs, write about their personal experiences, and so on. Instructors can use all, part, or none of this section, according to individual needs and schedules.

The text concludes with **Capítulo 20** (**En el extranjero**), which explores the experiences of students studying abroad.

Additional features of importance include:

- **Notas** (**comunicativas, lingüísticas, culturales**) New to this edition, these boxes highlight functional language and cultural material at logical points throughout all sections of the text.
- **¿Recuerda Ud.?** These brief review sections provide a link between previously studied grammar points and new material that builds on those grammar points.
- **Study Hints** These sections give students specific advice about how to acquire language skills: how to learn vocabulary, how to use a bilingual dictionary, and so on. Hints are placed at logical points throughout the text.
- **Voces del mundo hispánico/Repaso** These review sections follow every third chapter. They include new-to-this-edition cultural materials, interviews (**Entrevistas**), and role-play activities (**Situaciones**) that recycle the major language functions of the previous chapters.

Statement of Purpose

The authors believe that students' *class* time is best spent in *using* Spanish: listening to and speaking with the instructor and each other. For that reason, grammar explanations in ***Puntos de partida*** have been written to be self-explanatory, and sample answers have been provided in the back of the book for many exercises so that students can check their own work before coming to class. Thus, instructors might spot-check text exercises in class but devote more time to their marginal-note extensions and variations, creating new material to maintain student interest and provide fresh language input.

All exercises and activities in the program have been designed to help students develop proficiency in Spanish rather than simply display their grammatical knowledge. The authors believe that the process of attempts to use language provides an optimal language-learning situation—one that will prepare students to function in Spanish in the situations they are most likely to encounter outside the classroom.

Puntos de partida and Developing Language Proficiency

The conceptualization of all editions of ***Puntos*** makes it an appropriate text to use for developing language proficiency.

- an insistence on the acquisition of vocabulary during the early stages of language learning (**Ante todo**) and then in each chapter throughout the text
- an emphasis on personalized and creative use of language to perform various functions or achieve various goals
- careful attention to skills development rather than only grammatical knowledge
- a cyclical organization in which vocabulary, grammar, and language functions are consistently reviewed and re-entered
- an integrated cultural component that embeds practice in a wide variety of culturally significant contexts
- content that aims to raise student awareness of the interaction of language, culture, and society

Within each chapter, text materials are sequenced to facilitate and maximize progress in communication skills: from vocabulary acquisition activities, to grammar practice, to divergent activities that stimulate student creativity. The overall text organization progresses from a focus on formulaic expressions; to vocabulary and structures relevant to the "here and now" (descriptions, student life, family life) to survival situations (ordering a meal, travel-related activities) to topics of broader conceptual interest (current events, the environment). Some material is introduced functionally in small chunks before the entire paradigm is presented. Major grammar topics such as the past tenses and the subjunctive are introduced, then re-entered later in the text; most grammar topics and language functions are continually reviewed and re-entered throughout the text and its ancillaries.

Major Changes in the Third Edition: Student Text

Keeping the chapter structure of the first and second editions, the authors have effected a serious and thorough revision of all features of the text.

Language: Skills Development and Content

- The conceptual "fit" between the vocabulary and grammar of many chapters and their cultural themes has been refined so that grammar, vocabulary, and culture work together better as interactive units.
- Starting with **Capítulo 13**, instructors will find the grammar sequence to be simplified and more coherently organized.
- Grammar sections are more functionally oriented. Some points have been omitted, others treated as lexical items with emphasis on their use in practical situations. Aspects of some grammar points are presented for recognition only. Many structures are used passively, in controlled situations, before their formal introduction. The authors believe that instructors who wish to do so should not hesitate to eliminate the grammar content from at least the last four grammar chapters (16–19) of the text, especially if their beginning language sequence comprises only one academic year.
- A substantial portion of the exercises have been rewritten to tell a story or form a logical sequence. Inferential follow-up activities will allow students to verify their comprehension of such exercises and also serve as a starting point for discussion. Interview, partner, role-playing, realia-based, and problem-solving exercises and activities have been added to all parts of the chapters. Emphasis is on meaningful use of language throughout

the exercise sections. Pattern practice has been moved to the *Instructor's Edition* marginal glosses.

- Review and re-entry continues to be emphasized, especially in the synthetic **Un poco de todo** sections and in the **Entrevistas** and **Situaciones** activities of the new **Repaso** sections, which occur every three chapters. Major topics that receive continuous attention in exercises and activities include **ser** and **estar**, preterite and imperfect, gender and gender agreement, and indicative and subjunctive.
- New **Situaciones** dialogues, replacing **Diálogo** from previous editions, are shorter and less dense than the **Diálogos**. The brevity and practical orientation of the **Situaciones** allow them—as well as the new functional minidialogues, two per chapter—to serve as models of language use.

Culture: An Integral Part of Language Learning

- Most of the cultural readings have been replaced with two kinds of material. One third of the readings are now in the form of authentic materials: brief magazine or newspaper articles, several sections from a driver-training manual, a page from an elementary school geography book, and so on. All these materials are easily accessible to beginning students within the context of the comprehension tasks that follow them (**Comprensión**). Another third of the cultural readings are now "testimony": brief paragraphs written by Hispanics in answer to a survey conducted by the coauthors. Thus, rather than the authors attempting to interpret the "Hispanic reality" of some cultural topics, Hispanic individuals are speaking for themselves.
- Realia from all parts of the Spanish-speaking world appears in all sections of the text. No attempt has been made to simplify or correct the language in these authentic pieces. Some may be viewed as merely decorative or serve as the basis for whole-class discussion or activities; others have exercises or activities based on them. It is hoped that instructors will discover that beginning students in particular can profit from exposure to such authentic materials and that students will not be frightened by them when it is clear that they are not expected to understand every word.
- The new **Voces del mundo hispánico** sections vividly present the wide variety of people, places, activities, and ideas of the Hispanic world. Here (and in the essays in **Ante todo**) the major groups within the Spanish-speaking world are presented, with special emphasis on Hispanic communities within the United States. These groups have not been interpreted for the students; rather, the groups are permitted to speak for themselves, in excerpts that are historically significant, timely, and—it is hoped—provocative.
- Some cultural themes from the second edition have been abbreviated and others elaborated, to enrich and expand the cultural content. Themes added or treated differently in the third edition include personal possessions and goals, computers and technology, and current events.

Supplementary Materials for the Third Edition

The effectiveness of ***Puntos de partida*** will be enhanced by adding any of the following components.

- The *Workbook*, by Alice Arana (Fullerton College) and Oswaldo Arana (California State University, Fullerton), continues the format of previous editions, providing additional practice with vocabulary and structures through a variety of controlled and open-ended exercises, review sections, and guided compositions. Realia and more review materials have been added in the third edition.

- The *Laboratory Manual* and *Tape Program*, by María Sabló-Yates, continues to emphasize listening-comprehension activities. More effective use is made of dialogue materials in the third edition, and each chapter now contains a number of interview and dialogue activities in which students interact with the speakers. Realia-based listening and speaking activities and more review materials have been added. A *Tapescript* is also available. Cassette tapes are free to adopting institutions and are also made available for student purchase upon request. Reel-to-reel tapes are available for copying.
- The *Instructor's Edition* of the text contains on-page suggestions, many supplementary exercises for developing listening and speaking skills, and abundant variations and follow-ups on student text materials. The number of marginal glosses has been slightly increased in the third edition. **¡OJO!** Note that most annotations for the **Vocabulario: Preparación** sections are bound into the back of the *Instructor's Edition*, rather than appearing directly on the page.
- The *Instructor's Manual* offers an extensive introduction to teaching techniques, general guidelines for instructors, suggestions for lesson planning and for writing semester/quarter schedules, sample tests and quizzes, models for vocabulary introduction, conversation cards, supplementary exercises, and suggestions for the **Situaciones, Lectura cultural,** and **Repaso** sections.
- The *Testing Package* reflects the revisions in the student text. It also includes selections for testing reading and listening comprehension and optional sections for testing oral proficiency.
- Two types of *computer-assisted instructional programs* are available with the third edition, both by John Underwood (Western Washington University) and Richard Bassein (Mills College). The first program, RHELT (Random House Electronic Language Tutor), includes most of the more controlled exercises from the student text, for IBM and Apple computers. (This specific program is new to the third edition.) The second, **Juegos comunicativos**, is an interactive program that stresses communication skills in Spanish: ordering a meal, giving directions, and so on.

The following supplementary materials are all new to the third edition.

- The *Instructor's Resource Kit*, coordinated with chapters of the student text, offers additional optional activities, transparency masters of realia, and transparency masters of text visuals.
- A set of *slides* from various parts of the Spanish-speaking world, with activities for classroom use, is available to each adopting institution.
- The *Random House Video Program for Spanish*, by Total Video (South San Francisco) offers functional language segments coordinated with most of the third edition themes, along with pre- and post-viewing exercises and activities. Video segments are noted in the *Instructor's Edition* of the text with a videocassette symbol.
- The *Electronic Puntos*, by John Underwood (Western Washington University) is an interactive HyperCard/Macintosh program that, when used with the videodisk version of the Random House Video Program for Spanish, allows students to explore the video materials in an innovative and nonlinear fashion.
- A *training/orientation manual* for use with teaching assistants, by James F. Lee (University of Illinois, Urbana–Champaign), offers practical advice for beginning language instructors and language coordinators.
- The *listening-comprehension tape*, with accompanying manual of comprehension and follow-up activities, by María José Ruiz Morcillo, provides additional listening practice with major sections of the student text. Tape segments are noted in the *Instructor's Edition* with an audio cassette symbol.

Acknowledgments

The coauthors would like to acknowledge the friends, students, and colleagues who contributed materials for the **Lectura cultural** sections that we have referred to as "testimony": Alma Margarita Alarcón Nagy (El Salvador), Marcial Beltrán (México), Eduardo Cabrera (Uruguay), Laura Chastain (El Salvador), Margarita Cuesta (España), Marianela Chaumiel (Argentina), Eva Martínez Torres (México), Manuel Mendoza (México), María José Ruiz Morcillo (España), Graciela Ramírez (México), Emilién D. Sabló (Panamá), José Luis Suárez (España), and M. L. Valencia (México).

Finally, although the following individuals are not included as coauthors of the text, the authors would especially like to acknowledge their contributions to the third edition. The work of Martha Marks and Ruth Ordas on several editions of ***¿Qué tal?*** continues to form an integral part of this text. Leslie J. Ford (Graceland College) and Laura Chastain thoughtfully collected current realia, magazines, and newspapers during their recent trips to Latin America and Spain, respectively; their contribution to this edition has been invaluable. Most of the **Situaciones** dialogues are the lively creations of María José Ruiz Morcillo, who is the "Maripepa" often referred to in activities and the author of the letters in **Capítulo 20**. Aspects of the work of Dr. Theodore V. Higgs (San Diego State University) on the second edition of ***Puntos*** have been incorporated into the third *Instructor's Edition*.

The publishers would again like to thank those instructors who participated in the various surveys that proved indispensable in the development of previous editions of ***Puntos de partida***. In particular, we would like to acknowledge the comments and suggestions of Professor Marie S. Rentz and the teaching assistants of the Spanish Department of the University of Maryland; their reactions to and commentary on aspects of the second edition of ***Puntos*** were invaluable in the formulation of the revision plan for this edition.

In addition, the publishers wish to acknowledge the input received from the following instructors and professional friends across the country. The appearance of their names does not necessarily constitute their endorsement of the text or its methodology.

Eloise Andries
Louisiana State University
Jim P. Artman
University of Oklahoma
Angela Ayres
Portland Community College
S. M. Bacon
University of Cincinnati
Thomas O. Bente
Temple University
Rea Berroa
George Mason University
Marilyn Bierling
Calvin College
Pedro Bravo-Elizondo
Wichita State University
Leon Bright
University of Southern Colorado
Vivana Brodey
Kapiolani Community College
Bob Brown
University of Toledo
Danielle Comby
University of Texas, Austin
Malcom Compitollo
Michigan State University
Stephen S. Corbett
Texas Tech University
Patricia P. Corcoran
University of Minnesota
Darren R. Crasto
Mississippi State University
Lucia Da Silveira
Mississippi State University
Philip M. Donley
University of Texas, Austin
Lee Dowling
University of Houston
Thomas Wayne Edison
University of Louisville
Bette L. Ervin
Ohio Dominican College
Anthony P. Espósito
Brandeis University
Joseph Farrell
California State Polytechnic University
Beatriz G. Faust
Houston Community College
David W. Foster
Arizona State University
Michelle A. Fuerch
Ripon College

Liz Ginsburg
Sacramento City College
John G. Gladstein
University of Louisville
Frank González-Mena
Solano Community College
Lynn C. Gorell
The Pennsylvania State University
Alessandra Graves
The Pennsylvania State University, Media Campus
Enrique Grönlund
The Pennsylvania State University, Ogontz Campus
Leonora Guinazzo
Portland Community College
Robert M. Hammond
Catholic University of America
Donald C. Harris
Cañada College
Deni Heyck
Mundelein College
Sam Hill
California State University, Sacramento
Renato Holguin
Castleton State College
Grace Holmen
University of Texas, Arlington
Cleveland Johnson
Spelman College
Irma Karam
Delta College
Thomas W. Kelly
The Pennsylvania State University
Joseph J. Kinkaid
University of Mississippi
Dale Koike
University of Texas, Austin
Roberta Z. Lavine
University of Maryland
Donna Reseigh Long
The Ohio State University
Mildred H. Lyon
Central State University
Kathleen N. March
University of Maine
Betty Mitchell
University of Louisville
Rose Anna Mueller
Morton College
Judith Némethy
Cornell University
Pennie Nichols
University of Texas, Austin
John R. O'Boyle
Bemidji State University
Rafael Ocasio
University of Kentucky
Laurie Ojeda
Los Medanos College
Mireya Pérez-Erdelyi
College of New Rochelle
Sue Petcher
Illinois Institute of Technology
Mariana Petrea
Portland State University
Manuel Puerta
Ferris State College
David Quinn
Western Illinois University
Barbara Rank
University of Illinois, Chicago Circle
Kay E. Raymond
The University of Alabama
Diane Ringer Uber
Rutgers University
Dorothy Rissel
Indiana University
Renate Robinson
Northwestern University
Hildebrando Ruiz
University of Georgia
A. T. Sallustio
Pace University
Paul Seaver
University of Hawaii
Helen A. Sharp
Mississippi State University
Kathleen Sheridan
University of Louisville
Victoria Smith
Brown University
Alfredo Torrejón
The Pennsylvania State University, Altoona Campus
K. V. Unruh
University of Wisconsin, Milwaukee
Bernardo Valdés
Iowa State University
Roberto Véguez
Middlebury College
Lida E. Wenzel
The Ohio State University, Mansfield Campus
Ann E. Wiltrout
Mississippi State University
John A. Yenchik
The Pennsylvania State University, Lehman Campus

Many other individuals deserve our thanks and appreciation for their help and support. Among them are the people who, in addition to the coauthors, read the manuscript to ensure its linguistic and cultural authenticity and pedagogical accuracy: Alice Arana (United States), Oswaldo Arana (Perú), Eduardo Cabrera (Uruguay), Laura Chastain (El Salvador), María José Ruiz Morcillo (España), and María Sabló-Yates (Panamá).

Special thanks are also due to Judith Macdonald and Axelle Fortier for their superb artwork; to Judy Mason, for another round of thoughtful photo research; to Mark Accornero, for his help in selecting and singing the songs that appear in the tape program; to our editorial and production team at Random House—Jan deProsse, Jamie Brooks, Karen Judd, and Pattie Myers—for their careful guidance of the project through the various stages of production; to Juan Vargas, for his striking interior design and beautiful cover; to Edie Williams for her help in selecting realia and for her extraordinarily thoughtful job of putting the pages together; to Edith Brady and the rest of the Random House marketing and sales staff, for continuing to believe in the book; and to Judy Getty and Charlotte Jackson, for their help with various aspects of the contents of the third edition. Last but not least, special thanks to Lesley Walsh, whose behind-the-scenes presence keeps everything moving, to Eirik Børve, who inspired the project and brought some of us together, and, as always, to Random House for continuing to care about quality and for letting us do the book the way we want to do it.

Suggestions for first class meeting: See Teaching Techniques: First Day of Class in Instructor's Manual (IM).
Emphasis: Learning about culture is an integral part of learning a foreign language.

Suggestion: Use *Una invitación al mundo hispánico* (p. 30) as springboard for first-day discussion of students' current awareness of Hispanic peoples and culture.

Suggestions for *Ante todo* lesson plans: See Possible Lesson Plans (IM).

Communicative objectives for *Ante todo:* to "get used to" Spanish; to learn to communicate in basic situations with minimal knowledge of the language; to learn how to use cognates to expand communicative abilities.

ANTE TODO

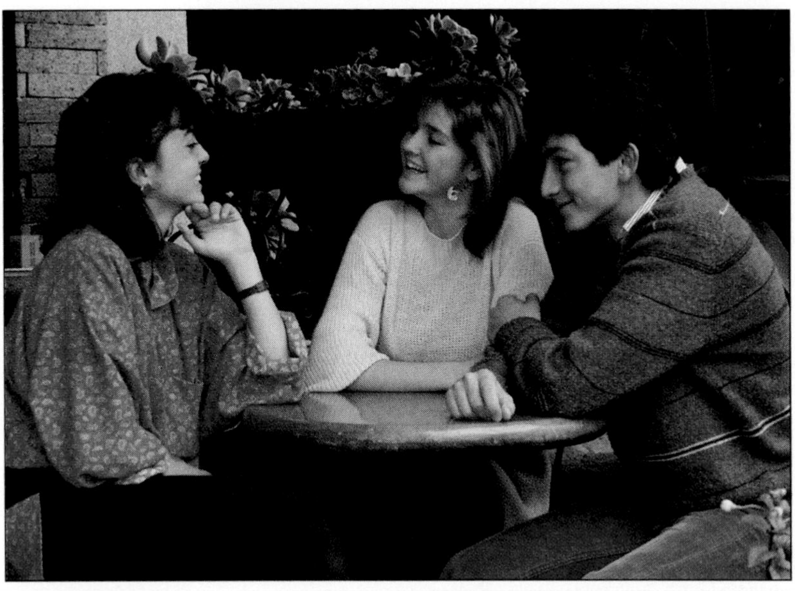

Bogotá, Colombia

Puntos de partida means *points of departure, starting places,* in Spanish. This textbook, called ***Puntos de partida***, will provide you with a way to begin to learn the Spanish language and to become more familiar with the many people here and abroad who use it.

Language is the means by which humans communicate with one another. To learn a new language is to acquire another way of exchanging information and of sharing your thoughts and opinions with others. ***Puntos de partida*** will help you use Spanish to communicate in various ways—and function in many kinds of real-life situations—to understand Spanish when others speak it, to speak it yourself, and to read and write it. This text will also help you to communicate in Spanish in nonverbal ways through an awareness of cultural differences.

Learning about a new culture is an inseparable part of learning a language. "Culture" can mean many things: everything from great writers and painters to what time people usually eat lunch. Throughout ***Puntos de partida*** you will have the opportunity to find out about the daily lives of Spanish-speaking people and the kinds of things that are important to them. Knowing about all these things will be important to you when you visit a Spanish-speaking country, and it may also be useful to you here. If you look around, you will see that Spanish is not really a foreign language, but rather a widely used language in the United States today.

Ante todo (*First of all*) is a three-part chapter that will introduce you to the Spanish language and to the format of ***Puntos de partida***.

PRIMERA PARTE

Suggestions for *Minidiálogo* 1:
- **Introduction:** How to greet and take leave of friends.
- **Point out:** English equivalent of *minidiálogos* will always appear at page bottom.
- Model *minidiálogo* and act it out with several students (see Teaching Techniques: *Minidiálogos*, IM).
- Multiple choral repetitions followed by individual repetitions.
- Small groups (see Teaching Techniques: Small Groups, IM). Students practice dialogue in pairs, using own names; then reverse roles.

Suggestions for *Minidiálogo* 2:
- **Introduction:** Discuss familiar (first-name-basis) vs. formal (last-name-basis) relationships. *Hola* and *¿Qué tal?* are appropriate with friends and family members, but usually *not* in last-name-basis relationships. Hence the more formal *Buenas tardes, ¿cómo está?*.
- Model *minidiálogo* and act it out with several students.
- Multiple choral repetitions followed by individual repetitions
- Small-group practice; students use own names.

Suggestions for *Minidiálogo* 3:
- **Introduction:** One way to ask someone's name.
- Model; act it out.
- Multiple choral repetitions followed by individual repetitions, avoiding *encantada*.
- **Point out:** formal *¿Cómo se llama usted?* vs. familiar *¿Cómo te llamas?*. Have students use *¿Cómo te llamas?* with other students.
- Chain Drill (see Teaching Techniques: Drills, IM). Student 1 asks, *¿Cómo te llamas?*; Student 2 answers, asks same question of Student 3, etc.
- **Point out:** *Encantado* for males and *Encantada* for females.

SALUDOS° Y EXPRESIONES DE CORTESÍA

°*Greetings*

Here are some words, phrases, and expressions that will enable you to meet and greet others appropriately in Spanish.

1.
ANA: Hola, José.
JOSÉ: ¿Qué tal, Ana? (¿Cómo estás?)
ANA: Así así. ¿Y tú?
JOSÉ: ¡Muy bien! Hasta mañana, ¿eh?
ANA: Adiós.

2.
SEÑOR ALONSO: Buenas tardes, señorita López.
SEÑORITA LÓPEZ: Muy buenas, señor Alonso. ¿Cómo está?
SEÑOR ALONSO: Bien, gracias. ¿Y usted?
SEÑORITA LÓPEZ: Muy bien, gracias. Adiós.
SEÑOR ALONSO: Hasta luego.

¿Qué tal?, **¿Cómo estás?**, and **¿Y tú?** are expressions used in informal situations with people you know well, on a first-name basis.

¿Cómo está? and **¿Y usted?** are used to address someone with whom you have a formal relationship.

---

[1] ANA: Hi, José. JOSÉ: How are you doing, Ana? (How are you?) ANA: So-so. And you? JOSÉ Fine! (Very well!) See you tomorrow, OK? ANA: Bye.

[2] MR. ALONSO: Good afternoon, Miss López. MISS LÓPEZ: 'Afternoon, Mr. Alonso. How are you? MR. ALONSO: Fine, thanks. And you? MISS LÓPEZ: Very well, thanks. Good-bye. MR. ALONSO: See you later.

- Model *Mucho gusto/Encantado/a* exchange with several students, reversing roles. Have students practice exchange.

Suggestions for *Otros saludos:*
- Model phrases in brief exchanges with students, using *señor*, *señora*, or *señorita*, as appropriate; help students use appropriate title for you.
- Have students interact with appropriate greetings and titles.
- **Point out:** Titles of respect are not capitalized when spelled out, but are when abbreviated: *señor Sánchez*; *Sr. Sánchez*.
- **Point out:** Lunchtime is often around 2 P.M.; evening meal may be as late as 8 or 9 P.M. in Mexico; 10 or 11 P.M. in Spain.

Suggestions for *Notas comunicativas:*
- Model phrases, creating situations in which expressions are appropriate: give student a book and "coach" him or her to say *gracias*; you respond *de nada*; and so on.
- **Optional:** *permiso* (without *con*); use of *con permiso* to take leave of someone; *cómo no* (as rejoinder); *perdone* (in addition to *perdón*); *perdón* to request permission to pass by or through.

3.

MARÍA: Buenos días, profesora.
PROFESORA: Buenos días. ¿Cómo se llama usted?
MARÍA: (Me llamo) María Sánchez.
PROFESORA: Mucho gusto.
MARÍA: Igualmente. (Encantada.)

¿Cómo se llama usted? is used in formal situations. **¿Cómo te llamas?** is used in informal situations—for example, with other students. The phrases **mucho gusto** and **igualmente** are used by both men and women when meeting for the first time. In response to **mucho gusto**, a woman can also say **encantada**; a man can say **encantado**.

Otros saludos y expresiones de cortesía

buenos días	good morning (*used until the midday meal*)
buenas tardes	good afternoon (*used until the evening meal*)
buenas noches	good evening, good night (*used after the evening meal*)
señor (Sr.)	Mr., sir
señora (Sra.)	Mrs., ma'am
señorita (Srta.)	Miss

- **Emphasis:** *buenos días* but *buenas tardes/noches.*

Note that there is no standard Spanish equivalent for *Ms.* Use **Sra.** or **Srta.**, as appropriate.

Notas comunicativas: Speaking Politely

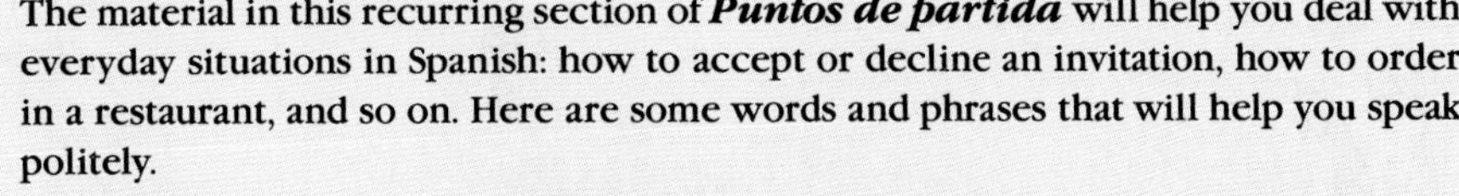

The material in this recurring section of ***Puntos de partida*** will help you deal with everyday situations in Spanish: how to accept or decline an invitation, how to order in a restaurant, and so on. Here are some words and phrases that will help you speak politely.

gracias	thanks, thank you
muchas gracias	thank you very much
de nada	you're welcome
por favor	please (*also used to get someone's attention*)
perdón	pardon me, excuse me (*to ask forgiveness or to get someone's attention*)
con permiso	pardon me, excuse me (*to request permission to pass by or through a group of people*)

---

[3]MARÍA: Good morning, professor. PROFESORA: Good morning. What's your name? MARÍA: (My name is) María Sánchez. PROFESORA: Pleased to meet you. MARÍA: Likewise. (Delighted.)

Práctica

A. Practice Dialogues 1 through 3 several times with another student, using your own names.

Suggestion B: Conduct as a Rapid Response Drill (see Teaching Techniques: Drills, IM), with students' books closed.

B. How many different ways can you respond to the following greetings and phrases?

1. Buenas tardes.
2. Adiós.
3. ¿Qué tal?
4. Hola.
5. ¿Cómo está?
6. Buenas noches.
7. Muchas gracias.
8. Hasta mañana.
9. ¿Cómo se llama usted?
10. Mucho gusto.

Conversación

Extension A: What would you say if you met . . . **5.** your Spanish professor, at 11 A.M.? **6.** your cousin, at 10 P.M.? **7.** the president of your university, at 4 P.M.?

Note B: More than one answer is possible for some items.

Extension B: As you walk through class, act out situations requiring the rejoinders *con permiso*, *perdón*, *por favor*. Then encourage a student to do same.

A. **Situaciones.** If the following persons met or passed each other at the times given, what might they say to each other? Role-play the situations with a classmate.

1. Mr. Santana and Miss Pérez, at 5:00 P.M.
2. Mrs. Ortega and Pablo, at 10:00 A.M.
3. Ms. Hernández and Olivia, at 11:00 P.M.
4. you and a classmate, just before your Spanish class

B. Are these people saying **por favor**, **con permiso**, or **perdón**?

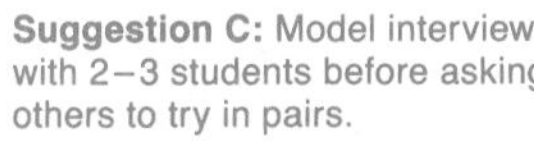

Suggestion C: Model interview with 2–3 students before asking others to try in pairs.

Emphasis C: Informal expressions in student exchanges, but formal expressions when addressing instructor.

C. **Entrevista** (*Interview*). Turn to the person sitting next to you and do the following.

- Greet him or her appropriately.
- Find out his or her name.
- Ask how he or she is.
- Conclude the exchange.

Now have a similar conversation with your instructor, using the appropriate formal forms.

EL ALFABETO ESPAÑOL

There are thirty letters in the Spanish *alphabet* (**el alfabeto**)—four more than in the English alphabet. The **ch**, **ll**, and **rr** are considered single letters even though they are two-letter groups; the **ñ** is the fourth extra letter. The letters **k** and **w** appear only in words borrowed from other languages.

Listen carefully as your instructor pronounces the names listed with the letters of the alphabet.

Note: Common Hispanic first names and place names are used as examples of letters.

Variation (listening): Use common Hispanic last names: Álvarez, Hernández, Fernández, Gómez, Pérez, etc.

Point out:
- *ce, ci* → [s] sound
  ca, co, cu → [k] sound
- *ga, go, gu* → [g] sound
  ge, gi → like Spanish *j*
- *r* at beginning of word pronounced like trilled (double) *r*
- letter *v* pronounced like Spanish *b*
- letter *x* sometimes pronounced like [ks], sometimes like [s], and sometimes like Spanish *j* (México, Texas)
- Castillian *ce, ci, z* → *th* sound [θ]

LETTERS	NAMES OF LETTERS	EXAMPLES		
a	a	*A*ntonio	*A*n*a*	(l*a*) *A*rgentin*a*
b	be	*B*enito	*B*lanca	*B*olivia
c	ce	*C*arlos	*C*e*c*ilia	*C*á*c*eres
ch	che	Pan*ch*o	Con*ch*a	*Ch*ile
d	de	*D*omingo	*D*olores	*D*urango
e	e	*E*duardo	*E*l*e*na	(*e*l) *E*cuador
f	efe	*F*elipe	*F*rancisca	(la) *F*lorida
g	ge	*G*erardo	*G*loria	*G*uatemala
h	hache	*H*éctor	*H*ortensia	*H*onduras
i	i	*I*gnac*i*o	*I*nés	*I*b*i*za
j	jota	*J*osé	*J*uana	*J*alisco
k	ca (ka)	(*K*arl)	(*K*ati)	(*K*ansas)
l	ele	*L*uis	*L*o*l*a	*L*ima
ll	elle	Gui*ll*ermo	Gui*ll*ermina	Sevi*ll*a
m	eme	*M*anuel	*M*aría	*M*éxico
n	ene	*N*icolás	*N*ati	*N*icaragua
ñ	eñe	Í*ñ*igo	Bego*ñ*a	Espa*ñ*a
o	o	*O*ctavi*o*	*O*livia	*O*vied*o*
p	pe	*P*ablo	*P*ilar	*P*anamá
q	cu	Enri*q*ue	Ra*q*uel	*Q*uito
r	ere	Álva*r*o	Cla*r*a	(el) Pe*r*ú
rr	erre *or* ere doble	*R*afael	*R*osa	Monte*rr*ey
s	ese	*S*alvador	*S*ara	*S*an Juan
t	te	*T*omás	*T*eresa	*T*oledo
u	u	Ag*u*stín	L*u*cía	(el) *U*r*u*guay
v	ve *or* uve	*V*íctor	*V*ictoria	*V*enezuela
w	doble ve, ve doble, *or* uve doble	Os*w*aldo	(*W*ilma)	(*W*ashington)
x	equis	*X*avier	*X*imena	E*x*tremadura
y	i griega	Pela*y*o	*Y*olanda	(el) Paragua*y*
z	ceta (zeta)	Gon*z*alo	Esperan*z*a	*Z*aragoza

Note A: See Index for Ch. references to pronunciation practice with specific sounds/letters. Vowel sounds are presented in *Ante todo: Segunda parte*. This exercise is intended only for immediate practice with sounds/letters that may be "strange" to students.

Point out: To distinguish *b* and *v*, Spanish speakers sometimes call the letter *b be grande* or *be de burro*, and the letter *v ve chica* or *ve de vaca*.

Note CH: Monterey (California), but Monterrey (México)

Optional CH: Introduce *¿Cómo se deletrea... ?*.

Variation CH (listening for cognate recognition): Pronounce these place names; students identify them: *el río Grande, Puerto Rico, Cuba, San Antonio, Sacramento, Nevada, Albuquerque, San José, Nueva York*, etc.

Follow-up: Have students think of other U.S. place names of Hispanic origin and spell them aloud in Spanish. Other students give the place names spelled. **Alternative:** Others try to guess place names before the student finishes spelling.

Práctica

A. The letters below represent the Spanish sounds that are the most different from their English counterparts. You will practice the pronunciation of some of these letters in upcoming sections of ***Puntos de partida***. For the moment, pay particular attention to their pronunciation when you see them. Can you match the Spanish spelling with its equivalent pronunciation?

Spelling

1. **ch**
2. **g** before **e** or **i**; also **j**
3. **h**
4. **g** before **a**, **o**, or **u**
5. **ll**
6. **ñ**
7. **r**
8. **r** at the beginning of a word or **rr** in the middle of a word
9. **v**

Pronunciation

a. like the *g* in English *garden*
b. similar to *dd* of *caddy* or *tt* of *kitty* when pronounced very quickly
c. like *ch* in English *cheese*
ch. like Spanish **b**
d. similar to a "strong" English *h*
e. like *y* in English *yes* or like the *li* sound in *million*
f. a trilled sound, several Spanish **r**'s in a row
g. similar to the *ny* sound in *canyon*
h. never pronounced

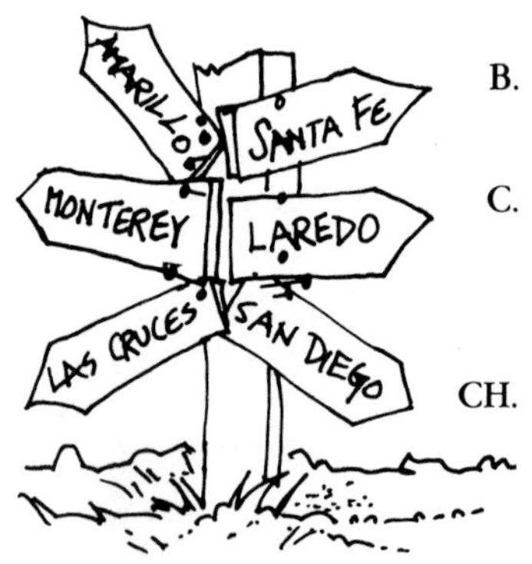

B. Spell your own name in Spanish, and listen as your classmates spell their names. Try to remember as many of their names as you can.

C. Identify as many of your classmates as you can, using the phrase **Te llamas** _____ (*Your name is* _____). Then spell the name in Spanish.

MODELO: Te llamas María: **M** (eme) **A** (a) **R** (ere) **Í** (i acentuada) **A** (a).

CH. Spell these U.S. place names in Spanish. All of them are of Hispanic origin: Toledo, Los Angeles, Texas, Montana, Colorado, El Paso, Florida, Las Vegas, Amarillo, San Francisco. Pronounce the names in Spanish before you begin to spell them.

Follow-up: Students spell abbreviations written on board: TWA (pronounced *túa*), IBM, ONU (*Organización de las Naciones Unidas*), CIA (pronounced *sía*), OVNI (*objeto volante no identificado*, or UFO).

LOS COGNADOS

Note: This section offers opportunities for pronunciation practice, as well as being a vehicle to make students "comfortable" with Spanish and to encourage self-expression.

Note: Additional ways to express cognate: *las cognadas, las palabras cognadas*.

Many Spanish and English words are similar or identical in form and meaning. These related words are called *cognates* (**los cognados**). Spanish and English share so many cognates because a number of words in both languages are derived from the same Latin root words and also because Spanish and English are "language neighbors," especially in the southwestern United States. Each language has borrowed words from the other and adapted them to its own sound system.

Realia: See IM for suggestions and exercises for handling authentic materials that are not accompanied by exercises in the student text.

EL SUPERTEST

Las preguntas de nuestro Supertest de enero son bastante fáciles. ¡Pon a prueba tus conocimientos y contesta rápidamente!

Enunciado	Sí	No
1. Los habitantes de Teruel son turolenses	☐	☐
2. Camacho fue el capitán de la selección española en el Mundial 86 de México..............	☐	☐
3. La «Rendición de Breda» fue pintada por Goya..	☐	☐
4. Marco Polo escribió «El libro de las maravillas»..	☐	☐
5. La última Olimpiada se celebró en San Francisco..	☐	☐
6. El chihuahua es la raza de perro más pequeña..	☐	☐
7. El archipiélago canario se compone de nueve islas..	☐	☐
8. Berlín es la capital de la RFA	☐	☐
9. Los nacidos entre el 20 de febrero y el 20 de marzo pertenecen al signo de Picis...........	☐	☐
10. El jugador de ajedrez Karpov es soviético.....	☐	☐
11. El caballo de Alejandro Magno se llamaba Bucéfalo..	☐	☐
12. Saturno es el segundo planeta más grande del sistema solar..	☐	☐

Soluciones del supertest: 1. Sí.–2. Sí.–3. Velázquez.–4. Sí.–5. En Los Angeles.–6. Sí.–7. De siete.–8. Bonn.–9. Sí.–10. Sí.–11. Sí.–12. Sí.

Optional: Present vowel sounds (p. 12–13) before beginning section. Present *soy*, *es*.

Emphasis:
- Words may look alike but not *sound* alike to beginning students.
- Students should *not* try to memorize all words presented in this section.

Suggestion: Model pronunciation of adjectives in brief sentences about yourself: *cruel... cruel... No soy cruel*, etc.

Suggestion: It is often helpful to have students pronounce only the vowels of a cognate before saying the complete word.

Optional: Useful for pronunciation or listening practice: *legal*, *superior*, *normal*, *diligente*, *excelente*, *impresionante*, *natural*, *horrible*, *prudente*, *popular*, *inferior*, *intelectual*, *indiferente*

Emphasis: Show adjective agreement in sentences about yourself and students in class. No need to discuss grammatical concept of agreement at this time.

Thus, the English word *leader* has become Spanish **líder**, and Spanish **el lagarto** (*the lizard*) has become English *alligator.* The existence of so many cognates will make learning some Spanish vocabulary words easier for you and increase the number of words that you can recognize immediately. Many cognates are used in **Ante todo**. Don't try to memorize all of them—just get used to the sound of them in Spanish.

Here are some Spanish adjectives (words used to describe people, places, and things) that are cognates of English words. Practice pronouncing them, imitating your instructor. These adjectives can be used to describe either a man or a woman.

cruel	independiente	pesimista
eficiente	inteligente	realista
egoísta	interesante	rebelde
elegante	liberal	responsable
emocional	materialista	sentimental
idealista	optimista	terrible
importante	paciente	valiente

The following adjectives change form. Use the **-o** ending when describing a man, the **-a** ending when describing a woman.

extrovertido/a	introvertido/a	serio/a
generoso/a	religioso/a	sincero/a
impulsivo/a	romántico/a	tímido/a

Conversación

Variation B: Suggest several familiar figures (real or fictional); students describe them. **Optional:** Introduce *¿Cómo es... ?*

Variation B: Introduce question forms via questions based on real or fictional people (*¿Es romántico Tom Selleck?*, etc.). Students can answer *sí* or *no* or in short sentences.

A. Describe Don Juan, the famous lover, in simple Spanish sentences that begin with **Don Juan es** (*is*)... or **Don Juan no es** (*is not*)...

B. Think of a well-known person—real or imaginary—and describe him or her. Try to describe as many qualities of the person as you can. For example:

El presidente es/no es...
Jane Fonda es/no es...

Suggestions
- Introduce forms of *ser* in context of brief sentences using adjectives just presented in *Los cognados*.
- No need to emphasize subject pronouns at this time.

¿CÓMO ES USTED?°

¿Cómo... *What kind of person are you?*

You can use these forms of the verb **ser** (*to be*) to describe yourself and others.

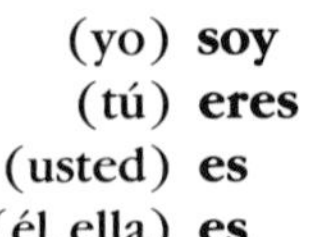

(yo)	**soy**	*I am*
(tú)	**eres**	*you* (familiar) *are*
(usted)	**es**	*you* (formal) *are*
(él, ella)	**es**	*he/she is*

- Make sure students connect *eres/es* forms with informal/formal concepts already discussed for greetings.

Note: This is a preliminary introduction of *ser* only. No need to contrast *ser* with *estar* at this time.

Conversación

A. **¿Cómo es usted?** Describe yourself, using adjectives from **Los cognados: Yo soy... Yo no soy...**

B. **Entrevista.** Use the following adjectives, or any others you know, to find out what a classmate is like. Follow the model.

MODELO: —¿Eres generoso? (¿Eres generosa?)
—¿Sí, soy generoso/a. (No, no soy generoso/a.)

Adjetivos: sincero/a, eficiente, emocional, inteligente, impulsivo/a, liberal

Now find out what kind of person your instructor is, using the same adjectives. Use the appropriate formal forms.

MODELO: **¿Es usted** optimista (generoso/a)?

Extension A: Encourage students to listen to each other by asking them to repeat what another student says about self. *¿Susie es _____? ¿Cómo es Bob?*, etc.

Suggestion B: Model interview with 2–3 students before asking others to try it in pairs. Model with both male and female students to emphasize gender agreement of adjectives, but do not expect accuracy with gender agreement in student speech at this time. Correct by restating incorrect student speech correctly.

Emphasis B: Double *no* in negative answer. Formal forms in questions to you.

Follow-up: Begin practice of listening for general meaning. Students will not understand every word in the following questions, but should be able to grasp concepts. They indicate comprehension with simple *sí* or *no* responses. Form questions with rising intonation. **1.** *¿Usted es profesor(a) en la universidad? ¿Es estudiante?* **2.** *¿Estudia matemáticas? ¿Estudia literatura? ¿Estudia física nuclear?* **3.** *¿Las clases son malas?* (Use thumbs down gesture to convey meaning.) *¿Son buenas?* (Thumbs-up gesture.) **4.** *¿La universidad es interesante? ¿Los estudiantes son inteligentes?*

SPANISH AS A WORLD LANGUAGE

Although no one knows exactly how many languages are spoken around the world, linguists estimate that there are between 3,000 and 6,000. Spanish, with 296 million native speakers, is among the top five languages. It is the language

Note: Top 12 languages (source: World Almanac 1987):
Chinese (Mandarin), 788 million
English, 420 million
Hindi–Urdu (in Pakistan and Northern India), 300 million
Spanish, 296 million
Russian, 285 million
Arabic, 177 million
Bengali, 171 million
Portuguese, 164 million
Malay–Indonesian, 128 million
Japanese, 122 million
German, 118 million
French, 114 million

Follow-up: Use map to continue pronunciation practice. Write names of countries on board as students say them; then use list as basis for choral repetition drill.

spoken in Spain, in all of South America (except Brazil and the Guyanas), in most of Central America, in Cuba, in Puerto Rico, and in the Dominican Republic—in approximately twenty countries in all.

Like all languages spoken by large numbers of people, modern Spanish varies from region to region. The Spanish of Madrid is different from that spoken in Mexico City or Buenos Aires, just as the English of London differs from that of Chicago or Dallas. Although these differences are most noticeable in pronunciation ("accent"), they are also found in vocabulary and special expressions used in different geographical areas. In Great Britain one hears the word *lift,* but the same apparatus is called an *elevator* in the United States. What is called an **autobús** (*bus*) in Spain may be called a **guagua** in the Caribbean. Although such differences are noticeable, they result only rarely in misunderstandings among native speakers, since the majority of structures and vocabulary are common to the many varieties of each language.

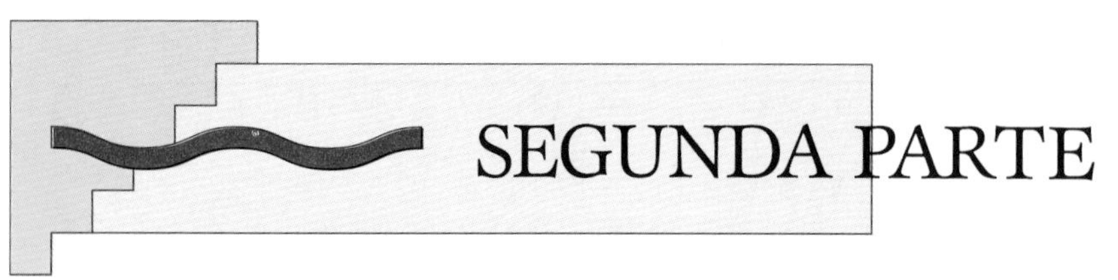

SEGUNDA PARTE

Optional: Expand cognate study with presentation of predictable categories of cognates; do as listening or pronunciation practice.
- -tion → *-ción, -sión*
  conversación, educación, sensación, repetición
- -ty → *-dad, -tad*
  identidad, libertad, sinceridad, universidad
- -ive → *-ivo, -iva*
  motivo, activo, impresivo, pasivo
- -ure → *-ura*
  literatura, arquitectura, cultura, temperatura

MÁS COGNADOS

Extension A (listening): ***Materias*** (Subjects): *sociología, biología, fisiología, filosofía, literatura, historia* ***Filosofía y política:*** *marxismo, materialismo, pesimismo, optimismo, capitalismo, comunismo*

Extension A: Students give as many adjectives as they remember from *Los cognados* (p. 7). Review forms of *ser* by basing simple questions on adjectives they mention: *¿Es usted ____?*

Although some English and Spanish cognates are spelled identically (*idea, general, gas, animal, motor*), most will differ slightly in spelling: *position*/**posición**, *secret*/**secreto**, *student*/**estudiante,** *rose*/**rosa**, *lottery*/**lotería**, *opportunity*/**oportunidad**, *exam*/**examen**.

The following exercises will give you more practice in recognizing and pronouncing cognates. Remember: don't try to learn all of these words. Just get used to the way they sound.

¿Cuántos (*How many*) cognados hay (*are there*) en esta (*this*) foto de un camping de Córdoba, España?

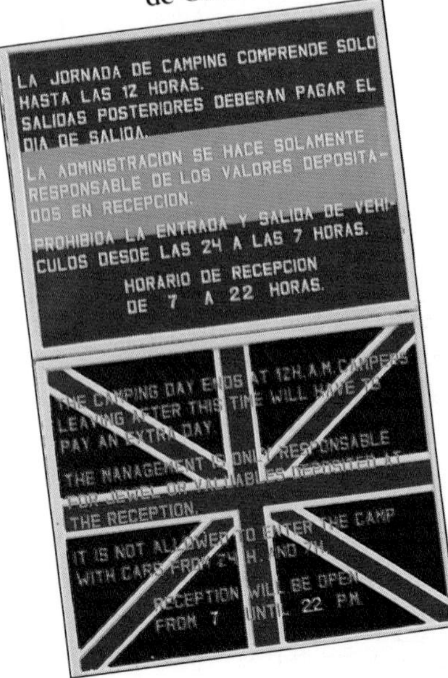

Práctica

A. Pronounce each of the following cognates and give its English equivalent.

Naciones: la Unión Soviética, el Japón, Italia, Francia, España, el Brasil, China, el Canadá
Personas: líder, profesor, actriz, pintor, político, estudiante
Lugares:° restaurante, café, museo, garaje, banco, hotel, oficina, océano, parque
Conceptos: libertad, dignidad, declaración, contaminación
Cosas:° teléfono, fotografía, sofá, televisión, radio, bomba, novela, diccionario, dólar, lámpara, yate
Animales: león, cebra, chimpancé, tigre, hipopótamo
Comidas y bebidas:° hamburguesa, cóctel, patata, café, limón, banana
Deportes:° béisbol, tenis, vólibol, fútbol americano
Instrumentos musicales: guitarra, piano, clarinete, trompeta, violín

Places
Things
Comidas... *Food and drink*
Sports

Emphasis B: Students should note gender distinctions (*un, una*) but not try to memorize them. They are not expected to know distinctions until material is formally presented in Ch. 1.

B. **¿Qué es esto?** (*What is this?*) Being able to tell what something is or to identify the group to which it belongs is a useful conversation strategy that will come in handy when you don't know the specific word for something in Spanish. Begin to practice this strategy by pronouncing these cognates and identifying the category from **Práctica A** to which they belong. Use the following sentences as a guide.

Es **un** lugar (concepto, animal, deporte, instrumento musical).*
Es **una** nación (persona, cosa, comida, bebida).*

MODELO: béisbol → Es un deporte.

1. calculadora
2. burro
3. sándwich
4. golf
5. México
6. actor
7. clase
8. limonada
9. elefante
10. refrigerador
11. universidad
12. fama
13. terrorista
14. Cuba
15. turista
16. rancho
17. serpiente
18. chocolate
19. básquetbol
20. acordeón
21. democracia

Conversación

Follow-up A: Bring in magazine or newspaper ads featuring cognates. Ask students to guess meanings of most obvious cognates; encourage contextual guessing with less obvious ones.

A. With a classmate, practice identifying words, using the categories given in **Práctica B**, above.

MODELO: —¿Qué (*What*) es un hospital? →
—Es un lugar.

1. un saxofón
2. un autobús
3. una estación
4. un doctor
5. Bolivia
6. una Coca-Cola
7. una enchilada
8. una jirafa

Suggestions B:
- Model pronunciation of words in *Personas*, *Categorías*, and *Naciones* lists.
- Model interview with 2–3 students before asking others to do it in pairs.

Extension B: Figures from the past: Pablo Picasso, Francisco Pizarro, Juan Perón, Roberto Clemente, Emiliano Zapata

Variation B: Do as question-answer exercise, asking students questions beginning with *¿Quién es ____? ¿De dónde es ____?*.

B. **Situaciones.** Can you identify these figures from the Spanish-speaking world? With a classmate, role-play conversations about them according to the model. Use the names, categories, and countries given below as a guide. Use **Soy**... to identify yourself and **Soy de**... to tell where you are from.

*The English equivalent of these sentences is *It is a place* (*concept* . . .); *It is a country* (*person* . . .). Note that Spanish has two different ways to express *a* (*an*): **un** and **una**. All nouns are either masculine (*m.*) or feminine (*f.*) in Spanish. **Un** is used with masculine nouns, **una** with feminine nouns. You will learn more about this aspect of Spanish in **Capítulo 1**. Don't try to learn the gender of nouns now, and note that you do not have to know the gender of nouns to do this activity.

ME LLAMO...
Irene es un nombre griego que significa «paz».
Rafael es un nombre de origen hebreo que significa «Dios ha sanado».
Cora es un nombre griego que significa «bella, adornada».
Guillermo es un nombre de origen germánico que significa «voluntad y yelmo» y que podría interpretarse como «protector voluntarioso».

MODELO: ESTUDIANTE 1 (uno): ¿Cómo se llama usted?
ESTUDIANTE 2 (dos): (Me llamo) Juan Carlos.
ESTUDIANTE 1: Y ¿quién (*who*) es usted?
ESTUDIANTE 2: Soy rey (*king*).* Soy de España.

Personas	**Categorías**	**Naciones**
Diego Rivera	actor (actriz)	México
Fernando Valenzuela	primer ministro	España
Geraldo Rivera	cantante (*singer*)	los Estados Unidos
Fidel Castro	muralista	Puerto Rico
Rita Moreno	jugador (*player*) de béisbol	Cuba
Ricardo Montalbán	jugador de golf	
Lee Treviño	reportero	
Julio Iglesias		
Severiano Ballesteros		

Realia: See IM for suggestions and exercises for handling authentic materials that are not accompanied by exercises in the student text.

PRONUNCIACIÓN

Point out: Different pronunciations of English vowel *a*: far, fat, fate, fall, sofa. Silent letter *e*: make, mate, crate.

Suggestion: emphasize diphthongized pronunciation of English *a* and *o* in ate, make, same; oh, gold, note. Pronounce each word slowly, calling attention to movement of your lips. Contrast with Spanish *me*, *te*, *de*; *lo*, *no*.

Point out: If students draw out a single Spanish vowel sound into two, they will have a noticeable "accent" in Spanish.

Preliminary Sound Discrimination Exercise: ***¿Español o inglés?*** Pronounce these English and Spanish words in random order. Students identify each as *español* or *inglés*.

English		Spanish	
me	may	*mi*	*me*
Fay	no	*fe*	*no*
ace	Sue	*es*	*su*
cone	lay	*con*	*le*
tea	two	*ti*	*tú*
low	say	*lo*	*se*
dose	day	*dos*	*de*
sea	Kay	*si*	*que*

You have probably already noted that there is a very close relationship between the way Spanish is written and the way it is pronounced. This makes it relatively easy to learn the basics of Spanish spelling and pronunciation.

Many Spanish sounds, however, do not have an exact equivalent in English, so you should not trust English to be your guide to Spanish pronunciation. Even words that are spelled the same in both languages are usually pronounced quite differently. It is important to become so familiar with Spanish sounds that you can pronounce them automatically, right from the beginning of your study of the language.

Las vocales (*Vowels*): *A, E, I, O, U*

Unlike English vowels, which can have many different pronunciations or may be silent, Spanish vowels are always pronounced, and they are almost always pronounced in the same way. Spanish vowels are always short and tense. They are never drawn out with a *u* or *i* glide as in English: **lo** ≠ *low*; **de** ≠ *day*.

¡OJO! The *uh* sound or schwa (which is how all unstressed vowels are pronounced in English: c*a*nal, wait*e*d, at*o*m) does not exist in Spanish.

a: pronounced like the *a* in *father*, but short and tense
e: pronounced like the *e* in *they*, but without the *i* glide

*Note that the indefinite article (**un**, **una**) is not used before unmodified nouns of profession.

i: pronounced like the *i* in *machine,* but short and tense*
o: pronounced like the *o* in *home* but without the *u* glide
u: pronounced like the *u* in *rule,* but short and tense

A. Pronounce the following Spanish syllables, being careful to pronounce each vowel with a short, tense sound.

1. ma fa la ta pa
2. me fe le te pe
3. mi fi li ti pi
4. mo fo lo to po
5. mu fu lu tu pu
6. mi fe la tu do
7. su mi te so la
8. se tu no ya li

Extension B: Present last names in the following sentences; practice phrases and then complete sentences. Emphasize clear diction and use of mouth muscles.
a: *Hasta mañana, señora Santana.*
e: *De nada, señor Pérez.*
i: *Así así, señora Martínez.*
o: *Con permiso, señor Ortega.*
u: *¿Y usted, señora Cruz?*

Follow-up: Write long words containing many vowel sounds on board; students practice sounding them out: *contemporáneo, aeróbico, unanimidad, movimiento, solemnemente, neoimpresionismo.*

B. Pronounce the following words, paying special attention to the vowel sounds.

1. hasta tal nada mañana natural normal fascinante
2. me qué Pérez usted rebelde excelente elegante
3. así señorita así así permiso diligente imposible tímido
4. yo con cómo noches profesor señor generoso
5. uno usted tú mucho Perú Lupe Úrsula

Here is part of a rental car ad in Spanish. Can you find the following information in it?

- How many cars does the agency have available?
- How many offices does the agency have?
- What Spanish word expresses the English word *immediately*?
- If not confirmed immediately, when are reservations confirmed by the agency?

ai Ansa International
RENT A CAR
Si necesita un coche para su trabajo o placer, nosotros tenemos el adecuado para Vd.
Con una flota de 40.000 coches y 1.000 oficinas, estamos a su servicio en los siguientes países;
ALEMANIA
ARABIA SAUDITA
ARGENTINA
AUSTRIA
BELGICA
BRASIL
CHIPRE
DINAMARCA
ESPAÑA
FINLANDIA
FRANCIA
GRAN BRETAÑA
GRECIA
HOLANDA
IRLANDA
ISLANDIA
ITALIA
JAMAICA
LUXEMBURGO
MALASIA
MARRUECOS
MARTINICA
PARAGUAY
PORTUGAL
SUECIA
SUIZA
URUGUAY
U.S.A.
En la mayoría de los casos, podemos confirmar su reserva inmediatamente.
Cuando esto no sea posible, su reserva le será confirmada en un plazo máximo de 48 horas.

*The word **y** (*and*) is also pronounced like the letter **i**.

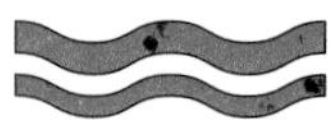

LOS NÚMEROS 0–30

Canción infantil*

Dos y dos son cuatro,
cuatro y dos son seis,
seis y dos son ocho,
y ocho dieciséis.

Suggestions:
- Practice *Canción infantil.*
- Practice numbers 0–10: count forward; count by twos in evens and odds; count backward 10–0.
- Practice numbers 11–20; evens 0–20.
- Practice numbers 21–30; odds 0–30.
- Count 0–30 by threes; by fives; by tens.
- **Point out:** Written accents on 16, 23, 26; final *-e* of *veinte* and final *-a* of *treinta*.

Listening Exercises:
- Write numbers on board and identify them (sometimes incorrectly). Students indicate comprehension with *sí* or *no*.
- Students number from 1–12 on paper. Using numerals, they write these numbers as you say them in Spanish: 7, 15, 20, 24, 30, 19, 14, 12, 2, 11, 28, 13.

Point out: The combined forms are somewhat more common in contemporary Spanish (see footnote).

Emphasis:
- *Hay* means both *there is* and *there are.*
- Question form is same (*¿Hay* ____ ?), with rising intonation.

Preliminary Listening Exercise: Say these pairs of numbers; students repeat the larger one: *dos/doce*, *once/uno*, *treinta/veinte*, *tres/trece*, *cuatro/catorce*, *quince/cinco*, *diez/once.*

0	cero				
1	uno	11	once	21	veintiuno
2	dos	12	doce	22	veintidós
3	tres	13	trece	23	veintitrés
4	cuatro	14	catorce	24	veinticuatro
5	cinco	15	quince	25	veinticinco
6	seis	16	dieciséis†	26	veintiséis
7	siete	17	diecisiete	27	veintisiete
8	ocho	18	dieciocho	28	veintiocho
9	nueve	19	diecinueve	29	veintinueve
10	diez	20	veinte	30	treinta

The number *one* has several forms in Spanish. **Uno** is the form used in counting. **Un** is used before masculine singular nouns, **una** before feminine singular nouns: **un señor, una señora**. Note, also, that the number **veintiuno** becomes **veintiún** before masculine nouns and **veintiuna** before feminine nouns: **veinti*ún* señores, veinti*una* señoras**.

Use the word **hay** to express both *there is* and *there are* in Spanish. **No hay** means *there is not* and *there are not.* **¿Hay... ?** asks *Is there . . . ?* or *Are there . . . ?*

—¿Cuántos estudiantes **hay** en la clase? —(**Hay**) Treinta.	—*How many students are there in the class? —(There are) Thirty.*
—¿**Hay** osos panda en el zoo? —¿**Hay** veinte osos, pero **no hay** osos panda.	—*Are there any panda bears at the zoo? —There are twenty bears, but there aren't any pandas.*

*__A children's song__ Two and two are four, four and two are six, six and two are eight, and eight (makes) sixteen.

†The numbers 16 to 19 and 21 to 29 can be written as one word (**dieciséis... veintiuno**) or as three (**diez y seis... veinte y uno**).

Suggestion A: Students read aloud, practicing pronunciation.

Variation A: Use this or similar exercise for in-class dictation (see Teaching Techniques: Dictation, IM).

Extension A: *18 museos, 17 jirafas, 26 autobuses, 21 señoras, 28 bebidas, 30 días, 16 ceros, 29 oficinas, 25 naciones*

Variations B:
- Do as pair exercise.
- Write additional problems on large flash cards. Students read problems aloud and give answers.
- Teach *¿Cuántos son?*; give additional problems orally.

Extension B: 1 + 4 = ? 1 − 1 + 3 = ? 8 + 7 = ? 13 − 9 = ? 2 + 3 + 10 = ? 28 − 6 = ? 30 − 17 = ? 28 − 5 = ? 7 + 19 = ?

Follow-up: *Un problema para Einstein:* 10 + 5 + 7 − 4 + 12 − 15 + 9 − 11 + 17 − 24 + 16 = ? (Answer: 22)

Emphasis A:
- Students may answer in complete sentences.
- Double *no* in negative answers when complete sentence.

Suggestion A3: Encourage students to estimate numbers.

Extension A4: Use same items, but ask questions about your campus, using *muchos/muchas* plus plural forms of nouns.

Follow-up: Using magazine or newspaper ads or photos, ask *¿Hay ____?* questions with previous cognate vocabulary.

Suggestion B: Do first as listening comprehension exercise; then as pair exercise.

Suggestion B: Bring in coins and currency from Hispanic countries and practice with numbers and cognates.

Práctica

A. Practique los números.

1. 4 señoras
2. 12 noches
3. 1 café (*m.*)
4. 21 cafés (*m.*)
5. 14 días
6. 1 clase (*f.*)
7. 21 ideas (*f.*)
8. 11 tardes
9. 15 estudiantes
10. 13 teléfonos
11. 28 bebidas
12. 5 guitarras
13. 1 león (*m.*)
14. 30 señores
15. 20 oficinas

B. Problemas de matemáticas: + (y) − (menos) = (son)

MODELO: 2 + 2 = 4 → Dos y dos son cuatro.
4 − 2 = 2 → Cuatro menos dos son dos.

1. 2 + 4 = ?
2. 8 + 17 = ?
3. 11 + 1 = ?
4. 3 + 18 = ?
5. 9 + 6 = ?
6. 5 + 4 = ?
7. 1 + 13 = ?
8. 15 − 2 = ?
9. 9 − 9 = ?
10. 13 − 8 = ?
11. 14 + 12 = ?
12. 23 − 13 = ?

Conversación

A. **Preguntas** (*Questions*)

1. ¿Cuántos estudiantes hay en la clase de español? ¿Cuántos estudiantes hay en clase hoy (*today*)? ¿Hay tres profesores o un profesor?
2. ¿Cuántos días hay en una semana (*week*)? ¿Hay seis? (No, no hay...) ¿Cuántos días hay en un fin de semana (*weekend*)? Hay cuatro semanas en un **mes**. ¿Qué significa **mes** en inglés? ¿Cuántos días hay en el mes de febrero? ¿en el mes de junio? ¿Cuántos meses hay en un año?
3. Hay muchos (*many*) animales en un zoo. ¿Hay un zoo en esta ciudad (*this city*)? ¿Cuántos elefantes hay en el zoo? ¿cuántas jirafas? ¿cuántos osos? ¿cuántos osos panda? ¿Hay muchos animales exóticos?
4. Hay muchos edificios (*buildings*) en una universidad. En esta (*this*) universidad, ¿hay una cafetería? ¿un teatro? ¿un cine (*movie theater*)? ¿un laboratorio de lenguas? ¿un bar? ¿una clínica? ¿un hospital? ¿un museo? ¿muchos estudiantes? ¿muchos profesores?

B. **¿Cuánto es?** (*How much does it cost?*) You have asked a clerk the prices of three different models or brands of something you want to buy. In each case you want to buy the least expensive model. What is the price of the item you finally select?

1. tres pesos, trece pesos, treinta pesos
2. dieciocho dólares, veintiocho dólares, ocho dólares
3. veintidós pesos, doce pesos, quince pesos
4. dieciséis pesetas, catorce pesetas, diecisiete pesetas

5. veintiún dólares, veintisiete dólares, veintinueve dólares
6. once pesetas, veintiuna pesetas, veintisiete pesetas

Now make up five similar sets of prices and present them orally to your classmates, who will select the lowest price.

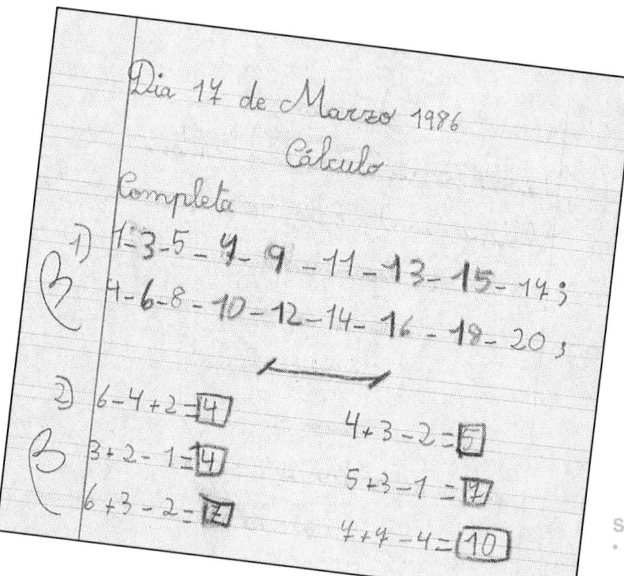
Dia 17 de Marzo 1986
Cálculo
Completa
1) 1-3-5-7-9-11-13-15-17;
4-6-8-10-12-14-16-18-20;
B
2) 6-4+2=4 4+3-2=5
3+2-1=4 5+3-1=7
6+3-2=7 4+4-4=10
B

Here is a page from a Spanish child's workbook. Can you find the Spanish word for *arithmetic*? What numbers are written differently in Spain? The letter **B** was written twice by the child's teacher. What do you think it stands for?

Suggestions:

- Encourage students to learn all of the *gustar* phrases as set expressions. There is no need for you to explain the *gustar* construction at this time. Exercises and activities will not require students to use *gustan*, although you may wish to use it in your speech.
- Be sure students relate *te/le gusta* to the informal/formal concept discussed in *Ante todo*, *Primera parte*.
- Contrast indefinite articles (practiced earlier) with definite articles (practiced here), but do not require mastery of the concept.

GUSTOS° Y PREFERENCIAS

°*Likes*

—¿Te gusta el béisbol?
—¿Sí, me gusta, pero (*but*) me gusta más (*more*) el vólibol.

To indicate that you like something in Spanish, say **Me gusta** _____. To indicate that you don't like something, use **No me gusta** _____. Use the question **¿Te gusta** _____? to ask a classmate if he or she likes something. Use **¿Le gusta** _____? to ask your instructor the same question.

In the following conversations, you will use the word **el** to mean *the* with masculine nouns and the word **la** with feminine nouns. Don't try to memorize which nouns are masculine and which are feminine. Just get used to using the words **el** and **la** before nouns.

Note: Introduction of infinitives with *gustar*, to expand communicative use of *gustar* phrases as well as to introduce the concept of the infinitive (formally presented in Ch. 1).

You will also be using a number of Spanish verbs in the infinitive form, which always ends in **-r**. Here are some examples: **estudiar** = *to study*; **comer** = *to eat.* Try to guess the meanings of the infinitives used in these activities from context. If someone asks you, for instance, **¿Te gusta beber Coca-Cola?**, it is a safe guess that **beber** means *to drink.*

Conversación

Extension A: Use other names of currently popular actresses and actors; use other cognate sports—*el béisbol*, *el vólibol*, etc.

A. Indicate whether you like the following things or like to do the following activities.

MODELOS: ¿la clase de español? → (No) Me gusta la clase de español.
¿estudiar mucho? → (No) Me gusta estudiar mucho.

1. ¿la música moderna? ¿la música clásica? ¿la música punk?
2. ¿la universidad? ¿la cafetería de la universidad? ¿la librería (*bookstore*)?
3. ¿la actriz Joan Collins? ¿el actor Emilio Estévez? ¿la cantante Madonna? ¿el grupo U-2? ¿el presidente de los Estados Unidos?
4. ¿estudiar español? ¿estudiar en la cafetería? ¿estudiar en la residencia (*dorm*)? ¿en la biblioteca (*library*)?
5. ¿esquiar (*to ski*)? ¿jugar al tenis? ¿jugar al fútbol americano? ¿jugar al golf? ¿jugar a la lotería?
6. ¿beber vino? ¿beber café? ¿beber té? ¿beber limonada? ¿beber chocolate?

Option B: Students expand each interview to three sentences by adding rejoinders like *a mí* and *también*: *A mí me gusta nadar en el océano también.*

Emphasis: Formal forms in questions to you.

B. **Entrevista.** Ask another student if he or she likes the following activities.

MODELO: nadar (*to swim*) en el océano →
—¿Te gusta nadar en el océano?
—Sí, me gusta nadar en el océano.
(No, no me gusta nadar.)
(Sí, pero me gusta más jugar al tenis.)

1. ¿comer piza? ¿comer hamburguesas? ¿comer en la cafetería? ¿comer en un restaurante elegante?
2. ¿hablar (*to speak*) español? ¿hablar otras lenguas? ¿hablar por teléfono? ¿hablar ante (*in front of*) muchas personas?
3. ¿tocar la guitarra? ¿tocar el piano? ¿tocar el violín?
4. ¿ir a (*to go to*) clase? ¿ir al cine? ¿ir al bar? ¿ir al parque? ¿ir al museo?

Now use the preceding cues to interview your instructor about his or her likes and dislikes.

MODELO: ¿**Le** gusta comer piza?

Suggestion: Ask students to give examples of uses of Spanish in the U.S.: place and street names, restaurants, advertising, music, friends of Hispanic descent, television programs about Hispanics or with Hispanic characters, etc. Explain derivations, if you know them.

Optional:

- Between 1980 and 1987, the U.S. Hispanic population grew from 14.5 million to 18.8 million. Hispanics accounted for 7.9% of the U.S. population in 1987 (compared to 6.4% in 1980).
- Between 1982 and 1987, Central and South Americans experienced the greatest growth

HISPANICS IN THE UNITED STATES

You don't need to go abroad to find evidence of the importance of Spanish. The Spanish language and people of Hispanic descent have been an integral part of United States life for centuries, and Hispanics are currently one of the fastest-growing cultural groups in this country. In fact, based on information obtained from the 1980 census, the United States is now the sixth largest Spanish-speaking country in the world!

Who are the almost 19 million people of Hispanic descent living in the United States today? If we are tempted to think of all U.S. Hispanics as similar, we soon discover that nothing could be farther from the truth! In fact, they are characterized by great diversity, the result of their ancestors' or their country of origin, the area of this country in which they live, socioeconomic-professional factors, and, of course, individual talents and aspirations.

People of Hispanic origin were among the first colonizers of what is now the United States. A visitor to the states of Montana, Idaho, and Nevada, for example, would meet many descendants of Spanish settlers—as well as many Basques, more recent immigrants—and in the Southwest many Mexican-Americans can trace their ancestors back several centuries.

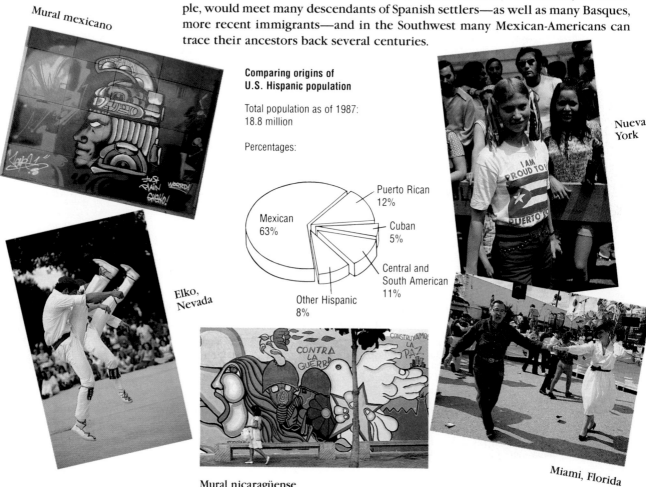

Mural mexicano

Comparing origins of U.S. Hispanic population

Total population as of 1987: 18.8 million

Percentages:

Mexican 63%
Puerto Rican 12%
Cuban 5%
Central and South American 11%
Other Hispanic 8%

Nueva York

Elko, Nevada

Mural nicaragüense

Miami, Florida

increase. Cubans experienced the smallest.

For additional information about U.S. Hispanics; see Supplementary Exercises and Materials: *Ante todo* and *Voces del mundo hispánico* (IM).

Optional: Most Hispanics still live in eight states (in order of Hispanic population as percentage of total state population): New Mexico, Texas, Arizona, California, Colorado, New York, Florida, Illinois.

For additional information, see Supplementary Exercises and Materials: *Ante todo* and *Voces del mundo hispánico* (IM).

Point out: Not all people of Hispanic origin have Spanish surnames. Many people with Spanish surnames do not consider themselves to be of Hispanic origin.

Note: This group focuses exclusively on Mexican Americans.

Large groups of more recent arrivals can be found in New York (where the Puerto Rican population is the largest) and in Florida (the home of many Cubans and Central Americans). And there has been a substantial increase in the number of Hispanics even in areas not usually thought of as having large Hispanic populations—Minneapolis–St. Paul, Seattle, Chicago, and New Orleans, to name only a few. Political and social changes in Central America have produced a recent influx of Nicaraguans and Salvadorans, who have established large communities in many U.S. cities, among them San Francisco and Los Angeles. Predominant among people of South American descent in this country are Colombians, Argentines, and Ecuadorans.

Many U.S. Hispanics strive to maintain aspects of their unique heritage while entering the mainstream of American culture at the same time. Although not all people of Hispanic origin speak Spanish, many are in fact bilingual and bicultural, able to move back and forth between their own and the mainstream culture with ease. This dual cultural identity is being increasingly recognized by the media and by the business community. Many major U.S. cities have one or more Spanish-language newspapers as well as television and radio stations. A wide variety of businesses are of course owned and operated by Hispanics, and major corporations in the food, clothing, entertainment, and service fields appeal to Hispanic clients . . . in both English and Spanish!

Perhaps the most important contributions of Hispanic culture to the United States come from individuals who make up the actual Hispanic population. It is easy to call to mind Hispanics who have achieved national prominence in all walks of life, but we should also keep in mind the many Hispanics, not in the public eye, who regularly make meaningful contributions in the fields of education, law, science, social work, and so on. Their efforts to create a better world are an integral part of the fabric of this country.

How many of these Mexican-Americans can you identify?

Note: Pictured are (left to right) James Edward Olmos (actor), Henry Cisneros (mayor of San Antonio, Texas), Nancy López (golf star), and Luis Valdez (director).

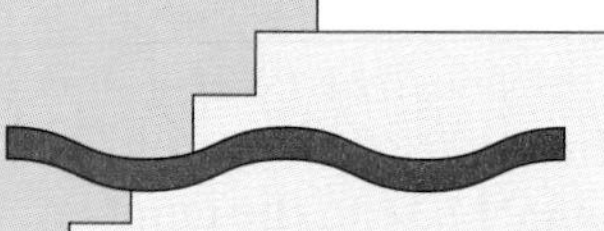

TERCERA PARTE

Suggestions: • The TV schedule is from *El País* (Spain).
• Give students a few minutes to scan the realia, telling them in advance that they will not understand every word. Note use of 24-hour clock for program times.

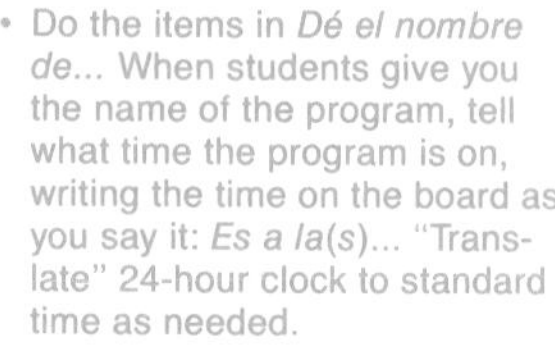

• Do the items in *Dé el nombre de...* When students give you the name of the program, tell what time the program is on, writing the time on the board as you say it: *Es a la(s)...* "Translate" 24-hour clock to standard time as needed.

• Additional questions for *Dé el nombre de...* : *un programa cómico, un programa educativo, un programa de detectives, una telenovela* (soap opera), *un documental cultural*.
• Additional items for *¿Qué significa en inglés... ?*: *cuerpo* (context = *gimnasia*), *imperdonable, perro mecánico* (in context), *conexión, espectáculos, cine, precio justo* (with *concurso*).

¿QUÉ HORA ES?

lunes 29

TVE-1

8.00 Buenos días (informativo). A las 8.00, avance informativo; a las 8.10, dibujos animados; a las 8.20, *Con tu cuerpo* (gimnasia). El tiempo.
9.00 Por la mañana *(magazine)*. — De 10.00 a 10.50: *Lo imperdonable.* — De 12.00 a 12.35: *Gabriela.*
13.00 Benito y Cecilio (dibujos animados). *Rintintín Ladín, el perro mecánico.*
13.30 Tres por cuatro (concurso).
14.30 Informativos territoriales.
14.55 Conexión con la programación nacional.
15.00 Telediario 1.
15.35 Los Colby (II). *Engaños.*
16.30 Tal cual (información y espectáculos).
17.55 Avance telediario.
18.00 Barrio Sésamo (infantil). *Gambas con gabardina.*
18.30 Fraguel Rock (dibujos animados). *El funeral de Musi.*
19.00 A media tarde. *Año bisiesto.*
19.30 De película. *Cine español actual.*
20.30 Telediario 2.
21.00 El tiempo.
21.15 El precio justo (concurso).
22.45 Alfred Hitchcock presenta... *Accidente imprevisto.*
23.10 Documentos TV. *Radio Bikini* (60 minutos) (repetición, sábado 5, a las 5.45). Este documento obtuvo el primer premio de la sección Tiempo de Historia del Festival de Cine de Valladolid de 1987.
0.10 Telediario 3.
0.30 Teledeporte.

Dé (*Give*) el nombre de...	¿Qué significa en inglés... ?
un programa infantil	dibujos animados (dibujo = *drawing*)
un melodrama	telediario (diario = *newspaper*)
un programa de aventuras	concurso (*con...*)
un programa de deportes (*sports*)	
un documental	

All students will not know all items immediately, but chances are that at least one person in the class will know each item.

Es la una.

Son las dos.

Son las cinco.

¿Qué hora es? is used to ask *What time is it?* In telling time, one says ***Es* la una** but ***Son* las dos (las tres, las cuatro**, and so on).

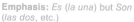

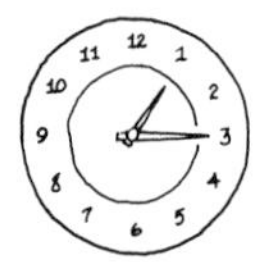

Es la una **y** {**cuarto.** / **quince.**}

Son las dos **y** {**media.** / **treinta.**}

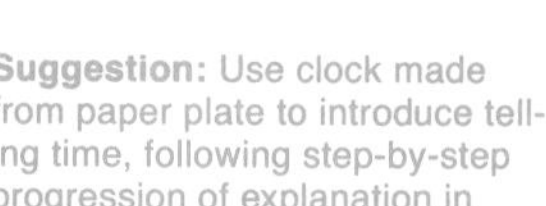

Suggestion: Use clock made from paper plate to introduce telling time, following step-by-step progression of explanation in text.

Emphasis: *Es* (*la una*) but *Son* (*las dos*, etc.)

Point out: *Son* is the plural form of *es*.

Note: In Mexico and some parts of Central America, one frequently hears *¿Qué horas son?*

Son las cinco **y diez.**

Son las ocho **y veinticinco.**

Note that from the hour to the half-hour, Spanish, like English, expresses time by adding minutes or a portion of an hour to the hour.

Son las dos **menos** { **cuarto.** / **quince.** }   Son las ocho **menos diez**.   Son las once **menos veinte.**

From the half-hour to the hour, Spanish usually expresses time by subtracting minutes or a part of an hour from the *next* hour.

Preliminary Listening Exercise: Holding up clock face, arrange hands to show various times and simultaneously say them, correctly or incorrectly. Students respond *sí* or *no*.

Suggestion: Practice telling time with most basic forms before presenting *Otras expresiones útiles*.

Suggestions: *Otras expresiones útiles*
- Model expressions with various times shown on your clock.
- **Point out:** *De la mañana* is used until lunch and *de la tarde* until evening meal. Make sure students associate this information with greetings *buenos días* and *buenas tardes/noches*.
- **Optional:** *mediodía*, *medianoche*, *hora de* + inf.
- **Emphasis:** *Es/Son* vs. *A la(s)*...
- **Ask:** *¿A qué hora es la clase de español?* Students respond; you repeat answer, adding *en punto*. Repeat question for a number of shared experiences: *la sesión de laboratorio*, *la clase de historia*, etc.

Follow-up B (listening): *¿Sí o no?* **(Note:** Vary hours as needed for your students. Reentry of infinitives from p. 17; pantomime as needed to convey meaning.) **1.** *Son las once de la noche. Es hora de estudiar.* **2.** *Son las siete de la mañana. Es hora de hablar español.* **3.** 8 A.M.: *beber café en la cafetería* **4.** 11:00 A.M.: *ir a la clase de español* **5.** 6:30 P.M.: *comer en un restaurante elegante*

Otras expresiones útiles

de la mañana	A.M., in the morning
de la tarde (noche)	P.M., in the afternoon (evening)
en punto	exactly, on the dot, sharp
¿a qué hora?	(at) what time?
a la una (las dos, ...)	at 1:00 (2:00, . . .)

Son las cuatro de la tarde **en punto**.	*It's exactly 4:00 P.M.*
¿A qué hora es la clase de español?	*(At) What time is Spanish class?*
Hay una recepción **a las once** de la mañana.	*There is a reception at 11:00 A.M.*

¡OJO! Don't confuse **Es/Son la(s)**... with **A la(s)**... The first is used for telling time, the second for telling when something happens (when class starts, when one arrives, and so on).

Práctica

A. ¿Qué hora es?

1. 1:00
2. 6:00
3. 11:00
4. 1:30
5. 3:15
6. 6:45
7. 4:15
8. 11:45 exactly
9. 9:10 on the dot
10. 9:50 sharp

B. Exprese la hora, usando **de la mañana (tarde, noche)**.

1.

2.

3.

4.

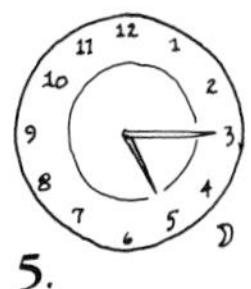
5.

6.

7.

8.

Conversación

Suggestion A: Model dialogue before asking students to do it.

Optional A: Point out use of 24-hour clock for official railroad time.
0:00 = midnight
8:00 = 8:00 A.M.
13:15 = 1:15 P.M.
22:30 = 10:30 P.M.
If you practice telling time with 24-hour clock, control items carefully; students do not yet know numbers over 30.

A. **Situaciones.** You are a travel agent. Your clients want to know when (**¿cuándo?**) they're going to arrive at their destinations. With a classmate, role-play this situation, according to the model.

MODELO: Guanajuato / 9:00 A.M. →
—¿Cuándo llegamos a (*do we get to*) Guanajuato?
—A las nueve de la mañana.

1. Sevilla / 11:00 A.M.
2. Buenos Aires / 11:54 P.M.
3. Los Ángeles / 1:15 P.M.
4. Miami / 8:31 P.M.
5. Málaga / 5:35 A.M.
6. Cali / 2:30 A.M. exactly

Optional B: Expand exchange with *a mí* and *también: A mí me gusta estudiar español a las ocho de la noche también.*

Follow-up (listening): Put following schedule of TV programs on board. Read incomplete sentences; students respond with *a la(s)*... . 7:00—*El show de Carol Burnett* 7:30—*El Zoo de Barcelona* 8:00—*¡Festival de música!* 8:30—*Dibujos animados* (Cartoons) 9:00—Hill Street Blues 10:00—*Cine Club: Historia de amor* Model for incomplete sentences: *Hay un programa (cómico, romántico, dramático, de animales, de música, para toda la familia, interesante) a* _____ .

Follow-up (optional): Return to TV schedule on p. 20 and ask questions like: *¿A qué hora hay un programa... (cómico, educativo...)? ¿A qué hora ponen... (un melodrama, una telenovela...)?*

B. **Entrevista.** Ask a classmate what time the following events or activities take place. He or she will answer according to the cue or will provide the necessary information.

MODELO: la clase de español (10:00 A.M.) →
—¿A qué hora es la clase de español?
—A las diez de la mañana... ¡en punto!

1. la clase de francés (1:45 P.M.)
2. la sesión de laboratorio (3:10 P.M.)
3. la excursión (8:45 A.M.)
4. el concierto (7:30 P.M.)

Now ask what time your partner likes to perform these activities. He or she should provide the necessary information.

MODELO: estudiar español →
—¿A qué hora te gusta estudiar español?
—Me gusta estudiar español a las ocho de la noche.

1. comer (*to eat*)
2. mirar (*to watch*) la televisión
3. jugar al (vólibol, tenis, ...)
4. ir (*to go*) a la cafetería

Suggestion C: Several pairs of students present brief dialogues in front of class. Encourage others to listen to skits by asking brief comprehension questions based on them.

C. **Situaciones.** How might the following people greet each other if they met at the indicated time? With a classmate, create a brief dialogue for each situation.

1. el profesor Martínez y Gloria, a las diez de la mañana
2. la Sra. López y la Srta. Luna, a las cuatro y media de la tarde
3. usted y su (*your*) profesor(a) de español, en la clase de español
4. Jorge y María, a las once de la noche

EL MUNDO° HISPÁNICO (PARTE 1)

world

Antes... *Before reading*

Note: Reading introduces *está* for location. Point out this usage but do not present *ser*/*estar* contrast at this time.

Antes de leer:° Recognizing Interrogative Words and *estar*

In the following brief reading, note that the word **está** means *is located*; **está** and other forms of the verb **estar** (*to be*) are used to tell where things are. You will learn more about the uses of **estar** in **Capítulo 4**.

The reading also contains a series of questions with interrogative words. You are already familiar with **¿cómo?**, **¿qué?**, and **¿cuántos?** (and should be able to guess the meaning of **¿cuántas?** easily). The meaning of other interrogatives may not be immediately obvious to you, but the sentences in which the words appear may offer some clues to meaning. You probably do not know the meaning of **¿dónde?** and **¿cuál?**, but you should be able to guess their meaning in the following sentences.

Suggestions:
- Students look at maps while you use reading as a "script" for improvising listening comprehension material and questions on maps.
- **Note:** Population figures for Mexico and Spain cannot be produced by students, who know only numbers through 30.
- **Emphasis:** *millones de habitantes*

Cuba está en el Mar Caribe. ¿Dónde está la República Dominicana?
Managua es la capital de Nicaragua. ¿Cuál es la capital de México?

Use the statements in the reading as models and the geographical and population information in the maps to answer the questions.

Las naciones del mundo hispánico

¿En cuántas naciones de la América Central se habla español? Hay setenta y dos (72) millones de habitantes en México. ¿Cuántos habitantes hay en Guatemala? ¿en El Salvador? ¿en las demás (*other*) naciones de la América Central? ¿Cuál es la capital de México? ¿de Costa Rica?

Cuba está en el Mar Caribe. ¿Dónde está la República Dominicana? ¿Qué parte de los Estados Unidos está también (*also*) en el Mar Caribe? ¿Dónde está el Canal de Panamá?

¿En cuántas naciones de Sudamérica se habla español? ¿Se habla español o portugués en el Brasil? ¿Cuántos millones de habitantes hay en Venezuela? ¿en Chile? ¿en las demás naciones? ¿Cuál es la capital de cada (*each*) nación?

España está en la Península Ibérica. ¿Qué otra nación está también en esa (*that*) península? ¿Cuántos millones de habitantes hay en España? No se habla español en Portugal. ¿Qué lengua se habla allí (*there*)? ¿Cuál es la capital de España? ¿Está en el centro de la Península?

Follow-up:
- Listening: *¿Sí o no?* ***Modelo:*** (capital) *está en* (country).
- Speaking: ***Modelos:*** *¿Dónde está* (capital)? *¿Dónde está* (country)?

Optional: Present names for inhabitants of Hispanic countries. Ask: *¿De dónde es un* _____? Students respond with name of country. ***Habitantes:*** *mexicano, cubano, dominicano, puertorriqueño, guatemalteco, hondureño, salvadoreño, nicaragüense, costarricense, panameño, venezolano, colombiano, ecuatoriano, peruano, boliviano, chileno, argentino, paraguayo, uruguayo, brasileño, español, portugués*

LAS PALABRAS INTERROGATIVAS
Un resumen

Interrogatives—Suggestion for using art: As a whole-class activity, invent a brief story about the drawing by having students respond *sí* or *no* to these statements:
- *Los hombres están... en casa* (draw house on board), *en un hospital, en una cafetería, en un hotel*, etc.
- *El hombre a la izquierda* (pantomime) *es... terrorista, profesor, fotógrafo, turista*, etc.
- *El hombre a la derecha* (pantomime) *es... policía, estudiante, recepcionista*, etc.
- *El turista es... tímido, agresivo, español, norteamericano, introvertido...*
- *El recepcionista es... impaciente, paciente; sincero...*

You have already used a number of interrogative words and phrases to get information. (You will learn more in subsequent chapters of ***Puntos de partida***.) Note the accent over the vowel you emphasize when you say the word, and the use of the inverted question mark.

¿a qué hora?	¿A qué hora es la clase?
¿cómo?	¿Cómo estás? ¿Cómo es Don Juan? ¿Cómo te llamas?
¿cuál?*	¿Cuál es la capital de Colombia?
¿cuándo?	¿Cuándo es la fiesta?
¿cuánto?	¿Cuánto es?
¿cuántos?, ¿cuántas?	¿Cuántos días hay en una semana? ¿Cuántas naciones hay en Sudamérica?
¿dónde?	¿Dónde está España?
¿qué?*	¿Qué es un hospital? ¿Qué es esto? ¿Qué hora es?
¿quién?	¿Quién es usted?

Note that in Spanish the voice falls at the end of questions that begin with interrogative words.

¿Qué es un tren?   ¿Cómo estás?

---

*Use **¿qué?** to mean *what?* when you are asking for a definition or an explanation. Use **¿cuál?** to mean *what?* in all other circumstances. See also Grammar Section 18.

Emphasis: This section is a review only. Students have seen and probably heard all of these forms already.

Note: Plural forms of most interrogatives are not presented until Ch. 5.

Point out: Difference in meaning between *¿cuánto?* and *¿cúantos/as?*

Optional: *¿Cómo?* to indicate non-comprehension, not *¿Qué?* or *¿Cuál?*.

Extension A: 13. *En la clase.* **14.** *Son las tres y media.* **15.** *Es inteligente.* **16.** *Es un animal.* ***¡OJO!*** A2 requires students to produce *está*.

Práctica 

A. What interrogative words do you associate with the following information?

1. ¡A las tres en punto!
2. En el centro de la península.
3. Soy profesor.
4. Muy bien, gracias.
5. ¡Es muy arrogante!
6. Hay 5 millones (de habitantes).
7. Dos pesos.
8. (La capital) Es Caracas.
9. Es un instrumento musical.
10. Mañana, a las cinco.
11. Son las once.
12. Soy Roberto González.

B. Now ask the questions that would result in the answers given in **Práctica A**.

Conversación

Suggestion: Use drawings as springboard for questions that re-enter all of *Ante todo* material. Encourage students to listen to questions for meaning only and respond with one word or phrase. Drawing #1: *¿Cómo se llama el hombre? ¿De dónde es? ¿Dónde está el cine? ¿Qué hora es? ¿A qué hora es la próxima función?*

Optional: Have students form questions about the drawings. Then have students answer questions asked by others, inventing details. "Coach" students to keep sequence of questions going.

What question is being asked by each of the following persons?

MODELO: El hombre pregunta (*is asking*): ¿______?
La mujer (*woman*) pregunta: ¿______?

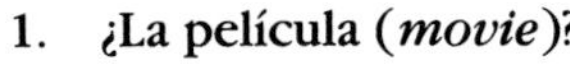

1. ¿La película (*movie*)?
2. ¿El libro?
3. ¿El regalo (*gift*)?

4. ¿La capital de España?
5. ¿El libro?
6. ¿El fantasma?

Suggestions:
- Before students begin the reading, review definite and indefinite articles (for recognition) with them. Emphasize *un* → *el* and *una* → *la*. Present plural definite articles (*los*, *las*).

EL MUNDO HISPÁNICO (PARTE 2)

Antes de leer: Guessing Meaning from Context

You will recognize the meaning of a number of cognates in the following reading about the geography of the Hispanic world. In addition, you should be able to guess the meaning of the underlined words from the context (the words that surround them); they are the names of geographical features. The photo captions at the bottom of the page will also be helpful. You have learned to recognize the meaning of the word **¿qué?** in questions; in this reading, **que** (with no accent mark) means *that* or *which.*

- Call students' attention to the need to guess the underlined words from context, and do the first such guess word (*pampas*) with them.

La geografía del mundo hispánico

La geografía del mundo hispánico es impresionante y muy variada. En algunas° regiones hay de todo.° Por ejemplo, en la Argentina hay pampas extensas en el sur° y la cordillera de los Andes en el oeste. En partes de Venezuela, Colombia y el Ecuador, hay regiones tropicales de densa selva, y en el Brasil está el famoso río Amazonas. En el centro de México y también en El Salvador, Nicaragua y Colombia, hay volcanes activos que a veces° producen erupciones catastróficas. El Perú y Bolivia comparten° el enorme lago Titicaca, situado en una meseta entre los dos países.°

some / de... *a bit of everything*
south
a... *sometimes*
share
naciones

Cuba, Puerto Rico y la República Dominicana son tres islas situadas en el Mar Caribe. Las bellas° playas° del Mar Caribe y de la península de Yucatán son populares entre° los turistas de todo el mundo.

beautiful / *beaches*
among

España, que comparte la Península Ibérica con Portugal, también tiene° una geografía variada. En el norte están los Pirineos, la cordillera que separa a España del° resto de Europa. Madrid, la capital del país, está situada en la meseta central, y en las costas del sur y del este hay playas tan bonitas como las de° Latinoamérica y el Caribe.

has
from the
tan... *as pretty as those of*

Es importante mencionar también la gran diversidad de las ciudades del mundo hispánico. En la Argentina está la gran° ciudad de Buenos Aires. Muchos consideran a Buenos Aires «el París» o «la Nueva York» de Sudamérica. En Venezuela está Caracas, y en el Perú está Lima, la capital, y Cuzco, una ciudad antigua de origen indio.

great

En fin,° el mundo hispánico es diverso respecto a la geografía. ¿Y Norteamérica?

En... *In short*

(*Top*) Una meseta de la Mancha, España
(*middle*) La ciudad de Caracas, Venezuela
(*bottom*) La cordillera de Los Andes, el Ecuador

Comprensión

Demonstrate your understanding of the words underlined in the reading and other words from the reading by giving an example of a similar geographical feature found in the United States or close to it. Then give an example from the Spanish-speaking world.

MODELO: un río → *the Mississippi,* el río Amazonas

1. un lago
2. una cordillera
3. un río
4. una isla
5. una playa
6. una costa
7. un mar
8. un volcán
9. una península

MANDATOS° Y FRASES COMUNES EN LA CLASE

°*Commands*

Note: Material presented in this section is *not* active vocabulary.

Suggestions:
- Model phrases in *Los estudiantes.*
- Choral and individual repetition
- With books closed, students give English equivalent of Spanish phrase read by instructor.
- Students give Spanish equivalent of English phrase read by instructor.
- Model phrases in *Los profesores.*
- With books closed, students give English equivalent of Spanish phrase read by instructor.

Optional: Say the following commands and questions. Students respond with an appropriate action or rejoinder. **1.** *Abra el libro en la página 20.* **2.** *¿Hay preguntas?* **3.** *Repita la oración: Soy estudiante.* **4.** *Escriba: Hola. ¿Qué tal?* **5.** *Escuche.* **6.** *Lea una oración.*

Here are some phrases that you will hear and use frequently during class. Don't try to memorize all of them. You will learn to recognize them gradually, with practice.

Los estudiantes

Practice saying these sentences aloud. Then try to give the Spanish as you look at the English equivalents.

Tengo una pregunta (que hacer).	*I have a question (to ask).*
¿Cómo se dice *page* en español?	*How do you say "page" in Spanish?*
Otra vez, por favor. No entiendo.	*(Say that) Again, please. I don't understand.*
¡(Espere) Un momento, por favor! No sé (la respuesta).	*(Wait) Just a minute, please! I don't know (the answer).*
(Sí,) Cómo no.	*(Yes,) Of course.*

Los profesores

After you read these Spanish sentences, cover the English equivalents and say what each expression means.

¿Hay preguntas?	*Are there any questions?*
¿Qué opina (cree) usted?	*What do you think?*
Escuche. Repita.	*Listen. Repeat.*
Lea (en voz alta).	*Read (aloud).*
Escriba/Complete (la siguiente oración).	*Write/Complete (the next sentence).*

(continúa)

Una clase bilingüe en Austin, Texas

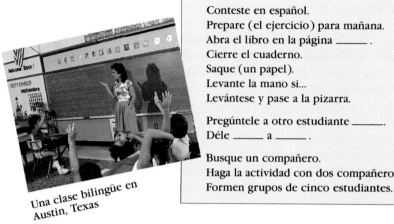

Conteste en español.	*Answer in Spanish.*
Prepare (el ejercicio) para mañana.	*Prepare (the exercise) for tomorrow.*
Abra el libro en la página ____ .	*Open your book to page ____ .*
Cierre el cuaderno.	*Close your notebook.*
Saque (un papel).	*Take out (a sheet of paper).*
Levante la mano si...	*Raise your hand if . . .*
Levántese y pase a la pizarra.	*Get up and go to the blackboard.*
Pregúntele a otro estudiante ____ .	*Ask another student ____ .*
Déle ____ a ____ .	*Give ____ to ____ .*
Busque un compañero.	*Look for a partner.*
Haga la actividad con dos compañeros.	*Do the activity with two classmates.*
Formen grupos de cinco estudiantes.	*Get into groups of five students.*

VOCABULARIO: ANTE TODO

Emphasis: Students are *not* expected to know every word they have used in *Ante todo.* Active vocabulary is listed here.

Although you have used and heard many words in this preliminary chapter of ***Puntos de partida***, the following words are the ones considered to be active vocabulary. Be sure that you know all of them before beginning **Capítulo 1**.

SALUDOS Y EXPRESIONES DE CORTESÍA

Buenos días. Buenas tardes. Buenas noches.
Hola. ¿Qué tal? ¿Cómo está(s)?
Así así. (Muy) Bien.
¿Y tú? ¿Y usted?
Adiós. Hasta mañana. Hasta luego.
¿Cómo te llamas? ¿Cómo se llama usted? Me llamo ____ .
señor (Sr.), señora (Sra.), señorita (Srta.)
(Muchas) Gracias. De nada.
Por favor. Perdón. Con permiso.
Mucho gusto. Igualmente. Encantado/a.

¿CÓMO ES USTED?

soy, eres, es

LOS NÚMEROS

cero, uno, dos, tres, cuatro, cinco, seis, siete, ocho, nueve, diez, once, doce, trece, catorce, quince, dieciséis, diecisiete, dieciocho, diecinueve, veinte, treinta

GUSTOS Y PREFERENCIAS

¿Te gusta ____? ¿Le gusta ____? Sí, me gusta ____. No, no me gusta ____.

OTRAS PALABRAS INTERROGATIVAS

¿cómo?, ¿cuál?, ¿cuándo?, ¿cuánto?, ¿cuántos/as?, ¿dónde?, ¿qué?, ¿quién?

¿QUÉ HORA ES?

es la... , son las... y/menos cuarto, y media, en punto, de la mañana (tarde, noche), ¿a qué hora?, a la(s)...

PALABRAS ADICIONALES

sí yes
hay there is/are
está is (*located*)
no no
no hay there is not/are not
hoy today
mañana tomorrow
y and
en in; at
o or
de of; from
también also
a to; at (*with time*)

INTRODUCTION TO *PUNTOS DE PARTIDA*

Suggestion: For four- and five-day plans for Ch., see Possible Lesson Plans, IM.

Suggestion: Look at *Ch. 1* and *Un paso más 1;* point out chapter structure and function of each part.

Puntos de partida is divided into nineteen grammar chapters, each followed by a section called **Un paso más** (*One more step*). Each chapter has its own theme—university life here and abroad, foods, daily routines, and so on. Following an initial brief dialogue, important vocabulary and expressions related to the themes are included in **Vocabulario: Preparación** and are then used throughout the chapter. **Pronunciación** (in the first five chapters) will introduce you to more aspects of the Spanish sound system.

The grammar section, **Minidiálogos y gramática**, contains brief dialogues, drawings, or readings, which introduce new grammar points, as well as two groups of exercises and activities, with the grammar. You have already seen materials of these kinds in **Ante todo**. The first group, **Práctica**, consists of basic step-by-step practice with each new grammar point. (The answers to many of these exercises are in Appendix 4.) The second group, **Conversación**, is exactly that—a stimulus for speaking. Here you can practice expressing yourself in Spanish by answering questions, interviewing others and being interviewed, describing pictures and cartoons, and so on. You will often be asked to work with another student or in small groups in the **Conversación** sections.

Realia: See IM for suggestions and exercises for handling authentic materials that are *not* accompanied by exercises in the student text.

Throughout the text there will be material you would actually find in Spanish-speaking countries—ads, tickets, forms, clippings from newspapers and magazines, and the like. (You have already seen authentic materials of this kind in **Ante todo**, and you may have been surprised by how much you could understand in them!) Also throughout all sections of the text are brief sections called **Notas...** There are **Notas comunicativas**, which offer hints for communicating more successfully with others in Spanish; **Notas lingüísticas**, which offer insights into interesting aspects of the Spanish language; and **Notas culturales**, with additional cultural information. The word **¡OJO!** (*Watch out!*) will call your attention to areas where you should be especially careful when using Spanish.

Situaciones: See IM for suggestions and additional exercises.

The dialogues (**Situaciones**) that immediately follow the grammar section offer models for interaction with others about aspects of the chapter theme. While containing much material that you will be very familiar with, they also include new material that is particularly useful for handling situations you might encounter in a Spanish-speaking country or areas of the United States. The **Notas comunicativas** sections that accompany the dialogues will highlight this new material for easy reference.

Un poco de todo (*A little of everything*) is a review that emphasizes everything you have learned in the chapter as well as aspects of previous chapters. In the **Vocabulario** you will find a complete list of the new (active) words for the chapter.

Another kind of review section that appears throughout the text is called **¿Recuerda Ud.?** (*Do you remember?*). These brief sections will help you review grammar points you have already studied and make it easier for you to learn new grammar based on those points. (The answers to the exercises in **¿Recuerda Ud.?** appear in Appendix 5.) In addition, the **Repaso** sections that appear every three chapters will focus on the most important grammar topics and language functions presented in those chapters.

Un paso más is very informal. Each of these sections contains a series of activities in which you will use your new language skills to communicate your ideas and opinions to others. In addition to cartoons, questionnaires, role-plays, and suggestions for conversations, there will be more authentic material that you would actually find in Spanish-speaking areas as well as additional hints for successful communication in the sections called **A propósito...** (*By the way . . .*). Finally, in the **Lectura cultural** (*Cultural reading*), you will become acquainted with aspects of everyday life in the Hispanic world by reading brief narratives and authentic readings and also by "listening" as real people tell you about some of their experiences, opinions, and beliefs.

Lectura: See IM for suggestions and additional exercises.

UNA INVITACIÓN AL MUNDO HISPÁNICO

One aspect of understanding another people's culture is understanding what they do all the time without thinking about it. Many times a familiar action—a particular gesture, for example—has a different meaning in another culture. Sometimes you see people doing things that just seem "wrong" to you. You will find shops closed when your culture tells you they "should" be open, and open when they "should" be closed.

In learning about another culture, you also learn more about your own. A culture is a structure that provides for basic human needs: personal safety, making and maintaining friendships, dealing with strangers, and so on. Each culture meets these needs in its own way. Your job as a visitor to another culture is to learn to observe this structure without immediately judging it, to compare by using the terms "same/different" and not "right/wrong." As you do this, your understanding and appreciation of yourself and of other people will continually grow, and you will be increasingly able to participate actively in many new and exciting experiences.

The photographs, dialogues, **Lectura cultural** sections, and authentic materials in ***Puntos de partida*** will help you develop your understanding of Hispanic cultures. In addition, **Voces del mundo hispánico** in the **Repaso** sections that occur every three chapters will focus on specific areas of the Spanish-speaking world and on ethnic groups that speak Spanish.

Voces del mundo hispánico: See IM for suggestions.

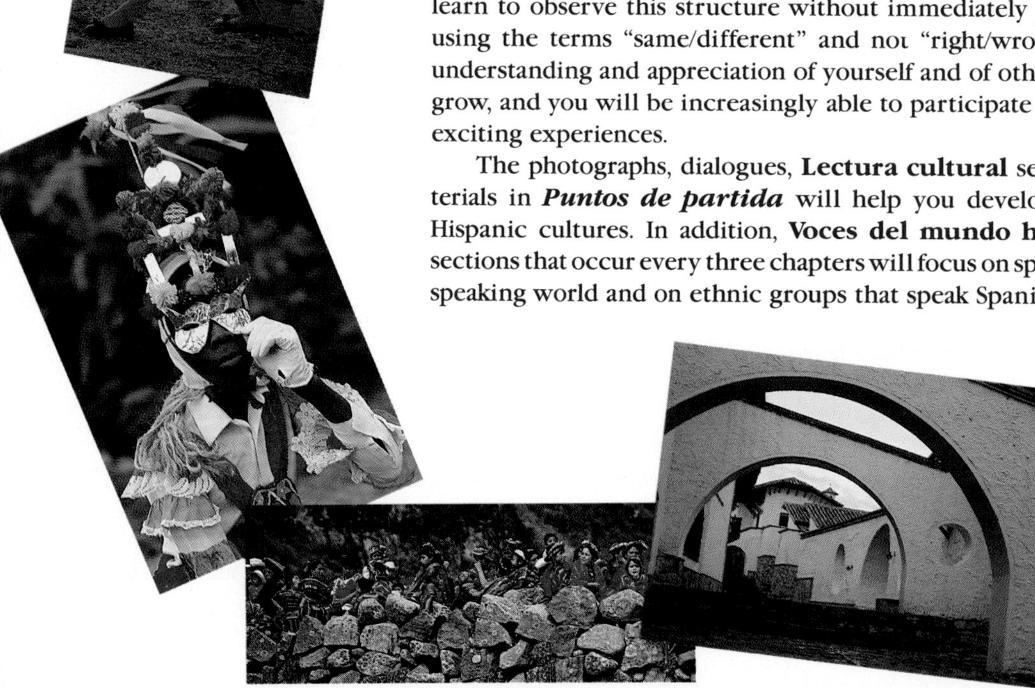

(*from top*) España, Panama, Guatemala, Colombia

CAPÍTULO UNO

EN LA UNIVERSIDAD

UNAM: Universidad Nacional Autónoma de México

▲ **En el *campus***

– Por favor, ¿dónde está el departamento de Historia?

– Está en el edificio Bolívar... allí mismo.[a]

– Gracias, ¿eh?

– De nada.

[a]allí... *right over there*

VOCABULARIO: PREPARACIÓN

• See also [video icon] and [audio icon]

Realia: See IM for suggestions and exercises for handling authentic materials that are not accompanied by exercises in the student text.

¿Dónde? La universidad

la biblioteca	the library	**la librería**	the bookstore
la clase	the class	**la oficina**	the office
el edificio	the building	**la residencia**	the dormitory

¿Qué? Cosas

el bolígrafo	the pen	**el lápiz**	the pencil
la calculadora	the calculator	**el libro**	the book
el cuaderno	the notebook	**la mesa**	the table
el diccionario	the dictionary	**la mochila**	the backpack
el dinero	the money	**el papel**	the paper
el escritorio	the desk	**la silla**	the chair

¿Quién? Personas

el consejero	the (male) advisor	**el profesor**	the (male) professor
la consejera	the (female) advisor	**la profesora**	the (female) professor
el estudiante	the (male) student	**el secretario**	the (male) secretary
la estudiante	the (female) student	**la secretaria**	the (female) secretary

Vocabulario: Preparación:
- See detailed supplementary materials and exercises for this section bound into the back of this Annotated Instructor's Edition.
- See model for vocabulary presentation and other materials in Supplementary *Vocabulario: Preparación* Materials, chapter by chapter, IM.

Point out A: Use of *están* for location

A. **¿Dónde están?** (*Where are they?*) Indique el edificio o lugar (*place*). Luego (*Then*) identifique las cosas y las personas usando las letras.

1. Están en _____.

_____ la profesora
_____ la estudiante
_____ el papel
_____ el lápiz
_____ el bolígrafo
_____ la mesa
_____ la silla
_____ la calculadora

2. Están en _____.

_____ el libro
_____ el diccionario
_____ el cuaderno
_____ el bolígrafo
_____ la mesa
_____ el estudiante
_____ la silla

Variation A: *¿Qué hay en ___?* Students identify persons and objects, using short complete sentences: *Hay una profesora, Hay un... .* Present *el → un, la → una* before doing variation.

Variation A: Students tell where objects and persons are, using short complete sentences: *El estudiante está en la biblioteca.*

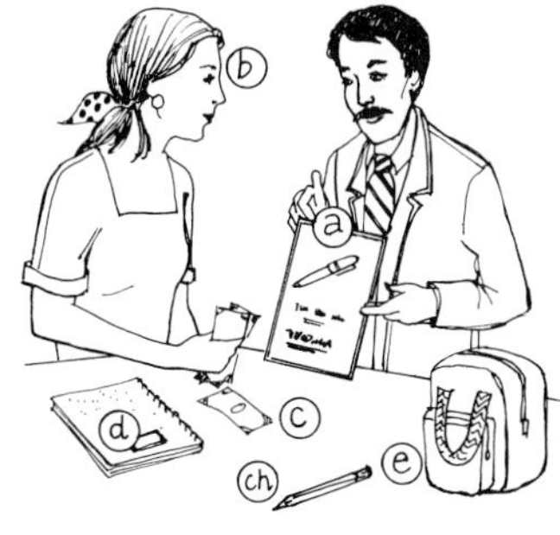

3. Están en ___.

___ la estudiante ___ el bolígrafo
___ el lápiz ___ el dinero
___ el cuaderno ___ la mochila

4. Están en ___.

___ la secretaria
___ la consejera
___ el profesor
___ el escritorio
___ el diccionario

Follow-up B: Students give male counterpart of *La profesora, la secretaria, la estudiante, la consejera;* female counterpart of *el profesor, el secretario, el consejero, el estudiante.*

B. **Identificaciones.** ¿Es hombre o mujer (*man or woman*)?

MODELO: ¿La consejera? → Es mujer.

1. ¿El profesor? 2. ¿La estudiante? 3. ¿El secretario? 4. ¿El estudiante?

Las materias

las ciencias	the sciences	**la historia**	history
el comercio	business	**el inglés**	English
la computación	computer science	**las matemáticas**	mathematics
el español	Spanish	**la sicología**	psychology

Note A: Introduction of *para* = intended for. Uses of *por* and *para* are introduced gradually throughout the text, then summed up in Ch. 19.

Extension A:
- Optional *materias* work well here.
- Hold up students' books; they identify books by course, as in model.
- Additional titles: *Introducción a Pascal, La revolución de los zares, Mein Kampf, La familia, Cómo usar el telescopio, Los microbios.*

Suggestions B:
- Model names of academic subjects, especially if you haven't introduced optional *Más materias.*
- Encourage students to listen to what others say and use ___ *estudia* ___ to repeat what they have heard.

A. Identifique los libros.

MODELO: *Los insectos de Norteamérica* →
Es para (*for*) una clase de ciencias.

1. *El cálculo 1*
2. *Romeo y Julieta*
3. *México en crisis*
4. *Programación básica*
5. *Skinner y Freud*
6. *Don Quijote*
7. *Análisis crítico de la economía mexicana*
8. *La caída* (fall) *del imperio romano*

B. **¿Qué estudias?** (*What are you studying?*) The right-hand column lists a number of university subjects. Tell about your academic interests by

Optional B: Students play role of *consejero/a* advising incoming freshmen on what to study, depending on their majors. Follow these models: *Usted necesita estudiar* ____. *Usted necesita tomar* ____ *créditos de* ____. Sample majors: *un estudiante de inglés, un estudiante de biología, un estudiante de ciencias políticas, un estudiante de francés*

creating sentences using one word or phrase from each column. You will be telling what you study, want to study, need to study, and like to study.

(No) Estudio ____.	español, francés, inglés
(No) Deseo estudiar ____.	arte, filosofía, literatura, música
(No) Necesito estudiar ____.	ciencias políticas, historia, sicología, sociología
(No) Me gusta estudiar ____.	biología, física, química
	comercio, matemáticas, computación

Note C: Introduction of subject pronouns *él* and *ella*. If students do not use these pronouns in their answers, rephrase answers with the pronouns.

Suggestion C: If students do not spontaneously recall the subjects studied by others, expand your cues by adding subjects: *¿Y Ted? ¿Estudia literatura?*, etc.

Follow-up: Have students practice the chapter-opener dialogue, using the names of *materias* they have learned in this section and the names of real buildings on your campus.

C. **¿Qué estudian los otros?** (*What are others studying?*) As you listened while other students described their academic interests in Exercise B, you learned a lot about what they are studying, want to study, and so on. How much do you remember? When your instructor asks about people in the class, give as much information as you can recall, following these models.

MODELOS: —¿Qué estudia Jorge?
—Él estudia historia.*
—¿Y Paula?
—Ella desea estudiar computación.* Necesita estudiar ciencias.

When information is given about you, be sure it is correct.

MODELO: —¿Y Ted?
—Él estudia literatura.
—¿Yo?† No estudio literatura. Estudio programación.

Realia: See IM for suggestions and exercises for handling authentic materials that are not accompanied by exercises in the student text.

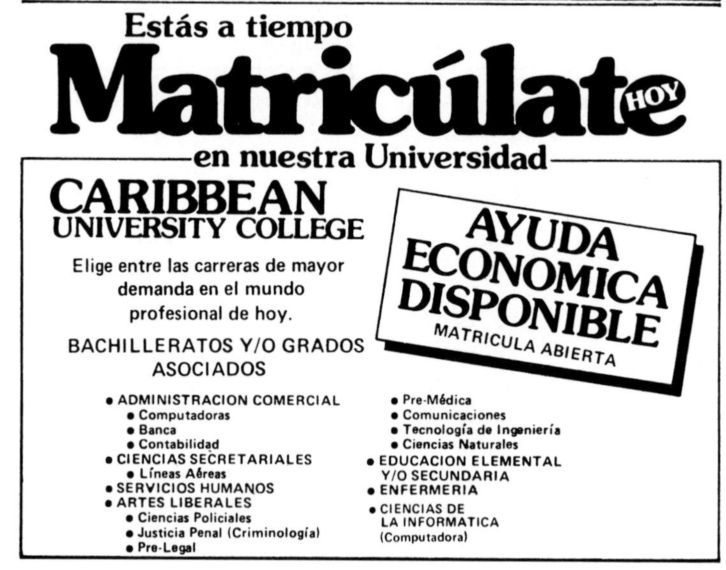

*Note the use of the words **él** (*he*) and **ella** (*she*) for emphasis in these sentences.
†Note that Spanish uses **¿Yo** (*I*)? in this context to express English (*Who*) *Me?*

Study Hint: Learning New Vocabulary

Vocabulary is one of the most important tools for successful communication in a foreign language. What does it mean to "know vocabulary"? And what is the best way to learn vocabulary?

1. Memorization is only part of the learning process. Using new vocabulary to communicate requires practicing that vocabulary in context. What do you associate with this word? When might you want to use it? Create a context—a place, a situation, a person, or a group of people—for the vocabulary that you want to learn or use a context from the text. The more associations you make with the word, the easier it will be to remember. Practice useful words and phrases over and over—thinking about their meaning—until you can produce them automatically. You may find it useful to "talk to yourself," actually saying aloud the words you want to learn.
2. Carefully study the words in vocabulary lists and drawings. If a word is a cognate or shares a root with an English word, be especially aware of differences in spelling and pronunciation. For example, note that **clase** is spelled with only one **s**; that there is no *th* in **matemáticas**; and that **ciencias** does not begin with an **s**. Keep in mind that an "almost but not quite perfect" spelling may lead to a miscommunication: **el libro** (*the book*) versus **la libra** (*the pound*); **la mesa** (*the table*) versus **el mes** (*the month*); **el consejero** (*male advisor*) versus **la consejera** (*female advisor*). You also need to remember which words require **el** and which require **la** to express *the,* as well as which words require a written accent—**el lápiz**, **el bolígrafo**, for example—and where the accent occurs.
3. After studying the list or drawing, cover the English and give the English equivalent of each Spanish word.
4. When you are able to give the English without hesitation and without error, reverse the procedure; cover the Spanish and give the Spanish equivalent of each English word. Write out the Spanish words (using **el** or **la** where appropriate) once or several times and say them aloud.
5. Vocabulary lists and flash cards can be useful as a review or as a self-test.

Point out in Study Hint: (1) A good knowledge of vocabulary can help compensate for grammatical errors when attempting communication in Spanish. **(2)** However, one must know both vocabulary and grammar in order to communicate effectively.

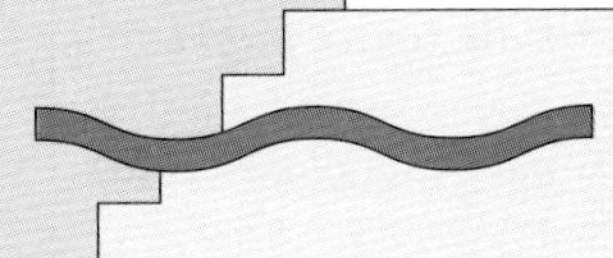

PRONUNCIACIÓN: DIPHTHONGS AND LINKING

Point out: Letter *y* pronounced like vowel *i* when standing alone (*y* = and) or when ending a word (*¡ay!*, *hay*).

Note: Hint for remembering weak vowels: *U* and *I* are weak.

Suggestion A: Review pronunciation of single vowel sounds before beginning exercise.

***¡OJO!* A:** *Hombre* should not be pronounced as *hambre* (hunger); *dólares* should not sound like *dolores* (pains).

Two successive weak vowels (**i, u**) or a combination of a strong vowel (**a, e,** or **o**) and a weak vowel (**i** or **u**) are pronounced as a single syllable, forming a *diphthong* (**un diptongo**): **L*ui*s**, **s*ie*te**, **l*ue*go**.

When words are combined to form phrases, clauses, and sentences, they are linked together in pronunciation. In spoken Spanish, it is usually impossible to hear the word boundaries—that is, where one word ends and another begins.

A. Más práctica con las vocales.

1.	hablar	pagar	cantar	trabajar
2.	trece	clase	papel	general
3.	dinero	oficina	bolígrafo	libro
4.	hombre	profesor	dólares	los
5.	universidad	gusto	lugar	mujer

Follow-up: Students sound out vowels and diphthongs first; then add consonant sounds: **1.** *la civilización india* **2.** *los negocios internacionales* **3.** *una bibliotecaria* (librarian) *italiana* **4.** *una especialidad fascinante* **5.** *los tiempos verbales*

Extension C: **9.** *Hay siete edificios en la universidad.* **10.** *Estudio historia y comercio.* **11.** *Deseo estudiar computación y matemáticas.* **12.** *Necesito un diccionario y una mochila.*

B. Practique las siguientes palabras.

1.	historia	secretaria	gracias	estudiante	materia
2.	bien	Oviedo	siete	ciencias	diez
3.	secretario	biblioteca	adiós	diccionario	Antonio
4.	cuaderno	Eduardo	el Ecuador	Guatemala	Managua
5.	bueno	nueve	luego	pueblo	Venezuela

C. Practice saying each phrase as if it were one long word, pronounced without a pause.

1. el papel y el lápiz
2. la profesora y la estudiante
3. las ciencias y las matemáticas
4. la historia y la sicología
5. la secretaria y el profesor
6. el inglés y el español
7. la clase en la biblioteca
8. el libro en la librería

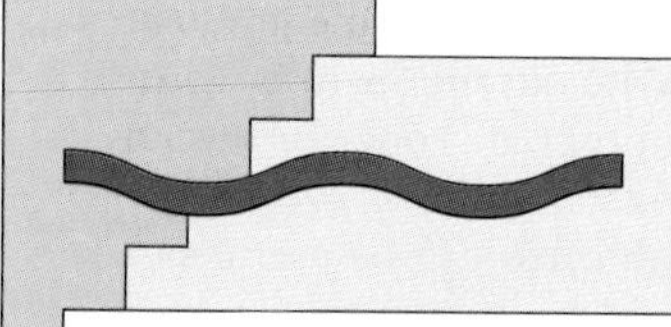

MINIDIÁLOGOS Y GRAMÁTICA

Communicative objectives for Grammar Sections 1 and 2: how to name persons, places, and things around you

En *la clase*: *el primer día*

PROFESORA: ... y para *mañana,* es necesario traer *los libros* de texto, *papel, un cuaderno* y *un diccionario.*

ANA: Perdón, *profesora,* pero... ¿ya están *los libros* para esta *clase* en *la librería*?

PROFESORA: Creo que sí.

ANA: ¿Y *diccionarios*?

PROFESORA: ¿No hay en *la librería*?

PEDRO: Sí, hay... pero *el problema* es *el precio.*

Note: Minidialogue introduces material from *both* Grammar Sections 1 and 2. Continue to use previous guidelines for presentation of minidialogues.

Follow-up (discussion): **1.** *¿Dónde están las personas del diálogo?* **2.** *¿Quiénes son?* **3.** *¿Qué estudian en esta clase?* **4.** *¿Hay profesor o profesora en esta clase?* **5.** *¿Cuántos estudiantes hay en la clase en total? ¿más o menos?*

Complete las oraciones lógicamente.

1. Para mañana es necesario traer _____.
2. En la librería hay _____.
3. El problema con (*with*) los diccionarios es _____.

Follow-up (personalization): Use comprehension questions as basis for forming personalized questions.

In class: the first day INSTRUCTOR: . . . and for tomorrow, it's necessary to bring the textbooks, paper, a notebook, and a dictionary. ANA: Pardon me, ma'am [professor], but . . . are the books for this class in the bookstore already? INSTRUCTOR: I think so. ANA: And (what about) dictionaries? INSTRUCTOR: Aren't there any in the bookstore? PEDRO: Yes, there are . . . but the problem is the price.

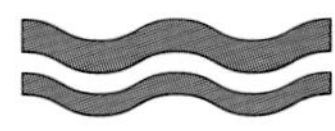

1. IDENTIFYING PEOPLE AND THINGS
Singular Nouns: Gender and Articles*

To name persons, places, things, or ideas, you need to be able to use nouns. In Spanish, all *nouns* (**los sustantivos**) have either masculine or feminine *gender* (**el género**). This is a purely grammatical feature of nouns; it does not mean that Spanish speakers perceive things or ideas as having male or female attributes.

Note: Spanish equivalents for English grammatical terms will be given throughout this text.

	MASCULINE NOUNS	FEMININE NOUNS
DEFINITE ARTICLES	**el** hombre *the man* **el** libro *the book*	**la** mujer *the woman* **la** mesa *the table*
INDEFINITE ARTICLES	**un** hombre *a (one) man* **un** libro *a (one) book*	**una** mujer *a (one) woman* **una** mesa *a (one) table*

A. Nouns that refer to male beings and most nouns that end in **-o** are *masculine* (**masculino**) in gender: **hombre**, **libro**.

Nouns that refer to female beings and most nouns that end in **-a**, **-ción**, **-tad**, and **-dad** are *feminine* (**femenino**): **mujer**, **mesa**, **nación** (*nation*), **libertad** (*liberty*), **universidad**.

¡OJO! A common exception is the word **día**, which ends in **-a** but is masculine in gender: **el día**. Many words ending in **-ma** are also masculine: **el problema**, **el programa**, **el drama**, and so on.

Optional with *¡OJO!*
- Also explain that *-pa* and *-ta* words are masculine: *el mapa*, *el cometa*, *el planeta*, *el poeta*. They are of Greek origin.
- ***la** persona*

Nouns that have other endings and that do not refer to either males or females may be masculine or feminine. Their gender must be memorized: **el lápiz**, **la clase**, **la tarde**, **la noche**, and so on.

B. In English, *the* is the *definite article* (**el artículo definido**). In Spanish, the definite article for masculine singular nouns is **el**; for feminine singular nouns it is **la**.

C. In English, the singular *indefinite article* (**el artículo indefinido**) is *a* or *an*. In Spanish, the indefinite article, like the definite article, must agree with the gender of the noun: **un** for masculine nouns, **una** for feminine nouns. **Un** and **una** can also mean *one* as well as *a* or *an*. Context determines the meaning.

Point out C: This "matching" (masculine singular article with masculine singular noun, feminine with feminine) is called agreement (*la concordancia*).

Point out C: Context often serves same function in English: for example, word *will*. Will you do it? vs. In his will he left everything to his mother.

[Práctica A–B]†

*The grammar sections of ***Puntos de partida*** are numbered consecutively throughout the book. If you need to review a particular grammar point, the index will refer you to its page number.

†This type of reference is a regular feature of some grammar sections of ***Puntos de partida***. This reference means that you are now prepared to do exercises A and B in the **Práctica** section.

CH. Some nouns that refer to persons indicate gender according to the following patterns:

Optional CH: *el/la decano* (dean)

Note CH: Many Spanish speakers use *cliente/clienta.*

If the masculine ends in **-o**, the feminine ends in **-a**:

el niño *the boy* → **la** niña *the girl*
el amigo *the (male) friend* → **la** amiga *the (female) friend*

If the masculine ends in a consonant, the feminine has a final **-a**:

un profesor *a (male) professor* → **una** profesora *a (female) professor*

Many other nouns that refer to people have a single form. Gender is indicated by the article: **el estudiante**, **la estudiante**; **el cliente** (*the male client*), **la cliente** (*the female client*). A few nouns that end in **-e** have a feminine form that ends in **-a**: **el dependiente** (*the male clerk*), **la dependienta** (*the female clerk*).

D. Since the gender of all nouns must be memorized, it is best to learn the definite article along with the noun; that is, learn **el lápiz** rather than just **lápiz**. The definite article will be given with nouns in vocabulary lists in this book.

[Conversación]*

Práctica

Follow-up A: *Cambie* (Change): *artículo definido → artículo indefinido*
artículo indefinido → artículo definido.
1. *el diccionario* **2.** *la librería* **3.** *el profesor* **4.** *la residencia* **5.** *el bolígrafo* **6.** *el consejero* **7.** *la ciencia* **8.** *el edificio* **9.** *la mesa* **10.** *el lápiz* **11.** *una silla* **12.** *una residencia* **13.** *un cliente* **14.** *un estudiante* **15.** *una oficina* **16.** *una biblioteca* **17.** *un secretario* **18.** *una clase* **19.** *una mochila* **20.** *un escritorio*

Variation B:
Modelo: *El estudiante está en la librería.*

A. Dé el artículo definido (**el**, **la**).

1. escritorio
2. biblioteca
3. bolígrafo
4. mochila
5. hombre
6. diccionario
7. universidad
8. dinero
9. mujer
10. nación
11. secretario
12. calculadora

Dé el artículo indefinido (**un**, **una**).

13. día
14. mañana
15. problema
16. lápiz
17. clase
18. noche
19. papel
20. condición
21. programa

B. **Escenas de la universidad.** Haga una oración con las palabras (*words*) indicadas. Luego haga otra oración lógica, cambiando (*changing*) el lugar.

MODELO: estudiante / librería → Hay un estudiante en la librería.
Hay un estudiante en la residencia.

1. consejero / oficina
2. profesora / clase
3. lápiz / mesa
4. cuaderno / escritorio
5. libro / mochila
6. bolígrafo / silla
7. palabra / papel
8. oficina / biblioteca

*You are now prepared to do **Conversación**.

Conversación

Point out A: The indefinite article is not used with professions.

Suggestion A: Use as cues place and person names from your campus and city.

A. **¿Quién es?** Give the male or female counterpart of each of the following persons.

MODELO: Pablo Ortiz es consejero. (Paula Delibes) →
Paula Delibes es consejera también.

1. Camilo es estudiante. (Conchita)
2. Carmen Leal es profesora. (Carlos Ortega)
3. Juan Luis es dependiente. (Juanita)
4. Josefina es mi amiga. (José)

Now identify as many people as you can in your class and on your campus.

Emphasis B: ***la** persona*

Extension B: **7** *¿la librería?* **8.** *¿el profesor?* **9.** *¿la historia?*

Optional Extension B: Present *una cosa/un objeto* as category. Items: **10.** *¿el cuaderno?* **11.** *¿el libro?* **12.** *¿el bolígrafo?*

Suggestion B: Use as cues place and person names from your campus and city.

B. **Definiciones.** Con un compañero (una compañera), defina estas palabras en español según el modelo.

MODELO: biblioteca / edificio → —¿La biblioteca?
—Es un edificio.

1. cliente / persona
2. inglés / materia
3. residencia / edificio
4. dependiente / ¿ ?
5. hotel (*m.*) / ¿ ?
6. comercio / ¿ ?
7. ¿ ? / ¿ ?

Notas comunicativas: Working with a Partner

As you have already seen, many of the exercises and activities in ***Puntos de partida*** work well with a classmate. It is likely that you did the preceding partner activity with the person sitting next to you. This time, when your instructor says **Busque un compañero**, find a different partner. Here are some phrases to use.

—¿Tienes compañero?	—*Do you have a partner?*
—Todavía no.	—*Not yet.*
—¿Deseas / —¿Te gustaría } trabajar conmigo?	—*Do you want / —Would you like } to work with me?*
—Sí, cómo no.	—*Yes, of course.*

You and your partner will probably feel comfortable talking at a distance of two or three feet from each other. If you were native speakers of Spanish, you would probably stand closer together. Spanish speakers generally maintain less distance between themselves and the person to whom they are speaking, often as little as 12 to 16 inches.

Emphasis (Working with a Partner): Have students work with a variety of partners rather than constantly working with the person who sits next to them. Doing this is one way to ensure that a real "information gap" exists in partner/pair exercises; that is, students really do need to ask the question to find the information.

Follow-up C: Have several students report back the information they have learned. You will need to present the following model: *A* __*nombre*__ *(no) le gusta... Le gusta...*

C. **Entrevista. ¿Te gusta... ?** Find out whether a classmate likes the following things. Remember to use the definite article.

MODELO: comida (*food*) en la residencia →
—¿Te gusta **la** comida en la residencia?
—Sí, me gusta. (No, no me gusta.)

1. comida en la residencia (en la cafetería, en...)
2. clase de español (de historia, de...)
3. programa *General Hospital* (*All My Children, . . .*)
4. drama *Dallas* (*L.A. Law, . . .*)

2. IDENTIFYING PEOPLE AND THINGS
Nouns and Articles: Plural Forms

Suggestion: Review minidialogue that precedes Grammar Section 1 before presenting material in this section.

CLASES-LECCIONES

SE DAN clases de Peluqueria. Plazas limitadas, matrículas gratuitas 100%. Prácticas reales de 3 a 7 en la c/ Antonio Susillo, 25.

● **DOY** clases, de parapsicología y control mental, experiencia, alto nivel. **27 21 25**

● **UNIVERSITARIO,** daría clases particulares EGB, BUP **36 30 07** y F.P.

● **ESTUDIANTE** universitario, daría clases particulares EGB, horas comidas. José **21 77 25** Luis.

● **DARIA** clases de inglés, profesor titulado con experiencia. De 2 a 5 h. **63 55 98**

● **ESTUDIANTE** Filologia, da clases de inglés, 250 ptas/h. Experiencia. Traduccio- **41 59 91** nes.

● **ESTUDIANTE** de COU, se ofrece para dar clases. EGB y **61 50 02** BUP. Barato.

● **CLASES** de Astrologia. **62 55 52**

● **SE DAN** clases de sevillanas y palillos. **51 50 35 - 76 15 01**

● **PARA** chicos/as de EGB. Clases particulares. Exito **45 33 04** seguro.

● **SE DAN** clases de Francés, con 22 años de expe- **57 12 16** riencia.

● **PROFESOR** EGB daria clases particulares. Econó- **64 11 10** mico.

● **DOY CLASES** a domicilio de EGB, mañanas y tardes. **41 86 90**

● **PROFESOR** titulado da clases de guitarra clásica en mi domicilio. Sector Macare- **38 35 25** na.

● **ESTUDIANTE** de Filología da clases de inglés, 250 ptas/h. Experiencia. También **41 59 91** traducciones.

● **SE DAN** clases particulares zona Nervión desde 225 ptas/H a 400 ptas/h. EGB y BUP. Especialidad en Cien- **63 14 60** cias.

● **PROFESOR** titulado da clases de inglés, BUP y COU. Experiencia. Economía. De 3 **41 90 56** a 5 horas.

● **DOY** clases de inglés a nivel de EGB y 1° de BUP. Sábados por la mañana, 500 pts. Grupos reducidos. Est- **62 66 25** her. De 3 a 6 h.

● **PROFESOR** de informática daría clases particulares. **43 26 53**

● **ESTUDIANTE** de Empresariales da clases de Matemáticas hasta 3° de BUP. **21 75 95** Pedro.

● **PROFESORA** de EGB daría clases particulares. **35 93 11**

● **PROFESOR** titulado nativo con experiencia. **63 55 98**

Realia: See IM for suggestions and exercises for handling authentic materials that are not accompanied by exercises in the student text.

	SINGULAR	PLURAL	
NOUNS ENDING IN A VOWEL	**el** libro **la** mesa **un** libro **una** mesa	**los** libros **las** mesas **unos** libros **unas** mesas	*the books* *the tables* *some books* *some tables*
NOUNS ENDING IN A CONSONANT	**la** universidad **un** papel	**las** universidad**es** **unos** papel**es**	*the universities* *some papers*

A. Spanish nouns that end in a vowel form plurals by adding **-s**. Nouns that end in a consonant add **-es**. Nouns that end in the consonant change the **-z** to **-c** before adding **-es**: **lápiz** → **lápices**.

B. The definite and indefinite articles also have plural forms: **el** → **los**, **la** → **las**, **un** → **unos**, **una** → **unas**. **Unos** and **unas** mean *some, several,* or *a few.*

C. In Spanish, the masculine plural form of a noun is used to refer to a group that includes both males and females.

los amigos	*the friends* (both male and female)
unos extranjer**os**	*some foreigners* (males and females)

Optional: Stress does not shift when plurals are formed. Pronunciation pattern of singular form is maintained. Since word stress and accentuation have not yet been formally presented, you might wait until Ch. 2 to discuss addition/deletion of accent marks in plurals.

Emphasis C: Even if group includes only one male (example: 1 male, 1,000 females), masculine plural form will be used.

Práctica

Preliminary Exercise (listening): *¿Singular o plural?* 1. *el diccionario* 2. *la librería* 3. *los papeles* 4. *el lápiz* 5. *unos bolígrafos* 6. *las clases* 7. *una profesora* 8. *las universidades*

A. Dé la forma plural.

1. la mesa
2. el libro
3. el amigo
4. la oficina
5. un cuaderno
6. un lápiz
7. una extranjera
8. un bolígrafo
9. un edificio

Dé la forma singular.

10. los profesores
11. las calculadoras
12. las niñas
13. los lápices
14. unos papeles
15. unas tardes
16. unas residencias
17. unas sillas
18. unos escritorios

Extension B: 4. *la Srta. Rodríguez: estudiante, mujer, amigo, consejera* 5. *Ana y Teresa: amigas, estudiantes, profesores, hombres* 6. *el Sr. García: hombre, profesora, amigo, secretario*

Follow-up B: Give plurals. 1. *Juana, una niña; Juana y Elena...* 2. *Ramón, un extranjero; Ramón y Ricardo...* 3. *Ramón, un extranjero; Ramón y Raquel...* 4. *David, un amigo; David y Cecilia...* 5. *David, un amigo; David y Robert...*

B. **Identificaciones.** Which of the words listed to the right might be used to refer to the person(s) named on the left?

1. Ana María: consejero mujer dependiente estudiante
2. Tomás: niño consejera profesor secretaria
3. Margarita y Juan: extranjeros amigos hombres estudiantes

C. **¿Cómo se dice en español?** Express in Spanish these phrases that describe people and buildings that you might see on your campus.

1. the (male and female) students
2. some dormitories
3. a (female) clerk in the bookstore
4. the foreigners
5. the (male) secretaries
6. some (female) professors

Conversación

Suggestion A: Use questions *¿Quién es?* (*¿Quiénes son?*) and *¿Dónde está(n)?* to elicit more conversation from students.

A. Identifique las personas, las cosas y los lugares.

MODELO: Hay _____ en _____. → Hay unos estudiantes en la clase.

Extension B: *¿Qué hay en nuestra* (our) (*sala de*) *clase?*

B. ¿Qué hay en el cuarto (*room*) de Ernesto? Use el artículo indefinido.

MODELOS: Hay _____ en el cuarto de Ernesto.
En el escritorio hay _____ .

¿Qué hay en su propio (*your own*) cuarto?

MODELOS: Hay _____ en mi cuarto.
En mi escritorio hay _____.

Preparation C: Do as whole-class activity: What things do you associate with... *una oficina típica de la universidad. ¿Qué hay en una clase que no hay en una oficina?*

Suggestion C: Introduce *muchos/muchas* and encourage students to use them in answers, in preparation for the introduction of gender agreement with adjectives in Ch. 2.

Palabras útiles: la computadora, la máquina de escribir (*typewriter*), la cama (*bed*), la lámpara

Optional C: Students work in groups, then compare answers to see which group came up with the greatest number of items in each category. Give a time limit of 5 minutes for the group work.

C. Working with your classmates, give as many nouns as you can that fit into these categories. Before you begin, you may wish to review the cognates presented in the explanations and exercises in **Ante todo.**

1. lugares de la universidad
2. cosas en una librería
3. personas en una librería
4. cosas en una clase típica
5. problemas de los estudiantes

Communicative objectives for 3: how to use words other than names to refer to people; first step in learning how to talk about actions and activities.

Note: Minidialogue introduces material from both major sections of Grammar Section 3. You may prefer to focus on subject pronouns alone before introducing the minidialogue. Continue to use previous guidelines for mini presentation.

3. EXPRESSING ACTIONS
Subject Pronouns, Present Tense of *-ar* Verbs, Negation

Una fiesta para los estudiantes extranjeros

CARLOS: ¿No *desean* Uds. *bailar*?
ALFONSO: ¡Cómo no! Yo *bailo* con Mary. Ella *habla* inglés.
TERESA: Yo *hablo* francés y *bailo* con Jacques.
CARLOS: Y yo *bailo* con Gretchen.
GRETCHEN: Sólo si *pagas* las cervezas. ¡*Bailas* muy mal!

Who made—or might have made—each of the following statements?

1. Yo bailo con Jacques.
2. Yo hablo inglés.
3. Yo hablo alemán (*German*).
4. Nosotros (*We*) hablamos francés.
5. Yo bailo con Alfonso.
6. ¡Yo no bailo mal!

Follow-up (listening): Ask students if these statements are true for them (*¿sí o no?*): **1.** *Yo hablo francés* (*inglés*). **2.** *Nosotros hablamos español* (*francés*) *en esta clase.* (**Suggestion:** introduce *un poco.*) **3.** *Nosotros bailamos en esta clase.* **4.** *Yo bailo muy mal* (*muy bien*).

In **Ante todo** and the first pages of **Capítulo 1**, you have already used a number of Spanish verbs—and some subject pronouns—to talk about actions and states of being. In this section you will learn more words for expressing actions.

Follow-up: Personalized completion: 1. *Yo hablo _____ y bailo con _____.* **2.** *¡Bailo muy _____!*

A party for foreign students CARLOS: Don't you want to dance? ALFONSO: Of course! I'll dance with Mary. She speaks English. TERESA: I speak French and I'll dance with Jacques. CARLOS: And I'll dance with Gretchen. GRETCHEN: Only if you buy (pay for) the beers! You dance very badly!

Suggestion: Review what students already know about informal/formal usages by asking them to address these questions to either you or another student, as appropriate. 1. *¡Hola! ¿Qué tal?* 2. *Buenas tardes. ¿Cómo está?* 3. *¿Le gusta la universidad?* 4. *¿Te gusta la clase de español?* 5. *¿Cómo se llama usted?* 6. *¿Cómo te llamas?*

hablar (*to speak*): **habl-**					
SINGULAR			PLURAL		
(*I*)	yo	habl**o**	(*we*)	nosotros / nosotras	habl**amos**
(*you*)	tú	habl**as**	(*you*)	vosotros / vosotras	habl**áis**
(*you*) / (*he*) / (*she*)	usted (Ud.)* / él / ella	habl**a**	(*you*) / (*they*)	ustedes (Uds.)* / ellos / ellas	habl**an**

Optional:

- The subject (*el sujeto*) of a sentence is the word or group of words about which something is said or asserted. Usually the subject indicates who or what performs the action of the sentence: The girl threw the ball.
- Have students indicate the subjects in the following sentences: 1. Olga is going to write the letter. 2. The car ran off the road. 3. Have Jack and Joyce arrived yet? 4. Love conquers all.
- A pronoun (*un pronombre*) is a word used in place of a noun: She [the girl] threw the ball.
- Students indicate the English pronouns to use in place of the subjects in the preceding four sentences.

Subject Pronouns

The preceding chart shows a number of Spanish subject pronouns you already know (**yo**, **tú**, **usted**, **él**, **ella**) with the corresponding forms of **hablar**. Here are some additional comments about these *pronouns* (**los pronombres**).

- Several subject pronouns have masculine and feminine forms: **nosotros**, **nosotras** (*we*); **vosotros**, **vosotras** (*you*); **ellos**, **ellas** (*they*). The masculine plural form is used to refer to a group of males as well as to a group of males and females.
- Spanish has two different words for *you* (singular): **tú** and **usted**. **Usted** is generally used to address persons with whom the speaker has a formal relationship. Use **usted** with people whom you call by their title and last name (**Sr. Gutiérrez**, **profesora Hernández**), or with people you don't know very well. Students generally address their instructors with **usted**. In some parts of the Spanish-speaking world, children use **usted** with their parents.

  Tú implies a familiar relationship. Use **tú** when you would address a person by his or her first name, with close friends or relatives, and with children and pets. Students usually address each other as **tú**. If you are unsure about whether to use **tú** or **usted**, it is better to use **usted**. The native speaker can always suggest that you use **tú** if that form is more appropriate.
- The plural of **usted** is **ustedes**. In Latin America, as well as in the United States, **ustedes** also serves as the plural of **tú**. In Spain, however, the plural of **tú** is **vosotros/vosotras**, which is used when speaking to two or more persons whom you would call **tú** individually.

Subject pronouns are not used as frequently in Spanish as they are in English. You will learn more about the uses of Spanish subject pronouns in **Capítulo 3**.

Suggestion: Teach singular pronouns first. Emphasize difference between *tú* and *Ud.*, explaining that the kind of relationship between two people determines the form they will use.

Note: No Spanish equivalent for *it* as subject.

Note: *Vosotros* will only be used actively as last item in mechanical exercises.

Preliminary exercises (subject pronouns):
A. What subject pronoun would you use to speak *about* the following persons? 1. yourself 2. two men 3. a female child 4. yourself (*m.*) and a female friend 5. yourself (*f.*) and a female friend

*__Usted__ and **ustedes** are frequently abbreviated in writing as **Ud.** or **Vd.**, and **Uds.** or **Vds.**, respectively. ***Puntos de partida*** will use **Ud.** and **Uds.**

¿Que... *What the devil is that?* / vos-tú en la Argentina y el Uruguay
¿Comprendes?

6. your uncle Jorge 7. your aunts Ana and Elena
B. What subject pronoun would you use to speak *to* the following persons? 1. *una profesora* 2. *unos consejeros* 3. *un niño* 4. *unas amigas* 5. *un dependiente* 6. *un estudiante* 7. *mamá*
C. What subject pronoun would you *substitute* for each of the following persons? 1. *Eva* 2. *Luis* 3. *Fausto y yo* (*m.*) 4. *tú* (*m.*) *y Cecilia* 5. *Vicente y David* 6. *Graciela y yo* (*f.*).

Suggestion C4: Use item to focus on difference between usage in Spain and in Latin America.

Infinitives and Personal Endings

A. The *infinitive* (**el infinitivo**) of a verb indicates the action or state of being, with no reference to who or what performs the action or when it is done (present, past, or future). In English the infinitive is indicated by *to*: ***to** run*, ***to** be*. In Spanish all infinitives end in **-ar**, **-er**, or **-ir**.

B. To *conjugate* (**conjugar**) a verb means to give the various forms of the verb with their corresponding subjects: *I speak, you speak, he* (*she, it*) *speaks,* and so on. All regular Spanish verbs are conjugated by adding *personal endings* (**las terminaciones personales**) that reflect the subject doing the action. These are added to the *stem* (**la raíz** or **el radical**): the infinitive minus the infinitive ending (**habl~~ar~~ → habl-**). These personal endings are added to the stem of all regular **-ar** verbs: **-o**, **-as**, **-a**, **-amos**, **-áis**, **-an**.

Point out B: The English present tense is relatively easy for Spanish speakers to learn, since the conjugated forms of the regular verbs do not vary a great deal. In fact, there are only two forms—for example, *speak* and *speaks*. (Compare with the six Spanish present tense forms of *hablar*.)

C. Some important **-ar** verbs in this chapter include:

bailar	to dance	**hablar**	to speak; to talk
buscar	to look for	**necesitar**	to need
cantar	to sing	**pagar**	to pay (for)
comprar	to buy	**practicar**	to practice
desear	to want	**regresar**	to return (*to a place*)
enseñar	to teach	**tomar**	to take; to drink
estudiar	to study	**trabajar**	to work

¡OJO! In Spanish the meaning of the English word *for* is included in the verbs **pagar** (*to pay for*) and **buscar** (*to look for*).

Suggestions:
- Model pronunciation of each infinitive several times. Then use *yo* form of each in brief, simple sentence about yourself, repeating several times (pantomiming as appropriate). Transform base sentence into simple *Ud.* question directed to a student, "coaching" him/her to answer using *yo* form. Example: *bailar... bailar... Me gusta bailar. Bailo muy bien... Bailo muy bien. Y Ud., ¿baila bien?*
- After going through infinitive list, ask students to generate all forms of *bailar*; write on board. It may help to write subject pronouns on board first and then put verb forms in appropriate slots.
- Ask: *¿Cómo se dice?* I/we dance; I/we sing; I/we buy; he teaches/they teach; he studies/they study; she/they pay; she returns/they return.

CH. As in English, when two Spanish verbs are used in sequence and there is no change of subject, the second verb is usually in the infinitive form.

Necesito **trabajar**.	*I need to work.*
También desean **bailar**.	*They want to dance, too.*

Optional verbs: *besar, caminar, escuchar, fumar, hablar por teléfono, mirar* (*la televisión*), *tocar*

English Equivalents for Present Tense

Point out: Use of present-tense questions to indicate near-future actions: *¿Hablo con Juan mañana?* (Will I speak to Juan tomorrow?).

Point out: *por la noche* vs. *de la noche* (used when hour is specified). Note introduction of this use of *por*.

In both English and Spanish, conjugated verb forms also indicate the *time* or *tense* (**el tiempo**) of the action: *I speak* (present), *I spoke* (past).

The present tense forms of Spanish verbs correspond to four English equivalents.

hablo	*I speak*	Simple present tense
	I am speaking	Present progressive to indicate an action in progress
	I do speak	Emphatic present to give special emphasis
	I will speak	Near future action

Preliminary exercises:
- **Oral Rapid Response Drill:** Give corresponding forms.
  yo: bailar, estudiar, trabajar, necesitar
  tú: buscar, hablar, pagar, tomar
  Ud./él/ella: cantar, necesitar, regresar, enseñar
  nosotros: comprar, pagar, estudiar, buscar
  vosotros: desear, regresar, cantar, bailar
  Uds./ellos/ellas: practicar, tomar, desear, comprar
- **Listening Exercise:** Give corresponding subject pronouns: *enseño, cantamos, estudian, paga, trabajan, desear, buscas, compra, habláis, regresas, bailan, tomo, necesitamos.*
- **Pattern Practice:** Explain its purpose (see Teaching Techniques: Drills, IM) and how you want students to do it.
  En la clase de español
  1. *—Ud. estudia mucho.* (*nosotros, yo, ellos, Juan, tú, vosotras*)
  2. *—Sara necesita un diccionario.* (*yo, Carlos y tú, tú, nosotras, Ada, vosotros*)

Note that another word or phrase may indicate future time when the present is used to describe near future actions.

Hablo con Juan **mañana**. — *I'll speak with John tomorrow.*
¿Estudiamos **por la noche**? — *Shall we study at night?*

Negation

Emphasis: Double use of *no*, second *no* being equivalent of English *not* with verb (we do not need)

A Spanish sentence is made negative by placing the word **no** before the conjugated verb. No equivalent for the English words *do* or *does* in negative sentences exists.

El señor **no** habla inglés. — *The man doesn't speak English.*
No, **no** necesitamos dinero. — *No, we don't need money.*

En una fiesta en la residencia
1. *—Clara toma Coca-Cola.* (*tú, Ud., él, Uds., Elena y yo, vosotras*)
2. *—Tú cantas y bailas.* (*nosotros, los amigos, Uds., Eva y Diego, yo, vosotros*)
Optional base sentences for each situation: ***En la clase de español:*** *Los estudiantes practican el español.* ***En una fiesta en la residencia:*** *Hablo con unos amigos.*

Note *Práctica* Section: There is more emphasis on *tú* forms in the exercises and activities of Grammar Section 4.

Suggestion A: Explain that this type of exercise is called a "dehydrated sentence." Explain its purpose (see Teaching Techniques: Drills, IM).

Emphasis A: Nonuse of subject pronouns in parentheses.

Práctica 

A. **Mis compañeros y yo.** Form complete sentences about yourself, your classmates, and your professor, based on the cues given. When the subject pronoun is given in parentheses, do not use it in the sentence. If any statement is not true for you or your class, make it negative or change it to make it correct.

1. (yo) necesitar / dinero
2. (nosotros) cantar / en francés
3. (nosotros) desear / practicar el español
4. (yo) trabajar / en la biblioteca
5. profesor(a), Ud. enseñar / muy bien
6. (nosotros) tomar / cerveza en clase
7. (yo) tomar / ocho clases este semestre
8. profesor(a), Ud. hablar / muy bien el alemán

Suggestion B: Have students scan through the paragraph for meaning before they attempt to do the items.

B. **En la residencia.** Complete the following paragraph with the correct form of the infinitives.

Esta noche° hay una fiesta en el cuarto de Marcos y Julio. Todos° los estudiantes (*cantar*[1]) y (*bailar*[2]). Jaime (*buscar*[3]) una Coca-Cola. Marta (*hablar*[4]) con un amigo. María José (*desear*[5]) enseñarles a todos° un baile° de Colombia. Todas las estudiantes desean (*bailar*[6]) con el estudiante mexicano—¡él (*bailar*[7]) muy bien! La fiesta es estupenda, pero todos (*necesitar*[8]) regresar a casa° o a sus° cuartos temprano.° ¡Hay clases mañana!

Esta... *Tonight* / *All*

enseñarles... *to teach everyone* / *dance*

a... *home* / *their* / *early*

After individual items are done, have one student read through the entire paragraph. Then do the comprehension questions.

Tell whether these statements are true (**cierto**) or false (**falso**), based on information in the paragraph.

1. Marcos es un profesor de español.
2. A Jaime le gusta la cerveza.
3. María José es de Colombia.
4. A los estudiantes les gustan las fiestas.

Note (comprehension): The majority of the items in exercises of this kind are inferential; that is, students need to apply their knowledge of the paragraph to the individual items in order to decide if an item is *cierto o falso*. Suggestion: Ask students to explain their answers in simple sentences. Example: 1. *Falso. Marcos está en la residencia con los estudiantes.* It is "OK" for students to disagree about and discuss items of this kind. For example, another student may say: *¡Sí! Hay profesores en las fiestas de los estudiantes.* and so on.

Optional Follow-up to *Práctica* section: Do orally or as dictation.

Cambie por el plural. **1.** *Él no desea tomar una cerveza.* **2.** *Ud. baila con un estudiante.* **3.** *¿Compro el lápiz mañana?* **4.** *Hablas con la dependienta.* **5.** *¿Hay sólo una extranjera en la clase?*

Conversación

A. Form complete sentences by using one word or phrase from each column. The words and phrases may be used more than once, in many combinations. Be sure to use the correct form of the verbs. Make any of the sentences negative, if necessary.

Cambie por el singular. **6.** *Ellas no busca* *dinero.* **7.** *¿Enseñan Uds. sólo dos clase* *español?* **8.** *Necesitamos unos libros de* **9.** *Las mujeres estudian sicología.* **10.** *¿* *Uds. sólo treinta pesos?*

MODELO: Yo no estudio francés.

yo
(estudiante), tú
nosotros (los miembros de esta clase)
los estudiantes de aquí (*here*)
el extranjero

un secretario
un profesor de español
un dependiente

(no)
comprar
regresar
buscar
trabajar
hablar
enseñar
pagar
tomar
estudiar

desear
necesitar

el edificio de ciencias
en la cafetería, en la universidad
en una oficina, en una librería
a casa por la noche
a la biblioteca a las dos
francés
bien el español
los libros de texto con un cheque
libros y cuadernos en la librería

tomar una clase de computación
hablar bien el español
estudiar más (*more*)
comprar una calculadora, una mochila
pagar la matrícula (*tuition*) en septiembre

Point out A: This kind of exercise is called a "sentence builder." Each subject and verb can be used with more than one item from right-hand column—many sentences are possible. The use of *no* is optional. Emphasize that forms of *desear* and *necesitar* must be followed by an infinitive.

B. Tell where these people are (using **está** or **están**) and what they are doing. Note that the definite article is used with titles—**el señor, la señora, la señorita, el profesor, la profesora**—when you are talking about a person.

Emphasis B: Use of definite article with title when talking about persons, as in *El Sr. Ramírez habla español.* Contrast with *Bueños días, Sr. Ramírez.* No article is used when speaking directly to a person.

Variation B: Using *¿quién(es)?*, ask questions based on drawings: *¿Quién busca el libro?*, etc. Students respond with name of person only.

Emphasis C4: *Uds.* + verb becomes *nosotros* + verb. Parallels English usage: you (all) becomes we. Additional similar items: *¿Qué estudian Uds. en esta* (this) *clase? ¿Qué lengua hablan en clase? ¿Hablan inglés en la clase de español? ¿Desean hablar español muy bien?*

Variation C: In pairs or small groups, students ask each other questions. If you use this technique, review intonation with question words; briefly present intonation for yes-no questions (in next grammar section).

Follow-up activity C: Ask representative question of several individual students; then ask them to report answers to others. Example: *Juan, ¿Ana estudia mucho o poco?* → *Ana estudia mucho.*

Extension C: *¿Quién enseña la clase mañana? ¿los estudiantes? ¿la consejera? ¿el presidente de la universidad? ¿el presidente de México?*

Optional exercises:

- Complete *las oraciones lógicamente.* **1.** *Deseo bailar con* _____, *pero no* _____. **2.** *En clase (no) hay* _____. **3.** *En clase necesitamos* _____. **4.** *En clase no deseamos* _____. **5.** *En la librería busco* _____ *y también* _____. **6.** *Regreso a* _____ *todos los días.* **7.** *(No) Deseo hablar con* _____. **8.** *Profesor(a), Ud. necesita* _____.
- Make the following statements. If students believe you, they respond with *Es verdad.* If they think you are lying, they say *Es falso.* **1.** *Hablo español, inglés y francés.* **2.** *Bailo muy bien.* **3.** *No regreso a casa hoy.* **4.** *Por la noche, enseño a estudiantes extranjeros.* Encourage students to make up original statements of their own to say to class.

MODELO: La Sra. Martínez _____. →
La señora Martínez está en la oficina. Busca un libro, trabaja...

1. Los estudiantes extranjeros _____.

2. La cliente _____.

3. La profesora Gil _____.

4. Los amigos _____.

5. El Sr. Miranda _____.

6. Los estudiantes _____.

C. **Preguntas**

1. ¿Ud. estudia mucho o poco? ¿Dónde estudia, en casa (*at home*), en la residencia o en la biblioteca? ¿Cuándo estudia, por la tarde o por la noche? ¿Con quién practica español? ¿Con quién desea practicar?
2. Preguntas «indiscretas»: ¿Canta Ud. muy bien o muy mal? ¿Baila muy bien o muy mal? ¿Toma mucho o poco? ¿Regresa a casa tarde (*late*) o temprano?
3. En una fiesta, ¿qué *no* desean Uds. hacer (*to do*)? ¿Desean estudiar? ¿cantar? ¿trabajar? ¿bailar con el profesor (la profesora)?
4. ¿Cuántas lenguas habla el profesor (la profesora)? ¿Qué lenguas enseña? ¿Trabaja en una oficina de la universidad? ¿Enseña por la mañana o por la tarde?
5. ¿Quién paga la matrícula, los estudiantes o los profesores? ¿Qué más necesitan pagar los estudiantes? ¿los libros de texto? ¿También necesitan comprar lápices? ¿diccionarios? ¿calculadoras?

Notas comunicativas: Expressing Preferences

In **Ante todo** you learned to combine the phrases **me gusta** and **te gusta** with infinitives to express what you like—or don't like—to do. In this chapter, you have seen that verbs like **desear** and **necesitar** can also be followed by infinitives. Here are two other verbs to express preferences that are followed by infinitives. Learn to use their **yo** forms now.

(no) quiero + *infinitive*	*I (don't) want to ...*
prefiero + *infinitive*	*I prefer to ...*
Quiero comprar una calculadora.	*I want to buy a calculator.*
Prefiero estudiar más tarde.	*I prefer to study later.*

Note (Expressing Preferences): Only the *yo* forms of *querer* and *preferir* are introduced here. There is no need to discuss the concept of stem-changing verbs at this time.

CH. **Gustos y preferencias.** Complete the following sentences by using infinitives you have learned plus any other necessary words. You may also wish to look back at the infinitives you used in the exercise on page 17 in **Ante todo** before you begin this exercise.

1. Prefiero _____ temprano. No me gusta _____ tarde.
2. No quiero _____ hoy. Prefiero _____.
3. Me gusta _____ los fines de semana (*weekends*), pero este (*this*) fin de semana necesito _____.
4. Quiero tomar _____ (materia), pero necesito tomar _____.
5. No quiero tomar más clases de _____ (materia).

Communicative objectives for 4: two more ways to ask questions of and get information from others.

4. GETTING INFORMATION
Asking Yes/No Questions

Follow-up activity: Students react (*¿sí o no?*) to the desirability of taking the following courses at the following times: *el inglés por la mañana/por la noche, el cálculo por la mañana/por la tarde, la sicología por la tarde/por la mañana, las ciencias por la noche.*

En una universidad: La oficina de matrícula

ESTUDIANTE: Necesito una clase más. *¿Hay sitio* en la clase de sicología 2?
CONSEJERO: Imposible, señorita. No hay.
ESTUDIANTE: *¿Hay un curso* de historia o de matemáticas?
CONSEJERO: Sólo por la noche. *¿Desea Ud. tomar* una clase por la noche?
ESTUDIANTE: Trabajo por la noche. Necesito una clase por la mañana.
CONSEJERO: Pues... ¿qué tal el francés 10? Hay una clase a las diez de la mañana.
ESTUDIANTE: *¿El francés 10?* Perfecto. Pero, *¿no necesito tomar* primero el francés 1?

At a university registration office STUDENT: I need one more class. Is there space in Psychology 2? COUNSELOR: Impossible, Miss. There's no room. STUDENT: Is there a history or math class? COUNSELOR: Only at night. Do you want to take a night course? STUDENT: I work at night. I need a class in the morning. COUNSELOR: Well . . . what about French 10? There's a class at 10 in the morning. STUDENT: French 10? Perfect. But don't I need to take French 1 first?

1. ¿Necesita la señorita dos clases más?
2. ¿Hay sitio en sicología 2?
3. ¿Hay cursos de historia o de matemáticas por la mañana?
4. ¿A qué hora es la clase de francés 10?
5. ¿Cuál es el problema con la clase de francés 10?

There are two kinds of questions: information questions and yes/no questions. Questions that ask for new information or facts that the speaker does not know often begin with *interrogative words* such as *who, what,* etc. (You learned many interrogative words in **Ante todo**.) *Yes/no questions* are those that permit a simple *yes* or *no* answer.

Preliminary exercise: Ask: Which of the following are yes-no questions? Which are information questions?
1. Do you dance well? **2.** Does she teach well? **3.** Where do you work? **4.** When do you study? **5.** Are you a student?

Do you speak French? → No, I don't (speak French).

Rising Intonation

A common way to form yes/no questions in Spanish is simply to make your voice rise at the end of the question.

Point out: English also puts a verb form in front of subject in forming yes-no questions. You work here. → Do you work here?

Statement

Ud. trabaja aquí todos los días.
You work here every day.

El niño regresa a casa hoy.
The boy is returning home today.

Question

¿Ud. trabaja aquí todos los días?
Do you work here every day?

¿El niño regresa a casa hoy?
Is the boy returning home today?

There is no Spanish equivalent to English *do* or *does* in questions. Note also the use of an inverted question mark (¿) at the beginning of a question.

Inversion

Another way to form yes/no questions is to invert the order of the subject and verb, in addition to making your voice rise at the end of the question.

Point out: If subject is very long, something else (adverb, object, prepositional phrase, etc.) may come between verb and subject. *¿Baila Ud. con Guillermo?* but *¿Baila con Guillermo la estudiante alemana?*

Statement: **Ud.** trabaja aquí todos los días. **El niño** regresa a casa hoy.

Question: ¿Trabaja **Ud.** aquí todos los días? ¿Regresa **el niño** a casa hoy?

Práctica

A. **En la librería (Parte 1).** With a classmate, look carefully at the following drawing. Then, as your classmate looks away from the drawing, ask him or her questions about it based on the following statements. Your classmate should try to answer without looking at the drawing.

Preliminary Listening Exercise: Statement or question? 1. ¿Regresa Ud. mañana? 2. Pepe necesita un bolígrafo. 3. ¿Hablamos bien? 4. ¿Bailas con Carmen? 5. Uds. estudian mucho. 6. ¿Desean regresar ahora?

Preliminary Speaking Exercise: Write sentences on board or on a transparency.
Forme dos preguntas, según el modelo.

Modelo: Irma habla español. →
¿Irma habla español?
¿Habla Irma español?
1. *Ud. regresa a clase mañana.* 2. *Elvira busca un cuaderno también.* 3. *Ramón toma café.* 4. *Ud. paga aquí.* 5. *Uds. estudian historia.* 6. *Ellos bailan todos los días.* 7. *Ella trabaja mañana.*

MODELO: El dependiente toma café. →
—¿El dependiente toma café? (¿Toma café el dependiente?)
—No. Ramón toma café.

1. Miguel habla con el dependiente.
2. Irma desea pagar la mochila.
3. Hildebrando busca un libro de historia.
4. Irma también busca un libro de historia.
5. Alicia estudia historia.
6. Ramón es una persona impaciente.
7. Hay tres dependientes en la librería hoy.

Suggestion A: Do as whole class activity before allowing students to work in pairs. After students have worked in pairs, ask for additional questions based on the drawing.

B. **En la librería (Parte 2).** Ask the questions that lead to the following answers you have just overheard. Follow the model.

MODELO: Sí, estudio con él (*him*). → ¿Estudia Ud. con Guillermo?
¿Estudias (tú) con Guillermo?

1. No, no trabajo aquí todos los días.
2. Sí, ella habla muy bien.
3. No, no regreso a casa hoy.
4. Sí, estudiamos mucho para esa (*that*) clase.
5. Sí, él busca un diccionario español-inglés.
6. No, no necesitamos lápiz.

Suggestion B: Point out to students that the answer and the question need not contain identical information. Note that *Guillermo* is replaced by *él* in the model. See how many different questions students can invent.

Conversación

Suggestion A, B: Point out to students that it is not necessary to use *tú* repeatedly in these questions. When students report back information to the class, they should not overuse *él* or *ella*.

A. **Entrevista.** Find out some information about a classmate, using the following cues as a guide.

1. estudiar en la biblioteca con frecuencia
2. practicar el español con un amigo
3. tomar café por la mañana

Situaciones

Follow-up activity A: Directed Dialogue (see Teaching Techniques: Drills, IM). *Pregúntele a (otro estudiante) si...* **1.** *regresa a casa hoy.* **2.** *necesita dinero.* **3.** *baila mucho.* **4.** *compra muchos libros.* **5.** *estudia sicología (cálculo).* **6.** *trabaja.* **7.** *desea hablar español.* **8.** *estudia en la biblioteca.*

4. bailar mucho en las fiestas
5. regresar a clase mañana
6. regresar a casa muy tarde a veces (*sometimes*)

Now find out the same information from your Spanish instructor. Begin each question with "**Profesor(a)** _____, ..." Remember to use **usted**.

Note B3: Provide students with model for sharing back information: *Le gusta más/menos la clase de...*

Suggestion B: Small group: Allow several minutes for students to interview each other. Ask them to report at least one thing they learned about another, or ask individual students specific questions, such as *David, ¿trabaja Luisa? ¿Dónde?*—or ask general questions (such as *¿Quién estudia matemáticas?*) so students can report information about others in class: *María estudia matemáticas.*

B. **Entrevista.** Without taking notes, interview a classmate by asking the following questions or any others that occur to you. Then present as much of the information as you can to the class.

MODELO: David toma cuatro clases. Prefiere la clase de literatura. Trabaja en McDonald's.

1. ¿Cuántas clases tomas este (*this*) semestre/trimestre?
2. ¿Estudias matemáticas? ¿literatura? ¿sicología? ¿química?
3. ¿Qué clase te gusta más? ¿Qué clase te gusta menos?
4. ¿Quieres estudiar ciencias naturales? ¿matemáticas? ¿comercio? ¿computación?
5. ¿Practicas español fuera de (*outside of*) la clase? ¿con quién?
6. ¿Trabajas? ¿Dónde? ¿Te gusta el trabajo (*job*)?

Bogotá, Colombia

Hablando (*Speaking*) de clases

—¿Cuántos estudiantes hay en tu (*your*) clase de física?
—Creo que hay quince o dieciséis.
—Y ¿quién es el profesor?
—La doctora Ortega.

SITUACIONES

Situaciones: See IM for suggestions, additional exercises, and supplementary dialogues and exercises.

En la biblioteca: Estudiando° con un amigo

—Oye,° ¿cuándo es tu clase de cálculo?
—A las once. ¿Qué hora es?
—Son las diez y veinte.
—Hay tiempo° todavía.° ¿No quieres estudiar diez minutos más?
—Está bien. Entonces,° ¿qué tal si tomamos un café antes de° tu clase?
—¡De acuerdo!

Studying / *Hey* / *time* / *still* / *Then* / antes... *before*

Notas comunicativas sobre el diálogo

To get a friend's attention: **Oye...**
To suggest activities to a friend:

¿Quieres... + *infinitive*
¿No quieres... + *infinitive*
¿Qué tal si + **nosotros** *verb form*

To express agreement or to accept an invitation.

Está bien.
De acuerdo.

Note (Notas comunicativas): Material in these boxes is not regarded as "active" material that students are expected to master. However, reference is made to these sections in the end-chapter vocabulary list for the first few chapters. You should make this material optional at your discretion.

Conversación

Practice the dialogue with a classmate. When you are familiar with it, vary some of the details:

- Mention a class you are taking this term.
- Give the time the class meets.
- Invite your friend to have a soft drink (**un refresco**) or an ice cream (**un helado**).

UN POCO DE TODO

Suggestion A: *biblioteca, clase (de ____), librería, oficina, residencia, cafetería, edificio de ciencias, centro de las computadoras, ...*

A. **Asociaciones.** Your instructor will name a place and a student will mention a noun at random. React by saying whether or not it is likely that the person or thing would be found in the place mentioned.

MODELOS: cafetería... exámenes... →
¡Imposible! (No. Creo que no.) No hay exámenes en la cafetería.
biblioteca... libros... →
Sí. (Creo que sí.) Hay libros en la biblioteca.

B. **Conversaciones en la cafetería.** Form complete questions based on the words given, in the order given. Conjugate the verbs and add other words if necessary. Do not use the subject pronouns in parentheses.

1. ¿buscar (tú) / diccionario?
2. ¿no trabajar / Paco / aquí / en / cafetería?
3. ¿necesitar / Uds. / calculadora / para / clase de cálculo?
4. ¿qué tal si / tomar (nosotros) / Coca-Cola?
5. ¿no desear (tú) / estudiar / minutos / más?

Now answer the questions in the negative, incorporating the following information into your responses.

1. mi mochila
2. biblioteca
3. química
4. no quiero / prefiero
5. quiero / regresar a casa

C. Describe the following persons by telling what they do and, if possible, where they do it.

1. un secretario
2. una profesora
3. un estudiante
4. una dependienta
5. Julio Iglesias
6. Madonna

CH. **Las actividades de la universidad.** Complete the following paragraphs from Tomás Gutiérrez's letter home from college. Give the correct form of the words in parentheses, as suggested by the context. When two possibilities are given in parentheses, select the correct word.

... Tomo cinco materias, y la que° más° (*me/te*[1]) gusta es (*el/la*[2]) español. Todos (*los/las*[3]) días estudio español con Jaime y Luisa. Nosotros (*practicar*[4]) el vocabulario y (*el/la*[5]) pronunciación y hablamos con Micaela, (*un/una*[6]) estudiante de Buenos Aires. Ella (*hablar*[7]) español más rápido que° nosotros. Micaela, Jaime, Luisa y yo también (*cantar*[8]). Yo (*cantar*[9]) muy mal, pero Jaime y Micaela (*cantar*[10]) bien.

la... *the one / most*
más... *faster than*

En este momento° estoy° en la cafetería. A (*los/las*[11]) tres y media quiero regresar a (*una/la*[12]) biblioteca para estudiar. Necesito (*buscar*[13]) un libro para (*el/la*[14]) clase de sicología. Prefiero no (*comprar*[15]) más° libros, si no es necesario.

En... *Right now / I am*
any more

Este° fin de semana hay (*un/una*[16]) fiesta en la residencia. Los estudiantes de (*el/la*[17]) universidad trabajan mucho, pero sólo cinco días por° semana. ¡(*Los/Las*[18]) fines de semana son para divertirse°!

This
per / to have a good time

With which of these statements would Tomás's parents agree after reading his letter? Change incorrect statements to make them true.

1. Los amigos de Tomás son todos de habla inglesa (*English-speaking*).
2. Tomás prefiere la clase de español.
3. No estudia con frecuencia.

VOCABULARIO

Point out: Re-entry of words learned in fixed expressions in *Ante todo* or used passively as cognates.

VERBOS

bailar to dance
buscar to look for
cantar to sing
comprar to buy
desear to want
enseñar to teach
estudiar to study
hablar to speak; to talk
necesitar to need
pagar to pay (for)
practicar to practice
regresar to return
  regresar a casa to go home
tomar to take; to drink
trabajar to work

LUGARES

la biblioteca library
la clase class
el cuarto room
el edificio building
la fiesta party
la librería bookstore
la oficina office
la residencia dormitory
la universidad university

PERSONAS

el/la amigo/a friend
el/la consejero/a advisor
el/la dependiente/a clerk
el/la estudiante student
el/la extranjero/a foreigner
el hombre man
la mujer woman
el/la niño/a boy/girl
el/la profesor (a) professor
el/la secretario/a secretary

MATERIAS Y CURSOS

el alemán German (language)
las ciencias sciences
el comercio business
la computación computer science
el español Spanish (language)
el francés French (language)
la historia history
el inglés English (language)
las matemáticas mathematics
la sicología psychology

COSAS

el bolígrafo pen
la calculadora calculator
el cuaderno notebook
el diccionario dictionary
el dinero money
el escritorio desk
el lápiz (*pl.* **lápices**) pencil
el libro (de texto) (text)book
la mesa table
la mochila backpack
el papel paper
la silla chair

OTROS SUSTANTIVOS

la cerveza beer
el día day
la matrícula registration fees

¿CUÁNDO?

con frecuencia frequently
el fin de semana (on) the weekend
tarde/temprano late/early
por la mañana (tarde, noche) in the morning (afternoon, evening)
todos los días every day

PALABRAS ADICIONALES

aquí here
con with
luego then, next
mal badly
más more
mucho much, a lot
muy very
para (intended) for; in order to
pero but
poco little; a little bit
pues... well . . .
si if
sólo only

Frases útiles para la comunicación

creo que sí (no)	I think so (*don't think so*)
(no) quiero + *infinitive*	I want (*don't want*) to (*do something*)
prefiero + *infinitive*	I prefer to (*do something*)

See also the words and phrases in **Notas comunicativas sobre el diálogo.**

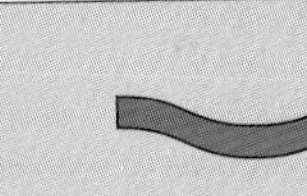

UN PASO MÁS 1

This and all subsequent *Un paso más* sections are optional.

Suggestion A (first part): Give more place names than listed in text, adding *en la librería*, *en la clase de* (*historia*), and local place names that students know.

Actividad A. ¿Qué pasa y dónde?

Suggestion A (with visual):
- Cover material in *A propósito...* before having students work with drawing.
- Students work in pairs. One describes drawing; other (with book closed) writes down information he/she hears. When finished, they compare written sentences to drawing to see how accurately drawing was described and how accurately description was "received."

***Mafalda:* Conversation Questions:** *¿Dónde están las personas? ¿Qué hay en la clase?*

Tell what you and your friends do in each of the following places. Use the verbs you have already learned plus some of those listed here.

mirar (películas, la televisión)	to watch (movies, TV)
escuchar (música, discos, cintas)	to listen to (music, records, tapes)
fumar	to smoke
descansar	to rest
tocar (la guitarra, el piano)	to play (the guitar, the piano)

1. en la biblioteca
2. en una fiesta
3. en casa por la noche
4. en casa durante las vacaciones
5. en el laboratorio de lenguas
6. en un bar estudiantil
7. en el pasillo (*hallway*) antes de (*before*) clase
8. en ¿?

Now tell what is happening in the following scene. Use complete sentences and describe as many details as possible so that a person who has not seen it could visualize it.

MODELO: Dos personas, un hombre y una mujer, bailan.

Actividad B. Las correcciones de la profesora

¿Qué hace Mafalda, recita o escucha? ¿Qué hacen los otros estudiantes? La clase de Mafalda, ¿es como nuestra clase? ¿Recitan Uds. muchos verbos? ¿Necesitan Uds. recitar como Mafalda?

As Professor Jiménez corrects the compositions of her first-year Spanish students, she finds that the following pairs of sentences are all grammatically correct, but they could be combined. Consider the probable relationship between the two sentences and, using the words given in **A propósito...** , combine them as you think she might.

Yo... *I trust*
Qué... *How gullible can you get?*

Suggestions B:
- Ask students to create items similar to those in text and present them orally.
- Student A creates sentence about someone or something; student B follows with connector and his or her own ending for sentence. This might best be done in writing, with students writing first part of sentence and exchanging papers.

1. Hans habla alemán. Estudia inglés.
2. Gina habla italiano y francés. No habla español.
3. Necesitamos comprar un diccionario. Buscamos una librería.
4. Marta estudia ciencias. Necesita estudiar matemáticas.
5. Julio canta mal. Baila bien.
6. Ellos estudian el capítulo uno. Nosotros estudiamos el capítulo dos.
7. Delia necesita pagar la matrícula. Trabaja todas las tardes.

Now use the same connecting words to add a comment about yourself to each of the following sentences.

8. Muchos estudiantes no desean estudiar lenguas.
9. Los éstudiantes de Harvard pagan mucho de matrícula.
10. Mi amigo (amiga) toma mucha cerveza.
11. En una clase típica de español, hay muchos estudiantes.
12. Algunos (*Some*) estudiantes necesitan tomar cursos de ciencias.

A propósito... : Using Linking Words

When you first begin to study Spanish, you may think that you can speak only in very simple sentences because your knowledge of Spanish vocabulary and grammar seems limited. The following words can help you to form more interesting sentences by linking together two or more words, phrases, or short sentences.

y and **también** also **pero** but **por eso** therefore

Note the different impression made by the following sentences.

- María enseña inglés. Estudia francés. → María enseña inglés **y** (**pero**) estudia francés.
- Pepe canta bien. José canta mal. → Pepe canta bien **pero** José canta mal.
- No bailo bien. No bailo esta noche (*tonight*). → No bailo bien; **por eso** no bailo esta noche.

La Universidad de Salamanca data del año 1220. Es una de las más antiguas universidades de España.

Notas culturales: The Hispanic Educational System

The educational system in Hispanic countries differs considerably from that of the United States. The **escuela primaria**—sometimes called the **colegio**—corresponds to our elementary school and consists of from five to seven years of instruction. The **escuela secundaria** (also called **liceo**, **instituto**, or **colegio**) provides secondary education. Students who complete their secondary education receive the **bachillerato**. In some countries, students attend an additional year or two of **preparatorio** before entering the university.

At the university, students immediately begin specialized programs leading to a professional degree (**título**) in areas such as law, medicine, engineering, or the humanities. These university-level programs of study are established by ministries of education, and there are almost no electives. Students are required to take as many as eight different subjects in a single academic term. The lecture system is even more prevalent than it is in the United States, and university students take oral exams as well as written ones. In most countries, performance is evaluated on a scale of one to ten, with seven considered passing.

A number of universities in Spain and Latin America have arranged special courses for foreign students (**cursos para extranjeros**). Such courses are designed for students whose special interest is the study of Spanish language, literature, and culture.

Point out C: Academic year does not begin until October in many parts of the world.

Suggestion C: Model Spanish words in matching exercise before asking students to do activity.

▲ Actividad C. Cursos para extranjeros

The **Universidad de Salamanca** is an old and famous Spanish university. In addition to its regular course of studies for native students, it offers a number of **cursos para extranjeros**.

Acompañar 3 fotografías tamaño pasaporte

Por favor, escriba con letra de imprenta

Cursos Internacionales de Verano - Universidad de Salamanca

HOJA DE INSCRIPCION

Apellido (Nom, last name)

Nombre (Prénom, first name)

Nacionalidad

Lugar de nacimiento

Fecha de nacimiento: Día | Mes | Año

Dirección actual (Present adress)

Residencia habitual (Home adress)

Profesión (Ocupation)

ENVIESE ESTA HOJA DE INSCRIPCION A (SEND THIS APPLICATION TO): **CURSOS INTERNACIONALES DE VERANO. PATIO DE ESCUELAS MENORES. UNIVERSIDAD DE SALAMANCA**

CURSOS OFRECIDOS (1)

	Julio	Agosto
I. Curso de lengua y cultura españolas:		
a) Iniciación		
b) Medio		
c) Superior		
II. Curso intensivo de lengua española:		
a) Iniciación		
b) Medio		
c) Superior		
III. Curso Superior de filologia:		

INSCRIPCIONES OPCIONALES

	Colegio	Familia	No desea
¿Alojamiento?[1]			
¿Abono piscina?[2]			
¿Seguro médico?[2]			
¿Actividades culturales?[2]			
¿Clases de guitarra?[2]			
¿Bailes regionales?[2]			
¿Ha asistido a los Cursos de esta Universidad en años anteriores?			

(1) Ponga una cruz en el recuadro que convenga (Write an X in the apropiate box)
(2) Póngase SI o NO en el recuadro correspondiente. (Write in SI or NO in the corresponding box)

By looking at the form from the **Universidad de Salamanca**, match these English words with their Spanish equivalents.

1. size
2. please print
3. nationality
4. place of birth
5. month
6. beginning/elementary level
7. intermediate level
8. advanced level
9. lodging (note: here, **colegio** = *dormitory*)
10. medical insurance

a. alojamiento
b. nacionalidad
c. tamaño
ch. Por favor, escriba con letra de imprenta
d. iniciación
e. mes
f. superior
g. seguro médico
h. medio
i. lugar de nacimiento

Now ask another student for the required information. You don't need to ask complicated questions. To find out the other student's last name, simply ask, **¿Apellido?** using the rising intonation that tells the listener that you are asking a question.

LECTURA CULTURAL

Lectura: See IM for suggestions and additional exercises and activities.

Antes de leer: More on Guessing Meaning from Context

As you learned in **El mundo hispánico** (**Ante todo**), you can often guess the meaning of unfamiliar words from the context (the words that surround them) and by using your knowledge about the topic in general. Making "educated guesses" about words in this way will be an important part of your reading skills in Spanish.

What is the meaning of the underlined words in these sentences?

1. En una lista alfabetizada, la palabra **grande** aparece antes de la palabra **grotesco**.
2. El edificio no es moderno; es viejo.
3. Me gusta estudiar español, pero detesto la biología. En general, odio las ciencias como materia.

Some words are underlined in the following reading (and in the readings in subsequent chapters). Try to guess their meaning from context.

Las universidades hispánicas

En el mundo hispánico—y en los Estados Unidos—hay universidades grandes y pequeñas, públicas, religiosas y privadas, modernas y antiguas. Pero el concepto de «vida° universitaria» es diferente.

Por ejemplo, en los países° hispánicos la universidad no es un centro de actividad social. No hay muchas residencias estudiantiles. En general, los estudiantes viven en pensiones* o en casas particulares° y llegan a la universidad en coche o en autobús. En algunas° universidades hay un *campus* similar a los de° las universidades de los Estados Unidos. En estos casos se habla° de la «ciudad° universitaria». Otras universidades ocupan sólo un edificio grande, o posiblemente varios edificios, pero no hay zonas verdes.

Otra diferencia es que en la mayoría° de las universidades hispánicas no se da° mucha importancia a los deportes. Si los estudiantes desean practicar un deporte—el tenis, el fútbol° o el béisbol—hay clubes deportivos pero éstos° no forman parte de la universidad.

Como se puede ver,° la forma y la organización de la universidad son diferentes en las dos

life
naciones
private / unas
los... *those of* / se... *one speaks*
city
majority / se... *is given*
soccer
they (lit. *these*)
Como... *As you can see*

*A **pensión** is a boarding house where students rent bedrooms and share a common bathroom with other boarders. Many students take their meals at the **pensión** as well.

culturas. Pero los estudiantes estudian y se divierten° en todas partes.° A los estudiantes hispanos—así como° a los norteamericanos—les gusta mucho toda clase de música: la música moderna, la nacional° y la importada (y hay para todos: Madonna, Durán-Durán, Ray Charles...), la música clásica y la música con raíces° tradicionales. Otras diversiones preferidas por los estudiantes son las discotecas y los cafés. Hay cafés ideales para hablar con los amigos. También hay exposiciones de arte, obras de teatro y películas° interesantes.

Los días favoritos de muchos jóvenes° hispánicos son los fines de semana. ¿Realmente son muy distintos los estudiantes hispanos?

se... *have a good time* / en... *everywhere*
así... *like*
(*music*) *from their own country*
roots
movies
young people

Comprensión

¿Cierto o falso? Corrija (*Correct*) las oraciones falsas. Todas las oraciones se refieren a la vida universitaria y a los estudiantes hispánicos.

1. La vida universitaria es similar a la (*that*) de los Estados Unidos.
2. Hay pocas residencias para los estudiantes.
3. Una «ciudad universitaria» es una ciudad grande donde hay una universidad.
4. Siempre hay un equipo (*team*) de fútbol.
5. No hay interés en la música norteamericana.
6. Hay pocas diversiones culturales.

Para escribir

In this exercise, you will write a description of your own **vida universitaria**. First, answer the following questions in short but complete sentences.

1. ¿Es grande o pequeña la universidad? (Mi universidad...)
2. ¿Es pública or privada?
3. ¿Cuántas residencias hay en el *campus*?
4. En general, ¿viven los estudiantes en residencias, en apartamentos o con su (*their*) familia?
5. ¿Cuáles son los dos edificios más grandes (*biggest*)? ¿la biblioteca? ¿la administración? ¿el *student union*?
6. ¿Se da mucha importancia a los deportes? ¿a la música? ¿al teatro?
7. ¿Dónde vive Ud.? (Yo vivo...)
8. ¿Cómo llega Ud. al *campus*? ¿en coche o en autobús? ¿O camina Ud.? (*Or do you walk?*)
9. ¿En qué edificios del *campus* estudia Ud.?
10. ¿Qué materia le gusta más?

Now take your individual answers and form two coherent paragraphs (using items 1–6 and 7–10) with them. Use the words from **A propósito...** (page 56) to make your paragraphs flow smoothly.

CAPÍTULO DOS

LA FAMILIA

España

▲ Hablando[a] de la familia

—Tienes una familia muy grande. ¿Cuántos son?

—Bueno, tengo seis hermanas y un hermano.

—Y ¿cuántos primos?

—¡Uf! Tengo un montón. Más de veinte.

[a]*Speaking*

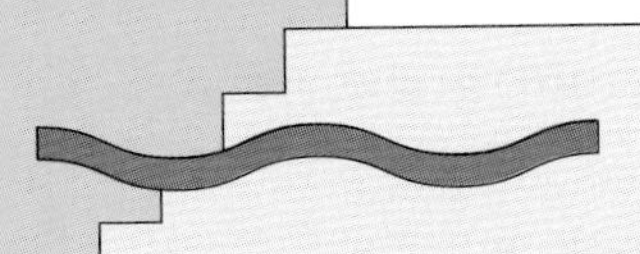

VOCABULARIO: PREPARACIÓN

• See also and

Vocabulario: Preparación:
• See detailed supplementary materials and exercises for this section bound into the back of this Annotated Instructor's Edition.

La familia y los parientes° *relatives*

la madre (mamá)	mother (mom)	**la nieta**	granddaughter
el padre (papá)	father (dad)	**el nieto**	grandson
la hija	daughter	**la prima**	cousin (female)
el hijo	son	**el primo**	cousin (male)
la hermana	sister	**la tía**	aunt
el hermano	brother	**el tío**	uncle
la esposa	wife	**la sobrina**	niece
el esposo	husband	**el sobrino**	nephew
la abuela	grandmother		
el abuelo	grandfather		

¡A EDUCAR TOCAN!

¿QUIEN PIENSA USTED QUE SE OCUPA MAS DE LA EDUCACION DE LOS HIJOS?

	%
El padre	2.8
La madre	41.5
Ambos, por igual	51.3
Ninguno	1.2
N.S./N.C.	3.2
	100.0

CUANDO HAY QUE HABLAR «SERIAMENTE» CON UN HIJO, ¿QUIEN LO HACE CON MAS FRECUENCIA?

	%
El padre	26.6
La madre	24.9
Ambos, por igual	42.2
Ninguno	0.9
N.S./N.C.	5.4
	100.0

• See model for vocabulary presentation and other materials in Supplementary *Vocabulario: Preparación* Materials, chapter by chapter, IM.

A. **Quiénes son?** (*Who are they?*)

los abuelos (*grandparents*)

los padres (*parents*)

los hijos (*children*)

Suggestion A: Focus on one family member and review his/her relationship to others in family: *¿Cómo se llama* (*¿Quién es*) *el padre de Juanito?*, etc.

Point out A: Use of diminutive. Similar to English John → Johnny and Ann → Annie.

Suggestion A: Students invent details about the family as you ask questions using *-ar* verbs from Ch. 1: *¿Quién trabaja? ¿Dónde trabaja ___? ¿A qué hora regresa a casa ___? ¿Qué lengua hablan? ¿Quiénes estudian en la escuela primaria? ¿Quién estudia en la universidad?*, etc.

Suggestion B: Do as listening comprehension exercise, or do as pair exercise.

B. ¿Cierto o falso? Corrija las oraciones falsas.

1. Juan es el hermano de Elena.
2. Josefina es la abuela de Elenita.
3. Carmencita es la sobrina de Joaquín.
4. Carmencita y Juanito son (*are*) primos.
5. Luis es el tío de Elenita.
6. Juanito es el sobrino de Juan.
7. Elena es la esposa de Luis.

C. **¿Quiénes son?** Identifique los miembros de cada (*each*) grupo, según el modelo.

MODELO: los hijos → el hijo y la hija

1. los abuelos
2. los padres
3. los hermanos
4. los nietos
5. los tíos
6. los sobrinos

Suggestion CH: Do as listening comprehension exercise, with students providing completion.

Follow-up: Imagine you are *Juanito* or *Elenita*. Identify members of your family, according to drawing on page 61. Then describe your family.

CH. **¿Quién es?** Complete las oraciones lógicamente.

1. La madre de mi* padre es mi _____.
2. El hijo de mi tío es mi _____.
3. La hermana de mi padre es mi _____.
4. El esposo de mi abuela es mi _____.

Ahora (*Now*) defina estas (*these*) personas, según el mismo (*same*) modelo.

5. prima 6. sobrino 7. tío 8. abuelo

Suggestion D: Model dialogue with several students before allowing the class to work in pairs. Model options for a small family.

D. **Entrevista.** With a classmate, discuss the members of your family, following the model of the photo caption on page 60. Use **tengo** (*I have*) and **tienes** (*you have*) as in the caption. Use **cuántos** before masculine nouns and **cuántas** before feminine nouns.

Adjetivos

guapo	handsome, good-looking	**listo**	smart, clever	**rico**	rich
bonito	pretty	**tonto**	silly, foolish	**pobre**	poor
feo	ugly				
		casado	married	**delgado**	thin, slender
corto	short (*length*)	**soltero**	single	**gordo**	fat
largo	long				
		simpático	nice, likeable		
bueno		**antipático**	unpleasant		
malo					

To describe a masculine singular noun, use **alto**, **bajo**, and so on; use **alt*a***, **baj*a***, and so on, for feminine singular nouns.

---

*Use **mi** to mean *my* with singular nouns and **mis** with plural ones. You will learn more about using words of this type in Grammar Section 14.

A. **Preguntas.** Conteste según los dibujos.

1. Einstein es listo. ¿Y el chimpancé?

2. Roberto es trabajador. ¿Y José?

3. Pepe es bajo. ¿Y Pablo?

4. El ángel es bueno y simpático. También es guapo. ¿Y el demonio?

5. Ramón Ramírez es casado. También es viejo. ¿Y Paco Pereda?

6. El libro es viejo y corto. ¿Y el lápiz?

7. Elena es gorda y morena. ¿Y Marta? (**¡OJO!**)

8. La familia Pérez es grande y rica. ¿Y la familia Gómez? (**¡OJO!**)

B. **¿Cómo son?** Your elderly uncle Guillermo is not familiar with these famous personalities. Describe them to him, using as many adjectives as possible. Don't forget to use cognate adjectives you have seen in **Ante todo** and in previous chapters.

1. Michael J. Fox 2. J. R. Ewing 3. la princesa Diana 4. Jane Fonda

***¡OJO!* A7 and 8:** These require production of female forms of adjectives.

Follow-up A: Name famous people or people in class. Students give adjectives they associate with each. Verify correct adjectives by repeating them in complete sentences (*Sí, Miss Piggy es bonita.*) and making adjectives agree where necessary.

Suggestions B:

- Additional names for expansion: Lucy, Charlie Brown, Snoopy (from Peanuts), Phyllis Diller, Ellie Ewing, George Burns, Michael Jackson, Dudley Moore, Joan Collins, Bo Dereck, Martina Navratilova, Elizabeth Taylor, Julio Iglesias, Sylvester Stallone, Madonna
- Students describe themselves.

Variation B: Give names of famous couples and partners who are complete opposites or exactly alike. Students describe them using *pero* and *también: Laurel y Hardy*, *Cagney y Lacey*, *Popeye y Olive Oyl*, *Archie e Edith Bunker*, etc.

Follow-up B (listening comprehension): Give brief (2–3 sentences) descriptions of famous personalities (orally, or as dictation). Students guess who is being described.

1. *Es actor; es rubio y muy guapo. No es muy alto, pero tampoco* (pantomime) *es muy bajo. En una película reciente, le gusta jugar al béisbol. También le interesa África.* (Robert Redford)
2. *Es profesor y también autor de varios libros sobre el universo. Es muy inteligente.* (Carl Sagan)
3. *Es gordo y viejo. Tiene muchos amigos pequeños. Es muy generoso en el mes de diciembre.* (Santa Claus)
4. *Es hispánico y es actor. Es muy moreno y es delgado. Es muy serio. Trabaja con dos detectives, en la Florida.* (James Edward Olmos)

Los números 31–100

En casa, por la noche

treinta y uno,
treinta y dos...
ochenta y cuatro,
ochenta y cinco...

Continúe la secuencia:

treinta y uno, treinta y dos...
ochenta y cuatro, ochenta y cinco...

31	treinta y uno	40	cuarenta
32	treinta y dos	50	cincuenta
33	treinta y tres	60	sesenta
34	treinta y cuatro	70	setenta
35	treinta y cinco	80	ochenta
36	treinta y seis	90	noventa
37	treinta y siete	100	cien, ciento
38	treinta y ocho		
39	treinta y nueve		

Beginning with 31, Spanish numbers are *not* written in a combined form; **treinta y uno**,* **cuarenta y dos**, **sesenta y tres**, and so on, must be three separate words. **Cien** is used before nouns and in counting.

cien casas	*a (one) hundred houses*
noventa y ocho, noventa y nueve, **cien**	*ninety-eight, ninety-nine, one hundred*

Follow-up A (listening): Which would you rather have? *¿25 dólares o 35 dólares? ¿100 dólares o 80 dólares? ¿67 pesos o 76 pesos? ¿84 pesos o 44 pesos?*, etc.

A. Más problemas de matemáticas

1. 30 + 50 = ?
2. 45 + 45 = ?
3. 32 + 58 = ?
4. 77 + 23 = ?
5. 100 − 40 = ?
6. 99 − 39 = ?
7. 84 − 34 = ?
8. 78 − 36 = ?
9. 88 − 28 = ?

Point out B: Two last names used in Mexican phone book. You may prefer to postpone any discussion of this topic until Ch. 4.

Follow-up B: Students practice asking for telephone numbers. Put model dialogue on board or on a transparency and use *La guía telefónica* as a guide.

Operador(a): *Información.* ***Turista:*** *El número de la familia* _____ *, por favor.* **O:** *Cómo no. ¿Dónde vive* (lives) *la familia?* **T:** *En la calle/avenida* _____ . **O:** *Muy bien, señor*(a) (*señorita*). *El número es el* _____-_____-_____-_____ . **T:** *Muchas gracias. También necesito el número de* _____. You should play role of *operador*(a) several times; then encourage students to work in pairs.

B. Telephone numbers in many countries are written and said slightly differently than in the United States. Here are parts of several pages from Hispanic telephone books. Do you notice anything different about the names? (The **Nota cultural** on the next page will give you information about them.) Following the model, give the phone numbers.

MODELO: 9-72-64-87 → nueve–setenta y dos–sesenta y cuatro–ochenta y siete.

---

*Remember that when **uno** is part of a compound number (**treinta y uno**, **cuarenta y uno**, and so on), it becomes **un** before a masculine noun and **una** before a feminine noun: **cincuenta y** ***una*** **mesas**; **setenta y** ***un*** **coches**.

LAZARO AGUIRRE, A. —Schez Pacheco, 17	415 0046
LAZCANO DEL MORAL, A. —E. Larreta, 14	215 8194
LAZCANO DEL MORAL, A. —Ibiza, 8	274 6868
LEAL ANTON, J. —Pozo, 8	222 3894
LIEBANA RODRIGUEZ, A. Guadarrama, 10	463 2593
LOPEZ BARTOLOME, J. —Palma, 69	232 2027
LOPEZ CABRA, J. —E. Solana, 118	407 5086
LOPEZ CABRA, J. —L. Van, 5	776 4602
LOPEZ GONZALEZ, J. A. —Ibiza, 27	409 2552
LOPEZ GUTIERREZ, G. —S. Cameros, 7	478 8494
LOPEZ LOPEZ, J. —Alamedilla, 21	227 3570
LOPEZ MARIN, V. —Illescas, 53	218 6630
LOPEZ MARIN, V. —N. Rey, 7	463 6873
LOPEZ MARIN, V. —Valmojado, 289	717 2823
LOPEZ NUÑEZ, J. —Pl. Pinazo, s/n	796 0035
LOPEZ NUÑEZ, J. —Rocafort, Bl. 321	796 5387
LOPEZ RODRIGUEZ, C. —Pl. Jesus, 7	429 3278
LOPEZ RODRIGUEZ, J. —Pl. Angel, 15	239 4323
LOPEZ RODRIGUEZ, M. E. B. Murillo, 104	233 4239
LOPEZ TRAPERO, A. —Cam. Ingenieros, 1	462 5392
LOPEZ VAZQUEZ, J. —A. Torrejón, 17	433 4646
LOPEZ VEGA, J. —M. Santa Ana, 5	231 2131
LORENTE VILLARREAL, G. —Gandia, 7	252 2758
LORENZO MARTINEZ, A. —Moscareta, 5	479 6282
LORENZO MARTINEZ, A. —P. Laborde, 21	778 2800
LORENZO MARTINEZ, A. Av. S. Diego, 116	477 1040
LOSADA MIRON, M. —Padilla, 31	276 9373
LOSADA MIRON, M. —Padilla, 31	431 7461
LOZANO GUILLEN, E. Juan H. Mendoza, 5	250 3884
LOZANO PIERA, F. J. —Pinguino, 8	466 3205
LUDEÑA FLORES, G. —Lope Rueda, 56	273 3735
LUENGO CHAMORRO, J. Gral Ricardos, 99	471 4906
LUQUE CASTILLO, J. —Pto Arlaban, 121	478 5253
LUQUE CASTILLO, L. —Cardeñosa, 15	477 6644
LLANES FERNANDEZ CAPALLEJA, R. Galileo, 93	234 7204
LLOMBART GALIANO, J. —Cavanilles, 37	433 6711
LLOVEZ FERNANDEZ, R. Av. N. Sra Fátima, 17	461 7935

Variation B: Do as Dictation, with several students working at board.

La guía telefónica

Fierro Aguilar	Amalia	Avenida Juárez 86	7-65-03-91
Fierro Navarro	Teresa	Calle Misterios 45	5-86-58-16
Fierro Reyes	Gilberto	Avenida Miraflores 3	5-61-12-78
Figueroa López	Alberto	Calle Zaragoza 33	5-32-97-77
Figueroa Pérez	Julio	Avenida Iglesias 15	5-74-55-34
Gómez Pérez	Ana María	Calle Madero 7	7-94-43-88
Gómez Valencia	Javier	Avenida Córdoba 22	3-99-45-52
Guzmán Ávila	José Luis	Avenida Montevideo 4	6-57-29-40
Guzmán Martínez	Josefina	Avenida Independencia 25	2-77-22-70

Now give your phone number according to the model.

MODELO: —¿Cuál es tu teléfono?
—Es el siete–veinticuatro–ochenta y tres–sesenta y uno (724-8361).

Optional:
- *Dictado:* Dictate cognate nouns and numbers, with several students working at the board: *100 estéreos, 76 trombones, 65 saxofones, 92 guitarras, 56 pianos*, etc.
- *¿Es Ud. muy listo? ¿Cuál es el próximo número en la serie?* **1.** 1, 4, 7, 10, ¿___? (13) **2.** 0, 1, 10, 2, 3, 32, ¿___? (4, 5, 54) **3.** 10, 15, 13, 18, 16, 21, ¿___? (19, 24) **4.** 2, 4, 3, 9, 4, 16, 5, 25, 6, ¿___? (36)
- *Preguntas: ¿Cuántos segundos hay en un minuto? ¿Cuántos minutos hay en una hora? ¿Cuántas horas hay en un día? ¿Cuántos días hay en una semana? ¿Cuántas semanas en un mes? ¿Cuántos meses en un año?*

Notas culturales: Hispanic Last Names

As you probably noted in the preceding excerpts from Hispanic telephone books, two last names (**apellidos**) were given for each entry: **Amalia *Fierro Aguilar***. The first last name (**Fierro**) is that of the person's father; the second (**Aguilar**) is her mother's. This system for assigning last names is characteristic of all parts of the Spanish-speaking world, although it is not widely used by Hispanics living in the United States. You will learn more about this system in the **Lectura cultural** in **Capítulo 4**.

Notas comunicativas: Expressing Age

—¿Cuántos años tienes, abuela?
—Setenta y tres, Nora.
—¿Y cuántos años tiene el abuelo?
—Setenta y cinco, mi amor. Y ahora, dime,° ¿cuántos años tienes tú? *°tell me*
—Pues... creo que tengo tres.

In Spanish, age is expressed with the phrase **tener... años** (literally, *to have . . . years*). You have now seen all the singular forms of **tener**: **tengo**, **tienes**, **tiene**.

C. Complete las oraciones lógicamente.

1. Un hombre que (*who*) tiene noventa años es muy ___.
2. Un niño que tiene sólo un año es muy ___.
3. La persona más vieja (*oldest*) de mi familia es mi ___. Tiene ___ años.
4. La persona más vieja de esta clase es ___. Tiene ___. La persona más joven es ___. Tiene ___.

Suggestion C4: Have students ask at least five students their age before completing this item.

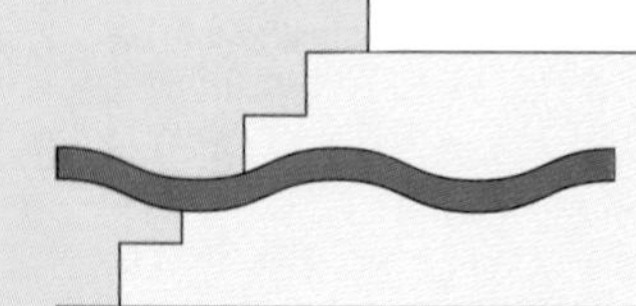

PRONUNCIACIÓN: STRESS AND WRITTEN ACCENT MARKS

In the words **habl*a*r**, **pap*á***, **matr*í*cula**, and **sobr*i*no**, the italicized vowel is stressed (given more emphasis than the others). In Spanish, *stress* (**la acentuación**) can be predicted based on the written form of the word.

Listening Exercise: Is stress on last syllable or on next-to-last syllable? *hable, hablé doblo, dobló bajé, baje espere, esperé pasó, paso pasé, paso*

Listening Exercise: Is stress on next-to-last or third-from-last (antepenultimate) syllable? *como, cómico, político, polo, pero, período, cinco, simpático*

Optional: Accent marks are added or deleted to preserve original stress pattern when words are made plural: accent deleted: *nación → naciones; francés → franceses;* accent added: *joven → jóvenes.*

- If a word ends in a *vowel*, *n*, or *s*, stress normally falls on the next-to-the-last syllable.

  ha-blo **ca**-sa **cla**-se **jo**-ven ne-ce-**si**-tan ha-**bla**-mos **pri**-mas

- If a word ends in any other consonant, stress normally falls on the last syllable.

  us-**ted** es-pa-**ñol** tra-ba-**jar** doc-**tor** ac-**triz** ha-**blar** tra-ba-ja-**dor**

- Any exception to these two rules will have a *written accent mark* (**un acento ortográfico**) on the stressed vowel.

  a-**quí** pa-**pá** na-**ción** fran-**cés** **lá**-piz **dó**-lar ma-**trí**-cu-la

- When one-syllable words have accents, it is to distinguish them from other words that sound like them. For example: **tú** (*you*)/**tu** (*your*); **él** (*he*)/**el** (*the*); **sí** (*yes*)/**si** (*if*).

- Interrogative and exclamatory words have a written accent on the stressed vowel. For example: **¿quién?** (*who?*); **¿dónde?** (*where?*); **¡cómo no!** (*of course!*).

Follow-up A (*Dictado*): 1. *José es rico.* 2. *Ramón es romántico.* 3. *El señor Gómez es simpático.* 4. *David es perezoso y antipático.* 5. *Joaquín es alto y guapo.* 6. *El señor Pérez es bajo y viejo.*
- Suggestion: Have several students write dictation on board while rest of class works at seats. Correct errors on board, paying special attention to accents and why they are needed/not needed.
- Suggestion: Go back over dictation, changing names to female names and having students tell you where to make changes for adjective agreement.

A. Practique las siguientes palabras.

1. hija alto bajo prima madre padre grande
   hermana bonito pequeño sobrina interesante
   buscan cantan enseñan hablas pagas trabajas
2. pagar comprar desear regresar mujer trabajador
   libertad universidad papel español general sentimental
3. práctico matrícula romántico simpático antipático
   José así así Ramón nación perdón adiós francés inglés
   lápiz Gómez Pérez Ramírez Jiménez

B. Indicate the stressed vowel of each word in the list that follows. Give the rule that determines the stress of each word.

1.	examen	5.	actitud	9.	compramos	13.	lugar
2.	lápiz	6.	acción	10.	hombre	14.	natural
3.	necesitar	7.	hermana	11.	peso	15.	plástico
4.	perezoso	8.	compran	12.	mujer	16.	sobrinos

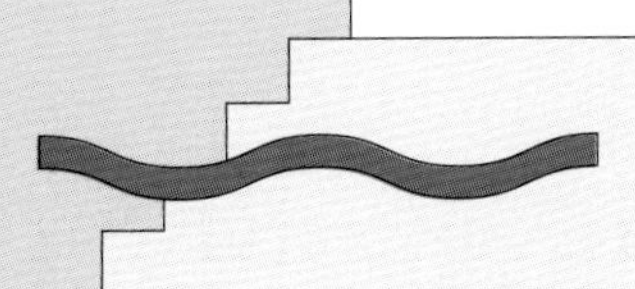

MINIDIÁLOGOS Y GRAMÁTICA

¿Recuerda Ud.?

Before beginning Grammar Section 5, review the forms and uses of **ser** that you have already learned by answering these questions.

1. ¿Eres estudiante o profesor(a)?
2. ¿De dónde eres?
3. ¿Eres una persona sentimental?
4. ¿Cómo es el profesor (la profesora) de español? ¿Es inteligente? ¿paciente? ¿elegante?
5. ¿Qué hora es? ¿A qué hora es la clase de español?
6. ¿Qué es un hospital? ¿Es una persona? ¿una cosa? ¿un edificio?

Communicative objectives 5: different things you can express with verb *ser:* who someone/something is, whom something is for, etc. *¡OJO!* Most uses of *ser* in this section are review of material formally presented or used in *Ante todo.* **Note:** use of *ser* to tell what something is made of is presented in Ch. 3; *ser* = to take place is in ch. 10. The *ser*/*estar* contrast is in Ch. 5.

5. EXPRESSING *TO BE*

Present Tense of *ser*; Summary of Uses

En la oficina de la profesora Castro

PROFESORA CASTRO: *¿Es* éste su examen, Sr. Bermúdez?
RAÚL BERMÚDEZ: *Es* posible. *¿Es* el examen de Raúl Bermúdez o de Jaime Bermúdez? *Somos* hermanos.
PROFESORA CASTRO: *Es* de Jaime Bermúdez, y *es* un suspenso.
RAÚL BERMÚDEZ: Pues el suspenso *es* de Jaime. ¡Yo *soy* Raúl!

1. ¿Con quién habla Raúl Bermúdez?
2. ¿Raúl y Jaime son primos?
3. ¿Es Jaime profesor o estudiante?
4. ¿Es el examen de Raúl o de Jaime?

Follow-up (Conversation): *¿Cómo se llama la profesora? ¿el estudiante? ¿Dónde están la ¿Quién es Jaime? ¿Es listo* (*trabajador, perezoso,* etc.) *Jaime? ¿Y Raúl?*

There are two Spanish verbs that mean *to be*: **ser** and **estar**. They are not interchangeable; the meaning that the speaker wishes to convey determines their use. In this chapter, you will review the uses of **ser** you already know and learn some new ones. Remember to use **está(n)** to express location. You will learn its complete conjugation and uses later.

Point out: Students have already used forms of *estar* in expression *¿cómo está(s)?* and for telling location. (No need to go into any more detail about *estar* at this time.)

In Professor Castro's office PROFESSOR: Is this your exam, Mr. Bermúdez? RAÚL: It's possible. Is it Raúl Bermúdez's exam or Jaime Bermúdez's? We're brothers. PROFESSOR: It's Jaime Bermúdez's, and it's an F. RAÚL: Well, the F is Jaime's. I'm Raúl!

Variation: Students practice minidialogue in small groups.

ser (*to be*)			
yo	**soy**	nosotros/as	**somos**
tú	**eres**	vosotros/as	**sois**
usted, él, ella	**es**	ustedes, ellos, ellas	**son**

Here are some basic language functions of **ser**. You have used all of them already in this and previous chapters.

Note: Telling time is not explicitly listed or reviewed in this section. You may wish to add it.

Emphasis (identify):
- Noun + *yo* → *nosotros* form of verb; similarly, pronoun + *yo*. Point out this is true for any verb.
- *Ser* is used when subject = predicate.
- The indefinite article is not used after *ser* before unmodified (undescribed) nouns of profession.

- To *identify* people and things

  Yo soy **estudiante**.
  La doctora Ramos es **profesora**.
  Alicia y yo somos **amigas**.
  Esto es **un libro**.

  [Práctica A]

- To *describe* people and things*

  Soy **sentimental**. — *I'm sentimental (a sentimental person).*
  El coche es **muy viejo**. — *The car is very old.*

- With **de**, to express *origin*

  Somos **de los Estados Unidos**, pero nuestros padres son **de la Argentina**. **¿De dónde** es Ud.? — *We're from the United States, but our parents are from Argentina. Where are you from?*

  [Práctica B–C]

- With **para**, to tell *for whom or what something is intended*

  ¿Romeo y Julieta? Es **para la clase de inglés**. — Romeo and Juliet*? It's for English class.*
  —**¿Para quién** son todos los regalos? —(Son) **Para mi nieto**. — *—Who are all the presents for? —(They're) For my grandson.*

  [Conversación A]

Emphasis (*para*): Stress meaning of *para* in this context.

- To express *generalizations* (**es**)

  Es **importante** estudiar, pero no es **necesario** estudiar todos los días. — *It's important to study, but it's not necessary to study every day.*

  [Conversación B–C]

Optional (generalizations): Some students may find the term "impersonal expressions" more understandable.

---

*You will practice this language function of **ser** in Grammar Section 6 in this chapter and in subsequent chapters.

Preliminary Exercises A:
- Review classroom vocabulary and practice *ser* + noun. Hold up or point to classroom objects, asking *¿Qué es esto?* Elicit plural forms by holding up two books, pencils, etc.
- *Identificaciones: ¿Quién es estudiante? Dé oraciones nuevas según las indicaciones. —Ana es estudiante.* (*yo, Mario y Juan, Uds., Lilia y yo, tú, vosotros*)

Suggestion B: Model pronunciation of names of countries.
Extension B:
- Present names of languages (*francés, español, italiano, inglés, alemán*). Students expand answers by telling where people are from and what language they speak.
- Name real or fictitious people from countries listed, asking *¿De dónde es ____?*
- Imagine you are a friend of persons listed in B. Tell where both of you are from: *John Doe y yo somos de...* . (Add language spoken if you introduced languages.)

Follow-up: *Más personas famosas del mundo hispánico* (similar to exercise on p. 19, *Ante todo*). Put information on board in columns. Do as sentence builder, with students forming own sentences, or ask cue questions *¿De dónde es ____?*.
Personas: *Jorge Luis Borges, Cantinflas, Lee Treviño, Guillermo Vilas, Salvador Dalí, Julio Iglesias, James Edward Olmos*
Categorías: *atleta, pintor, cantante, escritor* (writer), *actor*
Naciones: *la Argentina, los Estados Unidos, España*

Práctica

A. **Situaciones.** With a classmate, choose a fictitious family relationship, imagining that you are cousins, aunts of the same person, and so on. Another student will ask you questions until he or she determines your identity.

MODELO: —¿Son Uds. primos?
—No, no somos primos.
—¿Son... ?

Suggestion A: Do as whole class activity, with instructor taking part the first two times.

B. ¿De dónde son, según los nombres y apellidos?

Francia	Italia	Inglaterra (*England*)
México	los Estados Unidos	Alemania (*Germany*)

1. John Doe
2. Karl Lotze
3. Graziana Lazzarino
4. María Gómez
5. Claudette Moreau
6. Timothy Windsor

¿De dónde es Ud.? ¿de los Estados Unidos? ¿De dónde son sus (*your*) padres? ¿Son norteamericanos? (Mis padres...) ¿sus abuelos? (Mis abuelos...)

C. ¿Quiénes son, de dónde son y dónde trabajan ahora?

MODELO: Teresa: actriz / de Madrid / en Cleveland →
Teresa es actriz. Es de Madrid. Ahora trabaja en Cleveland.

1. Carlos Miguel: médico / de Cuba / en Milwaukee
2. Maripili: extranjera / de Burgos / en Miami
3. Mariela: dependienta / de Buenos Aires / en Nueva York
4. Juan: dentista* / de Lima / en Los Ángeles

Now tell about a friend of yours, following the same pattern.

Conversación

Note:
- Be sure students understand that simple explanations are sufficient for their level. There is no need for them to try to be complex.
- Introduction of *por eso* (expression with *por*).

Notas comunicativas: Explaining Your Reasons

In conversation, it is often necessary to explain a decision, tell why someone did something, and so on. Here are some simple words and phrases that speakers use to offer explanations.

porque	because
para	in order to
por eso	that's why; for that reason

(continúa)

*A number of professions end in **-ista** in both masculine and feminine forms. The article indicates gender: **el/la dentista**, **el/la artista**, and so on.

Preliminary exercises A:

- Create sentence-builder exercise on board or on transparency.
- first column: *el diccionario, los tíos, yo, Uds., Carla y yo, tú, la fiesta, Madrid, esto*
- second column: (*no*)
- third column: forms of *ser* (out of order): *eres, soy, es, son, somos*
- fourth column: *para Ernesto, un coche, de Chile, hermanas, la capital de España, de San Francisco, consejeros*

Add blanks to end of first and fourth columns and encourage students to fill in with names of real people and other words they know. This helps personalize exercise.

—¿Por qué necesitamos un televisor nuevo? ¡No comprendo! —Pues... **para** mirar el partido de fútbol... ¡Es el campeonato!	—*Why do we need a new TV set? I don't understand! —Well... (in order) to watch the soccer game... It's the championship!*
—¿Por qué trabajas tanto? —¡**Porque** necesitamos el dinero!	—*Why do you work so much? —Because we need the money!*
—¿No tomas el autobús 54 para llegar a la universidad? —No. El número 54 no llega a la universidad. **Por eso** espero el 32.	—*Don't you take bus 54 to get to the university? —No. The number 54 doesn't go to the university. That's why I'm waiting for number 32.*

Note the differences between **porque** (one word, no accent) and the interrogative **¿por qué?**

The words and phrases in this section are as important in listening as they are in speaking. Be alert to their use when others are talking to you; noting them will help you understand more completely what someone wants to say.

In addition, many activities in ***Puntos de partida*** will ask that you explain your decisions, tell why you acted in a certain way, and so on. Try to keep your explanations simple—especially at the beginning—and use only vocabulary and structures that you are familiar with. You will be able to explain your reasons more completely as your familiarity with Spanish increases.

Suggestion A: Provide several additional models with simple explanations, using *porque* and *por eso*.

A. **¿Para quién son los regalos?** The first column is a list of possible gifts. The second column lists some members of your imaginary family. Decide who should receive which gift, then use the additional information about each family member to explain your reasons.

MODELOS: _____ es para _____. → El dinero es para mi prima Anita. Ella es estudiante. Por eso necesita dinero.

el dinero (para comprar una mochila, para pagar la matrícula, para ¿ ?)	mis abuelos Ernesto y Lupita: pasan todos los días en casa
la camioneta (*station wagon*)	mi tío Juan: le gusta mirar los partidos de fútbol
el coche, un Mercedes	mi hermano Raúl y su (*his*) esposa: ¡tienen (*they have*) seis niños!
la cerveza	mi prima Anita: estudia en la universidad
la silla mecedora (*rocking chair*)	mi primo Marcos: le gusta mucho la música moderna
los discos (*records*) de Sade y Bruce Springsteen	mi tía Juana: es médica
el televisor	mis padres: desean comprar una casa en Phoenix
los cien mil (*100,000*) dólares	
¿ ?	

Suggestion B: Encourage students to guess the meaning of *fumar cigarrillos* from context.
Follow-up B:
- When students disagree with what others have said, ask them to tell what they prefer, using (*No*) *Prefiero* + infinitive, or *Quiero* + infinitive.

Optional B: Present phrases such as *¿Ah sí?*, *No me digas*, *¿De veras?*, *No, hombre*, and so on, for students to use to respond to answers given by others.

Follow-up: Have students present information about themselves, their families, and where they are from. Remind them not to overuse *yo*: *Yo soy Carlos. Soy de Garfield Heights. Tengo tres hermanos y una hermana. Mis abuelos son de Rusia.* **Suggestion:** Have students prepare this information as a brief composition, which you correct before they present to the class.

B. **¿Qué crees?** (*What do you think?*) Exprese opiniones originales, afirmativas o negativas, con estas palabras.

(No)	Es importante	mirar la televisión todos los días
	Es muy práctico	hablar español en la clase
	Es necesario	comer (*to eat*) tres veces (*times*) al día
	Es tonto	llegar a clase puntualmente
	Es fascinante	tomar cerveza en clase
	Es posible	hablar con los animales/las plantas
		tomar mucho café y fumar cigarrillos
		trabajar dieciocho horas al día

C. **Una fiesta familiar.** Imagine que Ud. está en una fiesta familiar, en la casa de sus (*your*) padres. ¿A qué hora llegan todos? ¿Quién llega tarde? ¿Quién no llega? ¿Qué toman Uds.? ¿Es posible bailar? ¿cantar? ¿hablar con muchos (*many*) parientes? ¿Es necesario ser amable con todos? ¿Le gusta hablar con sus parientes? ¿A qué hora termina la fiesta?

Study Hint: Learning Grammar

Learning a language is similar to learning any other skill; knowing *about* it is only part of what is involved. Consider how you would acquire another skill—swimming, for example. If you read all the available books on swimming, you would probably become an expert in talking *about* swimming and you would know what you *should* do in a pool. Until you actually got into a pool and practiced swimming, however, you would probably not swim very well. In much the same way, if you memorize all the grammar rules but spend little time *practicing* them, you will not be able to communicate very well in Spanish.

As you study each grammar point in ***Puntos de partida***, you will learn how the structure works; then you need to put your knowledge into practice. First, read the grammar discussion, study and analyze the examples, and pay special attention to any **¡OJO!** sections, which will call your attention to problem areas. Then begin to practice, first in the **Práctica** section. Do the exercises and check your answers. When you are certain that your answers are correct, practice doing each exercise several times until the answers sound and "feel" right to you. As you do each item, think about what you are conveying and the context in which you could use each sentence, as well as about spelling and pronunciation. Then move on to the **Conversación** section and continue to practice, this time in a more open-ended situation in which, in general, there are no "right" or "wrong" answers.

Always remember that language learning is cumulative. This means that you are not finished with a grammar point when you go on to the next chapter. Even though you are now studying the material in **Capítulo 2**, you must still remember how to conjugate **-ar** verbs and how to form yes/no questions, because **Capítulo 2** builds on what you have learned in **Capítulo 1**—and as all subsequent chapters will build on the material leading up to them. A few minutes spent each day reviewing "old" topics will increase your confidence—and success—in communicating in Spanish.

Communicative objectives for 6: describing people, places, and things

6. DESCRIBING
Adjectives: Gender, Number, and Position

Adjectives (**Los adjetivos**) are words used to talk about nouns or pronouns. Adjectives may describe (***large*** *desk*, ***tall*** *woman*) or tell how many there are (***a few*** *desks*, ***several*** *women*).

You have been using adjectives to describe people since **Ante todo**. In this section, you will learn more about describing the people and things around you.

Un poema sencillo

Amigo
Fiel
Amable
Simpático
¡Bienvenido!

Amiga
Fiel
Amable
Simpática
¡Bienvenida!

According to their form, which of the adjectives below can be used to describe each person? Which can refer to you?

Marta: fiel bienvenido simpática
Mario: amable simpático bienvenida

Suggestion: Read both versions of poem. Point out there is only one English equivalent given. Ask what differences are between two versions and who is described in each.
¡OJO! Gender agreement with adjectives has been used by students since beginning of *Ante todo*. Handling of this grammar section will depend on how much you have stressed agreement.
Follow-up:
- Students tell which adjectives could be used to describe themselves.
- Ask questions about couple in photo: *¿Quiénes son? ¿Dónde están? ¿De dónde son? ¿Son hermanos* (*amigos*, *estudiantes*, etc.)? *¿Qué hacen? ¿Cómo son? ¿Son ____?* (Cue students with adjectives.) *¿Les gusta hablar* (*bailar*, *estudiar*, etc.)?

Adjectives with *ser*

In Spanish, forms of **ser** are used with adjectives that describe basic, inherent qualities or characteristics of the nouns or pronouns they modify.

Alternate explanation: *Ser* establishes norm, what is considered to be objective reality: Snow is cold. Water is wet.

Antonio **es interesante**.	*Antonio is interesting.* (*He's an interesting person.*)
Tú **eres amable**.	*You're nice.* (*You're a nice person.*)
El diccionario **es barato**.	*The dictionary is inexpensive.*

Forms of Adjectives

Spanish adjectives agree in gender and number with the noun or pronoun they modify. Each adjective has more than one form.

- Adjectives that end in **-e** (**inteligente**) or in most consonants (**fiel**) have only two forms, a singular form and a plural form. The plural of adjectives is formed in the same way as that of nouns.

Optional: Adjectives that end in *-í* or *-a* also have two forms only: *israelí*(*s*), *iraní*(*s*), *realista*(*s*), *optimista*(*s*), etc.

	MASCULINE	FEMININE
Singular	amigo inteligente amigo fiel	amiga inteligente amiga fiel
Plural	amigos inteligente**s** amigos fiel**es**	amigas inteligente**s** amigas fiel**es**

A Simple Poem Friend Loyal Kind Nice Welcome!

- Adjectives that end in **-o** (**alto**) have four forms, showing gender and number.*

	MASCULINE	FEMININE
Singular	amigo alt**o**	amiga alt**a**
Plural	amigos alt**os**	amigas alt**as**

[Práctica A–C]

- Most adjectives of nationality have four forms:

	MASCULINE	FEMININE
Singular	el doctor mexicano español alemán inglés	la doctor**a** mexican**a** español**a** aleman**a** ingles**a**
Plural	los doctor**es** mexican**os** español**es** aleman**es** ingles**es**	las doctor**as** mexican**as** español**as** aleman**as** ingles**as**

The names of many languages—which are masculine in gender—are the same as the masculine singular form of the corresponding adjective of nationality: **el español**, **el inglés**, **el alemán**, and so on. Note that in Spanish the names of languages and adjectives of nationality are not capitalized, but the names of countries are: **español**, but **España**.

[Práctica CH]

Emphasis: Concept of agreement. Feminine singular adjective must be used to describe feminine singular noun; masculine plural adjective to describe masculine plural noun, etc.

Optional: Adjectives must agree with the gender of the nouns that they modify *grammatically,* not with the person one is talking or thinking about. Some Spanish words that refer to people are masculine, while others are feminine: *el individuo*, *la persona*, and so on. The adjectives that modify *persona* will always be feminine, and those that modify *individuo* will always be masculine, regardless of the sex of the person that they refer to.
- *El amigo de José es una persona muy lista.*
- *Luisa es un individuo muy independiente.*
- *¡Ay, Elena, mi amor divino! Tú eres un ángel.*

Point out: Accent marks dropped in feminine singular and in plural forms.

Optional: *-e* nationality adjectives have only two forms, singular and plural: *canadiense(s)*, *estadounidense(s)*.

Point out: Use of nationality adjectives as nouns—e.g., *el español* (the Spaniard), *los ingleses* (the English), etc.

Summary of agreement: (1) *-o* adjectives have four forms; **(2)** most nationality adjectives have four forms; **(3)** most other adjectives have two.

Forms of *this/these*

The demonstrative adjective *this/these* has four forms in Spanish.†

est**e** hijo	*this son*	est**a** hija	*this daughter*
est**os** hijos	*these sons*	est**as** hijas	*these daughters*

You have already used the neuter demonstrative **esto**. It refers to something that is as yet unidentified: **¿Qué es esto?**

[Práctica D]

Note: Whole system of demonstrative adjectives is presented in Ch. 4. Students should use only *este* forms, but you may want to use *ese* and *aquel* forms when talking to students, to cue natural use of *este.*

Point out: Unlike most other adjectives ending in *-e, este* has four forms.

---

*Adjectives that end in **-dor**, **-ón**, **-án**, and **-ín** also have four forms: **trabajador**, **trabajador*a***, **trabajador*es***, **trabajador*as***.

†You will learn all the forms of the Spanish demonstrative adjectives (*this, that, these, those*) in Grammar Section 15.

Placement of Adjectives

Adjectives that describe the qualities of a noun generally follow the noun they modify. Adjectives of quantity and demonstratives precede the noun.

Hay **cinco** sillas y **un** escritorio.	*There are five chairs and one desk.*
Y **este** edificio, ¿qué es?	*And this building, what is it?*
Busco **otro** carro.*	*I'm looking for another car.*

Point out: *Otro* = other or another; thus, does not require indefinite article. Refer students to footnote.

The interrogative adjectives **¿cuánto/a?** and **¿cuántos/as?** also precede the noun: **¿cuánto dinero?**, **¿cuántas hermanas?**

Bueno, **malo**, and **grande** may precede the nouns they modify. When **bueno** and **malo** precede a masculine singular noun, they shorten to **buen** and **mal**, respectively.

un recuerdo **bueno** / un **buen** recuerdo	*a good (pleasant) memory*
una niña **buena** / una **buena** niña	*a good girl*

When **grande** appears after a noun, it means *large* or *big*. When it precedes a singular noun—masculine or feminine—it is shortened to **gran** and means *great* or *impressive.*

Suggestion: Ask *¿Cómo se dice en inglés?: una ciudad grande, una gran ciudad; un estado grande, un gran estado. ¿Cómo se dice en español?*: a large book; a large university, a great university.

una ciudad **grande** / una **gran** ciudad	*a big city / a great (impressive) city*
un libro **grande** / un **gran** libro	*a big book / a great book*

[Práctica E–F]

Preliminary exercise: *Descripciones: ¿Cómo son? Dé oraciones nuevas según las indicaciones.* **1.** *¿Su* (Your) *familia?* —*(No) Es una familia grande.* (*interesante, importante, amable, intelectual*) **2.** *¿Los perros* (dogs)? —(No) *Son valientes.* (*fiel, impaciente, inteligente, importante*) **3.** *¿Su* (Your) *universidad?* —(No) *Es nueva.* (*viejo, grande, pequeño, bueno, famoso, malo*)

Extension A (listening): *¿Sí o no?:* **5.** *Los actores son* (*guapo/pobres/alto/buenos*). **6.** *La mujer es* (*inteligente/rubia/romántico/simpática*). **7.** *Las estudiantes son* (*sinceras/altos/perezosa/delgadas*).

Práctica 

A. Complete each sentence with all the adjectives that are appropriate according to form and meaning.

1. La tía Anita es _____. (morena / casado / jóvenes / lista / bonito / trabajadora)
2. El padre de Ernesto es _____. (viejo / alto / nueva / grande / fea / interesante)
3. Los abuelos son _____. (rubio / antipático / inteligentes / viejos / religiosos / práctica)
4. Las niñas son _____. (malo / cortas / sentimental / buenas / casadas / joven)

B. **Descripciones.** Describa a su (*your*) familia y su universidad, haciendo oraciones completas con estas palabras.

***Otro** by itself means *another* or *other.* The indefinite article is not used with **otro**.

Emphasis B: *ser* + adjective, *tener... años.*

Suggestion B: Before beginning exercise, ask students for additional adjectives used to describe family members, animals, and university. Encourage students to use the additional adjectives in their sentences.

Follow-up B: Ask several students to give four sentences with the first four sentence cues, to describe their families.

Mi familia Mi padre/madre Mi ¿ ? (otro pariente) Mi perro/gato (*dog*/*cat*) Esta universidad	(no) ser tiene	interesante, importante, amable, (im)paciente, grande, ¿ ? intelectual, fiel, ¿ ? nuevo, viejo, pequeño, bueno, malo, famoso, ¿ ? ... años

Note C: Encourage students to guess meaning of *hacer ejercicio* in context.

Follow-up C: *¿Juan o Juana?* (Students listen both for information and for gender agreement.) **1.** *Es trabajadora.* **2.** *Es casada.* **3.** *Tiene veinte años.* **4.** *Es guapo.* **5.** *No es gorda porque le gusta hacer ejercicio.*

C. Juan and Juana, fraternal twins, are totally different. Tell what Juana is like, changing details as necessary.

Juan tiene veinte años. Es soltero. Es alto y moreno y también muy guapo. Es muy perezoso—¡no le gusta estudiar! También es un poco gordo—¡no le gusta hacer ejercicio! No es como (*like*) su hermana Juana, pero es muy simpático de todos modos (*in any case*).

Extension CH: Name famous people; imagine they are all alive. What language do they speak, and what is their nationality? (Optional: Where are they from?) Examples: *Pablo Picasso, François Mitterand, Carlos y Diana, Fernando Valenzuela, Willy Brandt y Helmut Schmidt, Gina Lollobrigida y Sofía Loren, Pancho Villa, Juan y Eva Perón*

CH. Tell what nationality the following persons could be and where they might live: **Portugal**, **Alemania**, **Inglaterra**, **España**, **Francia**, **Italia**.

1. Monique habla francés; es _____ y vive (*she lives*) en _____.
2. José habla español; es _____ y vive en _____.
3. Greta y Hans hablan alemán; son _____ y viven en _____.
4. Gilberto habla portugués; es _____ y vive en _____.
5. Gina y Sofía hablan italiano; son _____ y viven en _____.
6. Winston habla inglés; es _____ y vive en _____.

Variation D: Students describe magazine pictures to class, pointing out individuals pictured as they speak. Suggestion: Bring in magazine pictures you have selected, making sure students have vocabulary necessary to describe several individuals in each.

D. **Una reunión familiar.** You and your friend Julio are looking at some photos of a family gathering. Julio does not know any of the members of your family. Point out some of them and tell him something about them. Begin each sentence with a demonstrative, as in the model, and use the correct form of **ser**. Add details if you can.

MODELO: fiesta / para mi hermano Manolo →
Esta fiesta es para mi hermano Manolo. Es profesor.

1. mujer / la esposa de Manolo
2. primos / de San Francisco
3. nietas / de California también
4. joven morena / mi hermana Cecilia
5. hombre guapo / el tío Julián

Preliminary E: *Vacaciones en Acapulco.* Create new phrases about your last vacation by changing the position of the adjectives. Be sure to use the appropriate form of the adjective. **1.** *un recuerdo bueno* **2.** *una ciudad grande* **3.** *unos parientes buenos* **4.** *un hotel malo* **5.** *unos niños malos*

Note E: *Do not* ask students to insert all adjectives into the sentences at same time.

E. **Variaciones.** You have heard the following sentences in the places indicated. Who is most likely to have said each, **un empleado** (*employee*) or **un cliente**? After you have identified the speaker, create new sentences by inserting the adjectives in parentheses into them, one at a time. Can you add any other adjectives that are appropriate in meaning?

1. En la agencia de automóviles: Busco un coche. (pequeño / francés / grande)
2. En la librería: Por favor, quiero comprar un diccionario. (completo / barato / nuevo)

3. En la biblioteca: Estas novelas son buenas. (alemán / nuevo / mexicano)
4. En la agencia de viajes (*travel agency*): ¿Buscan una excursión? (fascinante / largo / barato)

Follow-up F: *¿Cierto o falso?* **1.** *A Miguel no le gusta estudiar.* **2.** *Miguel es de Sudamérica.* **3.** *No estudia aquí.* **4.** *Prefiere estar aquí, en los Estados Unidos.* **5.** *Es una persona muy simpática.*

F. Cambie: Miguel → María

Miguel es un buen estudiante. Es listo y trabajador y estudia mucho. Es argentino, de la gran ciudad de Buenos Aires; por eso habla español. Quiere ser profesor de español; por eso estudia en esta universidad.

Miguel es alto y guapo; también es muy delgado, pues hace (*he does*) mucho ejercicio. Le gustan las fiestas grandes de la universidad y tiene buenos amigos aquí, pero también tiene buenos recuerdos de sus amigos y parientes argentinos.

Conversación

Suggestions A:
- Encourage students to give simple explanations using *porque* and *por eso.*
- Re-enter or introduce expressions such as *¿Ah sí?, ¿De veras?*, etc., and encourage students to use them in their reactions.

A. **Asociaciones.** With several classmates, how many names can you associate with the following phrases? Everyone in the group must agree with the names you decide on. Use the words and phrases you know to agree with the suggestions of others. To disagree, simply say: **No estoy de acuerdo.**

1. una gran mujer
2. una buena clase
3. un gran hombre
4. una persona mala
5. un mal restaurante

Emphasis B:
- Introduction of *¿verdad?* (tag question); reentered in Ch. 3.
- Introduction of *por lo general* (expression with *por*).

Preliminary B: *¿Es Ud. alto/a? ¿listo/a? ¿antipático/a? ¿rico/a? ¿rubio/a? ¿moreno/a? ¿sentimental? ¿religioso/a?*

Variation B: Ask students to form small groups and complete each sentence with as many different adjectives as possible.

Follow-up: Review *¿tienes?* → *tengo* and *mi(s)*. Working in pairs, students find out about each others' families: how many (brothers, cousins, etc.), what they are like, where they work, what they do, etc. ***Modelo:*** *¿Tienes una madre generosa?* → *Sí, mi madre es generosa.*

B. **Entrevista.** Ask a classmate questions that will elicit information to complete the following statements. Use adjectives, when appropriate, in your questions, and remember that you know a number of ways to ask questions. Another simple way to ask questions is to add the tag word **¿verdad?** (*right?*) to the end of a statement.

MODELO: El profesor (La profesora) es _____. →
—¿Cómo es la profesora? (¿Es inteligente la profesora? La profesora es simpática, ¿verdad?)
—La profesora es inteligente.

1. El profesor (La profesora) es _____.
2. Por lo general (*In general*), las mujeres (madres, hermanas) son _____.
3. Por lo general, los hombres (padres, hermanos) son _____.
4. Los buenos amigos son _____.
5. Yo soy _____.
6. Mi mejor (*best*) amigo/a es _____.

Now compare your classmate's answers with those of other students. Is there general agreement on the adjectives used to complete these sentences?

Hablando (*Talking*) de fotos

—¿Quién es el joven alto y moreno en esta foto?
—Es mi hermano Julio.
—¡Qué guapo es!
—¿Te gustaría conocerlo?*
—¡Sí! ¡Claro que sí! (*Of course!*)

Torreón, México

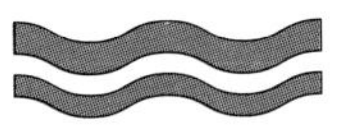

7. EXPRESSING POSSESSION AND DESTINATION
Ser Plus *de*; Contractions *del* and *al*

Amalia and Emily are describing family customs. Which one do you think made each statement?

MODELO: El número _____ es el comentario *de* Amalia/Emily.

1. Uso el apellido *de* mi padre y también el *de* mi madre.
2. Hasta en los documentos oficiales, generalmente la esposa usa sólo el apellido *del* esposo.
3. Por lo general, hay un sistema de familia extendida.
4. Los niños participan en casi todas las actividades familiares.

Extension (mini): **5.** *Es muy fácil divorciarse.* **6.** *Muchas madres trabajan fuera de casa* (outside of the home). **7.** *Los miembros de una familia pasan mucho tiempo juntos* (together).

Expressing Possession

In Spanish, **ser** is used with the preposition **de** to express possession.

Es el dinero **de Carla**.	*It's Carla's money.*
Son los abuelos **de Jorge**.	*They're Jorge's grandparents.*
¿De quién es el examen?	*Whose exam is it?*

Emphasis: *¿de quién?* = whose? (lit. of whom?)

Note that there is no *'s* in Spanish.

[Práctica A]

*This sentence means: *Would you like to meet him?* To use the sentence to talk about a woman, change **-lo** to **-la**: **¿Te gustaría conocer*la*?**

1. I use my father's last name and also my mother's (that of my mother). **2.** Even in official documents, a wife generally uses only the husband's last name. **3.** In general, there's an extended family system. **4.** Children participate in almost all family activities.

Contractions *del* and *al*

Suggestion: Write on board and point out different forms:

Es la casa
del niño.
de la niña.
de los niños.
de las niñas.

Regreso
al mercado.
a la tienda.
a los hoteles.
a las tiendas.

¡OJO! de + él never contract

A *contraction* (**una contracción**) is the joining of two words that may also be said or written separately. In English, contractions are optional: *Pam* ***is not*** / ***isn't*** *a student; They* ***are not*** / ***aren't*** *here.*

In Spanish there are only two contractions, and they are obligatory. The masculine singular article **el** contracts with the prepositions **de** and **a** to form **del** and **al**. No other articles contract with **de** or with **a**.

Es la casa **del** joven.	*It is the young man's house.*
Es la casa **de los** jóvenes.	*It is the young people's house.*
Llego **al** edificio a las dos.	*I'll get to the building at 2:00.*
Llego **a la** oficina a las tres.	*I'll get to the office at 3:00.*

[Práctica B–C]

Preliminary Exercise: *¿Qué es esto? Identifique estas cosas.* **1.** *Es la mesa del estudiante.* (*el coche, la casa, el dinero, el bolígrafo, la guitarra*) **2.** *Es el libro del niño.* (*la niña, los abuelos, el tío, las nietas, el primo Juan*)

Suggestion A: After several answers, change *de Luisa* to *de ella* to avoid redundancy and to have students start to use prepositional pronouns.

Follow-up A: "Steal" possessions from students in the class. Ask: *¿De quién es ____?* Another student answers: *Es el/la ____ de ____.*

Práctica

A. Este dibujo representa la familia de Luisa. ¿Quiénes son los parientes de Luisa?

MODELO: Alfonso es el abuelo de Luisa.

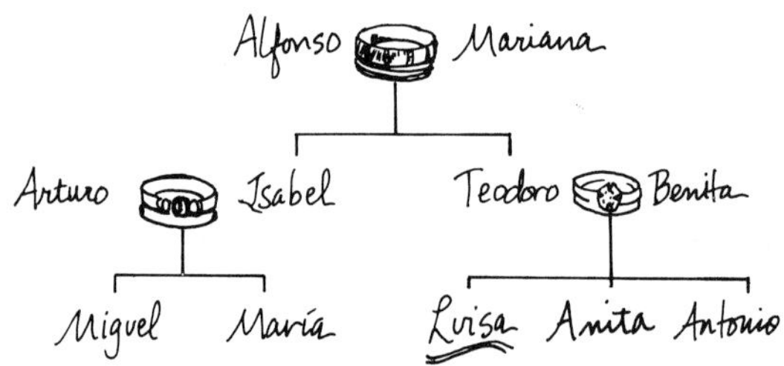

Suggestion B: Students give simple explanations using *porque, por eso.*

B. **¡Seamos (*Let's be*) lógicos!** ¿De quién son estas cosas? Con un compañero, haga y conteste preguntas según los modelos.

MODELOS: —¿De quién es el perro?
—Es de...

—¿De quién son las mochilas?
—Son de...

Personas: las estudiantes, la actriz, el niño, la familia con diez hijos, el estudiante extranjero, los señores Schmidt

1. la casa en Beverly Hills
2. la casa en Viena
3. la camioneta
4. el perro
5. las fotos de la Argentina
6. las mochilas con todos los libros

C. A veces, después de (*after*) trabajar todo el día, es necesario trabajar más por la noche. ¿Adónde regresan estas personas si necesitan trabajar más?

Extension C: Ask *¿Por qué?* (Why?) after each complete sentence. Answer based on model: *Porque* (Because) *trabaja en la universidad.*

Optional: *¿Cuál es la capital del estado de Colorado? ¿del estado de Nuevo México? ¿del estado de Arizona? ¿del estado de Montana? ¿del estado de Nevada? ¿del estado de Florida? ¿del estado de California?* If necessary, write cities on board: Sacramento / Denver / Phoenix / Carson City / Tallahassee / Helena / Santa Fe.

Lugares: el hospital, la biblioteca, la oficina, la librería, el cuarto en la residencia

1. el médico
2. el dependiente
3. la profesora
4. el estudiante
5. el decano (*dean*)

Conversación

Complete las oraciones lógicamente.

1. Si una persona llega temprano al baile es porque ______.
2. El doctor regresa al hospital todos los días porque ______.
3. Esta noche regreso a la universidad porque ______.
4. Todos los días llegamos a la clase de español a la(s) ______.
5. Si un profesor enseña una clase a las siete de la noche, regresa ______.

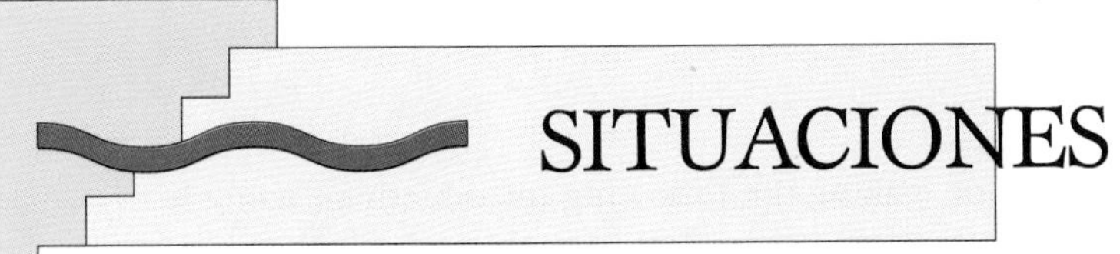

SITUACIONES

Situaciones: See IM for suggestions, additional exercises, and supplementary dialogues and exercises.

Presentaciones

En casa...

—Abuelo, quiero presentarle a Adolfo... Adolfo Álvarez Montes. Somos compañeros de clase en la universidad.
—Encantado, don Antonio.*
—Igualmente, Adolfo. Bienvenido a nuestra° casa. *our*

En clase...

—Profesora Benítez, quisiera presentarle a Laura Sánchez Trujillo. Es mi amiga salvadoreña.° de El Salvador
—Mucho gusto en conocerla, Laura.
—El gusto es mío, profesora.

En la cafetería...

—Quico, te presento a Adela. Es amiga de Julio, ¿sabes?° *you know?*
—Mucho gusto, Adela.
—Igualmente.
—¿Qué tal si tomamos un café?
—¡De acuerdo!

*Note the use of the title **don** with a man's first name to express respect. **Doña** is used with a woman's name.

Notas comunicativas sobre el diálogo

In **Ante todo** you learned some basic phrases to use when meeting someone for the first time. Here are some phrases to use to make introductions in formal and informal situations, as well as some additional responses.

Formal: Quiero / Quisiera } presentarle a...	*I want / Allow me* } *to introduce you to...*
Mucho gusto en { conocer**lo**. / conocer**la**.	*Pleased to meet you.*
El gusto es mío.	*The pleasure is mine.*

With **Mucho** gusto... , use **-lo** when speaking to a man, **-la** when speaking to a woman.

Informal: _____, te presento a...	_____, *this is...*
Mucho gusto en conocerte.	*Pleased to meet you.*

Conversación

With other students, practice making the following introductions, using **le** (*formal*) or **te** (*informal*), as appropriate. Tell something about the person you are introducing.

1. You are at home, and a good friend stops by for a few minutes. Introduce him or her to your family.
2. You are in the library and happen to run into two of your professors at the circulation desk. Introduce them to each other.
3. You are at a party. Introduce one good friend to another.
4. Introduce the student next to you to another student.

UN POCO DE TODO

A. **La familia del nuevo nieto.** The following sentences will form a description of a family in which there is a new grandchild. The name of the person described is given in parentheses after each description (if necessary). Form complete sentences based on the words given, in the order given. Conjugate the verbs and add other words if necessary.

As you create the sentences, complete the family tree given below with the names of the family members. Hint: Hispanic families pass on family names just like families in the United States.

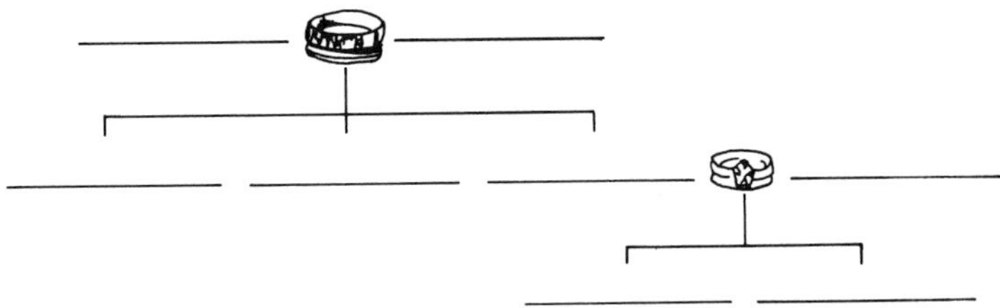

1. yo / ser / abuela / panameño (Anita)
2. nuevo / nieto / ser / de / Estados Unidos (Juan José)
3. Juan José / ser / padre / nieto
4. Juan José / también / ser / hijo / abuelo / panameño
5. uno / de / tías / de / nieto / ser / médico (Pilar)
6. otro / tía / ser / profesor / famoso (Julia)
7. madre / niño / ser / norteamericano (Paula)
8. hermana / niño / se llama / Concepción

Ahora conteste estas preguntas según la descripción de la familia.

1. ¿De dónde son los abuelos y tíos?
2. ¿De dónde es la madre del niño?

emocracia en familia

Ese deseo de igualdad se complementa con de una integración de los jóvenes en los pro- lemas de la familia. De cada tres mujeres, os propugnan una plena participación de los ijos en la problemática familiar, frente a só- o un 20.1 por ciento cuya opinión es que los ijos deben de *«permanecer al margen»* de di- chos problemas.

Casadas y solteras —frente a viudas y se- paradas— son las más partidarias de la «de- mocracia familiar».

Esa mayoría favorable a la participación de os hijos sólo muestra una reserva: los problemas directamente referidos a la pareja. Esa limitación la establecen, además, todos los grupos de mujeres con independencia incluso de su afinidad ideológica, puesto que alcanza al 87.4 por ciento de las socialistas, al 88.2 por ciento de las aliancistas y al 90 por ciento de las comunistas.

Educar es cosa de hombres, mujeres y de...

Casi la mitad exacta de las mujeres encuestadas —51.3 por ciento— cree que ellas como sus maridos se ocupan por igual de la educación de los hijos. Sin embargo, cuando se declaran diferencias, el 41.5 por ciento de las mujeres opina que ellas se ocupan más de la educación frente a tan sólo un 2.8 por ciento que reconoce la mayor dedicación del hombre. Esa diferencia en la dedicación a los hijos es mayor si se trata de mujeres que han superado los 65 años.

¿Se presenta la mujer ante los hijos como la última depositaria de la autoridad familiar? Esta es la cuestión que planteaba la encuesta formulada así: «Cuando hay que hablar ''seriamente'' con un hijo, ¿quién lo hace con más frecuencia?» Una mayoría —el 42.2 por ciento— opina que esta tarea también está repartida por igual entre ellas mismas y sus maridos. Sin embargo, un 26.6 por ciento reconocen que son sus maridos los que con más frecuencia se dirigen a los hijos en momentos «cumbre», frente al 24.9 por ciento de mujeres que se atribuyen tal función.

El reconocimiento del padre como representante máximo de autoridad en la familia és paralelo a la edad de las encuestadas.

B. **Quién es?** Identifique estos miembros de su (*your*) familia imaginaria, la familia Pérez.

1. Tiene setenta años y es jubilado (*retired*). Es casado y es padre de tres hijos. Uno de estos hijos es mi padre. Es mi ______.
2. Es joven—tiene sólo cinco años. Es la hija de tío Carlos y tía Matilde. Es mi ______.
3. Es el hijo de los señores Pérez (mis padres). Hay más hijos en la familia. Es mi ______.
4. Es el esposo de la Sra. Pérez. Es mi ______.
5. Es la hija de los abuelos. También, es la hermana de mi padre. Es mi ______.

C. **¿De dónde eres tú?** With two classmates, ask and answer questions according to the model.

Point out C: Italicized words indicate elements that will change as substitutions are made.

MODELO: Atlanta → ENRIQUETA: ¿De dónde eres tú?
AGUSTÍN: Soy de *Atlanta.*
EVA: Ah, eres *norteamericano.*
AGUSTÍN: Sí, por eso hablo *inglés.*

1. Guadalajara
2. París
3. Roma
4. San Francisco
5. Madrid
6. Londres
7. Berlín
8. Lima (peruano)

CH. **La familia hispánica típica: ¿Existe?** Complete the following paragraphs about families. Give the correct form of the words in parentheses, as suggested by the context. When two possibilities are given in parentheses, select the correct word.

Muchas personas creen° que (*todo*[1]) las familias (*hispánico*[2]) son (*grande*[3]), pero no es así.° Como en todas las partes (*de/del*[4]) mundo,° el concepto (*del/de la*[5]) familia ha cambiado° mucho últimamente,° sobre todo° en las ciudades (*grande*[6]).

Es verdad° que la familia campesina° (*típico*[7]) es grande, pero es así en casi (*todo*[8]) las sociedades° rurales del mundo. Ya que° los hijos (*trabajar*[9]) la tierra con sus° padres, es bueno y (*necesario*[10]) tener° muchos niños.

Pero en los grandes centros (*urbano*[11]), las familias con sólo dos o tres hijos (*ser*[12]) cada día° más comunes. Es caro° mantener a* (*mucho*[13]) hijos en una sociedad (*industrializado*[14]). Cuando la madre (*trabajar*[15]) fuera de° casa, nadie se queda° en casa con los niños. Esto pasa especialmente en las familias de clase (*medio*[16]) y de clase (*alto*[17]).

Pero es realmente difícil° (*hablar*[18]) de una sola° familia (*hispánico*[19]) típica. ¿Hay una familia (*norteamericano*[20]) típica?

believe
no... *that isn't so* / *world*
ha... *has changed* / *lately*
sobre... especialmente
true / *country*
societies / Ya... *Since*
their / *to have*
cada... *every day* / *expensive*
fuera... *outside* / nadie... *no one stays*
difficult / *single*

¿Cierto o falso? Corrija las oraciones falsas.

1. Todas las familias hispánicas son iguales.
2. Las familias rurales son grandes en casi todas partes del mundo.
3. Las familias rurales necesitan muchos niños.
4. Por lo general, las familias urbanas son más pequeñas.

VOCABULARIO

VERBOS

llegar to arrive
mirar to look (at)
ser (*irreg.*) to be

LA FAMILIA Y LOS PARIENTES

el/la abuelo/a grandfather/grandmother
los abuelos grandparents
el/la esposo/a husband/wife
el/la hermano/a brother/sister
el/la hijo/a son/daughter
los hijos children
la madre (mamá) mother (mom)
el/la nieto/a grandson/granddaughter
el padre (papá) father (dad)
los padres parents
el/la primo/a cousin
el/la sobrino/a niece/nephew
el/la tío/a uncle/aunt

OTROS SUSTANTIVOS

el apellido last name
la camioneta station wagon
la casa house, home
la ciudad city
el coche car
el examen test, exam
el gato cat
el/la médico/a (medical) doctor
el nombre (first) name
el perro dog
el recuerdo memory
el regalo present

*Note the use of the word **a** before a direct object that refers to a specific person or persons. This **a** has no equivalent in English. You will learn to use the word **a** in this way in Grammar Section 20.

ADJETIVOS

alemán, **alemana** German
alto/a tall
amable kind; nice
antipático/a unpleasant
bajo/a short (*in height*)
barato/a inexpensive
bienvenido/a welcome
bonito/a pretty
buen, bueno/a good
casado/a married
corto/a short (*in length*)
delgado/a thin, slender
español(a) Spanish
este/a this; **estos/as** these
familiar family-related, of the family
feo/a ugly
francés, francesa French
gordo/a fat
gran(de) large, big; great
guapo/a handsome; good-looking
inglés, **inglesa** English
joven young
largo/a long
listo/a smart; clever
mal, **malo/a** bad
mexicano/a Mexican
moreno/a brunette
mucho/a a lot of, many
necesario/a necessary
norteamericano/a North American; from the U.S.
nuevo/a new
otro/a other, another
pequeño/a small
perezoso/a lazy
pobre poor
posible possible
rico/a rich
rubio/a blond(e)
simpático/a nice; likeable
soltero/a single (*not married*)
todo/a all, every
tonto/a silly, foolish
trabajador(a) hardworking
viejo/a old

LOS NÚMEROS

treinta, cuarenta, cincuenta, sesenta, setenta, ochenta, noventa, cien(to)

PALABRAS ADICIONALES

ahora now
casi almost
¿de dónde es Ud.? where are you from?
¿de quién? whose?
en casa at home
esta noche tonight
por lo general in general, generally
que that; who
tener... años to be . . . years old
¿verdad? right?

Frases útiles para la comunicación

¿por qué?	why?
porque	because
por eso	that's why
no estoy de acuerdo	I don't agree
tengo, tienes, tiene	I have, you have, he/she/it has

See also the words and phrases in **Notas comunicativas sobre el diálogo.**

OPTIONAL SECTION

UN PASO MÁS 2

Suggestions A:
- *Compare el padre del dibujo con su (your) padre. ¿Son similares o son diferentes? ¿En qué?*
- *Invente una madre para esta familia. ¿Cómo es? ¿Es como su madre?*
- *¿Cómo es la madre ideal? ¿el padre ideal?*
- Students describe own families, using questions as guide. Review *mi(s)* if not heavily used already.

▲ Actividad A. ¿Una familia típica?

Describa la familia del dibujo.

1. ¿Es grande o pequeña la familia? ¿Cuántas personas hay en el dibujo?
2. ¿Hay muchas niñas en la familia? ¿Cuántas? ¿Cuántos niños hay? ¿Cuántos hijos en total? ¿Cuántos años tienen, más o menos?
3. Describa a los hijos, usando estos adjetivos o cualquier otro: **serio**, **estudioso**, **bueno**, **cómico**, **trabajador**, **malo**.
4. ¿Cómo es o *no* es el padre? ¿Es similar a los hijos? Descríbalo (*Describe him*) usando estos adjetivos y frases: **serio**, **buen padre**, **cariñoso** (*affectionate*), **paciente**, **cómico**, **egoísta**, **agradable**, **comprensivo** (*understanding*).
5. ¿Estudian mucho los hijos? ¿Trabajan mucho? ¿Hablan con el padre? ¿Habla el padre con ellos?
6. La familia del dibujo, ¿es una familia típica de los Estados Unidos? ¿Es una típica familia hispánica? Explique.

A propósito... Giving the Opposite

When you want to disagree with something that someone has said, it is often easiest to do so by contradicting or giving the opposite. Examine the contrasts in these sentences.

No es **rico** sino **pobre**.	*He isn't rich but (rather) poor.*
No es **mexicana** sino **salvadoreña**.	*She isn't Mexican but (rather) Salvadorean.*

The word that established the contradiction or contrast in each of these sentences is **sino**, which means *but*, implying *but rather*. Use **sino** in **Opiniones** in the following activity.

Optional (*A propósito...*): *Complete las oraciones con **pero** o **sino**.* **1.** *La casa que me gusta no es blanca ______ amarilla.* **2.** *No tengo bolígrafo ______ lápiz.* **3.** *Tengo un lápiz ______ no tengo bolígrafo.* **4.** *El idioma materno de Carlos no es el inglés ______ el español.* **5.** *Pepe no tiene mucho dinero ______ tiene un Porsche.* **6.** *El abogado no es simpático ______ es muy inteligente.* **7.** *Ramón no trabaja mucho ______ tiene mucho dinero.* **8.** *El Canadá no es su tierra natal ______ su país de exilio.*
Complete las oraciones en una forma lógica. **1.** (nombre) *no es soltero/a sino ______.* **2.** (nombre) *no es antipático/a sino ______.* **3.** *Yo no soy ______ sino ______.* **4.** *Yo no soy de ______ sino de ______.*

▲ Actividad B. Antónimos

Sometimes Spanish *antonyms* (words that are opposite in meaning) are not at all similar in form: **bueno/malo**, **trabajador/perezoso**. In Spanish, as in English, however, many antonyms are formed by adding negative prefixes, such as **ir-**, **des-**, **in-**, **im-**, and **anti-**, to the adjective.

Antónimos

(ir)regular	(im)paciente	(im)perfecto/a	(in)competente	(des)cortés
(ir)racional	(ir)reverente	(anti)comunista	(im)probable	(in)discreto/a
(in)justo/a	(des)agradable	(ir)religioso/a	(anti)patriótico/a	(im)práctico/a
(in)útil	(in)activo/a	(des)leal	(ir)responsable	(anti)poético/a

Suggestion B: Students choose one family member and describe him/her to class in as much detail as possible.

Autodefiniciones. Describe yourself, using as many adjectives as possible: Soy **religiosa**. No soy **irreverente**.

Definiciones. What is your idea of an ideal friend? Use as many of the preceding adjectives as you can in your definitions.

MODELO: Un amigo ideal es paciente. No es descortés. No importa (*It doesn't matter*) si es guapo o no.

PADECE USTED DE NEUROSIS?
RESPONDA UD. MISMO CONFIDENCIALMENTE AL PRESENTE TEST MARCANDO DONDE DICE SI, PARA SABER SI ES O NO NEUROTICO

¿Es usted supersensible? .... ___
¿Le gusta conmiserarse? .... ___
¿Trata siempre de justificarse o defenderse? .... ___
¿Padece de ansiedad, en ciertos momentos? .... ___
¿Es Ud. autoconsciente? (cree que todo mundo lo observa) .... ___
¿Es inseguro, celoso y desconfiado? .... ___
¿Le gusta criticar? .... ___
8-¿Exagera pequeños problemas? .... ___
9-¿Tiende a exagerar sus estados de optimismo y depresión? .... ___

Opiniones. ¿Sí o no? Corrija las opiniones falsas usando **sino**.

1. Mi madre (hermano, tía, abuelo) es impaciente.
2. Es necesario ser rico/a para ser alegre (*happy*).
3. Mis clases este semestre son desagradables.
4. Los estudiantes son irresponsables.
5. Los ejercicios (*exercises*) de este libro son útiles.
6. Es importante ser religioso.
7. La clase de español es muy grande.
8. El mejor automóvil es práctico y pequeño.

Variation B: *Opiniones.* Students restate false sentences so their own opinions are expressed.

▲ Actividad C. ¡Firma aquí, por favor!

Suggestions C:
- Be sure that students understand the format of this "autograph" activity before allowing the class to begin. Space has been provided for students to write their questions before beginning the activity.
- Set a time limit for the activity and stick to it: 5 minutes for the first time.
- Whole-class follow-up: Who found six people who answered in the same way? five persons? etc.

Complete these sentences in a logical and truthful manner. Then, for each item, write a question (using **tú** forms) and use it to try to find one person in the class who answered exactly—or almost exactly—the way you did. Have that person sign his or her name. Do not ask any individual more than two questions in a row. No one may sign your list more than once.

MODELO: No me gusta estudiar historia. → —No, no me gusta.
—¿Te gusta estudiar historia? —Firma (*Sign*) aquí, por favor.

Nombres

1. No me gusta estudiar ______________________.
   ¿______________________? ______________
2. Algún día (*Someday*), quiero tener ______________ hijos.
   (¿Quieres... ?) ¿______________________? ______________
3. Me gusta mucho mirar ______________ (programa de televisión).
   ¿______________________? ______________
4. Mi primera (*first*) clase es a la(s) ______________. (¡OJO! **tu** = *your*)
   ¿______________________? ______________
5. Soy ______________ y no me gusta.
   ¿______________________? ______________

LECTURA CULTURAL

Lectura: See IM for suggestions and additional exercises and activities.

Antes de leer: Connecting Words

Some words or phrases indicate the general type of information that they introduce. For example, as you know, **por eso** (*for this reason, that's why*) is a signal that the information following it is a justification or a reason for the information that came before.

Necesito dinero. **Por eso** trabajo en la librería.

What kinds of clues do these words and phrases give you about the information that follows?

1. Por otra parte, ... (*On the other hand, . . .*) 2. También... 3. En cambio, ... (*On the other hand, . . .*) 4. ...porque... 5. Por ejemplo, ... 6. Por lo general, ... 7. ¡Hasta... ! (*Even. . . !*)

The following reading contains a number of cognates that you should be able to guess in context, including some verb forms with endings different from those you have learned about. You will recognize the meaning of most of those verbs easily, however. A verb whose meaning may not be immediately obvious to you is **vivir**. Associate it with *vivisection*, and *vivid*. Then read it in this context and guess its meaning.

Mi amigo Julio vive en la Argentina, en Buenos Aires.

La unidad familiar

Cuando un hispano observa la estructura de la familia norteamericana, puede° llegar muy pronto a esta conclusión: La familia ya no° existe en los Estados Unidos. ¿Por qué cree esto?

Los padres e hijos norteamericanos no se quieren.° Cuando los hijos tienen unos 18 años, sus padres los mandan° a vivir a otra parte. A veces° los hijos trabajan en otras ciudades y, a veces, abandonan la casa familiar sólo porque sí.° Los padres ancianos viven solos porque cuando sus hijos ya tienen otra familia los padres son para ellos una gran molestia. ¡Hasta hay hospicios para los viejos! No están en casa donde deberían° estar.

Por otra parte, un norteamericano que mira la estructura de la familia hispánica puede concluir lo siguiente: La influencia de la familia es demasiado fuerte.° ¿Por qué cree esto?

Los padres no confían° en sus hijos, y no los° preparan para la vida. Por ejemplo, hay hijos ya mayores—de 30 años o más—que todavía viven con sus padres en la casa familiar. Estos hijos tienen buenos trabajos y suficiente dinero para vivir aparte. Obviamente los padres no desarrollan° en ellos la capacidad de vivir independientemente y por eso los hijos no salen del nido.°

he can
ya... *no longer*
no... *don't love each other*
los... *send them off* / A... *Sometimes*
sólo... *just because they want to*
they should
demasiado... *too strong*
trust / *them*
develop
salen... *leave the nest*

¿Son válidas estas conclusiones? El concepto de la unidad familiar existe en las dos culturas. En los Estados Unidos la independencia personal tiene gran importancia social. Es una gran responsabilidad de los padres el hacer° independientes a sus hijos. La integridad de la familia depende menos de la cercanía° física y geográfica. En cambio, en la cultura hispánica es muy importante mantener intacto el grupo familiar. En muchos casos, los hijos salen° de la casa cuando contraen matrimonio y no cuando terminan sus estudios o comienzan a trabajar. Las dos sociedades tienen perspectivas diferentes; es imposible evaluar una cultura según las normas de otra.

el... *to make*
closeness
leave

Comprensión

Complete las oraciones lógicamente.

1. El hispano cree que hay ____ en los Estados Unidos.
   a. gran unidad familiar b. poca unidad familiar c. buenas relaciones familiares
2. Para el hispano, es bueno para los viejos ____.
   a. vivir con los hijos b. no depender de los hijos c. estar en un lugar aparte.
3. El norteamericano cree que la estructura familiar hispana ____.
   a. no es unida (*united*) b. da (*gives*) confianza a los hijos
   c. desarrolla la dependencia
4. Las diferencias expresadas aquí reflejan ____.
   a. factores económicos b. diferencias de edad c. valores culturales

¿Quién habla, probablemente, según la lectura, un hispano o un norteamericano?

1. Tengo 28 años. Soy soltero y vivo con mis padres.
2. Necesito visitar a mi madre. Tiene 72 años y vive en Meadowbrook Home.
3. La independencia es un factor importante en mi vida. No quiero depender de mis padres el resto de mi vida.
4. Mi hijo tiene muy buen trabajo en la IBM. Ahora vive solo en su propio (*own*) apartamento.

Para escribir

Answer the following questions in short sentences. Then take the individual sentences to form a coherent paragraph, using connecting words from the **A propósito**... in **Capítulo 1** and from the **Antes de leer** section in this chapter to make your ideas flow smoothly.

1. ¿Cuántos años tiene Ud.? 2. ¿Vive con sus padres o ya es Ud. independiente? (Vivo...) 3. ¿Qué tipo de relación hay entre los parientes de su familia? ¿una relación íntima? ¿cariñosa? ¿fría? ¿cariñosa pero con cierta distancia?
4. ¿Puede Ud. depender de sus padres en cualquier (*any*) situación? (Puedo...)
5. Según Ud., ¿qué palabra describe a su familia? ¿Es una molestia? ¿una limitación? ¿un refugio? ¿un factor estabilizador en su vida?

CAPÍTULO TRES

DE COMPRAS

Buenos Aires, Argentina

▲ **¡Vamos de compras!**[a]

—Necesito comprar un abrigo nuevo.

—¿Adónde vas? ¿Al centro comercial?

—Sí. ¿Quieres ir conmigo?

—¡Cómo no! ¿A qué hora vas?

—Pues... a las tres. ¿Qué te parece?[b]

—Perfecto. Nos vemos[c] a las tres.

[a]¡Vamos... *Let's go shopping!*
[b]¿Qué... *What do you think?*
[c]Nos... *See you* (*We'll see each other*)

VOCABULARIO: PREPARACIÓN

• See also [video icon] and [audio icon]

Vocabulario: Preparación:
• See detailed supplementary materials and exercises for this section bound into the back of this Annotated Instructor's Edition.

De compras°

°De... *Shopping*

comprar	to buy	**el almacén**	department store
llevar	to wear; to carry; to take	**el centro**	downtown
regatear	to haggle, bargain	**el centro comercial**	shopping mall
vender	to sell	**la tienda**	shop, store
venden de todo	they sell everything	**el precio**	price
		el precio fijo	fixed (set) price
		barato/a	inexpensive
		caro/a	expensive

• See model for vocabulary presentation and other materials in Supplementary *Vocabulario: Preparación* Materials, chapter by chapter, IM.

La ropa

un par de (zapatos, medias...)	a pair of (shoes, stockings, . . .)
es de (lana, algodón, seda)*	it is made of (wool, cotton, silk)
¡Es de última moda!	It's the latest style!

*Note another use of **ser** + **de**: to tell what material something is made of.

A. ¿Qué ropa llevan estas personas?

1. El Sr. Rivera lleva ___.

2. La Srta. Alonso lleva ___.
El perro lleva ___.

3. Sara lleva ___.

4. Alfredo lleva ___.
Necesita comprar ___.

Generalmente, ¿qué artículos de ropa son para los hombres? ¿para las mujeres? ¿para hombres *y* mujeres?

Extension A: *¿para los preppies? ¿para los punkers? ¿los cantantes country-western? ¿los líderes militares? ¿los detectives? ¿los personajes* (characters) *bíblicos?*

Follow-up B: ***Preguntas personales:***
1. *¿Dónde compra Ud. la ropa generalmente, en una tienda o en un almacén?* **2.** *En esta ciudad, ¿hay tiendas o mercados donde regateen los clientes?* **3.** *¿Lleva Ud. ___ hoy?* **4.** *¿Necesita Ud. comprar ropa nueva? ¿Qué necesita comprar? ¿Qué tipo de ropa compra con más frecuencia?* **5.** *Imagine que Ud. es (un profesor conservador, un estudiante típico, el presidente, un famoso artista de Hollywood). ¿Qué lleva hoy?* **6.** *Por lo general, ¿le gusta llevar ropa elegante o ropa vieja?*

B. Complete las oraciones lógicamente.

1. Un ___ es una tienda grande.
2. No es posible ___ cuando hay precios fijos.
3. Quiero ___ el coche, pero el ___ es muy alto.
4. En la librería ___ de todo: textos y otros libros, cuadernos, lápices...
5. Para ir a bailar (*to go dancing*) a una discoteca me gusta llevar ___.
6. A una fiesta de etiqueta (*formal*) llevo ___.
7. En las playas (*beaches*) de Hawai los turistas llevan ___ todos los días.
8. Muchos ejecutivos llevan ___.
9. Muchas ejecutivas llevan ___.
10. Nunca (*Never*) llevo ___ a la clase.
11. En casa siempre (*always*) llevo ___.
12. La ropa de ___ es muy elegante. La ropa de ___ es muy práctica.
13. ___ de una ciudad es la parte céntrica.
14. Siempre hay *boutiques* en los ___.

Notas comunicativas: More About Getting Information

You have already used the tag phrase **¿verdad?** at the end of statements to change them into questions. Another common Spanish tag phrase is **¿no?**

Venden de todo aquí, { **¿no?** / **¿verdad?** }	*They sell everything here, right? (don't they?)*
No necesito impermeable hoy, **¿verdad?**	*I don't need a raincoat today, do I?*

¿Verdad? is found after affirmative or negative statements; **¿no?** is usually found after affirmative statements only. The inverted question mark comes immediately before the tag question, not at the beginning of the statement.

C. **Preguntas.** Using tag questions, ask a classmate questions based on the following statements. He or she will answer, based on general information, or as truthfully as possible, if the question is about aspects of his or her life.

1. En un almacén hay precios fijos.
2. Regateamos mucho en los Estados Unidos.
3. En México no hay muchos mercados.
4. Los *bluejeans* Calvin Klein son muy baratos.
5. Es necesario llevar traje y corbata a clase.
6. Estudias en la biblioteca por la noche.
7. Buscas un perro o un gato.
8. Eres una persona muy independiente.
9. Tienes una familia muy grande.
10. No hay examen mañana.

¿De qué color es?

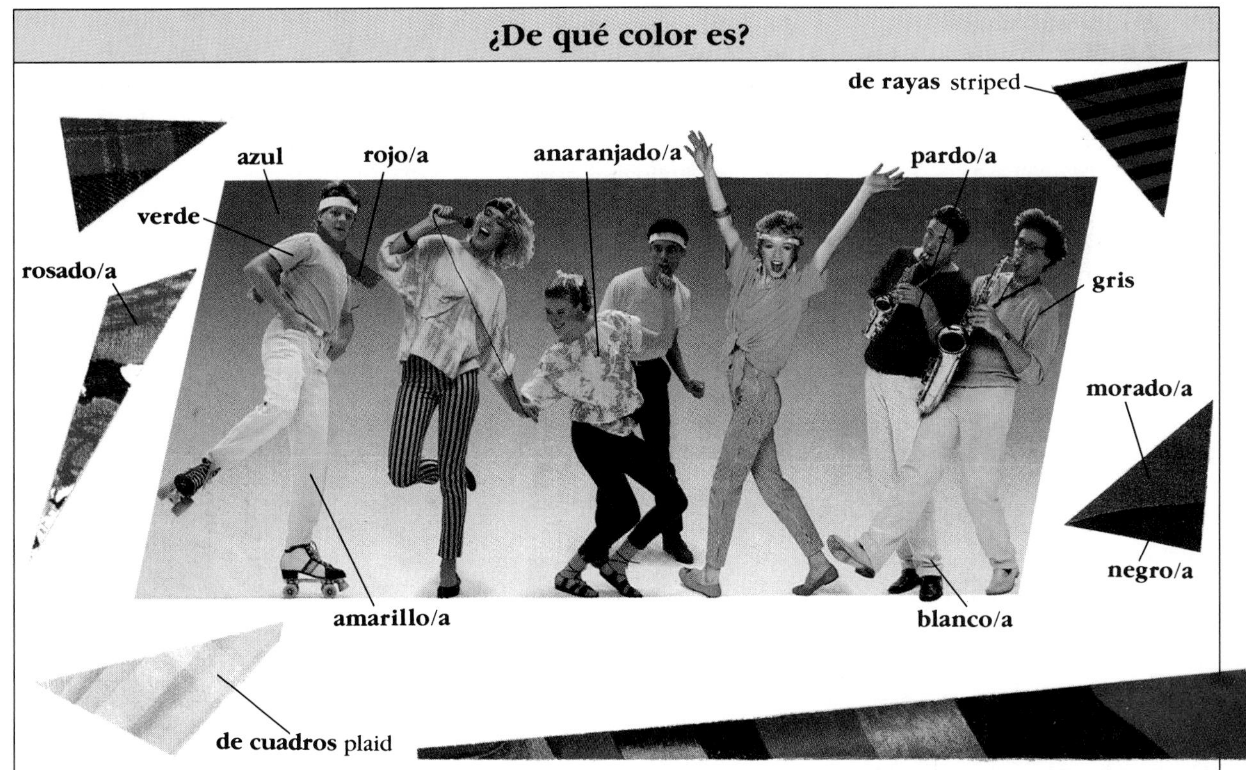

Extension A: *¿un lápiz? ¿el vino? ¿las violetas? ¿los zapatos de tenis? ¿los bluejeans? ¿una rosa? ¿una mañana bonita/fea?*

Follow-up (*Dictado* + listening comprehension):

- Dictate items: **1.** *una camisa negra* **2.** *un impermeable viejo* **3.** *medias blancas* **4.** *una falda de cuadros* **5.** *una camisa de rayas* **6.** (colors of your university) **7.** *una camisa o chaqueta verde militar,* etc.
- *¿Qué asocia Ud. con... ?* (Students give items from *Dictado.*) **1.** *un detective famoso de la televisión* **2.** *una persona que se llama McTavish* **3.** *un cantante* (country-western) *famoso* **4.** *un estudiante de* (university) **5.** *un grupo de beisbolistas* **6.** *un prisionero* **7.** *Fidel Castro*

A. **Asociaciones.** ¿Qué colores asocia Ud. con... ?

¿el dinero? ¿la una de la mañana? ¿una mañana bonita? ¿una mañana fea? ¿el demonio? ¿los Estados Unidos? ¿una jirafa? ¿un pingüino? ¿un limón? ¿una naranja? ¿un elefante? ¿las flores (*flowers*)?

B. **¿De qué color es?** Tell the color of things in your classroom, especially the clothing your classmates are wearing.

MODELOS: El bolígrafo de Anita es amarillo.
Los calcetines de Roberto son azules. Los de Jaime* son pardos.
Los de Julio...

Now describe what someone is wearing, without revealing his or her name. Using your clues, can your classmates guess whom you are describing?

Los números 100 y más

Continúe la secuencia: ciento, ciento uno, ...
mil, dos mil, ...
un millón, dos millones, ...

100	cien, ciento	700	setecientos/as
101	ciento uno/una	800	ochocientos/as
200	doscientos/as	900	novecientos/as
300	trescientos/as	1.000	mil
400	cuatrocientos/as	2.000	dos mil
500	quinientos/as	1.000.000	un millón
600	seiscientos/as	2.000.000	dos millones

- **Ciento** is used in combination with numbers from 1 to 99 to express the numbers 101 through 199: **ciento uno**, **ciento dos**, **ciento setenta y nueve**, and so on. **Cien** is used in counting and before numbers greater than 100: **cien mil**, **cien millones**.
- When the numbers 200 through 900 modify a noun, they must agree in gender: **cuatrocientas niñas**, **doscientas dos casas**.
- **Mil** means *one thousand* or *a thousand.* It does not have a plural form in counting, but **millón** does. When used with a noun, **millón** (**dos millones**, and so on) must be followed by **de**.[†]

1.899	mil ochocientos noventa y nueve
3.000 habitantes	tres mil habitantes
14.000.000 de habitantes	catorce millones de habitantes

*You can avoid repeating the noun **calcetines** just by dropping it and retaining the definite article. Here are some other examples of the same construction: **la camisa de Janet y la camisa de Paula → la camisa de Janet y *la de* Paula; el sombrero del niño y el sombrero de Pablo → el sombrero del niño y *el de* Pablo.** For more information on this topic, see Appendix 1, Using Adjectives as Nouns.

[†]In many parts of the Spanish-speaking world, a period in numerals is used where English uses a comma and a comma is used to indicate the decimal where English uses a period: **$10,45**.

A. **¿Cuánto es?** Diga los precios.

el dólar (los Estados Unidos, Canadá)
el peso (México)
el bolívar (Venezuela)
la peseta (España)
el quetzal (Guatemala)

1. 7.345 pesetas
2. $100
3. 5.710 quetzales
4. 670 bolívares
5. 2.486 pesetas
6. $1.000.000
7. 528 pesos
8. 836 bolívares
9. 101 pesetas
10. $4.000.000,00
11. 6.500.000,00 pesos
12. 25.000.000,00 pesetas

B. **Situaciones.** Imagine that you have recently made the following purchases. With a classmate, ask and answer questions about the amount you paid. Follow the model, using the prices indicated or inventing your own.

Note B: Introduction of *por* for price paid, in exchange for.

Follow-up B: Tell what you paid for some personal objects you have with you. Then ask students *¿Cuánto pagaste por... ?* questions about possessions they have with them (*la mochila, la falda, el abrigo,* etc.)

Optional: Guessing Game: ***¿Más o menos?:*** Instructor or student thinks of a number; others try to guess it. After each guess, leader tells whether number is *más* or *menos*. ***Modelo:*** *¿500? → Más. ¿700? → Menos. ¿600? → Más. ¿650? → Eso es.* (That's right.)

Palabras útiles: pagaste (*did you pay*), fue (*it was*), una ganga (*bargain*), una compra (*purchase*)

MODELO: la radio ($100) →
—¿Cuánto pagaste por la radio?
—Cien dólares.
—¡Uy! ¡Qué (*How*) cara!
¡Es/Fue una ganga!
Fue una buena compra.

1. la calculadora ($20)
2. tu (*your*) coche nuevo ($5,600)
3. tu estéreo ($1,500)
4. la computadora ($2,400)
5. el coche usado ($1,850)
6. el reloj ($350)

LO «IN»... PUESTO

Lo que más domina e incluso manda este año en la moda veraniega son, sin duda, los colores blanco y negro. La verdad es que para lucir la piel morena no hay nada como el blanco, con la ventaja de que se puede mezclar con casi todos los colores. Los naranjas y amarillos también están en alza, y los lunares que no falten. Las faldas son estrechas, minis o largas, acompañadas de grandes chaquetas con solapas. Los pantalones ceñidos y estrechos, en los bajos, con camisas grandes, blusones y túnicas que se deben llevar siempre con cinturón, porque estilizan la figura. Los vestidos muy «sexy», por encima de la rodilla, y con los hombros descubiertos, o bien camiseros. Son imprescindibles los pendientes muy largos, con el pelo muy corto y llevar muchas pulseras y collares dorados...

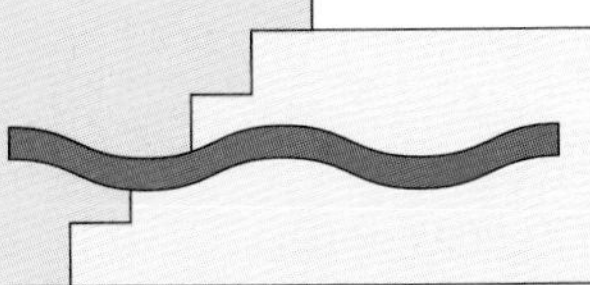

PRONUNCIACIÓN: *D*

Some sounds, such as English [b], are called *stops* because, as you pronounce them, you briefly stop the flow of air and then release it. Other sounds, such as English [f] and [v], pronounced by pushing air out with a little friction, are called *fricatives.*

Spanish **d** has two basic sounds. At the beginning of a phrase or sentence or after **n** or **l**, it is pronounced as a stop [d] (similar to English *d* in *d*og). Like the Spanish [t], it is produced by putting the tongue against the back of the upper teeth. In all other cases, it is pronounced as a fricative [đ], that is, like the *th* sound in English *they* and *another.*

Point out: At the end of a word fricative [đ] is very weak, sometimes not even pronounced—e.g., *usted → usté, verdad → verdá.*

A. Practique las siguientes palabras y frases.

1. [d] diez dos doscientos doctor ¿dónde? el doctor el dinero venden
2. [đ] mucho dinero adiós usted seda ¿adónde? la doctora cuadros todo

B. Pronuncie. ¿Dónde está el dinero? David Dávila es doctor. Dos y diez son doce. ¿Qué estudia Ud.? Venden de todo, ¿verdad?

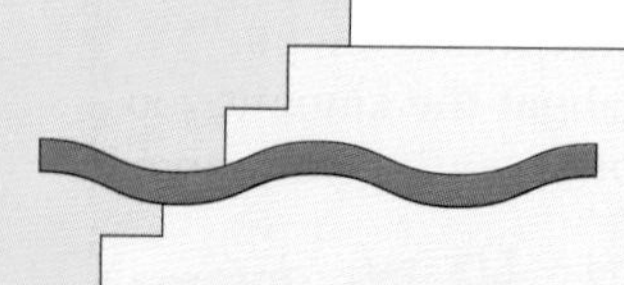

MINIDIÁLOGOS Y GRAMÁTICA

> **¿Recuerda Ud.?**
>
> The personal endings used with **-ar** verbs share some characteristics of those used with **-er** and **-ir** verbs, which you will learn in the next section. Review the endings of **-ar** verbs by telling which subject pronoun(s) you associate with each of these endings.
>
> 1. **-amos** 2. **-as** 3. **-áis** 4. **-an** 5. **-o** 6. **-a**

Communicative objectives 8: another set of verbs to talk about activities and actions

8. EXPRESSING ACTIONS

Present Tense of *-er* and *-ir* Verbs; More About Subject Pronouns

Por la tarde, en casa de la familia Robles

EL SR. ROBLES: Paquita, *debes* estudiar más ahora. *Insisto* en eso.

PAQUITA: Pero, papá, *asisto* a todas mis clases y saco buenas notas. Además, todos mis amigos están en el centro comercial esta tarde.

EL SR. ROBLES: Tus amigos no son mis hijos. Nunca *abres* los libros en casa. Nunca *lees* el periódico. Nunca...

PAQUITA: ¡Ay, papá! ¡No me *comprendes*! ¡Eres terrible a veces!

Point out in mini: *debes, abres, lees, comprendes* are *tú* forms. How are they similar to/different from *-ar* verb forms you already know?

Afternoon at the Robles' house MR. ROBLES: Paquita, you should study more now. I insist on that. PAQUITA: But, Dad, I go to all of my classes and I get good grades. Besides, all my friends are at the mall this afternoon. MR. ROBLES: Your friends aren't my children. You never open your books at home. You never read the newspaper. You never . . . PAQUITA: Oh, Dad! You don't understand me! You're terrible sometimes!

Follow-up: Who do you say these things to? Who says them to you? (Optional: *nadie*.) 1. *¡No me comprendes!* 2. *Debes estudiar más.* 3. *Nunca asistes a tus clases.* 4. *¡Eres terrible a veces!*

¿Quién...

1. debe estudiar más hoy?
2. insiste en imponer su voluntad (*his or her will, way*)?
3. asiste a todas las clases?
4. nunca abre los libros en casa?
5. no comprende la situación?

Verbs that End in *-er* and *-ir*

comer (*to eat*)		**vivir** (*to live*)	
como	com**emos**	vivo	viv**imos**
comes	com**éis**	vives	viv**ís**
come	com**en**	vive	viv**en**

The present tense of **-er** and **-ir** verbs is formed by adding personal endings to the stem of the verb (the infinitive minus its **-er**/**-ir** ending). The personal endings for **-er** and **-ir** verbs are the same except for the first and second person plural.

Remember that the Spanish present tense has a number of present tense equivalents in English and can also be used to express future meaning:

como { *I eat* — simple present; *I am eating* — present progressive; *I do eat* — emphatic present; *I will eat* — future }

Some important **-er** and **-ir** verbs in this chapter include the following:

aprender	to learn	**abrir**	to open
beber	to drink	**asistir (a)**	to attend, go to (*a class, function*)
comer	to eat	**escribir**	to write
comprender	to understand	**insistir (en + *inf.*)**	to insist (*on doing something*)
creer (en)	to think, believe (in)	**recibir**	to receive
deber (+ *inf.*)	should, must, ought to (*do something*)	**vivir**	to live
leer	to read		
vender	to sell		

[Práctica A–C]

Suggestions:
- Introduce *comer* as model *-er* verb. Talk through conjugation, using forms in complete sentences/questions but writing only verb forms on board.
- Introduce meaning of *leer* and use forms in questions to students, writing only verb forms on board.
- Follow same procedure with *vivir* and *escribir* (*-ir* verbs). **Point out:** only *nosotros* and *vosotros* forms differ from those of *-er* verbs.

Suggestions:
- Model pronunciation of each infinitive several times. Use *yo* form of each in brief simple sentence about yourself; then in *Ud.* and *Uds.* questions to students. (See Suggestions for *-ar* verbs.)
- *¿Cómo se dice?* I/we learn; I/we understand; he/she/they believe(s); he/she/they sell(s); I/we open; I/we insist; he/she/they receive(s); he/she/they live(s).

Emphasis: *deber*/*insistir en* + infinitive

Use and Omission of Subject Pronouns

In English, a verb must have an expressed subject (a noun or pronoun): ***he/she/ the train** returns*. In Spanish, however, as you have probably noticed, an expressed subject is not required. Verbs are accompanied by a subject pronoun only for clarification, emphasis, or contrast.

- *Clarification:* When the context does not make the subject clear, the subject pronoun is expressed ***Ud./él/ella* vende**; ***Uds./ellos/ellas* venden**. This happens most frequently with third person singular and plural verb forms.
- *Emphasis:* Subject pronouns are used in Spanish to emphasize the subject when in English you would stress it with your voice.

  ¡**Yo** no leo el periódico! — *I don't read the newspaper!*
- *Contrast:* Contrast is a special case of emphasis. Subject pronouns are used to contrast the actions of two individuals or groups.

  Ellos comen mucho; **nosotros** comemos poco. — *They eat a lot; we eat little.*

[Práctica CH]

Emphasis: Omission of subject pronouns is norm in Spanish except for situations requiring **(1)** clarity, **(2)** emphasis, or **(3)** contrast. Be alert for students' tendency to overuse subject pronouns. Correct by suggesting *No es necesario usar* (*yo, tú* etc.).

Preliminary exercises:
- Give corresponding forms:
  yo: *aprender, vender, comprender, escribir*
  tú: *comer, leer, beber, insistir*
  Ud./él/ella: *beber, creer, abrir, recibir*
  nosotros: *comprender, deber, asistir, vivir*
  vosotros: *deber, vender, aprender, abrir*
  Uds./ellos/ellas: *creer, leer, comer, escribir*
- Transformation exercise: *Ud./tú* → *yo*. **Modelo:** *¿Come Ud.?* → *Sí, como. ¿Comen Uds.?* → *Sí, comemos.*, etc.
- *Dé oraciones nuevas según las indicaciones.*
  Escenas de la sala de clase
  1. *Yo asisto a clase todos los días.* (*tú, nosotros, Ud., todos los estudiantes, Carlos, vosotros*) **2.** *Aprendes español en clase, ¿verdad?* (*nosotros, yo, Ud., la estudiante francesa, Uds., vosotros*)

Práctica

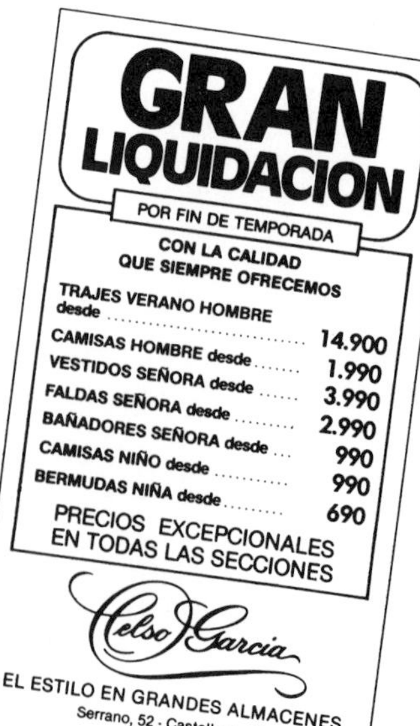

A. **Un día de compras.** Form complete sentences about a day of shopping with a friend, based on the cues given. When the subject pronoun is given in parentheses, do not use it in the sentence.

1. (yo) leer / periódico / por / mañana
2. hay / grande / rebajas (*sales*) / en / almacén Celso García
3. mi amigo / Anita / insistir / en / ir conmigo (*to go with me*) / a / centro
4. (ella) creer / que / (nosotros) deber / llegar / temprano
5. (ellos) abrir / almacén / las diez
6. rebajas / ser / estupendo: ¡(ellos) vender / de todo!
7. todos / comprar / algo (*something*)
8. Anita / creer / que / yo / no / deber / comprar / mucho...
9. ... pero / (yo) comprar / uno / camiseta / y / dos / par / sandalias
10. más tarde / Anita y yo / comer / juntas (*together*) / en / café

Now retell the story as if you were Anita, using the same cues as a guide and making the necessary adjustments: **1. Mi amiga lee...**

B. **Unas diferencias familiares: Habla Paquita.** The following paragraphs tell Paquita's side of the disagreement you read about in the minidialogue. Complete them with the correct form of the infinitives.

Según° mi padre, los jóvenes (*deber*[1]) asistir a clase todos los días. Papá también (*creer*[2]) que nosotros (*deber*[3]) estudiar con frecuencia. Papá (*insistir*[4]) en que no es necesario mirar la televisión. Según él, es más interesante (*leer*[5]) el periódico. Él sólo trabaja, (*comer*[6]) y (*leer*[7]).

°*According to*

Yo no soy como papá. Prefiero mirar la televisión todas las noches. (*Yo: abrir*[8]) los libros a veces° y (*leer*[9]) cuando es necesario, pero... tengo muchos amigos y (*creer*[10]) que es más interesante estar con ellos.

°a... *at times*

Es Navidad (Christmas) *y hay una fiesta en casa. ¿Qué pasa?* **1.** *Todos comen y beben. (yo, los tíos, tú, Uds., la prima y yo, Ud., vosotras)* **2.** *Los niños reciben regalos. (papá, tú, nosotras, los hijos de Juan, Alicia, los nietos, vosotros)*

Follow-up A: *¿Cierto o falso?* (Students imagine that they are *yo.*) **1.** *Anita lee el periódico por la mañana.* **2.** *No hay rebajas hoy.* **3.** *Anita compra mucho.* **4.** *Anita y yo comemos en un restaurante.*

Suggestion B: Have students scan through the paragraph for meaning before they attempt to do the items. After individual items are done, have one student read through the entire paragraph. Then do the comprehension questions.

Emphasis C: *Uds. → nosotros.*

Follow-up C: ***Preguntas:*** *¿Insiste Ud. en hablar inglés en esta clase? ¿en comprender todo? ¿en cantar en clase? ¿en aprender todo? ¿en practicar español un poco todos los días? ¿en tomar exámenes todos los días?*

Based on the preceding paragraphs and the minidialogue, who would have made the following statements, Paquita or her father (**su padre**)?

1. ¡No comprendo tu obsesión con los centros comerciales!
2. ¡Los programas de televisión son fascinantes!
3. ¡No comprendes a los jóvenes de hoy!
4. Esta noche quiero leer un buen libro.

C. **Las obligaciones universitarias.** ¿Qué deben o no deben hacer (*do*) Uds., los estudiantes de esta clase?

1. comer durante la clase
2. asistir a clase todos los días
3. llevar traje de baño a clase
4. aprender las palabras nuevas

¿En qué insiste su profesor(a) de español?

5. hablar español en clase
6. explicar toda la gramática
7. dar (*to give*) exámenes con frecuencia
8. llevar traje y corbata / un vestido elegante a clase

Follow-up CH: ***Dictado:*** **1.** *Uds. comprenden todo, ¿no?* **2.** *Debemos escribir los ejercicios, ¿no?* **3.** *Vendes la casa, ¿no?* **4.** *No asisten a clase, ¿verdad?* **5.** *No debo comprar la chaqueta verde, ¿verdad?*

CH. ¿Cómo se dice en español?

1. "Does *he* understand Spanish?" "I don't believe so, and *she* doesn't understand English." "What language (**lengua**) should we speak, then (**entonces**)?"
2. Anita has two children, Pablo and Teresa. He doesn't believe in Santa Claus, but she still (**todavía**) believes in him (**él**).

Córdoba, España

En la calle (*street*)

—Oye, quiero hablar un momento contigo (*with you*).

—No puedo ahora... tengo prisa... ¡Hay unas rebajas estupendas en Celso García! Hablamos después (*later*), ¿eh?

—¡Hombre, siempre tienes prisa!

—¡Tú, tranquila! ¡Nos vemos mañana!

Suggestion A: Personalize by encouraging students to use the _____ in first column to talk about someone they know.

Conversación

A. Form complete sentences using one word or phrase from each column. Be sure to use the correct form of the verbs. Make any of the sentences negative if you wish.

yo	abrir	novelas de ciencia ficción / de horror
(estudiante), tú	leer	la situación / los problemas de los estudiantes
Ud., profesor(a)	escribir	el periódico / una revista (*magazine*) todos los días
los estudiantes de aquí	beber	Coca-Cola / café antes de (*before*) la clase
los hombres	vender	muchas / pocas cartas (*letters*)
un consejero	comprender	muchos/pocos ejercicios
me gusta	recibir	llegar a casa temprano esta noche
	vivir	los libros al final del semestre
	deber	mirar mucho la televisión
	¿ ?	en una casa / un apartamento / ¿ ?
		regalos
		la puerta (*door*) para las mujeres
		mucho / poco

Optional: *Su* (Your) *amigo Carlos hace* (asks) *muchas preguntas... y a veces son absurdas. Conteste sus* (his) *preguntas con mucha paciencia, en oraciones completas.* 1. *Vivimos in Nueva York, ¿no?* 2. *Los estudiantes no beben en clase, ¿verdad?* 3. *Siempre recibes un suspenso en los exámenes, ¿no?* 4. *Escribo los ejercicios* (exercises) *en italiano, ¿no?* 5. *Muchos actores viven en Pocotella, Idaho, ¿no?* 6. *Aprendemos francés en clase, ¿no?* 7. *Los profesores no insisten en recibir muchos regalos, ¿verdad?* 8. *El profesor no comprende el problema, ¿verdad?* 9. *Todos los niños creen en Santa Claus, ¿no?* 10. *Venden cosas muy caras en el mercado, ¿no?*

Suggestion: Reenter rejoinders like *Hombre, claro*; *No me digas*; *No, hombre*; and so on.

Follow-up: Ask students to invent their own sentences to present to the class.

B. **Una noche en casa.** ¿Qué hacen estas personas? ¿Qué ropa llevan?

Palabras útiles: el refrigerador, la comida (*food*)

Suggestion B: Use these questions before asking students to describe activities depicted: 1. *¿Quiénes son estas personas?* 2. *¿Dónde están?* 3. *¿Son una familia típica?* Discuss drawing, cueing student responses when necessary. Then follow up with these questions: 1. *¿Qué otras actividades son típicas de las familias?* 2. *De las personas que se ven en el dibujo, ¿quién es como tú?*

Notas comunicativas: Telling How Frequently You Do Things

Use the following words and phrases to tell how often you perform an activity.

todos los días	*every day*
con frecuencia	*frequently*
a veces	*at times*
una vez / dos veces a la semana / al mes	*once/twice a week/month*
casi nunca	*almost never*
nunca	*never*

Hablo con mis amigos **todos los días**. Hablo con mis padres **una vez a la semana**. **Casi nunca** hablo con mis abuelos. Y **nunca** hablo con mis tíos que viven en Italia.

Use the expressions **casi nunca** and **nunca** only at the beginning of a sentence. You will learn more about how to use them in Grammar Section 19.

Emphasis: Use *casi nunca* and *nunca* at beginning of sentence only.

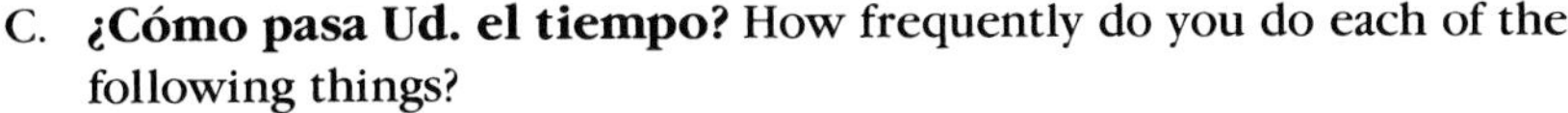

Extension C: Students add 3 original questions to list before doing interview.

C. **¿Cómo pasa Ud. el tiempo?** How frequently do you do each of the following things?

1. Escribo una carta.
2. Hablo por teléfono.
3. Como con todos los parientes.
4. Leo novelas.
5. Miro la televisión.
6. Bebo Coca-Cola.
7. Leo el periódico.
8. Aprendo palabras nuevas en español.
9. Compro regalos para papá y mamá.
10. Escribo un poema.
11. Insisto en hablar inglés en esta clase.
12. Recibo un suspenso (*F*) en un examen.
13. Llevo zapatos sin (*without*) calcetines.
14. Llevo una camiseta de rayas.

Now interview another student, asking him or her questions based on the sentences given above. Begin each question with **¿Con qué frecuencia... ?**

MODELO: ¿Con qué frecuencia escribes una carta?

Now use the same phrases to describe the activities of at least one member of your family.

MODELO: Mi padre nunca escribe cartas. Habla por teléfono con frecuencia...

CH. **Entrevista.** Hold a brief conversation with a classmate based on the following questions. Note that you will be using the **tú** forms of some expressions you learned in **Capítulo 1**.

MODELO: —¿Qué (no) quieres estudiar hoy?
—(No) Quiero estudiar español (filosofía, biología, ruso, ...).

1. ¿Qué (no) quieres leer?
2. ¿A qué hora prefieres comer?
3. ¿Prefieres aprender español o alemán?
4. ¿Qué no quieres hacer (*do*) hoy?
5. ¿Qué (no) debes hacer en clase?
6. ¿Qué te gusta escribir?
7. ¿Quieres asistir a un concierto esta noche?
8. ¿Prefieres hablar inglés o español?

9. EXPRESSING ACTIONS AND STATES
Tener, venir, preferir, querer, and *poder;* Some Idioms with *tener*

Communicative objectives for 9: how to talk about some states using idioms

tener (*to have*)	**venir** (*to come*)	**preferir** (*to prefer*)	**querer** (*to want*)	**poder** (*to be able, can*)
tengo	vengo	prefiero	quiero	puedo
tienes	vienes	prefieres	quieres	puedes
tiene	viene	prefiere	quiere	puede
tenemos	venimos	preferimos	queremos	podemos
tenéis	venís	preferís	queréis	podéis
tienen	vienen	prefieren	quieren	pueden

You have been using forms of some of these verbs for several chapters. The **yo** forms of **tener** and **venir** are irregular: **tengo**, **vengo**. In other forms of **tener**, **venir**, **preferir**, and **querer**, when the stem vowel **e** is stressed, it becomes **ie**: ***tie*nes**, ***vie*nes**, **pref*ie*res**, **qu*ie*res**, and so on. Similarly, the stem vowel **o** in **poder** becomes **ue** when stressed. In vocabulary lists these changes are shown in parentheses after the infinitive: **poder (ue)**. You will learn more verbs of this type in Grammar Section 16.

Point out (drawing): Caption = "Where there's a will there's a way." Ask: *¿Dónde está el hombre? ¿De dónde es? ¿Qué idiomas habla? ¿Es extranjero? ¿Qué idiomas habla la dependienta?*

Suggestions:
- Model infinitives and talk through conjugations, using forms in complete sentences/ questions.
- **Point out:** similarities and differences. Note *yo* forms of *tener* and *venir*, *nosotros* and *vosotros* forms with same stem as infinitive. Emphasize diphthongization of *e* → *ie* and *o* → *ue* when stressed (exceptions: *tengo*/*vengo*).

Some Idioms with *tener*

An *idiom* (**un modismo**) is a group of words that has meaning to the speakers of a language but that does not necessarily appear to make sense when examined word by word. Idiomatic expressions are often different from one language to another. For example, in English, *to pull Mary's leg* usually means *to tease her*, not *to grab her leg and pull it.* In Spanish, *to pull Mary's leg* is **tomarle el pelo a María** (literally, *to take María's hair*).

Point out: There is no one-to-one correspondence of words of idioms between two languages.

Alternate example: Her eyes were glued to the television.

Many ideas expressed in English with the verb *to be* are expressed in Spanish with idioms using **tener**. You have already learned one **tener** idiom: **tener... años**. Here are some additional ones. Note that they describe a condition or state that a person can experience.

tener miedo (de)	*to be afraid (of)*
tener prisa	*to be in a hurry*
tener razón	*to be right*
no tener razón	*to be wrong*

Other **tener** idioms include **tener ganas de** (*to feel like*) and **tener que** (*to have to*). The infinitive is always used after these two idiomatic expressions.

Note: *tener calor/frío* in Ch. 5 with weather, *tener hambre/sed* in Ch. 6 with foods, *tener sueño* in Ch. 9 with daily activities.

Suggestions:
- Model idioms in complete sentences about yourself.
- **Optional:** *mucha prisa, mucho miedo.*

Tengo ganas de trabajar.	*I feel like working.*
¿No tienes ganas de descansar?	*Don't you feel like resting?*
Tienen que ser prácticos.	*They have to be practical.*
¿No tiene Ud. que estudiar ahora mismo?	*Don't you have to study right now?*

Emphasis: *De* and *que* must be used even though there is no corresponding word in English (similar to use of *a* with *ir* + *a* + inf.). *¿Cómo se dice en español?*: **1.** I don't feel like bargaining (talking). **2.** We don't feel like studying (working). **3.** I hate to eat (read).

Preliminary exercises A:
- *Es la semana de los exámenes. Por eso ocurren las siguientes situaciones. Dé oraciones nuevas según las indicaciones.* **1.** *Sara tiene muchos exámenes.* (*Pepe, nosotros, Alicia y Carlos, yo, tú, vosotras*) **2.** *Ramón viene a la biblioteca todas las noches. Prefiere estudiar aquí.* (*yo, los estudiantes, tú, Uds., nosotras, vosotros*) **3.** *Silvia quiere estudiar más, pero no puede.* (*yo, ella, nosotros, todos, tú, vosotros*)
- *Conteste según las indicaciones.* **1.** *—¿Qué tiene Ud. que hacer* (to do) *esta noche? —Tengo que llegar a casa temprano.* (*asistir a una clase a las siete, aprender unas palabras en español, estudiar la Lección 4, leer toda la noche, hablar con un amigo,* __?__) **2.** *—Pero... ¿qué tiene ganas de hacer? —Tengo ganas de descansar.* (*abrir una botella de vino, mirar la televisión, comer en un buen restaurante, ¡no estudiar más!,* __?__)

Preliminary Exercises B: *Dictado* **and listening:**
- **Dictado: 1.** *Tiene prisa y miedo.* **2.** *Tiene toda la razón.* **3.** *Nunca tiene razón.* **4.** *No tienen ganas de estudiar.* **5.** *Tenemos que trabajar.*
- **Asociaciones:** *¿Con qué expresión asocia Ud. ... ?* **1.** *el cliente* **2.** *los tres cochinitos* (draw pig face or tail on board) **3.** *el conejo blanco* (draw rabbit ears on board)

Follow-up C: What *tener* idiom do you associate with *tres exámenes mañana, King Kong, 2 + 2 = 4, 2 + 2 = 5, no quiero comer ahora.*

Optional: *¿Qué se hace esta tarde? ¿Cómo se dice en español?*
1. Alicia feels like going shopping. **2.** We have to study for the exam. **3.** I don't feel like watching television. **4.** Do you have to go home now? **5.** Jorge has to buy another hat.

Práctica

A. **Es la semana de los exámenes.** Haga oraciones con las palabras indicadas para describir un día de Sara.

Sara...

1. tener / mucho / exámenes
2. por eso / (ella) venir / a / universidad / todo / días
3. (ella) preferir / estudiar / en / biblioteca / porque / allí (*there*) / no / hay / mucho ruido (*noise*)
4. hoy / trabajar / hasta / ocho / noche
5. querer / leer / más / pero / no / poder
6. por eso / regresar / a / residencia
7. tener / ganas / de / descansar / un poco...
8. ...pero / ser / imposible / porque / uno / amigos / venir a mirar / la tele

Now retell the same sequence of events twice, first as if they had happened to you, then as if they had happened to you and your roommate, using **nosotros/as**. Supply an appropriate name for your roommate.

B. **Situaciones.** Expand the situations described in these sentences by using a related idiom with **tener**.

MODELO: Tengo un examen mañana. → ¡Tengo que estudiar!

1. ¿Cuántos años? ¿40? No, yo sólo...
2. Esta calle es peligrosa (*dangerous*) de noche. Por eso...
3. ¿Ya son las tres de la mañana? Por eso...
4. ¡Hasta luego! ¡Me voy (*I'm leaving*)!
5. No, mi hijo, dos y dos no son cinco.

C. Listen as a classmate reads the following paragraphs to you and complete them with the appropriate **tener** idioms.

1. De repente (*Suddenly*) hay un terremoto (*earthquake*). Todos tienen ____.
2. Ernesto regresa a la universidad. Son las tres menos cinco y tiene una clase de matemáticas a las tres. Ernesto tiene ____.
3. Hay una fiesta porque hoy es el cumpleaños (*birthday*) del primo Antonio. Tiene 29 ____. Todos ____ de ir a la fiesta.
4. En la fiesta, hay muchos paquetes para Antonio. Son regalos para él y por eso tiene ____ abrir los regalos.

5. PROFESOR: ¿Y la capital de la Argentina?
   MARCIA: Buenos Aires.
   CELIA: Cuzco.

   Marcia tiene _____ y Celia no _____. Celia _____ estudiar más.
6. ¿Los exámenes de la clase de español? ¡Son siempre muy fáciles! Yo no tengo _____.

Conversación

Suggestion A: Coach students to help them invent situation for/story about drawing.

Follow-up: ***Preguntas personales:*** **1.** *¿Qué tiene Ud. miedo de comer? ¿ganas de comer? ¿ganas de tomar? ¿ganas de hacer ahora?* **2.** *¿De qué o de quién tiene Ud. miedo?* **3.** *¿Cuántos años tiene Ud.? ¿su abuelo/a? ¿su padre/madre? ¿el profesor/la profesora?* **4.** *¿Tiene Ud. razón siempre? En clase* (*En su familia*), *¿quién siempre tiene razón?* **5.** *¿Qué tiene Ud. que hacer ahora mismo* (right now)*? ¿después de* (after) *la clase? ¿mañana?* **6.** *¿Tiene Ud. muchos hermanos/as? ¿muchos primos/as? ¿muchos amigos/as?* **7.** *¿Tiene Ud. mucho dinero en la cartera/bolsa hoy? ¿Cuánto dinero tiene?* (*dólares/centavos*) **8.** *¿Tenemos clase todos los días? ¿Vienen Uds. a clase todos los días? ¿Tenemos muchos exámenes?* **9.** *¿Puede Ud. hablar alemán? ¿francés? ¿italiano? ¿Puede Ud. bailar bien? ¿cantar bien?* **10.** *¿Quiere Ud. ser profesor(a)? ¿tener muchos hijos? ¿tener una casa grande? ¿comprar un coche italiano? ¿trabajar en una oficina? ¿tomar un café ahora? ¿cantar en clase hoy?*

Suggestion B: After students have used items to ask you questions, reverse the situation, using the same items or different ones.

Follow-up C: Have selected students report back information they have learned. You may wish to help them organize their presentations.

A. Give advice to this person, who needs to make some clothing purchases immediately.

   ¡Qué horror! Tiene que comprar...
   No puede asistir a...

B. **Entrevista: Preferencias.** Using tag questions, try to predict the way your instructor will complete these sentences. He or she will answer as truthfully as possible.

   1. Ud. prefiere... los gatos / los perros
      la ropa elegante / la ropa informal
   2. Ud. quiere comprar...
      un coche deportivo, por ejemplo, un Porsche / una camioneta
      un abrigo / un impermeable
   3. Ud. viene a la universidad...
      todos los días / sólo tres veces a la semana
      en coche / en autobús
   4. Esta noche Ud. tiene ganas de...
      mirar la tele / leer
      comer en un restaurante / preparar la cena (*dinner*)
   5. Esta noche Ud. *no* puede...
      asistir a una fiesta / descansar

C. **Entrevista: Más preferencias.** With a classmate, explore preferences in a number of areas by asking and answering questions based on the following cues. Form your questions with expressions like these:

   ¿Prefieres... o... ?
   ¿Te gusta más (*infinitive*) o (*infinitive*)?

   If you have no preference, express that by saying **No tengo preferencia.** Be prepared to report some of your findings to the class. If you both agree, you will express this by saying **Preferimos...** If you do not agree, give the preferences of both persons: **Yo prefiero... pero Cecilia prefiere...**

   1. Los animales: ¿los gatos siameses o los persas? ¿los perros pastores alemanes o los perros de lanas (*poodles*)?

2. El color de la ropa informal: ¿el color negro o el blanco? ¿el rojo o el azul?
3. La ropa informal: ¿las camisas de algodón o las de seda? ¿los *bluejeans* de algodón o los pantalones de lana?
4. La ropa de mujeres: ¿las faldas largas o las minifaldas? ¿los pantalones largos o los pantalones cortos?
5. La ropa de hombres: ¿las camisas de cuadros o las de rayas? (¿o las camisas de un solo color?) ¿chaqueta y pantalón o un traje formal?
6. Las actividades en casa: ¿mirar la televisión o leer una novela? ¿escribir cartas o hablar con unos amigos?

CH. Complete the following sentences as the persons listed below might have. Be creative!

Quiero llevar _____,
Tengo ganas de llevar _____, } pero tengo que llevar _____.

1. una estudiante que asiste a una escuela privada muy conservadora
2. un *punk* que trabaja en una oficina
3. un niño que tiene que asistir a la fiesta de cumpleaños (*birthday*) de un amiguito
4. un profesor de inglés muy liberal que enseña por un año en Irán

Study Hint: Studying and Learning Verbs

Knowing how to use verb forms quickly and accurately is one of the most important parts of learning how to communicate in a foreign language. These suggestions will help you recognize and use verb forms in Spanish.

1. Study carefully any new grammar section that deals with verbs. Are the verbs regular? What is the stem? What are the personal endings? Don't just memorize the endings (**-o**, **-as**, **-a**, and so on). Practice the complete forms of each verb (**hablo**, **hablas**, **habla**, and so on) until they are "second nature" to you. Be sure that you are using the appropriate endings: **-ar** endings with **-ar** verbs, for example. Be especially careful when you write and pronounce verb endings, since a misspelling or mispronunciation can convey inaccurate information. Even though there is only a one-letter difference between **hablo** and **habla** or between **habla** and **hablan**, for example, that single letter makes a big difference in the information communicated.
2. Are you studying irregular verbs? If so, what are the irregularities? Practice the irregular forms many times so that you "overlearn" them and will not forget them: **tengo**, **tienes**, **tiene**, **tienen.**
3. Once you are familiar with the forms, practice asking short conversational questions using **tú/Ud.** and **vosotros/Uds.** Answer each question, using the appropriate **yo** or **nosotros** form.

   ¿Hablas español?
¿Habla español? } Sí, hablo español.

   ¿Comen Uds. en clase?
¿Coméis en clase? } No, no comemos en clase.

4. It is easy to become so involved in mastering the *forms* of new verbs that you forget their *meanings.* However, being able to recite verb forms perfectly is useless unless you also understand what you are saying. Be sure that you always know both the spelling *and* the meaning of all verb forms, just as you must for any new vocabulary word. Practice using new verb forms in original sentences to reinforce their meaning.
5. Practice the forms of all new verbs given in the vocabulary lists in each chapter. Any special information that you should know about the verbs will be indicated either in the vocabulary list or in a grammar section.

Communicative objectives for 10: one way to talk about future, about what you are going to do

10. EXPRESSING DESTINATION AND FUTURE ACTIONS

Ir; *ir* + *a* + Infinitive

Un regalo para la «mamá» ecuatoriana

ALLEN: Esta tarde *voy a ir* de compras. ¿Quieres *ir* conmigo?
LORENZO: Sí, con mucho gusto. ¿Qué *vas a comprar*?
ALLEN: Un regalo para mi mamá ecuatoriana... algo bueno pero barato—como una tostadora, por ejemplo.
LORENZO: Los aparatos eléctricos son muy caros aquí, Allen. ¿Por qué no compras una blusa bordada a mano?
ALLEN: Todos los artículos hechos a mano son también muy caros, ¿no?
LORENZO: Pues... no. Normalmente aquí son muy baratos.

¿Qué va a pasar hoy por la tarde? Conteste completando las oraciones.

1. Allen y Lorenzo van a ir ____.
2. Allen va a buscar ____.
3. Allen no va a comprar ____.
4. Sí va a comprar ____ porque ____.

Follow-up: *Preguntas:* 1. *Allen y Lorenzo, ¿son hermanos? ¿Son ecuatorianos los dos?* 2. *¿Realmente tiene Allen una mamá ecuatoriana? ¿Por qué usa él esta expresión? ¿Tiene Ud. a una persona que* **no** *es su mamá/papá pero es como una mamá/un papá?* 3. *¿Qué sería* (would be) *un buen regalo para una «mamá» norteamericana?*

Suggestion: *Imagine la situación al revés: Lorenzo está en los Estados Unidos y desea comprar un regalo para su mamá estadounidense.*

ir (*to go*)	
voy	**vamos**
vas	**vais**
va	**van**

The first person plural of **ir**, **vamos** (*we go*, *are going*, *do go*), is also used to express *let's go*.

Vamos a clase ahora mismo. — *Let's go to class right now.*

Ir + **a** + *infinitive* is used to describe actions or events in the near future.

Van a venir a la fiesta esta noche. — *They're going to come to the party tonight.*
Voy a ir de compras esta tarde. — *I'm going to go shopping this afternoon.*

A gift for one's Ecuadorian "mother" ALLEN: I'm going shopping this afternoon. Do you want to go with me? LORENZO: Yes, I'd really like to (*lit.* With much pleasure). What are you going to buy? ALLEN: A present for my Ecuadorian mother . . . something nice but inexpensive, like a toaster, for example. LORENZO: Electrical appliances are very expensive here, Allen. Why don't you buy a hand-embroidered blouse? ALLEN: All handmade things are also very expensive, aren't they? LORENZO: Well . . . no. Normally they're very inexpensive here.

Práctica

A. ¿Adónde van Uds. los viernes (*on Fridays*) después de (*after*) la clase? Haga oraciones completas usando **ir**.

1. yo / residencia
2. Francisca / almacén para trabajar
3. tú / otra clase
4. Jorge y Carlos / bar (*m.*)
5. nosotros / biblioteca
6. el profesor (la profesora) / ¿ ?

Emphasis B: Use of *a* in *ir* + *a* + inf. The *a* is required, even though no "extra" word is needed in English. *¿Cómo se dice?*: I'm going to work. They're going to eat.

Variation B: Personalize sequence, having students do all items with *yo* forms; then change details as necessary.

Follow-up: Make statements true for students right now, varying information according to individuals in your class. Using time cue, students tell what they will do in future. **1.** *Este semestre Ud. toma clases muy fáciles. ¿Y el próximo semestre?* **2.** *Ud. vive ahora en la residencia. ¿Y el próximo semestre?* **3.** *Ahora _____ es el presidente. ¿Y en cuatro años?* **4.** *Ud. lleva ropa muy vieja hoy. ¿Y mañana?* **5.** *Ud. tiene problemas económicos ahora. ¿Y en cinco años?* **6.** *Este año Ud. escucha música* punk (New Wave). *¿Y en el futuro?*

B. **¡Vamos de compras!** Describa la tarde, usando **ir** + **a** + el infinitivo, según el modelo.

MODELO: Raúl compra un regalo para Estela. →
Raúl va a comprar un regalo para Estela.

1. Llegamos al centro a las diez de la mañana.
2. Los niños quieren comer algo.
3. Compro unos chocolates para Lupita.
4. Raúl busca una blusa de seda.
5. No compras esta blusa de rayas, ¿verdad?
6. Tenemos que buscar algo más barato.
7. ¿Puedes ir de compras mañana también?

C. **¡Qué negativos!** Exprese en español, usando **ir** + **a** + el infinitivo.

1. I'll go to the market with you (**Uds.**), but I'm not going to bargain!
2. We'll sell the old car, but we won't buy another, right?
3. You'll look for bargains, but the things won't be cheap.

Conversación

Optional: *Ir* and *venir* are used somewhat differently than are their English equivalents. This telephone conversation shows the differences. *—¿Vas a venir a mi casa esta noche a las ocho? —A las ocho, no. ¿Puedo ir a las nueve? —¡Claro que sí! Hasta luego.* *Venir* means "come to where I am when I use the word *venir*." *¿Vas a venir a mi casa?* tells you immediately that the speaker is at home when he/she calls you. *Ir*—whether it means come or go in English—refers to some place other than where the speaker is when he/she uses the word *ir*. *«Voy a hacer una fiesta en mi casa el viernes. ¿Puedes ir?»* tells you that the speaker is not at home when the invitation is extended. Note also that *¡Ya voy!* means "I'm coming," not "I'm going."

A. **¿Adónde vas si... ?** ¿Cuántas oraciones puede Ud. hacer?

Me gusta
- leer revistas
- ir de compras—¡no importa el precio!
- buscar gangas y regatear
- bailar
- comer en restaurantes elegantes
- mirar programas de detectives

Por eso voy a _____.

B. **Entrevista: ¿Qué hay en tu futuro?** Complete las oraciones lógicamente. Luego úselas (*use them*) para entrevistar a un compañero (una compañera) de clase.

1. Un día voy a tener (ser, comprar, poder) _____. (¿Qué vas a tener tú? ...)
2. Esta noche voy a regresar a casa a las _____. Voy a estudiar _____. Voy a comer en _____. Y voy a mirar _____ en la tele. (¿Qué vas a... ?)
3. Mañana voy a llegar a la universidad a la(s) _____. Voy a tener mi primera clase a la(s) _____. A la(s) _____ voy a asistir a la clase de español. (¿A qué hora... ?)

Communicative objectives for 11: talking about the duration of an action or state

11. TELLING HOW LONG SOMETHING HAS BEEN HAPPENING

Hace... que: Another Use of the Present Tense

—*Cuánto tiempo hace que miran* la tele?
—Sólo unos minutos...

Follow-up (drawing): *¿Qué hacen los padres? (¿Adónde van?) ¿Qué hacen los niños? ¿Cuándo (¿En cuántas horas) regresan los padres? ¿Qué hacen los niños? ¿Cuánto tiempo hace que miran la televisión, según ellos? ¿Y de verdad?*

In the **Notas comunicativas** section on page 98, you learned to talk about the frequency of actions in Spanish. It is also useful to be able to tell how long an action has been going on.

In Spanish, the phrase **hace** + *period of time* + **que** + *the present tense* is used to express an action that has been going on over a period of time and is still going on.

Hace dos horas **que leo**.	*I've been reading for two hours.*
Hace tres años **que vivimos** en esta calle.	*We've been living on this street for three years.*

Use the phrase **¿Cuánto tiempo hace que... ?** to ask how long something has been going on. To answer a question posed in this way, it is sufficient to state the period of time.

—**¿Cuánto tiempo hace que** vives en esta residencia?	—*How long have you been living in this dorm?*
—**Dos meses**.	—*Two months.*

Suggestion: Use the *hace... que* + present tense structure as frequently as possible in your speech. Some (but not all) students will begin to use it spontaneously if they hear it enough.

Preliminary exercises:
- Dictado: 1. *Hace tres años que vivo aquí.* 2. *Hace un año que no vemos a los nietos.* 3. *Hace una semana que no hablo con mis padres.* 4. *Hace tres semanas que estudiamos español.*
- Listening: *¿Qué sugerencias tiene Ud. para estas personas?* 1. *Hace una semana que Juan no abre su libro de español... y tiene un examen mañana.* 2. *Hace dos días que Amanda no come. Está a dieta.* 3. *Hace treinta años que Julio vive con sus padres.* 4. *Hace cuarenta años que el señor Vargas trabaja para la misma* (same) *compañía.*

Práctica

- Speaking: *Haga oraciones según el modelo.* **Modelo:** *Julio/trabajar/una hora → Hace una hora que Julio trabaja.* 1. *yo/descansar/una hora* 2. *tú/cocinar/media hora* 3. *Jaime/estudiar/dos horas* 4. *nosotros/leer/hora y media* 5. *niños/escribir cartas/dos horas* 6. *Tina/hablar por teléfono/veinte minutos*
- Tell how long your classmates have been studying (at this university, Spanish, history, . . .).

Suggestion: Have three students model the exchanges for the class before allowing groups to work on their own.

Reacciones: ¿Qué tienen ganas de hacer? ¿Qué van a hacer? En grupos de tres estudiantes, hagan preguntas y contesten.

MODELO: Están en la biblioteca. Hace cuatro horas que (*estudiar*). →

—Uds. están en la biblioteca. Hace cuatro horas que estudian. ¿Qué tienen ganas de hacer?

—¡No puedo estudiar más! Quiero ir a la cafetería.

—Yo tengo ganas de estudiar una hora más. Luego voy a regresar a la residencia.

1. Están en casa. Hace tres horas que (*escribir*) ejercicios de español.
2. Hace dos meses que (*vivir*) en la residencia y siempre hay mucho ruido.

3. Están en casa. Hace media hora que (*mirar*) un programa de televisión muy aburrido (*boring*).
4. Hace diez años que (*tener*) un coche viejo que no funciona bien.
5. Hace unos meses que (*querer*) comprar un estereo nuevo. Tienen uno muy viejo.
6. Están en una discoteca. Hace media hora que (*bailar*).

Conversación

Suggestion A: Go through items with the class as a whole before allowing students to work through the interview on their own.

A. **Entrevista.** Find out the following information from a classmate. How long he or she has been . . .

1. living in this state (**estado**)
2. living in this city
3. living in his or her (**tu**) house/apartment/dorm
4. attending this university
5. studying Spanish
6. working at (**en**) . . . / looking for a job (**un trabajo**)

Suggestion B: Model five items yourself before asking students to answer. This exercise can be assigned for homework.

B. **¿Qué tienes ganas de hacer?** We all have things we've wanted to do for some time but never get around to doing or have the chance to do. Express at least five things you've wanted to do for some time, using the model provided.

MODELO: Hace tiempo que tengo ganas de...

Palabras útiles: leer, ver (*to see*), mirar, ir a... , comprar, ¿ ?

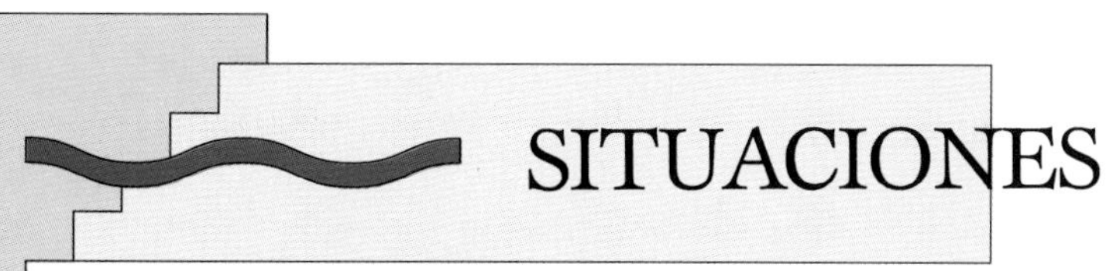

SITUACIONES

Situaciones: See IM for suggestions, additional exercises, and supplementary dialogues and exercises.

En una tienda de ropa

—¿Le atienden°? ¿Qué desea?
—Hola, buenas. Busco un pantalón de algodón de color oscuro,° para mí.
—¿Qué talla° usa?
—La trece, por lo general.
—¿Qué le parece este pantalón negro?
—No está mal. Y ¿qué tal una blusa de seda también?
—Cómo no. En su talla tenemos blusas de seda en color beige, rojo y gris perla. Son perfectas para este pantalón.
—¿Dónde me los puedo probar°?
—Allí están los probadores.° Si necesita algo, mi nombre es Méndez.
—Gracias.

¿Le... *Is someone waiting on you?*
¿ ? (*Guess the meaning.*)
size
me... *can I try them on?*
¿ ? (*Guess the meaning.*)

Más tarde, hablando con una amiga

—¿Cuánto pagaste por esta blusa?
—Fue muy barata... sólo mil pesetas. ¿Te gusta?
—Sí, me gusta mucho.
—¿Verdad? Pues... yo creo que el color no me va° muy bien.
—¡Qué va°! Te va estupendamente.

no... *doesn't suit me*
¡Qué... *Nonsense!*

Notas comunicativas sobre el diálogo

Here are some other phrases that will be useful when you go shopping.

DEPENDIENTE:

¿Qué desea (Ud.)? ¿En qué puedo servirle? Dígame.	*Can I help you?*
¿Qué talla usa?	*What size do you need? (clothing)*
¿Qué número usa?	*What size do you need? (shoes)*
¿De qué color?	*What color?*
No hay. No tenemos.	*We don't have any.*
Lo siento.	*I'm sorry.*
No nos quedan.	*We don't have any left.*

CLIENTE:

Deseo comprar un regalo para...	*I want to buy a gift for . . .*
¿Tienen Uds. ... ?	*Do you have . . . ?*
¿Cuánto es/son? ¿Cuánto vale(n)? ¿Qué precio tiene(n)?	*How much is it/are they?*
Es muy caro/a.	*It's very expensive.*
Necesito algo más barato.	*I need something cheaper.*
¿Se aceptan tarjetas de crédito?	*Do you take credit cards?*

Conversación

Although it is often possible—and lots of fun—to bargain over the price of an item in a shop or open-air market, merchandise is normally sold at a fixed price in many, if not most, Hispanic stores.

With your instructor acting as the salesperson, try to make the purchases described in one of the following situations. Use the phrases and expressions from **Notas comunicativas sobre el diálogo** as a model. Not everyone will get the chance to act out a shopping scene, so pay close attention to how your classmates interact with the salesperson to see if you would have said or done the same thing. You may have to make some educated guesses about what the Spanish-speaking salesperson says.

1. Ud. está en un almacén de Bogotá (Colombia). Desea comprar un suéter para su (*your*) mamá. Quiere un color y un estilo específicos.
2. Ud. está en un almacén de Madrid. Necesita comprar un traje elegante / un vestido de noche para asistir a una fiesta muy elegante.
3. Ud. está en un almacén de la Ciudad de México. Necesita comprar los siguientes objetos, pero no sabe (*you don't know*) las palabras en español.

   a. shoelaces b. an umbrella c. a bow tie ch. tennis shoes

Now, with another student, take the roles of customer and salesperson in the following situations. Use the phrases from **Notas comunicativas** as well as strategies that you learned from listening to the preceding dialogues.

1. En la librería de la universidad: Ud. desea comprar dos cuadernos pequeños.
2. En una tienda pequeña: Ud. desea comprar una blusa azul para su hermana (madre, amiga, tía).
3. En un almacén: Ud. quiere comprar un regalo para un amigo.
4. En una tienda de flores: Ud. necesita comprar seis rosas rojas.

Notas culturales: Talking About Sizes

Shoe and clothing sizes are quite different in Hispanic countries from those used in the United States. If you need to buy clothing abroad, it is a good idea to ask the clerk to help you with sizes. The simple question **¿Qué talla/número necesito?** will let the clerk know that you are not familiar with the size system.

UN POCO DE TODO

A. **Se busca dependiente.** (*Clerk needed.*) Form complete questions based on the words given in the order given. Conjugate the verbs and add other words if necessary. Use subject pronouns only when needed.

INTERVIEWER:

1. ¿tener / Ud. / experiencia / trabajando (*working*) / en / tienda de ropa?
2. ¿cuánto / años / tener / Ud.?
3. Ud. / asistir / clases / en / universidad / todo / mañanas / ¿no?

APPLICANT:

4. ¿poder / yo / trabajar / siempre / por / noche?
5. ¿hora / abrir / Uds. / almacén?
6. yo / no / tener / llegar / ocho / ¿verdad?

Now answer the questions.

Notas lingüísticas: Using *mucho* and *poco*

In the first chapters of ***Puntos de partida***, you have used the words **mucho** and **poco** as both adjectives and adverbs. *Adverbs* (**Los adverbios**) are words that modify verbs, adjectives or other adverbs: ***quickly***, ***very** smart*, ***very** quickly*. In Spanish and in English, adverbs are invariable in form.

Adverb:	Rosario compra **mucho** hoy.	*Rosario is buying a lot today.*
Adjective:	Rosario tiene **mucha** ropa.	*Rosario has a lot of clothes.*
	Sobre todo tiene **muchos** zapatos.	*She especially has a lot of shoes.*

B. **Las obligaciones y preferencias universitarias.** Describe the things you have to do as students. Follow the model, giving as many examples as you can for each item.

MODELO: escribir: Como estudiantes, tenemos que... → Como estudiantes, tenemos que escribir mucho. Escribimos muchos ejercicios, muchas...

Palabras útiles: oraciones, palabras, composiciones, ejercicios, cartas, novelas, periódicos, revistas, poemas, reglas (*rules*), diálogos, personas, estudiantes, compañeros, amigos, ...

1. escribir: Como estudiantes, tenemos que...
2. leer: Debemos...
3. estudiar: También es necesario...
4. hablar con: Y es importante...
5. Pero realmente preferimos...
6. Y este fin de semana, ¡tenemos ganas de... !

C. **¿Somos tan diferentes?** Answer the following questions. Then ask the same questions of other students in the class to find at least one person who answered a given question the way you did.

1. ¿Tienes mucha o poca ropa?
2. ¿Te gusta ir de compras, por lo general? ¿Te gusta comprar ropa?
3. ¿Cuál es tu color favorito?
4. ¿Qué tienda prefieres para comprar ropa? ¿Por qué vas allí? ¿Es barata la ropa allí? ¿Es de última moda?
5. De la siguiente lista, ¿qué cosa tienes ganas de tener? ¿Por qué? (**¡OJO!** También es posible contestar: **No quiero tener ninguna**.)
   - un abrigo de pieles (*fur*)
   - unas botas de cuero (*leather*)
6. ¿Cuál de las siguientes cosas que dicta la moda es la más tonta, en tu opinión?
   - las minifaldas
   - los relojes Swatch
   - los *bluejeans* de los grandes diseñadores como Calvin Klein y Guess
   - la ropa de estilo *punk*

CH. **Pero, ¿no se puede regatear?** Complete the following paragraph with the correct form of the words in parentheses, as suggested by the context. When two possibilities are given in parentheses, select the correct word.

Cuando Ud. va (*de/a*[1]) compras en (*un/una*[2]) ciudad hispánica, (*ir*[3]) a ver° una (*grande*[4]) variedad de tiendas. Hay almacenes (*elegante*[5]) como (*los/las*[6]) de los Estados Unidos, donde los precios siempre (*ser*[7]) (*fijo*[8]). También hay (*pequeño*[9]) tiendas que se especializan° en un solo° producto. En (*un/una*[10]) zapatería, por ejemplo, venden solamente zapatos. (*El/La*[11]) sufijo **-ería** se usa° para formar el nombre (*del/de la*[12]) tienda. ¿Dónde (*creer*[13]) Ud. que venden papel y (*otro*[14]) artículos de escritorio? ¿A qué tienda (*ir*[15]) Ud. a comprar fruta?

Si Ud. (*poder*[16]) pagar el precio que piden,° (*deber*[17]) comprar los recuerdos° en (*los/las*[18]) almacenes o *boutiques*. Pero si (*tener*[19]) ganas o necesidad de (*regatear*[20]), tiene (*de/que*[21]) (*ir*[22]) a un mercado: un conjunto° de tiendas (*pequeño*[23]) o locales° donde el ambiente° es más (*informal*[24]) que° en los (*grande*[25]) almacenes. Ud. no (*deber*[26]) (*pagar*[27]) el primer° precio que mencione (*el/la*[28]) vendedor°—¡casi siempre va (*de/a*[29]) ser muy alto!

to see
se... *specialize* / *single*
se... *is used*
they ask
souvenirs
group / *stalls* / *atmosphere*
than
first / *seller*

¿Cierto o falso? Corrija las oraciones falsas.

1. En el mundo hispánico, todas las tiendas son similares.
2. Uno puede regatear en un almacén hispánico.
3. Es posible comprar limones en una papelería.
4. En un mercado, el vendedor siempre ofrece un precio bajo al principio (*beginning*).

En España hay muchas rebajas y los españoles somos muy aficionados a comprar en estas ocasiones. Las empresas se quitan de encima sus excedentes y los consumidores aprovechan para adquirir los artículos más baratos. Todo el mundo parece satisfecho. Trajes de baño, camisas, blusas y faldas son los productos más vendidos en las rebajas de verano. El Corte Inglés, en el primer día de esta locura consumista de verano, ingresó la cifra de 2.600 millones de pesetas superando, incluso, sus propias previsiones.

En la guerra de las rebajas todos resultan vencedores

Theme vocabulary previously listed as active: *comprar, barato/a*

VOCABULARIO

VERBOS

abrir to open
aprender to learn
asistir (a) to attend, go to
beber to drink
comer to eat
comprender to understand
creer (en) to think, believe (in)
deber (+ *inf.*) should, must, ought to (*do something*)
descansar to rest
escribir to write
insistir (en + *inf.*) to insist (on *doing something*)
ir (*irreg.*) to go; **ir a** + *inf.* to be going to (*do something*)
leer to read
llevar to wear; to carry; to take
poder (ue) to be able, can
preferir (ie) to prefer
querer (ie) to want
recibir to receive
regatear to haggle, bargain
tener (*irreg.*) to have

vender to sell
venir (*irreg.*) to come
vivir to live

LA ROPA

el abrigo coat
los *bluejeans* jeans
la blusa blouse
la bolsa purse
la bota boot
los calcetines socks
la camisa shirt
la camiseta T-shirt
la cartera wallet
el cinturón belt
la corbata tie
la chaqueta jacket
la falda skirt
el impermeable raincoat
las medias stockings
los pantalones pants
el par pair
el reloj watch
la sandalia sandal
el sombrero hat
el suéter sweater
el traje suit
el traje de baño swimsuit
el vestido dress
el zapato shoe

LOS COLORES

amarillo/a yellow
anaranjado/a orange
azul blue
blanco/a white
gris gray
morado/a purple
negro/a black
pardo/a brown
rojo/a red
rosado/a pink
verde green

DE COMPRAS

de cuadros plaid
de rayas striped
de última moda the latest style
el precio (fijo) (fixed) price
las rebajas sales, reductions
venden de todo they sell (have) everything

MATERIALES

es de... it is made of . . .
  algodón cotton
  lana wool
  seda silk

LOS LUGARES

el almacén department store
el café café, coffee shop
la calle street
el centro downtown
el centro comercial shopping mall
el mercado market(place)
la tienda shop

OTROS SUSTANTIVOS

el café coffee
la carta letter
el ejercicio exercise
la novela novel
la puerta door
la revista magazine
el periódico newspaper
el ruido noise

ADJETIVOS

caro/a expensive
poco/a little

¿CON QUÉ FRECUENCIA... ?

a veces sometimes, at times
nunca never
siempre always
una vez (dos veces)... once (twice) . . .
  a la semana a week
  al mes a month

LOS NÚMEROS

cien(to), doscientos/as, trescientos/as, cuatrocientos/as, quinientos/as, seiscientos/as, setecientos/as, ochocientos/as, novecientos/as, mil, un millón

PALABRAS ADICIONALES

¿adónde? where (to)?
algo something
allí there
hace + *period of time* + **que** + *present tense* to have been doing something for a period of time
ir de compras to go shopping
¿no? right? don't they (you, etc.)?
por ejemplo for example
tener...
  ganas de + *inf.* to feel like (*doing something*)
  miedo (de) to be afraid (of)
  prisa to be in a hurry
  que + *inf.* to have to (*do something*)
  razón to be right

Frases útiles para la comunicación

Vamos a...	Let's go to . . .	**¿Cuánto pagaste por... ?**	How much did you pay for . . . ?
¡Nos vemos!	See you around!	**Fue una ganga.**	It was a bargain (steal).
conmigo	with me		

See also the words and phrases in **Notas comunicativas sobre el diálogo**.

OPTIONAL SECTION

UN PASO MÁS 3

▲ Actividad A. Ojo alerta

Note A: Adjective form *alerta*, invariable in singular, is used to modify both masculine and feminine nouns.

Expansion A: *Describa las diferencias entre los siguientes almacenes: Penney's y Saks Fifth Avenue; Macy's y K-Mart.*

¿Cuáles son las diferencias entre el dibujo A y el dibujo B? Hay ocho diferencias en total.

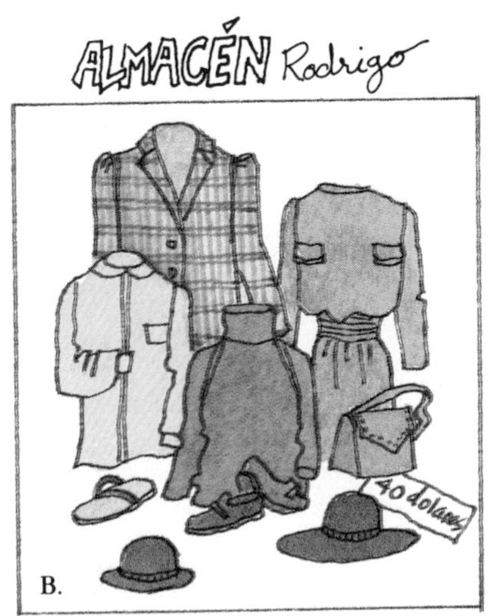

MODELO: En el dibujo A hay _____; en el dibujo B hay _____.

▲ Actividad B. Lavandería y tintorería

Suggestions B:
- Model *Frases útiles* before beginning activity.
- With student, do first part of activity in front of class, going through several items of clothing.
- Students do form once; then reverse roles.

You are staying at a hotel in Mexico City, and you need to have laundry and dry cleaning done. A person from the hotel staff comes to pick up your clothing and to fill out the laundry form on the following page. Working with another student, play the roles of hotel guest and staff member.

Frases útiles	
Su nombre, por favor.	*Your name, please.*
¿El número de su habitación?	*Your room number?*
¿Cuántos/as _____ hay?	*How many _____ are there?*
Muy bien, señor/señora/señorita. Regreso mañana.	*Fine, Sir/Ma'am/Miss. I'll return tomorrow.*

Cuenta del Húesped Guest's Count	Nuestra Cuenta Our Count	LAVANDERÍA — TINTORERÍA / *LAUNDRY — DRY CLEANING*	Tarifa Rates Pesos	TOTAL
		Batas—Robes	36.00	
		Blusas—Blouses	20.00	
		Calcetines—Socks	7.00	
		Camisones—Nightgowns	23.00	
		Camisas—Shirts	18.00	
		Camisas sport—Sport shirts	18.00	
		Corbatas—Neckties	14.00	
		Chaquetas—Jackets	30.00	
		Faldas—Skirts	28.00	
		Impermeables—Raincoats	45.00	
		Pantalones—Slacks	28.00	
		Pañuelos—Handkerchiefs	5.00	
		Pijamas—Pajamas	23.00	
		Ropa interior—Underwear	10.00	
		Sacos—Coats	28.00	
		Smoking—Tuxedos	65.00	
		Suéteres—Sweaters	28.00	
		Trajes—Suits	56.00	
		Trajes de noche—Evening dresses	CONVENCIONAL	
		Vestidos—Dresses	49.00	

A propósito... Expressing Agreement and Disagreement

You have already learned many words and phrases to use to accept an invitation and to react to what someone has said: **De acuerdo. (No) Estoy de acuerdo,** and so on. Here are some additional phrases to use to agree or disagree with an opinion that someone has expressed.

¡claro que sí!	*of course!*
¡claro que no!	*of course not!*
¡en absoluto!	*of course not!*
¿Cómo puedes creer eso?	*How can you think that?*
¡Qué horror!	*How horrible!*
¡Qué barbaridad!	*What a terrible thing!*

▲ Actividad C. Gustos y preferencias

Suggestion C: Can be done as "autograph" activity.

Read the following statements and indicate the extent to which you agree or disagree with them according to the following scale.

5 = sí enfático
4 = sí
3 = no tengo opinión
2 = no
1 = no enfático

La clase de español

_____ 1. Comprendo todo cuando el profesor (la profesora) habla.
_____ 2. Debemos leer más y hablar menos en clase.
_____ 3. El laboratorio debe ser obligatorio.
_____ 4. Yo asisto al laboratorio con frecuencia.

Los colores y la ropa

_____ 5. Las personas mayores (*older*) deben llevar siempre ropa de colores oscuros, como negro, gris, etcétera.
_____ 6. Una mujer que tiene más de 30 años nunca debe llevar minifalda.
_____ 7. Sólo las mujeres deben usar arete(s) (*earring*[*s*]).
_____ 8. Cuando la moda cambia (*changes*), es necesario comprar mucha ropa nueva.

When you have finished, compare your responses with those of your classmates. Did most respond in the same way that you did?

LECTURA CULTURAL

Lectura: See IM for suggestions and additional exercises and activities.

Antes de leer: Finding the Main Parts of a Sentence

When reading Spanish, it's easy to "get lost" in long sentences. Here is a way to get around that difficulty. First omit the words and information set off by commas and concentrate on the main verb and its subject. Try this strategy in the following sentence.

> En muchos lugares del mundo hispánico, especialmente en las tierras templadas o frías, los hombres casi siempre llevan una camisa con corbata y una chaqueta.

Once you have located the subject and verb (**los hombres**, **llevan**), you can read the sentence again, adding more information to the framework provided by the phrase *men wear*. . . Men from what part of the world? What, specifically, do they wear? Try the strategy again in this sentence.

> Aunque mi mamá parece tímida, es una mujer independiente con ideas fijas que no tiene miedo de ofrecer su opinión.

Now apply the strategy to the reading.

Las modas

Por lo general, los hispanos desean lucir bien.° Claro que los *bluejeans* son muy populares entre los jóvenes de todo el mundo. Pero para casi toda ocasión los hispanos se visten° con más esmero que° los norteamericanos. Cuando uno está en la calle, es decir,° cuando no está en casa, es preferible estar elegante.

En muchos lugares del mundo hispánico, especialmente en las tierras templadas o frías, los hombres por lo general llevan camisa con corbata y una chaqueta. Los colores preferidos para los pantalones y las chaquetas son azul, negro o gris, y las camisas son casi siempre blancas. En cambio, las mujeres usan ropa de colores vivos y alegres.°

lucir... *look nice*
se... *dress*
con... *more carefully than* / es... *that is*
happy

En los climas cálidos, el estilo de ropa se relaciona con el tiempo.° En ciudades como Cartagena, Veracruz o Guayaquil, por ejemplo, no todos los hombres llevan siempre chaqueta y corbata. Es muy común en estos lugares llevar una guayabera* para ir a la oficina o la universidad. Las guayaberas pueden ser muy elegantes; hay algunas muy bonitas, bordadas a mano.° También son muy cómodas.°

Si usted va a visitar un país hispánico, debe llevar ropa apropiada. Así° usted siempre va a causar una buena impresión.

weather

bordadas... *band-embroidered*

comfortable

That way

Comprensión

¿Cierto o falso? Corrija las oraciones falsas.

1. Los hispanos tienen poco interés en lucir bien.
2. A veces el clima determina el tipo de ropa que una persona lleva.
3. Al hombre hispano típico le gusta llevar ropa de colores vivos.
4. Cartagena y Veracruz son ciudades con un clima templado.
5. La guayabera es una camisa que se lleva solamente en casa.

Para escribir

A. Complete el siguiente párrafo sobre las modas en los Estados Unidos.

En los Estados Unidos la individualidad es importante en las modas. Por ejemplo, los estudiantes llevan _____, pero los profesores _____. También son diferentes los estilos de los jóvenes y los viejos. Las madres llevan _____ y los padres _____. Pero yo, cuando bailo en una discoteca (estudio en la biblioteca, trabajo en casa), llevo _____.

B. Use the following phrases as a guide to describe an imaginary shopping excursion in Madrid. Form complete sentences and add as many details as you can.

1. ir al centro en (coche, autobús, ...)
2. entrar en (un almacén, una tienda pequeña, ...)
3. leer las etiquetas (*labels*)
4. no poder creer los precios porque...
5. querer regatear pero...
6. por fin decidir comprar...
7. pagar _____ pesetas por el/la...
8. tener que escribir un cheque

REPASO 1:
Note: All *Repaso* sections follow this format:
- A photo/text essay (*Voces del mundo hispánico*) that focuses on a major group within the Spanish-speaking world.
- *Entrevista:* Interview activity that provides a vehicle for reviewing a major "system" presented in the preceding three chapters.
- *Situaciones...* : Role-play situations that focus on the major vocabulary groups presented in the preceding chapters.

Note: Corresponding chapters of the Workbook and Laboratory Manual offer focused vocabulary and grammar activities.

Repaso 1: See IM for detailed suggestions for handling *Entrevistas*, *Situaciones*, and the specific *Voces* sections.

---

*A **guayabera** is a man's shirt made to wear outside the trousers, not tucked in.

REPASO 1 VOCES DEL MUNDO HISPÁNICO

OPTIONAL SECTION

MÉXICO Y LA AMÉRICA CENTRAL

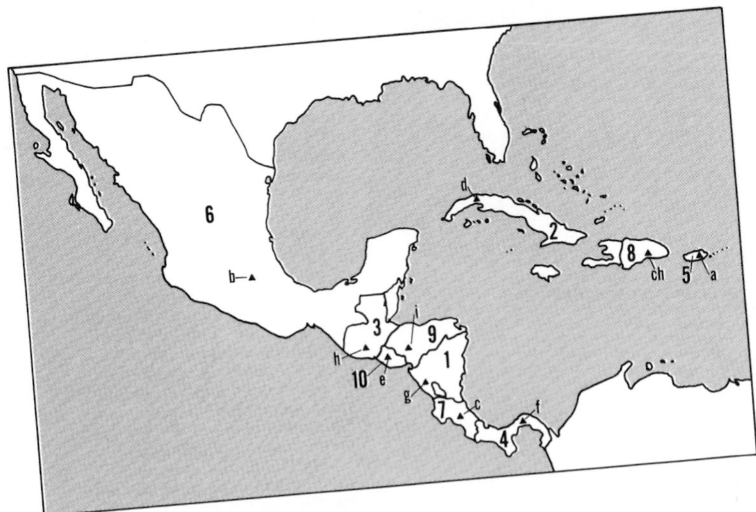

¿Cuánto sabe Ud. de la geografía de esta región? Identifique los siguientes países en el mapa: **México**, **Honduras**, **Costa Rica**, **Guatemala**, **Nicaragua**, **Panamá**, **El Salvador**. Luego ponga los nombres de estas capitales con sus países respectivos: **Managua**, **San José**, **la Ciudad de Panamá**, **la Ciudad de México**, **la Ciudad de Guatemala**, **San Salvador**, **Tegucigalpa**.

Ahora use la siguiente lista para nombrar los habitantes de cada país: **mexicano/a**, **hondureño/a**, **guatemalteco/a**, **salvadoreño/a**, **panameño/a**, **costarricense**, **nicaragüense**. Siga el modelo.

MODELO: Una persona de _____ es _____.

La ciudad de Tenochtitlán, con 300.000 (trescientos mil) habitantes, fue la capital del imperio azteca. Fue destruida por los españoles en 1521 (mil quinientos veintiuno). Sobre (*On top of*) sus ruinas se fundó la moderna Ciudad de México. Lo siguiente (*The following*) es parte de la descripción de Tenochtitlán por Hernán Cortés, en una carta al rey español.

Esta gran ciudad de Tenochtitlán está fundada en esta laguna salada,° y desde° la tierra firme hasta el cuerpo° de la ciudad... hay dos leguas°... Es tan° grande la ciudad como Sevilla y Córdoba. Son las calles de ella muy anchas° y muy derechas°... Tiene esta ciudad muchas plazas, donde hay continuos mercados y trato° de comprar y vender.

salty / from / body
legua = *5572 meters / as*

wide / straight

dealings

La llegada de Cortés a Tenochtitlán, mural de Diego Rivera

Ciudad de México: ¿la urbe más grande del mundo?

Carlos Brambila Paz

El propósito° de este ensayo es analizar la información disponible sobre la población de las principales metrópolis mundiales y ubicar° a la ciudad de México dentro de esta jerarquía urbana. La importancia de este análisis radica en el hecho de que, de acuerdo con las proyecciones internacionales más recientes, la ciudad de México será° la metrópoli más poblada del mundo a finales del presente siglo°.

De acuerdo con las proyecciones de la ONU°, las metrópolis más pobladas en 1990 serán Tokio, con 23.4 millones de habitantes; la ciudad de México, con 22.9; Nueva York, con 21.8; São Paulo, con 19.9, y Shanghai, con 17.7. Otras ciudades con más de 10 millones de habitantes serán Beijing, Río de Janeiro, Bombay, Calcuta, Seúl, Buenos Aires, Yakarta y El Cairo, dentro de los países subdesarrollados°. En los países desarrollados se contarán Los Ángeles, París, Osaka-Kobe y Londres.

Finalmente, de acuerdo con las estimaciones de la ONU que se reportan en el cuadro 1, las aglomeraciones más pobladas en el año 2000 serán la ciudad de México, con 31 millones de habitantes; São Paulo, con 25.8, y Tokio, con 24.2. Según las mismas proyecciones, las tasas de crecimiento° de las metrópolis de los países desarrollados deben de ser cercanas a cero, de modo que se espera que Nueva York sea la segunda metrópoli desarrollada que exceda los 20 millones de habitantes. [...]

purpose / *locate, place* / *will be* / cien años / Organización de Naciones Unidas / *underdeveloped* / tasas... *growth rate*

La gran Ciudad de México

Semblanza de Oscar Arias Premio Nobel de la Paz

SAN JOSE, Costa Rica (UPI) — Oscar Arias Sánchez, un abogado° y escritor elegido el año pasado como el presidente más joven de Costa Rica, que ayer° ganó el Premio Nobel de la Paz, comenzó su lucha° por la paz en Centroamérica desde el momento mismo que asumió su cargo.°

Después de varias tentativas fracasadas,° los presidentes de El Salvador, José Napoleón Duarte; de Guatemala, Vinicio Cerezo Arevalo; de Honduras, José Azcona Hoyo; de Nicaragua, Daniel Ortega Saavedra y el propio Arias acordaron° reunirse en Guatemala el 6 y 7 de agosto para discutir el plan de paz.

Tras la reunión presidencial, Arias declaró que 'éste es uno de los días más felices° de mi vida'. 'Para muchos esto era° un sueño° irrealizable, una utopía, una quijotada, una ilusión...pero, hay momentos en que las ideas tienen tanta fuerza° que llegan a plasmarse en realidad'.

Arias está casado con Margarita Penon. La pareja tiene dos hijos, Eugenia, de 9 años, y Oscar Felipe, de 7.

lawyer / *yesterday* / *fight* / *position* / *failed* / *agreed* / *happiest* / *was* / *dream* / *force*

«A Roosevelt»

... esa° América
que tiembla de huracanes y que vive de amor:
hombres de ojos° sajones y alma bárbara,° vive.
Y sueña.° Y ama, y vibra; y es la hija del Sol.°
Tened cuidado.° ¡Vive la América española!

that / *eyes* / alma... *wild soul* / *it dreams* / *Sun* / Tened... *Be careful.*

Rubén Darío, poeta nicaragüense
(1867–1916)

Manifestación en Nicaragua

ENTREVISTA

In the first chapters of ***Puntos de partida***, you have frequently practiced asking questions and getting information from others. This activity will help you review much of what you have learned so far.

First, working with a classmate, create questions you can use to get information about the topics indicated below. Add other questions that occur to you about these topics. Then find someone in the class you have either spoken with infrequently or not at all, and use the questions to interview him or her. Finally, write down the information you have learned, using words like those in **A propósito**... (**Un paso más**, **Capítulo 1**) to help you write paragraphs that flow smoothly.

Datos personales y familiares

Hint: Use **tu(s)** to express *your*.

1. name and age
2. where he or she lives now and how long he or she has lived there
3. where his or her family lives and how long the family has lived there
4. if he or she has a large or small family
5. how many brothers and sisters he or she has and some information about them
6. where the parents work
7. where the grandparents are from

Datos escolares y profesionales

8. the number of courses he or she is taking this semester
9. how long he or she has been studying at this university
10. how many languages (**lenguas**) he or she speaks
11. if he or she likes to go to the language lab (**laboratorio de lenguas**)
12. if he or she works now and, if so, where
13. what he or she would like to be some day (**algún día**)

Gustos y preferencias

14. what he or she likes to do (**hacer**) on weekends
15. what he or she doesn't like to do
16. where he or she prefers to study
17. what he or she prefers to wear on weekends
18. the color of his or her favorite shirt, blouse, or T-shirt

Entrevista: Focus: Putting the present tense of regular verbs of all classes together with irregular verbs presented so far, along with *gusta* + infinitive and *hace... que* + present tense.

SITUACIONES DE LA VIDA ESTUDIANTIL

Listen as your instructor role-plays some of the following situations with one or more of your classmates. Pay close attention to how your classmates interact with your instructor, to see if you would have said or done the same thing. You may have to make some educated guesses about what your instructor says as he or she plays the situation. After you have watched each situation at least once, act out the situations with another classmate. Try to use as much as possible of the vocabulary that you know.

1. You are a freshman (**Estoy en el primer año**...) at the university and don't know anyone yet. Introduce yourself to the student sitting next to you and try to find out about him.
2. You find yourself waiting in line at the bookstore behind one of your professors. Strike up a conversation with her. Tell the professor something interesting about yourself and ask her some questions about her family.
3. You have just begun preregistering for next term's classes when you discover that all the Spanish classes are closed. Explain to the secretary why you want to get into one of them.
4. Your best friend has just invited you to go downtown with her. Find out what time you will leave, where you will go, what you will do, and all other pertinent information.
5. You have gone to a department store to buy some clothing. Explain to the salesclerk exactly what you are looking for.

C A P Í T U L O CUATRO

NOSOTROS Y LOS DEMÁS

España

▲ Una cita para esta noche

—Oye, tengo dos boletos[a] para el concierto de Billy Joel esta noche. ¿Quieres ir conmigo?

—¡Sí! Hace tiempo que tengo ganas de asistir a uno de sus conciertos.

—Paso por ti a las siete, ¿vale?[b]

—¡De acuerdo!

[a] *tickets*
[b] ¿está bien?

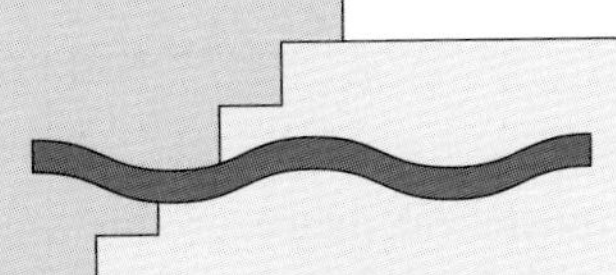

VOCABULARIO: PREPARACIÓN

• See also [video] and [cassette]

¿Qué día es hoy?

lunes	Monday	**viernes**	Friday
martes	Tuesday	**sábado**	Saturday
miércoles	Wednesday	**domingo**	Sunday
jueves	Thursday		

el lunes, el martes...	on Monday, on Tuesday . . .
los lunes, los martes...	on Mondays, on Tuesdays . . .
Hoy (Mañana) es viernes.	Today (Tomorrow) is Friday.
el fin de semana	(on) the weekend
pasado mañana	the day after tomorrow
el próximo (martes, miércoles, ...)	next (Tuesday, Wednesday, . . .)
la próxima semana	next week

Except for **el sábado/los sábados** and **el domingo/los domingos**, all the days of the week use the same form for the plural as they do for the singular. The definite articles are used to express *on* with the days of the week. The days are not capitalized in Spanish.

Vocabulario: Preparación:
- See detailed supplementary materials and exercises for this section bound into the back of this Annotated Instructor's Edition.
- See model for vocabulary presentation and other materials in Supplementary *Vocabulario: Preparación* Materials, chapter by chapter, IM.

Optional A1: Stress use of *ayer. Fue* is active vocabulary from Ch. 3.

Follow-up A: *Dictado* and *¿Sí o no?* **1.** *Los viernes por la tarde hay muy pocas personas en la biblioteca.* **2.** *Por lo general los lunes son días fenomenales.* **3.** *Los días del fin de semana son martes y miércoles.* **4.** *Muchas personas no tienen que trabajar los sábados.*

Suggestion B: Do as pair exercise; then partners report each other's activities to class.

A. **Preguntas**

1. ¿Qué día es hoy? ¿Qué día es mañana? Si hoy es sábado, ¿qué día es mañana? Si hoy es jueves, ¿qué día es mañana? ¿Qué día fue ayer?
2. ¿Qué días de la semana tenemos clase? ¿Qué días no?
3. ¿Estudia Ud. mucho durante (*during*) el fin de semana? ¿y los domingos por la noche?
4. ¿Qué le gusta hacer (*to do*) los viernes por la tarde? ¿Le gusta salir (*to go out*) con los amigos los sábados por la noche?

B. Tell at least one thing you want, need, have, like to do, or can do each day this week. Then tell about next week.

MODELO: El lunes quiero (necesito, tengo que, puedo) asistir a clase.
Los lunes me gusta estudiar en la biblioteca por la noche.
El próximo lunes voy a...

Palabras útiles: dormir (*to sleep*) hasta muy tarde, jugar (*to play*) al tenis, al golf, al vólibol, al...), ir al cine (*movies*), ir al bar (al parque, al museo, a...), ¿ ?

Las relaciones sentimentales

el novio boyfriend; fiancé; groom
la novia girlfriend; fiancée; bride

el esposo husband
la esposa wife

cariñoso/a affectionate

A. **Definiciones.** Match these words with their definitions.

1. el matrimonio
2. el amor
3. el divorcio
4. la boda
5. la amistad

a. relación cariñosa entre dos personas
b. posible resultado de un matrimonio desastroso
c. relación sentimental y especial entre dos personas
ch. una ceremonia (religiosa o civil) en que la novia a veces lleva un vestido blanco
d. relación legal entre dos personas

B. Complete las oraciones lógicamente.

1. Mi abuelo es el _____ de mi abuela.
2. Muchos novios tienen un largo _____ antes de (*before*) la boda.
3. María y Julio tienen _____ el viernes para comer en un restaurante y luego van a bailar.
4. La _____ de Juan y Marta es el domingo a las dos de la tarde, en la iglesia (*church*) de San Martín.
5. En una _____, ¿quién debe pagar o comprar los boletos, el hombre o la mujer?
6. La _____ entre estos exesposos es imposible. No pueden ser amigos.
7. Ramón tiene miedo del _____; no quiere tener esposa.
8. ¡El _____ es ciego (*blind*)!

Notas culturales: Relaciones de la vida social

Dos palabras españolas que no tienen equivalente exacto en inglés son **amigo** y **novio**. En el diagrama se indica cuándo es apropiado usar estas palabras para describir relaciones sociales en la cultura hispana y en la norteamericana.

friend — *girl/boyfriend* — *fiancée/fiancé* — *bride/groom*

amiga/amigo (*friend*, *girl/boyfriend*) — novia/novio (*girl/boyfriend*, *fiancée/fiancé*, *bride/groom*)

Como en todas partes del mundo, los enamorados hispanos usan muchos términos de cariño: **mi amor**, **mi vida**, **viejo/vieja**, **querido/querida** (*dear*), **cielo**, **corazón**. Es también frecuente el uso afectuoso de las frases **mi hijo/mi hija** entre esposos y aun (*even*) entre buenos amigos.

Optional C: Ask students to explain their answers. Stress the use of *porque, por eso*.

Follow-up C: Introduce (*No*) *Estoy de acuerdo*. Students react to following statements: **1.** *El matrimonio (La luna de miel) es un concepto muy anticuado.* **2.** *Si el noviazgo es corto, el matrimonio va a ser corto también.* **3.** *Las mujeres son más románticas que los hombres.* **4.** *El noviazgo debe ser largo y formal.* **5.** *El matrimonio es una obligación social necesaria.*

C. ¿Cierto o falso? Conteste cierto, falso o depende.

1. El amor verdadero (*real*) no existe.
2. El matrimonio es una institución social necesaria.
3. Un novio / Una novia es una limitación.
4. Las bodas grandes y formales son una tontería (*foolish thing*).
5. Un novio debe ser alto, moreno y guapo.
6. La luna de miel es un concepto anticuado.

¿Dónde está?: Las preposiciones

Prepositions express relationships in time and space:

The book is *on* the table. The food is *for* tomorrow.

- Some common Spanish prepositions you have already used include **a**, **con**, **de**, **en**, and **para**. Here are some others.

cerca de	close to	**encima de**	on top of	**entre**	between, among
lejos de	far from	**debajo de**	below	**durante**	during
				sin	without
antes de	before	**delante de**	in front of		
después de	after	**detrás de**	behind	**a la izquierda (derecha) de**	to the left (right) of

- In Spanish, the pronouns that serve as objects of prepositions are identical in form to the subject pronouns, except for **mí** and **ti**.

Ella va a comprar un regalo para **mí**. *She's going to buy a gift for me.*
Buscamos algo para **ti**. *We're looking for something for you.*

- As you know, **conmigo** expresses *with me*. Use **contigo** to express *with you* (*fam. sing.*).

No puedo hablar **contigo** ahora. *I can't talk with you now.*

(continúa)

- Subject pronouns are used after the preposition **entre**.

  Entre tú y yo, Horacio es un tipo antipático. — *Between you and me, Horace is an unpleasant guy.*

- The infinitive is the only verb form that can follow a preposition.

  ¿Adónde vas después de estudiar? — *Where are you going after you study?*

A. **¿Dónde está(n) ____?**

MODELO: el hospital →
El hospital está a la derecha del cine.

1. el bar
2. la ambulancia
3. el cine
4. la iglesia
5. el cura (*priest*)
6. los novios
7. el niño
8. los árboles (*trees*)
9. la mamá
10. el parque

Preliminary A:
- Model pronunciation of items.
- Review *está(n)*.
- Give true/false statements with vocabulary, based on the drawing.

Follow-up A: *¿Dónde están?*: Students tell where these objects or persons are in relation to you. **1.** *la pizarra* **2.** *la puerta* **3.** *los estudiantes* **4.** *la(s) ventana(s)* (window[s]) **5.** *la mesa* (*el escritorio*)

B. ¿Qué hace Ud. (*do you do*) antes de la clase de español? ¿y después? ¿y durante la clase? ¿Tiene otra clase después de ésta (*this one*)? ¿Adónde va Ud. después de estudiar en la biblioteca toda la tarde?

Extension B: *¿Qué día viene después de miércoles? ¿y después de jueves? ¿y después de domingo? ¿Qué día viene antes de martes? ¿y antes de miércoles? ¿y antes de viernes?*

C. Complete las oraciones lógicamente, usando un pronombre apropiado.

1. Sí, sí, Teresa es muy simpática, pero casi nunca hablo con ____.
2. Sin ____ no puedo vivir, mi cielo (*beloved*). Siempre quiero vivir con ____.
3. Jaimito no puede ver (*see*) bien porque hay un hombre delante de ____.
4. —Entre ____ y ____, no puedo aguantar (*stand*) las fiestas de Paula.
   —No estoy de acuerdo con ____. ¿Por qué siempre hablas mal de (*about*) ____?
5. Declaración de amor: Nunca voy a bailar con otro hombre (otra mujer). Siempre voy a bailar con ____. Tampoco (*Neither*) voy a cantar para otro/a. Sólo voy a cantar para ____.

Follow-up C: Students invent a context for the sentences or exchanges.

CH. **Situaciones.** You and a friend are discussing what is easy (**fácil**) and difficult (**difícil**) for each of you to do. Ask and answer questions according to the model, adding more information when possible.

MODELO: hablar en público →
—Para ti, ¿es fácil o difícil *hablar en público*?
—Para mí es difícil *hablar en público*.
—Pues, para mí es muy fácil. ¡Me gusta *hablar en público*!

1. asistir a clase todos los días
2. aprender el vocabulario
3. comer menos (*less*)
4. regatear en un mercado
5. estudiar los sábados por la noche
6. gastar (*to spend*) menos dinero en (ropa, libros, discos...)

Preliminary CH: Give objects (dollar bill, dictionary, pencil, etc.) to different students. Say, e.g., *El dólar es para Ud.* Then ask, *¿Para quién es el dólar?* (→ *Es para mí.*) Take objects back and give them to other students. *¿Es para Ud. o para él/ella? ¿Es para Ud. o para mí?* Give at least one object to two students: *¿Es para Uds. o para ellos/ellas?*

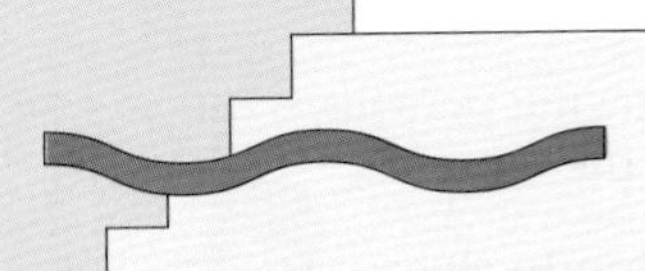

PRONUNCIACIÓN: *B/V*

In Spanish, the pronunciation of the letters **b** and **v** is identical. At the beginning of a phrase or sentence—that is, after a pause—or after **m** or **n**, the letters **b** and **v** are pronounced just like the English stop [b]. Everywhere else they are pronounced like the fricative [ƀ], produced by creating friction when pushing the air through the lips. This sound has no equivalent in English.

Suggestion: Articulate an English *b*, showing how lips are tightly closed and how flow of air is stopped briefly before being released.

Point out: English *v* is a labiodental fricative, i.e., it is produced by friction of air passing between lower lip and upper teeth. Spanish fricative *b* is bilabial; it is produced by friction of air passing between lips.

Follow-up: 1. *Viven bien en Venezuela.* **2.** *Vicente viene a Venezuela el sábado.* **3.** *Bárbara trabaja en la biblioteca.* **4.** *Victor es el abuelo de Vicente.*

Practique las siguientes palabras y frases.

1. [b] bueno viejo verde venir barato Vicente boda viernes también hombre sombrero bienvenido bota
2. [ƀ] novio llevar libro pobre abrir abrigo universidad abuelo
3. [b/ƀ] bueno / es bueno busca / Ud. busca bien / muy bien en Venezuela / de Venezuela vende / se vende en Bolivia / de Bolivia
4. [b/ƀ] beber bebida vivir biblioteca Babel vívido

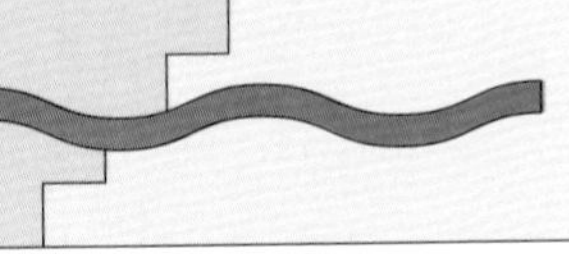

MINIDIÁLOGOS Y GRAMÁTICA

Communicative objectives for 12: how to describe what you are doing right now

Suggestions:
- Use visuals to teach concept of progressive; students should be able to produce progressive forms by following models given.
- First visual: Say: (Student) *baila* (*habla español*). Have student act out. Observe: *Ahora está bailando* (*hablando español*). *¿Qué significa "está ____"?* Complete first visual exercise. Emphasize *ahora mismo*.

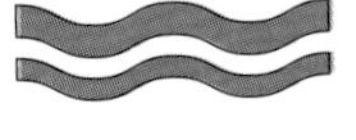

12. ¿QUÉ ESTÁS HACIENDO?
Estar; Present Progressive: *estar* + *-ndo*

The sentences in the left-hand column tell what the following persons are able to do. Following the example, tell what they are doing right now (**ahora mismo**).

Dolores baila muy bien.	→	Dolores **está bailando** ahora ahora mismo.
Soledad canta muy bien.	→	Soledad **está** ____.
Yo hablo español muy bien.	→	Yo **estoy** ____.
El profesor enseña muy bien.	→	Él **está** ____.

(continúa)

The sentences in the left-hand column tell what the following persons want to do. Following the example, tell what they are doing at the moment.

Santiago quiere comer algo. → Santiago **está comiendo** algo en este momento.
Nati quiere beber algo. → Nati **está bebiendo** algo en este momento.
Yo quiero escribir una carta. → Yo **estoy** _____.
Tú quieres abrir el regalo. → Tú **estás** _____.

- Similar presentation for second visual. Emphasize *en este momento.*
- **Follow-up:** *¿Cuáles son algunas actividades que Ud. puede hacer pero que no está haciendo en este momento?* Coach students, based on activities they mentioned in previous class discussion: *Carlos, ¿estás mirando la televisión en este momento?*

Forms and Uses of *estar*

Suggestion: Review what students know about *estar* by asking *¿Cómo está*(s)? and *¿Dónde está?* Emphasize *estoy* in answers.

Point out: irregular *yo* form, accents on other forms.

estar (*to be*)	
estoy	estamos
estás	estáis
está	están

You need to use forms of **estar** to tell where someone or something is located, and to talk about how someone is feeling, one's condition or state of health.

Emphasis: Use of *estar* for **(1)** condition or state of health, **(2)** location. Students have used *estar* to express both concepts since *Ante todo.*

¿Dónde **está** el parque? — *Where is the park?*

—¿Cómo **está** Ud.? — *—How are you?*
—**Estoy** bien (mal, enfermo). — *—I'm fine (not well, sick).*

Estar de acuerdo (**con**) means *to be in agreement* (*with*).

¿No **están** Uds. **de acuerdo con** Pablo? — *Don't you agree with Pablo?*

[Práctica A]

Uses of the Progressive

As you saw in the drawings that open this section, you need to use special verb forms in Spanish to describe an action in progress—that is, something actually happening at the time it is being described. These Spanish forms, called **el progresivo**, correspond in form to the English *progressive*: *I am walking, we are driving, she is studying*. But their use is not identical. Compare the Spanish and English verb forms in the following sentences.

Emphasis: Spanish progressive is used only for describing actions actually in progress. Ask which of following sentences would be expressed with progressive forms in Spanish: **1.** They are reading the newspaper now. **2.** Mary is typing all her homework this year. **3.** I'm speaking English now. **4.** We're going to San Francisco next summer.

Ramón **está comiendo** ahora mismo. — *Ramón is eating right now.*
Compramos la casa mañana. — *We're buying the house tomorrow.*

Ella **estudia** química este semestre. *She's studying chemistry this semester.*

In Spanish, the present progressive is used primarily to describe an action that is actually in progress, as in the first example. The simple Spanish present is used to express other English usages of the present progressive: to tell what is going to happen (the second sentence) and to tell what someone is doing over a period of time but not necessarily at this very moment (the third sentence).

Preliminary exercises:
- *¿Cómo están Uds. hoy? Haga oraciones según las indicaciones.* **1.** *yo / muy bien* **2.** *tú / bien / ¿no?* **3.** *el profesor (la profesora) / muy bien* **4.** *nosotros / no / enfermo* **5.** *Julio / mal / ¿verdad?* **6.** *Uds. / bien / también*
- *¿Dónde están las siguientes ciudades?* **1.** *¿Amarillo? ¿Los Ángeles? ¿San Agustín? ¿Toledo? ¿Sante Fe? ¿Reno?* **2.** *¿Managua? ¿Guadalajara? ¿Buenos Aires? ¿La Habana? ¿Quito? ¿La Paz? ¿Bogotá?* **Suggestion:** Give students names of states and countries, if necessary
- *Dé oraciones nuevas según las indicaciones.* *—Todos los amigos de Ud. están en una fiesta. Ud. quiere asistir también. ¿Por qué? —Todos están bailando. (tomar, cantar, comer, abrir botellas de champán, hablar mucho) —Pero Ud. no puede ir. ¿Por qué no? —Estoy estudiando. (trabajar, escribir los ejercicios, leer el periódico, mirar un programa muy interesante, aprender el vocabulario nuevo)*

Point out: *todos* (everyone, all of them) → plural verb.

Formation of the Progressive

The Spanish present progressive (**el progresivo**) is formed with **estar** plus the present participle (**el gerundio**), which is formed by adding **-ando** to the stem of **-ar** verbs and **-iendo** to the stem of **-er** and **-ir** verbs.* The present participle never varies; it alwavs ends in **-o.**

tomar	→	**tomando**	*taking; drinking*
comprender	→	**comprendiendo**	*understanding*
abrir	→	**abriendo**	*opening*

Spelling hint: Unaccented **i** represents [y] in the participle ending **-iendo**: **comiendo**, **viviendo**. Unaccented **i** between two vowels becomes **y**: **leyendo**, **creyendo**.

[Práctica B–C]

Práctica

Note A: The progressive forms are not used in this exercise.

A. **Una película** (*movie*) **extranjera.** Form complete sentences about making plans to go to a movie with a friend, based on the words given, in the order given. Do not use the subject pronouns in parentheses.

1. (yo) estar / en la residencia / por la tarde
2. leer / en / periódico / que / hay / película / español / en / cine Avenida
3. película / estar / doblado (*dubbed*) / en inglés
4. (yo) no / querer / estar / en / cuarto / todo / tarde
5. por eso / (yo) invitar / a Gloria†
6. ella / estar / enfermo; / no / poder / ir / con / (yo)
7. luego / (yo) hablar / por teléfono / con / Carlos
8. él / estar / libre (*free*) / este / tarde

***Ir**, **poder**, and **venir**—as well as several other verbs that you will learn later—have irregular present participles: **yendo**, **pudiendo**, **viniendo**. These three verbs, however, are seldom used in the progressive.

†Note again the use of the word **a** before a direct object that refers to a specific person or persons: **invitar a Gloria**. This **a** has no equivalent in English. You will learn to use the word **a** in this way in Grammar Section 20.

Footnote†: Purpose of this footnote is to call students' attention to the presence of the personal *a*. There is no need to ask students to learn the concept at this time.

9. ¡(nosotros) estar / en / cine / a / seis!
10. a / nueve / (nosotros) estar / en / café / hablando / de / película

Now retell the story as if you were **Carlos**, using the same cues as a guide and making the necessary adjustments: **1. Mi amigo está...**

Follow-up B: *Preguntas orales:* **1.** *¿Está Ud. hablando español ahora? ¿cantando? ¿tomando Coca-Cola? ¿escribiendo?* **2.** *¿Están Uds. bailando ahora? ¿regresando a casa? ¿regateando? ¿leyendo? ¿hablando con el profesor (la profesora)?*

B. What is happening right now that makes tonight different from other evenings? Answer by completing each sentence with the progressive form of the verb in parentheses.

1. Generalmente miro la televisión por la noche, pero esta noche... (leer un libro)
2. María Cristina prepara la cena (*dinner*) casi siempre, pero esta noche ella y su (*her*) esposo Juan Carlos... (comer en un restaurante)
3. Generalmente los niños estudian por la noche, pero ahora mismo... (descansar)
4. Por lo general, comemos a las seis. Esta noche... (comer a las cinco)
5. Mi esposa generalmente trabaja en casa por la noche, pero en este momento... (escribir cartas)
6. Casi todas las noches los nietos visitan a los abuelos, pero esta noche... (visitar a los tíos)

Suggestion C: Encourage students to supply their own verbs.

C. **El sábado por la tarde.** Haga oraciones según las indicaciones.

Todos los amigos de Ud. están en el parque. Ud. quiere ir también. ¿Por qué?

todos	estar	comer, beber
mi amigo/a ____		hablar mucho
		jugar al tenis, al vólibol, al béisbol, al ¿ ?
		tomar el sol (*to sunbathe*)

Pero Ud. no puede ir. ¿Por qué no?

yo	estar	trabajar, estudiar (en ____)
		escribir cartas, ¿ ?
		leer la lección para el lunes, ¿ ?
		mirar un programa de televisión
		aprender el vocabulario nuevo, ¿ ?
		terminar una composición, ¿ ?

Conversación

Suggestion A: Have students read silently the items in *Práctica A* before beginning this activity.

A. The following drawings represent the brief story you told, based on the cues in **Práctica A**. Tell the story again based on the drawings. Add as many details as you can about the new people you see.

Extension B: Part 1: 5. *en la librería* **6.** *en el laboratorio de lenguas* **7.** *en la oficina del profesor* **Part 2: 5.** *comprando ropa* **6.** *buscando unos libros* **7.** *regateando*

Follow-up B: Listening: ***¿Dónde estamos? Modelo:*** *Vamos a bailar. → Estamos en una fiesta. Vamos a mirar la televisión* (*bailar, leer, descansar, comer, aprender el vocabulario, mirar las plantas y los animales, tomar cerveza, hablar español, pagar la comida*).

B. **Situaciones. ¿Qué vamos a hacer?** With another student, form sentences that tell where you are and one thing that you are going to do there. Follow the model.

MODELO: en la clase → Estamos en la clase.
Vamos a cantar en español.

1. en una boda (fiesta)
2. en el parque
3. en casa
4. en un restaurante (bar)

Now reverse the situation. Tell what you're doing, then tell where you are.

MODELO: cantando en español → Estamos cantando en español.
Estamos en la cafetería con unos amigos colombianos.

1. leyendo
2. celebrando una fiesta
3. comiendo espaguetis
4. hablando por teléfono

C. ¿Con qué o con quién está Ud. de acuerdo?

Suggestion C1: If your class is interested in politics, give them cognate vocabulary like *capitalista*, *socialista*, and so on, and encourage students to defend their statements.

1. (No) Estoy de acuerdo con las ideas políticas de... (el presidente, los republicanos, los demócratas, el senador _____, Karl Marx, los capitalistas, ¿ ?)
2. (No) Estoy totalmente de acuerdo con las ideas de... (mis padres, mis abuelos, mis profesores, todos mis amigos, las instituciones religiosas, ¿ ?)

CH. **Actividades de personas famosas.** ¿Qué están haciendo (*doing*) ahora mismo estas personas? ¿Qué cree Ud.? Use la forma progresiva de los verbos a la derecha.

Julia Child	cantar
Clint Eastwood	buscar criminales
los empleados (*employees*) de McDonald's	escribir...
el presidente de este país (*country*)	cocinar (*to cook*)
la esposa del presidente	pintar
J. R. Ewing	leer...
Stephen King	vender hamburguesas
Mikhail Baryshnikov	comer...
Andrew Wyeth	bailar
Elizabeth Taylor	hablar (por teléfono) con...
David Letterman	beber en un bar
¿ ?	conspirar
	actuar
	¿ ?

Communicative objectives for 13: a review of all uses of *ser* and *estar* presented so far; how to use *ser* and *estar* to describe people, places and things

Point out: use of *aló*, *bueno* (Mexico), and *diga* (Spain) in answering the phone

13. ¿SER O ESTAR?
Summary of the Uses of *ser* and *estar*

Aquí hay un lado de una conversación entre una esposa que está en un viaje de negocios (*business trip*) y su esposo, que está en casa. Habla el esposo.

Aló [...] ¿Cómo *estás*, mi amor? [...] ¿Dónde *estás* ahora? [...] ¿Qué hora *es* ahí? ¡Uyy!, *es* muy tarde. Y el hotel, ¿cómo *es*? [...] ¿Cuánto cuesta por noche? [...] *Es* bien barato. Oye, ¿qué *estás* haciendo ahora? [...] Ay, pobre, lo siento. *Estás* muy ocupada. ¿Con quién *estás* citada mañana? [...] ¿Quién *es* el dueño de esa compañía? [...] Ah, él *es* de Cuba, ¿verdad? [...] Bueno, mi vida, ¿adónde vas luego? [...] ¿Y cuándo vas a regresar? [...] *Está* bien, querida. Hasta luego, ¿eh? [...] Adiós.

Ahora imagine las palabras de la otra persona.

Aló. [...] → **Aló, buenas noches, querido.** → ¿Cómo estás, mi amor? [...] etcétera.

Variation: Have students work in pairs and pretend to have phone conversation.

Follow-up: Conversation: 1. *¿Quiénes son las dos personas?* 2. *¿Dónde están?* 3. *¿Qué están haciendo en este momento?* 4. *¿A la esposa le gusta viajar* (to travel)?

Hello . . . How are you, dear? . . . Where are you now? . . . What time is it there? . . . My, it's very late. And how's the hotel? . . . How much is it per night? . . . It's very inexpensive. Hey, what are you doing now? . . . Poor dear, I'm sorry. You're very busy. Whom do you have an appointment with tomorrow? . . . Who is the owner of that company? . . . Ah, he's from Cuba, isn't he? . . . Well, dear, where are you going next? . . . And when are you coming home? . . . OK, dear. Talk to you soon . . . 'Bye.

Summary of the Uses of *ser*

• To *identify* people and things	Ella **es doctora**.
• To express *nationality*; with **de** to express *origin*	**Son cubanos**. **Son de** la Habana.
• With **de** to tell of what *material* something is made	Este bolígrafo **es de plástico**.
• With **para** to tell *for whom something is intended*	El regalo **es para** Sara.
• To tell *time*	**Son las once. Es la una y media.**
• With **de** to express *possession*	**Es de Carlota.**
• With *adjectives* that describe *basic, inherent characteristics*	Ramona **es inteligente**.
• To form many *generalizations*	**Es necesario** llegar temprano. **Es importante** estudiar.

Suggestions:
- Review uses of *ser* and *estar*.
- Ask students to give additional examples of each use listed, where possible.
- Ask students to explain why *ser* and *estar* are used each time in minidialogue.

Optional: *Ser* is used to tell where an event takes place—e.g., *El baile* (*la fiesta, la reunión*) *es en la calle Goya*.

Summary of the Uses of *estar*

• To tell *location*	El libro **está en la mesa**.
• To form the *progressive*	**Estamos tomando** un café ahora.
• To describe *health*	Paco **está enfermo**.
• With *adjectives* that describe *conditions*	**Estoy** muy **ocupada**.
• In a number of *fixed expressions*	**(No) Estoy de acuerdo. Está bien. Está claro.**

Ser and *estar* with Adjectives

Ser is used with adjectives that describe the fundamental qualities of a person, place, or thing.

La amistad es **importante**.	*Friendship is important.*
Son **cariñosos**.	*They are affectionate (people).*
Esta mujer es muy **baja**.	*This woman is very short.*

Alternate explanation: *ser* + adj. represents norm; *estar* + adj. represents change from norm.

Estar is used with adjectives to express conditions or observations that are true at a given moment but that do not describe inherent qualities of the noun.

furioso/a	furious	**sucio/a**	dirty
nervioso/a	nervous	**limpio/a**	clean
cansado/a	tired	**abierto/a**	open
ocupado/a	busy	**cerrado/a**	closed
aburrido/a	bored	**triste**	sad
preocupado/a	worried	**alegre, contento/a**	happy

Optional: *de buen humor, de mal humor*, *estar alegre* (to be tipsy)

Alternate: *Estar* is used to express unexpected quality: *¡Qué fría está el agua!* vs. *El agua es fría.* (Speaker expects it to be cold.)

Emphasis: looks, tastes, feels, appears (subjective personal evaluation) → *estar*. Contrast following pairs of sentences and meanings.

Many adjectives can be used with either **ser** or **estar**, depending on what the speaker intends to communicate. In general, when *to be* implies *looks, tastes, feels*, or *appears*, **estar** is used. Compare the following pairs of sentences:

Daniel **es** guapo.	*Daniel is handsome. (He is a handsome person.)*
Daniel **está** muy guapo esta noche.	*Daniel looks very nice (handsome) tonight.*
Este plato mexicano **es** muy rico.	*This Mexican dish is very delicious.*
Este plato mexicano **está** muy rico.	*This Mexican dish is (tastes) great.*
—¿Cómo **es** Amalia? —**Es** simpática.	*—What is Amalia like (as a person)? —She's nice.*
—¿Cómo **está** Amalia? —Está enferma todavía.	*—How is Amalia (feeling)? —She's still feeling sick.*

Note: *Daniel está muy guapo esta noche* does not imply he is by nature ugly, but rather comments on his appearance at a given point in time (he is especially handsome) or expresses surprise of speaker at how handsome he is *tonight*.

Práctica

Note A: Purpose of this exercise is to give students practice with the "new" adjectives presented in the preceding section. No *ser* versus *estar* decisions are called for.

A. **¡Una boda desastrosa!** Describa la boda, cambiando por antónimos los adjetivos indicados.

1. La novia no está *bien*; está _____.
2. El traje del novio no está *limpio*; está _____.
3. Cuando todos llegan a la iglesia, no está *abierta*; está _____.
4. El padre de la novia no está *contento*; está _____.
5. El novio no está muy *tranquilo*; ¡está _____!

Suggestion B: Ask students to justify choice of *ser/estar* in each case.

Optional: Bring in magazine pictures and ask a series of questions involving *ser/estar* (similar to items in B) about each.

B. Haga oraciones completas con una palabra o frase de cada grupo.

1. Hay un regalo en la mesa de su cuarto. ¿Qué es? Es un florero (*vase*).

El florero	es está	un regalo de boda / para Alicia y Jorge del Almacen Carrillo / de cristal / grande y verde en una caja (*box*) bonita / un regalo caro pero... ¡Alicia y Jorge son buenos amigos!

2. Hay también una fotografía en la mesa de su cuarto. ¿Quiénes son los jóvenes que aparecen en la foto?

Los jóvenes	son están	mis primos argentinos / de Buenos Aires / visitando a los parientes norteamericanos este mes a la derecha de los abuelos en la foto / muy simpáticos / en San Francisco esta semana muy contentos con el viaje (*trip*) en general / un poco cansados después del viaje

Suggestion C: Follow previous suggestions for handling contextual paragraph exercises.

C. **Actividades sociales.** Complete the following description with the correct form of **ser** or **estar**, as suggested by the context.

LAS FIESTAS: Las fiestas (*ser/estar*[1]) populares entre los jóvenes de todas partes del mundo. Ofrecen una buena oportunidad para (*ser/estar*[2]) con los amigos y conocer° a nuevas personas. Imagine que Ud. (*ser/estar*[3]) en una fiesta con muchos hispanos en este momento: todos (*ser/estar*[4]) comiendo, hablando y bailando... ¡Y (*ser/estar*[5]) las dos de la mañana!

to meet

LA PANDILLA:° Ahora en el mundo hispánico no (*ser/estar*[6]) necesario tener chaperona. Muchas de las actividades sociales se dan° en grupos. Si Ud. (*ser/estar*[7]) miembro de una pandilla, sus° amigos (*ser/estar*[8]) el centro de su vida social y Ud. y su novio o novia salen° frecuentemente con otras parejas° o personas del grupo.

group of friends
se... occur
your
go out
couples

¿Sí o no? ¿Son éstas las opiniones de un joven hispano?

1. Me gustan mucho las fiestas.
2. Nunca bailamos en las fiestas.
3. Es necesario salir con chaperona.
4. La pandilla tiene poca importancia para mí.

Suggestion CH: Ask students to tell which verb would most frequently be used in each case and to justify their choice. Ask if there are some items that might be used with either *ser* or *estar.*

Extension CH: 11. *¿El vestido que voy a comprar? (rojo)* 12. *¿El árabe? (difícil)* 13. *¿La biblioteca? (cerrada esta noche)* 14. *¿Yo? (muy alegre en este momento)* 15. *¿Nosotros? (muy, muy cansados)*

Notas Sociales

Club Español

Como es tradicional, el Club Español organiza este año las celebraciones de año nuevo en su clásico estilo familiar, en el cual siempre los socios y amigos que asisten son acogidos favorablemente.

Como la demanda excede la capacidad, se pide efectuar las reservas con la debida anticipación.

Al pedir la cena se puede solicitar el horario que más acomode al socio. El valor es de cinco mil pesos por persona.

Hermandad de la Montaña

En los salones del Club Alemán de Valparaíso, se efectuará mañana martes 29 la "Fogata Término del año 87", organizada por la Hermandad de la Montaña y con lo que se pone fin a las actividades del año.

En esta oportunidad, a las 20 horas, habrá una proyección de diapositivas y una charla sobre la estada en Francia del "encordado" Manuel González.

Posteriormente, a las 21 horas, se realizará la "fogata", la que al final será con intercambios de regalos.

Bautizo

En la Parroquia San Benito de Viña del Mar, fue bautizada el sábado 26 de diciembre Bárbara Moreno Santibáñez. Fueron sus padrinos el señor Juan Santibáñez Cos y la señora Marisol Araya de Santibáñez.

CH. Haga oraciones completas, usando las palabras entre paréntesis y la forma correcta de **ser** o **estar**, según el modelo.

MODELO: ¿El vestido de la novia? (muy elegante) → Es muy elegante.

1. ¿John? (norteamericano)
2. ¿Mi escritorio? (sucio)
3. ¿Los Hernández? (ocupados esta noche)
4. ¿Yo? (muy bien hoy)
5. ¿Su abuelo? (viejo, muy viejo)
6. ¿El problema? (muy difícil)
7. ¿La clase de computación? (muy interesante)
8. ¿Maricarmen? (no de acuerdo con nosotros)
9. ¿Los hijos de Francisco? (rubios y cariñosos)
10. ¿La tienda? (abierta esta tarde)

D. **Escenas de la primera (*first*) cita**. ¿Cómo se dice en español?

1. These flowers (**flores**, *f.*) are for you.
2. I'm a little nervous.
3. You look very pretty tonight!
4. It's necessary to be home by (**para**) 12:00. Is that clear?
5. Oh, the restaurant is closed.
6. These tacos are (taste) good!
7. The movie is excellent, isn't it?
8. It's 11:00, but I'm not tired yet.

Expansion CH: Expand each item into mini-conversation, making initial phrase cue into a complete sentence and then asking a follow-up question after students answer.

Follow-up CH: Conversation: 1. *¿Cómo es su* (your) *compañero/a de cuarto?* 2. *¿Cuánto tiempo hace que vive con él/ella?* 3. *¿Cómo es el cuarto de Uds.? ¿Es grande o pequeño? ¿viejo o moderno? ¿elegante o simple?* 4. *¿Cómo está, normalmente? ¿Está limpio o sucio? ¿Está siempre en buenas condiciones?*

Conversación

A. Describa este dibujo de un cuarto típico de la residencia. Invente los detalles necesarios. ¿Quiénes son las dos compañeras de cuarto? ¿De dónde son? ¿Cómo son? ¿Dónde están en este momento? ¿Qué hay en el cuarto? ¿En qué condición está el cuarto? ¿Están ordenadas o desordenadas las dos?

Extension B: List useful *estar* adjectives on the board and expand exercise as long as student interest lasts.

Extension B: 7. *Cuando otra persona habla y habla y habla,* _____. **8.** *Cuando estoy con mi familia,* _____. **9.** *Cuando estoy de vacaciones,* _____. **10.** *Cuando tengo problemas con mi coche,* _____. **11.** *Cuando voy al consultorio del dentista,* _____.

Variation B: Students complete sentences, telling what they are usually doing if they are (adj.): **1.** *Estoy preocupado/a cuando* _____. **2.** *Estoy aburrido/a cuando* _____. **3.** *Estoy furioso/a cuando* _____. **4.** *Estoy de buen/mal humor cuando* _____.

Follow-up C: *Describa su casa ideal:* **1.** *¿Dónde está?* **2.** *¿De quién es?* **3.** *¿Cómo es?* **4.** *¿De qué es?*

B. **Sentimientos.** Complete the following sentences by telling how you feel in the situations described. Then ask questions of other students in the class to find at least one person who completed a given sentence the way you did.

MODELO: Cuando saco (*I get*) una A en un examen, estoy alegre. →
¿Cómo te sientes (*do you feel*) cuando tienes una A en un examen?

1. Cuando saco una A en un examen, estoy _____.
2. Cuando tengo mucho trabajo, estoy _____.
3. Cuando no puedo estar con mis amigos, estoy _____.
4. Por lo general, cuando estoy en clase, estoy _____.
5. Los lunes por la mañana, estoy _____.
6. Los viernes por la noche, estoy _____.

C. **Entrevista.** Assume the identity of a famous person (television or movie personality, recording artist, or sports figure, for example). Your classmates will ask you yes/no questions in order to determine your identity. They may ask about your place of origin, your basic personal characteristics, your nationality, your profession, and so on. Here are some possible questions.

1. ¿Es Ud. hombre? ¿mujer? ¿niño/a? ¿animal?
2. ¿Es Ud. viejo/a? ¿joven? ¿guapo/a? ¿rubio/a? ¿moreno/a?
3. ¿Es de los Estados Unidos? ¿del Canadá?
4. ¿Es casado/a? ¿soltero/a? ¿Está separado/a de su esposo/a?
5. ¿Está en (lugar) hoy?
6. ¿Está muy ocupado/a estos días? ¿muy contento/a con su vida?
7. ¿Está en (programa de televisión)? ¿en (película)?

Note (Después de clase, p. 135): 4 options given for explaining why the individual cannot accept the invitation. Expand options by asking students to suggest other reasons for not being able to accept an invitation; rephrase their suggestions if necessary.

¿Recuerda Ud.?

Before beginning Grammar Section 14, review what you already know about expressing possession. Use **de** + *noun* to express these sentences in Spanish.

1. Whose presents are these?
2. They're Carmen's.
3. Carmen's wedding is *today*?!
4. Yes, and all of Miguel's relatives are coming.

Después de clase

—¿Tienes tiempo ahora para tomar un café?
—Gracias, pero no puedo.

- Tengo un examen mañana y tengo que estudiar.
- Ya (*Already*) tengo otros planes. Lo siento.
- Estoy citado/a con unos amigos en la biblioteca.
- Tengo que estar en el centro a las tres hoy.

—Tal vez (*Perhaps*) mañana, ¿eh?
—Sí, cómo no.

Universidad de los Andes, Bogotá, Colombia

Communicative objectives for 14: another way to tell to whom something belongs

14. EXPRESSING POSSESSION
Possessive Adjectives (Unstressed)*

En el periódico

Querida Antonia,

Tengo un problema con mis padres. Me gusta ir de compras con mi hermana menor, pero nuestros padres creen que no se debe gastar dinero. ¡Nuestra situación es desesperante! ¿Cuál es tu consejo?

Sin Zapatos

Querida Sin Zapatos,

Tu situación es difícil pero no es imposible de solucionar. Debes contraer matrimonio con un ladrón porque casi siempre son ricos y no les importa gastar mucho dinero. Por otro lado, casi siempre tienen un par de esposas...†

Antonia

¿Qué escribe Sin Zapatos, **mi** o **mis**?

1. _____ padres tienen mucho dinero.
2. _____ ermana también quiere ir de compras.
3. ¡_____ situación es terrible!

¿Qué contesta Antonia, **tu** o **tus**?

4. _____ zapatos son muy viejos.
5. _____ padre no tiene razón.
6. _____ problema tiene solución.

Point out: *mis padres* vs. *mi hermana*. Ask, *¿Cuál es la diferencia entre **mi** y **mis** en este caso?*

Follow up: 1. *¿Es imposible la situación de Sin Zapatos?* **2.** *¿Qué debe hacer?* **3.** *¿Debe hablar con sus padres?*

In the newspaper Dear Antonia, I have a problem with my parents. I like to go shopping with my younger sister, but our parents think that one should not spend money. Our situation is desperate! What is your advice? Shoeless
Dear Shoeless, Your situation is difficult but it isn't impossible to solve. You should marry a thief because they're almost always rich and they don't mind spending a lot of money. On the other hand, they almost always have a couple of wives (handcuffs*) . . . Antonia

*There is another set of possessives called the Stressed Possessive Adjectives. They can be used as nouns. For information on them, see Appendix 1, Using Adjectives as Nouns.

†The plural form **esposas** means *handcuffs,* as well as *wives.*

You have already learned **mi(s)**, one of the possessive adjectives in Spanish. Here is the complete set.

POSSESSIVE ADJECTIVES				
my	**mi** libro/mesa **mis** libros/mesas	*our*	nuestr**o** libro nuestr**os** libros	nuestr**a** mesa nuestr**as** mesas
your	**tu** libro/mesa **tus** libros/mesas	*your*	vuestr**o** libro vuestr**os** libros	vuestr**a** mesa vuestr**as** mesas
your, his, her, its	**su** libro/mesa **sus** libros/mesas	*your, their*	**su** libro/mesa **sus** libros/mesas	

In Spanish, the ending of a possessive adjective agrees in form with the person or thing possessed, not with the owner/possessor. Note that unstressed possessive adjectives are placed before the noun.

Son {mis / tus / sus} zapatos. Es {nuestra / vuestra / su} casa.

The possessive adjectives **mi(s)**, **tu(s)**, and **su(s)** show agreement in number only with the nouns they modify. **Nuestro/a/os/as** and **vuestro/a/os/as**, like all adjectives that end in **-o**, show agreement in both number and gender.

Suggestions:
- Present *mi(s)*, *tu(s)*, *su(s)*.
- **Emphasis:** Possessive adjectives must agree with noun they modify.
- **Point out:** *tu libro* (your book) versus *su libro* (your book.)
- **Oral drill: 1.** *Dé el plural: mi coche, mi casa, mi abrigo, mi camisa.* **2.** *Dé el singular: mis trajes, mis tiendas, mis primos, mis exámenes.*
- **Preguntas orales: 1.** *¿De qué color es su camisa* (*blusa, suéter, chaqueta*)? **2.** *¿De qué color son sus pantalones* (*zapatos, calcetines*)? Repeat questions, asking students about other students: *¿De qué color es la camisa de ____?*

Notas lingüísticas: Clarifying Meaning with Possessives

Su(s) can have several different equivalents in English: *your* (*sing.*), *his, her, its, your* (*pl.*), *their.* Usually its meaning will be clear in context. For example, if you are admiring the car of someone whom you address as **Ud.** and ask, **¿Es nuevo su coche?**, it is clear from the context that you mean *Is your car new?* When context does not make the meaning of **su(s)** clear, **de** and a pronoun are used instead, to indicate the possessor.

{el coche / la casa / los libros / las mesas} de él (de ella, de Ud., de ellos, de ellas, de Uds.)

¿Son jóvenes los hijos **de él**?	*Are his children young?*
¿Dónde vive el abuelo **de ellas**?	*Where does their grandfather live?*

- **Point out:** ambiguity of *su(s)*. *Su hijo* = your/his/her/their son. ***¿Cómo se dice?*** (your/his/her/their) mother, (your/his/her/their) parents. For clarity, use *la madre de él* (*ella*, etc.).
- **Note:** *de* + *él* do not contract.
- **Point out:** *Nuestro* and *vuestro* have four forms, like all *-o* adjectives.
- **Oral Drill: 1.** *Dé el singular: nuestros coches, nuestras casas, nuestros amigos, nuestras camisas.* **2.** *Dé el plural: nuestro traje, nuestra tienda, nuestro primo, nuestro examen.*

Práctica

Note A: Focus is on forms only, not on meaning.

A. Which nouns can these possessive adjectives modify without changing form?

1. **su:** problema / pantalones / dinero / exámenes / amor / medias
2. **tus:** camisetas / idea / novias / falda / chaquetas / mercado
3. **mi:** cita / ejercicios / suéter / coche / boda / amistad
4. **sus:** trajes / periódico / limitaciones / zapato / país / boda
5. **nuestras:** blusa / noviazgo / camisas / cine / tienda / nieta
6. **nuestro:** tacos / calcetines / parientes / puerta / clase / sombrero

B. ¿Cómo son los parientes de Isabel? Conteste según el modelo.

MODELO: familia / grande → Su familia es grande.

1. primo Julián / cariñoso
2. hermanitos / travieso (*mischievous*)
3. tíos / generoso
4. prima / pequeño / todavía
5. abuela / viejo / ya
6. esposo / muy trabajador

Ahora imagine que Ud. es Isabel y describa a sus parientes, usando las mismas palabras como guía.

MODELO: familia / grande → Mi familia es grande.

C. **¡Propaganda!** Your store has the following characteristics. Explain them to a prospective client, following the model.

MODELO: tienda / extraordinaria → ¡Nuestra tienda es extraordinaria!

1. precios / bajos
2. ropa / elegante
3. dependientes / amables
4. estacionamiento (*parking*) / gratis

Follow-up CH: Touch or point to various objects in class, asking questions such as: *Este libro, ¿es de ____?* Follow-up also serves to review forms of *este*, expanded in next grammar section.

CH. **Cosas de la boda.** ¿Cómo se dice en español?

1. Our love is impossible!
2. Your (*form.*) engagement was very long, no?
3. His fiancée is charming, isn't she?
4. Your (*fam.*) wedding is going to be expensive.
5. Their relatives are quite nice.
6. I like his mother in particular (**especialmente**).

Conversación

Notas comunicativas: Asking for Repetition

As the exchanges you are able to have with others in Spanish become more complex, there is a greater chance that you will not always understand completely what the person you are speaking to has said. In **Ante todo** you learned to use the following sentences in that context: **Otra vez, por favor. No entiendo.** Here are some additional simple phrases you can use to ask for a repetition or to express a lack of understanding.

(continúa)

Repite,* por favor. No entendí.	*Repeat, please, I didn't get it.*
Favor de repetir.	*Please repeat.*
¿Cómo?	*What? I didn't catch that.*

Note in particular the use of **¿Cómo?** (and not **¿Qué?**) to indicate a real lack of understanding.

Emphasis A: *Tu* forms with a classmate, *su* forms with instructor. Also, students will need to use *su* forms to report information to the class (even though they use *tu* forms to speak directly to a partner).

A. **Entrevista.** You have already learned a great deal about the families of your classmates and instructor. This interview will help you gather more information. Use the questions as a guide to interview your instructor or a classmate and take notes on what he or she says. Then report the information to the class.

1. ¿Cómo es su familia? ¿grande? ¿pequeña? ¿Cuántas personas viven en su casa?
2. ¿Son norteamericanos sus padres? ¿hispanos? ¿De dónde son?
3. ¿Son simpáticos sus padres? ¿generosos? ¿cariñosos?
4. ¿Trabaja su padre (madre)? ¿Dónde? ¿Cuánto tiempo hace que trabaja allí?
5. ¿Cuántos hijos tienen sus padres? ¿Cuántos años tienen?
6. ¿Cómo son sus hermanos? ¿listos? ¿traviesos? ¿trabajadores? Si son muy jóvenes, ¿prefieren estudiar o mirar la televisión? Si son mayores (*older*), ¿trabajan o estudian? ¿Dónde?
7. ¿Viven sus padres en una casa o en un apartamento? ¿Cuánto tiempo hace que viven allí? ¿Cómo es su casa/apartamento?
8. ¿Sus abuelos/tíos viven también en la casa (el apartamento)?
9. ¿De dónde son sus abuelos? ¿Cuántos años tienen? ¿Cuántos hijos tienen?
10. ¿Tiene Ud. esposo/a o novio/a? ¿Quién es? ¿Cuánto tiempo lleva con él/ella? ¿Cómo es? ¿Trabaja o estudia?

B. **Asociaciones.** With several classmates, how many words can you associate with the following phrases? Everyone in the group must agree with the associations decided on. Remember to use the words and phrases you know to agree or disagree with the suggestions of others.

MODELO: nuestro país →
Nuestro país es _____.
En nuestro país hay _____.
En nuestro país uno puede _____.

1. nuestro país
2. nuestra clase de español
3. nuestra universidad (librería)
4. nuestra ciudad
5. el centro de nuestra ciudad (los centros comerciales de nuestra ciudad)

***Repite** is the informal command form. Use it with a classmate or with someone you know well. **Repita** is the formal command.

¿Recuerda Ud.?

You have already learned the forms of **este** (*this*), one of the Spanish demonstrative adjectives. Review them by describing the color of the articles that are near to you and the clothing you are wearing.

MODELO: Esta camisa es de rayas. Estos papeles son blancos...

Communicative objectives for 15: More about pointing out people and things

15. POINTING OUT PEOPLE AND THINGS
Demonstrative Adjectives

Depende del punto de vista...

Delante de una iglesia

PANCHITO: Pero no tengo ganas de asistir a *esta* boda, papá. Las bodas son una tontería.

SR. MARTÍNEZ: Basta ya, Panchito. Todos están entrando ya en la iglesia y tú vas a entrar conmigo.

En la iglesia, un poco más tarde

SR. MARTÍNEZ: Mira, Panchito, *esas* mujeres son las damas de honor y *aquella* señorita del vestido blanco es la novia.

PANCHITO: ¿Y *aquel* hombre mayor? ¿Es su padre? ¿Por qué está con ella?

SR. MARTÍNEZ: Porque su padre también es el padrino y los padrinos acompañan a la novia al altar. Debe estar muy contento hoy.

PANCHITO: ¿Por qué?

SR. MARTÍNEZ: Porque el novio tiene una buena posición social y está muy bien económicamente. ¿Qué más puede desear un padre para su hija?

Y Ud., ¿cree que sí o que no?

1. Las bodas son una tontería.
2. La novia siempre debe llevar un vestido blanco.
3. La cosa más importante para los padres debe ser la posición social y económica del novio (de la novia).
4. Los niños deben asistir a las bodas con sus padres... aun (*even*) cuando no conocen (*they don't know*) a los novios.

Follow-up (mini): Comprensión. Who might have made each of the following statements? *Panchito, el señor Martínez, el padre de la novia* **1.** *Hoy soy padre y padrino.* **2.** *No tengo ganas de entrar en la iglesia.* **3.** *¡Ay, este niño es un desastre!* **4.** *Me gusta mucho el novio de mi hija.*

It depends on your point of view *In front of a church* PANCHITO: But I don't feel like going to this wedding, Papa. Weddings are silly (a foolish thing). SR. MARTÍNEZ: That's enough, Panchito. Everyone is going into the church already and you're going to go in with me. *In the church, a bit later.* SR. MARTÍNEZ: Look, Panchito, those women are the maids of honor and that young woman in the white dress is the bride. PANCHITO: And that older man? Is that her father? Why is he with her? SR. MARTÍNEZ: Because her father is also the best man and the best men always take the bride to the altar. He must be very happy today. PANCHITO: Why? SR. MARTÍNEZ: Because the bridegroom is well placed socially and well off economically. What more can a father want for his daughter?

DEMONSTRATIVE ADJECTIVES		
this	**este** libro	**esta** mesa
these	**estos** libros	**estas** mesas
that	**ese** libro aque**l** libro (allí)	**esa** mesa aque**lla** mesa (allí)
those	**esos** libros aque**llos** libros (allí)	**esas** mesas aque**llas** mesas (allí)

Suggestion: Hold up book and say *este libro*. Place book near student and say *ese libro*. Place book distant from both self and student and say *aquel libro*. **¡OJO!** Masc. sing. forms are *este*, *ese*, and *aquel*; they do not end in *-o*.

Demonstrative Adjectives

Demonstrative adjectives (**los adjetivos demostrativos**) are used to point out or indicate a specific noun or nouns. In Spanish, demonstrative adjectives precede the nouns they modify. They also agree in number and gender with the nouns.

- **Este**, **esta**, **estos**, **estas** (*this, these*)

Este coche es de Francia.	*This car is from France.*
Estas señoritas son argentinas.	*These women are Argentinean.*

  Forms of **este** are used to refer to nouns that are close to the speaker in space or time.

- **Ese**, **esa**, **esos**, **esas** (*that, those*)

Esas blusas son baratas.	*Those blouses are cheap.*
Ese hombre (cerca de Ud.) es abogado.	*That man (close to you) is a lawyer.*

  Forms of **ese** are used to refer to nouns that are *not* close to the speaker. Sometimes nouns modified by forms of **ese** are close to the person addressed.

- **Aquel**, **aquella**, **aquellos**, **aquellas** (*that* [over there], *those* [over there])

Aquel coche (allí en la calle) es rápido.	*That car (there in the street) is fast.*
Aquella casa (en las montañas) es del hermano de Ramiro.	*That house (in the mountains) belongs to Ramiro's brother.*

  Forms of **aquel** are used to refer to nouns that are even farther away.

Point out: Distance may be physical (*aquella casa en México*) or temporal (*en aquella época*).

Note that Spanish speakers use forms of **ese** and **aquel** interchangeably to indicate nouns that are at some distance from them: **esa/aquella casa en las montañas**, **esa/aquella ciudad en Sudamérica**. However, if a form of **ese** has been used to indicate a distant noun, a form of **aquel** must be used to indicate a noun that is even farther away in comparison: **esa señora allí y aquel hombre en la calle**.

[Práctica A–B]

Neuter Demonstratives

Optional: Present demonstrative pronouns. (See Appendix 1.) Demonstrative pronouns will appear for recognition only throughout text. Students should grasp their meaning easily.

The neuter demonstratives **esto**, **eso**, and **aquello** mean *this*, *that* (not close), and *that* (farther away), respectively.

¿Qué es **esto**? *What is this?*
Eso es todo. *That's all.*
¡**Aquello** es terrible! *That's terrible!*

They refer to a whole idea, concept, situation, or statement, or to an as yet unidentified object. They never refer to a specific noun. Compare: **este libro y ese bolígrafo**, **esa mesa y aquella silla**, and so on.

[Práctica C]

Práctica

Preliminary exercise: 1. *Dé el plural* (hold up objects): *este lápiz*, *este libro*, *este bolígrafo*; *esta mesa*, *esta bolsa*, *esta carta*. 2. *Dé el singular: estos libros*, *estos bolígrafos*, etc. 3. *Dé el plural* (point to articles of clothing worn by students): *ese zapato*, *ese traje*, *ese abrigo*, *esa chaqueta*, *esa falda*, *esa camisa*, etc. Expand to practice with other objects and articles of clothing in classroom.

A. **Comentarios en la recepción, después de la boda.** Haga oraciones completas para describir la recepción.

1. este / sala (*hall*) / ser / muy bonito
2. ¡este / regalos / deber / ser / de / familia / de / novio!
3. este / recepción / ser / muy elegante
4. ese / jóvenes / ser / amigos de la novia
5. ese / señora / no / poder / bailar / bien
6. ese / niños / no / tener / ganas / estar / en la recepción
7. ¡este / champán (*m.*) / estar / delicioso!
8. ese / mujer / mayor / no / estar / muy contento

Variation B: Following same model, students construct new sentences about places they know.

B. **Situaciones.** Imagine that you were in Mexico recently and had a good trip. With another student, ask and answer the following questions, using the cues in parentheses. Follow the model.

MODELO: —¿Recuerdas (*Do you remember*) cómo es el restaurante La Independencia? (excelente)
—¡Ah, aquel restaurante es excelente!

1. ¿Recuerdas si es cara la ropa del Mercado de la Merced? (barata)
2. ¿Recuerdas cómo son los periódicos de la capital? (magníficos)
3. Y el Hotel Libertad, ¿recuerdas qué tal es? (fenomenal)
4. ¿Y los dependientes del hotel? (simpáticos)
5. ¿Recuerdas si se puede (*one can*) regatear en los almacenes? (precios fijos)

Variation C: Students provide cues (similar to those in right-hand column) for expressions in left-hand column. They read them to other students, who react appropriately.

C. Match the questions or statements in the left-hand column with the situations described on the right.

1. ¿Qué es esto?
2. ¿Todo eso?
3. Eso es terrible.
4. ¿Qué es aquello?

a. En la montaña hay una cosa que Ud. no puede ver (*see*) muy bien.
b. El profesor dice (*says*), «Uds. tienen que estudiar para un examen mañana y tienen que escribir una composición para el lunes.»
c. Ud. abre un regalo y descubre una cosa interesante y curiosa.
ch. La hermana de un amigo está en el hospital por (*because of*) un accidente de coche.

Suggestion: Model the first item with one student. Then let students work in pairs.

Optional: 1. *¿Qué va a hacer Ud. esta noche? ¿Y este fin de semana?* 2. *¿Cómo es esta universidad? ¿Cómo es esta clase? Y este libro, ¿cómo es?* 3. *¿Cómo es esta ciudad? ¿y este estado?* 4. *¿Cómo se llama el decano* (dean) *de esta facultad? ¿el rector* (president) *de esta universidad? ¿el presidente de este país?* 5. *¿Cuántos estados hay en este país?* 6. *¿Tiene Ud. muchos exámenes esta semana? ¿Tiene que estudiar mucho esta noche?*

Conversación

Situaciones. You are visiting several stores with your friend Alice. Help her decide what to buy in each situation.

MODELO: Pues me gusta mucho aquel abrigo rojo. Pero también me gusta este gris.* ¿Qué te parece? →

- Debes comprar el rojo.* Va muy bien con tu personalidad.
- Vas a comprar el rojo, ¿verdad? Es más barato.
- A mí me gusta más el gris porque es más elegante.

1. Hay una camisa azul que me gusta. Pero aquella amarilla también es bonita.
2. Aquí venden un diccionario inglés-alemán muy barato, pero en aquella tienda tienen otro que sólo cuesta dos dólares más... y es más grande.
3. Aquí hay una planta grande muy bonita. Aquélla es más pequeña.
4. Esta blusa de seda es elegante. Aquella otra, de algodón, es mucho más barata.

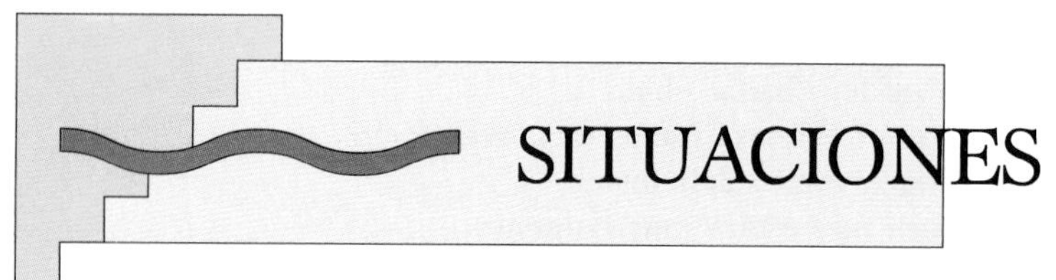

Situaciones: See IM for suggestions, additional exercises, and supplementary dialogues and exercises.

Cita para el fin de semana

—¡Por fin° es viernes! ¡Qué alegría°!
—¿Qué vas a hacer° este fin de semana?
—El sábado Luisa y yo vamos a la playa,° pero regresamos temprano. Ven° con nosotros, si quieres.
—Gracias, pero no puedo. Hace tiempo que tengo ganas de ir a la playa, pero tengo varias cosas que hacer mañana. Tal vez otro fin de semana.
—¿Por qué no cenas° con nosotros por lo menos°? Tenemos mesa en el restaurante La Olla. ¿Sabes° dónde está?
—Sí, y es una gran idea. ¿A qué hora?
—Entre las siete menos cuarto y las siete. La mesa está en mi nombre.
—Muy bien y... muchas gracias por insistir. Hasta mañana, ¿eh?
—¡Sí, mañana!

Por... *Finally* / ¡Qué... *Great!*
¿ ?
beach / *Come*
cenar = *to have dinner* / por... *at least*
¿ ?

---

*Note the *article* + *adjective* or *demonstrative* + *adjective* combination that can be used as a noun: **la camisa roja** (*the red blouse*) → **la roja** (*the red one*); **aquellos pantalones azules** (*those blue pants*) → **aquellos azules** (*those blue ones*). For more information on this topic, see Appendix 1, Using Adjectives as Nouns.

Notas comunicativas sobre el diálogo

Extending and accepting or rejecting invitations takes practice in any language. In **Situaciones** and in the functional minidialogues in this chapter, you have seen a number of ways to perform those language functions. Here are some additional useful phrases.

¿Estás libre { esta tarde / hoy? / para + *infinitive*	*Are you free* { *this afternoon / today?* / *to (do something)?*
Ven a + *infinitive* con nosotros.	*Come (do something) with us.*
Claro. Perfecto.	*Of course. Great.*
Lo siento, pero...	*I'm sorry, but . . .*
Es una lástima, pero...	*It's a shame (too bad), but . . .*
Es imposible porque...	*It's impossible because . . .*
tengo (que)...	*I have (to) . . .*
ya tengo planes	*I already have plans*
estoy invitado/a a (comer en casa de unos amigos, salir con unos amigos, ...)	*I'm invited to (eat at the home of some friends, go out with some friends, . . .)*

Correspondencia entre nuestros lectores

• Somos dos chicas de 20 y 18 años, respectivamente, deseamos mantener correspondencia con chicos de 19 a 25 años para intercambiar amistad. Susana Mateos Estrade. Valdepajuelas, 14. Jerez de la Frontera (Cádiz).

• Somos dos chicas españolas de 20 y 22 años, y nos gustaría mantener correspondencia con chicos-as italianos, ya que pensamos ir de vacaciones este verano a Italia y nos gustaría conocer gente. Sólo exigimos simpatía. María del Carmen Salaberry Rueda. Bono Guarner, 21, piso 12 M. 03005-Alicante.

• Soy una señora divorciada de 50 años, vivo en Londres, me gusta leer, viajar, la pintura, etcétera, profesión: locutora de radio, aunque por el momento no trabajo, me gustaría encontrar caballero culto, con sentido del humor de 50 a 65 años, preferible que viva en Madrid. Carmen Tiseornia. 42 Huddlestone Road, London., N.W. 2. England.

Conversación

With your instructor, use the preceding phrases—or variations on them—to accept or decline an invitation that he or she will present to you. Then, with another student, create a dialogue illustrating one or more of the following situations.

1. Una persona quiere ir al cine (tomar un café), pero la otra rechaza (*declines*) la invitación.
2. Dos personas están en un museo. Los dos miran una pintura muy famosa. Él quiere hablar con ella y ella con él. Uno de ellos inicia la conversación y luego invita a la otra persona a tomar café.
3. Un joven de catorce años invita a una chica de trece años a una fiesta. Los dos están muy nerviosos.
4. Dos personas van a una fiesta. Tienen que arreglar (*to arrange*) todos los detalles: ¿a qué hora van, qué ropa van a llevar, cómo van, etcétera?

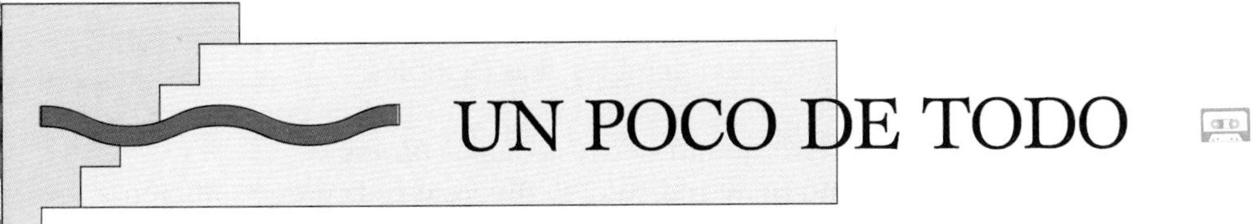

UN POCO DE TODO

A. **En esta foto familiar...** Imagine that the following persons appear in a family photograph. Identify them according to the model, then give one detail about them, using either **ser** or **estar**.

MODELO: abuelo: México → Este hombre es mi abuelo. Es de México.

1. madre: doctora
2. padre: una persona muy generosa
3. tías Elena y Eugenia: en España este año
4. novio/a: estudiando en México ahora
5. abuela: muy vieja pero simpática
6. perro: contento porque está con la familia

B. Practice accepting and declining invitations by responding to these questions from your friend Alfonso, who is calling from the place or event he mentions. How many different ways can you respond?

MODELO: Vienes a la fiesta, ¿no? →
- No puedo porque estoy...
- No tengo ganas de ir esta noche. Tengo que...
- ¡Sí, cómo no! ¿Qué debo llevar?
- Yo no, pero creo que Anita quiere ir.

1. Vienes a la fiesta, ¿no?
2. ¿Qué es esto? ¿No vienes al baile?
3. Vienes al café esta tarde, ¿verdad?
4. Vienes a la biblioteca a estudiar hoy, ¿no?

C. **¿Realmente está muy claro este caso?** Working as a class, answer these questions about the situation presented in the dialogue. Invent as much information as possible.

En el consultorio matrimonial

FEDERICO: ... y nunca estás en casa cuando yo regreso de la oficina.
MARICARMEN: Estoy de acuerdo, pero no puedo estar en casa con los niños todo el santo día. A veces voy al parque o a la...
SR. ALONSO: Perdón. El caso está muy claro...

1. ¿Quién es el Sr. Alonso? Y Federico y Maricarmen, ¿quiénes son? ¿De dónde son? ¿Cómo son? ¿Cuántos hijos tienen?
2. ¿Dónde están todos en este momento? ¿De qué están hablando? ¿Están muy contentos Federico y Maricarmen con su matrimonio?
3. ¿Cuál es la queja (*complaint*) de Federico? ¿Cómo reacciona Maricarmen? ¿Está de acuerdo con su esposo?
4. ¿Cuál va a ser el consejo del Sr. Alonso? ¿Por qué?
   - Los dos tienen que aprender a ser más flexibles.
   - Maricarmen, debes regresar a la casa de tus padres por un mes.
   - Federico, está claro que tú tienes la culpa (*blame*).
   - Este problema no tiene remedio. El divorcio es la única solución.

CH. With another student, play the roles of **los señores Gimeno**, a well-to-do Latin American couple. The two of you will be interviewed by the other members of the class, who will ask you about your possessions and about your family. Answer your classmates' questions by inventing details about yourselves and your married life together. You can talk about your children, your relatives, your houses, your cars, and so on.

MODELO: —¿Cómo es su hijo Carlos? —Es inteligente y guapo.

D. **De compras y amistades.** Complete the following paragraphs with the correct forms of the words in parentheses, as suggested by the context. When two possibilities are given in parentheses, select the correct word.

(*Me/Mí*[1]) gusta ir de (*comprar/compras*[2]) con mi amiga Margarita cuando ella tiene (*gastar/ganas*[3]) de acompañarme.° Este fin de semana, necesito (*buscar*[4]) unos regalos para los hijos (*del/de el*[5]) Sr. Suárez, que (*trabajar*[6]) con mi madre en el hospital. (*Mi*[7]) padres y los Suárez (*ser/estar*[8]) muy buenos amigos, aunque° no (*ser/estar*[9]) siempre de acuerdo con sus opiniones (*político*[10]), y la familia Suárez (*venir*[11]) a (*nuestro*[12]) casa con frecuencia.

go with me / *although*

Este mes° todos los niños de los Suárez (*celebrar*[13]) su cumpleaños.° Por (*ese/eso*[14]) tengo que (*ir*[15]) de compras antes (*de/en*[16]) su visita. Ana, (*el/la*[17]) mayor,° es una chica muy simpática. (*Yo: querer*[18]) comprarle° un vestido de cuadros o de rayas si encuentro° uno bonito en el centro. Ya tiene (*dos/doce*[19]) años y está (*comenzar*°[20]) a tener interés en la ropa elegante. (*Su*[21]) hermanos son muy niños todavía —casi siempre (*llevar*[22]) camisetas y pantalones cortos. Por eso no (*yo*: *ir*[23]) a comprarles° ropa; creo que (*ellos*: *tener*[24]) más interés en los juguetes.°

month / birthday / *eldest / buy her* / *I find* / *to begin* / *buy them / toys*

Más tarde, por teléfono

—¿Diga°?

—Margarita, ¿eres tú?

—Sí, chica. ¿Qué hay°? ¿Cómo (*ser/estar*[25])?

—Muy bien. Oye, ¿qué (*ser/estar*[26]) haciendo° en este momento?

—Ahora mismo estoy (*leer*[27]) una novela para la clase de literatura (*inglés*[28]). ¿Qué pasa?

¿Qué te parece si (*ir*[29]) al centro? Hay (*mucho*[30]) gangas en las tiendas (*este*[31]) días y tengo que comprar (*los/unos*[32]) regalos.

—¡(*Encantado*[33])! En este momento yo (*ser/estar*[34]) abriendo la puerta para salir.°

Hello? (*on the telephone*) / ¿Qué... *What's up?* / *doing* / *leave*

Who might have said the following things? Look for possible names in the story. Call the person who is speaking **la autora de la historia**. Hint: More than one answer is possible for some items.

1. Tengo que comprar muchos regalos esta semana.
2. Voy a estar en casa toda la tarde, leyendo un libro.
3. ¡Necesitamos más juguetes!
4. Trabajo con el Sr. Suárez. Es un tipo simpático, pero... sus ideas políticas son otra cosa.
5. Antes no necesitaba (*I didn't use to need*) mucha ropa, pero ahora sí.
6. ¡Paso por ti en unos minutos!
7. Celebro mi cumpleaños este mes.

VOCABULARIO

Theme vocabulary previously listed as active: *el esposo/la esposa, el fin de semana, hoy, mañana*

VERBOS

contestar to answer
entrar (en) to enter
estar (*irreg.*) to be
gastar to spend (*money*)
invitar to invite
pasar to spend (*time*); to pass
pasar por to come by to pick up (*someone, something*)
terminar to finish
visitar to visit

LAS RELACIONES SOCIALES

la amistad friendship
el amor love
la boda wedding
la cita date; appointment
el divorcio divorce
la iglesia church
la luna de miel honeymoon
el matrimonio marriage
el noviazgo courtship, engagement
el/la novio/a boy/girlfriend; fiancé/fiancée; groom/bride
la vida life

OTROS SUSTANTIVOS

el boleto ticket
el cine movies; movie theatre
el consejo (piece of) advice
la montaña mountain
el país country, nation
el parque park
la película movie
la tontería foolishness, silly thing

ADJETIVOS

abierto/a open
aburrido/a bored
alegre happy
cansado/a tired
cariñoso/a affectionate
cerrado/a closed
citado/a booked up, committed
contento/a content, happy
difícil difficult
enfermo/a sick
fácil easy
furioso/a angry
invitado/a invited
libre free
limpio/a clean
nervioso/a nervous
ocupado/a busy
preocupado/a worried
próximo/a next (*in time*)
querido/a dear
sucio/a dirty
travieso/a mischievous
triste sad

FORMAS POSESIVAS

mi(s), tu(s), su(s), nuestro/a(s), vuestro/a(s)

FORMAS DEMOSTRATIVAS

aquel, aquella, aquellos/as that, those (over there)
ese/a, esos/as that, those
esto, eso, aquello this, that, that (over there)

PREPOSICIONES

a la derecha de to the right of
a la izquierda de to the left of
antes de before (*with time*)
cerca de close to, near
debajo de under(neath)
delante de in front of
después de after (*with time*)
detrás de behind
durante during
encima de on top of
entre between; among
lejos de far from
sin without

¿CUÁNDO?

ahora mismo right now
en este momento right now, at this very moment
pasado mañana the day after tomorrow
la próxima semana next week
el próximo (martes, miércoles...) next (Tuesday, Wednesday . . .)
todavía still
ya already
los días de la semana: lunes, martes, miércoles, jueves, viernes, sábado, domingo

PALABRAS ADICIONALES

contigo with you (*fam.*)
está bien it's okay (fine)
está claro it's clear
mí me (*obj. of prep.*)
tal vez perhaps
ti you (*fam.*) (*obj. of prep.*)

Frases útiles para la comunicación

Repite. (*fam.*)	Repeat.
¿Cómo?	What? I didn't catch that.
Favor de repetir.	Please repeat.
Lo siento.	I'm sorry.

OPTIONAL SECTION

UN PASO MÁS 4

▲ Actividad A. Opiniones

Variation A: After doing as in-class activity, students survey friends and family and report results to class next day.

Suggestion A: Find out if there was great disagreement (no consensus) about any item, then discuss.

Read the following statements and indicate the extent to which you personally agree or disagree with them, according to the following scale.

5 = sí enfático 4 = sí 3 = no tengo opinión 2 = no 1 = no enfático

_____ 1. Es importante tener un noviazgo largo.
_____ 2. Los hombres deben trabajar; las mujeres deben estar en casa con los niños.
_____ 3. Un matrimonio no debe tener más de (*more than*) dos hijos.
_____ 4. Vivir con el novio (la novia) es una buena alternativa al matrimonio.
_____ 5. Los novios deben practicar la misma (*same*) religión.
_____ 6. El divorcio es una solución buena y lógica para los problemas matrimoniales.
_____ 7. La opinión que tienen los padres del novio (de la novia) es muy importante.
_____ 8. Las mujeres deben tener los mismos derechos que (*same rights as*) los hombres.

When you have finished, the class will divide into groups of four or five. Circulate within each group a piece of paper with the numbers 1–8 and corresponding blanks, on which each person will write anonymously, for each item, the number he or she wrote to express a personal opinion. When all the answers for the group have been collected, add up the numbers written for each item. The highest number will show which statement the group as a whole agrees with most emphatically; the lowest number will show which it disagrees with most emphatically.

Then, working as a group, write three or four sentences that serve to justify the group's two strongest opinions. The words and phrases in the **A propósito...** in this section will be useful. When the group has finished, compare your answers with those of other groups. Did most groups respond the way yours did?

a. *nice* b. por... *ahead of your* c. ¡A... *Everything is waiting for you!* ch. *graduate* d. *get married* e. lo... *all the rest* f. *old folk's home*

A propósito... More Ways to Describe Social Relationships

You have already learned a good deal of vocabulary useful for describing friendships, marriage, and other kinds of social relationships. Here are some additional useful phrases.

conocer a una persona	*to meet someone*
llegar a conocer a una persona	*to get to know someone*
llegar a conocerse bien/mejor	*to get to know each other well/better*
llevarse bien (con)	*to get along (with)*
mayor/menor	*older/younger*
encontrar: encuentro	*to find: I find*
casarse con	*to marry*
divorciarse	*to get a divorce*

You probably noticed that some of these phrases contain **-se**, a word that often signals a reflexive construction in Spanish. You will learn to use reflexives in **Capítulo 9**. For now, limit your use of these phrases to sentences that express generalizations or are in the third person, as in these examples. Your instructor can help you use all these phrases correctly.

Creo que **es necesario casarse** con una persona de la misma religión.
Los noviazgos largos son buenos porque así (*that way*) **los novios llegan a conocerse** mejor.

Variation B:
- Do as written paragraph.
- Oral Composition: Whole class works together to create single story.

Variation: Students talk about *un mal amigo*, *un mal novio*, *un mal suegro*, etc.

▲ Actividad B. Más opiniones

Prepare una descripción de lo que (*what*) pasa en el dibujo. Use las siguientes preguntas como guía e (*and*) invente los detalles necesarios. Al describir (*As you describe*) la escena, va a expresar algunas (*some*) de sus ideas sobre el matrimonio.

Palabras útiles: la escalera (*ladder*), la suegra (*mother-in-law*)

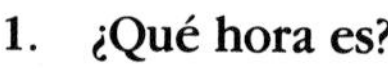

1. ¿Qué hora es?
2. ¿Quién es el novio? ¿Cómo es?
3. ¿Quién es la novia? ¿Cómo es ella?
4. ¿Por qué no quieren tener una boda grande?
5. ¿A quién lleva la novia? (Lleva a...) ¿Por qué?
6. ¿Adónde van después de la boda para su luna de miel?
7. ¿Van a vivir felices (*happy*) para siempre o van a tener problemas? Explique.

Ahora describa lo que son para usted los aspectos más importantes de las relaciones sociales. ¿Cuál es su concepto de la amistad? ¿del noviazgo? ¿del matrimonio? ¿Cómo es un buen amigo (una buena amiga)? ¿el novio perfecto (la novia perfecta)? ¿el suegro ideal? ¿la suegra perfecta?

Frases útiles

guardar (*to keep*) un secreto
ser una limitación
mostrar (*to show*) el cariño libremente (*freely*)
tener mucha paciencia
expresar todos sus sentimientos
ganar (*to earn*) todo el dinero
necesitar mucha atención
escuchar (*to listen to*) todos mis problemas
querer (*to love*) mucho a los niños
cuidar a (*to take care of*) los nietos
causar muchos problemas

Suggestion: The whole class works as a group to "answer" one of the ads on behalf of one of the people in the activity.

MODELO: Para mí, un buen amigo es/debe ____, porque ____.
Para mí, la suegra ideal es/debe ____, porque ____.

CENTRO CONTINENTAL
Solteros/as, viudos/as, divorciados/as, separados/as. No anden por el mundo solos.
CENTRO CONTINENTAL
le formaliza la persona adecuada.
GARANTIA – FORMALIDAD
Tel. 232 52 90

•**BUSCO** amiga o compañera para convivencia estable, que al igual que yo, no tenga problemas familiares (sin padres ni hijos) que sea mujer cariñosa y edad de 39 a 44 años, soy legalmente libre y tengo trabajo seguro.
Aptado. 1.074 Leganés.
•**UNIVERSITARIO** 32 años, buena presencia y posición, desea amistad con chica imprescindible cultura, buen físico y mida entre 1,65 y 1,70. Enviar fotografía y teléfono.
Aptado. 53.093 Madrid.
•**TENGO** 35 años, soy funcionario del estado y practicamente de yoga, deseo escribirme con fines serios con señoritas que también practique yoga y vida natural.
Apatado. 14.089 Madrid.
•**MUJER** acude a mi quiero darte mi cariño, amor y afecto sin condicines, ni reparos. Escribe al
Aptado. 150.138 Madrid.
•**DESEO** tener correspondencia con señores cultos nivel universitario de 60 a 65 años, de edad, sin problemas, familiares y con situación económica definida, escribir

EMPRESARIO
maduro, de aspecto y trato agradables, dinámico y juvenil, para convivencia estable inmediata.
BUSCA MUJER
joven, atractiva, alegre, cariñosa, de buen carácter, con cierta cultura mínima. No importa tenga niño pequeño, ni estado civil.
Enviar foto, no imprescindible.
Aptdo. 29.087 Madrid

•**CABALLERO** formal, sincero, cariñoso, soltero, 1,72 mts. que dirige empresa agricola propia, desea casarse con mujer de físico agradable no mayor de 48 años, escribir
Aptado. 50.724 Madrid.
•**JEUN** homme offre amitie et peut être quelque chose de plus aux damines authentiques.
Aptado 10.169 Madrid.
•**MAESTRO** estatal, 40 años, solero, desea conocer mujer igual situación.
Aptado. 169 Coslada.
•**SOLTERO,** 42 años trabajo propio desea conocer señorita viva en Madrid, fines serios, abstenerse casadas o separadas. Charly.
Aptado. 47.014 Madrid.
•**RETIRADO** viudo, 60 años, solo, presencia, trato agradable, desea relacionarse con señora educada agradable sin problemas, con ilusión hayar felicidad estable, formal.
Aptado. 15.200 Madrid.
•**SI ERES** culto y cariñoso, estatura media, buen nivel económico, te guste el diálogo, cine, teatro, etc. puedes escribirme y enviar teléfono. Soy divorciada y tengo 46 años.
Aptado. 50.308 Madrid.
•**SOLTERO** 28 años, 1,80 buena presencia, y valores tradicionales, desea amistad, con señorita 22-28, católica, culta y sincera, escribir:
Aptado. 49.040 Madrid.
•**UNIVERSITARIO** soltero, 30 años, buen nivel económico y cultural, busca amistad chicas agradables, características similares.
Aptado. 50.735
•**SEÑORITA** buena, cultura, presencia y posición... Desea encontrar hombre libre, entre 50 y 55 años con las mismas condiciones, para matrimonio o convivencia.
Aptado. 8.198 Madrid.
•**A TI** mujer de 27-37 años, sincera, desinteresada, me agradaría conocerte y tal vez con el tiempo no lleve a caminar por el mismo sendero.
Aptdo. 38.020

▲ Actividad C. ¡Busco amigo/a!

"Personals" ads, placed by people who want to meet others for various reasons, are common in newspapers and magazines throughout the world. Here are some ads from the personal ads section of a Madrid newspaper. Scan the ads to get a general sense of the kinds of relationships being sought. Then tell which ad(s) the following individuals should answer.

1. Un hombre de 62 años quiere mantener correspondencia con una mujer independiente en todos los sentidos, con educación universitaria.
2. Una joven que habla francés busca amistad con un joven.
3. Una persona no quiere contestar ninguno (*any*) de los anuncios concretos pero sí busca amistad.
4. Una mujer de 30 años, con interés en las filosofías orientales, quiere casarse con un hombre que tenga intereses similares.
5. Un hombre de 50 años, bien situado económicamente, tiene mucho interés en toda clase de espectáculos (*shows*).

Alternative: Students take roles (some as placer of the ads, some as respondents) and write to each other.

LECTURA CULTURAL

Lectura: See IM for suggestions and additional exercises and activities.

Antes de leer: *Recognizing Cognate Patterns*

You already know that cognates are words that are similar in form and meaning from one language to another: for example, English *poet* and Spanish **poeta**. The more cognates you can recognize, the more easily you will read in Spanish.

The endings of many Spanish words correspond to English word endings according to fixed patterns. Learning to recognize these patterns will increase the number of close and not-so-close cognates that you can recognize. Here are a few of the most common.

-dad → -ty **-ción** → -tion **-ico** → -ic, -cal **-mente** → -ly **-sión** → -sion **-oso** → -ous

What are the English equivalents of these words?

1. unidad
2. reducción
3. explosión
4. idéntico
5. dramático
6. estudioso
7. famoso
8. reacción
9. recientemente
10. frecuentemente
11. religioso
12. religiosidad

Try to spot cognates in the following reading, and remember that you should be able to guess the meaning of underlined words from context.

Los apellidos hispánicos

Suggestion: Return to telephone book activity on page 65, Ch. 1.

En español, generalmente, las personas tienen dos apellidos: el apellido paterno y también el materno. Cuando un individuo usa solamente uno de sus apellidos, casi siempre es el paterno.

Imagine que Ud. tiene una amiga, Gloria Gómez Pereda. El **nombre** de esta persona es «Gloria» y sus **apellidos** son «Gómez» y «Pereda». «Gómez» es el apellido paterno y «Pereda» es el materno. En situaciones oficiales o formales, ella usa los dos apellidos. En ocasiones informales, usa solamente el paterno. Cuando uno habla con ella, la llama° «Señorita Gómez» o «Señorita Gómez Pereda», pero nunca «Señorita Pereda».

Ahora imagine que su amiga Gloria va a casarse con un señor que se llama Eduardo Cabrera Meléndez. El nombre de casada° de Gloria será° Gloria Gómez de Cabrera, pues ella va a usar su apellido paterno (Gómez) y el apellido paterno de su esposo (Cabrera). En ocasiones formales Gloria será «la señora Gómez de Cabrera» o «la señora de Cabrera», pero nunca «la señora Gómez».

Es importante comprender el sistema de apellidos cuando Ud. usa una lista alfabetizada. Lo primero° que determina el orden en la lista es el apellido paterno, y después el materno. En una guía telefónica, el señor Carlos Martínez Aguilar aparece cerca del comienzo° de la lista de todos los Martínez.* Su padre, el señor Alfonso Martínez Zúñiga, aparece cerca del final de la lista. En la guía telefónica de la Ciudad de México, hay más de veinticinco páginas—con más de 8.000 personas—que tienen el apellido paterno «Martínez». Si usted busca el número de teléfono de un señor Martínez y no sabe° su apellido materno, ¡va a tener un gran problema!

la... *one calls her*

de... *as a married woman* / *will be*

Lo... *The first thing*

beginning

no... *you don't know*

*Last names are made plural in Spanish simply by putting the plural definite article in front of the name: **los Martínez** (*the Martínez family*), **los García** (*the Garcías*), and so on.

Comprensión

Complete las oraciones 1 a 3 según la lectura. Después conteste la pregunta 4.

1. Un hispano tiene dos apellidos: ____.
   a. el materno y el paterno
   b. dos paternos
   c. dos maternos
2. En una fiesta de amigos y colegas, una persona usa ____.
   a. su apellido materno
   b. su apellido paterno
   c. los dos apellidos
3. Si Ud. busca el nombre de un amigo en la guía telefónica, necesita saber (*to know*) ____.
   a. solamente el apellido paterno
   b. solamente el apellido materno
   c. los dos apellidos
4. ¿En qué orden aparecen estos nombres en una guía telefónica?
   ____ Benito Pérez Galdós
   ____ Jaime García Jiménez
   ____ Baldomero Pérez Almena
   ____ Juan Pereda García
   ____ Virginia Pérez García

Para escribir

A. Write a brief paragraph about the Hispanic system of names as it would apply to your own family. Use the following sentences as a guide.

1. Me llamo ____.
2. Mi apellido paterno es ____ y ____ es mi apellido materno.
3. En situaciones informales me llamo ____.
4. ____ es el nombre completo de mi padre.
5. ____ es el nombre completo de mi madre.
6. Si me caso con (*If I marry*) Juan(a) García Sandoval, el nombre completo de mi hijo Carlos será (*will be*) Carlos ____.

B. **Querida Antonia...** Antonia offers free advice in her column to the lovelorn and to those with problems of almost all types (see letter from "**Sin Zapatos**" on page 135). Write a letter to Antonia about one specific problem. Create an original problem or write about one of the following situations. Then write Antonia's answer to your letter, or trade letters with another student and write appropriate responses.

1. Ud. necesita hablar con sus padres sobre un problema, pero ellos no quieren hablar con Ud.
2. Su novio/a y Ud. quieren una boda familiar, con poca gente (*people*); sus padres quieren una boda grande, con unos quinientos invitados.
3. Sus padres creen que su novio/a es feo/a (que es perezoso/a, que no es muy inteligente, ...)
4. Su novio/a cree que el matrimonio es una tontería.
5. Sus padres creen que Ud. es muy joven para tener novio/a. Ud. tiene doce años.
6. Su novio/a quiere tener ocho o nueve niños. ¡Ud. no!

CAPÍTULO CINCO

LAS ESTACIONES Y EL TIEMPO

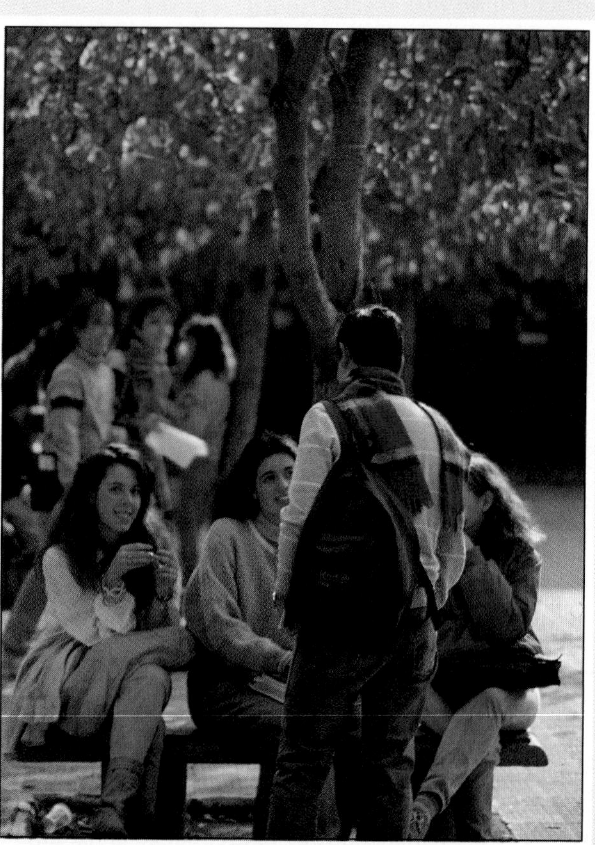

Santiago, Chile

▲ **¡Hablemos[a] del tiempo!**

—De todas las estaciones, ¿cuál es tu favorita?

—Creo que el otoño.

—¿El otoño? ¿Por qué?

—Porque hace calor durante el día y fresco durante la noche. Y porque llueve... ¡Me gusta la lluvia!

[a]*Let's talk*

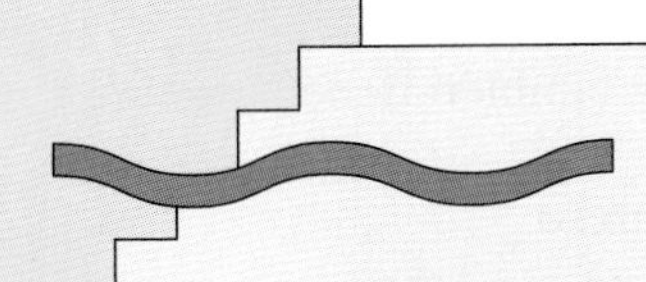

VOCABULARIO: PREPARACIÓN

• See also [video] and [cassette]

¿Qué tiempo hace hoy?°

¿Qué... *What's the weather like today?*

Hace frío.

Hace calor.

Hace viento.

Hace sol.

Está (muy) nublado.

Llueve. Está lloviendo.

Nieva. Está nevando.

Hay mucha contaminación.

Hace (mucho) frío (calor, viento, sol).	It's (very) cold (hot, windy, sunny).
Hace fresco.	It's cool.
Hace (muy) buen/mal tiempo.	It's (very) good/bad weather. The weather is (very) good/bad.

In Spanish, many weather conditions are expressed with **hace**. Note that the adjective **mucho** is used with the nouns **frío**, **calor**, **viento**, and **sol** to express *very*.

Pronunciation hint: Remember that, in most parts of the Spanish-speaking world, **ll** is pronounced exactly like **y**: **llueve**, **está lloviendo**.*

Vocabulario: Preparación:
- See detailed supplementary materials and exercises for this section bound into the back of this Annotated Instructor's Edition.
- See model for vocabulary presentation and other materials in Supplementary *Vocabulario: Preparación* Materials, chapter by chapter, IM.

A. Diga qué tiempo hace, según la ropa de cada persona.

1. San Diego: María lleva pantalones cortos y una camiseta.
2. Madison: Juan lleva suéter, pero no lleva chaqueta.
3. Toronto: Roberto lleva suéter y chaqueta.

*Because **ll** = the sound **y**, pronunciation alone will not tell you whether a word is spelled with **y** or **ll**. In many areas of Spain, **ll** is a sound made with the middle of the tongue against the palate. This resembles the [ly] sound of English *million*, but is one sound, not an [l] plus a [y].

4. Guanajuato: Ramón lleva impermeable y botas y también tiene paraguas (*umbrella*).
5. Buenos Aires: Todos llevan abrigo, botas y sombrero.

Follow-up B: 1. *¿Dónde prefiere Ud. vivir, donde hace calor o donde hace fresco?* 2. *¿Le gusta vivir donde llueve mucho? ¿donde nieva mucho?* 3. *Describa la diferencia entre el clima de Michigan y el de Texas.* 4. *¿Prefiere Ud. vivir en un lugar con cuatro estaciones o con solamente una?* 5. *¿En qué partes de los Estados Unidos hay solamente una estación?*

B. **¿Dónde debe vivir Joaquín?** Joaquín es de Valencia, España. El clima allí es moderado y hace mucho sol. Hay poca contaminación. Va a venir a los Estados Unidos y quiere vivir en un lugar con un clima similar. ¿Dónde debe—o *no* debe—vivir?

MODELO: Joaquín, (no) debes vivir en _____ porque allí _____.

1. Seattle
2. Los Ángeles
3. Phoenix
4. New Orleans
5. Buffalo
6. ¿ ?

Notas lingüísticas: More *tener* Idioms

Several other conditions expressed in Spanish with **tener** idioms—not with *to be,* as in English—include the following:

tener (mucho) calor	to be (very) warm
tener (mucho) frío	to be (very) cold

These expressions are used to describe people or animals only. To be comfortable—neither hot nor cold—is expressed with **estar bien**.

C. **¿Tienen frío o calor? ¿Están bien?** Describe the following weather conditions and tell how the people pictured are feeling.

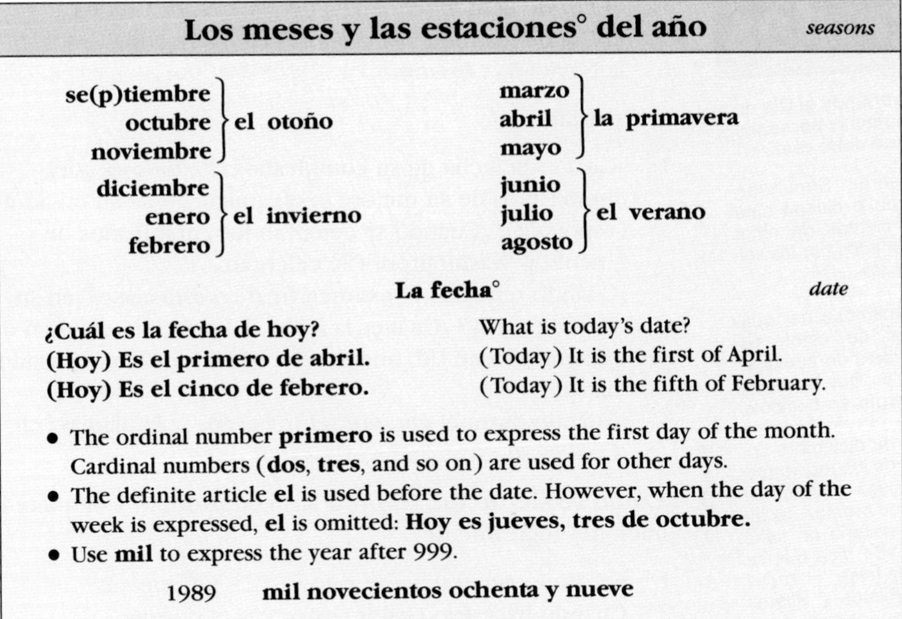

Los meses y las estaciones° del año

°*seasons*

se(p)tiembre, **octubre**, **noviembre**	**el otoño**	**marzo**, **abril**, **mayo**	**la primavera**
diciembre, **enero**, **febrero**	**el invierno**	**junio**, **julio**, **agosto**	**el verano**

La fecha°

°*date*

¿Cuál es la fecha de hoy?	What is today's date?
(Hoy) Es el primero de abril.	(Today) It is the first of April.
(Hoy) Es el cinco de febrero.	(Today) It is the fifth of February.

- The ordinal number **primero** is used to express the first day of the month. Cardinal numbers (**dos**, **tres**, and so on) are used for other days.
- The definite article **el** is used before the date. However, when the day of the week is expressed, **el** is omitted: **Hoy es jueves, tres de octubre.**
- Use **mil** to express the year after 999.

1989 **mil novecientos ochenta y nueve**

A. ¿Qué día de la semana es el 12 (1, 20, 16, 11, 4, 29) de noviembre?

B. Exprese estas fechas en español.

1. March 7
2. August 24
3. December 1
4. June 5
5. September 19, 1989
6. May 30, 1842
7. January 31, 1660
8. July 4, 1776

C. Lea los siguientes (*following*) años en español. ¿A qué dato (*fact, event*) corresponden?

1. 1492	a. el año de mi nacimiento (*my birth*)
2. 1776	b. la Declaración de la Independencia
3. 1945	c. el asesinato de John F. Kennedy
4. 2001	ch. Cristóbal Colón descubre América
5. 1963	d. la bomba atómica
6. 1984	e. una película famosa
7. ¿ ?	f. la novela de George Orwell
	g. este año

Point out CH: Hispanic *Día de los Inocentes* is December 18: a religious holiday commemorating the day King Herod had all babies slaughtered.
Extension CH: *¿Qué acciones asociamos con estas fiestas?* Cues: **1.** *desfiles* (parades) **2.** *fiesta la noche antes del Día del Año Nuevo, tomar/beber champán* **3.** *mandar* (to send) *tarjetas, chocolates, flores* **4.** *barbacoas y picnics en el parque, fuegos artificiales* (fireworks) **5.** *bromas* (jokes) **6.** *el árbol de la Navidad, abrir regalos*

CH. **¿Cuándo se celebran?***

1. el Día de la Raza (*Columbus Day*)
2. el Día del Año Nuevo
3. el Día de los Enamorados (de San Valentín)

¡OJO!** Note that the word **se** before a verb changes the verb's meaning slightly. **¿Cuándo se celebran?** = ***When are they celebrated? You will see this construction throughout ***Puntos de partida***. Learn to recognize it, for it is frequently used in Spanish.

Día de Inocentes

En todo el mundo cristiano se celebra hoy el Día de los Santos Inocentes. Por esto, muchas personas suelen hacer bromas a los demás, lo que debe realizarse antes del mediodía.

El 28 de diciembre se considera Día de los Inocentes debido a que recuerda la fecha que el Rey Herodes mandó a matar a todos los niños recién nacidos en la ciudad, debido a que él se había enterado de que iba a nacer un Mesías, y temiendo ser destronado no encontró mejor recurso que acabar con todas las criaturas que habían llegado al mundo en esa fecha.

Debido a esta decisión del Rey Herodes de matar a los niños, fue que María y José huyeron de la ciudad y se dirigieron a Belén. Este pequeño poblado estaba lleno de visitantes, así es que no encontraron alojamiento. Es por esto que el Niño Jesús fue a nacer en un pesebre. Simultáneamente, en la ciudad natal de José cientos de niños eran asesinados por los soldados del rey.

Es en memoria de todas las almas de estos pequeños, libres de cualquier tipo de culpa, que las personas que profesan cualquier tipo de fe cristiana recuerdan el 28 de diciembre como el Día de los Inocentes. Cómo se llegó a constituir en un día de bromas, es algo que la historia no tiene muy claro. Se dice que se origina en la frase "Herodes mandó a Pilatos y Pilatos mandó a su gente", a lo que se ha agregado "el que presta en este día pasa por inocente".

4. el Día de la Independencia de los Estados Unidos
5. el Día de los Inocentes (*Fools*) en los Estados Unidos*
6. la Navidad (*Christmas*)

D. **Preguntas**

1. ¿Cuál es la fecha de su cumpleaños (*birthday*)? ¿del cumpleaños de su mejor (*best*) amigo/a? ¿de su novio/a (esposo/a)? ¿Cuándo se celebran los cumpleaños de Lincoln y Washington? (Se celebran...)
2. ¿Cuándo tenemos el examen final en esta clase? ¿en su clase de _____? ¿Cuál es la fecha del próximo examen de español? ¿Tiene Ud. una prueba (*quiz*) mañana? ¿pasado mañana?
3. ¿Cuándo entra el verano? ¿el invierno? ¿y la primavera? ¿Cuál es su estación favorita? ¿Por qué?

E. **¿Cómo se siente Ud.** (*do you feel*) **cuando... ?** Complete las oraciones lógicamente.

1. En otoño generalmente estoy _____ porque _____.
2. Cuando hace frío (calor) estoy _____ porque _____.
3. En verano estoy _____ porque _____.
4. Cuando llueve (nieva) estoy _____ porque _____.

Expressing Actions: *hacer*, *poner*, and *salir*

hacer (*to do; to make*)		**poner** (*to put; to place*)		**salir** (*to leave; to go out*)	
hago	hacemos	pongo	ponemos	salgo	salimos
haces	hacéis	pones	ponéis	sales	salís
hace	hacen	pone	ponen	sale	salen
haciendo		poniendo		saliendo	

- ***hacer:*** ¿Por qué no **haces** los ejercicios? — *Why aren't you doing the exercises?*

Two common idioms with **hacer** are **hacer un viaje** (*to take a trip*) and **hacer una pregunta** (*to ask a question*).

Quieren **hacer un viaje** al Perú. — *They want to take a trip to Peru.*
Los niños siempre **hacen muchas preguntas**. — *Children always ask a lot of questions.*

*In Hispanic countries, **el Día de los Inocentes** is celebrated on December 28.

- ***poner:*** Siempre **pongo** mucho azúcar en el café. *I always put a lot of sugar in my coffee.*

Many Spanish speakers use **poner** with appliances to express *to turn on.*

Voy a **poner** el televisor. *I'm going to turn on the TV.*

- ***salir:*** **Salen de** la clase ahora. *They're leaving class now.*

Note that **salir** is always followed by **de** to express leaving a place. **Salir para** expresses destination. **Salir con** can mean *to go out with, to date.*

Salimos para la playa mañana. *We're leaving for the beach tomorrow.*

Salgo con el hermano de Cecilia. *I'm going out with Cecilia's brother.*

A. **¿Qué hacemos esta noche?** Haga oraciones completas con una palabra o frase de cada grupo.

yo		hacer	ejercicio en el gimnasio
mi amigo/a (nombre)	(no)	poner	el televisor a las seis para las noticias (*news*)
(profesora), Ud.		salir	con unos amigos, con...
			ejercicios para la clase de español
			para casa hasta las siete o las ocho
			para la universidad otra vez, para estudiar en la biblioteca

Follow-up B: Suggestion: ***¿Cómo se dice?:*** **1.** I'm going to turn on the TV (the heat). I want to turn on the radio. **2.** She's going out with her boyfriend. He wants to go out with Margarita. **3.** She's leaving for Rome tomorrow. I'm leaving for Bogotá on Friday. **4.** We have to take a trip. They should ask a question.

B. **Consecuencias lógicas.** ¿Qué va Ud. a hacer en estas condiciones? Use las siguientes frases en su respuesta.

poner el aire condicionador / la calefacción (*heat*)
poner el televisor / la radio
salir de / para...
hacer un viaje a...
hacer una pregunta

1. Me gusta esquiar. Por eso...
2. Tengo frío y hace frío afuera (*outside*). Por eso...
3. Tenemos calor y hace calor afuera. Por eso...
4. Hay un programa interesante en la televisión.
5. ¡Estoy cansada de trabajar!
6. Estamos aburridos.
7. Quiero escuchar (*to listen to*) música y bailar.
8. No comprendo.

C. **Preguntas**

1. ¿Qué pone Ud. en el café? ¿en el té? ¿en una limonada? ¿Pone Ud. hielo (*ice*) en los refrescos (*soft drinks*) en invierno? ¿y en verano?
2. ¿Qué hace Ud. en verano? ¿en invierno? ¿el día de su cumpleaños? ¿en septiembre? ¿los sábados?
3. ¿Qué quiere Ud. hacer esta noche? ¿Qué necesita hacer? ¿Qué va a hacer? ¿Va a salir con sus amigos? ¿Adónde van?

Extension C: 5. *¿Cuánto tiempo hace que Ud. estudia español? ¿que asiste a esta universidad? ¿que vive en esta ciudad? ¿este estado?*

4. ¿A qué hora sale Ud. de la clase de español? ¿de otras clases? ¿A veces sale tarde de clase? ¿Por qué? ¿Le gusta salir temprano? ¿Siempre sale Ud. temprano para la universidad? ¿Sale tarde a veces?

Suggestion CH: If it becomes too hard for students to remember entire list after 7 or 8 items, stop; start new list with different students.

CH. **Un viaje.** You're going to take a trip, and you have to pack your suitcase. Tell what you're going to pack, using the model given below. The next person will repeat what you said and add one item, and so on. See how long you can keep the sentence going.

MODELO: Voy a hacer un viaje, y en mi maleta voy a poner _____.

PRONUNCIACIÓN: *R* and *RR*

Spanish has two *r* sounds, one of which is called a *flap,* the other a *trill.* The rapid pronunciation of *tt* and *dd* in the English words *Betty* and *ladder* produces a sound similar to the Spanish flap **r**: the tongue touches the alveolar ridge (behind the upper teeth) once. Although English has no trill, when people imitate a motor, they often produce the Spanish trill, which is a rapid series of flaps.

The trilled **r** is written **rr** between vowels (**carro**, **correcto**) and **r** at the beginning of a word (**rico**, **rosa**). Any other **r** is pronounced as a flap. Be careful to distinguish between the flap **r** and the trilled **r**. A mispronunciation will often change the meaning of a word—for example, **pero** (*but*) / **perro** (*dog*).

Preliminary exercise: Listening: Flap or trill? *para, pero, parra, perro, ahora, ahorra, carro, caro, rico, coro, corro, Roberto*

Follow-up: 1. *Roberto quiere ir.* 2. *Ramón es rico.* 3. *Raquel Ramírez tiene un perro.* 4. *El perro es rebelde.* 5. *Roberto es el amigo de Ramón.* 6. *Raquel es de Puerto Rico.*

Note. This is the last *Pronunciación* section in the student text of *Puntos de partida. Pronunciación* sections continue in the Laboratory Manual and tape program, however.

A.

inglés:	potter	ladder	cotter	meter	total	motor
español:	para	Lara	cara	mire	toro	moro

B.
1. rico
2. ropa
3. roca
4. Roberto
5. Ramírez
6. rebelde
7. reportero
8. real
9. corro
10. carro
11. corral
12. barra

C.
1. coro/corro
2. coral/corral
3. pero/perro
4. vara/barra
5. ahora/ahorra
6. caro/carro
7. cero/cerro

CH.
1. el nombre correcto
2. un corral grande
3. una norteamericana
4. Puerto Rico
5. rosas amarillas
6. un libro negro y rojo
7. una mujer refinada
8. Enrique, Carlos y Rosita
9. El perro está en el corral.
10. Estos errores son raros.
11. Busco un carro caro.
12. Soy el primo de Roque Ramírez.

MINIDIÁLOGOS Y GRAMÁTICA

¿Recuerda Ud.?

The change in the stem vowels of **querer** and **poder** (**e** and **o**, respectively) follows the same pattern as that of the verbs in the next section. Review the forms of **querer** and **poder** before beginning that section.

querer: **e** → ¿ ?	qu__ro	queremos	poder: **o** → ¿ ?	p__do	podemos
	qu__res	queréis		p__des	podéis
	qu__re	qu__ren		p__de	p__den

16. EXPRESSING ACTIONS
Present Tense of Stem-Changing Verbs

Haciendo planes

PADRE: Mira, Esteban, *empiezo* a perder la paciencia contigo. No comprendo por qué no *quieres* hacer este viaje a Sudamérica con nosotros.
ESTEBAN: Estoy muy bien aquí...
MADRE: Pero, hijo, aquí *nieva* todos los días y allí hace muy buen tiempo ahora. ¡Con lo que a ti te gusta nadar... !
ESTEBAN: Pero es que aquí *jugamos* al básquetbol en invierno y si nosotros no *volvemos* hasta febrero *pierdo* el campeonato. *Prefiero* no ir.
PADRE: Lo *siento*,* Esteban, pero no *pensamos* dejarte aquí. ¡Y se acabó!

1. ¿Adónde va la familia?
2. ¿Qué tiempo hace este mes donde viven? ¿Y en Sudamérica?
3. ¿A qué juegan los amigos de Esteban en invierno?
4. ¿Qué va a perder Esteban si acompaña a sus padres?
5. En la opinión de Ud., ¿qué va a decir (*say*) ahora Esteban?
   - Bueno, está claro que no tengo alternativa.
   - ¿No puedo volver un poco antes que Uds.?
   - ¡No quiero ir y no voy!

Follow-up: 1. *¿Hace Ud. muchos viajes? ¿Adónde viaja con frecuencia? ¿Cuánto tiempo hace que no visita ese lugar?* **2.** *Cuando viaja, ¿prefiere viajar solo/a, con un grupo de amigos o con su familia?* **3.** *¿Le gusta viajar con los niños? ¿Por qué sí o por qué no?* **4.** *Imagine que Ud. es Esteban. ¿Quiere o no hacer el viaje?* **5.** *Imagine que Ud. es el padre de Esteban. ¿Qué va a hacer?*

Making plans FATHER: Look, Esteban, I'm starting to lose patience with you. I don't understand why you don't want to take this trip to South America with us. ESTEBAN: I'm just fine here . . . MOTHER: But son, here it's snowing every day, and there the weather is very nice now. Considering how much you like to swim . . . ! ESTEBAN: But it's just that we play basketball here in the winter and if we don't come back until February, I'll miss the championship game. I'd rather not go. FATHER: I'm sorry, Esteban, but we don't intend to leave you here. And that's that!

***Siento** is the first person singular form of the stem-changing verb **sentir** (*to regret*). You will learn to use other forms of **sentir** in later chapters.

e → ie		o (u) → ue		e → i	
pensar (ie) (*to think*)		**volver (ue)** (*to return*)		**pedir (i)** (*to ask for, order*)	
pienso	pensamos	vuelvo	volvemos	pido	pedimos
piensas	pensáis	vuelves	volvéis	pides	pedís
piensa	piensan	vuelve	vuelven	pide	piden
pensando		volviendo		pidiendo	

Suggestions:
- Review *querer* and *poder* (*¿Recuerda Ud.?*). Point out *e → ie* and *o → ue* in stressed position (i.e., everywhere except *nosotros* and *vosotros* forms).
- Present *pensar* (*ie*), *volver* (*ue*), and *pedir* (*i*), modeling forms and changing to questions asked of students. Write forms on board as you produce them.

A. You have already learned three *stem-changing verbs* (**los verbos que cambian el radical**): **querer**, **preferir**, and **poder**. In these verbs the stem vowels **e** and **o** become **ie** and **ue**, respectively, in stressed syllables. The stem vowels are stressed in all present tense forms except **nosotros** and **vosotros**. All three classes of stem-changing verbs follow this regular pattern in the present tense. In vocabulary lists, the stem change will always be shown in parentheses after the infinitive: **volver (ue)**.

Some stem-changing verbs practiced in this chapter include the following.

- Model infinitives you have not yet presented, creating a brief conversational exchange with each.
- *¡OJO! perder* vs. *pedir*

e → ie		o (u) → ue		e → i	
cerrar (ie)	*to close*	almorzar (ue)	*to have lunch*	pedir (i)	*to ask for, order*
empezar (ie)	*to begin*	dormir (ue)	*to sleep*	servir (i)	*to serve*
entender (ie)	*to understand*	jugar (ue)*	*to play* (a game, sports)		
pensar (ie)	*to think*				
perder (ie)	*to lose; to miss* (a function)	volver (ue)	*to return*		

- When used with an infinitive, **empezar** is followed by **a**.

  Uds. **empiezan a hablar** muy bien el español. — *You're beginning to speak Spanish very well.*

- When followed directly by an infinitive, **pensar** means *to intend, plan to.*

  ¿Cuándo **piensas contestar** la carta? — *When do you intend to answer the letter?*

[Práctica A–C]

- **Emphasis:** *empezar a* + inf.; *pensar* + inf.
- **Note:** infinitives for *llueve* (*llover*) and *nieva* (*nevar*) are not listed but are in end-of-chapter active vocabulary list.

B. The stem vowels in the present participle of **-ir** stem-changing verbs also show a change. When listed in the vocabulary, all **-ir** stem-changing verbs will show two stem changes in parentheses: **dormir (ue, u)**. The first stem change occurs in the present tense, the second in the present participle (and also in another tense that you will learn later on).

dormir (ue, **u**)→ **du**rmiendo preferir (ie, **i**)→ pref**i**riendo
pedir (i, **i**)→ p**i**diendo servir (i, **i**)→ s**i**rviendo

[Práctica CH]

- **Emphasis:** second stem change of *-ir* stem-changing verbs
- **Note:** This change will appear in *-ndo* form as well as in forms students have not yet learned: third-person sing. and pl. of preterite, *nosotros* and *vosotros* forms of pres. subj.

*__Jugar__ is the only **u** → **ue** stem-changing verb in Spanish. **Jugar** is often followed by **al** when used with the name of a sport: **Juego *al* tenis**. Some Spanish speakers, however, omit the **al**.

Preliminary exercises: Subject/verb correspondence:
yo: cerrar, empezar, entender, almorzar, pedir
tú: pensar, preferir, jugar, dormir
Ud./él/ella: perder, empezar, volver, servir
nosotros: empezar, preferir, jugar, volver
vosotros: pensar, cerrar, entender, dormir, servir
Uds./ellos/ellas: preferir, almorzar, jugar, pedir

- *Dé oraciones según las indicaciones.*
  1. *Sara y Anita almuerzan en el patio.* (*Ud., nuestros hijos, nosotros, tú, yo, vosotros*) **2.** *Felipe pide un refresco.* (*yo, nosotros, ellos, Lisa, tú, vosotras*) **3.** *Yo prefiero descansar en la playa* (beach). (*Sergio, nosotros, Ana, ellas, tú, vosotras*) **4.** *El equipo* (team) *pierde muchos partidos* (games). (*ellos, yo, Fernando, tú, los niños, vosotros*) **5.** *Los González* vuelven de su viaje el sábado. (*yo, nosotras, mis primas, Manuel, tú, vosotros*)

Suggestion B: Follow up each exercise item with *Ud.* or *Uds.* question directed at students.

Follow-up C:
- Put infinitives on board. Students invent original sequence based on infinitives.
- Vary subject: *yo, Julio, nosotros,* etc.

Práctica

A. **Una tarde de verano.** Hace buen tiempo hoy. ¿Cuáles son las actividades de estas personas? Haga oraciones completas con una palabra o frase de cada grupo.

yo		almorzar	descansar en la playa, en el patio
el equipo (*team*)		volver	en el parque, en el patio
mi padre/madre		preferir	toda la tarde
los niños	(no)	perder	varios partidos (*games*)
mi amigo/a ____ y yo		jugar	al golf (tenis, vólibol, etcétera)
los perros		pedir	muchos refrescos
		dormir	a casa muy tarde
			afuera
			la siesta
			helados (*ice-cream cones*)

B. **¿Qué prefieren?**

MODELO: Ignacio pide café, pero nosotros pedimos un refresco.

1. Tomás y Julia piensan viajar (*to travel*) a Sudamérica este otoño, pero nosotros ____ viajar a España.
2. Tú vuelves a la estación (*station*) mañana, pero nosotros ____ allí el jueves.
3. Nosotros empezamos a trabajar a las ocho, pero Reynaldo ____ a las nueve.
4. Nosotros dormimos ocho horas todas las noches, pero Lucía sólo ____ seis horas.
5. Nosotros servimos comida mexicana en casa y Susana también ____ comida mexicana, especialmente en las fiestas.
6. Nosotros jugamos al tenis hoy y Paula ____ con nosotros.
7. Tú cierras la tienda a las ocho, pero nosotros no ____ hasta las diez.
8. María y Teresa prefieren esquiar en Vail, pero nosotros ____ ir a Aspen. Ellas no entienden por qué vamos a Aspen, y nosotros no ____ por qué van a Vail.

C. Using the following verbs as a guide, tell about a visit to a restaurant. Use **yo** as the subject except where otherwise indicated.

1. pensar comer comida (*food*) española
2. entrar en un restaurante en la calle Bolívar
3. pedir el menú
4. preferir comer paella, un plato español
5. (ellos) no servir comida española
6. pedir tacos y un refresco
7. (ellos) servir la comida en diez minutos
8. comer y volver a casa
9. dormir un poco porque hace calor

Suggestion CH: Before students begin exercise, ask what verb form is most appropriate to use (pres. prog.).

Follow-up CH: Ask questions that follow each item: **1.** *¿Qué programa está mirando? ¿Le gusta? ¿Por qué sí o por qué no?* and so on.

Follow-up: Interview: *¿Con qué frecuencia... ?* Write infinitive phrases on board. Students form questions based on them. **1.** *dormir en clase* **2.** *almorzar en restaurantes elegantes.* **3.** *pensar mucho en las notas* (grades) **4.** *pensar en el futuro* **5.** *cerrar la puerta de tu cuarto cuando estudias* **6.** *tener problemas románticos* **7.** *ir al cine* **8.** *volver a casa muy tarde* **9.** *hacer algo* (something) *totalmente loco* **10.** *no entender algo importante en clase* **11.** *jugar al fútbol*

Suggestions for answers: *siempre / casi siempre / a veces / casi nunca / nunca*

CH. Hace frío hoy y hay mucha nieve. Por eso todos están en casa. Son las tres de la tarde. ¿Qué están haciendo estas personas? Haga oraciones según las indicaciones.

1. Nora / mirar la televisión
2. papá / pedir la comida
3. el perro / dormir en el sofá
4. Pepito y Carlos / jugar / en sus cuartos
5. (ellos) hacer / mucho ruido
6. mamá / empezar / perder la paciencia

Conversación

Note A: Use of *se* construction in 1. Students need only repeat forms; no transformation necessary.

Suggestion A: Small groups. Students use *tú* forms in 2–4.

A. **Preguntas**

1. ¿A qué hora se cierra la biblioteca? ¿A qué hora se cierra la cafetería? ¿Están abiertas toda la noche durante el semestre/trimestre? ¿Y durante la época de los exámenes finales?
2. ¿Almuerza Ud., por lo general? ¿A qué hora? ¿Dónde le gusta almorzar? ¿Con quién? ¿Piensa Ud. almorzar hoy? ¿mañana? Cuando almuerza en la cafetería de la universidad, ¿qué pide? ¿una hamburguesa? ¿un taco? ¿una ensalada? ¿un refresco? ¿Sirven la comida en la cafetería o hay auto-servicio?
3. ¿Es Ud. un poco olvidadizo/a? Es decir, ¿pierde las cosas con frecuencia? ¿Qué cosa pierde Ud.? ¿el dinero? ¿su cuaderno? ¿su mochila? ¿sus llaves (*keys*)?
4. Los días de entresemana, ¿a qué hora sale Ud. de casa (de su cuarto/apartamento), por lo general? ¿A qué hora vuelve? ¿A qué hora empieza a comer? ¿a estudiar? ¿a mirar la tele? Y los fines de semana, ¿en qué forma es diferente su rutina?

Notas comunicativas: What Do You Think About . . . ?

One way to ask for someone's opinion with the verb **pensar** is to use the phrase **¿Qué piensas de...?** (*What do you think about . . .?*). The answer can begin with **Pienso que...** (*I think that . . .*).

—**¿Qué piensas de** la clase de química?
—**¡Pienso que** es muy difícil!

Emphasis *Notas...*: Contrast *pensar de* (opinion) and *pensar en* (to have on one's mind).

Suggestion B: Additional option for expressing disagreement: *A mí me gusta más (el café), pero Juan prefiere (el té) y Cecilia prefiere (la Coca-Cola).*

B. **Entrevista: Otras preferencias.** With a classmate, explore preferences in a number of areas by asking and answering questions based on the following cues. Form your questions with expressions like these:

¿Prefieres... o... ?
¿Te gusta más (*infinitive*) o (*infinitive*)?
¿Qué piensas de... ?
¿Piensas que... o... ?

Follow-up B: Using *Hablando de...* as lead-in, encourage students to give reasons for choices, where appropriate. Model for 1: *Hablando de clases, ¿por qué prefieren Uds. las clases fáciles?* **Suggestion:** introduce simple comparative forms for adjectives: *más/menos* + adj. + *que*.

If you have no preference or opinion, express that by saying **No tengo preferencia/opinión**. Be prepared to report some of your findings to the class. If you both agree, you will express this with phrases like: **Pensamos que... Preferimos...** If you do not agree, give the preferences of both persons: **Yo prefiero/pienso... pero Gustavo prefiere/piensa...**

1. Las clases: ¿las clases fáciles o las difíciles? ¿las clases que empiezan a las ocho o las que empiezan a la una? ¿hacer preguntas o contestar en clase? ¿hablar en inglés o en español en la clase de español? (¿o no hablar?)
2. Las bebidas: ¿el café con azúcar o sin azúcar? ¿el café con o sin cafeína? ¿la Coca-Cola con hielo o sin hielo? ¿los refrescos con calorías o los dietéticos? ¿los refrescos con o sin cafeína?
3. Cuando hace mucho calor: ¿beber agua (*water*), refrescos o cerveza? ¿estar en casa o estar afuera? ¿estar en el parque o en la playa? ¿jugar al tenis (al golf, etcétera) o dormir?
4. Las estaciones: ¿los días cortos del invierno o los días largos del verano? ¿el tiempo del otoño o el de la primavera? ¿las actividades de verano o las de invierno?
5. Los viajes: ¿hacer un viaje largo en autobús o en tren? ¿en tren o en avión (*plane*)? ¿en avión o en coche? ¿hacer los viajes en invierno o en verano? ¿tomar las vacaciones en invierno o en verano? ¿ir de vacaciones con su familia o con sus amigos?
6. Miscelánea: ¿la música clásica? ¿la música *punk*? ¿el presidente actual (*current*)? ¿Bruce Springsteen? ¿las películas extranjeras no dobladas?

Suggestions (Tipos y estereotipos):
- Use drawings as vehicle for presentation of regular comparative forms of adjectives. Expansion: Use *inteligente, simpático.*
- **Point out:** agreement of adjective with noun modified
- Ask several students to stand up: Ask (*¿sí o no?*): *¿ ____ es más/menos alto* (*rubio, moreno, bajo*) *que ____? ¿ ____ es tan ____ como ____?*
- Use drawings to present comparison of *nouns*. Expansion: Use *dinero.*
- Ask several students to stand up holding book(s) and other objects. Ask similar *sí/no* questions.

17. DESCRIBING
Comparisons

Tipos y estereotipos

Adolfo es muy atlético y extrovertido, pero estudia poco.

- Es una persona **más** atlética **que** Raúl y Esteban.
- Es **menos** estudioso **que** Raúl.
- Es **tan** extrovertido **como** Esteban.

Y Raúl, ¿cómo es?

- Es menos extrovertido que ____.
- Es más estudioso que ____.
- No es una persona tan atlética como ____.

(continúa)

Esteban trabaja en la cafeteria y también estudia—tiene cinco clases este semestre.

- Tiene **tantas** clases **como** Raúl.
- No tiene **tanto** tiempo libre **como** Adolfo.
- Tiene **más** amigos **que** Raúl pero **menos** amigos **que** Adolfo.

Y Adolfo, ¿cómo es?

- No tiene tantas clases _____.
- Tiene más tiempo libre _____.
- Tiene más amigos _____.

As you have just seen while you were describing Adolfo, Raúl, and Esteban, comparative forms enable you to compare and contrast people, things, and characteristics or qualities. Similar—but not identical—forms are used with adjectives and nouns.

¡*OJO!* Be careful to use *tan* + adj. and *tanto/a/os/as* + noun.

with adjectives	**with nouns**
más/menos... que	más/menos... que
tan... como	tanto/a/os/as... como

Regular Comparisons of Adjectives

Alicia es **más perezosa que** Marta.	*Alicia is lazier than Marta.*
Julio es **menos listo que** Pablo.	*Julio is less bright than Pablo.*
Enrique es **tan trabajador como** Alicia.	*Enrique is as hardworking as Alicia.*

The *comparative* (**el comparativo**) of most English adjectives is formed by using the adverbs *more* or *less* (***more** intelligent, **less** important*), or by adding *-er* (*tall**er**, long**er***).

In Spanish, unequal comparisons are usually expressed with **más** (*more*) + *adjective* + **que** or **menos** (*less*) + *adjective* + **que**.

Equal comparisons are expressed with **tan** + *adjective* + **como**.

[Práctica A–B]

Irregular Comparative Forms

Point out: irregular comparisons and their pl. forms.

Note: *Más grande* and *más pequeño* refer to size; contrast with *mayor* and *menor* (for age).

Spanish has the following irregular comparative forms:

mejor(es)	better	**mayor(es)**	older
peor(es)	worse	**menor(es)**	younger

Estos dulces son **buenos**, pero ésos son **mejores**.	*These candies are good, but those are better.*

[Práctica C]

Comparison of Nouns

Point out: *más de* + numbers

Optional: ***No** tengo **más que** un hijo* (only one).

¿Cómo se dice?: **1.** more than $10 **2.** more than 100 students **3.** less than $20 **4.** fewer than 50 students

Optional: Have students add *más de* + number to the chart if you intend to stress that structure.

Alicia tiene **más/menos** bolsas **que** Susana.	*Alicia has more/fewer purses than Susana.*
Nosotros tenemos **tantas** revistas **como** ellas.	*We have as many magazines as they (do).*

Nouns are compared with the expressions **más/menos** + *noun* + **que** and **tanto/a/os/as** + *noun* + **como. Más/menos *de*** is used when the comparison is followed by a number: **Tengo más *de un* hijo. Tanto** must agree in gender and number with the noun it modifies.

[Práctica CH–E]

Práctica

Suggestion A:
- Follow up questions 2, 3, and 5 by asking students to explain why.
- Ask follow-up questions involving comparisons with nouns: *¿Quién tiene más libros? ¿Quién practica más deportes?* and so on.

A. Conteste según el dibujo.

1. Emilia, ¿es más alta o más baja que Sancho?
2. ¿Es tan tímida como Sancho? ¿Quién es más extrovertido?
3. Sancho, ¿es tan atlético como Emilia?
4. ¿Quién es más intelectual? ¿Por qué cree Ud. eso?
5. ¿Es Emilia tan estudiosa como Sancho? ¿Es tan trabajadora?
6. ¿Quién es más listo? ¿Por qué cree Ud. eso?

Suggestions B:
- Do as listening comprehension exercise.
- **Extension: 7.** *Los seniors son tan serios como los freshmen.* **8.** *Aquí el otoño es tan bonito como la primavera.*
- Follow up each item with a question, if possible, to have students explain their response.

B. **Opiniones.** Cambie, indicando su opinión personal: **tan... como** → **más/menos que**.

1. La primavera es tan verde como el invierno.
2. Los niños siempre están tan ocupados como sus padres.
3. También siempre están tan preocupados como sus padres.
4. El dinero es tan importante como la amistad.
5. El vólibol es tan difícil como el golf.
6. Hacer un viaje es tan interesante como estudiar para un examen.

C. Complete, haciendo una comparación.

1. La comida italiana es buena, pero la mexicana es _____.
2. Las pruebas son malas, pero los exámenes son _____.
3. Pepito tiene 17 años. Demetrio, que tiene 20 años, es su hermano _____.
4. Luisita es muy joven; el bebé de la familia es su hermano _____.
5. La Argentina es grande, pero el Brasil es _____.
6. El elefante es grande. El chimpancé es _____.

CH. Conteste, comparando las cosas de Alfredo con las de Graciela.

1. ¿Cuánto dinero tiene Alfredo?
2. ¿Cuántas cervezas tiene Graciela?
3. ¿Cuántos libros tiene Alfredo?
4. ¿Cuántos bolígrafos tiene Graciela?
5. ¿Cuántos cuadernos tiene Alfredo?
6. ¿Cuántas cartas tiene Graciela?

Suggestions D: Follow suggestions for B.

D. **Más opiniones.** Cambie, indicando su opinión personal: **tanto... como** → **más/menos... que**, o vice versa.

1. Los profesores trabajan más que los estudiantes.
2. En esta universidad las artes son tan importantes como las ciencias.
3. Aquí el béisbol es tan importante como el fútbol americano.
4. Hay más hombres que mujeres en esta clase.
5. Hay tantos exámenes en la clase de español como en la clase de historia.
6. En esta ciudad hace tanto calor en verano como en invierno.
7. Yo bebo menos café que el profesor (la profesora).
8. Las mujeres pueden practicar tantos deportes (*sports*) como los hombres.

E. ¿Cómo se dice en español?

1. more than $10
2. fewer than 100 students
3. fewer than 20 chairs
4. Are you over 18 years old?
5. She's over 90 years old!
6. I'm younger than she is.

Conversación

A. Conteste las preguntas lógicamente. ¿Es Ud...

1. tan guapo/a como Tom Cruise/Christie Brinkley?
2. tan rico/a como los Rockefeller?
3. tan fiel como su mejor amigo/a?
4. tan inteligente como Einstein?
5. tan romántico/a como su novio/a (esposo/a, amigo/a)?

¿Tiene Ud...

6. tanto dinero como los Ford?
7. tantos tíos como tías?
8. tantos amigos como amigas?
9. tantas ideas buenas como _____?
10. tantos años como su profesor(a)?

B. Comparative forms are used in many Spanish sayings (**dichos**). Several are given below. What are the English equivalents of these sayings? Can you think of another way to end them?

1. Más feo que el coco (*bogeyman*).
2. Pesar (*To weigh*) menos que un mosquito... o más que el matrimonio.
3. Dormir como un tronco.
4. Más bueno que el pan (*bread*).*
5. Más viejo que Matusalén.
6. Más claro que el agua.
7. Más alto que un pino.
8. Más vale (*is worth*) tarde que nunca.
9. Más largo que un día sin pan.

---

*Note the special usage of **más bueno**, similar to the use of "gooder" in English.

Chile

En la biblioteca
Hablan dos compañeros de cuarto.

—Hace mucho frío hoy, ¿verdad?
—Sí. Hace dos horas que nieva.
—¿Por qué no vamos a esquiar este fin de semana? Seguro que hay mucha nieve en las montañas.
—¡Excelente idea! ¿Qué coche usamos, el mío o el tuyo?

18. GETTING INFORMATION
Summary of Interrogative Words

Grammar Section 18 Note: Students have used actively all interrogatives in this section. Treat section as summary, using it to emphasize variations of interrogative forms (*¿dónde?* versus *¿de/a-?*, etc.).

¿Cómo	How?	**¿Quién(es)?**	Who?
¿Cuándo?	When?	**¿De quién(es)?**	Whose?
¿A qué hora?	At what time?	**¿Dónde?**	Where?
¿Qué?	What? Which?	**¿De dónde?**	From where?
¿Cuál(es)?	What? Which one (ones)?	**¿Adónde?**	Where (to)?
		¿Cuánto/a?	How much?
¿Por qué?	Why?	**¿Cuántos/as?**	How many?

You have been using interrogative words to ask questions and get information since the preliminary chapter of ***Puntos de partida***. The preceding chart shows all of the interrogatives you have learned so far. Be sure that you know what they mean and how they are used. If you are not certain, the index will help you find where they are first introduced. Only the specific uses of **¿qué?** and **¿cuál?** represent "new" material.

Point out (in box): plural forms of *¿cuál?*, *¿quién?*; difference in meaning between *¿cuánto/a?* and *¿cuántos/as?*

Optional: *¿Cómo?* to request repetition or clarification

Using *¿qué?* and *¿cuál?*

¿Qué? asks for a definition or an explanation.

¿Qué es esto?	*What is this?*
¿Qué quieres?	*What do you want?*
¿Qué tocas?	*What do you play?*

¿Qué? can be directly followed by a noun.

¿Qué traje necesitas?	*What (Which) suit do you need?*
¿Qué playa te gusta más?	*What (Which) beach do you like most?*
¿Qué instrumento musical tocas?	*What (Which) musical instrument do you play?*

¿Cuál(es)? expresses *what?* or *which?* in all other cases.*

¿Cuál es la clase más grande?	*What (Which) is the biggest class?*
¿Cuáles son tus actrices favoritas?	*What (Which) are your favorite actresses?*
¿Cuál es la capital de Uruguay?	*What is the capital of Uruguay?*
¿Cuál es tu telefono?	*What is your phone number?*

Note: See footnote. In Latin America, *¿cuál?* and *¿cuáles?* may be used as adjectives—e.g., *¿Cuál libro quieres?* In Spain they are used only as pronouns.

Preliminary exercise: *¿Qué? or ¿Cuál?*: 1. What is an aardvark? **2.** What is the capital of Bolivia? **3.** What are the colors of the U.S. flag? **4.** What's that?

Follow-up A: *Preguntas orales:* **1.** *¿Cuál es la capital de ____?* **2.** *¿Cuál es su teléfono?* **3.** *¿Qué es esto?* (indicate object or use visual) **4.** *¿Qué es un elefante* (*en español, claro*)*? ¿un restaurante? ¿una discoteca? ¿Qué son sandalias?*

Optional (review): *¿Quien, quiénes o de quién?: Preguntas orales:* **1.** *¿Quién es su actor/actriz favorito/a?* **2.** *En esta clase, ¿quiénes tienen muchos hermanos? ¿hablan mucho? ¿llevan* bluejeans *hoy?* **3.** *De quién es* (object)? ***¿Dónde, de dónde o adónde?: Preguntas orales:*** **1.** *¿Dónde está Managua? ¿San Juan? ¿Santiago? ¿Barcelona?* **2.** *¿De dónde es Ud.? ¿De dónde son sus padres? ¿sus abuelos? ¿sus bisabuelos* (great-grandparents)? **3.** *¿Adónde va Ud. después de clase? ¿esta noche? ¿el sábado?* ***¿Cuándo, a qué hora, cuánto/a o cuántos/as?: Preguntas orales:*** **1.** *¿Cuándo hace frío en ____? ¿Cuándo hace calor?* **2.** *¿A qué hora llega Ud. a la universidad? ¿a clase? ¿A qué hora regresa a casa?* **3.** *¿Cuántos hermanos (coches) tiene Ud.? ¿Cuántas materias estudia este semestre?* **4.** *¿Cuánto dinero tiene Ud. en el banco? ¿Cuánto cuesta un cuaderno (un bolígrafo, una camiseta)?*

Suggestions B, C:
- Students work in pairs to form questions.
- Students exchange questions with other pairs or ask questions directly.
- Students ask questions of the whole class.

Práctica

A. **¿Qué? o ¿cuál(es)?**

1. ¿____ es esto? —Un peso mexicano.
2. ¿____ es Sacramento? —Es la capital de California.
3. ¿____ es tu clase preferida? —Pues, yo creo que es la de sicología.
4. ¿____ guitarra vas a tocar? —La de Juanita.
5. ¿____ son los cines más modernos? —Los del centro.
6. ¿____ camisa debo llevar? —La azul.
7. ¿____ es un «tambor»? —Es un instrumento musical.
8. ¿____ es el novio de Alicia? —Es el hombre moreno.

B. **Una tarjeta postal de Buenos Aires.** Here is a postcard that Sara has sent to Alfonso in the United States. Read the postcard. Then, using interrogative words, form as many questions as you can about its content to ask your classmates. You can ask questions about what it actually says as well as about what it implies.

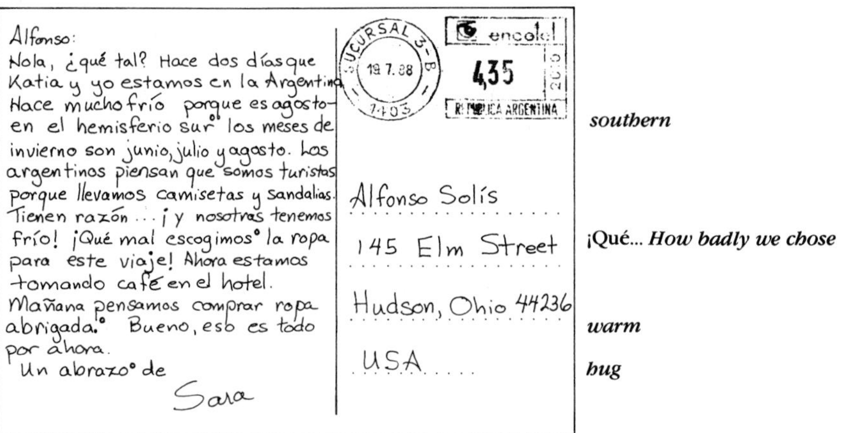
Alfonso:
Hola, ¿qué tal? Hace dos días que Katia y yo estamos en la Argentina. Hace mucho frío porque es agosto—en el hemisferio sur° los meses de invierno son junio, julio y agosto. Los argentinos piensan que somos turistas porque llevamos camisetas y sandalias. Tienen razón ... ¡y nosotras tenemos frío! ¡Qué mal escogimos° la ropa para este viaje! Ahora estamos tomando café en el hotel. Mañana pensamos comprar ropa abrigada.° Bueno, eso es todo por ahora.
Un abrazo° de
Sara

Alfonso Solís
145 Elm Street
Hudson, Ohio 44236
USA

southern

¡Qué... *How badly we chose*

warm

hug

*The **¿cuál(es)** + *noun...* structure is not used by most speakers of Spanish: **¿Cuál de los dos libros** quieres? *Which of the two books do you want?* BUT **¿Qué libro** quieres? *Which (What) book do you want?*

C. **El invierno.** On the opposite page is a description of the winter season, written by an eight-year-old Mexican girl. Very little language has been changed, and you will be able—with glosses—to read it easily. After you read the description, form as many questions about it as you can, as you did in the preceding exercise.

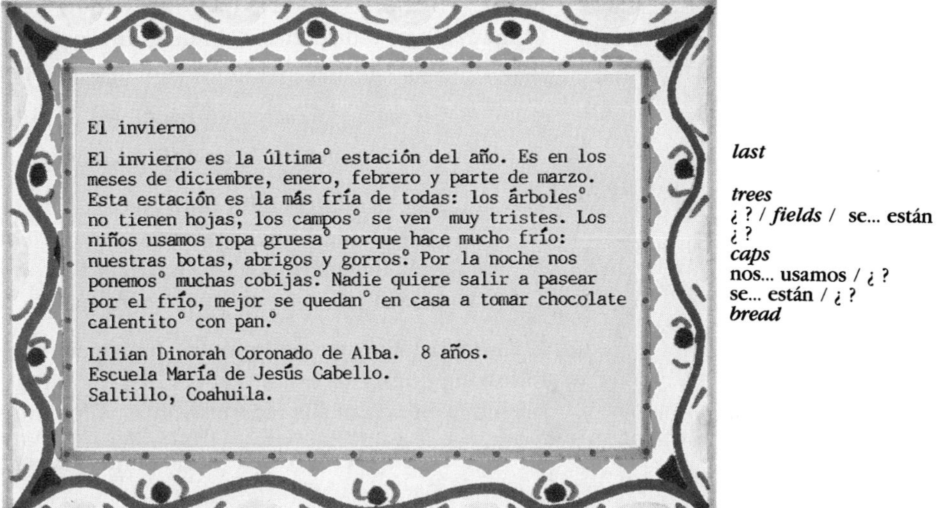

El invierno

El invierno es la última° estación del año. Es en los meses de diciembre, enero, febrero y parte de marzo. Esta estación es la más fría de todas: los árboles° no tienen hojas°, los campos° se ven° muy tristes. Los niños usamos ropa gruesa° porque hace mucho frío: nuestras botas, abrigos y gorros°. Por la noche nos ponemos° muchas cobijas°. Nadie quiere salir a pasear por el frío, mejor se quedan° en casa a tomar chocolate calentito° con pan°.

Lilian Dinorah Coronado de Alba. 8 años.
Escuela María de Jesús Cabello.
Saltillo, Coahuila.

last

trees
¿ ? / *fields* / se... están
¿ ?
caps
nos... usamos / ¿ ?
se... están / ¿ ?
bread

Follow-up: Game format: Divide students into two teams. Instructor gives answer; students must form question that results in answer. *Modelo: Bogotá → ¿Cuál es la capital de Colombia?*

Follow-up: Working in pairs, students prepare list of questions (trying to use as many interrogatives as possible) to find out as much as they can about the following topics, from the persons indicated: **1.** from the instructor: the next major exam **2.** a foreign exchange student: weather/geography of his/her country **3.** a new acquaintance: what he/she does at the university **4.** a foreign student who now lives in this country: his/her family **5.** parent of a friend: where he/she is and when you should call back

Suggestion A: This activity will work well if you provide a ditto with a grid on which students can write the information they gather.

Conversación

A. **Una encuesta** (*poll*). Practice getting information from others by getting the following information from at least three classmates. You may want to compare the results obtained to see if there is a consensus in the class on any of these topics. Note that you will be asking two different kinds of questions: one to determine a preference between two choices, the other to determine a general preference. Following the model, ask questions based on the cues suggested, then invent a category of your own.

MODELO: grupos musicales: U-2 / los Beatles →
¿Cuál prefieres, el grupo U-2 o los Beatles?
¿Qué grupo musical prefieres entre todos?

Hint: If you like neither of the choices offered in the first question when you are being interviewed, simply answer by saying: **Ninguno/a** (*Neither*).

1. grupo musical: U-2/los Beatles
2. tipo de música: la música clásica / la música rock
3. bebida (*beverage*) en la mañana: el café / el té
4. bebida con el almuerzo: un refresco / una limonada
5. deporte individual: el esquí / el tenis
6. deporte de equipo: el béisbol / el fútbol americano

7. equipo de fútbol americano: los ____ / los ____
8. estación del año: el otoño / el verano
9. ¿ ?

B. **Las preguntas indiscretas de Guillermina.** Guillermina, una niña de cinco años, es su prima favorita. Como todos los niños, siempre hace muchas preguntas. A veces pregunta lo que (*what*) no debe, y a veces sus preguntas son indiscretas. Con un compañero (una compañera), ¿cuántas preguntas de Guillermina puede Ud. inventar para estas situaciones?

MODELO: Su madre presenta (*introduces*) a Guillermina al Sr. Vargas. → ¿Quién es el Sr. Vargas? ¿De dónde es? ¿Tiene esposa? etcétera.

1. Su madre presenta Guillermina a la Sra. de Inza.
2. Su madre anuncia que el primo Octavio viene mañana.
3. La abuela llega a la casa de Guillermina con un regalo muy grande.
4. Ud. pone el televisor después de almorzar.

Note C: The material in this **Entrevista** is material with which students should be quite familiar. If you have not tried many interview activities up till now, this would be a good one to start with.

Emphasis C: *tu* → *su* when students are reporting information back to the class.

C. **Entrevista.** Without taking notes, interview another student by asking the following questions or any others like them that occur to you. Then present as much of the information as you can to the class.

1. ¿De dónde eres? ¿Dónde vives ahora? ¿Cuánto tiempo hace que vives allí? ¿Por qué vives allí?
2. ¿Qué materias tienes este semestre/trimestre? ¿Por qué estudias español? ¿Lo entiendes todo en clase?
3. ¿Cuántos primos tienes? ¿Cuántos tíos?
4. ¿Qué tipo de persona eres?
5. ¿Qué instrumento musical tocas? (el piano, la guitarra, la trompeta, los tambores...)
6. ¿Cuál es tu color favorito? ¿Tienes mucha ropa de ese color?
7. ¿Tienes novio/a (esposo/a)? ¿un amigo (una amiga) especial? ¿Cómo es?
8. ¿Con quién te gusta salir los sábados? ¿Adónde van?
9. ¿Adónde quieres viajar algún dia (*someday*)? ¿Por qué quieres hacer un viaje a ese lugar?

Situaciones: See IM for suggestions, additional exercises, and supplementary dialogues and exercises.

SITUACIONES

Pronóstico del tiempo

—Oye, ¿sabes° qué tiempo va a hacer en San Sebastián la próxima semana? ¿Qué dice° la televisión?
—Supongo° que fresco, pero no estoy seguro. Nunca miro la tele para saber qué tiempo hace. No confío en sus predicciones.

do you know
¿ ?
I imagine, suppose

—Fantástico, pero... ¿qué ropa debo llevar? Es la primera vez que voy a San Sebastián. Tú, ¿qué crees?

—En diciembre hace frío en toda España, pero San Sebastián está en la costa.

—¿Y qué?° — *¿Y... So what?*

—Pues que la temperatura es siempre más suave.° Lleva° una buena chaqueta y un impermeable. Llueve bastante. — ¿ ? / (*command form*)

—¿Estás seguro? Mira° que sólo tengo una hora para hacer la maleta. El tren sale a las siete. — (*command form*)

—No te preocupes.° En cuanto a° las predicciones sobre el tiempo, tengo razón con más frecuencia que la tele. — No... *Don't worry.* / En... *As far as ... are concerned*

Más tarde, en el tren, en la radio

«Como ya se comunicó en anteriores° servicios informativos, un frente frío de gran intensidad azota° las costas del norte. La nieve sigue° cayendo en Bilbao y San Sebastián y esta noche se espera que las temperaturas bajarán a un grado bajo cero.» — *previous* / *whips* / está todavía

Notas comunicativas sobre el diálogo

As happens in English, the Spanish vocabulary used in talking about the weather in everyday conversations is quite different from the more scientific vocabulary used in weather forecasts. With a classmate, try to figure out the meaning of the preceding forecast. Hint: The brief forecast refers to three different periods of time: past, present, and future.

Conversación

In the preceding dialogue, note the number of different questions used to get information about the weather. Then, with your instructor playing the role of friend/advisor, try to get as much information as you can for the following situations.

1. Ud. quiere ir a la playa (a las montañas) este fin de semana.
2. Ud. tiene planes para hacer un viaje a San Francisco en el mes de julio.

UN POCO DE TODO

A. **Rosario y sus compañeros.** Take the role of Rosario as she compares herself and her study habits to those of her classmates. Form complete sentences based on the words given, in the order given. Conjugate the verbs and add other words if necessary. Use subject pronouns only when needed.

1. yo / empezar / ser / estudiante / ejemplar (*exemplary*)
2. yo / volver / casa / con / más / libros / Elena
3. yo / no / perder / tanto / tiempo / cafetería / Raúl
4. próximo / semestre / yo / pensar / tomar / tanto / cursos / difícil / Estela
5. yo / pedir / menos / consejos / Felipe
6. yo / hacer / mejor / preguntas / Antonio

¿Qué pasó en Roma el 6 de octubre de 1582?

Casi caemos en la trampa pero, en fin, no ha habido que consultar demasiados libros de Historia: esa fecha no existió nunca. A raíz de la reforma del calendario *gregoriano* —que abolió el anterior *juliano*, implantado por Julio César en el año 46 antes de Cristo— las fechas *saltaron*, por decreto del Papa Gregorio XIII, del 4 al 15 de octubre de 1582. Así de sencillo fue borrar, lisa y llanamente, diez días de la Historia. ■

Marta and Solimar, Rosario's friends, are not good students at all. Describe them, using the preceding cues and changing the information as needed. Here are the first two items.

1. Rosario / empezar / ser / estudiante / ejemplar / pero / ¡nosotras, no!
2. (nosotras) volver / casa / con / menos / libros / Elena

B. **¿Qué llevas en tu maleta?** With another student, ask and answer questions based on the places listed below. Follow the model, providing appropriate weather information.

MODELO: San Francisco / impermeable →
—¿Piensas hacer un viaje a San Francisco?
—Sí, salgo para allí el domingo.

—¿Cuánto tiempo hace que planeas el viaje?
—Un año.

—¿No hace (mucho) _____ allí en _____?
—Sí, por eso pienso llevar mi impermeable.

1. Mallorca / traje de baño
2. el Polo Norte / suéteres
3. San Juan, Puerto Rico / camisetas
4. Vermont / abrigo
5. Acapulco / raqueta de tenis

C. **¿Somos tan diferentes?** Answer the following questions. Then ask the same questions of other students in the class to find at least one person who answered a given question the way you did.

1. ¿A qué hora almuerzas generalmente, y dónde?
2. ¿Adónde piensas ir hoy después de la clase?
3. ¿Estás triste cuando llueve? ¿Qué haces cuando llueve?
4. ¿Qué estación del año prefieres? ¿Por qué?
5. ¿Qué día prefieres, el lunes o el sábado? ¿Por qué?
6. ¿Cuánto tiempo hace que vives en esta ciudad?
7. Generalmente, ¿cuántas horas duermes por la noche?
8. ¿Cuántos hermanos tienes en total? ¿Son mayores o menores que tú?

CH. **En este momento**... Select one of the individuals listed and tell where that person is, what he or she is doing, and how he or she feels at the times indicated. Invent any details you need.

- sus padres
- su profesor(a)
- su (novio/a, esposo/a, mejor amigo/a)
- Ud.

1. el sábado por la noche
2. el domingo por la mañana
3. un día típico de verano
4. un día típico de otoño
5. un día en que hace mucho frío y nieva

Notas culturales: The Southern Hemisphere

As you know, seasons are reversed in the Southern Hemisphere, where many Spanish-speaking countries lie. This means, of course, that when it is summer in the United States, it is winter in Argentina, and vice versa. You may never have thought about the effect of this phenomenon on the celebration of many traditional holidays. Christmas and New Year's Eve, winter holidays for residents of the United States, are generally associated with snow and ice, snow figures, winter sports, and so on. What does this ad for a Chilean hotel reveal about the kind of holiday New Year's Eve is in the Southern Hemisphere?

D. **Dos hemisferios.** Complete the following paragraphs with the correct forms of the words in parentheses, as suggested by the context. When two possibilities are given in parentheses, select the correct word.

Hay (*mucho*[1]) diferencias entre el clima del hemisferio norte y el del hemisferio sur. Cuando (*ser/estar*[2]) invierno en los Estados Unidos, por ejemplo, (*ser/estar*[3]) verano en la Argentina, en Bolivia, en Chile... Cuando yo (*salir*[4]) para la universidad en enero, con frecuencia tengo que (*llevar*[5]) abrigo y botas. En (*los/las*[6]) países del hemisferio sur, un estudiante (*poder*[7]) asistir (*a/de*[8]) clases en enero llevando sólo pantalones (*corto*[9]), camiseta y sandalias. En muchas partes de los Estados Unidos, (*antes de/durante*[10]) las vacaciones en diciembre, casi siempre (*hacer*[11]) frío y a veces (*nevar*[12]). En (*grande*[13]) parte de Sudamérica, al otro lado del ecuador, hace calor y (*muy/mucho*[14]) sol durante (*ese*[15]) mes. A veces en enero hay fotos, en los periódicos, de personas que están (*tomar*[16]) el sol y nadando (*swimming*) en las playas sudamericanas.

Tengo un amigo que (*ir*[17]) a (*hacer/tomar*[18]) un viaje a Buenos Aires. Él me dice° que allí la Navidad (*ser/estar*[19]) una fiesta de verano y que todos (*llevar*[20]) ropa como la que° llevamos nosotros en julio. Parece increíble, ¿verdad?

Él... *He tells me*
la... *that which*

¿Probable o improbable? Conteste según el párrafo.

1. Los estudiantes argentinos están en la playa en julio.
2. Muchas personas sudamericanas hacen viajes de vacaciones en enero.
3. Hace frío en Santiago (Chile) en diciembre.

VOCABULARIO

Note: All interrogatives from Grammar Section 18 previously active.

VERBOS

almorzar (ue) to have lunch
cerrar (ie) to close
dormir (ue, u) to sleep
empezar (ie) to begin
entender (ie) to understand
escuchar to listen (to)
hacer (*irreg.*) to do; to make
jugar (ue) to play (*sports*)
pedir (i, i) to ask for, order
pensar (ie) to think; to intend
perder (ie) to lose
poner (*irreg.*) to put, place
salir (*irreg.*) to leave, go out
servir (i, i) to serve
tocar to play (*a musical instrument*)
viajar to travel
volver (ue) to return

SUSTANTIVOS

el agua (*f.*) water
el azúcar sugar
el clima climate
la comida food
el equipo team
el hielo ice
la maleta suitcase
la playa beach
la prueba quiz
la radio radio (set)
el refresco soft drink
el teléfono telephone; telephone number
el televisor TV (set)
el tiempo weather; time

ADJETIVOS

mayor older
mejor better; best
menor younger
peor worse
siguiente next, following

¿QUÉ TIEMPO HACE?

está nublado it's cloudy, overcast
hace...
buen/mal tiempo it's good/bad weather
calor it's hot
fresco it's cool
frío it's cold
sol it's sunny
viento it's windy
hay contaminación there's pollution
llover (ue) to rain
nevar (ie) to snow

¿CUÁL ES LA FECHA?

el cumpleaños birthday
el primero de... the first of...

LOS MESES DEL AÑO

enero, febrero, marzo, abril, mayo, junio, julio, agosto, se(p)tiembre, octubre, noviembre, diciembre

LAS ESTACIONES DEL AÑO

la primavera, el verano, el otoño, el invierno

PALABRAS ADICIONALES

afuera outside
hacer un viaje to take a trip
hacer una pregunta to ask a question
más/menos... que more/less than
tan... como as . . . as
tanto/a... como as much/many . . . as

Frases útiles para la comunicación

tener calor	to be warm, hot
tener frío	to be cold
estar bien	to be comfortable (*temperature*)
¿Qué piensas de... ?	What do you think of. . . ?
Pienso que...	I think that . . .

OPTIONAL SECTION

UN PASO MÁS 5

Optional: *el básquetbol, el golf, el hockey, el vólibol, el boxeo, pasear en bicicleta (el ciclismo), el ping pong, jugar en la nieve, remar* (to row), *hacer gimnasia*

Point out: difference between *el fútbol* and *el fútbol (norte)americano.*

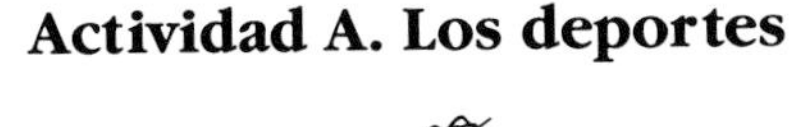

▲ Actividad A. Los deportes

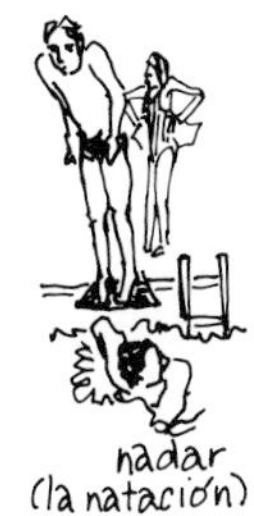

Preliminary exercise:
- ***¿Cierto o falso?*** **1.** *Se asocia el patinar con el verano.* **2.** *Es mejor correr cuando llueve.* **3.** *Se puede jugar al tenis con solamente dos personas.* **4.** *Se practica el esquí en la Florida.*

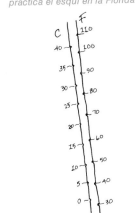

How interested are you and your classmates in sports? Are you active participants or do you prefer to watch? Use the following questions to interview another student. Take notes and report what you learn to the class.

1. ¿Juegas al béisbol? ¿al vólibol? ¿al básquetbol? ¿al fútbol norteamericano? ¿al fútbol? De estos deportes, ¿cuál es tu favorito? ¿Con quiénes practicas este deporte?
2. ¿Juegas al tenis? ¿al ping-pong? ¿al golf? ¿Cuál prefieres?
3. En invierno, ¿qué prefieres, jugar en la nieve, patinar o esquiar?
4. ¿Te gusta correr? ¿pasear en bicicleta? ¿nadar? ¿Cuál prefieres?
5. ¿Qué deportes hay en la televisión? ¿Cuáles miras tú con frecuencia? ¿Cuál es tu favorito?
6. En tu opinión, ¿uno de los deportes es más peligroso (*dangerous*) que los otros? ¿Cuál? ¿Uno es más violento que los otros? ¿más interesante? ¿más aburrido? ¿más sano (*healthful*) que los otros?

5. *El* (deporte) *es más popular en los Estados Unidos que el* (deporte). **6.** *Jugamos al* (deporte) *en* (mes). **7.** *Es más difícil* (verbo) *que* (verbo). **8.** *Cuando hace calor* (frío), *podemos* (verbo).

▲ Actividad B. El 21 de julio en Europa

El termómetro indica las equivalencias entre los grados Celsius, o centígrados de Europa, y los grados Fahrenheit de los Estados Unidos. Imagine que Ud. y sus compañeros de clase son habitantes de varias ciudades del mundo. A base de (*Based on*) las temperaturas indicadas para el 27 de enero (página 176), ¿cómo van a contestar las siguientes preguntas para las ciudades indicadas?

¿Qué tiempo hace? ¿Qué ropa van a llevar? ¿Qué deportes van a practicar? ¿Qué otras cosas van a hacer?

1. Madrid 2. París 3. Caracas 4. Miami 5. Nueva York

Option B: Students tell a Spanish speaker what people are doing in the following locations and what the weather is like on *el primero de mayo:* Toronto, *Nueva York,* Miami, San Francisco, (your location).

TEMPERATURAS		MAX.	MIN.
Amsterdam	I	3	–5
Atenas	Q	16	11
Barcelona	T	15	7
Beirut	T	19	14
Bonn	I	4	–1
Bruselas	I	4	–1
Buenos Aires *	D	27	15
Cairo, El	A	20	9
Caracas *	Q	26	16
Copenhague	I	8	–5
Estocolmo	F	–12	–19
Francfort	I	4	0
Ginebra	Q	7	–4
Lisboa	Q	13	–1
Londres	Q	4	–4
Madrid	I	10	–2
México *	D	23	8
Miami *	Q	20	16
Moscú	I	–2	–5
Nueva York *	D	–1	–3
Oslo	F	–18	–20
París	I	6	–1
Rabat	T	15	7
R. de Janeiro *	P	27	18
Roma	P	15	11
Tokio *	Q	5	–1
Viena	Q	5	–2
Zúrich	Q	4	–2

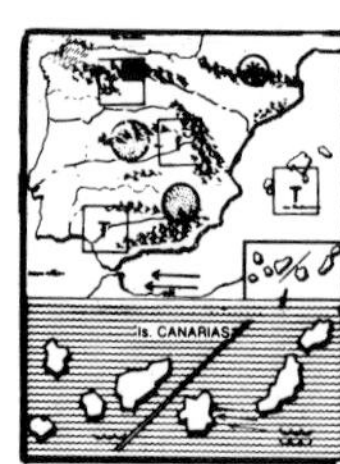

A, agradable / C, mucho calor / C, calor / D, despejado / F, mucho frío / I, frío / H, heladas / N, nevadas / P, lluvioso / Q, cubierto / S, tormentas / T, templado / V, vientos fuertes.
* Datos del domingo 27.

Ahora explique lo que (*what*) Ud. hace cuando el tiempo está como sigue.

1. Es el 12 de octubre. Llueve todo el día.
2. Es el 24 de diciembre. Hace mucho frío y hay mucho viento. Nieva, pero las calles y carreteras (*highways*) están en buenas condiciones.
3. Es el 15 de mayo. Hace sol. Realmente es un día estupendo, pero Ud. tiene clases toda la tarde.

Point out: Hispanic letters, even to friends, tend to sound more formal than North American letters: e.g., *muy estimado amigo.* This is not a sign of distance.

A propósito... Writing Personal Letters

The following greetings (**saludos**) and closings (**despedidas**) are used in writing non-business letters.

Saludos:	(Muy) Estimado amigo / Estimada amiga	*Dear friend*
	Querido Juan / Querida Juana	*Dear Juan / Juana*
Despedidas:	Tu amigo / a, Su amigo / a	*Your friend*
	Con mucho cariño	*Affectionately*
	Abrazos	*Hugs*
	Recibe un fuerte abrazo de...	*Here's a big hug from . . .*

Querido is more likely to be used among close friends and relatives; **estimado** is used to show deference or respect. **Abrazos** and **Recibe un fuerte abrazo de**... are intimate closings, used by people who know each other well. Holiday greetings and greetings for other special occasions include the following:

Feliz Navidad y Próspero Año Nuevo	*Merry Christmas and Happy (Prosperous) New Year*
Con los mejores deseos para la Navidad y el Año Nuevo	*With best wishes for Christmas and the New Year*
Felices Pascuas	*Merry Christmas*
Feliz cumpleaños	*Happy Birthday*
Feliz aniversario	*Happy Anniversary*

Optional: *un abrazo de*

▲ Actividad C. Muy estimada amiga...

Tell how you would open and close a letter to the following persons.

1. your good friend Jim
2. your great-aunt (**tía abuela**) Laura
3. your parents
4. your Spanish professor
5. someone you met once at a meeting
6. a spouse or fiancé(e)

The letter on the following page was sent from Spain as a thank-you note for a gift. What can you guess about the relationship of the two persons involved? (How close are they? How do you think they know each other?)

Santander, 16 de enero

Muy estimada amiga:

Le mando° un recuerdo muy cariñoso y le° deseo mucha felicidad en este Año Nuevo.

También le mando mis más° sinceras gracias por el regalo maravilloso de Navidad, que es la cinta° cassette con su música preciosa de jazz. Recuerdo° con mucho afecto° aquellas conversaciones del verano pasado sobre° esta música.

En la televisión estos días ponen escenas de varias ciudades de Norteamérica que pasan un frío muy intenso. Aquí en el Norte de España no estamos pasando mucho frío--las temperaturas más bajas son de 6 ó 7 grados sobre° cero.

Deseándole muchas felicidades en este año, le mando un saludo muy cariñoso.

Mercedes

Le... *I send you / you*

most

tape

I remember / affection

about

above

Now use the letter as a model to write a thank-you note for a gift (Christmas, baby, graduation . . .). Be sure to comment on the weather. If you are writing to someone with whom you have a close relationship, use **te** where **le** is used in the model letter; if writing to two or more persons, use **les**.

LECTURA CULTURAL

Lectura: See IM for suggestions and additional exercises and activities.

Antes de leer: *Getting a General Idea About Content*

Before starting a reading, it is a good idea to try to get a general sense of the content. The more you know about the reading before you begin to read, the easier it will seem to you. Here are some things you can do to prepare yourself for readings.

1. Make sure you understand the title. Think about what it suggests to you and what you already know about the topic. Do the same with any subtitles that the reading contains.
2. Look at the drawings, photos, or other visual cues that accompany the reading. What do they indicate about the content?
3. Read the comprehension questions before starting to read. They will tell you what kind of information you should be looking for.

The reading in this chapter is taken from a grade school geography book from Venezuela. No words have been changed in the reading to make it easier for you. You should be able to get the general meaning if you apply the preceding strategies and keep in mind some important information.

The title and subtitles. The reading, **Las Américas**, is divided into two subsections. You already know most of the words in the subtitles. Guess the meaning of **Lo que...** from context.

Lo que América debe a Europa
Lo que el mundo debe a América

If you guessed *what*, you are correct.

The art. The reading is accompanied by a drawing and a brief caption. What information is communicated by the drawing? As you do the reading, check back periodically to the drawing to see whether the items in it give you clues to the meanings of words you will find in the reading text.

The tense. Now that you have a sense of where the reading is going, can you predict what tense (present or past) the majority of the reading will be written in? Most of the reading is written in the past tenses of Spanish. You already know the Spanish past tense verb form **fue**. If you pay attention to the root meaning of other verbs and ignore the verb endings, many of which will be unfamiliar to you, you should be able to derive meaning from the forms themselves. You probably do not know the meaning of the word **colonizaron**, but you probably recognize its root in *to colonize*. If you see the verb in this context and you know the reading is talking about the past, what does the verb mean?

Los europeos *colonizaron* las Américas.

The comprehension questions. Finally, scan the items in **Comprensión.** What clues do they give you about some of the information contained in the reading?

Las Américas

Lo que America debe a Europa

América fue colonizada por europeos, como ya sabes. El traspaso° de las lenguas, religiones, costumbres y formas de vida de Europa a América se realizó con relativa facilidad, pues todos los pueblos° indígenas americanos sumaban apenas° diez millones en la época del descubrimiento. Sólo algunos° pueblos, como los mayas, los méxicas o aztecas, los chibchas y los quéchuas, poseían un alto nivel de civilización. Por el resto de las tierras de América había numerosas tribus dispersas cuya existencia era pobre, debido a su atraso° cultural.

transfer
peoples / barely
some
backwardness

Los españoles, los ingleses, los portugueses, los franceses y los demás europeos que colonizaron las Américas, comenzaron la explotación de los grandes recursos naturales de nuestras tierras, mejoraron° la agricultura, crearon industrias y establecieron el comercio con Europa y demás partes del mundo.

improved

Entre los grandes aportes° traídos a América por los europeos figuran muchas plantas útiles, originarias del Viejo Mundo, como el trigo, el arroz, la caña de azúcar y el café, y también animales como el caballo, la vaca, el cerdo, el carnero y numerosas especies de aves de corral.

contribuciones

Tres siglos° después de comenzada la colonización europea, casi todos los pueblos de América se independizaron, pero la labor realizada por los europeos ha sobrevivido,° ya que de Europa nos llegaron nuestros idiomas, nuestras creencias religiosas y los otros elementos fundamentales de nuestra cultura actual.

un siglo = cien años
survived

Lo que el mundo debe a América

América no se ha limitado a recibir la herencia de la cultura europea. Nuestros pueblos han contribuido al progreso del mundo, provocando cambios° en la forma de vivir de los pueblos

changes

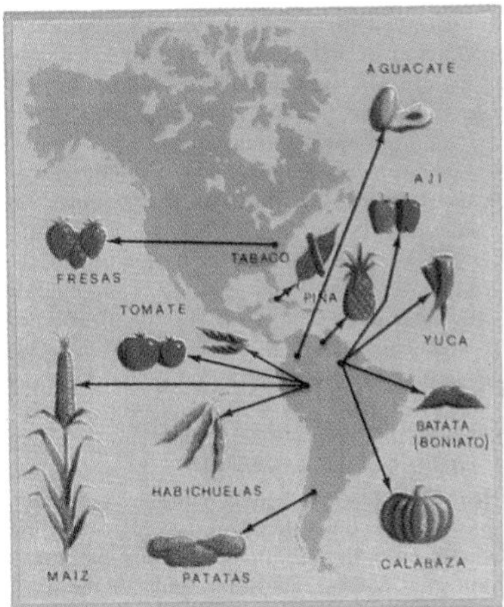

Algunas de las valiosas plantas oriundas de América, cuyo cultivo se ha extendido por todo el mundo.

de Europa y de otros continentes.

En los primeros tiempos coloniales fueron llevadas de América a Europa muchas plantas útiles que hoy cultivan los pueblos de varios continentes. Entre estas plantas figuran la papa, el maíz, el cacao, el tomate, la vainilla y la quina. El caucho,° uno de los más valiosos productos forestales del mundo actual, es también americano.

caucho: *rubber*

El tabaco, cuyo uso se ha generalizado° en todo el mundo, es originario de América, y fue descubierto en Cuba durante el primer viaje de Colón.°

generalizado: *spread*; Colón: *Columbus*

En los tiempos más recientes se han logrado o han sido perfeccionados en América, especialmente en Estados Unidos, numerosas invenciones que hoy disfrutan° todos los pueblos del mundo. Entre estas invenciones pueden citarse el buque° de vapor, la luz eléctrica, el fonógrafo, el telégrafo, el teléfono, el avión, la radio y la televisión.

disfrutan: *enjoy*; buque: barco

Comprensión

A. Complete la siguiente tabla según la lectura.

Lo que América debe a Europa

1. Número aproximado de habitantes indígenas en 1492: _____
2. Nombres de algunas civilizaciones indias importantes: _____, _____, _____, _____.
3. Nombres de algunos países colonizadores: _____, _____, _____, _____.
4. Contribuciones de los europeos a América: ¿Sí o no? Conteste exclusivamente según la lectura.

_____ algunas plantas
_____ el sistema de educación
_____ aspectos de la agricultura
_____ el sistema político
_____ algunos animales
_____ la religión
_____ el idioma
_____ el concepto de la explotación de la tierra

Lo que Europa debe a América

Nombres de algunas contribuciones de América a Europa:
algo que se come: _____
una planta que era (*was*) importante para los coches: _____
una planta que forma la base de una industria norteamericana muy importante: _____
dos invenciones modernas: _____, _____

B. Según la lectura, ¿en qué consiste América?

_____ sólo los países de habla española
_____ sólo los países de Norteamérica
_____ todos los países de los dos continentes del hemisferio

Cuando *Ud.* usa la palabra **América**, ¿qué quiere decir (*what do you imply*)?

Study Hint: Using a Bilingual Dictionary

A Spanish–English/English–Spanish dictionary or vocabulary list is an excellent study aid, but one that should be used very carefully. Follow these guidelines to minimize the pitfalls.

1. If you are looking for a Spanish word in the Spanish-English part of the dictionary, remember that in the Spanish alphabet the letters **ch**, **ll**, and **ñ** follow the letters **c**, **l**, and **n**, respectively. The word **coche** is found after the word **cocina**; **calle** comes after **calma**; and **caña** follows **candidato**.
2. When you look in the English-Spanish section for the Spanish equivalent of an English word, keep in mind the part of speech—noun, verb, adjective, and so on—of the word you are looking for. By doing so, you will avoid many mistakes. Imagine the confusion that would arise if you chose the wrong word in the following cases:

   can: **lata** (noun, *tin can*), but **poder** (verb, *can, to be able*)

   light: **luz** (noun, *electric light, daylight*), but **ligero** (adjective, *light, not heavy*), and **claro** (adjective, *light in color*).
3. If the Spanish word that you find is not familiar to you, or if you simply want to check its meaning and usage, look up the new word in the Spanish-English section. Do the English equivalents given there correspond to the meaning you want to convey?
4. Remember that there is rarely a one-to-one equivalency between Spanish and English words. **Jugar** means *to play* a sport or game, but the verb **tocar** must be used to talk about *playing* a musical instrument. **Un periódico** is a paper (a *news*paper) and **un papel** is a *sheet* of paper.
5. Minimize the number of "dictionary words" you use when writing in Spanish. It is best to limit yourself to words you know because you have used them in class. And when you do have to use the dictionary, try to check your word choice with your instructor or someone else who knows Spanish.

Para escribir

A. Write a brief paragraph introducing a Latin American to the geography and climate of the United States. You may want to give an overview, or you may prefer to describe the area in which you live. Some of the following questions may help you to organize your ideas. You should also look back to **El mundo hispánico (Parte 2)** in **Ante todo**, where you will find the names for a number of geographical phenomena.

   1. ¿Hay mucha variedad geográfica en los Estados Unidos?
   2. ¿Cuáles son algunos de los diferentes fenómenos geográficos de los Estados Unidos? ¿Dónde están situados? En su opinión, ¿uno de estos fenómenos es más interesante (hermoso [*beautiful*], importante) que los otros? ¿Cuál es? ¿Por qué?
   3. ¿Cómo es el clima de los Estados Unidos? ¿Hay mucha variedad? ¿Dónde hay extremos de clima?
   4. ¿Qué tiempo hace en su estado? ¿Cuándo llegan las diferentes estaciones?
   5. ¿Cómo afectan las estaciones la vida en las diferentes regiones del país?
   6. ¿Prefiere Ud. vivir en su estado o en otra parte del país? ¿Por qué?

B. Write a brief paragraph about your favorite season by completing the following sentences. Describe your attitudes and activities during this season, as well as the weather.

   Yo prefiero _____ porque _____. Durante esta estación _____.

CAPÍTULO SEIS

EN UN RESTAURANTE

Guadalajara, México

▲ **¿Dónde vamos a comer?**

—Vamos al Mesón de las Tres Hermanas.

—No conozco ese restaurante.

—Pues allí sirven un bistec exquisito.

—¿Y no es muy caro?

—Al contrario. Los precios son muy razonables.

—¡Eso espero! ¡A comer! ¡Tengo hambre!

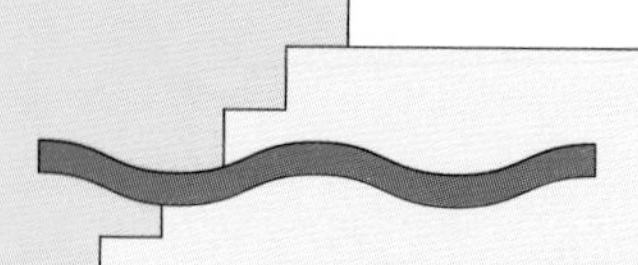

VOCABULARIO: PREPARACIÓN

• See also [video icon] and [audio icon]

Vocabulario: Preparación:
- See detailed supplementary materials and exercises for this section bound into the back of this Annotated Instructor's Edition.
- See model for vocabulary presentation and other materials in Supplementary *Vocabulario: Preparación* Materials, chapter by chapter, IM.

La comida

las bebidas

el café, el té, la leche, el refresco, el agua (mineral)
el jugo (de fruta), la cerveza, el vino blanco, el vino tinto

la carne

el jamón, el pollo
el bistec, las chuletas (de cerdo)
la hamburguesa

los mariscos

los camarones
la langosta

el pescado

el atún
el salmón

las verduras

las papas (fritas), la zanahoria, los frijoles, las arvejas

otros platos y comidas

la ensalada (de lechuga y tomate), la sopa, los huevos
el arroz, el pan, el queso, el sándwich

la fruta

la manzana, la naranja, la banana

los postres

el pastel, el helado, el flan, la galleta

Las comidas

desayunar: el desayuno	to have breakfast: breakfast
almorzar (ue): el almuerzo	to have lunch: lunch
cenar: la cena	to have dinner: dinner

¡OJO! The Spanish equivalents for *breakfast/lunch/dinner* given here do not express exactly the U.S. concept of these meals, nor are the meals eaten at the same time of day. See **Nota cultural** (page 199) for more information about mealtimes in Hispanic countries.

Variation A: Do exercise once, according to directions. Then, with books closed, instructor gives food item and students give definition, following model of items in **A**.

A. **Definiciones.** ¿Qué es esto?

1. un líquido caliente (*hot*) que se toma* con cuchara (*spoon*)
2. un plato de lechuga y tomate
3. una bebida alcohólica blanca o roja

*Remember that placing **se** before a verb form can change its English equivalent slightly: **usa** (*he/she/it uses*) → **se usa** (*is used*).

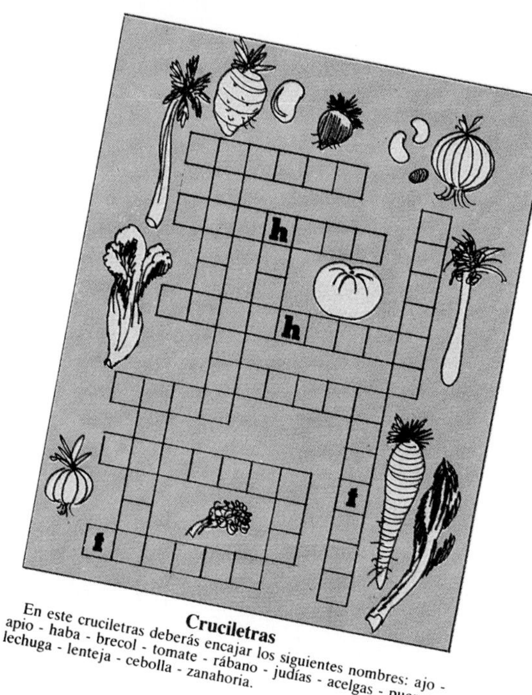

Cruciletras
En este cruciletras deberás encajar los siguientes nombres: ajo - apio - haba - brecol - tomate - rábano - judías - acelgas - puerro - lechuga - lenteja - cebolla - zanahoria.

4. una verdura anaranjada
5. la carne típica para barbacoa en los Estados Unidos
6. una comida muy común en China y en Japón
7. la comida favorita de los ratones
8. una verdura frita que se come con las hamburguesas
9. una fruta roja o verde
10. una fruta amarilla de las zonas tropicales
11. un líquido de color blanco que se sirve especialmente a los niños
12. la bebida tradicional de los ingleses
13. se usa para preparar sándwiches
14. un postre muy frío
15. un postre que se sirve en las fiestas de cumpleaños
16. una cosa que se come y que tiene el centro amarillo y el resto blanco

Notas lingüísticas: More *tener* idioms

Here are two additional ***tener*** idioms related to foods and eating.

tener (mucha) hambre	*to be (very) hungry*
tener (mucha) sed	*to be (very) thirsty*

Notas lingüísticas: Note the introduction of two more *tener* idioms.

B. **Consejos a la hora de comer.** ¿Qué debe Ud. comer o beber en las siguientes situaciones?

1. Ud. quiere comer algo ligero (*light*) porque no tiene hambre.
2. Ud. quiere comer algo fuerte (*heavy*) porque tiene mucha hambre.
3. Ud. tiene un poco de sed y quiere tomar algo antes de la comida.
4. Ud. quiere comer algo antes del plato (*dish*) principal.
5. Ud. quiere comer algo después del plato principal.
6. Después de jugar al tenis, Ud. tiene mucha sed.
7. Ud. está a dieta.
8. Ud. es vegetariano/a; come en un restaurante con unos amigos.
9. Ud. está de vacaciones en Maine (o Boston).
10. Ud. está enfermo/a.

Extension B: 10. *cuando Ud. tiene mucho calor?* **11.** *cuando hace mucho frío?* **12.** *cuando Ud. está en* (local restaurant)?

C. **Asociaciones.** ¿Qué palabras asocia Ud. con estas frases y oraciones?

1. comer bien
2. un bistec
3. cenar
4. engordar (*to gain weight*)
5. el desayuno
6. el almuerzo

Extension C: Mention not only food items but other words as well. **7.** *un sándwich* **8.** *estar a dieta* **9.** *los postres* **10.** *una comida barata* **11.** *el verano* **12.** *la cafetería de esta universidad*

CH. **Entrevista.** Use the following patterns to find out what several classmates had to eat last night. Take notes on what you learn.

MODELO: —¿Qué **comiste** anoche?
—**Comí** una hamburguesa con papas fritas.

Now use this pattern to report what you learned to the class and to add information about what you had to eat.

MODELO: Juanita **comió** una hamburguesa con papas fritas anoche.
Yo **comí** pescado.

Expressing Actions: *oír*, *traer*, and *ver*

oír (*to hear*)	**traer** (*to bring*)	**ver** (*to see*)
oigo oímos oyes oís oye oyen oyendo	traigo traemos traes traéis trae traen trayendo	veo vemos ves veis ve ven viendo

- ***oír:*** No oigo bien por el ruido. *I can't hear well because of the noise.*

English uses *listen*! or *hey*! to attract someone's attention. In Spanish the command forms of **oír** are used: **oye (tú)**, **oiga (Ud.)**, **oigan (Uds.)**.

Oye, Juan, ¿vas a la fiesta así? *Hey, Juan, are you going to the party like that?*

¡**Oiga Ud.**, por favor! *Listen (Pay attention), please!*

- ***traer:*** ¿Por qué no **trae** la cuenta el camarero? *Why doesn't the waiter bring the check?*
- ***ver:*** No **veo** bien por la contaminación. *I can't see well because of the pollution.*

A. **¡Un restaurante desastroso!** You're eating dinner with friends at a new restaurant . . . and things are not working out well. Describe what is happening by completing the following sentences in as many ways as you can.

- Hay tanto ruido que no oigo . . .
- Hay tan poca luz (*light*) que no veo bien...
- El camarero (no) trae... cuando debe.
- ¡Qué desgracia! Yo no traigo...

Palabras útiles: mi cartera, la cuenta, la música, a mis amigos, los platos, los platos del día (*specials*), el menú, el vino, la comida, dinero

B. **Una comida en común.** Imagine que los estudiantes de la clase van a hacer una comida todos juntos (*together*). ¿Qué van a traer todos para los siguientes tipos de comida?

1. un almuerzo en la sala de clase para celebrar el cumpleaños del profesor (de la profesora)
2. una comida mexicana, en casa de uno de los estudiantes
3. un *picnic* en el parque

El infinitivo: Preposition + Infinitive

Acaban de pedir la cena.	*They've just ordered dinner.*
Acabo de almorzar con Tina.	*I've just had lunch with Tina.*
La niña **vuelve a pedir** dulces.	*The little girl is asking for candy again.*
¡Nunca **vuelvo a comer** allí!	*I'll never eat there again!*

The infinitive is the only verb form that can follow a preposition in Spanish. You have already learned to use the following constructions in which prepositions are followed by an infinitive: **ir a**, **empezar a**, **tener ganas de**. Two other useful expressions with prepositions are **acabar de** + *infinitive* (*to have just done something*) and **volver a** + *infinitive* (*to do something again*).

A. **Situaciones.** Pregúntele a otro/a estudiante...

- qué acaba de hacer si sale de los siguientes lugares

MODELO: un restaurante →
—Si sales de un restaurante, ¿qué acabas de hacer?
—Acabo de comer.

Extension A: 5. *el estadio* (name university stadium) 6. *el laboratorio de lenguas* 7. *una clase de inglés*

1. un mercado
2. una discoteca
3. una librería
4. una tienda de ropa

- dónde está si acaba de hacer las siguientes cosas

MODELO: almorzar →
—¿Dónde estás si acabas de almorzar?
—Estoy en la cafetería.

Extension A: 7. *hablar con la secretaria del departamento de español* 8. *presenciar* (to witness) *una boda* 9. *comprar ropa muy elegante* 10. *comer una cena excelente*

1. ver una película
2. escribir los ejercicios de español
3. escuchar música en la radio
4. dormir ocho horas
5. hacer una pregunta en español
6. salir para la universidad

B. **Reacciones.** Ud. está en los siguientes lugares o situaciones. ¿Qué quiere volver a hacer?

MODELO: Ud. está en una discoteca con unos amigos. Están hablando ahora, pero empiezan a tocar una música encantadora. →
¡Quiero volver a bailar!

1. Ud. está en las montañas. Hace cuatro horas que esquía. Está descansando ahora, pero empieza a nevar.
2. Ud. está en la playa. Acaba de nadar (*to swim*) un poco, pero ahora está tomando el sol. ¡Hace mucho calor!

Follow-up: *Ud. está en los siguientes lugares. ¿Qué acaba de pedir?* **1.** *un restaurante elegante* **2.** *la cafetería de la universidad* **3.** *su restaurante favorito de comida rápida* **4.** *un restaurante mexicano (chino)*

3. Ud. está en la cama (*bed*). Son las seis de la mañana y acaba de oír el despertador (*alarm clock*). Ud. quiere descansar un poco más.
4. Ud. está en la clase de historia y acaba de sacar (*to receive*) una D en un examen.
5. Ud. está mirando un programa interesante en la tele y su amigo Julio llama por teléfono. Ud. contesta.
6. Ud. acaba de salir del cine. No vio (*you didn't see*) los primeros diez minutos.

Notas comunicativas: More About Expressing Likes and Dislikes

You have been using the phrase **me gusta/no me gusta** since the beginning of this course. Here are two simple ways to express *intense* likes and dislikes.

¡Me gusta **muchísimo**!	*I like it a lot!*
¡No me gusta **(para) nada**!	*I don't like it at all!*

C. **Una encuesta.** Read the following categories and jot down your answers. Then pick the four items that interest you the most and ask questions of four classmates to determine how they answered each one. Try to get additional information and be prepared to share your answers with the class.

MODELO: un restaurante que no me gusta nada →
¿Qué restaurante no te gusta nada?
¿Acabas de comer en ese restaurante?
¿Qué comiste allí?
¿Vas a volver a comer allí?

1. un programa de televisión que veo con frecuencia y que me gusta muchísimo
2. un programa de televisión que no me gusta nada
3. una película (nueva o vieja) que acabo de ver y que es estupenda
4. una película nueva que quiero ver
5. una estación de radio que escucho con frecuencia
6. un restaurante estupendo donde comí recientemente / donde acabo de comer
7. un restaurante que no me gusta nada
8. un plato que no vuelvo a comer nunca

¿Qué comen los astronautas?

Remitida por Elvira Gallart, Zaragoza.

Durante los primeros vuelos tripulados al espacio, a principios de los años sesenta, los astronautas se alimentaban de comida concentrada y congelada y de semilíquidos, todo ello transportado en unos tubos parecidos a los de la pasta de dientes. Además de no ser muy apetitosa, esta comida tenía el inconveniente de desprender migas que quedaban flotando por la nave.

Durante el proyecto Gemini, los astronautas comen a la carta: pollo con verduras, coctel de gambas, zumos, etcétera. Las migas se eliminan cubriendo con gelatina los cubitos de comida deshidratada. Los tripulantes de las naves Apollo, ya pueden consumir alimentos sólidos y bebidas calientes y utilizan cucharas. En los laboratorios espaciales se utilizan las latas para los líquidos, y se impone la comodidad: los astronautas se sientan a la mesa y hacen uso de sus cubiertos magnéticos que se adhieren a la bandeja. Durante las misiones conjuntas Soyuz-Apollo (EE UU-URSS), dado lo corto de los vuelos, los tripulantes consumieron alimentos frescos como pan y queso. Ya en los recientes vuelos de los transbordadores, se calientan los alimentos y es posible aderezarlos con pimienta y sal líquidas, mostaza o mahonesa. La carta de «estos restaurantes espaciales» cuenta con más de ochenta posibles platos y veinte bebidas diferentes. ■

NASA

Con los años, la comida espacial ha presentado un variado menú.

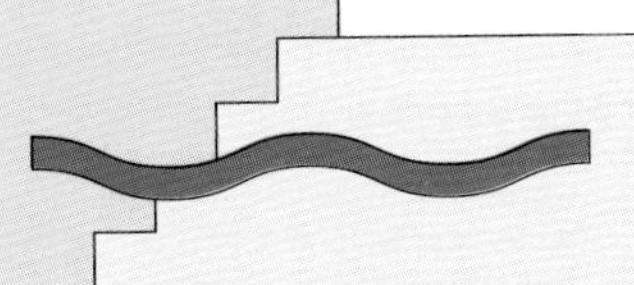

MINIDIÁLOGOS Y GRAMÁTICA

19. EXPRESSING NEGATION
Indefinite and Negative Words

Communicative objectives for **19:** how to express negatives with words other than *no* alone

Imagine que Ud. vive en Lima este año. ¿Cómo contesta Ud. en estas situaciones?

SU AMIGO ALFONSO: Ya son las diez de la noche. Vamos a comer *algo* en El Perico Negro. ¡Tengo hambre!

USTED:
- No, gracias, casi *nunca* ceno fuera.
- Pero... ¡*nadie* cena a estas horas!
- Sí, pero... ¿*no* hay *ningún* otro restaurante cerca de la facultad?

EL CAMARERO: *También* tenemos ceviche, camarones...

USTED:
- Pues... creo que *no* voy a comer *nada*, gracias.
- ¡Qué bien! Quiero probar *algunos* platos típicos.
- Aquí *siempre* pido el ceviche.

Aquí hay otras situaciones. ¿Qué respuestas puede Ud. improvisar, siguiendo el modelo de las respuestas anteriores (*preceding*)?

SU AMIGA ROSA: ¿Algo para beber? Pues, tenemos agua mineral... y también hay vino tinto, si quieres.

SU AMIGO MEXICANO RAÚL: Hoy para el desayuno quiero comer huevos rancheros, frijoles y tortillas.

algo	something, anything	**nada**	nothing, not anything
alguien	someone, anyone	**nadie**	no one, nobody, not anybody
algún (alguno/a/os/as)	some, any	**ningún (ninguno/a)**	no, none, not any
siempre	always	**nunca, jamás**	never
también	also	**tampoco**	neither, not either

YOUR FRIEND ALFONSO It's already ten P.M. Let's eat something at the Black Parakeet. I'm hungry! YOU: • No, thanks, I almost never have dinner out. • But . . . nobody eats dinner at this hour! • OK, but . . . isn't there any other restaurant close to campus? WAITER: We also have ceviche (*raw marinated fish*), shrimp . . . YOU: • Well . . . I don't think I'll have anything, thank you. • Great! I want to try some typical dishes! • I always have the ceviche here.

You have been using many indefinite and negative words since the early chapters of ***Puntos de partida***.

Suggestions:
- Model affirmative and negative words in situations similar to those shown in *Práctica B*. Students first show comprehension and then produce sentences that describe the situations that you are setting up. Hint: move a book/several books around to show something/nothing, some books/no book, etc.

Casi **nunca** ceno fuera los días de entre semana.	*I almost never have dinner out on weekdays.*
Queremos comer **algo** diferente esta noche.	*We want to have (eat) something different tonight.*
¿**Nadie** trae dinero?	*No one has (Doesn't anyone have) any money?*

Pronunciation hint: Remember to pronounce the **d** in **nada** and **nadie** as a fricative: **na đa**, **na đie**.

Pay particular attention to the following aspects of using negative words.

- When a negative word comes after the main verb, Spanish requires that another negative word—usually **no**—be placed before the verb. When a negative word precedes the verb, **no** is not used.

- Optional: *o, ni... ni*

¿**No** estudia **nadie**? ¿**Nadie** estudia?	*Isn't anyone studying?*
No estás en clase **nunca**. **Nunca** estás en clase.	*You're never in class.*
No quieren cenar aquí **tampoco**. **Tampoco** quieren cenar aquí.	*They don't want to have dinner here, either.*

- The adjectives **alguno** and **ninguno** shorten to **algún** and **ningún**, respectively, before a masculine singular noun, just as **uno** shortens to **un** and **bueno** to **buen**. The plural forms **ningunos** and **ningunas** are rarely used.

Emphasis: Plural forms *ningunos/as* are rarely used. As in example, affirmation questions with plural *algunos/as* frequently require singular *ningún/ninguna* in negative answers. Exceptions: nouns usually used in plural in Spanish: *pantalones, medias, vacaciones*, etc.

—¿Hay **algunas** cartas para mí hoy? —Lo siento, pero hoy no hay **ninguna** carta para Ud.	*—Are there any letters for me today? —I'm sorry, but there are no letters for you today. (There is not a single letter for you today.)*

Práctica

Preliminary exercises: Give the opposite: *algo, alguien, alguno, siempre, también, nada, nadie, ninguno, nunca, tampoco.* *¡OJO!* A2: *No tienen ningún plato...*

A. **¡Por eso no come nadie allí!** Exprese negativamente, usando la negativa doble.

1. Hay algo interesante en el menú.
2. Tienen algunos platos típicos.
3. El profesor cena allí también.
4. Mis amigos siempre almuerzan allí.
5. Preparan algo especial para grupos grandes.
6. Siempre hacen platos nuevos.
7. Y también sirven paella, mi plato favorito.

B. Answer each question, first affirmatively, then in the negative. The first question is done for you in each set. If you can, expand each response by explaining the situation. Model explanations are given in parentheses.

1. ¿Hay **algo** en la pizarra? (palabras) →

   Sí, hay **algo**. Hay unas **palabras** en la pizarra. (Hay clase hoy en esta sala [*room*]).
   No, **no** hay **nada**. (**No** hay **ninguna** clase aquí hoy.)

   ¿en la mesa? (periódico)
   ¿en la calle? (carro)
   ¿en la montaña? (pueblo)

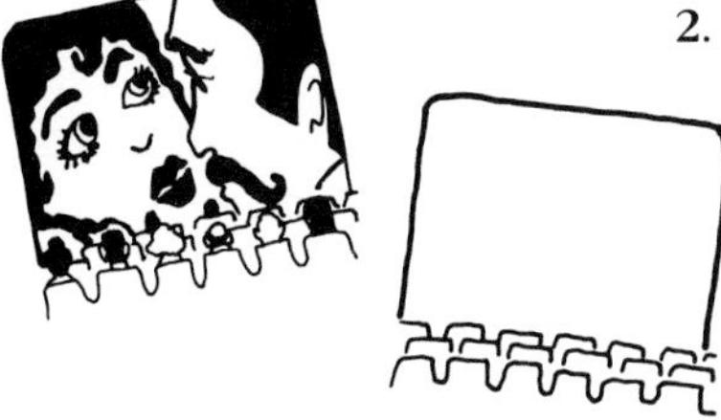

2. ¿Hay alguien en el cine? (muchas personas) →

   Sí, hay **alguien**. Hay **muchas personas**. (Hay una película muy buena hoy.)
   No, **no** hay **nadie**. (¡La película es muy mala!)

   ¿en el restaurante? (varias familias)
   ¿en el parque? (niños)
   ¿en la biblioteca? (muchos estudiantes)

C. ¿Cómo se dice en español?

Suggestion: Use *Práctica B* as inductive exercise to present and practice double negative.

Extension B: Using several books, set up similar pattern with *¿Hay algunos libros en el suelo* (floor)? → *Sí, hay algunos. No, no hay ninguno.* Expand by using other classroom objects at hand.

A la hora de la cena

1. Is there anything special tonight?
2. They serve dinner at six at (**en**) their house, too.
3. No one is eating at home tonight, right?
4. We don't want to order anything right now.
5. There's no restaurant on that street.

En la residencia, antes del examen

1. No one understands that.
2. Marcos can't write this sentence, either.
3. You never study with Carmen. Why not?
4. No one is as tired as I am!
5. Doesn't anybody feel like sleeping?

Conversación

A. Rosa es una persona muy positiva, pero su hermano Rodolfo tiene ideas muy negativas. Aquí hay unas oraciones que expresan las ideas de Rosa sobre varios temas. ¿Cuáles son las opiniones de Rodolfo?

Sobre las clases y la vida universitaria

- Hay algunos estudiantes excelentes en mi clase de sicología.
- Hay algunas personas muy listas en la clase de español.
- Por lo general, ¡me gusta muchísimo mi compañera de cuarto!
- Salgo con mis amigos con frecuencia.

Extension A: *En casa*
- *Quiero escuchar algo en la radio.*
- *Siempre me gusta escuchar música popular.*
- *Hay algunas ideas fascinantes en este libro.*
- *Tengo algunos libros muy interesantes.*

Las actividades de esta noche

- Tengo hambre. ¿Por qué no comemos algo?
- Vamos a beber algo antes de cenar.
- Sirven algunos platos estupendos aquí.
- Hay algo interesante en la tele esta noche.

Ahora invente Ud. algunos comentarios de Rodolfo sobre su familia y la ciudad donde vive. ¿Cómo reacciona Rosa?

B. **Ningún cumpleaños es perfecto.** Using the words and phrases given under **Posibilidades** and some of the negative words you have just learned, tell someone about a terrible birthday.

MODELOS: cartas → No hay ninguna carta para mí.
bailar → Nadie quiere bailar conmigo.

Posibilidades: regalos, tarjetas (*cards*), cena especial, telegramas, flores, platos especiales, llamar por teléfono, cenar, salir, cantar para mí

Extension C: **4.** *¿Hay algo más importante que el dinero? ¿que la amistad? ¿que el amor?* **5.** *En la clase, ¿hay alguien más inteligente que el profesor (la profesora)? ¿más estudioso/a que Ud.? / ¿más rico/a que Ud.?* **6.** *La perfección es una meta* (goal) *imposible, ¿verdad? ¿Hay alguna clase perfecta en esta universidad? ¿Hay alguna residencia perfecta? ¿alguna familia perfecta? ¿Tiene Ud. algún hermano perfecto? ¿un plan perfecto para esta noche?*

C. **Preguntas**

1. ¿Vamos a vivir en la luna algún día? ¿Vamos a viajar a los otros planetas? ¿Vamos a vivir allí algún día? ¿Vamos a establecer contacto con seres (*beings*) de otros planetas algún día?
2. ¿Algunos de los estudiantes de esta universidad son de países extranjeros? ¿De dónde son? ¿Algunos de sus amigos son de habla española? ¿De dónde son?
3. En esta clase, ¿quién... ? ¿siempre tiene algunas ideas buenas? ¿tiene algunos amigos españoles? ¿no entiende nada nunca? ¿nunca contesta ninguna pregunta? ¿va a ser muy rico/a algún día? ¿nunca tiene tiempo para tomar un café después de la clase? ¿nunca ve la televisión?

Communicative objectives for 20: how to talk about who and what you know

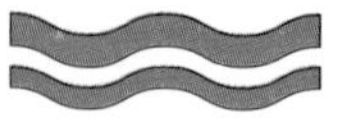

20. ¿QUÉ SABES Y A QUIÉN CONOCES?
Saber and *conocer*; Personal *a*

Venezuela

Delante de un restaurante

AMALIA: ¿Dónde vamos a almorzar?
ERNESTO: (Entrando en el restaurante.) ¿Por qué no aquí mismo?
AMALIA: ¿*Conoces* este restaurante?
ERNESTO: Sí, lo *conozco* y *sé* que es excelente.
AMALIA: ¿Y cómo *sabes* que es tan bueno?
ERNESTO: *Conozco* muy bien a la dueña. ¡Es mi tía! ¿Nos sentamos?

In front of a restaurant AMALIA: Where are we going to have lunch? ERNESTO: (Entering the restaurant.) Why not right here? AMALIA: Do you know (Are you familiar with) this restaurant? ERNESTO: Yes, I know it, and I know that it's excellent. AMALIA: And how do you know that it's so good? ERNESTO: I know the owner very well. She's my aunt! Shall we sit down?

Follow-up: 1. *¿Qué restaurantes conoce Ud. muy bien?* 2. *¿Es excelente la comida allí?* 3. *¿Come Ud. allí con frecuencia?* 4. *¿Conoce Ud. al dueño/a la dueña?* 5. *¿Cómo es?*
Point out: irregular *yo* forms

1. ¿Qué hora es, aproximadamente?
2. ¿Conoce Ernesto el restaurante?
3. ¿Cuál es su opinión del restaurante?
4. ¿Cómo sabe Ernesto que el restaurante es muy bueno?
5. ¿Por qué conoce a la dueña del restaurante?

Saber and *conocer*

saber (*to know*)		**conocer** (*to know*)	
sé	sabemos	cono**z**co	conocemos
sabes	sabéis	conoces	conocéis
sabe	saben	conoce	conocen
sabiendo		conociendo	

Saber means *to know* facts or pieces of information. When followed by an infinitive, **saber** means *to know how* to do something.

Note: "gray" areas (knowing a language, history, poetry, etc.), where only context and meaning speaker wishes to convey determine whether *saber* or *conocer* is appropriate.

No **saben** el teléfono de Alejandro. — *They don't know Alejandro's phone number.*
¿**Saben** Uds. dónde vive Carmela? — *Do you know where Carmela lives?*
¿**Sabes** tocar el piano? — *Do you know how to play the piano?*

Conocer means *to know* or *to be acquainted* (*familiar*) *with* a person, place, or thing. It can also mean *to meet.* Note the **a** used before a specific person.

No **conocen** a la nueva estudiante todavía. — *They don't know the new student yet.*
¿**Conocen** Uds. el restaurante mexicano en la calle Goya? — *Are you familiar with* (*Have you been to*) *the Mexican restaurant on Goya Street?*
¿Quieren **conocer** a aquel joven? — *Do you want to meet that young man?*

[Práctica A–C]

Personal *a*

Suggestion: Illustrate concept of indirect object by pretending to hit someone/throwing an eraser/breaking a piece of chalk. Ask: Who/what is directly affected by the action? → person, eraser, chalk.

A. In English and in Spanish, the *direct object* (**el complemento directo**) of a sentence answers the question *what?* or *whom?* in relation to the subject and verb.

Ann is preparing dinner.	Ann is preparing *what*? *What* is Ann preparing?	*dinner*
They can't hear the baby.	They can't hear *whom*? *Whom* can't they hear?	*the baby*

Indicate the direct objects in the following sentences:

1. I don't see Betty and Mary here.
2. Give the dog a bone.
3. No tenemos dinero.
4. ¿Por qué no pones la sopa en la mesa?

B. In Spanish, the word **a** immediately precedes the direct object of a sentence when the direct object refers to a specific person or persons. This **a**, called the **a personal**, has no equivalent in English.*

Note: Personal *a* has been used passively in text for some time.

Vamos a visitar **al profesor**.	*We're going to visit the professor.*
but	
Vamos a visitar **el museo**.	*We're going to visit the museum.*
Necesitan **a la camarera**.	*They need the waitress.*
but	
Necesitan **la cuenta**.	*They need the bill.*

¡OJO! The verbs **esperar** (*to wait for*), **escuchar** (*to listen to*), **mirar** (*to look at*), and **buscar** (*to look for*) include the sense of the English prepositions *for*, *to*, and *at*. These verbs take direct objects in Spanish (not prepositional phrases, as in English).

¿Cómo se dice?: **1.** I'm looking at the TV (at María). **2.** We're listening to the radio (to the professor). **3.** She's looking for her pen (for her brother). **4.** They're waiting for the bus (for the doctor).

Estoy buscando **mi abrigo**.	*I'm looking for my overcoat.*
Estoy esperando **a mi hijo**.	*I'm waiting for my son.*

C. The personal **a** is used before the interrogative words **¿quién?** or **¿quiénes?** when these words function as direct objects.

¿A quién llama?	*Whom are you calling?*
¿Quién llama?	*Who is calling?*

CH. The personal **a** is used before **alguien** and **nadie** when these words function as direct objects.

¿Vas a invitar **a alguien**?	*Are you going to invite someone?*
—¿A quién llamas?	*—Whom are you calling?*
—No llamo **a nadie**.	*—I'm not calling anyone.*

[Práctica CH]

*The personal **a** is not generally used with **tener**: **Tengo cuatro hijos.**

Preliminary exercises:

- *Saber, conocer*
  La familia de Julita. Dé oraciones nuevas según las indicaciones. 1. *Conocemos muy bien a Julita.* (*yo, Uds., Juan y yo, Raúl y Mario, vosotros*) 2. *Sabemos que su familia es de Chile.* (*ellos, yo, Elvira, Uds., Ana y tú, vosotros*)
- *A personal*
  En este momento... Dé oraciones nuevas según las indicaciones. 1. *—¿A quién o qué ve? —Veo el texto.* (*profesor, pizarra, estudiantes, mesa, mi amigo/a, puerta*) 2. *—¿A quién o qué busca? —Estoy buscando a mi amigo José.* (*mi libro, Felipe, el amigo de Tomás, el profesor, un cuaderno*)
- *¿Saber o conocer?:* 1. I know the truth. 2. She knows the vice-president. 3. They know how to swim. 4. Do you know New York (i.e., Are you familiar with it)? 5. We don't know the answer. 6. Everyone wants to meet the new student in the class.

Extension A: Use names with *conocer: ¿José Feliciano conoce a Julio Iglesias?*, etc.

Follow-up A: *¿Sabe Ud. mi nombre?* (→ *Sí, lo sé.*) *¿los nombres de todos los estudiantes de la clase? ¿la fecha de hoy? ¿la fecha de mi cumpleaños? ¿las formas del verbo* **saber**? *¿todo el nuevo vocabulario?*

Extension B: *¿Conoce Ud. a* (someone in the class)? (→ *Sí, lo/la conozco.*) *¿a Linda Evans? ¿a Michael Jackson? ¿al presidente y su esposa? ¿a los padres de* (someone in the class)? *¿a la novia de* (someone in the class)?

Follow-up B: *¿Sabe Ud. o conoce Ud....? ¿esta ciudad? ¿a mis padres? ¿que dos y dos son cuatro? ¿el arte abstracto? ¿la música clásica? ¿tocar la guitarra?*

Práctica

A. ¿Qué saben hacer estas personas famosas?

José Feliciano		jugar al béisbol
Mikhail Baryshnikov		hacer ejercicios gimnásticos
Fernando Valenzuela		cantar en español
Mary Lou Retton	sabe	cocinar (*to cook*) bien
James Michener		jugar al tenis
Chris Evert		escribir novelas
Julia Child		bailar

B. **Parejas famosas.** ¿A quién conoce... ?

Adán		Marta
Romeo		Cleopatra
Rhett Butler	conoce a	Eva
Antonio		Julieta
Jorge Washington		Scarlett O'Hara

C. Complete las siguientes oraciones con **conozco** o **sé**.

1. _____ al nuevo novio de Marta pero no _____ de dónde es.
2. _____ un excelente restaurante chino pero no _____ en qué calle está.
3. Sí, sí, _____ a Julio pero no _____ su teléfono.
4. _____ jugar muy bien al tenis pero no _____ a ningún otro tenista (*player*) en esta residencia.
5. No _____ muy bien la Ciudad de México pero _____ que quiero regresar este verano.
6. ¡Qué problema! _____ que hay una prueba en esa clase mañana pero no _____ sobre qué capítulo es y no _____ a nadie de la clase que me pueda informar (*who can tell me*)...

CH. ¿Qué hace Roberto los martes? Describa su rutina, haciendo oraciones según las indicaciones.

1. martes / Roberto / nunca / salir / apartamento / antes / doce
2. esperar / su amigo Samuel / delante / su casa
3. los dos / esperar / juntos / autobús (*m.*)
4. cuando / (ellos) llegar / universidad, / buscar / su amiga Ceci / en / cafetería
5. ella / acabar / empezar / estudios / allí / y / no / conocer / mucha gente (*people*) / todavía
6. a veces / (ellos) ver / profesora de historia en / cafetería / y / hablar / un poco / con ella
7. (ella) ser / persona / muy interesante / que / saber / mucho / de / ese / materia
8. a / dos / todos / tener / clase / de / sicología

9. siempre / (ellos) oír / conferencias (*lectures*) / interesante / y / hacer / alguno / pregunta
10. a veces / tener / oportunidad de / conocer / conferenciante (*m.*) (*lecturer*)
11. las cinco / Roberto y Samuel / volver / esperar / autobús
12. cuando entrar / apartamento, / Roberto / siempre / buscar / compañero Raúl / para / hablar / un poco / con / él
13. los dos / preparar / cena / juntos / y / luego / mirar / televisión

¿Quién habla?

1. Quiero conocer a más gente. ¡Casi no conozco a nadie todavía!
2. Algunos estudiantes hacen buenas preguntas.
3. ¡Acabo de llegar! ¿Dónde estás?
4. ¡Ay! Ya veo a Roberto por la ventana (*window*) y todavía tengo que buscar mis libros.

Ahora vuelva a contar la historia desde el punto de vista de Roberto, usando **yo** o **nosotros** como sujeto donde sea apropiado.

****
* L A D O R A D A *
RESESA CIF:A41-098989
****
TICKET N.PERS. NOTA
1 4 6317
26.06.87 * 65* 22.50
1 GAMBAS.... 1220
1 AGUA MIN.1/2 65
4 CERVEZA.... 360
TOTAL 1645

Conversación

Suggestion A: Use the drawing as a vehicle for reentering all of the chapter's grammar so far: irregular verbs, food vocabulary, questions with affirmative and negative words, and so on.

A. **Una noche típica en El Mesón Fuentes.** Describa este dibujo de una noche típica en este restaurante popular. Invente los detalles (***details***) necesarios. ¿Quiénes son todas estas personas? ¿Qué hacen? ¿Qué buscan? ¿Qué necesitan?

Follow-up B: *Sus compañeros de clase acaban de hablar de varios detalles de su vida en el ejercicio B. Además, Ud. ya conoce a varios de ellos muy bien. ¿Qué sabe Ud. de sus vidas? ¿Qué recuerda* (do you remember) *de lo que acaba de oír? Describa a varios compañeros de clase, según el modelo.* **Modelo** *Conozco a _____. Sé que (él/ella) _____.*

Suggestion: If you are going to do Follow-up B, alert students to listen carefully while you are asking the questions in B.

B. **Preguntas**

1. ¿Qué restaurantes conoce Ud. en esta ciudad? ¿Cuál es su restaurante favorito? ¿Por qué es su favorito? ¿Es buena la comida de allí? ¿Qué tipo de comida sirven? ¿Es agradable el ambiente (*atmosphere*)? ¿Come Ud.

Un lugar atractivo en el corazón de Buenos Aires, frente al Obelisco. Exactamente, C. Pellegrini y Lavalle, en el 1er piso del:

Lo esperamos para satisfacer sus gustos y probar nuestros exquisitos platos internacionales o la moderna cocina española e italiana.

Restaurante abierto hasta las 24 hs.
Noche: Coffee-shop

También para cualquier exigencia empresaria en sus 4 amplios salones para convenciones, banquetes o eventos especiales.

C. Pellegrini 507 - 1° Piso/ Bs.As.
Tel: 393-1717/1417/ 1017/1117/1167

allí con frecuencia? ¿Conoce a los dueños del restaurante? ¿De dónde son?

2. ¿Conoce Ud. a alguna persona famosa? ¿Quién es? ¿Cómo es? ¿Qué detalles sabe Ud. de su vida?
3. ¿Qué platos sabe Ud. preparar? ¿tacos? ¿enchiladas? ¿pollo frito? ¿hamburguesas? ¿Le gusta cocinar? ¿Cocina con frecuencia? ¿Por qué sí o por qué no?
4. ¿Qué habilidades especiales tiene Ud.? ¿Sabe jugar al tenis? ¿a otros deportes? ¿Sabe tocar un instrumento musical? ¿bailar muy bien? ¿cantar? ¿hablar otra lengua?
5. ¿Espera Ud. a alguien para ir a la universidad? ¿Espera a alguien después de la clase? ¿A quién busca cuando necesita ayuda con el español? ¿Dónde busca a sus amigos por la noche?

Study Hint: Practicing Spanish Outside of Class

The few hours you spend in class each week are not enough time for practicing Spanish. But once you have done your homework and gone to the language lab (if one is available to you), how else can you practice your Spanish outside of class?

1. Practice "talking to yourself" in Spanish as you walk across campus, wait for a bus, and so on. Have an imaginary conversation with someone you know, or simply practice describing what you see or what you are thinking about at a given moment. Write notes to yourself in Spanish.
2. Hold a conversation hour—perhaps on a regular basis—with other students of Spanish. Or make regular phone calls to practice Spanish with other students in your class. It is difficult to communicate on the phone, because you can't rely on gestures and facial expressions, but it's an excellent way to improve your skill.
3. See Spanish-language movies when they are shown on campus or in local movie theaters. Check local bookstores, libraries, and record stores for Spanish-language newspapers, magazines, and music. Read the radio and television listings. Are there any Spanish-language programs or any stations that broadcast partially or exclusively in Spanish?
4. Practice speaking Spanish with a native speaker—either a Hispanic American or a foreign student. Is there an international students' organization on campus? An authentic Hispanic restaurant in your town? Spanish-speaking professors at your university? Try out a few phrases—no matter how simple—every chance you get. Every bit of practice will enhance your ability to speak Spanish.

Oiga, señor...

—Camarero, esta sopa está fría.
—No es posible, señor. Acaban de prepararla.
—De todas maneras, está fría.
—Lo siento (Disculpe), señor. Le traigo otro plato inmediatamente.

Barcelona, España

21. EXPRESSING *WHAT* OR *WHOM*
Direct Object Pronouns

Follow-up: Who might have made the following statements? 1. *Aquí vienen Agustín y Mariela.* 2. *A mi esposa le gusta cenar fuera con frecuencia.* 3. *No quiero cocinar esta noche.*

¿Dónde vamos a comer?

AGUSTÍN: Estoy empezando a tener hambre. ¿Qué te parece si cenamos fuera esta noche?

MARIELA: ¡Buena idea! A propósito, ¿conoces a los Velázquez?

AGUSTÍN: Claro que sí. Hace años que *los* conozco. ¿Por qué me *lo* preguntas? Estamos hablando de comidas.

MARIELA: Pues acabo de oír que tienen un restaurante en la Avenida Bolívar.

AGUSTÍN: ¡Qué suerte! ¡A ver si *nos* invitan* a comer!

1. ¿Quién tiene hambre?
2. ¿Quién conoce a los Velázquez?
3. ¿Por qué habla Mariela de ellos?
4. ¿Quiere pagar la comida Agustín?

DIRECT OBJECT PRONOUNS			
me	*me*	**nos**	*us*
te	*you* (fam. sing.)	**os**	*you* (fam. pl.)
lo[†]	*you* (form. sing.), *him, it* (m.)	**los**	*you* (form. pl.), *them* (m., m. + f.)
la	*you* (form. sing.), *her, it* (f.)	**las**	*you* (form. pl.), *them* (f.)

Suggestions:
- Introduce third-person direct object pronouns first. Put a number of objects on the desk (*un libro, una flor, un coche* [toy car]) and model sentences with a noun to pronoun transformation: *Estoy mirando el libro.* → *Lo estoy mirando.*
- Follow a similar sequence with feminine singular nouns, then masculine plural and feminine plural.
- After presenting third-person object pronouns with visual, expand use to include meaning *you*, having students stand up, as appropriate: *Yo lo veo* (a *Ud., Roberto*), etc. *¿Ud. me ve* (*a mí*)? → *Sí, profesor*(*a*), *lo*/*la veo.*
- **Point out:** Like subject pronoun *ellos*, direct object pronoun *los* can refer to group either masculine or combination of masculine/feminine.

A. Like direct object nouns, *direct object pronouns* (**los pronombres del complemento directo**) answer the questions *what?* or *whom?* in relation to the subject and verb. Direct object pronouns are placed before a conjugated verb and after the word **no** when it appears. Direct object pronouns are used only when the direct object noun has already been mentioned.

¿El libro? Diego no **lo** necesita.	*The book? Diego doesn't need it.*
¿Dónde están la revista y el periódico? **Los** necesito ahora.	*Where are the magazine and the newspaper? I need them now.*
Ellos **me** ayudan.	*They're helping me.*

Note A: In the third example, the use of the direct object pronoun (*me*) implies that the referent is clear in conversation.

Where are we going to eat? AGUSTÍN: I'm starting to get hungry. What do you think about eating out tonight? MARIELA: Great! By the way, do you know the Velázquezes? AGUSTÍN: Of course I do. I've known them for years. Why do you ask? We're talking about food (meals). MARIELA: Well, I've just heard that they have a restaurant on Bolivar Avenue. AGUSTÍN: What luck! Let's see if they invite us to a free meal!

*¡OJO! **Invitar** is a cognate that has somewhat different connotations in Spanish and in English. In English, *to invite* someone is a request for that person's company. In Spanish, **te invito**, **nos invitan**, and similar phrases imply that the person who is inviting will also pay.

[†]In Spain and in other parts of the Spanish-speaking world, **le** is frequently used instead of **lo** for the direct object pronoun *him*. This usage will not be followed in ***Puntos de partida***.

B. The direct object pronouns may be attached to an infinitive or a present participle.

Emphasis: Position of object pronouns.

Las tengo que leer. / Tengo que leer**las**. — *I have to read them.*

¿**Nos** están buscando? / ¿Están buscándo**nos**? — *Are you looking for us?*

When a pronoun object is attached to a present participle, a written accent is needed on the stressed vowel: **buscándonos**.

[Práctica A–D]

C. The direct object pronoun **lo** can refer to actions, situations, or ideas in general. When used in this way, **lo** expresses English *it* or *that*.

Lo comprende muy bien. — *He understands it (that) very well.*
No **lo** creo. — *I don't believe it (that).*
Lo sé. — *I know (it).*

[Práctica E]

Preliminary exercises: (listening): Do you hear a masculine or a feminine object pronoun? 1. *María lo tiene.* 2. *Las buscan.* 3. *No lo necesitamos.* 4. *Teresa las lee.* 5. *Ellos no la escuchan.*
Singular or plural? 6. *Lo leemos.* 7. *Ramón los compra.* 8. *Ellas la venden.* 9. *Tú la necesitas.* 10. *Ella no lo cree.*
(speaking)
—¿Quién me mira? ¿(Student)? *—Sí,* (student) *lo/la mira.* *¿Quién nos mira* (student stands with instructor)? ¿(Student)? *—Sí, _____ los/las mira.*
Suggestion A: Students do as partner/pair activity, after you demonstrate the first item with a student.

Práctica

A. **Situaciones.** Imagine you are in the following situations, performing the indicated tasks. A friend asks you about particular items. Answer logically—you will not need some items at all! Follow the models.

1. Ud. está haciendo la maleta para un viaje a Acapulco.
   —¿El traje de baño? —¡Claro que *lo* necesito!

Artículos: las sandalias, las gafas de sol (*sunglasses*), los pantalones cortos, las camisetas, la crema bronceadora, el reloj

2. Ud. está preparando un pastel para el cumpleaños de un amigo.
   —¿La harina (*flour*)? —Sí, tengo que usarla.

Ingredientes: los huevos, la leche, el azúcar, el chocolate, la vainilla

3. Ud. está en un restaurante y es hora de pedir.
   —¿El vino blanco? —Sí, voy a pedirlo.

Platos: la sopa de espárragos, el pan, las chuletas de cerdo, las patatas fritas, el café, el helado de vainilla

B. **Escenas en un restaurante.** The following description of a dinner out at a restaurant contains much repetition. Rephrase sentences, changing direct object nouns to pronouns as needed.

1. El camarero trae los vasos y pone los vasos en la mesa.
2. Luego trae el menú y los señores leen el menú.
3. ¿Los platos del día? Voy a explicar los platos del día ahora mismo.
4. Al señor le gusta el bistec y va a pedir el bistec.
5. La señora prefiere el pescado fresco pero no tienen pescado fresco hoy.

Follow-up B: *¿Qué come Ud. cuando está a dieta? ¿el helado? (→ No, no lo como.) ¿la ensalada? ¿los pasteles? ¿las papas fritas? ¿el pollo? ¿la piza? ¿el queso? ¿el pan?*

6. Ernestito, debes comer con el tenedor (*fork*). ¿Por qué no usas el tenedor?
7. El niño necesita tenedor y el camarero trae el tenedor.
8. Todos prefieren vino tinto. Por eso el señor pide vino tinto.
9. ¿La cuenta? El dueño está preparando la cuenta en este momento.
10. El señor quiere pagar con tarjeta de crédito pero no trae su tarjeta de crédito.
11. Por fin la señora toma la cuenta y paga la cuenta.

C. **Más invitaciones.** Con otro/a estudiante, haga y conteste preguntas según el modelo.

MODELO: comer en tu casa → —¿Cuándo me invitas a comer en tu casa?
—Te invito a comer el sábado.

1. cenar en tu casa
2. almorzar contigo
3. nadar en tu piscina (*pool*)
4. ver una película
5. ir contigo a la playa

Ahora repita el ejercicio en plural, según el modelo.

MODELO: comer en tu casa → —¿Cuando nos invitas a comer en tu casa?
—Los invito a comer el sábado.

Note CH: Reentry of *comí/comiste.*

CH. **¿Qué comiste anoche?** Con otro/a estudiante, haga y conteste preguntas según el modelo.

MODELO: tacos → —¿Comiste tacos anoche?
—Sí, los comí. (No, no los comí.)

1. jamón
2. zanahorias
3. papas fritas
4. salmón
5. enchiladas
6. helado

Note D7: *comprarla* (*el agua*, but fem.).

Suggestion D: Students write similar items and present them orally.

Variation D: *—Ya lo hice. ¡No vuelvo a (escribirla)!*

Variations E:
- Create context for each question: ***Modelo:*** *Los profesores son muy trabajadores. Trabajan mucho más que los estudiantes. ¿Creen Uds. eso?* **1.** *No vamos a tener el examen mañana. Lo vamos a tener hoy. ¿Prefieren Uds. eso?*
- Students create own brief contexts and questions and present them to the class. ***Modelo:*** *Mi hermana es artista de cine. ¿Creen Uds. eso?*

D. Your roommate (**compañero/a de cuarto**) is constantly suggesting things for you to do, but you've always just finished doing them. How will you respond to each of the following suggestions? Follow the model.

MODELO: —¿Por qué no escribes la composición para la clase de español?
—¡Porque *acabo de* escribirla!

1. ¿Por qué no estudias la lección ahora?
2. ¿Por qué no visitas el museo conmigo?
3. ¿Por qué no aprendes las palabras nuevas?
4. ¿Por qué no compras el periódico de hoy?
5. ¿Por qué no pagas las cervezas?
6. ¿Por qué no preparas las arvejas?
7. ¿Por qué no compras agua mineral?
8. ¿Por qué no me ayudas más?

E. **Situaciones.** Ud. y sus amigos están muy negativos hoy. ¿Cómo van a responder a las preguntas siguientes?

MODELO: ¿Creen Uds. eso? → ¡No, no lo creemos!

1. ¿Prefieren Uds. eso?
2. ¿Comprenden Uds. eso?
3. ¿Desean Uds. eso?
4. ¿Piensan Uds. eso?
5. ¿Aceptan Uds. eso?
6. ¿Esperan Uds. eso?

Conversación

Follow-up A: *Imagine que Ud. es el/la presidente/a de los Estados Unidos y puede invitar a cualquier* (any) *persona a la Casa Blanca. ¿A quién quiere Ud. invitar?* **Modelo:** *Quiero invitar a _____. Lo/La quiero conocer porque _____.*

- *Este sábado Ud. va a dar* (to have) *una fiesta y puede invitar a una persona famosa. ¿A quién va a invitar Ud.? Voy a invitar a _____. Lo/La quiero invitar porque _____.*
- *¿A quién va a llamar Ud. esta noche? ¿Por qué? Voy a llamar a _____. Necesito llamarlo/la porque _____. ¿Y quién lo/la va a llamar a Ud.? ¿Por qué? Creo que _____ me va a llamar. Necesita llamarme porque _____.*

A. **Preguntas**

1. ¿Quién lo/la invita a Ud. a... ? ¿A quién invita Ud. a... ?

   Actividades: cenar, tomar café, salir los sábados por la noche, bailar, ver una película, jugar al básquetbol, hacer un *picnic*

2. Todos necesitamos la ayuda (*help*) de alguien, ¿verdad? ¿Sus padres los ayudan a Uds.? (**Sí, nuestros padres...**) ¿Quién más los ayuda? ¿sus amigos? ¿sus compañeros de cuarto? ¿sus profesores? ¿sus consejeros? ¿sus _____?
3. Imagine que Ud. es un actor muy famoso (una actriz muy famosa)... ¡y muy vanidoso/a! ¿Qué cree Ud. que opinan de Ud. los demás? ¿Lo/La miran con envidia? ¿Lo/La admiran? ¿Lo/La quieren? ¿Lo/La escuchan con interés? ¿Lo/La adoran?

B. **Una encuesta sobre la comida.** Haga preguntas a sus compañeros de clase para saber si comen las comidas indicadas y con qué frecuencia. Deben explicar también por qué comen o *no* comen cierta comida.

MODELO: la carne →
—¿Comes carne?
—No la como casi nunca porque tiene mucho colesterol.

1. la carne
2. los mariscos
3. el yogur
4. la piza
5. las hamburguesas
6. el pollo
7. el café
8. el vino
9. el alcohol
10. el atún

Palabras útiles: la grasa (*fat*), el colesterol, las calorías, la cafeína, la salud (*health*), ser alérgico/a a, me pone (*it makes me*) nervioso/a, estar a dieta

Notas culturales: Meals in the Spanish-Speaking World

Hispanic eating habits are quite unlike those in the United States. Not only does the food itself differ somewhat, but the meals occur at different times.

There are three fundamental meals: **el desayuno**, **la comida/el almuerzo** (*midday meal*), and **la cena** (*supper*). Breakfast, which is eaten around seven or eight o'clock, is a very simple meal, frugal by most U.S. standards: **café con leche** or **chocolate** (*hot chocolate*) with a plain or sweet roll or toast; that is all. The **café con leche** is heated milk with very strong coffee to add flavor and color.

The main meal of the day, **la comida/el almuerzo**, is frequently eaten as late as two P.M., and it is a much heartier meal than the average U.S. lunch. It might consist of soup, a meat or fish dish with vegetables and potatoes or rice, a green salad, and then dessert (often fruit or cheese). Coffee is usually served after the meal.

The evening meal, **la cena**, is somewhat lighter than the noon meal. It is rarely eaten before eight o'clock, and in Spain is commonly served as late as ten or eleven P.M. Because the evening meal is served at such a late hour, it is customary to eat a light snack or **merienda** about five or six P.M. The **merienda** might consist of a sandwich or other snack with **café con leche** or **chocolate**. Similarly, a snack is often eaten in the morning between breakfast and the midday meal.

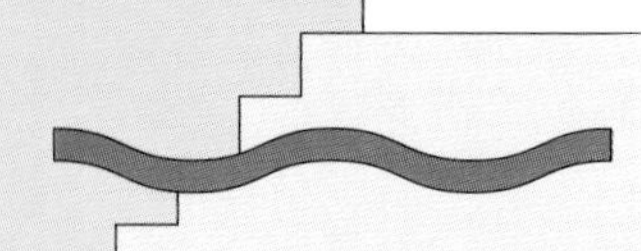

SITUACIONES

Situaciones: See IM for suggestions, additional exercises, and supplementary dialogues and exercises.

En un restaurante español

MANUEL: ¿Nos sentamos°? Creo que aquí se está° bien.
ANA MARÍA: Perfecto. Aquí viene el camarero. ¿Por qué no pides tú la cena ya que° conoces este restaurante?
CAMARERO: Buenas noches, señores. ¿Desean algo de aperitivo?
MANUEL: Para la señorita un vermut;° para mí un jerez.° Los trae con jamón, queso y anchoas,° por favor. ¿Y qué recomienda Ud. de comida?
CAMARERO: El solomillo a la parrilla° es la especialidad de la casa. Como plato del día hay paella°...
MANUEL: Bueno. De entrada, el gazpacho.° De plato fuerte,° el solomillo con patatas y guisantes.° Ensalada de lechuga y tomate. Y de postre, flan. Vino tinto y, al final, dos cafés.
ANA MARÍA: Manolo, basta° ya. ¡Estoy a dieta y he merendado más de la cuenta°!
MANUEL: Chica,* ¿qué importa? Luego vamos a bailar.

¿Nos... *Shall we sit down?* / se... *one is*
ya... *since*
vermouth / *sherry*
anchovies
solomillo... *grilled filet mignon*
Spanish dish of rice, seafood, often chicken; flavored with saffron
chilled tomato soup / plato... *main*
arvejas
enough / he... *I snacked more than I should have*

Notas comunicativas sobre el diálogo

Here are some useful words and expressions related to eating at home and in restaurants. You will be familiar with many of them already.

El camarero/La camarera:

¿Qué desea Ud. de entremés? ¿de plato principal? ¿de postre? ¿para beber?	*What would you like as an appetizer? as a main course? for dessert? to drink?*
¿Algo más?	*Something else?*

El/La cliente:

Favor de traerme un(a) _____. / ¿Me trae un(a) _____, por favor?	*Would you please bring me a _____?*
¿Qué recomienda Ud.?	*What do you recommend?*
Un(a) _____ más, por favor.	*One more _____, please.*
Psst. Oiga. Señor/Señorita.	Used to get a waiter's/waitress's attention. **Psst** is not used in formal settings.
La cuenta, por favor.	*The check, please.*

Palabras y frases útiles:

el tenedor, el cuchillo, la cuchara, la cucharita	*fork, knife, soup spoon, teaspoon*
Buen provecho.	*Enjoy your meal.*

*Note that Manolo calls Ana María **chica**. The words **chico/chica** (*boy/girl*) are commonly used in Spanish by friends of all ages.

¡Me muero de hambre!	*I'm starving. (I'm dying of hunger.)*
la especialidad de la casa	*specialty of the house*
el plato del día	*special of the day*
¿Nos sentamos?	*Shall we sit down?*

Conversación

Using the menu on page 203 and the **Situaciones** dialogue as a model, answer the following questions that a waiter/waitress would ask. Try to answer each question in several different ways.

MODELO: ¿Qué desea Ud. de postre? →

- Para mí, la fruta.
- Me trae un helado, por favor.
- Favor de traerme un helado.
- ¿Todavía hay flan?
- ¿Qué tal los pasteles?
- No deseo nada, gracias.

1. ¿Qué desean Uds. de entremés?
2. ¿Va a tomar sopa?
3. ¿Qué desea Ud. de plato principal?
4. ¿Y para beber?
5. ¿Qué quiere de postre?
6. ¿Prefiere Ud. té o café?

Now, with your instructor acting as waiter/waitress, order a meal as if you were at El Charro. (Pay close attention as your classmates act out the role of client. What would you have said?) You may want to include some, but not all, of the following common situations in your scene.

- You need ice for your Coke.
- Your spoon is dirty and you need another one.
- You want something that you don't see on the menu.
- There are items on the menu that you don't understand.

UN POCO DE TODO

A. Con un compañero (una compañera), haga y conteste las siguientes preguntas. Puede contestar negativa o afirmativamente. La persona que contesta debe añadir (*add*) más información, explicando la respuesta.

Para hablar de la clase y de los estudiantes

1. ¿Ves algo en la pizarra en este momento?
2. ¿Traes algunos libros a clase hoy?
3. ¿Ves a alguien nuevo en la clase?
4. ¿Sabes algo de la historia de Puerto Rico?
5. ¿Sabes algo de la comida de Sudamérica?
6. ¿Qué clase no vuelves a tomar nunca?

Para hablar de sus amigos

7. ¿Conoces a alguien de la Argentina? ¿de Cuba?
8. ¿Conoces a algunos atletas?
9. ¿Tienes algunos amigos de habla española?
10. ¿Acabas de conocer a alguien interesante?

B. **Hablando de comidas.** A friend is asking your advice about the following dishes. Answer, based on your actual eating habits. Use the model as a guide.

MODELO: las chuletas → —¿Qué tal las chuletas de aquí?
—No lo sé. Nunca las pido.
—¿Qué tal el pollo frito?
—¡Estupendo! ¡Riquísimo! Yo lo voy a pedir.

1. el bistec
2. la paella
3. las gambas al ajillo (*garlic sauce*)
4. el mole poblano (*turkey in spicy chocolate sauce*)
5. el atún a la parrilla (*grilled*)
6. los chiles rellenos
7. la sangría (*wine punch*)
8. el ceviche (*marinated raw fish*)

Note C: This activity will work well if students are given the questions on a ditto.

EL SUPERTEST

Las preguntas de nuestro Supertest de febrero son bastante fáciles. ¡Pon a prueba tus conocimientos y contesta rápidamente!

Enunciado	Sí	No
1. La mayor parte de la vitamina C de los vegetales se destruye al congelarlos........	☐	☐
2. Los atletas necesitan mucha proteina extra........	☐	☐
3. La sal engorda........	☐	☐
4. Los melocotones son una buena fuente de vitamina A........	☐	☐
5. Los aditivos alimentarios sirven para conservar sanos los alimentos........	☐	☐
6. El zumo de naranja tiene mucha vitamina C........	☐	☐
7. No es bueno comer muchos cereales........	☐	☐
8. De la soja se obtiene aceite y harina........	☐	☐
9. La vitamina A es esencial para los ojos........	☐	☐
10. Un zumo de limón, tomado antes del desayuno, adelgaza........	☐	☐

C. **¡Firma aquí, por favor!** Find someone in the class about whom the following descriptions are true; have that person sign his or her name.

MODELO: Conozco a mucha gente latina. →
—¿Conoces a mucha gente latina?
—¡Sí! Tengo amigos argentinos, bolivianos,...
—Firma (*Sign*) aquí, por favor.

	Nombres
1. Conozco a mucha gente latina.	________
2. Sé hablar *muy muy* bien el español.	________
3. No me gusta nada comer.	________
4. Nunca tengo muchas ganas de trabajar.	________
5. Siempre traigo mucho dinero a la clase.	________
6. Veo *Miami Vice* con frecuencia.	________
7. Conozco a una persona famosa, _____.	________
8. Oigo las noticias (*news*) en la radio; nunca las veo en la televisión.	________

CH. **Gustos y preferencias.** Survey some of the members of your class to determine their tastes and preferences in food. Tabulate the responses to find the most/least popular foods, restaurants, and so on.

1. ¿Prefieres cenar en casa, en un restaurante o en la cafetería estudiantil?
2. ¿Hay días en que no cenas?
3. ¿Prefieres comer una hamburguesa o un bistec con papas fritas?
4. ¿Prefieres comer en McDonald's (o en otro restaurante donde se sirve la comida rápidamente) o en un restaurante de lujo (*deluxe*)?

5. ¿Qué comes—y dónde—cuando tienes mucha prisa?
6. ¿Qué comes—y dónde—cuando tienes mucho dinero? ¿poco dinero?
7. ¿Qué plato comes con frecuencia? ¿Qué plato no comes nunca? ¿Qué plato comes solamente en casa de tus padres?
8. ¿Qué bebida prefieres?
9. Cuando tienes hambre a las tres de la tarde, ¿qué prefieres comer o beber? ¿Un yogur? ¿galletas y leche? ¿zanahorias? ¿un jugo de tomate? ¿chocolate? ¿un sándwich y una cerveza? ¿un pastel y un vaso de leche? ¿otra cosa?
10. ¿Qué comes cuando tienes hambre a las once de la noche?

D. **Comentarios de un camarero.** Complete the following paragraphs with the correct forms of the words in parentheses, as suggested by the context. When two possibilities are given in parentheses, select the correct word.

(Yo: *ser*/*estar*[1]) camarero en un excelente restaurante mexicano que se llama El Charro. El dueño del restaurante (*ser*/*estar*[2]) mi tío Rodrigo. (Él: *llegar*[3]) al restaurante cada° mañana (*son*/*a*[4]) las ocho en punto. (*Nada*/*Nunca*[5]) puede llegar tarde porque él tiene (*que*/*de*[6]) (*abrir*[7]) las puertas y (*hacer*[8]) los preparativos para el día. Entra en la oficina y (*cerrar*[9]) la puerta tan pronto como llega. Nunca lo (*yo: ver*[10]) salir antes de (*los*/*las*[11]) once y media.

every

Pasa tres horas y media (*preparar*[12]) el menú del día. Todo depende de° los productos disponibles° en el mercado. En primavera y verano, por ejemplo, hay más verduras y frutas frescas (*como*/*que*[13]) en las otras estaciones. Durante el otoño hay mucho guajolote° o carne de res.° Los vendedores° del mercado (*conocer*/*saber*[14]) que (*nosotros*/*nuestros*[15]) clientes esperan lo mejor° que hay.

on / *available*
turkey / carne... *beef*
merchants
lo... *the best*

Durante todas las estaciones del año (nosotros: *ofrecer*[16]) platos tradicionales de (*nuestro*[17]) país: tacos con salsa picante,° mole poblano, enchiladas de pollo, guacamole... (*Este*[18]) platos (*ser*/*estar*[19]) los favoritos de todos. Si los clientes (*ser*/*estar*[20]) satisfechos, nosotros (*ser*/*estar*[21]) contentos también.

hot, spicy

RESTAURANTE EL CHARRO

Desayuno (de 8:00 a 11:00) precio fijo —
Huevos rancheros (eggs with tomatoes, onions, and chiles) o Huevos con jamón
Frutas o jugo extra
Pan dulce o Pan tostado (Sweet rolls or toast)
Café Té chocolate

Comida (de 1:00 a 4:00) precio fijo —
Antojitos (appetizers):
Guacamole o cóctel de camarones (shrimp cocktail)
Sopas:
Sopa de albóndigas (meatball soup) o
Sopa de tortillas
Bebidas: Café Té Leche Refrescos
Agua mineral
Cerveza o vino (blanco, tinto o rosado) extra
Postres: Helado o pastel de chocolate
Platos fuertes (main courses):
• Tacos «El Charro» con salsa picante (hot sauce)
• Bistec con papas fritas
• Mole poblano de guajolote (turkey in a spicy sauce of chiles and chocolate)
• Pescado veracruzano (fish in a spicy sauce of tomatoes, chiles, onions and green olives)
Tortillas o Bolillos (rolls)

¿Probable o improbable?

1. Al camarero le gusta trabajar en el restaurante de su tío.
2. El camarero es un trabajador entusiasta.
3. El trabajo del dueño de un restaurante es muy duro (*hard*).
4. El restaurante de la historia es uno de los más baratos de la ciudad.
5. El menú es igual todos los días.

VOCABULARIO

Theme vocabulary previously listed as active: *el café*, *la cerveza*, *el refresco*. Also previously active: *algo*, *nunca*, *siempre*, *también*.

VERBOS

acabar de (+ *inf.*) to have just (*done something*)
ayudar to help
cenar to have dinner
cocinar to cook
conocer (**conozco**) to know, be acquainted with
desayunar to have breakfast
esperar to wait (for); to expect
llamar to call
nadar to swim
oír (*irreg.*) to hear
saber (*irreg.*) to know; to know how
traer (*irreg.*) to bring
ver (*irreg.*) to see
volver a (+ *inf.*) to do (*something*) again

LA COMIDA

el arroz rice
las arvejas peas
el atún tuna
la bebida drink; beverage
el bistec steak
los camarones shrimp
la carne meat
la chuleta (**de cerdo**) (pork) chop
el flan custard
el frijol bean
la galleta cookie
el helado ice cream
el huevo egg
el jamón ham
el jugo juice
la langosta lobster
la leche milk
la lechuga lettuce
la manzana apple
los mariscos shellfish
la naranja orange
el pan bread
la papa (**frita**) (French fried) potato
el pastel cake, pie
el pescado fish
el pollo chicken
el postre dessert
el queso cheese
la sopa soup
las verduras vegetables
el vino (**blanco**, **tinto**) (white, red) wine
la zanahoria carrot

COGNADOS

la banana, la ensalada, la fruta, la hamburguesa, el sándwich, el salmón, el té, el tomate

LAS COMIDAS

el almuerzo lunch
la cena dinner, supper
el desayuno breakfast

EN EL RESTAURANTE

el/la camarero/a waiter/waitress
la cuenta check, bill
el menú menu
el plato plate; dish

UTENSILIOS DE COMER

la cuchara spoon
la cucharita teaspoon
el cuchillo knife
el tenedor fork

OTROS SUSTANTIVOS

el/la compañero/a de cuarto roommate
el detalle detail
el/la dueño/a owner
la gente people
la pizarra blackboard
la respuesta answer

ADJETIVOS

algún (**alguno/a/os/as**) some, any
juntos/as together
ningún (**ninguno/a**) no, none, not any

PALABRAS ADICIONALES

a dieta (*with* **estar**) on a diet
alguien someone, anyone
fuera out (as in **cenar fuera**)
jamás never
nada nothing, not anything
nadie no one, nobody, not anybody
tampoco neither, not either

Frases útiles para la comunicación

tener (mucha) hambre	to be (very) hungry
tener (mucha) sed	to be (very) thirsty
comí, comiste, comió	I ate, you ate, he/she/it ate
¡me gusta muchísimo!	I like it a lot!
¡no me gusta (para) nada!	I don't like it at all!

OPTIONAL SECTION

UN PASO MÁS 6

A propósito... Shopping for Food in Hispanic Countries

Going shopping for food in a Spanish-speaking country can be quite different from shopping in the United States. In some cities you can go to a central **mercado**, where you can buy items from separate stands and also purchase prepared foods. Or you can go to small shops that specialize in separate items. **Las tiendas de comestibles** are somewhat similar to small U.S. grocery stores; there, canned and packaged goods are sold, along with fresh produce, beverages, and so on.

As you saw in **Capítulo 3** about clothing stores, the suffix **-ería** is often used to form the name of a store where something is sold: **el papel** → **la papelería**.

La Argentina

▲ Actividad A. De compras

Where would you go to buy the following food items?

MODELO: Para comprar leche, voy a una lechería.

1. carne
2. un pastel
3. nata (*whipped cream*)
4. huevos
5. jamón
6. una trucha (*trout*)
7. queso
8. vino
9. naranjas
10. arvejas
11. pan
12. agua mineral
13. sardinas enlatadas (*canned*)

a. una panadería
b. una pescadería
c. una lechería
ch. una carnicería
d. una pastelería
e. una frutería
f. una cervecería
g. una tienda de comestibles

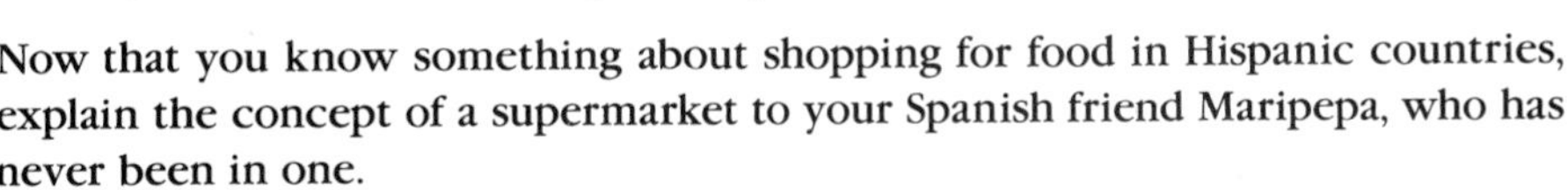

Now that you know something about shopping for food in Hispanic countries, explain the concept of a supermarket to your Spanish friend Maripepa, who has never been in one.

Palabras útiles: el supermercado, el departamento (*section*), el pasillo (*aisle*), el carrito (*cart*)

▲ Actividad B. Mi familia y la comida

Suggestion B: Divide students into groups and have them tabulate the answers to the questions. When groups are finished, share group results as a whole-class activity. It will help if you put a grid for the answers on the chalkboard. Example for Item 1:
1. *una vez*
   dos veces
   tres veces
   más
   hora: 8 9 10 11 12 1
   5 6 7 8 9

A la hora de comer, las costumbres (*habits*) de todas las familias son distintas. Conteste las siguientes preguntas sobre las costumbres de su familia. Luego se van a comparar las respuestas de todos para saber si en la clase hay algunas costumbres en común.

¡OJO! Se entiende (*It is understood*) que todas las preguntas se refieren a lo que (*what*) se acostumbra en general, aunque no necesariamente todos los días.

1. ¿Cuántas veces comen al día? ¿A qué hora?
2. ¿Comen juntos, a la misma (*same*) hora y en la misma mesa?
3. ¿Quién prepara la comida?
4. ¿Alguien sirve la comida o se sirve cada uno (*does everyone serve him/herself*)?
5. ¿Hablan mucho mientras (*while*) comen? ¿Quién habla más? ¿menos?
6. ¿Miran la televisión mientras comen?
7. ¿Qué bebidas toman con la cena?
8. ¿Cómo son los modales (*manners*) de todos? ¿muy correctos? ¿aceptables? ¿ordinarios (*average*)?
9. ¿Cómo son los modales de todos cuando hay invitados?
10. ¿Con qué frecuencia hay invitados para comer?

COMER VERDURA CRUDA

PARA preparar las verduras en crudo lo más importante es el lavado, pues hay que eliminar cualquier parásito o bichito. Las lechugas, escarolas, berros, etc., se ponen en un colador, bajo el chorro del agua fría, para quitarles la tierra. Luego, se inspecciona hoja por hoja y se lavan también al chorro. Se pican a continuación en un recipiente hondo lleno de agua con unas gostas de lejía –una gota por cada litro de agua– y se dejan un rato. La lejía es un desinfectante muy eficaz. Pasado este tiempo se escurre y se prepara como más guste. Las zanahorias crudas no necesitan ponerse en lejía, pues ya se pelan o raspan. Las verduras, una vez en casa, hay que consumirlas en el día o, a lo sumo, en dos. Conservarlas en la parte baja del frigorífico. También se pueden conservar en cacharros de plástico que cierren bien. En ellos, la lechuga limpia y lavada dura cuatro o cinco días.

▲ Actividad C. ¿Sopa fría?

Suggestions C:
- Try working through one or more scenes with your better students without letting them prepare a text ahead of time.
- Do as written exercise only.

The cartoon on the facing page elaborates on a theme typically found in "restaurant jokes." With one or more students, write a short dialogue that presents some problem related to meals; it may take place either in a restaurant or at home. Work up to the "critical moment," ending your dialogue as soon as you have presented a problem to be resolved. Present your dialogue to the other students in your class, who should then suggest as many solutions to the problem as they can. For the problem shown in the cartoon they might suggest:

—¿Sopa fría? Parece que está aún bastante templada°...

°bastante... *rather warm (lukewarm)*

- Los clientes pueden ir a otro restaurante.
- El camarero debe traer otro plato de sopa.
- Deben pedir otro plato, y no deben pagar la sopa.
- Los clientes pueden hablar con el dueño del restaurante.

You may base your skit on one of the following problems or on one of your own creation.

En un restaurante

1. Hay una mosca (*fly*) en mi sopa.
2. El camarero trae la cuenta; los clientes no pueden pagar.
3. Un violinista da un concierto al lado de la mesa de los clientes. Ellos quieren hablar; no quieren oír música. Además, el violinista toca muy mal.
4. El niño no come sus verduras pero sí pide postre.
5. El hijo (La hija) de la familia invita a unos amigos a comer. No hay bastante (*enough*) comida.

LECTURA CULTURAL

Lectura: See IM for suggestions and additional exercises and activities.

Antes de leer: Words with Multiple Meanings

It is easy to get "off the track" while reading if you assign the wrong meaning to a word that has multiple English equivalents. The word **como** can cause confusion because it can mean *how*, *like*, *the way that*, *as*, *since*, and *I eat*, depending on the context in which it occurs. Other common words with multiple meanings include **que** (*what*, *that*, *who*), **clase** (*class meeting*, *course*, *kind* or *type*), and **esperar** (*to wait for*, *to hope*, *to expect*).

You must rely on the context to determine which meaning is appropriate. Practice by telling what **como** means in each of the following sentences.

1. En España, como en Francia, se come mucho pescado.
2. No me gusta como habla el profesor; necesita hablar más despacio.
3. Como tú no deseas estudiar, ¿por qué no tomamos una cerveza?

Besides containing a number of words with multiple meanings, the following reading selection has some additional special characteristics. Each part of the selection is a separate **receta** (*recipe*) typical of a Hispanic country. The style of writing recipes varies in different parts of the Spanish-speaking world and from writer to writer. The recipes in this reading selection are authentic: the cook's style has not been changed!

Scan this vocabulary list before you begin the readings. You will not find all these words in the recipes in exactly the same form as in the list, but you should be able to infer the meaning of the words in most cases.

el aceite	*oil*	agregar	*to add*
el ají	*pepper*	apagar	*to turn off*
el ajo	*garlic*	cortar	*to cut*
la cebolla	*onion*	echar	*to add, put on*
la manteca	*lard, oil*	(es)polvorear	*to sprinkle*
la mantequilla	*butter*	freír	*to fry*
la nuez	*nut*	mezclar	*to mix, beat*
la papa	*potato*	picar	*to chop*
el plátano	*plantain*	rallar	*to grate*
		saltar	*to brown*
la charola	*casserole*	tapar	*to cover*
el horno	*oven*		
la olla	*pot*	doradito	*lightly browned*
el pedazo, pedacito	*piece, small piece*	duro	*hard*

Algunas recetas hispánicas

Suggestion: Ask students what verb form is generally used in recipes (command).

Receta A

$\frac{1}{2}$ taza mantequilla
$\frac{1}{2}$ taza manteca
1 cucharita vainilla
2 tazas harina
$\frac{3}{4}$ taza nueces picadas

Mezcla bien la mantequilla, la manteca y la vainilla. Añade la harina y las nueces. Forma bolitas; pon éstas en una charola sin grasa. Cocina en el horno a 425 grados por 10 minutos. Polvorea con azúcar mientras están calientes. Salen como 5 docenas, pero depende del tamaño.

María Luisa Valencia, México

Receta B

1 kg de carne picada
1 cebolla grande
perejil (un poco)
1 diente de ajo
2 huevos duros
1 ají verde
$\frac{1}{2}$ taza de pasas de uva (opcional)
5 papas medianas
sal
ají molido
orégano
queso rallado (un poco)

Saltar la cebolla en aceite, agregar el ají verde cortado en pedacitos, el diente de ajo picado y el perejil picado. Saltar estos ingredientes. Agregarles la carne y saltarla un poco con lo anterior, no muy cocinada. Condimentar a gusto.

Agregar los huevos duros picados y las pasas de uva. Tapar la olla para que la carne suelte jugo un ratito y apagar el fuego.

Poner la preparación en un molde de 3 o 4 centímetros de alto y echar sobre ésta las papas hechas puré.

Espolvorearlo con queso rallado. Colocar la preparación en el horno ya caliente por unos 10 minutos.

Marianela Chaumiel, Argentina

Receta C

2 plátanos verdes aceite o manteca sal	Pele los plátanos y córtelos en tajadas delgadas. Caliente el aceite o la manteca hasta que esté bien caliente y fría las tajadas de plátano hasta que estén doraditas. Sáquelas y écheles sal a su gusto. María Sabló-Yates, Panamá

Comprensión

A. ¿A qué categoría general pertenecen (*belong*) estas recetas?

_____ un plato principal _____ un postre
_____ una tapa o entremés (*appetizer*) _____ una ensalada

B. Busque el equivalente en español de estas palabras inglesas.

1. salt (*noun*)
2. to season
3. heat, flame
4. hot (*temperature*)
5. to peel
6. to one's taste
7. slice (*noun*)
8. little balls
9. to put (*not* **poner**)
10. fry (*command*)
11. cup

Para escribir

A. Create your own composition about eating and drinking habits in the United States by completing the sentences of the following paragraph.

En los Estados Unidos la gente no da (*give*) gran importancia a las comidas. La vida norteamericana es tan rápida que _____. Muchas veces el padre o la madre _____ y no puede _____. También los niños _____. Por eso cada miembro de la familia norteamericana _____.

B. Write a brief paragraph about your eating preferences or those of your family. Use the following questions as a guide in developing your paragraph. You may also wish to refer to the questions in **Actividad B**.

1. ¿Cuántas veces comen al día? ¿A qué horas?
2. ¿Comen juntos?
3. ¿Quién(es) prepara(n) la comida?
4. ¿Qué prepara(n)? ¿Es excelente la comida? ¿buena? ¿mala? ¿regular?
5. ¿Qué comida prefieren cuando comen en un restaurante? ¿comida china? ¿mexicana? ¿italiana? ¿hamburguesas? ¿En qué restaurantes comen?
6. ¿Comen allí con frecuencia? ¿Cuántas veces al año? ¿Cuándo van a volver?

REPASO 2

OPTIONAL SECTION

VOCES DEL MUNDO HISPÁNICO

Note: Corresponding chapters of the Workbook and the Laboratory Manual offer focused vocabulary and grammar activities.

Repaso 2: See IM for detailed suggestions for handling *Entrevistas*, *Situaciones*, and the specific *Voces* sections.

LOS HISPANOS EN LOS ESTADOS UNIDOS
La comunidad mexicanoamericana

La gran mayoría de los mexicanoamericanos viven a lo largo de (*along*) la frontera (*border*) de los Estados Unidos y México—de Texas a California—y también en otros estados del oeste. Los antepasados (*ancestors*) de algunos fueron (*were*) los dueños de estos territorios muchos años antes de que llegaran (*arrived*) los anglosajones. De hecho (*In fact*), la patria (*motherland*) legendaria de los aztecas, la «tierra blanca» de Aztlán, hoy forma parte del sudoeste de los Estados Unidos. La frontera es solamente una línea artificial para la gente de la región fronteriza; es una realidad política, pero no divide dos pueblos.

SUSANA RENDON

Presidenta y Directora del Consejo Ejecutivo, Empresas Rendon Ltda. Publicidad/Promociones/ Mercadotecnia° — *Marketing*

Northwestern Univ., Evanston, Ill.

Comenzó° su trayectoria profesional como ingeniera en la industria de la televisión, 1976 - Publicista de TV — *She began*

Primera Ingeniera Telefónica con licencia de FCC

Fundó REL en 1982.

Miembro de la Asociación Latina de Negocios,° Cámara° de Comercio Hispano-Americana, Consejo Consultor de la Asociación México-Americana de Almacenes, Club de Publicidad de Los Angeles, y Consulado de la Archidiócesis de Los Angeles, Parroquia San Vicente. — *Businesseses / Chamber*

La tradición oral: Refranes y adivinanzas (*riddles*)

- Plata° no es. Oro° no es. ¿Qué es? — *Silver / Gold*
- A buen hambre, no hay pan duro.
- Más vale un hoy que diez mañanas.

Unos niños juegan con una piñata en Texas.

Las Posadas, San Antonio, Texas

Las posadas:° Una tradición navideña — *inn, lodging*

¿Quién les da° posada — *les... gives*
a estos peregrinos,° — *pilgrims*
que vienen cansados
de andar caminos°? — *andar... walking the roads*

Una ninã mexicanoamericana, Austin, Texas

Dos tradiciones... y ahora una tercera (*third*)

Yo soy hijo de la tierra,
y heredero° de la raza°; *heir / Spanish-speaking people*
tengo rasgos° de españoles *traces*
y de aztecas en mi alma.° *soul*

Mario A. Benítez, poeta chicano, «Yo soy hijo de la tierra»

César Chávez

¡Viva la Causa! ¡Viva la Raza! ¡Viva la UFWA (*United Farm Workers Association*)!

De colores, de colores se visten° los campos° en la primavera — se... *dress* / *fields*
De colores, de colores son los pajaritos° — *little birds*
que vienen de afuera
De colores, de colores es el arco iris° — arco... *rainbow*
que vemos lucir° — *to shine*
Y por eso los grandes amores de muchos colores me gustan a mí.

«Cuando el sol se baja° y los bolillos° dejan° sus tiendas, el pueblo americano se duerme para no despertar° hasta el día siguiente. (se... *sets* / *Anglos* / *leave*; to wake up)

Cuando el sol se baja y la gente ha cenado,° el pueblo mexicano se aviva y se oyen las voces del barrio: la gente mayor, los jóvenes, los chicos, los perros... (ha... *have had dinner*)

El barrio puede llamarse el Rebaje, el de las Conchas, el Cantarranas, el Rincón del Diablo, el Pueblo Mexicano—verdaderamente los títulos importan poco.

Lo importante, como siempre, es la gente.

Rolando Hinojosa, «Voces del barrio»

«Cake-Walk», de Carmen Lomas Garza, pintora mexicano-americana de Kingsville, Texas, que ahora vive en San Francisco

Richard "Cheech" Marin

Richard «Cheech» Marin, actor, cómico, director de cine y de vídeo; su última película es «Nacido (*Born*) en el este de Los Ángeles».

«Nacido en el este de Los Ángeles» es una parodia del éxito de Bruce Springsteen «Nacido en Los Estados Unidos». Y está basada en un incidente verdadero que ocurrió en 1984 cuando un ciudadano americano de ascendencia mexicana fue aprehendido en una redada de migra (*immigration raid*) y fue deportado a México por no tener ningún documento de identificación.

CHEECH: «[En "Nacido en el este de Los Ángeles"] Sólo estoy presentándolas [cuestiones] para que la gente tome sus propias (*own*) decisiones. Estas cuestiones no son tan claras como lo blanco y lo negro. Alguna gente del I.N.S. (*Immigration and Naturalization Service*) es buena y otra no tanto, y algunos se quedan (*are*) atrapados entre la espada y la pared (*a rock and a hard place*).»

Américas 2001

Entrevista: Focus: Using regular, irregular, and stem-changing verbs, as well as using models (*ir a*, *acabar de*, etc.); pronouns and possessives.

ENTREVISTA

In the last three chapters of ***Puntos de partida***, you have continued to practice asking questions, and the number of topics you can discuss in Spanish has increased dramatically. This activity will help you review the major topics you have worked with so far.

First, read over the following topics and think about what your answers will be when someone asks you questions about them in Spanish. You may want to jot down things to say or additional points to raise about the same questions. Then find someone in the class with whom you have spoken only infrequently and interview him or her based on these topics. Finally, organize the information you have learned about your classmate into a brief presentation.

Hint: Remember to use **te gusta** + *infinitive* to ask what someone likes to do. Answer using **me gusta** + *infinitive*. When you describe what the person you interviewed has told you, use this structure: **a (nombre) le gusta** + *infinitive*.

Aspectos de la vida social

1. si es casado/a o soltero/a
2. para los casados: cuánto tiempo tiene de casado/a
   si tiene hijos y cuántos
   algunos datos sobre su esposo/a
   para los solteros: si tiene o busca novio/a
   algunos datos sobre su novio/a (verdadero [*real*] o ideal)
   si la cosa va en serio
3. el nombre de su mejor amigo
4. qué actividad(es) prefiere hacer con sus amigos
5. adónde va con sus amigos con frecuencia
6. el nombre de una persona que para él/ella es muy especial y por qué (lo/la admira mucho, lo/la quiere [*loves*] mucho, etcétera)
7. el nombre de una persona interesante a quien acaba de conocer

Aspectos temporales

8. cuándo es su cumpleaños
9. cuál es su estación favorita y por qué
10. una cosa que hace en cada (*each*) estación del año
11. adónde quiere hacer un viaje algún día y por qué

Aspectos culinarios

12. la clase de comida que prefiere cuando come fuera
13. la clase de comida que prefiere cuando come en casa
14. una cosa que comió una vez y que no va a volver a comer nunca
15. el nombre de su restaurante favorito y el del plato que prefiere allí
16. si le gusta probar (*to try*) comidas exóticas

SITUACIONES PRÁCTICAS

Listen as your instructor role-plays some of the following situations with one or more students. Pay close attention to how your classmates interact with your instructor to see if you would have said or done the same thing. You may have to make some educated guesses about what your instructor says as he or she plays the situation. After you have watched each of the situations at least once, act out the situations with another student. Try to use as much as possible of the vocabulary that you know.

1. You meet someone at a college party and learn that she is a graduate of your high school (**Me gradué en... ¿Cuándo te graduaste?**). It's possible that you know many of the same people. Ask each other questions about teachers and students at your high school.
2. You go to a French/Mexican/American restaurant. The other student will take the role of waiter. Ask for a table near a window (**ventana**), away from the kitchen (**cocina**), and order a meal.
3. You have become friendly in class with another person, but you have never dated him. Now you want to invite him to a party at your dormitory or home next Saturday night. Arrange a time and place to meet and discuss the kind of clothing to wear.
4. You are a travel agent (**un[a] agente de viajes**) in the northern part of Spain. A customer comes to you in January asking for information about the weather in New York, Buenos Aires, and Acapulco.

CAPÍTULO SIETE

DE VACACIONES

Acapulco, México

▲ **¡Por fin[a] estamos de vacaciones!**

—¿Cuántos días te dan de vacaciones?

—Este año, tres semanas.

—¿Vas a ir a algún lugar?

—¡Claro! Es posible que vayamos a la playa.

[a]Por... *Finally*

• See also  and 

VOCABULARIO: PREPARACIÓN

• See model for vocabulary presentation and other materials in Supplementary *Vocabulario: Preparación* Materials, chapter by chapter, IM.

Vocabulario: Preparación:
• See detailed supplementary materials and exercises for this section bound into the back of this Annotated Instructor's Edition.

¡Vamos de vacaciones! ¡Buen viaje!

Ir en avión

el aeropuerto	airport
la azafata	female flight attendant
el/la camarero/a	flight attendant
la sala de espera	waiting room
la sección de (no) fumar	(non)smoking section
el vuelo	flight

Ir en tren/en autobús/en barco

el barco	boat
la cabina	cabin
la estación	station
del tren	train station
de autobuses	bus station
el maletero	porter

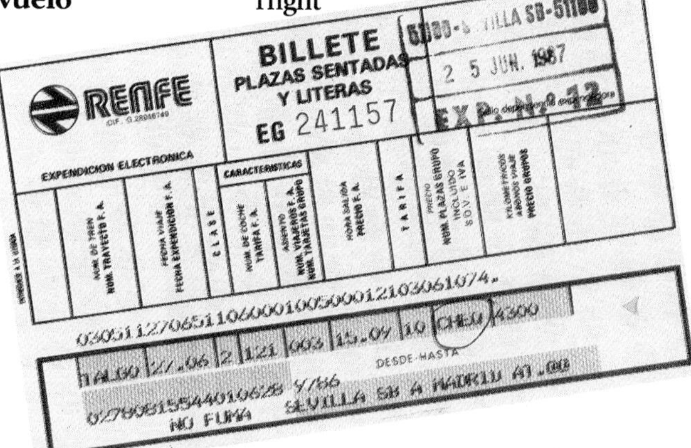

Vamos a hacer un viaje

el asiento	seat
el billete/el boleto*	ticket
de ida	one-way
de ida y vuelta	round-trip
la demora	delay
la llegada	arrival
el pasaje	passage, ticket
el/la pasajero/a	passenger
la salida	departure

bajar (de)	to get down (from, off of)
estar atrasado/a	to be late
facturar el equipaje	to check one's bags
guardar (un puesto)	to watch over; to save (a place)
hacer cola	to stand in line
hacer escalas	to make stops
hacer la(s) maleta(s)	to pack one's suitcase(s)
ir/estar de vacaciones	to go/be on vacation
subir (a)	to go up; to get on (*a vehicle*)

*Throughout Spanish America, **boleto** is the word used for a *ticket for travel.* **Billete** is commonly used in Spain. The words **entrada** and **localidad** are used to refer to tickets for movies, plays, or similar functions.

A. Ud. va a hacer un viaje en avión. El vuelo sale a las siete de la mañana. Usando los números 1 a 9, indique en qué orden van a pasar las siguientes cosas.

_____ Subo al avión.
_____ Voy a la sala de espera.
_____ Hago cola para comprar el boleto de ida y vuelta y facturar el equipaje.
_____ Llego al aeropuerto a tiempo (*on time*) y bajo del taxi.
_____ Por fin se anuncia la salida del vuelo.
_____ Estoy atrasado/a. Salgo para el aeropuerto en taxi.
_____ La azafata me indica el asiento.
_____ Pido asiento en la sección de no fumar.
_____ Hay demora. Por eso todos tenemos que esperar el vuelo allí antes de subir al avión.

B. ¿Qué va Ud. a hacer en estas situaciones?

Variation B: Situations may be used as starting points for mini-role playing.

1. Ud. no tiene mucho dinero. Si tiene que viajar, ¿qué clase de pasaje va a comprar?
   a. clase turística b. primera clase c. un pasaje en la sección de fumar
2. Ud. quiere pedir dos asientos juntos—uno para Ud., el otro para su amigo/a. Él/Ella tiene alergia a los cigarrillos (*cigarettes*). ¿Qué pide Ud.?
   a. Dos boletos, sección de fumar, por favor.
   b. Dos pasajes, sin escala, por favor.
   c. Dos asientos, sección de no fumar, por favor.
3. Ud. es una persona muy nerviosa y tiene miedo de viajar en avión. Necesita ir desde Nueva York a Madrid. ¿Qué pide Ud.?
   a. una cabina en un barco
   b. un vuelo sin escalas
   c. un boleto de tren
4. Ud. tiene muchas maletas. Pesan (*They weigh*) mucho y no puede llevarlas. ¿Qué hace Ud.?
   a. Compro boletos. b. Guardo un asiento. c. Facturo el equipaje.
5. Su vuelo está atrasado, pero Ud. está tranquilo/a. ¿Qué dice Ud. (*do you say*)?
   a. Azafata, insisto en hablar con el capitán.
   b. Una demora más... no importa.
   c. Si no salimos dentro de (*within*) diez minutos, bajo del avión.

C. ¿Cuántas cosas y acciones puede Ud. identificar o describir en este dibujo?

Suggestion C: Do as whole-class activity or as whole-class composition, with you or a student writing sentences on the board.

Extension CH: 8. *Con frecuencia, sus padres le pagan el boleto.* 9. *Le gusta tomar varios cocteles durante el vuelo.*

Follow-up CH:

- Imagine you want to take a trip to visit a friend during vacation. You need to call a travel agency to get information. What are some questions you might ask?
- You are working in a travel agency; person who speaks Spanish (but very little English) calls to book flight. What questions might you ask person to make sure he/she gets ticket for right flight?

CH. ¿A quién se describe, a don Gregorio, vicepresidente de la IBM, o a Harry, típico estudiante universitario?

1. Siempre viaja en clase turística porque es más económica.
2. No le (*to him*) importan nada las demoras; no tiene prisa.
3. Nunca hace cola para comprar el boleto porque su secretaria le arregla (*arranges for him*) todo el viaje.
4. Cuando viaja en avión, es porque está de vacaciones.
5. Por lo general, prefiere viajar en tren porque es más económico.
6. Muchas veces no lleva equipaje porque hace viajes de un solo día.
7. Siempre que (*Whenever*) viaja, lleva traje y corbata.

Notas comunicativas: Hablando de los viajes

Here are a few phrases that will enable you to talk about some aspects of trips you have taken in the past.

¿Adónde fuiste/fue (el verano pasado)?	*Where did you go (last summer)?*
Fui a...	*I went to . . .*
¿Adónde (¿Cómo) has/ha viajado?	*Where (How) have you traveled?*
He viajado a/en...	*I've traveled to/in . . .*

Extension D: *¿Cómo reacciona Ud. cuando hay una demora de treinta minutos? ¿Está furioso/a? ¿irritado/a? ¿indiferente? ¿Y cuando hay una demora de una hora?*

Lo que no debe hacer durante el verano: dejar que se le acumule el correo, mantener el garaje abierto, dejar cubos de basura vacíos a la puerta de su vivienda, dejar ventanas y persianas abiertas, fijar notas o avisos en la puerta de su domicilio, olvidar una escalera de mano fuera de la casa.

D. **Preguntas**

1. Por lo general, ¿cuándo está Ud. de vacaciones? ¿en invierno? ¿en verano? En las vacaciones, ¿le gusta viajar o prefiere no salir de su ciudad? ¿Le gusta ir de vacaciones con su familia? ¿Prefiere ir solo/a, con un amigo (una amiga) o con un grupo de personas?
2. ¿Cuáles son las actividades que Ud. normalmente asocia con las vacaciones? ¿En qué mes fue de vacaciones el año pasado? ¿Adónde fue? ¿Con quién(es) fue?
3. De los medios de transporte mencionados en **¡Vamos de vacaciones!**, ¿cuáles conoce Ud. personalmente? Conteste usando esta oración: He viajado en (avión, tren, autobús, barco, coche). De estos medios de transporte, ¿cuál es el más rápido? ¿el más económico? ¿Cuáles hacen más escalas o paran (*stop*) con más frecuencia? ¿Cómo prefiere Ud. viajar?

Follow-up: Discussion: 1. *Es peligroso* (dangerous) *volar.* 2. *Las personas que fuman son la parte más molestosa de los vuelos largos.* 3. *Es mejor viajar en primera clase.* 4. *Es más interesante viajar por la noche.* 5. *Me gusta cuando hay niños en el vuelo.* 6. *Es buena idea ver la película durante un vuelo largo.*

4. Imagine que Ud. va a viajar en avión. ¿Pide primera clase o clase turística? ¿Por qué? ¿Pide asiento en la sección de fumar o en la de no fumar? ¿Pide asiento en la cola (*tail*) o lo más adelante posible (*as far up front as possible*)? ¿Cómo paga el pasaje? ¿con cheque? ¿con tarjeta de crédito? ¿Paga al contado (*cash*)? Imagine que la aerolínea pierde su equipaje. ¿Cómo reacciona Ud.?
5. Por lo general, cuando Ud. viaja en avión (tren, autobús), ¿cómo pasa el tiempo durante el viaje? ¿Habla con los otros pasajeros? ¿Lee? ¿Duerme? ¿Mira el paisaje (*scenery*)? ¿Trabaja? ¿Estudia? ¿Escribe cartas? ¿Mira la película? ¿Escucha música?

Nueva York

Notas lingüísticas: *¿Cómo se dice... ?*—Impersonal *se*

Se estudia mucho aquí, ¿verdad? *You (They) study a lot here, right?*

In English several subjects—*you, one, people, they*—can refer to people in general instead of to one person in particular. In Spanish these impersonal subjects are commonly expressed by using the word **se** followed by the third person singular of the verb.* There is no expressed subject.

A. **Situaciones.** ¿Qué se hace (*is done*) y qué no se hace en... ? Conteste con un compañero (una compañera).

MODELO: la biblioteca →
—En la biblioteca, se estudia, se lee... No se habla en voz alta (*loudly*), ...
—Tienes razón. Tampoco se come en la biblioteca.

1. la clase de español
2. un mercado al aire libre
3. un avión
4. una discoteca
5. una tienda de ropa
6. una fiesta
7. la calle (caminar [*to walk*])
8. la cafetería de los estudiantes

B. Se usa la expresión **¿Cómo se dice...?** cuando se quiere aprender una palabra nueva. Repase Ud. (*Review*) el vocabulario nuevo de esta lección, preguntando a las otras personas de la clase, **¿Cómo se dice ____ en inglés?** o **¿Cómo se dice ____ en español?**

***Se habla español aquí** is a similar construction: *Spanish is spoken here; One speaks Spanish here.*

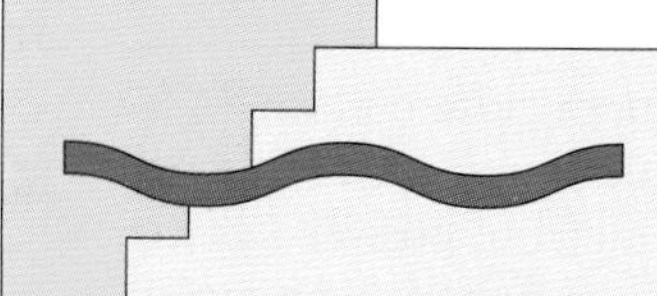

MINIDIÁLOGOS Y GRAMÁTICA

Note: Direct object pronouns were presented in preceding chapter. Review briefly with exercise similar to Option A (*Vocabulario: Preparación*, this chapter).

22. EXPRESSING *TO WHOM* OR *FOR WHOM*
Indirect Object Pronouns; *dar* and *decir*

En la sala de espera del aeropuerto

HIJO: Mamá, tengo hambre. ¿*Me das* un caramelo?
MAMÁ: No, hijo. No *te* voy a *dar* un caramelo. Acabas de comer.
HIJO: Mamá, quiero leer. ¿*Me* compras un librito?
MAMÁ: No, no *te* voy a comprar más libros. Ya tienes tres.
HIJO: Mamá...
MAMÁ: No, hijo. Te quiero mucho, pero no *te doy* nada más.
HIJO: Pero mamá...
MAMÁ: ¡*Te digo* que no!
HIJO: Pero mamá, ¿no oyes? ¡Acaban de anunciar nuestro vuelo!

¿Qué dicen el niño y su mamá, **me** o **te**?

Point out: *me/te* → to me/you, *nos* → from us in mini.

EL NIÑO:	LA MAMÁ:
1. ¿_____ das un caramelo?	No, no _____ doy más dulces (*sweets*).
2. ¿_____ compras un librito?	No, no _____ voy a comprar nada más.
3. ¿_____ quieres mucho?	¡Claro que _____ quiero!, pero _____ haces demasiadas preguntas.

Indirect Object Pronouns

Follow-up: Summarize and invent information about mini. **1.** *¿Quiénes son las personas que hablan?* **2.** *¿Dónde están?* **3.** *¿Son pasajeros o esperan la llegada de un vuelo? ¿Cómo sabe Ud. eso? ¿Cuánto tiempo hace que esperan?* **4.** *¿Qué está haciendo el niño?* **5.** *En su opinión, ¿es un niño típico? ¿Por qué sí o por qué no?* **6.** *Y su madre, ¿es una mamá típica?*

me	*to, for me*	**nos**	*to, for us*
te	*to, for you* (fam. sing.)	**os**	*to, for you* (fam. pl.)
le	*to, for you* (form. sing.), *him, her, it*	**les**	*to, for you* (form. pl.), *them*

Point out: IO pronouns have the same form as DO pronouns except in third-person singular and plural: *le* and *les*. Gender is not reflected in third-person IO pronouns.

A. *Indirect object* nouns and pronouns usually answer the questions *to whom?* or *for whom?* in relation to the verb. The word *to* is frequently omitted in English. Note that indirect object pronouns have the same form as direct object pronouns, except in the third person: **le, les**.

In the airport waiting room SON: Mom, I'm hungry. Will you give me a piece of candy? MOM: No, son. I will not give you a piece of candy. You just ate. SON: Mom, I want to read. Will you buy me a little book? MOM: No, I'm not going to buy you any more books. You already have three. SON: Mom . . . MOM: No, son. I love you a lot, but I'm not giving you anything else. SON: But Mom . . . MOM: I'm telling you no! SON: But Mom, don't you hear? They've just announced our flight!

Suggestion: Illustrate concept of indirect object by suggesting that student has asked you to hit other student for him/her. Pretend to hit student: I hit John for Tom. Ask, Who is directly affected? → John, direct object. Who is indirectly affected (indirectly benefits from action)? → Tom, indirect object.

Note: DO and IO pronouns are not used together until Grammar Section 27 (Ch. 8).

Indicate the direct and indirect objects in the following sentences.

1. I'm giving her the present tomorrow.
2. Could you tell me the answer now?
3. El profesor nos va a hacer algunas preguntas.
4. ¿No me compras el librito ahora?

B. Like direct object pronouns, *indirect object pronouns* (**los pronombres del complemento indirecto**) are placed immediately before a conjugated verb. They may be attached to a present participle—with the addition of an accent mark—or to an infinitive.

No, no **te** presto el coche.	*No, I won't lend you the car.*
Están facturándo**me** el equipaje. **Me** están facturando el equipaje.	*They're checking my bags for me.*
Voy a guardar**te** el asiento. **Te** voy a guardar el asiento.	*I'll save your seat for you.*

C. Since **le** and **les** have several different equivalents, their meaning is often clarified or emphasized with the preposition **a** and the pronoun objects of prepositions (see **Las preposiciones, Capítulo 4**).

Emphasis: Use of seemingly redundant *le*(*s*) with *a* + noun/pronoun is norm rather than exception. In general, *le*(*s*) is obligatory and *a* + noun/pronoun optional, even though it conveys more information than *le*(*s*).

Voy a mandar**le** un telegrama **a Ud.** (**a él, a ella**).	*I'm going to send you* (*him, her*) *a telegram.*
Estoy haciéndo**les** una comida **a Uds.** (**a ellos, a ellas**).	*I'm making you* (*them*) *a meal.*

CH. When there is an indirect object noun in a sentence, the indirect object pronoun is almost always used in addition. This construction is very common in Spanish.

Vamos a decir**le** la verdad **a Juan.**	*Let's tell Juan the truth.*
¿**Les** guardo los asientos **a Jorge y Marta**?	*Shall I save the seats for Jorge and Marta?*

D. Verbs frequently used with indirect objects include **dar** (*to give*), **decir** (*to say; to tell*), **escribir**, **explicar**, **hablar**, **mandar**, **pedir**, **preguntar** (*to ask*), **prestar**, **regalar** (*to give as a gift*), and **servir**.

Optional: *contar* (*ue*), *permitir.*

Dar and *decir*

Note: Introduction of *dar* and *decir* has been delayed so these verbs could be used naturally, with IO pronouns.

Point out: irregular *yo* form of *dar*; *-g-* in *yo* form of *decir* plus similarity to stem-changing verbs

dar (*to give*)		**decir** (*to say; to tell*)	
doy	damos	digo	decimos
das	dais	dices	decís
da	dan	dice	dicen
dando		diciendo	

Dar and **decir** are almost always used with indirect object pronouns in Spanish.

¿Cuándo **me das** el dinero?	*When will you give me the money?*
¿Por qué no **me dice** Ud. la verdad, señor?	*Why don't you tell me the truth, sir?*

¡OJO! In Spanish it is necessary to distinguish between the verbs **dar** (*to give*) and **regalar** (*to give as a gift*). Do not confuse **decir** (*to say* or *to tell*) with **hablar** (*to speak*).

Emphasis: *dar* vs. *regalar; decir* vs. *hablar* (*charlar*)

Preliminary exercises (speaking):

- *De vacaciones con los amigos. Dé oraciones nuevas según las indicaciones.* **1.** *Les escribo tarjetas postales a mis padres.* (*a ti, a Ud., a Andrés, a Uds., a Alicia, a vosotros*) **2.** *Ahora estoy comprándole un recuerdo a Jorge.* (*a Sergio, a ti, a Eva, a Uds., a Martín y Rosa, a vosotros*) **3.** *El conductor le dice la hora de la llegada.* (*yo, ellos, tú, nosotros, Uds.*) **4.** *Juan le da el billete, ¿verdad?* (*tú, nosotros, yo, Uds., ellas*)
- Act out with students: *¿Ud. me da el libro? ¿Ud. nos da el dinero* (student standing with you)? *¿Uds. me dicen siempre la verdad? ¿la hora? ¿las respuestas correctas? ¿Yo les digo siempre la fecha de los exámenes? ¿la tarea* (homework) *para mañana? ¿cosas interesantes sobre la cultura hispánica?*

Variations A:

- Repeat the same items, using *les... a los* (*clientes, estudiantes*).
- Students do items in pairs, asking questions based on the cue items: *¿Quién te trae el menú?* (*El camarero me...*)

Práctica

A. **¿Quién te... ?** Who does the following things for you? Follow the model.

MODELO: En el restaurante: traer el menú (camarero) →
En el restaurante, el camarero **me** trae el menú.

1. En el restaurante: traer el menú (camarero), explicar los platos del día (camarero), preparar la comida (cocinero [*cook*]), servir la comida (camarero), dar la cuenta (dueño)
2. En clase: explicar la gramática (profesor[a]), hacer preguntas (otros estudiantes), dar exámenes (profesor[a]), prestar un lápiz o un papel (un compañero)

Now repeat the same items, using **nos**: **En el restaurante, el camarero *nos* trae el menú.**

B. Your friends the Padillas, from Guatemala, need help arranging for and getting on their flight back home. Explain how you will help them, using the cues as a guide.

MODELO: comprar el boleto → Les compro el boleto.

1. llamar un taxi
2. bajar (*to carry down*) las maletas
3. guardar el equipaje
4. facturar el equipaje
5. guardar el puesto en la cola
6. guardar el asiento en la sala de espera
7. buscar el pasaporte
8. por fin decir adiós

Now explain the same sequence of actions as if you were talking about your friend Guillermo: ***Le* compro el boleto.** Then tell your friend Guadalupe how you will help her: ***Te* compro el boleto.**

C. **¿Qué va a pasar?** Dé varias respuestas.

Palabras útiles: medicinas, Santa Claus, tarjetas navideñas (*Christmas cards*), flores (*flowers*), juguetes (*toys*)

1. Su amiga Elena está en el hospital con un ataque de apendicitis. Todos le mandan... Le escriben... Las enfermeras (*nurses*) le dan... De comer, le sirven...

2. Es Navidad. Los niños les prometen (*promise*) a sus padres... Les piden... También le escriben... Le piden... Los padres les mandan... a sus amigos. Les regalan...
3. Hay una demora y el avión no despega (*takes off*) a tiempo. La azafata nos sirve... El camarero nos ofrece... El piloto nos dice...
4. Mi coche no funciona hoy. Mi amigo me presta... Mis padres me preguntan... Luego me dan...
5. Es la última semana de clases y hay exámenes finales la próxima semana. En la clase de computación, todos le preguntan al profesor... El profesor les explica a los estudiantes...

Follow-up CH: Ask questions based on the story. Students answer as if they were *Benjamín*.

CH. Your little cousin Benjamín has never eaten in a restaurant before. Explain to him what will happen, filling in the blanks with the appropriate indirect object pronoun.

Primero el camarero _____ indica una mesa desocupada. Luego tú _____ pides el menú al camarero. También _____ haces preguntas sobre los platos y las especialidades de la casa y _____ dices tus preferencias. El camarero _____ trae la comida. Por fin papá _____ pide la cuenta al camarero. Si tú quieres pagar, _____ pides dinero a papá y _____ das el dinero al camarero.

Conversación

A. **Dos fiestas.** Describa las escenas que se ven en los dibujos, añadiendo todos los detalles que pueda. Por ejemplo, puede explicar por qué cada persona escogió (*chose*) su regalo.

1. Hoy es el cumpleaños de Marcos. ¿Qué le dice Ud. (a él)? ¿Qué le regala Julio? ¿Por qué? ¿Qué le regala Ana? ¿Ernesto? ¿María? ¿Qué les dice Marcos a todos? ¿Le da Ud. algunos regalos a Marcos? ¿Por qué no? ¿No lo conoce Ud.? Y a Ud., ¿qué le van a regalar sus amigos este año el día de su cumpleaños?
   - un libro
   - un regalo grande
   - una radio portátil
   - una camisa
2. Hoy es el aniversario de los Sres. González. ¿Qué les dice Ud. a ellos? ¿Qué les regala Inés? ¿Irma? ¿Pepe? ¿Rodolfo? ¿Qué les va a regalar Ud. a sus padres para su aniversario?
   - un televisor
   - unos boletos para un viaje
   - una pintura bonita
   - un regalo pequeño

¡OJO! **A1:** *¿No* ***lo*** *conoce Ud.?* (DO)

Extension A: Use DO pronouns to discuss persons pictured: **1.** *¿Conoce Ud. a los Sres. González?* **2.** *¿Sabe dónde viven?* **3.** *¿Cuántos hijos tienen? ¿Los conoce Ud.?* **4.** *¿Conoce Ud. a Inés? ¿a Irma?*, etc.

Optional: What would you like to "get off your chest"? Tell to whom you would write and what you would say, following this model. ***Modelo*** *Quiero escribirle(s) a _____ para decirle(s)...* Put possible problems and people to write to on board as guide for students. ***Problemas:*** *la contaminación del aire, la matrícula, el precio de (un pasaje a _____, la gasolina, los libros)* ***Personas:*** *el presidente de (los Estados Unidos, Shell, American Airlines), el rector de la universidad, el dueño de la librería.* Vary problems and information according to campus and current events/problems.

Follow-up B: 1. *¿A quién le manda Ud. flores? ¿Quién le manda flores a Ud.?* **2.** *¿A quién le escribe Ud. cartas? ¿Qué tipo de cartas escribe Ud.? ¿cartas políticas? ¿amistosas? ¿románticas? ¿Quién le escribe cartas a Ud.?* **3.** *¿Les va a comprar algo a sus padres este año? ¿a su mejor amigo/a? ¿a su profesor(a)?*

Extension C: Students report to class at least two interesting things they learned about partner.

B. Complete las oraciones lógicamente.

1. ¡Estoy furioso/a! Voy a escribirle(s) a _____ para decirle(s) que _____.
2. Los hombres deben abrirles la puerta a _____, ¿verdad? Y en un autobús, deben ofrecerles su asiento a _____.
3. Nunca le presto a nadie mi(s) _____ porque _____. Pero sí les presto _____ a mis amigos porque _____.
4. _____ es mi restaurante favorito en esta ciudad. Allí, les recomiendo a Uds. _____. No les recomiendo _____.
5. Para mi cumpleaños, mi mejor amigo/a (esposo/a, ...) siempre me manda _____. Para su cumpleaños, yo le doy (voy a dar) _____.

C. **Entrevista.** Find out to whom or for whom a classmate does the following things. Then find out who does them to or for him or her.

MODELO: darle consejos → —¿A quién le das consejos?
—Pues... con frecuencia le doy consejos a mi compañero de cuarto.
—Y ¿quién te da consejos a ti?
—¡Mis padres me dan muchos consejos! Mi mejor amiga también...

1. darle consejos (dinero)
2. pedirle ayuda académica (dinero)
3. prestarle la ropa (el coche, dinero)
4. mandarle flores (dulces)
5. decirle secretos (mentiritas [*little white lies*])
6. hacerle favores (regalos especiales)
7. escribirle cartas románticas (tarjetas postales)

¿Recuerda Ud.?

You have already used forms of **gustar** to express your likes and dislikes (**Ante todo, Segunda parte**). Review what you know by answering the following questions. Then use them, changing their form as needed, to interview your instructor.

1. ¿Te gusta el café (el vino, el té, ...)?
2. ¿Te gusta jugar al béisbol (al golf, al vólibol, al...)?
3. ¿Te gusta viajar en avión (fumar, viajar en tren, ...)?
4. ¿Qué te gusta más, estudiar o ir a fiestas (trabajar o descansar, cocinar o comer)?

Communicative objectives for 23: more about expressing likes and dislikes

Note: Students have been using *gustar* construction since *Ante todo.*

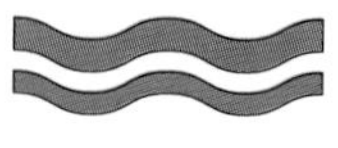

23. EXPRESSING LIKES AND DISLIKES *Gustar*

1. ¿Dónde están sentados (*seated*) los dos hombres?
2. Al hombre de la derecha, ¿qué le gusta hacer?

Parece que a Ud. no le gusta el humo.

3. ¿Qué cosa no le gusta al hombre de la izquierda?
4. ¿Dónde debe estar sentado el hombre de la izquierda?
5. ¿Les gusta a todos el humo de los cigarrillos?
6. ¿A Ud. le gusta fumar?

Follow-up: listening: *¿Quién lo dice, el que fuma o el que no fuma?* **1.** *A mí no me gusta el humo.* **2.** *¿Le molesto si fumo?* **3.** *No fume Ud. más.* **4.** *Tengo ganas de fumar.* **5.** *Fume Ud. en otro lugar, por favor.*

Constructions with *gustar*

SPANISH	EQUIVALENT	ENGLISH
Me gusta la playa.	The beach is pleasing to me.	*I like the beach.*
No le gustan sus cursos.	His courses are not pleasing to him.	*He doesn't like his courses.*
Nos gusta correr.	Running is pleasing to us.	*We like to run.*

As you already know, the verb **gustar** is used to express likes and dislikes. However, **gustar** does not literally mean *to like*. **Gustar** means *to be pleasing* (to someone).

Gustar is always used with an indirect object pronoun: someone or something is pleasing *to* someone else. It is most commonly used in the third person singular or plural (**gusta/gustan**), and must agree with its subject, which is the person or thing liked, *not* the person whose likes are being described. Note that an infinitive (**correr** in the final sentence in the box above) is viewed as a singular subject in Spanish.

Note: Similarity to English construction: The (very) idea disgusts me.

Point out: Use of definite article to refer to something in general: *los tacos* = *tacos*. I don't like it (them) = *No me gusta(n)*.

Note: Grammatical subject of Spanish sentence (thing liked) comes after verb.

A mí me gustan las arvejas. **A Ud.** no **le** gustan, ¿verdad?	*I like peas. You don't like them, do you?*
¿A ellos les gusta nadar?	*Do they like to swim?*

As in the preceding sentences, **a mí** (**a ti**, **a Ud.**, and so on) may be used in addition to the indirect object pronouns for clarification or emphasis.

The indirect object pronoun *must* be used with **gustar** even when an indirect object noun is expressed. A common word order is as follows:

(*a* + pronoun/ noun)	**indirect object pronoun**	***gustar* + subject**
A Juan	le	gustan las fiestas.
(A ellas)	Les	gusta esquiar.

Suggestion: *¿Cómo se dice en español?* To make sure this construction is clear, ask students to give literal English equivalents of Spanish sentences. **1.** I like the car. (→ The car is pleasing to me.) **2.** We/he/you/I like(s) the car. **3.** I/we/she/they like(s) to read. **4.** She likes the soup/chicken/coffee. **5.** He likes tomatoes/tacos/movies/to go to the movies. (*¡OJO!* Use of definite articles.)

Suggestion: *¿Cómo se dice en español?* Use to stress redundancy of IO pronoun and IO noun. **1.** My father likes to eat. **2.** My mother likes fish. **3.** The boys like steak. **4.** María likes salads.

Would Like/Wouldn't Like

What one *would* or *would not* like to do is expressed with the form **gustaría*** + *infinitive* and the appropriate indirect objects.

Note: *Gustaría* will be used with infinitives only until all forms of conditional are presented in Ch. 18.

---

*This is one of the forms of the conditional of **gustar**. You will study all of the forms of the conditional in Grammar Section 50.

A mí me gustaría viajar a Colombia.	*I would like to travel to Colombia.*
Nos gustaría hacer *camping* este verano.	*We would like to go camping this summer.*

Optional: Verbs with constructions similar to that of *gustar*: *importar, faltar, quedar, parecer, encantar.*

Práctica

Emphasis A: Use of definite article to refer to something in general.

Optional A: Reenter *muchísimo*/*nada* with *gustar* expressions.

A. **Gustos y preferencias.** ¿Le gusta o no le gusta? Siga los modelos.

MODELOS: ¿el café? → (No) Me gusta el café.
¿los pasteles? → (No) Me gustan los pasteles.

1. ¿el vino?
2. ¿los niños pequeños?
3. ¿la música clásica?
4. ¿los discos de Barbra Streisand?
5. ¿el invierno?
6. ¿hacer cola?
7. ¿las clases que empiezan a las ocho?
8. ¿el chocolate?
9. ¿las películas de horror?
10. ¿cocinar?
11. ¿las clases de este semestre?
12. ¿la gramática?
13. ¿los vuelos con muchas escalas?
14. ¿bailar en las discotecas?

Emphasis B: Redundant use of IO pronoun and IO noun.

B. **¿Adónde vamos este verano?** The different members of the Soto family all have favorite vacation activities and, of course, would prefer to go to different places this summer. Imagine that you are one of the Sotos and describe the family's various preferences, following the model.

MODELO: padre / nadar: ir a la playa →
A mi padre le gusta nadar. Le gustaría ir a la playa.

1. padre / el océano: ir a la playa
2. hermanitos / nadar también: ir a la playa
3. hermano Ernesto / correr: ir al campo (*country*)
4. abuelos / descansar: estar en casa
5. madre / la tranquilidad: visitar un pueblecito (*small town*) en la costa
6. hermana Elena / discotecas: pasar las vacaciones en una ciudad grande
7. mí / ¿ ? : ¿ ?

Now, remembering what you have learned about the vacation preferences of your imaginary family, answer the following questions.

1. ¿A quién le gustaría ir a Nueva York?
2. ¿A quién le gustaría estar en Acapulco?
3. ¿Quién no quiere salir de casa?
4. ¿A quién le gustaría ir a Hyannis Port?
5. ¿Quién quiere ir a un club deportivo (*sports*) en las montañas?

C. **Seleccionando una piza.** ¿Cómo se dice en español?

1. My father likes anchovies (**las anchoas**), but he doesn't like sausage (**el chorizo**).
2. My mother likes sausage, but she doesn't like cheese much.

3. My brothers like cheese, but they don't like mushrooms (**los champiñones**).
4. I like everything (**todo**), and I would like to have a pizza right now!

CH. **De viaje.** ¿Cómo se dice en español?

1. My mother likes to fly (to travel by plane), but she doesn't like long flights. She wouldn't like to go to China (**la China**) by plane.
2. My father doesn't like to wait in line, and he doesn't like delays.
3. My brothers like to get on the plane right away (**en seguida**), but they don't like to save a place for anyone.
4. And I like to travel with all of them!

Escriba Ud. en español un párrafo parecido sobre los gustos y preferencias de los miembros de su familia (sus compañeros de clase, de la residencia, etcétera).

Conversación

A. **Los gustos de los señores Trujillo.** ¿Qué les gusta hacer a los señores Trujillo? Conteste según el dibujo. ¿Puede Ud. inventar otros detalles sobre su vida? Por ejemplo, ¿cuántos años tienen? ¿Tienen niños? ¿Dónde viven? etcétera.

Suggestion A: Do as whole-class discussion or whole-class composition, with you or a student writing sentences on the board. Use as vehicle for review of major structures presented so far (verbs of all classes, modals, possessives, pronouns, etc.).

Options B: Use *me molesta(n)* instead of *odio*. Reenter *no me gusta nada*.

B. **¿Qué te gusta? ¿Qué odias?** (*What do you hate?*) Almost every situation has aspects that one likes or dislikes—even hates. React to the following situations by telling what you like or don't like about them. Follow the model and the cues, but add your own words as well and expand your responses, using **me gustaría** if you can.

MODELO En la playa: el agua, el sol, nadar, la arena (*sand*) →
- Me gusta mucho el agua pero no me gusta nada el sol. Por eso no me gustaría pasar todo el día en la playa.
- Me gusta nadar pero odio la arena. Por eso me gustaría más nadar en una piscina (*pool*).

Follow-up: Students describe likes and dislikes of various family members on various topics. In addition to *gustar*, encourage students to use *preferir*, *odiar*, *molestar*.

1. En el avión: viajar en avión, la comida, las películas, la música
2. En la discoteca: la música, bailar, el ruido, el humo
3. En el parque: los animales, los insectos, las flores, la hierba (*grass*)
4. En el coche: manejar (*to drive*), el tráfico, los camiones (*trucks*), los policías, el límite de velocidad
5. En el hospital: las inyecciones, los médicos, los enfermeros (las enfermeras) (*nurses*), los visitantes, recibir flores

Otros sitios: en una fiesta; en la biblioteca; en clase; en una cafetería; en un gran almacén; en casa, con sus padres; en un autobús/tren

Suggestion C: Model answers to several questions with another student, to give students guidelines about explaining their preferences.

Variations:
- Students invent own interview topics.
- Poll entire class on answer to one or several questions.
- Encourage use of *gustaría* where appropriate.

C. **Entrevista: ¿Qué te gusta más?** Use the following cues to determine what another student likes or dislikes about the topics, asking him or her to give reasons, if possible. When the interview is over, report the most interesting information you have learned to the class.

MODELO: el rojo, el azul o el verde →
—¿Qué color te gusta más—el rojo, el azul o el verde?
—Pues... yo creo que me gusta más el azul.
—¿Puedes explicarme por qué te gusta más ese color?
—Sí, me gusta porque es el color de los ojos (*eyes*) de mi novio/a.

1. el cine o la televisión
2. el verano, el invierno, el otoño o la primavera
3. vivir solo/a o vivir con un compañero (una compañera)
4. viajar en clase turística o en primera
5. viajar en avión, en tren, en autobús, en barco o en coche
6. vivir en la residencia, en un apartamento o en la casa de sus padres
7. las fiestas grandes o las pequeñas
8. las fiestas improvisadas o las bien organizadas
9. comer en casa o salir a comer en un restaurante
10. ir de compras a un almacén o a una tienda especializada

Bogotá, Colombia

En el aeropuerto
—Perdón, ¿sabe Ud. si el vuelo 638 va a salir a tiempo?
—Sí, eso dicen. A las tres y cuarto.
—Pues, ¡qué bien! Así tengo tiempo para tomar algo.
—Si quiere, deje (*leave*) sus cosas aquí. Le puedo guardar el puesto.
—Muchísimas gracias. ¿Quiere que le traiga algo?
—No, nada. Gracias.

Communicative objectives for 24: Various ways to tell people to do things.

24. INFLUENCING OTHERS
Present Subjunctive: An Introduction; Formal Commands

Note: This section emphasizes formal commands and the forms of the present subjunctive, as one system. Ch. 9 focuses on uses of the subjunctive.

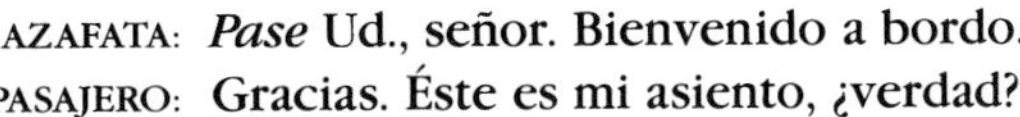

Un pasajero distraído

AZAFATA: *Pase* Ud., señor. Bienvenido a bordo.
PASAJERO: Gracias. Éste es mi asiento, ¿verdad?
AZAFATA: Sí, es el 5A. Es necesario que *tome* asiento ahora mismo. Y, por favor, no *olvide* el cinturón de seguridad.
PASAJERO: ¿Puedo fumar?
AZAFATA: Se puede fumar en esta sección, pero no queremos que *fume* ahora. Vamos a despegar pronto para Quito y...
PASAJERO: ¿Para Quito? Pero... el vuelo ciento doce va a Cuzco.
AZAFATA: Sí, señor, pero éste es el vuelo ciento dos. ¡*Baje* Ud. ahora mismo! Todavía es posible que *llegue* a su avión a tiempo.

1. ¿Qué dice la azafata cuando el pasajero entra en el avión?
2. ¿El pasajero encuentra (*finds*) su asiento? ¿Cuál es?
3. ¿Por qué no debe fumar ahora el pasajero?
4. ¿Cuál es el error del pasajero?
5. ¿Qué debe hacer el pasajero?

Point out:
- Similarity in pronunciation of 102 and 112, source of passenger's confusion.
- Forms *pase*, *tome*, *no olvide*, *fume*, *baje*. Ask: What is infinitive of each verb? (→ *pasar*, etc.). Ending for new verbal system (→ *-e*). Ask: What might the ending for *-er*/*-ir* verbs be? (*-a*)

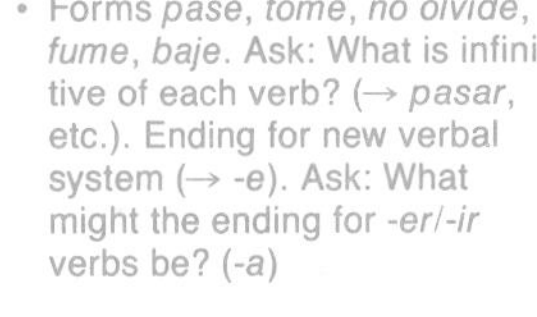

Subjunctive: An Overview

The present tense forms you have already learned are part of a verb system called the *indicative mood* (**el indicativo**). In both English and Spanish, the indicative is used to state facts and to ask questions. It is used to express objectively most real-world actions or states of being.

> ***She's writing** the letter.*
> ***We are** already there!*

Both English and Spanish have another verb system called the *subjunctive mood* (**el subjuntivo**). The subjunctive is used to express more subjective or conceptualized actions or states: things we want to happen, things we try to get others to do, and events that we are reacting to emotionally.

An absent-minded passenger FLIGHT ATTENDANT: Come in, sir. Welcome aboard. PASSENGER: Thank you. This is my seat, isn't it? FLIGHT ATTENDANT: Yes, it's 5A. You must take your seat (It's necessary that you take your seat) right now. And, please, don't forget your seat belt. PASSENGER: Can I smoke? FLIGHT ATTENDANT: Smoking is permitted (One can smoke) in this section, but we don't want you to smoke now. We've going to take off soon for Quito and . . . PASSENGER: For Quito? But . . . flight 112 goes to Cuzco. FLIGHT ATTENDANT: Yes, sir, but this is flight 102. Get off right now! It's still possible for you to get to your plane on time.

I recommend that ***she write*** *the letter immediately.*
I wish (that) ***we were*** *already there.**

In later chapters, you will learn more about the concepts associated with the Spanish subjunctive as well as about the structure of sentences in which it is used. This chapter focuses on the forms of the subjunctive and on a use of the subjunctive with which you are already familiar. In Spanish, many command forms are part of the subjunctive, identical in form to the third person singular and plural. You have seen command forms in several contexts: in **Mandatos y frases comunes en la clase** (**Ante todo**) and in direction lines throughout the chapters of this text (**Haga**..., **Complete**..., **Conteste**..., and so on).

Note: Section is intended *only* as introduction to present subjunctive. **Emphasis:** give students orientation to concept of subjunctive and to subjunctive constructions; present forms.

Suggestions:
- Review *Ud.* commands that students are familiar with (see *Ante todo* and think about the commands you use regularly in class).
- **Emphasis: (1)** relationship of *Ud.* commands to subjunctive; **(2)** similarity of personal endings (*-s*, *-mos*, etc.) to present indicative.
- Working within brief-sentence context, present subjunctive forms of *trabajar*: *Yo quiero que Uds. trabajen mucho. ¿Quieren que yo trabaje mucho?* (Write forms on board as they are produced.) *¿Quiero que John trabaje mucho?*, etc. Do same with *beber*, *recibir*. **Note:** Emphasize forms of subjunctive only for student production, but use full syntax in your input.
- Present verbs with spelling changes briefly, pointing out spelling change in all persons of conjugation.
- Briefly enter subjunctive forms of irregular verbs in same conversational context, asking 1–2 questions with each. Continue to use only *Quiero que...* as semantic cue, or introduce *Ojalá que*.

Forms of the Present Subjunctive

PRESENT SUBJUNCTIVE OF REGULAR VERBS		
hablar: **hablø → habl-**	**comer:** **comø → com-**	**vivir:** **vivø → viv-**
habl**e** habl**emos**	com**a** com**amos**	viv**a** viv**amos**
habl**es** habl**éis**	com**as** com**áis**	viv**as** viv**áis**
habl**e** habl**en**	com**a** com**an**	viv**a** viv**an**

- The personal endings of the present subjunctive are added to the first person singular of the present indicative minus its **-o** ending. **-Ar** verbs add endings with **-e**, while **-er**/**-ir** verbs add endings with **-a**.
- Verbs ending in **-car**, **-gar**, and **-zar** have a spelling change in all persons of the present subjunctive, in order to preserve the **-c-**, **-g-**, and **-z-** sounds.

  -car: c → **qu** buscar: bus**que**, bus**que**s, ...
  -gar: g → **gu** pagar: pa**gu**e, pa**gu**es, ...
  -zar: z → **c** empezar: empie**c**e, empie**c**es, ...

- Verbs with irregular **yo** forms show the irregularity in all persons of the present subjunctive.

  decir: **diga**, ... poner: **ponga**, ... traer: **traiga**, ...
  hacer: **haga**, ... salir: **salga**, ... venir: **venga**, ...
  oír: **oiga**, ... tener: **tenga**, ... ver: **vea**, ...

- A few verbs have irregular present subjunctive forms.

  dar: **dé, des, dé, demos, deis, den** ir: **vaya**, ...
  estar: **esté**, ... saber: **sepa**, ...
  haber (hay): **haya** ser: **sea**, ...

- **Emphasis:** subjunctive of *hay* (*haya*).

*Subjunctive has lessened in modern English, and many English speakers no longer use it.

- **-Ar** and **-er** stem-changing verbs follow the stem-changing pattern of the present indicative.

  pensar (ie): **pie**nse, **pie**nses, **pie**nse, pensemos, penséis, **pie**nsen
  poder (ue): **pue**da, **pue**das, **pue**da, podamos, podáis, **pue**dan

- **-Ir** stem-changing verbs show the first stem change in four forms and the second stem change in the **nosotros** and **vosotros** forms.

  dormir (ue, u): d**ue**rma, d**ue**rmas, d**ue**rma, d**u**rmamos, d**u**rmáis, d**ue**rman
  preferir (ie, i): pref**ie**ra, pref**ie**ras, pref**ie**ra, pref**i**ramos, pref**i**ráis, pref**ie**ran

[Práctica A]

• Present subjunctive forms of stem-changing verbs. **Emphasis:** second stem change (students know it from *-ndo* forms) in the *nosotros* and *vosotros* forms of *-ir* stem-changing verbs.

Meanings of the Present Subjunctive; Use with *querer*

Like the present indicative, the Spanish present subjunctive has several English equivalents: **(yo) hable** can mean *I speak, I am speaking, I do speak, I may speak,* or *I will speak.* The exact English equivalent of the Spanish present subjunctive depends on the context.

An English infinitive is frequently used to express the Spanish subjunctive.

Quieren que **estemos** allí a las dos.	*They want us **to be** there (that we be there) at 2:00.*
Quiero que **hables** con él en seguida.	*I want you **to speak** to him immediately.*

Note that there are two conjugated verbs in the preceding sentences. The subjunctive form is the second of the two verbs, while a form of the verb **querer** occurs at the beginning of the sentence.

This use of the verb **querer** is one of the cues for the use of the subjunctive in the second part of the sentence. In this section you will practice the forms of the subjunctive mainly with **querer**. You will learn additional frequent uses of the subjunctive in the remaining chapters of this book and will see still other instances of the Spanish subjunctive wherever appropriate, though you may not know the rule or generalization that governs a particular occurrence. Now that you know how the subjunctive is formed, however, you will *always* be able to recognize it and understand its general meaning.

[Práctica B–C]

Discuss meaning (English equivalents) of subjunctive forms. Note there are several English equivalents.

Emphasis: Present subjunctive will be used in appropriate situations from this point on in ***Puntos de partida***, whether or not students have learned "reason" for use. (They will never be asked to produce subjunctive, however, unless particular use in question has been presented.)

Formal Commands

Commands (imperatives) are verb forms used to tell someone to do something. In Spanish, the *formal commands* (**los mandatos formales**) are used with people whom you address as **Ud.** or **Uds.** The command forms for **Ud.** and **Uds.** are the corresponding forms of the present subjunctive.

	hablar	comer	escribir	volver	decir
Singular	hable hables hable (Ud.)	coma comas coma (Ud.)	escriba escribas escriba (Ud.)	vuelva vuelvas vuelva (Ud.)	diga digas diga (Ud.)
Plural	hablemos habléis hablen (Uds.)	comamos comáis coman (Uds.)	escribamos escribáis escriban (Uds.)	volvamos volváis vuelvan (Uds.)	digamos digáis digan (Uds.)
English equivalent	*speak*	*eat*	*write*	*come back*	*tell*

Using **Ud.** or **Uds.** after the command forms makes the command somewhat more formal or more polite. Since the formal commands are part of the subjunctive system, they reflect all the irregularities you have seen listed on pp. 228–29.

- Formal commands of stem-changing verbs will show the stem change.

  p**ie**nse Ud.   vu**e**lva Ud.   p**i**da Ud.

- Verbs ending in **-car**, **-gar**, and **-zar** have a spelling change.

  buscar: bus**que** Ud.   pagar: pa**gue** Ud.   empezar: empie**ce** Ud.

- The **Ud./Uds.** commands for verbs that have irregular **yo** forms will reflect the irregularity.

  conocer → **conozca Ud.**
  decir → **diga Ud.**
  hacer → **haga Ud.**
  oír → **oiga Ud.**
  poner → **ponga Ud.**
  salir → **salga Ud.**
  tener → **tenga Ud.**
  traer → **traiga Ud.**
  venir → **venga Ud.**
  ver → **vea Ud.**

- A few verbs have irregular **Ud./Uds.** command forms.

  dar: **dé Ud.**
  estar: **esté Ud.**
  ir: **vaya Ud.**
  saber: **sepa Ud.**
  ser: **sea Ud.**

[Práctica CH–D]

Suggestions:
- Present regular command forms.
- **Rapid Response Drill:** *¿Cuál es el mandato* (**Ud.**) *de ____?* *bailar, comprar, estudiar, hablar, descansar, entrar, mirar, llamar, preparar, escuchar, regresar; aprender, beber, comer, leer, vender; abrir, asistir, escribir.*
- Present commands of stem-changing verbs. Point out stem change in *yo* form.
- **Rapid Response Drill:** *¿Cuál es el mandato* (**Ud.**) *de ____?* *cierro, recomiendo, vuelvo, duermo, prefiero, sirvo, pido.*
- Present commands with spelling changes. Additional verbs: *tocar; llegar, jugar; almorzar.*
- Present irregular commands. Review irregular *yo* forms: **(1)** Instructor gives *Ud.* command; students give infinitive. **(2)** Instructor gives infinitive; students give *Ud.* command.
- **Point out:** only five irregular commands. Accent on *dé* (to differentiate from preposition *de*) but not on *den*; accents on *esté* and *estén*.

Position of Object Pronouns with Formal Commands

Direct and indirect object pronouns must follow affirmative commands and be attached to them. In order to maintain the original stress of the verb form, an accent mark is added to the stressed vowel if the original command has two or more syllables.

Léalo Ud. — *Read it.*
Búsquele el bolígrafo. — *Look for the pen for him.*

Direct and indirect object pronouns must precede negative commands.

No lo lea Ud.	*Don't read it.*
No le busque el bolígrafo.	*Don't look for the pen for him.*

[Práctica E–F]

Práctica

Preliminary exercise: listening: *¿Presente de indicativo o presente de subjuntivo?* **-ar:** *baile, cena, lleguemos, pago, pague, hablemos, vuele, miramos, buscan, busquen* **-er/-ir:** *aprende, aprenda, lea, leemos, escribamos, coma, asisten, recibo, beban* **irreg. yo forms:** *digo, diga, dices, pongamos, traigan, sabe, sepan, sea, salgas, va, vaya, vienen, haya*

Note A: Exercise calls for passive use of subjunctive forms and structures only.

A. **Al aeropuerto, por favor. ¡Tenemos prisa!** En el siguiente diálogo, identifique los verbos del subjuntivo.

ESTEBAN: ¡Más rápido, Carlota! ¡Quiero que lleguemos al aeropuerto a tiempo!
CARLOTA: ¿Quieres que te ayude con las maletas?
ESTEBAN: No. Quiero que subas al taxi. Estamos atrasados. No quiero que perdamos el vuelo, como la última vez.
CARLOTA: ¡Y yo no quiero que te dé un ataque al corazón (*heart*)! Si el avión despega sin nosotros, ¿qué importa? Tomamos el próximo vuelo y llegamos unas horas más tarde.

Ahora, conteste según el diálogo.

1. Esteban quiere que (ellos)...
   a. lleguen a tiempo b. lleguen en dos horas
2. Según Esteban, parece que Carlota...
   a. no tiene prisa b. no encuentra sus maletas
3. Esteban quiere que Carlota...
   a. suba al taxi b. suba al autobús
4. No quiere que Carlota...
   a. lo ayude con las maletas b. lo ayude con el taxista
5. No quiere que (ellos)...
   a. pierdan el taxi b. pierdan el vuelo
6. Según Carlota, es más importante...
   a. estar tranquilo b. estar en el aeropuerto a tiempo

Y Ud., ¿es como Carlota o como Esteban?

Emphasis B: First verb requires indicative, as written; second verb requires subjunctive.

¡OJO! **B3–7:** Object pronouns precede conjugated verb forms, indicative or subjunctive. Contrast with direct *Ud.* commands (which use subjunctive forms): *Tráigalo* vs. *Quiero que lo traiga.*

Variation B: Vary semantic cue: **2.** *¿Prefieres...* **3.** *Ud. insiste...* **4.** *No me gusta...* **5.** *Es necesario...* **6.** *Dudo...* **7.** *¿Es posible...*

B. Haga oraciones según las indicaciones. **¡OJO!** Cambie sólo el infinitivo.

1. Quiero que (tú)... (bailar, cenar, mirar esto, llegar a tiempo, buscar a Anita)
2. ¿Quieres que el niño... ? (aprender, escribir, leer, responder, asistir a clases)
3. Ud. quiere que (yo)... , ¿verdad? (empezar, jugar, pensarlo, servirlo, pedirlo)
4. No quieren que (nosotros)... (pedir eso, almorzar ahora, perderlos, dormir allí, cerrarla, encontrarlo aquí)
5. Queremos que Uds... (conocerlo, hacerlo, traerlo, saberlo, decirlo)
6. Yo no quiero que Ana... (venir, salir ahora, ponerlo, oírlo, ser su amiga)
7. ¿Quieres que (yo)... ? (tenerlo, verlo, estar allí, dar una fiesta, ir al cine contigo)

Note C: Infinitives on which commands should be based are indicated in italics.

Optional Follow-up C: *¿Qué quiere que haga Ud. su amigo/a Carlos (Carlota)? Siga el modelo:* **Modelo:** *Carlos (Carlota): ¡No fume Ud.! → Carlota no quiere que yo fume.* **1.** *Facture el equipaje.* **2.** *No crea eso.* **3.** *No olvide los boletos.* **4.** *Traiga el pasaporte.* **5.** *No diga eso.* **6.** *No me llame.* **7.** *Escúchela.* **8.** *Espérelo.* **9.** *No nos busque.* **10.** *Sírvalos.*

Variation C: Put infinitives on board. Working in pairs, one student forms command, second tells what Carlos (Carlota) wants him/her to do/not do.

Un bronceador natural
La zanahoria posee más vitamina A que cualquier otra hortaliza conocida. De cara al verano, y para los amantes del bronceado que reniegan de cremas y potingues, tiene también la propiedad de activar la producción de melanocitos, responsables del «moreno» como respuesta a la agresión del sol.
La zanahoria acelera el proceso del bronceado.

C. **Más sugerencias para las vacaciones.** Aquí están los miembros de la familia Soto otra vez. ¿Qué quiere cada uno que hagan todos de vacaciones? Haga oraciones según el modelo.

MODELO: papá: ir a la playa → Papá quiere que **vayamos** a la playa.

1. hermanitos: ir a la playa también
2. Ernesto: volver a hacer *camping* en las montañas
3. abuelos: no salir de la ciudad en todo el verano
4. mamá: sólo hacer unas excursiones cortas
5. Elena: visitar Nueva York

Y Ud., ¿adónde quiere que su familia vaya este verano?

CH. El Sr. Casiano no se siente (*feel*) bien. Lea la descripción que él da de algunas de sus actividades.

«*Trabajo* muchísimo—¡me gusta trabajar! En la oficina, *soy* impaciente y *critico* bastante (*a good deal*) a los otros. En mi vida personal, a veces *soy* un poco impulsivo. *Fumo* bastante y también *bebo* cerveza y otras bebidas alcohólicas, a veces sin moderación... *Almuerzo* y *ceno* fuerte, y casi nunca *desayuno*. Por la noche, con frecuencia *salgo* con los amigos—me gusta ir a las discotecas—y *vuelvo* tarde a casa.»

¿Qué *no* debe hacer el Sr. Casiano para estar mejor? Aconséjele sobre lo que (*what*) no debe hacer, usando los verbos indicados o cualquier (*any*) otro, según los modelos.

MODELOS: *trabajo* → Sr. Casiano, no trabaje tanto.
soy → Sr. Casiano, no sea tan impaciente.

D. Imagine que Ud. es el profesor (la profesora) hoy. ¿Qué mandatos debe dar a la clase?

MODELO: hablar español → Hablen Uds. español.
hablar inglés → No hablen Uds. inglés.

1. llegar a tiempo
2. leer la lección
3. escribir una composición
4. abrir los libros
5. pensar en inglés
6. estar en clase mañana
7. traer los libros a clase
8. olvidar los verbos nuevos
9. ¿ ?

E. **Situaciones.** La Sra. Medina quiere tener solamente clases fáciles este semestre. ¿Debe o no debe tomar las siguientes clases? Con otro estudiante, haga y conteste preguntas según el modelo.

MODELO: la física → —¿Física?
—No, no la tome.

1. Inglés 1
2. Ciencias políticas
3. Química orgánica
4. Historia de Latinoamérica
5. Cálculo 1
6. Comercio
7. Español 2
8. ¿ ?

Note CH: *lo que*, introduced and made active, for use in direction lines only, not for student production. If you want the *que/lo que* contrast to be active, you may wish to present it now.

Note E, F: The "other" student takes the role of *Medina/Casiano*.

Preliminary Exercise F: *Dé el mandato negativo:* **1.** *Cómprelo.* **2.** *Estúdielas.* **3.** *Mírelo.* **4.** *Llámeme.* **5.** *Apréndalo.* **6.** *Escríbame.*

Dé el mandato afirmativo. **7.** *No me diga.* **8.** *No lo coma.* **9.** *No lo lea.* **10.** *No lo haga.* **11.** *No lo sirva.* **12.** *No lo traiga.*

Extension F: **11.** *pasteles* **12.** *queso* **13.** *yogur* **14.** *patatas fritas*

Variation F: Instead of question, as in model, first student says: *A mí me gustaría comer ensalada.* Second student replies: *Pues, cómala.*

Follow-up F: *Luisa y Carlos llegan a su primer día de escuela en la clase del primer grado. La maestra les explica las reglas de conducta, especialmente la conducta prohibida. ¿Qué mandatos les da?*

Suggestions: *no comer en el salón de clase, no hablar cuando habla la maestra, no pegar* (to hit) *a los amiguitos, no traer animales a clase, no escribir en las paredes* (walls), *no llegar tarde. ¿Qué otros mandatos—afirmativos o negativos—recuerdan Uds. de la escuela primaria?*

Variations A:
- Arrange classroom furniture to represent airport. One student walks through "airport," following directions given by others.
- Use map of campus, city, or building for similar exercise. Prepare dittoed hand-out or transparency or draw on board.

F. **Situaciones.** El Sr. Casiano ha decidido (***has decided***) adelgazar (***lose weight***). ¿Debe o no debe comer o beber las siguientes cosas? Con otro estudiante, haga y conteste preguntas según los modelos.

MODELOS: ensalada → —¿Ensalada? —Cómala. postres → —¿Postres? —No los coma.

1. alcohol (*m.*)
2. verduras
3. pan
4. dulces
5. leche
6. hamburguesas con queso
7. frutas
8. refrescos dietéticos
9. pollo
10. carne

Conversación

A. **Situaciones.** You are a clerk at a ticket counter (**el mostrador**) in a small airport. Someone has asked you how to get to the waiting room (**la sala de espera**) for Gate 2. Give him or her directions in Spanish.

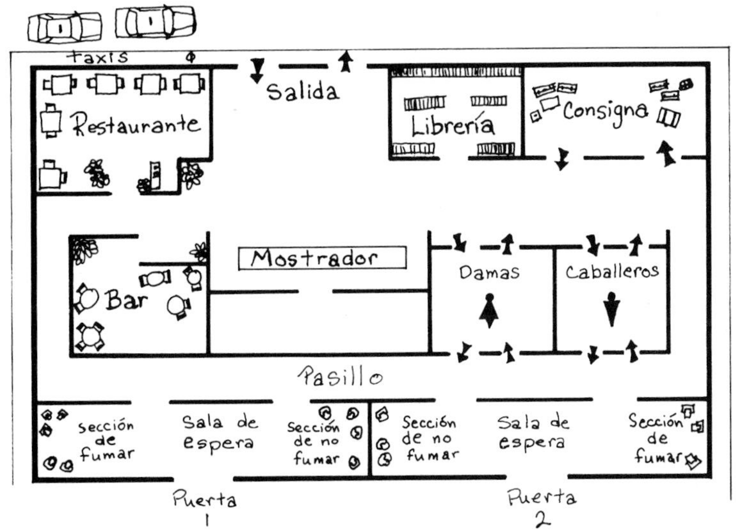

Frases útiles: ir: vaya Ud. (*go*), doblar: doble Ud. (*turn*), seguir (i, i): siga Ud. (*continue*), pasar: pase Ud. por (*pass through/by*), (todo) derecho ([*straight*] *ahead*), a la derecha (*to the right*), a la izquierda (*to the left*), el pasillo (*the hall, corridor*)

Now, if you are in/at . . .	tell someone how to get to . . .
la sala de espera	el bar
la consigna (*baggage claim area*)	la librería
el restaurante	los servicios (*restrooms*)
la puerta 2	la parada (*stand*) de taxis

Notas culturales: Los mandatos

Los mandatos formales son de verdad mandatos, y a veces pueden parecer un poquito bruscos. Si usted está en un restaurante, por ejemplo, es importante no ofender al camarero para no quedar mal (*to make a bad impression*). Si le dice, «Tráigame otra cerveza», puede resultar maleducado (*impolite*).

Hay varias maneras de suavizar (*softening*) un mandato. La más fácil es la de decir también «por favor» o «si me hace el favor». Otra forma es la de usar simplemente el presente del verbo: «Me trae, por favor, otra cerveza». Más suave aún es la forma interrogativa: «¿Me trae otra cerveza, por favor?» Si usted quiere estar seguro de no ofender a nadie, pregúntele: «¿Puede Ud. traerme otra cerveza, por favor?»

Follow-ups B:
- *¿Qué le aconseja? Dé mandatos afirmativos o negativos a la persona que dice lo siguiente.* **1.** *Estoy cansado.* **2.** *Tengo sed.* **3.** *Tengo hambre.* **4.** *No puedo dormir.* **5.** *No entiendo el ejercicio.* **6.** *Necesito más dinero.* **7.** *Mis padres quieren saber cómo estoy.* **8.** *No puedo encontrar mi libro de español.*
- Return to drawing on p. 223. What commands would you give to smoker? What commands might smoker give to you?
- (Oral or written): What commands would you like to give to the following persons? **1.** *el presidente* **2.** *los candidatos políticos* **3.** Johnny Carson, Howard Cosell (or any other person on TV or in news) **4.** *sus amigos* **5.** *el/la profesor(a)*

B. **En la oficina del consejero.** Imagine that you are a guidance counselor. Students consult you with questions of all kinds, some trivial and some important. Offer advice to them in the form of affirmative or negative commands. How many different commands can you invent for each situation?

1. EVELIA: No me gusta tomar clases por la mañana. Siempre estoy muy cansada durante esas clases y además (*besides*) a esa hora tengo hambre. Pienso constantemente en el almuerzo... y no puedo concentrarme en las explicaciones.
2. FABIÁN: En mi clase de cálculo, ¡no entiendo nada! No puedo hacer los ejercicios que el profesor nos da de tarea (*as homework*) y durante la clase tengo miedo de hacerle preguntas, porque no quiero parecer (*seem*) tonto.
3. FAUSTO: Fui a México el verano pasado y me gustó (*I liked it*) mucho. Quiero volver a México este verano. Ahora que lo conozco mejor, quiero manejar (*drive*) mi coche y no ir en autobús como el verano pasado. Desgraciadamente no tengo dinero para hacer el viaje.
4. PILAR: Mis padres no están muy contentos conmigo. Dicen que no los llamo nunca, que no les escribo y que los visito con poca frecuencia.

¡OJO! **C:** *Ojalá* is invariable in form and always followed by subjunctive.

C. La palabra **ojalá** significa *I wish* o *I hope*; nunca cambia de forma. Se usa con el subjuntivo para expresar deseos.

Ojalá que haya paz (*peace*) en el mundo algún día.
Ojalá que mis abuelos estén bien.

Imagine que Ud. desea tres cosas: una para Ud. personalmente, otra para algún miembro de su familia y otra para el país o la humanidad. ¿Qué desea Ud.? Exprese sus deseos empezando con **Ojalá que...**

Palabras útiles: ganar (*to win*) (las elecciones, el partido, ...), la guerra (*war*), terminar (*to end*), el millonario (la millonaria), resolver (ue)

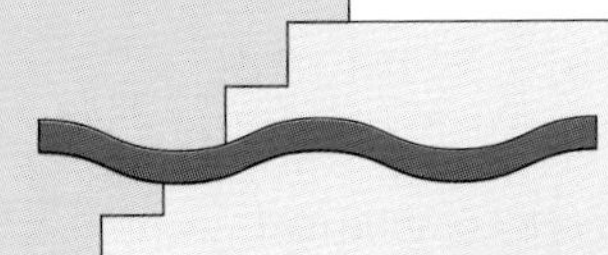

SITUACIONES

Situaciones: See IM for suggestions, additional exercises, and supplementary dialogues and exercises.

UN FIN de semana QUE JUSTIFICA LOS MEDIOS.
Un fin de semana en el AL ANDALUS EXPRESO. Madrid-Córdoba-Sevilla con toda la magia y esplendor de un tren fantástico que pone a su disposición todos los medios del más lujoso hotel.
Haga este itinerario por gusto. Viaje en un maravilloso hotel sobre raíles. Es un placer que Ud. recordará siempre.

RENFE
MEJORA TU TREN DE VIDA
AL ANDALUS EXPRESO
UN FIN DE SEMANA INOLVIDABLE.
Desde 39.000 pts. Infórmese en su agencia de viajes.

Buscando transporte

En el aeropuerto

—Buenas tardes, señor.
—Muy buenas. Aquí están mi boleto y mi pasaporte.
—Perfecto. ¿Éste es todo el equipaje que va a facturar?
—Sí, sólo esas dos maletas.
—Y ¿dónde quiere sentarse°? *be seated*
—Me gustaría que me ponga en la sección de los no fumadores. Quiero la ventanilla° y lo más adelante posible,° por favor. *window seat* / lo... *as far forward as possible*
—Muy bien. Tiene el asiento 23A. Ya puede seguir a la puerta de embarque° número 7. El vuelo está atrasado veinticinco minutos solamente. ¿ ?

En la estación del tren

—Quisiera° un billete Madrid–Sevilla. *May I please have*
—¿Para qué tren?
—Quiero viajar de noche.
—En ese caso tiene un expreso a las 20:45,° y otro a las 23.° las nueve menos cuarto de la noche / las once de la noche
—Bien. Déme uno para el tren de las 23.

En la estación de autobuses

—Por favor, un boleto para Guanajuato.
—Ya no quedan° boletos para esta mañana. Tiene que esperar hasta la tarde. no... ¿ ?
—¿A qué hora sale el primero?
—Tiene autobús a las cuatro y media, a las seis, a las siete, a las nueve y a las diez y cuarto.
—Muy bien. Déme un boleto para las cuatro y media. ¿Puedo comprar ahora un boleto de regreso° para esta misma noche? vuelta
—Por supuesto.° El último sale de Guanajuato a las diez. Por... *Of course.*

Notas comunicativas sobre el diálogo

In class you are frequently asked to use complete sentences. But when you speak Spanish outside of the classroom, you don't always speak in complete sentences—sometimes because you do not know or cannot remember how to say something. And when you try to say a long sentence, such as "*Would you be so kind as to tell me how I can get to the train station?*", it is easy to get tongue-tied, to omit something, or to mispronounce a word. When this happens, the listener often has trouble understanding. A shorter, more direct phrase or sentence often yields more effective results. A simple **perdón** or **por favor** followed by **¿la estación del tren?** is both adequate and polite.

To accomplish something more complicated, such as buying two first-class tickets on Tuesday's 10:50 A.M. train for Guanajuato, you might begin by saying, «**Dos boletos para Guanajuato, por favor.**» After that you can add other information, often in response to the questions that the ticket agent will ask you. By breaking the message down into manageable bits of information, you simplify the communication process for both parties.

A word of caution, though: You may streamline your message, but native speakers may answer using complex sentences and words that are unfamiliar to you. Be prepared to guess, relying on context and on real-world information. You can also use the following strategies.

Repita, por favor. No comprendo.	*Repeat, please. I don't understand.*
Por favor, repita ____.	*Please, repeat* ____. (If you can, repeat or approximate the word or phrase you didn't understand.)
Más despacio, por favor.	*More slowly, please.*
¿Me lo escribe, por favor?	*Will you write it down for me, please?*

Conversación

How would you go about getting the following information? Prepare a series of short statements and questions that will help you get all the information you need. Your instructor will play the role of ticketseller, travel agent, or flight attendant.

MODELO: You need to buy two first-class tickets on Tuesday's 10:50 A.M. train for Guanajuato. → Dos boletos para Guanajuato, por favor. Para el martes, el tren de las 10:50. De primera clase, por favor.

1. You need to buy two second-class (**segunda clase**) train tickets for today's 2:50 P.M. train for Barcelona.
2. You are at the train station and need to find out how to get to the university—which you understand is quite some distance away—by 10:00 A.M.
3. The flight you are on is arriving late, and you will probably miss your connecting flight to Mexico City. You want to explain your situation to the flight attendant and find out how you can get to Mexico City by 7:00 this evening.
4. You are talking to a travel agent and want to fly from Santiago, Chile, to Quito, Ecuador. You are traveling with two friends who prefer to travel first class, and you need to arrive in Quito by Saturday afternoon.

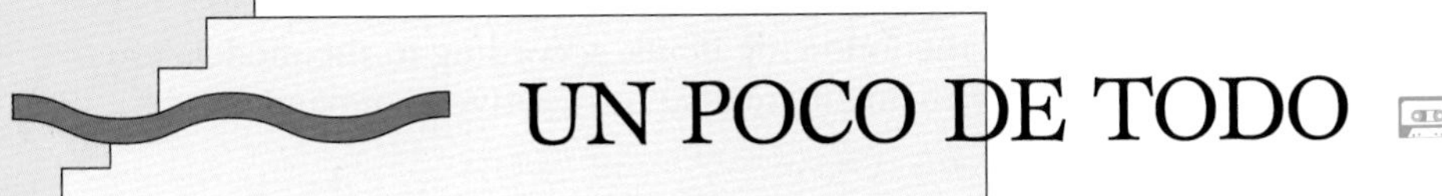

UN POCO DE TODO

A. **En el aeropuerto.** Form complete sentences based on the words given, in the order given. Conjugate the verbs and add other words if necessary. Use subject pronouns only when needed. Use the subjunctive forms or an **Ud.** command of the italicized verbs.

1. (yo) querer / que / (tú) *comprar*me / boleto / primero / clase; / yo / esperarte / aquí
2. ojalá que / no / *haber* / mucho / pasajeros; / mí / no / gustar / nada / hacer cola
3. no / *fumar* / Uds., / por favor; / mi / compañero / no / gustar / humo
4. nosotros / querer / que / vuelo / *llegar* / tiempo; / nosotros / no / gustar / esperar
5. (yo) no / querer / que Ud. / *facturar*me / equipaje; / mi / maletas / ser / nuevo / y / yo / no / querer / que / Uds. / *perder*las

B. **Preparativos para un viaje.** ¿Cómo se dice en español?

1. Pack (**Ud.**) your bags. I want you to (**Quiero que...**) pack your bags.
2. Don't forget your wallet. I don't want you to (**No quiero que...**) forget your wallet.
3. Go to the airport. I want you to (**Quiero que...**) go to the airport.
4. Don't be (**llegar**) late. I don't want you to be late.
5. Buy your round-trip ticket. I want you to buy your round-trip ticket.
6. Check your bags. I want you to check your bags.
7. Wait in line. I want you to wait in line.
8. Give your ticket to the flight attendant. I want you to give your ticket to the flight attendant.
9. Get on the plane. I want you to get on the plane.
10. Find your seat. I want you to find your seat.

Notas lingüísticas: Exclamations

Strong reactions can be expressed in Spanish with a simple formula.

¡**Qué** libro!	*What a book!*
¡**Qué** libro **más** largo!	*What a long book!*
¡**Qué** día!	*What a day!*
¡**Qué** día **más** bonito!	*What a pretty day!*

Note that there is no Spanish equivalent for English *a* (*an*) in these expressions.

Note (*Notas lingüísticas*): *¡qué* + noun! = what a + noun!

Variation C: Students provide situations on which exclamations are based.

C. **Situaciones.** React to the following items, according to the model. Your partner will respond with an affirmative or negative command, as appropriate.

MODELO: canción / bonito →
—¡Qué canción más bonita! ¡Me gusta muchísimo!
—¿Ah, sí? Pues, cántela (tóquela, escúchela).

1. ¡Qué canción más fea!
2. ¡Qué vestido más elegante!
3. ¡Qué abrigo más caro!
4. ¡Qué novela más interesante!
5. ¡Qué libro más aburrido!
6. ¡Qué pintura más estupenda!
7. ¡Qué ciudad más interesante!
8. ¡Qué viaje más largo!

Suggestion CH: Refer students to photo of *Machu-Picchu* in *Repaso 5.*

CH. **Recomendaciones para las vacaciones.** Complete the following vacation suggestion with the correct form of the words in parentheses, as suggested by the context. When two possibilities are given in parentheses, select the correct word.

(*Les/Los*[1]) quiero decir (*algo/nada*[2]) sobre (*el/la*[3]) ciudad de Machu-Picchu. ¿Ya (*lo/la*[4]) (*saber/conocer*[5]) Uds.? (*Ser/Estar*[6]) situada en los Andes, a unos ochenta kilómetros° de la ciudad de Cuzco (Perú). Machu-Picchu es conocida° como (*el/la*[7]) ciudad escondida° de los incas. Se (*decir*[8]) que (*ser/estar*[9]) una de las manifestaciones (*más/tan*[10]) importantes de la arquitectura incaica. Era° refugio y a la vez ciudad de vacaciones de los reyes° (*incaico*[11]).

Yo (*querer*[12]) que Uds. la (*visitar*[13]) porque (*ser/estar*[14]) un sitio inolvidable.° (*Ir*[15]) Uds. a Machu-Picchu en primavera o verano—son las (*mejor*[16]) estaciones para visitar este lugar. Pero (*comprar*[17]) Uds. los boletos pronto, porque (*mucho*[18]) turistas de todos los (*país*[19]) del mundo (*visitar*[20]) este sitio extraordinario. ¡(*Saber/Conocer*[21]) que a Uds. (*los/les*[22]) va a (*gustar*[23]) el viaje!

50 millas
known / hidden
It was
kings
unforgettable

¿Cierto o falso? Conteste según la descripción.

1. Machu-Picchu está en Chile.
2. Fue un lugar importante en el pasado.
3. Todavía es una atracción turística de gran interés.
4. Sólo los turistas latinoamericanos conocen Machu-Picchu.

Preliminary D: Formulate questions to use in the interviews, with students working as a class. Write questions on the board.

D. **¿Has viajado a Machu-Picchu?** Do you know where your classmates have traveled and how they have traveled? Interview a classmate to find out the following information.

1. una gran ciudad o centro turístico de los Estados Unidos a la que fue una vez (o varias veces)
2. una ciudad o centro turístico que le gustaría visitar
3. si ha viajado a Europa (¿A qué país?) / a Latinoamérica (¿A qué país?) / a Asia, África, Centroamérica, otro país de Norteamérica
4. el país que más le gustaría visitar y por qué

After completing the survey, compile the results of all of the interviews to determine the following:

1. el lugar visitado por la mayoría (*majority*) de la gente
2. el lugar que la mayoría de la gente quiere visitar
3. la persona que ha visitado el mayor número de continentes

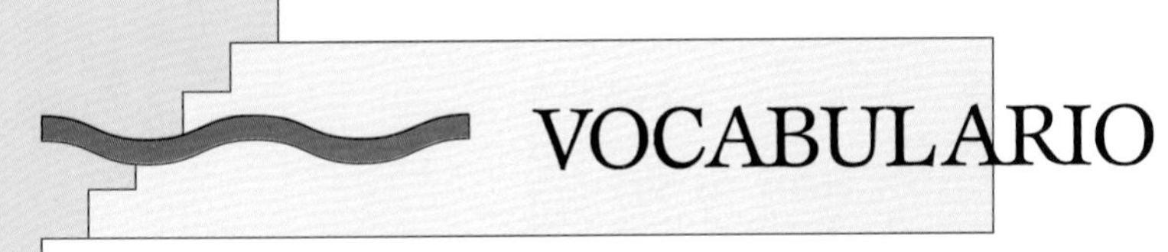

VOCABULARIO

VERBOS

anunciar to announce
bajar (de) to get down (from); to get off (of)
correr to run
dar (*irreg.*) to give
decir (*irreg.*) to say; to tell
despegar to take off (*airplane*)
doblar to turn (*a corner*)
encontrar (ue) to find
explicar to explain
facturar to check (*baggage*)
fumar to smoke
guardar to watch over; to save (*a place*)
gustar to be pleasing
mandar to send
olvidar to forget
parecer to seem
preguntar to ask, inquire
prestar to lend
querer (ie) to love
regalar to give (*as a gift*)
seguir (i, i) to continue; to follow
subir (a) to go up; to get on (*a vehicle*)

LOS VIAJES

el aeropuerto airport
el asiento seat
el autobús bus
el avión airplane
la azafata female flight attendant
el barco boat, ship
el billete/boleto ticket; **de ida** one-way; **de ida y vuelta** round-trip
la cabina cabin (*in a ship*)
el/la camarero/a flight attendant
la demora delay
el equipaje baggage, luggage
la estación station
del tren train station
de autobuses bus station
el humo smoke
la llegada arrival
el maletero porter
el pasaje passage, ticket
el/la pasajero/a passenger
el puesto place (*in line, etc.*)
la sala de espera waiting room
la salida departure
la tarjeta (postal) (post)card
el tren train
el vuelo flight

OTROS SUSTANTIVOS

la ayuda help, assistance
el dulce piece of candy; *pl.* sweets

ADJETIVOS

atrasado/a (*with* **estar**) late
solo/a alone
tranquilo/a calm, tranquil

PALABRAS ADICIONALES

a tiempo on time
la clase turística tourist class
derecho straight ahead
hacer cola to stand in line; **hacer escalas** to have stopovers; **hacer las maletas** to pack one's suitcases
lo que what, that which
por fin finally, at last
la primera clase first class
la sección de (no) fumar (non)smoking section

estar de vacaciones to be on vacation
ir de vacaciones to go on vacation

Frases útiles para la comunicación

fui, fuiste, fue	I, you, he/she/it went
he, has, ha + viajado	I, you have traveled, he/she/it has traveled
me gustaría...	I would really like . . .
ojalá que + *subjunctive*	I wish, hope that (*something happens*)
¡qué + *noun***!**	What a . . . !

UN PASO MÁS 7

OPTIONAL SECTION

A propósito... Saying What You Don't Know How to Say

Even in our native language we find ourselves in situations in which we don't know the word or phrase to express a concept. We cope with situations like this by paraphrasing: using synonyms, explaining what the item or concept is like, what it is used for or made of, and so on.

Learning to paraphrase in Spanish will help you get your message across even when you don't know the exact word or words you need. Here are some simple phrases that will help you say something in different words.

Es una persona que...
Es algo que se usa (una cosa) para... + *infinitive*
Es lo que uso cuando...
Es un lugar donde la gente...

Extension A: Kleenex, gloves, stationery, a mechanical pencil, a television set

▲ Actividad A. Necesito comprar...

Imagine that you need to buy the following items but do not know—or have forgotten—the words in Spanish. Try to get your idea across to a Spanish-speaking clerk by paraphrasing, using synonyms, telling what the item is like, what it is used for, what it is made of, and so on.

MODELO: *a suitcase* → Necesito comprar algo para mi viaje. Lo uso para llevar mi ropa y mis otras cosas. Cuando tengo demasiada ropa y demasiadas cosas, otra persona me ayuda a cerrarlo.

1. a wallet
2. motion-sickness pills
3. a bread box
4. a music box
5. a hammock
6. postcards
7. a briefcase

▲ Actividad B. ¿Dónde está mi maleta?

You arrive at your destination, but your luggage does not. When you go to the baggage claim area, you are required to fill out a form. With another student, play the roles of **agente** and **pasajero/a**. The **agente** will ask the following questions in order to fill out the form. The list will help you describe your suitcase.

IBERIA
LÍNEAS AÉREAS DE ESPAÑA S.A.

PARTE DE IRREGULARIDAD DE EQUIPAJE
PROPERTY IRREGULARITY REPORT
P. I. R.

Apellido(s) del Pasajero *Passenger's name* | Inicial(es) del Nombre *Initial(s)*

Itinerario del pasajero según su cupón *Passenger's itinerary as per passenger coupon* ** | Compañía *Airline* | N.° de Vuelo *Flight N°* | Mes *Month* | Día *Day* | De *From* | A *To*

Etiqueta de equipaje n.° de serie *Baggage Tag-Serial N.°* | Compañía *Airline* | 4 últimos digitos *Last 4 digits*

Tipo de equipaje y Código de Colores *Baggage Type and Colour Codes* | Tipo *Type* | Color *Colour* | Tipo *Type* | Color *Colour* | Tipo *Type* | Color *Colour*

Contenido (Cualquiera de los artículos más corrientes indicados en el reverso) *Contents (Any of the distinct items listed overleaf)*

Instrucciones para la entrega local *Local delivery instructions* | Peso total del equipaje facturado *Total weight of checked baggage*

Título del pasajero *Passenger's title* | Correspondencia con el pasajero *Correspondence with the passenger* Idiomas: *Languages:* Español *Spanish* ☐ Inglés *English* ☐ Otro *Other* ☐ | Llaves adjuntas al PIR-*Keys attached to PIR* ☐ Llaves no adjuntas al PIR-*Keys not attached to PIR* ☐

Dirección permanente del pasajero y n.° de teléfono *Passenger's permanent address and telephone n°* | Direccion temporal y n.° de teléfono. A partir de/hasta *Temporary address telephone n°. Date from/to*

Fecha-*Date* | Firma del empleado autorizado por la Compañía *Company official's signature* | Este informe no supone ninguna aceptación de responsabilidad por parte de IBERIA. *This report does not involve any acknowledgement of liability for IBERIA.* | Firma del pasajero *Passenger's signature*

EQUIPAJE
Baggage

Color: *Colour:*	Use el siguiente Código de colores. *Use following colour codes.*
ALU	Plateado (*Aluminum, Silver*).
BLU	Azul (*Blue*).
BLK	Negro (*Black*).
BRN	Marrón, Tostado, del Cervato, Bronce, Cobre, Óxido de hierro, Rojo oscuro (*Brown, Tan, Fawn, Bronze, Copper, Rust, Oxblood*).
CLR	Claro, Traslúcido, Opaco, Plástico (*Clear, Translucent, Opaque, Plastic*).
CRM	Beige, Crema, Marfil, Ante (*Beige, Cream, Ivory, Buff*).
GRN	Verde (*Green, Olive*).
GRY	Gris (*Grey*).
PLD	Cuadros escoceses, Ajedrezado, Jaspeado (*Plaid, Checked, Tweed*).
RED	Rojo, Castaño, Rosa (*Red, Maroon, Pink*).
STR	Listado (*Striped*).
TPY	Tapizado, Floreado, Moteado (*Tapestry, Floral, Spotted*).
WHT	Blanco (*White*).
YLW	Amarillo, Naranja (*Yellow, Orange*).

Material: Para describir la clase de material, utilice una de las siguientes palabras:
Material: For the description of the material, use one of the following.

CUERO	— *LEATHER*
FIBRA	— *FIBRE*
METAL	— *METAL*
PLÁSTICO	— *PLASTIC*
MADERA	— *WOOD*
LONA	— *CANVAS*
CARTÓN	— *CARDBOARD*

AGENTE:

1. ¿Cuál es su apellido, por favor? ¿y sus iniciales?
2. ¿De dónde salió (*left from*) su vuelo? ¿Cuál es el número de su vuelo?
3. ¿Cuál es el número de la etiqueta (*tag*) de su maleta?
4. ¿De qué material es? ¿de qué color?
5. ¿Qué contiene su maleta?
6. ¿Cuál es su dirección (*address*) permanente? ¿y su teléfono?
7. ¿Cuál es su dirección temporal aquí? ¿y el nombre de su hotel? ¿hasta qué fecha?

LECTURA CULTURAL

Lectura: See IM for suggestions and additional exercises and activities.

Antes de leer: Accessing Background Information

Before beginning a reading, it is sometimes helpful to think about the information the reading might contain in order to review important background information you already know about the topic. For example, if you are reading a newspaper account of a traffic accident, what kinds of information and details would you expect to find in it? What kinds of information would you find in a magazine article about drugs? In a manual for the owner of a car or a computer?

Working with a partner, spend three minutes "brainstorming" about ideas and information you think will be presented in the following advertisements about vacation spots. You can talk in English or in Spanish. Then, working as a class, share your ideas and select the ten most frequently mentioned ideas. How many of the ideas actually appear in the reading?

¡Venga con nosotros a... !

Los siguientes anuncios son de revistas y periódicos sudamericanos y caribeños. Léalos para saber dónde y cómo la gente latinoamericana puede pasar sus vacaciones.

este verano
viva la naturaleza
en
TERMAS de CHILLAN

SALUD, DESCANSO Y ENTRETENCION PARA TODA LA FAMILIA

NATURALEZA Y ENTRETENCION
- PISCINA
- PASEOS A CABALLO
- CAMINATAS A PRECIOSOS LUGARES
- TENIS
- PASEOS EN TELESILLA
- JUEGOS INFANTILES
- ASADOS

EXCELENTE HOTEL
- TELEVISION Y VIDEO-CINE
- JUEGOS ELECTRONICOS
- PARVULARIA
- ORQUESTA
- DISCOTHEQUE

SALUD Y TERMALISMO
- BAÑOS TERMALES DE AZUFRE, FIERRO Y VAPOR NATURAL
- FANGOTERAPIA
- SAUNA, HIDROMASAJES
- COSMETOLOGIA
- MASAJES KINESICOS
- SERVICIO MEDICO

ACTIVIDADES CULTURALES
- OBRAS DE TEATRO
- CONCIERTOS
- RECITALES
- MUSICA CLASICA
- EXPOSICIONES
- CHARLAS CULTURALES Y CIENTIFICAS

VENGA CON SU FAMILIA Y VIVA LA NATURALEZA EN TERMAS DE CHILLAN.

CREDITO HASTA 12 MESES

SANTIAGO: PROVIDENCIA 2237 LOCAL P. 41 ☎ 2515776-2512685.
CONCEPCION: O'HIGGINS 734 LOCAL 14 ☎ 234981.
CHILLAN: ARAUCO 600 ☎ 223664.

B&G

Disfrute con Lan Chile las mejores vacaciones de su vida.

Punta del Este, un lugar pleno de atracciones para usted y su familia. Maravillosas playas, casino, vida nocturna. Un lugar que usted y los suyos pueden disfrutar ahora intensamente con Lan Chile y su programa espectacular.
Consulte a su Agente de Viajes o a Lan Chile.

Programa Espectacular Incluye:
- Recepción y traslados aeropuerto-hotel-aeropuerto.
- Alojamiento por 7 noches con desayuno, en hotel de su elección.
- City tour.
- Opcional/arriendo de auto (kilometraje ilimitado).
- Seguro médico y asistencia jurídica gratuita los tres primeros días. I.T.C. (Travellers Assistance Ltd.).

*Precio por persona en base habitación doble.

Una buena razón para ser los mejores.

Comprensión

A. ¿Cuál de los tres sitios de los anuncios...

- se caracteriza por sus fenómenos naturales?
- tiene interés histórico?
- es un lugar de veraneo muy moderno?

B. ¿Adónde van a querer viajar las siguientes personas? Conteste según los anuncios. Algunas preguntas tienen más de una respuesta correcta.

1. una persona a quien le interesa mucho la antropología
2. una persona a quien le gusta practicar varios deportes
3. una persona que tiene pasión por el juego (*gambling*)
4. un matrimonio que tiene que pasar las vacaciones con sus niños
5. una persona que sobre todo (*especially*) quiere pasar el tiempo en la playa
6. una persona para quien los aspectos culturales del lugar son de gran importancia

Para escribir

Imagine you are writing out some travel tips for a Spanish-speaking friend who is going to visit the United States. How will you complete each sentence?

1. Si quieres visitar una gran ciudad, te recomiendo la ciudad de _____. Allí puedes ver _____.
2. Si te interesa nadar y pasar el tiempo en la playa, ¿por qué no vas a _____? Tiene _____.
3. Entre las atracciones turísticas de este país, la que más me gusta es _____. Te recomiendo este lugar porque _____.
4. Una vez fui a _____ y no me gustó. Por eso no te recomiendo que vayas allí.
5. Un fenómeno natural que tienes que ver es _____ porque _____.

CAPÍTULO OCHO

LO QUE TENGO Y LO QUE QUIERO

a. *saving*
b. *logré... I was able to accumulate*
c. *feel*
ch. *being*

▲ **En la residencia**

—¿Qué necesitas todavía para tu cuarto?

—Prácticamente, lo necesito todo.

—Entonces, ¿por qué no vamos de compras esta tarde?

—Pues... el problema es que mi cheque de ayuda financiera no llega hasta la semana que viene.

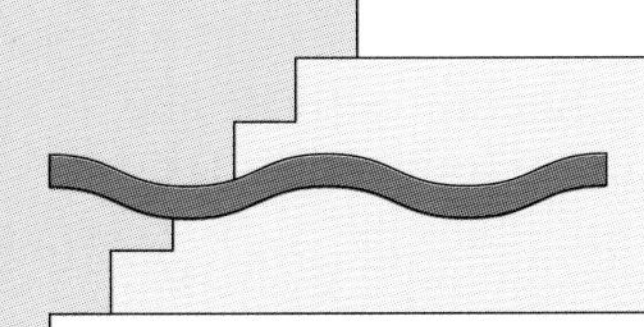

Vocabulario: Preparación:
- See detailed supplementary materials for this section bound into the back of this Annotated Instructor's Edition.

VOCABULARIO: PREPARACIÓN

- See model for vocabulary presentation and other materials in Supplementary *Vocabulario: Preparación* Materials, chapter by chapter, IM.

- See also [video icon] and [audio icon]

Los cuartos, los muebles° y las otras partes de una casa

°*furniture*

la alcoba*	bedroom
el baño	bathroom
la cocina	kitchen
el comedor	dining room
el garaje	garage
la pared	wall
el patio	patio; yard
la piscina	swimming pool
la sala	living room

la alfombra	rug
la cama (de agua)	(water) bed
la cómoda	bureau
el escritorio	desk
el estante	bookshelf
la lámpara	lamp
la mesa	table
la mesita	end table
la silla	chair
el sillón	armchair
el sofá	sofa

A. Identifique las partes de esta casa y diga lo que hay en cada (*each*) cuarto.

B. ¿A qué parte de la casa se refiere? Identifique el lugar y luego explique quién habla y con quién habla. Invente todos los detalles necesarios.

Palabras útiles: la criada (*maid*), las visitas (*guests*)

1. Por favor, ponga la leche en el refrigerador.
2. Tu hermanito está jugando afuera.
3. El niño está durmiendo. Por favor, no hagan tanto ruido.
4. ¡Este perro está muy sucio! Tenemos que lavarlo (*to wash him*).
5. El médico quiere que hagas más ejercicio. Y aquí estás, sentado en el sofá como siempre.
6. Pasen Uds., por favor. ¡Bienvenidos a esta casa!
7. ¿Por qué no invitas a Carmen y Jorge a cenar el sábado?
8. ¿Cómo es posible? Todavía tienes las manos (*hands*) sucias y es la hora de comer.

Note B: More than one answer is possible for many of these items. Encourage students to give several answers and to explain their reasons.

*Other frequently used words for *bedroom* include **el dormitorio** and **la habitación**.

Follow-up C: *¿Qué le gustaría tener en su casa (apartamento) ideal?* Students present their ideal residence to the class, followed by comprehension questions asked by you based on the presentation. **Suggestion:** Assign as brief composition, which you correct before students read to the class.

C. ¿Qué muebles o partes de la casa asocia Ud. con las siguientes actividades? Compare sus asociaciones con las de otros estudiantes. ¿Tienen todos las mismas costumbres?

1. estudiar para un examen importante
2. dormir la siesta por la tarde
3. pasar una noche en casa con la familia
4. comer con las visitas

Tengo... Quiero... Necesito...

Los bienes personales°

°Los... *Possessions*

el cartel	poster
la pintura	painting
el trofeo	trophy
el acuario	aquarium
el pájaro	bird
el pez	fish
el compact disc	compact disc (player)
el equipo estereofónico	stereo equipment
el equipo fotográfico	photographic equipment
el grabador de vídeo	VCR
la radio (portátil)	(portable) radio
el televisor	TV set
la bicicleta	bicycle
la camioneta	station wagon
el coche (descapotable)	car (convertible)
la motocicleta	motorcycle

Es época de adviento navideño y, con toda seguridad, usted quiere regalarse algo para disfrutarlo en familia... Una buena posibilidad es incorporarse al mundo del video. Pensando en ello es que en esta edición le entregamos una completa guía de compras de videograbadores, video-reproductores, cámaras y equipos de grabación y cintas para su equipo. En suma, todo lo que usted podrá encontrar de equipamiento de videos.

Pero como la adquisición de uno de estos aparatos implica una decisión de cierta relevancia, hemos querido también explicarle todo lo que usted debe tener presente en el momento de la compra. El mundo del video se ha expandido aceleradamente en nuestro país y en todo el planeta, a raíz de las infinitas posibilidades culturales y de entretención que pone al alcance de quienes entran en él.

En la oficina

la computadora (el ordenador)*	computer
la impresora	printer
la máquina de escribir	typewriter
el aumento	raise
el cheque	check
los impuestos	taxes
el/la jefe/a	boss
el sueldo	salary
el trabajo	job, work; written work; (term) paper

Verbos útiles

cambiar (de cuarto, de puesto, de ropa...)	to change (rooms, jobs, clothing, . . .)
conseguir (i, i)	to get, obtain
funcionar	to function, operate, work
ganar	to earn; to win
manejar	to drive
sacar fotos	to take photos

*Note: **La computadora** is the term most commonly used in Hispanic America. **El ordenador** is used primarily in Spain.

A. ¿Qué acción o descripción corresponde a los sustantivos que están a la izquierda?

1. el grabador de vídeo
2. el cartel
3. el aumento de sueldo
4. el trabajo
5. el acuario
6. el equipo fotográfico
7. el trofeo
8. los impuestos

a. Es necesario si queremos combatir la inflación.
b. Son todas las cosas que necesitamos si nos gusta sacar fotos.
c. Es la parte de nuestro sueldo que le pagamos al gobierno (*government*).
ch. Lo que nos dan cuando ganamos una competencia.
d. El lugar donde viven los peces que tenemos en casa.
e. Algo que colgamos (*we hang*) en la pared.
f. Lo usamos cuando hay un programa de televisión que queremos ver pero estamos ocupados en ese momento.
g. Puede tener mucho prestigio y ser muy interesante o puede ser algo monótono.

Notas comunicativas: More About Expressing Interests

You already know how to use the verb **gustar** to talk about what you and others like. Here are some additional verbs that are used in exactly the same way.

interesar: No **me interesa** nada el arte moderno.
Me interesan mucho las ciencias.
encantar: ¡**Me encanta** cocinar!
Me encantan las películas extranjeras.

Suggestion B: Use drawing as a springboard for the activity. Ask students to read all the descriptions, then tell which one corresponds to drawing, explaining their reasons. Then let them work in pairs to create rooms for the remaining three items.

B. ¿Qué tienen las siguientes personas en casa, en su cuarto o en su oficina? Con otros dos compañeros, contesten, inventando todos los detalles posibles. Luego comparen sus descripciones con las de otros grupos. Estén preparados para explicar sus respuestas. Si dicen que una persona tiene un equipo fotográfico, tienen que decir por qué: le gusta sacar fotografías, lo necesita para su trabajo, etcétera.

1. Maripepa tiene un trabajo de tiempo parcial por las tardes, en el centro. Hace la correspondencia para un dentista y les manda las

cuentas a sus pacientes. Por las mañanas toma clases en un «community college» que está en los suburbios. Este semestre estudia literatura inglesa. Tiene que leer mucho y hacer muchos trabajos académicos. Le interesa mucho la fotografía.

2. Teresa tiene una vida muy activa. Le gusta participar en los deportes y también sigue los deportes profesionales con gran interés. Le encanta pasar tiempo fuera de casa, en el campo (*country*) o en el parque. También escucha mucho la música y le encanta visitar el zoo.
3. Francisco no tiene una vida muy activa. Es contador (*accountant*). Maneja su coche a la oficina por la mañana y regresa a casa por la noche. Le interesan mucho el arte y la música y también le encantan las telenovelas (*soap operas*).
4. Los Fuentes tienen cinco hijos. Aunque (*Although*) los dos esposos trabajan, pasan mucho tiempo con los niños por las noches y durante los fines de semana. Los ayudan mucho con su tarea (*homework*). No les gusta que los niños pasen mucho tiempo mirando la televisión pero sí les interesa que vean películas y vídeos de interés cultural. Creen que los niños deben llevar una vida muy activa y que es una buena experiencia para un niño tener la responsabilidad de cuidar de (*take care of*) un animal.

Suggestion C:
- Have students suggest other solutions for each problem.
- Working in groups, students select or invent solutions and explain reasons. To save time, have each group work on just one problem.

C. Escoja (*Choose*) el mejor consejo para cada situación. Luego justifique su respuesta.

1. Su jefe es muy antipático.
   a. Cambie de puesto, porque los jefes no cambian nunca.
   b. Sea muy simpático/a para ver si él empieza a cambiar de actitud con Ud.
   c. ¿ ?
2. Su compañero/a de cuarto en la residencia es una persona muy desordenada... ¡y Ud. es todo lo contrario!
   a. Cambie de cuarto. No es posible que una persona desordenada aprenda a ser organizada.
   b. Insista en que su compañero/a cambie de cuarto, porque a Ud. le encanta el cuarto que tiene ahora.
   c. ¿ ?
3. Ud. gana un sueldo muy bajo.
   a. Explíquele su situación a su jefe y pídale un aumento.
   b. Consiga un trabajo de tiempo parcial por las noches.
   c. ¿ ?
4. Su coche es muy viejo y no funciona muy bien.
   a. Pídales dinero a sus padres para conseguir otro coche.
   b. No vuelva a manejarlo. Véndalo y empiece a tomar el autobús.
   c. ¿ ?

Notas lingüísticas: More About Describing Things

You already know that the verb **ser** can be used with **de** + a *noun* to tell what something is made of: **La falda es *de algodón*. La camisa es *de lana*.** These descriptions could also be expressed in this way: **Es una falda de algodón. Es una camisa de lana.** The English equivalent of these phrases is *a cotton skirt*, *a wool shirt*.

As you can see in these examples, an English noun can modify another noun, to express the material of which something is made: ***a gold watch***. The same *noun* + *noun* structure is used in English to describe the nature of a place or thing: *the language lab*, *a summer day*.

In Spanish, this structure can only be expressed by using a *noun* + **de** + *noun* phrase: **un reloj *de* oro, el laboratorio *de* lenguas, un día *de* verano**. You have seen this structure in some of the new vocabulary for this chapter: **una cama de agua, un grabador de vídeo, una máquina de escribir**.

Zoquetes de streech femenino con logo.
Artículo 038.
Set de 4 pares de colores diferentes.
Precio del set: ₳ 14.
UNIQUE
Maletín. De goma negra, art. 011 precio: ₳ 160.
De cocodrilo negro art. 012a y marrón 012b. Precio: ₳ 200.

Suggestion CH: Be sure that students know what the *Objetos* mean. Encourage guessing in context with these words especially: *las piezas*, (*agua*) *salada*, *el saco* (*de dormir*).

CH. ¿De quiénes son los siguientes objetos? Explique su respuesta.

Objetos: la alarma de seguridad, las piezas de cerámica, el acuario de agua salada, los trofeos de tenis, la tienda de campaña (*tent*), el saco de dormir

1. A Adela le encantan los deportes. De hecho (*In fact*), es campeona de golf, tenis y vólibol.
2. A Geraldo le gusta hacer *camping* en las montañas.
3. Los señores de Inza son muy ricos. Tienen una casa magnífica y una colección de pinturas de un valor incalculable.
4. Laura tiene una pequeña colección de figuras de animales.
5. A Ernestito le interesan mucho los peces. Tiene más de 100 peces tropicales.

Suggestion D: Assign as written composition, asking students to select one of the three topics.

D. **Tengo... Necesito... Quiero...** Consulte la lista de **Palabras útiles** (página 250) antes de contestar las siguientes preguntas.

1. ¿Qué tiene Ud. en su cuarto (apartamento, casa)? ¿Qué necesita con urgencia? ¿Qué quiere tener algún día?
2. ¿Qué hay en la casa de sus padres (de un amigo o una amiga) que a Ud. le gustaría tener? ¿Por qué quiere Ud. tener lo/la?
3. Imagine que Ud. puede pedirle cualquier cosa a un amigo (una amiga)... ¡y recibirla! ¿Qué le va a pedir?

MODELO: Quiero que ____ me des un(a) ____ de ____.

Palabras útiles:

Materiales: oro, plata (*silver*), diamantes, cristal, porcelana, cerámica, madera (*wood*); cuero (*leather*), ante (*suede*), pieles (*fur*); pana (*corduroy*), dril (*denim*), mezclilla (*tweed*).

Objetos: anillo (*ring*), cadena (*chain*), reloj, pendientes (*earrings*), pulsera (*bracelet*); pieza, figura, vaso, escultura

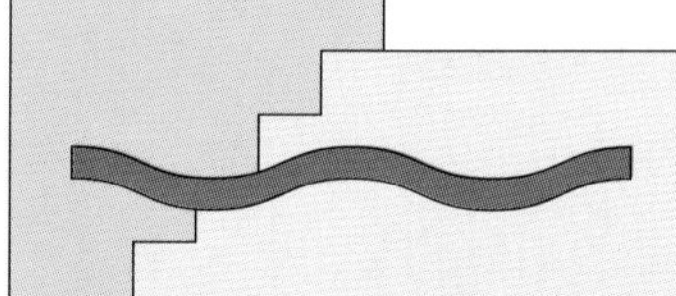

MINIDIÁLOGOS Y GRAMÁTICA

Suggestion: Ask students to pick out subjunctive and subjunctive cues in mini. Ask: What do cues have in common? (→ asking someone to do something).

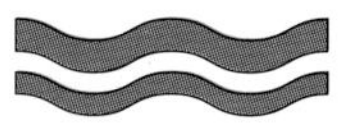

25. EXPRESSING DESIRES AND REQUESTS
Use of the Subjunctive in Noun Clauses: Concepts; Influence

El viernes, por la tarde

JEFE: Tenemos que trabajar el sábado, señores, y tal vez el domingo. *Es necesario* que el inventario *esté* listo el lunes.

EMPLEADO: Ud. *quiere* que *lleguemos* a las ocho, como siempre, ¿verdad?

JEFE: No, una hora más temprano. Y si quieren comer, *recomiendo* que *traigan* algo de casa. No va a haber tiempo para salir.

EMPLEADO: (A la empleada.) ¡Ay! Mis planes para el fin de semana... *Ojalá* que el jefe *cambie* de idea.

EMPLEADA: ¡Lo más probable es que tengas que cambiar de planes!

¿Qué va a pasar este fin de semana? Use el subjuntivo de las palabras entre paréntesis.

1. El jefe quiere que los empleados (*preparar*)...
2. Va a ser necesario que todos (*llegar*)...
3. Va a ser necesario que los empleados (*traer*)...
4. Va a ser necesario que el empleado (*cambiar*)...

Follow-up: 1. *¿Quién quiere que todos trabajen el fin de semana?* **2.** *¿Por qué tienen que trabajar?* **3.** *¿Qué otras recomendaciones hace el jefe?* **4.** *¿Al empleado le gusta la idea del trabajo extra?* **5.** *¿Qué puede pasar si el empleado no cambia de planes?* **6.** *Si Ud. trabaja, ¿cómo es su jefe/a? ¿Es como el jefe del diálogo?* **7.** *¿Tiene Ud. que trabajar cuando no quiere? ¿Tiene que cambiar de planes cuando su jefe/a lo quiere?*

Friday afternoon BOSS: We'll have to work on Saturday, people, and maybe on Sunday. It's necessary that the inventory be ready on Monday. EMPLOYEE: You're going to want us to be here at eight as usual, right? BOSS: No, an hour earlier. And if you want to eat, I recommend that you bring something from home. There won't be any time to go out. EMPLOYEE: (*To female employee.*) Oh, my plans for the weekend! I hope that the boss changes his mind. FEMALE EMPLOYEE: It's more likely that you'll have to change your plans!

Subjunctive: Sentence Structure

Independent Clause		**Dependent Clause**
I recommend	that	she write the letter.
I wish	(that)	we were already there.

Emphasis: Syntactic requirements for subjunctive: **(1)** two clauses; **(2)** a different subject in each clause.

As you saw in Grammar Section 24 (**Capítulo 7**), the subjunctive is used in the preceding English sentences. In addition, the sentences share another characteristic. Each has two clauses: an independent clause with a conjugated verb and subject that can stand alone (*I recommend, I wish*), and a dependent (subordinate) clause that cannot stand alone (*that she write, that we were there*). The subjunctive is used in the independent clause.

Indicate the independent and dependent clauses in the following sentences.

1. I don't think (that) they're very nice.
2. We feel (that) you really shouldn't go.
3. He suggests (that) we be there on time.
4. We don't believe (that) she's capable of that.

Note: "That" is often optional in English, but *que* is required in Spanish.

The Spanish subjunctive also occurs primarily in *dependent clauses* (**las cláusulas subordinadas**). Note that each clause has a different subject and that the clauses are linked by **que**.

Independent Clause		**Dependent Clause**
first subject + *indicative*	(that)	second subject + *subjunctive*
Quiero	**que**	subas al taxi.
No quiero	**que**	perdamos el vuelo.

Subjunctive: Concepts

Emphasis: Three main semantic triggers for subjunctive: influence, emotion, doubt.

In addition to the sentence structure typical of many sentences that contain the subjunctive in Spanish, the use of the subjunctive is associated with the presence, in the independent clause, of a number of concepts or conditions—influence, emotion, and doubt—that trigger the use of the subjunctive in the dependent clause.

- ***What** does the boss want?*
  Quiere que los empleados lleguen a tiempo. (*direct object*)
- ***What** does the boss like?*
  Le gusta que los empleados lleguen a tiempo. (*subject*)
- ***What** does the boss doubt?*
  Duda que los empleados siempre lleguen a tiempo. (*direct object*)

These uses of the subjunctive fall into the general category of the subjunctive in noun clauses. The clause in which the subjunctive appears functions like a noun (subject or direct object) in the sentence as a whole.

Subjunctive in Noun Clauses: Influence

Emphasis: A noun clause functions like a noun in a sentence.

Optional: Influence = willing

Independent Clause		**Dependent Clause**
first subject + *indicative* (expression of influence)	**que**	second subject + ***subjunctive***

La jefa **quiere** que los empleados **estén** contentos. — *The boss wants the employees to be happy.*

¿**Prefieres** tú que (yo) **compre** un compact disc o un grabador de vídeo? — *Do you prefer that I buy a compact disc player or a VCR?*

Es necesario que Álvaro **estudie** más. — *It's necessary that Álvaro study more.*

A. Expressions of influence are those in which someone, directly or indirectly, tries to influence what someone else does or thinks: *I suggest that you be there on time; It's necessary that you be there.* In Spanish, expressions of influence, however strong or weak, are followed by the subjunctive mood in the dependent clause.

Emphasis: Word *que* may not be omitted.

B. Some verbs of influence include **decir**, **desear**, **insistir (en)**, **mandar** (*to order* or *to send*), **pedir (i, i)**, **permitir** (*to permit*), **preferir (ie, i)**, **prohibir** (*to prohibit* or *forbid*), **querer (ie)**, and **recomendar (ie)**. Because it is impossible to give a complete list of all Spanish verbs of influence, remember that verbs that convey the sense of influencing—not just certain verbs—are followed by the subjunctive.

Point out: **(1)** When an expression of influence is followed by subject change, subjunctive is required: *La jefa quiere que los empleados estén contentos.* Ask, Who wants? (→ *la jefa*) Who is happy? (→ *los empleados*) **(2)** When there is no subject change, infinitive is used, just as in English: *Quiero estar contento.* Who wants? (→ *yo*) Who is happy? (→ *yo*, same person). Infinitive, not subjunctive, is used.

¡OJO! The subjunctive is used in the dependent clause after **decir** and **insistir en** when they convey an order. The subjunctive is *not* used when they convey information. Compare the following:

Carolina nos dice que **lleguemos** a las siete en punto. — *Carolina says (that) we should arrive at 7:00 sharp.*

Carolina dice que **son** simpáticos. — *Carolina says (that) they're nice.*

Point out: Accents on forms of *prohibir: prohíbo, prohíbes, prohíbe, prohíben.*

Additional example: *Insisto en que son/sean amigos.*

C. Remember to use the infinitive—not the subjunctive—after verbs of influence when there is no change of subject:

Desean cenar ahora.
but
Desean que **Luisa y yo cenemos** ahora.

[Práctica A]

Discrimination exercise: Influence or information? **1.** They say that it will rain. **2.** She's telling them to go away. **3.** She always tells me what she thinks. **4.** He says for you to wash the car tomorrow.

Note: The use of indirect object pronouns with verbs like *decir*, *pedir*, *prohibir*, and *recomendar* is treated in Ch. 14. You may wish to call students' attention to this usage now, however, but do not require them to produce it at this time.

CH. As you know, generalizations are followed by infinitives: **Es necesario *estudiar*.** When a generalization of influence is personalized (made to refer to a specific person), it is followed by the subjunctive in the dependent clause. **Es necesario *que estudiemos*. Es importante *que***

¡OJO! Contrast *es necesario estudiar* (no expressed subject) and *es necesario que yo estudie*.

¿Cómo se dice?: **1.** It's important to do it. **2.** It's important for Alice to do it. **3.** It's necessary to leave now. **4.** It's necessary that we leave now.

Note: Subjunctive with generalizations of influence, emotion, and doubt will be presented concurrently with those concepts rather than in a separate section.

***consiga* el puesto.** Other generalizations of influence include **es urgente**, **es preferible**, and **es preciso** (*necessary*).

[Práctica B–D]

Práctica

Preliminary exercise: *Sugerencias y recomendaciones. Dé oraciones nuevas según las indicaciones.* **1.** *En clase: El profesor no quiere que Uds. fumen (yo, nosotros, tú, los estudiantes, Lupe, vosotros)* **2.** *En casa, el día antes de la fiesta: Es necesario que alguien llame a nuestros amigos. (comprar los refrescos, buscar unos discos nuevos, invitar a nuestros amigos, traer la comida)*

Follow-up A: *¿Qué le piden a Ud. siempre sus amigos? Mis amigos siempre me piden que _____. (estudiar con ellos, salir con ellos, explicarles la gramática, ir al cine, no tomar tanto café, ¿ ?)*

A. **En la oficina.** ¿Qué recomendaciones hace la jefa? Haga oraciones completas según el modelo. Use el pronombre sujeto sólo si es necesario.

MODELO: Paco / trabajar el sábado →
La jefa quiere que Paco trabaje el sábado.

La jefa (no) quiere que...
Recomienda que...
Insiste en que...
Pide que...
Prohíbe que...

1. yo / no hablar tanto por teléfono
2. Alicia / empezar a llegar a las ocho
3. el Sr. Morales / buscar otro puesto
4. todos / ser más cuidadosos (*careful*) con los detalles
5. nosotros / tener el inventario listo para el miércoles
6. los empleados / fumar en su oficina
7. la Sra. Medina / llevar un trabajo importante a casa este fin de semana
8. los empleados / pedirle aumentos este año

¿Qué opina Ud. de esta jefa? ¿Qué tipo de persona es? ¿Es muy exigente (*demanding*)? ¿muy comprensiva? ¿Es una amiga para sus empleados? ¿Le gustaría tenerla como jefe? ¿Por qué sí o por qué no?

Optional B: Other verb phrases: *Prefiero, Es importante, Recomiendo*

Follow-up B: Students listen to statements and offer as many suggestions as possible with *Es necesario que Ud.* _____. **1.** *Tengo hambre.* **2.** *Tengo sed.* **3.** *Necesito más dinero.* **4.** *Quiero ir a Bolivia.* **5.** *Me gustaría renunciar a mi trabajo.* **6.** *Voy a casarme* (to get married) *en (mes).*

B. **Preparativos para una fiesta.** Imagine que Ud. y un grupo de amigos van a dar una fiesta en su apartamento. ¿Qué es necesario hacer para tenerlo todo preparado? Haga oraciones con una palabra o frase de cada grupo.

es necesario	que alguien	invitar a los otros amigos
es preciso	tú	comprar los refrescos
quiero	¿ ?	buscar unos discos nuevos
		ayudarme a preparar la comida
		traer un estéreo
		avisar a los vecinos (*neighbors*)
		sacar fotos durante la fiesta

C. Complete las oraciones, usando el subjuntivo de los verbos indicados.

1. No nos gusta *pagar* los impuestos, pero es preciso que (nosotros) los _____.
2. Quiero *ir* a Albania, pero nuestro gobierno prohíbe que los ciudadanos (*citizens*) de los Estados Unidos _____ a ese país.

3. Quiero *tomar* seis clases este semestre, pero el consejero no permite que ____ tantas.
4. Amanda no le quiere *regalar* nada a su primo, pero su madre insiste en que le ____ algo.
5. El abuelo está enfermo y el niño quiere *ver*lo, pero sus padres no permiten que (el niño) lo ____.
6. Nunca *descanso* mucho. Ahora todos están insistiendo en que (yo) ____ más.
7. Quiero *ir* de vacaciones este año, pero mi situación económica no permite que (yo) ____.

Suggestion CH: Do as whole-class activity. Or have students do the first sentence working individually, then work as a class to come up with explanations.

CH. **El día de mudanza** (*moving*). Ud., su esposo/a y sus hijos acaban de llegar, con todas sus cosas, a un nuevo apartamento. ¿Dónde quieren Uds. que se pongan los siguientes muebles? Siga el modelo, explicando por qué quiere cada cosa en el sitio indicado. Empiece cada oración con frases como: **Queremos que...** , **Preferimos que...** , **Es necesario que...** , **Es preciso que...**

MODELO: los trofeos de Julio / sala: verlos todos los días →
Queremos que los trofeos de Julio estén el la sala. ¡Nos gusta verlos todos los días!

1. el nuevo televisor / sala: ver la tele todos juntos
2. el televisor portátil / cocina: ver la tele mientras (*while*) cocina
3. el equipo estereofónico / alcoba de Julio: escuchar música mientras estudia
4. el sillón grande / sala: leer el periódico allí
5. las bicicletas de los niños / patio: jugar allí
6. la computadora / oficina: hacer las cuentas allí
7. el acuario / alcoba de Anita: mirar los peces

Optional Follow-up D: *Trabajo del guía* (guide). *¿Cómo se dice en español?* **1.** I want him to buy the tickets. **2.** Do you want him to check the bags? **3.** He doesn't want us to stand in line. **4.** He doesn't want us to be late.

D. **Recomendaciones del director.** ¿Cómo se dice en español?

1. I want you to do the inventory.
2. I insist that it be ready by (**para**) tomorrow.
3. If you can't do it by then (**para entonces**), I want you to work this weekend.
4. It's urgent that it be on my desk at 8 A.M.
5. I recommend that you begin it immediately (**en seguida**).

Conversación

Follow-up A: *¿Qué quiere Ud. que hagan los demás* (others)*? Complete la oración en una forma lógica, haciendo todas las oraciones posibles: Quiero que mi(s)* (*padres, novio/a, esposo/a, mejor amigo/a*) ____.

A. ¿Qué cree Ud. que ocurre en las siguientes situaciones? Primero lea las oraciones incompletas. Luego, identifique el lugar y complete las oraciones lógicamente. Compare sus respuestas con las de otros compañeros de clase. ¿Vieron todos (*Did everyone see*) la misma cosa?

1. El cliente _____. No tiene _____.
   El dependiente _____
   Siempre es preciso _____.

¿Quieres que lo haga ahora o mañana?

2. La jefa _____.
   La empleada _____.
   Parece que es urgente _____.
   Los jefes siempre _____.

3. La madre _____. Los niños _____.
   Yo creo que es necesario _____.
   Los padres siempre _____.

Optional: *Situaciones y consejos.* Students give advice in form of commands or sentences with *Quiero que...* . **1.** *Hace dos días que el hijo de la Sra. Cruz está enfermo.* **2.** *Los hijos de los Sres. Fuentes necesitan un pasaje para el vuelo 774.* **3.** *Francisco tiene sed y la azafata le pregunta qué quiere tomar.*

B. **¡Dos padres muy distintos!** Nati y Tomás tienen dos hijos: una niña de ocho años que se llama Nora y un niño de nueve años que se llama Joaquín. A los dos padres les encantan sus hijos, pero tienen ideas muy distintas sobre la mejor manera de educarlos. Tomás tiene ideas muy tradicionales, pero Nati es más moderna: cree que los niños deben crecer (*grow up*) en un ambiente de libertad y con ciertas responsabilidades, para que (*so that*) aprendan a ser adultos responsables.

Describa las ideas de Nati y Tomás sobre los siguientes temas, usando las frases como guía. Empiece sus descripciones con frases como: **Nati quiere que...**, **Tomás prefiere...**, **Nati nunca permite que...**, etcétera. Siga el modelo.

MODELO: Nora: jugar sólo con muñecas (*dolls*), tener coches también si los quiere → Tomás quiere que Nora juegue sólo con muñecas. Nati prefiere que tenga coches también, si los quiere.

1. Joaquín: tener muñecas, jugar con soldados y coches
2. Nora: ser profesora o médica algún día, ser esposa y madre
3. los niños: no tocar la computadora, aprender a usarla
4. los niños: tener animales en casa, no tener ningún animal
5. los niños: jugar en la piscina, no jugar allí solos
6. los niños: no tocar el grabador de vídeo, permitir que lo usen
7. Joaquín: aprender a cocinar, no aprender a hacerlo
8. Nora: aprender a arreglar (*repair*) el coche, no saber nada de coches
9. los niños: no ver la televisión nunca, verla cuando quieran
10. los niños: estar con ellos los fines de semana, estar con sus amigos

C. Working in groups, make a list of five things you would like someone else to do. Then present each request to someone in the class, who must either do it, promise to do it, or give a good excuse for not doing it.

MODELO: Queremos que Roberto nos traiga *donuts* mañana. →
ROBERTO: No les voy a traer *donuts* porque no tengo dinero.

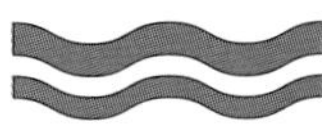

26. EXPRESSING FEELINGS

Use of the Subjunctive in Noun Clauses: Emotion

Suggestion: Ask students to pick out subjunctive and subjunctive cues in mini. Ask: What do cues have in common? (→ emotional responses)

Buenos Aires, la Argentina

Un futuro peatón

ANITA: ¿Qué tal el tráfico en la carretera esta mañana?

CARLOS: Un desastre, un verdadero desastre. Dos horas al volante, una multa y ahora un coche que no funciona como debe. *Tengo miedo* de que la transmisión no *esté* totalmente bien.

ANITA: ¡Hombre, hace años que tienes problemas de este tipo! *Me sorprende* que no *busques* un apartamento más cerca de la oficina.

JULIO: ... ¡o que no *compres* un carro nuevo!

1. Para Carlos, ¿es fácil llegar a la oficina?
2. ¿De qué tiene miedo Carlos ahora?
3. ¿Dónde vive Carlos, cerca o lejos de la oficina?
4. ¿Qué le recomiendan Anita y Julio?

Follow-up (Conversation): **1.** *¿Qué es un peatón?* (new verb: *caminar*) **2.** *¿Cuál de las tres personas puede ser un peatón en el futuro? ¿Por qué?* **3.** *¿Vive Ud. cerca de la universidad* (*cerca de su trabajo*)*?* **4.** *¿Le gustaría vivir más cerca?*

Independent Clause		**Dependent Clause**
first subject + *indicative* (expression of emotion)	**que**	second subject + *subjunctive*

Esperamos que Ud. **pueda** asistir. — *We hope (that) you'll be able to come.*

Tengo miedo (de) que mi abuelo **esté** muy enfermo. — *I'm afraid (that) my grandfather is very ill.*

Es lástima que no **den** aumentos este año. — *It's a shame they're not giving raises this year.*

¿Cómo se dice?: **1.** I'm afraid that they're not coming/that he can't do it. **2.** It surprises me that you can't do it/that he won't permit it.

A. Expressions of emotion are those in which speakers express their feelings: *I'm glad you're here*; *It's good that they can come.* Such expressions of emotion are followed by the subjunctive mood in the dependent clause.

B. Some expressions of emotion are **esperar**, **gustar**, **sentir (ie, i)** (*to regret or feel sorry*), **me (te, le,** and so on**) sorprende** (*it is surprising to me* [*you, him, her*]), **temer** (*to fear*), and **tener miedo (de)**. Since not all expressions of emotion are given here, remember that any expression of emotion—not just certain verbs—is followed by the subjunctive.

Suggestions:
- **Point out:** similarity to subjunctive after expressions of influence with change of subject
- **Emphasis:** Use infinitive—not subjunctive—after expressions and generalizations of emotion when there is no change of subject. **Examples:** *Siento estar tan cansado* vs. *Siento que estés tan cansado. Es mejor esperar* vs. *Es mejor que esperen.*

A future pedestrian ANITA: What was the traffic like on the highway this morning? CARLOS: Terrible, just terrible. Two hours at the wheel, a ticket, and now a car that isn't working as it should. I'm afraid that the transmission isn't quite right. ANITA: Man, you've had problems like these (of this kind) for years. I'm surprised you don't look for an apartment closer to the office. JULIO: . . . or buy a new car!

C. When generalizations of emotion are personalized, they are followed by the subjunctive in the dependent clause. Some expressions of emotion are **es terrible**, **es ridículo**, **es mejor/bueno/malo**, **es increíble** (*incredible*), **es extraño** (*strange*), **¡qué extraño!** (*how strange!*), **es lástima** (*shame*), and **¡qué lástima!** (*what a shame!*).

Práctica

Suggestion A: Encourage students to use the ¿ ? option to personalize the exercise.

A. **Sentimientos.** ¿Cuáles son algunas de las cosas que le gustan o que le dan miedo a Ud.?

1. Me gusta mucho que _____. (*estar contentos mis amigos, funcionar bien mi equipo estereofónico, venir todos a mis fiestas, estar bien mis padres, ¿ ?*)
2. Tengo miedo de que _____. (*haber mucho tráfico en la carretera mañana, no venir nadie a mi fiesta, haber una prueba* [quiz] *mañana, ocurrir una crisis internacional, no darme el jefe un aumento, ¿ ?*)

Suggestion B: Students invent similar situations and present them to the class.

B. **Chismes** (*Gossip*) **de la oficina.** Haga oraciones completas de dos cláusulas, según el modelo.

MODELO: Juan / no gustar / tenemos que trabajar los fines de semana →
A Juan no le gusta que tengamos que trabajar los fines de semana.

1. Sara / esperar / le dan un aumento
2. a ti / sorprender / hay tanto trabajo
3. Armando / temer / lo van a despedir (*fire*)
4. a nosotros / no gustar / son tan altos los impuestos
5. a mí / no gustar / nos dan sólo dos semanas de vacaciones
6. todos / tener miedo / no hay aumentos este año
7. jefe / sentir / tener / despedir / cinco / empleados

C. Complete las oraciones con la forma apropiada del verbo entre paréntesis.

1. Dicen en la agencia que mi carro nuevo es económico. Por eso me sorprende que (*usar tanta gasolina*). Temo que el coche (*no funcionar totalmente bien*).
2. ¡Qué desastre! El jefe dice que me va a despedir. ¡Es increíble que (*despedirme*)! Es terrible que (yo) (*tener que buscar otro puesto*). Espero que (él) (*cambiar de idea*).
3. Generalmente nos dan un mes de vacaciones, pero este año sólo tenemos dos semanas. Es terrible que sólo (*darnos dos semanas*). No nos gusta que (*ser tan breves las vacaciones*). Es lástima que (*no poder ir a ningún sitio*).
4. A los niños no les gustan sus regalos de Navidad este año. ¡Qué lástima que no (*gustarles los regalos*)! Siento que (ellos) (*estar tan triste*). Espero que (ellos) (*recibir lo que pidan*) el año que viene.

Optional CH: Noticias familiares. ¿Cómo se dice en español? **1.** I'm sorry your daughter is sick. **2.** It's incredible that Johnny is already twelve years old! **3.** What a shame that Julio isn't feeling well. **4.** How strange that Jorge never calls you. **5.** I'm glad that you're going to invite John to the wedding.

CH. **El equipo más moderno.** ¿Cómo se dice en español?

1. I'm sorry your stereo isn't working.
2. It's incredible that you don't have a compact disc player yet!
3. What a shame that they cost so much!
4. How strange that they bring out (**sacar**) new models every year!
5. I'm glad you don't have to have the most modern equipment.

Conversación

A. Las siguientes personas están pensando en otra persona o en algo que van a hacer. ¿Qué emociones sienten? ¿Qué temen? Conteste las preguntas según los dibujos.

1.

2.
3.

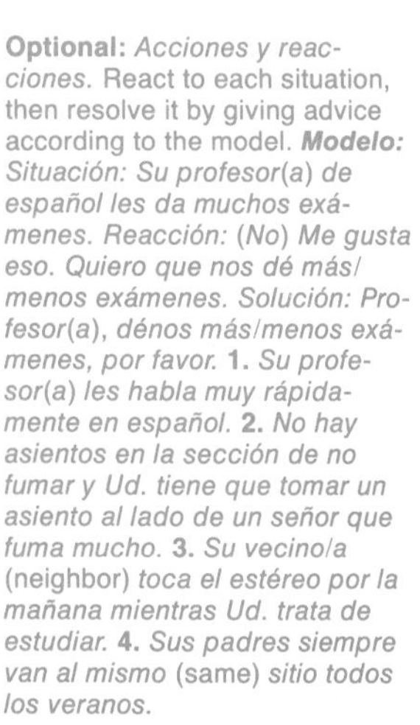
Optional: *Acciones y reacciones.* React to each situation, then resolve it by giving advice according to the model. ***Modelo:*** *Situación: Su profesor(a) de español les da muchos exámenes. Reacción: (No) Me gusta eso. Quiero que nos dé más/menos exámenes. Solución: Profesor(a), dénos más/menos exámenes, por favor.* **1.** *Su profesor(a) les habla muy rápidamente en español.* **2.** *No hay asientos en la sección de no fumar y Ud. tiene que tomar un asiento al lado de un señor que fuma mucho.* **3.** *Su vecino/a* (neighbor) *toca el estéreo por la mañana mientras Ud. trata de estudiar.* **4.** *Sus padres siempre van al mismo* (same) *sitio todos los veranos.*

1. Jorge piensa en su amiga Estela. ¿Por qué piensa en ella? ¿Dónde está? ¿Qué siente Jorge? ¿Qué espera? ¿Qué espera Estela? ¿Espera que la visiten los amigos? ¿que le manden algo? ¿que le digan algo?
2. Fausto quiere comer fuera esta noche. ¿Quiere que alguien lo acompañe? ¿Dónde espera que cenen? ¿Qué teme Fausto? ¿Qué le parecen los precios del restaurante? ¿Dónde quiere él que coman los dos?
3. ¿Dónde quiere pasar las vacaciones Mariana? ¿Espera que alguien la acompañe? ¿Dónde espera que pasen los días? ¿Qué teme Mariana? ¿Qué espera?

B. **Los valores de nuestra sociedad.** Express your feelings about the following situations by restating them, beginning with one of the following phrases or any others you can think of: **es bueno/malo que**, **es extraño/increíble que, es lástima que**.

Extension B: 10. *Los hombres generalmente no reciben* paternity leave *después del nacimiento de un bebé.* **11.** *Hay discriminación contra la gente mayor para ciertas profesiones.*

Follow-up: Similar to Exercise B, but with real-world statements related to class members. **1.** *(Estudiante) está enfermo/a.* **2.** *No tenemos clase el sábado.* **3.** *(Estudiante) se gradúa en junio.* **4.** *El coche de* ____ *no funciona bien.* **5.** *Los profesores (no) reciben un salario más alto.* **6.** *Llueve mucho/poco este año.*

1. Muchas personas viven para trabajar. No saben descansar.
2. Somos una sociedad de consumidores.
3. Siempre queremos tener el último modelo de todo... el coche de este año, el grabador de vídeo que acaba de salir...
4. Juzgamos (*We judge*) a los otros por las cosas materiales que tienen.
5. Las personas ricas tienen mucho prestigio en esta sociedad.
6. Las mujeres generalmente no ganan tanto como los hombres cuando hacen el mismo trabajo.
7. Los plomeros ganan más que los profesores.
8. Los jugadores profesionales de fútbol norteamericano ganan salarios fenomenales.
9. Muchas personas no tienen con quién dejar a los niños cuando trabajan.

Guadalajara, México

Hablando del trabajo

—¿Cuánto tiempo llevas en tu nuevo empleo?
—Casi dos meses.
—¿Y cómo te va? (*And how's it going?*)
—No muy bien. Me piden que trabaje los fines de semana... , y el salario no es muy bueno.
—Me imagino que vas a buscar otro puesto, ¿no?
—Sí. Sólo espero que termine el mes para hacerlo.

¿Recuerda Ud.?

Review the direct (Grammar Section 21) and indirect (Grammar Section 22) object pronouns before beginning Grammar Section 27. Remember that direct objects answer the questions *what* or *whom* and that indirect objects answer the questions *to whom* or *for whom* in relation to the verb.

Direct:	me	te	**lo/la**	nos	os	**los/las**
Indirect:	me	te	**le**	nos	os	**les**

Identifique los complementos directo e (*and*) indirecto en las siguientes oraciones.

1. Nos mandan los libros mañana.
2. ¿Por qué no los vas a comprar?
3. ¿Me puedes leer el menú?
4. Hágalo ahora, por favor.
5. Juan no te va a dar el dinero hoy.
6. Quiero que lo tenga para mañana, por favor.
7. Sí, claro que te voy a invitar.
8. ¿Me escuchas?

27. EXPRESSING DIRECT AND INDIRECT OBJECTS TOGETHER

Double Object Pronouns

¡ES MUY LINDO!...¿ME LO PRESTÁS?

¡PEATONA!

Pedestrian!

Suggestions for cartoon: *La niña morena se llama Mafalda, la rubia Susanita.* **1.** *¿Quién tiene triciclo?* **2.** *¿Qué le pide Susanita a Mafalda?* **3.** *¿Mafalda le presta el triciclo a Susanita?* (rephrase student answer: *Es verdad. Mafalda se lo presta.*) **4.** *Susanita debe darle las gracias a Mafalda, ¿verdad?* (rephrase student answer: *Es verdad. Susanita debe dárselas, pero no se las da.*) **5.** *¿Qué le dice Susanita a Mafalda?*

When both an indirect and a direct object pronoun are used in a sentence, the indirect object pronoun (**I**) precedes the direct (**D**): **ID**. Note that nothing comes between the two pronouns. The position of double object pronouns with respect to the verb is the same as that of single object pronouns.

Suggestion: Treat section 27 as a topic for passive recognition only.

Suggestion: Students identify direct (verb + what/whom) and indirect (to/for whom) objects.

Emphasis: indirect before direct

—¿La fecha del examen? ¡Claro que la sé! —¿Por qué no **nos la** dices? — *—The date of the exam? Of course I know it! —Why don't you tell us?*

—¿Tienes el trofeo? —Sí, acaban de dár**melo**. — *—Do you have the trophy? —Yes, they just gave it to me.*

—Mamá, ¿cuándo nos das la cena? —**Os la** estoy preparando ahora mismo. — *—Mom, when is (will you give us) dinner? —I'm getting it ready for you right now.*

Suggestion: Remind students that *os* = form used in Spain.

[Práctica A–B]

When both the indirect and the direct object pronouns begin with the letter **l**, the indirect object pronoun always changes to **se**. The direct object pronoun does not change.

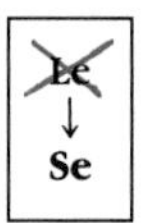

Le compra unos zapatos. — *He's buying her some shoes.*

Le → **Se** los compra. — *He's buying them for her.*

Les mandamos la blusa. — *We'll send you the blouse.*

Les → **Se** la mandamos. — *We'll send it to you.*

Emphasis: *le(s)* → *se* before *lo/la/los/las*

Hint: In sentences with both direct and indirect third-person object pronouns students need focus only on gender of direct object pronoun, since indirect object pronoun will always be *se*.

Since **se** stands for **le** (*to/for you* [sing.], *him, her*) and **les** (*to/for you* [pl.], *them*), it is often necessary to clarify its meaning by using **a** plus the pronoun objects of prepositions.

Se lo escribo (**a Uds.**, **a ellos**, **a ellas...**). — *I'll write it to (you, them...).*

Se las doy (**a Ud.**, **a él**, **a ella...**). — *I'll give them to (you, him, her...).*

[Práctica C–D]

Práctica

A. El jefe está muy exigente hoy. ¿A qué se refiere (*What is he talking about*) cuando dice lo siguiente? Fíjese en (*Pay attention to*) los pronombres y en el sentido de la oración. **Note A:** Students do not need to produce the double object pronouns in this exercise.

una computadora unos contratos una carta
un nuevo trabajo un aumento unas cuentas

1. ¡No! ¡No quiero que se lo expliquen ahora.
2. ¿Me los trae ahora, por favor?
3. ¡Es necesario que Ud. se las mande ahora mismo!
4. Prefiero que Ud. *no* me lo pida este mes.
5. Es necesario que me la escriba a máquina inmediatamente.
6. Es preciso que Ud. nos la arregle hoy. ¡La necesitamos!

Preliminary exercise: listening: 1. Which sentences could refer to *el dinero*? (*¿sí o no?*) *¿Me lo prestas? Voy a dársela. Te lo mando mañana.* **2.** Which could refer to *las recomendaciones? Te los doy, si quieres. ¿Cuánto tiempo hace que se las pides? Sí, quiero que me las traiga Ud.*

Note B: Use of present indicative statement (*Me la pasas...*) as command equivalent.

B. Ud. acaba de comer pero todavía tiene hambre. Pida más comida, según el modelo. Fíjese en (*Note*) el uso del tiempo presente como sustituto para el mandato.

MODELO: ensalada → ¿Hay más ensalada? Me la pasas, por favor.

1. pan 2. tortillas 3. tomates 4. fruta 5. vino 6. jamón

C. **En el aeropuerto.** Cambie: sustantivos → pronombres para evitar (*avoid*) la repetición.

1. ¿La hora de la salida? Acaban de decirnos la hora de la salida.
2. ¿El horario? Sí, quiero que me leas el horario, por favor.
3. ¿Los boletos? No, no tiene que darle los boletos aquí.
4. ¿El equipaje? Claro que estoy guardándole el equipaje.
5. ¿Los pasajes? ¿No quieres que te compre los pasajes?
6. ¿El puesto en la cola? No te preocupes. Te puedo guardar el puesto.
7. ¿La clase turística? Sí, les recomiendo la clase turística, señores.
8. ¿La cena? La azafata nos va a servir la cena en el avión.

Suggestion CH:
- Before students give answers for each item, ask for appropriate infinitives to use in each.
- **Follow-up:** Students give advice to *Raúl* for keeping his apartment in better order. ***Modelo:*** *Es necesario que laves los platos después de usarlos.*

CH. **Situaciones.** La casa de su amigo Raúl es un desastre... y sus padres vienen a visitarlo este fin de semana. Un compañero (Una compañera) va a hacer el papel (*role*) de Raúl. Dígale cómo va a ayudar a poner la casa en orden. Use el verbo apropiado para cada caso.

MODELO: —¡Todos los platos están sucios! →
—¡No te preocupes! (*Don't worry!*) Yo te los lavo.

Verbos: lavar (*to wash*), comprar, arreglar

1. También están sucias las paredes de la sala.
2. No hay refrescos en casa.
3. Tampoco hay leche.
4. Hay un montón de ropa sucia en la alcoba.
5. El televisor no funciona.
6. Tampoco funciona el refrigerador.

Note D: The last person named in each sequence is the one pictured.

D. Answer the questions, basing your answers on what you observe happening in the drawings. Use double object pronouns.

1. ¿A quién le está vendiendo el coche el empleado? ¿Se lo está vendiendo a María? ¿a los Sres. Benítez? ¿a Ud.? ¿a Esteban?

2. ¿A quién le está sirviendo una cerveza el camarero? ¿Se la está sirviendo a Carlos? ¿a unos señores? ¿a Uds.? ¿a Emilia?

3. ¿A quién le va a mandar flores Ramiro? ¿a Tomás? ¿a los Sres. Padilla? ¿a ti? ¿a Carmen?

4. ¿A quién le recomienda los tacos Carolina? ¿a Raúl y Celia? ¿a Pilar? ¿a Ud.? ¿a Lucas?

Suggestion D: Extend each set of questions with questions about people in the class.

Conversación

Follow-up: Your neighbor Mr. Martínez always forgets to return things he has borrowed. When he asks if he should return something right away or another day, you answer: Today.
Modelo:
—Los discos, ¿se los traigo hoy o mañana? —Quiero que me los traiga hoy, por favor.
Artículos: los diez dólares, el café, el azúcar, las sillas, las maletas, el periódico, el suéter

A. **Situaciones.** Someone has just mentioned the following items to you. React in as many ways as you can. Be creative!

MODELO: la novela *Guerra* (War) *y paz* →

No quiero que me la prestes. ¡Es demasiado larga! Prefiero que se la des a mi hermano. A él le gusta leer.

1. un millón de dólares
2. una camioneta usada del año ochenta
3. dos entradas (*tickets*) para un concierto de la orquesta sinfónica
4. unas flores
5. unos dulces
6. un nuevo grabador de vídeo

B. **Entrevista.** Find out another student's opinion about the topics listed, following the model.

MODELO: Profesiones: la carrera de maestro (*grade school teacher*) →
—¿Me recomiendas la carrera de maestro?
—No, no te la recomiendo porque tienes que pasar todo el día con niños, y sé que a ti no te gustan mucho.
—¿Y la carrera de... ?

1. Profesiones: la carrera de maestro, de profesor universitario, de jefe de oficina, de consejero, de piloto, de agente de policía
2. La música: los discos de Sting, las canciones de Bob Dylan, los conciertos de Michael Jackson, la ópera, los conciertos sinfónicos
3. Las vacaciones: una semana en Buenos Aires, un mes en Madrid, una excursión a la Ciudad de México, dos semanas en las islas del Caribe

4. La comida: McDonald's, el ceviche, la paella, (nombre de un restaurante)

Otros temas: clases de la universidad, películas recientes, residencias, actividades, programas de televisión, tiendas

a. ¡Bueno!
b. *hands*
c. *put*
ch. *Go*

SITUACIONES

Situaciones: See IM for suggestions, additional exercises, and supplementary dialogues and exercises.

En busca de un cuarto

—¿Qué te pasa? Pareces muy preocupado.
—Llevo dos semanas buscando cuarto y... ¡nada!
—¿Qué tipo de cuarto buscas?
—Pues... quiero un cuarto para mí solo, que sea grande. Además° necesito muchos estantes para poner libros y un armario° bien grande. También me gusta que el cuarto tenga mucha luz y que sea tranquilo.
—¿Nada más?
—Además quiero que esté cerca de la universidad, que tenga garaje, con derecho° a usar la cocina, con teléfono... y ¡claro!, que sea barato.
—Hombre, no pides mucho... Pero no te preocupes. Ahora que me lo dices, creo que hay uno en el edificio donde vive Rosario. No sé por qué no se me ocurrió antes°! ¿Sabes dónde está?
—Creo que sí. La voy a llamar ahora mismo. Gracias, ¿eh?

Además° *Also*
armario° *closet*
derecho° *right*
no... *I didn't think of it before*

Notas comunicativas sobre el diálogo

Many common expressions in Spanish contain double object pronouns that are used in a fixed pattern. Try to use them in conversation, without thinking about the specific meaning of the pronouns.

Ahora que **me lo** dices...	*Now that you mention it . . .*
No **se me** ocurrió.	*It didn't occur to me.*
¿**Se te** ocurre algo?	*Does anything occur to you?*

Conversación

Think about the things you would want if you were looking for a room, apartment, or house to rent. Then, with a classmate, practice the preceding dialogue, substituting real information wherever possible.

UN POCO DE TODO

A. Ud. es jefe/a de una oficina. Hoy viene un empleado a la oficina por primera vez. ¿Qué le va a decir? ¿Qué consejos le va a dar?

Recomiendo que Ud... Espero que los otros empleados... Es necesario que Ud... Me gusta que todos... Prefiero que... Quiero que Ud.... Ojalá que...	trabajar todos juntos aquí conocer a los otros empleados llegar puntualmente por la mañana no usar el teléfono en exceso no dejar (*to leave*) para mañana el trabajo de hoy ayudarlo a acostumbrarse (*to get used to*) a la rutina no estar ausente con frecuencia hacer preguntas cuando no comprenda algo no querer cambiar de puesto pronto

B. **Situaciones: Se lo di a...** (*I gave it to . . .*) Con otro/a estudiante, haga y conteste preguntas, según el modelo. Use el nombre de la persona más apropiada.

MODELO: discos de música *punk* →
—Oye, ¿me prestas tus discos de música *punk*?
—Lo siento, pero no puedo. Se los di a Roberto.

Amigos y parientes

- Susana tiene una nueva computadora que no funciona.
- A Hildebrando le gusta mucho la música... y especialmente las canciones en español.
- El televisor de sus padres no funciona.
- A Roberto le interesa mucho todo tipo de arte.
- Teresa piensa hacer un viaje.
- A su hermanito le encanta ir al campo.
- Su madre acaba de empezar a estudiar francés.

1. discos de Menudo o de Los Lobos
2. bicicleta vieja
3. libro de francés
4. máquina de escribir vieja
5. maleta vieja
6. televisor viejo

C. **De vacaciones.** Con otro/a estudiante, planee un viaje de vacaciones para este verano. Primero, hágale preguntas al compañero (a la compañera) para conocer sus preferencias. Luego, pónganse de acuerdo (*agree*) sobre el itinerario. Use las siguientes preguntas como guía.

1. ¿Quieres que vayamos a las montañas o a la playa? (¿al mar o al campo?)
2. ¿Prefieres que pidamos hoteles de lujo (*deluxe*) o de clase turística?
3. ¿Es mejor que vayamos en avión o en barco? ¿en coche?
4. ¿Qué lugares esperas que visitemos?
5. ¿Cómo es necesario que paguemos? ¿con tarjetas de crédito o al contado (*in cash*)?

Ahora describa el itinerario para la clase.

CH. **Entrevista.** Complete las oraciones lógicamente... ¡y sinceramente! Luego entreviste a otro/a estudiante para saber cómo él/ella completó las mismas oraciones.

MODELO: Mis padres siempre quieren que (yo) *los llame*. →
—¿Qué siempre quieren tus padres que hagas?
—Siempre quieren que yo estudie más. Y tus padres, ¿qué quieren que hagas?

1. Mis padres siempre quieren que (yo) _____.
2. Mi mejor amigo/a (esposo/a, novio/a, ...) siempre desea que (yo) _____.
3. Me gusta mucho que mis amigos _____.
4. No me gusta nada que mis amigos _____.
5. Es absolutamente ridículo que _____.
6. Una cosa que no tengo ahora pero que me gustaría muchísimo tener es _____.

D. **Una cuestión de suerte** (*luck*). Complete the following dialogue with the correct form of the words in parentheses, as suggested by the context. When two possibilities are given in parentheses, select the correct word.

CARLOS, estudiante colombiano que estudia comercio internacional en Arizona
FRED, estudiante estadounidense y compañero de Fred
LA SRA. CARRILLO, empleada de una oficina de empleos

En la residencia

CARLOS: ¿(*Saber/Conocer*[1]), Fred? va a (*ser/estar*[2]) necesario que (yo: *regresar*[3]) a Colombia sin (*terminar*[4]) el semestre. Temo que (*mí/mi*[5]) padres no me (*poder*[6]) ayudar más.

FRED: ¡Qué fatal, hombre! ¿Por (*que/qué*[7]) no buscas un trabajo (*en/de*[8]) tiempo parcial?

CARLOS: No (*saber/conocer*[9])... Hay (*tan/tanto*[10]) reglas° para los extranjeros...

°*rules*

FRED: Sí, pero también hay excepciones. (*Sólo/Solo*[11]) tienes (*de/que*[12]) demostrar° que hay circunstancias excepcionales. — *to show*

CARLOS: ¡Ojalá que (tú: *tener*[13]) razón! ¿(*Mí/Me*[14]) acompañas a Inmigración?

FRED: Cómo no.

En la oficina de empleos

SRA. CARRILLO: No sé... Sin título,° experiencia ni recomendaciones, temo que Ud. (*tener*[15]) muy (*poco*[16]) posibilidades de (*conseguir*[17]) un buen trabajo. ¿Tiene (*alguno*[18]) oficio°? — *degree*; *trade*

CARLOS: No, señora, ni carrera tampoco. Todavía (*ser/estar*[19]) estudiante. Lo que necesito (*ser/estar*[20]) sólo un trabajo de tiempo parcial.

SRA. CARRILLO: Ah, ya comprendo. (*Esperar*[21]) Ud. un momento mientras veo en este fichero°... ¿(*Saber/Conocer*[22]) Ud. traducir contratos del inglés (*al/a la*[23]) español y vice versa? Una empresa° mercantil (*buscar*[24]) traductor. Ud. (*poder*[25]) traducir los documentos en (*tu/su*[26]) casa... y le pagan bastante (*bueno/bien*[27]). — *card file*; compañía

CARLOS: ¡Creo que (*ser/estar*[28]) la persona para ese empleo! Estudio comercio internacional.

SRA. CARRILLO: Pues (*ir*[29]) Ud. a la Sección de Personal de la empresa con estos papeles. Es necesario que (*se los/se las*[30]) presente al jefe en mi nombre. ¡Buena suerte en la entrevista!

CARLOS: Se lo agradezco° enormemente, señora Carrillo. ¡Adiós! — *I thank*

¿Quién lo dijo (*said*), Carlos, sus padres, la señora Carrillo o Fred? Conteste según el diálogo.

1. ¡Ay! No quiero regresar tan pronto.
2. Nos gusta que Carlos sea tan independiente.
3. No te preocupes. Sé lo que puedes hacer.
4. No sé por qué no se me ocurrió antes buscar empleo.
5. Me gusta que el joven sea tan cortés.
6. Creo que Ud. es la persona para este puesto.

Notas culturales: Working Abroad

Carlos is able to get special permission from the Immigration Department to seek a job in the United States, but in many cases it is not easy for a foreigner to get a work permit in this country. Normally a student visa does not permit one to work, and other regulations make it difficult for skilled or semiskilled foreigners to support themselves in this country. The situation in Hispanic countries is even more strict, and in many nations foreigners are strictly prohibited from holding jobs at all. All employment possibilities are reserved for citizens.

VOCABULARIO

Theme vocabulary previously listed as active: *la camioneta, el coche, el escritorio, la mesa, la oficina, la silla, el televisor*

VERBOS

arreglar to fix, repair
cambiar (de) to change
conseguir (i, i) to get, obtain
despedir (i, i) to fire
funcionar to function; to run, work (*machines*)
ganar to earn; to win
lavar to wash
mandar to order
manejar to drive
permitir to permit, allow
prohibir to prohibit, forbid
recomendar (ie) to recommend
sentir (ie, i) to regret, feel sorry
temer to fear

LOS CUARTOS Y LAS OTRAS PARTES DE UNA CASA

la alcoba bedroom
el baño bathroom
la cocina kitchen
el comedor dining room
el garaje garage
la pared wall
el patio patio; yard
la piscina swimming pool
la sala living room

LOS MUEBLES

la alfombra rug
la cama (de agua) (water) bed
la cómoda bureau
el estante bookshelf
la lámpara lamp
la mesita end table
el sillón armchair
el sofá sofa

LOS BIENES PERSONALES

el acuario aquarium
la bicicleta bicycle
el cartel poster
el compact disc compact disc (player)
la computadora computer (*L.A.*)
el equipo estereofónico stereo equipment
el equipo fotográfico photographic equipment
el grabador de vídeo VCR
la impresora printer
la máquina de escribir typewriter
la motocicleta motorcycle
la muñeca doll
el ordenador computer (*Spain*)
el pájaro bird
el pez (*pl.* **peces**) fish
la pintura painting
la radio (portátil) (*portable*) radio
el trofeo trophy

EL TRABAJO

el aumento raise, increase
la carrera career, profession
el cheque check
el/la director(a) manager, director
el/la empleado/a employee
el gobierno government
el impuesto tax
el inventario inventory
el/la jefe/a boss
el puesto job, position
el sueldo salary
el trabajo job, work; written work; (term) paper

OTROS SUSTANTIVOS

el campo country
la carretera highway
el/la maestro/a grade school teacher

ADJETIVOS

cada (*inv.*) each, every
descapotable convertible (*with cars*)
exigente demanding
listo/a (*with* **estar**) ready, prepared

PALABRAS ADICIONALES

aunque although
de tiempo parcial part-time
es extraño it is strange
  ¡qué extraño! how strange!
es...
  increíble incredible
  preciso necessary
  preferible preferable
  urgente urgent
es lástima it is a shame
  ¡qué lástima! what a shame!
me (te, le...) sorprende it is surprising to me (you, him . . .)
mientras while
sacar fotos to take pictures, photographs

Frases útiles para la comunicación

me interesa(n)...	. . . is/are interesting to me
me encanta(n)...	. . . is/are exciting to me
no te preocupes	don't worry (*fam.*)

UN PASO MÁS 8

OPTIONAL SECTION

Actividad A. Los bienes personales y la personalidad

Primera parte: Una casa sin muebles. Invente un cuento (*story*) que explique este dibujo. Use estas preguntas como guía.

—*¿Te has suscrito tú a una revista de decoración?*

¿Te... *Have you subscribed?*

1. ¿Quiénes son estos señores?
2. ¿Dónde viven? ¿Cuánto tiempo hace que viven allí?
3. ¿Por qué se suscribió (*subscribed*) la señora a una revista de decoración?
4. ¿Qué muebles necesitan?
5. ¿Por qué no tienen muebles?
6. ¿Es probable que tengan muebles más adelante (*later*)? Explique.
7. Si estos señores le piden a Ud. que les dé consejos para decorar su casa, ¿qué les aconseja Ud.? ¿Deben comprar muebles nuevos o usados? ¿antigüedades (*antiques*)? ¿Qué colores deben emplear? ¿Cuáles son las cosas que deben hacer o comprar primero para decorar la sala? ¿por último (*last*)?

Segunda parte: ¿Cómo es la persona que... ? En la primera parte, Ud. fue capaz (*able*) de explicar ciertos aspectos de la vida de dos personas juzgándolas por lo que *no* tienen. Ahora, la pregunta es distinta. ¿Qué se puede decir de la personalidad o las circunstancias de una persona juzgándola por lo que tiene o hace?

Tomando como base estas descripciones breves, ¿cómo cree Ud. que son las siguientes personas? No olvide consultar la lista de **Palabras útiles**.

1. una mujer que tiene en casa ¡cinco! perros pastores alemanes
2. un matrimonio que tiene tres coches, una casa grande y elegante en el centro y otra en las montañas, una colección de arte impresionante... y ningún hijo
3. una persona que vive en el campo, aislada de la civilización
4. un hombre que está todo el día en casa con los niños, mientras su esposa sale a trabajar
5. una joven que tiene en su casa una colección de libros de astronomía

Palabras útiles: materialista, liberado/a, temeroso/a, solitario/a, raro/a, egoísta, perezosa/a, científico/a, tímido/a

Ahora compare sus respuestas con las de algunos compañeros de clase. ¿Sacaron todos (*Did all of you arrive at*) las mismas conclusiones?

Follow-ups A:
- *Describa el cuarto típico de un estudiante. ¿Qué hay en él? ¿Qué no hay en él?*
- *¿Hay una sala formal en la casa de sus padres? Descríbala.*
- *¿En qué son similares y en qué son diferentes la casa de los Rockefeller y la de Ud.?*

A propósito... More About What to Do When You Don't Understand

You've already learned a number of words and phrases to use when you haven't understood what someone has said to you in Spanish. Remember in particular that it is inappropriate to use **¿qué?** in Spanish to express English *what?* in this context. If you want a speaker to repeat what he or she has said, use one of these expressions.

¿Cómo? ¿Mande? (México)	*What? How's that again?*
¿Qué (me) dice(s)?	*What did you say?*
Perdón, no entendí bien.	*Excuse me, I didn't understand.*
¿Puede(s) hablar más despacio, por favor?	*Could you speak more slowly, please?*

If you understand most of what is said but miss a single important word or phrase, you can repeat what you *did* understand, leaving it to the speaker to fill in the part you missed: **¿El autobús para León sale a... ? ¿Quieres que yo... ?** Or you can simply use an interrogative such as **¿cuántos?**, **¿cuál(es)?**, **¿quién(es)?**, **¿dónde?**, or **¿cuándo?** to elicit the missing information.

Variation B: Instructor reads aloud a simple short story or cultural reading (or uses materials from Tape Program). Students listen and, as group, piece together as much information as they can. Students confirm understanding by listening to selection a second time.

Actividad B. ¿Cómo?

You hear the following sentence fragments. How can you get the entire message in each situation? Give as many different responses as possible to each fragment, using the expressions in the **A propósito...** section.

1. Cuesta... pesos el kilo.
2. Primero vaya Ud. a la calle Princesa, después... y por fin doble a la derecha.
3. ...no tienen que tomar el examen final.
4. ...lo puede hacer.
5. Es necesario que... y después Ud. puede hablar con el jefe.
6. La entrevista es a las...
7. Siento decirte que tu amigo...
8. Ahora quiero que Ud.... Podemos hablar más tarde.

Actividad C. ¡Ay!

Los padres del dibujo experimentan (*are feeling*) una ansiedad típica de muchas personas: temen que se estén poniendo (*becoming*) viejos demasiado rápidamente. ¿Teme Ud. esto también? ¿Qué ansiedad o ansiedades tiene Ud.? Mencione por lo menos cinco, siguiendo estos modelos.

MODELO: Tengo miedo de que ____. Temo que ____.

¿Qué ansiedades tienen las siguientes personas?

1. el presidente de los Estados Unidos
2. una bailarina muy famosa
3. un millonario
4. un estudiante durante un examen final
5. un profesor sin experiencia, el primer día de clases en su primer puesto
6. un niño de cinco años en el primer día de clases de la escuela primaria

LECTURA CULTURAL

Lectura: See IM for suggestions and additional exercises and activities.

Antes de leer: Word Families

Guessing the meaning of a word from context is easier if it has a recognizable root, or a relation to another word that you already know. For example, if you know **llover**, you should be able to guess the meaning of **lluvia** and **lluvioso** quite easily in context. Can you guess the meaning of these words?

la pobreza La pobreza es un problema muy grave en muchas partes de la India y Latinoamérica.

la enseñanza Muchos datos indican que la calidad de la enseñanza actual en los Estados Unidos es inferior a la del año 1960.

If you know the meaning of the following words, you will be able to guess the approximate meaning of the related words you will encounter in the reading: **el lápiz**, **estudiar**, **iluminar**, **marcar**, **la playa**, **la ingeniería**, **la formación**, **el papel**, **usar**.

«Tengo... Necesito... Quiero... »

En una de las primeras actividades del **Capítulo 8**, Ud. terminó° la serie de oraciones incompletas que constituye el título de esta lectura. Escuche ahora mientras tres hispanos terminan las mismas oraciones. Tres estilos distintos... tres individuos. ¿Qué nos revelan estas respuestas sobre la vida de estas tres personas? ¿Son sus respuestas similares a las que Ud. dio°?

completed

las... *those you gave*

MARGARITA CUESTA, España

Tengo una casa donde vivir, un coche pequeño, bastante ropa, estatuillas de Italia, Guatemala y España, cacharros de cocina, etcétera. En cuanto a entretenimiento,° tengo una tienda de campaña con linternas, saco de dormir y cocina.

En... *As for entertainment*

Necesito una cuna muy grande para mi bebé, que se haga° cama cuando él sea mayor, pero como es bastante cara me tengo que conformar con una cuna normal y corriente.

se... *can be made into*

Quiero un Fiat descapotable rojo, un reloj y una pulsera de oro.

MARCIAL BELTRÁN, México

Tengo dos pantalones de mezclilla, ocho playeras,° dos camisas, diez calzoncillos,° diez pares de calcetines, un cinturón, tres pares de tenis, dos calzones para correr, muchas cosas de higiene personal, platos, vasos, cucharas, cuchillos y tenedores, dos ollas° para cocer° frijoles, una estufa, un refrigerador, un televisor, un sofá, una mesa con cuatro sillas, una lámpara y un «sleepbag», seis trofeos de carreras° y cinco medallas.

T-shirts / shorts, underwear

pots / cocinar

racing

Necesito mucho, pero lo más importante es comprar material escolar para poder seguir mis estudios y un lugar seguro° donde vivir.

stable, permanent

También **quiero** mucho, pero hay tres cosas principales en mi vida. La primera, llegar a ser ingeniero. Segunda, formarme como individuo en la sociedad. Y tercera, correr en la Olimpiada.

MARÍA JOSÉ RUIZ MORCILLO, España

Tengo una cámara de fotos bastante buena pero todavía no tengo un equipo fotográfico muy completo. Tengo una buena colección de posters y de carteles (que ya no sé en dónde colgar). Tengo bastantes libros e° infinidad de artículos de papelería (cuadernos, lapiceros, bolígrafos, *clips*, carpetas,° etiquetas,° tarjetas, sobres° de distinto color y formato, marcadores de lectura...), ¡muchos de los cuales no he usado nunca!

y

files / labels / envelopes

Necesito una impresora y no es necesario que sea muy sofisticada (de lo que se deduce que tengo un ordenador personal). Necesito un buen traje de chaqueta pues casi toda mi ropa es bastante informal.

Me gustaría **tener** un buen equipo estereofónico y una buena colección de música. También quiero tener una casa no muy grande pero que sea tranquila y luminosa.

Comprensión

Hay más de una respuesta posible. De estas tres personas, ¿quién... ?

1. es esposa y madre
2. es estudiante ahora
3. escribe muchos trabajos académicos
4. lleva una vida muy activa
5. pasa mucho tiempo en la cocina
6. vive ahora en un apartamento
7. no está muy contenta con el sitio donde vive ahora
8. aspira a tener fama internacional

De las tres, ¿a quién le interesa(n)... ?

1. el arte
2. los deportes
3. estar fuera de casa
4. las diversiones que se hacen en casa
5. las matemáticas
6. sacar fotos

Para escribir

Vuelva Ud. a completar las tres oraciones del título de la lectura, incorporando en sus respuestas algunas de las palabras y frases que acaba de leer. Por ejemplo:

En cuanto a... (*As far as . . . is concerned*)
Necesito... pero me tengo que conformar con...
Necesito mucho, pero lo más importante es...
Hay... cosas principales en mi vida: ...
Necesito... pues...
Tengo... de lo que se puede deducir que (yo)...

CAPÍTULO NUEVE

EN CASA

Panamá, Panamá

▲ **¡Qué apartamento más lindo![a]**

—¿Hace mucho tiempo que vives aquí?

—Casi tres años. ¿Te gusta?

—¡Sí! ¡Es un apartamento fenomenal!

—Pues lo decoré yo misma y casi no gasté nada.

[a]bonito

Vocabulario: Preparación:
- See detailed supplementary materials for this section bound into the back of this Annotated Instructor's Edition.

VOCABULARIO: PREPARACIÓN

- See model for vocabulary presentation and other materials in Supplementary *Vocabulario: Preparación* Materials, chapter by chapter, IM.

- See also [video] and [audio]

Los quehaceres° domésticos

°*tasks*

barrer (el suelo)	to sweep (the floor)
dejar	to leave (something) behind
hacer la cama	to make the bed
lavar (las ventanas, los platos)	to wash (the windows, dishes)
limpiar la casa (entera)	to clean the (whole) house
pasar la aspiradora	to vacuum
planchar la ropa	to iron clothing
poner la mesa	to set the table
preparar la comida/cocinar	to prepare food/to cook
sacar la basura	to take out the trash
sacudir los muebles	to dust the furniture†

la tostadora · la cafetera · el congelador · el refrigerador · el (aire) acondicionador · la lavadora · la secadora · la estufa* · la aspiradora · el lavaplatos

LOS APARATOS DOMÉSTICOS

A. ¿En qué cuarto o parte de la casa se hacen las siguientes actividades?

1. Se hace la cama en _____.
2. Se pone la mesa en _____.
3. Se saca la basura de _____ y se deja en _____.
4. Se prepara la comida en _____.
5. Se sacude los muebles de _____.
6. Se duerme en _____.
7. Uno se baña (*bathes*) en _____. Se baña al perro en _____.
8. Se barre el suelo de _____.
9. Se pasa la aspiradora en _____ y en _____.
10. Se lava la ropa en _____ y se plancha en _____.

B. ¿Para qué se usan los siguientes productos? Explíqueselo a su amigo hispano, que no los conoce.

1. Windex
2. Mr. Coffee
3. Endust
4. Glad Bags
5. Joy
6. Cascade
7. Tide
8. Lysol

LA COCINA

Los muebles de cocina se derivan hacia un diseño moderno y sencillo. Los materiales son las maderas lacadas y melaminas. El color base, el blanco y como detalle los tenedores en colores vivos o como en el caso de la imagen en un tono discreto y fácilmente combinable: el gris.

---

*The word for *stove* varies in the Hispanic world. Many Spanish speakers use **la cocina**. *Oven* is generally **el horno**.

†An alternative phrase used in some parts of the Spanish-speaking world is **quitar el polvo**.

C. **Familias de palabras.** Dé Ud. el verbo que corresponda al sustantivo (*noun*) indicado en cada oración.

MODELO: **preparación** → **preparar**

1. La **seca**dora sirve para _____ la ropa. La **plancha** sirve para _____ la.
2. Es necesario _____ la comida en un **refrigera**dor.
3. En la **cocina** se puede _____.
4. La **lava**dora sirve para _____ la ropa.
5. El **acondiciona**dor sirve para _____ el aire.

Notas comunicativas: Talking About Obligation

You already know several ways to express obligation, things you have to do.

Tengo que / **Necesito** / **Debo** } barrer el suelo. — *I have to* / *I need to* / *I should* } *sweep the floor.*

Of the three alternatives, **tener que** + *infinitive* expresses the strongest sense of someone's obligation.

The concept *turn to do* (*something*) is expressed in Spanish with the verb **tocar** plus an indirect object.

—**¿A quién le toca** lavar los platos esta noche? —**A mí me toca** solamente sacar la basura. Creo que **a papá le toca** lavar los platos.

—*Whose turn is it to wash the dishes tonight? —I only have to take out the garbage. I think it's Dad's turn to wash the dishes.*

Suggestion CH: Students do in pairs, then report what they learned about partner to class.

Follow-up CH: *En el palacio de los reyes de Inglaterra, hay muchas criadas y sirvientes. Por eso la reina Isabel no tiene ningún quehacer doméstico. Las criadas se lo hacen* **todo**. *Por ejemplo, la reina no hace su cama; se la hace la criada.* **1.** *La reina tampoco lava las ventanas. ¿Por qué?* **2.** *Y nunca lava los platos. ¿Por qué?* **3.** *Nunca tiene que preparar la comida. ¿Por qué?* **4.** *¿Por qué nunca saca la basura (sacude los muebles,...)?*

CH. **Entrevista.** ¿Es Ud. buen(a) ama de casa (*housekeeper*)? ¿Con qué frecuencia hace Ud. los siguientes quehaceres? Si Ud. no los hace, ¿a quién le toca? Otro/a estudiante lo/la va a entrevistar para evaluar sus hábitos domésticos. Si Ud. vive en una residencia estudiantil, imagine que vive en una casa o en un apartamento.

MODELO: lavar las ventanas →
—¿Con qué frecuencia lavas las ventanas? (¿A quién le toca lavar las ventanas?)
—Nunca me toca a mí lavarlas. Me las lava la criada (*maid*). (Las lavo frecuentemente. No me gusta que estén sucias.)

0 = nunca 1 = a veces 2 = frecuentemente 3 = todos los días

_____ 1. lavar las ventanas
_____ 2. hacer las camas
_____ 3. poner la mesa
_____ 4. preparar la comida
_____ 5. sacudir los muebles
_____ 6. lavar los platos
_____ 7. limpiar la casa entera
_____ 8. sacar la basura
_____ 9. pasar la aspiradora
_____ 10. limpiar el horno
_____ 11. planchar la ropa
_____ 12. barrer el suelo
_____ TOTAL

Interpretaciones

0–8 puntos:	¡Cuidado! (*Careful!*) Ud. estudia demasiado (*too much*). Por favor, ¡limpie su casa! O, por lo menos, haga que alguien se la limpie. ¡No lo deje para mañana!
9–17 puntos:	Ud. puede vivir en su casa, pero no debe invitar a otras personas sin limpiarla bien primero.
18–27 puntos:	Su casa, aunque no está perfecta, está limpia. Es un buen modelo para todos.
28–36 puntos:	¡Ud. es una maravilla y tiene una casa muy, muy limpia! Pero, ¿pasa Ud. todo el día limpiándola? ¿Tiene Ud. una criada? ¿Le pide a la criada que le limpie todo?

¿Dónde vive Ud.? ¿Dónde quiere vivir?

alquilar to rent
las afueras outskirts; suburbs
el alquiler rent
el centro downtown
la dirección address
el/la dueño/a owner; landlord, landlady
el gas gas; heat
el/la inquilino/a tenant, renter
la luz light; electricity
el/la portero/a building manager; doorman
el/la vecino/a neighbor
la vista view

la planta baja ground floor
el (primer, segundo, tercer) piso the (second, third, fourth) floor

Notas culturales: Naming the Floors of a Building

In English the phrases *ground floor* and *first floor* are used interchangeably in most dialects. In Spanish, however, there are separate expressions for these concepts. **La planta baja** can refer only to the *ground floor.* **El primer piso** (literally, *the first floor*) refers to what English speakers call *the second floor*. **El segundo piso** (literally, *the second floor*) is actually *the third floor* of the building, and so on.

Suggestion A: Students do as partner/pair activity. Then ask several pairs of students to report to the class what they learned about their partner.

A. ¿Qué prefiere Ud.?

1. ¿vivir en una casa o vivir en un edificio de apartamentos?
2. ¿vivir en el centro o en las afueras? ¿o tal vez en el campo?
3. ¿alquilar una casa/un apartamento o comprar una casa?
4. ¿pagar el gas y la luz—o pagar un alquiler más alto con el gas y la luz incluidos?
5. ¿ser el dueño del apartamento o ser el inquilino?
6. ¿que el portero/la portera lo arregle todo o arreglarlo todo Ud. mismo/a (*yourself*)?
7. ¿vivir en la planta baja o en un piso más alto?

8. ¿un apartamento pequeño con una vista magnífica o un apartamento más grande sin vista?
9. ¿un apartamento pequeño con una dirección elegante o un apartamento grande con una dirección más modesta?
10. ¿conocer muy bien a los vecinos o mantenerse a distancia (*keep your distance*)?

B. **Definiciones**

MODELO: la piscina →
Allí nadamos. (Se nada en una piscina.)

1. el inquilino
2. el centro
3. el alquiler
4. el portero
5. el vecino
6. el dueño
7. la criada
8. las afueras

Suggestion B: Reverse exercise; you give action or definition, students give the person, place, or thing described.

Más verbos útiles			
acostar (ue)	to put to bed	**levantar**	to lift, raise
afeitar	to shave	**quitar**	to remove, take away
bañar	to bathe	**sentar (ie)**	to seat, lead to a seat
despertar (ie)	to wake	**vestir (i, i)**	to dress
divertir (ie, i)	to amuse, entertain		

Complete las oraciones lógicamente, usando estas palabras o cualquier otra.

- el televisor, el ruido, una buena película, el sol, la clase de español, el despertador (*alarm clock*), el estéreo
- mi compañero/a, la enfermera (*nurse*), el camarero, el barbero, el dueño, el padre, la madre, un estudiante

1. _____ me despierta.
2. _____ me divierte.
3. _____ baña al bebé.
4. _____ nos sienta en el restaurante.
5. _____ nos afeita en la barbería.
6. _____ acuesta a los niños en el hospital.
7. _____ quita los platos después de la comida.
8. _____ viste a los niños.
9. _____ levanta la mano (*hand*).

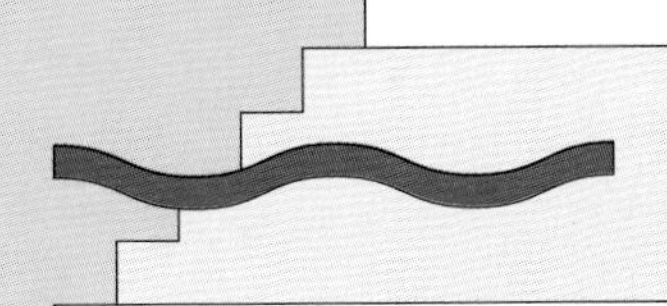

MINIDIÁLOGOS Y GRAMÁTICA

Communicative objectives for 28: includes expressing *-self* / *-selves* as well as talking about various daily activities (not all reflexive verbs are related to daily activities, however)

28. EXPRESSING *-SELF/-SELVES*
Reflexive Pronouns

Un día típico

Point out (mini):
- *Me llamo, me despierto,...* Ask, What is reflexive pronoun used with *yo* form?
- *Se levanta, se llama...* What is reflexive pronoun used with *Ud./él/ella* form?
- *Nos bañamos...* What is reflexive pronoun used with *nosotros* form?

Note: introduction of *tener sueño* in mini.

Follow-up: ***¿Cierto o falso?*** Students respond according to their own situations. **1.** *Me despierto temprano.* **2.** *Me levanto a las seis.* **3.** *El sábado me levanto a las siete.* **4.** *Prefiero bañarme por la mañana.* **5.** *Los días de clase me visto rápidamente.* **6.** *Siempre es necesario que me acueste a las diez.* **7.** *El sábado me acuesto a las doce.*

1. ***Me llamo*** Alicia; mi esposo ***se llama*** Miguel. 2. ***Me despierto*** y ***me levanto*** temprano, a las seis. Él también ***se levanta*** temprano. 3. ***Nos bañamos*** y ***nos vestimos.*** 4. Luego yo pongo la mesa y él prepara el desayuno. 5. Después él hace la cama y yo lavo los platos. 6. ¡Por fin! Estamos listos para salir para la oficina. 7. Pero... un momentito. ¡Es sábado! ¿Es demasiado tarde para ***acostarnos*** otra vez? No, pero... desgraciadamente, ¡ya no tenemos sueño!

Imagine que Ud. es Alicia y complete las oraciones.
1. _____ llamo Alicia y mi esposo _____ llama Miguel.
2. _____ levanto a las seis y Miguel _____ levanta a las seis y diez.
3. _____ baño; luego él _____ baña.
4. _____ visto y él _____ viste al mismo tiempo.

Ahora imagine que Ud. es Miguel y complete las oraciones describiendo las acciones de los dos.
1. Alicia y yo _____ levantamos temprano.
2. _____ bañamos y _____ vestimos con prisa (*quickly*) por la mañana.
3. Casi siempre _____ acostamos temprano también.

A typical day 1. My name is Alicia; my husband's name is Miguel. 2. I wake up and get up early, at six. He also gets up early. 3. We bathe and get dressed. 4. Then I set the table, and he makes breakfast. 5. Next he makes the bed, and I wash the dishes. 6. Finally! We're ready to leave for the office. 7. But . . . just a minute. It's Saturday! Is it too late to go back to bed? No, but . . . unfortunately, we're not sleepy any more!

Many English verbs that describe parts of one's daily routine—to get up, to take a bath, and so on—are expressed in Spanish with a reflexive construction: *I'm taking a bath* → **me baño** (literally, *I'm bathing myself*). In this section you will learn to use reflexive pronouns, as well as other verbs that are used reflexively, to talk about your daily routine.

Uses of Reflexive Pronouns

bañarse (*to take a bath*)		
(yo)	**me** baño	*I'm taking a bath*
(tú)	**te** bañas	*you're taking a bath*
(Ud.) (él) (ella)	**se** baña	*you're taking a bath* / *he's taking a bath* / *she's taking a bath*
(nosotros)	**nos** bañamos	*we're taking baths*
(vosotros)	**os** bañáis	*you're taking baths*
(Uds.) (ellos) (ellas)	**se** bañan	*you're taking baths* / *they're taking baths* / *they're taking baths*

Suggestions:
- Contrast I wash the car/I wash myself. **Point out:** In first sentence, subject and object are different; in second they are same person (object pronoun reflects subject).
- **Emphasis:** In vocabulary lists *-se* indicates that verb is used reflexively; pronouns that reflect subject must be used.
- **Point out:** Many reflexive verbs are also stem changing. The correctly conjugated form includes (1) appropriate reflexive pronoun, (2) correct stem, (3) appropriate personal ending.
- Model verbs in conversational setting, saying sentence about yourself and turning it into *Ud.* or *Uds.* question asked of students.

Emphasis: meaning change: *dormir* → *dormirse*; *ir* → *irse*.

In Spanish, whenever the subject does anything to or for him/her/itself, a *reflexive pronoun* (**un pronombre reflexivo**) is used. The Spanish reflexive pronouns are **me**, **te**, and **se** in the singular; **nos**, **os**, and **se** in the plural. English reflexives end in *-self/selves*: *myself, yourself,* and so on.

The pronoun **se** at the end of an infinitive indicates that the verb is used reflexively. When the verb is conjugated, the reflexive pronoun that corresponds to the subject must be used: **(*yo*) *me* baño**, **(*tú*) *te* bañas**, and so on.

The following Spanish verbs, which you have already used nonreflexively, are also frequently used with reflexive pronouns.* Many of them are stem-changing.

acostarse (ue)	to go to bed	**lavarse**	to wash oneself, get washed
afeitarse	to shave	**levantarse**	to get up; to stand up
bañarse	to take a bath	**llamarse**	to be named, called
despertarse (ie)	to wake up	**ponerse**	to put on (*clothing*)
divertirse (ie, i)	to have a good time, enjoy oneself	**quitarse**	to take off (*clothing*)
dormirse (ue, u)	to fall asleep	**sentarse (ie)**	to sit down
irse	to leave, go away	**vestirse (i, i)**	to get dressed

¡OJO! After **ponerse** and **quitarse**, the definite article—not the possessive—is used with articles of clothing.

Se pone **el** abrigo.	*He's putting on his coat.*
Se quitan **el** sombrero.	*They're taking off their hats.*

- **Rapid Response Drill:** *Ud.* → *yo*, *Uds.* → *nosotros.* **Modelo:** *¿Se baña? → Sí, me baño. ¿Se bañan? → Sí, nos bañamos.* Do with all infinitives in list.

Option: Present use of article with body parts (Chs. 11 and 12).

*Compare: **Juan se lava.** (John gets washed/washes himself.) **Juan lava la ropa.** (John washes his clothing.) **Juan la lava.** (John washes it.)

Placement of Reflexive Pronouns

Like direct and indirect object pronouns, reflexive pronouns are placed before a conjugated verb but after the word **no** in a negative sentence: **No *se* bañan.** They may either precede the conjugated verb or be attached to an infinitive or present participle.

Emphasis: use of appropriate reflexive pronoun with infinitive or present participle—e.g., *tengo que levantarme, tienes que levantarte,* etc.

Me tengo que levantar temprano. Tengo que levantar**me** temprano.	*I have to get up early.*
¿No **te** estás divirtiendo? ¿No estás divirtiéndo**te**?	*Aren't you having a good time?*

¡OJO! Regardless of its position, the reflexive pronoun reflects the subject of the sentence.

[Práctica A–C]

Reflexive pronouns are attached to affirmative commands, but they precede the verb in negative commands. When a reflexive and another object pronoun are used together, the reflexive comes first.

Point out: Position of pronouns is same for reflexive, indirect, and direct object: R I D

Preliminary exercise: *Hace calor. ¿Qué hacemos? Dé oraciones nuevas según las indicaciones. —Ellos se quitan el suéter.* (*yo, Carolina, nosotros, tú, todos, vosotros*)

Point out: *suéter* = singular (each person takes off only one). Repeat with *abrigo, chaqueta*.

Quíte**se** el suéter.	*Take off your sweater.*
Quíte**selo** Ud.	*Take it off.*
No **se** ponga esa blusa.	*Don't put on that blouse.*
No **se la** ponga Ud.	*Don't put it on.*

[Práctica CH–D]

Práctica

Variation A:
- Following sequence of infinitives as given, students answer based on own lives and family/roommates.
- Do sequence using *Juan Típico* as subject.
- Students use items as the basis for a partner/pair exercise, answering based on their own lives.

Follow-up A: 1. *Cuando hace mal tiempo, ¿qué lleva Ud.? ¿Se pone las sandalias?* (→ *Sí, me las pongo.*) *¿el impermeable? ¿las botas?* **2.** *Cuando hace calor, ¿qué se ponen los niños? ¿los pantalones cortos? ¿una corbata? ¿el abrigo? ¿el traje de baño?*

A. **Hábitos y costumbres.** ¿Qué acostumbran hacer los miembros de la familia Hernández? Conteste, imaginando que Ud. es el esposo (la esposa). Use el sujeto pronominal cuando sea necesario.

1. yo / levantarse / a las siete
2. mi esposo/a / levantarse / más tarde cuando puede
3. nosotros / bañarse / por la mañana
4. por costumbre / niños / bañarse / por la noche
5. yo / vestirse / antes de desayunar
6. mi esposo/a / vestirse / después de tomar un café
7. por la noche / niños / acostarse / muy temprano
8. yo / acostarse / más tarde, a las once
9. por lo general / mi esposo/a / acostarse / más tarde que yo

En la familia Hernández, ¿quién...

1. se levanta primero?
2. se acuesta primero?
3. no se baña por la mañana?
4. se viste antes de tomar el desayuno?

Ahora, con un compañero (una compañera), haga y conteste preguntas basadas en las frases anteriores, según el modelo. La persona que contesta puede cambiar los detalles.

MODELO: yo / levantarse / a las siete →
—¿A qué hora te levantas?
—Me levanto a las ocho.

B. Complete las oraciones, usando la forma correcta de los verbos de la derecha.

1. En la escuela primaria los niños _____ en el suelo con frecuencia. Generalmente los maestros prefieren _____ en una silla.
2. ¡Hace calor! Yo voy a _____ el abrigo. ¿No vas a _____ la chaqueta?
3. Voy a _____ antes de acostarme esta noche. Mi esposo/a, en cambio, _____ en la mañana.
4. Nosotros _____ muy temprano, a las seis de la mañana. Y tú, ¿a qué hora te gusta _____?
5. Hace un poco de frío. En este momento yo estoy _____ una chaqueta. Alfredo prefiere _____ un suéter.
6. ¡Tú siempre _____ en las fiestas! ¿Por qué no estás _____ ahora?
7. Yo _____ cuando tengo sueño; no importa la hora. En cambio mi compañero de cuarto siempre _____ a las once.

lavarse
sentarse
acostarse
despertarse
ponerse
quitarse
divertirse
bañarse

Emphasis C: preposition + infinitive.

Suggestion C: Do sequence using *Juan Típico* as subject, then *los señores Gómez*.

C. Complete las oraciones lógicamente, describiendo su propia rutina diaria. **¡OJO!** Después de una preposición, sólo puede usarse el infinitivo. Use pronombres reflexivos cuando sea posible.

1. Me levanto después de _____.
2. Me siento a la mesa antes de _____.
3. Me duermo después de _____.
4. Me baño antes de _____.
5. Me visto después de _____.
6. Me quito la ropa antes de _____.
7. Me pongo el abrigo antes de _____.
8. Por la noche, me divierto antes de _____.

Preliminary Exercise CH: *Dé el mandato negativo:* **1.** *Acuéstese.* **2.** *Aféitese.* **3.** *Lávese.* **4.** *Siéntese.* *Dé el mandato afirmativo.* **5.** *No se bañe.* **6.** *No se levante.* **7.** *No se quite los zapatos.* **8.** *No se ponga la chaqueta.*

CH. **Consejos.** Su vecino Pablo es una persona muy perezosa y descuidada (*careless*). No estudia mucho y tampoco hace los quehaceres que le tocan en el apartamento donde vive con un compañero. Déle consejos lógicos usando estos verbos, según el modelo.

MODELO: afeitarse → Es necesario que se afeite. ¡Aféitese!

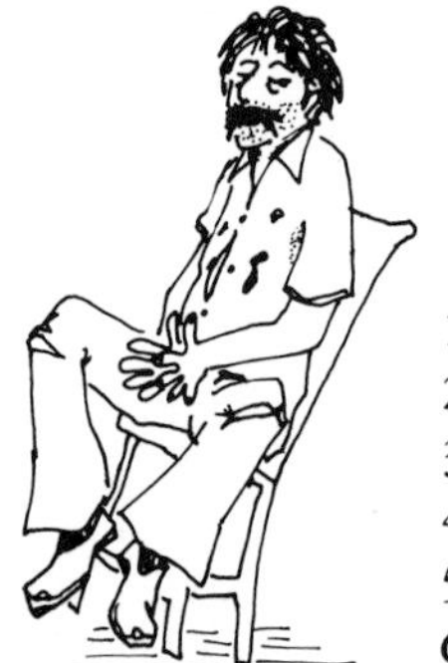

1. despertarse más temprano
2. levantarse más temprano
3. bañarse más
4. quitarse esa ropa sucia y ponerse ropa limpia
5. planchar su ropa y vestirse mejor
6. estudiar más
7. no divertirse tanto
8. ir más a la biblioteca
9. no acostarse tan tarde
10. ayudar con los quehaceres
11. sacar la basura, por lo menos
12. ¿ ?

D. **Situaciones: En el hospital.** Con un compañero (una compañera), hagan los papeles (*play the roles*) de paciente y enfermero/a, según el modelo.

MODELO: los zapatos → —¿Quiere Ud. que me quite los zapatos ahora?
—Sí, quíteselos, por favor.

1. el suéter
2. la camisa/la blusa
3. los pantalones
4. la camiseta
5. los calcetines/las medias
6. toda la ropa

¿Qué otros mandatos le puede dar la enfermera (el enfermero) al paciente?

Conversación

A. Aquí hay algunas escenas de un día típico de la vida de la familia Hernández. Describa los distintos momentos que se ven e* invente otros detalles, usando pronombres reflexivos cuando sea posible. Por ejemplo:

Dibujo 1: Los padres se despiertan muy temprano. El bebé se despierta aún (*even*) más temprano. Va a la cama de sus padres y los despierta.

Suggestion A: Do as whole-class composition, with you or a student writing sentences on the board. Alternatively, assign as written homework.

Optional: *Escenas domésticas. ¿Cómo se dice en español? (¡**OJO!** No se usan pronombres reflexivos en todas las oraciones.)* **1.** I'm going to put Johnny to bed now. **2.** I'll go to bed later. **3.** Wake up now! **4.** And wake up the kids, too! **5.** Their son's name is Agustín. **6.** He always calls his parents on weekends. **7.** They're putting on their slippers (*zapatillas*) now. **8.** Then they're going to put the coffeepot on the stove.

Follow-up: Ask students to explain why each construction is or is not reflexive.

Conteste estas preguntas en su descripción.

1. ¿Quiénes son los miembros de la familia Hernández? (¿Cuántos hijos hay en total? ¿Vive alguien más con la familia? etcétera)
2. ¿Necesitan un despertador los señores Hernández? ¿Por qué sí o por qué no?
3. ¿Dónde duerme cada miembro de la familia? ¿Dónde es necesario que duerma la niña?
4. ¿Cuáles son los «juguetes» del bebé?
5. ¿Qué parece ser el centro de la vida doméstica de esta familia?

Palabras útiles: la bañera (*bathtub*), la cuna (*crib, cradle*), el juguete (*toy*), la pelota (*ball*), los anteojos (*eyeglasses*)

---

*Note that the word **y** changes to **e** before the sound **i** (which can also be spelled **hi-**): **español *e* inglés**, **padres *e* hijos**.

Optional: Do as partner/pair activity, with students converting *Ud.* questions to *tú*.

B. **Preguntas**

1. ¿Prefiere Ud. bañarse por la mañana o por la noche? ¿Es necesario que los hombres se afeiten todos los días? ¿Se afeita Ud. todos los días? ¿Prefiere no afeitarse los fines de semana? ¿Cuántos años hace que se afeita?
2. ¿Dónde le gusta a Ud. sentarse para leer, en la sala o en la alcoba? ¿en un sofá, en un sillón o en la cama? ¿Es buena idea sentarse en la cama para estudiar? ¿Por qué sí o por qué no? ¿Es mejor que uno se siente a estudiar en un escritorio? ¿Dónde le gusta sentarse en las clases? ¿cerca o lejos del profesor? ¿cerca o lejos de la puerta?
3. ¿Le gusta a Ud. vestirse elegante o informalmente? ¿Qué ropa se pone cuando quiere estar elegante? ¿cuando quiere estar muy cómodo/a (*comfortable*)? ¿Qué se pone para ir a las clases? ¿para ir a la playa?
4. ¿A qué hora tiene que levantarse todos los días? ¿Es necesario que alguien lo/la despierte? ¿A qué hora se acuesta? ¿Cuál es la última cosa que hace antes de acostarse? ¿Cuál es la última cosa en que piensa antes de dormirse?
5. ¿Ud. se duerme fácilmente o con dificultad? ¿Qué hace cuando no puede dormirse? ¿Es necesario que Ud. piense en cosas agradables para poder dormir? ¿Qué hace cuando tiene sueño pero no debe dormirse?
6. ¿Cómo se llama el dueño (la dueña) de su casa de apartamentos? ¿el portero (la portera)? ¿Cómo se llama su vecino favorito (vecina favorita)? ¿Por qué le gusta esta persona?

Suggestion C:
- As preparation, do as whole-class rapid pattern drill, using *yo* as subject, then *nosotros*.
- Individual students tell about their typical day.
- Students tell what they will do tomorrow: *Voy a...* .
- Students explain some actions (cued by instructor) by saying: *Es necesario que... porque...* .

C. **Entrevista.** Using the following verbs as a guide, ask another student what he or she does during a typical day, and, when appropriate, where. Note the answers; then tell the class about his or her day.

MODELO: despertarse → ¿Te despiertas temprano? ¿tarde? ¿fácilmente? ¿A qué hora te despiertas?

1. despertarse
2. levantarse
3. bañarse
4. afeitarse
5. vestirse
6. desayunar
7. salir para la universidad
8. asistir a clases
9. almorzar
10. divertirse
11. volver a casa
12. cocinar
13. cenar
14. lavar los platos
15. limpiar la cocina
16. sacar la basura
17. sentarse a ver la televisión
18. quitarse la ropa
19. acostarse
20. dormirse
21. dormir _____ horas

29. TALKING ABOUT THE PAST (1)
Preterite of Regular Verbs and of *dar*, *hacer*, *ir*, and *ser*

Communicative objectives for 38: how to talk about things you did in the past

Note: Students have used some preterite forms since Ch. 3. Presentation of the entire preterite system, of the imperfect, and of the preterite/imperfect contrast is spread over the next four chapters and reentered throughout the text.

Un problema con la agencia de empleos

SRA. GÓMEZ: ¡La criada que Uds. me *mandaron* ayer fue un desastre!

SR. PARDO: ¿Cómo que *fue* un desastre? ¿Qué *hizo*?

SRA. GÓMEZ: Pues, no *hizo* nada. *Pasó* todo el día en la casa, pero no *lavó* los platos, no *limpió* la bañera, ni *recogió* los juguetes de los niños. Y cuando *se fue* a las tres, me *dio* las buenas tardes como si nada.

SR. PARDO: Trate de comprender, señora; cada persona tiene sus más y sus menos. Por lo menos esta criada *fue* mejor que la otra que le *mandamos* anteayer... que ni *llegó*.

Imagine que Ud. es la Sra. Gómez y descríbale al Sr. Pardo las acciones de la criada. Use el diálogo como guía.

1. Ella no... (lavar los platos, limpiar la bañera, recoger los juguetes)
2. Pero (ella) sí... (llegar temprano por la mañana, pasar todo el día en casa, salir a las tres)
3. Total que (ella)... (no hacer nada, ser un desastre)

¿Quiere la Sra. Gómez que esta criada vuelva mañana? ¿Va a querer que esta agencia le mande otra criada?

Follow-up: *Preguntas*. Students respond using object pronouns. *La criada de la agencia, ¿hizo el trabajo doméstico? ¿lavó los platos? ¿sacó la basura? ¿sacudió los muebles? ¿Qué hizo?*

Follow-up: Subjunctive. Students reconstruct commands that Sra. Gómez gave to maid: *Quiero que Ud....* .

In previous chapters of ***Puntos de partida***, you have already used a few past tense forms: **¿Qué *comiste* anoche?**, ***Fue* una ganga**, and so on. To talk about all aspects of the past in Spanish, you need to know how to use two simple tenses (tenses formed without an auxiliary or "helping" verb): the preterite and the imperfect. You will focus on the forms and uses of these tenses beginning in this chapter and continuing through **Capítulos 10**, **11**, and **12**.

The *preterite* (**el pretérito**) has several equivalents in English. For example, **hablé** can mean *I spoke* or *I did speak*. The preterite is used to report finished, completed actions or states of being in the past. If the action or state of being is viewed as completed—no matter how long it lasted or took to complete—it will be expressed with the preterite.

Follow-up: Dictation. Students should pay particular attention to oral stress and written accents. **1.** *Mandaron una criada ayer.* **2.** *Fue un desastre.* **3.** *No hizo nada.* **4.** *No lavó los platos.* **5.** *No sacó la basura ni sacudió los muebles.* **6.** *Pero fue mejor que la otra.* **7.** *La otra ni llegó.*

Option: Present adverbs commonly associated with preterite: *ayer, anteayer, anoche* (*¡OJO!* last night, not at night), *la semana pasada, el semestre pasado, una vez* (once).

A problem with the employment agency MRS. GÓMEZ: The maid you sent me yesterday was a disaster! MR. PARDO: What do you mean, a disaster? What did she do? MRS. GÓMEZ: Well, she didn't do anything. She spent all day at the house, but she didn't wash the dishes, clean the bathtub, or pick up the kids' toys. And when she left at 3:00, she said, "Good afternoon," as if nothing were wrong. MR. PARDO: Try to understand, madam; everyone has his or her good and bad points. At least this maid was better than the other one we sent you the day before yesterday—who didn't even arrive.

Preterite of Regular Verbs

hablar		comer		vivir	
hablé	*I spoke (did speak)*	comí	*I ate (did eat)*	viví	*I lived (did live)*
habl**aste**	*you spoke*	com**iste**	*you ate*	viv**iste**	*you lived*
habl**ó**	*you/he/she spoke*	comi**ó**	*you/he/she ate*	vivi**ó**	*you/he/she lived*
habl**amos**	*we spoke*	com**imos**	*we ate*	viv**imos**	*we lived*
habl**asteis**	*you spoke*	com**isteis**	*you ate*	viv**isteis**	*you lived*
habl**aron**	*you/they spoke*	com**ieron**	*you/they ate*	viv**ieron**	*you/they lived*

Note the accent marks on the first and third person singular of the preterite tense. These accent marks are dropped in the conjugation of **ver**: **vi**, **vio**.

Pronunciation hint: some English words are distinguished from each other solely by the position of stress: *objéct* (*to express disagreement*) or *óbject* (*thing*); *súspect* (*one who is suspected*) or *suspéct* (*to be suspicious*). The same is true in Spanish: **tomas** (*you take*) or **Tomás** (*Thomas*). It is particularly important to pay attention to stress in preterite verb forms since many of them are identical in form—except for the written accent—to other forms you have learned: **hablo** (*I speak*) versus **habló** (*he/she/it spoke*), **hable** (*speak*, **Ud.** command) versus **hablé** (*I spoke*), and so on.

Also, note the following about regular preterite forms.

- Verbs that end in **-car**, **-gar**, and **-zar** show a spelling change in the first person singular of the preterite.

  buscar: bus**qu**é, buscaste,...
  pagar: pag**u**é, pagaste,...
  empezar: empe**c**é, empezaste,...

- **-Ar** and **-er** stem-changing verbs show no stem change in the preterite: **desperté**, **volví**. **-Ir** stem-changing verbs do show a change.*
- As in the present participle, an unstressed **-i-** between two vowels becomes **-y-**.

  creer: creyó, creyeron   leer: leyó, leyeron

Suggestions:
- Model pronunciation of regular forms, emphasizing stress on *yo* and *Ud.* forms.
- **Point out:** *nosotros* forms of *-ar* and *-ir* verbs are identical to present-tense forms. Context clarifies meaning.
- Use *llamar*, *aprender*, and *recibir* in brief conversational exchanges with students, first generating sentence about yourself, then asking *Ud./Uds.* questions of students.

Listening Exercise: Discrimination.
- Give appropriate subject pronoun. Singular: *pregunté, bajó, ayudaste, fumé, llamé, anunció, mandaste, bebió, aprendí, comiste, contesté, ayudó* Plural: *escuchamos, terminaron, mirasteis, estudiamos, bailaron, regresaron, pagamos, bebieron, comimos, aprendisteis* Is verb present, past, or could it be both? *miró, mandé, escuché, escucha, escribimos, fumaste, bebió*, etc. Is verb subjunctive or preterite? *estudie, estudié, fumé, fumen*, etc.
- **Point out:** lack of accents on *vi/vio*; spelling changes in *-car/-gar/-zar* verbs same as in *Ud(s).* commands and in subjunctive

Irregular Preterite Forms

dar		hacer		ir/ser	
di	dimos	hice	hicimos	fui	fuimos
diste	disteis	hiciste	hicisteis	fuiste	fuisteis
dio	dieron	hizo	hicieron	fue	fueron

Emphasis: Preterite forms of *ir* and *ser* are identical. Context clarifies meaning.

Point out: lack of accent marks on *di/dio*

*You will practice the preterite of most stem-changing verbs in **Capítulo 10**.

The preterite endings for **dar** are the same as those used for regular **-er**/**-ir** verbs in the preterite, except that the accent marks are dropped. The third person singular of **hacer—hizo**—is spelled with a **z** to keep the [s] sound of the infinitive. **Ser** and **ir** have identical forms in the preterite. Context will make the meaning clear.

Fui profesora.	*I was a professor.*
Fui al centro anoche.	*I went downtown last night.*

Práctica

Preliminary Exercises:
- Rapid Response Drill: *Ud.* → *yo, Uds.* → *nosotros.* **Modelo:** *¿Llamó Ud.? → Sí, llamé. ¿estudió? ¿trabajó? ¿habló? ¿escuchó? ¿terminó? ¿mandó? ¿bajó? ¿cantó? ¿bailó? ¿comió? ¿bebió? ¿abrió? ¿asistió? ¿escribió? ¿preguntaron? ¿contestaron? ¿bajaron? ¿mandaron? ¿escucharon? ¿miraron? ¿bebieron? ¿comieron? ¿comprendieron? ¿vivieron? ¿recibieron?*
- *Preparativos para el examen de química. Dé oraciones nuevas según las indicaciones.* **1.** *Pepe estudió hasta muy tarde. (yo, Uds., tú, Graciela, nosotros, vosotros)* **2.** *Tú escribiste todos los ejercicios. (Rodrigo, yo, nosotras, ellas, Uds., vosotros)* **3.** *Julio fue al laboratorio. (yo, Paula, tú, nosotros, Estela y Clara, vosotras)* **4.** *Ana hizo los experimentos. (yo, nosotros, Uds., tú, Adolfo, vosotros)*

Suggestion A: Redo items using *tú* as subject, then *nosotros*.

A. **El día de dos compañeras.** Teresa y Evangelina comparten un apartamento en un viejo edificio de apartamentos. Ayer Teresa fue a la universidad mientras Evangelina se quedó (*stayed*) en casa. Describa lo que hicieron, según la perspectiva de cada una.

TERESA:

1. (yo) salir / apartamento / las nueve
2. llegar / biblioteca / las diez
3. estudiar / toda la mañana / para / examen de química
4. escribir / todo / ejercicios / de / libro de texto
5. las doce y media / almorzar / con / amigos / en / cafetería
6. la una / ir / laboratorio
7. hacer / todo / experimentos / de / manual (*m.*) de laboratorio
8. tomar / examen / las cuatro
9. comentarlo / con / amigos: ¡ser / horrible!
10. regresar / a casa / y / ayudar / a / Evangelina / preparar / cena

EVANGELINA:

1. (yo) quedarse / en casa / todo / día
2. por la mañana / ver / que / portero / no / sacar / basura
3. por eso / (yo) llamar / dueño / de / edificio
4. tomar / café / con / vecinos, / que / irse / las once y media
5. limpiar / casa / entero: sacudir / muebles, / pasar / aspiradora, / hacer / camas, / planchar / ropa / de las dos...
6. electricista / llegar / las dos
7. (él) arreglar / luz / de / comedor
8. (yo) barrer / suelo / otra vez / después de que / él / salir
9. ir / garaje / para / dejar / cajas (*boxes*) / allí
10. empezar / preparar / cena / las cinco

¿Quién lo dijo (*said*), Evangelina o Teresa?

1. A mi compañera de apartamento no le interesan los quehaceres domésticos.
2. ¡El examen fue desastroso!
3. Es cierto. El portero no sacó la basura otra vez.
4. ¿Qué estás preparando para la cena?

5. No funciona la luz del comedor.
6. No, no puedo cenar con Uds.; mi compañera de apartamento me espera para la cena esta noche.

Ahora vuelva a contar el día de Evangelina pero según la perspectiva de Teresa. Luego cuente el día de Teresa según Evangelina.

B. **¿Qué hicieron ayer?** Haga oraciones completas, usando los verbos en el pretérito.

1. **Julián:** hacer cola para comprar una entrada (*ticket*) de cine / comprarla por fin / entrar en el cine / ver la película / gustarle mucho / encontrar a unos amigos frente al cine / ir a un café con ellos / regresar a casa tarde
2. **mis compañeros de apartamento:** ir a la universidad por la mañana / regresar temprano a casa / sacudir los muebles de la sala / lavar la ropa / sacarla de la secadora / limpiar la casa entera / prepararlo todo para la fiesta de este fin de semana
3. **yo:** llegar a la universidad a las ¿ ? / asistir a clases / ir a la cafetería / almorzar con ¿ ?, prestarle un libro a ¿ ?, ¿ ?

C. **Un semestre en México.** Cuente la siguiente historia según la perspectiva de la persona indicada, usando el pretérito de los verbos.

1. (yo) pasar un semestre estudiando en México
2. mis padres: pagarme el vuelo...
3. ...pero yo trabajar para ganar el dinero para la matrícula y los otros gastos (*expenses*)
4. vivir con una familia mexicana encantadora
5. aprender mucho sobre la vida y la cultura mexicanas
6. visitar muchos sitios de interés turístico e histórico
7. mis amigos: escribirme muchas cartas
8. (yo) mandarles muchas tarjetas postales
9. comprarles muchos recuerdos a todos
10. volver a los Estados Unidos al final de agosto

Suggestion B: Vary subjects, as appropriate.

Follow-up B: Read whole paragraph out loud. Then repeat, phrase-by-phrase. Students retell story line-by-line. *Anoche Miguel volvió a casa a las siete. Preparó la comida. Cenó rápidamente y lavó los platos. Luego limpió la casa entera. Trabajó como un loco: sacudió los muebles, lavó las ventanas, sacó la basura. También hizo las camas. Terminó a las ocho menos cinco. Y a las ocho en punto llegaron sus padres.*

Optional: *¿Qué hicieron estas personas ayer? ¿Qué piensa Ud.? Invente los detalles necesarios.*
Personas: Dan Rather, el presidente, Julio Iglesias, Julia Child, el profesor (*la profesora*), *¿ ?*
Acciones: dar un discurso (speech), *leer las noticias* (news), *cocinar, cantar, enseñar, no hacer ninguno de sus quehaceres, ¿ ?*

Follow-up: Tell about daily lives of one of following people. Is his/her life very different from yours on a daily basis? Invent as many details as you can and don't be afraid to include trivial details—that is what daily life is all about. **1.** *un actor famoso/una actriz famosa* **2.** *la reina de Inglaterra, Isabel II* **3.** *las criadas de la Casa Blanca* **4.** *un(a) atleta profesional* **5.** *un bebé de dos años*

Suggestion C:
- Vary subject, as appropriate.
- Students read through paragraphs first, before starting.
- Have students do preterites as dictation while you read present tense version.

Conversación

A. **Preguntas**

1. ¿Qué le dio Ud. a su mejor amigo/a (esposo/a, novio/a) para su cumpleaños el año pasado? ¿Qué le regaló a Ud. esa persona para su cumpleaños? ¿Alguien le mandó a Ud. flores el año pasado? ¿Le mandó Ud. flores a alguien? ¿Le gusta a Ud. que le traigan chocolates? ¿otras cosas?
2. ¿Dónde y a qué hora comió Ud. ayer? ¿Con quiénes comió? ¿Le gustaron todos los platos que comió? ¿Quién se los preparó? Si comió fuera, ¿quién pagó?

Variation A: Working in small groups, students ask each other questions, using *tú* forms.

Follow-up A: For next class, students write down **(1)** 1–2 unusual things they did in past; **(2)** 1–2 unusual things they did *not* do. Students read statements in class; others judge *cierto* or *falso* for each statement.

3. ¿Cuándo decidió Ud. estudiar el español? ¿Cuándo lo empezó a estudiar? ¿Cuánto tiempo hace que lo estudia ahora? ¿Va a seguir estudiándolo el semestre (trimestre) que viene?
4. ¿Qué hizo Ud. ayer? ¿Adónde fue? ¿Con quién(es)? ¿Ayudó a alguien a hacer algo? ¿Lo/La llamó alguien? ¿Llamó Ud. a alguien? ¿Lo/La invitaron a hacer algo especial algunos amigos? Y anteayer, ¿qué hizo? ¿Lo mismo?
5. ¿Qué programa de televisión vio anoche? ¿Qué película vio la semana pasada? ¿Qué libro/novela leyó el año pasado? El año pasado, ¿pasó Ud. más tiempo leyendo o viendo la televisión? ¿trabajando o estudiando? ¿estudiando o viajando? Si hizo algún viaje, ¿adónde fue? ¿Qué tal fue el viaje?

Notas comunicativas: Putting Events in Sequence

When telling about what we did, we often want to emphasize the sequence in which events took place. You can use these phrases to put events into a simple sequence in Spanish. You will learn additional words and phrases of this kind as you learn more about the past tenses.

Primero...	First . . .
Luego... y...	Then . . . and . . .
Después... y...	Afterwards . . . and . . .
Finalmente (Por fin)...	Finally . . .

Suggestion B: Assign as written composition, or do as in-class oral composition.

—*Ah, pues... Naturalmente: Si le pasa usted el dedo°!...*

le... *you run your finger over it*

B. **¿Por qué no sacudió Ud. los muebles?** The housekeeper in the cartoon will have to explain why she did not dust the furniture. An able excuse-maker, she could point out all the other tasks that she *did* complete during the day. She could also indicate the many unexpected complications that kept her from dusting.

MODELO: ¿Por qué no sacudió Ud. los muebles? →
—No fue posible, señora, pero sí hice muchas otras cosas. Primero hice todas las camas. Luego lavé las ventanas y saqué la basura. Después preparé la cena y...
—No lo hice hoy, señora, porque—como Ud. sabe—llegó inesperadamente (*unexpectedly*) su hermana con sus diez niños. Primero les preparé el almuerzo. Luego los acompañé al museo de arte moderno. Después fui al mercado a comprar más carne y tuve que (*I had to*)...

Following the model of the housekeeper's excuses, give the most elaborate excuses that you can in response to the following questions.

1. EL JEFE: ¿Por qué llegó Ud. tarde a la oficina?
2. LA PROFESORA: ¿Por qué no terminó Ud. los ejercicios de hoy?

3. SU MEJOR AMIGO: ¿Por qué no me llamaste la semana pasada?
4. SU COMPAÑERO/A: ¿Por qué no le ayudaste a Juan a limpiar el apartamento? ¿Por qué no comiste nada esta mañana? ¿Por qué no fuiste a la fiesta anoche?
5. SUS PADRES: ¿Por qué no nos escribiste la semana pasada?

Suggestion C: Have students practice with the interview items by interviewing you first. You may wish to set an example by giving outrageous answers to all or some of the questions.

C. **Entrevista: Preguntas indiscretas.** Hágale preguntas personales a un compañero (una compañera), usando estas frases como guía. Invente otras «preguntas indiscretas» si quiere. Luego dígale a la clase algo interesante sobre su compañero/a.

1. ¿a qué hora? despertarse esta mañana
2. ¿a qué hora? volver a casa el sábado pasado (anoche, ...)
3. ¿por cuánto tiempo? mirar la televisión ayer
4. ¿a qué hora? acostarse anoche
5. ¿cuánto? pagar de gas (luz, alquiler) el mes pasado
6. ¿cuánto? pagar por la ropa que lleva hoy
7. ¿qué? comer anteayer
8. ¿de quién? enamorarse (*to fall in love*) el año pasado
9. ¿en qué clase? sacar una nota (*grade*) mala en la escuela secundaria
10. ¿qué? tocarle hacer ayer (anteayer, el mes pasado, ...) pero que no hizo

Bogotá, Colombia

¿A quién le toca? (*Whose turn is it?*)

—¿Quieres poner el televisor? Hay una película estupenda esta noche.
—Espérate. ¿A ti no te toca lavar los platos?
—A mí, no. Creo que le toca a Julio.
—Pero Julio no está. Ya salió.
–Vamos a dejarlos hasta que regrese.

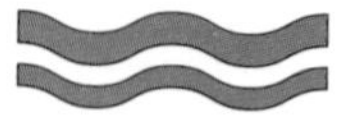

30. EXPRESSING *EACH OTHER*
Reciprocal Actions with Reflexive Pronouns

—*¿Tú crees que cada vez que nos encontramos tenemos que saludarnos dándonos la mano?*

Follow-up (cartoon): *Si los pulpos siguen conversando, ¿qué van a decir? ¿Cómo termina la conversación?*

1. ¿Dónde se encuentran los dos pulpos?
2. ¿Cómo se saludan (*do they greet each other*)?
3. ¿Se conocen? ¿Cómo se sabe?

The plural reflexive pronouns, **nos**, **os**, and **se**, can be used to express *reciprocal actions* (**las acciones recíprocas**). Reciprocal actions are usually expressed in English with *each other* or *one another.*

Nos queremos

Nos queremos.	*We love each other.*
¿**Os** ayudáis?	*Do you help one another?*
Se miran.	*They're looking at each other.*

Se miran

Preliminary exercises:
- *¿Cómo se dice?* 1. We help each other. (you, they) 2. We love each other. (you, they) 3. We write to each other. (you, them)
- *Exprese como acciones recíprocas.* 1. *Estela me mira a mí. Yo miro a Estela.* 2. *Eduardo habla con Pepita. Pepita habla con Eduardo.* 3. *El padre necesita a su hijo. El hijo necesita a su padre.* 4. *Tomás me conoce a mí. Yo conozco a Tomás.* 5. *Tú escribes a Luisa. Luisa te escribe a ti.* 6. *La profesora escucha a los estudiantes. Los estudiantes escuchan a la profesora.* 7. *Ud. quiere a su esposo. Su esposo la quiere también a Ud.* 8. *Jorge le da la mano a Mario. Mario le da la mano a Jorge.*

Práctica

Describa las siguientes relaciones familiares o sociales, haciendo oraciones completas con una palabra o frase de cada grupo.

los buenos amigos
los parientes
los esposos
los padres y los niños
los amigos que no viven en la misma ciudad
los profesores y los estudiantes
los jefes y los empleados

(no)

verse con frecuencia
quererse
ayudarse (con los quehaceres domésticos/con los problemas económicos/con los problemas personales)
hablarse (todos los días/con frecuencia/sinceramente)
respetarse
llamarse por teléfono (con frecuencia)
mirarse (en la clase/con cariño)
necesitarse
conocerse bien
escribirse
saludarse (en la clase/con cariño)
darse la mano

Follow-up: *Ud. y sus amigos/as, ¿se llaman por teléfono? ¿se ven frecuentemente? ¿se ayudan? ¿se escriben? ¿se mandan regalos?* etc.

Conversación

A. **Preguntas**

1. ¿Con qué frecuencia se ven Ud. y su novio/a (esposo/a, mejor amigo/a)? ¿Cuánto tiempo hace que se conocen? ¿Con qué frecuencia se dan regalos? ¿se escriben? ¿se telefonean? ¿Le gusta a Ud. que se vean tanto (tan poco)? ¿Es lástima que no se vean con más frecuencia?
2. ¿Con qué frecuencia se ven Ud. y sus abuelos (primos)? ¿Por qué se ven Uds. tan poco (tanto)? ¿Cómo se mantienen en contacto? Por lo general, ¿es bueno que los abuelos y los nietos se vean con frecuencia? ¿Ocurre esto con frecuencia en la sociedad norteamericana? En su opinión, ¿es esto común entre los hispanos?

Suggestion B: *El hombre no se mira en el espejo, es decir, no se puede ver. ¿Cuál de las siguientes explicaciones le parece a Ud. más razonable? ¿menos razonable? ¿Por qué? ¿Puede Ud. dar una mejor explicación? El hombre no se ve en el espejo porque...* 1. *es vampiro y los vampiros no tienen reflejo.* 2. *el espejo es un espejo mágico.* 3. *es un fantasma* (ghost). 4. *el espejo tiene un defecto.* 5. *es víctima del fenómeno «Twilight Zone» y realmente no existe en este mundo.* 6. *sufre de alucinaciones a causa de las drogas.*

B. **En el espejo** (*mirror*). Describa lo que pasa en el dibujo. Use oraciones cortas, pero sea imaginativo/a.

1. ¿Quiénes son las personas del dibujo?
2. ¿Dónde están y qué hacen?
3. ¿Quién trata de mirarse en el espejo?
4. ¿Se puede ver a sí mismo? ¿Por qué sí o por qué no?

SITUACIONES

Situaciones: See IM for suggestions, additional exercises, and supplementary dialogues and exercises.

La rutina cotidiana°

° de todos los días

Hablando con un buen amigo

—¿Qué tal? ¿Cómo llevas el curso?

—Muy bien, pero... no sé... Llevo una vida muy aburrida.

—¡No seas tan pesimista! Eso siempre sucede al final del semestre, ¿no?

—Sí, pero ahora es peor. Hago las mismas cosas todos los días. Tengo clases de las 8 a las 2. Después voy a la biblioteca y trato de hacer todos mis deberes.° A las 6 entro a trabajar y salgo a las 10. Por suerte° tengo libres los jueves y es cuando aprovecho° para ir de compras o a la lavandería.° Cuando llego a casa, estoy roto.° Me limito a leer un rato° y... a dormir.

° *assignments*
° Por... *Luckily*
° *I take the opportunity* / ¿ ?
° ¿ ? / breve período de tiempo

Note: *roto* (slang) = *agotado, muy cansado*

—¿A qué hora te levantas de costumbre?

—No te lo vas a creer, pero me levanto a las 6 todos los días. Hago un poco de ejercicio, me baño, desayuno, arreglo mi habitación y me preparo el almuerzo y a veces la cena. ¡Qué ganas tengo de empezar a trabajar y dejar ya los estudios!

Unos años más tarde

—¿Qué te pasa? Pareces cansado.

—Sí, lo estoy. Desde que soy jefe de sección en el banco, tengo muchísimo trabajo. Hay días que me quedo doce horas en la oficina.

—Y ¿cómo te organizas con la casa?

—De momento no me organizo para nada. Creo que voy a volver a la universidad por un semestre más. ¡Qué tiempos aquéllos!

Notas comunicativas sobre el diálogo

The dialogue contains another double object phrase that is useful in conversation: **No te lo vas a creer...** Note also the use of the verb **llevar** (*to wear; to bring*) to talk about how things are going.

¿Cómo **llevas** el curso?	*How is the term going for you?*
Llevo una vida...	*I have (lead) a _____ life.*
aburrida, fascinante, muy ocupada	*boring, fascinating, very busy*

Optional: *¿Cómo **va** el curso?*

Conversación

With a classmate, repeat the first part of the dialogue with these variations.

- Substitute real information about your daily routine.
- Illustrate your daily routine by telling what you did yesterday: **«Sí, pero ahora es peor. Hago las mismas cosas todos los días. Te voy a contar lo que hice ayer... »**

With a different classmate, repeat the second part of the dialogue with these variations.

- Expand the description of daily activities at the office.
- Select another occupation (university professor, grade school teacher, homemaker . . .) and invent a description of that person's daily routine, comparing it to that of a student.

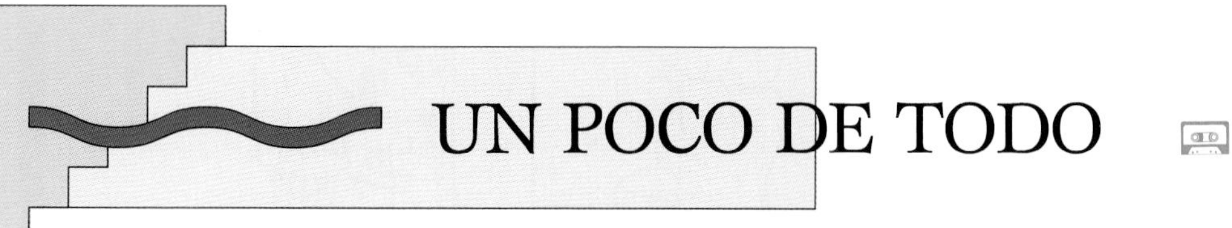

UN POCO DE TODO

A. **La triste historia de amor de Orlando y Patricia.** Descríbala, usando el pretérito de los siguientes verbos.

1. verse en clase
2. mirarse
3. saludarse
4. hablarse mucho
5. empezar a llamarse por teléfono constantemente
6. mandarse regalos
7. escribirse durante las vacaciones
8. ayudarse con los problemas
9. casarse (*to get married*)
10. no llevarse (*to get along*) bien
11. separarse
12. divorciarse

B. **¡Firma (*Sign*) aquí, por favor!** Complete estas oraciones usando información verdadera. Luego hágales preguntas a sus compañeros de clase para encontrar a alguien que contestó de la misma manera.

MODELO El año pasado, leí por lo menos cinco novelas. →
—¿Cuántas novelas leíste el año pasado?
—No sé exactamentae. Probablemente cinco.
—Firma aquí, por favor.

	Nombres
1. El año pasado leí por lo menos _____ novelas.	_________
2. Anoche volví a casa (a mi apartamento, a mi cuarto en la residencia) a las _____.	_________
3. Una vez fui a _____ (ciudad, estado, país) y me gustó muchísimo.	_________
4. Una vez fui a _____ (ciudad, estado, país) ¡y no me gustó nada!	_________

5. Me divierto más cuando mis amigos me invitan a _____. _______
6. Ayer me desperté y me levanté a las _____. _______
7. Un quehacer doméstico que siempre me toca hacer—y que no me gusta nada—es _____. _______
8. Mi _____ y yo nos queremos mucho. _______

C. **La hora de comer.** ¿Qué pasa en el dibujo? ¿Quiénes son las personas que aparecen? ¿Qué pasó y qué va a pasar? Use las preguntas como guía, inventando los detalles necesarios.

1. ¿Qué hora es? ¿En qué parte de la casa ocurre la escena?
2. ¿Quién se levantó primero? ¿Quién se despertó después y qué escuchó?
3. ¿Comió mucho el esposo para la cena? ¿Por qué no tiene sueño esa noche? ¿Qué necesidad física tiene en ese momento? ¿Qué está sacando del refrigerador?
4. ¿Qué está haciendo la esposa? ¿Al esposo le sorprende que su esposa le esté sacando una foto? ¿Qué quiere probar (*to prove*) la esposa? ¿Qué quiere que su esposo haga (o no haga)?
5. ¿Va a comer algo también la esposa? ¿A qué hora van a acostarse los dos otra vez?

—*Ahora no me podrás° negar que te levantas por la noche a saquear° el refrigerador.*

won't be able to

to plunder, raid

Follow-up CH: *Ahora imagine que estas personas cuentan los detalles de su día, como lo hizo Elvira. Cambie los detalles de la rutina diaria de acuerdo con la persona.*
- *el jefe/la jefa de una sección de banco*
- *el presidente/la presidenta de los Estados Unidos*
- *un actor/una actriz de cine o de televisión*
- *un personaje* (character) *de televisión muy conocido*

Palabras útiles: grabar (to film), *reunirse* (*con*) (to meet [with])

CH. **¡Pregúntame qué hice hoy!** Complete este diálogo con el pretérito de los verbos entre paréntesis.

ELVIRA: ¡Estoy cansada! ¿Por qué no cenamos fuera esta noche?
MANUEL: Elvira, tú sólo piensas en divertirte.
ELVIRA: ¿Divertirme? ¿Por qué no me preguntas qué hice hoy?
MANUEL: Vamos a ver. ¿Qué hiciste?
ELVIRA: (*Levantarse*[1]) a las seis, (*hacer*[2]) gimnasia por media hora, (*sacar*[3]) la basura y después (*despertar*[4]) a los niños. Los (*bañar*[5]) y les (*hacer*[6]) el desayuno. Luego (yo: *bañarse*[7]) y (*llevar*[8]) a los niños a la escuela...
MANUEL: Y cuando (tú: *volver*[9]), (*acostarse*[10]) otra vez...
ELVIRA: No, señor. (*Hacer*[11]) las camas, (*planchar*[12]) la ropa...
MANUEL: No sigas, Elvira. Tú siempre exageras las cosas. Ahora, cálmate y dime adónde quieres ir a cenar.

D. **Los anuncios.** Complete the following paragraphs with the correct form of the words in parentheses, as suggested by the context. When two possibilities are given in parentheses, select the correct word. Use the preterite of infinitives indicated with an asterisk.

Hay anuncios publicitarios por (*todo*[1]) partes (*del/de la*[2]) mundo° y los hay° de (*todo*[3]) tipos. Algunos (*aparecer*[4])* primero en los Estados Unidos, pero ahora (*ser/estar*[5]) internacionales.

world

los... *there are some*

- (*Beber*[6]) Ud. Coca-Cola, (*delicioso*[7]) y refrescante.
- ¿No (*ser/estar:* tú[8]) contento de usar Dial?
- La (*nuevo*[9]) sonrisa° Colgate... *smile*

Un estadounidense° que (*viajar*[10]) por Latinoamérica o España (*poder*[11]) (*tener*[12]) la impresión de que (*cada*[13]) hombre (*afeitarse*[14]) con Gillette y que todos (*bañarse*[15]) y (*lavarse*[16]) los dientes° con productos norteamericanos.

persona que vive en los Estados Unidos / *teeth*

Hay un caso famoso en el mundo de la propaganda° que (*demostrar* [*ue*][17]) el peligro° de tratar de vender un producto en el extranjero° (*con/sin*[18]) considerar bien su nombre. Se trata° (*del/de la*[19]) coche norteamericano *Nova*, que (*alguno*[20]) latinoamericanos malpensados° (*cambiar*[21])* a **No va**.° Ya que° (*este*[22]) nombre realmente no (*animar*[23]) al comprador de habla española, los fabricantes° lo (*cambiar*[24])* a *Caribe*.

advertising / *danger* / en... *abroad* / Se... *It's the case* / *malicious* / No... *It doesn't go* / Ya... *Since* / *manufacturers*

En los países hispanos también se ven muchos anuncios de lotería. Allí, como aquí, (*ser/estar*[25]) preciso que tales anuncios nos (*prometer*° [26]) un futuro mejor:

to promise

- Juan Fernández (*ganar*[27])* un millón de pesos en la lotería nacional. (*Ser/Estar*[28]) el sueño de todos comprar un décimo° o un billete entero° y ganar el premio gordo.°

tenth / billete... *whole sheet* / premio... *first prize*

¿Cierto o falso? Corrija las oraciones falsas.

1. No hay ningún anuncio publicitario internacional.
2. Hay productos norteamericanos que se venden en los países hispánicos.
3. Es muy difícil traducir los anuncios de una lengua a otra.
4. En las culturas hispánicas, los anuncios tienen un mensaje (*message*) menos materialista que los de los Estados Unidos.

La bacteria del frigorífico ataca

La descubrieron hace veinticinco años, pero sus efectos no eran preocupantes.

Hoy la *Yersinia enterocolitica* tiene en su haber miles de pacientes a los que ha producido problemas intestinales, artritis generalizadas y algunos casos mortales de septicemia.

Se la llama la bacteria del frigorífico, porque en él vive y se reproduce a sus anchas. Luego llega a nuestro cuerpo a través de las verduras crudas, la carne o la leche.

Su rarísima peculiaridad es reproducirse a temperaturas muy bajas –4° bajo cero–, cuando las bacterias patógenas para el hombre lo suelen hacer entre los 20 y 40 grados. Además, la reproducción a bajas temperaturas selecciona los mutantes más virulentos, con lo que la bacteria está ganando terreno y virulencia día a día. Los investigadores intentan ahora detener su avance y su peligrosidad. ■

VOCABULARIO

Theme vocabulary previously listed as active: *el centro, cocinar, la comida, el dueño, el plato, la ropa*

VERBOS

acostar (ue) to put to bed; **acostarse** to go to bed
afeitar to shave; **afeitarse** to shave (oneself)
alquilar to rent
bañar to bathe; **bañarse** to take a bath
dejar to leave behind
despertar (ie) to wake; **despertarse** to wake up
divertir (ie, i) to amuse, entertain; **divertirse** to have a good time, enjoy oneself
dormirse (ue, u) to fall asleep
irse to leave, go away
lavarse to wash oneself, get washed
levantar to lift, raise; **levantarse** to get up; to stand up
llamarse to be named, called
ponerse to put on (*clothing*)
preparar to prepare
quedarse to stay, remain
quitar to remove, take away; **quitarse** to take off (*clothing*)
saludar to greet
sentar (ie) to seat, lead to a seat; **sentarse** to sit down
vestir (i, i) to dress; **vestirse** to get dressed

ADJETIVO

mismo/a same

ALGUNOS APARATOS DOMÉSTICOS

el (aire) acondicionador air conditioner
la aspiradora vacuum cleaner
la cafetera coffeepot
el congelador freezer
la estufa stove
el horno oven
la lavadora washing machine
el lavaplatos dishwasher
el refrigerador refrigerator
la secadora clothes dryer
la tostadora toaster

ALGUNOS QUEHACERES DOMÉSTICOS

barrer (el suelo) to sweep (the floor)
hacer la cama to make the bed
lavar las ventanas to wash the windows
limpiar la casa (entera) to clean the (whole) house
pasar la aspiradora to vacuum
planchar to iron
poner la mesa to set the table
sacar la basura to take out the garbage
sacudir los muebles to dust the furniture

Frases útiles para la comunicación

tocarle a uno	to be someone's turn
después **finalmente**	later, afterward finally
tuve (que)...	I had (to) . . .

¿DÓNDE VIVE UD.?

las afueras outskirts, suburbs
el alquiler rent
la dirección address
el gas gas; heat
el/la inquilino/a tenant; renter
la luz (*pl.* **luces**) light; electricity
la planta baja ground floor, first floor
el/la portero/a building manager; doorman
el primer (segundo, tercer) piso second (third, fourth) floor up
el/la vecino/a neighbor
la vista view

OTROS SUSTANTIVOS

el anuncio ad; announcement
la bañera bathtub
el/la criado/a servant, maid
el despertador alarm clock
el/la enfermero/a nurse
el espejo mirror
el juguete toy
la mano hand
el producto product

¿CUÁNDO... ?

anoche last night
anteayer the day before yesterday
ayer yesterday

pasado/a past, last (*in time*)

PALABRAS ADICIONALES

demasiado too much
en cambio on the other hand
tener sueño to be sleepy
tratar de + *inf.* to try to (*do something*)

OPTIONAL SECTION

UN PASO MÁS 9

Suggestion A: Bring in Hispanic magazines or newspapers, and show students several authentic ads. When appropriate, discuss the cultural message conveyed by the ads. Bring in U.S. English language ads for comparison and contrast, when possible.

▲ Actividad A. Más sobre los anuncios

"Con Dove, mi piel se siente fantástica—no reseca como con el jabón."
Marta Margulies
North Hollywood, CA
Pruebe
Dove
No seca la cara como el jabón

Como se ve en este anuncio del jabón *Dove*, el testimonio personal puede ser una manera efectiva de anunciar un producto. Los anuncios de este tipo se ven en la televisión con gran frecuencia. Son especialmente frecuentes los anuncios en que aparecen personas famosas a quienes la mayoría de la gente puede reconocer: estrellas del cine y de la televisión, figuras del mundo de los deportes, políticos, etcétera. ¿Qué opina Ud. de los anuncios publicitarios en general y de los anuncios con formato de testimonio personal? Complete estas oraciones lógicamente. Luego compare sus respuestas con las de sus compañeros de clase.

1. Los anuncios comerciales de televisión que más me gustan son...
   a. los anuncios en que aparecen personas famosas
   b. los anuncios en que habla la gente común (*average people*)
   c. los anuncios con dibjujos animados
   ch. los anuncios que contienen mucha información científica
   d. los anuncios cómicos
2. Creo que las personas famosas que aparecen en los anuncios...
   a. lo hacen porque creen que el producto que representan es bueno... ¡y lo usan!
   b. lo hacen por el dinero que les pagan
3. Cuando interrumpen con un anuncio un programa que estoy viendo, ...
   a. me levanto para (ir al baño, buscar algo que comer, ¿ ?)
   b. empiezo a hacer otra cosa hasta que termina el anuncio
   c. lo veo con interés, por lo general
4. Un anuncio de televisión que me gusta mucho es ____. El anuncio me gusta porque ____. Puedo decir que...
   a. compro este producto... a veces / con frecuencia
   b. me gustaría comprar el producto (pero no puedo o nunca lo hago)
   c. nunca compré el producto ni pienso hacerlo en el futuro
5. Un anuncio de televisión que me molesta mucho es ____. El anuncio me molesta porque ____. Puedo decir que...
   a. me molesta tanto que nunca compro el producto

   b. me gustaría comprar el producto, pero no lo hago.
   c. nunca compré el producto y no pienso comprarlo nunca.

6. Creo que los anuncios tienen un efecto muy dañino (*harmful*) especialmente en...
   a. los niños
   b. la gente que tiene poco dinero
   c. la gente que es muy susceptible o poco informada
   ch. ¿ ?
7. De los siguientes productos, creo que éstos no deben ser anunciados en la televisión: _____.

Productos: los juguetes, los cigarrillos, la cerveza, otras bebidas alcohólicas, los servicios de los médicos y dentistas, los servicios de los abogados (*lawyers*), los coches, ¿ ?

Ahora imagine que a Ud. lo/la invitaron a aparecer en un anuncio de televisión, de tipo testimonio personal. Su profesor(a), haciendo el papel (*role*) de entrevistador(a), va a hacerle a Ud. éstas y otras preguntas similares. ¡Prepárese para la entrevista!

Suggestion: After doing the interview with one student, have students interview each other, working in pairs.

1. ¿Dónde compró Ud. este/a _____? ¿Cuándo lo/la compró?
2. ¿Cuánto pagó Ud. por él/ella?
3. ¿Quién se lo/la recomendó?
4. ¿Puede Ud. recomendárselo/la a nuestros televidentes (*viewers*)?
5. ¿Qué le gusta más de este producto?
6. ¿Es probable que lo/la compre otra vez? ¿Por qué sí o por qué no?

Cartoon: 1. *¿Adónde quiere ir Mafalda?* **2.** *¿Qué le recomienda su mamá?* **3.** *¿Qué hace Mafalda?* **4.** *¿Qué le dice luego a su mamá?* **5.** *¿Por qué quiere que compre esas cosas?* **6.** *¿Qué cree Ud. que su mamá le recomienda ahora?* **7.** *¿Por qué se lo recomienda?*

cera = ***wax***

A propósito... Talking About Everyday Life

The following phrases are useful for communicating about basic everyday matters while living with a Spanish-speaking family. They should help you to be a polite guest, to fit into the family schedule, to offer and ask for help and information.

¿A qué hora se cena?	What time do you eat?
Salgo ahora pero vuelvo a las dos.	I'm going out now but I'll be back at two.
Voy a cenar fuera esta noche.	I'm going to eat out tonight.
¿Cómo te/le puedo ayudar? (¿Pongo la mesa? ¿Saco la basura?)	How can I help you? (Shall I set the table? Shall I take out the garbage?)

Voy de compras. ¿Necesita(s) algo?	I'm going shopping. Do you need anything?
¿Me puede(s) prestar (enseñar, decir) _____ ?	Can you lend (show, tell) me _____ ?
No quiero molestarte/lo/la, pero _____ ?	I don't want to bother you, but _____ .
¿Dónde puedo comprar _____ ?	Where can I buy _____ ?
Me falta* jabón (papel higiénico).	I need soap (toilet paper).
Me faltan* toallas.	I need towels.
¿Está libre el baño?	Is the bathroom free? (Does anyone else want to use the bathroom?)
Quisiera lavarme el pelo. ¿Hay agua caliente?	I would like to wash my hair. Is there any hot water?
¿Se puede usar el teléfono (mirar la televisión) ahora?	Is it okay to use the phone (watch television) now?

▲ Actividad B. En familia

Variation B: Working in pairs, students determine whether or not they would be compatible roommates.

Using the phrases in **A propósito...**, give as many different questions or statements as possible about each of the following situations. Work with a partner and practice interviewing each other.

MODELO: Ud. acaba de llegar a México sin tener alojamiento (*lodging*). La universidad le da una lista de familias que ofrecen alojamiento a estudiantes extranjeros. Ud. va a la casa de una de ellas. ¿Qué les pregunta?

- ¿La habitación es para una persona o para dos?
- ¿Cuánto es?
- ¿Se incluyen las comidas?
- ¿Hay niños en la familia?
- Tengo una radio. (Toco la guitarra.) ¿Les va a molestar?

1. Ud. vive ya con una familia mexicana, pero acaba de llegar y todavía no sabe mucho de la familia, de su rutina, sus costumbres, sus gustos. ¿Qué necesita saber para hacerse parte de la familia? ¿Qué pregunta?
2. Ud. es como parte de la familia ya. Por eso Ud. quiere ayudarles a todos los miembros de la familia. ¿Qué les va a decir para ofrecer su ayuda?
3. Ud. también necesita pedirles ayuda a los miembros de la familia cuando no sabe algo o cuando necesita algo. ¿Qué les puede preguntar?
4. Ud. vive en un apartamento y busca un compañero (una compañera) de habla española para poder practicar el español. Al mismo tiempo, quiere compartir su apartamento con alguien que le sea simpático, que tenga algunos de sus mismos gustos, etcétera. ¿Qué preguntas les va a hacer a las personas que quieran compartir el apartamento con Ud.?

---

*The use of the verb **faltar** (*to be lacking*) is like that of **gustar**. It takes an indirect object, and the subject usually follows the verb.

Me **falta** un libro.	*I need a book. (A book is lacking to me.)*
Me **faltan** diez dólares.	*I need ten dollars. (Ten dollars are lacking to me.)*

APTO.
MODERNO
Piscina y club deportivo.
No amueblado.
Recientemente renovado.
Calle Alonso, 64

Se alquila apartamento amueblado. Sala. Baño. Dos alcobas. Teléfono 184-3345.

CASA PARTICULAR. Tres habitaciones. Ducha y baño. Buenas condiciones. 254-7812.

Magnífico apto. Para dos o tres personas. **244-8900**

Piso moderno. Todo elétrico. Baño incluso. Alquiler barato. Edificio Magallanes, centro.

APTO. Barrio residencial. Animales prohibidos. Llame 323-7892.

▲ Actividad C. Se alquila apartamento

Ads for housing in Spanish-language newspapers are usually easy to understand because they are written in somewhat telegraphic language. Since the authors of the ads are paying by the word or by the fraction of an inch, they try to write as briefly as possible. Rather than writing out **Se ofrece un apartamento en buenas condiciones**, the ad might simply say: **Apto. buenas condiciones**.

PISOS DE LUJO
C/ ALCALÁ, Nº 227
esquina Cardenal Belluga
☆ 3 dormitorios.
☆ 2 baños.
☆ Gran salón comedor.
☆ 13.500.000 Ptas.
☆ Precio y plazo de entrega cerrados.
FACILIDADES
OBRAS INICIADAS
Información y reservas
DOCASA
Gran Vía, nº 67,
planta 6ª, número 624
Tels. 247 69 43, 247 61 15

Piso = Apartamento

Read the accompanying ads, then do the following activities based on them.

1. You have just arrived in Mexico City and need a place to live for a year. Which of the ads would you respond to and why? Why would you *not* respond to the others? What questions would you ask the owner or landlord when you went to see the house or apartment, before renting it?
2. You need to sublet your house or apartment for the summer and want to place an ad in a Spanish-language newspaper. Write an ad of twenty-five words or less and present it to the class. What kinds of details should you include to get a lot of response to your ad?

RESIDENCIA
TERCERA EDAD
en ARANJUEZ
• Asistencia médica permanente.
• 2.000 metros de jardín. Inmejorable.
C/ Joaquín Rodrigo, 26. 91-891 09 44

Tercera... *Senior Citizens*

CHALET. PASEO HABANA
Chalet en construcción, adosado, con jardín y piscina privados, 450 m². Construcción de lujo
Información. Teléfono 250 43 07 / 08
Laborables, de 10 a 2 y de 5 a 8

Chalet = Casa

LECTURA CULTURAL

Lectura: See IM for suggestions and additional exercises and activities.

Variation C: Students prepare lists of 5 or more priorities for apartment hunting. What is most important/least important? Students present items to the class for comparisons.

Antes de leer: Recognizing Derivative Adjectives

In previous chapters you learned to recognize cognates, word endings, and new words that are related to familiar words. Another large group of adjectives derived from verbs ends in **-ado** or **-ido**: you can often guess the meaning of these adjectives if you know the related verb. For example: **conocer** (*to know*) → **conocido** (*known, famous*); **preparar** (*to prepare*) → **preparado** (*prepared*). Can you guess the meaning of the following italicized adjectives based on verbs you already know?

1. unas ideas bien *explicadas* 2. una mujer *desconocida* 3. su libro *preferido*

In the following reading there are many **-do** adjectives. Try to guess their meaning from context.

«Hogar, dulce hogar»

Una casa es una casa, ¿verdad? Pues, eso depende de la persona y también de su cultura. Es verdad que en ciertos aspectos la vida en una casa hispana no es muy diferente de la vida en una casa norteamericana: la gente duerme por la noche y se despierta por la mañana; se levanta, se baña, se viste y desayuna. Pero hay también diferencias interesantes: algunas tienen que ver con las cosas materiales y otras con el estilo de vida.

Note: Unglossed imperfect tense verbs should not pose problems of comprehension for students. Encourage them to guess, based on context.

«¿Qué te sorprendió cuando llegaste a los Estados Unidos, sobre todo en lo que a las casas y a la manera de vivir se refiere?» Ésta fue la pregunta que les hicimos a varias personas de descendencia hispana que ahora viven en los Estados Unidos. Las respuestas son interesantes... y se le ofrecen a Ud. sin mencionar el nombre de la persona que habla, sólo el de su país de origen.

la calefacción central
el extremo confort (microondas, *freezer*, alfombrado en toda la casa, secarropa, etcétera)
los productos congelados
la cantidad de canales en la TV
las lámparas que tienen regulador de intensidad
la cantidad de objetos descartables° — *disposable*
los pequeños vasos descartables del baño
el papel higiénico perfumado
los garajes grandes con más de un auto
el autoservicio en la mesa
los «dips» para las papas° fritas — patatas
la cantidad de enchufes° en cada pared — *plugs*

de la Argentina

A mi llegada a los Estados Unidos, el hecho de que° las casas estaban° cerradas, sin ventilación, en comparación con las de mi país, en donde siempre había° un patio lleno de plantas y flores, me sorprendió. Me parecía° que faltaba aire y que uno estaba propenso a asfixiarse.

el... *the fact that* / *were*
there was
Me... *It seemed to me*

de México

Una de las cosas que me sorprendió cuando vine° por primera vez a los Estados Unidos fue el orden, aseo° y disciplina de esta gente. Me fue muy grato observar que los carros o más bien dicho el tráfico se paraba° para dejar que los peatones cruzaran las calles.
También me sorprendió mucho ver las grandes calles solitarias y muertas° de ciudades como Beverly Hills.

pretérito de ***venir***
cleanliness
se... *stopped*
dead, not lively

de El Salvador

El culto a los animales domésticos: perros, gatos, ¡ratones!, etcétera.
Las industrias que se han originado° y se benefician de este culto: comidas especiales, juguetes, ropa, casas especiales para que vivan estos animales, hospitales, cementerios, agencias que se dedican a cuidar de estos animales cuando los dueños se ausentan, etc.
El aspecto retraído,° serio y a veces sombrío de la gente en la calle.
El aparente aislamiento en que vive la gente.

se... *have come from*
withdrawn

de El Salvador

Lo que más me sorprendió fue la preocupación y la necesidad de «privacidad»° de la gente. También es sorprendente el que° se espere que los hijos adolescentes se vayan de la casa familiar y tengan su propia casa a una edad relativamente temprana.
También me impresionó la mobilidad, la frecuencia con que las personas cambian de casa, ciudad o estado.
A otro nivel, me gustó la falta° de formalidad en las costumbres y en la vestimenta.°

del Uruguay

vida privada / el... *the fact that* / *lack* / ropa

Como en Panamá tenemos un clima tropical, las casas tienen más ventanas para que entre el aire fresco. Aunque las casas en los Estados Unidos tenían muchas ventanas, eran más pequeñas y algunas de ellas ni siquiera se podían° abrir.

de Panamá

ni... *couldn't even be*

Las casas no suelen° tener tantos aparatos electrodomésticos como en los Estados Unidos, o por lo menos no son tan grandes, en particular las neveras° y congeladores, las lavadoras y las secadoras (aparato, este último, de uso no muy extendido verdaderamente). Otra cosa de la que suelen carecer° las cocinas hispanas medias° es del triturador de basuras. ¡Es todo un ingenio que tenemos que aprender a manejar al llegar a los Estados Unidos!

de España

no... *don't usually* / refrigeradores / de... *that is usually lacking in* / *average*

Comprensión

¿Dónde está Ud., en una casa hispana o en una norteamericana?

1. Antes de una cena elegante, le ofrecen a Ud. como hors d'œuvre unas patatas fritas con una salsa hecha (*made*) con crema agria (*sour cream*) y cebollas (*onions*)... y tiene que servirse a sí mismo.
2. En la cocina hay algunos aparatos eléctricos, pero no muchos.
3. Todos los cuartos de la casa están ubicados (*located*) alrededor de un patio central, donde hay plantas, flores y pájaros.
4. Unos amigos llegan a la casa para cenar con la familia un domingo por la tarde. Llevan pantalones cortos, camiseta y sandalias.

Para escribir

Write two short paragraphs about your living accommodations. The first should give information about where you live: whether in a house, apartment, or dormitory; the number of rooms; a description of the furniture; and so on. You might also want to write about what you like or do not like about where you live. The second paragraph should include information about those you live with and about your and their personal habits: who gets up first, who takes care of domestic chores, who smokes or doesn't smoke, and so on.

OPTIONAL SECTION

REPASO 3

VOCES DEL MUNDO HISPÁNICO

Note: Corresponding chapters of the Workbook and the Laboratory Manual offer focused vocabulary and grammar activities.

Repaso 3: See IM for detailed suggestions for handling *Entrevistas*, *Situaciones*, and the specific *Voces* sections.

LOS HISPANOS EN LOS ESTADOS UNIDOS

La comunidad cubanoamericana

En su mayoría (*majority*), los cubanos son un grupo inmigrante. Comenzaron a llegar a los Estados Unidos en gran número alrededor del año 1960 debido a (*due to*) la situación política existente en la isla de Cuba. Esta inmigración es, en cierto sentido, única (*unique*) en la historia de los Estados Unidos.

Históricamente, siempre que ha habido (*there have been*) grandes inmigraciones a este país, la gente era (*was*) pobre y perteneciente a las clases más humildes. Pero en el caso de los cubanos, los inmigrantes de la década de los años 60 eran (*were*) en su mayoría profesionales de las clases media y alta. Llegaron sólo con su cultura y su educación.

En sólo una generación los inmigrantes cubanos han recuperado (*have gotten back*) casi todo lo que tuvieron que abandonar y ejercen ahora una enorme influencia en la vida del sur de la Florida en donde todavía están concentrados.

CUBA: Sube número de turistas extranjeros

Aproximadamente 250 mil turistas extranjeros visitaron Cuba en 1987, un diez por ciento más que el año pasado. El Instituto Nacional de Turismo informó que se esperaba° que los ingresos devengados° alcancen a 120 millones de dólares.

La Época (Santiago de Chile), 29 de diciembre de 1987

se... *it was hoped*
ingresos... *revenue generated*

Varadero, Cuba

«Así, nos encontramos con las familias Rodríguez y Montesino... El auto de la familia, casi tocando el mar de breves olas,° dos asientos bajo los pinos y la fresca brisa marina que resulta infantilmente acariciante proveen° a los Rodríguez y Montesino de ese ambiente° de paz revitalizante que tanto necesitan...
—¿De dónde son ustedes?
—De Pinar del Río.°
—Vinimos° porque el señor Montesino se está recuperando y este lugar vale un millón.
—¿Acostumbran a venir con frecuencia?
—Sí. Este lugar es mejor que un tónico.»

Ralph Rewes, «El entrepuente del sol», *Miami Mensual*

waves
provide
atmosphere
ciudad de Cuba
pretérito de ***venir***

«Yo soy un hombre sincero
de donde crece° la palma;
y antes de morirme,° quiero
echar mis versos del alma.

Mi verso es de un verde claro
y de un carmín encendido:°
mi verso es un ciervo herido°
que busca en el monte amparo.°»

José Martí (1853–1895), héroe nacional de Cuba y poeta, de *Versos sencillos*

grows
dying
fiery
ciervo... *wounded deer*
refugio

Un son° para Celia Cruz

son: typically Hispanic musical form

Celia Cruz canta que canta,
y de su canto diré° (*I will say*)
que el son, de Cuba se fue
escondido° (*hidden*) en su garganta.° (*throat*)

Hay en su voz, una santa
devoción por la palmera;
vibra en ella Cuba entera,
y es tan cubano su acento
que su voz, al darse al viento,° (al... *as it mixes with the wind*)
flota como una bandera°... (*flag*)

Canta, Celia Cruz, en tanto,° (en... *a little*)
ya que° (ya... *for*) no hay nada que vibre
y recuerde a Cuba libre
como el sabor de tu canto.

Ernesto Montaner, «El poeta del exilio», en *La Voz libre,* Los Ángeles, 11 de septiembre de 1987

La mundialmente famosa Celia Cruz, que ostenta el honroso título de "La Guarachera de Cuba" cuya estrella será (*will be*) colocada en el famoso Bulevar de la Fama, el próximo jueves 17 del actual, a las doce y media del día. Será un acontecimiento memorable.

XAVIER SUÁREZ, ALCALDE (*MAYOR*) DE MIAMI

- Nacido (*Born*) en Las Villas, Cuba, el noveno (*ninth*) de catorce hijos
- Llegó a los Estados Unidos, a los once años, después de la invasión de la Bahía de los Cochinos
- Aprendió inglés en dos meses
- B.S. en ingeniería, Villanova University
- M.A. en administración pública, Harvard University
- Título de abogado (*lawyer*), Harvard University
- Cita de su discurso de inauguración: «Con los pobres de la tierra quiero yo mi suerte echar (*cast my fate*)»—José Martí

«Miami esencialmente se ha profesionalizado en general. Esto se refleja inclusive en la manera en la que visten las personas... Estamos llegando a nivel de gran metrópolis internacional. Nosotros como arquitectos nos damos cuenta de° (nos... *we realize*) eso... La combinación de idiomas, la combinación de ideologías sociales y políticas... todo esto ha hecho que° (ha... *has made*) muchos describan a Miami como la Suiza del Hemisferio.»

Hilario Candela, arquitecto cubano, en *Miami Mensual*

MI CARRETA CUBANA
EL MEJOR RESTAURANTE DE ESTA AREA
Fw. 101
Sunset Blvd.
Rowena
Sta. Ana Freeway
ESPECIALES
Ropa Vieja. Fricasé de pollo. Boliche. Picadillo. Carne con Papas,De Lunes a Viernes.
Cerramos los Martes
ABIERTO todos los días de 11:30 de la mañana a 8:30 de la noche.
2924-2926 Rowena Ave, L.A.
(213) 669-2752

La famosa Calle Ocho, Miami

«Ricco tiene 15 años, el cabello° rubio oscuro y los ojos color castaño.° Es un muchachón fuerte° y ágil y habla ayudado con las manos, como cualquier otro latino...
—Y tú, ¿cómo te sientes, Ricco, americano o miamense?, le pregunto. Sin la menor vacilación, me contesta con un fuerte acento cubano:
—Chico, a la verdad que yo me siento cubano.
—¿Cómo fue que te empezaste a interesar en hablar español? ¿Fue la curiosidad o qué? ...
—Primero fue porque, yo parezco° cubano, tú sabes. Y todo el mundo me hablaba° en español. Empecé a entender ya mucho, pero no hablaba casi nada. Después en la escuela me empecé a reunir con cubanitos, y me gustó el ambiente, tú sabes.»

hair / *brown* / *strong* / *look* / *would speak*

Ralph Rewes, «El bilingüismo en Hialeah», *Miami Mensual*

«Hermanita nacida en estas tierras»

...No es un reproche
hermana
hermanita nacida° en estas tierras — *born*
Es que tú sólo tienes
la alegría° — *joy, happiness*
de los héroes de Disney
Porque sonreirás° — *you will smile*
cuando el señor genial
de los muñecos° — *dolls (from Disney movies)*
haga de ti
de cada niño
un payasito° plástico — *little clown*
y ridículo

Al escurrirte° — Al... *As you slip away*
lenta y cariñosa
sin poder inventarte
otra niñez° — *childhood*
regalarte la mía° — regalarte... (*I wish I could*) *give you mine*
que aunque también
se alimentó de héroes
tuvo sabor° a palma — *taste, flavor*
y mamoncillo° — *papaya*
Y no sufrió la burla° — *joke* (*in a negative sense*)
de los juguetes caros
que te regala
el fantasma engañoso° — *deceitful*
de diciembre

Elías Miguel Muñoz, novelista y poeta cubanoamericano; poema de *En estas tierras/In This Land,* Bilingual Review Press, 1989

Niños cubanoamericanos, la Pequeña Habana, Florida

"It's one thing to speak English, even to require it. It's quite another to *think and feel English*, and *that* you can't legislate.

"I am blessed, and I mean that sincerely, in that I can think and feel in both circles. But I cannot, and I shall not, forget that my father died in Cuba because he loved it so, and that I am part of that land that he loved so much."

María C. García, periodista cubanoamericana, *Hispanic Link,* March 2, 1986

ENTREVISTA

***Entrevista:* Focus:** Integrating preterite forms learned so far with other verb forms students know.

In the last three chapters of ***Puntos de partida***, you have expanded your ability to interact with others in Spanish and begun to talk about things that happened in the past. This activity will help you review the major topics you have worked with so far.

In the course of this activity, you will interview a classmate. Imagine that you have just met him or her at a social function. Try to find out as much information as you can about this person.

First, read over the following topics and think about what your answers will be when someone asks you questions about them in Spanish. You may want to jot down things to say or additional points to raise about the same questions. Then find someone in the class with whom you have spoken only infrequently and interview him or her based on these topics. Finally, organize the information you have learned about your classmate into a brief paragraph about aspects of his or her high school experience.

Hint: Remember that **tuve** is the first person singular preterite form of **tener**. The **tú** and **Ud.** forms, respectively, are **tuviste** and **tuvo**.

Información general

1. su nombre
2. por qué está en esta fiesta
3. dónde vive ahora
4. el año en que se graduó en la escuela secundaria y dónde vivió aquel año
5. qué hizo después de graduarse

Aspectos de la vida social en la secundaria

6. en qué actividades/deportes participó
7. quién fue su mejor amigo
8. adónde fueron una vez después de las clases (y qué les molestó mucho a sus padres)
9. que hizo una vez con los amigos para divertirse un fin de semana
10. si tuvo novio/a
11. a qué hora regresó a casa un fin de semana (y que les molestó mucho a sus padres)

Aspectos de la vida escolar en la secundaria

12. si siempre sacó notas (*grades*) buenas, regulares o malas
13. si tuvo que tomar _____ (varios cursos)
14. si le gustó el curso (si lo tomó)
15. quién fue el profesor del curso

Más información general

16. si tuvo que trabajar antes o después de las clases y qué tipo de trabajo hizo
17. si tuvo que ayudar en casa con los quehaceres domésticos
18. si le gustaría estar en la escuela secundaria otra vez
19. si regresó alguna vez a visitar la escuela
20. qué quieren sus padres que haga ahora

Note: Questions have been carefully selected to avoid potential need for imperfect forms (not yet presented).

SITUACIONES DE LA VIDA DIARIA

With a classmate, act out the following role-play situations as fully as possible. Try to use vocabulary that you know.

1. A reporter (**un reportero/una reportera**) from another country is interviewing you about the everyday lives of students at your university. Explain in detail what you normally do from the moment you get up to the moment you go to bed, stressing things that are special to your university.
2. A journalist from another country is interviewing a young professional who also has a spouse and two young children. Play the role of the professional, answering the journalist's questions about how you and your spouse handle the responsibilities of your personal and professional lives.
3. Your roommate (spouse, friend) has just found a marvelous apartment in the city and is very excited about it. Ask questions about its location, how big it is, what it looks like, what kinds of public transportation are available, what the neighborhood (**el barrio**) is like, how much the rent is, if light and heat are included in the rent, if you can have a dog, and so on.
4. Imagine that you are the personnel manager of a large office. Today you are interviewing a candidate for a secretarial position. Find out all you can about the applicant: education, experience, ambitions, interests, family, and so on.

CAPÍTULO DIEZ

DÍAS FESTIVOS

México, D.F.

▲ **La Nochebuena**

—¿Cómo pasaste la Nochebuena?

—Estuve bailando en casa de unos amigos. Lo pasamos muy bien. ¿Y tú?

—Tuve una invitación de mis tíos y fui a cenar con ellos.

—¿Te divertiste?

—Sí. Comí, bailé y me reí[a] mucho.

[a]me... *I laughed*

Vocabulario: Preparación:
• See detailed supplementary materials for this section bound into the back of this Annotated Instructor's Edition.

VOCABULARIO: PREPARACIÓN

• See model for vocabulary presentation and other materials in Supplementary *Vocabulario: Preparación* Materials, chapter by chapter, IM.

• See [cassette]

Los días festivos y las fiestas

la Noche Vieja	New Year's Eve	**dar/hacer una fiesta**	to give/have a party
el Día del Año Nuevo	New Year's Day	**faltar**	to be absent, lacking
la Pascua	Passover	**llorar**	to cry
la Pascua (Florida)	Easter	**pasarlo bien/mal**	to have a good/bad time
el Día de los Muertos	All Souls' Day	**reírse (i, i)**	to laugh
el Día de Gracias	Thanksgiving	**sentirse (ie, i) feliz/triste**	to feel happy/sad
la Nochebuena	Christmas Eve	**sonreír (i, i)**	to smile
la Navidad	Christmas	**ser + en +** lugar	to take place at (*location*)
los entremeses	hors d'œuvres		
¡felicitaciones!	congratulations	—**¿Dónde es** la fiesta?	—*Where is the party?*
los refrescos	refreshments	—**Es en** casa de Julio.	—*It's at Julio's house.*
la sorpresa	surprise		

¡OJO! You will see the names of the preceding holidays throughout ***Puntos de partida***. Learn to use those that are particularly important or interesting to you. The entire list will not be considered "active" vocabulary that you will be expected to say or write spontaneously.

¿CUAL DE ESTAS FIESTAS ES MAS IMPORTANTE?

%	Total
Nochebuena	30,8
Navidad	19,4
Nochevieja	19,4
Año Nuevo	3,7
Reyes Magos	3,6
Todas por igual	21,2
NS/NC	2,0

ACTOS RELIGIOSOS

Aparte de las celebraciones, ¿en estos días asiste usted a oficios religiosos navideños?

%	Total
Sí	42,7
No	55,2
NS/NC	2,2

A. ¿Qué palabra corresponde a estas definiciones?

1. el día en que se celebra el nacimiento (*birth*) de Jesús
2. algo que alguien no sabe o no espera
3. algo de comer que se sirve en las fiestas (dos respuestas)
4. el día en que los hispanos visitan el cementerio para honrar la memoria de los difuntos (*deceased*)
5. reacción emocional cuando se reciben muy buenas noticias (*news*) (tres respuestas)
6. reacción emocional cuando se recibe la noticia de una tragedia (dos respuestas)
7. la noche en que se celebra el pasar de un año a otro
8. palabra que se dice para mostrar una reacción muy favorable, por ejemplo, cuando un amigo recibe un gran aumento de sueldo

B. Explique cómo se divierte Ud. en estas fiestas y en otras ocasiones. ¿Qué hace para pasarlo bien? ¿Qué desea Ud. que ocurra, idealmente?

1. el día de su cumpleaños
2. durante las vacaciones de invierno o de Semana Santa (*Easter Week*)
3. en una fiesta que dan sus padres (sus hijos)... y los amigos de ellos están presentes

¿QUE ES LA NAVIDAD?

¿Cuál de estas frases se ajusta más a la forma en que usted pasa las Navidades?

	% Total
Es una fiesta fundamentalmente religiosa	9,5
Es una fiesta esencialmente familiar	73,6
Es una fiesta para consumir y gastar dinero	7,3
Son unas vacaciones de invierno, sin ningún otro significado	3,2
Es una época triste y deprimente que preferiría que no existiera	6,1
NS/NC	0,4

4. los viernes por la noche
5. el Día de Gracias
6. la Navidad/la Pascua

Ahora describa una situación típica en la que Ud. lo pasa mal.

C. Explíquele a un amigo hispano los siguientes días festivos. ¿Qué hace la gente en estos días en los Estados Unidos?

Palabras útiles: el pavo (*turkey*), dar las doce (*to strike 12*), el trébol (*four-leaf clover*), hacerle una broma a alguien (*to play a trick on someone*), el corazón (*heart*), hacer un *picnic* (*to have a picnic*), el desfile (*parade*)

1. el Día de Gracias
2. *Labor Day*
3. *Saint Patrick's Day*
4. la Noche Vieja
5. el Día de los Enamorados
6. *April Fools' Day*

Más emociones

enojarse	*to get angry*	**olvidarse (de)**	*to forget (about)*
portarse	*to behave*	**quejarse**	*to complain*
bien/mal	*well/badly*	**recordar (ue)**	*to remember*

To Become (Get)

¿Por qué **te pones** tan furioso?	*Why are you getting (becoming) so angry?*
Vamos a **ponernos** muy tristes.	*We're going to get (become) very sad.*
Se hizo / **Llegó a ser** } directora de la compañía.	*She became director of the company.*
Quiere { **hacerse** / **llegar a ser** } rico.	*He wants to become rich.*

Ponerse + *adjective* is used to indicate physical, mental, or emotional changes. **Hacerse** and **llegar a ser** + *noun* indicate a change as the result of a series of events or effort. They are also frequently used with the adjectives **rico** and **famoso**.

Being Emphatic

To emphasize the quality described by an adjective or an adverb, speakers of Spanish often add **-ísimo/-a/-os/-as** to it, adding the idea *extremely* (*exceptionally; very, very; super*) to the quality. You have already used one emphatic form of this type: **Me gusta muchísimo.**

Estos entremeses son **dificilísimos** de preparar.	*These hors d'œuvres are very hard to prepare.*
Durante la época navideña, los niños son **buenísimos**.	*At Christmastime, the kids are extremely good.*

(continúa)

If the adjective ends in a consonant, **-ísimo** is added to the singular form: **difícil → dificilísimo** (and any accents on the accent stem are dropped). If the adjective ends in a vowel, the final vowel is dropped before adding **-ísimo**: **bueno → buenísimo**. Spelling changes occur when the final consonant of an adjective is **c**, **g**, or **z**: **riquísimo**, **larguísimo**, **felicísimo**.

Suggestion A: Do as listening comprehension only.

Optional A: *de buen/mal humor, impaciente*

Extension A: **11.** *Llueve todo el día.* **12.** *No sé la respuesta, pero el profesor me pide que hable.* **13.** *Sé la respuesta y levanto la mano, pero el profesor no me presta atención.* **14.** *Quiero bañarme y no hay agua caliente.* **15.** *Estoy solo/a en casa y oigo un ruido.* **16.** *Ud. le pide a alguien que no fume, pero la persona sigue fumando.* **17.** *Su madre le muestra a su novio/a algunas fotos de Ud.... de niño/a.*

¿QUE DIA HACE USTED LOS REGALOS?

%	Total
Día de Reyes Magos	64,0
Día de Navidad	9,9
Días de Navidad y de Reyes Magos	6,8
No hay día fijo para dar regalos	9,3
No hacemos regalos	8,9
NS/NC	1,0

A. ¿Cómo reacciona o cómo se pone Ud. en estas situaciones? Use estos adjetivos o cualquier otro, y también los verbos que describen las reacciones emocionales. No se olvide de usar las formas enfáticas cuando sea apropiado.

serio/a	feliz/triste	avergonzado/a (*embarrassed*)
nervioso/a	furioso/a	contento/a

1. Es Navidad y alguien le regala a Ud. un reloj muy, muy caro.
2. Es Navidad y sus padres se olvidan de regalarle algo.
3. En una fiesta, alguien acaba de contarle (*to tell you*) un chiste (*joke*) muy cómico.
4. Ud. está completamente aburrido/a en una fiesta que sus amigos le están dando. Tiene ganas de estar en otro sitio, pero no quiere ofender a sus amigos.
5. Ud. está dando una fiesta pero la gente no lo está pasando bien, es decir, no se ríen, no sonríen, no cuentan chistes, están aburridos, etcétera.
6. Hay un examen muy importante esta mañana, pero Ud. no estudió nada anoche.
7. Ud. acaba de terminar un examen difícil (fácil) y cree que lo hizo bien (mal).
8. En un examen de química, Ud. se olvida de una fórmula muy importante.
9. Sin querer, Ud. se portó en una forma muy descortés con un buen amigo.
10. Se acaban (*run out*) los entremeses durante su fiesta de Noche Vieja, y sólo son las diez de la noche.

B. ¿Qué ambiciones tiene Ud.? Complete las oraciones lógicamente. Luego explique sus decisiones. (Consulte la lista de profesiones y oficios de la página 488.)

Yo quiero hacerme _____ algún día.
Nunca quiero llegar a ser _____.

¿CON QUE FAMILIA CELEBRA USTED ESTAS FIESTAS?

%	Nochebuena	Navidad	Nochevieja	Año Nuevo	Reyes Magos
Propia familia	67,1	66,2	62,5	67,1	72,3
Familia (padres)	17,5	15,9	11,6	12,5	12,4
Familia (suegros)	3,7	4,6	3,7	3,9	1,6
Todos juntos	5,7	6,2	6,1	5,6	3,9
No en familia	1,0	1,8	10,9	6,2	5,1
NS/NC	5,0	5,3	5,2	4,6	4,7

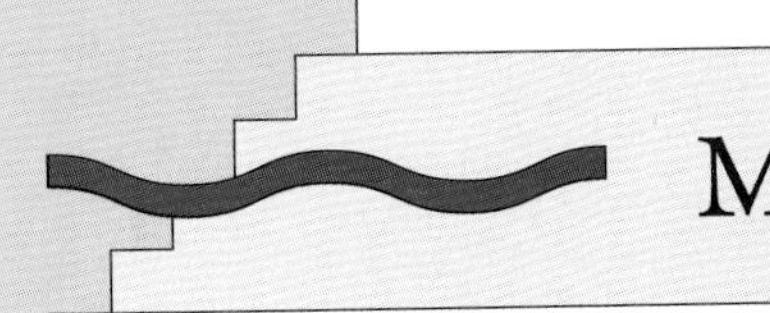

MINIDIÁLOGOS Y GRAMÁTICA

Follow-up: **1.** *¿Puede Ud. pronunciar el nombre de la niña vasca? ¿el apellido?* **2.** *¿Conoce Ud. otros apellidos largos? ¿Son difíciles de pronunciar? ¿de escribir?* **3.** *¿Se considera difícil el apellido de Ud.? ¿Hay personas que pronuncian (escriben) mal el apellido de Ud.? ¿Lo pronuncian bien los profesores?*

31. TALKING ABOUT THE PAST (2)
Irregular Preterites

Pronóstico de un nombre

FÉLIX: ¿Por qué faltaste al bautizo de la nieta de don Pepe ayer?
BEGOÑA: *Quise* ir pero no *pude* por el trabajo. ¿Qué tal *estuvo*?
FÉLIX: La fiesta *estuvo* estupenda. ¡Cuánta gente! ¡Y qué divertido todo!
BEGOÑA: ¿Qué nombre le *pusieron* a la niña?
FÉLIX: Arántzazu Gazteizgogeascoa. Son vascos, sabes.
BEGOÑA: ¡Por Dios! Con un nombre así, tiene que hacerse oculista. ¡No hay más remedio!

1. ¿Por qué faltó Begoña al bautizo?
2. ¿Qué tal estuvo la fiesta?
3. ¿Qué nombre le pusieron a la niña?
4. ¿Por qué es preciso que ella llegue a ser oculista?

Note: (1): Use of *estuvo* (*¿Qué tal estuvo?*) to ask other's opinion (How did it seem to you?). **(2)** Spanish speakers consider many Basque names long and hard to pronounce.

You have already learned the irregular preterite forms of **dar**, **hacer**, **ir**, and **ser**. The following verbs are also irregular in the preterite. Note that the first and third person singular endings, which are the only irregular ones, are unstressed, in contrast to the stressed endings of regular preterite forms.

¡OJO! Unstressed *-o* indicates third-person singular in irregular preterites, not *yo* form, as in present indicative.

estar: **estuv-**
poder: **pud-**
poner: **pus-**
querer: **quis-**
saber: **sup-**
tener: **tuv-**
venir: **vin-**
} **-e, -iste, -o, -imos, -isteis, -ieron**

decir: **dij-**
traer: **traj-**
} -e, -iste, -o, -imos, -isteis, **-eron**

estar	
estuve	**estuvimos**
estuviste	**estuvisteis**
estuvo	**estuvieron**

Prognosis for a name FÉLIX: Why weren't you at the baptism of don Pepe's granddaughter yesterday? BEGOÑA: I tried to go, but I couldn't because of work. How was it? FÉLIX: The party was marvelous. So many people! And what fun! BEGOÑA: What name did they give the child? FÉLIX: Arántzazu Gazteizgogeascoa. They're Basques, you know. BEGOÑA: Heavens! With a name like that, she has to become an eye doctor. She has no choice!

When the preterite verb stem ends in **-j-**, the **-i-** of the third person plural ending is omitted: **dijeron**, **trajeron**.

The preterite of **hay** (**haber**) is **hubo** (*there was/were*).

Several of these Spanish verbs have an English equivalent in the preterite tense that is different from that of the infinitive.

saber:	Ya lo sé.	*I already know it.*
	Lo **supe** ayer.	*I found it out (learned it) yesterday.*
conocer:	Ya la conozco.	*I already know her.*
	La **conocí** ayer.	*I met her yesterday.*
querer:	Quiero hacerlo hoy.	*I want to do it today.*
	Quise hacerlo ayer.	*I tried to do it yesterday.*
	No quise hacerlo anteayer.	*I refused to do it the day before yesterday.*
poder:	Puedo leerlo.	*I can (am able to) read it.*
	Pude leerlo ayer.	*I could (and did) read it yesterday.*
	No pude leerlo anteayer.	*I couldn't (did not) read it the day before yesterday.*

Point out: Special meaning of preterite forms of certain verbs.

Preliminary Exercises:
Preguntas:
- **1.** *¿Cuál es el infinitivo?: quise, estuve, vine, tuve, puse, pude, supe, dije, traje* **2.** *¿Cuál es el sujeto,* ***yo, tú*** *o* ***Ud.?:*** *vine, tuviste, tuvo, pudo, supo, estuvo, trajiste, dijo, puse, dije, supiste, puso, quise, vino, estuviste*
- *¿Qué verbo se puede usar en cada situación? Use la forma de* ***yo.*** **1.** *...un examen ayer.* (*Tuve*) **2.** *...enfermo/a la semana pasada.* (*Estuve*) **3.** *...a clase todos los días el semestre pasado.* (*Vine*) **4.** *...hacer todo el trabajo.* (*No pude*) **5.** *...varios chistes a mis amigos.* (*Dije*) **6.** *...la radio.* (*Puse*) **7.** *...un viaje.* (*Hice*) **8.** *...razón.* (*Tuve*) **9.** *...los libros a clase.* (*Traje*)

Preliminary Exercises:
- ***Dé el pretérito.***
yo: estar, poder, poner
tú: querer, saber, tener
Ud.: decir, traer, estar
nosotros: poder, poner, saber
Uds.: tener, decir, traer
- *La fiesta del Día del Año Nuevo. ¿Qué pasó? Dé oraciones nuevas según las indicaciones.*
1. *Todos estuvieron en casa de Mario.* (*yo, Raúl, Uds., tú, nosotros, vosotras*) **2.** *Muchos vinieron con comida y bebidas.* (*Ud., nosotros, tú, Rosalba, Uds., vosotros*) **3.** *Todos dijeron que la fiesta estuvo estupenda.* (*tú, Anita, Uds., yo, ellas, vosotros*)

Preguntas: **1.** *¿Tuvo Ud. una entrevista ayer? ¿un examen? ¿una cita con el dentista?* **2.** *¿Estuvo Ud. en España (México, etc.) el verano pasado?* **3.** *¿Ud. se puso rojo/a ayer? ¿Por qué?* **4.** *¿Quién no pudo dormir bien anoche? ¿Esto es un problema común?* **5.** *¿Quién dijo una mentira* (lie) *ayer? ¿a quién?* **6.** *¿Quién vino temprano hoy? ¿Quién no vino ayer? ¿Estuvo enfermo/a el día entero?*

Extension A: Students tell what happened on Christmas Day.

Variation A: Students use exercise items as guide in describing their own Christmas (or other holiday) celebrations.

Optional: Dictate in present tense. Students transform verbs to preterite.

Práctica

A. **Una Nochebuena en casa de los Ramírez.** Describa lo que pasó en casa de los Ramírez, haciendo el papel (*role*) de uno de los hijos. Haga oraciones en el pretérito según las indicaciones, usando el sujeto pronominal cuando sea necesario.

1. todos / estar / en casa / abuelos / antes de / nueve
2. (nosotros) poner / mucho / regalos / debajo / árbol (*tree*)
3. tíos y primos / venir / con / comida y bebidas
4. niños / querer / dormir / pero / no / poder
5. yo / tener / que / ayudar / a / preparar / comida
6. haber / cena / especial / para / mayores
7. más tarde / alguno / amigos / venir / a / cantar / villancicos (*carols*)
8. niños / ir / a / alcoba / a / diez y / acostarse
9. a / doce / todos / desearse / «¡Feliz Navidad!»
10. al día siguiente / todos / decir / que / fiesta / estar / estupendo

¿Cierto, falso o no lo dice? Corrija las oraciones falsas.

1. Hubo muy poca gente en la fiesta.
2. Sólo vinieron miembros de la familia.
3. Todos comieron bien... ¡y mucho!
4. Los niños abrieron sus regalos antes de las doce.

B. **Un sábado por la tarde.** Complete el siguiente diálogo con el pretérito de los infinitivos. Use el sujeto pronominal cuando sea necesario.

P1: Oye, ¿y dónde (*estar:* tú) toda la mañana?
P2: (Yo: *Tener*) que ir a la oficina a terminar un trabajo.

¿Qué pasó anoche? Cambie por el pretérito.
1. *El nieto de Ana viene a visitarnos. El niño se porta muy bien. Está en casa una hora; luego dice adiós y se va.* **2.** *Los Sres. Torres hacen la cena y ponen la mesa a las seis. Luego tienen que lavar los platos. No pueden ir al cine hasta muy tarde.*
3. *Quiero estudiar pero no puedo porque mi amigo Octavio viene a casa con un amigo ecuatoriano. Tengo que ver las fotos que traen.*

Follow-up (listening): *¿Presente o pretérito? dice, dije, decimos, dijimos, estuve, estamos, estuvimos, puede, podemos, pudimos, pude, ponemos, pusimos, pone, puse, tuve, tenemos, tuvimos, traigo, trajo, traemos, trajimos, vinimos, venimos, vinieron, vienen*

Note B: Follow-up questions should focus students' attention on stereotypical sex roles.

P1: ¿Por qué no me lo (*decir:* tú) antes de irte?
P2: ¡Qué memoria! ¿Nunca recuerdas nada? Te lo (*decir:* yo) anoche.
P1: Puede ser, pero se me olvidó (*I forgot*).
P2: ¿(*Venir*) tus padres?
P1: Sí, y los chicos y yo (*tener*) que arreglar la sala. ¡Qué lata (*pain*)!
P2: No te quejes. Tú también puedes hacer algunos de los quehaceres.
P1: ¿Por qué? Nunca los (*hacer:* yo) en casa de mis padres y no quiero empezar ahora.

¿Quién lo dijo, la persona 1 o la persona 2?

1. Mañana tengo que regresar a la oficina, aunque es sábado.
2. Mis padres no me hicieron ayudar con los quehaceres.
3. No me gustan los quehaceres domésticos, pero los hago.
4. ¡Levántense, niños! Aquí están los abuelos... ¡y la casa es un desastre!

Es probable que hablen dos esposos, pero... ¿quién es la persona 1 y quién es la persona 2? Conteste, explicando su respuesta.

C. A la persona perezosa del diálogo anterior le tocó ayudar hoy con los quehaceres de la casa, pero se le olvidó (*forgot*) hacer ciertas cosas. Hágale preguntas según el modelo.

MODELO: estar: garaje / sacar la basura →
Estuviste en el garaje. ¿Por qué no sacaste la basura?

1. estar: comedor / poner la mesa
2. ir: garaje / sacar la ropa de la secadora
3. pasar por: alcoba / hacer las camas
4. estar: sala / poder pasar la aspiradora
5. ir: cocina / poner los platos en el lavaplatos

Suggestion CH: Talk about recent current events and/or people in the news.

CH. Describa Ud. estos hechos (*events*) históricos, usando una palabra o frase de cada grupo. Use el pretérito de los verbos.

en 1969 los estadounidenses	traer	un hombre en la luna
Adán y Eva	saber	en Valley Forge con sus soldados
Jorge Washington	conocer	«que coman (*let them eat*) pasteles»
los europeos	decir	que las serpientes son malas
Stanley	estar	a Livingston en África
María Antonieta	poner	el caballo (*horse*) al Nuevo Mundo

Conversación

Follow-up A1: *Ahora que Ud. conoce bien al profesor (a la profesora), ¿cree que ese día presentó una clase típica?*

A. **Preguntas**

1. ¿En qué mes conoció Ud. al profesor (a la profesora) de español? ¿A quién(es) más conoció ese mismo día? ¿Tuvo Ud. que hablar español el primer día de clase? ¿Cuánto tiempo hace que ya lo habla? ¿Qué les

dijo a sus amigos después de esa primera clase? ¿Qué les va a decir hoy?

Follow-up A2: *¿Qué hizo Ud. para prepararse para el examen?* (Encourage use of object pronouns.) *¿Estudió los verbos? ¿Aprendió el vocabulario? ¿Escribió las terminaciones varias veces? ¿Leyó las explicaciones gramaticales?*

2. ¿Hubo una prueba ayer en la clase de español? ¿Cuándo hubo examen? ¿Le fue difícil a Ud. aprenderlo todo para ese último examen? ¿Cuánto tiempo estudió Ud.? ¿Qué dijo cuando supo la nota que tuvo en ese examen? ¿Cuándo va a haber otra prueba en esta clase? ¿Le gusta a Ud. que haya tantas pruebas?
3. ¿Dónde estuvo Ud. el fin de semana pasado? ¿Con quiénes estuvo? ¿Adónde fue con ellos? ¿Qué hicieron? ¿Lo pasaron bien? ¿Dónde estuvo Ud. la última Noche Vieja? ¿el último Día de Gracias? ¿Dónde piensa estar este año para celebrar esos días festivos?

Follow-up A4: *¿Le hizo Ud. una fiesta de cumpleaños a algún amigo/pariente?* (Encourage use of object pronouns.) *¿Quién preparó la comida? ¿Dio la fiesta en su casa o en casa de otra persona? ¿Puso Ud. adornos* (decorations)? *¿Invitó a sus amigos? ¿Preparó una sangría? ¿Bebieron Coca-Cola sus invitados? ¿Lo pasaron bien todos?*

4. ¿Le dio alguien a Ud. una fiesta de cumpleaños este año? ¿Qué le trajeron sus amigos? ¿Qué le regalaron sus padres? ¿Le hizo alguien un pastel? ¿Qué le dijeron todos? ¿Y qué les dijo Ud.? ¿Quiere que le den otra fiesta el próximo año?
5. ¿Dónde puso su coche ayer? ¿Lo puso en el garaje o lo dejó en la calle? ¿Dónde puso el abrigo cuando se lo quitó? ¿Dónde puso los libros cuando llegó a casa? ¿Se olvida a veces de dónde pone las cosas? ¿De qué otra cosa se olvida Ud. a veces?

Notas comunicativas: Telling How Long Ago . . .

Tell how long ago something happened by using the word **hace** + *period of time.*

—¿Cuándo fuiste a Bogotá con tu familia? —**Hace tres años**.	—*When did you go to Bogota with your family? —Three years ago.*

The preterite is the verb form most commonly used with this **hace** expression. Note also the use of **que** when the **hace** phrase comes at the beginning of the sentence.

Fui a Bogotá con mi familia hace tres años.
Hace tres años **que** fui a Bogotá con mi familia.

Preguntas: Hace diez años... **1.** *¿adónde fuiste de vacaciones?* **2.** *¿con quién pasaste la Nochebuena?* **3.** *¿qué te dieron tus padres el día de Navidad?* **4.** *¿cómo celebraste tu cumpleaños?*

Emphasis: *hace* structure with preterite.

Suggestion B: Cover *A propósito...* in *Un paso más 10* and encourage students to use conversation extension techniques as they conduct interviews.
- Provide several full models before students begin exercise.

B. **Entrevista.** With another student, ask and answer questions to determine the first or last time the following situations occurred. Answer using the **hace** + *time* structure and give some additional details.

MODELO: —¿Cuándo fue la última vez (la primera vez) que tú... ?
—Pues, la verdad es que, hace dos años, en...

1. decir tonterías en una clase
2. estar contentísimo/a
3. estar muy enfermo/a
4. tener que pedirle ayuda a alguien
5. traer mucho dinero a clase
6. dar una fiesta
7. ir a un centro comercial
8. enamorarse (*to fall in love*)
9. enojarse
10. faltar a una clase
11. quejarse de algo
12. ¿ ?

Notas culturales: Celebraciones

En la vida de uno hay muchas ocasiones para dar fiestas. Claro que todos los años hay que celebrar el cumpleaños. Pero en partes del mundo hispánico se celebra también el día del santo. En el calendario religioso católico cada día corresponde al nombre de un santo. Si usted se llama Juan, por ejemplo, el día de su santo es el 24 de junio, y lo celebra igual que el día de su cumpleaños.

Para las señoritas, la fiesta de los quince años, la quinceañera, es una de las más importantes, porque desde esa edad a la niña se le considera ya mujer. Para los muchachos, la fiesta de los dieciocho o veintiún años representa la llegada a la mayoría de edad (*coming of age*).

ESPECIALMENTE PARA TI
En El Día
De Tu Santo

Deseando disfrutes todo
Cuanto pueda serte grato
Y te rodeen el cariño
Las atenciones y halagos
De familiares y amigos
En el día de tu santo.
Muchas Felicidades

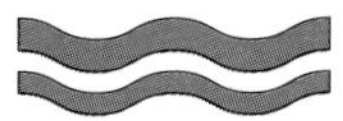

32. TALKING ABOUT THE PAST (3)
Preterite of Stem-Changing Verbs

El cumpleaños de Mercedes

Siguiendo las indicaciones, invente Ud. una descripción de la fiesta de sorpresa que se celebró para Mercedes el año pasado.

1. Llegaron todos a ___(hora)___ .
2. Mercedes {sonrió / se rió / empezó a llorar} cuando los vio.

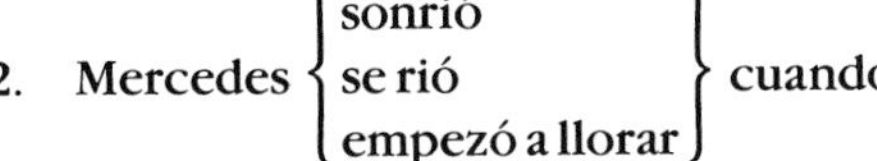

3. Sus amigos le trajeron muchos regalos. Su amigo Raúl le regaló un libro de dibujos cómicos. Su prima Julita le regaló un diccionario de español. Su hermano...
4. Mercedes {sonrió / se rió / le dijo ____} cuando abrió el regalo de ____.
5. Su compañera de cuarto sirvió (¿un pastel? ¿helados?).
6. Se despidieron (*said goodbye*) todos a ___(hora)___ , y Mercedes se durmió, muy contenta, a ___(hora)___ .

Point out: Ask students to compare *yo* vs. *ella* forms of verbs. Ask, What pattern occurs in the third-person form? Where else does this change occur?

Ahora repita Ud. algunos de los detalles, pero desde el punto de vista de Mercedes.

1. Yo {sonreí / me reí / empecé a llorar} cuando llegaron todos.
2. Cuando ____ me dio ____, (yo) {sonreí / me reí / le dije ____}.
3. Comí y bebí ____.
4. Me dormí, muy contenta, a ___(hora)___ .

Follow-up: Students tell what happened at last birthday party. Use verbs in mini as guide to keep narration in preterite (recounting actions, not describing).

As mentioned in **Capítulo 9**, the **-ar** and **-er** stem-changing verbs have no stem change in the preterite.

recordar (ue)		**perder (ie)**	
recordé	recordamos	perdí	perdimos
recordaste	recordasteis	perdiste	perdisteis
recordó	recordaron	perdió	perdieron
recordando		perdiendo	

The **-ir** stem-changing verbs have a stem change in the preterite, but only in the third person singular and plural, where the stem vowels **e** and **o** change to **i** and **u** respectively. This is the same change that occurs in the present participle of **-ir** stem-changing verbs.

pedir (i, i)		**dormir (ue, u)**	
pedí	pedimos	dormí	dormimos
pediste	pedisteis	dormiste	dormisteis
pidió	pidieron	durmió	durmieron
pidiendo		durmiendo	

These are the **-ir** stem-changing verbs that you already know or have seen:

(con)seguir (i, i)
despedir(se) (i, i)
divertir(se) (ie, i)
dormir(se) (ue, u)
pedir (i, i)
preferir (ie, i)
reír(se) (i, i)*
sentir(se) (ie, i)
servir (i, i)
sonreír (i, i)*
vestir(se) (i, i)

Another **-ir** stem-changing verb is **morirse** (**ue**, **u**) (*to die*).

Suggestions:
- **Point out:** no stem change in preterite of *-ar* and *-er* stem-changing verbs
- **Exercise:** Give third-person singular and plural: **1.** (*ue*): *contar, recordar, encontrar, jugar, volver, llover* (third sing. only) **2.** (*ie*): *empezar, recomendar, cerrar, despertarse, nevar* (third sing. only)
- **Point out:** Second stem change occurs in third sing. and pl. preterite of *-ir* stem-changing verbs. *dormir: durmió, durmieron* (also *durmiendo, durmamos, durmáis*) *preferir: prefirió, prefirieron* (also *prefiriendo, prefiramos, prefiráis*)

Preliminary Exercises: Give third person sing. and pl. **1.** (*ue, u*) *dormir, morir, dormirse* **2.** (*i, i*) *pedir, despedir, seguir* **3.** (*ie, i*) *preferir, sentir, sentirse, divertirse*

Todos pasaron un día fatal ayer. ¿Qué les pasó? Dé oraciones nuevas según las indicaciones. **1.** *Dormimos muy mal anoche.* (*yo, todos, Irma, tú, Ud., vosotros*) **2.** *No recordaste traer los ejercicios.* (*Raúl, nosotros, Ud., ellos, vosotros*) **3.** *Raúl perdió las llaves* (keys) *del coche.* (*tú, Horacio y Estela, yo, Ud., vosotras*) **4.** *Pedimos mariscos pero no había* (they were out of them). (*yo, Jacinto, tú, Uds., vosotros*) **5.** *Todos se rieron mucho de Nati.* (*nosotros, Esteban, yo, Uds., vosotras*)

Práctica

A. **Un día fatal.** En casa de sus amigos Alicia y Raúl, todos lo pasaron muy mal ayer. Ayúdeles a describir lo que pasó, haciendo oraciones según las indicaciones.

1. niños / dormir / muy mal
2. bebé / despertarse / tres / mañana
3. tú / no recordar / traerme / libro / que / (yo) pedirte
4. Raúl / perder / llaves (*keys*) / de / coche
5. criada / les / servir / niños / pastel para la fiesta
6. yo / empezar / perder / paciencia / con / ella
7. Raúl / reírse / de / jefe / y / jefe / lo / despedir
8. abuelos / no despedirse / hasta / once

*Note the simplification: **ri-ió → rió**; **ri-ieron → rieron**; **son-ri-ió → sonrió**; **son-ri-ieron → sonrieron**.

Suggestion B: Have students read through each sequence first before beginning exercise.

B. Cuente las siguientes historias breves en el pretérito. Luego continúelas, si puede.

1. En un restaurante: Juan (*sentarse*) a la mesa. Cuando (*venir*) el camarero, le (*pedir*) una cerveza. El camarero no (*recordar*) lo que Juan (*pedir*) y le (*servir*) una Coca-Cola. Juan no (*querer*) beber la Coca-Cola. Le (*decir*) al camarero: «Perdón, señor. Le (*pedir:* yo) una cerveza.» El camarero le (*contestar*): _____.
2. Un día típico: Rosa (*acostarse*) temprano y (*dormirse*) en seguida. (*Dormir*) bien y (*despertarse*) temprano, a las siete. (*Vestirse*) y (*salir*) para la universidad. En el autobús (*ver*) a su amigo José y los dos se (*sonreír*). A las nueve _____.
3. Dos noches diferentes: Yo (*vestirse*), (*ir*) a una fiesta, (*divertirse*) mucho y (*volver*) tarde a casa. Mi compañero de cuarto (*decidir*) quedarse en casa y (*ver*) la televisión toda la noche. No (*divertirse*) nada. (*Perder*) una fiesta excelente y lo (*sentir*) mucho. Yo _____.

C. Describa Ud. estos hechos pasados, usando una palabra o frase de cada grupo. Use el pretérito de los verbos.

durante la primavera pasada	llover	buenos puestos después de graduarse
Romeo	recordar	en Acapulco
la segunda guerra mundial	divertirse	en 1939
Rip Van Winkle	dormir	por Julieta
los turistas	morir	muchos años
mis amigos	empezar	todo el vocabulario en el último examen
yo	conseguir	mucho
	nevar	

Conversación

Suggestion A: Encourage use of object pronouns whenever possible.

A. **Preguntas**

1. ¿Dónde almorzó Ud. ayer? ¿Qué pidió? ¿Quién se lo sirvió? ¿Quién pagó la cuenta? ¿Cuánto dejó Ud. de propina (*tip*)? La última vez que cenó en un restaurante, ¿qué pidió? ¿Prefiere Ud. que otra persona pague en un restaurante elegante?
2. ¿A qué hora se acostó Ud. anoche? ¿Cuántas horas durmió? ¿Durmió bien? ¿Se sintió descansado/a (*rested*) cuando se despertó? ¿Cómo se vistió esta mañana, elegante o informalmente? ¿Se levantó con el pie izquierdo (*on the wrong side of the bed*)?
3. ¿Qué película o programa de televisión le divirtió más el año pasado? ¿Se rió Ud. mucho cuando vio _____? ¿Les gustó también a sus amigos? ¿Qué película quiere ver este mes?

Suggestion B, C: Have students ask you questions first as a model for the interviews. You may wish to give outrageous answers to the questions in B.

B. **Entrevista.** Ask another student **preguntas indiscretas** based on these cues. He or she should invent some equally outrageous answers. Then report what you have learned to the class, which will decide whether the information is true or false.

MODELO: dormirse → —¿A qué hora te dormiste anoche?
—Me dormí a las tres de la mañana... y me levanté a las siete, muy descansada.
—Alicia se durmió a las tres... y se levantó a las siete.

1. dormir(se): ¿a qué hora? ¿dónde?
2. servir: ¿qué, en su última (fiesta, cena)? ¿quién? ¿a quién?
3. despedirse: ¿de quién, anoche? ¿a qué hora?
4. perder: ¿qué cosa? ¿cuánto dinero? ¿dónde?

C. **Entrevista.** ¿Cómo celebró Ud. las siguientes fiestas hace dos años? ¿Y hace diez años? ¿Dónde pasó el día y con quién(es) lo pasó? ¿Faltó alguien importante? ¿Qué sirvieron? ¿Se divirtió mucho? ¿A qué hora se despidieron todos? Con un compañero (una compañera), haga y conteste preguntas para comparar sus experiencias.

1. su cumpleaños
2. el Día de los Muertos (*Halloween*)
3. el Día de Gracias
4. la Noche Vieja

Santiago, Chile

Conociendo a otras personas
—Éste es mi hermano Luis. Está visitándome unos días.
—Hola, Luis. ¿Qué tal? Gusto de conocerte.
—Luis, ellos son mis mejores amigos: Antonio, Rafael y Carmen. Te dejo con ellos un momento, ¿eh?
—Luis, ¿cuánto tiempo llevas por aquí?
—Llegué el miércoles, pero es la segunda vez que visito a mi hermana desde que estudia aquí.
—Sí, creo que nos conocimos en una fiesta hace un año.

¿Recuerda Ud.?

Before beginning Grammar Section 33, review Grammar Section 17, Comparison of Adjectives.

¿Cómo se dice en español?

1. Christmas is more interesting than Thanksgiving.
2. Our Christmas tree is taller than the tree outside the house.
3. This party is better than a present!
4. My brothers are older than I (am).

Suggestion: Review comparative forms and structures before presenting superlatives. *¿Cómo se dice?* 1. taller than John 2. bigger than an apple 3. better than Johnny. 4. easier than Spanish 5. older than my grandmother

33. EXPRESSING EXTREMES
Superlatives

Communicative objectives for 33: more about how to talk about the ultimate (continuation of Absolute Superlatives, *Vocabulario: Preparación*)

Otro aspecto del mundo del trabajo

TERESA: ¿Por qué cambiaste de puesto? ¿No me escribiste que era *el* trabajo *más fácil* del mundo?

TOMÁS: Sí, eso dije, pero me equivoqué. El trabajo resultó malísimo. Tuve *el peor* jefe, *las* condiciones *más incómodas* y *el* sueldo *más bajo de* toda la oficina.

TERESA: ¿Y los días festivos?

TOMÁS: ¡Poquísimos! ¡Ni siquiera nos dieron libre la Semana Santa! Así no se puede, mujer. El trabajo es necesario, pero para mí, la cosa *más importante del* mundo es estar con mi familia, sobre todo los días de fiesta. Este nuevo puesto me permite pasar más tiempo en casa y estoy contentísimo con el cambio.

Imagine que Ud. es Tomás y que todavía tiene el trabajo anterior. Describa su trabajo, usando estas palabras como guía y refiriéndose al diálogo.

- ¿Mi trabajo? (malo)
- ¿Mi jefe? (peor, oficina)
- ¿Las condiciones? (incómodo, oficina)
- ¿Mi sueldo? (bajo, oficina)
- ¿Los días festivos? (poco)
- ¿Estar con la familia? (importante)
- ¿Yo ahora? (no/contento)

Emphasis: use of article, of *de*

article + *noun* + **más/menos** + *adjective* + **de**
article + **mejor/peor** + *noun* + **de**

David es **el** estudiante **más inteligente de** la clase.	*David is the smartest student in the class.*
Son **los mejores** doctores **de** aquel hospital.	*They're the best doctors at that hospital.*

The *superlative* (**el superlativo**) is formed in English by adding *-est* to adjectives or by using expressions such as *the most, the least*, and so on, with the adjective. In Spanish, this concept is expressed in the same way as the comparative but is always accompanied by the definite article. In this construction **mejor** and **peor** tend to precede the noun; other adjectives follow. *In* or *at* is expressed with **de**.

Another side to the working world TERESA: Why did you change jobs? Didn't you write me that it was the easiest job in the world? TOMÁS: Yes, that's what I said, but I was wrong. The job turned out to be extremely bad. I had the worst boss, the most uncomfortable conditions, and the lowest salary in the whole office. TERESA: And what about holidays? TOMÁS: Very few. They didn't even give us Holy Week off! You just can't put up with that, my friend. Work is necessary, but for me the most important thing in the world is to be with my family, especially on holidays. This new job lets me spend more time at home, and I'm very happy with the change.

Preliminary Exercise: (Listening) *¿Cierto o falso?:* 1. _____ *es la persona más alta/baja/joven de la clase.* **2.** *Los perros/gatos son los animales más fieles/cariñosos.* **3.** *El* _____ *es el mejor/peor coche del mundo.* **4.** _____ *es el mejor periódico de los Estados Unidos.* **5.** *Los exámenes de* _____ *son los más difíciles/fáciles de todos.* **6.** _____ *es el actor más guapo del mundo.* **7.** _____ *es la actriz más bonita del mundo.* **8.** *Uds. son los estudiantes más trabajadores/amables/perezosos/simpáticos de la universidad.*

Extension: 10. *El Presidente Reagan fue un presidente viejo.* **11.** *El Presidente Kennedy fue un presidente joven.* **12.** *El Everest es un pico alto.* **13.** *Rip Van Winkle fue un hombre dormilón.* **14.** *El chihuahua es un perro pequeño.*

Práctica

Expand the information in these sentences, according to the model.

MODELO: Carlota es una estudiante muy inteligente. (la clase) →
En efecto, es la estudiante más inteligente de la clase.

En la oficina

1. Olga y Paula son empleadas muy trabajadoras. (todas)
2. La Sra. Gómez es una secretaria muy buena. (la oficina)
3. Es una oficina muy eficiente. (la compañía)

En la excursión

4. Es una plaza muy pequeña. (la ciudad)
5. Son ciudades muy grandes. (el país)
6. Es un metro muy rápido. (mundo)

En la universidad

7. Son capítulos muy importantes. (el texto)
8. Es una residencia muy ruidosa. (la universidad)
9. ¡Es una clase muy mala! (el departamento)

Note: Integration of superlative and absolute superlative forms through *Conversación* section.

Conversación

A. **Situaciones.** A su amigo Rodolfo le gusta exagerar. Cuando Ud. lo llama el día de Navidad, él contesta sus preguntas pero exagerándolo todo, como de costumbre. Con un compañero (una compañera), haga y conteste preguntas, inventando las respuestas exageradas de Rodolfo. Luego compare sus respuestas con las de otros estudiantes. ¿Quién exageró más... pero manteniéndose dentro de los límites de la realidad?

MODELO: —¿Es importante para tu familia la fiesta de este día? → ¡Hombre! ¡Es un día importantísimo! (Es la fiesta más importante del año.) (Es la única fiesta que celebramos en la familia.)

1. Tu árbol de Navidad, ¿cómo es? ¿Es grande? ¿elegante?
2. Tus hermanitos, ¿están felices?
3. Los platos que preparó tu mamá, ¿cómo son? ¿Son ricos? ¿Son difíciles de preparar?
4. ¿Hay muchos regalos para todos? ¿Cómo son? ¿Son caros?
5. Y tú, ¿cómo estás?

Follow-up B: Working as a group, students describe the following, using superlatives. **1.** Alaska **2.** Rhode Island **3.** John F. Kennedy **4.** *el monte Everest* **5.** *el río Amazonas* **6.** *esta universidad* **7.** *la comida de la residencia/cafetería estudiantil*

B **Entrevista.** With another student, ask and answer questions based on the following phrases. Then report your opinions to the class. Report any disagreements as well.

1. la persona más guapa del mundo
2. la noticia más seria de esta semana

3. un libro interesantísimo y otro pesadísimo (*very boring*)
4. el mejor restaurante de la ciudad y el peor
5. el cuarto más importante de la casa y el menos importante
6. un plato riquísimo y otro malísimo
7. un programa de televisión interesantísimo y otro pesadísimo
8. un lugar tranquilísimo, otro animadísimo y otro peligrosísimo (*very dangerous*)
9. la canción más bonita del año y la más fea
10. la mejor película del año y la peor

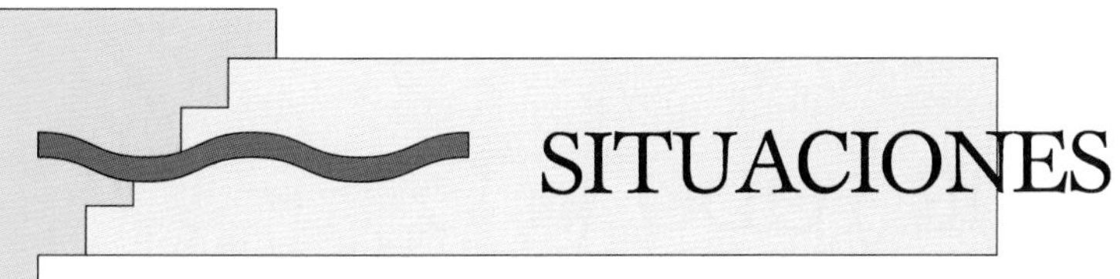

SITUACIONES

Situaciones: See IM for suggestions, additional exercises, and supplementary dialogues and exercises.

En una fiesta de Navidad

A la llegada

—¡Chicos, cuánto gusto! ¡Felices Pascuas!* Pasen, pasen.
—¡Hola, Antonieta! ¡Felices Pascuas!
—¿Por qué no vino Alejandro?
—Se me olvidó° decirte que no pudo regresar. Perdió el vuelo de la tarde. — se... *I forgot*
—Lo siento. Ahora pónganse cómodos y vamos a divertirnos. ¿Qué quieren tomar?
—Una bebida sin alcohol, por favor. Pero, primero, ¿dónde podemos dejar estas cosillas° que trajimos? — *little things* (*i.e., gifts of food*)
—¡Ay, muchas gracias! ¡Muy amables! Pueden dejarlas en la cocina. Ahora bien: José Antonio preparó un ponche muy rico que a todos nos gusta.
—Oye, esta fiesta está estupenda. La música es fabulosa y ¡cuánta comida deliciosa!
—¡Pobre Alejandro. Se está perdiendo la mejor fiesta del año.

A la despedida

—Muchas gracias por venir.
—Gracias a ti. ¡Lo pasamos estupendamente!
—Y, como ya te dijimos, mañana vamos a estar aquí a las nueve para ayudarte a limpiar la casa.
—No es necesario que se molesten.° Se lo agradezco,° de verdad. — se... *you go to that trouble* / *I thank*
—No es molestia.° — *a bother*
—Bueno, si insisten... Seguro que entre todos vamos a terminar pronto.

*Although **Pascua** is the word for *Easter* or *Passover,* many Spanish speakers use the phrase **Felices Pascuas** as a holiday greeting at Christmas time.

Conversación

With a classmate, repeat the first part of the dialogue with these variations.

- Imagine that the party is taking place at the apartment or home of a friend.
- Substitute the names of real people and other real information.

With another classmate, create a brief dialogue in which a friend of the host(ess) asks how the party was. Base the details of the reply on the preceding dialogue and on the minidialogue on page 309. Use the preterite tense as much as possible and keep sentences simple.

UN POCO DE TODO

A. **Un día en la vida de Domingo Meléndez.** Domingo es un estudiante graduado en la Universidad de Sevilla. Los siguientes verbos sirven de base para hacer una descripción de un día típico de su vida. Úselos para describir lo que Domingo hizo ayer. Luego, con los mismos verbos, diga lo que Ud. hizo ayer. **¡OJO!** Hay toda clase de verbos en la lista: regulares (Sección 29), irregulares (Secciones 29 y 31) y verbos que cambian el radical (Sección 33). Haga un repaso (*review*) del pretérito antes de empezar esta actividad.

despertarse a las ocho
levantarse
bañarse
vestirse
desayunar
tomar sólo un café con leche
ir a la universidad
asistir a clases toda la mañana
almorzar con unos amigos a las tres en la cafetería estudiantil
divertirse hablando con ellos
despedirse de ellos
ir a la biblioteca
quedarse allí estudiando toda la tarde
volver a casa a las ocho
ayudar a su madre a preparar la cena
poner la mesa
cenar con la familia
poner los platos en el lavaplatos
tratar de estudiar
no poder (estudiar)
mirar la televisión
decirle buenas noches a su madre
salir a las once a reunirse con unos amigos en un bar
tomar unas copas (*drinks*) con ellos
bailar un poco con una amiga
volver a casa a la una
quitarse la ropa y acostarse
leer un poco
poner el despertador
dormirse pronto

Algunos detalles de la descripción de la vida de Domingo le pueden parecer raros. Vamos a verlos.

- Desayunar sólo un café con leche es un desayuno español muy típico. —¿Qué desayunó Ud. esta mañana? ¿Qué debe desayunar? ¿Es más grande el desayuno de Ud. o el de Domingo?

- Almorzar a las dos o tres y cenar a las nueve o diez es un horario muy típico de España.
  —¿A qué hora almuerza y cena Ud., generalmente? ¿A qué hora almorzó y cenó ayer? En su opinión, ¿qué horario (*schedule*) es mejor para un estudiante, el de España o el de los Estados Unidos?
- Aunque es un estudiante graduado, Domingo todavía vive con su familia. Si estudian o trabajan en la misma ciudad, los jóvenes españoles suelen (*usually*) vivir con sus padres hasta que se casan, aunque esta costumbre está cambiando poco a poco.
  —¿Dónde vive Ud.? ¿Dónde vive la mayoría de sus amigos? Para la mayoría de los estudiantes estadounidenses, ¿es importantísimo independizarse de la familia?
- Domingo sale de casa a las once de la noche. Por lo general, el horario de los españoles incluye horas más avanzadas que el de los estadounidenses. No es nada raro salir de casa para reunirse con los amigos a las diez o a las once de la noche.
  —¿A qué hora se reúne Ud. con sus amigos, generalmente? ¿Se reunió con alguien ayer?
- Los amigos se reúnen en un bar: la palabra *bar* no tiene en español las conotaciones negativas que puede tener en inglés.
  —¿Hay muchos bares estudiantiles en su universidad? ¿Cuál es el mejor, en su opinión? ¿Estuvo Ud. allí ayer?

B. **Costumbres de Navidad.** Con un compañero (una compañera), haga oraciones completas según las indicaciones para formar un diálogo entre dos madres (padres).

E1: ¿ / qué / esperar / tu / niños / que / les / traer / Santa Claus / este año?
E2: ¿Santa Claus? mi / niños / no / lo / conocer; / en / nuestro / casa / los Reyes Magos / les / traer / regalos / a / niños
E1: ¿ah, sí?
E2: sí / y / no / llegar / en / Nochebuena / sino (*but rather*) / el / seis / enero

De las dos personas que hablan, ¿cuál no es hispánica? ¿Cuál es posible que sea hispánica?

C. **Situaciones y reacciones.** Imagine que ocurrieron las siguientes situaciones en algún momento en el pasado. ¿Cómo reaccionó Ud.? ¿Sonrió? ¿Lloró? ¿Se rió? ¿Se enojó? ¿Se puso triste, contento/a, furioso/a? ¿Qué hizo?

MODELO: Su compañero de cuarto hizo mucho ruido anoche. ¿Cómo reaccionó Ud.? →

- Me enojé.
- Me puse furiosísimo/a.
- Salí de casa y fui a la biblioteca a estudiar.
- Hablé con él.

Situaciones

1. Una amiga le regaló un libro pesadísimo. Luego su mejor amigo hizo lo mismo.
2. El profesor le dijo que no hay clase mañana.

3. Ud. rompió las gafas (*eyeglasses*).
4. Su hermano perdió la cartera.
5. Su mejor amigo lo/la llamó a las seis de la mañana el día de su cumpleaños.
6. Nevó muchísimo y Ud. tuvo que hacer un viaje en auto.
7. Ud. recibió el aumento de sueldo más grande de la oficina.
8. Durante el último examen, Ud. no pudo recordar las formas del pretérito.
9. Ud. preparó una cena para algunos amigos y todo le salió horrible.

Ahora, usando las formas del pretérito, invente otras situaciones y pídales a sus compañeros de clase que le indiquen sus reacciones.

CH. **Más días festivos.** Complete the following paragraphs with the correct form of the words in parentheses, as suggested by context. When two possibilities are given in parentheses, select the correct word. Use the preterite of infinitives indicated with an asterisk.

La fiesta de la Virgen de Guadalupe

En (*alguno*[1]) países hispánicos los días de (*cierto*[2]) santos (*ser/estar*[3]) fiestas nacionales. El día 12 (*de/del*[4]) diciembre se (*conmemorar*[5]) a la santa patrona de México, la Virgen de Guadalupe. (*Mucho*[6]) mexicanoamericanos celebran (*este*[7]) fiesta también. Se (*creer*[8]) que la Virgen María se le (*aparecer*[9])* (*a/de*[10]) Juan, un humilde pastor,° en el pueblo (*a/de*[11]) Guadalupe. La Virgen (*dejar*[12])* su imagen en un rebozo° que todavía se puede (*ver*[13]) en la Catedral de la Ciudad de México.

°*shepherd* °*shawl*

La fiesta de San Fermín

No (*todo*[14]) las fiestas hispánicas (*ser/estar*[15]) religiosas. Esta fiesta de Pamplona (España) lleva (*el/la*[16]) nombre de un santo y (*ser/estar*[17]) de origen religioso, pero es esencialmente secular. Durante diez días—entre (*el/la*[18]) 7 y (*el/la*[19]) 17 de julio—se interrumpe la rutina diaria° (*del/de la*[20]) ciudad. (*Llegar*[21]) personas de todas partes de España e inclusive de (*otro*[22]) países para beber, cantar, bailar... y (*pasarlo*[23]) bien en general. Todas las mañanas se (*permitir*[24]) que algunos toros (*correr*[25]) sueltos° por (*el/la*[26]) calle de la Estafeta, en dirección (*al/a la*[27]) plaza de toros. (*Alguno*[28]) personas atrevidas° (*correr*[29]) delante de ellos. No (*haber*[30]) duda que (*este*[31]) demostración de brío° (*ser/estar*[32]) bastante peligrosa. Luego por (*el/la*[33]) tarde se celebra una corrida° en la famosa plaza de toros que (*describir*[34])* Ernest Hemingway en (*su*[35]) novela *The Sun Also Rises.* En Pamplona todavía (*ser/estar*[36]) posible (*hablar*[37]) con personas que (*saber/conocer*[38])* a este famoso escritor estadounidense que (*tener*[39])* tanto interés por las culturas (*hispánico*[40]).

°*daily* °*free* °*daring* °*courage* °*bullfight*

¿Cierto o falso? Corrija las oraciones falsas.

1. Todas las fiestas hispánicas son religiosas.
2. Sólo los mexicanos celebran la fiesta de la Virgen de Guadalupe.
3. La fiesta de San Fermín es esencialmente para los niños.
4. Algunos españoles todavía recuerdan a Hemingway.

fiestas del mundo cristiano *Celebraciones del Corpus Christi, San Pedro y San Pablo, y San Juan Bautista*

Para la Iglesia, el día de San Pedro y San Pablo es una fiesta de guardar, cuya santificación es estrictamente obligatoria, y encierra un doble precepto: el de no trabajar en obras serviles y el de oír misa entera.

Fiesta importante del mundo católico y ortodoxo oriental que, aunque movible, suele caer en el mes de junio, es la del Corpus Christi. Los fieles reciben la sagrada comunión para conmemorar la última cena de Jesús con los doce apóstoles, cuando les ofreció su cuerpo y sangre en las formas del pan y del vino. En numerosos países, el Corpus Christi es celebrado, además, con procesiones a través de pueblos y ciudades. En España e Hispanoamérica, la ruta de estas procesiones es generalmente decorada con motivos florales alegóricos.

La otra gran festividad del mes de junio es la de San Juan Bautista, la cual, por antiquísimas tradiciones que incluso se remontan a tiempos anteriores al cristianismo, incorpora diversas ceremonias. En casi toda Europa, por ejemplo, se encienden hogueras (en ciertos pueblos españoles, la gente camina sobre brasas); en Moravia (Che.), las muchachas forman guirnaldas con nueve clases de flores y las ponen bajo la almohada para soñar con el hombre que desposará; en Barcelona, los enamorados se regalan una rosa y un libro. La francófona provincia de Québec (Can.) celebra el día de su santo patrón con hogueras, desfiles y bailes.

La institución de las Fiestas Cristianas no obedece a un capricho de la Iglesia, sino a razones muy serias y profundas. Todas ellas tienen un valor santificador y educativo. Las fiestas del Señor invitan a imitar su vida ejemplar; las fiestas de los Santos y Apóstoles son estímulos para mover al hombre a la práctica del deber y la virtud.

El martirio de los santos apóstoles Pedro y Pablo era festejado en Roma en tiempos del papa San León (440-461), no obstante su observancia se remonta a los primeros siglos de la Era Cristiana. Dicha fiesta tiene como objeto venerar a San Pedro —llamado el príncipe de los apóstoles— y San Pablo —llamado el apóstol de las gentes o gentiles—, pilares de la iglesia cristiana y cabezas del colegio apostólico instituido por Cristo.

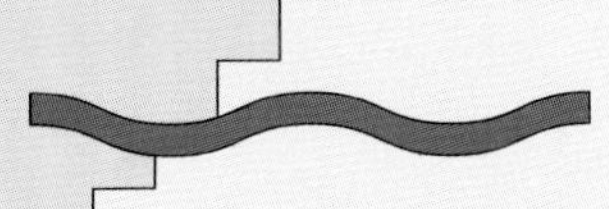

VOCABULARIO

Theme vocabulary previously listed as active: *triste*

VERBOS

celebrar to celebrate
contar (ue) to tell about
despedirse (i, i) (de) to say goodbye (to), take leave (of)
enojarse to get angry
faltar to be absent, lacking
hacerse (*irreg.*) to become
llegar a ser to become
llorar to cry
morirse (ue, u) to die
olvidarse (de) to forget (about)
pasarlo bien/mal to have a good/bad time
ponerse (*irreg.*) to become, get
portarse to behave
quejarse to complain
reaccionar to react
recordar (ue) to remember
reírse (i, i) to laugh
sentirse (ie, i) to feel
sonreír (i, i) to smile

SUSTANTIVOS

el árbol tree
el chiste joke
la emoción emotion
los entremeses hors d'œuvres
el hecho event
la nota grade
la noticia piece of news
los refrescos refreshments
la sorpresa surprise

ADJETIVOS

avergonzado/a embarrassed
feliz (*pl.* **felices**) happy
peligroso/a dangerous
pesado/a boring
(in)cómodo/a (un)comfortable

PALABRAS ADICIONALES

así thus, like that, in that way
dar/hacer una fiesta to give a party
¡felicitaciones! congratulations!
no hay más remedio nothing can be done about it
por because of
ser en + *place* to take place in/at (*place*)

ALGUNOS DÍAS FESTIVOS

la Noche Vieja, la Pascua (Florida), la Nochebuena, la Navidad

Frases útiles para la comunicación

hace + *time* (+ *preterite*)	(*time*) ago
Se fue **hace dos años**.	*He left two years ago.*

UN PASO MÁS 10

OPTIONAL SECTION

Actividad A. Chistes

In all countries there are jokes about children, families, and aspects of family life. Here are a number of cartoons without captions. Can you match them with appropriate captions from the list following them?

Captions

1. ¿Vieron como sin mí no son nadie?
2. ¡Y los que quieran llamarme cuando yo sea un señor muy ocupado sin tiempo para atenderlos, ¡Joróbense (*To heck with them*)!
3. ¿Novios? Lo siento, pero me dijeron que Bo Derek se va a divorciar... Comprende que no voy a dejar pasar la oportunidad...
4. ¿Que si te gusta el casco (*helmet*) espacial que me trajeron los Reyes?
5. Lo siento, la señora no está en casa.

Suggestions A:
- Bring in additional cartoons from Spanish magazines, newspapers, and books, and expand exercise, working as a group.
- Working in small groups, students provide own captions for cartoons, then present them to the class.

- Students tell story of cartoon strips. Can be done as small-group or whole-class activity.

Point out: Best *not* to use jokes that depend on play on words for their humor.

Here are some jokes that do not depend on visual appeal for their humor.

JAIMITO: Abuelita, ¿quién trajo a Pepito?
ABUELITA: Una cigüeña (*stork*) lo trajo.
JAIMITO: ¿Y por qué no lo trajo directamente a la casa en vez de dejarlo en el hospital?

ROSITA: Abuelito, ¿de dónde vienen los niños?
ABUELITO: De París, guapa, de París.
ROSITA: Y si yo vine de París, ¿cómo es que no hablo francés?

Write in simple Spanish an English joke that does not involve a play on words. If you need to use a dictionary, follow the suggestions in the **Study Hint** on page 180. Practice reading your joke aloud; then present it to the class.

A propósito... Keeping the Conversation Going

Carrying on a conversation in a second language requires effort. When you are speaking to someone in Spanish, you may be making such an effort to understand everything or to formulate even simple answers that you forget to say the things that you would automatically say in English.

A conversation is somewhat like a tennis game: it is important to keep the ball moving. But to keep a conversation going, you need to do more than just answer the other person's questions mechanically. If you volunteer a comment or ask a question in return, you not only provide more information but let the other person know that you are interested in continuing the conversation. For example, in answer to the question **¿Juegas al béisbol?**, the words **Sí** or **Sí, juego al béisbol** do little more than hit the ball back. They are factually and grammatically correct, but since they provide no more new information, they return the burden of carrying the conversation to the other person. Answers such as **Sí, soy el pícher** or **Sí, ¿a ti te gusta también? ¿Quieres jugar con nosotros el domingo?** or **No, pero juego al tenis** demonstrate your willingness to keep on talking.

Suggestions B:
- Alternate roles with students so that *Ud.* questions are formed as well.
- Conduct as whole-class activity. Students generate as many different discussion-sustaining responses as possible for each question.

▲ Actividad B. Dime más (*Tell me more*)

With another student, ask and answer the following questions. After answering the questions with a minimal amount of information, volunteer an additional comment or ask your partner a follow-up question. Using the suggestions in the **A propósito...** section, keep each conversation going for a minimum of three or four exchanges before going on to the next questions.

1. ¿A ti te gusta bailar el chachachá?
2. ¿Conoces la ciudad de Nueva York?
3. ¿Dónde vive tu familia?
4. ¿Tienes coche?
5. ¿Por qué estudias español?
6. ¿Cuál es tu programa de televisión favorito?
7. ¿Quieres viajar por México?
8. ¿Qué hiciste el verano pasado?

▲ Actividad C. Entrevistas

Suggestion C: May be done as written assignment

Many U.S. families have special traditions that come from their ethnic or cultural heritage. Other family customs originate in special events that have meaning only to individual families. Explain some of your family traditions to the class by answering the following questions.

1. ¿De dónde viene su familia? 2. ¿Se habla otra lengua en casa? ¿Cuál? 3. ¿Algún miembro de su familia nació en otro país? ¿Cuál? 4. ¿Cuáles son las fiestas que se celebran en su familia con reuniones (*gatherings*) familiares o con costumbres especiales? ¿la Navidad? ¿la Pascua? ¿la Pascua Florida? ¿el Día de Gracias? ¿el 4 de julio? ¿el cumpleaños de alguien? 5. ¿Cómo se celebra esta fiesta? ¿Dónde es la fiesta? ¿Hay comida especial? ¿Quiénes vienen a casa? ¿Van Uds. a casa de otro pariente?

Lectura: See IM for suggestions and additional exercises and activities.

LECTURA CULTURAL

Suggestion: Before assigning the reading, review with students the most important strategies they have worked with thus far: **1.** Look at the pictures, titles, and subtitles of a reading before beginning it. **2.** Look at the questions at the end to see what kinds of information to watch for. **3.** Skip some words, guess others. **4.** Break long sentences down into their "main parts," etc.

There are no additional **Antes de leer** sections before the remaining cultural readings. Remember to apply the strategies you have learned in previous chapters to each reading, and keep trying to guess the meaning of words underlined in the reading texts.

La Navidad

«Los Reyes Magos»

Llegaron ya los reyes
y eran tres,
Melchor, Gaspar
y el negro Baltazar.
Arrope[a] y miel[b]
le llevarán[c]
y un poncho blanco
de alpaca real.[ch]

Changos[d] y chinitas
duérmanse,
que ya Melchor,
Gaspar y Baltazar
todos los regalos
dejarán[e]
para jugar mañana
el Redentor.

El niño Dios
muy bien lo agradeció;
comió la miel
y el poncho lo abrigó.[f]
Y fue después
que los miró,
y a medianoche[g]
el sol se alumbró.[h]

de la Argentina

a. *Syrup*
b. *honey*
c. le... they will bring him
ch. *fine*
d. Niños
e. *they will leave*
f. *kept warm*
g. *midnight*
h. se... *lit up the sky*

En el mundo hispánico hay diferentes costumbres navideñas. Es importante recordar que para los hispanos la Navidad es generalmente una fiesta religiosa que celebra el nacimiento de Jesucristo en Belén.* En realidad, en algunos países las celebraciones navideñas comienzan el 16 de diciembre. Durante nueve días hay una mezcla° de actividades religiosas y sociales. Es costumbre reunirse en grupos primero a rezar° la novena—una serie de oraciones dirigidas a María, a José y al Niño Jesús—y a cantar villancicos. Después hay una fiesta con comida y música. Este período

mezcla° *mixture*
rezar° *to pray*

*También es importante recordar que hay hispanos—judíos, ateos, agnósticos, indios, etcétera—que *no* celebran la Navidad.

culmina con la gran cena y la fiesta familiar que se celebra en la noche del 24 de diciembre. A veces la familia va a la iglesia a medianoche para oír la Misa del Gallo.° (Misa... *Midnight Mass*)

Las costumbres navideñas varían de país en país. En algunas partes de México, por ejemplo, se celebra la Navidad más o menos como es celebrada en los Estados Unidos: se reciben los regalos la Nochebuena o el mismo día de Navidad y se conoce al Papá Noel. Es también frecuente ver árboles de Navidad decorados con ángeles y bolas de colores.

En Colombia se reciben los regalos en la Nochebuena a las doce. Siempre hay una fiesta con toda la familia, incluyendo a los niños chiquitos. Los niños creen que los regalos son enviados° por el Niño Dios y que el Papá Noel los reparte,° ayudado por los ocho venaditos. Después de abrir los regalos, hay una gran cena. En cuanto a° las decoraciones, es muy importante el pesebre: figuras de barro° o de porcelana que representan en miniatura a la Sagrada° Familia, a los Reyes Magos y a algunos animalitos. Pero en las calles es común ver representado el pesebre con personas y animales de verdad. En otros países al pesebre se le llama «Nacimiento» o «Belén». (*sent* / distribuye; En... *Concerning*; *clay* / *Holy*)

En España también se celebra la Navidad con fiestas religiosas y familiares, pero no se reciben los regalos ese día. Éstos llegan el día de los Reyes: el 6 de enero. Se dejan los zapatos cerca de una ventana de la casa, y todos madrugan° para ver qué les dejaron los Reyes. Si los niños no se portan bien se les da carbón° en vez de dulces y otros regalos. Para hacer una broma,° a veces se les pone un «dulce de carbón» en el zapato. Éste es un verdadero dulce, pero en forma de un pedazo° de carbón. (se levantan muy temprano; *coal*; *practical joke*; *piece*)

Comprensión

¿Cierto o falso? Corrija las oraciones falsas.

1. Todos los hispanos celebran la Navidad de la misma manera.
2. En general, la Navidad es una fiesta religiosa *y* social para los hispanos.
3. Una figura similar a Santa Claus no existe en la tradición hispana.
4. El pesebre es una fiesta para la Nochebuena.
5. Para los niños españoles, los Reyes Magos son más importantes que el Papá Noel.

Para escribir

Imagine that you are writing a note to a friend on a holiday greeting card. Describe how the holiday season is being celebrated by your friends and family this year, and pass along other holiday greetings. Use the model.

20 de diciembre de ______.

Querido Juan (Querida Juana),
Ya casi pasó otro año, ¿verdad? Parece que el tiempo vuela (*flies*). Aquí estamos haciendo preparativos para ______. Anoche ______ y hoy ______. Los niños ya le escribieron a ______. Quieren que les traiga ______. Esperamos que todos Uds. ______. Si puedes, ______. ¡Feliz Navidad!

Un abrazo de tu amigo/a

Julio

CAPÍTULO ONCE

¡HUY, PERDÓN!

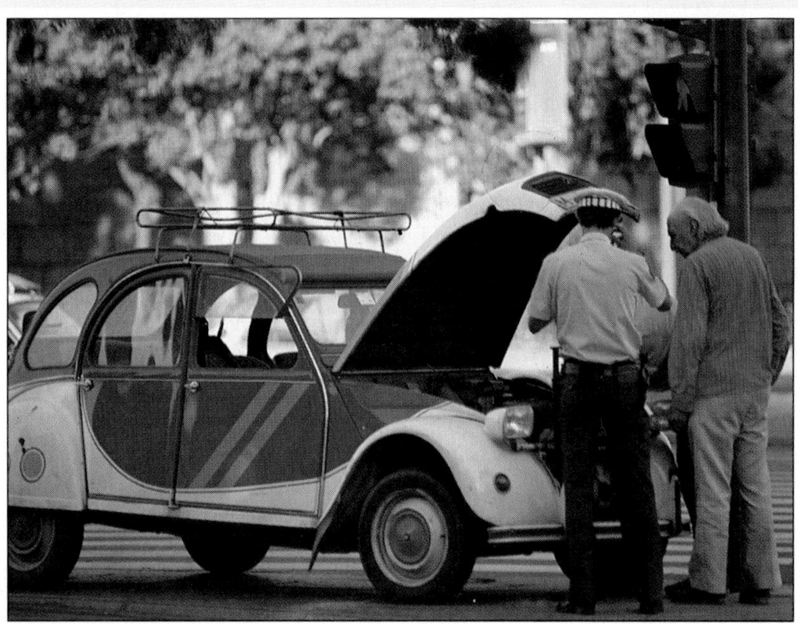

Madrid, Espãna

▲ **Discúlpeme, por favor**

—Perdone, fue sin querer.

—No se preocupe.

—De verdad, no lo vi. Déjeme ayudarlo.

—No, si no es nada[a]... Estoy bien.

[a]si... *it wasn't* (lit. *isn't*) *anything*

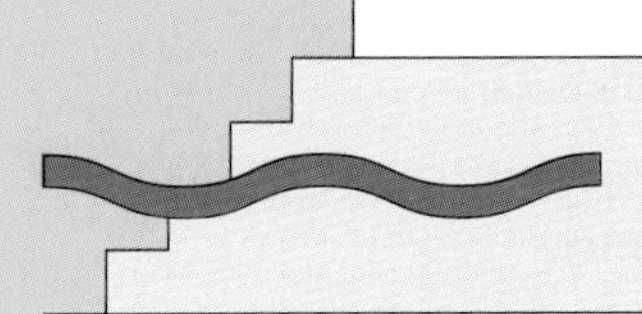

Vocabulario: Preparación:
- See detailed supplementary materials for this section bound into the back of this Annotated Instructor's Edition.

VOCABULARIO: PREPARACIÓN

- See model for vocabulary presentation and other materials in Supplementary *Vocabulario: Preparación* Materials, chapter by chapter, IM.
- See also [video] and [cassette].

Me levanté con el pie izquierdo° *con... on the wrong side of the bed*

acordarse (ue) de	to remember
apagar	to turn off (*lights or an appliance*)
caerse (me caigo)	to fall down
cambiar de lugar	to move (*something*)
doler (ue)	to hurt
Me duele la cabeza.	I have a headache.
equivocarse	to make a mistake
hacerse daño	to hurt oneself
pegar	to hit, strike
romper	to break
sufrir muchas presiones	to be under a lot of pressure
tropezar (ie) con	to bump into
Fue sin querer.	It was unintentional. I (he, we...) didn't mean to do it.
¡Qué mala suerte!	What bad luck!

¡POBRE SR. MARTÍNEZ!

Le duele la cabeza. · la cabeza · Está distraído. · la mano · el brazo · DAMAS · Se equivoca. · el pie · la pierna · Se hace daño en el pie.

ALGUNAS PARTES DEL CUERPO° *body*

las aspirinas	aspirin
la llave	key
distraído/a	absent-minded
torpe	clumsy

Variation A: Students cover up second column and invent their own responses.

A. Indique una respuesta para cada pregunta o situación. Luego invente un contexto para cada diálogo. ¿Dónde están las personas que hablan? ¿en casa de un amigo? ¿en una oficina? ¿Qué van a decir después?

A

1. ¡Ay, estoy sufriendo muchas presiones en el trabajo!
2. Anoche no me acordé de poner el despertador.
3. ¡Ay! ¡Me pegaste!
4. Nunca miro por donde camino (*I'm going*). Esta mañana me caí otra vez.
5. Lo siento, señores, pero ésta no es la casa de Lola Pérez.
6. No cambié de lugar el coche y el policía me puso una multa (*fine*).
7. Anoche en casa de unos amigos rompí su lámpara favorita.

B

a. ¿Vas a comprarles otra?
b. Perdón, señora. Nos equivocamos de casa.
c. ¿Otra vez? ¡Qué distraído eres! ¿Te hiciste daño?
ch. Huy, perdón. Fue sin querer.
d. ¿Te olvidaste otra vez? ¿A qué hora llegaste a la oficina?
e. ¡Qué mala suerte! ¿Cuánto tienes que pagar?
f. ¿Sí? Por qué no te tomas unos días de vacaciones?

TETANOS

Es una infección muy peligrosa que actúa sobre el sistema nervioso de forma generalizada y aguda a través de una toxina.

El tétanos sólo se reconoce cuando se manifiestan los síntomas externos. No hay ninguna otra alteración detectable mediante radiografía o análisis de sangre —a excepción de un ligero aumento de los leucocitos— que permita tomar medidas precoces.

F. Navarro

B. **Asociaciones.** ¿Qué verbos asocia Ud. con estas palabras?

la llave	la mano	la aspirina	la luz	el despertador
la pierna	el brazo	la cabeza	los pies	

Posibilidades: despedirse, doler, apagar, caminar, levantar, correr, preguntar, pegar, escribir, pensar, tomar, caerse, hacerse daño, poner, tropezar, perder

C. ¿Qué puede Ud. hacer o decir—o qué le puede pasar—en cada situación?

1. A Ud. le duele mucho la cabeza.
2. Ud. le pega a otra persona sin querer.
3. Ud. se olvida del nombre de otra persona.
4. Ud. está muy distraído/a y no mira por donde camina.
5. Ud. se hace daño en la mano/el pie.

CH. ¿Se refieren a Ud. estas oraciones? Conteste diciendo «**Sí, así soy**» o «**No, no soy así**».

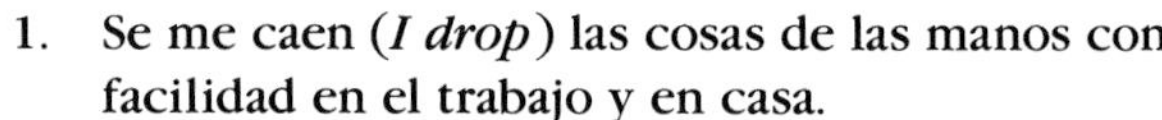

1. Se me caen (*I drop*) las cosas de las manos con facilidad en el trabajo y en casa.
2. Con frecuencia no me acuerdo de hacer la tarea (*homework*) para la clase de español.
3. Cuando oigo el despertador, lo apago y me duermo otra vez.
4. Rompo los platos y los vasos cuando los lavo.
5. Se me pierden (*I misplace*) ciertos objetos, como las llaves, los cuadernos, la cartera...
6. Con frecuencia tropiezo con los muebles.
7. Algunas veces me hago daño en las manos mientras preparo la cena.
8. En las fiestas, me olvido de los nombres de las personas que acabo de conocer.

Variation B: Game format: divide class into teams. Allow one minute for each word; team with most associations wins round; team with most rounds won is winner.

Variation CH: Students give each item a number, corresponding to following scale: 1 = *con frecuencia*; 2 = *algunas veces*; 3 = *nunca*. Then score total points according to this system: 8–12: *¡Quédese en cama y no salga de casa!* 13–19: *Ud. no es perfecto/a, pero lleva una vida típica.* 20–24: *Ud. es una persona ideal... pero... ¡qué vida más aburrida!*

Notas comunicativas: Talking About What Doesn't Matter

In the previous chapters of ***Puntos de partida***, you have learned a number of ways to express likes, dislikes, interests, and so on. Our reactions to particular situations, however, are sometimes quite neutral or indifferent, even when others have strong opinions. Here are some expressions you can use to express neutrality or indifference. Note that some of them are quite colloquial, not appropriate in formal situations.

(Eso) Me da igual.	*(That's) It's all the same to me.*
No (me) importa (nada).	*It doesn't matter (to me) (at all).*
No vale la pena (molestarse por eso).	*It's not worth it (to get upset about that).*
¿Eso? Ni fu ni fa. (*colloquial*)	*That? I'm indifferent about it.*

You may find some of these expressions useful in doing the following activity.

Follow-up CH: As appropriate, ask students to comment on specific problems, asking questions such as *¿Cuándo ocurrió esto la última vez? ¿Qué pasó? ¿Y qué pasó después? ¿Fue un problema grande?*

Suggestion D: Students do as written assignment for homework, then read answers to class the next day, as basis for class discussion of appropriate/inappropriate/funny reactions.

D. ¿Cómo se debe o se puede reaccionar en estas situaciones? Compare sus respuestas con las de los otros miembros de la clase. ¿Quién tiene la solución más original?

1. Son las seis de la mañana. Ud. oye el despertador, pero todavía tiene sueño.
2. Ud. quiere despedirse, pero la persona con quien está hablando quiere hablar más.
3. Ud. pierde su cartera y con ella todo su dinero y el pasaporte.
4. El vecino siempre deja su carro delante del garaje de Ud. y Ud. no puede sacar su carro.
5. Ud. rompe un objeto muy caro y muy querido (*beloved*) en la casa de un amigo.
6. Ud. está preparándose para salir con unos amigos cuando lo/la llama Jaime. Ud. se olvidó de la cita que tenía (*had*) con él para esta tarde.
7. Ud. sufre muchas presiones a causa de los exámenes finales.
8. En el trabajo, Ud. se equivoca en un asunto (*matter*) muy importante.
9. En casa Ud. se equivoca en un pequeño detalle... pero resulta que es algo muy importante para su compañero de cuarto (esposo, hermanito, ...).

Study Hint: False Cognates

Not all Spanish and English cognates are identical in meaning. Here are a few important "traps" to be aware of: **sano** is *healthy*; **renta**, *income*; **pariente**, *relative*; **gracioso**, *funny*; **actual**, *current, up to date*; **fábrica**, *factory*; **colegio**, *elementary* or *secondary school*; **una molestia**, *a bother*; **sopa**, *soup*; **ropa**, *clothing*; **real**, *real* or *royal*; **sensible**, *sensitive*; **éxito**, *success*—and **constipado** means *suffering from a head cold.* These words are *false*, or misleading, *cognates* (**amigos falsos**).

Occasionally such words can lead to communication problems. The American tourist who, feeling embarrassed, describes himself or herself as **embarazado/a** may find people chuckling at the remark, since **embarazada** means not *embarrassed* but *pregnant.*

Talking About How Things Are Done: Adverbs

You already know some of the most common Spanish *adverbs* (**los adverbios**): **bien**, **mal**, **mejor**, **peor**, **mucho**, **poco**, **más**, **menos**, **muy**, **pronto**, **a tiempo**, **tarde**, **temprano**, **siempre**, **nunca**, **sólo**. The form of adverbs is invariable.

Adverbs that end in *-ly* in English usually end in **-mente** in Spanish. The suffix **-mente** is added to the feminine singular form of adjectives. Adverbs ending in **-mente** have two stresses: one on the adjective stem and the other on **-mente**. The stress on the adjective stem is the stronger of the two.

(continúa)

ADJECTIVE	ADVERB	ENGLISH
rápido	**rápidamente**	*rapidly*
fácil	**fácilmente**	*easily*
valiente	**valientemente**	*bravely*

In Spanish, adverbs modifying a verb are placed as close to the verb as possible. When they modify adjectives or adverbs, they are placed directly before them.

Hablan **estupendamente** el español.	*They speak Spanish marvelously.*
Ese libro es **poco** interesante.*	*That book is not very interesting.*
Vamos a llegar **muy tarde**.	*We're going to arrive very late.*

Follow-up A: *¿Qué acción personal asocia Ud. con los siguientes adverbios?* (Students create sentences about themselves.) **1.** *infrecuentemente* **2.** *lentamente* **3.** *tristemente* **4.** *felizmente* **5.** *fielmente* **6.** *fabulosamente*

Follow-up C: Completion. Model answer, then expand to question. **1.** *Yo ____ rápidamente, pero no ____ rápidamente.* **2.** *Yo siempre ____ tranquilamente.* **3.** *Yo ____ mejor que mis padres.* **4.** *Yo ____ peor que mi mejor amigo/a.*

A. Complete estas oraciones lógicamente con adverbios basados en los siguientes adjetivos.

Adjetivos: directo, inmediato, paciente, posible, rápido, fácil, puntual, tranquilo, total, constante

1. La familia está esperando ____ en la cola.
2. Hay examen mañana y tengo que empezar a estudiar ____.
3. Se vive ____ en aquel pueblo en la montaña.
4. ¿Las enchiladas? Se preparan ____.
5. ¿El hombre va a vivir en la luna algún día? Mi hermana contesta, «____».
6. ¿Qué pasa? Estoy ____ confundido.
7. Un vuelo que hace escalas no va ____ a su destino.
8. Cuando mira la tele, mi hermanito cambia el canal ____.
9. Es necesario que las clases empiecen ____.

B. **Entrevista.** Con un compañero (una compañera), haga y conteste preguntas para obtener la siguiente información.

MODELO: algo que hace pacientemente →
—¿Qué haces pacientemente? (Dime algo que haces pacientemente.)
—Pues... espero a mi esposo pacientemente cuando se viste para salir. ¡Lo hace tan lentamente! También...

1. algo que hace pacientemente
2. algo que su (compañero/a, mejor amigo/a, esposo/a, ...) hace constantemente y que le molesta muchísimo a la persona entrevistada (*interviewed*)
3. algo que le toca hacer inmediatamente
4. algo que hizo (comió, escuchó, ...) solamente una vez y que no le gustó nada

*Note that in Spanish one equivalent of *not very* + *adjective* is **poco** + *adjective*.

5. algo que hizo (comió, escuchó, ...) solamente una vez y que le gustó muchísimo
6. algo que hace fácilmente pero que para los otros es difícil

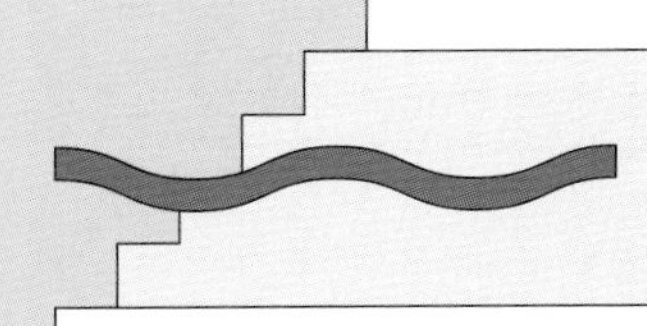

MINIDIÁLOGOS Y GRAMÁTICA

Communicative objectives for 34: how to talk about what used to happen.

34. DESCRIPTIONS AND HABITUAL ACTIONS IN THE PAST

Imperfect of Regular and Irregular Verbs

Torreón, Mexico

La nostalgia

MATILDE: ...y todos los hijos *eran* chiquitos. *Entraban* y *salían* de casa como locos. ¡Qué ruido *había* siempre! ¿Te acuerdas?

ARMANDO: Sí, sí, sí, aquéllos *eran* otros tiempos.

MATILDE: Y luego en verano *íbamos* siempre a la playa con todos los tíos y tus padres y dos criados y los amigos de los niños. *Teníamos* aquella casita tan linda... ¡Casi la puedo ver! ¿No la ves?

ARMANDO: Sí, sí, sí, aquellos *eran* otros tiempos.

MATILDE: Dime una cosa, Armando. De verdad, ¿que prefieres, aquella época o estos tiempos más tranquilos?

ARMANDO: Sí, sí, sí, aquéllos *eran* otros tiempos.

MATILDE: Ay, querido, parece que las cosas nunca cambian. ¡Tampoco me *escuchabas* en aquel entonces!

1. ¿Qué hacían los niños de Matilde y Armando?
2. ¿Su casa era muy tranquila?
3. ¿Adónde iban siempre en verano? ¿Iban solos?
4. ¿Qué le pregunta Matilde a Armando? ¿Cómo responde él?
5. ¿Armando escucha lo que Matilde dice? Y antes, ¿la escuchaba?

Follow-up: *¿Cierto o falso?* Are these statements true or false for your childhood? **1.** *Siempre había mucho ruido en casa.* **2.** *Los niños de la familia entraban y salían de casa como locos.* **3.** *Los niños de los* ____ *también entraban y salían.* **4.** *En verano todos íbamos a la playa/a las montañas.* **5.** *Los niños escuchaban a sus padres.* **6.** *Papá escuchaba a mamá y vice versa.* **7.** *Yo siempre hacía lo que mis padres me mandaban.* **8.** *Me gustaba mucho ir a la escuela.* **9.** *Me gustaban mucho los niños del sexo opuesto.*

Nostalgia MATILDE: . . . and all the kids were little. They went in and out of the house like mad. There was always so much noise! Remember? ARMANDO: Yes, yes, yes, those were different times. MATILDE: And then in the summer we would go to the beach with all the uncles and aunts and your parents and two servants and the kids' friends. We used to have that pretty little house . . . I can almost see it! Don't you see it? ARMANDO: Yes, yes, yes, those were different times. MATILDE: Tell me something, Armando. Honestly, which do you prefer—those times or these more peaceful times? ARMANDO: Yes, yes, yes, those were different times. MATILDE: Well, dear, I guess things never change. You never used to listen to me back then, either!

The *imperfect* (**el imperfecto**) is the second simple past tense in Spanish. In contrast to the preterite, which is used when you view actions or states of being as finished or completed, the imperfect tense is used when you view past actions or states of being as habitual or as "in progress." The imperfect is also used for descriptions.

The imperfect has several English equivalents. For example, **hablaba**, the first person singular of **hablar**, can mean *I spoke*, *I was speaking*, *I used to speak*, or *I would speak* (when *would* implies a repeated action). Most of these English equivalents indicate that the action was still in progress or was habitual, except *I spoke*, which can correspond to either the preterite or the imperfect.

Suggestions:
- **Point out:** Imperfect = second of two simple past tenses. This section presents and practices only imperfect. Section 36 (Ch. 12) contrasts the two, but some exercises in intervening sections will combine the two tenses in controlled situations.
- Present regular imperfect forms, using *trabajar, beber,* and *vivir* in conversational exchanges with students.

Forms of the Imperfect

hablar		comer		vivir	
habl**aba**	habl**ábamos**	com**ía**	com**íamos**	viv**ía**	viv**íamos**
habl**abas**	habl**abais**	com**ías**	com**íais**	viv**ías**	viv**íais**
habl**aba**	habl**aban**	com**ía**	com**ían**	viv**ía**	viv**ían**

- **Point out: (1)** *Yo* form is identical to *Ud./él/ella* form. Context will often make meaning clear, but subject pronouns are more frequently used with imperfect forms for that reason. **(2)** No stem change in imperfect.
- Present irregular forms of *ser*, *ir*, and *ver*.

Stem-changing verbs do not show a change in the imperfect: **almorzaba**, **perdía**, **pedía**. The imperfect of **hay** is **había** (*there was*, *there were*, *there used to be*).

Only three verbs are irregular in the imperfect: **ir**, **ser**, and **ver**.

ir		ser		ver	
iba	íbamos	era	éramos	veía	veíamos
ibas	ibais	eras	erais	veías	veíais
iba	iban	era	eran	veía	veían

Uses of the Imperfect

The imperfect is used for the following.

- To describe *repeated habitual actions* in the past

Siempre **nos quedábamos** en aquel hotel.	*We always stayed (used to stay, would stay) at that hotel.*
Todos los veranos **iban** a la costa.	*Every summer they went (used to go, would go) to the coast.*

- To describe an *action that was in progress*

Pedía la cena.	*She was ordering dinner.*
Buscaba el carro.	*He was looking for the car.*

- Present uses of imperfect. *¿Cómo se dice?* (vary subjects of sample sentences) **A.** I always used to stay... Every summer we used to go... etc.
- **Emphasis:** English "cues" associated with imperfect: used to, would (habitual action), every (day/month, etc.), was/were ____ing.

- To describe two *simultaneous past actions in progress*, with **mientras**

Tú **leías mientras** Juan **escribía** la carta.	*You were reading while John was writing the letter.*

- To describe ongoing *physical, mental, or emotional states* in the past

Estaban muy distraídos.	*They were very distracted.*
La **quería** muchísimo.	*He loved her a lot.*

- To tell *time* in the past and to express age with **tener**

Era la una.	*It was one o'clock.*
Eran las dos.	*It was two o'clock.*
Tenía dieciocho años.	*She was eighteen years old.*

¡OJO! Just as in the present, the singular form of the verb **ser** is used with one o'clock, the plural form from two o'clock on.

[Práctica A]

- To form a *past progressive*: imperfect of **estar** + *present participle**

Estábamos cenando a las diez.	*We were having dinner at ten.*
¿No **estabas estudiando**?	*Weren't you studying?*

[Práctica B–CH]

- **Emphasis:** *mientras*, *mientras que* as cue for simultaneous actions
- **Point out:** *Saber*, *conocer*, *querer*, and *poder* retain base meaning of infinitive (in contrast to preterite meaning). See Section 36 for more detail.
- **Suggestion:** Contrast action in progress and past progressive, reentering simple present vs. present progressive.

Optional: The imperfect is used to project into the future from a specific point in the past. Contrast: *Va a ser una larga noche. Sabíamos que iba a ser una larga noche.*

Preliminary Exercises:

- **Rapid Response Drill:** *Dé el imperfecto.*
  yo: cerrar, escuchar, mirar, querer, asistir, recibir
  tú: pensar, visitar, entrar, tener, vivir, pedir
  Ud./él/ella: preguntar, comprar, enseñar, volver, abrir, servir
  nosotros: jugar, bailar, tomar, aprender, preferir, venir
  Uds./ellos/ellas: trabajar, ganar, creer, divertir, ser

- *Dé oraciones nuevas según las indicaciones.*
  En la escuela primaria...
  1. *Tina estudiaba y jugaba mucho.* (*yo, Uds., tú, nosotros, Julio, vosotros*) **2.** *Todos bebían leche y dormían la siesta.* (*Tina, tú, nosotros, Alicia, yo, vosotros*) *¿Qué hacían Uds. anoche a las doce?*
  3. *Ceci veía un programa interesante.* (*tú, yo, Uds., Pablo, ellas, vosotros*) **4.** *Mis padres iban a acostarse.* (*tú, yo, nosotros, Hernando, ellas, vosotros*) **5.** *Yo (no) estaba ____.* (*leer, mirar la televisión, escribir una carta, dormir, llorar, comer, apagar las luces, ¿ ?*)

Follow-up A: *En la escuela primaria:* **1.** *¿Cantaba/Jugaba Ud. mucho en la primaria?* **2.** *De niño/a, ¿bebía mucha leche/Coca-Cola? ¿Dormía la siesta? ¿De qué hora a qué hora?* **3.** *Anoche a las doce... ¿Veía Ud. programas interesantes en la televisión cuando era niño/a? ¿Cuáles le gustaban más?* **4.** *¿A qué hora se acostaba Ud. cuando tenía (3, 7, 12) años? ¿Le gustaba acostarse tan temprano/tarde? ¿Leía Ud. a veces en la cama?*

Práctica 

A. **De niño/a.** (*As a child.*) Describa la vida de Tina cuando era muy joven, haciendo oraciones según las indicaciones.

La vida de Tina era muy diferente cuando tenía ocho años.

1. vivir / en / casa / de / padres
2. todos los días / asistir / a / escuela primaria
3. caminar / a / escuela / con / mejor / amigo
4. por / mañana / aprender / a / leer / y / escribir / en / pizarra
5. a / diez / beber / leche / y / dormir / un poco
6. ir / a / casa / para / almorzar / y / regresar / a / escuela
7. estudiar / geografía / y / hacer / dibujos
8. jugar / vólibol / con / compañeros / en / patio / de / escuela
9. camino de (*on the way*) casa / comprar / dulces / y / se los / comer
10. frecuentemente / pasar / por / casa / de / abuelos
11. cenar / con / padres / y / ayudar / a / lavar / platos
12. ver / tele / un rato (*short while*) / y / acostarse / a / ocho

---

*A progressive tense can also be formed with the preterite of **estar**: ***Estuvieron* cenando hasta las doce**. The use of the progressive with the preterite of **estar**, however, is relatively infrequent, and it will not be practiced in ***Puntos de partida***.

Suggestion C: Personalize items: *De niño/a, ¿creía Ud. en Santa Claus?* (See chapter opener photo for *los Reyes Magos.*) *¿Estudiaba mucho?*, etc.

Optional: Dictate in present tense. Students write imperfect forms.
¿Qué pasaba? Cambie los verbos indicados por el imperfecto. **1.** *Olga va a la universidad todos los días. Siempre asiste a sus clases. Pregunta mucho porque es inteligente. Sus profesores están muy contentos con ella.* **2.** *Yo trabajo para el gobierno. Mi jefe, que se llama Ángel, nos hace trabajar mucho. Siempre almorzamos juntos en el mismo restaurante y a veces jugamos al básquetbol por la tarde.* **3.** *Vivo en Sacramento. Siempre llueve mucho en invierno y en primavera, pero me gusta mucho el clima. Además* (Besides), *las montañas están cerca y puedo esquiar.*

Follow-up: Using verbs in the imperfect, personalize sequences given. **1.** *El semestre pasado, ¿venía Ud. a la universidad todos los días? ¿Asistía a todas sus clases? ¿Hacía muchas preguntas?* **2.** *En la secundaria, ¿trabajaba Ud. después de las clases? ¿los fines de semana? ¿durante las vacaciones? ¿Dónde? ¿Cómo se llamaba su jefe? ¿Cuántas horas trabajaba la semana?* **3.** *De niño/a, ¿dónde vivía Ud.? ¿Llovía mucho allí? ¿Le gustaba el clima?*

¿Cierto, falso o no lo dice? Corrija las oraciones falsas.

1. Tina no tenía hermanos.
2. Iba a la escuela en autobús.
3. Tenía un perro que se llamaba Júpiter.
4. Generalmente, almorzaba y cenaba en casa.
5. Le gustaba estar con los abuelos.
6. Era una niña muy distraída.

Ahora vuelva a hacer la descripción pero usando el sujeto **yo** para describir su propia infancia. Si es posible, dé detalles auténticos.

B. **¿Que pasó?** Anoche se apagaron todas las luces de la vecindad (*neighborhood*) a las nueve. ¿Qué **estaban haciendo** los miembros de la familia de Tina a esas horas? Conteste usando formas progresivas.

1. Tina / dormir
2. padre / leer / periódico
3. hermano mayor / jugar / con / Júpiter
4. madre / hablar por teléfono
5. abuelos / mirar / álbum (*m.*) de fotos

C. ¿Cómo eran o qué hacían estas personas de niños?

O. J. Simpson		ser	con frecuencia/siempre
todos		cantar	fútbol americano/béisbol/tenis
Michael Jackson		tocar	música moderna
Elizabeth Taylor		estudiar	mucho/poco
Fernando Valenzuela		jugar al/con	el piano/la guitarra
Chris Evert	(no)	creer en	el señor Wilson
yo		acostarse	temprano/tarde
Ann Landers		equivocarse	guapo/a, pobre, rico/a
Tom Selleck		levantarse	con el pie izquierdo
Daniel el Travieso (*Dennis the Menace*)		dar	Santa Claus/los Reyes Magos
		caerse	consejos
¿ ?		molestar	¿ ?

CH. **Descripciones**

- **La vida en New Hampshire.** Complete la descripción con la forma correcta del imperfecto del verbo apropiado.
  Cuando (yo: _____[1]) veinticinco años, (_____[2]) en New Hampshire. Allí siempre (_____[3]) mucho en invierno y en primavera, pero me (_____[4]) mucho el clima. Además (*Besides*), las montañas (_____[5]) cerca y (yo: _____[6]) esquiar. En verano no (_____[7]) muchísimo calor y (nosotros: _____[8]) a la playa con frecuencia.
- **Una noche tranquila en casa.** ¿Cómo se dice en español?
  It was eight o'clock, and I was reading while my friend was writing a letter. There was little noise, and it was snowing outside. We weren't expecting (**esperar**) anyone, and we thought that it was going to be a quiet evening.

Ayer

Hoy

Variation A: Students invent statements that describe current times; class gives description of past. Topics: *los precios, las computadoras, la sencillez/complejidad de la vida, la seguridad personal, el impacto del gobierno en la vida diaria*

Suggestion B: Remind students to use conversation-extending techniques practiced in last chapter.

Follow-up: Completions: Model answer, then expand to question. 1. *En otra época siempre me gustaba ______. No me gustaba nada ______.* 2. *Anoche a las (10, 12), yo estaba ______.* 3. *Siempre veía (programa de televisión), pero ahora prefiero ______.* 4. *De niño/a, siempre leía ______, pero ahora leo ______.*

Conversación

A. **Los tiempos cambian.** Muchas cosas y costumbres actuales son diferentes de las del pasado. Las oraciones siguientes describen algunos aspectos de la vida de hoy. Después de leer cada oración, invente Ud. otra, describiendo cómo eran las cosas antes, en otra época.

MODELO: Ahora casi todos los bebés nacen en el hospital. →
Antes casi todos los bebés nacían en casa.

1. Ahora muchas personas viven en apartamentos.
2. Se come con frecuencia en los restaurantes.
3. Muchísimas mujeres trabajan fuera de casa.
4. Muchas personas van al cine y miran la televisión.
5. Ahora las mujeres—no sólo los hombres—llevan pantalones.
6. Ahora hay enfermeros y maestros—no sólo enfermeras y maestras.
7. Ahora tenemos coches pequeños que gastan (*use*) poca gasolina.
8. Ahora usamos más máquinas y por eso hacemos menos trabajo físico.
9. Ahora las familias son más pequeñas.
10. Muchas parejas viven juntas sin casarse (*to get married*).

B. **Entrevista.** Using the following questions as a guide, interview another student about his or her childhood. Then report the information to the class.

1. ¿Dónde vivías y con quién? ¿Tenías un apodo (*nickname*)?
2. ¿Cómo se llamaba tu escuela primaria? ¿y tu maestro/a en el primer grado?
3. ¿Cuál era tu materia favorita? ¿Por qué te gustaba esa materia?
4. ¿Cómo se llamaba tu mejor amigo/a? ¿Dónde vivía? ¿Siempre se llevaban bien (*did you get along*)?
5. ¿Perdías o rompías muchas cosas? ¿Eras un niño distraído (una niña distraída)?
6. ¿Practicabas algunos deportes? (**Sí, jugaba [al] ______.**)
7. ¿Te caías con frecuencia? ¿Siempre te hacías daño?
8. ¿Tenías un perrito? ¿un gato? ¿Cómo se llamaba?
9. ¿Cómo era la casa o el apartamento en que vivías?
10. ¿Cómo era tu cuarto? ¿Tenías allí un objeto muy especial? ¿muchos juguetes?
11. ¿Qué bebías (comías) cuando eras niño/a que ahora no bebes (comes)?
12. ¿Qué programas de televisión veías que ahora no ves?

En busca de la casa de unos amigos

Mijas, España

—¡Ay! Se nos quedó la dirección en casa.
—Pero ¿no la recuerdas? Acabas de buscarla en la guía telefónica.
—Es verdad, pero siempre se me olvidan esas cosas.
—No hay tiempo para volver. Ojalá que podamos reconocer la casa.

Communicative objectives for 35: talking about accidents

35. EXPRESSING UNPLANNED OR UNEXPECTED EVENTS

Another Use of *se*

Se me cayó el vaso.
I dropped the glass. (The glass fell from my hands.)

A Mario se le perdieron los libros.
Mario lost his books. (Mario's books were lost to him.)

Unplanned or unexpected events (*I dropped, we lost, you forgot*) are frequently expressed in Spanish with **se** and the third person of the verb. In **Situaciones** in **Capítulo 10**, for example, you saw the phrase **Se me olvidó**. In this structure, the occurrence is viewed as happening *to* someone—the unwitting performer of the action. Thus the victim is indicated by an indirect object pronoun, often clarified by **a** + *noun* or *pronoun*. In such sentences, the subject (the thing that is dropped, broken, forgotten, and so on) usually follows the verb.

Point out:
- Subject of English sentences is Spanish IO pronoun: I = *se me*; Mario = *se le*. Similarity to *gustar*-type construction.
- Optional emphasis or clarification of IO (*a mí, a Mario*).
- Sing. vs. pl. verbs: depends on English DO.

¿Cómo se dice? **1.** I dropped the glasses/plate/books. **2.** Robert lost the book/keys/alarm clock.

(A + NOUN OR PRONOUN)	SE	INDIRECT OBJECT PRONOUN*	VERB	SUBJECT
(A mí)	Se	me	cayó	el vaso.
A Mario	se	le	perdieron	los libros.

Preliminary Exercises:
- What IO pronoun do you hear? **1.** *Se me olvidó el bolígrafo.* **2.** *Se le rompieron los platos.* **3.** *Se nos cayeron las flores.* **4.** *Se te acabó la gasolina.* **5.** *Se nos quedaron en casa los boletos.*
- ***Dictado:*** **1.** *Se me cayeron las llaves.* **2.** *Se nos rompieron los vasos.* **3.** *A Pepe se le rompió el despertador.* **4.** *A María se le olvidaron las aspirinas.*
- **Follow-up:** *¿Qué significa cada frase en inglés?*
- *¡Qué distraídos estuvimos*

The verb agrees with the grammatical subject of the Spanish sentence (**el vaso, los libros**), not with the indirect object pronoun. **No** immediately precedes **se**: **A Mario *no se* le perdieron los libros.**

As with **gustar**, the clarification of the indirect object pronoun is optional. But the indirect object pronoun itself is always necessary whether or not the victim is named: ***A la mujer* se *le* rompió el plato**. Some verbs frequently used in this construction include the following.

acabar	to finish; to run out of	**olvidar**	to forget	**quedar**	to leave behind
caer	to fall	**perder (ie)**	to lose	**romper**	to break

Práctica

A. **Hablando de desastres.** Complete las siguientes descripciones con la forma correcta de una frase de esta lista.

olvidó llenar el tanque	perdieron las gafas (*glasses*)	rompieron muchos platos y vasos
quedó la cartera en casa	rompió la pierna	acabó el vino

*While the verb form is always third person singular or plural in this construction, all of the indirect object pronouns can be used: **¿A Uds. *se les* perdió todo el dinero?**; **A los niños *se les* perdió el perro.** However, the exercises in ***Puntos de partida*** will focus on sentences containing **se me...**, **se te...**, and **se le...** .

todos ayer! Dé oraciones nuevas según las indicaciones. **1.** *A Pablo se le olvidó la cartera. (mí, nosotros, Inés, ti, los chicos, vosotros)* **2.** *¡Se te perdieron las llaves otra vez! (Ernesto, Uds., niña, mí, vosotros)* **3.** *María fue la más distraída de todos. Se le olvidó/olvidaron ____. (tomar el desayuno, las gafas* [glasses]*, estudiar para el examen, los cheques, venir a clase)*

Suggestion A: Students create a context for each situation.

Suggestion A: Turn items into personalized questions, when appropriate.

Suggestion B: You may want to supply sentences for students to complete with the *porque se le...* phrase.

- *Pablo se levantó tarde, a las ocho...*
- *Salió de casa descalzo...*
- *No pudo abrir la puerta del coche...*
- *No pudo tomar el autobús...*
- *Su jefe se ofendió porque a Pablo...*
- *Su primer cliente se enojó porque*
- *Pablo tenía muchísima hambre a las diez...*
- *El vicepresidente se puso furioso...*

1. ¡Pobre camarero! Lo despidieron porque se le ____.
2. Carmen no pudo pagar la cuenta en el restaurante anoche porque se le ____.
3. Tú esquías mucho, ¿no? ¿Se te ____ alguna vez?
4. Anoche tuve invitados (*guests*) para cenar y les serví champán porque se me ____.
5. Señor, el problema es que el coche no tiene gasolina. ¿Se le ____?
6. ¡Qué distraído eres, niño! ¿Se te ____ otra vez?

B. Pablo pasó un día fatal ayer. Lea la siguiente descripción de su día. Luego explique cada acción o circunstancia, usando la frase **Porque se le...**

Pablo no se levantó a las siete, como siempre, sino (*but rather*) muy tarde, a las ocho. Se vistió rápidamente y salió de casa descalzo (*barefooted*). Entró en el garaje pero no pudo abrir la puerta del coche. Por eso trató de tomar el autobús para llegar a la oficina, pero cuando el conductor le pidió la tarifa, no tenía dinero. Por eso tuvo que irse caminando.

Cuando por fin entró en la oficina, su jefe se ofendió porque Pablo lo trató descortésmente. Su primer cliente se enojó porque Pablo no tenía toda la información necesaria para resolver su caso. Para las diez de la mañana, Pablo tenía muchísima hambre. Por eso fue a la cafetería para comer algo. Se sentó con el vicepresidente de la compañía, quien se levantó furioso de la mesa, diciendo que Pablo le arruinó la chaqueta de su traje. Pablo se levantó y regresó a casa. ¡Ya no pudo más!

MODELO: Pablo se levantó tarde, a las ocho, porque se le...

	tomar el desayuno
	las llaves del coche
olvidar	la cartera
perder	todos los papeles en casa
caer	una taza (*cup*) de café
quedar	saludar al jefe
	poner el despertador
	ponerse los calcetines y zapatos

Ahora, déle un consejo a Pablo: La próxima vez que Pablo se levante con el pie izquierdo, debe...

Conversación

Suggestion A: Limit students to simple answers to question, to avoid need to use imperfect. Or ask students guiding questions that can be answered in same tense as question, to use both preterite and imperfect together.

A. ¿Qué les pasó a estas personas?

1.

2.

3.

4.

B. **Al mono más vivo se le cae la banana de vez en cuando.** (*Even the brightest monkey drops his banana sometimes.*) ¿Qué desastres le han ocurrido (*have happened*) a Ud.? Después de completar las oraciones, use sus propias respuestas como guía para entrevistar a un compañero (una compañera) de clase.

MODELO: Una vez durante las vacaciones se me perdió/perdieron ____. → Una vez durante las vacaciones se me perdió el dinero. ¿Se te perdió el dinero alguna vez? ¿Qué te pasó?

1. Una vez durante las vacaciones se me perdió/perdieron ____.
2. Una vez se me cayó/cayeron ____.
3. A veces se me olvida(n) ____. De niño/a, siempre se me olvidaba(n) ____.
4. Nunca/Casi siempre se me acaba(n) ____.
5. Una vez se me rompió/rompieron ____.
6. A veces se me queda(n) ____ en casa.
7. El año pasado se me perdió/perdieron ____.

Follow-up B: As appropriate, ask follow-up questions such as *Entonces, ¿qué pasó? ¿Qué hizo Ud.?*, etc.

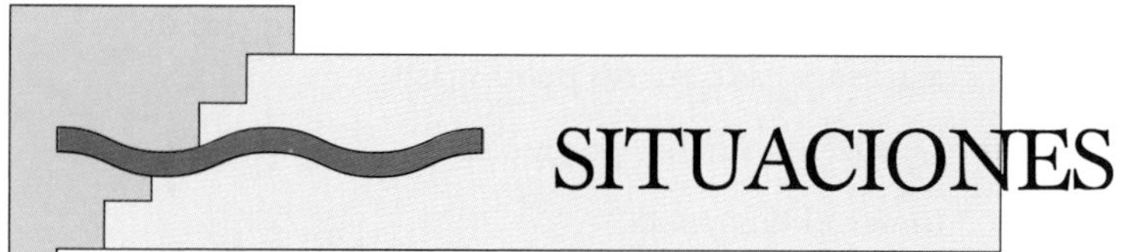

SITUACIONES

Situaciones: See IM for suggestions, additional exercises, and supplementary dialogues and exercises.

Incidentes de la vida diaria

En una mesa o dondequiera° que sea — *wherever*

¡Oh! Discúlpeme. ¡Qué torpeza°! Permítame que le limpie la camisa. — *clumsiness*
—No se preocupe. No es nada.
—Lo siento muchísimo.

En el autobús o en el metro

—Sígueme.° Hay un sitio en el fondo.° — *Follow me. / back*
—¡Hombre! Es imposible llegar allí.
—¿Tú crees? Mira... Con permiso... Disculpe, señora, fue sin querer... Con permiso... Perdone... Permiso, gracias... (Al pisar° a una señora.) ¡Huy! Perdón, lo siento, señora. — Al... *Upon stepping on*
—¡Mal educado°! — *How rude!*

Al llegar tarde a una cita

—¡Uf! Lo siento. Créeme que no era mi intención llegar tan tarde. De verdad. Fue culpa° del autobús. — *fault*
—Anda°... No te voy a regañar° por diez minutos de retraso. No importa. — *Come on / scold*

Al olvidar° algo

—Oye, ¿trajiste los apuntes° que te pedí?
—¿Los apuntes? ¿Qué apuntes? ¡Ay! Si ya decía yo que se me olvidaba algo. Se me ha pasado por completo.° Lo lamento. Te los llevo el lunes, sin falla.°
—Bueno, bueno... No es para tanto.°

Al... *When you forget*
(*class*) *notes*
Se... *I completely forgot about it.* / ¿ ?
para... ¿ ?

Conversación

Con un compañero (una compañera) practique las conversaciones anteriores. Trate de variar las expresiones de cortesía. Si quiere, lea primero **A propósito**... en la página 345.

Notas culturales: Más sobre la cortesía

El pisarle los pies a alguien, sobre todo en el transporte público, es algo que ocurre todos los días. En **Situaciones**, la señora que llamó «¡Mal educado!» al joven que le pisó los pies tal vez se exaltó demasiado (*got too worked up*), pero usó una frase hispánica muy típica para expresar su disgusto con el comportamiento (*behavior*) de alguien. La frase **mal educado** significa *ill mannered, rude, poorly brought up*, lo opuesto de **educado**, que significa *well mannered, polite, cultured.*

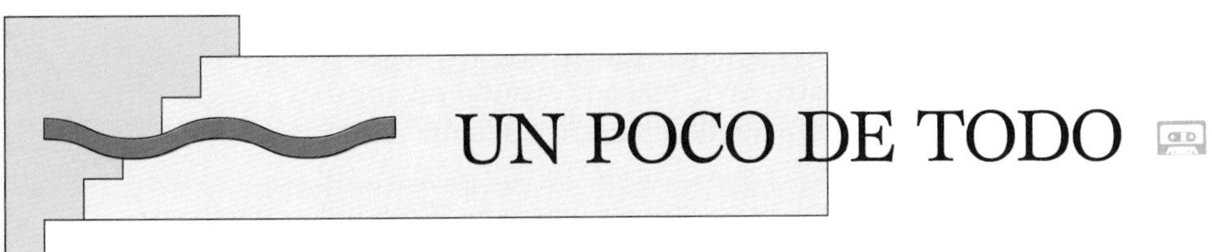

Note A: Students will use preterite tense verbs with the dehydrated items, then imperfect tense verbs to complete the sentences.

A. Use the following words in the order given to form incomplete sentences that relate a completed action in the past. What verb tense will you use? Then use the phrases given below to complete each sentence logically, describing the background circumstances for the action. What tense will you use in the second part of the sentence?

1. anoche / señora Ochoa / servir / cena / temprano / porque...
2. durante / cena / niños / reírse / mucho / porque...
3. (nosotros) apagar / luces / diez / porque...
4. Cecilia / acostarse / tarde / porque...
5. Lorenzo / se / olvidar / poner / despertador / porque...
6. a la mañana siguiente / (nosotros) no salir / para / montañas / porque...

Posibles circunstancias: hacer buen tiempo, estar muy contento, estar muy distraído, todos/tener mucha hambre, llegar tarde su esposo, nevar mucho, tener sueño y querer dormir, tener que terminar un trabajo, estar triste, haber una película interesante en la tele

Note B: Students will use imperfect tense verbs to complete the sentences.

B. Complete las oraciones lógicamente, usando un verbo para describir los sentimientos, la condición o las emociones de la persona nombrada. **¡OJO!** ¿Qué tiempo verbal se debe usar, el imperfecto o el pretérito?

1. A Cristina el trabajo para la clase de historia se le quedó en casa porque _____.
2. Ayer Roberto tropezó con un sillón y se cayó porque _____.
3. Cuando se le murió la abuela, Leopoldo _____.
4. Cuando se despidió de su novio, Ángela _____.
5. Gregorio volvió temprano a casa anoche porque _____.
6. A Angelito se le rompió el reloj que le regalaron sus padres. Por eso (él) _____.
7. El niño se hizo mucho daño cuando se cayó en la calle. Por eso _____.
8. Alfonso se tomó dos aspirinas porque _____.

Note C: Students will use preterite tense verbs.

¿Por qué nos salen chichones?

Al recibir el cuerpo un golpe puede producirse la rotura de un vaso sanguíneo, con la consiguiente salida de sangre que circula a través de él. Esta sangre, como es sabido, posee una presión determinada. Sucede además que cuando se produce un traumatismo, la afluencia de sangre en esa zona es aún mayor, debido a la respuesta que el organismo ofrece ante cualquier agresión de este tipo.

A consecuencia de esto, la sangre comienza a hacerse un hueco entre los tejidos. En caso de que el golpe haya tenido lugar en una zona próxima a algún hueso (cráneo, espinillas, rodilla, etc.), la sangre presionará hacia afuera –dada la resistencia que ofrece el hueso– produciéndose un abultamiento hasta que la flexibilidad de la piel lo permita. Aun entonces, la sangre seguirá presionando hasta igualar su presión con la de la sangre que circula por la arteria. A partir de entonces, la sangre liberada comienza a descomponerse en otras sustancias más simples y a ser reabsorbida mediante un proceso metabólico. A esta fase corresponden los sucesivos cambios de color de la piel: rojo, azul, verde, amarillo... Y en unos cuantos días, todo vuelve a su estado normal. ■

C. Complete estas oraciones lógicamente, usando un verbo para contar una acción. **¡OJO!** ¿Qué tiempo verbal se debe usar, el imperfecto o el pretérito?

1. La semana pasada yo estaba muy ocupado/a (preocupado/a). Por eso yo (no) _____.
2. Era tarde y tenía que estudiar más todavía. Por eso yo _____.
3. Eran las cuatro de la mañana cuando mi amigo/a _____.
4. Yo estaba manejando mi carro a setenta millas por hora. Por eso el policía _____.
5. El carro estaba en un lugar marcado «Prohibido estacionarse». Por eso yo lo _____.
6. Me dolían los pies. Por eso yo _____.
7. Todos tenían mucha sed. Por eso yo les _____.
8. Me dolía la cabeza. Por eso yo _____.

Note CH: This retelling of the Snow White story is an authentic version from Spain. You and students may be familiar with other versions of the story. Encourage students to add additional details.

CH. **Blancanieves y los siete enanitos.** Complete the following fairy tale with the correct form of the infinitives—preterite (**P**) or imperfect (**I**)—as indicated. When an adjective is given in parentheses, give the adverb derived from it. When two possibilities are given in parentheses, select the correct word.

The narrative starts with the Spanish equivalent of the words typically used to begin to tell a tale. Can you guess the meaning of the phrase? In addition, you should be able to guess the meaning of the words marked with "¿ ?," from context and on the basis of the drawings and your prior knowledge of the story.

Érase una vez una linda princesita blanca como la azucena,° hija de un rey casado por segunda vez.
lily

Su madrastra,° la reina,° (*tener:* I[1]) un espejo mágico. (*Diario*[2]) la reina le (*preguntar:* I[3]) al espejo:—¿Quién es la más hermosa?
¿ ? / ¿ ?

Un día el espejo le (*contestar:* P[4]):—¡Blancanieves! Llena° de envidia y de maldad° la reina (*mandar:* P[5]) a un criado que matara° a la princesa.
Full / ¿ ? / que... *to kill*

El criado la (*llevar:* P[6]) al bosque° y por compasión la (*dejar:* P[7]) abandonada. Una ardilla° la (*llevar:* P[8]) (*alegre*[9]) a una casita.
¿ ? / ¿ ?

En la casita (*vivir:* I[10]) siete enanitos. Cuando (*ellos: volver:* P[11]) a casa por la noche, (*encontrar:* P[12]) a Blancanieves dormida° en sus camitas.
¿ ?

En el palacio, la madrastra (*volver:* P[13]) a consultar el espejo:—Y ahora, ¿quién es la más bella°? El espejo le (*contestar:* P[14]) sin vacilar:—¡Blancanieves!
¿ ?

Por eso la reina (*planear:* P[15]) matarla. (*Llegar:* P[16]) a la casa de los enanitos una tarde, disfrazada° de vieja, y le (*ofrecer:* P[17]) a Blancanieves una manzana envenenada.°
¿ ? / ¿ ?

Cuando (*ella: morderla:*° P[18]), Blancanieves (*caer:* P[19]) desvanecida.° Por la noche, los enanitos la (*encontrar:* P[20]) tendida° en el suelo.
to bite it / ¿ ? / *lying*

Un príncipe muy guapo, quien (*enterarse:*° P[21]) de lo que (*ocurrir:* P[22]), (*ir:* P[23]) a verla. Cuando el príncipe la (*besar:*° P[24]), Blancanieves (*recobrarse:* P[25]) (*inmediato*[26]).
to find out / ¿ ?

Enamorados,° los dos (*salir:* P[27]) (*feliz*[28]) hacia el castillo del príncipe, donde (*casarse:* P[29]) con gran alegría de los enanitos.
¿ ?

¿Quién lo dijo?

1. ¡Ay! ¿Qué vamos a hacer? ¡Parece que se murió!
2. Sé que no te gusta que me vuelva a casar. Lo siento sinceramente.
3. No sabía que la manzana estaba envenenada.

4. ¡Te quiero desesperadamente! Quiero que te cases conmigo.
5. Yo estaba más contenta antes de la segunda boda de papá.
6. Ay, aquí viene otra vez a hacerme la misma pregunta... ¡Qué molestia!
7. No importa lo que me diga la reina. No lo puedo hacer.
8. ¿Cómo es posible que me conteste de la misma manera? Debe ser que todavía está viva...
9. En esta casita viven unos amigos míos que te van a gustar.
10. No hay nadie más linda que nuestra Blancanieves.

VOCABULARIO

Theme vocabulary previously listed as active: *la mano*

VERBOS

acabar to finish; to run out of
acordarse (ue) de to remember
apagar to turn off (*lights or appliances*)
caer (caigo) to fall; **caerse** to fall down
cambiar de lugar to move (*something*)
caminar to walk
casarse (con) to marry
doler (ue) to hurt
equivocarse to be wrong, make a mistake
hacerse daño to hurt oneself
pegar to hit, strike
quedar to remain, be left
romper to break
sufrir muchas presiones to be under a lot of pressure
tropezar (ie) con to bump into

¡HUY, PERDÓN!

discúlpeme pardon me
fue sin querer it was unintentional
levantarse con el pie izquierdo to get up on the wrong side of the bed
perdone pardon
¡qué mala suerte! what bad luck!

ALGUNAS PARTES DEL CUERPO

el brazo arm
la cabeza head
el pie foot
la pierna leg

OTROS SUSTANTIVOS

la aspirina aspirin
la época era, time (*period*)
la escuela school
la llave key
la multa fine, ticket
la tarea homework
la taza cup

ADJETIVOS

actual current
chico/a small
distraído/a absent-minded
lento/a slow
lindo/a pretty
loco/a crazy
propio/a own, one's own
torpe clumsy

PALABRAS ADICIONALES

además besides, in addition
de niño/a as a child
de verdad really
de vez en cuando from time to time
en aquel entonces back then, in those days
solamente only

Frases útiles para la comunicación

(Eso) Me da igual.	(*That's*) It's all the same to me.
No (me) importa (nada).	It doesn't matter (*to me*) (*at all*).
No vale la pena (molestarse por eso).	It's not worth it (*to get upset about that*).
Dime (algo, una cosa). (*fam.*)	Tell me (*something, one thing*).

OPTIONAL SECTION

UN PASO MÁS 11

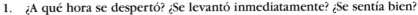

Suggestion A: Do as written assignment. Students answer questions and then develop them into a paragraph.

Follow-up: *La vergüenza* (embarrassment): Conduct as interview of appropriate student. **Note:** Not all students will be comfortable answering questions; choose student carefully, perhaps consulting him/her beforehand. You may wish to initiate follow-up by telling about embarrassing incident in your own life. *¿Cuándo fue la última vez que Ud. realmente tuvo vergüenza?* **1.** *¿Dónde estaba Ud.?* **2.** *¿Estaba solo/a o con otras personas? ¿Lo/La estaban mirando/escuchando?* **3.** *¿Qué hizo Ud. o qué le pasó que le causó vergüenza?* **4.** *¿Cómo reaccionaron los demás? ¿Se rieron de Ud.? ¿Le dijeron algo o trataron de no darle importancia al incidente?* **5.** *¿Cuál fue la reacción de Ud.? ¿Se puso rojo/a? ¿Salió corriendo? ¿Tuvo que explicar su acción o disculparse* (to excuse yourself)? **6.** *¿Le contó Ud. más tarde la historia a otra persona o se la guardó como secreto?*

▲ Actividad A. Me levanté con el pie izquierdo

A mí... nada me sale a derechas.°

sale... *turns out right*

Hay días en que nada sale a derechas, como dice el paracaidista (*parachutist*) del dibujo. Usando las siguientes preguntas como guía, describa Ud. un día de la vida de una persona que se levantó con el pie izquierdo. Puede describir un día de su propia vida o de la vida de otra persona—un amigo (una amiga), un actor/una actriz, una ama de casa, el presidente, etcétera.

1. ¿A qué hora se despertó? ¿Se levantó inmediatamente? ¿Se sentía bien?
2. ¿Tuvo tiempo para comer y vestirse bien? ¿Le faltaba algo? ¿Qué no podía encontrar?
3. ¿Hubo problemas con los otros miembros de la familia? ¿con el coche?
4. ¿Qué tiempo hacía? ¿Llovía? ¿Nevaba?
5. ¿Dónde estaba por la mañana? ¿por la tarde? ¿Qué le pasó en cada lugar?
6. ¿Se le perdió algo?
7. ¿Tuvo problemas con los amigos (el director, los otros actores, los niños)?
8. ¿Recordó todo lo que tenía que hacer ese día? ¿Se le olvidó algo?

A propósito... Extending and Accepting Apologies

Familiarity with the following expressions can help smooth over embarrassing moments. Use the expressions given below on the left when you need to apologize to someone. You can follow these phrases by a brief explanation of what caused the problem. To accept someone else's apology graciously, use one of the expressions on the right.

Perdón, me equivoqué.	Lo hice sin querer.	Está bien.
Perdón, es que...	No quise decir eso.	No se preocupe.°
¿Me perdona(s)?	Perdón. No sabía que...	No te preocupes.
Lo siento mucho.	No sé qué decirle.	No importa.
¡Cuánto lo siento!	Mil disculpas.	Tranquilo/a.
Me equivoqué de...		No es para tanto.
Fue sin querer.		

Don't worry.

▲ Actividad B. ¡Huy, perdón!

How would you respond in each of the following situations? Keep in mind the persons involved, the place or situation, and the degree of severity of what you have done.

1. En el autobús, Ud. le pisa el pie a una viejecita. Ella grita, «¡Ay!» y todos los pasajeros se vuelven (*turn around*) para mirarlos.
2. Ud. bosteza (*yawn*), haciendo mucho ruido, en la clase de español.
3. En una fiesta, Ud. tropieza con una silla y se le cae la bebida encima del vestido nuevo de la anfitriona (*hostess*).
4. Se le olvidó el cumpleaños de su (novio/a, hermano/a, etcétera).
5. En la cafetería Ud. habla con unos amigos nuevos. Al mencionarse el nombre de alguien, Ud. inmediatamente dice, «¿Ésa? Es tonta y aburrida.» Una de las personas que lo/la escucha dice, «¡Qué insulto! Es mi hermana.»
6. Ud. le pregunta a un amigo por (*about*) el padre de él. Su amigo le contesta: «¿No lo sabías? Mi padre murió en un accidente hace dos semanas.»

▲ Actividad C. Refranes

Proverbs often focus on extremes—the very good and the very bad aspects of life, the positive and the negative. Tell why you agree or disagree with one of the following proverbs, or tell about an incident from your own life that illustrates it.

1. Después de la tempestad (*storm*) viene la calma.
2. Con amor y aguardiente (*brandy*), nada se siente.
3. Cada día que amanece (*dawns*), el número de tontos crece (*grows*).
4. Quien (*He/She who*) nunca subió no puede caer.
5. Poco a poco se va lejos.
6. No hay mal que por bien no venga.

LECTURA CULTURAL

Lectura: See IM for suggestions and additional exercises and activities.

Las supersticiones

¿Ud. piensa que sólo los niños creen que el mundo es un sitio mágico? ¡Está equivocado! Casi todos nosotros—aun cuando no lo admitimos—tenemos algunas creencias que no se diferencian en mucho de las creencias infantiles que nos hacen sonreír cuando las escuchamos de boca de los niños. En boca de adultos, estas creencias se llaman supersticiones.

Hay muchas creencias supersticiosas que son comunes en las culturas hispanas y anglosajonas. ¿Reconoce Ud. las siguientes?

- Trae mala suerte...
  - pasar debajo de una escalera
  - derramar sal
  - el número trece
  - abrir un paraguas dentro de la casa
  - romper un espejo
  - cruzarse con un gato negro, sobre todo en la oscuridad.° *dark*
- Trae buena suerte...
  - derramar el vino en el mantel° *tablecloth*
  - encontrar un trébol de cuatro hojas° *leaves*
  - cruzar el dedo° índice y el mayor *finger*

Un remedio bastante usado en el mundo hispánico parece ser el de la escoba.° Cuando una visita se alarga mucho más de lo que se desea, se pone una escoba detrás de la puerta, preferiblemente de la puerta de entrada. Dentro de poco tiempo la visita se irá.° (¡OJO! En algunos países, también es necesario echar° sal al fuego.°)

broom
se... *will go away*
to throw / *fire*

Aquí hay otras creencias y supersticiones. Éstas son características del país de la persona que las explica. Claro que, como también ocurre en los Estados Unidos, hay creencias diferentes en distintas partes del mundo hispánico.

«El día de mala suerte en España no es el viernes trece sino el martes trece. Recuerdo que la primera vez que vine a este país, estaba un poco asustado° de viajar porque era martes trece, pero pensé que llegaría° a los Estados Unidos en un día en que eso no representaba nada. Entonces, me calmé. También recuerdo cuando pusieron la película *Viernes 13* en España y casi nadie sabía que eso era como el martes trece español.»

José Luis Suárez, España

scared
I would arrive

«En mi país abundan las vacas° y, por lo tanto,° también abundan los <u>huesos</u> y esqueletos de vacas muertas. Éstos despiden° fósforo de alguna forma y durante la noche se pueden ver, si hay viento, efectos parecidos a una estrella fugaz.° Se creía, y en el campo todavía se cree, que son almas° de personas que tuvieron una mala vida y todavía penan,° caminando por los campos.»

Eduardo Cabrera, Uruguay

cows / por... *for that reason*
give off
estrella... *shooting star*
souls / sufren

Comprensión

Aquí hay algunas supersticiones más del mundo hispánico. ¿Qué tipo de suerte traen, buena o mala? (Las respuestas se dan al pie de la página.)

1. tener un buho (*owl*) vivo o una representación de uno (El Salvador)
2. llevar ropa de color rosa (algunas partes de México)
3. matar a un gato (El Salvador)
4. barrerle los pies a una señorita (varios países)
5. ver un cuervo (*crow*) o cualquier pájaro nocturno (varios países)
6. posársele (*land on*) a uno una mariposa (*butterfly*) (España)

Para escribir

¿Qué supersticiones tiene Ud.? Piénselo bien antes de decir que no tiene ninguna. ¿Hay algún objeto que siempre lleve (en la bolsa o en la cartera) que cree que trae buena suerte? ¿Tiene algunas costumbres características antes de los exámenes? ¿antes de entrar en una conversación o situación difícil? ¿Tiene alguna superstición algún miembro de su familia? En tres o cuatro oraciones, describa sus supersticiones o las de su familia. Si está seguro/a de no tener ninguna, trate de explicar por qué no las tiene.

Respuestas: 1. buena 2. mala (La persona puede tener una tragedia de muerte.) 3. mala 4. mala (para su futuro matrimonio) 5. mala 6. buena 7. buena

CAPÍTULO DOCE

LA SALUD

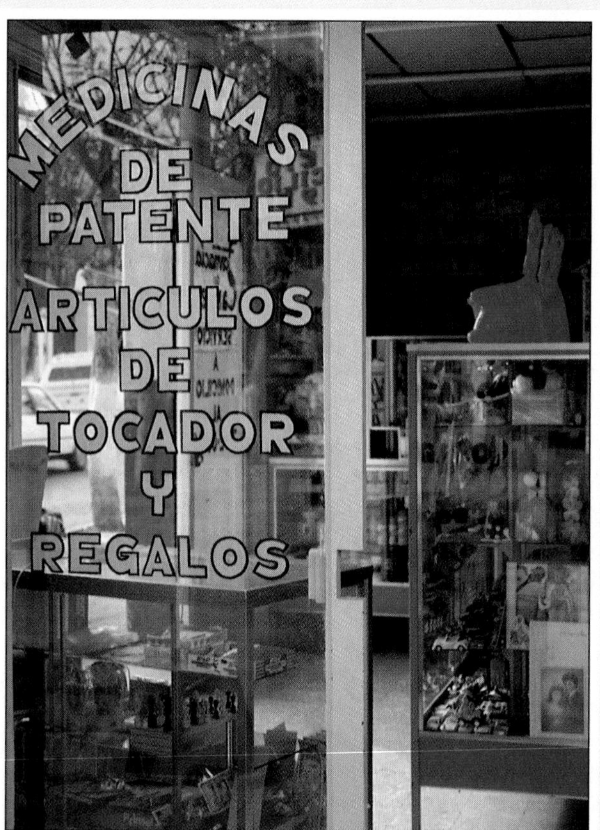

México

▲ **¿Cómo te encuentras?**

—¿Es cierto que estuviste enfermo ayer?

—Sí, me dolía todo el cuerpo y no pude dormir nada anoche.

—Bueno, por lo menos ya estás un poco mejor hoy, ¿no?

—¡Qué va! Esta mañana todavía tenía fiebre.

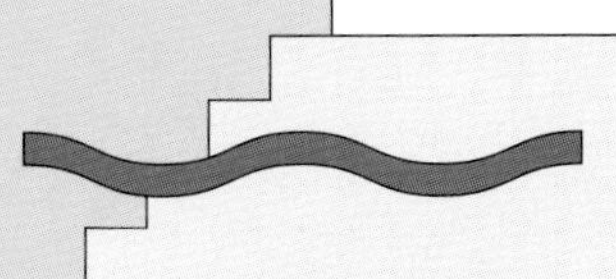

VOCABULARIO: PREPARACIÓN

• See also [video] and [audio cassette]

Vocabulario: Preparación:
• See detailed supplementary materials for this section bound into the back of this Annotated Instructor's Edition.
• See model for vocabulary presentation and other materials in Supplementary *Vocabulario: Preparación* Materials, chapter by chapter, IM.

La salud° y el bienestar°

health / well-being

caminar	to walk
comer bien	to eat well
correr	to run
dejar de + *inf.*	to stop (*doing something*)
dormir lo suficiente	to sleep enough
hacer ejercicio	to exercise, get exercise
llevar gafas/lentes (de contacto)	to wear glasses/contact lenses
llevar una vida tranquila (sana)	to lead a calm (healthy) life
practicar deportes	to participate in sports

Visadron®
Combate el enrojecimiento y la irritación ocular.
Usar los medicamentos adecuadamente y siguiendo sus instrucciones.

Más partes del cuerpo

la boca	mouth	**la nariz**	nose
el corazón	heart	**el ojo**	eye
el estómago	stomach	**los pulmones**	lungs
la garganta	throat		

Variation A: *¿Qué verbos asocia Ud. con cada parte del cuerpo?*

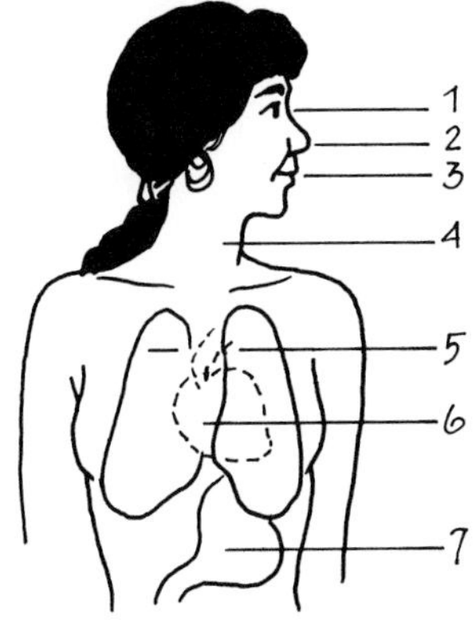

A. ¿Cómo se llaman las partes del cuerpo indicadas en el dibujo?

B. Imagine que Ud. es Richard Simmons; explique cada una de las siguientes oraciones.

Variation B: "Richard" gives answers in form of *Ud.* commands.

MODELO: Se debe comer bien. →
RICHARD: ¡Sí, eso es! Eso quiere decir (*means*) que es necesario comer muchas verduras, que...

1. Se debe dormir lo suficiente todas las noches.
   RICHARD: ¡Exacto! Esto significa que... También...
2. Hay que hacer ejercicio.
3. Es necesario llevar una vida tranquila.
4. En general, uno debe cuidarse mucho.

Variation C: Do as whole-class discussion.

C. **Entrevista.** Use las siguientes frases como guía para entrevistar a un compañero (una compañera) de clase. ¿Cree él/ella que estas acciones son buenas o malas para la salud? Pídale que explique su punto de vista. ¿Traen algún beneficio para la salud de uno? ¿Hacen algún daño? ¿En qué parte del cuerpo?

Extension C: 13. *correr seis millas todos los días* **14.** *comer menos de tres comidas al día* **15.** *dormir diez a doce horas al día*

1. fumar tres o cuatro cigarrillos al día
2. fumar dos paquetes de cigarrillos al día
3. preocuparse mucho y no descansar
4. gritar (*to shout*) y enojarse con frecuencia
5. leer con poca luz
6. hacer ejercicio sin llevar zapatos
7. salir sin chaqueta cuando hace frío
8. no llevar las gafas—¡por vanidad!—aunque uno tiene miopía o astigmatismo
9. correr todos los días hasta el punto de agotarse (*to exhaust oneself*)
10. beber uno o dos vasos de vino al día
11. dejar de tomar bebidas alcohólicas por completo
12. dejar de comer por completo para adelgazar (*to lose weight*)

En el consultorio° del médico

°*office*

el/la enfermero/a	nurse	**enfermarse**	to get sick
el/la paciente	patient	**guardar cama**	to stay in bed
congestionado/a	congested, stuffed-up	**ponerle una inyección**	to give someone a shot
mareado/a	dizzy, nauseated	**resfriarse**	to get/catch a cold
el antibiótico	antibiotic	**respirar**	to breathe
el jarabe	(cough) syrup	**sacar (la lengua)**	to stick out (the tongue)
la pastilla	pill	**tener dolor (de)**	to have a pain (in)
la receta	prescription	**tener fiebre**	to have a fever
el resfriado	cold	**tomarle la temperatura**	to take someone's temperature
la tos	cough	**toser**	to cough

A. **Estudio de palabras.** Complete las siguientes oraciones con una palabra de la misma familia de la palabra en *letras cursivas.*

1. Si me *resfrío*, tengo _____.
2. La *respiración* ocurre cuando alguien _____.
3. Si me _____, estoy *enfermo/a*; un(a) _____ me toma la temperatura.
4. Cuando alguien *tose*, se oye una _____.
5. Si me *duele* el estómago, tengo un _____ de estómago.

Extension B: 8. *los cigarrillos* **9.** *el amor* **10.** *conversar*

B. **Asociaciones.** ¿Qué partes del cuerpo asocia Ud. con las siguientes palabras?

1. un ataque
2. la digestión
3. comer
4. respirar
5. congestionado
6. ver
7. mareado

Note C: Subjunctive syntax in some items.

C. Describa Ud. la situación de estas personas. ¿Dónde están y con quiénes? ¿Qué síntomas tienen? ¿Qué les recomienda Ud.?

1. Anamari está muy bien de salud. Nunca le duele(n) _____. Nunca tiene _____. Siempre _____. Es bueno que _____.
2. Martín tiene un resfriado. Le duele(n) _____. Tiene _____. El médico le dice que _____. Le va a _____. Es mejor que _____.
3. Inés tiene apendicitis. Le duele(n) _____. Tiene _____. El médico y la enfermera mandan que _____. Es necesario que _____.

Suggestion CH: Students rehearse dialogue and act it out in front of class. After several times, instructor acts as either doctor or patient and varies situation, interacting with one of better students in class.

Note CH: Conversion formulas:
- A meter equals 39.39 inches, and a kilo equals 2.2 pounds.
- To convert Celsius to Fahrenheit, use the formula: F = 9/5C + 32.

CH. Ud no se siente bien y va al consultorio del médico. Complete el diálogo entre Ud. y el médico.

PACIENTE: Buenas tardes, doctor.
DOCTOR: Buenas tardes. ¿Qué le pasa? ¿Qué tiene?
PACIENTE: Es que me _____ muy mal. Me _____ la cabeza y tengo una _____ muy alta.
DOCTOR: Entonces, ¿tiene un resfriado?
PACIENTE: Bueno, Ud. es el médico.
DOCTOR: ¿Se tomó la temperatura antes de venir?
PACIENTE: No, pero la _____ me la tomó y tenía 38,5.
DOCTOR: ¿Tiene dolor de estómago? ¿Se siente _____?
PACIENTE: No, pero respiro con dificultad; estoy muy _____. Toso tanto que me duelen también los _____. Es que me duele el _____ entero.
DOCTOR: Vamos a ver. Abra Ud. la _____, por favor, y _____ la lengua. Hmm... tiene la _____ bastante (*rather*) inflamada. Ahora la respiración... _____ Ud. profundamente... Me parece que está bien. ¿Tiene alergia a los antibióticos?
PACIENTE: No, no creo.
DOCTOR: Bueno, aquí tiene Ud. una _____. Vaya a la farmacia y compre este _____ para la tos. Tómeselo cuatro veces al día. Para la fiebre, tome un par de _____ cada cuatro horas y este _____ para combatir la infección. Si todavía se siente mal la semana que viene, venga a verme otra vez. Y cuídese, ¿eh?
PACIENTE: Muchas gracias, doctor. Adiós.

Notas comunicativas: The Good News . . . The Bad News . . .

Use **lo** with the masculine singular form of an adjective to describe general qualities or characteristics.

lo bueno / lo malo   lo más importante   lo mejor / lo peor   lo mismo

This structure has a number of English equivalents, especially in colloquial speech.

lo bueno = the good thing/part/news, what's good

D. A nadie le gusta estar enfermo, pero también es cierto que, cuando no se trata de (*it's not a question of*) algo grave, el estar enfermo puede tener ventajas. Con un compañero (una compañera), conteste las siguientes preguntas. Luego compare sus respuestas con las de otros compañeros. ¿Quién pudo reunir el mayor número de ventajas y desventajas?

1. En su opinión, ¿qué es lo bueno de tener un resfriado muy grave? ¿Y lo malo?
2. Para un niño, ¿qué es lo bueno de tener fiebre y dolor de estómago? ¿Y lo malo?
3. Para un niño, ¿qué es lo malo de tener amigdalitis (*tonsilitis*)? ¿Y lo bueno?
4. ¿Qué es lo bueno de estar en el consultorio del médico / del dentista? ¿Y lo malo?

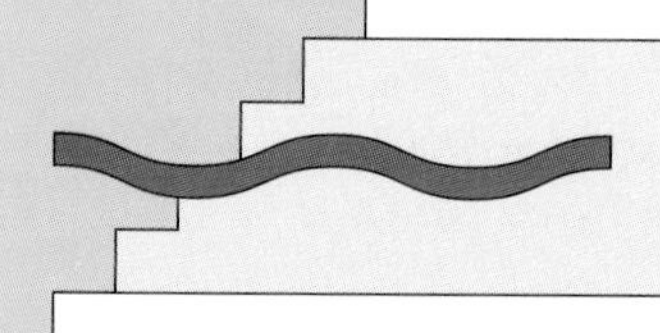

MINIDIÁLOGOS Y GRAMÁTICA

36. NARRATING IN THE PAST
Using the Preterite and Imperfect

Communicative objectives for 36: using both the preterite and the imperfect to talk about past events, tell complete stories, and so on

No es para tanto...

CARMEN: Yo no *sabía* lo que *tenía*, pero la doctora me lo *diagnosticó* en seguida.

PILAR: ¿Y qué te *dijo* que *tenías*?

CARMEN: Pues... que tengo insomnio... y que tengo los ojos muy irritados... Pero de todos modos todavía tengo que terminar las investigaciones para el proyecto que necesitan mañana en la oficina.

1. ¿Quién acaba de tener una consulta con la doctora?
2. ¿Pudo la doctora diagnosticar la enfermedad?
3. ¿Qué dijo la doctora que tenía Carmen?

Suggestion: Review preterite and imperfect forms quickly. **1.** *respirar: Ud.* **2.** *sacar: yo* **3.** *toser: nosotros* **4.** *romper: ellos* **5.** *ser: tú* **6.** *ir: nosotros* **7.** *querer: yo* **8.** *dormir: él* **9.** *jugar: yo* **10.** *poner: ellos* **11.** *despedirse: Ud.* **12.** *saber: nosotros*

It's not that serious... CARMEN: I didn't know what I had, but the doctor diagnosed it for me immediately. PILAR: And what did she say you had? CARMEN: Well . . . that I have insomnia . . . and that my eyes are very irritated . . . But in any case I still have to finish the research for the project (that) they need at the office tomorrow.

Ahora invente respuestas para las siguientes preguntas.

1. ¿Cuánto tiempo hace que no duerme bien Carmen?
2. ¿Por qué tiene los ojos muy irritados?
3. ¿Qué recomienda la doctora que haga?
4. ¿Qué quiere el jefe que Carmen haga?
5. ¿Qué cree Ud. que va a hacer ella?

When speaking about the past in English, you choose which past tense forms to use in a given context: *I wrote letters, I did write letters, I was writing letters, I used to write letters,* and so on. Usually only one or two of these options will convey exactly the idea you want to express. Similarly, in many Spanish sentences either the preterite or the imperfect can be used, but the meaning of the sentence will be different, depending on which tense you use. The choice between the preterite and imperfect depends on the speaker's perspective: how does he or she view the action or state of being?

Suggestions:
- **Note:** This section focuses on uses of preterite versus uses of imperfect and provides practice in deciding which to use. Students have been using both in controlled situations for a number of Chs.
- **Emphasis:** Importance of speaker's perspective. Many sentences are equally "correct" in either imperfect or preterite, but will "mean" something different to native speaker of Spanish.

Optional presentation: Every action (or state) can be seen as having three phases or aspects: a beginning, a middle, and an end. When focus is on the beginning of an action or on its ending, the preterite is used. When focus is on the middle, or on the repetitive nature of an action, the imperfect is used.

Note: Beginning of action is also usually expressed with preterite: *Empezó a llover. Comenzaron el ejercicio.* Exception: *Isabel empezaba el ejercicio cuando su hermano entró.*

A. The PRETERITE is used to report *completed* actions or states of being in the past, no matter how long they lasted or took to complete; focus may be on the beginning or end of the action or state. The IMPERFECT is used, however, if the *ongoing* or *habitual nature* of the action is stressed, with no reference to its beginning or termination.

Escribí las cartas.	*I wrote (did write) the letters.*
Escribía las cartas cuando...	*I was writing the letters when . . .*
Carlos **fue** estudiante.	*Carlos was a student* (at that time).
Carlos **era** estudiante.	*Carlos was (used to be) a student.*
Anita **estuvo** nerviosa.	*Anita was (became) nervous.*
Anita **estaba** nerviosa.	*Anita was (used to be) nervous.*

B. *A series of completed actions that take place in sequence* will be expressed in the PRETERITE (unless it refers to habitual actions).

Optional B: Contrast meaning of *pensó* (he thought, it occurred to him) versus *pensaba* (he was of the opinion, planned/intended to). Use *creer* forms in a similar contrast.

Me **levanté**, me **vestí** y **desayuné**.	*I got up, got dressed, and ate breakfast.*

Actions or states *in progress* are expressed with the IMPERFECT. The IMPERFECT is also used to express most *descriptions; physical, mental, and emotional states; the time* (with **ser**); and *age* (with **tener**).

Escribía las cartas **mientras** Ana **leía**.	*I was writing letters while Ann was reading.*
Estaban cansados.	*They were tired.*
Eran las ocho.	*It was eight o'clock.*
Tenía ocho años.	*She was eight years old.*

C. Certain words and expressions are frequently associated with the preterite, others with the imperfect.

Words often associated with the preterite:

ayer, anteayer, anoche	el año pasado, el lunes pasado, . . .
una vez, dos veces (*twice*), . . .	de repente (*suddenly*)

Words often associated with the imperfect:

todos los días, todos los lunes, . . .
siempre, frecuentemente
mientras
de niño/a, de joven
was ____*-ing*, *were* ____*-ing* (in English)
used to, *would* (when *would* implies *used to* in English)

¡OJO! The words do not automatically cue either tense, however. The most important consideration is the meaning that the speaker wishes to convey.

Ayer cenamos temprano.	*Yesterday we had dinner early.*
Ayer cenábamos cuando Juan llamó.	*Yesterday we were having dinner when Juan called.*
De niño jugaba al fútbol.	*He played football as a child.*
De niño empezó a jugar al fútbol.	*He began to play football as a child.*

[Práctica A–B]

Emphasis: "Cue" words associated with preterite and imperfect. Discuss how words relate to concepts of preterite and imperfect and thus "cue" tense.

¡OJO! Dos veces (*tres veces, etc.*) is associated with preterite (not imperfect) because it refers to completed past actions. Contrast with *todos los días* (open-ended repetition): *dos veces* is repeated but not habitual.

CH. Remember the special English equivalents of the preterite forms of **saber**, **conocer**, **poder**, and **querer**: **supe** (*I found out*), **conocí** (*I met*), **pude** (*I could and did*), **no pude** (*I couldn't and didn't*), **quise** (*I tried*), **no quise** (*I refused*).

[Práctica C]

Point out: English equivalents of preterite of *saber*, *conocer*, *poder*, and *querer* vs. base meaning of inf. in imperfect.

D. The preterite and the imperfect frequently occur in the same sentence.

Miguel **estudiaba** cuando **sonó** el teléfono.	*Miguel was studying when the phone rang.*
Olivia **comió** tanto porque **tenía** mucha hambre.	*Olivia ate so much because she was very hungry.*

In the first sentence the imperfect tells what was happening when another action—conveyed by the preterite—broke the continuity of the ongoing activity. In the second sentence, the preterite reports the action that took place because of a condition, described by the imperfect, that was in progress or in existence at that time.

E. The preterite and imperfect are also used together in the presentation of an event. The preterite narrates the action while the imperfect sets the stage, describes the conditions that caused the action, or emphasizes the continuing nature of a particular action.

[Práctica CH–E]

Optional: Continuation of preterite/imperfect discussion: *Estos dos tiempos dan imágenes muy diferentes de una acción. Si Ud. dice, por ejemplo, «Cuando visité a mi tío, me desperté a las seis de la mañana», yo entiendo que Ud. lo visitó solamente una vez. En cambio, si Ud. dice: «Cuando visitaba a mi tío, me despertaba a las seis de la mañana», entiendo que iba a visitar a su tío con cierta frecuencia y que habla de algo rutinario que ocurría en todas sus visitas. Las dos oraciones son gramaticalmente correctas, pero sólo Ud. puede saber cuál comunica «la verdad». Si Ud. dice, «Ayer por la tarde íbamos a la tienda», su oyente espera que Ud. siga hablando, que le cuente qué pasó mientras iban. Normalmente no lo va a interrumpir con un comentario. En cambio, si Ud. dice, «Ayer* *fuimos a la tienda por la tarde», su oyente puede interrumpirlo con una pregunta porque él va a creer que Ud. ya acabó una parte de su narración. Otra vez, las dos oraciones son «correctas». El uso del imperfecto o del pretérito depende totalmente de lo que Ud. quiere expresar.*

Preliminary Exercise: *¿Pretérito o imperfecto?* Have students give reason for each choice. **1.** She used to eat eggs every day. **2.** I ate breakfast, brushed my teeth, and left for the university. **3.** He was tall and blond. **4.** She was playing the piano. **5.** They began to sing. **6.** Thomas was playing tennis while I was studying. **7.** It was three o'clock. **8.** The car was yellow and black.

Suggestion A: Students give the reasons for their choices.

Práctica

A. Give the preterite or the imperfect of the verbs in parentheses, basing your decision on the clues in the sentences.

1. Cuando (*ser*) niños, Jorge y yo (*vivir*) en la Argentina. Siempre (*ir*) al Mar del Plata para pasar la Navidad. Allí casi siempre (*quedarse*) en el Hotel Fénix.
2. ¡(*Ser*) las once de la noche cuando de repente se nos (*apagar*) todas las luces de la casa! (Yo: *dejar*) de leer y (*levantarse*) para investigar la causa del incidente.
3. Antonio (*trabajar*) en aquella farmacia todos los lunes. ¿No lo (*ver*) tú allí alguna vez?
4. La tía Anita (*resfriarse*) la semana pasada pero (*guardar*) cama y ahora se siente mucho mejor.
5. ¡Qué mala suerte tengo! El año pasado (*enfermarse*) durante las vacaciones. (*Estar*) muy mal durante todo el viaje.
6. El niño (*toser*) mientras la enfermera le (*hablar*). La madre del niño (*esperar*) pacientemente. Por fin (*venir*) la doctora. Le (*tomar*) la temperatura, le (*examinar*) la garganta y le (*dar*) un jarabe.

Note B: preterite in the questions (first item in each pair), imperfect in the answers (second item in each pair).

B. **Situaciones.** With another student, ask and answer questions based on the cues. The questions ask for an explanation of an action. What tense should be used in them? The answers explain the reason for the actions. What tense do they require?

En un restaurante: El dueño habla con un camarero torpe.

1. ¿por qué / irse / sin pedir nada / esos clientes ?
   porque / yo / no / atenderlos / como / deber
2. ¿por qué / se le / caer / vasos ?
   porque / llevar / mucho / en / bandeja (*tray*)
3. ¿por qué / equivocarse / tanto / con / pedidos (*orders*) ?
   porque / no saber / bien / detalles / de / menú

En casa: Los padres de un niño le hablan sobre su comportamiento.

4. ¿por qué / dormirse / en clase / hoy ?
   porque / tener / mucho / sueño
5. ¿por qué / se te / olvidar / hacer / tarea / para hoy ?
   porque / estar / distraído / con / nuevo perrito
6. ¿por qué / reírse / tanto / que / maestra / mandarte / a / oficina / de / director ?
   porque / mi / amigos / hacer / cosas cómicas

Note C: Emphasis is on *saber, conocer, querer,* and *poder.*

C. **Los hijos de los Quintero.** ¿Cómo se dice en español?

1. When I met Mr. and Mrs. Quintero, I already knew their son.
2. He knew how to read when he was five.

3. And he could play the piano before starting (to go to) school.
4. They tried to teach their daughter to play when she was five.
5. But she refused to practice ten hours a (**al**) day.
6. How did you find all of that (**todo eso**) out?

Suggestion CH: Create brief additional narratives in Spanish and read to class. Students explain use of preterite vs. imperfect. Or ask students to write additional narratives, based on these models.

CH. Explain the reasons for the use of the preterite or the imperfect for each verb in the following paragraph.

Cuando Ester se levantó, hacía mucho frío en su apartamento. Cerró con cuidado todas las ventanas, pero todavía tenía frío. Parecía que la calefacción (*heat*) no funcionaba. Se preparó una taza de té, se puso otro suéter y llamó al dueño del edificio para decirle lo que pasaba. Éste le dijo que ya lo sabía y que un técnico iba a venir en seguida. Mientras Ester lo esperaba, llamó a su amiga, que vivía en el apartamento vecino, para saber qué estaba haciendo para abrigarse (*keep warm*).

Which Spanish past tense should be used to express each verb in the following paragraph? Explain why in each case.

We were walking down Fifth Street when we caught sight of him. He looked very tired and his clothes were very dirty. He said he was hungry and he asked us for money. We gave him all the money that we had because he was an old friend.

Emphasis D: Read the entire paragraph to "see where story is going" before decisions on preterite vs. imperfect can be made. Recall importance of speaker's perspective.

D. Read the following paragraph at least once to familiarize yourself with the sequence of events in it. Then read it again, giving the proper form of the verbs in parentheses in the preterite or the imperfect, according to the needs of each sentence and the context of the paragraph as a whole.

Rubén (*estar*) estudiando cuando Soledad (*entrar*) en el cuarto. Le (*preguntar*) a Rubén si (*querer*) ir al cine con ella. Rubén le (*decir*) que sí porque se (*sentir*) un poco aburrido con sus estudios. Los dos (*salir*) en seguida para el cine. (*Ver*) una película cómica y (*reírse*) mucho. Luego, como (*hacer*) frío, (*entrar*) en El Gato Negro y (*tomar*) un chocolate. (*Ser*) las dos de la mañana cuando por fin (*regresar*) a casa. Soledad (*acostarse*) inmediatamente porque (*estar*) cansada, pero Rubén (*empezar*) a estudiar otra vez.

Answer the following questions based on the paragraph about Rubén and Soledad. **¡OJO!** A question is not always answered in the same tense as that in which it is asked.

1. ¿Qué hacía Rubén cuando Soledad entró?
2. ¿Qué le preguntó Soledad a Rubén?
3. ¿Por qué dijo Rubén que sí?
4. ¿Les gustó la película? ¿Por qué?
5. ¿Por qué tomaron un chocolate?
6. ¿Regresaron a casa a las tres?
7. ¿Qué hicieron cuando llegaron a casa?

E. Read the following paragraphs once for meaning. Then read them again, giving the proper form of the verbs in parentheses in the present, preterite, or imperfect.

Durante mi segundo año en la universidad, yo (*conocer*) a Roberto en una clase. Pronto nos (*hacer*) muy buenos amigos. Roberto (*ser*) una persona muy generosa que (*organizar*) una fiesta en su apartamento todos los viernes. Todos nuestros amigos (*venir*). (*Haber*) muchas bebidas y comida, y todo el mundo (*hablar*) y (*bailar*) hasta muy tarde.

Una noche algunos de los vecinos de Roberto (*llamar*) a la policía y (*decir*) que nosotros (*hacer*) demasiado ruido. (*Venir*) un policía al apartamento y le (*decir*) a Roberto que la fiesta (*ser*) demasiado ruidosa. Nosotros no (*querer*) aguar (*to spoil*) la fiesta, pero ¿qué (*poder*) hacer? Todos nos (*despedir*) aunque (*ser*) solamente las once de la noche.

Aquella noche Roberto (*aprender*) algo importantísimo. Ahora cuando (*hacer*) una fiesta, siempre (*invitar*) a sus vecinos.

Suggestion E: Have students write *short*, simple paragraph using imperfect and preterite for homework. Choose best and "edit," making exercises on dittos or overhead transparencies with them. Paragraphs in Exercises D and E are based on actual student paragraphs.

Conversación

A. Dé Ud. sus impresiones del primer día de su primera clase universitaria. Use estas preguntas como guía.

1. ¿Qué hora era cuando llegó Ud. a la universidad? ¿Por qué llegó tan tarde/temprano?
2. ¿Cuál fue la clase? ¿A qué hora era la clase y dónde era?
3. ¿Vino Ud. a clase con alguien? ¿Ya tenía su libro de texto o lo compró después?
4. ¿Qué hizo Ud. después de entrar en la sala de clase? ¿Qué hacía el profesor (la profesora)?
5. ¿A quién conoció Ud. aquel día? ¿Ya conocía a algunos miembros de la clase? ¿A quiénes?
6. ¿Aprendió Ud. mucho durante la clase? ¿Ya lo sabía todo?
7. ¿Le gustó el profesor (la profesora)? ¿Por qué? ¿Cómo era?
8. ¿Cómo se sentía durante la clase? ¿nervioso/a? ¿aburrido/a? ¿cómodo/a? ¿Por qué?
9. ¿Les dio tarea el profesor (la profesora)? ¿Pudo Ud. hacerla fácilmente?
10. ¿Cuánto tiempo estudió Ud. la materia antes de la próxima clase?
11. Su primera impresión de la clase y del profesor (de la profesora), ¿fue válida o cambió con el tiempo? ¿Por qué?

Suggestions A and C: Students choose one situation and give oral presentation using questions as guide. Or do as written exercise only.

Extensions A: **1.** *¿Qué ropa llevaba?* **4.** *¿Cuántos estudiantes había en la clase? ¿Qué hacían cuando Ud. entró?* **5.** *¿Ya sabía Ud. el nombre del profesor? ¿Sabía qué tipo de profesor era?* **6.** *¿Sabían todos más que Ud.? ¿Habló Ud. durante la clase? ¿Le hizo algunas preguntas al profesor?* **8.** *¿Tenía ganas de regresar a clase o quería dejarla?*

B. **Caperucita Roja.** Retell this familiar story, based on the drawings and the sentences and cues that accompany each drawing. Add as many details as you can.

Note B: This retelling of the Little Red Riding Hood story is an authentic version from Spain. You and students may be familiar with other versions of the story. Encourage students to add additional details.

Palabras útiles: abalanzarse sobre (*to pounce on*), avisar (*to warn*), dispararle (*to shoot at someone/something*), esconderse (*to hide*), enterarse de (*to find out about*), huir (*to flee*), saltar (*to jump*)

Érase una vez una niña hermosa que (*llamarse*[1]) Caperucita Roja. Todos los animales del bosque (*ser*[2]) sus amigos y Caperucita Roja los (*querer*[3]) mucho.

Un día su mamá le (*decir*[4]): —Quiero que (*llevar*[5]) en seguida esta jarrita de miel a casa de tu abuelita. Ten cuidado con el lobo feroz.

En el bosque, el lobo (*salir*[6]) a hablar con la niña. Le (*preguntar*[7]): —¿Adónde vas, Caperucita? Ésta le (*contestar*[8]) dulcemente: —Voy a casa de mi abuelita.

—Pues, si vas por este sendero, vas a llegar antes. —(*decir*[9]) el malvado lobo, que (*irse*[10]) por otro camino más corto.

El lobo: (*llegar*[11]) primero a la casa de la abuelita / (*entrar*[12]) La abuelita: (*tener*[13]) mucho miedo / (*saltar*[14]) de la cama / (*correr*[15]) a esconderse

Caperucita: (*llegar*[16]) por fin a la casa de la abuelita / (*encontrar*[17]) a su "abuelita" / (*decir*[18]): —¡Qué dientes tan largos tienes! —¡Son para comerte mejor!

Una ardilla del bosque: (*enterarse*[19]) del peligro que (*correr*[20]) Caperucita / (*avisar*[21]) a un cazador

El lobo: (*saltar*[22]) de la cama / (*abalanzarse*[23]) sobre Caperucita Caperucita: (*salir*[24]) de la casa corriendo y pidiendo socorro desesperadamente

El cazador: (*ver*[25]) lo que (*ocurrir*[26]) / (*dispararle*[27]) al lobo / (*hacerle*[28]) huir

Caperucita: (*regresar*[29]) a casa de su abuelita / (*abrazarla*[30]) / (*prometerle*[31]) escuchar siempre los consejos de su mamá

Note B: Complete sentences are given for drawings 1–4; skeletal cues for remaining drawings.

Hay varias versiones del cuento de Caperucita Roja. La que Ud. acaba de leer termina felizmente, pero otras no. Con otros dos compañeros, vuelva a contar la historia, empezando por el dibujo número 7. Invente un diálogo más largo entre Caperucita y el lobo y cambie por completo el final del cuento.

Más palabras útiles: comérselo/la (*to eat something up*), atacar, matar (*to kill*)

Extensions C: **7.** *¿Le enojó el precio de la medicina?* **8.** *¿Qué era lo peor de estar enfermo/a?*

C. **Entrevista.** Lea las siguientes preguntas sobre su última enfermedad y piense en las respuestas que Ud. daría (*would give*). Luego use las preguntas para entrevistar a un compañero (una compañera) de clase, haciendo los cambios necesarios.

1. ¿Cuándo empezó Ud. a sentirse mal? ¿Dónde estaba Ud.? ¿Qué hacía?
2. ¿Cuáles eran sus síntomas? ¿Cómo se sentía? ¿Estaba mareado/a? ¿congestionado/a? ¿Le dolía alguna parte del cuerpo? ¿Tenía fiebre? ¿Se tomó la temperatura?
3. ¿Qué hizo? ¿Regresó a casa? ¿Se quitó la ropa? ¿Tosía mucho? ¿Se acostó?
4. ¿Fue al consultorio del médico? ¿Lo/La examinó? ¿Cuál fue su diagnóstico?
5. ¿Le puso una inyección el médico? ¿Le dio una receta? ¿Llevó Ud. la receta a la farmacia? ¿Cuánto le costó la medicina?
6. ¿Cuándo se sintió bien por fin? ¿Empezó a cuidarse más?

En la sala de urgencia (de emergencias)

—¿Qué le ocurre?

—Me caí por la escalera (*staircase*) y ahora me duele mucho el tobillo (*ankle*).

—A ver... Lo tiene bastante inflamado... pero no parece que haya fractura.

—Lo peor es que no lo puedo mover.

—Bueno, lo voy a mandar a radiología para que le saquen una radiografía.

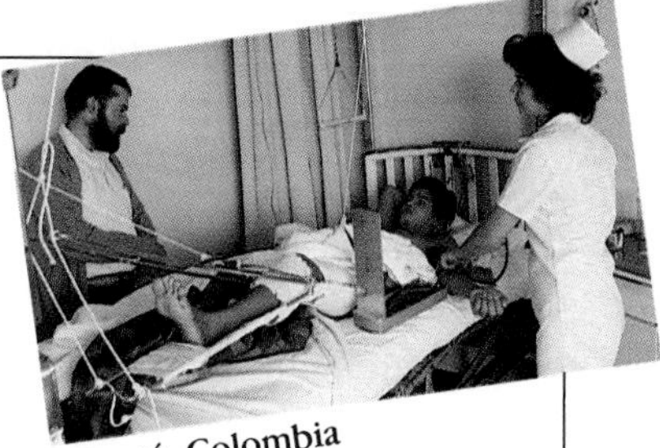

Bogotá, Colombia

37. *QUE, QUIEN(ES), LO QUE*
Relative Pronouns

Lo que **dijo el doctor Matamoros**

ISABEL: ¿Y qué más te dijo este médico *que* tanto sabe?

BEATRIZ: Que lo más importante es guardar cama y descansar.

ISABEL: Mira, la próxima vez *que* te pongas enferma, la primera persona con *quien* debes hablar es conmigo. Te digo lo mismo... ¡y sin cobrar!

1. La persona con quien habla Isabel es _____.
2. El médico de quien hablan es _____.
3. El médico recomienda que Beatriz _____.
4. Isabel le recomienda que _____.
5. Yo creo que lo que debe hacer Beatriz es lo siguiente: _____.

Follow-up (mini drawing): **1.** *¿Quién es la mujer del dibujo?* **2.** *¿Dónde está ahora?* **3.** *¿Qué está leyendo?* **4.** *¿De quién es la carta (= cuenta)?* **5.** *¿La va a pagar o no?*

What Dr. Matamoros said ISABEL: And what did this doctor who knows so much tell you? BEATRIZ: That the most important thing is to stay in bed and rest. ISABEL: Look, the next time you get sick, the first person you should talk to is me. I'll tell you the same thing . . . and without charging!

There are four principal relative pronouns in English: *that*, *which*, *who*, and *whom*. They are usually expressed in Spanish by the following relative pronouns:

que	refers to things and people
quien	refers only to people
lo que	refers to a situation

Note:
- The word students have learned to use in subjunctive constructions is a relative conjunction, used to introduce noun clauses (clauses that function as nouns).
- *Lo que* has been active since Ch. 7, for use in direction lines primarily.

que = *that, which, who*

Tuve una cita con el médico **que** duró una hora.	*I had an apointment with the doctor that lasted an hour.*
Es un buen médico **que** sabe mucho.	*He's a good doctor who knows a lot.*

Note: Relative pronoun *que* introduces adjective clauses (clauses that modify nouns). Use of subjunctive in such clauses is presented in Ch. 15. Point out here how clauses modify nouns *cita* and *médico*.

quien(es) = *who/whom* after a preposition or as an indirect object

La mujer con **quien** hablaba era mi hermana.	*The woman with whom I was talking was my sister.*
Éste es el hombre de **quien** te hablaba.	*This is the man about whom I was talking to you.*
Ése es el niño a **quién** no le gustan los helados.	*That's the boy who doesn't like ice cream.*

Optional: *quien* after a comma in restrictive clauses.

Emphasis: *Lo que* is relative pronoun, *not* used to express direct questions (*¿Qué es esto? ¿Cuál es tu teléfono?*).

Note: *Lo que* refers to single word only when word has not been mentioned yet: *Lo que necesito es dinero.*

lo que = *what, that which*

No entiendo **lo que** dice.	*I don't understand what he is saying.*
Lo que no me gusta es su actitud hacia los pobres.	*What I don't like is his attitude toward poor people.*

The antecedent of **lo que** is always a sentence, a whole situation, or something that hasn't been mentioned yet: **Lo que necesito es estudiar más.**

Práctica

A. Complete las oraciones lógicamente, usando **que**, **quien** o **lo que**.

En la sala de emergencias

1. ¿Quién fue el hombre ____ la trajo aquí?
2. Desgraciadamente no podemos localizar a la mujer con ____ vive.
3. ¡____ necesitamos es más tiempo!
4. Quiero saber el nombre de la medicina ____ Ud. tomaba.
5. ¿Dónde está el ayudante ____ empezó a trabajar ayer?

En el consultorio del médico

—Pues ____[6] Ud. tiene es exceso de peso (*weight*). Debe perder por lo menos 10 libras.

—Pero, doctor... Es cierto que como mucho, pero... Dígame, ¿a ____[7] no le gusta comer?

—De ahora en adelante, Ud. puede comer todo ____[8] le guste... ¡y aquí está la lista de ____[9] le debe gustar!

Variation B: Students define first word in each example, using *lo que*. ***Modelo:*** *El bisturí es lo que usa el cirujano para cortar.*

Suggestion B: Do as whole-class activity; one person takes role of person with problems so suggestions can be directed to a real individual. As students give advice, following models given, mix in suggestions and recommendations with dependent noun clauses introduced by *que*.

B. **Situaciones.** Imagine que Ud. es el doctor (la doctora) Matamoros. Explíquele a la enfermera lo que Ud. necesita.

MODELO: bisturí (*m.*, *scalpel*) / mesa → —Lo que necesito es el bisturí.
—¿Cuál?
—El bisturí que está en la mesa.

1. termómetro / armario (*closet*)
2. jarabe / consultorio
3. frasco (*bottle*) / bolsa
4. bolsa / escritorio
5. teléfono del especialista / mi agenda
6. nombre del hospital / ese pueblo

Conversación

Problemas y consejos. Déle varios consejos a la persona que tiene los siguientes problemas. Use estas frases como guía.

- La persona con quien debes hablar es...
- Lo que debes hacer es...
- Lo que creo es que debes...

1. Tengo un resfriado terrible.
2. Necesito descansar y tengo tres días libres la semana que viene.
3. Tengo ganas de comer comida china esta noche.
4. No sé qué clases debo tomar el semestre que viene.
5. ¡Sufro tantas presiones en mi vida privada!
6. Vivo muy lejos de la universidad. Pierdo una hora en ir y venir todos los días.
7. Se me cayó el vaso favorito de mi abuela y se rompió, pero no se lo dije cuando pasó.

Ahora invente Ud. problemas semejantes—o cuente un problema real—y pídales consejos a sus compañeros de clase.

Notas culturales: La medicina en los países hispánicos

Como regla general los hispanos tienen como costumbre consultar no sólo a los médicos sino a otros profesionales con sus problemas de salud. Por ejemplo, ya que (*since*) muchas drogas se venden sin receta en los países hispánicos, es posible que una persona enferma le explique sus síntomas a un farmacéutico, que le pueda recomendar una medicina. Aun le puede recomendar y poner inyecciones al paciente. Los farmacéuticos reciben un entrenamiento riguroso y están al tanto (*up to date*) en farmacología. También se puede consultar a un practicante. Éstos tienen tres años de entrenamiento médico y pueden aplicar una serie de tratamientos, incluyendo inyecciones.

Otra característica del sistema médico hispánico es que es fácil y barato conseguir los servicios de una enfermera particular (*private*) que cuide a un enfermo, ya sea en la casa o en el hospital. Las enfermeras no tienen que tener tantos conocimientos teóricos como las de los Estados Unidos, pero tienen mucha experiencia en su campo.

SITUACIONES

Situaciones: See IM for sugg[estions], additional exercises, an[d] supplementary dialogues and exercises.

CENTRO ANTITABACO

TRATAMIENTO PARA FUMADORES. Instituto Médico Laennec, 1 Poniente 331, Viña del Mar. 972677 - 972941. 31 dic

BRONCOPULMONARES

INSTITUTO MEDICO LAENNEC ENFERMEDADES RESPIRATORIAS Y ALERGICAS. Viña: 1 Poniente 331. Fonos 972677, 972941, 978320. Valparaíso: Pedro Montt 2034 Depto. 503 Fono: 210347. 31 dic

CENTROS MEDICOS

"CENTROMED". Diagnóstico y tratamiento integral. Rayos X, Laboratorio, Fisioterapia, Pabellón Cirugía Menor y Yeso. Urgencias de llamada. Atención Fonasa. Cajas. Isapres. Bienestares. 4 Poniente 332. Fono: 976947. 31 dic

CIRUGIA INFANTIL

DR. LORENZO MORALES. Viña: Clínica 3 Norte Fono 977149. Valparaíso: Centro Brasil Fono 213879. 31 dic

DR. HUMBERTO VERDUGO. Mañanas: Hospital de Niños. Fono 683714. Urgencias: 681497. 31 dic

En el consultorio del médico

Hablando con la enfermera

—Siéntese, por favor. ¿Cómo se llama?
—Tomás Hernández Rodríguez.
—¿Qué es lo que tiene?
—Un resfriado muy grave.
—¿Cuándo empezó a sentirse mal?
—Ayer por la noche tenía fiebre. Tosía mucho y me dolía todo el cuerpo. Hoy me siento peor.
—¿Tiene otros síntomas?
—Por suerte, no.
—Dígame su edad, su peso° y su estatura,° por favor.
—Tengo veintiún años, mido° un metro ochenta y cinco y peso ochenta kilos.°
—Muy bien. Ahora, lo que voy a hacer es tomarle la temperatura... Hmm... todavía tiene Ud. fiebre: treinta y ocho grados.° Súbase la manga° derecha, que le voy a tomar la presión.°
—¿Todo esto por un resfriado?
—Es rutinario. Ahora pase Ud. al consultorio de la doctora.

weight / height
I am (measure) / 6' 3/4", 176 lbs.
100.4° F / Súbase... *Roll up your sleeve*
blood pressure

Hablando con la doctora

—Siéntese. Saque la lengua. Abra bien la boca y diga: «Aaaaa... aaa...». La garganta está un poco inflamada. Ahora respire profundamente. Diga: «treinta y tres».
—Treinta y tres.
—Bien. Ud. no tiene nada serio en los pulmones.
—Pero toso mucho, doctora. Ya tosía antes de resfriarme.
—Lo que pasa es que fuma demasiado. Ahora calle° mientras le ausculto° el corazón. Humm... ¿hace Ud. mucho ejercicio físico?
—Fui campeón° de natación° en el colegio. Todavía practico varios deportes.
—Bueno, en general, Ud. está en muy buen estado físico.
—¿Y para este resfriado?
—Pues, unas aspirinas y... paciencia. Para su salud en general, deje de fumar. No es necesaria otra receta.

no diga nada / *I listen to (medical)*
champion / swimming

Conversación

Con otros dos compañeros, describa lo que pasa en esta serie de dibujos. Invente todos los detalles que pueda, incluyendo todo lo que el doctor le explica al paciente. Luego compare su descripción con la de otros grupos.

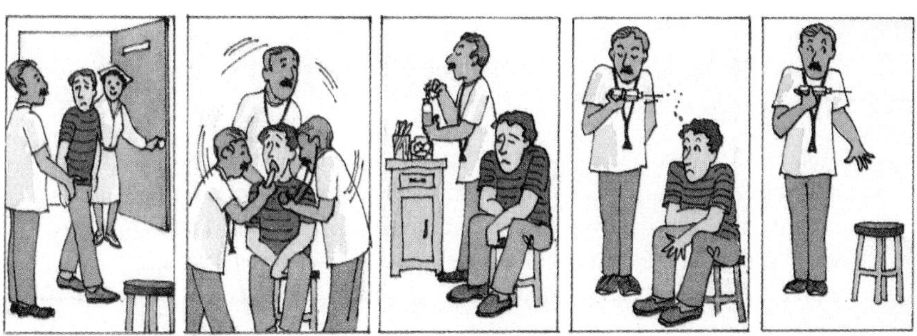

UN POCO DE TODO

A. Form complete sentences based on the words given in the order given. Conjugate the verbs in the preterite or the imperfect and add other words if necessary. Use subject pronouns only when needed.

1. cuando / yo / ser / niño / pensar / que / mejor / de / estar enfermo / ser / guardar cama
2. peor / ser / que / con frecuencia / yo / resfriarse / durante / vacaciones
3. una vez / yo / ponerme / muy / enfermo / durante / Navidad / y / mi / madre / llamar / a / médico / con / quien / tener / confianza
4. Dr. Matamoros / venir / casa / y / darme / antibiótico / porque / tener / mucho / fiebre
5. ser / cuatro / mañana / cuando / por fin / yo / empezar / respirar / sin dificultad
6. desgraciadamente / día / de / Navidad / yo / tener / tomar / jarabe / y / no / gustar / nada / sabor (*taste*)
7. bueno / de / este / enfermedad / ser / que / mi / padre / tener / dejar / fumar / mientras / yo / estar / enfermo

Ahora vuelva a contar la historia desde el punto de vista de la madre del niño.

B. **¿Qué pasó?** Complete the following narrative with the proper form—preterite or imperfect—of the verbs in parentheses, and fill in the blanks with **que**, **quien(es)** or **lo que**, as needed.

El muchacho (_____[1]) se hizo daño fue Daniel. (*Estar*[2]) jugando con Guillermo, con (_____[3]) (*jugar*[4]) todas las tardes. Los dos (*llamar*[5]) a una vecina, (_____[6]) (*venir*[7]) en seguida a ayudarlos. Le (*preocupar*[8]) a la vecina la cantidad de sangre (*blood*) que (*perder*[9]) Daniel. Pero no (*ser*[10]) muy seria la herida (*wound*). Por eso no (*llamar*[11]) a los padres de Daniel, a (_____[12]) la vecina no (*conocer*[13]) muy bien.

C. **Entrevista.** Use the following questions to interview another student about his or her childhood and about specific events in the past, as well as what is currently happening in his or her life. Report the most interesting information to the class.

1. ¿A qué escuela asistías (cuando tenías ____ años)? ¿Asististe a esta universidad el año pasado? ¿Cuánto tiempo hace que estudias aquí?
2. ¿Qué lenguas estudiabas? ¿Estudiaste latín en la secundaria? ¿Cuánto tiempo hace que estudias español?
3. ¿Qué hacías cuando te enfermabas? ¿Cuántas veces te resfriaste el año pasado? ¿Es necesario que empieces ahora a llevar una vida más sana?
4. ¿Qué películas te gustaban más? ¿Te gustó la última película que viste? ¿Qué nueva película quieres ver este mes?
5. En la secundaria, ¿qué era lo más importante de tu vida? ¿Qué cosa importante te pasó el año pasado? ¿Qué esperas que pase este año?
6. ¿Qué hacías durante los veranos? ¿Qué hiciste el verano pasado? ¿Qué vas a hacer este verano?

CH. **Un accidente que salió bien.** Complete the following paragraphs with the correct form of the verbs in parentheses—preterite or imperfect—as suggested by the context. When two possibilities are given in parentheses, select the correct word. When an adjective is given in parentheses, give the nominalized form of it.

Cuando yo (*tener*[1]) doce años, (*caerse*[2]) de la bicicleta en que (*montar*[3]) y se me (*romper*[4]) el brazo derecho. Las personas (*que/quien*[5]) (*ver*[6]) el accidente (*llamar*[7]) una ambulancia (*que/lo que*[8]) me (*llevar*[9]) al hospital. Me (*doler*[10]) mucho el brazo y (*tener*[11]) mucho miedo, pero no (*querer*[12]) portarme como un niño. Por fin, cuando (*ver*[13]) la sala de urgencia, (*empezar*[14]) a llorar.

La recepcionista (*llamar*[15]) a mi madre, pero ella no (*estar*[16]) en casa; (*trabajar*[17]) en la oficina. Cuando por fin la (*localizar*[18]), ella les (*dar*[19]) permiso para tratarme. Yo (*dejar*[20]) de llorar muy pronto porque los médicos me (*contar*[21]) chistes mientras me (*examinar*[22]) el brazo. (*Más divertido*[23]) (*ser*[24]) cuando ellos (*cubrirse*[25]) de yeso° al° ponerme la enyesadura.°

plaster / when
cast

(*Ser*[26]) las siete de la noche y ya (*estar*[27]) oscuro cuando mi madre y yo (*llegar*[28]) a casa. Yo (*tener*[29]) mucha hambre y (*querer*[30]) comer, pero mi mamá no (*sentirse*[31]) muy bien. Utilizando sólo el brazo sano, le (*hacer*[32]) una taza de té y me (*preparar*[33]) un sándwich.

¿Qué (*ser*[34]) (*bueno*[35]) del accidente? Pues, ahora soy completamente ambidextro.

¿Quién lo dijo?

1. Por favor, ¿trabaja en su oficina la Sra. Hernández?
2. ¡Me duele muchísimo el brazo!

3. Tenemos que llamar una ambulancia. Parece que el niño se hizo daño.
4. No te molestes. Yo te preparo la cena.
5. Pues ya que te gusta tanto esta enyesadura, te vamos a poner otra en el brazo izquierdo. ¿Qué te parece?

Theme vocabulary previously listed as active: *caminar, comer bien, correr, dormir, el/la enfermero/a, llevar, practicar, tomar, tranquilo*

LA SALUD Y EL BIENESTAR

cuidarse to take care of oneself
dejar de + *inf.* to stop (*doing something*)
enfermarse to get sick
examinar to examine
guardar cama to stay in bed
hacer ejercicio to exercise, get exercise
llevar una vida... to lead a . . . life
ponerle una inyección to give (*someone*) a shot, injection
resfriarse to get/catch a cold
respirar to breathe
sacar to stick out (*the tongue*)
tener dolor de to have a pain in
toser to cough

ALGUNAS PARTES DEL CUERPO

la boca mouth
el corazón heart
el estómago stomach
la garganta throat
la lengua tongue
la nariz nose
el ojo eye
los pulmones lungs

LAS ENFERMEDADES Y LOS TRATAMIENTOS

el antibiótico antibiotic
el consultorio (medical) office
la farmacia pharmacy
la fiebre fever
las gafas glasses
el jarabe (cough) syrup
los lentes (de contacto) contact lenses
la medicina medicine
el/la paciente patient
la pastilla pill
la receta prescription
el resfriado cold
(**urgencia**) emergency room
la sala de emergencias (**urgencia**) emergency room
el síntoma symptom
la temperatura temperature
la tos cough

OTROS SUSTANTIVOS

el deporte sport
la escalera ladder

ADJETIVOS

congestionado/a congested
cualquier(a) any
mareado/a nauseated
sano/a healthy

PALABRAS ADICIONALES

de joven as a youth
de repente suddenly
en seguida immediately
ya que since, considering that

Frases útiles para la comunicación

lo + *adjective* (*masc. sing.*)	the . . . thing/part/news
lo bueno / lo malo	the good news / the bad news
lo suficiente	enough

UN PASO MÁS 12

OPTIONAL SECTION

¡LO CONTENTOS QUE SE VAN A PONER FELIPE, SUSANITA Y MAFALDA CUANDO ME VEAN LEVANTADO!

¡AMIGOS!... ¡ME HE SACADO ESA MALDITA GRIPE DE ENCIMA!... ¿DONDE ESTÁN TODOS?

Cartoon: *¿Cómo está Manolo al principio? ¿Cómo estaba la semana anterior? ¿A quiénes espera ver hoy? ¿Dónde están ellos? ¿Qué tienen? ¿Se contagiaron de Manolo?*

out of bed, up

sacar de encima *to get rid of:*
me he sacado *I got rid*

▲ Actividad A. ¿Te importa tu salud?

Variations A:
- Students report what they have learned to class. Then whole class decides whether or not average student *lleva una vida sana o no.*
- Using questions as guide, students describe lifestyle of one of individuals depicted.

A pesar de nuestros esfuerzos para cuidarnos, a veces nos enfermamos. Y todos tenemos creencias propias sobre la medicina y la mejor manera de tratar una enfermedad. ¿Está Ud. de acuerdo con las siguientes oraciones? Conteste según la siguiente escala.

5 = sí enfático
4 = sí
3 = no tengo opinión
2 = no
1 = no enfático

1. Me pongo muy nervioso/a en el consultorio del médico.
2. No me molesta ir al médico, pero sí me pongo muy nervioso/a en el consultorio del dentista.
3. No hay nada peor que las inyecciones. ¡No las aguanto (*I can't stand them!*)
4. Si una persona sentada (*seated*) a mi lado empieza a toser, me cambio de lugar... ¡Los resfriados son muy contagiosos!
5. Cuando mi compañero/a de cuarto (esposo/a, etcétera) tiene un resfriado, me voy a dormir a otro sitio.
6. Cuando tengo un resfriado, nunca tomo pastillas ni antibióticos ni jarabes. Creo que los resfriados deben seguir su curso natural.
7. Mente (*Mind*) sana en cuerpo sano.
8. Si Ud. quiere vivir muchos años, acuéstese y levántese temprano, no fume ni beba y coma con moderación.
9. Músculos de Sansón (*Sampson*) con cerebro de mosquito.
10. La mayoría de las enfermedades se curan sin intervención médica.

Compare sus respuestas con las de otros compañeros de clase. ¿Hay común acuerdo—o desacuerdo—sobre algunas ideas?

A propósito... Speaking with Medical Personnel

It is important to be able to communicate accurately when you are in need of medical or dental attention. English-speaking doctors and dentists are available in most large cities in Spanish-speaking countries. But if you do need to speak Spanish with medical personnel, the following words and phrases will be useful.

¿Cuánto tiempo hace que Ud. está enfermo/a?	*How long have you been ill?*
Hace (dos días) que estoy enfermo/a.	*I've been sick for (two days).*
¿Cuándo se enfermó?	*When did you get sick?*
¿Padece de algo más?	*Is anything else wrong?*
Sí, padezco de _____.	*Yes, I'm also suffering from _____.*
¿Ha tenido Ud. _____?	*Have you had _____?*
Sí, he tenido / No, no he tenido ___.	*Yes, I've had / No, I haven't had ___.*
¿Toma Ud. alguna medicina?	*Are you taking any medicine?*
Vamos a sacar los rayos equis/las radiografías.	*We're going to take X-rays.*
Tenemos que sacarle el diente (la muela).	*We have to pull the tooth (molar).*

Remember that any temperature above 37 degrees Celsius (98.6 degrees Fahrenheit) constitutes a fever.

Preliminary exercise B: Working in groups, students make up lists of questions they are likely to be asked during first visit to new physician who wants to get complete information on their health background.

▲ Actividad B. Dramas médicos

Con su profesor(a), hagan los papeles de paciente (Ud.) y doctor(a) o enfermero/a (su profesor[a]) en las siguientes situaciones.

1. Ud. está en el consultorio del médico. Le duele muchísimo la garganta.
2. Ud. visita al médico porque tiene dolor de cabeza desde hace (*for*) una semana. Tampoco respira bien—le es casi imposible bajar y subir las escaleras.
3. Ud. visita al dentista porque hace varios días que le duele una muela. Pero Ud. es cobarde y no quiere que el dentista se la saque.
4. Ud. lleva a su hijo a una consulta con la doctora. Tiene fiebre y vomita con frecuencia.
5. Ud. está en el hospital, en la sala de urgencia. Acaba de tener lo que parece ser un ataque de apendicitis y lo/la van a operar. Habla con una enfermera.

—Pero ¿cómo quiere que le opere, si no tiene usted nada?
—Mejor, doctor. Así la operación le será más fácil...

▲ Actividad C. Estereotipos sobre la salud

Su amigo hispano es muy observador... por lo menos así lo cree él. Le gusta mirar a la gente y después hacer comentarios. Hace un año que observa las costumbres de los estadounidenses referentes a la comida y la salud. ¿Qué le va a decir Ud. cuando él haga los siguientes comentarios?

1. Uds. los norteamericanos tienen una verdadera manía por el *jogging*.
2. Creo que las comidas favoritas de los norteamericanos son el yogur y el *wheat germ*.
3. Uds. los norteamericanos trabajan demasiado. No saben descansar y divertirse.
4. ¿Por qué toman Uds. tantas vitaminas? Vitamina C, vitaminas de alta potencia... ¿Es realmente tan mala la comida de este país?
5. Me fascina el hecho de que (*the fact that*) en cada esquina (*corner*) haya un gimnasio pequeño. Allí veo a muchas personas que levantan pesas y hacen ejercicio. ¿Qué significa *shape up*?

Extension C:
• Students name and discuss other aspects of our preoccupation with health.

• ***Pregunta:*** *¿Hay personas que se preocupen demasiado por la salud? Describa a estas personas.*

LECTURA CULTURAL

Lectura: See IM for suggestions and additional exercises and activities.

¿Está Ud. resfriado/a?

No hay nada más común que el resfriado común... y nada más raro que un remedio seguro. Ya que, tarde o temprano, todos sufrimos los efectos de un resfriado, el folklore de todos los países del mundo ofrece varios remedios. Aquí se dan algunos remedios que se usan en el mundo hispano. ¿Cómo se comparan con los de su familia?

- Para los resfríos es bueno tomar antes de acostarse leche bien caliente con miel y alguna bebida fuerte.° Se abriga uno bien y se pone dos o tres frazadas° para transpirar° durante la noche.

  de la Argentina

- Para «sudar la calentura»° de una gripe, se usa una mezcla caliente de jugo de limón (con todo el bagazo°), canela,° miel y un poco de licor, con dos aspirinas, antes de acostarse.

  de El Salvador

- Un remedio que se acostumbraba usar era el de la cáscara de naranja para bajar la fiebre. Se pone una porción de la cáscara en agua y se deja hervir.° Una vez hervida el agua, se separa la cáscara y se toma el agua más o menos caliente.

  de Panamá

- Para los catarros:° leche caliente con miel. También puede tomarse café con leche, y es muy popular añadirle un poquito de coñac. Esto y una aspirina ayudan a sudar bastante, lo cual es muy recomendable cuando se tiene fiebre.

  de España

bebida... *alcohol* (*in some form*) / *blankets* / *sweat*

fiebre

pulp / *cinnamon*

to boil

resfriados

- Para curar el resfriado es bueno tomar una limonada caliente con bastante limón, con un poquito de tequila y unas dos aspirinas antes de acostarse.

  de México

Comprensión

¿Cierto o falso? Corrija las oraciones falsas.

1. En general los resfriados no se tratan con ningún tipo de medicina en el mundo hispánico.
2. Se recomienda con frecuencia tomar una bebida con un poco de alcohol como medicina (no para emborracharse).
3. Parece que los hispanos aguantan los resfriados sin acostarse.
4. Es frecuente el uso de las frutas tropicales como la papaya y la piña para curar un resfriado.

Study Hint: Writing

You can develop a more mature writing style in Spanish by using transition words to link shorter sentences. Follow these suggestions.

1. Write a first draft of your composition, trying to express your ideas in short, simple sentences. Be sure that each sentence contains at least a subject and a verb.
2. Determine which sentences have a logical relationship and can be linked together. Choose transition words that show these relationships.
3. Rewrite the composition, adding the transition words and making changes, if necessary. For example, if you link the following sentences together with **cuando**, the word **ella** will not be necessary.

Vimos a Jacinta. Ella estaba en la cafetería. →
Cuando vimos a Jacinta, estaba en la cafetería.

Remember to use words with which you are familiar because you have used them before, and avoid using the dictionary too much (**Study Hint**, **Capítulo 5**).

Transition Words

además	*besides*	pero	*but*
así	*thus, so*	por ejemplo	*for example*
cuando	*when*	por eso	*therefore, for that reason*
de vez en cuando	*from time to time*		
en cambio	*on the other hand*	por fin	*at last, finally*
es decir	*that is*	pues	*well; since*
luego	*then, next*	sin embargo	*nevertheless*
mientras	*while*	también	*also*

Para escribir

Answer the following questions about your last visit to the doctor, adding as many details as possible. Then, using the words in **Study Hint: Writing** and any others you know, join the sentences together to form three paragraphs that flow smoothly.

Párrafo A

1. ¿Cuándo fue la última vez que Ud. consultó con un médico?
2. ¿Por qué lo hizo? ¿Cuáles eran sus síntomas?

Párrafo B

1. En el consultorio, ¿tuvo Ud. que esperar mucho tiempo? ¿Esperaban también otros pacientes?
2. Cuando por fin entró en el consultorio, ¿cuánto tiempo duró la consulta? ¿Qué actitud mostró el médico? ¿compasión? ¿humor? ¿preocupación? ¿indiferencia?
3. ¿Le recetó alguna medicina? ¿Qué otras recomendaciones le dio? ¿Las siguió Ud.? ¿Por qué sí o por qué no?

Párrafo C

1. ¿Cuándo se mejoró Ud. por fin?
2. ¿Qué hace ahora para mantenerse en buen estado de salud?

OPTIONAL SECTION

REPASO 4 VOCES DEL MUNDO HISPÁNICO

Note: Corresponding chapters of the Workbook and the Laboratory Manual offer focused vocabulary and grammar activities.

Repaso 4: See IM for detailed suggestions for handling *Entrevistas*, *Situaciones*, and the specific *Voces* sections.

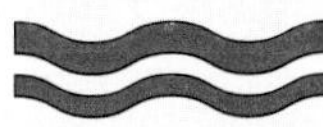

LOS HISPANOS EN LOS ESTADOS UNIDOS
La comunidad puertorriqueña

"American Feast", pintado por Ibsen Espada

Como los mexicanoamericanos, los puertorriqueños no son extranjeros. La isla de Puerto Rico es un Estado Libre Asociado de los Estados Unidos, y las personas que allí nacen son ciudadanos (*citizens*) norteamericanos.

Las grandes concentraciones de puertorriqueños se encuentran en Nueva York, Nueva Jersey y Pensilvania. Hay mucho movimiento entre las ciudades del noreste de los Estados Unidos y la Isla (como los puertorriqueños llaman a Puerto Rico), ya que muchas personas tienen amigos y familiares en las dos partes.

La mayoría de los puertorriqueños que se han establecido (*have settled*) en el continente vinieron en busca de mejores condiciones económicas y educativas para ellos y sus hijos. Mientras muchos quieren que Puerto Rico se incorpore a los Estados Unidos, para ser el estado número cincuenta y uno, otros prefieren que se independice. Otros desean que se mantenga el *status quo*.

Cuando a sus playas llegó Colón,
exclamó, lleno de admiración,
¡Oh! ¡Oh! ¡Oh!
Ésta es la linda tierra
que busco yo,
es Borinquen,° la hija
del mar y el sol.

de «La boriqueña», himno nacional de Puerto Rico

°nombre indio de la isla de Puerto Rico

San Juan, Puerto Rico

Por una celebración navideña, típicamente puertorriqueña
¡Feliz Navidad y un alegre Día de Reyes!
Lic. Ismael Cuevas

Hermoso° *bouquet*,
Aquí te traemos
Bellísimas flores
Del jardín riqueño.
De todas las flores
Yo te traigo un ramo.°
Recíbelas bien
Que éste es mi aguinaldo.°

de «El Aguinaldo de las flores», canción de la tradición popular

°Bonito
°*bouquet*
°*Christmas gift*

Marta Istomín

Marta Istomín

- Directora artística del John F. Kennedy Center for the Performing Arts
- Casada con Pablo Casals por 17 años, hasta la muerte de éste en 1973
- Con Casals, ayudó a fundar el Festival de Música Casals, que se celebra anualmente en San Juan
- Profesora de violoncelo
- Participante en muchos festivales musicales
- Nacida en Puerto Rico
- Empezó a tocar el violín y el violoncelo a los cinco años

El Maestro Rafael Frübeck de Burgos y la Orquesta Sinfónica de Puerto Rico, en el Festival Casals, 1986

We drank hot cocoa and talked about summertime. Momma talked about Puerto Rico and how great it was, and how she'd like to go back one day, and how it was warm all the time there and no matter how poor you were over there, you could always live on green bananas, *bacalao*, and rice and beans. "*Dios mío*," she said, "I don't think I'll ever see my island again."

"Sure you will, Mommie," said Miriam, my kid sister. She was eleven. "Tell us, tell us all about Porto Rico."

"It's not P*o*rto Rico, it's P*ue*rto Rico," said Momma.

"Tell us, Moms," said nine-year-old James, "about Puerto Rico . . ."

Moms copped that wet-eyed look and began to dream-talk about her *isla verde*, Moses' land of milk and honey.

"When I was a little girl," she said, "I remember getting up in the morning and getting the water from the river and getting the wood for the fire and the quiet of the greenlands and the golden color of the morning sky, the grass wet from the *lluvia . . . ai, Dios,* the *coquís* and the *pajaritos* making all the *música . . .*"

Piri Thomas, autor puertorriqueño, *Down These Mean Streets*

Willie Colón

Nueva York

San Juan, Puerto Rico

ROGELIO NARANJO/*Actualidad, Mexico*

puerto rico 1974
this is not the place where i was born
remember—as a child the fantasizing images my mother planted
within my head—
the shadows of her childhood recounted to me many times
over welfare loan on *crédito* food from *el bodeguero*
i tasted *mango* many years before the skin of the fruit
ever reached my teeth . . .

i was born on an island where to be puerto rican meant to be
part of the land & soul & *puertorriqueños* were not the
minority
puerto ricans were first, none were second
no, i was not born here . . .
no, i was not born in the attitude & time of this place

Miguel Piñero, poeta puertorriqueño, «this is not the place where i was born», de *La Bodega Sold Dreams*

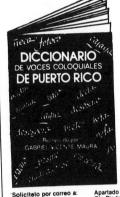

Carta a Los Hispanos

a mis alumnos

Quiero escribir un poema tipo colectivo
donde cada latino meta° mano — ponga
y recite sobre el papel veinticinco tristezas° — *sorrows*
o unos cuantos sueños ya olvidados.

Quiero redactar° un verso tipo cesta° abierta — escribir / *basket*
donde cada cual deposite lo que trajo
y se deshaga° con ello de limosnas cotidianas, — se... *get rid of*
welfare cards, los food-stamps, la yerba° y to's° los hang-ups. — marihuana / todos

Quiero unos versos escritos por manos negras,
manos callosas y llenas de trabajo,
ni la tinta° ni el papel ya nos importan — *ink*
sino el relief de dejarlo todo a un lado.

Ay, quiero escribir un poema tipo colectivo.
Se solicitan escribientes,
Favor de contestarme para atrás,° HERMANO. — para... *back*

Luz María Umpierre, poeta puertorriqueña y profesora de español, Rutgers University

Estudiantes puertorriqueños de secundaria

ENTREVISTAS

***Entrevistas:* Focus:** Asking questions with all verb forms and tenses presented so far, in particular preterite and imperfect.

In the last three chapters of ***Puntos de partida***, you have gained a good deal of experience in talking about the past as well as in asking others questions about past experiences and activities. This activity will allow you to put those skills to use in a different context.

First, read the descriptions of the following persons and of an incident in their recent past. Try to come to some conclusions about the reasons for each person's behavior. Then, working in groups of three or four, compare your conclusions and make up a list of questions you would ask the person to determine which explanation is correct.

Finally, a classmate or your instructor will play the part of each person named. Ask him or her your questions and come to a conclusion in each group. Compare the decisions of all the groups and then compare them to those of each person, who will reveal his or her motivation or explanation of the incident after all groups have spoken.

1. María Luisa es estudiante en esta universidad. Se especializa en química orgánica. Acaba de salir mal en un examen de química; salieron mal también un 40 por ciento de los estudiantes de la misma clase. María Luisa nunca había salido mal (*had failed*) en un examen de química antes. De hecho (*In fact*), nunca ha salido mal (*has failed*) en ningún examen en toda su vida.
2. John es un amigo de todos ustedes que estudia aquí y es de otro estado. Esta Navidad no fue a la casa de sus padres, como de costumbre. En cambio, pasó aquí todas las vacaciones navideñas. En enero, cuando Ud. le preguntó cómo pasó las vacaciones, trató de evitar (*to avoid*) la pregunta. Estos días no se reúne con ustedes y no se le ve mucho por la universidad.
3. Mientras manejaba, el Sr. Ramírez, un vecino de usted, chocó con otro coche en la calle enfrente de su casa. Aunque es una calle residencial, el Sr. Ramírez manejaba a unas 60 millas por hora. Por suerte, no hubo víctimas, pero el Sr. Ramírez no lo supo, pues tan pronto como recobró el control del coche, se fue a toda velocidad.

SITUACIONES EXTRAORDINARIAS

With another student, act out the following role-play situations as fully as possible. Try to use as much as possible of the vocabulary that you know.

1. A reporter (**Un reportero/Una reportera**) from another country is interviewing you about holiday customs of people in the United States. Tell the journalist in detail what you and your family normally do to celebrate a holiday of your choice, stressing activities special to your family and including details typical of most families in this country.
2. You have just witnessed an accident in which a car struck (**chocar con**) a small child on a bicycle. Stop to help, asking the child questions about his or her injuries, asking someone to call an ambulance, getting information from the driver of the car, and so on. Accompany the child to the emergency room of a nearby hospital and explain what happened to the parent who has met you there.
3. You run into a friend who is obviously feeling out of sorts, whose eyes are red and who can barely talk. Ask questions to find out why your friend is in such bad shape. Your friend should invent details of the problem: an illness, a term paper (**un trabajo**) written and then lost (**perdido**) before it was handed in, a problem in the family or with a class, and so on.

CAPÍTULO TRECE

EL COCHE

Bogotá, Colombia

▲ **En la gasolinera**

—Buenos días, señora.

—Hola, buenos. Lléneme el tanque, por favor. Aquí tiene la llave.

—¿Gasolina super o normal?

—Super. ¿Puede revisar el aceite[a]?

—Sí. Ábrame el capó.[b].... Está un poco bajo, pero todavía tiene.

—Muy bien.

[a] *oil*
[b] *hood*

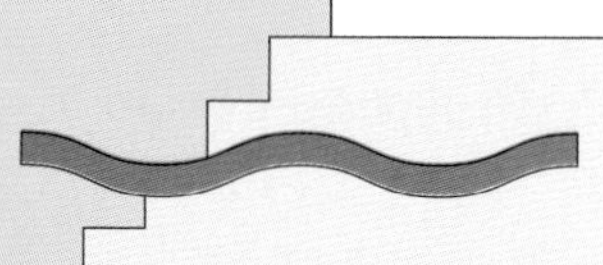

VOCABULARIO: PREPARACIÓN

Vocabulario: Preparación:
- See detailed supplementary materials for this section bound into the back of this Annotated Instructor's Edition.
- See model for vocabulary presentation and other materials in Supplementary *Vocabulario: Preparación* Materials, chapter by chapter, IM.

- See also [cassette icon].

Los coches

la autopista	freeway
el camino	street, road
la carretera	highway
la circulación, el tráfico	traffic
el conductor/la conductora	driver
la esquina	(street) corner
la licencia (de manejar / conducir)	driver's license
el semáforo	traffic light
la estación de gasolina, la gasolinera	gas station
los frenos	brakes
una llanta desinflada	a flat tire
el taller	(repair) shop

Revisamos las llantas.
GASOLINERA GÓMEZ
Sí, señor, aquí recibe Ud. un servicio completo.
Llenamos el tanque con gasolina.
Revisamos el aceite y la batería.
Lo arreglamos todo.
Limpiamos el parabrisas.
CARRETERA 66
CENTRO CIUDAD
Y Ud. puede continuar su viaje.

arrancar	to start up (*a car*)	**gastar (mucha gasolina)**	to use (a lot of gas)
arreglar	to fix, repair	**manejar, conducir (conduzco)**	to drive
contener (*like* **tener**)	to contain	**parar**	to stop
chocar (con)	to run into, collide (with)	**revisar**	to check
doblar	to turn	**seguir (i, i) (todo derecho)**	to keep on going; to go (straight ahead)
estacionar	to park		

Variation A: Students work in pairs, one covering column A, other column B.

A. **Definiciones.** Busque Ud. la definición de las palabras de la columna de la derecha.

1. Se pone en el tanque.
2. Se llenan de aire.
3. Lubrica el motor.
4. Es necesaria para arrancar el motor.
5. Cuando se llega a una esquina hay que hacer esto o seguir todo derecho.
6. No contiene aire suficiente y por eso es necesario cambiarla.
7. Es un camino público ancho (*wide*) donde los coches circulan rápidamente.
8. Se usan para parar el coche.
9. El policía nos la pide cuando nos para en el camino.
10. Allí se revisan y se arreglan los carros.

a. los frenos
b. doblar
c. la carretera
ch. la batería
d. el taller
e. una llanta desinflada
f. la gasolina
g. las llantas
h. el aceite
i. la licencia

Ahora, siguiendo el modelo de las definiciones anteriores, ¿puede Ud. dar una definición de las siguientes palabras?

1. el semáforo
2. la circulación
3. estacionarse
4. gastar gasolina
5. la gasolinera
6. la autopista

B. **Mientras Ud. conducía...** Invente los detalles para explicar lo que pasó en las siguientes situaciones. ¿Qué necesitaba o qué debía hacer Ud.? ¿Qué hizo?

1. De repente Ud. oyó un *flop flop.*
2. Su coche se paró y no volvió a arrancar.
3. Ud. llegó a una esquina donde había otro coche parado (*stopped*) a la derecha.
4. En una esquina, Ud. vio dos coches, una ambulancia y varios policías.
5. Ud. manejó solamente 20 millas y gastó un cuarto de tanque de gasolina.

Suggestion C: Focus in preceding chapters and in preceding exercises in this Ch. has been on preterite/imperfect usage. Take advantage of drawing to cue students back into use of present subjunctive in noun clauses, anticipating the use of the subjunctive for expressing uncertainty: *Es posible que la gasolina cueste ______ el litro; Es necesario que el dueño del coche cambie... ; Es posible que los mecánicos de esta estación sean... .*

C. **En la gasolinera.** Describa Ud. las cosas y acciones que se ven en el dibujo.

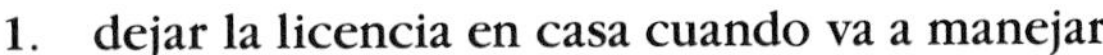

CH. **Entrevista.** Usando las siguientes frases como guía, entreviste a un compañero (una compañera) de clase para determinar con qué frecuencia hace las siguientes cosas.

1. dejar la licencia en casa cuando va a manejar
2. acelerar (*to speed up*) cuando ve a un policía
3. manejar después de beber alcohol
4. respetar o exceder el límite de velocidad
5. estacionar el coche donde dice «Prohibido estacionarse»
6. revisar el aceite y la batería
7. seguir todo derecho a toda velocidad cuando no sabe llegar a su destino
8. adelantar (*to pass*) tres carros a la vez (*at the same time*)

Ahora, según lo que Ud. averiguó (*learned*), describa la forma de manejar de su compañero/a. ¿Es un buen conductor (una buena conductora)?

Follow-up CH:
- Students rank question items in order of importance.
- *¿Es símbolo de mucho prestigio social tener un Ferrari? ¿un Volkswagen? ¿un BMW? ¿un Toyota? ¿una camioneta? ¿un pick-up? ¿Cómo es el típico dueño (la típica dueña) de cada uno de estos coches?*
- *¿Qué tipo de coche recomienda Ud. que compre una persona que... ?* **1.** *necesite un coche barato?* **2.** *no sepa nada de coches y no quiera preocuparse por el coche que maneja?* **3.** *tenga un puesto importante y quiera impresionar a sus clientes?* **4.** *quiera impresionar a sus clientes pero* **no** *tiene mucho dinero?*

Putting Things in Rank Order: Ordinals

primer(o)	first	**quinto**	fifth	**octavo**	eighth
segundo	second	**sexto**	sixth	**noveno**	ninth
tercer(o)	third	**séptimo**	seventh	**décimo**	tenth
cuarto	fourth				

Ordinal numbers are adjectives and must agree in number and gender with the nouns they modify.* Ordinals usually precede the noun: **la cuarta lección, el octavo ejercicio.**

Like **bueno**, the ordinals **primero** and **tercero** shorten to **primer** and **tercer**, respectively, before masculine singular nouns: **el primer niño**, **el tercer mes**.

---

*Ordinal numbers are frequently abbreviated with superscript letters that show the adjective ending: **las 1as lecciones**, **el 1er grado**, **el 5° estudiante**.

A. ¿En qué grado están estos niños?

1. Manuel—5°
2. Teresa—3er
3. Eduardo—7°
4. Jesús—1er
5. Pablo—10°
6. Evangelina—2°

B. Conteste las preguntas según el dibujo.

1. ¿Quién es la décima persona? ¿la quinta? ¿la tercera? ¿la segunda?
2. ¿En qué posición está Ángela? ¿Cecilia? ¿Juan? ¿Simón? ¿Linda?

Follow-up B: ***Preguntas:*** **1.** *¿Quién fue el primer presidente de los Estados Unidos? ¿el segundo? ¿el tercero? ¿El primer presidente de este siglo* (century)*? ¿el segundo?*, etc. **2.** *¿En qué año empezó la Primera Guerra Mundial? ¿En qué año terminó la Segunda Guerra Mundial?* **3.** *¿Cuántos hijos hay en su familia? ¿Cómo se llama el primero? ¿el segundo?*, etc. **4.** *¿Cuál fue su primera clase hoy? ¿la segunda?* **5.** *¿Cómo se llamaba su maestro/a del quinto grado? ¿Cómo era? ¿Quién fue su maestro en el sexto grado? ¿Era semejante o diferente al del quinto grado?*

Notas comunicativas: Telling What You Would Do

You have already learned to use the form **me gustaría...** to talk about what you would like—or not like—to do. You can use a similar form, **sería** (*would be*), to talk about what you would do in a given situation.

El primer factor sería... El segundo sería...
Lo mas importante para mí sería...
Para mí, la primera consideración sería...

Extension C: **3.** *Ud. tiene que aceptar o no una invitación para ir al cine con un compañero/una compañera: su apariencia física/su inteligencia/su sentido de humor / si tiene coche / si tiene mucho dinero y quiere pagarlo todo / si le gusta la película o no / si le interesa llegar a conocer mejor a esta persona / si es de su misma nacionalidad / religión* **4.** *Ud. tiene que escoger una universidad: la matrícula / la distancia de su casa / la fama académica de la universidad / el aspecto físico del campus / si tiene "fraternities"* **y** *"sororities" / si hay residencias estudiantiles / si Ud. puede asistir a clases* **y** *seguir viviendo donde vive ahora / si son importantes los deportes / si hay muchas fiestas*

Suggestion C: Do items in text (1 and 2) with students working in pairs or in groups. Do extension as whole-class exercise.

C. Imagine que Ud. tiene que tomar las siguientes decisiones. ¿En qué orden de importancia colocaría (*would you put*) los siguientes factores? ¿Por qué?

MODELO: Lo más importante para mí sería la materia del curso.

1. Ud tiene que eligir los cursos para el próximo semestre.
   _____ la hora de la clase
   _____ el profesor (la profesora)
   _____ la materia del curso
   _____ la posibilidad de sacar una buena nota
2. Ud. tiene que escoger entre dos puestos.
   _____ el sueldo
   _____ el prestigio de la compañía
   _____ la ciudad
   _____ la posibilidad de ascenso (*promotion*)
   _____ la personalidad del jefe (de la jefa)
   _____ las condiciones físicas de la oficina

Suggestion CH: Model completions for *No me importan estos factores...* including subjunctive use: *...que sea nuevo, que tenga aire acondicionado,* etc.

Follow-up CH: Have students pass their information to a partner, who will look at it and complete the following: *Según esta información, tú comprarías un ____ o posiblemente un ____. Seguramente un ____ no sería el coche ideal para ti.* Then students tell whether the predictions were correct.

CH. Su viejo carro no arrancó esta mañana y en el taller le dicen que no lo pueden arreglar. Es hora de comprar un carro nuevo. ¿Qué tipo de carro desea Ud.? Lea la siguiente lista de factores y póngalos en orden de importancia según sus preferencias. Luego describa el carro que va a comprar, según el modelo.

MODELO: Primero, deseo un carro ____ porque ____.
Segundo, ...
No me importan estos factores: si es grande o no, ...

____ grande / económico
____ nuevo / usado
____ con una transmisión automática / de cambios (*manual shift*)
____ con llantas convencionales / con llantas radiales
____ con aire acondicionado / sin aire acondicionado
____ con radio AM / con radio AM/FM / sin radio
____ con frenos normales / con frenos de disco
____ de color / marca ____
____ hecho (*made*) en USA / importado
____ con cassette / sin cassette

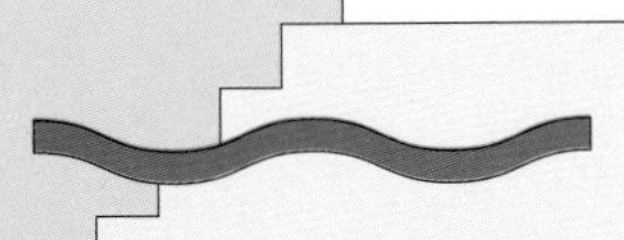

MINIDIÁLOGOS Y GRAMÁTICA

Suggestions: Point out subjunctive cues in sentences that accompany art. Ask, What do they have in common?

38. EXPRESSING UNCERTAINTY
Use of the Subjunctive in Noun Clauses: Doubt and Denial

Communicative objectives for 38: how to express doubt and denial

—¡*No es posible* que *pidan* diez mil!
—*Dudo* que *tenga* una batería nueva.
—*No creo* que el interior *esté* en buenas condiciones.
—Estoy seguro de que tiene más de 40 mil millas.

Continúe las especulaciones de los compradores.

- ¡Es imposible que...
- No creo que...
- Dudo que...
- Estoy seguro/a de que... (¡OJO!)

Independent Clause		**Dependent Clause**
first subject + *indicative* (expression of doubt or denial)	**que**	second subject + *subjunctive*

No creo que **sean** estudiantes. — *I don't believe they're students.*
No están seguros de que Roberto **tenga** razón. — *They're not sure that Roberto is right.*
Es imposible que **esté** con él. — *It's impossible for her to be with him.*

Suggestions:
- **Point out:** similarity to subjunctive after expressions of influence/emotion with change of subject
- **Optional:** When there is no subject change, Spanish uses either subjunctive or infinitive after expressions of doubt or denial. Generalizations are followed by infinitive only when there is no subject change. *Dudo que tenga el dinero./ Dudo tener el dinero.* = I doubt that I have the money. *Es imposible tener el dinero para mañana.*

A. Expressions of doubt and denial are those in which speakers express uncertainty or negation: *I doubt he's right*; *It's not possible for her to be here.* Such expressions, however strong or weak, are followed by the subjunctive in the dependent clause in Spanish.

B. Expressions of doubt and denial include **no creer**, **dudar** (*to doubt*), **no estar seguro/a**, and **negar (ie)** (*to deny*). Not all Spanish expressions of doubt are given here. Remember that any expression of doubt is followed by the subjunctive in the dependent clause.

C. When generalizations of doubt are personalized, they are followed by the subjunctive in the dependent clause. Some generalizations of doubt and denial are **es posible**, **es imposible**, **es probable**, **es improbable**, **no es verdad**, **no es cierto** (*certain*), and **no es seguro** (*a sure thing*).*

Indicative Versus Subjunctive

No creer, **dudar**, **no estar seguro/a** and **negar** are followed by the subjunctive. However, **creer**, **no dudar**, **estar seguro/a**, and **no negar** are usually followed by the indicative, since they do not express doubt, denial, or negation. Compare the following:

No niego (No dudo) que **es** simpático. — *I don't deny (doubt) that he's nice.*
Niego (Dudo) que **sea** simpático. — *I deny (doubt) that he's nice.*

Estamos seguros (Creemos) que el examen **es** hoy. — *We're sure (believe) the exam is today.*
No estamos seguros (No creemos) que el examen **sea** hoy. — *We're not sure (We don't believe) that the exam is today.*

- **Emphasis:** Contrast *no creer* and *dudar* (subjunctive) with *creer* and *no dudar* (usually imply affirmation → indicative).
- ***¿Cómo se dice?:*** **1.** I doubt that they are rich/ that they are coming. **2.** I don't believe that they are rich/that they are coming. **3.** I believe that they are rich/that they are coming.

Optional: In questions with *creer*, use of indicative or subjunctive in dependent clause reflects opinion of person asking question:
Indicative: *¿Crees que los Ramírez son ricos?* (Speaker believes they are.)
Subjunctive: *¿Crees que los Ramírez sean ricos?* (Speaker doubts they are.)

- **Emphasis:** indicative after *es verdad, es cierto, es seguro*

*Generalizations that express certainty are not followed by the subjunctive: ***Es verdad* que *cocina* bien; *No hay duda* de que el inquilino lo *paga*.**

Preliminary Exercises:

- *¿Sí o no?:* 1. *Es probable que Ud. compre un coche nuevo este año.* 2. *Es probable que terminemos el libro esta semana.* 3. *Es probable que Ud. cambie de trabajo mañana.* 4. *Es probable que yo vaya a* (country) *este verano.* 5. *Es probable que nieve* (*llueva*) *hoy.* 6. *Es probable que* (make up statement about a student in class). 7. *Es probable que* (make up statement about current events).
- *¡El coche no funciona! ¿Hay un mecánico aquí? Dé oraciones nuevas según las indicaciones.* 1. *Dudo que Luis sepa mucho de coches.* (*tú, el tío, Uds., Ud., vosotros*) 2. *No creo que sea la transmisión.* (*creo, dudo, estoy seguro/a, niego, no dudo, no estoy seguro/a*) 3. *Es necesario que Ud. compre otro carro.* (*mejor, posible, seguro, probable, verdad, imposible*)

Práctica

¡El coche no funciona! Ésta es una conversación que ocurrió ayer en el taller cuando Ud. llevó allí su «nuevo coche viejo». Haga oraciones según las indicaciones. Use el pretérito de los verbos marcados con asterisco (*).

1. es verdad / que / (yo) sólo / pagar* / mil / dólar / por / coche
2. es cierto / que / coche / funcionar* / bien / por / dos / mes
3. ahora / dudo / que / carro / arrancar / otra vez
4. ¿creer / Ud. / que / ser / transmisión?
5. es mejor / que / Ud. / dejarlo / aquí / hasta / mañana
6. (yo) no / estar / seguro / de que / (yo) poder / arreglarlo
7. (yo) creer / que / es probable / Ud. / tener / que / comprar / otro / coche
8. es posible / que / en / agencia / (ellos) darle / ciento / dólar / por / coche

¿Cierto, falso o no lo dice? Corrija las oraciones falsas.

1. Es verdad que Ud. tiene un coche nuevo.
2. Es seguro que Ud. tiene que comprar otro coche.
3. Ud. manejó el coche a casa ayer.

Conversación

Suggestion A: Use drawing as a vehicle for reviewing major structures presented so far.

A. **Escenas de la carretera.** Describa lo que pasa en el siguiente dibujo, contestando las preguntas e inventando otros detalles.

Palabras útiles: el hombre/la mujer de negocios (*businessman/woman*), el recipiente (*container*)

¿Por qué hay tanto tráfico ahora? ¿Qué le pasa al coche de la señora? ¿Es posible que sea la transmisión? ¿Adónde iba la señora? ¿Qué pasa con el coche del señor? ¿Qué lleva el señor? ¿Es probable que tenga una llanta desinflada? ¿De dónde viene el señor? ¿Adónde iba? ¿Es probable que alguien pare para ayudarlos?

Variations B:
- Make up statements about yourself/your family or about class members, to which students react using phrases given. Some statements should be false/outrageous.
- Substitute more controversial statements for those given in text. ***Modelos:*** *Creo que el aborto debe ser legal. No creo que se deba fumar marihuana.*

B. Algunos creen que las oraciones siguientes describen el mundo de hoy. ¿Qué cree Ud.? Reaccione Ud. a estas oraciones, empezando con una de estas expresiones:

Dudo que...	Es bueno/malo que...
(No) Es verdad que...	Es lástima que...
No hay duda que...	Es increíble que...
Es probable que...	(No) Me gusta que...

1. Los niños miran la televisión seis horas al día.
2. Hay mucha pobreza (*poverty*) en el mundo.
3. En los Estados Unidos, gastamos mucha energía.
4. Hay mucho sexo y violencia en la televisión y en el cine.
5. Se come poco y mal en muchas partes del mundo.
6. Los temas de la música ***punk*** son demasiado violentos.
7. Hay mucho interés en la exploración del espacio.
8. El fumar no es malo para la salud.
9. Los deportes para las mujeres no reciben tanto apoyo (*support*) financiero como los de los hombres.
10. No se permite el uso de la marihuana.

Indique Ud. soluciones para algunos de los problemas. Empiece las soluciones con estas frases:

Es urgente que...	Es necesario que...
Es preferible que...	Es importante que...
Quiero que...	Insisto en que...

Notas culturales: Variaciones lingüísticas

Las palabras que se usan para hablar de caminos y vehículos y de la acción de manejar varían en las diferentes partes del mundo de habla española. Aquí hay algunos ejemplos.

car = coche, auto, automóvil (uso generalizado)
carro (Centroamérica y los Estados Unidos)
¡OJO! carro = *cart* en España

bus = autobús (uso generalizado)
guagua (Cuba)
camión (México)
¡OJO! camión = *truck* en la mayoría del mundo de habla española

tire = llanta (uso generalizado)
rueda (España)

Note: This is primarily a summary section. The only new material presented is use of indirect object pronouns with verbs like *decir.*

39. EXPRESSING INFLUENCE, EMOTION, DOUBT AND DENIAL

Uses of the Subjunctive in Noun Clauses: A Summary

Suggestion: Ask students to explain uses of the subjunctive in the mini.

Follow-up (mini): Students predict what will happen when the client comes back to pick up his car in two hours.

En el taller

CLIENTE: *Temo* que mi carro *tenga* algo serio. ¿Podría revisarlo, por favor?

EMPLEADO: Sí, señor. Entre por aquí y apague el motor, por favor.

CLIENTE: Esta mañana tuve dificultad en hacerlo arrancar.

EMPLEADO: Puede ser la batería.

CLIENTE: Pues... la verdad... *me sorprende* que *sea* la batería. Es nueva; la cambié hace dos semanas, ¿sabe?

EMPLEADO: En ese caso, le *recomiendo* que lo *deje* para poder revisarlo con cuidado.

CLIENTE: Está bien. También *quiero* que le *revise* las llantas delanteras y las bujías.

EMPLEADO: Sí, señor. Eso es parte de nuestro servicio normal.

CLIENTE: ¿Por cuánto tiempo debo dejar el carro aquí?

EMPLEADO: Lo puede venir a buscar en dos horas. *No creo* que *sea* nada que requiera más tiempo.

1. ¿Qué teme el dueño del carro?
2. ¿Está de acuerdo el empleado del taller?
3. ¿Qué posibilidad sugiere el empleado?
4. ¿Cuál es la reacción del dueño?
5. ¿Qué recomienda el empleado?
6. ¿Cuánto tiempo se requiere para revisar el coche?

Independent Clause		**Dependent Clause**
first subject + *indicative*	**que**	second subject + *subjunctive*
expression of { influence / emotion / doubt, denial }		

At the shop CLIENT: I'm afraid there is something seriously wrong with my car. Could you take a look at it, please? EMPLOYEE: Yes, sir. Come in through here and shut off the motor, please. CLIENT: I had trouble getting it to start this morning. EMPLOYEE: Maybe it's the battery. CLIENT: Well, the truth is . . . I'm surprised that it could be the battery. It's new; I changed it two weeks ago, you know? EMPLOYEE: In that case, I recommend that you leave it to be checked out carefully. CLIENT: O.K. I also want you to check the front tires and the spark plugs. EMPLOYEE: Yes, sir. That's part of our normal service. CLIENT: How long should I leave the car here? EMPLOYEE: You can come to get it in two hours. I don't think it will take any longer.

A. Remember that, in Spanish, the subjunctive occurs primarily in two-clause sentences with a different subject in each clause. If there is no change of subject, an infinitive follows the first verb. Compare the following:

Quiero Es necesario	} que él revise el carro.	*I want* *It's necessary for*	} *him to check the car.*
Quiero Es necesario	} revisar el carro.	*I want* *It's necessary*	} *to check the car.*

The independent clause, in addition to fulfilling the preceding conditions, must contain an expression of influence, emotion, or doubt in order for the subjunctive to occur in the dependent clause. If there is no such expression, the indicative is used.* Compare the following:

Dicen que maneje Julio.	*They say that Julio should drive.*
Dicen que Julio **maneja** muy mal; por eso quieren que maneje Carlota.	*They say that Julio drives very badly; that's why they want Carlota to drive.*

Note: Use examples to emphasize use of subjunctive or indicative after certain verbs, depending on particular connotations of verb. Here *decir* is followed by both indicative and subjunctive in dependent clause, depending on meaning conveyed: *decir* = to say → indicative; *decir* = to tell, order → subjunctive.

B. Some verbs of influence are frequently used with indirect object pronouns.

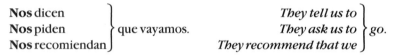

Nos dicen **Nos** piden **Nos** recomiendan } que vayamos.	*They tell us to* *They ask us to* *They recommend that we* } *go.*

The indirect object indicates the subject of the dependent clause, as in the preceding sentences: **nos** → **vayamos.**

Point out: Function of IO pronouns in Spanish sentences; omission of subject pronouns in subordinate clause.

¿Cómo se dice? 1. They tell us to study. 2. They tell us to work. 3. They tell him to come. 4. They tell them to come.

Práctica

Suggestion A: Students supply their own completions.

A. **Un coche: ¿Una compra esencial?** Si Ud. quiere comprar un coche para su uso personal, tiene que ir a una agencia de automóviles. Allí va a ver todos los nuevos modelos. ¿Qué quiere Ud. que pase en la agencia?

Quiero que el vendedor...

- enseñarme los últimos modelos
- explicarme cómo funciona cada coche
- decirme cuáles son las ventajas y las desventajas de cada modelo

Claro está que Ud. va a aprender mucho. ¿Qué es lo que le va a sorprender?

Me va a sorprender que...

- costar tanto los coches hoy día
- ser tan fáciles de manejar
- haber tantos modelos distintos

Después de examinar muchos coches, es probable que Ud. por fin decida comprar uno. Si no puede pagar al contado (*in cash*), es posible que le hagan unas sugerencias en la agencia.

---

*See Grammar Sections 24, 25, 26, and 38 for a more detailed presentation of the uses of the subjunctive in noun clauses.

Es posible que el vendedor...

- proponerme un plan para pagar a plazos (*in installments*)
- pedirme mi tarjeta de crédito
- decirme que espere hasta el mes que viene, pues va a haber unas rebajas

Si Ud. decide pagar a plazos, firme los papeles necesarios y ya puede tener su coche nuevo. ¡Buena suerte!

Optional:

- *En esta era de la tecnología avanzada, hay máquinas para todo. Imagine que Ud. tiene en casa un robot de último modelo. Complete las oraciones según las indicaciones.* **1.** *Quiero que el robot (me)* ____. *(lavar los platos, hacer las camas, mantener el carro en buenas condiciones, pagar las cuentas, ¿ ?)* **2.** *Me alegro de* (I'm glad) *que el robot* ____. *(ayudarme tanto, funcionar bien casi siempre, no quejarse nunca, no pedirme un aumento de sueldo, ¿ ?)* **3.** *Me sorprende que el robot* ____. *(hablar tan bien y tan lógicamente, ser tan inteligente, parecer tan humano, saberlo todo, ¿ ?)* **4.** *Dudo que los robots* ____ *algún día. (reemplazar* [to replace] *a los seres humanos, controlarlo todo, ¿ ?)*
- *¿Qué va a pasar en clase mañana? ¿Cómo se dice en español?* **1.** There's a quiz (*prueba*), but I'm not sure that it's tomorrow. **2.** I doubt that the subjunctive is (*entrar*) on the test. **3.** Is it possible there will be commands? **4.** I don't think it will be easy! **5.** It's probable that John won't come to class!

B. Imagine que Ud. tiene en casa un robot de último modelo que va a hacer lo que Ud. le diga. ¿Qué le va a mandar al robot que haga?

Le digo que... lavarme los platos, hacerme las camas, mantener el carro en buenas condiciones, cambiarme el aceite cada tres meses, escribir todos los cheques, ¿ ?

Conversación

A. **Situaciones.** Ud. es mecánico/a y encuentra muchos problemas con el coche de un cliente. ¿Cuáles son? Ud. y el cliente pueden hablar de los frenos de disco, la transmisión, el aire acondicionado, las llantas, la batería, el radiador, el aceite, etcétera. Use estas palabras como guía. ¿Cuántas oraciones puede Ud. inventar?

Temo que	revisarme ____
Recomiendo que	su ____ estar roto/a (*broken*)
Me sorprende que	no funcionar bien ____
¿Cómo es posible que... ?	poner un(a) ____ nuevo/a
Quiero que	arreglar ____
	ir a costarle ____
	usar un(a) ____ reconstruido/a (*rebuilt*)
	no hay ____ en ____
	¿ ?

B. **Si yo fuera...** (*If I were . . .*) With a classmate, adopt the identity of each of the following persons, and tell at least two things about which you might be happy or concerned. Begin your sentences with phrases such as these:

Temo que ____. Me alegro de (*I'm glad*) que ____. No creo que ____.

Then complete the following statement the way each person might.

Lo que más me preocupa es ____. (*infinitive or singular noun*)
son ____. (*plural noun*)

1. una persona de noventa años
2. un turista hispano que viaja por los Estados Unidos
3. un turista norteamericano que viaja por México
4. un policía que trabaja en Nueva York
5. un padre/una madre que tiene un hijo de 16 años
6. una persona que acaba de graduarse en esta universidad

México, D.F.

Pidiendo información

—Dígame, por favor, ¿cómo se llega al parque San Marcos?

—Siga todo derecho en esta calle por dos cuadras (*blocks*). Luego doble a la derecha en el semáforo y siga una cuadra más. Allí lo va a encontrar.

—Gracias, y perdone la molestia.

—No hay de qué.

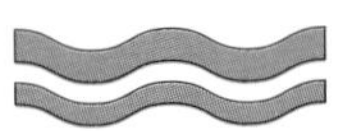

40. EL INFINITIVO

Verb + Infinitive; Verb + Preposition + Infinitive

Ventajas y desventajas de la era de la tecnología

Algunos de los inventos del siglo (*century*) XX nos traen problemas a la vez que nos facilitan otros aspectos de la vida. Mire el dibujo y lea el comentario del señor. Luego, usando las frases como guía, invente la historia de este señor, que es una víctima del progreso. Use infinitivos con cada frase.

1. Este señor tenía que...
2. Quería...
3. Cuando llegó a la oficina, trató de...
4. Pero no pudo...
5. Por eso tuvo que...
6. Una vez en casa, decidió...
7. En este momento, acaba de...
8. El señor con quien habla va a...

—Yo quería ir a su oficina a pagar la tasa de estacionamiento,° pero no pude hacerlo porque no encontré sitio para estacionar.

tasa... *parking fee*

As you have already learned, when two verbs occur in a series, the second verb is usually in the infinitive form. The infinitive is also the only verb form that can follow a preposition. You have already used many of the constructions that are presented in this section.

A. Many Spanish verbs require no preposition before an infinitive.

Prefieren poner la mesa. — *They prefer to set the table.*

deber	**gustar**	**poder (ue)**
decidir	**necesitar**	**preferir (ie)**
desear	**parecer**	**querer (ie)**
esperar	**pensar (ie)** (*to intend*)	**saber**

B. Some Spanish verbs require a preposition or **que** before an infinitive.

1. Some verbs require **a** before an infinitive.

La profesora nos **enseña a bailar**. — *The professor is teaching us to dance.*

Follow-up B: *¿Cuáles son las ventajas y desventajas (lo bueno y lo malo) de los robots?*

Follow-up: Students tell which verbs take preposition or other word (*que*) and which not when followed by infinitive.

Follow-up: *¿Cuáles son las ventajas y desventajas (lo bueno y lo malo) de los siguientes inventos?* **1.** *el teléfono* **2.** *el coche* **3.** *la computadora personal*

Note: Students have used virtually all verbs presented in this section, along with their respective prepositions/other words. Treat section as summary only, not as new information to be learned.

Option B1: verbs of motion + *a* + inf.

aprender a **ayudar a** **empezar (ie) a** **enseñar a** **invitar a** **ir a** **venir (ie) a** **volver (ue) a**

2. Other verbs or verb phrases require **de** before an infinitive.

Siempre **tratamos de llegar** puntualmente. *We always try to arrive on time.*

acabar de **acordarse (ue) de** **dejar de** **olvidarse de** **tener ganas de** **tratar de**

Note B2: contrast: *olvidar* + inf. vs. *olvidarse de* + inf.; *acordarse de* + inf. vs. *recordar* + inf.

3. **Insistir**, a frequently used verb, requires **en** before an infinitive.

Insisten en venir esta noche. *They insist on coming over tonight.*

Option B3: *pensar* + inf. versus *pensar de/en/que*

4. Two verbs require **que** before an infinitive: **haber que**, **tener que**.

Hay que sacar la basura. *It's necessary to take out the garbage.*

Preliminary exercise: ***¿Cómo se dice?:*** **1.** He's learning to read (to write, to play tennis). **2.** She helps me wash the dishes (dust, cook). **3.** We're beginning to understand it (to read it, to explain it). **4.** They always invite us to go to the theater (to the movies, to the museum). **5.** They're coming to eat (to visit us, to see us). **6.** He's trying to help (to cook, to see). **7.** I just ate (arrived, called). **8.** He insists on doing it (bringing it, listening to it). **9.** It's necessary to work more (to eat more, to sleep more). **10.** I have to leave now (to eat supper, to eat breakfast).

Suggestion A: Emphasize personal completions. Be alert to potential for confusion with subjunctive syntax (noun clauses).

Práctica

A. Haga oraciones completas y lógicas. Use **no** cuando sea necesario.

mi profesor(a) de español (me)	invitar	a	hablar español
mis padres (me)	querer	de	pagar (la matrícula, ¿ ?)
mis amigos (me)	ayudar	en	salir con ellos
¿ ?	deber		divertirse
	tratar		ser (tolerante, ¿ ?)
	insistir		llegar a ser ¿ ?
	enseñar		fumar
	dejar		acostarse (temprano, ¿ ?)
	aprender		sacar la basura
	¿ ?		equivocarse (nunca)
			viajar (a... , con... , ¿ ?)
			quejarse (de ¿ ?)
			¿ ?

B. Complete las oraciones lógicamente usando infinitivos.

1. A un mecánico le gusta _____ con los coches. Trata de _____lo todo con cuidado y a veces tiene que _____ a arreglar algo si no le sale bien la primera vez. A veces nos dice que hay que _____ el coche hasta el día siguiente.

2. Un niño de un año empieza a _____ y a _____. Un niño de cinco años aprende a _____ y a _____ en la escuela. Le gusta _____ con sus amigos en el patio de la escuela. A los trece años, no tiene ganas de _____. Sólo quiere _____ con los amigos.
3. Si un estudiante sale de la biblioteca a las once de la noche, acaba de _____ mucho. Es probable que piense _____ a un bar estudiantil o al apartamento de unos amigos para _____. No va a volver a _____ esa noche.
4. Mi abuelo tiene que _____ a cuidarse mejor. Tiene que dejar de _____ y _____ tanto, y el médico le dijo que debe empezar a _____ ejercicio y _____ mejor. Espero que mi abuelo trate de _____ los consejos del médico.
5. Los novios acaban de _____. Piensan _____ a Hawai para su luna de miel. Allí desean _____ todo el día en la playa y por la noche van a _____ a comer y _____.
6. En el avión, hay que _____ de fumar cuando el avión despega. Durante el vuelo, los pasajeros pueden _____ una película o _____ música. Algunos prefieren _____ revistas o periódicos y otros tienen que _____ porque están en un viaje de negocios.

Conversación

A. **Preparativos para un viaje en carro.** ¿Qué tiene Ud. que hacer en las siguientes situaciones? Use las palabras que Ud. ya sabe y las que se dan a continuación (*below*). Use también **a**, **de**, **en** o **que**, si es necesario.

1. Pienso viajar durante la época de las lluvias. Por eso debo _____.
2. Quiero hacer un viaje por las montañas de Colorado en el mes de diciembre. Por eso tengo _____.
3. Vamos al desierto a hacer *camping* este fin de semana. Parece que una de las llantas está un poco desinflada. Por eso hay _____.
4. Antes de empezar un viaje largo, debo consultar con _____. Él/Ella va _____.
5. Yo no sé _____. Por eso siempre me lo/la cambia _____.

Palabras útiles: las cadenas (*chains*), el filtro del aire (del aceite, del combustible), hacer una revisión de _____, los limpiaparabrisas (*windshield wipers*), la llanta de repuesto (*spare*), el radiador

B. **Entrevista.** Use las frases como guía para entrevistar a un compañero (una compañera) de clase. Empiece sus preguntas con **Dime...**

1. algo que él/ella dejó de hacer el año pasado
2. algo que le gustaría aprender a hacer
3. algo que empieza a hacer muy bien
4. la razón por la cual (*the reason why*) tuvo que guardar cama una vez
5. algo que sus padres (hijos) le ayudan a hacer

Follow-up B:
- *¿Qué trata Ud. de hacer todos los días? ¿Qué tiene que hacer todos los días? ¿Qué no le gusta hacer todos los días? ¿Qué se olvida de hacer todos los días? ¿Qué le gustaría hacer todos los días?*
- Students answer preceding series of questions as if they were a famous person.

6. algo que siempre se olvida de hacer (y que le molesta mucho a su compañero/a [esposo/a, madre/padre, ...])
7. algo que piensa hacer después de graduarse
8. lo que prefería comer para el almuerzo cuando era niño/a

Study Hint: Listening

When you are listening to someone speaking Spanish, try to pick out cognates and to guess the meaning of unfamiliar words from context, just as you do when you are reading. The following suggestions will also help you to understand more of what you hear in Spanish.

1. Remember that it is not necessary to understand every word to get the gist of the conversation. You may feel uncomfortable if you cannot understand absolutely everything, but chances are good that you will still be able to handle the conversational situation.
2. Watch the speaker's facial expressions and gestures—they will give you a general idea about what he or she is saying. For example, if there is a pause and the speaker is looking at you expectantly, it is reasonable to guess that he or she has just asked you a question.
3. Use brief pauses in the conversation to digest the words that you have just heard.
4. The more familiar you are with the vocabulary being used, the easier it will be to understand what you are hearing. Listen for familiar words—and be flexible: they may appear with a different meaning in a new context. Listen also for specific clues, such as the following.

- *gender of nouns and adjectives:* Is the speaker talking about **un chico alto** or **una chica alta**? Here you have three chances—with the article, the noun itself, and the adjective—to catch the gender of the person being described.
- *verb endings:* Who did what to whom? If you hear **habló**, for example, you know that the speaker is not talking about himself or herself, since the **-ó** ending signals another person.
- *object pronouns:* The sentence **La vi en el restaurante** can only refer to a woman or to a feminine noun.
- *intonation:* Did you hear a question or a statement?

Above all, if you really have not understood what someone said to you, react: ask questions, admit that you haven't understood, and ask him or her to repeat. You will find some phrases to help you do this politely in the **A propósito...** section on page 394.

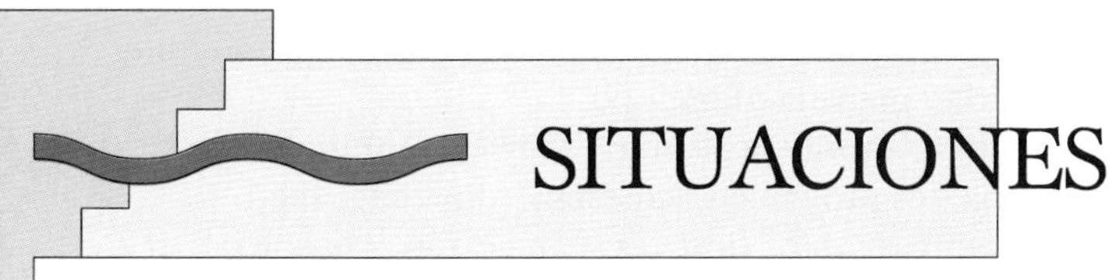

SITUACIONES

Situaciones: See IM for suggestions, additional exercises, and supplementary dialogues and exercises.

Hablando de coches

Un servicio extraordinario

—Buenas. ¿Qué desea?
—Necesito que me arreglen la llanta de repuesto.
—Puede dejarla y pasar mañana a recogerla.°
—Pero... es que salgo de viaje ahora mismo... y quisiera tenerla en seguida.
—De acuerdo. Se lo hacemos en diez minutos.

° *to pick it up*

El servicio normal

—Buenos días.
—Buenos días. ¿Le lleno el tanque?
—Sí, primero haga eso, pero después necesito que revise el agua del radiador y el aceite, por favor.
—Sí, cómo no.

—¿En qué puedo servirle?
—Lléneme el tanque, por favor.
—¿Quiere que le revise el aceite?
—Sí, por favor, y el agua de la batería y del radiador. Y otra cosa, ¿podría° mirarme la presión de las ruedas?
—De acuerdo. Lleve el coche allí delante. Voy en seguida.

°could you. . . ?

Conversación

Con un compañero (una compañera) practique las conversaciones anteriores. Trate de variar las expresiones de cortesía. Si quiere, lea primero **A propósito**... en la página 394.

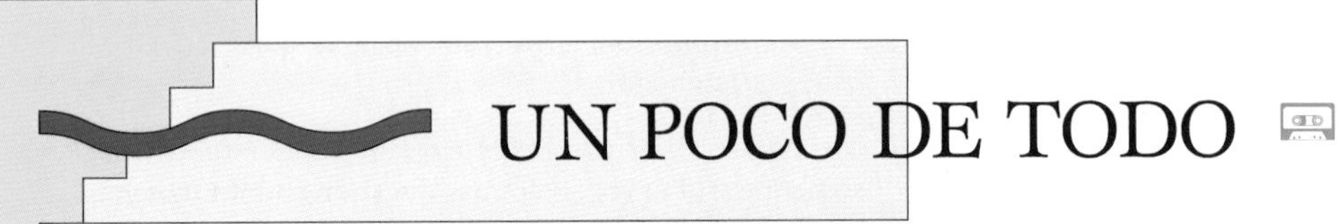

UN POCO DE TODO

A. **Los compañeros de cuarto.** Form complete sentences based on the words given, in the order given. Conjugate the verbs and add other words if necessary. Use subject pronouns only when needed. The double slashes (//) mark the end of one sentence and the beginning of the next.

1. yo / dudar / Marcos / limpiar / todo / casa / hoy // yo / saber / él / no / ir / querer / limpiarla / mañana / tampoco
2. yo / no / creer / compañero/a / acostarse / muy / temprano / este / noche // ¡y / mañana / es probable / acostarse / dos / mañana !
3. no / es posible / nosotros / dar / fiesta / este / sábado // nosotros / ir / tratar / hacer / uno / fin de semana que viene
4. yo / estar / seguro / Enrique / no / hacer / cama / todo / días // yo / dudar / él / hacerla / hoy
5. ojalá / yo / despertarse / a tiempo / mañana // ayer / yo / no / despertarse / hasta / once

B. **Recomendaciones.** Ud. es miembro de los siguientes grupos y les quiere pedir (recomendar, etcétera) muchas cosas—el número mayor posible—a las personas indicadas. ¿Qué va a decir? Use los siguientes verbos y frases.

Follow-up B: Working in groups or at home, students prepare telegrams they would like to send to the President or other government official. E.g., *Recomiendo que* ___. *Le pido que* ___. Students read telegrams to class.

pedir que	insistir en que	preferir que
recomendar que	prohibir que	querer que
es importante que	es preciso que	es urgente que

1. un grupo de empleados (todos miembros de un sindicato [*union*]), a los jefes
2. un grupo de prisioneros, al director de la prisión
3. un grupo de niños mimados (*spoiled*), a los padres
4. un grupo de viejos militantes (como los «Panteras Grises»), al gobierno
5. los ciudadanos de los Estados Unidos, al presidente
6. los consejeros, a un grupo de estudiantes nuevos
7. ___, a ___

C. **De vacaciones.** Cuando menos se espera, las cosas pueden no ir bien—sobre todo cuando se trata de coches (*where cars are concerned*). La escena en este dibujo no es una excepción. Describa la situación, contestando las preguntas y añadiendo otros detalles cuando sea posible.

1. ¿Quiénes son estas personas?
2. ¿Adónde es probable que vayan? ¿De dónde vienen?
3. ¿Por qué tienen que empujar (*to push*) el coche?
4. ¿Qué se les cae del coche?
5. ¿Qué quiere cada miembro de la familia que hagan?
6. ¿Qué cree Ud. que deben hacer?
7. ¿Cómo va a terminar el episodio?

CH. **El coche nuevo: ¿una ganga o un desastre?** Complete the following dialogue with the correct form of the words in parentheses, as suggested by the context. When two possibilities are given in parentheses, select the correct word. Begin with the present indicative.

Margarita, (un/una[1]) *joven de veinticinco años que* (acabar[2]) (de/que[3]) *comprarse un carro nuevo*
Alberto, un amigo de Margarita (quien/que[4]) *sabe* (mucho/muchos[5]) *de coches*

Camino a° una fiesta en casa de unos amigos

Camino... *On the way to*

A: (Al volante°) Margarita, perdona (*que / lo que*[6]) te interrumpa, pero a sólo 3 kilómetros de tu casa, no es posible que el termómetro (*marcar*[7]) una temperatura (*tan/tanto*[8]) alta en el motor. Ya (*ser/estar*[9]) en la zona roja.

wheel

M: No te (*preocupar*[10]); debe (*que/—*[11]) estar roto como el cuentakilómetros y (*el/la*[12]) reloj, que tampoco (*funcionar*[13]).

A: Pronto te vas a (*quedas/quedar*[14]) sin coche. Mira, en cosa de pocos minutos se (*poder*[15]) localizar (*el/la*[16]) problema. En (*ese*[17]) estación de servicio (*haber*[18]) un mecánico y un electricista. ¿Quieres que (yo: *parar*[19])?

M: ¡Ay, Alberto! Ahora no vamos a (*un/una*[20]) taller sino° a una fiesta. Conduce más (*rapido*[21]), por favor, o vamos a (*llegamos/llegar*[22]) tarde.

but rather

Unos minutos después

A: Margarita, quieras o no, tengo (*de/que*[23]) (*veo/ver*[24]) lo que le pasa al motor. Ni con las luces plenas° puedo (*veo/ver*[25]) el camino. Y la calefacción no (*calentar [ie]*[26])... déjame probar° la bocina°... ¡ay, tampoco suena!

M: Alberto, ¡hoy (*ser/estar*[27]) imposible! (*Primer/Primero*[28]), el termómetro; segundo, el taller; tercero, (*los/las*[29]) luces; cuarto, la calefacción; (*quinto/quinta*[30]), la bocina... Vamos a llegar tarde.

A: No me importa que (nosotros: *llegar*[31]) tarde o temprano. Lo único que (yo: *querer*[32]) es que (nosotros: *llegar*[33]). (Apaga el motor y se baja del coche.)

luces... *high beams*
try / *horn*

Follow-up CH: Ask students: *¿Cómo cree Ud. que va a terminar el episodio?*

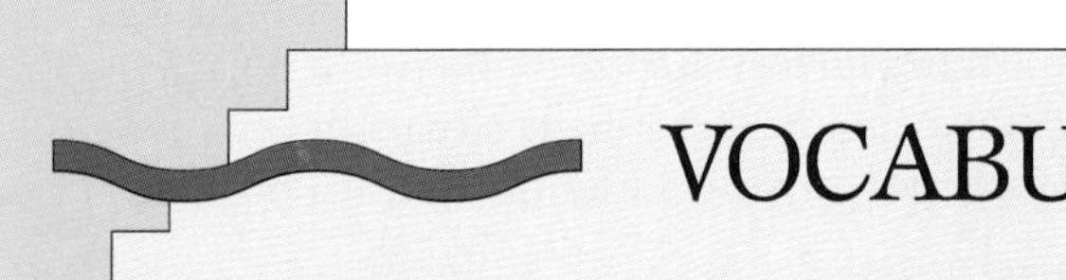

VOCABULARIO

Theme vocabulary previously listed as active: *arreglar, la carretera, doblar, manejar, seguir.*

VERBOS

alegrarse (de) to be happy (about)
costar (ue) to cost
decidir to decide
dudar to doubt
haber *infinitive form of* **hay** (there is/are)
negar (ie) to deny

HABLANDO DE COCHES

arrancar to start (*a motor*)
contener (contengo) to contain, hold
gastar to use, expend
llenar to fill (up)
mantener (mantengo) to maintain, keep up
revisar to check

el aceite oil
el automóvil car, automobile
la batería battery
el capó hood
la estación de gasolina gas station
los frenos brakes
la gasolina gasoline
la gasolinera gas station
la llanta tire
una llanta desinflada a flat tire
el/la mecánico/a mechanic
el servicio service
el tanque tank
el taller (repair) shop

EN EL CAMINO

conducir (conduzco) to drive
chocar (con) to run into, collide (with)
estacionar(se) to park
parar to stop

la autopista freeway
el camino street, road
la circulación traffic
el/la conductor(a) driver
la esquina corner (*of a street*)
la licencia license
la milla mile
el/la policía police officer
el semáforo traffic signal
el tráfico traffic
la velocidad speed

OTROS SUSTANTIVOS

la desventaja disadvantage
la ventaja advantage

ADJETIVOS

raro/a strange
roto/a broken
verdadero/a true, real

LOS ADJETIVOS ORDINALES

primer(o/a), segundo/a, tercer(o/a), cuarto/a, quinto/a, sexto/a, séptimo/a, octavo/a, noveno/a, décimo/a

PALABRAS ADICIONALES

a la vez at the same time
es cierto it's certain
es seguro it's a sure thing
estar seguro/a to be sure, certain
hay que + *inf.* it is necessary to (*do something*)
prohibido estacionarse no parking
todo derecho straight ahead

Frases útiles para la comunicación

sería — it would be
¿podría (Ud.) ... ? — Could you . . . ?

OPTIONAL SECTION

UN PASO MÁS 13

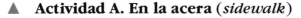

▲ Actividad A. En la acera (*sidewalk*)

Point out: Need to have valid driver's license in order to rent car and drive in other countries. Simplest way is to secure International Driver's License at an American Automobile Association office before leaving U.S.

Hints: Maximum Speed *80 kilómetros por hora; Tránsito* = Traffic (one-way traffic); no parking; stop; yield right of way; no turns; railroad (*ferrocarril*), detour (from *desviar*).

Describa lo que pasa en el dibujo del hombre que espera junto al cruce para peatones (*pedestrians*). Conteste las siguientes preguntas y añada otros detalles.

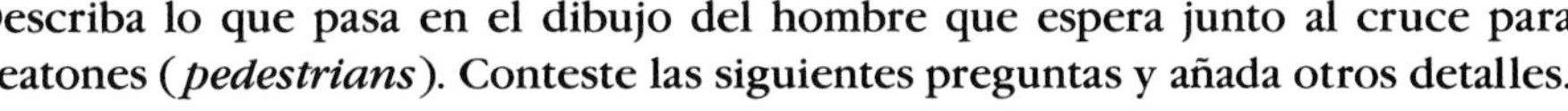

1. ¿Quién es el hombre? ¿Dónde trabaja?
2. ¿Es un conductor o un peatón? ¿Por qué camina y no maneja?
3. ¿Dónde está ahora? ¿Qué hace?
4. ¿Qué prohíbe la señal de tráfico?
5. ¿Qué cree Ud. que significan los números que se ven en la señal?
6. ¿Tiene miedo el hombre? ¿de qué?

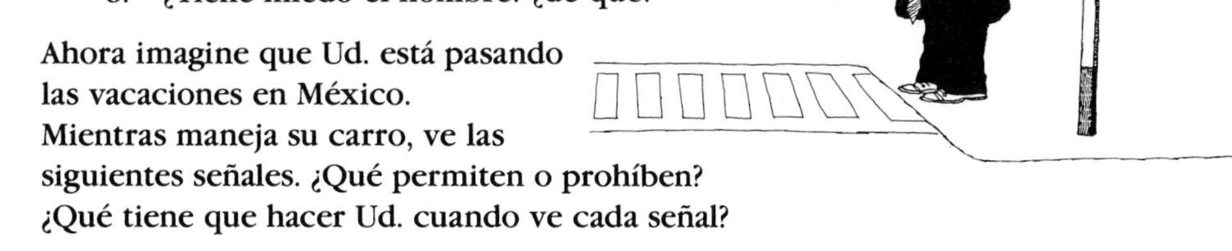

Ahora imagine que Ud. está pasando las vacaciones en México. Mientras maneja su carro, ve las siguientes señales. ¿Qué permiten o prohíben? ¿Qué tiene que hacer Ud. cuando ve cada señal?

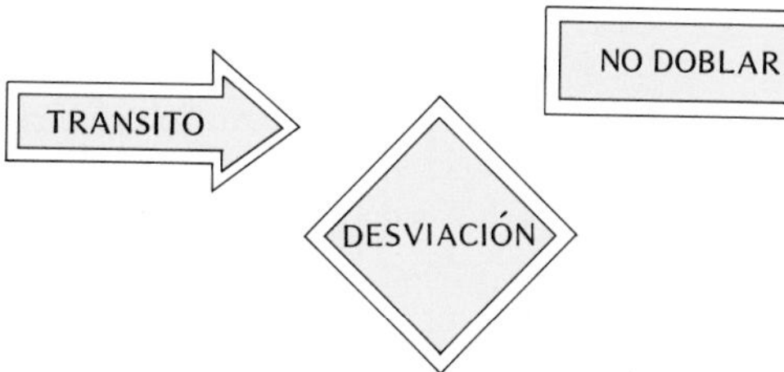

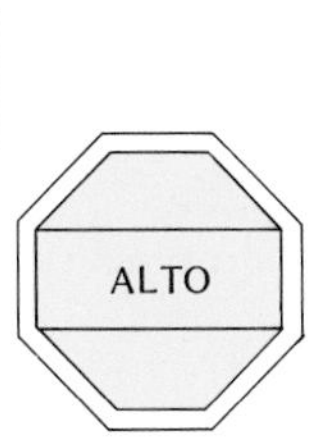

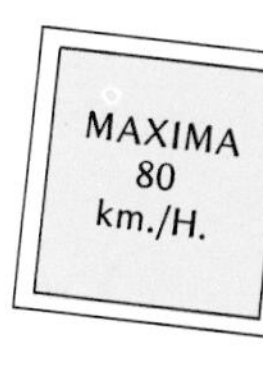

▲ Actividad B. ¿Qué se debe decir?

Variation B: Do as written exercise only.

What would you say to be especially courteous in each of the following situations? How would you thank the person for helping you? Try to use the phrases in **A propósito**... on page 394.

1. You need to return an article of clothing to a department store because it is the wrong size. You want the clerk to help you select the right size.
2. You know that you need to catch the number 17 bus to get to the **Museo de Arte**, but you don't know where to catch it. You ask a police officer on the street corner.
3. You have lost the key to your hotel room and need to tell the clerk. You also need to get another key.
4. The waiter has just brought you a cup of coffee. You ordered tea.

5. Something is wrong with your car. You want the mechanic to fix it as quickly and as cheaply as possible.
6. You have gone to the doctor with a routine ailment. After the doctor has examined you and you have received a prescription, you discover that you have left your money and checkbook at home and cannot pay at this moment.

A propósito... More About Being Polite

When you are searching for words to express the exact nature of a problem or situation or when you are trying to make a request, it is possible to sound abrupt or impolite, even though that is not your intention. The use of phrases such as **por favor**, **perdón**, and **con permiso** will show that you want to be polite, even when you may not be able to express yourself as precisely or as eloquently as a native speaker of Spanish.

In addition to direct commands—often with **por favor**—Spanish speakers use a number of other ways of expressing requests.

Quisiera + *infinitive*	*I would like to* + verb
¿Podría Ud. ... ?	*Could you . . . ?*
Necesito que Ud. + *subjunctive*	*I need you to* + verb

All of these alternatives are more polite than just saying **quiero** (*I want*). This usage, of course, parallels that of English.

Here are some additional phrases that will help you communicate respect and politeness.

Es Ud. muy amable.	You are very kind.
Mil gracias. Ud. me ha ayudado muchísimo.	Thanks a million. You've helped me a lot.
Ha sido un placer hablar con Ud.	It's been a pleasure to talk to you.

LECTURA CULTURAL

Lectura: See IM for suggestions and additional exercises and activities.

Manual para el conductor

Aunque los caminos y carreteras son diferentes en algunos aspectos en los distintos países del mundo de habla española, también es cierto que las normas generales de seguridad, dictadas por el buen sentido común al conducir, son universales. Las siguientes páginas son de un manual de conductores de Nicaragua. Va a ver que Ud. tiene mucho en común con el típico conductor nicaragüense.

SIETE CONSEJOS PARA CONDUCIR BIEN

1. Saber, cuidar y mantener el vehículo en condiciones mecánicas seguras y excelentes: Lubricación, frenos, llantas, volante, luces y amortiguadores.

2.- Saber manipular el vehículo diestramente.

3.- Conocer y usar las reglas y prácticas de conducir vehículos.

4.- Saber como usar correctamente sus ojos.

5.- Saber como conducir en toda clase de caminos, rectos, con curvas, pendiente, ascendente y descendente, secos, mojados, resbaladizos, con hojas mojadas, aceitosos.

6.- Conocer los peligros y evitar el beber y conducir.

7.- Sea un conductor que conduce a la defensiva; tenga buena actitud; asuma responsabilidad de conducir sin accidentes.

EL ACCIDENTE INEVITABLE

La gran mayoría de los accidentes que le ocurran a los vehículos de motor podrían llamarse colisiones-choques y los pocos restantes podrían considerarse más correctamente como accidentes. En este último grupo se incluyen los que realmente son accidentes por su naturaleza, los que son casi inevitables. En otras palabras, la inmensa mayoría de los choques son evitables, son innecesarios y reflejan errores o faltas de parte de los conductores afectados.

FALTA DE ATENCION AL CONDUCIR SU VEHICULO.

BUSCANDO LA DIRECCION MIENTRAS SE GUIA EL AUTO

Invitando al enterrador
"Mira Juan, que bonita está aquella tumba"

EL CAMINO HACIA EL INFIERNO ESTA PAVIMENTADO CON FALTA DE ATENCION

Los conductores están sujetos a sufrir muchas distracciones mientras guían. Ellos son responsables, sin embargo, de no permitir que estas distracciones les hagan apartar la atención y descuidar su obligación fundamental: guiar dentro de las normas de seguridad.

1. Hable poco cuando vaya guiando y no vuelva nunca la cabeza para hablar con un pasajero.

2. Cuando los reglamentos permitan fumar, tenga el mayor cuidado al encender un cigarrillo, especialmente si es de noche, porque ello puede producirle una ceguera momentánea.

3. Saliéndose de la carretera hacia el hombrillo, detenga el auto siempre que vaya a consultar los mapas o su libreta de direcciones.

Pasajeros en el asiento posterior. Los estudios sobre las causas de accidentes revelan claramente que los conductores que llevan pasajeros que saben manejar en el asiento posterior sufren más accidentes que los conductores que llevan pasajeros silenciosos. ¿Puede haber una razón mejor para que los conductores en el asiento posterior permanezcan callados? ¡No sólo es desagradable, es peligroso!

No levante caminantes. Levantar personas que van por las carreteras ha resultado en atracos y en otras experiencias desagradables para el conductor. Estos transeúntes tienen derecho a exigir también compensación si resultaren lesionados. Por esto es que muchas compañías advierten a los conductores de autos o camiones que "NO LEVANTEN CAMINANTES"

Comprensión

A. De los «Siete consejos para conducir bien», ¿cuál trata de (*deals with*)... ?

_____ el alcohol
_____ la condición física del vehículo
_____ la necesidad de ser un conductor responsable
_____ la vista (*vision*)
_____ el acto de manejar
_____ el conocimiento del reglamento de tránsito
_____ la condición del camino

B. En «El accidente inevitable», busque el equivalente español de las siguientes frases en inglés.

1. Don't pick up hitchhikers.
2. Don't turn your head.
3. backseat driver
4. temporary blindness

Para escribir

¿Es Ud. un buen conductor (una buena conductora)? Conteste en tres párrafos.

Primer párrafo: ¿Cómo, cuándo y dónde aprendió Ud. a conducir? Añada algunos detalles interesantes.
Segundo párrafo: Evaluación de su estilo de manejar según los «Siete consejos para conducir bien». Añada los detalles necesarios.
Tercer párrafo: Su *record* de conducir: multas, accidentes, etcétera.

Si Ud. no sabe conducir, describa el estilo de conducir de otra persona.

CAPÍTULO CATORCE

EL MUNDO DE HOY

Guadalajara, México

▲ **En una tienda de computadoras**

—Quiero comprar una computadora personal, pero no sé cuál. ¿Puede recomendarme alguna?

—¿Tiene experiencia?

—Realmente no.

—Entonces le sugiero que compre este modelo. Es fácil de manejar y tiene muchas funciones.

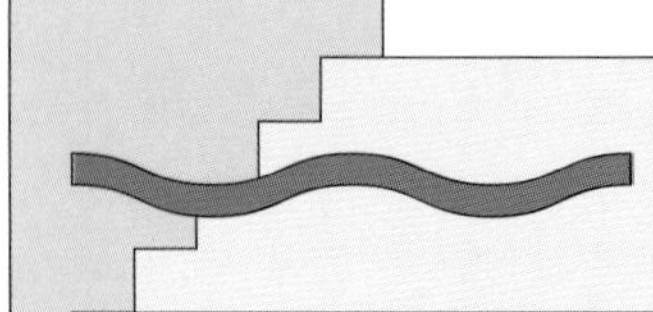

VOCABULARIO: PREPARACIÓN

Vocabulario: Preparación:
- See detailed supplementary materials for this section bound into the back of this Annotated Instructor's Edition.
- See model for vocabulary presentation and other materials in Supplementary *Vocabulario: Preparación* Materials, chapter by chapter, IM.

- See also

Nueva tecnología: Las computadoras/Los ordenadores

la informática/computación	data processing
el lenguaje	(computer) language
el manejo/uso	operation, use (*of a machine*)
la memoria	memory
la microcomputadora	microcomputer
el ordenador personal	personal computer, PC
archivar la información	to store information
diseñar programas	to design, write programs
escribir a máquina	to type
manejar/usar	to use, operate (*a machine*)

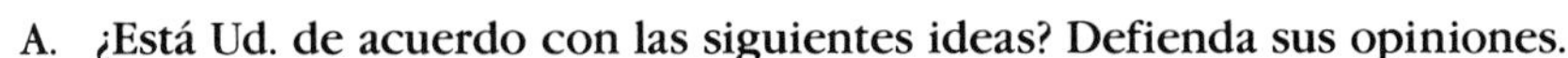

A. ¿Está Ud. de acuerdo con las siguientes ideas? Defienda sus opiniones.

1. Saber manejar una computadora es un requisito indispensable para conseguir un buen empleo hoy en día.
2. Es difícil aprender a manejar un ordenador. Es mucho más fácil escribir a máquina.
3. La informática es una ciencia muy útil. Saber algo de informática debe ser un requisito para graduarse en esta universidad.
4. El precio de los microordenadores personales baja todos los años. Por eso no pienso comprarme uno todavía.
5. Las computadoras nos controlan a nosotros; nosotros no las controlamos a ellas.
6. Es bueno que tengamos acceso a información médica, bancaria y educativa por medio (*means*) de las computadoras.

Suggestion B: Encourage students to begin their reactions with phrases like: *No creo que...* , *Creo que...* , *Dudo que...* , *Es cierto que...* , and so on.

B. ¿Cómo se llaman las partes de la computadora que se ven en el dibujo?

Suggestion C: Students present their definitions to the class; classmates give the words defined.

C. **Definiciones.** Dé Ud. una definición de estas palabras.

MODELO: la memoria → Es lo que se archiva en un ordenador.

1. la pantalla
2. las teclas
3. el disco
4. la impresora
5. el lenguaje
6. el programador

CH. **Preguntas.** De niño/a, ¿tenía Ud. mucho contacto con las computadoras? ¿Aprendió a manejar una computadora en la escuela primaria? ¿en la secundaria? ¿Es necesario que aprenda la informática en la universidad? ¿Qué lenguajes sabe Ud.? ¿PASCAL? ¿BASIC? ¿Tiene una computadora personal? ¿Cuánto le costó? ¿Cuándo la usa?

Notas culturales: Hablando de la tecnología

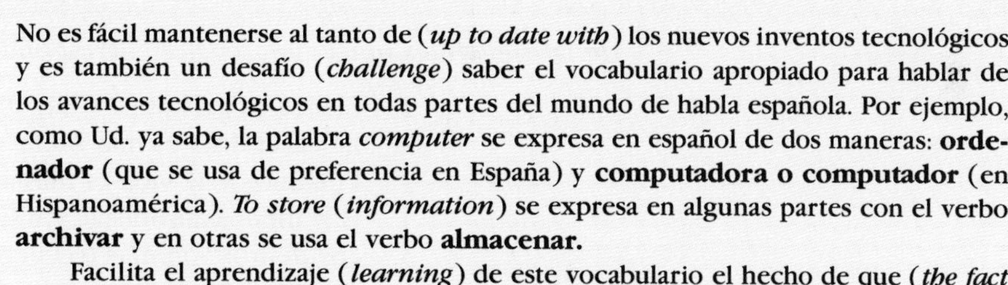

No es fácil mantenerse al tanto de (*up to date with*) los nuevos inventos tecnológicos y es también un desafío (*challenge*) saber el vocabulario apropiado para hablar de los avances tecnológicos en todas partes del mundo de habla española. Por ejemplo, como Ud. ya sabe, la palabra *computer* se expresa en español de dos maneras: **ordenador** (que se usa de preferencia en España) y **computadora o computador** (en Hispanoamérica). *To store* (*information*) se expresa en algunas partes con el verbo **archivar** y en otras se usa el verbo **almacenar.**

Facilita el aprendizaje (*learning*) de este vocabulario el hecho de que (*the fact that*) gran parte de las palabras o se derivan del inglés o son cognados de esa lengua. ¿Puede Ud. adivinar el significado de las palabras indicadas en estas frases?

...la **capacidad** de memoria RAM es el principal determinante de la **potencia** de un ordenador...

...el **átomo de hidrógeno** está compuesto por un **protón** y un **electrón**...

...se obtiene por **evaporación**, como **producto residual** de los procesos de **electrólisis**...

El medio ambiente°

medio... *environment*

la energía	energy	**acabar**	to run out, use up completely
la escasez	lack, shortage	**conservar**	to save, conserve
la fábrica	factory	**construir***	to build
el gobierno	government	**contaminar**	to pollute
la naturaleza	nature	**desarrollar**	to develop
la población	population	**destruir***	to destroy
los recursos naturales	natural resources	**proteger (protejo)**	to protect

*Note the present indicative conjugation of **construir**: **construyo**, **construyes**, **construye**, **construimos**, **construís**, **construyen**. **Destruir** is conjugated like **construir**.

¿La ciudad o el campo?

el árbol	tree	**la vivienda**	housing
la autopista	freeway	**bello/a**	beautiful
el/la campesino/a	farm worker; peasant	**denso/a**	dense
el delito	crime	**puro/a**	pure
la finca	farm	**encantar**	enchant
el ranchero	rancher	**me encanta(n)**	I like very much
el rascacielos	skyscraper	**madrugar**	to get up early
el ritmo (acelerado) de la vida	(fast) pace of life	**montar a caballo**	to ride horseback
los servicios públicos	public services	**recorrer**	to pass through; to cover (*territory, miles, etc.*)
la soledad	solitude		
el transporte	(means of) transportation		

A. De las siguientes oraciones, ¿cuáles corresponden al campo? ¿a la ciudad?

1. El aire es más puro y hay menos contaminación.
2. La naturaleza es más bella.
3. El ritmo de la vida es más acelerado.
4. Hay menos autopistas y menos tráfico.
5. Los delitos son más frecuentes.
6. Los servicios financieros y legales son más asequibles (*available*).
7. Hay pocos transportes públicos.
8. La población es menos densa.
9. Hay escasez de viviendas.
10. Hay más árboles y zonas verdes.

B. **Definiciones.** Dé Ud. una definición de estas palabras.

MODELO: ranchero → Es el dueño de una finca (un rancho).

1. fábrica 3. delito 5. naturaleza 7. soledad
2. campesino 4. finca 6. población 8. rascacielos

Follow-up A: ***Preguntas:*** *1. ¿Hay mucha contaminación en esta ciudad? ¿En qué lugares hay mucha contaminación? ¿En dónde se encuentra aire puro? 2. ¿Cómo es el ritmo de vida en (ciudad), acelerado o lento? ¿Qué ritmo de vida prefiere Ud.? ¿Le gusta recorrer la ciudad durante la noche? 3. ¿Trata Ud. de conservar la energía? ¿Hay ahora una escasez de energía? Si una persona realmente quiere conservar energía, ¿qué puede hacer? 4. ¿Hay muchos delitos y crímenes en esta ciudad? ¿Qué lugares son famosos por la frecuencia de sus delitos? ¿Tiene*

C. ¿Está Ud. de acuerdo con las ideas siguientes? Defienda sus opiniones.

1. Para conservar energía debemos bajar la calefacción en invierno y usar menos el aire acondicionado en verano.
2. Es mejor calentar la casa con una estufa de leña (*wood stove*) que con gas o electricidad.
3. Debemos proteger nuestras «zonas verdes» y crear (*to create*) más parques públicos para las futuras generaciones.
4. Es más importante explotar los recursos naturales que proteger el medio ambiente.
5. Para gastar menos gasolina, debemos tomar el autobús, caminar más y formar *car pools.*

Ud. miedo de visitar estos lugares? **5.** *¿Va Ud. al campo con frecuencia? ¿Sabe Ud. montar a caballo? ¿Lo hace con frecuencia? ¿Tiene su familia una finca en el campo? ¿La visita Ud.? ¿Cuándo? Descríbala. ¿Le gustaría vivir en una finca? ¿Cómo es el ritmo de vida en una finca típica?*

6. No debemos importar petróleo de otros países a menos que se acaben nuestras propias reservas.
7. El gobierno debe poner multas muy fuertes a las compañías y a los individuos que contaminen el aire.
8. Debemos adoptar una manera de vivir más sencilla.
9. No es necesario destruir la naturaleza para construir centros urbanos bien planeados.
10. Se deben explotar todos nuestros recursos naturales al máximo para satisfacer las necesidades que la población tiene en la actualidad (*right now*).

CH. Pancho cree que la vida del campo es ideal. Para él, vivir en la ciudad no ofrece ni una sola ventaja. Gabriela, la amiga de Pancho, es una mujer muy cosmopolita. Le encanta la ciudad y no puede decir nada bueno de la vida del campo. ¿Quién dijo las siguientes oraciones? ¿Qué desventaja puede citar la otra persona en cada caso?

1. No hay buenos servicios públicos.
2. Hay más actividades culturales—teatro, conciertos y museos.
3. Allí es posible vivir en paz y en tranquilidad.
4. No me gusta levantarme temprano; allí hay que madrugar para terminar el trabajo.
5. Me encanta recorrer las autopistas de la ciudad por la noche.
6. Necesito vivir en contacto con la naturaleza.
7. Cuando la nieve cubre (*covers*) las calles, las ciudades están paralizadas.

Ahora adopte el punto de vista de Pancho/Gabriela. ¿Qué va Ud. a decir sobre los siguientes temas?

1. el ritmo de la vida
2. la explotación de la tierra
3. la gente/los vecinos
4. el gobierno

Suggestion CH: Once again, encourage the use of phrases such as *No creo que...* .

Extension CH: Students tell whether they agree with Pancho or with Gabriela.

COLEGIO DE INGENIEROS TÉCNICOS DE OBRAS PÚBLICAS ZONA DE MADRID

CURSOS DE MICROORDENADOR EN LOS LENGUAJES PASCAL, FORTH LOGOS Y ADA

- **PASCAL:** Comienzo, 6 de febrero.
- **FORTH:** Comienzo, 27 de febrero.
- **LOGOS:** Comienzo, 26 de marzo.
- La duración de los cursos es de 24 horas, y corresponde al primer nivel de estos lenguajes.
- Precio: 12.000 pesetas. Colegiados de colegios oficiales: 25% descuento.
- Diploma del Colegio de Ingenieros Técnicos de Obras Públicas.
- Curso especial de sábados.
- Abierta la matrícula para dichos cursos.

CURSO ESPECIAL PARA JÓVENES (E.G.B., B.U.P. y F.P.)

- Duración: 24 horas en 8 sábados.
- Precio: 5.000 pesetas.
- Comienzo: 28 de enero.

INFORMACIÓN: Secretaría del Colegio San Hermenegildo, 3 MADRID-8. Teléfono 448 59 98

D. **¿Qué piensa Ud. de la tecnología?** Express your opinions about this topic by completing the following sentences in a logical manner, selecting topics from the right-hand column and adding appropriate information. Then ask other students how they responded (**¿Qué esperas de... ?** etc.) until you find some who share your hopes and/or uncertainties.

MODELO: Espero que la tecnología ayude a resolver el problema del hambre mundial. Y tú, ¿qué esperas de la tecnología?

1. Espero que _____.
2. Estoy seguro/a de que _____.
3. Dudo que _____.
4. Me alegro de que _____.
5. Tengo miedo de que _____.
6. Creo que _____.

las computadoras
el progreso científico
la tecnología
la energía nuclear
la escasez de energía
la comunicación instantánea
los robots
¿ ?

Extension D: May be done as written exercise; students expand answers into coherent paragraph.

Suggestion D: Model several question/answer pairs with a student before letting students begin activity.

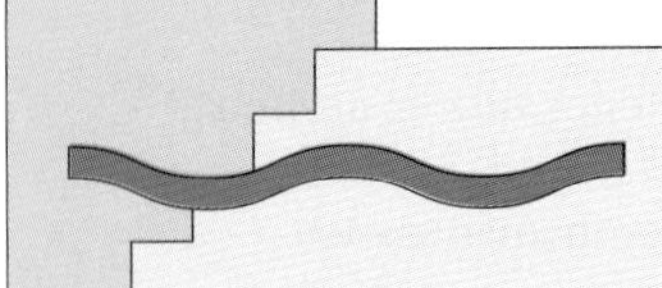

MINIDIÁLOGOS Y GRAMÁTICA

Note: Students have been using a number of past participles (with *estar*) since early chapters: *casado, cansado, ocupado, aburrido, preocupado, abierto, cerrado*, and so on.

41. MÁS DESCRIPCIONES
Past Participle Used as an Adjective

Unos refranes y dichos en español

1. En boca *cerrada* no entran moscas.
2. *Aburrido* como una ostra.

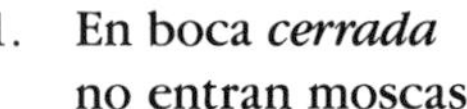

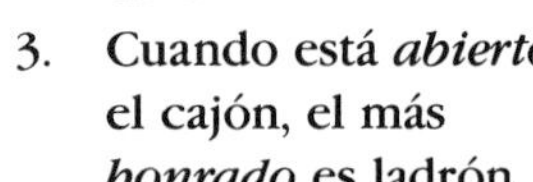

3. Cuando está *abierto* el cajón, el más *honrado* es ladrón.

1. A veces, ¿es mejor no decir nada? ¿Qué le puede pasar a uno cuando tiene la boca abierta?
2. ¿Llevan una vida muy interesante las ostras? ¿Sufren de muchas presiones?
3. ¿Cometen todos los delitos (*crimes*) los criminales? ¿Es posible que una persona honrada llegue a ser un criminal?

Suggestion (art): Ask, What do *cerrada, aburrido*, and *honrado* have in common? (→ *-do/a* ending).

Variation: Students give equivalent English proverbs for these Spanish *refranes.*

Forms of the Past Participle

hablar	comer	vivir
habl**ado** (*spoken*)	com**ido** (*eaten*)	viv**ido** (*lived*)

Suggestions:
- Present formation of past participle.
- **Rapid Response Drill:** Students give past participles of *comprar, pagar, mandar, terminar, preparar, llamar, recomendar, invitar, arreglar, visitar, vender, conocer, leer, llover, perder, comer, recibir, pedir, dormir, seguir.*
- Model pronunciation of irregular past participles. You give participle, students give infinitive; then reverse procedure.
- ***¿Cómo se dice?:*** broken, seen, covered, discovered, returned, written, said, dead, made, done, open(ed), put

The past participle of most English verbs ends in *-ed*: for example, *to walk → walked*; *to close → closed*. Many English past participles, however, are irregular: *to sing → sung*; *to write → written*. In Spanish the *past participle* (**el participio pasado**) is formed by adding **-ado** to the stem of **-ar** verbs, and **-ido** to the stem of **-er** and **-ir** verbs. An accent mark is used on the past participle of **-er/-ir** verbs with stems ending in **-a**, **-e**, or **-o**.

caído **creído** **leído** **oído** **(son)reído** **traído**

The following Spanish verbs have irregular past participles.

abrir:	**abierto**	escribir:	**escrito**	resolver:	**resuelto**
decir:	**dicho**	hacer:	**hecho**	romper:	**roto**
cubrir:	**cubierto**	morir:	**muerto**	ver:	**visto**
descubrir:	**descubierto**	poner:	**puesto**	volver:	**vuelto**

A few Spanish proverbs and sayings 1. Into a closed mouth no flies enter. 2. As boring as an oyster. 3. When the drawer is open, the most honest person is (can become) a thief.

The Past Participle Used as an Adjective

- **Point out:** Agreement of past participle (used as adj.) with noun modified.
- ***Ejercicio:*** Agreement: *hecho: bolsas, vestidos, camisa* *escrito: carta, ejercicio, libros* *roto: tazas, silla, disco*
- **Emphasis: (1)** use of past participle with *estar* to describe resulting condition (reentry of material from Ch. 5); **(2)** contrast of English simple past and past participle.

In both English and Spanish, the past participle can be used as an adjective to modify a noun. Like other Spanish adjectives, the past participle must agree in number and gender with the noun modified.

Tengo una bolsa **hecha** en El Salvador.	*I have a purse made in El Salvador.*
El español es una de las lenguas **habladas** en los Estados Unidos.	*Spanish is one of the languages spoken in the United States.*

The past participle is frequently used with **estar** to describe conditions that are the result of a previous action.

La puerta **está abierta**.	*The door is open.*
Todos los lápices **estaban rotos**.	*All the pencils were broken.*

¡OJO! English past participles often have the same form as the past tense: *I* closed *the book. The thief stood behind the* closed *door.* The Spanish past participle is never identical in form or use to a past tense. Compare the following:

Cerré la puerta.	*I* closed *the door.*
Ahora la puerta está **cerrada**.	*Now the door is* closed.

Preliminary exercise: ***¿Cómo se dice en español?:*** **1.** money earned **2.** the lost luggage **3.** a repeated sentence **4.** the fired employee **5.** dead flies **6.** the broken cup

Note A: Language in the exercise is quite close to that of the original ad.

Práctica

A. Los siguientes consejos y recomendaciones son de un anuncio del Ministerio de Industria de España. Complételos con la forma correcta del participio pasado de los verbos indicados.

como... *as if*

Consuma electricidad como si quedara poca.

Queda poca.
Es increíble. Dá la sensación de que el interruptor es una fuente inagotable de energía, ¿no es verdad?

No es verdad. Porque las fuentes de producción de energía eléctrica son limitadas. Bien es cierto que estamos aún muy lejos de un agotamiento, de una insuficiencia eléctrica. Pero prevenir es curar. Y prevenir es fácil en este caso.

Basta con acostumbrarnos a unos pequeños gestos cotidianos: cerrar las neveras mientras nos servimos la cerveza, tener las luces de la casa apagadas mientras vemos a Kojak, desconectar el tocadiscos o bajar el termostato del radiador al acostarse.

Pequeños hábitos que asegurarán una vida más plena a nuestros hijos y unas facturas más llevaderas a nuestra economía. Moderémonos. Ahora.

Campaña Nacional de Ahorro de Energía.
Centro de Estudios de la Energía.
Ministerio de Industria.

Aunque usted pueda pagarla, España no puede.

1. Las fuentes (*sources*) de energía no están _____ todavía. (agotar = *to exhaust*)
2. Pero las fuentes son _____. (limitar)
3. Todavía no estamos _____ a conservar energía diariamente. (acostumbrar)
4. Cuando nos servimos la comida, la puerta de la nevera (= refrigerador) debe estar _____. (cerrar)
5. Las luces de la casa deben estar _____ mientras vemos la televisión. (apagar)
6. El tocadiscos debe estar _____ y el termostato del radiador debe estar _____ cuando nos acostamos. (desconectar, cerrar)

Variation B: Give a result statement based on items. Students give action that will occur.
- *La carta no está escrita todavía.* (→ *Natalia tiene que escribir la carta.*)
- *La tienda no está abierta todavía.* (→ *Los Sres. García tienen...*)

Note B4: *cubierta* **de** *nieve.*

B. Las siguientes oraciones describen las obligaciones o los deseos de algunas personas. ¿Cuál es la situación del momento presente? Conteste, siguiendo el modelo.

MODELO: Natalia les tiene que *escribir* una carta a sus abuelos. →
La carta no está *escrita* todavía.

1. Los Sres. García deben *abrir* la tienda más temprano. ¡Ya son las nueve!
2. David y Marta quieren *casarse*. Hace dos años que andan juntos.
3. Pablo tiene que *cerrar* las ventanas; entra un aire frío.
4. Los niños siempre esperan que la tierra se *cubra* de nieve para la Navidad.
5. Los turistas tienen que *facturar* el equipaje. No les permiten llevarlo con ellos al avión.
6. Delia debe *poner* la mesa. Los invitados llegan a las nueve y ya son las ocho.
7. Claro está que la contaminación va a contribuir a la *destrucción* del medio ambiente.
8. Es posible que los ingenieros *descubran* el error de construcción del reactor nuclear.
9. Se debe *resolver* pronto el problema de la escasez de energía.

Conversación

Suggestion A: List appropriate verbs and adjectives on the board before students begin the activity: *acostar, poner, cocinar, encender, cansar; limpio, sucio.*

Variations A:
- Using preterite/imperfect, students invent story based on drawing.
- Students complete these sentences based on drawing. **1.** *Los esposos trabajan mucho para que...* **2.** *Se duermen antes de que...* **3.** *No van a despertarse a menos que...*

A. Describa Ud. el siguiente dibujo, tratando de mencionar todos los detalles que han ocasionado (*have caused*) la situación presentada. Use el participio pasado donde sea posible.

MODELO: Todo está preparado
para la cena...

Extension B: **6.** *¿Está abierta la ventana/puerta de la clase en este momento? ¿Está abierto su libro de español/cuaderno? ¿Está abierta su boca? ¿sus ojos?* **7.** *¿Está Ud. sentado/a ahora?* (*sentado* = seated, sitting) *¿dormido/a?* **8.** *¿Están Uds. preparados para el próximo examen?* **9.** *¿Tiene Ud. algún libro escrito en español? ¿en francés? ¿en alemán?*

B. **Preguntas**

1. ¿Tiene Ud. algo (ropa, perfume, un auto, ...) hecho en Francia? ¿en un país latinoamericano? ¿en España? ¿en el Japón? ¿algo hecho a mano?
2. ¿Sabe Ud. el título de un libro escrito por un autor latinoamericano? ¿por un autor español?
3. En su casa o garaje, ¿hay algo roto? ¿algo sucio?
4. En su casa, ¿el televisor está puesto constantemente? ¿el estéreo? ¿la radio?
5. ¿El Nuevo Mundo ya estaba descubierto en 1700? ¿La penicilina ya estaba descubierta en 1960?

Suggestion C: Select 1 item and have students work in groups, with a time limit, to see which group can come up with the greatest number of associations for the item.

C. Dé Ud. el nombre de...

1. algo contaminado
2. una persona muy/poco organizada
3. un programa de computadora bien diseñado
4. un edificio bien/mal construido
5. un grupo humano explotado
6. algo que pueda estar cerrado o abierto
7. un curso acelerado
8. un servicio necesitado por muchas personas
9. un tipo de transporte usado por muchas personas
10. algo deseado por muchas personas
11. un programa visto por muchas personas
12. un problema resuelto por un árbitro

Note CH: Purpose of activity is to remind students about *he/has/ha*, which they began to use in Ch. 7, in preparation for the presentation of the present perfect in next section.

CH. Use el participio pasado para expresar algo inolvidable (*unforgettable*) que Ud. haya hecho (*have done*), siguiendo el modelo.

MODELO: ver → He visto un concierto de Bruce Springsteen.

1. oír
2. comer
3. romper
4. hacer un viaje
5. leer
6. olvidar
7. ¿?

Ventajas y desventajas

—¿Prefieres vivir en el campo o en la ciudad?
—Me encantan las ciudades... el bullicio (*hubbub*), la animación...
—También tienen sus inconvenientes, ¿no?
—¡Por supuesto! Por eso... vivo en el campo.

Yucatán, México

Communicative objectives for 42: how to express what has happened in the past

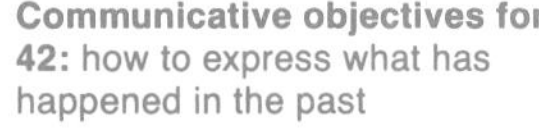

42. ¿QUÉ HAS HECHO?
Perfect Forms: Present Perfect Indicative and Present Perfect Subjunctive

Suggestion: Reenter *he/has/ha viajado* (from Ch. 7) if you have not used them recently.

¿Cambio de ritmo?

RAFAEL: Como tú sabes, Aurelia, yo siempre *he vivido* en grandes ciudades. Siempre *he usado* el carro para todo. Nunca *he tenido* tiempo de apreciar la naturaleza. ¡Y nunca *he madrugado* con regularidad! Por eso me extraña tanto la vida que Uds. llevan aquí.

AURELIA: Pues... como yo siempre *he vivido* en una finca, no *he conocido* otro estilo de vida. Nunca *he visto* las autopistas en que tú *has conducido* todos los días. Y nunca *he conocido* la vida cultural de que me hablas tanto. Por eso no la echo de menos. (continúa)

RAFAEL: La ciudad tiene muchas ventajas, es cierto. Pero... creo que estoy empezando a sentirme a gusto aquí.
AURELIA: ¡Y me decías que no podrías acostumbrarte!
RAFAEL: Bueno, bueno... eso fue antes de mudarme. Como dicen, ¡no hay nada escrito sobre gustos, ¡tú sabes!

Exprese las opiniones de Rafael y Aurelia, buscando las formas apropiadas en el minidiálogo.

Note: Mini contains only present perfect indicative forms. Follow-up exercise leads students into use of present perfect subjunctive.

Follow-up: ***Preguntas:*** **1.** *De los dos, ¿hay alguien que haya vivido toda la vida en la ciudad o en el campo?* **2.** *¿Adónde es posible que Rafael se haya mudado? ¿Y Aurelia? ¿Qué ciudades/regiones tienen las cualidades que ellos mencionan?*

RAFAEL: Siento que Aurelia siempre *haya*... (vivir/finca)
Es raro que no *haya*... (conocer/estilo de vida)
Me parece increíble que nunca *haya*... (ver/autopistas)
Es lástima que no *haya*... (conocer/vida cultural)
AURELIA: Para mí, es extraño que Rafael siempre *haya*... (vivir/grandes ciudades)
Es imposible que siempre *haya*... (usar/coche)
Es improbable que no *haya*... (tener/tiempo)
No creo que no *haya*... (madrugar/con regularidad)

Present Perfect Indicative

he hablado	*I have spoken*	**hemos** hablado	*we have spoken*
has hablado	*you have spoken*	**habéis** hablado	*you* (pl.) *have spoken*
ha hablado	*you have spoken, he/she has spoken*	**han** hablado	*you* (pl.) *have spoken, they have spoken*

In English, the present perfect is a compound tense consisting of a present tense form of the verb *to have* plus the past participle: *I have written*, *you have spoken*, and so on.

In the Spanish *present perfect* (**el presente perfecto**) the past participle is used with present tense forms of **haber**, the equivalent of English *to have* in this construction. **Haber**, an auxiliary verb, is not interchangeable with **tener**.

In general, the use of the Spanish present perfect parallels that of the English present perfect.

No **hemos estado** aquí antes. — *We haven't been here before.*
Me he divertido mucho. — *I've had a very good time.*
Ya **le han escrito** la carta. — *They've already written her the letter.*

Suggestions:
- Present the present tense of *haber* and formation of present perfect.
- **Emphasis:** use of masculine singular form of past participle with *haber* vs. use of past participle as adjective
- **Listening comprehension:** Students give subject pronoun: *he corrido, hemos caminado, han perdido, has dormido, habéis dicho, ha visto*
- ***¿Cómo se dice?:*** **1.** I have studied/eaten/read/gotten up. **2.** (S)He has answered/promised/lived/opened. **3.** We have called/lost/written. **4.** They have traveled/run/discovered.
- **Point out:** In both English and Spanish, present perfect often used as alternative for simple past tense: *¿Leíste/Has leído el periódico?* Usage is particularly frequent in Spain, where it can seem that no one uses preterite anymore (exaggerated perception).

A change of pace? RAFAEL: As you know, Aurelia, I've always lived in big cities. I've always used the car for everything. I've never had time to appreciate nature. And I've never gotten up at dawn on a regular basis! That's why the life you people lead here is so strange to me. AURELIA: Well . . . since I've always lived on a ranch, I've never known another lifestyle. I've never seen the freeways that you drove (on) every day. And I've never known the cultural life that you talk about so much. That's why I don't miss it. RAFAEL: The city has a lot of advantages, that's for sure. But . . . I think I'm beginning to feel at home here. AURELIA: And you used to tell me that you would never be able to adjust! RAFAEL: O.K., O.K. . . . that was before I moved. As they say, there's no accounting for tastes, you know!

The form of the past participle never changes with **haber**, regardless of the gender or number of the subject. The past participle always appears immediately after the appropriate form of **haber** and is never separated from it. Object pronouns and **no** are always placed directly before the form of **haber**.

The present perfect of **hay** is **ha habido** (*there has/have been*).

¡OJO! Remember that **acabar** + **de** + *infinitive*—not the present perfect tense—is used to state that something *has just* occurred.

Acabo de mandar la carta.	*I've just mailed the letter.*

[Práctica A–B]

Suggestion: Before beginning, review basic uses of subjunctive: (1) influence, (2) emotion, (3) doubt.
- Review forms of present subjunctive.
- Emphasis: These are subjunctive counterparts of present indicative (*he hablado, has hablado*, etc.).
- Point out: *yo* form = *Ud./él/ella* form
- Listening comprehension: Students give subject pronoun: *haya dicho, hayamos perdido, hayan escuchado, hayáis llamado*

Preliminary Exercises:
- Rapid Response: *Dé las formas del perfecto.*
  yo: llegar, terminar, bañarse, acostarse
  tú: comer, prometer, romper, volver
  Ud./él/ella: asistir, insistir, sonreír, divertirse
  nosotros: abrir, decir, cubrir, descubrir
  Uds./ellos/ellas: escribir, poner, ver, hacer
- *¿Qué hemos hecho hoy? Dé oraciones nuevas según las indicaciones.*
  1. *José se ha preparado muy bien para la clase.* (*tú, el profesor, los estudiantes, Luis, Carmen y Pilar, vosotros*) 2. *Yo he empezado la lección para hoy.* (*leer, escribir, estudiar, comprender, aprender*) 3. *Lidia se ha despertado.* (*levantarse, bañarse, vestirse, desayunar, correr a la facultad, leer en la cafetería, reírse con los amigos, ir a su primera clase*)

Present Perfect Subjunctive

haya hablado	**hayamos** hablado
hayas hablado	**hayáis** hablado
haya hablado	**hayan** hablado

The *present perfect subjunctive* (**el perfecto del subjuntivo**) is formed with the present subjunctive of **haber** plus the past participle. It is used to express *I have spoken* (*written*, and so on) when the subjunctive is required. Although its most frequent equivalent is *I have* + *past participle*, its exact equivalent in English depends on the context in which it occurs.

Es posible que lo **haya hecho**.	*It's possible (that) he may have done (he did) it.*
Me alegro de que **hayas venido**.	*I'm glad (that) you have come (you came).*
Es bueno que lo **hayan construido**.	*It's good that they built (have built) it.*

Note that the English equivalent of the present perfect subjunctive can be expressed as a simple or as a compound tense: *did/have done*; *came/have come*; *built/have built*.

[Práctica C–CH]

Follow-up A: *Preguntas:*
1. *¿Qué ha hecho Ud. hoy? ¿Ha hablado con un amigo (una amiga)? ¿Ha estudiado? ¿Ha comido?* 2. *¿Qué ha hecho Ud. esta semana? ¿Ha ido a una fiesta? ¿Ha bailado? ¿Ha cantado? ¿Ha tomado Coca-Cola/cerveza/vino? ¿Ha visto una película?* 3. *¿Ha escrito una carta este mes? ¿Ha visitado un museo? ¿Ha salido de la ciudad? ¿Se ha levantado antes de las 6? ¿antes de las 5? ¿Por qué tan temprano? ¿Ha depositado dinero en el banco? ¿Ha vendido/comprado algo?*

Suggestion: Extend all questions in Follow-up A with *¿Qué más ha hecho Ud. hoy/esta semana/este mes?*

Práctica

A. Ud. y su amigo/a están visitando un rancho. Es el segundo día de su visita. ¿Qué han hecho Uds.? Haga oraciones basadas en las siguientes palabras.

1. recorrer la finca entera
2. ver las vacas (*cows*) y los toros
3. montar a caballo
4. hablar con los campesinos
5. respirar el aire puro
6. ver los efectos del desarrollo industrial

B. **Situaciones.** Margarita lo/la llama a Ud. por teléfono. Quiere saber lo que Ud. está haciendo. Con otro/a estudiante, haga y conteste preguntas, según el modelo.

Preliminary C:
- **Listening comprehension: *¿Subjuntivo o indicativo?:*** *1. Dice que ha hablado con ella. 2. Es posible que haya hablado con ella. 3. No, no han repetido las palabras. 4. No creo que hayan repetido las palabras. 5. Me alegro de que me hayas escrito. 6. No vengas a menos que me hayas escrito antes. 7. Es de alguien que ya me ha escrito antes.*
- Students give subjunctive equivalents of *he hablado, he repetido, has comido, has manejado, ha mandado, ha venido, hemos podido, hemos alquilado, han comprendido, se han acostado.*

Follow-up CH: Using same expressions as in parentheses or any others, students answer these questions. 1. *¿Ha sacado sólo A's este semestre su compañero/a de cuarto?* 2. *¿Han servido hoy una comida excelente en la cafetería/en la residencia estudiantil?* 3. *¿Le han mandado dinero este mes sus padres?* 4. *¿Le han dado muchos exámenes este semestre sus profesores?*

Optional: *El viaje de David. ¿Cómo se dice en español?* 1. He's just returned from his year in Uruguay. 2. I hope he's brought us a souvenir. 3. I don't think he's found a new apartment yet. 4. I doubt that he's looked for one in the city. 5. It's more likely (probable) that he's gone back to the country. 6. He's always preferred the tranquility of life there.

Suggestion A: Prompt students if they have trouble coming up with responses. Example 1: *¿Qué ha hecho el estudiante? Ha estudiado (leído varias lecciones, hecho varios ejercicios). Se ha preparado muy bien para el examen. Ha estudiado toda la noche. ¿Qué no ha hecho todavía? Todavía no ha tomado el examen.*

MODELO: cenar → MARGARITA: Estás cenando, ¿no?
UD.: No, ya he cenado.

1. cocinar
2. descansar
3. lavar los platos
4. leer el periódico
5. poner la mesa

Ahora Margarita tiene unos recados (*messages*) de Jorge.

MODELO: llamarlo → MARGARITA: Jorge dice que lo llames.
UD.: Pero ya lo he llamado.

6. mandarle una invitación a Pablo
7. hablar con Concepción
8. ir a su casa
9. ver (película)
10. escribir la composición esta tarde

C. Imagine que se descubrió el año pasado un caso de contaminación ambiental en su ciudad. ¿Qué ha dicho la gente sobre el caso? Haga oraciones completas según las indicaciones. Use **Uds.** como sujeto y el perfecto del subjuntivo en la cláusula dependiente.

1. es probable: ya estudiar el problema
2. no creo: descubrir la solucíon todavía
3. es posible: ya consultar con unos expertos
4. es dudoso: ya arreglar la situación
5. espero: ya reconocer la necesidad de evitar (*to avoid*) situaciones parecidas en el futuro

CH. Imagine que Ud. es dueño/a de una casa de apartamentos. Conteste las siguientes preguntas, empezando sus respuestas con las palabras entre paréntesis.

1. ¿Han alquilado todos los apartamentos? (Dudo que...)
2. ¿Han vuelto de su viaje los inquilinos del primer piso? (Es posible que...)
3. ¿Se han mudado ya los inquilinos ruidosos? (Sí, y me alegro mucho de que...)
4. ¿Han pagado todos el gas y la luz este mes? (No creo que...)
5. ¿Se ha arreglado ya la ventana? (Es probable que...)
6. Se ha muerto la esposa del portero. (¡Ay, siento que... !)

Conversación

A. **Situaciones.** ¿Qué han hecho ya estas personas? ¿Y qué no han hecho todavía? Invente todos los detalles posibles.

1. antes del examen

2. en el restaurante Cinco Estrellas

3. una carta al exnovio

Follow-up A: *Imagine que hoy es un día típico para Ud. Ya son las dos y media. ¿Qué ha hecho Ud.? ¿Qué no ha hecho todavía? ¿Qué va a hacer más tarde? ¿Qué es posible que haga por la noche?*

Follow-up B: *¿Qué es posible que hayan hecho las siguientes personas?* **1.** *Un hombre que lleva máscara sale corriendo de un banco, con una bolsa en la mano.* **2.** *Un joven está saliendo de una lavandería con un montón de ropa limpia.* **3.** *Un sábado de otoño, a las cuatro y media de la tarde, muchas personas están saliendo de un estadio.* **4.** *Unos turistas están hablando ansiosamente con un policía. La mujer no lleva bolsa.* **5.** *Una familia está saliendo del McDonald's.*

Variation C: Do as listening comprehension, saying statements yourself: students react to you. Include statements based on current events. Additional items. **9.** *Recibí el Premio Nobel de Literatura el año pasado.* **10.** *Me puse furioso/a con mis estudiantes después del último examen.* **11.** *Trabajé anoche hasta las tres de la mañana.*

Note (Notas lingüísticas): Present perfect is presented here and practiced in *Conversación E.* Here are some additional exercises and activities, if you wish to stress this tense.

- *Jaimito es un niño acusón* (tattle-tale). *Siempre le dice a su madre las cosas que ha hecho—y que no ha hecho—Laura, su hermana mayor. ¿Qué le dijo a su madre ayer? Dé oraciones nuevas según las indicaciones.*
  —Jaimito le dijo que Laura había dicho una mentira. (mirar la televisión toda la tarde, no estudiar, perder sus libros, romper un plato, faltar a clase, comer todo el pastel, pegarle, ¿ ?)
- *¿Qué cosas habían hecho—o no habían hecho—Uds. antes de 1980? Dé oraciones nuevas según las indicaciones.*
  —Antes de 1980 (no) habíamos... (estudiar español, asistir a esta universidad, graduarnos en la escuela superior, escuchar un concierto, ver una comedia española, comer flan, ¿ ?)

B. **Entrevista.** Con un compañero (una compañera), haga y conteste preguntas con estos verbos. La persona que contesta debe decir la verdad.

MODELO: visitar México → —¿Has visitado México?
—Sí, he visitado México una vez. (No, no he visitado México nunca. Sí, he visitado México durante las últimas vacaciones.)

1. comer en un restaurante hispánico
2. estar en Nueva York
3. manejar un Alfa-Romeo
4. correr en un maratón
5. abrir hoy tu libro de español
6. escribir un poema
7. actuar en una comedia
8. ver un monumento histórico
9. conocer a una persona famosa
10. romperse la pierna alguna vez

C. Con un compañero (una compañera), reaccione a las siguientes oraciones. La persona que reaccione debe empezar con frases como **Lo siento,** (nombre), **pero dudo que...** ; **No, es imposible que...** ; **Estoy seguro/a que...** ; **Es obvio que...** ; etcétera.

MODELO: —Anoche hice un viaje a la luna.
—Lo siento, Harry, pero dudo que hayas hecho un viaje a la luna.

1. Escribí una novela este fin de semana.
2. Leí *Lo que el viento se llevó* (*Gone with the Wind*) en veinte minutos.
3. Anoche salí con Robert Redford/Emilio Estévez/Ally Sheedy/Madonna.
4. Vi un OVNI (objeto volador no identificado) esta mañana.
5. Tom Selleck/Jessica Lange me mandó una carta de amor.
6. Hice algo estúpido en una ocasión.
7. En mi otra vida fui rey/reina de Inglaterra.
8. Anoche tomé ocho botellas de cerveza y una de vino.

CH. Todos somos «diferentes» en el sentido de que hemos hecho algo que los otros no han hecho. Es posible que hayamos visitado un sitio que los otros no conocen, ganado alguna vez un concurso (*contest*), inventado o preparado un plato especial (u otra cosa), etcétera. ¿Qué ha hecho Ud. que lo/la hace diferente? Complete la siguiente oración. Sus compañeros de clase le van a hacer preguntas para saber más detalles sobre lo que ha hecho: **Soy diferente. (No) He...**

Notas lingüísticas: Talking About What You Had Done

Use the past participle with the imperfect form of **haber** (**había**, **habías**, ...) to talk about what you had—or had not—done before a given time in the past. This form is called the past perfect.

Antes de graduarme en la escuela secundaria, no **había estudiado** español.	*Before graduating from high school, I hadn't studied Spanish.*
Antes de 1985, siempre **habíamos vivido** en Kansas.	*Before 1985, we had always lived in Kansas.*

¿Qué cosas no habían hecho... y no han hecho todavía? —No habíamos... ¡Y no lo hemos hecho todavía! (visitar la Patagonia, viajar a Moscú, aprender ruso, conocer a Julio Iglesias, ¿ ?)

Follow-up D:
- *Describa Ud. su juventud* (youth). *Antes de cumplir dieciocho años, ¿qué había hecho? ¿Qué no había hecho?*
- *Complete las oraciones en una forma lógica.* **1.** *Antes de 1492 Cristóbal Colón no ____.* **2.** *Antes de 1938 la Segunda Guerra Mundial no ____.* **3.** *Antes de 1500 Shakespeare no ____.* **4.** *Antes de 1950 mis padres (no) ____.* **5.** *Antes de 1975 yo (no) ____.*

D. **Entrevista.** Use the following cues to interview a classmate about his or her activities before coming to this campus. Begin your questions with **Dime...**

MODELO: algo / no haber aprendido a hacer todavía →
—Dime algo que no habías aprendido a hacer todavía antes de estudiar aquí.
—Pues... no había aprendido a nadar. Aprendí a nadar en mi clase de natación.

1. algo / no haber aprendido a hacer todavía
2. una materia / no haber estudiado todavía
3. un deporte / haber practicado mucho
4. un viaje / haber hecho varias veces
5. un libro / no haber leído todavía
6. una decisión / no haber tomado todavía
7. ¿ ?

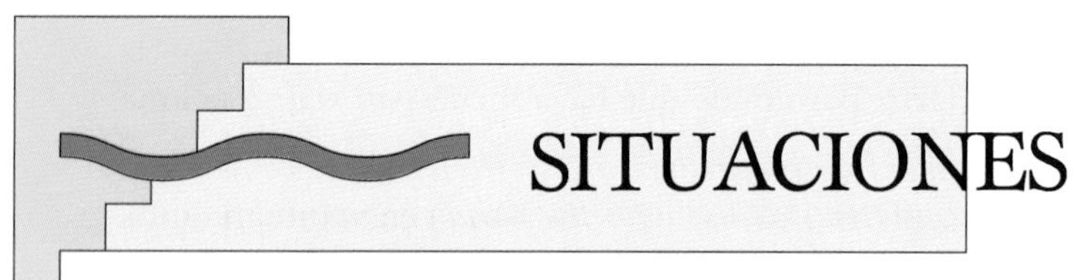

SITUACIONES

Situaciones: See IM for suggestions, additional exercises, and supplementary dialogues and exercises.

Facetas de la ciudad y del campo

Un viaje al campo

—Estoy entusiasmado con este viaje, ¿sabes? Siempre me ha encantado el campo.
—A mí también, pero sólo para los fines de semana. Prefiero estar en la ciudad, donde hay más servicios públicos y posibilidades de trabajo.
—¿Y qué me dices del aire contaminado, el ritmo acelerado de la vida, las viviendas amontonadas,° los delitos... ?
—No te lo puedo negar. Y si estamos contando todo lo malo, hay que admitir que la ciudad siempre ha explotado al campo y a los campesinos. A éstos se les paga muy poco por las cosechas.° Pero en la ciudad hay mejores posibilidades: la educación, los negocios...

amontonadas: ¿ ?
cosechas: *harvests, crops*

Entre la ciudad y el campo

—¿Qué tal el verano en la urbanización°? ¿No cambiaste° casa con mis primos por un mes?
—Sí, pero Juan Antonio regresó a nuestro piso° al cabo° de una semana.
—¿Ha pasado algo?
—No, el sitio es verdaderamente ideal y la casa es preciosa. Pero Juan Antonio no conseguía pegar ojo° por las noches. Cualquier ruidito le despertaba: el murmullo de los árboles, los grillos,° todo. Y por el día tanta paz y calma lo ponía nerviosísimo.
—¡Qué desastre!

suburb / cambiar = *to exchange, tra*
apartamento / *end*
pegar... ¿ ?
insectos

Conversación

Con un compañero (una compañera), exprese sus opiniones sobre los siguientes temas en diálogos de cinco a seis oraciones.

1. la energía nuclear: ventajas y desventajas
2. las computadoras: ¿un beneficio o una amenaza?
3. los coches: ¿una bendición (*blessing*) o un desastre?

UN POCO DE TODO

A. **Cosas de la vida.** Form complete sentences based on the words given. Use the present perfect of both verbs.

1. yo / madrugar / este / mañana // (yo) nunca / levantarse / tan temprano
2. ellos / preocuparse / mucho / por / niños // nunca / preocuparse / tanto
3. hoy / Juan / faltar / trabajo / primero / vez // nunca / faltar / antes
4. nosotros / divertirse / mucho / aquel / película // nunca / reírse / tanto
5. tú / pedir / vino / con / comida // antes / siempre / beber / leche

B. Con un compañero (una compañera), haga y conteste preguntas según el modelo.

MODELO: escribir la carta →
—¿Ya *está escrita* la carta?
—No, no la *he escrito.*
—¡Hombre! Es imposible que no la *hayas escrito* todavía.

1. hacer las maletas
2. comprar los boletos
3. preparar la cena
4. facturar el equipaje
5. sacudir los muebles
6. archivar los datos

C. **Entrevista.** With two other students, react to the following statements by telling whether you believe them to be possible or not. Use the present perfect indicative or subjunctive, as needed.

MODELO: —Hoy tuve que madrugar. Me levanté a las cinco. →
—Bueno, yo creo que te has levantado hoy a las cinco.
—No, no te creo. Es imposible (No es probable) que te hayas levantado hoy a las cinco.

1. A veces digo cosas estúpidas y absurdas.
2. Nunca digo cosas estúpidas y absurdas.
3. Nunca duermo.
4. Hoy me levanté a las tres de la mañana.
5. Puedo leer quince libros en una hora.
6. He leído muchos libros este año.
7. Mis padres me mandaron mil dólares la semana pasada.
8. Fui al Japón el año pasado.
9. Fui a Nueva York el mes pasado.
10. Siempre salgo bien en los exámenes difíciles.

11. He comprado algo hecho en México.
12. Nunca he conocido a una persona nacida en el Canadá.
13. Esta semana he ido a cuatro fiestas.
14. Siempre he creído en Santa Claus.

CH. Describa el dibujo, usando las preguntas como guía.

1. Describa la ciudad que se ve en el dibujo.
2. ¿Qué mira la gente? ¿Por qué mira con tanto interés?
3. Para construir la ciudad, ¿qué han hecho? ¿Qué han destruido? (Es posible que...)
4. ¿Cuál es su reacción personal frente a esta situación? (Creo que...)
5. ¿Cree Ud. que se ve el mundo de hoy o el mundo del futuro en el dibujo? ¿Por qué?

D. **Cambio de ritmo.** Complete the following paragraphs with the correct form of the words in parentheses, as suggested by the context. When two possibilities are given in parentheses, select the correct word.

Ayer yo pasé el día recorriendo mi nueva finca. Toda la vida he (*admirar*[1]) la naturaleza, pero creo que (*ser*[2]) la primera vez que había (*ver*[3]) (*tan/tanto*[4]) belleza en (*tan/tanto*[5]) poco tiempo. En el lago había unos patitos° y sus padres (*les/los*[6]) estaban (*enseñar*[7]) a nadar. La buganvilla, que (*florecer*[8]) la semana pasada, estaba (*cubrir*[9]) de flores de colores (*brillante*[10]). (*Oír:* yo[11]) la canción de un pájaro y (*ver:* yo[12]) que uno estaba (*construir*[13]) su nido° en (*un/una*[14]) árbol cerca del lago.

°*ducklings*
°*nest*

(*Pasar:* yo[15]) todo el día a caballo hasta la hora de (*cenar*[16]) y luego, después de (*comer*[17]), (*descansar*[18]) un rato bajo los árboles. Antes de (*mudarse*[19]) al campo, (*hablar:* nosotros[20]) constantemente de las ventajas del aire puro y del ritmo lento de la vida, pero no (*pensar*[21]) en la tranquilidad y la belleza de las cosas (*cotidiano*[22]). Ahora (*ser/estar:* nosotros[23]) (*tan/tanto*[24]) contentos que no es posible que nuestra decisión (*haber ser*[25]) un error.

Nueva demanda por detención de una vaca

BAYONA (Pontevedra), 21. (Efe.) — José Costas Martínez, propietario de la vaca "Pinta", que hace tres años fue detenida por la Policía Municipal de Bayona, demandó hoy a su depositario, al que reclama la devolución y una indemnización de millón y medio de pesetas.

José Costas había demandado con anterioridad al Ayuntamiento de Bayona por el mismo motivo, procedimiento que está pendiente de sentencia en el juzgado número uno de Vigo.

Los hechos se iniciaron hace tres años cuando la vaca "Pinta" estaba pastando en los jardines públicos de La Palma, y dos guardias municipales, por orden del alcalde, la llevaron a un depósito municipal. Como la vaca inició una "huelga de hambre" el alcalde se la entregó en custodia al cartero de la parroquia de Belesar, José Rodríguez Juncal.

Según el propietario de la vaca, durante estos tres años el animal produjo beneficios por importe de millón y medio de pesetas entre leche, crías y abono, cantidad que ahora reclama, al margen de la devolución del animal.

El pasado día 22 de enero, el alcalde de Bayona, Benigno Rodríguez Quintas, solicitó en el pleno la autorización para comparecer en el pleito que, pocos días antes, había iniciado José Costas para la recuperación de su vaca, recibiendo respuesta afirmativa.

El depositario de la vaca, José Rodríguez Juncal, y sus familiares impidieron recientemente el acceso a su cuadra de periodistas gráficos que tenían intención de fotografiar a la "Pinta".

¿Cierto, falso o no lo dice? ¿O se infiere? Corrija las oraciones falsas y explique su punto de vista usando palabras del párrafo.

1. La persona que habla es una mujer.
2. Esta persona acaba de comprar un rancho.
3. A la persona que habla le interesan los animales.
4. La persona y su compañero/a vivían antes en la ciudad.
5. La persona que habla debe ser bastante acomodada (*well off*).

VOCABULARIO

Theme vocabulary previously listed as active: *acabar, el árbol, la autopista, explotar, el gobierno, la impresora, (el ordenador) personal, el servicio, la vida*

VERBOS

conservar to conserve
construir to build
contaminar to pollute
cubrir to cover
desarrollar to develop
descubrir to discover
destruir to destroy
encantar to enchant
evitar to avoid
explotar to exploit
madrugar to get up early
montar a caballo to ride horseback
mudarse to move
preocuparse to worry
proteger (protejo) to protect
recorrer to pass through; to cover (*territory, miles, and so on*)
resolver (ue) to solve, resolve

LAS COMPUTADORAS

el disco computer disc
la impresora printer
la informática data processing
el lenguaje (computer) language
el manejo/uso operation, use (*of a machine*)
la memoria memory
la microcomputadora microcomputer
el monitor monitor, screen
la pantalla screen
las teclas keys
archivar la información to store information
diseñar programas to design, write programs
escribir a máquina to type
manejar/usar to use, operate (*a machine*)

EL MEDIO AMBIENTE

el aire air
el desarrollo development
la energía energy
la escasez (*pl.* **escaseces**) lack, shortage
la fábrica factory
la naturaleza nature
la población population
los recursos naturales natural resources

¿LA CIUDAD O EL CAMPO?

el/la campesino/a farm worker; peasant
el delito crime
la finca farm
el negocio business
el ranchero rancher
el rascacielos skyscraper
el ritmo rhythm, pace
la soledad solitude
el transporte (means of) transportation
la vivienda housing

OTROS SUSTANTIVOS

la actualidad right now
el requisito requirement

ADJETIVOS

acelerado/a fast, accelerated
bello/a beautiful
denso/a dense
público/a public
puro/a pure

Frases útiles para la comunicación

había (**habías**, **había**, etc.) + *past participle*	*I* (*you, he/she/it*) *had* (*done something*)
Antes de 1985, yo no **había estudiado** español todavía.	*Before 1985, I hadn't studied Spanish yet.*

UN PASO MÁS 14

OPTIONAL SECTION

▲ Actividad A. Una noche misteriosa

Variation A: May be done as written exercise.

Imagine que Ud. está haciendo *camping* con un grupo de amigos. Alguien pregunta: «¿Por qué no contamos un cuento (*story*) de misterio?» ¿Cómo es el cuento que se va a contar? Para empezar, puede usar una de las siguientes situaciones. Luego, use las preguntas para continuar su cuento.

¡OJO! Debe tratar de contar una historia que realmente capte la atención de todos.

Una noche de invierno dos jóvenes entraron en una casa abandonada, una casa que estaba en una zona aislada en las afueras de la ciudad. Los jóvenes estaban hablando de _____ cuando de repente...

Una noche de verano un grupo de jóvenes fue al Parque Transilvania porque se decía que era muy bonito de noche. Habían caminado mucho cuando...

1. ¿Quiénes son los personajes (*characters*) del cuento? ¿Dónde estaban?
2. ¿Qué hora era?
3. ¿Qué tiempo hacía?
4. ¿Qué hacían los personajes?
5. ¿Qué oyeron?
6. ¿Cómo se sintieron?
7. ¿Qué hicieron?
8. ¿Qué pasó después?
9. ¿Y después?
10. ¿Cómo terminó su aventura?

A propósito... Talking About What You Need or Have Left

Two Spanish verbs frequently used with indirect object pronouns will allow you to express what you don't have (and need!) or what you do have (what is left or remaining). They are **faltar** (*to need; to miss, not attend*) and **quedar** (*to remain*).

—¿Cuánto dinero **te falta** todavía para comprar el nuevo ordenador? —Pues, después de pagar la matrícula, **me quedan** sólo doscientos dólares para este mes. **Me falta** mucho dinero todavía.	*—How much money do you still need to buy the new computer? —Well, after paying the tuition, I have only $200 left for this month. I still need a lot more money.*

Note that, like **gustar**, the verbs **quedar** and **faltar** agree with the thing needed or lacking, not with the person.

▲ Actividad B. Es cuestión de prioridades...

Variation B: May be done in either debate or forum format, with several students playing role of interest groups while student "committee" listens and responds to pleas.

Imagine que Ud. es miembro de un comité imaginario: COPAMA (el Comité del Presidente para la Preservación de Animales y del Medio Ambiente). El comité se ha reunido porque varios grupos le han solicitado fondos para ciertos casos de urgencia. Al comité le queda muy poco dinero que distribuir antes del primero del mes. En su opinión, ¿qué grupo(s) debe(n) recibir los fondos? ¿Por qué? Use algunas de las frases que aparecen en **A propósito...**

1. un grupo dedicado a la preservación del cóndor
2. el grupo que se llama «Salve las ballenas (*whales*)»
3. un grupo de víctimas de la contaminación ambiental
4. un municipio que busca fondos para la renovación del centro de su ciudad
5. el Club Sierra

▲ Actividad C. Volver a la tierra

O MUCHAS GANAS DE TRABAJAR, ya sea en
)o o en alguna casa o restaurante vegetariano. Tengo
es sobre cocina y sé algo de francés. Mari Ripollés. c/.
nando, 12. Oliva (Valencia).

ARÍA TRABAJAR en un restaurante vegetariano
ble en Barcelona o Valencia). No tengo ninguna expe-
razón por la cual quiero aprender. Merçè Vallès Figue-
a. de la Estación, 6. Santa Bárbara (Tarragona). Tel.
1 81 19.

SITO LUGAR con buena agua y buen aire para vivir
hija de 5 años. Haría cualquier trabajo campestre, arte-
oméstico, docente, musical, administrativo o sanitario.
carnet de conducir. M.ª Luz Gil. Sta. Otilia, 28. 08032
na. Tel. 358 03 99.

OS UN MATRIMONIO con cuatro hijos de 8 a 13
los ofrecemos para llevar granja y huerta en Catalunya
ar como cocineros en una casa de colonias (durante to-
ño). Tenemos experiencia como granjeros. Ignacio Vila-
. San Pedro, 13, Artés (Barcelona). Tel. 873 57 58 (de-
ado).

MESTRA I VEGETARIANA; vull treballar en qual-
cosa. Angela Buj i Alfara. c/. Campanar, 2. Alcanar.
; Tel. (977) 73 09 10 (dilluns).

USTARÍA TRABAJAR con gente sana y sincera en
granja-escuela en el extranjero, preferiblemente en In-
y a ser posible después del verano. No tengo expe-
Jesús María Sarries Napal. c/. Maruguete, 9. Navascues
a).

Note C: One of the ads is in *catalán*.

Follow-up C: Students write personal ads of their own, following the model of those in the text. Post the ads in class and have students answer one or more of them.

DESEO CONTACTO CON PERSONAS que quieran vivir en el campo. Tengo casa y tierra. Damián Carrasco. Lista de Correos. Mogón (Jaén).

LLEVAMOS 6 AÑOS VIVIENDO en el campo. Poseemos cabras, colmenas y huerta. Venden cerca de nosotros, en Guadalupe (Cáceres), 110 ha. de monte y algo de llano con mucha agua. Nos podríamos asociar y crear una cooperativa de quesos. José Luis Martín Martín. Navatrasierra (Cáceres).

DESEO CONOCER MÁS DE CERCA España, el país, su vida y su gente, por lo cual me interesaría poder trabajar en el campo durante un tiempo a fin de profundizar mis impresiones. Tengo 22 años, experiencia en el manejo de caballos y en trabajos de cestería. Renate Ginhold. Schyrenstr. 10, 8000 München. Rep. Fed. de Alemania.

BUSCO COMUNIDAD RURAL donde pueda trabajar en el campo unas semanas en agosto. Quiero trabajar de medio día por alojamiento y alimentación. Deseo mejorar tanto mi español como mis conocimientos de agricultura. Hanne Ziegler. Schumannstr. 10. 6000 Frankfurt 1. Rep. Fed. Alemania.

SOMOS UNA PAREJA VEGETARIANA de 23 y 21 años con un niño y nos gusta la vida de trabajo y búsqueda interna en contacto con la naturaleza y lejos de cualquier hábito nocivo. Yo doy clases de Hatha Yoga y ambos hemos trabajado en un restaurante macrobiótico vegetariano. Nos gustaría trabajar y vivir en una comunidad o similar, con búsquedas afines a las nuestras. Podemos contribuir económicamente. César Cacharrón Gómez. Apdo. 5104 Vigo. Tel. 23 91 67 (de 13 a 16 h.).

DOS FAMILIAS TENEMOS UNA FINCA de 6 ha. Podemos alojar alguna persona para trabajar en serio con animales, quesos, cultivos de cereales y hortalizas, viviendo una vida más o menos sencilla con los productos producidos aquí. Famille Rochart - Kauhs c/o Famille Waber. Ferme de Visargent. Sens sur Seille 71330 St. Germain du Bois - Saône et Loire, France.

En Europa, como en los Estados Unidos, ha sido muy popular el movimiento llamado «volver a la tierra». Los siguientes anuncios son de una revista para personas que se interesan en temas relacionados con la ecología y la naturaleza. Léalos rápidamente y diga por lo menos cinco temas que les interesan a las personas que leen esta revista, según los anuncios.

Ahora, con un compañero (una compañera), busque los siguientes anuncios. Un anuncio puesto por una persona (unas personas) que...

1. habla alemán
2. necesita ayuda con su finca
3. quiere trabajar en el campo durante sus vacaciones de verano
4. le interesa mucho la comida
5. vive en España pero habla y escribe otro idioma
6. tienen muchos hijos

Un anuncio que las siguientes personas deben contestar:

1. un matrimonio con muchos hijos que quiere vivir en el campo
2. una persona que busca un trabajo relacionado con los temas ecológicos
3. el dueño de una finca que tiene muchos caballos
4. una persona que se interesa en vivir con muchas otras personas

LECTURA CULTURAL

Lectura: See IM for suggestions and additional exercises and activities.

Estos consejos son de un folleto (*pamphlet*) de la Secretaría General de Turismo de España.

NORMAS BASICAS PARA LA PROTECCION DEL MEDIO AMBIENTE POR PARTE DEL TURISMO

Disfrute y observe la riqueza de fauna y flora españolas, pero no capture animales ni arranque plantas. No importe ni intente exportar objetos naturales sin autorización o información al respecto. • Visite nuestros nueve «Parques Nacionales» y once «Parques Naturales»: disfrute de ellos y evite su deterioro. • Los incendios forestales ocasionan en España graves pérdidas económicas y ecológicas. No encienda hogueras[a] en el campo, salvo en los lugares señalados para ello. Apague las colillas[b] y no las arroje por la ventanilla de su automóvil. • El agua es un bien escaso en la mayoría del territorio español. No la malgaste. • El vertido[c] de combustible y aceite de embarcaciones a motor es un importante factor de contaminación del agua. Mantenga en buen estado el motor de su embarcación. • Las aguas de lavado y desperdicios pueden contaminar gravemente los ríos. Evite realizar estas tareas fuera de las instalaciones adecuadas; en caso de que no le sea posible, vierta el agua sucia sobre el terreno. No acerque su vehículo a menos de 100 metros de arroyos, ríos, lagunas, etc. • El vertido de aceites de automóvil en el suelo puede producir una grave contaminación de aguas subterráneas. No cambie nunca el aceite de su vehículo en el campo. • Las rodaduras de automóvil son uno de los agentes de inicio de erosión más poderosas. No invada con su vehículo el césped y vegetación fuera de los caminos o carreteras. • Ochenta y tres decibelios es el nivel máximo de ruido permisible a un automóvil. Además es preciso mantener niveles mínimos de emisión de partículas y monóxido de carbono. Mantenga a punto[ch] el motor de su vehículo. • En sus viajes por carretera pare en las estaciones de servicio o puntos de estacionamiento señalados, donde podrá depositar basuras y residuos en los recipientes al efecto. Evite en todo caso arrojarlos en las márgenes de las carreteras. • El abandono de basuras en el medio natural constituye un atentado a la estética, además de un claro peligro en muchos casos. No deje jamás en el campo ningún tipo de residuo orgánico o inorgánico. Extreme su cuidado en zonas especialmente delicadas, como son las playas. • La excavación por parte de excursionistas en zonas naturales muy frecuentadas se traduce en notables alteraciones de la vegetación y de los horizontes superficiales del suelo. No excave nunca agujeros[d] en el suelo para ocultar residuos de ningún tipo. • La acampada libre es una de las causas más importantes de contaminación y deterioro del medio natural. No acampe fuera de las áreas dispuestas para ello. • El máximo nivel de ruido ambiental permisible es de cincuenta y cinco decibelios. Evite, en lo posible, elevar el volumen de su aparato de radio o TV., especialmente en lugares y transportes públicos, en el campo o medio natural, y siempre durante las horas de descanso. • Cumpla las normas sanitarias que afecten a los animales que traiga con Vd. Mantenga su perro sujeto por la correa en zonas públicas. Para hacer sus necesidades, condúzcalo a los desagües[e] practicados en los bordillos. • España es un país deficitario en energía. Sea moderado en el uso del agua caliente, luz y aparatos de calefacción y aire acondicionado. • Si adquiere Vd. terrenos o edificios en España, infórmese previamente de sus condiciones urbanísticas en los Ayuntamientos[f] respectivos. • Los monumentos y lugares históricos urbanos deben ser objeto de especial cuidado en cuanto al abandono de residuos. No arroje colillas, envoltorios u otros objetos que puedan deteriorarlos.

a. *bonfires* b. *butts* c. *spilling* ch. a... *tuned up* d. *holes* e. *drains* f. *city governments*

Comprensión

1. ¿Cuántos parques nacionales hay en España? ¿Cuántos parques naturales?
   En su opinión, ¿cuál es la diferencia entre los dos tipos de parques?
2. Según el anuncio, ¿cuáles de los siguientes sitios de interés turístico hay en España?

   _____ playas
   _____ volcanes
   _____ sitios para hacer *camping*
   _____ lagos y ríos
   _____ bosques (*forests*)
   _____ monumentos en la ciudad
   _____ cuevas (*caves*)
   _____ pirámides

3. Busque en el folleto algo que el turista sí debe hacer en relación con cada uno de los siguientes y algo que no debe hacer.

	sí	no
los animales y las plantas	______	______
los bosques	______	______
el agua	______	______
la basura	______	______
los coches	______	______

Para escribir

Describa la ciudad más grande que Ud. conoce. Su descripción debe incluir los siguientes detalles.

1. dónde está
2. su importancia nacional e internacional
3. población: tamaño (*size*), grupos étnicos o culturales
4. lugares de interés
5. industrias
6. política
7. si le gustaría a Ud. vivir allí y por qué (no)

NO CONTAMINES A NUESTRA COSTA
Las costas y las playas necesitan cuidado, defensa y protección.
El Ministerio de Obras Públicas y Urbanismo, desde 1983 hasta 1986, ha destinado 12.000 millones de pesetas para la regeneración de playas, accesos a las mismas y paseos marítimos.
También desde 1983, en colaboración con el Instituto Nacional de Empleo, está llevando a cabo un Programa de Limpieza de playas y vigilancia de costas. Este verano se realiza en 331 municipios, lo que, además de mejorar la calidad de nuestras playas, supone la creación de nuevos puestos de trabajo.
Para que las costas y las playas no se deterioren, mantengan su atractivo y sean un lugar de descanso y recreo.
Pero todo esfuerzo resultaría inútil sin tu colaboración.
Porque proteger la costa cuesta dinero, porque es necesaria una conducta responsable con un bien que es de todos.
MOPU
Ministerio de Obras Públicas y Urbanismo.

CAPÍTULO QUINCE

LOS PASATIEMPOS Y LA VIDA COTIDIANA

Madrid, España

▲ La vida de la gran ciudad

—¿Cómo pasas tus ratos[a] libres aquí en la capital?

—A veces voy al teatro o a ver una película. Soy muy aficionado al cine.

—¿No te gusta visitar los museos?

—Eso también. Sobre todo el Museo de Arte Moderno.

[a]momentos

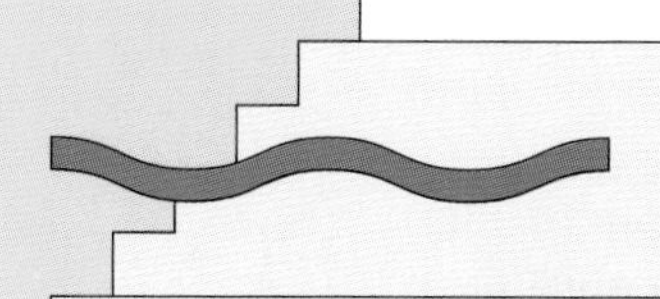

VOCABULARIO: PREPARACIÓN

Vocabulario: Preparación:
- See detailed supplementary materials for this section bound into the back of this Annotated Instructor's Edition.
- See model for vocabulary presentation and other materials in Supplementary *Vocabulario: Preparación* Materials, chapter by chapter, IM.

- See also and

Los pasatiempos

dar un paseo	to take a walk
hacer *camping*	to go camping
hacer planes para + *inf.*	to make plans to (*do something*)
ir al teatro/a ver una película	to go to the theater/ to see a movie
jugar (ue) a las cartas/ al ajedrez	to play cards/chess
pasarlo bien, divertirse (ie, i)	to have a good time
practicar un deporte	to participate in a sport
ser divertido/a	to be fun
tomar el sol	to sunbathe
visitar un museo	to visit a museum
la butaca	seat (*in a theater*)
el cine	movie theater
la comedia	play; comedy
la función	performance, show
la película (doblada)	(dubbed) movie
la trama	plot
los ratos libres	free time

Variation A: After putting items in order, change verbs to appropriate past tenses. Give students past-tense version of first sentence: *El viernes pasado, **hice** planes para ir al cine. Lo primero que hice fue consultar el periódico.*

A. Ud. quiere ir al cine. Usando los números del **1** al **9**, indique en qué orden va a hacer las siguientes cosas.

_____ Llamo a mi amigo/a para ver si quiere acompañarme.
_____ Cuando hago planes para ir al cine, lo primero que hago es consultar el periódico.

*The words **billete** and **boleto** can designate *tickets* for travel or theater tickets. **Entrada** can mean only *tickets* for an event or performance.

_____ Compramos las entradas en la taquilla.
_____ Subo al autobús para ir al centro, donde está el cine.
_____ Buscamos buenas butacas para poder ver bien.
_____ Compramos refrescos para tomar durante la película.
_____ Me fijo en (*I pay attention to*) la trama para tratar de adivinar (*to guess*) cómo va a terminar la película.
_____ Espero a mi amigo/a en la acera delante de la taquilla.
_____ Después de la función, vamos a un café a tomar algo.

Suggestion B: Emphasize the need to invent details. Not all of the questions will be answerable by just looking at the drawings.

Suggestion B: Assign as written composition. Compare answers in class.

B. Describa los dibujos, contestando las preguntas e inventando otros detalles.

1. VOCABULARIO: la pantalla, tener lugar (*to take place*)
¿Dónde tiene lugar esta escena? ¿Por qué han venido estas personas a este sitio? ¿Por qué están de pie esas dos personas? ¿Por qué han llegado tarde? ¿En qué país se hizo esta película? ¿Está doblada? ¿Por qué sí o por qué no? ¿Quiénes son el actor y la actriz principales? ¿Es una película de aventuras? ¿de horror? ¿romántica? Cuente Ud. un poco de la trama.

2. VOCABULARIO: la plaza central
¿Tiene lugar esta escena en los Estados Unidos? Explique su respuesta. ¿Qué tiempo hace? ¿Qué hace la familia ahora? ¿Qué ha hecho ya hoy? ¿Qué planes tiene para el resto de la tarde? ¿Qué hace el resto de la gente? ¿Se está divirtiendo?

3. VOCABULARIO: el río, el valle, el bosque (*forest*)
¿Qué hace esta familia? ¿Dónde están? ¿De dónde son? ¿Por qué han venido a este sitio? ¿Cuánto tiempo hace que están allí? ¿Cuánto tiempo van a pasar allí en total? ¿Por qué les gusta hacer esto? ¿En qué otros sitios lo han hecho?

4. VOCABULARIO: la pareja (*couple*), la exposición de arte
¿En qué tipo de edificio está la pareja? ¿Por qué han venido a este lugar? ¿Dónde viven? ¿Por qué cree Ud. esto? ¿Qué día de la semana cree Ud. que es? ¿Por qué está aquí la pareja? ¿Qué otras cosas han hecho hoy? ¿Qué van a hacer después?

C. **Asociaciones.** ¿Qué actividades o pasatiempos asocia Ud. con... ?

el verano, la primavera, el otoño, el invierno, una cita especial con (su novio/a, su esposo/a, ...), un día lluvioso

Notas culturales: La tertulia

Una costumbre muy común en muchas partes del mundo hispánico es la tertulia, que consiste en un grupo de amigos a quienes les gusta pasar el rato conversando. Los participantes se reúnen periódicamente, por ejemplo, a la misma hora de la tarde todos los días. Generalmente la tertulia se celebra en un bar o café donde se puede tomar vino o cerveza y hablar. Las conversaciones pueden abarcar (*cover*) muchos temas, pero sin duda dos de los más comunes son los deportes y la política. Ya que la gente hispánica se muda con menos frecuencia que en los Estados Unidos, muchos de estos grupos duran años y años, con los mismos amigos reuniéndose en el mismo sitio y a la misma hora.

Los deportes

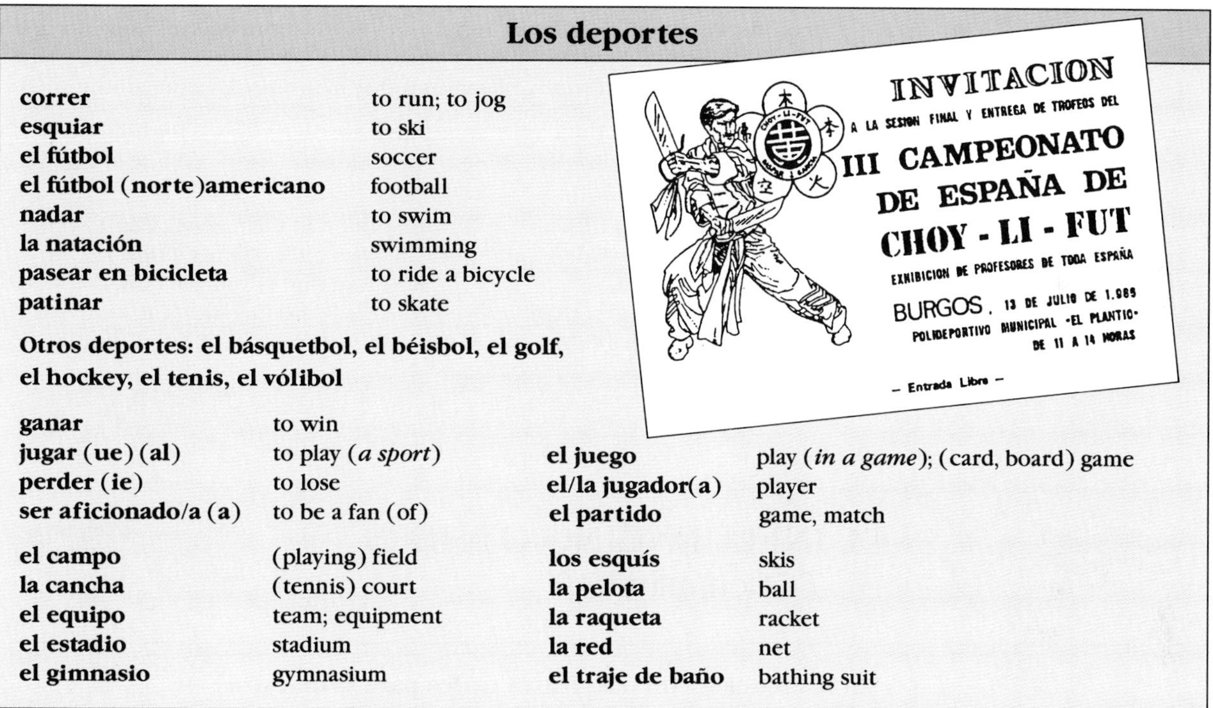

correr	to run; to jog
esquiar	to ski
el fútbol	soccer
el fútbol (norte)americano	football
nadar	to swim
la natación	swimming
pasear en bicicleta	to ride a bicycle
patinar	to skate

Otros deportes: el básquetbol, el béisbol, el golf, el hockey, el tenis, el vólibol

ganar	to win		
jugar (ue) (al)	to play (*a sport*)	**el juego**	play (*in a game*); (card, board) game
perder (ie)	to lose	**el/la jugador(a)**	player
ser aficionado/a (a)	to be a fan (of)	**el partido**	game, match
el campo	(playing) field	**los esquís**	skis
la cancha	(tennis) court	**la pelota**	ball
el equipo	team; equipment	**la raqueta**	racket
el estadio	stadium	**la red**	net
el gimnasio	gymnasium	**el traje de baño**	bathing suit

Follow-up A: **1.** *¿Cuál es la diferencia entre... ? ¿el fútbol y el béisbol? ¿el fútbol y el fútbol norteamericano? ¿un estadio y un gimnasio?* **2.** *¿Qué tienen en común... ? ¿el esquiar y el patinar? ¿pasear en bicicleta y dar un paseo? ¿la natación y el esquí acuático? ¿un campo y una cancha? ¿una raqueta y una red?*

A. ¿Qué palabra o frase no pertenece al grupo? Explique por qué.

1. la cancha la raqueta la pista la piscina
2. el ciclismo el correr el juego la natación
3. el traje de baño la pelota el jugador la raqueta
4. la red los esquís la bicicleta el equipo
5. la pista el equipo los aficionados los jugadores

B. ¿Dónde y cuándo se practican estos deportes? ¿Cómo es el jugador típico de cada deporte? ¿Qué tipo de persona es? ¿Le gusta jugar con un equipo o practicar el deporte individualmente? ¿Le interesa la competencia o prefiere competir consigo mismo (*with himself*)? ¿Cómo es el aficionado típico? Conteste estas preguntas sobre uno o dos de los siguientes deportes.

1. el golf 2. el fútbol norteamericano 3. el correr 4. el béisbol 5. el básquetbol 6. la natación 7. pasear en bicicleta 8. el esquiar

Follow-up B: Ask students: *¿Cuáles son sus deportes favoritos? ¿Por qué?*

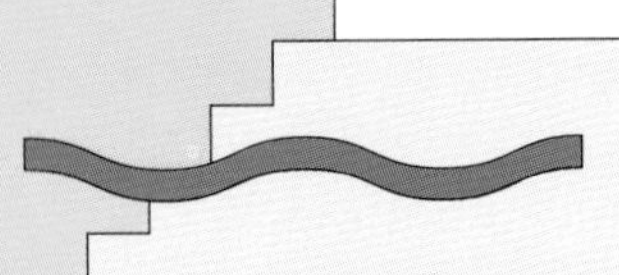

MINIDIÁLOGOS Y GRAMÁTICA

¿Recuerda Ud.?

Ud. and **Uds.** commands (Grammar Section 24) are the third persons (singular and plural) of the present subjunctive. Object pronouns (direct, indirect, reflexive) must follow and be attached to affirmative commands; they must precede negative commands.

Affirmative:	Háblele Ud.	Duérmase.	Dígaselo Ud.
Negative:	No le hable Ud.	No se duerma.	No se lo diga Ud.

¿Cómo se dice en español?

1. Bring me the book. (**Uds.**)
2. Don't give it to her. (**Uds.**)
3. Sit here, please. (**Ud.**)
4. Don't sit in that chair! (**Ud.**)
5. Tell them the truth. (**Uds.**)
6. Tell it to them now! (**Uds.**)
7. Never tell it to her. (**Uds.**)
8. Take care of yourself (**Ud.**)
9. Lead a healthy life. (**Ud.**)
10. Listen to me. (**Ud.**)

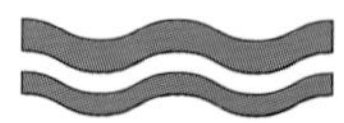

43. INFLUENCING OTHERS
Tú Commands

Communicative objectives for 43: how to give commands to people whom you know well

En la escuela primaria: frases útiles para la maestra

—Maritere, *toma* tu leche; *no tomes* la de Carlos.
—Cristina, *escribe* las oraciones en la pizarra; *no las escribas* en la pared.
—Joaquín, *escucha*; *no hables* tanto.
—Esteban, *siéntate* en tu silla; *no te sientes* en el suelo.
—Silvia, *quítate* el abrigo; *no te quites* el suéter.
—Graciela, *dale* el cuaderno a Ernesto; *no se lo des* a Joaquín.
—Mario, *ponte* el abrigo; *no olvides* tu calculadora.
—Ramón, *ten* cuidado; *no corras*, *no te caigas*.
—Juana, *no hagas* eso; *tráeme* el papel.

1. ¿Qué dice la maestra cuando Maritere no toma su leche? ¿cuando alguien debe escribir en la pizarra? ¿no escucha? ¿no se sienta en la silla? ¿no se

Point out in mini:
- Affirmative commands: Ask, Where have you seen these forms before? (→ third person sing. pres. ind.).
- Negative commands: Ask, Where have you seen these forms before? (→ *tú*, pres. subj.).

In grade school: Useful phrases for the teacher Maritere, drink your milk; don't drink Carlos's. Cristina, write the sentences on the board; don't write them on the wall. Joaquín, listen; don't talk so much. Esteban, sit in your chair; don't sit on the floor. Silvia, take off your coat; don't take off your sweater. Graciela, give the notebook to Ernesto; don't give it to Joaquín. Mario, put on your coat; don't forget your calculator. Ramón, be careful; don't run, don't fall. Juana, don't do that; bring me the paper.

quita el abrigo? ¿no le da el cuaderno a Ernesto? ¿no se pone el abrigo? ¿no tiene cuidado? ¿no trae el papel?

2. ¿Por qué la maestra da mandatos negativos? Por ejemplo, ¿por qué le dice la maestra a Maritere «no tomes la leche de Carlos»?
   - Porque Maritere tomó la leche de Carlos.
   - Porque no está tomando su propia leche.
   - Porque la maestra no quiere que Maritere la tome.

Informal commands (**los mandatos informales**) are used with persons whom you address as **tú**.

- **Emphasis:** Students already know all forms involved; position of object pronouns is identical to that with *Ud./Uds.* commands.

Negative *tú* Commands

Suggestion: Treat the material in this section for passive recognition only. Ask students to learn only high frequency irregular *tú* commands.

Suggestion: Explain to students that the command system in Spanish (although easy to understand when someone gives you a command) is difficult to master in speaking. They should not be discouraged if using the system correctly does not come easily.

Emphasis: All negative commands are expressed with corresponding subjunctive forms.

Preliminary exercise: *Un amigo dice que no quiere hacer las siguientes cosas. Dígale que no las haga.* **Modelo:** *No quiero cantarlo. → Pues no lo cantes. No quiero comprarlo/mirarlo/leerlo/beberlo/escribirlo/decidirlo.*

-ar *verbs*		**-er/-ir** *verbs*	
No hables.	*Don't speak.*	**No comas.**	*Don't eat.*
No cantes.	*Don't sing.*	**No escribas.**	*Don't write.*
No juegues.	*Don't play.*	**No pidas.**	*Don't order.*

Like **Ud.** commands (Grammar Section 24), the negative **tú** commands are expressed with the present subjunctive: **no hable Ud., no hables (tú)**. The pronoun **tú** is used only for emphasis.

No cantes **tú** tan fuerte. *Don't you sing so loudly.*

As with negative **Ud.** commands, object pronouns—direct, indirect, and reflexive—precede negative **tú** commands.

No lo mires. *Don't look at him.*
No les escribas. *Don't write to them.*
No te levantes. *Don't get up.*

[Práctica A–B]

Affirmative *tú* Commands*

Suggestion: Use preceding Preliminary Exercise to cue affirmative commands.

Preliminary exercise: *Un amigo dice que debe hacer las siguientes cosas. Déle mandatos afirmativos.* **Modelo:** *Debo hacer la cama. → Haz la cama. (Hazla.) Debo decir la verdad/hacer más tacos/ir a la biblioteca/poner los libros en la mesa/salir ahora/tener más paciencia/venir a clase todos los días/ser buen(a) estudiante*

-ar *verbs*		**-er/-ir** *verbs*	
Habla.	*Speak.*	**Come.**	*Eat.*
Canta.	*Sing.*	**Escribe.**	*Write.*
Juega.	*Play.*	**Pide.**	*Order.*

*Affirmative **vosotros** commands are formed by substituting **-d** for the final **-r** of the infinitive: **hablar → hablad**; **comer → comed**; **escribir → escribid**. There are no irregular affirmative **vosotros** commands. Negative **vosotros** commands are expressed with the present subjunctive: **no habléis/comáis/escribáis**. Placement of object pronouns is the same as with all other command forms: **Decídmelo**; **No me lo digáis**.

Unlike the other command forms you have learned, most affirmative **tú** commands have the same form as the third person singular of the present *indicative*. Some verbs have irregular affirmative **tú** command forms.

decir:	**di**	poner:	**pon**	tener:	**ten**
hacer:	**haz**	salir:	**sal**	venir:	**ven**
ir:	**ve**	ser:	**sé**		

Sé puntual pero **ten** cuidado. — *Be there on time, but be careful.*

¡OJO! The affirmative **tú** commands for **ir** and **ver** are identical: **ve**. Context will clarify meaning.

¡**Ve** esa película! — *See that movie!*
Ve a casa ahora mismo. — *Go home right now.*

As in affirmative **Ud.** commands, object and reflexive pronouns follow affirmative **tú** commands and are attached to them. Accent marks are necessary except when a single pronoun is added to a one-syllable command.

Dile la verdad. — *Tell him the truth.*
Léela, por favor. — *Read it, please.*
Póntelos. — *Put them on.*

[Práctica C–CH]

Práctica

Suggestion A: After giving cued command, students give affirmative commands that expand situation. *Ejemplo* with model: *Estaciónalo en la calle Sexta*.

A. **Un viaje con Raúl.** Durante un viaje en coche, su amigo Raúl insiste en hacer cosas que a Ud. no le gustan. Dígale que no las haga, según el modelo.

MODELO: Raúl estaciona el carro en medio (*middle*) de la calle. → Raúl, no lo estaciones aquí, por favor.

1. Raúl gasta mucho dinero en gasolina.
2. Raúl maneja rápidamente.
3. Cierra la ventana.
4. Dobla en la esquina.
5. Para en la esquina.
6. Lee el mapa.
7. Sigue todo derecho.
8. Dice que Uds. van a llegar tarde.
9. Es muy descortés con Ud.
10. Arranca rápidamente.

Follow-up B, C, CH: *Julita* tells what commands she would like to give to others.

B. Los señores Villarreal no están contentos con el comportamiento de su hija Julita. Continúe los comentarios de ellos con mandatos informales lógicos según cada situación. Siga el modelo.

MODELO: *Hablaste* demasiado ayer. → No *hables* tanto hoy, por favor.
Dejaste tu ropa en el suelo anoche. → No la *dejes* allí hoy, por favor.

1. También *dejaste* tus libros en el suelo.
2. ¿Por qué *regresaste* tarde a casa hoy después de las clases?
3. Ayer *usaste* mi toalla.

4. Tampoco quiero que *entres* en nuestro cuarto de baño para nada.
5. No es bueno que *corras* y *juegues* en la calle.
6. ¿Por qué *vas* al parque todas las tardes?
7. No es bueno que *mires* la televisión constantemente. ¿Y por qué quieres *ver* todos esos programas de detectives?
8. ¿Por qué le *dices* mentiras a tu papá?
9. Siempre *te olvidas* de sacar la basura, que es la única tarea que tienes que hacer.
10. Ay, hija, no te comprendemos. ¡*Eres* tan insolente!

C. La pobre Julita también escucha muchos mandatos de su maestra en clase. Invente Ud. esos mandatos según las indicaciones.

1. llegar / a / escuela / puntualmente
2. entrar / clase / sin / hacer tanto ruido
3. quitarse / abrigo / y / sentarse
4. sacar / libro de matemáticas / y / abrirlo / en / página 10
5. escribir / problema dos / en / pizarra
6. leer / nuevo / palabras / y / aprenderlas / para mañana
7. venir / aquí / a / hablar conmigo / sobre / este / composición
8. ayudar / Carlitos / con / su composición

¿Qué mandatos—positivos o negativos—recuerda Ud. de la escuela primaria?

CH. En casa, otra vez las acciones de la pobre Julita siguen disgustando a todos, hasta a Eufemia, su hermana mayor. Continúe los comentarios de todos con mandatos informales lógicos—positivos o negativos—según cada situación.

1. Siempre entras en mi cuarto y usas mis cosas sin permiso. No quiero que toques nada en este cuarto, ¿comprendes?
2. No ayudas nunca con las tareas domésticas. Por lo menos puedes poner la mesa, ¿no?
3. Siempre quieres hacer las cosas rápidamente. Nunca tienes paciencia ni cuidado.
4. Tienes que desayunar. No puedes salir para la escuela sin tomar algo.
5. No me escuchas nunca. ¿Qué te pasa? ¿Por qué no puedes poner atención?
6. No debes contestarme con ese tono de voz. Y cuando te hablo, quiero que me mires.
7. No le dijiste la verdad a papá sobre el disco roto.
8. Nunca te acuestas cuando yo te lo digo. ¿Por qué no puedes ser obediente, como Eufemia?

Conversación

CENTRO CULTURAL MAPOCHO

TALLERES INTENSIVOS DE VERANO

- DANZA MODERNA
  Prof. Fany Luengo
- ACTUACION TEATRAL
  Prof. Juan Carlos Nanjarl
- TEATRO INFANTIL
  Prof. Jaun Carlos Nanjarl
- PIANO
  Prof. José Hoffman
- GUITARRA
  Prof. Pita Barrios
- PINTURA INFANTIL
  Prof. Magdalena Labbé
- RETABLO
  Prof. Arnaldo Silva
- PERIODISMO POPULAR
  Prof. Eduardo Rossel
- FOTOGRAFIA
  Prof. Héctor López

Del 4 de enero al 5 de febrero de 1988. Tres veces por semana. Matrícula gratis.

Alameda 381 - Fono 336253

A. Algunos de sus amigos tienen que hacer ciertas cosas. Déles consejos sobre lo que van a hacer, en forma de mandatos informales.

1. Miguel tiene una entrevista con una compañía de computadoras para ser programador. Déle consejos para la entrevista.
2. Su amiga mayor, la señora Fuentes, quiere comprar un coche nuevo. Su viejo coche ya no arranca con facilidad por la mañana. ¿Adónde debe ir, con quién debe hablar y qué debe decir?
3. Paula quiere ser maestra de primaria. Sus padres quieren que se case pronto. ¿Qué debe decirles y que *no* les debe decir?
4. Su amigo Ernesto quiere empezar a llevar una vida más activa. Le interesan sobre todo el tenis y correr. ¿Qué debe comprar y dónde debe practicar esos deportes?
5. Unos amigos quieren asistir a unos talleres (*workshops*). ¿Qué talleres de la lista a la izquierda les recomienda?

B. Con dos compañeros, invente mandatos informales para las siguientes situaciones.

- para ser un esposo (una esposa) feliz
- para ser el compañero (la compañera) de cuarto ideal
- para estar en buena salud

Variations B: 1. *para cuando sale para su primera cita con un nuevo amigo (una nueva amiga) a quien quiere impresionar* **2.** *para cuando conoce a los padres del novio (de la novia) por primera vez* **3.** *para cuando un(a) policía lo/la para por ir demasiado rápido* **4.** *para un(a) freshman en esta universidad*

C. **Entrevista.** Con un compañero (una compañera), haga y conteste preguntas para saber los cinco mandatos que el otro escuchaba con más frecuencia en los lugares indicados cuando era niño/a. ¿Quién se los daba?

MODELO:

USTED: Cuando jugaba en la calle, siempre me decía mi madre: «Ten cuidado. No corras—te vas a caer.» Y era verdad; me caía con frecuencia. Era muy torpe. Y a ti, ¿te decía lo mismo tu mamá?

COMPAÑERO/A: No, no me decía eso cuando estábamos en la calle. Pero sí me decía con frecuencia...

Sitios: en la escuela, en el gimnasio, en la calle, en la iglesia, en la piscina, en una tienda, en el coche, durante una cena familiar

¡Malas noticias!

—Lo siento, pero tu equipo volvió a perder.

—No me hables. 3 a 0... ¡ y en casa!

—Si siguen así, es posible que pierdan la liga (*division title*).

—¡La culpa es de los árbitros!

—¡Claro! Siempre que pierde tu equipo, la culpa es del árbitro.

El jugador argentino de fútbol Diego Maradona

Communicative objectives for 44: how to talk about things that are indefinite in your mind or that do not exist.

44. ¿HAY ALGUIEN QUE... ? ¿HAY UN LUGAR DONDE... ?

Subjunctive After Nonexistent and Indefinite Antecedents

En la plaza central

Describa lo que pasa y lo que *no* ocurre en esta escena de la plaza principal de un pueblo mexicano.

- *Hay personas* que *conversan* con los amigos, que *pasan* aquí sus ratos libres todos los días, que... (jugar al ajedrez, vender/comprar periódicos/comida, tomar el sol, ¿ ?)
- *Hay niños* que *toman* helados, que... (jugar en la acera, dar un paseo con sus padres, ¿ ?)
- *No hay nadie* que *lleve* ropa de invierno, que *pasee* en bicicleta, que... (ser aficionado al golf, ser de los Estados Unidos, escuchar la radio, ¿ ?)

In English and Spanish, statements or questions that give or ask for information about a person, place, or thing often contain two clauses:

I have a **car** *that* **gets good mileage.**
Is there a **house** for sale *that* **is closer to the city?**

Each of the preceding sentences contains a main clause (*I have a car . . .* ; *Is there a house for sale . . .*). In addition, each sentence also has a dependent clause (*. . . that gets good mileage; . . . that is closer to the city?*) that modifies a noun in the main clause: *car*, *house*. The noun (or pronoun) modified is called the *antecedent* (**el antecedente**) of the dependent clause, and the clause itself is called an adjective clause, since—like an adjective—it modifies a noun (or pronoun).

In Spanish, when the antecedent of an adjective clause refers to someone (something, someplace, and so on) that does not exist in the speaker's experience or whose existence is indefinite or uncertain, the subjunctive must be used in the adjective (dependent) clause.

Suggestions:
- Use visual to present grammar inductively.
- Ask: What verb form—subjunctive or indicative—is used after *No hay nadie que _____?* Does clause *que lleve ropa de invierno* modify an existent antecedent (= *nadie*)? Contrast existent vs. nonexistent antecedents.
- **Variation:** *Imagine que Ud. está en esta plaza. ¿A quién busca o necesita?* Put beginning of answer on board: *Busco/Necesito a alguien que _____.* Stress use of subjunctive.
- **Contrast:** adjective vs. noun clauses

EXISTENT ANTECEDENT:	**Hay algo** aquí que me **interesa**.	*There is something here that interests me.*
NONEXISTENT ANTECEDENT:	**No hay nada** aquí que me **interese**.	*There is nothing here that interests me.*

DEFINITE ANTECEDENT:	**Hay muchos restaurantes** donde **sirven** comida mexicana auténtica.	*There are a lot of restaurants where they serve authentic Mexican food.*
INDEFINITE ANTECEDENT:	**Buscamos un restaurante** donde **sirvan** comida salvadoreña auténtica.	*We're looking for a restaurant where they serve authentic Salvadorean food.*

Note, as in the preceding examples, that adjective clauses of this type can be introduced with **donde...** rather than **que...**

¡OJO! The dependent adjective clause structure is often used in questions to find out information about someone or something the speaker does not know much about. Note, however, that the indicative is used to answer the question if the antecedent is known to the person who answers.

—¿**Hay algo** aquí que te **guste**? —Sí, **hay varias cosas** que me **gustan** y que **creo** que las voy a comprar.	*—Is there something here that you like? —Yes, there are several things that I like and that I think I'm going to buy.*

¡OJO! The personal **a** is not used with direct object nouns that refer to hypothetical persons.* Compare the use of the indicative and the subjunctive in the following sentences.

Busco **un señor** que lo **sepa**.	*I'm looking for a man who knows that (it).*
Busco **al señor** que lo **sabe**.	*I'm looking for the man who knows that (it).*

Suggestion: Relate these uses of subjunctive to general use of subjunctive to express conceptualized states/actions.
- **Emphasis:** Use of *donde* to introduce the adjective clause
- **Discrimination:** Existent or nonexistent? Do English first; then Spanish. **1.** There's nothing here that I like./*No hay nada aquí que me guste.* **2.** Here's something that you will like./*Aquí hay algo que te va a gustar.* **3.** I don't know anyone who can do it./*No conozco a nadie que lo pueda hacer.* **4.** I know many people who can do it./*Conozco a muchas personas que lo pueden hacer.* **5.** There's no car that is economical./*No hay ningún coche que sea económico.*
- **Discrimination:** Definite or indefinite? Do English first, then Spanish. **1.** I have a book that is interesting./*Tengo un libro que es interesante.* **2.** I want to buy a book that is interesting./*Quiero comprar un libro que sea interesante.* **3.** I'm looking for a secretary who speaks Spanish./*Busco un secretario que hable español.* **4.** I have a secretary who speaks Spanish./*Tengo un secretario que habla español.*
- **Point out:** *¿Hay algo que te* ***guste****? → No, no hay nada que me* ***guste****.* (nonexistent) but *Sí, hay algo que me* ***gusta*** (existent).

Práctica

A. Contradict the speakers in the following situations, using the cues in parentheses.

1. Ud. y su amigo Rodolfo están perdidos en un camino rural, por la noche. Además, parece que el coche empieza a fallar (*sputter*).
   RODOLFO: —Seguramente hay alguien en aquella casa que conoce el camino. (No, hombre, no hay nadie...)
   —Sin duda en aquella gasolinera hay alguien que puede arreglar el coche. (No, no hay nadie...)
2. En una oficina: son las cinco de la tarde y hay mucho trabajo que hacer todavía. Ud. habla con el jefe.
   JEFE: —Necesito al secretario que sabe español. (Pero, señor, aquí no tenemos ningún...)
   —Claro que hay alguien que tiene tiempo de terminarlo para mañana. (Siento decírselo, pero no hay...)

Variation A: Students supply own contradictions.
- *Buscando un restaurante, con unos amigos:* **1.** *Vamos a ese restaurante donde sirven comida china.* **2.** *En «El Toledano» hay un camarero que toca la guitarra, ¿verdad?*
- *En la agencia de viajes, hablando con el agente:* **1.** *¿No tienen alguna excursión que vaya a Machu Picchu?* **2.** *No veo aquí en esta lista ninguna excursión que sea muy interesante.* (***¡OJO!*** Contradiction requires indicative, breaking pattern of earlier responses.)

*Remember that **alguien** and **nadie** always take the personal **a** when they are used as direct objects: **Busco a alguien que lo sepa. No veo a nadie que sea norteamericano.**

• En el club deportivo, hablando con el dueño. **1.** *Me interesan las actividades que no sean demasiado arduas.* **2.** *Supongo que aquí no hay nadie que me pueda enseñar a nadar, ¿verdad?*

3. En la tienda de muebles: su esposo/a busca muebles para su casa.
   ESPOSO/A: —Pues, sí, aquí hay algunas cosas que me gustan. (No hay nada...)
   —Necesitamos un sillón que sea un poco más grande. (Pero si ya tenemos dos...)

B. Carmen acaba de llegar aquí de otro estado. Quiere saber algunas cosas sobre la universidad y la ciudad. Haga las preguntas de Carmen según el modelo.

MODELO: restaurantes / sirven comida latinoamericana →
¿Hay restaurantes que sirvan (donde sirvan) comida latinoamericana?

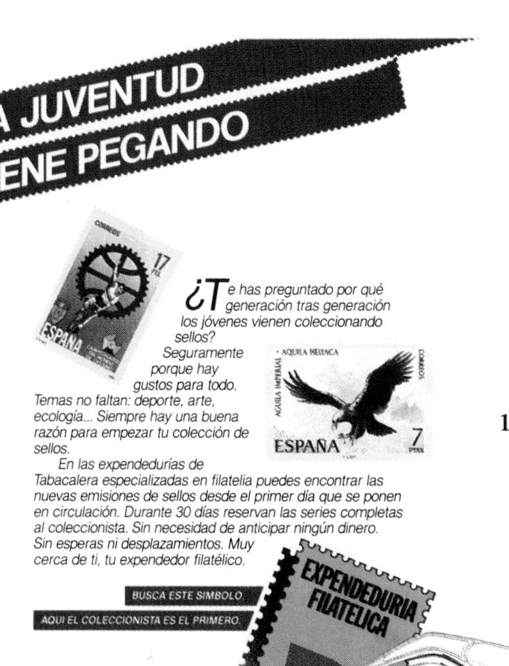

1. librerías / venden libros usados
2. tiendas / se puede comprar revistas de Latinoamérica
3. cafés cerca de la universidad / se reúnen muchos estudiantes
4. discotecas / se puede bailar
5. apartamentos cerca de la universidad / son buenos y baratos
6. cines / pasan películas en español
7. canchas de tenis / se puede jugar por la noche
8. un gimnasio en la universidad / se juega al ráquetbol
9. parques / la gente corre o da paseos
10. museos / hacen exposiciones de arte latinoamericana

Según las preguntas que le ha hecho Carmen, ¿son ciertas o falsas las siguientes declaraciones?

1. A Carmen no le interesa la cultura hispánica.
2. Carmen es una persona muy deportista.
3. Es posible que sea estudiante.
4. Este año piensa vivir con unos amigos de sus padres.

Ahora conteste las preguntas de Carmen con información verdadera sobre la ciudad donde Ud. vive y su universidad.

Conversación

A. **Una encuesta.** Las habilidades o características de un grupo de personas pueden ser sorprendentes. ¿Qué sabe Ud. de los compañeros de su clase de español? Por turno, pregunte a la clase quién sabe hacer lo siguiente o a quién le ocurre lo siguiente. Deben levantar la mano sólo los que puedan contestar afirmativamente. Luego la persona que hizo la pregunta debe hacer un comentario apropiado. Siga el modelo.

MODELO: hablar chino →
En esta clase, ¿hay alguien que hable chino? (Nadie levanta la mano.) No hay nadie que hable chino.

1. hablar ruso
2. saber tocar la viola
3. conocer a un actor (una actriz)
4. saber preparar comida vietnamita
5. tener el cumpleaños hoy
6. escribir poemas
7. ¿ ?

Suggestion B: Encourage students to use conversation-extending techniques to elicit more information.

Extension B: Write these question beginnings on the board. Students supply own details to form questions to use in interview situation. **8.** *¿Tienes algún amigo que ___?* **9.** *¿Tienes alguna clase que ___?* **10.** *Termina esta oración: En mi opinión, no hay nada/nadie ___.*

B. **Entrevista.** With another student, ask and answer the following questions. Then report what you have learned to the class.

1. ¿Hay alguien en tu vida que te quiera más que tus padres?
2. ¿Hay algo que te importe más que los estudios universitarios?
3. ¿Buscas una especialización (*major*) que sea interesante? ¿útil? ¿que lleve a un puesto bien remunerado?
4. Para el semestre que viene, ¿qué clases buscas? ¿una que empiece a las ocho de la mañana?
5. ¿Deseas vivir en un apartamento (una casa) que tenga piscina?
6. ¿Conoces a alguien que sepa patinar muy bien? ¿bailar muy bien? ¿nadar muy bien?
7. ¿Hay alguien en tu familia que sea campeón (campeona) de ajedrez? ¿de natación? ¿de esquí?

Communicative objectives for 53: how to express many kinds of cause-and-effect relationships: so that, unless, etc.

45. EXPRESSING CONTINGENCY AND PURPOSE
The Subjunctive After Certain Conjunctions

Unos verdaderos aficionados

SARA: No quiero ir al partido *a menos que juegue* David.
CARLOS: Estoy de acuerdo. *Antes de que compres* los boletos, pregunta si va a jugar.
JULIO: Y *en caso de que* no *juegue*, ¿qué?
CARLOS: ¡Hombre, pues entonces mejor nos quedamos en casa! Hay un estupendo partido en la televisión. Aquí tenemos cerveza y bocadillos y cojines y... ¡Y además está empezando a llover! ...¿No es hora de poner la tele?

Busque en el diálogo el equivalente de estas oraciones.

1. No voy al partido *si no juega David.*
2. *Antes de comprar* los boletos, quiero saber quién juega.
3. ¿Qué hacemos *si no juega*?

¿Son verdaderos deportistas Sara, Carlos y Julio? ¿Les interesa más el deporte o su amigo David? ¿Les interesa más el deporte o su propia comodidad (*comfort*)?

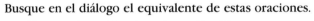

Follow-up (mini): 1. *¿Qué prefiere Ud., estar en el estadio o ver los partidos en la tele? ¿O le gusta hacer las dos cosas, estar en el estadio* **y** *tener la tele?*

Some real fans SARA: I don't want to go to the game unless David is playing. CARLOS: I agree. Before you buy the tickets, ask if he's going to play. JULIO: And if (in case) he's not playing, what shall we do? CARLOS: Well, then it's better to stay home! There's a great game on TV. We've got beer and snacks and cushions here . . . And besides, it's starting to rain! . . . Isn't it time to turn on the TV?

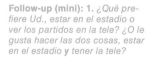

When one action or condition is related to another—X will happen provided that Y occurs; we'll do Z just in case A happens—we say that a relationship of *contingency* exists between the actions or conditions: one thing is contingent, or depends, on another.

The following Spanish *conjunctions* (**las conjunciones**) express relationships of contingency or purpose. The subjunctive always occurs in dependent clauses introduced by these conjunctions.

a menos que	unless	**en caso de que**	in case
antes (de) que	before	**para que**	so that
con tal (de) que	provided (that)		

Voy **con tal que** ellos me **acompañen**. — *I'm going, provided (that) they go with me.*
En caso de que llegue Juan, dile que ya salí. — *In case Juan arrives, tell him that I already left.*

Note that these conjunctions introduce dependent clauses in which the events have not yet materialized; the events are conceptualized, not real-world events. When there is no change of subject in the dependent clause, Spanish more frequently uses the prepositions **antes de** and **para**, plus an infinitive, instead of the corresponding conjunctions plus the subjunctive. Compare the following:

PREPOSITION:	Estoy aquí **para aprender**.	*I'm here to (in order to) learn.*
CONJUNCTION:	Estoy aquí **para que Uds. aprendan**.	*I'm here so that you will learn.*
PREPOSITION:	Voy a comer **antes de salir**.	*I'm going to eat before leaving.*
CONJUNCTION:	Voy a comer **antes (de) que salgamos**.	*I'm going to eat before we leave.*

2. *¿Cuáles son las ventajas de ver los partidos de fútbol americano en el estadio? ¿y las desventajas?* 3. *¿Cuántos partidos vio Ud. en el estadio el año pasado? ¿y en la tele? Y este año, ¿qué piensa hacer?*

Suggestions:
- Present 5 conjunctions always followed by subjunctive: A PACE = memory device for *a menos que*, *para que*, etc.
- **Emphasis:** Relate conjunctions to use of subjunctive to express conceptualized states/actions.
- **Optional:** Include the lower frequency *sin que* in your presentation: A SPACE
- ***¿Cómo se dice?:*** **1.** unless you go with me/ call me/ write to me **2.** in case they arrive/ leave/come **3.** provided that they go/eat dinner/have lunch **4.** in order for us to go/be there/arrive on time (***¡OJO!:*** subjunctive, not preposition)
- **Emphasis:** preposition + inf. (Grammar Section 40) (no second subject named) vs. conjunction + subjunctive (second subject indicated)

Práctica

A. Siempre es buena idea llegar un poco temprano al teatro o al cine. Sin embargo, su amigo Julio, quien va al cine con Ud. esta tarde, no quiere salir con un poco de anticipación. Trate de convencerle de que Uds. deben salir pronto.

—No entiendo por qué quieres que lleguemos al teatro tan temprano.
—Pues, para que (nosotros)...

Sugerencias: poder estacionar el coche, no perder el principio de la función, poder comprar entradas, conseguir buenas butacas, no tener que hacer cola, comprar palomitas (*popcorn*) antes de que empiece la película, hablar con Raúl y Ceci, ¿ ?

Follow-up B: Write the conjunctions on the board. Students use as appropriate to complete the following sentences. **1.** *El cielo está muy nublado hoy. Voy a llevar un impermeable...* **2.** *Nunca pienso casarme,...* **3.** *Es fácil*

B. **Un fin de semana en las montañas.** Hablan Manuel y su esposa Marta. Use la conjunción entre paréntesis para unir las oraciones, haciendo todos los cambios necesarios.

1. No voy. Dejamos a los niños en casa. (a menos que)
2. Yo también prefiero que vayamos solos. Pasamos un rato libre sin ellos. (para que)
3. Esta vez voy a aprender a esquiar. Tú me lo enseñas. (con tal que)
4. Quiero que salgamos temprano por la mañana. Nieva mucho. (a menos que)
5. Es importante que lleguemos a la cabaña. Empieza a nevar en las montañas. (antes de que)
6. Compra leña (*firewood*) aquí. No hay leña en la cabaña. (en caso de que)
7. Deja un recado (*message*). Tus padres nos llaman. (en caso de que)

¿Cierto, falso o no lo dice?

1. Manuel y Marta acaban de casarse.
2. Casi siempre van de vacaciones con los niños.
3. Los dos son esquiadores excelentes.
4. Son dueños de una cabaña que está en las montañas.

recibir una buena nota en esta clase,... **4.** *Vamos a las montañas este fin de semana,...*

Optional: *Una tarde en el parque. ¿Cómo se dice en español?* **1.** We go there to have fun. **2.** We also go there so that the kids can play baseball. **3.** They're going to swim before eating (they eat). **4.** Are they going to swim before *we* eat? **5.** Don't go without talking to your mother. **6.** And don't leave without your father giving you money.

Conversación

A. Cualquier acción humana puede justificarse. Explique Ud. las siguientes situaciones tan lógicamente como sea posible.

1. Cuando la familia es muy grande, los padres trabajan mucho para (que)...
2. Los profesores les dan tarea a los estudiantes para que...
3. Tenemos que pagar los impuestos federales para que...
4. Los dueños de los equipos profesionales les pagan mucho a algunos jugadores para (que)...
5. Les compramos juguetes a los niños para que...
6. Se doblan las películas extranjeras para (que)...
7. Cambiamos de lugar los muebles de vez en cuando para (que)...
8. Los padres castigan (*punish*) a los niños para (que)...

B. Complete las oraciones lógicamente.

1. Voy a graduarme en _____ a menos que _____.
2. Este verano voy a _____ a menos que _____.
3. Voy a seguir viviendo en esta ciudad con tal que _____.
4. Siempre me baño antes de (que) _____.

SITUACIONES

Situaciones: See IM for suggestions, additional exercises, and supplementary dialogues and exercises.

¿Qué quieres hacer?

Una tarde de verano

—Hace mucho que no paseo en bicicleta.
—Pues, si quieres, puedes usar la de mi hermano.
—¿Qué te parece si vamos hasta el lago?
—¡Estupendo! ... y podemos llevar la merienda.° — *snack*

Un fin de semana en la ciudad

—¿Qué hacen Uds. los fines de semana?
—Nos encanta pasear° por la mañana, cuando hay poco tráfico. — dar un paseo
—Sí, y a veces visitamos alguna exposición de arte y después tomamos el aperitivo° en un café. — ¿ ?
—¿Me invitan a ir con Uds. alguna vez?
—¡Encantados!

Delante del cine

—¡Hola, hombre! ¿Tú también vienes a ver *El museo de Drácula*?
—¡Qué va! Voy a ver *El Sol de Acapulco*.
—¿Por qué no nos acompañas? Está con nosotros Marisa, la prima de Carlos.
—Lo siento, pero voy a encontrarme con Elena Ortega... y además a mí me parecen pesadísimas las películas de horror.
—Hasta luego, entonces. Que lo pases bien.° — Que... ¿ ?
—Chau. ¡Y que se diviertan°! — Que... ¿ ?

Notas lingüísticas: Indirect Commands

You should be able to guess from context the meaning of the last two phrases glossed in the dialogue. They are both the approximate equivalent of English "*Hope you have a good time!*" Note that the subjunctive is used in both expressions.

Structures of this type are called indirect commands in Spanish. If they were *direct* commands, they would be: **Pásalo bien, Diviértanse.** Instead, their structure is like that of the dependent clause in a two-clause sentence that uses the subjunctive:

(Espero) Que lo pases bien.
(Ojalá) Que se diviertan.

Indirect commands of this kind are used frequently in Spanish. You should be able to understand them easily whenever you hear or read them.

Conversación

Con un compañero (una compañera), invente las siguientes conversaciones, siguiendo el modelo de los diálogos anteriores. Haga dos versiones de cada conversación: en una, la persona invitada acepta la invitación; en otra, dice que no, explicando por qué.

- invitar a un amigo a pasar la tarde en la playa
- invitar a un amigo a acompañarlo/la al cine con un pariente de su novio/a (esposo/a)

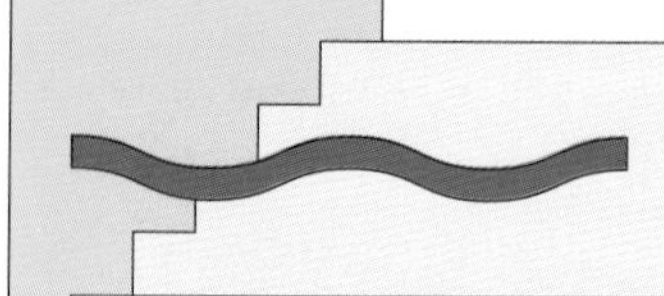

UN POCO DE TODO

A. **La rutina y las diversiones.** Form complete sentences based on the words given, in the order given. Give the informal command form of the verb in the main clause and add other words if necessary. Use subject pronouns only when needed.

1. tratar / despertarse / antes de que / sonar (ue) / despertador / por favor
2. buscar / alguien / que / levantarse / cinco / mañana / para correr
3. poner / mesa / y / tener / comida / preparado / antes de que / empezar / noticiero (*news*) / de / seis
4. en caso de que / tú / tener / rato libre / sábado, / comprar / entradas / para / cine
5. dormir / con / ventanas / abierto / para que / entrar / aire

B. Lea la siguiente sinópsis de algunas películas extranjeras que se exhibieron en Santiago (Chile) durante el mes de diciembre y complete las oraciones lógicamente, usando la información de la sinópsis o con información verdadera.

Sinopsis

- **Crónica de una muerte anunciada:** hermosa fotografía y ambientación, pero sin que el director Francesco Rosi logre recrear adecuadamente el libro de García Márquez. REGULAR.
- **Woodstock:** a más de un decenio de su estreno, mantiene su interés y sigue atrayendo a la juventud. RECOMENDABLE.
- **Robocop:** un policía, parte humano y parte robot, impone la ley y el orden; abundante violencia y acción. En su género, RECOMENDABLE.
- **Jardines de Piedra:** la guerra de Vietnam y la vida militar vistas desde una unidad ceremonial del ejército norteamericano. Dirigida por Coppola. RECOMENDABLE.
- **Tiempo de amar:** célebre violinista pierde su salud, su arte y su marido. A pesar de los esfuerzos de Julie Andrews, MENOS QUE REGULAR.
- **Mil veces adiós:** romance en tiempos de guerra (1942). Aviador norteamericano ama a hermosa sefardí en Jerusalén. La familia se opone. MENOS QUE REGULAR.
- **Camorra:** mujeres de Nápoles contra la mafia y las drogas, con la directora Lina Wertmuller en cuarto menguante. MENOS QUE REGULAR.
- **La familia:** ocho decenios de los placeres y pesares de una familia italiana. Muy buena interpretación de Vittorio Gassman. BUENA.
- **Los Intocables:** contra viento y marea, dos personajes muy disímiles imponen la ley en el Chicago de 1930, enviando a Al Capone a la cárcel. RECOMENDABLE.
- **Detective suelto en Hollywood:** Eddie Murphy otra vez hace de las suyas en Beverly Hills. Como entretención, sin mayores pretensiones. RECOMENDABLE.
- **Cita a ciegas:** farsa que no está a la altura de los buenos momentos en la trayectoria del realizador Blake Edwards. Con Kim Basinger. REGULAR.
- **"Cocodrillo" Dundee:** amena historia de un amable australiano dentro y fuera de su salsa. Con Paul Hogan. RECOMENDABLE.

Posibles terminaciones: italiano, francés, norteamericano

1. Hay varias películas que (ser) ____.
2. No hay ninguna película que (ser) ____.

Posibles terminaciones: recomendable, excepcional, bueno

3. Hay muchas películas que (ser) ____.
4. Hay pocas que (ser) ____.
5. No hay ninguna que (ser) ____.
6. Antes de que los niños (ir) ____ a ver una película, es bueno que los padres ____.
7. De estas películas, he visto ____ (no he visto ninguna). (No) Le recomiendo que ____ porque ____.

C. **Hablando de películas...** Complete the following dialogue and movie reviews with the correct form of the words in parentheses, as suggested by the context. When two possibilities are given in parentheses, select the correct word. Use the past participle of infinitives indicated with an asterisk.

Saliendo del cine

—Bueno, ¿qué piensas (*de/en*[1]) la película? ¿Te gustó?
—Pues, (*ser/estar*[2]) muy (*divertir*[3])*... pero quizás un poco superficial.
—Ah, ¿sí? ¿Por qué (*reírse*[4]) tanto?
—Hombre, no hay (*alguien/nadie*[5]) que no lo (*pasar*[6]) bien viendo una de estas historietas de vez en cuando. Pero (*que/lo que*[7]) yo realmente (*preferir*[8]) son las películas sobre temas más (*profundo*[9]). Como, por ejemplo, (*ese*[10]) película francesa (*que/lo que*[11]) (*ver:* nosotros[12]) la semana (*pasar*[13])*.
—Bueno, la próxima vez es mejor que tú (*escoger*°[14]) la película; pero no me (*llevar*[15]) a ver (*alguna/ninguna*[16]) película (*doblar*[17])*, ¿eh? Ya (*saber/conocer:* tú[18]) que no me (*gustar*[19]) nada.

to select (escojo)

El regreso del Jedi

Esta película (*ser/estar*[20]) la tercera parte de una serie muy famosa que se (*iniciar*[21]) con *La guerra de las galaxias* y (*continuar*[22]) con *El imperio* (*contraatacar*[23]). El rasgo° principal de *El regreso del Jedi* (*ser/estar*[24]) la acción emocionante, (*caracterizar*[25])* por complejos efectos (*especial*[26]). En *Jedi*, los personajes° principales, (*que/lo que*[27]) representan la Alianza Rebelde, (*volver*[28]) para enfrentarse° con las Fuerzas Imperiales de la Oscuridad, (*encabezar*°[29])* por el malévolo° Darth Vader.

característica
characters
to confront / to lead
malo

La Bamba

Esta película, (*escribir*[30])* y (*dirigir*°[31])* por Luis Valdez, se (*basar*[32]) en la vida de Ritchie Valens y (*los/las*[33]) ocho meses de su ascenso a la fama. *La Bamba* trata de° los sueños° «rocanroleros» de un joven chicano y de cómo su trágica muerte, (*ocurrir*[34])* en un accidente de aviación a la edad de 17 años, lo (*cambiar*[35]) todo. En ese accidente (*morir*[36]) también Buddy Holly y J. P. Richardson, más

to direct
trata... *deals with / dreams*

(*conocer*[37])* como «Big Bopper.» Verdaderamente, *La Bamba* es (*uno*[38]) película excelente que muestra° realidades de la vida que (*ir*[39]) más allá de° la historia de un joven chicano que logra° saborear las agridulces° experiencias del estrellato.°

shows / más... *beyond*
consigue / *bittersweet* / *stardom*

VOCABULARIO

Theme vocabulary previously listed as active: *ir, la película, el teatro, ver*

EL CINE Y EL TEATRO

la acera sidewalk
la butaca seat (*in a theater*)
la comedia play; comedy
la entrada ticket (*for an event or performance*)
la función performance, show
la taquilla box office
la trama plot

LOS PASATIEMPOS

dar un paseo to take a walk
hacer *camping* to go camping
hacer planes para + *inf.* to make plans to (*do something*)
jugar (ue) a las cartas/al ajedrez to play cards/chess
tomar el sol to sunbathe
visitar un museo to visit a museum

LOS DEPORTES

esquiar to ski
la natación swimming
pasear en bicicleta to ride a bike
patinar to skate

Otros deportes: el básquetbol, el béisbol, el fútbol (norteamericano), el golf, el hockey, el tenis, el vólibol

el campo (playing) field
la cancha (tennis) court
el estadio stadium
los esquís skis
el gimnasio gymnasium
el juego play (*in a game*); (card, board) game
el/la jugador(a) player
el partido game, match
la pelota ball
la raqueta racket
la red net

VERBOS

acompañar to accompany, go with
reunirse (con) to get together (with)

OTROS SUSTANTIVOS

el/la aficionado/a fan, enthusiast
el rato libre free minute; *pl.* spare, free time
el tema theme, topic

ADJETIVOS

cotidiano/a daily
deportista sports-minded
doblado/a dubbed

CONJUNCIONES

a menos que unless
antes (de) que before
con tal (de) que provided (that)
en caso de que in case
para que so that

PALABRAS ADICIONALES

quizá(s) perhaps
tener cuidado to be careful
tener lugar to take place

Frases útiles para la comunicación

que + *subjunctive*	I hope + *verb form*
Que lo **pases** bien. **Que** te **diviertas**.	I hope you have a good time.

OPTIONAL SECTION

UN PASO MÁS 15

▲ Actividad A. Las diversiones

Variation A: *Descríbale a un amigo hispánico recién llegado a esta ciudad lo que se puede hacer durante el fin de semana para pasarlo bien. ¿Qué actividades le recomienda Ud. y por qué?*

Aquí y en la página que sigue hay una serie de anuncios para toda clase de espectáculos. Con un compañero (una compañera), lea los anuncios y haga planes para este fin de semana. Deben decidir adónde van, qué van a hacer y cuándo van a regresar a casa. Luego describan su plan a la clase, explicando por qué decidieron asistir a unos espectáculos y no a otros.

Museos

MUSEO NACIONAL DE BELLAS ARTES — Av. del Libertador 1473. Salas y colecciones: Obras de arte de los más famosos plásticos: Gauguin, Corot, Degas, Hogarth, El Greco, Manet, Van Gogh, Bourdelle, etc. Obras vinculadas al pasado y costumbres argentinas: Palliére, Morel, Pellegrini, D'Hastrel, Monvoisin, Cándido López y otros. Posee biblioteca especializada en arte habilitada para el público los lunes y viernes de 14.30 a 19 horas. Y los jueves de 9 a 12,30 horas. HORARIO: jueves y martes de 9 a13.30 y de 14.30 a 19 horas. Visitas guiadas a las 17 horas.

COMPLEJO MUSEOLOGICO HISTORICO MUSEO HISTORICO NACIONAL — Defensa 1600. Tel. 27-4767 y 26-4588. Salas y colecciones: historia nacional. Salas: del Descubrimiento, de la Conquista, de las Misiones Jesuítas, del Virreinato, de las Invasiones Inglesas, de Mayo, etc.; de los Héroes y de hechos; símbolos nacionales, periodismo, etc.

CINES

VALPARAISO

NUEVO BRASILIA (P. Montt 1860, fono 259797) 15.00, 18.30, 21.30 horas. "Viaje insólito". $ 300. (Para todos).
CENTRAL (Condell 1459, fono 250705) Continuado desde las 14.30 horas. "Terciopelo azul", "Pasión sin límite". $ 200. (Mayores 21 años).
CONDELL (Condell 1585, fono 212027). Continuado desde las 14.30 horas. "Pecado a los 15 años", "La prima". $ 200. (Mayores 21 años).
IMPERIO (P. Montt 1955, fono 214567) Continuado desde las 14.30 horas. "Dos policías en Miami", "La bamba". $ 200. (Todo espectador).
METROVAL (P. Montt 2111, fono 253029) 15.00, 18.30, 21.30 horas. "Nacido para matar". $ 300. (Mayores 18 años).
VALPARAISO (Plaza Victoria 1646, fono 255522) 15.00, 19.00, 21.30 horas "Pie grande y los Henderson". $ 250 y $ 230. (Todo espectador).
VELARDE (Uruguay 410, fono 214654) 15.00, 18.30, 21.30 horas. "Amos del Universo". $ 250. (Mayores y menores).

VIÑA DEL MAR

CINE ARTE 15.30, 19.00, 22.00 horas. "La familia". $ 350. (Mayores 14 años).
OLIMPO Nº 1 (Quinta s/n, fono 882616). 15.30, 19.00, 22.00 horas. "Nacido para matar". $ 400. (Mayores 18 años).
OLIMPO Nº 2 (Quinta s/n, fono 882616) 15.30, 18.45, 21.45 horas. "Ishtar" $ 400. (Para todos).
PREMIER (Quillota 898, fono 973002) 15.00, 19.00, 21.30 horas "Pie grande". $ 200 y $ 250 (Todo espectador).
REX (Valparaíso 746, fono 685050) 15.30, 19.00, 22.00 horas "Tiburón, la venganza". $ 400. (Mayores y menores).

QUILPUE

VELARDE (A. Pinto 634, fono 910342). 15.00, 18.30, 21.30 horas. "Robocop". $ 200. (Mayores y menores).

VILLA ALEMANA

POMPEYA (Latorre 20, fono 950077). Continuado desde las 18.00 horas. "Un detective suelto en Hollywood" I y II partes. $ 180. (Todo espectador).

tv/programas

13.00 BALONVOLEA. Cometarios: Rafael Muro. Desde Palma de Mallorca, transmisión de la fase final de Spring Cup de Balonvolea.

15.00 TELEDIARIO.

15.15 VUELTA CICLISTA A ESPAÑA. En directo, final de la etapa correspondiente a esta día: Málaga-Elche.

16.00 MASADA. «Episodio número 5».

16.55 DOCUMENTAL. «En algún lugar de Europa: Goodwood Mansion». Goodwood Mansion, residencia de los duques de Richmond, es uno de los más bellos y extensos ejemplos de la arquitectura aristocrática inglesa. Este documental nos cuenta su historia, muestra sus hermosos paisajes, su valiosa pinacoteca y los problemas que presenta para habitarlo y conservarlo.

17.30 DIBUJOS ANIMADOS. «Trapito». El destino de Trapito, el espantapájaros, es triste y aburrido al tenerse que mantener siempre clavado en el suelo. Durante una gran tormenta salva la vida a un pequeño gorrión que, a partir de este momento, se convierte en su ilusión.

18.35 BARRIO SESAMO. «Circuitos y Espinete». Antonio y Matilde salen a cenar. Chema trae a Circuitos para que haga compañía a los niños. En un principio, el «humanoide» funcionará muy bien, pero al oír la radio se producirá el caos.

19.05 EL PLANETA IMAGINARIO. «Desperdicios».

19.30 LAS FABULAS DEL BOSQUE VERDE. «El pequeño Danielito». La nieve es la gran diversión de Danielito, y ahora que la pradera está totalmente cubierta se entretiene haciendo túneles en todas direcciones.

20.00 ANDY ROBSON. «Carrera entre dos caballos». Intérpretes: Jack Watling, Norman Jones y Tom Davidson. Durante el curso de una cacería surge un incidente entre George Grieve y Helga.

20.30 AL GALOPE. Comentarios: Daniel Vindel y Marisa Abad. Reportaje sobre el mundo de las carreras de caballos. Pronóstico de la Quiniela Hípica.

21.00 TELEDIARIO.

21.15 INFORMATIVO: VUELTA CICLISTA A ESPAÑA.

21.35 ESTRELLAS DEL BOLSHOI. «Paquita». De la actuación del ballet soviético Estrellas del Bolshoi les ofreceremos «Paquita», de Minkos, por la primera bailarina del teatro Kirov, de Leningrado, e Imijail Petujov, del Teatro de la Opera de Odesa.

22.05 LARGOMETRAJE. «El despertar» («The yearling»), 1964. Duración: 2 h. 7 m. Dirección: Clarence Brown. Intérpretes: Gregory Peck, Jane Wyman, Claude Jarman Jr. y Chill Wills. Un muchacho, hijo de un granjero de Florida forjado a la antigua usanza, encuentra un día a un cervatillo, al que convierte en su inseparable mascota.

00.15 CONCIERTO SENTIDO. La Orquesta Sinfónica de la RTVE, bajo la dirección de Miguel Angel Gómez Martínez, interpretará el «Concierto número 24 en do menor para piano y orquesta», de Mozart. Solista: Alicia Delarrocha (piano).

00.50 MEDITACION. «Mañana es Sábado Santo», por monseñor Narciso Jubany, cardenal arzobispo de Barcelona.

00.55 DESPEDIDA Y CIERRE.

Buenos Aires
TANGO SHOW
SU CONFITERIA BAILABLE
BULNES 1596
Cap. Fed.
Reservas 825-3740

Un lugar grande en Buenos Aires, para grandes, donde nos reencontraremos con los tangos y la música del 40.
Un lugar distinto del Viejo Palermo donde nuestra meta principal es la de pasar un momento de sana diversión.
Te esperamos, de elegante sport.
Jueves, viernes, sábado y domingo.

CALENDARIO

21 Viernes

19.30. Concierto de **Silvia Lester** en piano; obras de Mozart, Chopin, Debussy y otros. En *Cerrito 740, primer piso.* Entrada libre.
20.30. Proyección del filme **1789,** de la realizadora Ariane Mnouckhine. En *Sarmiento 2255.*
21. Proyección del filme **Bananas,** con Woody Allen. En la *sala Leopoldo Lugones.*

22 Sábado

20. Proyección del filme **Alphaville,** de Godard. En *Yerbal 2651.*
21. Juan Carlos Cirigliano y los **Músicos de Buenos Aires,** y el grupo **Maroma.** En el *teatro Santa María, Montevideo 842.*
22. Cóctel de sueños, espectáculo humorístico musical. En la *sala ADISYC, Malpú 523, subsuelo.*

23 Domingo

15.30. En el Monumental, **River Plate** recibe a **Ferro Carril Oeste** y en Avellaneda, **Independiente** a **Huracán.**
16. Visita al **Mercado de Pulgas** de la Plaza Dorrego. *Humberto I y Defensa.*
21. Proyección del filme **Dos extraños amantes,** de Woody Allen, con Diane Keaton. En la sala *Leopoldo Lugones.*

Suggestion B: Do as written exercise only.

▲ Actividad B. ¿Qué haces para pasarlo bien?

No todos nos divertimos de la misma manera. A veces el dinero y el tiempo imponen restricciones y otras veces es sencillamente una cuestión de gustos: lo que a otra persona le gusta mucho tal vez no le guste a Ud... y vice versa. ¿Qué cree Ud. que hacen para pasarlo bien las siguientes personas en un sábado típico? Use su imaginación pero manténgase entre los límites de lo que es posible en el mundo real de cada persona o grupo.

1. una persona rica que vive en Nueva York
2. un grupo de buenos amigos que trabajan en una fábrica en Michigan
3. un matrimonio joven con poco dinero y dos niños pequeños
4. un niño de ocho años que vive en el centro de una ciudad grande
5. dos amigas de mediana edad (*middle-aged*) que viven en los suburbios de Los Ángeles
6. un matrimonio viejo—él de ochenta años y ella de ochenta y dos—que vive en Texas

A propósito... Pausing and Taking a Position

In English we frequently use vocalized pauses ("uh," "um") and filler words ("well now," "okay," "let's see") when we don't quite know what to say or when we are looking for the right words. When you need a few seconds to collect your thoughts in Spanish, use one of the following expressions:

este	uh, um	**bien**	well, okay
pues	well	**a ver**	let's see
bueno	well, okay	**ahora bien**	well now

When you want to avoid taking a position on an issue, perhaps to avoid an argument, use one of these phrases:

En mi opinión...	In my opinion . . .	**Puede ser.**	That might be.
Depende.	It depends.	**Posiblemente.**	Possibly.
No sé.	I don't know.	**A veces.**	At times.
Tal vez. Quizá(s).	Perhaps.	**¿Ud. cree?** / **¿Tú crees?**	Do you think so?
Es posible.	It's possible.		

Point out: ***A propósito...:*** Many Spanish speakers do not consider it acceptable to use vocalized pause *este*, just as many Americans disapprove of "uh" and "um." *Pues*, *bueno*, and the other fillers are considered to be more appropriate.

▲ Actividad C. ¿Cómo responde Ud.?

Suggestion C: Will be most effective done as paired exercise.

Un amigo (Una amiga) o un miembro de la familia pregunta o expresa las siguientes opiniones. Ud. no está de acuerdo, pero no quiere ofender a la otra persona. ¿Cómo va a responder? Use algunas de las frases que aparecen en **A propósito...**

MODELO: Jorge trabaja mucho y debe recibir un aumento de salario. →
—Puede ser, pero hay otros empleados que trabajan más que él y por eso ellos van a recibir el aumento.
—Pues no sé. Me dicen que es un hombre muy simpático, pero, ¿de veras trabaja bien?

1. Es más interesante ir al teatro que ir al cine, ¿no crees?
2. Cher es una actriz excelente. Me gusta mucho.
3. Para descansar, no hay nada como sentarse delante del televisor.
4. Para echar raíces (*to settle down*), las ciudades grandes son mejores que las pequeñas.
5. Me encanta la comida japonesa, sobre todo el *sushi*.
6. No sé qué les pasa a los jóvenes de hoy. ¡Son tan descorteses! Y su ropa... y su pelo...
7. Creo que es mejor *no* tener hijos.
8. No me gustan los gatos. Los perros son infinitamente superiores.

LECTURA CULTURAL

Lectura: See IM for suggestions and additional exercises and activities.

Los pasatiempos

En el mundo hispánico las diversiones son tan variadas y numerosas como en los Estados Unidos. Las actividades pueden variar según la clase social y el lugar, pero hay aficiones que gozan de° gran aceptación popular en todas partes: el cine, las visitas y los deportes. Además, hay una serie de juegos o pasatiempos que se hacen en casa, para pasar el tiempo. Son populares, entre otros, el ajedrez, las damas,° las canicas,° los rompecabezas... Aquí les ofrecemos tres pasatiempos distintos: dos de niños y un juego de cartas. ¿Se parecen a algún juego norteamericano?

gozan... tienen

checkers / *marbles*

«Veo veo... »

Este juego de vocabulario es popular entre los niños. ¡También puede ayudar a los estudiantes de lenguas extranjeras!

El adulto (El profesor) dice: «Veo veo... » El niño (el estudiante) contesta: «¿Qué ves?» ADULTO: «Una cosita... » NIÑO: «¿Y qué cosita es?» ADULTO: «Empieza con la letra... » («Es de color... ») El niño tiene que pensar en las palabras que conoce que empiezan con la letra dada (y que son del color nombrado).

José Luis Suárez, España

«Los platillos»

Un pasatiempo muy popular cuando era niño era el juego de «platillos» (tapas° de botellas, especialmente las que encontramos en los refrescos como Coca-Cola). El juego consiste en marcar un círculo de tamaño° regular en la acera. Si el cemento es liso,° mejor todavía, porque de esta manera el platillo se desliza° fácilmente. Se colocan° los platillos de todos los jugadores en el centro del círculo y todos tratan de sacar del círculo, con su platillo, los platillos de los otros jugadores. Para impulsar el platillo, uno necesita colocar los dedos de tal forma que con un movimiento rápido de uno de los dedos el platillo se dirige al centro del círculo a fin de ir reduciendo gradualmente el número de platillos dentro del círculo. Al final, el jugador con el mayor número de platillos en su poder es el ganador.

caps

size / *smooth*

se... *slides* / Se... Se ponen

Emilién Sabló, Panamá

«La casita robada»

Se reparten° cuatro cartas a cada participante (no más de dos). Se ponen cuatro cartas boca arriba° sobre la mesa. El primer jugador ve si entre las cartas que tiene hay alguna igual a las que están sobre la mesa; si no hay, descarta° una carta suya.° Ahora es el turno del otro jugador.

Si alguno encuentra en la mesa una carta igual a la suya, la toma mostrando la suya y se la lleva, poniéndola a su lado boca arriba. Si el compañero de turno tiene en su mano la misma carta que el otro tiene a su lado, se la puede robar («casita robada») y ponerla en el lado suyo. Se puede robar de la mesa o del compañero.

Cuando se acaban las cartas que se tienen en la mano, se reparten otras cuatro, y así hasta que se acabe el mazo.° Gana el que tiene la mayor cantidad de cartas al finalizar el juego. **¡OJO!** Se juega con barajas° españolas (bastos, copas, oros y espadas).

Marianela Chaumiel, Argentina

Se... *Are distributed*
boca... *face (lit. mouth) up*
he discards / of his
deck
cartas

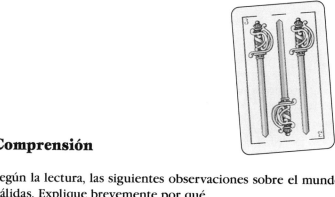

Comprensión

Según la lectura, las siguientes observaciones sobre el mundo hispánico no son válidas. Explique brevemente por qué.

1. Las diversiones más populares del mundo hispánico son totalmente distintas a las de los Estados Unidos.
2. El juego de los platillos no se parece a ningún juego norteamericano.
3. Se pueden jugar todos los juegos hispánicos usando cartas norteamericanas.
4. Los hispanos no se interesan en los juegos que tienen que ver con palabras.

Para escribir

Describa un juego o pasatiempo que Ud. recuerde de su niñez. Su breve párrafo debe incluir los siguientes detalles.

1. con quién y dónde jugaba Ud.
2. el número de participantes
3. en qué consistía el juego y algunas de sus reglas

OPTIONAL SECTION

REPASO 5

Note: Corresponding chapters of the Workbook and the Laboratory Manual offer focused vocabulary and grammar activities.

Repaso 5: See IM for detailed suggestions for handling *Entrevistas*, *Situaciones*, and the specific *Voces* sections.

VOCES DEL MUNDO HISPÁNICO

LA AMÉRICA LATINA

¿Cuánto sabe Ud. de la geografía de esta región del mundo de habla española (y también de habla portuguesa, porque en uno de los países latinoamericanos se habla ese idioma)? Identifique los siguientes países en el mapa: la Argentina, el Brasil, Bolivia, Colombia, Chile, el Ecuador, el Paraguay, el Perú, el Uruguay, Venezuela. Luego ponga estas capitales con sus respectivos países: Brasilia, Buenos Aires, Bogotá, Santiago, La Paz, Asunción, Quito, Caracas, Montevideo, Lima.

Ahora indique el nombre para los habitantes de cada país: paraguayo/a, brasileño/a, ecuatoriano/a, boliviano/a, argentino/a, peruano/a, uruguayo/a, colombiano/a, chileno/a, venezolano/a.

MODELO: Una persona de _____ es _____.

Himno de Manco Capac

Viracocha,
poderoso cimiento del mundo,
Tú dispones:
«Sea este varón,[a]
sea esta mujer.»
Tú gobiernas
hasta[b] al granizo.[c]
¿Dónde estás
—como si no fuera[ch]
yo hijo tuyo—
arriba,
abajo,
en el intermedio
o en tu asiento de supremo juez[d]?
Óyeme,
Tú que permaneces[e]
en el océano del cielo
y que también vives
en los mares de la tierra,
gobierno del mundo,
creador del hombre. [...]
Tú, que me mandaste
el cetro[f] real,
óyeme
antes de que caiga
rendido o muerto.

Traducido del quechua, lengua del Perú incaico

a. hombre b. *even* c. *hail* ch. no... *I weren't* d. *judge* e. *remain* f. *scepter, staff*

El Cuzco, el Perú

Machu Picchu, el Perú

Niños venezolanos

Buenos Aires, la Argentina

EL NUEVO PODER ECONÓMICO DE LAS MUJERES

LAS MUJERES ARGENTINAS FUNDARON 5 VECES MÁS EMPRESAS QUE LOS HOMBRES EN LOS ÚLTIMOS 10 AÑOS

- Como ejecutivas, ganan menos que sus colegas masculinos.
- A las mujeres siempre se les exige mayor rendimiento.
- El 50 por ciento de los coches vendidos en el último lustro fueron comprados por mujeres.
- Se les reconoce mayor capacidad de negociación que a los hombres.
- Entre las exitosas abundan las solteras y separadas.

compañias

productivity

período de cinco años

successful ones

La semana, Buenos Aires (Argentina)

Retorno para 54

Angel Parra

La ola de rumores anunciando que el gobierno daría a conocer una nueva lista de exiliados a los cuales se les permitiría el ingreso a Chile, tuvo su confirmación el miércoles pasado por la tarde. Ese día, el Ministerio del Interior hizo pública una cuartilla conteniendo 54 nombres de autorizados para volver, entre los cuales se cuentan los del cantautor Angel Parra; el ex ministro del Trabajo del gobierno de Allende, Jorge Godoy; el ex senador radical Hugo Miranda; Viviana Corvalán Castillo, hija del secretario general del Partido Comunista, Luis Corvalán; y los ex diputados socialistas Alejandro Giliberto y Andrés Sepúlveda. •

a. *entry* b. cantante

APSI, Santiago (Chile)

LA HISTORIA OFICIAL

En 1986 obtuvo el Oscar a la Mejor Película Extranjera y recibió veintisiete premios internacionales. Quizás esta presentación baste para referirse al filme del argentino Luis Puenzo, quien, en casi dos horas, retrata un período traumático de la vida de su país.

A través de la vida de "Alicia" (Norma Aleandro) –una profesora de historia estricta y conservadora– se va descubriendo lo que aconteció en Argentina durante los regímenes militares. La maestra, casada con un próspero hombre de negocios, "Roberto" (Héctor Alterio), vive feliz junto a "Gaby", a quien adoptaron al verse impedida ella de tener hijos. Hasta ese momento, su situación es ideal. Los tres conforman un hogar armónico, donde la niña es lo principal.

Sus angustias irrumpen cuando en la prensa abundan las informaciones respecto a menores, cuyos padres por razones políticas han desaparecido, que fueron entregados en adopción. Desde ese momento, "Alicia" no descansará. Quiere llegar a la verdad, y una vez que la obtiene ya no puede vivir con ella. La dramática trama se combina con lo que acontece en esos momentos en Buenos Aires, adquiriendo esta "Historia oficial" un carácter documental.

Argentina (1985)
Protagonistas: Norma Aleandro y Héctor Alterio
Director: Luis Puenzo
Censura: Mayores de 18 años
Duración: 112 minutos
Distribuidora: Villarrica Films Video
Hablada: En español

Videograma, Santiago (Chile)

a. *portrays* b. pasó
c. casa ch. *whose* d. pasa

Manifestación en Santiago, Chile, 1973

Los ex Presidentes de la República de Colombia juegan un papel político vital

REUTER, Bogotá

Un puñado de ex Presidentes colombianos juega un papel decisivo en la vida política del país, pero una nueva generación de dirigentes jóvenes y ambiciosos se encuentra impaciente por disputarles esa influencia. Estos veteranos estadistas pertenecen tanto al Partido Liberal como al Conservador.

handful

La Época, Santiago (Chile)

Verbo

Voy a arrugar° esta palabra — *wrinkle*
voy a torcerla,° — *twist it*
sí,
es demasiado lisa,° — demasiado... *too even or smooth*
como si un gran perro o un gran río
le hubiera repasado° lengua o agua — le... *had passed over it*
durante muchos años.

Quiero que en la palabra
se vea la aspereza,° — *harshness*
la sal ferruginosa,° — *iron-laden*
la fuerza desdentada° — *toothless*
de la tierra,
la sangre
de los que hablaron y de los que no hablaron.

Quiero ver la sed
adentro de las sílabas:
quiero tocar el fuego
en el sonido:
quiero sentir la oscuridad
del grito.° Quiero — *scream*
palabras ásperas
como piedras° vírgenes. — *stones*

Pablo Neruda, poeta chileno, Premio Nóbel de literatura, 1971

El petróleo, el "oro negro" del lago Maracaibo, Venezuela

Edificios modernos en Buenos Aires, la Argentina

Cartagena, Colombia

La obra se instalará en la ciudad sede,° Barcelona — *site*

Fernando Botero construirá° una gran escultura para las Olimpíadas de 1992

will build

El artista, que vive entre París, Colombia y Nueva York, criticó los remates° de obras de arte que organizan las casas de Christie's y Sotheby's. Actualmente no expone en galerías de arte; dice preferir los espacios abiertos "pues hay que acercar las esculturas a las plazas públicas". — *auctions*

La Época, Santiago (Chile)

CONTAMINACION DE PLAYAS

El final de un problema

☐ Autoridades de la quinta región analizan dos alternativas para terminar con la polución de las aguas del mar.

Si bien el problema de contaminación que afecta a las playas de Viña del Mar aún no está solucionado en forma definitiva, la situación este año parece más auspiciosa que en temporadas pasadas. En 1986, la comisión encargada de estudiar tanto la contaminación de playas (arena) como la calidad del agua (mar), que es presidida por el gobernador de Valparaíso, determinó la clausura de nueve balnearios de la ciudad jardín.

La medida no afectó el flujo turístico hacia la zona, pero sí provocó una natural preocupación entre los veraneantes. Según expresó a ERCILLA el jefe subrogante del Departamento de Programas del Ambiente de la quinta región, doctor Cristián Gutiérrez, en la actualidad se están haciendo los estudios pertinentes en los diferentes balnearios de la región.

Explicó el funcionario que con los datos en la mano se podrá hacer una evaluación que permita entregar un diagnóstico sobre el estado de contaminación que las playas puedan presentar.

Gabriel García Márquez, Premio Nóbel de literatura, 1982; autor de *Cien años de soledad*

—Norteamérica fue colonizada por los protestantes —gentes que ponen el acento en la propia responsabilidad frente a lo divino—, mientras que el continente latinoamericano fue pasto[a] del catolicismo, una confesión más dada a poner la salvación humana en manos de Dios. ¿Hasta qué punto ha influido esto en la profunda diferencia que existe entre ambos continentes?

—¡Claro! No te olvides tampoco que la colonización norteamericana fue una operación económica. Se van allí para mantener unas formas de vida ortodoxas y puras y, sobre todo, de gentes muy trabajadoras. Son gente que no tiene ninguna utopía, seres fundamentalmente pragmáticos. Todo lo contrario de lo que fue la conquista española.

—¿Como si los colonizadores norteamericanos fueran[b] más ejecutivos y los españoles más caóticos y también más románticos?

—La política que llevaron a cabo[c] los conquistadores españoles la puedes llamar romántica, cruel, ingenua e, incluso, vesánica.[ch] Pero lo cierto es que nunca fue realista. Los españoles hicieron todo lo que no hay que hacer, que es igualito a lo que seguimos haciendo los latinoamericanos.

—¿Qué es, según usted, lo que no hay que hacer?

—Lo que no existe en los países latinoamericanos es esa política pragmática,[d] esa política de resignación al mal menor, que es la que ha traído el éxito a los países anglosajones. Y después está esa relación frente al trabajo. Para la España de la conquista trabajar era algo despreciable, una especie de maldición.[e]

—Eso tampoco lo inventaron los conquistadores españoles, sino la Biblia...

—Efectivamente. Pero ese sistema de eludir el trabajo no es el mejor para desarrollar un país. La ética protestante, por el contrario, predica que el trabajo no solo dignifica, sino que es una de las señales de estar en...

—¿El buen camino?

—Sí, en el buen camino.

Mario Vargas Llosa, escritor peruano, en una entrevista en *Cambio 16*

a. *fuel* b. *were* c. La... *The policy put into practice by* ch. *crazy* d. *evil* e. *curse*

***Entrevista:* Focus:** Asking questions, using verb forms presented thus far in the text.

ENTREVISTA

In the last three chapters of ***Puntos de partida***, you have reviewed the uses of the subjunctive and have learned some new ones. You have also begun to talk about the past with some additional verb forms, the perfect tenses. Throughout these chapters, you have found out a good deal of information about your classmates, using the interview activities included in all sections of the text. The following activity will let you use your interviewing techniques in a different way.

Your instructor has invited a Spanish-speaking person (someone you do not know at all) to class. Look at this person and answer the questions below, based solely on the visual image that he or she presents. Indicate your answers with the number **1**. After answering the questions, the class will interact with the guest for about ten minutes. Ask anything you wish, although none of your questions should be *directly* related to those questions given below. (It is a good idea to think about questions to ask before the class period in which the interview is conducted.)

After the question period is over, answer the questions again, this time indicating your answer with the number **2**. After you have finished, the guest will go over the questions, giving his or her own answers to them. Here are the questions.

1. Cuando lee, es probable que esta persona lea...
   ______ novelas cómicas
   ______ novelas de Dostoievski
   ______ ensayos filosóficos
   ______ un manual sobre la reparación de coches
   ______ novelas populares románticas, como las de Bárbara Cartland
   ______ artículos científicos
   ______ novelas de éxito actual (*best-sellers*)
2. Es probable que esta persona prefiera...
   ______ las películas de detectives
   ______ las películas románticas
   ______ las películas del «Oeste»
   ______ las películas cómicas
   ______ las películas eróticas
   ______ las películas extranjeras
   ______ las películas de ciencia ficción
3. En cuanto a deportes, es posible que esta persona...
   ______ juegue al béisbol
   ______ juegue al tenis
   ______ juegue al golf
   ______ esquíe
   ______ no practique ninguno de esos deportes sino (*but rather*) otro
   ______ no practique ningún deporte
4. Creo que, cuando escucha música, esta persona prefiere...
   ______ la música clásica
   ______ la música *country and western*
   ______ la música disco
   ______ la música punk
   ______ el rock n'roll

5. En mi opinión, esta persona tiene... (hay más de una respuesta posible)
   ______ un coche norteamericano
   ______ un coche extranjero
   ______ un coche común y corriente
   ______ un coche deportivo
   ______ una camioneta

6. Yo supongo que a esta persona le interesa más...
   ______ el problema de la contaminación del medio ambiente
   ______ la escasez de energía
   ______ el problema del analfabetismo (*illiteracy*) en este país
   ______ los peligros de las industrias relacionadas con la energía nuclear
   ______ la tecnología genética

7. Esta persona busca (tiene) un esposo (una esposa) que sea (es)...
   ______ inteligente
   ______ guapo/a
   ______ rico/a
   ______ muy simpático/a, con una personalidad encantadora

8. Es muy probable que esta persona asista a...
   ______ un concierto de música rock, punk o popular
   ______ una exposición en un museo de arte
   ______ un partido de béisbol
   ______ una ópera
   ______ una obra teatral
   ______ una película

9. Yo creo que esta persona prefiere estar...
   ______ solo/a ______ con otra persona
   ______ en grupos grandes

10. Los siguientes adjetivos describen bien la personalidad de esta persona: (escoja un adjetivo de cada par)

______ introvertido/a	______ extrovertido/a
______ dinámico/a	______ tímido/a
______ emotivo/a	______ racional, práctico/a
______ energético/a	______ perezoso/a

Datos sobre esta persona:

Edad: ______	Posición económica: ______
Profesión: ______	Estado civil (casado/a, soltero/a, divorciado/a, viudo/a, vive con otra persona): ______
Educación: ______	

After listening to the stranger's answers and comparing them with yours, discuss as a class the following questions.

1. ¿Están Uds. más o menos de acuerdo sobre los intereses, gustos y características de la persona? ¿Qué correspondencia encontraron entre sus juicios y las respuestas de la persona?
2. ¿Son muy diferentes las opiniones que Uds. dieron antes de hablar con la persona de las que dieron después de escuchar sus respuestas? ¿Por qué cree Ud. que ocurrió esto?
3. ¿Qué cosas (palabras, manera de hablar, manera de actuar, etcétera) le ayudaron a formar sus opiniones?
4. ¿Dio Ud. algunas opiniones influenciado/a por ideas estereotípicas? ¿Cuáles?*

SITUACIONES SOCIALES

With a classmate, act out the following role-play situations as fully as possible. Try to use as much of the vocabulary as you can.

1. Your car is almost out of gas and needs some repair work. Ask a pedestrian where you can find a gas station and a repair shop.
2. You are the parent of a small child. Your child is playing outside when it begins to rain. Call the child in and help him or her find something else to do.
3. You meet a new neighbor who has just moved to your city. He or she is very interested in learning from you what activities are available and what activities you personally participate in.
4. You invite a friend to go to a movie with you. Discuss with him or her what film you want to see, where it's showing, how you will get there, how much tickets cost, etc.
5. You are a tour guide for prospective students at your college. One person on your tour is especially interested in the sports program. Discuss her interests and explain the campus sports options.

---

* Adapted from Joseph A. DeVito, *The Interpersonal Communication Book,* 4th ed. (New York: Harper & Row, 1986).

CAPÍTULO DIECISÉIS

LAS ÚLTIMAS NOVEDADES

Buenos Aires, la Argentina

▲ **Las noticias de hoy**

—¿Has oído las noticias de las cinco?

—No. ¿Qué pasó? Nada malo, espero.

—Pues, hubo un terremoto[a] en Centroamérica, pero no fue muy fuerte.

—Menos mal. Siempre esperamos lo peor de los desastres naturales.

[a]*earthquake*

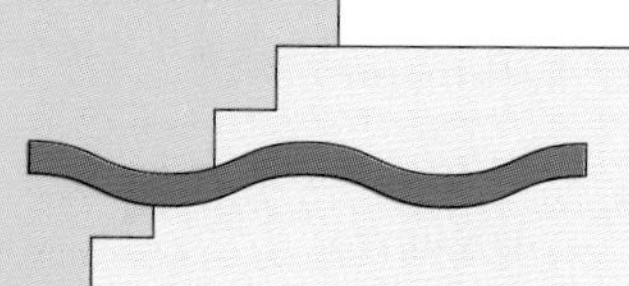

VOCABULARIO: PREPARACIÓN

Vocabulario: Preparación:
• See detailed supplementary materials for this section bound into the back of this Annotated Instructor's Edition.
• See model for vocabulary presentation and other materials in Supplementary *Vocabulario: Preparación* Materials, chapter by chapter, IM.

• See also [video icon] and [audio icon]

Las noticias

el acontecimiento event
la prensa press; news media
el/la reportero/a reporter
el/la testigo witness

el barrio neighborhood
el choque collision
el desastre disaster
la (des)igualdad (in)equality
la esperanza hope
la paz peace

enterarse (de) to find out, learn (about)
informar to inform
ofrecer (ofrezco) to offer

Y ahora, el canal 45 les ofrece a Uds. el NOTICIERO 45...
...Con las últimas novedades del mundo...

Asesinato de un dictador

Huelga de obreros en Alemania

Guerra en el Oriente Medio

"Erupción de un volcán en Centroamérica"

"Choque de trenes"

"Bombas en un avión"

El gobierno y la responsabilidad cívica

comunicarse (con) to communicate (with)
durar to last, endure
obedecer (obedezco) to obey
votar to vote

el/la ciudadano/a citizen
el deber responsibility; obligation
los demás others, other people
el derecho right
la dictadura dictatorship
la ley law
el rey/la reina king/queen

**EL FORTIN DIARIO Y USTED,
UN AMOR RENOVADO DIARIAMENTE.**

Usted quiere y necesita saber qué pasa
en Chile y en el mundo y quiere también compartir sus ideas con otros.
Para eso usted tiene que estar bien enterado.
Hágase amigo del Fortín Diario y verá cómo su diario se hará sumamente indispensable.
Recuerde que el amor es comunicación.
Para que no le cuenten cuentos, compre el **Fortín Diario.**
Cómprelo todos los días.

**El Fortín Diario
El diario popular a su medida.**

A. **Definiciones.** ¿Qué palabra se asocia con cada definición?

1. un programa que nos informa de lo que pasa en nuestro mundo
2. la persona que está presente durante un acontecimiento y lo ve todo
3. un medio importantísimo de comunicación
4. la persona que nos informa de las novedades
5. la persona que gobierna un país de una forma absoluta
6. la persona que emplea la violencia para cambiar el mundo según sus deseos
7. cuando los obreros se niegan a (*refuse*) trabajar
8. la frecuencia en que se transmiten y se reciben los programas de televisión
9. la confrontación armada entre dos o más países

a. el noticiero
b. la guerra
c. el/la terrorista
ch. el/la dictador(a)
d. el canal
e. el/la testigo
f. el/la reportero/a
g. la huelga
h. la prensa

Follow-up A: *¿Qué va a decir una persona ultra-liberal* (*una persona ultra-conservadora*) *sobre los siguientes conceptos?* **1.** *la libertad de prensa* **2.** *una dictadura en Centroamérica* **3.** *la pena capital* (death penalty) **4.** *la obediencia a las leyes* **5.** *las huelgas*

Ahora diga las palabras que Ud. asocia con los siguientes conceptos o dé una definición de cada uno.

1. el deber
2. la ley
3. el barrio
4. una monarquía

Suggestion B: Students select one item and report back to the class their opinions and recommendations.

Optional B: Written assignment.

B. **Entrevista.** With another student, exchange opinions about the news media and television in general. Tell whether you agree or disagree with the following statements and give examples to support your point of view. Then make suggestions for improvement, as appropriate.

1. Los reporteros de la televisión nos informan imparcialmente de los acontecimientos.
2. Por lo general ofrecen los programas más interesantes en el canal ____.
3. En este país la prensa es irresponsable. Nos da sólo los detalles que apoyan (*support*) sus posiciones políticas.
4. Las telenovelas (*soap operas*) reflejan la vida tal (*just*) como es.
5. Los anuncios son sumamente (*extremely*) informativos y más interesantes que muchos programas.
6. Me gusta que los reporteros y meteorólogos cuenten chistes durante el noticiero.

Note C: Subjunctive reentry, in preparation for Grammar Section 46.

C. Algunos creen que las siguientes declaraciones describen el estado del mundo actual. ¿Qué cree Ud.? Dé su opinión, empezando con una de estas expresiones.

(No) Dudo que...
(No) Es verdad que...
Es probable que...
Es bueno/malo que...
Es lástima que...
Es increíble que...
(No) Me gusta que...

1. En los Estados Unidos seguimos usando demasiado petróleo.
2. Debemos concederles todo lo que pidan a los terroristas que tienen rehenes (*hostages*).
3. Hay más catástrofes naturales actualmente que hace 50 años.
4. Es una buena idea asesinar a todos los dictadores del mundo.

5. No hay esperanza de una paz mundial.
6. En los Estados Unidos, la igualdad legal de todos los ciudadanos es una realidad, no sólo una esperanza.
7. Los policías, los bomberos (*firefighters*), los médicos y los enfermeros no tienen el derecho de declararse en huelga.
8. La guerra es un buen medio de resolver los conflictos internacionales.

Ahora invente una oración a la que van a responder sus compañeros de clase.

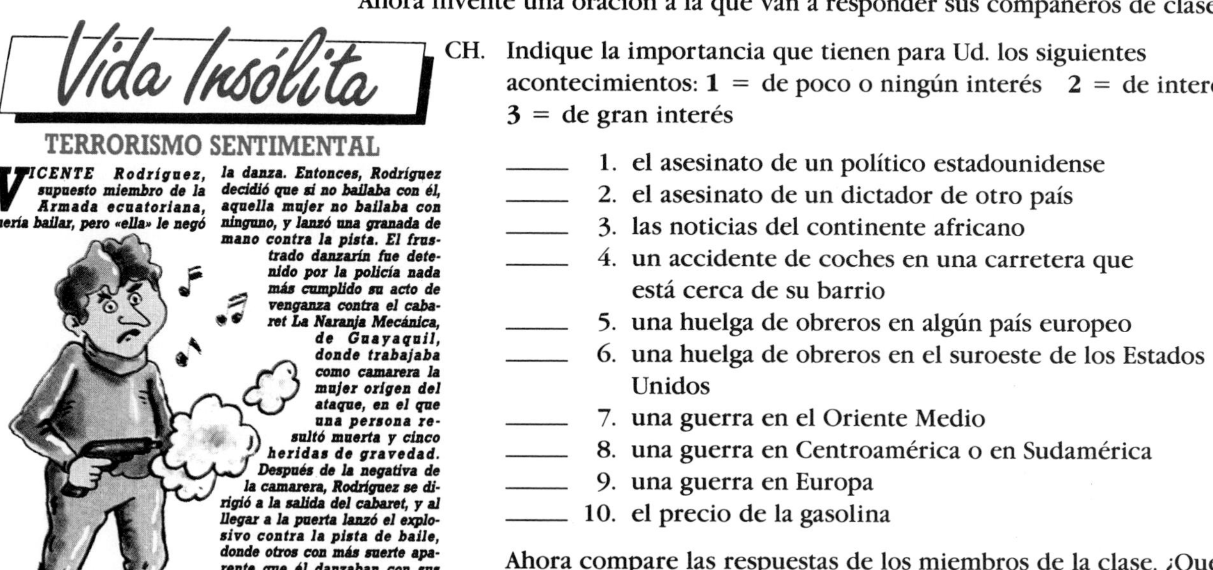

Vida Insólita

TERRORISMO SENTIMENTAL

VICENTE Rodríguez, supuesto miembro de la Armada ecuatoriana, quería bailar, pero «ella» le negó la danza. Entonces, Rodríguez decidió que si no bailaba con él, aquella mujer no bailaba con ninguno, y lanzó una granada de mano contra la pista. El frustrado danzarín fue detenido por la policía nada más cumplido su acto de venganza contra el cabaret La Naranja Mecánica, de Guayaquil, donde trabajaba como camarera la mujer origen del ataque, en el que una persona resultó muerta y cinco heridas de gravedad. Después de la negativa de la camarera, Rodríguez se dirigió a la salida del cabaret, y al llegar a la puerta lanzó el explosivo contra la pista de baile, donde otros con más suerte aparente que él danzaban con sus parejas. No contento con eso, los policías que llegaron al lugar de los hechos para detenerle, se encontraron con que el despechado danzarín les recibió a tiros, lo que no impidió su captura.

CH. Indique la importancia que tienen para Ud. los siguientes acontecimientos: **1** = de poco o ningún interés **2** = de interés **3** = de gran interés

_____ 1. el asesinato de un político estadounidense
_____ 2. el asesinato de un dictador de otro país
_____ 3. las noticias del continente africano
_____ 4. un accidente de coches en una carretera que está cerca de su barrio
_____ 5. una huelga de obreros en algún país europeo
_____ 6. una huelga de obreros en el suroeste de los Estados Unidos
_____ 7. una guerra en el Oriente Medio
_____ 8. una guerra en Centroamérica o en Sudamérica
_____ 9. una guerra en Europa
_____ 10. el precio de la gasolina

Ahora compare las respuestas de los miembros de la clase. ¿Qué indican sus respuestas sobre su interés en los acontecimientos mundiales?

Variation CH: Students survey 10 students outside class and report results to class in Spanish.

You may want to tabulate results of surveys as a whole and analyze.

D. **Preguntas**

1. Para Ud., ¿es importante estar informado/a de lo que pasa en el mundo? ¿Cómo se entera de las noticias locales o regionales? ¿Cómo se entera de lo que pasa en su barrio? ¿en su familia?
2. ¿Qué canal de televisión prefiere Ud. para enterarse de las noticias? ¿Cree Ud. que en ese canal le informan mejor? ¿O es que le gusta el locutor (la locutora) que se las ofrece? ¿Le interesan a Ud. mucho o poco las noticias del estado de California? ¿de Nueva York? ¿Por qué sí o por qué no?
3. ¿Le importan más a Ud. su autonomía e individualismo o los sentimientos de los demás? En una tienda, ¿hace cola con paciencia o primero trata de atraer la atención del dependiente? En una parada de autobús (*bus stop*), ¿hace cola o trata de subir primero?
4. Para Ud., ¿cuáles son los derechos más básicos de que todos debemos gozar (*enjoy*)? ¿Cuáles son los deberes de un buen ciudadano? ¿Es importante que todos votemos en todas las elecciones, sean nacionales o locales? ¿Por qué cree Ud. que muchas personas no votan?

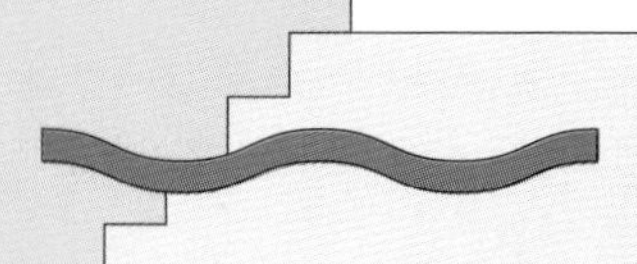

MINIDIÁLOGOS Y GRAMÁTICA

¿Recuerda Ud.?

In Grammar Secion 46, you will learn about and begin to use the forms of the past subjunctive. As you learn this new tense, you will be continually using the past tense forms you have already learned along with the new material, so this section presents many opportunities for review. The following brief exercises will help you get started.

A. To learn the forms of the past subjunctive, you will need to know the forms of the preterite well, especially the third person plural. Regular **-ar** verbs end in **-aron** and regular **-er/ir** verbs in **-ieron** in the third person plural of the preterite. Stem-changing **-ir** verbs show the second change in the third person: **servir (i, i) → sirvieron**; **dormir (ue, u) → durmieron**. Verbs with a stem ending in a vowel change the **i** to **y**: **leyeron**, **cayeron**, **construyeron**. Many common verbs have irregular stems in the preterite: **quisieron**, **hicieron**, **dijeron**, and so on. Four common verbs are totally irregular in this tense: **ser/ir → fueron**, **dar → dieron**, **ver → vieron**.
Change these verbs to the third person plural of the preterite.

1. habla
2. como
3. vives
4. juegan
5. pierde
6. dormimos
7. río
8. leemos
9. estoy
10. tenemos
11. vamos
12. visten
13. traigo
14. dan
15. sé
16. puedo
17. digo
18. destruimos
19. creo
20. mantienen

B. The forms of the imperfect are relatively regular, and there are only three verbs with irregular imperfect forms: **dar**, **ir**, and **ser**. Give their first person singular and plural forms.

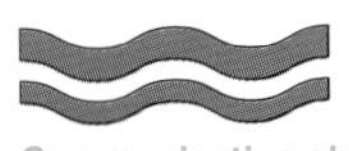

Communicative objectives for **46:** to be able to use subjunctive constructions to talk about things in past

46. ¡OJALÁ QUE PUDIÉRAMOS HACERLO!
Past Subjunctive

Aquéllos eran otros tiempos...

—¡Parece imposible que yo *dijera* eso! ¡Qué egoísmo!

—¡No es posible que *lucháramos* tanto!

Hace treinta años, era difícil que don Jorge y don Gustavo *hablaran* de las elecciones sin pelearse. Era imposible que se *pusieran* de acuerdo en política. ¡Qué lástima que *hubiera* tanta enemistad entre ellos!

—*VIEJOS VOTANTES.* ¿Recuerda cuánto tuvimos que discurrir° usted y yo antes de votar hace treinta años?

°*to discuss*

Point out: Forms of past subjunctive in reading. Ask, What past tense do some of these forms (*dijera, pusieran, hubiera*) resemble? (→ preterite)

Ahora es probable que no se acuerden de todas las peleas del pasado. También es posible que sus convicciones políticas sean menos fuertes... o simplemente que ahora tengan otras cosas de que hablar.

Hace diez años...

1. ¿de qué era difícil que Ud. hablara con sus padres?
2. ¿con quién era imposible que Ud. se pusiera de acuerdo?
3. ¿con quién era imposible que Ud. se comunicara?
4. ¿contra qué orden de sus padres era común que Ud. protestara?

Cuando Ud. era niño/a...

5. ¿era probable que discutiera (*you argued*) con alguien en la escuela primaria o en el barrio? ¿con quién?
6. ¿dónde le prohibían sus padres que jugara?
7. ¿qué era obligatorio que comiera o bebiera?
8. ¿de qué temía que sus padres se enteraran?

Follow-up: 1. *¿Habla Ud. de temas políticos con sus amigos? ¿Siempre están de acuerdo?* 2. *¿Hay otros temas que a veces sean difíciles de comentar con los amigos? ¿la religión? ¿la moralidad?* 3. *¿Tenía Ud. un amigo (una amiga) con quien siempre se peleara de niño/a? ¿un amigo (una amiga) con quien se pelee con frecuencia ahora?*

Although Spanish has two simple indicative past tenses (preterite and imperfect), it has only one simple subjunctive past tense, **el imperfecto del subjuntivo** (*past subjunctive*). Generally speaking, this tense is used in the same situations as the present subjunctive but, of course, when talking about past events. The exact English equivalent depends on the context in which it is used.

Suggestions:

- Students give third-person plural preterite forms of *caminar, terminar, usar, pensar, esperar, cerrar, nadar, ofrecer, resolver, correr, prometer, volver, leer, creer, abrir, escribir, subir, admitir.*
- Present formation of past subjunctive. All forms based on third-person plural preterite: no exceptions.
- Use past subjunctive forms of *trabajar, volver, abrir* in conversational exchanges.

Forms of the Past Subjunctive

PAST SUBJUNCTIVE OF REGULAR VERBS*					
hablar: hablar~~on~~		**comer: comier~~on~~**		**vivir: vivier~~on~~**	
hablar**a**	hablár**amos**	comier**a**	comiér**amos**	vivier**a**	viviér**amos**
hablar**as**	hablar**ais**	comier**as**	comier**ais**	vivier**as**	vivier**ais**
hablar**a**	hablar**an**	comier**a**	comier**an**	vivier**a**	vivier**an**

The past subjunctive endings **-a**, **-as**, **-a**, **-amos**, **-ais**, **-an** are identical for **-ar**, **-er**, and **-ir** verbs. These endings are added to the third person plural of the preterite indicative, minus its **-on** ending. For this reason, the forms of the past subjunctive reflect the irregularities of the preterite.

Those were the days . . . —It seems impossible that I said that. How selfish! —It's not possible that we fought that much!

Thirty years ago it was difficult for don Jorge and don Gustavo to talk about elections without fighting. It was impossible for them to come to any agreement about politics. What a shame that there was so much bad feeling between them!

Now it's probable that they don't remember all the fights of the past. It's also possible that their political convictions are less intense . . . or just that they have other things to discuss now.

*An alternate form of the past subjunctive (used primarily in Spain) ends in **-se**: **hablase**, **hablases**, **hablase**, **hablásemos**, **hablaseis**, **hablasen**. This form will not be practiced in ***Puntos de partida***.

Stem-changing Verbs

-Ar and **-er** verbs: no change

empezar (**ie**): empezar~~on~~ → **empezara**, **empezaras**, etc.
volver (**ue**): volvier~~on~~ → **voviera**, **volvieras**, etc.

-Ir verbs: all persons of the past subjunctive reflect the vowel change in the third person plural of the preterite.

dormir (**ue**, **u**): durmier~~on~~ → **durmiera**, **durmieras**, etc.
pedir (**i**, **i**): pidier~~on~~ → **pidiera**, **pidieras**, etc.

Spelling Changes

All persons of the past subjunctive reflect the change from **i** to **y** between two vowels.

i → **y** (caer, construir, creer, destruir, leer, oír)

creer: creyer~~on~~ → **creyera**, **creyeras**, **creyera**, **creyéramos**, **creyerais**, **creyeran**

Verbs with Irregular Preterites

dar: dier~~on~~ → **diera**, **dieras**, **diera**, **diéramos**, **dierais**, **dieran**

decir:	dijer~~on~~ → **dijera**	**haber**	hubier~~on~~ → **hubiera**
estar:	estuvier~~on~~ → **estuviera**	**hacer**:	hicier~~on~~ → **hiciera**
ir:	fuer~~on~~ → **fuera**	**saber:**	supier~~on~~ → **supiera**
poder:	pudier~~on~~ → **pudiera**	**ser:**	fuer~~on~~ → **fuera**
poner:	pusier~~on~~ → **pusiera**	**tener:**	tuvier~~on~~ → **tuviera**
querer:	quisier~~on~~ → **quisiera**	**venir:**	vinier~~on~~ → **viniera**

- Students give third-person plural preterite forms of *dar, hacer, ser, ir, decir, estar, poder, poner, querer, saber, tener, traer, venir, divertirse, servir, dormir, jugar, pedir*.
- Use past subjunctive forms of *servir*, *sentir*, *dar*, *decir*, *hacer*, *ir*, and *venir* in conversational exchanges.

Uses of the Past Subjunctive

The past subjunctive usually has the same applications as the present subjunctive, but is used for past events. Compare these pairs of sentences.

- Use of past subjunctive to describe past events where context requires subjunctive form.
- **Emphasis:** When verb in main clause is in past, past—never present—subjunctive is used in subordinate clause. Past → Past.

Quiero que **jueguen** por la tarde.	*I want them to play in the afternoon.*
Quería que **jugaran** por la tarde.	*I wanted them to play in the afternoon.*
Siente que no **estén** allí.	*He's sorry (that) they aren't there.*
Sintió que no **estuvieran** allí.	*He was sorry (that) they weren't there.*
Dudamos que se **equivoquen**.	*We doubt that they will make a mistake.*
Dudábamos que se **equivocaran**.	*We doubted that they would make a mistake.*

Remember that the subjunctive is used (1) after expressions of *influence*, *emotion*, and *doubt*; (2) after *nonexistent* and *indefinite antecedents*; and (3) after certain *conjunctions* (**a menos que**, **antes [de] que**, **con tal [de] que**, **en caso de que**, **para que**).

¿**Era necesario** que **regatearas**?	*Was it necessary for you to bargain?*
Sentí que no **tuvieran** tiempo para ver Granada.	*I was sorry that they didn't have time to see Granada.*
No había nadie que **pudiera** resolverlo.	*There wasn't anyone who could (might have been able to) solve it.*
Los padres trabajaron **para que** sus hijos **asistieran** a la universidad.	*The parents worked so that their children might go to the university.*

[Práctica A–CH]

Softening Requests or Statements

Emphasis: formation of polite requests with past subjunctive. Similarity to English *really should*, *would like you to* . . . to attenuate requests.

The past subjunctive forms of **deber**, **poder**, and **querer** are used to soften a request or statement.

Debieras estudiar más.	*You really should study more.*
¿**Pudieran** Uds. traérmelo?	*Could you bring it for me?*
Quisiéramos hablar con Ud. en seguida.	*We would like to speak with you immediately.*

[Práctica D]

Preliminary exercise: *Recuerdos. Dé oraciones nuevas según las indicaciones. —Cuando Ud. estudiaba en la secundaria, ¿qué le gustaba? —Me gustaba que nosotros ____. (estudiar idiomas, leer libros interesantes, ver películas en la clase de historia, hacer experimentos en la clase de física, bailar durante la hora del almuerzo, divertirnos después de las clases, ¿ ?)*

Práctica

A. **Recuerdos.** Haga oraciones con una frase de cada grupo para describir los siguientes aspectos de su niñez.

Mis padres (no) querían que yo...	portarse bien, ser bueno/a,...
Mis maestros me pedían que...	estudiar mucho, sacar buenas notas, ...
Yo buscaba amigos que...	creer en Santa Claus, tener un árbol de Navidad muy alto, ...
Yo siempre quería que los miembros de mi familia...	ponerse la ropa vieja para jugar, no jugar en las calles, no luchar con mis amigos, traer animales a casa, ...
	mirar mucho la televisión, comer muchos dulces, ...
	vivir en nuestro barrio, tener muchos juguetes, venir a mi casa a jugar, ...
	ir a la playa en verano, pasar juntos los día feriados, ...

Follow-up A: 1. *¿Qué no le gustaba **nada**?* 2. *¿Qué quería Ud. que sus padres (sus hermanos) hicieran?*

Suggestion B: Students tell why each sentence requires subjunctive rather than indicative.

B. **Las últimas novedades.** Cambie al pasado. Luego diga si la oración presenta un hecho (*fact*) o sólo es una opinión del locutor.

1. Los obreros quieren que les den un aumento de sueldo.
2. Es posible que los trabajadores sigan en huelga hasta las Navidades.

3. Es necesario que las víctimas reciban atención médica en la Clínica del Sagrado Corazón.
4. Es lástima que no haya espacio para todos allí.
5. Los terroristas piden que los oficiales no los sigan.
6. Parece imposible que el gobierno escuche sus demandas.
7. Es necesario que el gobierno informe a todos los ciudadanos del desastre.
8. Dudo que la paz mundial esté fuera de nuestro alcance (*reach*).
9. Lee Iacocca prefiere que la nueva fábrica se construya en México.
10. Temo que el número de votantes sea muy bajo en las próximas elecciones.

Suggestion C: Expand each item with questions about historical situation in question. Focus on imperfect/preterite in questions, not necessarily on use of imperfect subjunctive. ***Modelo:*** **1.** *¿En qué año llegaron al Nuevo Mundo los primeros colonos? ¿Había muchos indios aquí en aquel entonces* (back then)*? ¿Qué hicieron los colonos tan pronto como llegaron? ¿Tenían miedo de los indios?*, etc.

C. **Escenas históricas.** Dé una breve descripción de la historia de los Estados Unidos, haciendo oraciones según las indicaciones. Empiece en el pasado, pero tenga en cuenta (*keep in mind*) que la historia termina en el presente.

1. indios / temer / que / colonos / quitarles / toda la tierra
2. colonos / no / gustar / que / tener / pagarle / impuestos / rey
3. parecía imposible / que / joven república / tener éxito (*success*)
4. los del sur / no / gustar / que / gobernarlos / los del norte
5. abolicionistas / no / gustar / que / algunos / no / tener / mismo / libertades
6. era necesario / que / declararse / en huelga / obreros / para / obtener / alguno / derechos
7. era terrible / que / haber / dos / guerra / mundial
8. para que / nosotros / vivir / en paz / es cuestión de / aprender / comunicarse / con / demás naciones
9. también / es necesario / que / haber / leyes / que / garantizar / derechos / todos

ARCHIVO

Los helados aportaban, hasta ahora, un alto nivel calorífico.

La novedad para este verano

Se presentó en Jijona el helado "Light"

JIJONA, 29. — Una nueva variedad de refresco, el **"helado light"**, se presenta en la octava edición de la feria dedicada al helado artesanal, "Gelat'87" (Helado-87), que se celebra durante estos días en la localidad alicantina de Jijona.

El "helado light" se produce con fructosa, que le da un aporte calórico muy bajo, pero **"su aceptación, pese a la moda del light, depende del gusto del consumidor"**, según ha indicado el presidente de "Gelat'87", José Manuel Miquel.

La feria "Gelat'87", organizada por la Asociación Empresarial Nacional de Elaboradores Artesanos y Comerciantes de Helados y Horchateros, está dedicada este año a los productos, maquinaria y servicios para la elaboración del helado.

José Manuel Miquel ha explicado que "los sabores nuevos de los helados artesanos dependen de la demanda y los gustos del consumidor, ya que éstos pueden ser tantos como imaginación tenga el fabricante de helados".

El presidente de "Gelat'87" ha destacado también que "se pueden elaborar helados artesanos con sabor a ginebra, queso e incluso cava, para que, dado su contenido bajo en alcohol, puedan ser consumidos por los niños".

Sin embargo, siempre según José Manuel Miquel, "estos nuevos sabores no podrán desbancar nunca a los helados tradicionales elaborados con chocolate, vainilla, turrón, leche merengada, limón y mantecado, entre otros".

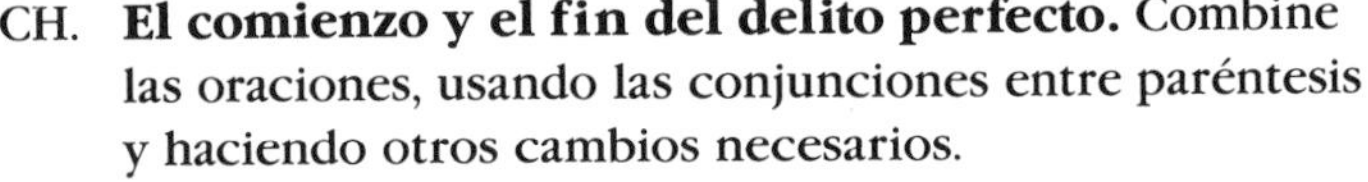

Suggestion CH: Students invent central part of story filling in details between 5 and 6.

CH. **El comienzo y el fin del delito perfecto.** Combine las oraciones, usando las conjunciones entre paréntesis y haciendo otros cambios necesarios.

1. El ladrón (*thief*) no pensaba entrar en la casa. No oía ningún ruido. (a menos que)
2. No iba a molestar a los dueños. Encontraba dinero y objetos de valor. (con tal que)
3. Un amigo lo acompañaba. Había alguna dificultad. (en caso de que)
4. El amigo rompió la ventana. El ladrón pudo entrar. (para que)
5. El ladrón entró silenciosamente. Los dueños no se despertaron. (para que)
6. Salió. Los dueños pudieron llamar a la policía. (antes de que)

D. **La situación es delicada...** ¿Cómo se dice en español?

1. You really should drive more slowly.
2. Couldn't you think about others this time?
3. We would like you to consider your obligations.
4. How would you like to pay, madam?
5. We really should protect their welfare first.

Conversación

A. **Me decía ayer Cristóbal...** ¿Cómo van a completar estas personas las siguientes oraciones?

1. *Cristóbal Colón:* Casi todos dudaban que...
2. *Neil Armstrong:* Yo esperaba que un día...
3. *Miss Piggy:* Mis padres esperaban que un día yo...
4. *Franklin Delano Roosevelt:* Yo temía que...
5. *El rey Tut:* Dudaba que...
6. *Marie Curie:* Pocos creían que yo...

a. hubiera otra guerra mundial
b. el mundo fuera redondo (*round*)
c. descubrieran mi tumba
ch. hiciera un descubrimiento magnífico
d. llegara a ser una actriz famosa
e. el hombre llegara a la luna

Variation A: Students supply complete items without naming speaker. Class identifies speaker.

¿Qué consejos cree Ud. que los demás les dieron a esas personas? Por ejemplo, ¿qué le aconsejaron a Cristóbal Colón antes de empezar su viaje? ¿Le dijeron que no lo hiciera? ¿que saliera con más de tres barcos? ¿que llevara mucha fruta? Invente todos los consejos que pueda.

B. **Preguntas**

1. ¿De qué tenía Ud. miedo cuando era pequeño/a? ¿Era posible que ocurrieran las cosas que Ud. temía? ¿Era probable que ocurrieran? ¿A veces temía que lo/la castigaran (*punish*) sus padres? ¿Lo merecía a veces? ¿Era necesario que Ud. los obedeciera siempre? ¿Va a querer que sus propios niños lo/la obedezcan de la misma manera? ¿Cree Ud. que lo van a hacer? ¿Por qué sí o por qué no?
2. ¿Qué tipo de clases buscaba para este semestre? ¿clases que fueran fáciles? ¿interesantes? ¿Las encontró Ud.? Según sus experiencias durante este semestre, ¿qué tipo de clases va a buscar para el semestre que viene?
3. ¿Qué quería el gobierno que hicieran los ciudadanos el año pasado? ¿Quería que gastaran menos gasolina? ¿que usaran menos energía? ¿que pagaran los impuestos? ¿que votaran en todas las elecciones? ¿que fueran ciudadanos responsables? ¿Hizo Ud. todo eso? ¿Por qué sí o por qué no? ¿Qué hizo por Ud. el gobierno?
4. ¿Qué buscaban los primeros inmigrantes que vinieron a los Estados Unidos? ¿un lugar donde pudieran practicar su religión? ¿un lugar donde fuera posible escaparse de las obligaciones financieras? ¿donde hubiera abundancia de recursos naturales? ¿menos leyes? ¿más libertad? ¿más respeto por los derechos humanos? ¿menos gente? ¿más espacio?

—Verás, quisiera un vaso de agua. Pero no te molestes, porque ya no tengo sed. Sólo quisiera saber si, en el caso de que tuviese otra vez sed, podría° venir a pedirte un vaso de agua.

° *I could*

Point out: In cartoon: *las formas verbales usadas por el niño en esta situación delicada*

C. Su tía Laura, quien asistió a la universidad en la década de los años cincuenta, le describe cómo eran entonces las normas de conducta. ¿Cuáles de estas normas todavía están vigentes (*viable*) en las universidades en la actualidad? Explíquele a Laura las diferencias. ¿Hay algunas antiguas normas que le parezcan a Ud. mejores que las modernas? ¿Cuál(es)? ¿Por qué?

1. Era necesario que los hombres y las mujeres vivieran separados en distintas residencias.
2. Para entrar en la cafetería de la universidad a cenar, era necesario que los hombres llevaran corbata y las mujeres, falda.
3. Había «horas de visita» en las residencias. Los hombres sólo podían visitar a sus amigas durante esas horas, y vice versa.
4. Era necesario que cada estudiante volviera a su propia residencia a una hora determinada de la noche (a las once, por ejemplo).

CH. **Entrevista.** Con un compañero (una compañera), haga y conteste preguntas para saber la siguiente información. Describa a la clase las opiniones más interesantes.

1. el tipo de amigos que buscaba de niño/a y los que tiene ahora
2. una cosa que le parecía imposible de niño/a y algo que le parece imposible ahora
3. lo que pensaba de la educación cuando era niño/a y lo que piensa ahora
4. una cosa de la que dudaba de niño/a y algo de lo que duda ahora
5. una cosa de la que tenía miedo de niño/a y algo que teme ahora

Follow-up C: 1. *¿Es diferente la vida universitaria de lo que Ud. esperaba? Explique.* **2.** *¿Esperaba que las clases fueran más pequeñas? ¿más fáciles?* **3.** *¿Esperaba que hubiera menos exámenes? ¿más fiestas?* **4.** *¿Qué es lo que más le gustaba mucho durante las primeras semanas del primer semestre/trimestre? ¿Qué es lo que no le gustaba para nada?*

Notas comunicativas: I Wish I Could . . . I Wish They Would

There are many ways to express wishes in Spanish. As you know, one of the most common is **ojalá (que)** with the subjunctive. The past subjunctive following **ojalá** is one of the most frequent uses of those verb forms.

Ojalá (que) pudiera acompañarlos, pero no es posible.	*I wish I could go with you, but it's not possible.*
Ojalá inventaran una máquina que hiciera todas las tareas domésticas.	*I wish they would invent a machine that would do all the household chores.*

Follow-up (cartoon): *¿Qué diría Ud. en las siguientes situaciones? Use el pasado de subjuntivo cuando sea posible.* **1.** *Ud. ha llamado a un amigo a las diez de la noche para invitarlo a salir... pero ya estaba dormido y Ud. lo ha despertado.* **2.** *Ud. llega a casa muy enfermo/a, con tos y fiebre. El médico le ha aconsejado que se quede en cama para descansar. Pero su compañero/a de cuarto, queriendo darle una sorpresa, le ha preparado una fiesta de cumpleaños... de sorpresa. Todos los amigos lo/la saludan cuando entra.*

D. Complete las oraciones lógicamente.

1. Ojalá que (yo) tuviera _____.
2. Ojalá que pudiera _____.
3. Ojalá pudiera _____ por _____.
4. Ojalá inventaran una máquina que _____.
5. Ojalá solucionaran el problema de _____.
6. Ojalá que en esta universidad fuera posible _____.

Hablando de las raíces° *roots*

—¿Por qué emigró tu familia?

—Por necesidad. La situación política de mi país era intolerable.

—Para ser extranjero hablas muy bien el inglés.

—¿Ves? La necesidad es la mejor maestra.

La Pequeña Habana, Miami

¿Recuerda Ud.?

Review the forms and uses of possessive adjectives (Grammar Section 14) before beginning Grammar Section 47.

Singular:	mi	tu	su	nuestro/a	vuestro/a	su
Plural:	mis	tus	sus	nuestros/as	vuestros/as	sus

Son mis libros.	*They're my books.*
Es su gobierno.	*It's his (her, your, their) government.*
Son nuestras casas.	*They're our houses.*

¿Cómo se dice en español?

1. It's his right.
2. What about (**¿Y...**) my rights?
3. It's our obligation.
4. It's your (**Uds.**) government, too!
5. Their press doesn't inform them well.
6. Our crimes were not serious.
7. Your (**Ud.**) welfare is important.
8. It's our country, too!

Communicative objectives for 47: another way to indicate what belongs to someone

47. MORE ABOUT EXPRESSING POSSESSION
Stressed Possessives

1. ¿Quién es el dueño del mundo en esta visión del futuro?
2. ¿A quién le va a dar todo el padre robot?

When in English you would emphasize the possessive with your voice, or when you want to express English *of mine* (*of yours, of his,* and so on), you will use the *stressed forms* (**las formas tónicas**) of the possessive in Spanish. As the term implies, they are more emphatic than the *unstressed forms* (**las formas átonas**).

Follow-up: 1. *¿Cómo cree Ud. que va a ser la vida del ser humano en un mundo como éste?* **2.** *¿Qué les quisiera Ud. dejar a los hijos suyos algún día? ¿mucho dinero? ¿una casa enorme? ¿buenos recuerdos?*

Suggestions:
- Review unstressed possessives
- *¿Cómo se dice?* He's my friend. It's her dog. Contrast: *Es un amigo mío. Es el perro suyo.*
- Present stressed forms and their use. **Point out:** Stressed forms follow noun.
- *¿Cómo se dice?* **1.** She's a friend of mine/of ours/ of his/ of theirs. **2.** We have some books of yours/of his/of theirs.

Point out: Ambiguity of *suyo* (similar to ambiguity of *su*). For clarification: *unos libros suyos → unos libros de él, de ellos,* etc.

Note: The text does not emphasize the adjective/nominalized form distinction. Most students will not have difficulty with it. You may wish to use the following optional explanation, if necessary.

Optional: Possessive Pronouns: Examples: *Éste es mi banco. ¿Dónde está el suyo? Sus bebidas están preparadas; las nuestras, no. No es el pasaporte de Juan; es el mío.* The stressed possessive adjectives—but not the unstressed possessives—can be used as possessive pronouns: *la maleta suya → la suya.*

FORMS OF THE STRESSED POSSESSIVE ADJECTIVES			
mío/a/os/as	my, (of) mine	**nuestro/a/os/as**	our, (of) ours
tuyo/a/os/as	your, (of) yours	**vuestro/a/os/as**	your, (of) yours
suyo/a/os/as	your, (of) yours; his, (of) his; her, (of) hers; its	**suyo/a/os/as**	your, (of) yours; their, (of) theirs

Es **mi** amigo. — *He's my friend.*

Es **un** amigo **mío**. — *He's **my** friend.* / *He's a friend of mine.*

Es **su** perro. / Es **un** perro **suyo**. Es **suyo**. — *It's **her** dog.* / *It's a dog of hers. It's hers.*

The stressed forms of the possessive adjective follow the noun, which must be preceded by a definite or indefinite article or by a demonstrative adjective. The stressed forms agree with the noun modified in number and gender. The stressed possessives are often used as nouns: **la maleta suya → la suya**; **el pasaporte tuyo → el tuyo.***

The article and the possessive form agree in gender and number with the noun to which they refer. The definite article is frequently omitted after forms of *ser: Es suya.*

Preliminary exercises:
- **Rapid Response Drill:** ***Modelo:*** *el coche mío → el mío; el traje tuyo, los libros míos, la casa suya, el pasaporte mío, los amigos nuestros, las maletas suyas*
- "Steal" objects from students. Ask, *¿Este _____ es mío o es suyo?*
- **Optional:** *¿Cuál es? ¿Es **el** mío?* vs. *¿De quién es? ¿Es mío?* (no article)
- *Con un compañero (una compañera), haga y conteste las siguientes preguntas.* **1.** *—El carro de Antonio está roto. ¿Y el tuyo? —¿El mío? Ya lo he arreglado.* (*lámparas, estéreo, cámara, frenos, transmisión*) **2.** *—¿Ya han encontrado todo el equipaje? —El maletín de Juan, sí, pero las maletas mías, no.* (*suyo, tuyo, nuestro, vuestro*)
- *Conteste según el modelo.* ***Modelo:*** *Voy a lavar mi carro esta tarde. ¿Y tú? → ¿Vas a lavar el tuyo también?* **1.** *No puedo pagar mis cuentas este mes. ¿Y tú?* (*¡**OJO!***

Práctica

A. **En el hotel.** Complete el siguiente diálogo con las formas apropiadas del posesivo.

—Perdone, señorita, pero esta maleta que Uds. me han dado no es (*mío*).
—¿No es (*suyo*)? ¿No es Ud. el doctor Méndez?
—Sí, soy yo, pero esta maleta no es (*mío*). Ud. todavía tiene la (*mío*). Está allí a la derecha.
—Ah, nos equivocamos. Ésta es de los señores Palma. Aquí tengo la (*suyo*). ¡Cuánto lo siento!

B. Ud. trata de encontrar una serie de objetos perdidos. ¿Son suyos los objetos que le ofrecen? Con un compañero (una compañera), haga y conteste preguntas según los modelos.

MODELO: —Esta maleta, ¿es *de Ud.*?
—No, no es mía.

1. de Juan 2. de Uds. 3. de Alicia 4. de Ud. 5. tuya

MODELO: —¿Y esta *radio*?
—No, no es mía. La mía es más pequeña.

6. despertador
7. zapatos
8. llave
9. televisor
10. pastillas
11. periódico

*For more information, see Appendix 1, Using Adjectives as Nouns.

tampoco) **2.** *Ya han hecho sus reservaciones para junio. ¿Y Juan?* **3.** *¡Ay, he dejado mis cheques en casa! ¿Y tú?* **4.** *No podemos encontrar nuestras llaves. ¿Y ellos? (¡**OJO!** tampoco)* **5.** *Vas a informar a tus padres, ¿verdad? ¿Y ellos?* **6.** *No, no perdimos el vuelo. ¿Y Uds.? (¡**OJO!** tampoco)* **7.** *Ya he hecho mis planes para las vacaciones. ¿Y Ud.?* **8.** *Claro que nos preocupamos por nuestro bienestar. ¿Y los demás? (¿No...)*

Variations A:

- *Comparen Uds. nuestra universidad con la de los estudiantes de ___.* **1.** *¿Qué universidad es más respetada académicamente, la nuestra o la suya?* **2.** *¿Qué equipos deportivos son mejores, los nuestros o los suyos?* **3.** *¿Qué matrícula es más cara, la nuestra o la suya?* **4.** *¿Qué campus es más bonito, el nuestro o el suyo?* **5.** *¿Qué estudiantes son más listos, los nuestros o los suyos?*
- Working in pairs, students write comparisons. ***Modelo:*** *los zapatos: Los míos son negros; los tuyos son blancos.* **1.** *clases* **2.** *horario* **3.** *coche* **4.** *casa/apartamento* **5.** *pelo* **6.** *camisa/blusa* **7.** *familia*

Suggestion B: After matches are made, ask students to tell about person named, using preterite and imperfect: in what century and where they lived, etc. *¡OJO!* Statements are not intended to be exact quotes, only approximations of individual's philosophy.

Conversación

A. **Entrevista.** Con un compañero (una compañera), haga y conteste las siguientes preguntas.

1. ¿Qué clases tienes este semestre (trimestre)? ¿Son interesantes? ¿Cuáles son más interesantes, mis clases o las tuyas?
2. ¿Cómo es tu horario este semestre (trimestre)? ¿Cuál es más fácil, mi horario o el tuyo?
3. ¿Tienes coche? ¿Cómo es? ¿Prefieres mi coche o el tuyo?
4. ¿Vives en un apartamento? ¿Cuánto pagas al mes? ¿Cuál es más barato, mi apartamento o el tuyo?
5. ¿Cuántas personas hay en tu familia? ¿Cuál es más grande, mi familia o la tuya?
6. ¿Trabajas? ¿Dónde? ¿Te gusta ese trabajo? ¿Cuál es mejor, mi puesto o el tuyo?

B. **Asociaciones.** ¿Con quién asocia Ud. estas ideas? Luego explique por qué Ud. (no) está de acuerdo con las ideas de esa persona.

MODELO: Habla ___. Estoy de acuerdo con estas ideas suyas porque ___. Otra idea (sugerencia) suya es (fue) ___.

Personas: Martín Lutero King, Ghandi, Carlos Marx, William Randolph Hearst, Thomas Jefferson, Gloria Steinem, Adolfo Hitler

1. El individuo debe trabajar para el bienestar del estado; el estado es más importante que el individuo.
2. La dictadura es la única manera de gobernar a las masas.
3. Todos tenemos que protestar contra la discriminación de las minorías.
4. La prensa es la voz (*voice*) del pueblo, no del gobierno.
5. Para protestar contra la represión de nuestros derechos, estoy en huelga de hambre.
6. Es evidente que el rey no toma en cuenta los derechos de los que vivimos aquí en las colonias.
7. Tenemos que garantizar los derechos y la libertad personal de todos.

SITUACIONES

Situaciones: See IM for suggestions, additional exercises, and supplementary dialogues and exercises.

Hablando de las noticias

En la televisión

—¿Oíste lo del último accidente de aviación?
—¿Te refieres al accidente en que murieron cerca de 150 personas?

—Sí. Dicen que sucedió° por pura negligencia. — pasó
—Es difícil creerlo, ¿no? Parece imposible que el piloto no pudiera hacer nada para evitarlo.° — *to avoid it*
—Bueno, hay que tomar en cuenta que es posible que el avión tuviera un desperfecto.° — ¿ ?
—No creo que fuera eso... Si las autoridades se interesaran más por proteger al público...
—Bueno. Es cuestión de opiniones. Personalmente creo que sí se interesan.
—¡Pero no lo suficiente! Yo creo que...

En el periódico

—¿Algo nuevo?
—¡Qué va! Centroamérica está a punto de estallar,° la tensión sigue creciendo° en el Golfo Pérsico, la situación en el Oriente Medio continúa igual de catastrófica... — *explode* / ¿ ?
—Ya veo. Lo de siempre.

Después de las elecciones

—Te digo de verdad que nunca creí que hubiera alguien que apoyara a ese candidato.
—Ya lo ves. No les importó su postura° sobre el desarme nuclear. — *position*
—¿Qué le vamos a hacer, pues?
—Bueno... esperar las próximas elecciones.

Conversación

Con un compañero (una compañera), exprese dos opiniones distintas sobre cada uno de los siguientes temas en diálogos de cinco a seis oraciones. **¡OJO!** *No* es necesario que expresen sus opiniones personales. Sólo deben presentar dos puntos de vista opuestos.

- la pena de muerte: ¿castigo (*punishment*) inhumano o freno necesario para el crimen?
- la censura de las canciones rock: ¿tema «de moda» o es necesaria para proteger a la juventud?
- el desarme nuclear: ¿amenaza a la libertad o compromiso inteligente?

Notas culturales: Formas de gobierno

No es por casualidad que los hispanoamericanos llaman a España la «madre patria». Cuando los conquistadores llegaron al Nuevo Mundo, instalaron un sistema de gobierno, controlado directamente desde España, que duró casi doscientos años. Pero a pesar de los vínculos (*in spite of the ties*) culturales, sociales y religiosos que existen entre estos países y España, ha habido también muchas diferencias entre ellos, sobre todo en el área de la política.

España tiene una larga tradición monárquica, empezando con la unificación política de la península que ocurrió cuando se casaron la reina Isabel y el rey Fernando en 1469. Esta tradición ha sido interrumpida sólo por dos períodos republicanos, una guerra civil (1936–1939) y la dictadura del general Francisco Franco (1939–1975). Según la Constitución Española de 1978, «La forma política del Estado español es la Monarquía parlamentaria.» El monarca actual, el rey don Juan Carlos, se inclina por las reformas democráticas.

En Hispanoamérica, el siglo XIX es la época de las guerras de independencia y de los libertadores. Se destaca (*stands out*) entre todos la figura de Simón Bolívar, quien es para Sudamérica lo que Jorge Washington es para los norteamericanos: el verdadero padre de la independencia. En la actualidad todavía continúan las luchas (*struggles*) en Hispanoamérica. Ha habido—y sigue habiendo (*there continue to be*)—guerras de guerrillas en algunos países y verdaderas revoluciones en otros. El objetivo de éstas es lograr (*achieve*) cambios políticos, económicos y sociales.

UN POCO DE TODO

A. **Siempre los mismos problemas.** Cambie por el pasado.

1. Es increíble que haya tantos problemas mundiales.
2. No creo que nadie sepa todas las soluciones.
3. Siento que no se pueda resolver todos los problemas.
4. Las autoridades siempre niegan que la culpa sea suya.
5. Los ciudadanos piden que alguien haga algo por ellos.

Siga con la historia, haciendo oraciones completas según las indicaciones.

6. ser / necesario / que / todos / cumplir (*to fulfill*) / con / responsabilidades / suyo
7. haber / suficiente / recursos / para que / nadie / sufrir / ninguno / privación
8. ¿haber / gobierno / que / ser / mejor / nuestro?
9. (yo) dudar / que / se / formar / nunca / sociedad / perfecto
10. (yo) sugerir / que / todo / ciudadanos / trabajar / junto / para / crear / mundo / mejor

B. **Situaciones.** Imagine that you are a member of the family featured in the following situations and describe what you wanted to happen. Begin your reactions with **Yo prefería que...** , **Yo quería que...** , or **Yo insistía en que...** Incorporate the information given in parentheses or equivalent information that is real for you.

1. El verano pasado, mi esposo/a y yo fuimos a las montañas con todos los niños. (playa; solos)
2. Durante las mismas vacaciones, alquilamos una casa vieja y en malas condiciones. Vinieron a visitarnos todos nuestros amigos. (nueva y con todas las comodidades; todos nuestros parientes)

3. El año pasado mi esposo/a quería que gastáramos mucho en comida y vivienda. (menos; más en la educación de los niños)
4. Anoche fuimos a ver una película italiana. Usamos el coche de mi esposo/a. (francesa; mi coche)
5. Pasamos la última Navidad con la familia de mi esposo/a. (mi familia; pasar la Nochebuena con los padres de él/ella)

C. Examine el siguiente dibujo de Mafalda, una niña argentina a quien no le gusta nada la sopa que su madre insiste en prepararle. Luego complete las oraciones para formar una historia completa.

Frases útiles: estar listo/a, soñar(ue) con (*to dream about*), soñar que (*to dream that*), llenar un plato

1. Anoche, mientras dormía, Mafalda ____.
2. Soñaba que estaba ____.
3. Cuando la sopa ____, Mafalda ____.
4. Llevó el plato ____ y ____.
5. Su ____ estaba sentada a la mesita.
6. Mafalda veía a su madre como si ésta (*as if the latter*) ____. (¡OJO! *past subjunctive*)
7. Mafalda quería que su madre ____.
8. Pero cuando su madre ____, ____.
9. Es probable que Mafalda soñara todo esto, porque con frecuencia su madre quiere que ____.

Ahora cuente Ud. lo que va a pasar después. ¿Que va a hacer la madre? ¿Qué va a hacer Mafalda?

CH. **El noticiero de las seis (Parte 1).** Complete the following news flashes with the correct form of the words in parentheses, as suggested by the context. When two possibilities are given in parentheses, select the correct word. Use the past participle of infinitives indicated with an asterisk.

Trenton, New Jersey, Estados Unidos

Se reveló ayer que los comandantes de las bases navales de los Estados Unidos han (*recibir*[1])* órdenes «supersecretas» de (*intensificar*[2]) las medidas de seguridad.° Se (*creer*[3]) que terroristas (*pensar*[4]) sabotear instalaciones norteamericanas. Estas órdenes, (*emitir*°[5])* por el jefe de operaciones navales, (*mandar*[6]) que los comandantes (*aumentar*[7]) las medidas de seguridad para que no (*ocurrir*[8]) otra tragedia como el ataque contra el cuartel de los marinos en Beirut.

medidas... *security measures*
to issue

Moscú

Hoy todo Moscú se está (*preguntar*[9]) si el jefe del Estado y del Partido Comunista va a (*asistir*[10]) mañana sábado (*por/de*[11]) la tarde a la solemne reunión (*organizar*[12])* por el Kremlin para (*celebrar*[13]) el aniversario (*del/de la*[14]) revolución bolchevique. Hace varios meses que el jefe no (*aparecer*[15]) en público y es posible que (*ser/estar*[16]) gravemente enfermo. Hasta este momento, claro, la prensa soviética no (*haber decir*[17]) nada al respecto.° Mañana sábado, a las 17 horas, no sólo el cuerpo° diplomático y los periodistas (*extranjero*[18]), sino° también la población soviética va a (*ser/estar*[19]) ante° los televisores para (*ver*[20]) si la directiva° del Partido hace su entrada° en la Sala de Congreso del Kremlin.

al... *about it* / *corps*
but
in front of / *leadership*
entrance

VOCABULARIO

VERBOS

apoyar to support
castigar to punish
comunicarse (con) to communicate (with)
durar to last
enterarse (de) to find out (about)
gobernar (ie) to govern, rule
informar to inform
luchar to fight
merecer (merezco) to deserve
obedecer (obedezco) to obey
ofrecer (ofrezco) to offer
protestar to protest
votar to vote

LAS ÚLTIMAS NOVEDADES

el acontecimiento event, happening
el asesinato assasination
el barrio neighborhood
el canal (TV) channel
el choque collision
el desastre disaster
la (des)igualdad (in)equality
la esperanza hope, wish
la guerra war
la huelga strike (*labor*)
la libertad liberty, freedom
las noticias news
el noticiero newscast
el/la obrero/a worker
la paz peace
la prensa press; news media
el/la reportero/a reporter
el/la testigo witness

EL GOBIERNO Y LA RESPONSABILIDAD CÍVICA

el/la ciudadano/a citizen
el deber responsibility; obligation
los demás others, other people
el derecho right
el/la dictador(a) dictator
la dictadura dictatorship
la ley law
el rey/la reina king/queen

PALABRAS ADICIONALES

tomar/tener en cuenta to keep/to have in mind, take into account

Frases útiles para la comunicación

ojalá + *past subjunctive*	*I wish... could/would*
¡Ojalá pudiera asistir!	*I wish I could attend.*
¡Ojalá llamaran esta noche!	*I wish they would call tonight!*

UN PASO MÁS 16

OPTIONAL SECTION

Optional A: ¿Está Ud. de acuerdo con las siguientes afirmaciones? ¿Hay situaciones en que se puedan justificar? Explique. **1.** *Debe constituir un delito el* **no** *ofrecer ayuda a una persona que se encuentra en grave peligro.* **2.** *Debe haber un límite legal en el número de hijos que un matrimonio puede tener.* **3.** *Todos debemos tener la libertad de decir lo que nos dé la gana (cualquier cosa).* **4.** *Deben ser prohibidas las manifestaciones* (demonstrations) *de los nazis y de los del KKK.* **5.** *Es la responsabilidad de la comunidad—y no del gobierno—el ayudar a los pobres.* **6.** *Cada comunidad tiene el derecho de censurar los libros y otro material didáctico usado en las escuelas públicas.* **7.** *El votar en las elecciones nacionales debe ser la obligación legal de todo ciudadano.* **8.** *Es un derecho del individuo* **no** *obedecer una ley que le parezca injusta o estúpida.*

Actividad A. Una elección difícil

Aquí hay una lista de los derechos que consideramos básicos en este país. Para Ud., ¿cuáles son los más importantes y cuáles son los menos importantes? Póngalos en orden de importancia (**1** = el más importante). Luego compare su lista con las de los otros miembros de la clase. ¿Hay algún derecho que tenga prioridad sobre los demás? ¿Por qué tiene tanta importancia para Uds.?

EL RESPETO
Respetar la zona de los otros animales, es algo muy claro en ellos. Este respeto se basa en la supervivencia, en la protección contra los depradadores y, los animales pequeños, tienen defensas exclusivas frente a los animales grandes que pueden llegar a vencer en un momento dado. Por eso hay respeto.
Si los animales se respetan, nosotros, ¿Por qué no?
Un mensaje
VICUÑA
40 AÑOS

_____ el derecho a la libertad de expresión
_____ el derecho a la asociación libre
_____ el derecho a no dar testimonio
_____ el derecho a ser juzgado (*judged*) por un jurado
_____ el derecho a llevar armas
_____ el derecho a la igualdad de oportunidades para todos en el mundo laboral
_____ el derecho a recibir una educación gratis

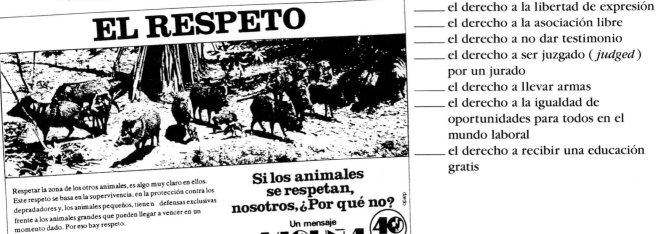

De los derechos anteriores, ¿cuáles pueden ser los más importantes para los siguientes individuos? Explique sus respuestas.

1. una mujer divorciada con tres hijos
2. un granjero (*farmer*) que vive en Kansas
3. un miembro de un grupo minoritario que vive en un barrio pobre de Los Ángeles
4. un senador en Washington, D.C.
5. un adolescente residente en Chicago

Follow-up A: ¿Con quién(es) está Ud. más de acuerdo con respecto a los derechos?

Actividad B. Continúa el noticiero de las seis

In this chapter you have read and talked about news events of all kinds—some international in scope, some local. Follow the model of those articles or news flashes and, working with another student, write three brief news items. Two of them should describe real events that have appeared recently in the news. The third should be imaginary, perhaps the invented perspective of someone who has appeared in a recent news item but whose "side of the story" has not been told. Present your news items to the class. Your classmates will determine which of the three news items is a fabrication.

A propósito... More About Influencing Others

Command forms and indirect requests with the subjunctive are not always the best way of getting someone to do something. Often a greater degree of politeness is necessary in order not to offend the person you are addressing.

Here are some examples of how to initiate a request that someone do—or stop doing—something.

Por favor, ¿puede/pudiera Ud... ? ¿quiere/quisiera Ud... ?
Por favor, ¿me trae... ? ¿me pasa... ? ¿me da... ? ¿me dice/explica... ?

The last series of questions can also be declarative statements: **Por favor, me trae el periódico**. To be even more polite, you could also add **...si (Ud.) es/fuera tan amable** to the end of the sentence.

The other side of making a request is responding to one. When someone asks a favor of you, you may or may not want—or even be able—to comply. Here are a few ways to indicate your willingness to help.

¡Sí, sí!	Sí, no hay problema.	¡Por supuesto!
¡Cómo no!	¡Claro!	¡Con mucho gusto!

If the favor is not one that you can grant, use phrases such as the following.

Lo siento. Realmente quisiera hacerlo, pero no puedo por(que)...
(Desgraciadamente) No es posible ahora por(que)...

▲ Actividad C. ¿Me hace el favor de... ?

Suggestion C: Instructor plays role of other person mentioned in situations.

The following are common situations in which you might need to ask for something or in which someone might make a request of you. What might you say in each situation? Try to offer several different responses, when possible.

1. En la mesa, durante la cena, Ud. necesita la sal, pero el salero está al otro lado de la mesa, cerca del señor de la casa.
2. Sus padres le han mandado un cheque desde los Estado Unidos, pero Ud. no lo ha recibido todavía. Ud. necesita un poco de dinero y habla con su amigo Jaime.
3. Ud. se encuentra en una esquina de Madrid y no sabe dónde está. Con el mapa en la mano, Ud. para a dos personas y les pregunta: ...
4. Su amiga Marta le pregunta si Ud. le puede prestar unos discos para una fiesta. Marta tiene fama de olvidarlo todo.
5. Un compañero le pide prestado un dólar y Ud. tiene diez. No es una molestia prestarle dinero.
6. Otro compañero acaba de pedirle prestados cincuenta dólares. Ud. no tiene disponible esa cantidad y tampoco tiene mucha confianza en él.
7. Alguien le pide prestado su coche. Pero el coche no es suyo; es de su papá y Ud. sabe que a él no le gusta que otras personas lo manejen.

LECTURA CULTURAL

Lectura: See IM for suggestions and additional exercises and activities.

Aspectos de la «mili»

Los siguientes artículos de España tratan dos aspectos muy diferentes de la vida militar. Antes de empezar a leerlos, lea los ejercicios de comprensión.

Un ex-combatiente de la guerra civil vivía en cuevas de montaña desde 1939

LA CORUÑA. — El ex-combatiente de la guerra civil española Manuel Durán Souto vivió en cuevas de las montañas lucenses de Ourol desde 1939.

Según un reportaje del matutino coruñés "La Voz de Galicia", Manuel Durán, fue legionario en Africa y combatió en el Ejército del general Franco, llegando a alcanzar el grado de sargento en la campaña de Asturias.

Cuando terminó la guerra se encontraba herido en Zaragoza y al ser dado de alta se trasladó° a las montañas de O Sixto, cerca de su pueblo natal de Ambosores, en una parte abrupta de la provincia de Lugo, donde decidió vivir como ermitaño.

Manuel Durán, que según el diario coruñés presenta síntomas de pérdidas de razón alternados con momentos de lucidez, estuvo durante 48 años vagando de cueva en cueva y alimentándose con hierbas y hiedras, hasta que hace seis meses, cuando padeció° una pulmonía, única enfermedad en todo ese período, fue convencido para que viva en una choza° próxima a la casa de sus parientes.

padeció: sufrió

choza: *hut*

Los vecinos de este ermitaño explicaron al periódico que, dos veces al año, hacía un viaje a pie hasta La Coruña, recorriendo más de un centenar de kilómetros por montes, sin acercarse a lugares habitados, solamente para ver el mar, tras lo cual retornaba a sus refugios lucenses.

El ex-combatiente estuvo dado por desaparecido durante muchos años, y recobró recientemente la identidad, poco antes de cumplir los 70, con el reconocimiento de una paga de 15.000 pesetas mensuales como herido de guerra, gracias a las gestiones de los familiares y del párroco de Ambosores.

se trasladó: se... se mudó

Precisamente este sacerdote lo convenció, recientemente, para que asistiera a la fiesta del patrón del pueblo,

Según una encuesta° del Centro de Investigaciones Sociológicas

survey

Los jóvenes quieren que la "mili" dure sólo seis meses

MADRID, 14. — Los jóvenes estiman que el servicio militar debe durar 6 meses, según se desprende de los datos de una encuesta que ha elaborado el Centro de Investigaciones Sociológicas.

Los 6 meses de "mili" es la media de tiempo ideal reflejada en las 2.500 entrevistas realizadas a jóvenes de 16 a 24 años pertenecientes a todas las provincias españolas excluidas las insulares y Ceuta y Melilla.

Un 49 por ciento de los encuestados se pronuncia a favor de un Ejército totalmente profesional, tanto en el personal de mando como en el de tropa y un 25 por ciento por un sistema mixto.

Este sistema mixto —para los jóvenes preguntados— debería mantener el servicio militar obligatorio pero todos los puestos que requieran una cualificación o especialización técnica serían cubiertos por militares profesionales, tanto en la escala de mando como en la tropa.

El 44 por ciento de los encuestados° afirma que con los 12 meses de servicio en filas, y debido a la complejidad de los medios militares actuales, es imposible que las tropas estén preparadas adecuadamente.

los... *the people interviewed*

La mayoría de los encuestados (52 por ciento) estima que la defensa de la Nación afecta a todos los españoles y que todos debemos prepararnos para realizarla y un 37 por ciento está en desacuerdo con esta idea.

Al ser preguntados sobre si participarían de una manera voluntaria en la defensa armada de España en el caso de que fuese atacada militarmente, el 23 por ciento dice que **"no, con toda seguridad"** y el 20 por ciento que **"sí, con toda seguridad"**.

Otro 29 por ciento manifiesta que **"probablemente sí"** y el 18 por ciento que **"probablemente no"**.

Comprensión

Complete las siguientes tablas según los artículos.

A. «Un ex-combatiente... »

1. Nombre y edad del soldado: _____
2. Nombre de la guerra en que participó: _____
3. Año en que empezó a vivir en una cueva: _____
4. Enfermedad que sufrió: _____
5. Su estado mental: _____
6. Cosa que quería ver cada dos años: _____
7. Donde vive ahora: _____
8. Recompensa recibida del gobierno: _____

B. «Los jóvenes quieren... »

1. Tiempo que el servicio militar debe durar, según los jovenes encuestados: _____
2. Porcentaje a favor de un ejército profesional: _____
3. ¿En qué consiste un sistema «mixto»? _____
4. Porcentaje que *no* está de acuerdo con la idea de que la defensa de España afecta a todos: _____ Porcentaje que dice que sí: _____
5. Opinión mayoritaria sobre la posible participación en la defensa de España en caso de ataque: _____

Para escribir

A. Imagine que Ud. va a entrevistar a Manuel Durán Souto. Escriba por lo menos 10 preguntas que le gustaría hacerle sobre su historia. Luego intercambie preguntas con otro estudiante y conteste sus preguntas como si Ud. fuera Manuel Durán.

B. Escriba preguntas para una encuesta según la información en «Los jóvenes quieren... » y hágala en su clase. ¿Cómo se comparan las respuestas de sus compañeros con las de los jóvenes españoles encuestados?

CAPÍTULO DIECISIETE

EL DINERO

San Juan, Puerto Rico

▲ **¡La vida es cara!**

—No sé qué pasa. El dinero nunca me alcanza.[a]

—¿En qué lo gastas?

—Pues... en el alquiler, en la luz, en la comida, en libros, en cassettes, en el cine...

—Yo creo que tengo menos gastos que tú.

—Claro, porque tú todavía vives con tus padres. Hace un año que tengo mi propio apartamento.

[a]El... *I never have enough money.*

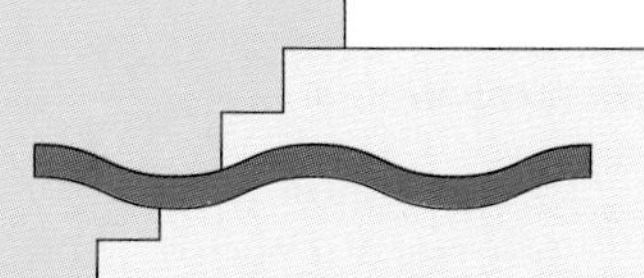

Vocabulario: Preparación:
• See detailed supplementary materials for this section bound into the back of this Annotated Instructor's Edition.
• See model for vocabulary presentation and other materials in Supplementary *Vocabulario: Preparación* Materials, chapter by chapter, IM.

VOCABULARIO: PREPARACIÓN

• See also

Una cuestión de dinero

el alquiler	rent	**ahorrar**	to save (*money*)
el banco	bank	**aumentar**	to increase
el/la cajero/a	cashier	**cargar** (**a la cuenta de uno**)	to charge (to someone's account)
la cuenta/factura	bill	**cobrar**	to cash (*a check*); to charge (*someone for an item or service*)
la cuenta corriente	checking account		
la cuenta de ahorros	savings account		
el cheque	(*bank*) check		
los gastos	expenses	**devolver** (**ue**)	to return (*something*)
la libreta de ahorros	bank book	**economizar**	to economize
el préstamo	loan	**gastar**	to spend (*money*)
el presupuesto	budget	**ingresar/sacar**	to put in, deposit/to take out
el talonario de cheques	checkbook	**pagar a plazos/al contado/con cheque**	to pay in installments/in cash/by check
la tarjeta de crédito	credit card	**prestar**	to lend
		quejarse (**de**)	to complain (about)

Suggestion A: Do as role play, with instructor taking role of Spanish-speaking clerk (left-hand column).

A. Indique una respuesta para cada pregunta o situación. Luego invente un contexto para cada diálogo. ¿Dónde están las personas que hablan? ¿en un banco? ¿en una tienda? ¿Quiénes son? ¿clientes? ¿cajeros? ¿dependientes?

1. ¿Cómo prefiere Ud. pagar?
2. ¿Hay algún problema?
3. Me da su pasaporte, por favor. Necesito verlo para que pueda cobrar su cheque.
4. ¿Quisiera usar su tarjeta de crédito?
5. ¿Va a depositar este cheque en su cuenta corriente o en su cuenta de ahorros?
6. ¿Adónde quiere Ud. que mandemos la factura?

a. En la cuenta de ahorros, por favor.
b. Me la manda a la oficina, por favor.
c. No, prefiero pagar al contado.
ch. Sí, señorita, Ud. me cobró demasiado por el jarabe.
d. Aquí lo tiene Ud. Me lo va a devolver pronto, ¿verdad?
e. Cárguelo a mi cuenta, por favor.

Variation B: Do as written exercise: students select 1–2 items to use as paragraph opening sentences.

Variation B: Do as written exercise.

B. **Situaciones.** ¿Quiénes son estas personas? ¿Dónde están? ¿Qué van a comprar? ¿Cómo van a pagar? ¿Qué van a hacer después?

1. 2.

3.

C. **Definiciones.** Dé una definición de estas palabras en español.

1. el presupuesto
2. economizar
3. el préstamo
4. la factura
5. el alquiler
6. pagar a plazos

Ahora explique la diferencia entre una cuenta corriente y una cuenta de ahorros; entre un talonario de cheques y una libreta de ahorros; entre ingresar dinero en una cuenta y sacarlo.

Follow-up CH: ***Preguntas:*** **1.** *¿Tiene Ud. un presupuesto?* **2.** *¿Cuáles son los gastos más grandes que Ud. tiene cada mes?* **3.** *Si Ud. tiene que economizar, ¿hay gastos que pueda eliminar fácilmente?* **4.** *¿Qué gasto es imposible eliminar?*

CH. De estas oraciones, ¿cuáles describen la situación económica suya?

1. Me resulta imposible ahorrar dinero. Siempre aumentan los gastos.
2. Uso demasiado mis tarjetas de crédito; por eso tengo muchas cuentas que pagar.
3. Es mejor pagar al contado que cargarlo todo a la cuenta.
4. Necesito dos empleos para poder pagar todas mis cuentas.
5. Si mi producto favorito sube un 50 por ciento de precio, dejo de comprarlo.
6. Si el dependiente de una tienda me cobra demasiado, me quejo en seguida.
7. Si no tengo dinero al final del mes, saco dinero de mi cuenta de ahorros.
8. En mi cuenta corriente siempre tengo mucho dinero al final del mes.
9. Siempre les pido dinero prestado (*borrow*) a mis amigos, pero nunca se lo devuelvo.
10. Tengo muchos amigos que no me devuelven nunca el dinero que les presto.

D. Haga Ud. una descripción de la situación económica de estas dos personas. Incluya todos los detalles que sean posibles.

1. el señor Rodríquez, presidente de la compañia «Universal, S.A.»*
2. Juan Típico (Juana Típica), estudiante de esta universidad

Notas culturales: El pluriempleo

En los países de habla española, como también en los Estados Unidos, el pluriempleo (*moonlighting*) es una faceta importante de la economía. Es común en casi todos los países y entre todas las clases sociales, pero sobre todo (*especially*) entre las familias de la clase pobre y la clase media.

Para algunas familias el pluriempleo representa una oportunidad para poder aumentar sus ingresos (*income*). El segundo salario les facilita la compra de artículos de lujo: un televisor, un coche. Para otras familias, en cambio, el pluriempleo es una necesidad impuesta por su situación económica. La familia no puede vivir bien con un solo salario. En vez de (*Instead of*) vivir estrechamente (*barely making ends meet*), uno de los miembros de la familia busca un trabajo por la noche o de tiempo parcial. Estas personas trabajan por necesidad, no por gusto.

El pluriempleo no corresponde a la idea que los estadounidenses tienen de los latinos. Sin embargo, la situación de un profesor que enseña durante el día y trabaja de camarero por la noche está más de acuerdo con la realidad hispánica que el estereotipo del indio con el burrito durmiendo la siesta junto al cacto.

***S.A.** is the abbreviation for **Sociedad Anónima**, the Spanish equivalent of *Incorporated* (*Inc.*).

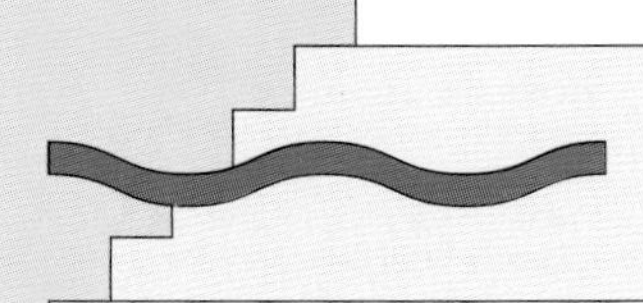

MINIDIÁLOGOS Y GRAMÁTICA

Communicative objectives for 48: another way to talk about future

48. TALKING ABOUT THE FUTURE
Future Verb Forms

Ask: What is stem for future? (→ infinitive)

¡Hay que reducir los gastos! ¿Qué vamos a hacer?

MADRE: *Tomaré* el autobús en vez de usar el carro.
ANDRÉS: *Comeremos* más ensalada y menos carne y pasteles.
PADRE: Los niños no *irán* al cine con tanta frecuencia.
JULIETA: Yo *dejaré* de fumar.
MADRE: Los niños *gastarán* menos en dulces.
PADRE: Y yo no *cargaré* nada a nuestras cuentas. Lo *pagaré* todo al contado.
JULIETA: *Bajaremos* la calefacción.
GABRIELA: Y yo me *iré* a vivir con los abuelos. Allí *habrá* de todo como siempre, ¿verdad?

1. ¿Quién dejará de usar el carro? ¿de fumar?
2. ¿Qué comerá la familia? ¿Qué no comerá?
3. ¿Cómo gastará menos dinero el padre? ¿y los niños?
4. ¿Adónde irá a vivir Gabriela? ¿Por qué?

Follow-up: Listening (*¿sí o no?*) or *Preguntas* (introduce -é ending for *yo* form) *Imagine que Ud. está en la misma situación económica que la familia en el diálogo: es necesario reducir los gastos. ¿Qué va a hacer Ud.?* **1.** *¿Tomará el autobús en vez de usar el carro?* **2.** *¿Comerá en casa con más frecuencia en vez de comer en restaurantes?* **3.** *¿Comerá más ensalada? ¿menos carne? ¿menos helado o dulces?* **4.** *¿Dejará de fumar? ¿de tomar cerveza?* etc.

You have already learned to talk about the future in a number of ways. The forms of the present can be used to describe the immediate future, and the **ir** + **a** + *infinitive* construction (Grammar Section 10) is very common in both spoken and written Spanish. The future can also be expressed, however, with future verb forms.

hablar		**comer**		**vivir**	
hablar**é**	hablar**emos**	comer**é**	comer**emos**	vivir**é**	vivir**emos**
hablar**ás**	hablar**éis**	comer**ás**	comer**éis**	vivir**ás**	vivir**éis**
hablar**á**	hablar**án**	comer**á**	comer**án**	vivir**á**	vivir**án**

Suggestions:
- Present future of regular verbs.
- Form brief questions with *comprar, beber, escribir.*
- **Listening: Discrimination.** *Dé el sujeto: tomaré, regresarán, mandará, necesitarás, llevarán, viajaremos, entrará,*

It's necessary to cut down on expenses! What are we going to do? MOTHER: I'll take the bus instead of using the car. ANDRÉS: We'll eat more salad and less meat and cake. FATHER: The kids won't go to the movies so much. JULIETA: I'll stop smoking. MOTHER: The kids will spend less on candy. FATHER: And I won't charge anything. I'll pay for everything in cash. JULIETA: We'll turn down the heat. GABRIELA: And I'll go to live with our grandparents. There they'll have (there will be) everything as usual, right?

In English, the future is formed with the auxiliary verbs *will* or *shall*: ***I will/shall** speak.* In Spanish, the *future* (**el futuro**) is a simple verb form (only one word). It is formed by adding the future endings **-é**, **-ás**, **-á**, **-emos**, **-éis**, **-án** to the infinitive. No auxiliary verbs are needed.

The following verbs add the future endings to irregular stems.

decir:	**dir-**	
hacer:	**har-**	**-é**
poder:	**podr-**	**-ás**
poner:	**pondr-**	**-á**
querer:	**querr-**	**-emos**
saber:	**sabr-**	**-éis**
salir:	**saldr-**	**-án**
tener:	**tendr-**	
venir:	**vendr-**	

decir	
diré	diremos
dirás	diréis
dirá	dirán

The future of **hay** (**haber**) is **habrá** (*there will be*).*

¡OJO! Remember that indicative and subjunctive present tense forms can be used to express the immediate future. Compare the following:

Llegaré a tiempo.	*I'll arrive on time.*
Llego a las ocho mañana. ¿Vienes a buscarme?	*I arrive at eight tomorrow. Will you pick me up?*
No creo que Pepe **llegue** a tiempo.	*I don't think Pepe will arrive on time.*

¡OJO! When English *will* refers not to future time but to the willingness of someone to do something, Spanish uses a form of the verb **querer**, not the future.

¿**Quieres** cerrar la puerta, por favor?	*Will you please close the door?*
¿**Quisieras** cerrar la puerta?	*Would you close the door?*

compraré, celebraremos, aprenderán, comprenderás, leeré, creerán, vivirá.

- Present irregular futures and *habrá* in brief conversational exchanges.
- **Point out:** similarities among irregular stems: **(1)** loss of vowel: *poder, querer, saber*; **(2)** loss of 2 letters: *decir, hacer*; **(3)** *-d-* substituted for theme vowel: *poner, salir, tener, venir*
- **Emphasis:** Will (→ willingness) = form of *querer*.
- **Note:** Future perfect is presented only in footnote. Active production is not required.
- **Preliminary Exercises: Rapid Response Drill:** *Dé el futuro.* *yo: cantar, visitar, acostarse, vender, asistir, escribir* *tú: estudiar, casarse, ayudar, aprender, recibir, divertirse* *Ud./él/ella: pagar, terminar, guardar, correr, pedir, dormir* *nosotros: regresar, esperar, gastar, comer, insistir, servir* *Uds./ellos/ellas: dejar, leer, abrir, vivir*
- *Son las tres de la tarde, un viernes, y todos han recibido el cheque semanal* (weekly). *Claro que todos tratarán de cobrar el cheque antes de que se cierren los bancos, pero... ¿qué harán después? Conteste según las indicaciones.* *—Algunos comprarán comestibles. Otros ______. (pagar las cuentas, volver a hacer un presupuesto, depositar un poco en la cuenta de ahorros, quejarse porque nunca tienen suficiente, decir que ya no usarán las tarjetas de crédito. ¿ ?)*

Práctica

Follow-up A: Students redo the items, changing them to describe a trip that they would like to take and adding additional information when possible.
***Modelo:** ver una presentación del Ballet Folklórico →*
Veré algunas presentaciones del Ballet Folklórico porque me interesan muchos aspectos de la cultura indígena.

A. **Un viaje en grupo.** Un grupo de amigos piensa hacer un viaje a México este verano. Imagine que Ud. forma parte de ese grupo y haga oraciones según las indicaciones para hacer algunos comentarios respecto al viaje.

1. yo
   - hablar sólo español
   - leer mucho en español: periódicos, revistas...
   - conocer a mucha gente joven
   - ver un programa del Ballet Folklórico

*The future forms of the verb **haber** are used to form the *future perfect tense* (**el futuro perfecto**), which expresses what *will have* occurred at some point in the future.

Para mañana, ya **habré hablado** con Miguel.	*By tomorrow, I will have spoken with Miguel.*

You will find a more detailed presentation of these forms in Appendix 2, Additional Perfect Forms (Indicative and Subjunctive).

CREDITO

En el acto, sin salir de la oficina, toda una innovación que aumenta la rapidez, la facilidad y la comodidad cuando usted desee obtener dinero en efectivo para gastar en lo que quiera, desde **100.000** hasta **2.000.000** de pesetas. Desde 6 meses a 3 años para pagarlo. Con sólo responder a un sencillo cuestionario, la concesión de su Crédito Personal Rápido es instantánea; usted tendrá el dinero que precise, incluso en cuestión de minutos.

BANCO CENTRAL

No pierda la oportunidad.

2. tú
   - levantarse temprano todos los días
   - comer comida típica
   - aprender mucho sobre la historia de México
   - visitar todos los museos
3. nosotros
   - cambiar mucho dinero en los bancos
   - escribir muchas tarjetas postales
   - comprar muchos recuerdos
   - regatear en los mercados
4. Uds.
   - no usar demasiado las tarjetas de crédito
   - querer pagarlo todo al contado
   - tratar de adaptarse a un presupuesto
   - regresar a los Estados Unidos con algún dinero
5. Gustavo
   - gastar todo su dinero muy pronto
   - pasar todo el tiempo con otros turistas
   - tener que volver pronto a los Estados Unidos
   - estar muy descontento con el viaje

¿Cierto o falso? Corrija las oraciones falsas.

1. Todos los miembros del grupo tendrán mucho cuidado con el dinero.
2. Nadie aprenderá nada sobre la cultura del país.
3. Todos harán por lo menos algunas de las cosas que siempre les interesan a los turistas.

Follow-up B: 1. *¿Pagará Ud. con atraso todas sus cuentas? ¿Cuándo las pagará?* **2.** *¿Tratará de adaptarse a un presupuesto? ¿Cómo lo hará?* **3.** *¿Tendrá que hacer un presupuesto para el próximo mes? ¿Por qué le será (o no le será) necesario hacerlo?* **4.** *¿Ingresará algo en su cuenta de ahorros? ¿Sacará algo?* **5.** *¿Se quejará de su situación económica? ¿Por qué?* **6.** *¿Usará sus tarjetas de crédito? ¿Cuándo las dejará de usar?* **7.** *¿A quién le pedirá dinero? ¿Se lo devolverá?* **8.** *¿Buscará trabajo? ¿Qué clase de trabajo?*

B. **Mi amigo Gregorio.** Describa Ud. las siguientes cosas que hará su compañero Gregorio. Luego indique si Ud. hará lo mismo (**Yo también... Yo tampoco...**) u otra cosa.

MODELO: no / gastar / menos / mes →
Gregorio no gastará menos este mes. Yo tampoco gastaré menos. (Yo sí gastaré menos este mes. ¡Tengo que ahorrar!)

1. pagar / tarde / todo / cuentas
2. tratar / adaptarse a / presupuesto
3. volver / hacer / presupuesto / próximo mes
4. no / ingresar / nada / en / cuenta de ahorros
5. quejarse / porque / no / tener / suficiente dinero
6. seguir / usando / tarjetas / crédito
7. pedirles / dinero / a / padres
8. buscar / trabajo / de tiempo parcial

¿Cuál de las siguientes oraciones describe mejor a su amigo?

1. Gregorio es muy responsable en cuanto a asuntos de dinero. Es un buen modelo para imitar.
2. Gregorio tiene que aprender a ser más responsable con su dinero.

C. **¿Cómo se dice en español?** Un grupo de turistas está en una tienda en Costa Rica. Explique cómo pagarán sus compras.

Follow-up C: Students give *tres cosas que harán hoy; tres cosas que harán mañana; tres cosas que harán este fin de semana; tres cosas que harán durante las vacaciones; tres cosas que harán después de graduarse.*

1. Mr. Adams says (that) he will pay in cash.
2. It's possible that Mrs. Walsh will use her credit card.
3. Ms. Berry will cash a check at (**en**) the bank.
4. It's necessary for the shop to send the bill to Karen's home.

Conversación

A. **Para conseguir más dinero.** What can you do to get extra cash or to save money? Some possibilities are shown in the following drawings. What are the advantages and disadvantages of each plan?

MODELO: dejar de tomar café →
Si dejo de tomar café estaré menos nervioso/a, pero será más difícil despertarme por la mañana. ¡Pero realmente quisiera dejar de tomar café!

1. pedirles dinero a mis amigos
2. cometer un robo
3. alquilar un cuarto de mi casa a otras personas
4. dejar de fumar
5. buscar un trabajo de tiempo parcial
6. ¿ ?

Follow-up B: ***Preguntas:*** **1.** *¿A qué hora llegará Ud. a casa esta noche?* **2.** *¿A qué hora cenará?* **3.** *¿A qué hora empezará a estudiar?* **4.** *¿Irá a la biblioteca?* **5.** *¿Mirará la televisión?* **6.** *¿Hablará por teléfono?* **7.** *¿Leerá mucho?* **8.** *¿Se bañará antes de acostarse?* **9.** *¿A qué hora se acostará?* **10.** *¿Se dormirá fácilmente?*

Option B: *¿Probable o improbable?* In small groups or for homework, students write realistic/unrealistic statements about what classmates and/or well-known people will be doing in 10 years. Students present statements; class indicates *probable* or *improbable.*

B. Imagine que Ud. es astrólogo/a y puede predecir (*predict*) el futuro. ¿Qué predicciones puede Ud. hacer usando una palabra o frase—en su forma correcta—de cada grupo? Use el futuro del verbo principal.

yo	conseguir	pagar todas las cuentas algún día
el profesor (la profesora)	querer	casarse, mudarse a, trabajar como ____, retirarse en (año)
mi amigo/a (nombre)	tener	un aumento de salario por fin
mis padres	(no) poder	en un país hispánico, en ____
¿ ?	ser	casado/a, soltero/a, rico/a, famoso/a, ____
	vivir	ahorrar dinero para comprar ____
	¿ ?	muchos/pocos/ningún hijo(s)
		¿ ?

Preliminary C: *Piensen en el mundo de ahora... en 25 años.* **1.** *¿Tendremos una mujer presidente?* **2.** *¿Eliminaremos las armas nucleares?* **3.** *¿Colonizaremos la luna?* **4.** *¿Tendrá computadora todo el mundo?* **5.** *¿Seremos todos bilingües?* **6.** *¿Limpiaremos el medio ambiente?* **7.** *¿Manejaremos coches todavía?* **8.** *¿Escucharemos música punk?* **9.** *¿Existirá el matrimonio todavía como institución social?*

C. Siga con sus predicciones, haciendo una descripción del mundo en el año 2500.

1. (No) Habrá ____. (pobreza [*poverty*], guerras, igualdad para todos, un gobierno mundial, gasolina, otros tipos de energía, ____)

2. La gente (no) vivirá en _____.
tendrá _____.
se quejará de _____.
hablará _____.
comerá _____.

3. Nosotros (no) viajaremos a/en _____.
usaremos más/menos _____.
podremos _____.
comeremos _____.

Point out: Future of probability in English: Cecilia must (will be) on her way here by now.

¿Está Ud. de acuerdo con las predicciones de sus compañeros de clase? Exprese su opinión, completando estas oraciones.

Estoy de acuerdo en que _____ en el futuro.
No creo que _____ en el futuro. (**¡OJO!** subjuntivo)

Suggestion: Use visuals with future of probability to speculate about the individuals pictured: *¿Quién será la mujer que espera? ¿Dónde estará esperando?* etc.

Optional exercises (future of probability):

- *Cambie por el futuro para expresar probabilidad o conjetura.*
  De compras
  1. *Cobran mucho en aquella tienda, ¿no crees?* **2.** *¿Cuánto es el precio de aquella estatua?* **3.** *Podemos usar las tarjetas de crédito aunque estamos en el extranjero.* **4.** *¡Las facturas llegan a casa antes que lleguemos nosotros!*
  Una visita de la doctora
  1. *Julito está enfermo.* **2.** *¿Cuántos grados de temperatura tiene?* **3.** *La doctora viene más tarde.* **4.** *Le da un antibiótico.*
- Los nuevos vecinos. *¿Cómo se dice en español? Use el futuro de probabilidad.*
  1. He's probably a teacher, and she must be a doctor. **2.** I wonder where she works. **3.** I wonder which one earns more money. **4.** They're probably from a big city. **5.** They probably have a lot of kids. **6.** They must be asking questions about (*acerca de*) us, too!
- *Explique las siguientes situaciones o acciones, usando el futuro de probabilidad.* **1.** *Un amigo está en la sala de espera de un hospital.* **2.** *Un amigo ha hecho una cita con el profesor(la profesora) de español.* **3.** *Un amigo está*

Notas comunicativas: Expressing Conjecture

En el aeropuerto

En la carretera

¿Dónde **estará** Cecilia?	*I wonder where Cecilia is. Where can Cecilia be?*
Cecilia **estará** en un lío de tráfico.	*Cecilia is probably (must be) in a traffic jam. I bet she's in a traffic jam.*
¿Qué le **pasará**?	*I wonder what's happening to her. I wonder what can be wrong.*
Estará tan preocupada como yo.	*She's probably (I'll bet she's) as worried as I am.*

The future can also be used in Spanish to express probability or conjecture about what is happening now. This use of the future is called the *future of probability* (**el futuro de probabilidad**). Note in the preceding examples that the English cues for expressing probability (*probably, I guess, I bet, I wonder*, and so on) are not directly expressed in Spanish. Their sense is contained in the future form of the verb.

CH. Imagine that you are a fortune teller (**un adivino/una adivina**). Using the future of probability, speculate about the current life of a member of your class or of a well-known person. Use these questions as a guide.

entrando en el banco. **4.** *Un amigo hace las maletas.* **5.** *Un amigo necesita llamar a sus padres.* **6.** *Un amigo está vestido elegantísimamente.*

1. ¿Dónde vivirá? ¿Cómo será su casa/apartamento?
2. ¿Cuántos años tendrá?
3. ¿Estará casado/a? ¿Tendrá hijos? ¿Cómo serán?
4. ¿Cuánto ganará?
5. ¿Ahorrará mucho dinero? ¿Cómo lo gastará?
6. ¿Qué le gustará hacer?
7. ¿Cuáles serán sus mayores preocupaciones?

Suggestions D:
- Bring in pictures of various parts of world. Working in small groups, students make conjectures about places, people, climates, etc.
- Students bring in pictures/photos. Class conjectures about what is happening or significance of picture.

D. Describa Ud. estas escenas.
¿Quiénes serán las personas?
¿Dónde estarán?
¿Qué estarán haciendo?
¿Qué les pasará?

1.

2.

Caracas, Venezuela

Entre amigos

—Oye, ¿me puedes prestar cien dólares?
—¡Hombre! Bueno... si me los devuelves lo antes posible.
—Cómo no. Pasado mañana a más tardar (*at the latest*).
—¿Para qué necesitas tanto dinero?
—Tengo unas cuentas atrasadas (*late*) que quisiera pagar.

Follow-up: Ask, What mood is used in dependent clause of completion questions? (→ subjunctive) Is use linked to any other subjunctive uses? (→ conceptualized, i.e., hasn't happened, action rather than description of real-world action)

49. EXPRESSING FUTURE OR PENDING ACTIONS

Subjunctive and Indicative After Conjunctions of Time

eres
salir... decir que

Complete las oraciones según el dibujo.

PADRE: Cuando yo sea anciano, Mafalda me va a preguntar...
MAFALDA: Cuando yo sea grande, papá me va a decir que...

Talking about future events in a two-clause sentence often involves the use of conjunctions of time.

cuando	when	**hasta que**	until
después (de) que	after	**tan pronto como**	as soon as
en cuanto	as soon as		

In a dependent clause after these conjunctions of time, the subjunctive is used to express a future action or state of being, that is, one that is still pending or has not yet occurred from the point of view of the main verb. The events in the dependent clauses are conceptualized—not real-world—events.

Pending Action (Subjunctive)

Saldremos **en cuanto llegue** Felipe.	*We'll leave as soon as Felipe arrives.*
Anoche, íbamos a salir **en cuanto llegara** Felipe.	*Last night we were going to leave as soon as Felipe arrived.*

The indicative is used after conjunctions of time to describe a habitual action or a completed action in the past. Compare the following:

Habitual Action (Indicative)

Siempre salimos **en cuanto llega** Felipe.	*We always leave as soon as Felipe arrives.*

Past Action (Indicative)

Anoche, salimos **en cuanto llegó** Felipe.	*Last night, we left as soon as Felipe arrived.*

The subject and verb are frequently inverted in the subordinate clause following conjunctions of time.

¡OJO! Even though it is a time conjunction, **antes de que** always requires the subjunctive (Grammar Section 45).

Suggestions:
- **Point out:** Subjunctive is always used **(1)** after certain conjunctions (Grammar Section 45); **(2)** after conjunctions of time only when they introduce future uncompleted—and therefore conceptualized—actions or states.
- **Contrast:** future action, habitual action, past action
- **Optional:** Subjunctive used with most time conjunctions even without change of subject in dependent clause: *Vamos a salir tan pronto como terminemos.* However, when no change of subject in dependent clause, *después de/hasta* + infinitive more frequently used: *Saldremos después de comer. No vamos a salir hasta terminar la tarea.*
- **Emphasis:** Subjunctive always used with *antes de que*, even though time conjunction. Because of meaning, always followed by future uncompleted action.

Preliminary Exercise: future uncompleted, habitual, or past? **1.** I'll do it when he gets here. **2.** They always write when they are abroad. **3.** We'll study until they arrive. **4.** As soon as I have the time, I'll do it. **5.** He studied until he fell asleep. **6.** She'll give us the answers after we hand in the test. **7.** We turn off the lights when we leave the house.

Preliminary Exercise: *Detalles del viaje al extranjero. Dé oraciones nuevas según las indicaciones.*
1. *En el avión, ¿qué les dice la azafata sobre las planillas* (forms) *de inmigración? —Entréguenlas ____ aterrice el avión.* (*tan pronto como, cuando, después de que, en cuanto, No... hasta que*) **2.** *Cuando el inspector quiere que Ud. le dé el pasaporte, ¿qué le dice Ud.? —Le doy el pasaporte tan pronto como (yo) ____.* (*encontrarlo, poder encontrar la llave de mi maleta, cerrar mi maleta, dármelo mi esposo/a, recordar dónde lo tengo*)

Suggestion A: Personalize each set of exercise items by asking questions of individual students. Push for detailed answers only if students are comfortable revealing this kind of information.

Práctica

A. **Hablando de dinero.** Haga oraciones completas, usando el presente del subjuntivo de los verbos indicados.

1. Julio empezará a ahorrar más en cuanto... (darle [ellos] un aumento de sueldo; dejar de gastar tanto)
2. Pagaré todas mis cuentas tan pronto como... (tener el dinero para hacerlo; ser absolutamente necesario)
3. Susana dice que dejará de usar sus tarjetas de crédito tan pronto como... (encontrar un buen trabajo; recibir el sueldo del primer mes)
4. Mis compañeros pagarán la matrícula después de que... (sus padres mandarles un cheque; cobrar su cheque en el banco)

5. No podré pagar el alquiler hasta que... (sacar dinero de mi cuenta de ahorros; ingresar el dinero en mi cuenta corriente)
6. Los García no van a retirarse hasta que su hijo... (terminar sus estudios universitarios; establecerse y casarse)
7. Vamos a volver a hablarle a Ernesto cuando... (devolvernos los cien dólares que le prestamos; dejar de pedirnos más dinero)

Note B: Review/Use of many tenses and moods.

Follow-up B: *¿Cierto o falso?* **1.** *Mariana estudia en la universidad ahora.* **2.** *En la universidad, ha seguido muchos cursos de matemáticas.* **3.** *Depende de la ayuda económica de sus padres hasta cierto punto.* **4.** *Le gusta mirar la televisión.*

B. **Dos momentos en la vida...** Compare Ud. lo que pasó y lo que pasará en el futuro en la vida de Mariana.

1. Hace cuatro años, cuando Mariana (*graduarse*) en la escuela secundaria, sus padres (*darle*) un reloj. El año que viene, cuando (*graduarse*) en la universidad, (*darle*) un coche.
2. Cuando (*ser*) niña, Mariana (*querer*) ser enfermera. Luego, cuando (*tener*) 18 años, (*decidir*) que quería estudiar computación. Cuando (*terminar*) su carrera este año, yo creo que (*poder*) encontrar un buen trabajo como programadora.
3. Generalmente Mariana no (*escribir*) cheques hasta que (*tener*) los fondos en su cuenta corriente. Sin embargo, el año pasado, (*escribir*) un cheque antes de que sus padres (*mandarle*) su cheque mensual (*monthly*). Este mes tiene muchos gastos, pero no (*ir*) a pagar ninguna cuenta hasta que le (*llegar*) el cheque.
4. Cuando (*estudiar*) en la secundaria, los padres de Mariana no le permitían mirar la tele hasta que (*terminar*) la tarea. Mariana aprendió bien la lección. Ahora nunca (*dejar*) su trabajo hasta que lo (*haber*) terminado. Yo creo que, cuando Mariana (*tener*) niños, les va a prohibir que vean la tele hasta que (*haber*) hecho sus deberes.

Conversación

A. Describa Ud. los dibujos, completando las oraciones e inventando un contexto para las escenas. Luego describa Ud. su propia vida.

Note A: Action on right of each pair indicates future uncompleted activity.

Extension A: Students complete: *Voy a ____ en cuanto ____. Siempre ____ en cuanto ____. De niño/a, ____ en cuanto ____.*

1. Pablo va a estudiar hasta que ____.

   Esta noche yo voy a estudiar hasta que ____.
   Siempre estudio hasta que ____.
   Anoche estudié hasta que ____.

2. Los señores Castro van a cenar tan pronto como ____.

   Esta noche voy a cenar tan pronto como ____.
   Siempre ceno tan pronto como ____.
   Anoche iba a cenar tan pronto como ____.

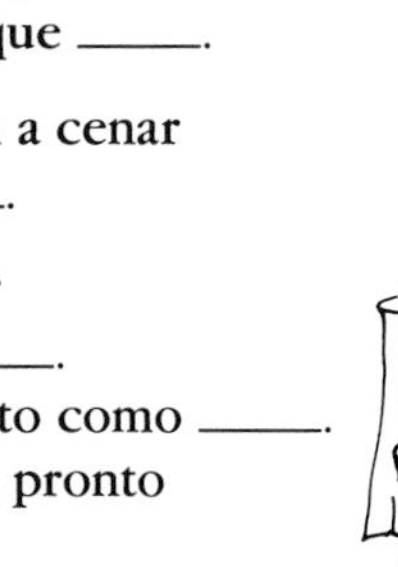

3. Lupe va a viajar al extranjero en cuanto ____.

   Voy a ____ en cuanto ____.
   Siempre ____ en cuanto ____.
   De niño/a, ____ en cuanto ____.

B. **Preguntas**

1. ¿Qué piensa Ud. hacer después de graduarse en la universidad? ¿Qué le van a regalar sus padres/amigos cuando Ud. se gradúe? ¿Qué recibió Ud. cuando se graduó en la escuela secundaria? ¿y en la primaria?
2. Cuando Ud. tenga el tiempo y el dinero, ¿adónde va a ir? ¿Adónde fue Ud. el año pasado cuando estaba de vacaciones? Cuando todavía vivía con su familia, ¿adónde iban Uds. de vacaciones?

C. ¿Qué piensa que pasará cuando se encuentre en estas situaciones en el futuro? Dígalo con tantos detalles como posible.

MODELO: Cuando sea anciano, ____. → Cuando sea anciano, no me va a gustar la música que escuchan los jóvenes.

1. Cuando por fin tenga un puesto que me guste mucho, ____.
2. Cuando tenga 40 años, ____.
3. Cuando tenga 65 años, ____.
4. Cuando sea anciano/a, ____.

SITUACIONES

Situaciones: See IM for suggestions, additional exercises, and supplementary dialogues and exercises.

Cambiando dinero en un banco

Al entrar

—Por favor. Quisiera cambiar moneda.° *money*
—Pase a la ventanilla 14, donde pone Cambio.° ¿ ?
—Gracias, ¿eh?
—De nada.

Hablando con el cajero

—Sí, dígame. ¿Qué desea?
—Quisiera cambiar unos cheques de viajero en dólares a pesetas.
—¿Cuántos dólares quiere cambiar?
—Doscientos dólares, por favor. ¿A cuánto está el cambio hoy?
—A ciento veinte. ¿Ya firmó los cheques?
—Sí.

—Su pasaporte, por favor.
—Aquí lo tiene.
(El cajero hace los trámites.°) *paperwork*
—Pase Ud. a la Caja° con este recibo.° La llamarán por este número. *Cashier's window / ¿ ?*
—¿Y cuándo me devuelven el pasaporte?
—En la Caja, señorita.

Conversación

Con un compañero (una compañera), invente las siguientes conversaciones, siguiendo el modelo del diálogo anterior. Busque en el periódico la tasa de cambio actual de la moneda indicada e incluya en el diálogo la cantidad en moneda nacional que el/la turista va a recibir.

- Un(a) turista quiere cambiar 500 dólares a pesetas (España).
- Un(a) turista quiere cambiar 100 dólares a pesos mexicanos.
- Un(a) turista quiere cambiar 200 dólares a pesos colombianos.

UN POCO DE TODO

A. **Los planes de la familia Alonso.** Haga oraciones completas según las indicaciones. Use el futuro donde sea posible.

1. ser / necesario / que / (nosotros) ahorrar / más
2. yo / no / usar / tanto / tarjetas / crédito
3. mamá / buscar / trabajo / donde / (ellos) pagarle / más
4. (nosotros) pedir / préstamo / en / banco
5. ¿creer (tú) / que / nos / lo / dar ?
6. papá / estar / tranquilo / cuando / todos / empezar / economizar
7. (tú) deber / pagar / siempre / al contado
8. no / haber / manera / de que / (nosotros) irse / de vacaciones / este verano

Según los comentarios de las personas anteriores, ¿cree Ud. que la familia Alonso está muy bien económicamente o no? Explique.

B. **Es una cuestión de bodas.** Use las conjunciones entre paréntesis para unir las dos oraciones. Haga todos los cambios necesarios. **¡OJO!** No se usa el subjuntivo en todas.

1. Miguel y Carmen se casaron. Los padres de Miguel volvieron a Colombia. (antes de que)
2. Te dije lo de la boda. Lo supe. (en cuanto)
3. Los padres se sorprendieron también. Miguel les dio la noticia. (cuando)
4. Miguel y Carmen pensaban ir de luna de miel. Terminó el semestre. (tan pronto como)
5. Les íbamos a dar una fiesta. Regresaron de su viaje. (después de que)
6. Tuvimos que cambiar de planes. Anunciaron que se habían separado por el momento. (cuando)
7. Carmen piensa esperar a Miguel. Éste regresa de Colombia. (hasta que)

Ahora conteste estas preguntas según la historia de Miguel y Carmen.

1. ¿Quién será la persona que habla?
2. ¿De dónde será Miguel? ¿y Carmen?
3. ¿Por qué Miguel no les dijo lo de la boda a sus padres antes?
4. ¿Por qué se separaron los dos?
5. ¿Cuándo regresará Miguel de Colombia?

C. **El noticiero de las seis (Parte 2).** Complete the following news flashes with the correct form of the words in parentheses, as suggested by the context. When two possibilities are given in parentheses, select the correct word. Use the past participle of infinitives indicated with an asterisk.

Santiago, Chile

Al final del próximo febrero, seis familias chilenas (*viajar*[1]) a la Antártida. Allí (*vivir*[2]) por un período de dos años como parte (*del/de la*[3]) programa de exploración y colonización del territorio antártico (*que/lo que*[4]) lleva a cabo° la Fuerza Aérea Chilena. Las seis familias (*vivir*[5]) en casas especialmente (*diseñar*[6])* y (*construir*[7])* por la Fuerza Aérea. También se (*construir*[8]) un centro comunitario donde los niños (*tener*[9]) algunas diversiones. Para poder (*participar*[10]) en la colonización de la Antártida, fue necesario que los profesionales (*estar*[11]) casados, (*tener*[12]) hijos pequeños y (*viajar*[13]) con su familia. El mayor de los niños (*que/quien*[14]) viajará a la Antártida (*tener/estar*[15]) actualmente siete años.

lleva... *is carrying out*

México

La Compañía Minera de Cananea, (*un/uno/una*[16]) de las minas de cobre° más importantes de México, fue (*vender*[17])* por el gobierno (*al/a la*[18]) consorcio (*privar*[19])* Protexa en 910 millones (*de/—*[20]) dólares, que serán (*utilizar*[21])* para el pago de la deuda° externa (*del/de la*[22]) país. El gobierno (*informar*[23]) que un conjunto° de bancos privados (*encabezar*°[24])* por el First Chicago Bank (*dar*[25]) al Grupo Protexa el financiamiento necesario para esta operación, que se (*formalizar*[26]) antes de 40 días.

copper

debt

grupo

to lead

1. **SIN LIMITES: Usted puede utilizarla en España y en todo el mundo sin límite de gastos.*** Miles de hoteles, restaurantes, establecimientos comerciales, líneas aéreas, compañías de alquiler de coches... aceptan la Tarjeta AMERICAN EXPRESS y dan la bienvenida a sus Titulares. Ya no necesitará llevar consigo importantes sumas de dinero.
2. **LA PERDIDA NO ES PROBLEMA: Su tranquilidad está garantizada si pierde o le roban la Tarjeta.** Incluso aunque no haya podido avisar a tiempo, su responsabilidad está siempre limitada a un máximo de 8.000 Ptas. Además, obtendrá una nueva Tarjeta, rápida y gratuitamente, en cualquier parte del mundo.
3. **UN SEGURO GRATUITO: Un Seguro de Accidentes de Viaje de 60.000.000 de Ptas.**** Le protege gratuitamente a usted, su cónyuge y sus hijos menores de 23 años cada vez que adquieran sus billetes de viaje con cargo a la Tarjeta.
4. **MAXIMA INFORMACION: Verificará y controlará sus gastos fácilmente,** al recibir todos los meses un Estado de Cuenta acompañado de las copias de todas las facturas. Posteriormente, el cargo le será presentado en la cuenta bancaria que usted haya designado.
5. **ASISTENCIA AMERICAN EXPRESS EN VIAJES:** Más de 1.200 Agencias de Viajes AMERICAN EXPRESS y sus Representantes en 160 países le prestarán la ayuda que necesite en sus planes de viaje o ante cualquier emergenci
6. **SU FAMILIA TAMBIEN CUENTA: Su familia también puede beneficiarse de todas estas ventajas,** disponiendo de Tarjetas Suplementarias emitidas a su nombre.

CH. **«La Tarjeta de Mayor Prestigio en el Mundo... »** Lea la siguiente descripción de las ventajas de tener una Tarjeta American Express y conteste las preguntas. **¡OJO!** Ud. no tiene que comprenderlo todo para poder contestar. Busque sólo la idea principal de cada ventaja.

¿Qué ventaja le interesará más a la persona... ?

1. que teme que le pase algún accidente mientras está viajando
2. a quien nunca le gusta pagarlo todo al contado
3. que tiene una familia grande
4. que tiene miedo de las emergencias
5. a quien siempre se le pierden las cosas
6. a quien le gusta saber exactamente lo que ha gastado

SOLICITE LA TARJETA DE
MAYOR PRESTIGIO EN EL MUNDO

VOCABULARIO

Theme vocabulary previously listed as active: *el alquiler, gastar, pagar, prestar, quejarse*

UNA CUESTIÓN DE DINERO

ahorrar to save (*money*)
aumentar to increase
cargar to charge (*to an account*)
cobrar to cash (*a check*); to charge (*someone for an item or service*)
devolver (ue) to return (*something*)
economizar to economize
ingresar to put in, deposit
pedir prestado/a to borrow

el banco bank
el/la cajero/a cashier
el cambio (rate of) exchange
la cuenta account
la cuenta corriente checking account
la cuenta de ahorros savings account
la factura bill
las ganancias earnings
los gastos expenses
la libreta de ahorros bank book
la moneda currency, money
el préstamo loan
el presupuesto budget
el talonario de cheques checkbook
la tarjeta de crédito credit card

a plazos in installments
al contado cash
con cheque by check

CONJUNCIONES

después (de) que after
en cuanto as soon as
hasta que until
tan pronto como as soon as

PALABRAS ADICIONALES

al final de at the end of
en vez de instead of
sobre todo above all, especially

Frases útiles para la comunicación

El futuro de probabilidad

¿Quién será?	Who can that be? I wonder who it is.
¿Dónde estará... ?	Where can . . . be? I wonder where . . . is.
Serán las ocho.	It must be (probably is) eight o'clock.

OPTIONAL SECTION

UN PASO MÁS 17

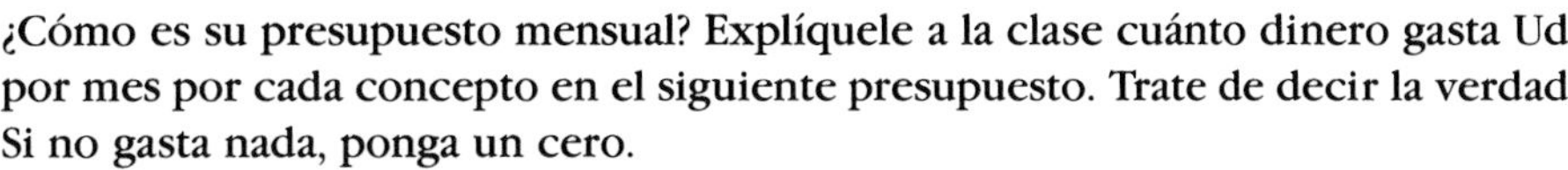

Actividad A. El presupuesto

Variations A:
- ¿Cómo será su presupuesto si su compañero/a pierde su puesto y sólo tienen Uds. novecientos dólares al mes?
- ¿Cómo será el presupuesto si Uds. tienen $5.000 al mes?

¿Cómo es su presupuesto mensual? Explíquele a la clase cuánto dinero gasta Ud. por mes por cada concepto en el siguiente presupuesto. Trate de decir la verdad. Si no gasta nada, ponga un cero.

LO ÚNICO QUE ME CONSUELA DE GANAR UN MAL SUELDO ES SABER QUE UN BUEN SUELDO TAMPOCO ALCANZA PARA NADA

1. Ropa _____
2. Casa (alquiler, hipoteca [*mortgage*]) _____
3. Gas, luz, agua, teléfono _____
4. Comida _____
5. Diversiones (cine, fiestas, restaurantes, etcétera) _____
6. Gastos médicos _____
7. Seguros (*Insurance*) (automóvil, casa, etcétera) _____
8. Automóvil (préstamos, reparaciones, gasolina, aceite, etcétera) _____
9. Educación (matrícula, libros, etcétera) _____
10. Impuestos _____
11. Ahorros _____
12. Miscelánea: _____ _____

TOTAL: _____

Ahora, con un compañero (una compañera) de clase, imagine que juntos ganan $1.500,00 al mes. ¿Cómo será su presupuesto? ¿Cómo gastarán el dinero? Conteste, usando las siguientes preguntas como guía.

1. ¿Cuánto gastarán por cada concepto (*category*)?
2. ¿Les será fácil o difícil ahorrar dinero? Expliquen.
3. Imaginen que alguien les da cinco mil dólares y Uds. pueden hacer cualquier cosa con ese dinero. ¿Qué harán con él? ¿Lo ahorrarán? ¿Comprarán algo? ¿Pagarán sus facturas? Expliquen.
4. ¿Qué harán para economizar? ¿En qué categoría podrán gastar menos? Comenten.

Actividad B. ¿Una ganga?

Activity B: Students do not need to understand every word of the application in order to do the activity.

Based on U.S. prices, are the following people getting a bargain, or are they paying an exorbitant price? Refer to the rates of exchange in the **A propósito...** section below.

1. Los señores Berriman visitan Acapulco donde alquilan una habitación en el Hotel Ritz. Pagan setenta mil pesos al día.

2. Karen Judd va a México y encuentra una habitación en un hostal de estudiantes. Paga catorce mil pesos al día. Está incluido el desayuno.
3. Pattie Myers vive en Madrid. Allí en una tienda de lujo paga cinco mil pesetas por una cartera de cuero (*leather*) para su padre.
4. Janet De Proso cena en un restaurante español. Aunque el restaurante no es de lujo, cena muy bien. Le cobran quinientas pesetas.
5. Wayne Curtis toma un taxi en Guadalajara, México. Hace un viaje de unos cuarenta kilómetros y paga ochenta y cinco mil pesos.
6. Eric Burlingame va a Colombia. Allí compra un suéter de lana por veinticuatro mil pesos.
7. Los señores Walsh van a ver la Pirámide del Sol en México. En una pequeña tienda compran un libro sobre las civilizaciones precolombinas. Es un libro grande, con muchas fotografías en colores. Pagan sesenta y dos mil quinientos pesos.

A propósito... Using Foreign Currency

Using foreign currency when traveling outside of the United States can be confusing. Often tourists have no concrete sense of what foreign currency is worth or how much they are paying for an item or a service, even though they know the current conversion factor used to exchange money at the bank.

Here are the exchange rates (**cambios**) for the currencies of several Spanish-speaking countries. These rates of exchange fluctuate; they may be different by the time you read this.

Suggestion: ***A propósito...* : Update** exchange rates before covering material in class: may have changed substantially since the summer of 1988 (when these materials were prepared).

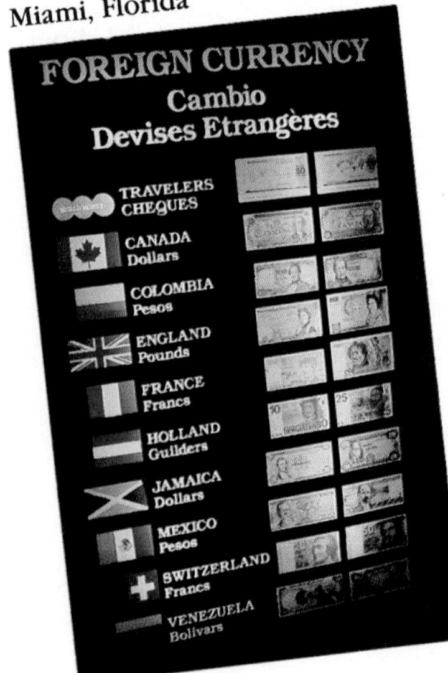

México: 1 peso = \$.0004 U.S.A. (100 pesos = \$.04)
($1.00 = 2.290 pesos; $10.00 = 22.900 pesos)
España: 1 peseta = \$.008 U.S.A. (100 pesetas = \$.87)
($1.00 = 113 pesetas; $10.00 = 1.139 pesetas)
Colombia: 1 peso = \$.003 U.S.A. (100 pesos = \$.33)
($1.00 = 295 pesos; $10.00 = 2.957 pesos)

Familiarize yourself with these exchange rates by determining the following equivalents.

¿Cuánto valen?

	a.	b.
1. 50 pesos (Méx.)	a. \$.02	b. \$1.00
2. 2.000 pesos (Méx.)	a. \$.87	b. \$1.14
3. 10.000 pesos (Méx.)	a. \$2,290	b. \$4.36
4. 300 pesetas	a. \$2.63	b. \$26.34
5. 1.000 pesetas	a. \$8.78	b. \$11,390
6. 20.000 pesetas	a. \$370	b. \$175.60
7. 500 pesos (Col.)	a. \$16.50	b. \$1.65
8. 3.000 pesos (Col.)	a. \$9.90	b. \$37.50
9. 40.000 pesos (Col.)	a. \$132	b. \$1,320

LECTURA CULTURAL

Lectura: See IM for suggestions and additional exercises and activities.

¿Cómo se ganan la vida los estudiantes?

La preocupación financiera es algo compartido por los estudiantes en todo el mundo. Aun cuando el sistema universitario esté a cargo del Estado, o sea, que es gratuito—cosa que ocurre en la mayor parte de los países de habla española—hay que tener dinero para los gastos personales, sin hablar ya de cines, cassettes, cafeterías y otras diversiones.

¿Cómo te ganas la vida, siendo estudiante? O, ¿cómo te ganabas la vida en tu época universitaria? Éstas fueron las preguntas que se hicieron a un grupo de hispanohablantes. A continuación aparecen algunas de sus respuestas.

«Desde los trece años empecé a trabajar en una oficina para así poder pagar la colegiatura de mis estudios. Trabajaba de día y estudiaba de noche.»

Eva Martínez Torres, México

«Trabajaba como ayudante en las escuelas especiales, o sea en escuelas para estudiantes incapacitados.»

María Luisa Valencia, México

«Cuando era estudiante me ganaba la vida como fotógrafo. Sacaba fotos de casamientos, bautismos, fiestas de cumpleaños y en cualquier ocasión en la que alguien estuviera dispuesto a pagarme por fotografiar.»

Eduardo Cabrera, Uruguay

Algunos de los entrevistados ofrecieron comentarios más largos. A continuación hay algunos de los más interesantes.

«Yo estudié en los Estados Unidos, pero mi sobrina, que ahora estudia para contadora° pública y que vive en Ciudad Juárez, gana su dinero juntando ropa usada de la gente rica y vendiéndola en El Paso. Los domingos mi sobrina y otras dos jovencitas alquilan un puesto° en un centro comercial y venden durante todo el día. Así ellas pagan su matrícula y gastos escolares.»

accountant

stand

Graciela Ramírez, México

«Ayudaba a enseñar a párvulos.° A los estudiantes en España, normalmente los padres les mantienen económicamente. Algunos trabajan, como por ejemplo: las chicas cuidan niños o ayudan en casa y los chicos trabajan en talleres. Pero, es raro que si los padres tienen dinero, los hijos trabajen hasta que no terminen su carrera.»

tots

Margarita Cuesta, España

«No olvidar que en la Argentina la enseñanza universitaria es gratuita. Si fuera pagada, el dinero no alcanzaría jamás° para estudiar. Claro que de todos modos los estudiantes siempre necesitan más de un trabajo y los padres ayudan con lo que pueden. Muchos no se van a otras ciudades sino que viven con sus padres y estudian en la universidad más cercana.»

no... *would never be enough*

Marianela Chaumiel, Argentina

«En la actualidad muchos estudiantes quieren independizarse de sus familias y desean vivir fuera de casa. Encontrar un trabajo es difícil para un estudiante en un país con un índice de paro° muy alto. Sin embargo hay bastantes estudiantes que trabajan fundamentalmente en bares, *pubs* o discotecas, y algunos otros trabajos.

°*unemployment*

«Otros estudiantes aprovechan la temporada turística (principalmente los meses de verano, en que la universidad está cerrada) y trabajan para ganar dinero para el curso escolar. También hay algunos que viajan a otros países como Francia para trabajar en el campo u otras cosas y vuelven para estudiar.

«En general hay que decir que es un poco más fácil para un hombre ganar dinero que para una mujer, pues estamos en una sociedad en la que domina el hombre a pesar de que la mujer se está igualando. Un ejemplo lo tenemos en que en España es bastante difícil encontrar mujeres que sean camareras.»

José Luis Suárez, España

Comprensión

Busque en la lectura por lo menos un trabajo que se relacione con las siguientes categorías.

1. Algo relacionado con los niños
2. Algo que tenga que ver con las diversiones
3. Un trabajo para la persona a quien le gusta estar al aire libre
4. Un trabajo ideal para una persona que sepa escribir a máquina
5. Algo que demuestre cierta aptitud artística
6. Algo que tenga que ver con la ropa

Para escribir

Aquí hay una lista de otros trabajos que hacen o han hecho otros estudiantes hispánicos. ¿Son trabajos que hacen también los estudiantes estadounidenses? Haga una encuesta (*survey*) entre sus compañeros, dentro o fuera de clase, o entre sus amigos o parientes para saber si alguien ha tenido o tiene los siguientes trabajos. Debe averiguar también qué clase de trabajo tienen—o tenían—si no es uno de los siguientes. Algunos estudiantes...

_____ trabajan pintando paredes en casas particulares
_____ dan clases privadas a los niños que tienen problemas en la escuela
_____ dan clases de música
_____ trabajan en negocios de venta de ropa, de comida, de zapatos, etcétera
_____ trabajan en bibliotecas
_____ venden productos de «Tupperware» o «Avon» u otros artículos de venta a domicilio
_____ realizan encuestas
_____ reparten propaganda (*advertising*)
_____ pasan trabajos a máquina (o procesan textos)

Después de hacer la encuesta, describa los resultados organizándolos en forma de que se pueda hacer una comparación entre los trabajos de los estudiantes hispánicos y los de los estadounidenses.

CAPÍTULO DIECIOCHO

HABLANDO DE CARRERAS

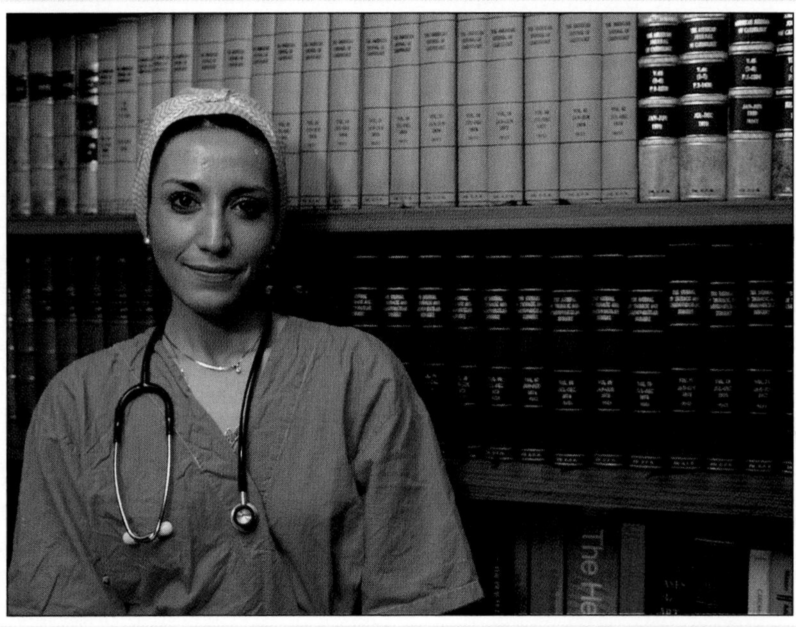

México, D.F.

▲ **¿Cuándo te gradúas?**

—¿Qué hace tu hermano? Se graduó el año pasado, ¿verdad?

—Sí, se graduó de abogado, pero no tiene trabajo todavía. Mis padres quieren que solicite un puesto en el gobierno.

—Y tú, ¿cuándo te gradúas?

—Espero que en junio.

Vocabulario: Preparación:
- See detailed supplementary materials for this section bound into the back of this Annotated Instructor's Edition.
- See model for vocabulary presentation and other materials in Supplementary *Vocabulario: Preparación* Materials, chapter by chapter, IM.

VOCABULARIO: PREPARACIÓN

- See also and

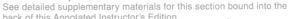

Profesiones y oficios°

°*trades*

In the preceding chapters of ***Puntos de partida***, you have learned to use a number of the words for professions and trades that appear below. Learn to use the new terms that are particularly important or interesting to you. Not all of these words will be considered "active vocabulary" that you will be expected to say or write spontaneously.

Profesiones

el/la abogado/a	lawyer
el/la analista de sistemas	systems analyst
el/la bibliotecario/a	librarian
el/la contador(a)	accountant
el/la dentista	dentist
el/la enfermero/a	nurse
el hombre/la mujer de negocios	businessman/woman
el/la ingeniero/a	engineer
el/la maestro/a	grade school teacher
el/la médico/a	doctor
el/la periodista	journalist
el/la profesor(a)	professor
el/la programador(a)	programmer
el/la siquiatra	psychiatrist
el/la trabajador(a) social	social worker
el/la traductor(a)	translator
el/la veterinario/a	veterinarian

Oficios

el/la cajero/a	cashier, teller
el/la cocinero/a	cook
el/la comerciante	merchant, shopkeeper
el/la electricista	electrician
el/la fotógrafo/a	photographer
el/la mecánico/a	mechanic
el/la obrero/a	worker, laborer
el/la peluquero/a	hairstylist
el/la plomero/a	plumber
el/la secretario/a	secretary
el soldado	soldier
el/la técnico/a	technician
el/la vendedor(a)	salesperson

Suggestion A: Do as listening comprehension exercise.

A. ¿A quién necesita Ud. en estas situaciones? ¿A quién llamará o con quién consultará?

Las empresas norteamericanas buscan humanistas

Las humanidades están de moda en las universidades norteamericanas ante el interés de las empresas por contratar "administradores flexibles, críticos y capaces de aprender continuamente", gentes con "una educación liberal" según publica la revista "Nuestro Tiempo" de la Universidad de Navarra.

Los empresarios norteamericanos pretenden aumentar los contactos de graduados en Humanidades en un 20%, en tanto que los de graduados en áreas muy especializadas crecen menos del 1%.

Por otra parte, al decir de los rectores de estos centros hoy en auge, los estudiantes han "descubierto" los clásicos y se entusiasman con ellos.

Extension B: Listening comprehension: *¿Qué profesión corresponde a cada descripción?* **1.** *Recibe muchas invitaciones para comer en buenos restaurantes. Es muy suceptible a los ataques el corazón. Viaja mucho.* **2.** *Compra y vende cosas. Pone anuncios de sus productos en la televisión, en los periódicos, etcétera. Está contento cuando los empleados venden mucho.* **3.** *Tiene que leer mucho. Tiene un puesto de mucho prestigio. A veces no sabe si su cliente es inocente o no.*

Variation B: Students give definitions of professions, following models given here.

Suggestion C: Model several recommendations before allowing students to begin the activity. Demonstrate the use of subjunctive syntax in your model.

1. Tiene problemas con la tubería (*plumbing*) de su cocina.
2. Ud. acaba de tener un accidente con el coche; el otro conductor dice que Ud. tuvo la culpa (*blame*).
3. Por las muchas tensiones y presiones de su vida profesional y personal, Ud. tiene serios problemas afectivos (*emotional*).
4. Ud. está en el hospital y quiere que alguien le dé una aspirina.
5. Ud. quiere que alguien le ayude con las tareas domésticas porque no tiene mucho tiempo para hacerlas.
6. Ud. quiere que alguien le construya una pared en el jardín.
7. Ud. conoce todos los detalles de un escándalo en el gobierno de su ciudad y quiere divulgarlos.

B. **Asociaciones.** ¿Qué profesiones u oficios asocia Ud. con estas frases? Consulte la lista de **Profesiones y oficios** y use las siguientes palabras también.

actor/actriz	carpintero/a	policía
ama de casa (*homemaker*)	consejero/a	político/a
arquitecto/a	cura/pastor(a)/rabino/a	presidente/a
azafata/camarero	detective	senador(a)
barman	pintor(a)	
camarero/a	poeta	

1. intelectual/aburrido
2. muchos/pocos años de preparación
3. sensible (*sensitive*)
4. mucho/poco dinero
5. mucho/poco poder (*power*)
6. mucha/poca responsabilidad
7. mucho/poco prestigio
8. mucha/poca prisa
9. mucho/poco peligro (*danger*)
10. mucho/poco trabajo
11. «de las nueve a las cinco»
12. en el pasado, sólo para hombres/mujeres
13. una carrera «nueva»
14. un programa de televisión

C. **¿Qué preparación se necesita para ser... ?** Imagine que Ud. es consejero universitario (consejera universitaria). Explíquele a un estudiante los cursos que debe tomar para prepararse para las siguientes carreras. Consulte la lista de cursos académicos de la página 33 y use la siguiente lista. Recomiéndele también lo que debe hacer durante los veranos y los trabajos de tiempo parcial que debe buscar para ganar experiencia en su campo.

Palabras útiles: la organización administrativa, la contabilidad (*accounting*), el márketing, la ingeniería, la pedagogía, el derecho (*law*), la sociología, la retórica (*speech*), las comunicaciones, la gerontología

1. traductor(a) en la ONU (Organización de las Naciones Unidas)
2. locutor(a) en la televisión, especializado/a en los deportes
3. contador(a) para un grupo de abogados
4. periodista en la redacción (*editorial staff*) de una revista de ecología
5. trabajador(a) social, especializado/a en los problemas de los ancianos
6. maestro/a de primaria, especializado/a en la educación bilingüe

Suggestion CH: Students report back what they learned to the class.

CH. **Entrevista.** Con un compañero (una compañera), haga y conteste preguntas para saber la siguiente información.

1. la profesión u oficio de sus padres
2. lo que hacían sus abuelos
3. si tiene un amigo o pariente que tenga una profesión extraordinaria o interesante y el nombre de esa profesión
4. lo que sus padres (su esposo/a) quiere(n) que Ud. sea
5. lo que él/ella quiere ser
6. la carrera para la cual (*which*) se preparan muchos de sus amigos

Notas culturales: Los nombres de las profesiones

En el mundo de habla española hay poco acuerdo sobre las palabras que deben usarse para referirse a las mujeres que ejercen ciertas profesiones. En gran parte, eso se debe al hecho de que (*the fact that*), en muchos de estos países, las mujeres *acaban de empezar* a ejercer esas profesiones; por eso el idioma todavía está cambiando para acomodarse a esa nueva realidad. En la actualidad se emplean, entre otras, las siguientes formas:

- Se usa el artículo **la** con los sustantivos que terminan en **-ista**.

  el dentista → **la dentista**
- En otros casos se usa una forma femenina.

  el médico → **la médica**
  el trabajador → **la** trabajadora
- Se usa la palabra **mujer** con el nombre de la profesión.

  el policía → **la mujer** policía
  el soldado → **la mujer** soldado

Escuche lo que dice la persona con que Ud. habla para saber las formas que él o ella usa. No se trata de (*It's not a question of*) formas correctas o incorrectas, sólo de usos y costumbres locales.

En busca de un puesto

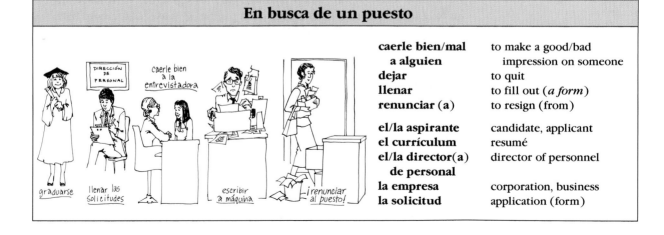

caerle bien/mal a alguien	to make a good/bad impression on someone
dejar	to quit
llenar	to fill out (*a form*)
renunciar (a)	to resign (from)
el/la aspirante	candidate, applicant
el currículum	resumé
el/la director(a) de personal	director of personnel
la empresa	corporation, business
la solicitud	application (form)

¡Participa en el mundo que has soñado!

La Escuela Internacional Tuñon te prepara para la carrera de Técnico o de Azafata en dos años de estudios.

- Una formación seria (cultura general, idiomas, informática).
- Numerosas prácticas en empresas durante la escolaridad.
- Posibilidad de intercambios entre las 23 escuelas durante el año.
- Múltiples salidas profesionales en los sectores del Turismo, Viajes, Hostelería...

Avenida Menendez Pelayo, 83 28007 MADRID Tel.: 433 80 48

ESCUELA INTERNACIONAL TUÑON 23 Escuelas en el Mundo

Fundada en 1964 Enseñanza Privada

Calle Tuset 23.25 08006 BARCELONA Tel.: 209 50 00

Suggestion: Encourage students to read all items before beginning the exercise.

Follow-up: Working in groups, students write brief dialogues that illustrate different parts of the sequence. Then have groups present their sections to the whole class.

Imagine que Ud. solicitó un puesto recientemente. Usando los números del **1** al **14**, indique en qué orden ocurrió lo siguiente.

_____ Se despidió de Ud. cordialmente, diciendo que lo/la iba a llamar en una semana.

_____ Fue a la biblioteca para informarse sobre la empresa: su historia, dónde tiene sucursales (*branches*), etcétera.

_____ Ud. llenó la solicitud tan pronto como la recibió y la mandó, con el currículum, a la empresa.

_____ El secretario le dijo que Ud. se iba a entrevistar con la directora de personal.

__1__ En la oficina de empleos de su universidad, Ud. leyó un anuncio para un puesto en su especialización.

_____ Le dijo que le iba a mandar una solicitud para llenar y tambien le pidió que mandara su currículum.

_____ Cuando por fin lo/la llamó la directora, ¡fue para ofrecerle el puesto!

_____ Mientras esperaba para hablar con el entrevistador en la Dirección de Personal, Ud. estaba nerviosísimo/a.

_____ La directora le hizo una serie de preguntas: cuándo se iba a graduar, qué cursos había tomado, etcétera.

_____ Llamó al teléfono que daba el anuncio y habló con un secretario en la Dirección de Personal.

_____ La mañana de la entrevista, Ud. se levantó temprano, se vistió con cuidado y salió temprano para la empresa para llegar puntualmente.

_____ Al entrar en la oficina de la directora, Ud. la saludó con cortesía, tratando de caerle bien desde el principio.

_____ También le pidió que hablara un poco en español, ya que la empresa tiene una sucursal en Santiago, Chile.

_____ En una semana lo/la llamaron para arreglar una entrevista.

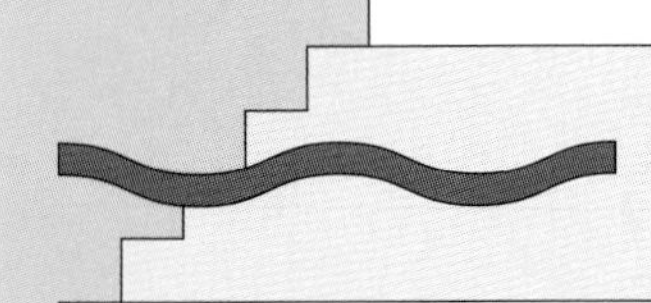

MINIDIÁLOGOS Y GRAMÁTICA

Communicative objectives for 50: how to talk about what you would like to do

Suggestion: Before beginning Grammar Section 50, lead into mini with *¿le gustaría* + infinitive questions, which have been active since Ch. 7.

50. EXPRESSING WHAT YOU WOULD DO

Conditional Verb Forms

La fantasía de la maestra de Mafalda

¡No aguanto este puesto! Creo que me *gustaría* ser abogada... *Pasaría* todo el día con tipos interesantes... *Ganaría* mucho dinero... *Viajaría* mucho, pues *tendría* clientes en todas partes del país... Me *llamarían* actores, actrices, políticos, hombres de negocios para consultar conmigo... También *haría* viajes internacionales para investigar casos en el extranjero... Todo el mundo me *respetaría* y me *escucharía*...

Y Ud., siendo la maestra (el maestro) de Mafalda, ¿cómo sería? Use **no** cuando sea necesario.

- estar contento/a → *Estaría* contento/a.
- ser un tipo (una tipa) coherente
- desorientar a los estudiantes
- mirarlos con ojos furiosos
- hacerlos morir de miedo (**¡OJO! har-**)
- poner una cara de poco sueldo (**¡OJO! pondr-**)
- hacer a los estudiantes llorar de lástima

hablar		**comer**		**vivir**	
hablar**ía**	hablar**íamos**	comer**ía**	comer**íamos**	vivir**ía**	vivir**íamos**
hablar**ías**	hablar**íais**	comer**ías**	comer**íais**	vivir**ías**	vivir**íais**
hablar**ía**	hablar**ían**	comer**ía**	comer**ían**	vivir**ía**	vivir**ían**

Point out: **(1)** infinitive used as stem, as with future; **(2)** *yo* form = *Ud./él/ella* form.

Note: Present *-ía* ending for infinitives to enable to do items in mini follow-up.

Mafalda's teacher's fantasy I can't take this job any more! I think I would like to be a lawyer . . . I would spend every day with interesting people . . . I would earn a lot of money . . . I would travel a lot, since I would have clients all over the country . . . Actors, actresses, politicians, businessmen would call me to consult with me . . . I would also take international trips to investigate cases abroad . . . Everyone would respect me and listen to me . . .

Like the English future, the English conditional is formed with an auxiliary verb: ***I would** speak*, ***I would** write*. The Spanish *conditional* (**el condicional**), like the Spanish future, is a simple verb form (only one word). It is formed by adding the conditional endings **-ía**, **-ías**, **-ía**, **-íamos**, **-íais**, **-ían** to the infinitive. No auxiliary verbs are needed.

Verbs that form the future on an irregular stem use the same stem to form the conditional.

Suggestions:
- Present forms of conditional.
- **Emphasis** Verbs irregular in future are irregular in same way in conditional.
- **Point out:** Endings are same as those for *-er*/*-ir* imperfect.
- Use conditional forms of *comprar*, *beber*, *escribir*, *decir*, *hacer*, *salir*, and *tener* in brief conversational exchanges.

decir:	**dir-**	**-ía**
hacer:	**har-**	**-ías**
poder:	**podr-**	**-ía**
poner:	**pondr-**	**-íamos**
querer:	**querr-**	**-íais**
saber:	**sabr-**	**-ían**
salir:	**saldr-**	
tener:	**tendr-**	
venir:	**vendr-**	

decir	
diría	diríamos
dirías	diríais
diría	dirían

The conditional of **hay** (**haber**) is **habría** (*there would be*).*

The conditional expresses what you would do in a particular situation, given a particular set of circumstances.

—¿**Hablarías** francés en México? —No, **hablaría** español.

—Would you speak French in Mexico? —No, I would speak Spanish.

¡OJO! When *would* implies *used to* in English, Spanish uses the imperfect.

Íbamos a la playa todos los veranos.

We would go (used to go) to the beach every summer.

- **Emphasis:** would (= habitual action) → imperfect
- **Optional:** Contrast future and conditional as used to quote people: *Estela dice que vendrá.* vs. *Estela dijo que vendría.*

Preliminary Exercise: Rapid Response Drill: *Dé el condicional.*
yo: mandar, necesitar, aprender, decir
tú: llevar, viajar, leer, hacer
Ud./él/ella: entrar, comprar, vivir, poner
nosotros: celebrar, comprender, ir, poder
Uds./ellos/ellas: regresar, creer, tener, venir

Práctica

A. **¿Es posible escapar?** Cuente Ud. la fantasía de esta trabajadora social, dando la forma condicional de los verbos.

Necesito salir de todo esto... Creo que me (*gustar*) ir a Puerto Rico o a algún otro lugar exótico del Caribe... No (*trabajar*)... (*Poder*) nadar todos los días... (*Tomar*) el sol en la playa... (*Comer*) platos exóticos... (*Ver*) bellos lugares naturales... El viaje (*ser*) ideal...

Pero... , tarde o temprano, (*tener*) que volver a lo de siempre... a los rascacielos de la ciudad... al tráfico... al medio ambiente contaminado... al

Suggestion A:
- Use conditional verb forms in paragraph as basis for personalized questions to students about what they would do on vacation to Puerto Rico.
- Students use same verbs as guide to tell about own vacations.

*The conditional forms of the verb **haber** are used to form the *conditional perfect tense* (**el condicional perfecto**), which expresses what *would have* occurred at some point in the past.

Habríamos tenido que buscarla en el aeropuerto.

We would have had to pick her up at the airport.

You will find a more detailed presentation of these forms in Appendix 2, Additional Perfect Forms (Indicative and Subjunctive).

mundo del trabajo... (*Poder*) usar mi tarjeta de crédito, como dice el anuncio—pero, al fin y al cabo, ¡(*tener*) que pagar después!

¿Cierto, falso o no lo dice? Corrija las oraciones falsas.

1. Esta persona trabaja en una ciudad grande.
2. No le interesan los deportes acuáticos.
3. Puede pagar este viaje de sueños al contado.
4. Tiene un novio con quien quisiera hacer el viaje.

Optional B: Students do exercise items in the future.

B. **¿Qué harías si pudieras?** Con un compañero (una compañera), haga y conteste preguntas según el modelo. Cambie los detalles, si quiere.

MODELO: estudiar árabe / japonés →
—¿Estudiarías árabe?
—No. Estudiaría japonés.

1. estudiar italiano / chino
2. renunciar a un puesto sin avisar / con dos semanas de anticipación
3. hacer un viaje a España / la Argentina
4. salir sin apagar el estéreo / las luces
5. seguir un presupuesto rígido / uno flexible
6. gastar menos en ropa / en libros
7. poner el aire acondicionado en invierno / en verano
8. alquilar un coche de lujo / uno económico

Ahora siga con el mismo modelo pero invente las respuestas.

9. dejar de estudiar / ¿ ?
10. vivir en otra ciudad / ¿ ?
11. ser presidente de los Estados Unidos / ¿ ?
12. gustarle conocer a una persona famosa / ¿ ?

Conversación

Extension A: **5.** *¿Dónde le gustaría a Ud. vivir? ¿Por qué?* **6.** *¿Votaría Ud. por Walter Cronkite para presidente? ¿por Bárbara Walters? ¿Por qué?*

Follow-up A: *Promesas del Año Nuevo. ¿Cuáles son algunas de las promesas del Año Nuevo que Ud. hace todos los años? ¿Qué promesas hizo Ud. el enero pasado?* Student model: *Dije que dejaría de fumar.* Instructor follows up with present perfect question, using object pronouns whenever possible. Instructor model: *¿Lo ha hecho Ud.?* (*¿Ha dejado de fumar?*)

A. **Preguntas**

1. ¿Qué le gustaría a Ud. comer esta noche? ¿Por qué quiere comerlo? ¿Le gustaba comerlo de niño/a? ¿Qué comió anoche? ¿Y qué comerá mañana?
2. ¿Qué lengua hablaría una persona de Pekín? ¿Cuál sería su nacionalidad? ¿y una persona de Moscú? ¿del Canadá? ¿de Lisboa? ¿de Guadalajara? ¿Podría Ud. hablar con todos ellos? ¿Qué lengua(s) tendría que aprender?
3. ¿Qué haría Ud. para obtener mucho dinero? ¿y para ahorrar mucho dinero? ¿y para gastar mucho dinero? ¿Siempre ha tenido Ud. mucho dinero? Como consecuencia, ¿qué tipo de vida ha llevado Ud. en cuanto al (*as regards*) aspecto económico? ¿Cuánto dinero necesitaría Ud. para pagar todas sus facturas actuales?

4. ¿Qué le gustaría decirle al presidente de los Estados Unidos? ¿al presidente de la universidad? ¿a ____ (actor/actriz, político, ¿ ?)? ¿Por qué le quiere decir eso?

Note B: Contrast between future and conditional.

B. **Entrevista.** ¿Cómo será su futuro? ¿Qué hará? ¿Qué haría? Con otro/a estudiante, haga y conteste las siguientes preguntas. Después de la entrevista, cada estudiante debe preparar un retrato (*portrait*) del otro para presentar a la clase.

MODELO: ¿Dejarás de fumar algún día? →
- ¡Ay, no! No dejaré de fumar nunca.
- Pues, creo que sí. Dejaré de fumar algún día.

Preguntas con el futuro

1. ¿Te graduarás en esta universidad (o en otra)?
2. ¿Vivirás en esta ciudad después de graduarte?
3. ¿Buscarás un empleo aquí?
4. ¿Te casarás pronto después de graduarte?
5. ¿Cuántos niños tendrás?
6. ¿Serás famoso/a algún día?
7. ¿Te pondrás gordo/a?
8. ¿Tendrás dificultades con la policía?

Preguntas con el condicional

1. ¿Te casarías con una persona de otra religión?
2. ¿Te mudarías con frecuencia?
3. ¿Estarías contento/a sin mirar la televisión?
4. ¿Ahorrarías el diez por ciento de tu sueldo?
5. ¿Vivirías en la misma ciudad para siempre?
6. ¿Te gustaría ayudar a colonizar otro planeta?
7. ¿Renunciarías a tu trabajo para viajar por el mundo?
8. ¿Podrías vivir sin usar nunca las tarjetas de crédito?

Note C: Activity introduces students to the *si...* structure, without requiring production of both parts of the clauses.

C. ¿Cómo sería el mundo si Ud. pudiera controlarlo todo? Haga oraciones con una palabra o frase de cada columna. También puede hacer oraciones con (**No**) **habría...** y una frase de la tercera columna.

yo		usar	(las) guerras
la gente		tener	(las) bombas atómicas
el gobierno		quejarse de	(la) (des)igualdad
nosotros		vivir en	un gobierno mundial
los terroristas	(no)	ser	(el) petróleo, (la) gasolina, otros tipos de energía
alguien		eliminar	(la) esperanza para un futuro mejor
(no) habría que		desarrollar	todos los dictadores
		matar	(las) tarjetas de crédito
		destruir	

Suggestion CH: Encourage use of *otra cosa* option.

Extension CH: 3. *Ud. tiene que economizar con respecto a la comida. ¿Qué haría Ud.?*
- *hacerse vegetariano/a*
- *invitarse a comer en casa de los amigos con frecuencia*
- *dejar de comer dos días a la semana*
- *hacerse miembro de una cooperativa*
- *otra cosa*

Follow-up CH: *Explique Ud. por qué* ***no*** *va a hacer estas cosas:* **1.** *Buscaría un trabajo, pero...* **2.** *Economizaría más, pero...* **3.** *Me mudaría de apartamento, pero...* **4.** *Tomaría francés el semestre que viene, pero...*

CH. **Situaciones.** ¿Qué haría Ud. en las siguientes situaciones? Conteste usando las palabras indicadas y explicando sus respuestas.

1. Sus gastos mensuales están aumentando y Ud. necesita dos trabajos. ¿Cuál sería su segundo empleo? ¿Por qué?
   a. camarero/a b. detective c. *barman*
   ch. dependiente/a en una tienda d. otra cosa
2. Su hijo le pide consejos sobre la carrera que debe seguir. ¿Qué consejos le daría sobre cada una de las profesiones siguientes?
   a. maestro de primaria b. programador de computadoras
   c. siquiatra ch. bibliotecario d. plomero

   Ahora es su hij**a** quien le pregunta sobre las mismas carreras. ¿Serán diferentes sus consejos? ¿Por qué sí o por qué no?

Notas comunicativas: More About Expressing Conjecture

The conditional is often used in Spanish to express probability or conjecture about past events or states of being, just as the future is used to indicate probability or conjecture about the present. This use of the conditional is called **el condicional de probabilidad.**

—¿Dónde **estaría** Cecilia? —**Estaría** en un lío de tráfico.	—*I wonder where Cecilia was.* (*Where could Cecilia have been?*) —*She was probably in a traffic jam.*

Optional: 1. I wonder where they went. 2. They probably went to the park. 3. I wonder what time it was. 4. It was probably 6.

Follow-up D: Bring in magazine photo or drawing with lots of action, interesting or mysterious persons, etc. Ask questions similar to those in CH to create story.

Optional: *Preguntas:* 1. *¿Qué persona famosa le gustaría ser? ¿Por qué?* 2. *¿Qué tipo de persona sería Abraham Lincoln? ¿Florence Nightingale? ¿Hernán Cortés? ¿Cristóbal Colón? ¿la reina Isabel? ¿Qué rasgos de su personalidad son similares a los de ellos? ¿Qué cosas o cualidades de ellos le gustaría tener a Ud.?* 2. *¿Dónde estaría _____ a las once anoche?* (Use this format to speculate on the activities of class members or your own.)

D. Lea el siguiente párrafo.

Había una mujer detrás de un mostrador (*counter*). Vino un hombre que llevaba una maleta porque iba a hacer un viaje. El hombre parecía nervioso y la maleta parecía pesar (*to weigh*) mucho. El hombre habló con la mujer y luego sacó dinero de su cartera. Se lo dio a la mujer, quien le dio un papelito (*small piece of paper*). El hombre le dio a la mujer la maleta y fue a sentarse. Parecía muy agitado. Escuchaba los avisos (*announcements*) que se oían periódicamente mientras que escribía rápidamente una tarjeta postal. Al escuchar un aviso en particular, se levantó el hombre y...

¿Qué pasaría aquí? Conteste, usando el condicional de probabilidad e inventando más detalles.

1. ¿Dónde estarían el hombre y la mujer?
2. ¿Quién sería la mujer? ¿y el hombre?
3. ¿Por qué estaría nervioso el hombre?
4. ¿Qué tendría el hombre en la maleta?
5. ¿Qué preguntaría el hombre a la mujer?
6. ¿Por qué le daría dinero a la mujer?
7. ¿Qué le daría la mujer al hombre?
8. ¿Por qué le daría el hombre la maleta a la mujer?
9. ¿Qué serían los avisos? ¿Qué dirían?
10. ¿A quién le escribiría el hombre?
11. ¿Qué haría el hombre después de levantarse?
12. ¿Qué pasaría después?

Bogotá, Colombia

Una preocupación universal

—Te digo que de verdad estoy preocupada. No he podido encontrar empleo todavía.

—¿No viste el anuncio en el Departamento de Lenguas? En dos semanas habrá puestos en la Compañía Palacios.

—¡No me digas! ¿Crees que pagarán bien?

—No lo dicen, pero piden varias lenguas y ofrecen la oportunidad de progresar y de viajar.

51. HYPOTHETICAL SITUATIONS: WHAT IF. . . ?

Conditional Sentences

Communicative objectives for 51: how to talk about hypothetical situations

Una entrevista en la dirección del Canal 45

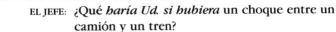

EL JEFE: ¿Qué *haría Ud. si hubiera* un choque entre un camión y un tren?

EL ASPIRANTE A REPORTERO: *Yo hablaría* con todos los testigos.

EL JEFE: ¿Y *si hubiera* una serie de bombas terroristas en algún país?

EL ASPIRANTE A REPORTERO: *Iría* al país y *me enteraría* de todos los detalles de la situación.

EL JEFE: ¿Y *si* aquí *hubiera* un terremoto?

EL ASPIRANTE A REPORTERO: *Me escondería* debajo de mi escritorio... ¡Los terremotos me inspiran más terror que los terroristas!

Point out: use of imperfect subjunctive and conditional in mini

Note: mini follow-up leads students into use of *si* clause sentences.

Complete las siguientes oraciones como si (*as if*) Ud. fuera el aspirante.

1. Si hubiera un choque de aviones, yo _____.
2. Si hubiera _____ en _____, yo iría al país para enterarme de los detalles.
3. Si hubiera un terremoto, yo _____.

Dependent Clause: *si* Clause	**Independent Clause**
si + *imperfect subjunctive*	*conditional*
Si yo **fuera** tú, no **haría** eso.	*If I were you, I wouldn't do that.**
Si se levantaran más temprano, **podrían** llegar a tiempo.	*If they got up earlier, they would be able to arrive on time.*
Iría a las montañas **si tuviera** tiempo.	*He would go to the mountains if he had the time.*

When a clause introduced by **si** (*if*) expresses a contrary-to-fact situation, **si** is always followed by the past subjunctive. In such sentences, the verb in the independent clause is usually in the conditional, since the sentence expresses what one *would do or say* if the **si** clause were true.*

An interview at Channel 45 headquarters THE BOSS: What would you do if there were a collision between a truck and a train? THE ASPIRING REPORTER: I would talk with all the witnesses. THE BOSS: And if there were a series of terrorist bombs in a country? THE ASPIRING REPORTER: I would go to the country and find out all the details of the situation. THE BOSS: And if there were an earthquake here? THE ASPIRING REPORTER: I would hide under my desk . . . Earthquakes scare me more than terrorists!

*The contrary-to-fact situations in these sentences express speculations about the present. The perfect forms of the conditional and the past subjunctive are used to speculate about the past: what *would have* happened if a particular event *had* or *had not occurred.*

Si hubiera tenido el dinero, **habría hecho** el viaje.	*If I had had the money, I would have made the trip.*

You will find a more detailed presentation of this structure in Appendix 2, Additional Perfect Forms (Indicative and Subjunctive).

When the **si** clause is in the present tense, the present indicative is used—not the present subjunctive.

Si tiene tiempo, **irá** a las montañas. — *If he has time, he'll go to the mountains.*

Como si (*as if, as though*) is always followed by the past subjunctive because it always indicates something contrary to fact.

Connie habla **como si fuera** española. — *Connie speaks as though she were Spanish.*

Emphasis: **(1)** present indicative to express conditions not contrary to fact; **(2)** past subjunctive to express conditions contrary to fact

Emphasis: *Como si* is always followed by imperfect subjunctive. ***¿Cómo se dice?*** **1.** as if he were rich **2.** as if they had a lot of time **3.** as if we were in Argentina **4.** as if they knew it all

Práctica

Preliminary Exercises: **Listening:** contrary to fact or not? **1.** *Si estoy en el centro, siempre almuerzo en «El Toledano».* **2.** *Si lloviera, no iríamos.* **3.** *Si estamos cansados, descansamos una hora por la tarde.* **4.** *Habla como si fuera argentina.* **5.** *Si yo tuviera esa clase, tendría que estudiar mucho.* **6.** *Si te veo mañana, te lo daré.* **Speaking:** *Su amigo Pablo necesita consejos. ¿Qué le dirá Ud.? Dé oraciones nuevas según las indicaciones. —Si yo ____, no lo haría.* (*ser tú, estar allí, tener ese problema, poder decidir, vivir allí*)

Variation A: Students provide interesting or provocative situations, as in C. Class reacts, completing *Si yo fuera* phrase.

Follow-up B: Students use items to tell what they would be doing if they were job hunting.

A. **¿Qué haría Ud.?** ¿Adónde iría? Complete las oraciones lógicamente.

1. Si yo quisiera comprar comida, iría a ____.
2. Si necesitara comprar un libro, iría a ____.
3. Si necesitara usar un libro, iría a ____.
4. Si tuviera sed en este momento, tomaría ____.
5. Si tuviera que emigrar, iría a ____.
6. Si quisiera ir a ____, viajaría en avión.
7. Si quisiera tomar ____, lo esperaría en la estación.
8. Si no funcionara(n) ____, compraría un coche nuevo.
9. Si me gustara(n) ____, iría a ver un concierto de Bruce Springsteen.
10. Si me gustara(n) ____, pasaría mucho tiempo mirando la televisión.

B. **Si buscara un puesto...** ¿Qué haría Ud. si necesitara un puesto? Haga oraciones según el modelo.

MODELO: si / necesitar / puesto, / leer / anuncios / en / periódico →
Si necesitara un puesto, leería los anuncios en el periódico.

1. si / encontrar / anuncio / interesante, / llamar / a / empresa
2. si / empresa / mandarme / solicitud, / llenarla
3. si / (ellos) pedirme / currículum, / mandárselo
4. si / interesarme / salario, / pedir / entrevista
5. si / (ellos) darme / entrevista, / tratar / caerle / bien / entrevistador
6. si / él / hacerme / mucho / preguntas, / contestar / honestamente
7. si / yo / tener / preguntas que hacer / sobre / empresa, / hacerlas / durante / entrevista
8. si / (ellos) ofrecerme / puesto, / estar / muy / contento/a

C. Su amiga Carlota exagera en todo. Describa sus exageraciones, usando oraciones que empiecen con **Habla como si...**, según el modelo. Incorpore las palabras sugeridas u otras si quiere.

MODELO: Carlota es de una familia de la clase media. (rica) →
Habla como si fuera de una familia rica.

1. Carlota vive en una casa bonita pero humilde. (palacio)
2. Se equivoca con frecuencia porque tiene mala memoria. (recordarlo todo)
3. No es experta en nada. (todo)
4. Tuvo una entrevista ayer, pero no le han ofrecido el puesto todavía. (tenerlo ya)
5. Tiene muy pocos amigos. (muchos)

CH. **¿Vamos a llegar a tiempo?** Cambie las oraciones según el modelo.

MODELO: Queremos *llegar* temprano a la fiesta, pero no *podemos* salir temprano. → Si *pudiéramos* salir temprano, *llegaríamos* temprano a la fiesta.

1. Queremos *comprar* flores, pero no *tenemos* tiempo.
2. Prefieres *usar* el nuevo coche, pero *está* en el taller.
3. Quiero *mirar* el mapa, pero no *hay* linterna (*flashlight*).
4. Creo que debemos *doblar* en esa esquina, pero no *puedo* ver el nombre de la calle.
5. Iba a *parar* aquí, pero no *reconozco* la casa.
6. *Puedes* estacionar aquí, si insistes, pero yo no *quiero* caminar tanto.
7. *Dejaría* de criticar tu manera de conducir, pero no me lo *pides* con calma.

Imagine que las personas que dijeron lo anterior son un matrimonio de ancianos. ¿Quién habla en cada oración, el esposo o la esposa? Explique su respuesta en cada caso.

Conversación

A. ¿Qué haría Ud. en estas situaciones? Explique su respuesta.

1. Los señores Medina están durmiendo. De repente se oye un ruido. Un hombre con máscara y guantes (*gloves*) entra silenciosamente en la alcoba. **Si yo fuera** el señor (la señora) Medina, _____. **Si yo fuera** el hombre, _____.
2. Celia está estudiando para un examen muy importante. Su compañera de cuarto se pone enferma y la tiene que llevar al hospital. No puede seguir estudiando para el examen y, a la mañana siguiente, no está lista para tomar el examen. **Si yo fuera** Celia, _____. **Si yo fuera** su compañera, _____.
3. Los padres de Ana no quieren que se case con su novio Antonio, que vive en otro estado. Un día, Ana recibe una carta de Antonio, la lee y de repente sale de la casa. Deja la carta, abierta, en la mesa. **Si yo fuera** Ana, _____. **Si yo fuera** el padre (la madre), _____.

B. **Entrevista. ¿Bajo qué circunstancias... ?** Entreviste a otro/a estudiante según el modelo.

MODELO: comprar un coche nuevo →
—¿Bajo qué circunstancias comprarías un coche nuevo?
—Compraría un coche nuevo si tuviera más dinero.

1. dejar de estudiar en esta universidad
2. emigrar a otro país
3. estudiar otro idioma
4. no obedecer a los padres
5. votar por _____ para presidente
6. ser candidato/a para presidente/a
7. casarse
8. no decirle la verdad a un amigo

Suggestion: Game: Half of class writes *si* clause using past subjunctive; other writes result clause using conditional. Collect *si* clauses in one box, result clauses in another. Draw clause from each box and read aloud resulting sentences.

C. Complete las oraciones lógicamente.

1. Si yo fuera presidente/a, yo _____.
2. Si yo estuviera en _____, _____.
3. Si tuviera un millón de dólares, _____.
4. Si yo pudiera _____, _____.
5. Si yo fuera _____, _____.
6. Si _____, (no) me casaría con él/ella.
7. Si _____, estaría contentísimo/a.
8. Si _____, estaría enojadísimo/a.

Situaciones: See IM for suggestions, additional exercises, and supplementary dialogues and exercises.

El mundo del trabajo

Hablando de la entrevista

—¿Qué tal te fue esta mañana?
—Pues no sé qué decirte. Me dijeron que me avisarían en una semana. ¿Y a ti?
—Lo mismo, pero no creo que me lo den. Tenían mucho interés en la experiencia que pudieran tener los candidatos, y como sabes, no tengo ninguna.

Hablando con los amigos

—¡Hola! ¿Ya tienes trabajo?
—¡Qué más quisiera! Me gustaría trabajar en lo mío,° pero de momento no hay nada.
—Por lo visto° los futuros biólogos no interesan demasiado...
—Hombre, a veces pienso que si volviera a entrar en la universidad, cambiaría de carrera, porque voy a tardar en colocarme° de biólogo.
—Pues, no es sólo en lo tuyo.° No sé si te acuerdas, pero yo tardé medio año° en colocarme. ¡Y ahora llevo siete meses trabajando! O sea, ¡ánimo°!

lo... *mine* (*i.e., my field*)
Por... *Apparently*
¿ ?
¿ ? / Yo... *It took me half a year*
¿ ?

Conversación

Hágale preguntas a un compañero (una compañera) de clase que ya tiene empleo (o a su profesor[a]) para saber la siguiente información.

- el nombre exacto del trabajo que tiene
- la carrera que hizo en la universidad
- el tiempo que tardó en colocarse (*getting a job*)
- la experiencia que tenía en ese campo cuando se colocó
- el tiempo que lleva en el empleo

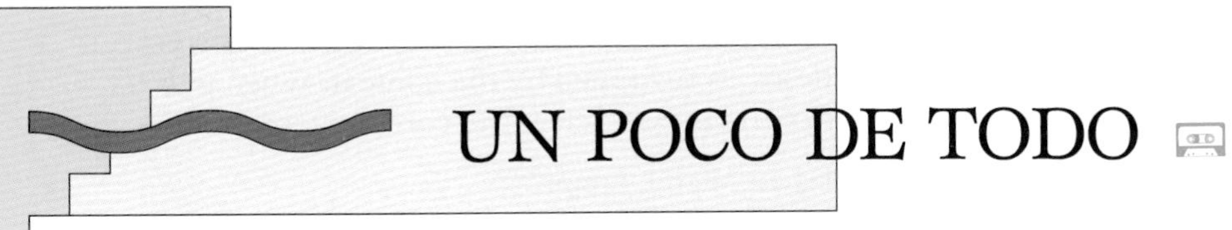

UN POCO DE TODO

A. **Si sólo fuera así...** Form complete sentences based on the words given, in the order given, to express contrary-to-fact conditions. Conjugate the verbs and add other words if necessary. Use subject pronouns only when needed.

1. si / yo / ser / tú, / (yo) no / hacer / eso
2. si / yo / estar / allí, / (yo) decírselo / claramente
3. si / yo / poder / viajar / a / España, / aprender / mucho
4. si tú / darme / dinero, / yo / poder / comprar / boleto
5. si / yo / no / tener / trabajar, / estar / contentísimo/a

B. **¡Entendiste mal!** Con un compañero (una compañera), haga y conteste preguntas según el modelo.

MODELO: llegar el trece de junio / tres →
- Llegaré el trece de junio.
- ¿No dijiste que llegarías el tres?
- ¡Que no! Dije que llegaría el trece. Entendiste mal.

1. estar en el bar a las dos / doce
2. estudiar con Juan / Juana
3. ir de vacaciones en julio / junio
4. verte en casa / en clase
5. comprar la blusa rosada / roja

C. **Si el mundo fuera diferente...** Adaptarse a un nuevo país o a nuevas circunstancias es difícil, pero también es una aventura interesante. ¿Qué ocurriría si el mundo fuera diferente?

MODELO: Si yo fuera la última persona en el mundo... →
- tendría que aprender a hacer muchas cosas
- sería la persona más importante—y más ignorante—del mundo
- me adaptaría fácilmente/difícilmente
- los animales y yo nos haríamos buenos amigos

1. Si yo pudiera tener solamente un amigo (una amiga), _____.
2. Si yo tuviera que pasar un año en una isla desierta, _____.
3. Si yo fuera (otra persona), _____.
4. Si el presidente fuera presidenta, _____.
5. Si viviera en la Argentina, _____.
6. Si fuera el año 2080, _____.
7. Si yo viviera en el siglo XIX (XV, etcétera), _____.
8. Si yo fuera la persona más poderosa (*powerful*) del mundo, _____.
9. Si los estudiantes fueran profesores y los profesores fueran estudiantes, _____.

CH. **Un exiliado cubano.** Complete the following story with the correct form of the words in parentheses, as suggested by the context. When two possibilities are given in parentheses, select the correct word.

Miguel García es un médico excelente que vive y trabaja en Miami. Emigró de Cuba (*después de/después de que*[1]) la revolución de Fidel Castro. Miguel (*querer*[2]) mucho a su patria, pero no le (*gustar*[3]) el nuevo sistema político. Así (*salir:* él[4]) de Cuba en 1963 y (*llegar*[5]) con su familia a los Estados Unidos. El gobierno cubano no permitió que (*traer:* ellos[6]) muchos bienes° personales; (*también/tampoco*[7]) les (*dejar*[8]) sacar dinero del país.

goods, belongings

Ser un refugiado político es como empezar una nueva vida. Al° establecerse en los Estados Unidos, Miguel (*experimentar*[9]) muchos cambios difíciles. (*El/La*[10]) idioma, (*por/para*[11]) ejemplo, (*representar*[12]) un obstáculo para él. Ya (*saber*[13]) bastante° gramática (*inglés*[14]) porque la (*haber estudiar*[15]) en el colegio en Cuba. Pero nunca (*haber aprender*[16]) a hablarlo con facilidad, y (*también/tampoco*[17]) tuvo muchos problemas en comprender (*al/a la*[18]) gente. Aunque Miguel (*haber ser*[19]) médico en Cuba, fue difícil encontrar trabajo. Tuvo que trabajar en una fábrica (*por/para*[20]) mantener a su mujer° y a sus tres hijos. Mientras tanto,° hizo la residencia en un hospital y (*tomar*[21]) el examen en el estado de Florida. (*Por/Para*[22]) fin (*conseguir*[23]) un (*bueno*[24]) puesto en un hospital de Miami.

Upon

a fair amount of

esposa / Mientras... *Meanwhile*

Además, era necesario que los García (*acostumbrarse*[25]) a una vida y a una cultura completamente diferentes. (*Decidir:* ellos[26]) adoptar una vida bilingüe: el español es (*que/lo que*[27]) usan en la casa, pero hablan inglés en el trabajo y en (*el/la*[28]) calle.

Hoy, después de muchos años de exilio, Miguel y su familia se (*haber acostumbrar*[29]) a la forma de vida en los Estados Unidos. (*Ser/Estar:* ellos[30]) ciudadanos de (*este/esto*[31]) país, aunque muchas veces añoran° su tierra natal. Sin embargo, saben que si todavía (*estar*[32]) en Cuba, su vida (*ser*[33]) muy diferente.

they miss

¿Cierto, falso o no lo dice?

1. Miguel tuvo que salir de Cuba; no pudo escoger.
2. Miguel y su familia sufrieron más al principio que ahora.

3. A Miguel no le gustó trabajar en la fábrica.
4. Tuvo que estudiar mucho para aprobar sus exámenes.
5. Los hijos de los Sres. García son bilingües.
6. No hay ningún aspecto de la sociedad cubana que prefieran a su equivalente en los Estados Unidos.

PAA: 115.000 inscritos

Para las 8.30 horas de este miércoles estaba programada la Prueba de Aptitud Académica, que este año será rendida por un total de 115.000 postulantes a la educación superior en todo el país. En tanto, a las 15.15 horas de la tarde se tomaba la prueba de Historia y Geografía de Chile, obligatoria para el proceso de admisión.

Los exámenes se iniciaron este martes con las pruebas específicas de Biología, Química y Física y concluían este jueves con las de Matemática, a las 8.30 horas, y Ciencias Sociales, a las 15.15 horas. Los cupos de las universidades e institutos superiores para el próximo año académico serán de aproximadamente treinta mil vacantes, incluyendo los planteles regionales. Seis corporaciones de Santiago ofrecerán 11.564 cupos.

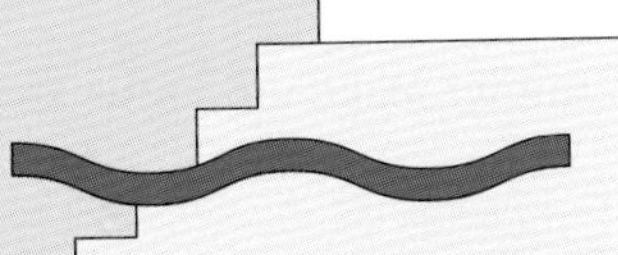

VOCABULARIO

Theme vocabulary previously listed as active: *el/la cajero/a, el/la enfermero/a, el/la maestro/a, el/la mecánico/a, el/la médico/a, el/la obrero/a, el/la profesor(a), el/la secretario/a*

PROFESIONES Y OFICIOS

el/la abogado/a lawyer
el/la bibliotecario/a librarian
el/la comerciante merchant, shopkeeper
el hombre/la mujer de negocios businessman/woman
el/la plomero/a plumber
el/la trabajador(a) social social worker
el/la vendedor(a) salesperson

EN BUSCA DE UN PUESTO

el/la aspirante candidate
el currículum resumé
la Dirección de Personal personnel, employment office
el/la director(a) de personal director of personnel
la empresa corporation, business
el/la entrevistador(a) interviewer
la solicitud application (form)
la sucursal branch (office)
caerle bien/mal a alguien to make a good/bad impression on someone
dejar to quit
ejercer (ejerzo) to practice (*a profession*)
entrevistar to interview
llenar to fill out (*a form*)
renunciar (a) to resign (from)

Frases útiles para la comunicación

Como si + *past subjunctive*	***as if . . .***
Habla **como si** lo **supiera** todo.	*He/She talks as if he/she knew everything.*

El condicional de probabilidad

¿Dónde **estaría?**	*Where could he (or she) have been?*
Estaría cansada.	*She was probably (must have been) tired.*

UN PASO MÁS 18

OPTIONAL SECTION

▲ Actividad A. Una llamada de la Dirección de Personal

Imagine that your friend Manuela has given your name as a personal reference on a job application. The person in charge of hiring for that position is calling you. What should you say about Manuela to help her get the job in the following situations? **Manuela quiere ser...**

1. abogada pública del condado (*county*)
2. vendedora de libros de texto para universidades
3. secretaria bilingüe
4. dependienta en un almacén
5. profesora de español en una escuela secundaria

Now imagine that you are trying to get information about an applicant for the jobs listed above. What would you want and need to know? Make up questions to elicit the information you need.

Palabras y frases útiles

la experiencia	experience	**maduro/a**	mature
los puntos débiles	weaknesses	**responsable**	responsible
los puntos fuertes	strengths	**llevarse bien/mal con los demás**	to get along well/badly with others
cuidadoso/a	careful	**preocuparse por los demás**	to be concerned about others
honrado/a	honest		
independiente	independent		

Suggestion A: Students discuss in groups; then role-play with instructor acting as caller.

Optional professions: *azafata/camarero, camarero/a*

Variation: What would you say if you really thought the person didn't do a good job?

Optional: Check newspapers and magazines for ads for jobs requiring bilingual skills. Use ads as context for A.

A propósito... How to Refuse to Answer a Question

When one is asked an inappropriate question, or when one simply doesn't want to answer a question that has been asked, it is useful to know how to avoid the question without making the person who has asked it feel uncomfortable. Here are some strategies for deflecting questions in a courteous manner.

Lo siento pero...	*I'm sorry but . . .*
realmente no quisiera comentar ese tema.	*I really don't want to discuss that topic.*
yo no creo que sea apropiado hablar de eso en esta situación.	*I don't think it's appropriate to talk about that in this context.*
Sé que Ud. quiere una respuesta, pero...	*I know that you want an answer, but . . .*
yo considero que esa información es confidencial.	*I consider that information to be confidential.*
no me siento cómodo/a hablando de eso.	*I don't feel comfortable talking about that.*

In informal situations, with close friends, you can afford to be a bit more direct.

¡Vaya pregunta! ¡No tienes por qué saber eso!	*What a question! You have no business knowing that!*
¡Sólo a mí me toca saberlo!	*That's my affair!*
¡No te metas en mis asuntos!	*Don't stick your nose into my affairs!*

▲ Actividad B. ¡Vaya pregunta!

Follow-up B: Have several students role-play the situations, with you taking the role of interviewer.

In recent years in the United States, legislation to protect the rights of all persons has substantially changed the nature of job interviews. Whereas prospective employers previously had the right to ask candidates almost anything, there are now certain questions that should not be asked and that, in fact, are illegal to ask during an interview. Of the following questions, which do you think a prospective employer may *not* ask during an interview?

1. ¿Cómo eran sus notas en la universidad?
2. ¿Está Ud. comprometido/a (*engaged*)? ¿casado/a?
3. ¿Qué aspiraciones tiene en esta empresa?
4. Su esposo/a está dispuesto/a (*willing*) a mudarse?
5. ¿Cuánto quiere ganar al año?
6. ¿Practica Ud. alguna religión? ¿Cuál?
7. ¿Está Ud. dispuesto/a a trabajar horas extra?
8. ¿Por quién votó en las últimas elecciones presidenciales?

With a classmate, imagine that you are in a job interview situation. As your classmate asks the preceding questions, answer or refuse to answer, using the phrases in **A propósito...** to help you courteously avoid inappropriate issues.

Expansion C: How are the following U.S. people stereotyped? What basis in reality has the stereotype, if any? How would you explain to a native speaker of Spanish how these persons are different from each other? **1.** Texans **2.** Californians **3.** people who live in New York City **4.** Southerners **5.** Bostonians **6.** Midwesterners **7.** Hawaiians

▲ Actividad C. Los estereotipos

Stereotypical ideas about individuals from a particular profession or national or ethnic background are extremely common. There may be a grain of truth in some stereotypical images, but most are inaccurate.

With a classmate, describe the stereotypes depicted in the following cartoons. Use the questions on page 506 as a guide.

—Ha ganado el primer premio en el baile de disfraces.° baile... *costume ball*

—Apenas° ha empezado sus estudios y ya está descontento, inquieto,° malhumorado... ¡Imagínate cómo estará cuando sea médico! *Scarcely* *uneasy*

- ¿Qué grupo aparece estereotipado en el dibujo?
- ¿De qué grupo son los individuos que usan el estereotipo?
- ¿Cuáles son las características esenciales del estereotipo?

With another classmate, describe the stereotype of people in the following professions, drawing on common knowledge as well as on the way these professions are portrayed in movies and on TV. When you have finished, compare your list of characteristics with those of others in the class to see if you share common stereotypical attitudes.

1. los bibliotecarios
2. los obreros que trabajan en la construcción de edificios
3. los maestros de primaria
4. los astronautas
5. los cantantes de música punk
6. los vendedores de coches usados

LECTURA CULTURAL

Lectura: See IM for suggestions and additional exercises and activities.

El breve artículo siguiente es de una revista española. En el artículo una serie de personas que ejercen varias profesiones contestan la pregunta que da título a esta lectura.

ENCUESTA

VIRGINIA MATAIX
(ACTRIZ)

Si no creyera no lo haría. Estoy muy satisfecha de mi trabajo como actriz y, ahora, como presentadora, donde también tengo que actuar. Soy muy entusiasta de lo que hago porque está muy relacionado con las emociones y la creatividad.

AMANDO DE MIGUEL
(SOCIOLOGO)

Qué pregunta más abstracta. Si no creyera sería como para volverse loco. Mi trabajo es muy apetecible° y, como no aspiro al poder, procuro hacer las cosas yo mismo y no delegar en los otros. Como sociólogo asimilo información, la digiero y luego la emito, procurando eliminar lo que me viene impuesto e imponer lo que me gusta.

ESPERANZA ROY
(ACTRIZ)

Absolutamente. Si no creyera en lo que estoy haciendo buscaría otra forma de creer, porque no me sentiría bien realizada°. Pienso que hay varias formas de realizarse en la vida, y una de ellas es creer en tu aportación personal.

¿CREES EN LO QUE HACES?

apetecible: tempting, attractive

realizada: fulfilled

FELIPE CAMPUZANO
(CANTANTE)

Hombre, claro que creo, porque sería absurdo no hacerlo, aunque fuera equivocadamente. Soy un Sagitario empedernido° y estoy seguro de que mi éxito se debe, en cierta forma, a creer en lo que hago.

stubborn

MAGDA ORANICH
(ABOGADA)

Sí, creo y mucho. A veces, demasiado. Pero no le veo un mérito especial, porque me resultaría muy difícil hacer algo si no creyera en ello. Tanto en el aspecto profesional, político, como en la vida cotidiana, mi actitud es tan importante para la sociedad como para mí misma. A veces me crea problemas pasajeros, pero la satisfacción de haber obrado° según mis convicciones supera cualquier otro inconveniente.

acted

MONCHO ALPUENTE
(PERIODISTA)

Creo en lo que hago, entre otras cosas, porque no tengo otro remedio. Nunca he cuestionado mi facultad fundamental, que es la de escribir, y lo hago instintivamente. Lo que sí me planteo° es su comercialización: qué escribo y para qué medio de comunicación.

me... *I ask myself about*

Comprensión

A. ¿Cierto, falso o no lo dice el artículo?

1. Todas las personas que aparecen en el artículo creen en lo que hacen.
2. La mayoría de ellos también afirman su profesión con entusiasmo.
3. La gran mayoría de las personas entrevistadas para el artículo dijeron que creían en lo que hacían.

B. De las personas del artículo, ¿quién... ?

_____ atribuye su satisfacción profesional a las características de su signo astrológico
_____ cree que contribuye al bienestar general de la sociedad con su trabajo
_____ cree que hace su trabajo casi sin pensar
_____ estaría loco si no creyera en lo que hace
_____ pone énfasis en la necesidad de poder contribuir con algo en esta vida
_____ pone énfasis en lo emocional y no en lo intelectual

Para escribir

Hágales la pregunta del artículo (¿Crees en lo que haces?) a una serie de amigos y parientes que ya ejercen una profesión o tienen un oficio. Si no son de habla española, hágales la pregunta en inglés. Luego escriba una serie de breves respuestas a la pregunta en español, siguiendo el modelo del artículo.

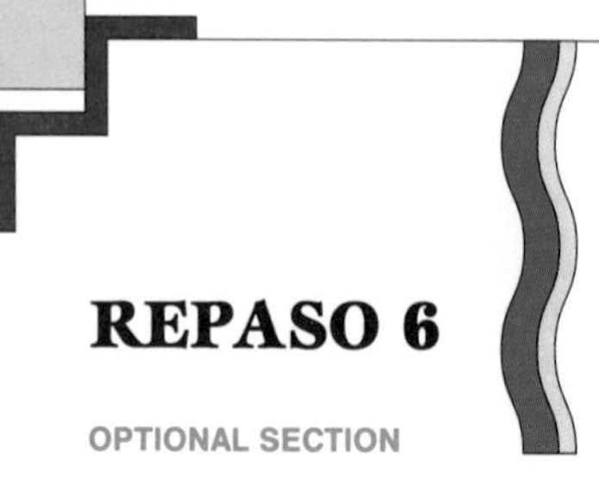

REPASO 6

OPTIONAL SECTION

VOCES DEL MUNDO HISPÁNICO

Note: Corresponding chapters of the Workbook and the Laboratory Manual offer focused vocabulary and grammar activities.

Repaso 6: See IM for detailed suggestions for handling *Entrevistas*, *Situaciones*, and the specific *Voces* sections.

ESPAÑA

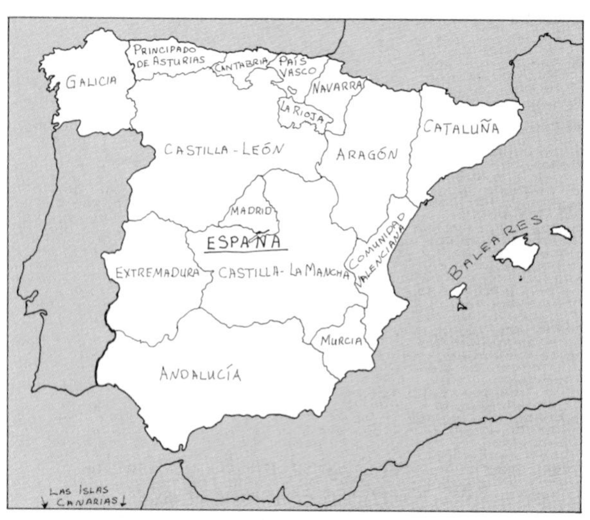

Situada con Portugal en la Península Ibérica, España es de un gran interés histórico y turístico por su diversidad geográfica y cultural. A causa de la influencia de la larga dominación árabe (711–1492), su cultura es diferente de la de los otros países de Europa. Actualmente forma parte de la Comunidad Económica Europea y de la Organización del Tratado del Atlántico Norte (OTAN) y, además, mantiene muy buenas relaciones con los países de Hispanoamérica.

Políticamente España se divide en 17 comunidades autónomas. Se habla español en todas partes de España, pero se hablan otras lenguas en algunas comunidades. ¿En qué comunidad cree Ud. que se hablan estas lenguas?

el vascuence (euskera) el gallego el catalán

¿Qué comunidad se asocia con las siguientes frases?

la capital del país Don Quijote las naranjas

«La transición democrática española es un capítulo excepcional en la historia de nuestro país y una experiencia singular en el contexto nacional. Los últimos diez años de la política española han representado un giro° radical en el itinerario de nuestra vida colectiva en la época contemporánea. En el plano internacional el modelo español de transición pacífica a la democracia por su originalidad ejerce una profunda influencia en los complejos procesos de cambio por los que atraviesan° las sociedades iberoamericanas en la actualidad.»

Felipe González, Presidente del gobierno socialista de España

turn

por... *through which are passing*

Plaza de Cataluña, Barcelona

La Familia Real Española

Callao | Carlos III | Roxy "A"

¡¡¡MAÑANA, JUEVES, ESTRENO!!!

La trama golpista que provocó el estallido de la guerra civil española

☆

DRAGON RAPIDE, el avión que cambió el rumbo de la Historia de España

☆

Por primera vez el personaje de Franco llevado al cine

☆

AUTORIZADA PARA TODOS LOS PUBLICOS

DRAGON RAPIDE
JUAN DIEGO · VICTORIA PEÑA · MANUEL DE BLAS
PEDRO DIAZ DEL CORRAL · LAURA GARCIA LORCA · MIGUEL MOLINA
JAIME CAMINO

CONSTITUCION

TITULO PRELIMINAR

Artículo 3.

1. El castellano es la lengua española oficial del Estado. Todos los españoles tienen el deber de conocerla y el derecho a usarla.
2. Las demás lenguas españolas serán también oficiales en las respectivas Comunidades Autónomas de acuerdo con sus Estatutos.
3. La riqueza de las distintas modalidades lingüísticas de España es un patrimonio cultural que será objeto de especial respeto y protección.

de la Constitución Española, aprobada por las Cortes el 31 de octubre de 1978
Referéndum Nacional del 6 de diciembre

TV-3

12.45 Resum Calgary.
13.00 Esports.
14.30 Gol a gol.
15.00 Telenotícies migdia.
15.30 Batman.
16.00 Simon i Simon.
16.50 El signe dels quatre.
18.30 Bàsquet.
20.00 Gol a gol.
20.30 Telenotícies.
21.00 30 Minuts.
21.30 A cor obert.
22.30 Gol a gol.

ETB

10.30 Meza.
11.30 Hi heu.
12.00 Luzemetrala: ETA Robin Hood Deitzen Zioten. *"...Y le llamaban Robin Hood".*
13.35 Busterren mundua. Telesaila.
14.00 Gaur egun. Albistegia.
14.15 Filemon Katuaren mundu Harrigarria.
14.40 Don don kikilikon.
15.40 Bazkal osteko zinea. *Gau ETA Egun.*
17.40 Pottokiak. Marrazki bizidunak.
18.05 Aste ero.
18.35 Perry Mason. Telesaila.
19.25 Krimenaren inguruan. Dokumentala.
20.15 Xanfarin eta andere king. Telesaila.
21.00 Gaur egun. Albistegia.
21.15 Ipuin Harrigarriak. Telesaila.
21.45 Cincinnati. Telesaila.
22.10 Kiroiez kirol.
23.40 Azken Txokoa.

TVG

11.30 Mira de axuste.
11.32 Santa misa.
12.00 Deportes. Baloncesto. Caixa Ourense-Cajamadrid.
13.30 Deportes. Campeonato de Natación.
14.00 Sky Channel (musical).
14.30 Telexornal mediodía.
15.00 Deportes.
15.30 Viva o domingo *(magazine).*
19.00 Cine de domingo.
20.50 En xogo.
21.00 Telexornal serán.
21.30 Doutor Cándido Pérez, médico de señoras.
22.00 En xogo.
24.00 Sky Channel.

TV-3 = Televisión Cataluña
ETB = País Vasco
TVG = Televisión Gallega

La otra cara de Euskadi°

País Vasco

Euskadi prepara una ofensiva para cambiar en Europa su imagen de violencia

LAS autoridades del País Vasco quieren cambiar la imagen de desolación económica que desde 1985 ha provocado la desaparición del trece por ciento de las empresas vascas y del veintiséis por ciento de los empleos.

En los últimos cinco años se han perdido en Euskadi más de cuarenta mil puestos de trabajo y la tasa de desempleo, el veintidós por ciento de la población activa, es una de las más altas de España.

La violencia, el terrorismo y la crisis económica han hecho huir° a los inversores extranjeros. El Gobierno autónomo ha lanzado una ofensiva a través de la Sociedad para la Promoción y Reconversión Industrial (SPRI) para cambiar, de cara al exterior, esta imagen negativa.

to flee

«Tenemos que dar una nueva visión del País Vasco —afirma Ramón Jáuregui, vicelendakari del Gobierno vasco—, no podemos seguir viviendo en el horror de la violencia y el conflicto permanente.»

Campo cerca de El Escorial, en la meseta central

NOS GUSTA ESPAÑA

"Nos gusta España porque no en vano fueron los Españoles quienes descubrieron California, donde dejaron como huella° el nombre de nuestras ciudades, las Misiones y la cultura Española."

trace

"Nos gusta España porque creemos en el futuro de la Economía Española."

"Nos gusta España porque creemos en sus empresas con las cuales colaboramos hace tiempo y a partir de ahora podemos colaborar a través de nuestra Sucursal Operativa en Madrid."

"Nos gusta España porque creemos en ella."

de un anuncio del *First Interstate Bank of California*

La tecnología del láser, Madrid

El Cid Campeador, Burgos

Castilla miserable, ayer dominadora,
envuelta° en sus andrajos° desprecia cuanto ignora. *wrapped / rags*
¿Espera, duerme o sueña? ¿La sangre derramada° *spilled*
recuerda cuando tuvo la fiebre de la espada°? *sword*
Todo se mueve, fluye, discurre,° corre o gira;° *rambles / turns*
cambian la mar y el monte y el ojo que los mira.

Antonio Machado, «A orillas del Duero,» *Campos de Castilla*

El Alcázar, Segovia

Cantar° de Mío Cid Poema

Mío Cid Ruy Díaz en Burgos entró,
sesenta pendones° lleva alrededor; *banners*
salían a verle mujer y varón
y en cada ventana se escucha un clamor,
los ojos llorando cuenta su dolor.
De todas sus bocas sale un razón:° oración
«¡Dios, qué buen vasallo, si tuviese buen señor°!» *master*

—Yo sé quién soy—respondió Don Quijote—, y sé que puedo ser, no sólo los que he dicho, sino todos los doce Pares de Francia,° y aun todos los nueve de la Fama, pues a todas las hazañas° que ellos todos juntos y cada uno por sí hicieron se aventajarán° las mías.

doce... *French knights*
deeds, feats
se... *will surpass*

Miguel de Cervantes Saavedra, *El ingenioso hidalgo Don Quijote de la Mancha*

El Alcázar, Sevilla

Allí respondiera el moro,
bien oiréis lo que decía:
—No te la° diré, señor, se refiere a una mentira
aunque me cueste la vida,
porque soy hijo de un moro
y una cristiana cautiva;
siendo yo niño y muchacho
mi madre me lo decía:
que mentira no dijese,
que era grande villanía;° muy malo (decir una mentira)
por tanto,° pregunta, rey, por... por eso
que la verdad te diría.
—Yo te agradezco, Abenámar,
aquésa° tu cortesía. ésa
¿Qué castillos° son aquéllos? *castles*
¡Altos son y relucían°! *they are shining*
—El Alhambra era, señor,
y la otra la mezquita°... *mosque*

Romance de Abenámar

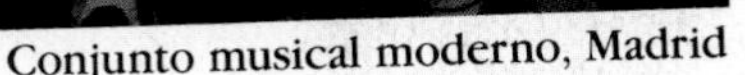
Conjunto musical moderno, Madrid

Ministerio de Cultura
Museo Nacional del Prado
Casón
Guernica
Serie F
Entrada
Casón
Salas Siglo XIX

«Tres músicos», del pintor español Pablo Picasso

ENTREVISTA

Entrevista: Focus: Asking questions, getting information, using all verb tenses and moods encountered in the text.

In the last three chapters of ***Puntos de partida***, you have learned about additional ways to use the subjunctive and you have begun to use additional verb forms to talk about the future, to make speculations, and to tell what would happen. This activity will give you the chance to explore the topics you have been talking about with a new person.

Your instructor will invite to class a Spanish-speaking person from your campus: another faculty member or teaching assistant in the Spanish Department, a professor from another department, an individual from the Hispanic community. Working in groups, make up questions to use in an interview in which you want to find out the following information about the person: his or her background, training and profession, and opinions in some areas. Try to invent questions that will motivate the person to talk about his or her life.

Training and Profession

- where he or she went to school, from the beginning of his or her education through the present
- his or her professional history, including all jobs held and how long they were held
- what he or she would study if he or she could start over again
- what he or she would do if money and natural ability were not a concern

Background

- where he or she is from and how long he or she has been here
- some details about significant persons in his or her life: spouse, children, fiancé(e), circle of friends and acquaintances
- where his or her parents are/were from and some details about them, as well as some details about other family members

Opinions

- what he or she thinks about an issue that is important on your campus at the moment: the sports program, funding to humanities programs (**las humanidades**), a controversial (**controvertible**) new program or topic, and so on
- what he or she thinks about an issue in the national or international spotlight at the moment
- what he or she thinks about an issue related to Hispanic cultures in the national or international spotlight at the moment

SITUACIONES ACTUALES

With a classmate, act out the following role-play situations as fully as possible. Try to use as much of the vocabulary that you know as possible.

1. You are on vacation in Lima, Peru. There you meet a young Peruvian who has a lot of questions about economic life in the United States. Answer as well as you can in Spanish.
2. You have a friend who has been quite ill lately and who doesn't know anything about world events. Explain to him or her what has been happening in the United States and abroad during the last two months.
3. You have just met a Mexican doctor (computer programmer, grade school teacher, . . .) at a party. He or she asks a lot of questions about how one prepares for that profession in the United States. Answer as well as you can.

CAPÍTULO DIECINUEVE

DE VIAJE

Caracas, Venezuela

▲ **En la aduana**[a]

—¿Tiene Ud. algo que declarar? ¿alcohol, tabaco, frutas, verduras... ?

—No, nada.

—Está bien. Pase.

—Sólo unas cositas que compré en Santiago.

—Lo siento, pero tendré que registrarle las maletas.

[a]*customs*

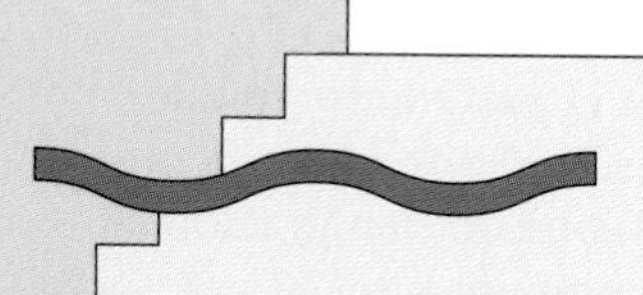

Vocabulario: Preparación:
- See detailed supplementary materials for this section bound into the back of this Annotated Instructor's Edition.

VOCABULARIO: PREPARACIÓN

- See model for vocabulary presentation and other materials in Supplementary *Vocabulario: Preparación* Materials, chapter by chapter, IM.

- See also [video] and [audio]

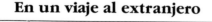

En un viaje al extranjero

ir al extranjero	to go abroad
tener algo que (declarar, decir, hacer)	to have something to (declare, say, do)
viajar al/en el extranjero	to travel abroad
la aduana	customs
los derechos de aduana	customs duty
la multa	fine, penalty
la nacionalidad	nationality
el pasaporte	passport
la planilla (de inmigración)	(immigration) form

A. **Definiciones.** Dé una definición de las siguientes palabras.

1. la aduana
2. el pasaporte
3. los derechos de aduana
4. la frontera
5. la multa
6. registrar
7. la planilla de inmigración

Follow-up B: After filling in information, students act out scenes they have created.

B. **Pasando por la aduana.** ¿Qué dice o pregunta el inspector en este diálogo?

BIENVENIDO A LOS ESTADOS UNIDOS

DEPARTMENTO DEL TESORO
SERVICIO DE ADUANAS DE LOS ESTADOS UNIDOS
DECLARACION DE ADUANAS

FORM APPROVED
OMB NO. 1515-0041

Todo viajero o jefe de familia que llega a los Estados Unidos debe facilitar la información siguiente (basta con una declaración por familia):

1. Nombre: ______________________ (Apellido / Nombre / Inicial del segundo nombre)
2. Número de familiares que viajan con usted ______________________
3. Fecha de nacimiento: ___ | ___ | ___ (Mes / Día / Año)
4. Línea aérea y número del vuelo: ______________

INSPECTOR: ¿ ______?
VIAJERA: Soy española, de Toledo.
INSPECTOR: ¿ ______?
VIAJERA: Aquí lo tiene, señor.
INSPECTOR: ¿ ______?
VIAJERA: Solamente estos libros y estos cigarrillos para uso personal.
INSPECTOR: ¿ ______?
VIAJERA: Espere Ud. un momento. Mi esposo trae la llave.
INSPECTOR: ¡ ______!
VIAJERA: ¡Oh, no! ¡No sabía que { tenía que declararlo! / era ilegal! }
INSPECTOR: ______ .
VIAJERA: ¿Cuánto tengo que pagar, pues?
INSPECTOR: ______ .

C. Explíquele a su amigo Paul, que nunca ha viajado en el extranjero, lo que pasa cuando uno toma un vuelo internacional. Empiece desde el momento de subir al avión hasta el momento de salir de la Oficina de Inmigración. Si Ud. nunca ha hecho un viaje al extranjero, hágale preguntas a su profesor(a) para saber los detalles.

El alojamiento°

lodging

confirmar	to confirm	**la pensión**	boarding house
quedarse	to remain, stay (*as a guest*)	**pensión completa**	room and full board (all meals)
reservar	to reserve	**media pensión**	room with breakfast and one other meal
los cheques de viajero	traveler's checks	**la propina**	tip
la habitación	room	**la recepción**	front desk
para una persona	single	**con (____ días de) anticipación**	(____ days) in advance
con/sin baño/ducha	with(out) bath/shower	**desocupado/a**	vacant, unoccupied, free
el hotel (de lujo)	(luxury) hotel		
el/la huésped(a)	(hotel) guest		
el mozo (el botones)	bellhop		

Variation A: Do as listening comprehension only.

A. **¿El Hotel María Cristina o la Pensión Libertad?** De estas oraciones, ¿cuáles describen un hotel grande e internacional? ¿y una pensión pequeña y modesta?

1. Tiene todas las comodidades (*comforts*) que se encuentran en los mejores hoteles.
2. Los botones llevan el equipaje a la habitación.
3. Muchos de los huéspedes y del personal hablan solamente una lengua, el español, por ejemplo.
4. Hay que reservar una habitación con muchos días de anticipación.
5. Los dependientes confirman la reservación del huésped.
6. Generalmente se puede llegar sin reservaciones y encontrar una habitación desocupada.
7. Hay que gastar mucho dinero en propinas.
8. Los huéspedes suben (*carry up*) su equipaje, o el dueño los ayuda a subirlo.
9. Hablan muchos idiomas en la recepción.
10. Todas las habitaciones tienen ducha y, a veces, baño completo con ducha.
11. Se puede pedir una habitación con todas las comidas incluidas.
12. Generalmente es necesario compartir (*to share*) el baño con otros huéspedes.
13. Tiene un comedor grande y elegante.
14. Es posible que los huéspedes coman con la familia, en el comedor o en la cocina.

Variation B: Use situations as basis for role-plays; instructor acts as clerk in all cases.

B. **¿Qué se puede hacer?** Si Ud. se encuentra en estas situaciones, ¿cómo va a resolver el problema? Hay más de una respuesta posible.

1. Ud. reservó una habitación, pero el recepcionista no puede encontrar la reservación.
   a. Me voy a otro hotel.
   b. Insisto en hablar con el gerente (*manager*).
   c. Me quejo en voz alta mientras el recepcionista la sigue buscando.
   ch. ¿ ?
2. Ud. llega al único hotel del pueblo y encuentra que la única habitación desocupada cuesta muchísimo más de lo que quiere pagar.
   a. Regateo con el hotelero, pidiéndole que baje el precio.
   b. Busco a alguien para compartir el cuarto.
   c. Duermo en el coche.
   ch. ¿ ?

DESAYUNO Crillón

___ Café americano *American coffee*	___ Jugo naranja *Orange juice*	___ Fritos *Fried*
___ Café express *Express coffee*	___ Jugo pomelo *Grapefruit juice*	___ Revueltos *Scrambled*
___ Café con leche *Coffee with milk*	___ Jugo tomate *Tomato juice*	___ Omelette
___ Té *Tea*	___ Jugo ananá *Pineapple juice*	___ Con: *With:*
___ Chocolate	___ Yoghurt	___ Panceta *Bacon*
___ Cereales *Corn flakes*	___ Huevos *Eggs*	___ Jamón *Ham*
___ Ensalada de frutas *Fruit salad*	___ Pasados por agua *Boiled*	___ Salchicha *Sausage*

Incluye: faturas, tostadas, manteca y mermelada
Rolls, toast, butter and marmalade included.
CON ESTE DESAYUNO SE SABOREA EL RICO CAFE "MARTINEZ"

Pedido especial ....
Special request ....

N° Hab. .... Firma del cliente: ....
Guest's signature: ....
ROOM NUMBER: .... Aclaración de firma: ....

3. Ud. está viajando con un amigo. Ud. quiere quedarse en un hotel de lujo con todas las comodidades—con aire acondicionado, televisor y refrigerador en la habitación—pero su amigo quiere quedarse en una pensión y prefiere una habitación sin baño porque es más barata.
   a. Lo dejo lo más pronto posible.
   b. Voy a la pensión pero me pongo de muy mal humor.
   c. Insisto en que nos quedemos en un hotel de lujo, pero pago más de la mitad (*half*) de la cuenta.
   ch. ¿ ?
4. Ud. quiere pagar su cuenta y salir, pero sólo tiene cheques de viajero. El hotel no los acepta. Además, es domingo y los bancos están cerrados.
   a. Me quedo un día más.
   b. Salgo sin pagar.
   c. Le pido al gerente que me haga el favor de aceptar los cheques de viajero y lloro tanto que no me lo puede negar.
   ch. ¿ ?
5. La pensión en que Ud. quiere quedarse ofrece tres posibilidades. ¿Cuál va a escoger?
   a. habitación sin comida
   b. pensión completa
   c. media pensión

Notas culturales: El alojamiento en el extranjero

En los países de habla española hay muchos tipos de hospedaje (*lodging*) entre los cuales el viajero puede escoger. Desde luego (*Of course*), un hotel de lujo ofrece todas las comodidades: piscina, canchas de tenis, restaurantes, discoteca, etcétera. Pero éstos son siempre muy caros. En cambio, los hoteles de segunda clase son más baratos y también muy buenos. Cada habitación tiene su baño, y hay comedor, bar y otras comodidades.

Si uno va a pasar una temporada (*period of time*) larga en un lugar, es una buena idea buscar una pensión.

(continúa)

En una pensión cada persona tiene su propio cuarto aunque puede ser necesario tener que compartir el baño con los demás huéspedes. Normalmente se sirve un desayuno sencillo y la cena. Todos los huéspedes viven como en una gran familia.

Lo mejor para un estudiante que va a pasar un semestre o un año en una ciudad es tratar de hospedarse en la casa de una familia. Al principio puede ser necesario hacer un esfuerzo (*effort*) especial para adaptarse a la rutina y las costumbres de la familia, pues al fin y al cabo (*after all*) la casa es de ellos y uno sólo es un huésped. Pero no hay mejor forma de aprender otro idioma y conocer otra cultura.

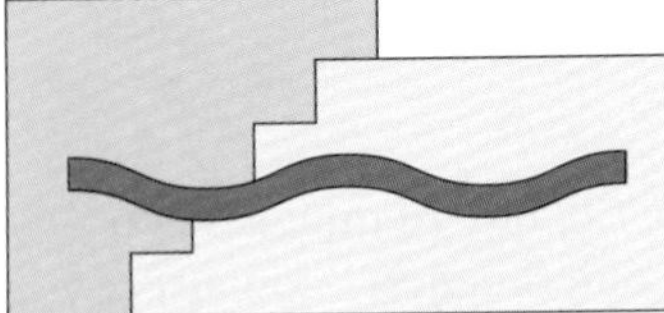

MINIDIÁLOGOS Y GRAMÁTICA

52. ¿*POR* O *PARA*? A Summary of Their Uses

Antes de aterrizar

AZAFATA: Atención, *por favor*, señoras y señores. *Por fin* estamos empezando el descenso para aterrizar en Bogotá. Ha sido nuestro placer servirles durante el vuelo. En preparación *para* nuestra llegada, dentro de unos momentos el camarero Ortega y yo vamos a estar pasando *por* la cabina para entregarles las planillas de inmigración y de la declaración de aduana. *Por favor,* llénenlas antes de que aterricemos y ténganlas a mano con sus pasaportes. Se los van a pedir al pasar *por* inmigración y la aduana. Muchas gracias.

VIAJERO: Señorita, *por favor.* ¿Es necesario que declare las cámaras fotográfica y la grabadora? No son para vender...

AZAFATA: Con tal que no las traiga de regalo o *para* comerciar, no tiene que pagar derechos. *Por lo menos* esto es lo que yo tengo entendido. Pero declárelas *por si acaso*, aunque son *para* su uso personal.

VIAJERO: ¿Y hasta cuántas cámaras se permiten *para* uso personal?

AZAFATA: No sé exactamente, pero... ¡creo que menos de las diez que Ud. tiene! *Por eso* es mejor declararlas... *para* estar seguro.

Follow-up (mini): 1. *¿Tiene Ud. una cámara fotográfica? ¿Es una Kodak? ¿Es alemana/japonesa/americana? ¿Saca Ud. buenas fotos con ella?* **2.** *¿Saca Ud. muchas fotos cuando viaja? ¿Saca fotos de edificios? ¿de personas? ¿de la naturaleza?* **3.** *¿Saca alguno de Uds. diapositivas* (slides)*? ¿Tiene diapositivas de un viaje en el extranjero?* **4.** *¿Cuántos tienen grabadora? ¿La usa con frecuencia? ¿Usa la grabadora para divertirse o como ayuda en sus estudios?*

Suggestion (mini): Students explain uses of *para* and *por.*

Before landing ATTENDANT: Your attention, please, ladies and gentlemen. We are finally beginning our descent for landing in Bogotá. It has been our pleasure serving you during the flight. In preparation for our arrival, in just a few minutes Steward Ortega and I will be passing through the cabin to hand out the immigration and customs forms. Please fill them out before we land and have them within easy reach, along with your passports. You will be asked to produce them in immigration and customs. Thank you very much. TRAVELER: Please, miss. Is it necessary for me to declare my cameras and tape recorder? I don't intend to sell them . . . ATTENDANT: As long as you're not bringing them as a gift or for business reasons, you don't have to pay duty. That's what I understand anyway. But declare them just in case, even though they are for your personal use. TRAVELER: And (up to) how many cameras are permitted for personal use? ATTENDANT: I don't know exactly, but . . . I think fewer than the ten you have! That's why it's better to declare them . . . to be safe.

¿Quién lo dijo? ¿Quién lo dirá? ¿la azafata, el camarero, el viajero o el inspector de aduanas?

1. Y ¿por qué trae Ud. estas diez cámaras?
2. Chicas, no van a creer lo que acaba de preguntarme uno de los pasajeros.
3. Pero... me dijo la azafata que se permitía entrar todo lo que fuera para uso personal...
4. Ya debes empezar el anuncio sobre las planillas, ¿no crees?

¿Quién será el viajero? ¿turista? ¿fotógrafo profesional? ¿contrabandista? ¿Qué cree Ud.? Explique.

You have been using the words **por** and **para** right from the very beginning of your study of Spanish. The major uses of these two words have been presented gradually throughout the chapters of ***Puntos de partida***. Thus, the majority of the information in this section will be review for you, a chance to put together everything you have learned about them so far. As you read this section, keep in mind that, as with **ser** and **estar**, it is quite easy to determine whether to use **por** or **para** in most contexts, since both words have a number of clearly different areas of use.

Por

The preposition **por** has the following English equivalents.

¿Cómo se dice? (Coordinated with uses of *por*) **1.** by train/plane; by phone/letter **2.** through the campus/plaza; along the river/street **3.** in the afternoon/evening; at 2 in the afternoon (*¡OJO!* → *de la tarde*) **4.** because of the test/accident **5. a.** Thanks for the book/pen/money. **b.** I'm doing it for you/him/us. **c.** I studied for 4 hours/2 days. **Optional:** in order to get, in search of: *Van por pan*.

- *by, by means of*

  Vamos **por avión** (**tren**, **barco**, etcétera). — *We're going by plane (train, ship, and so on).*
  Le voy a hablar **por teléfono**. — *I'll talk to him by phone.*

- *through, along*

  ¿No quieres caminar **por el parque**? — *Don't you want to walk through the park?*
  Recomiendan que caminemos **por la playa**. — *They suggest that we walk along the beach.*

- *during, in* (the morning, afternoon, and so on)

  Por la mañana jugamos al tenis. — *We play tennis in the morning.*

- *because of*

  Estoy nervioso **por la entrevista**. — *I'm nervous because of the interview.*

- *for*, when *for* means the following:
  a. *in exchange for*

  ¿Cuánto me das **por este sombrero**? — *How much will you give me for this hat?*
  Gracias por el regalo. — *Thanks for the gift.*

b. *for the sake of, on behalf of*

Lo voy a hacer **por ti**. — *I'm going to do it for you (for your sake).*

c. *for a period of time*

Elena manejó (**por**) tres horas esta tarde. — *Elena drove for three hours this afternoon.*

Many native speakers of Spanish do not use **por** in this and similar sentences; **tres horas** implies ***for*** *three hours*.

Preliminary Exercise: Use expressions with *por* to respond to these questions or comments. **1.** *¿Es necesario estudiar 30 minutos cada día para la clase de español?* **2.** *Parece que va a llover hoy. ¿Debo llevar impermeable?* **3.** *¿Le paso la carne? ¿la ensalada?* **4.** *Me dicen que Ud. toma ocho clases este semestre.* **5.** *Empecé a leer este libro el año pasado; lo terminé esta mañana.* **6.** *¡Me robaron el coche anoche!* **7.** *¿Le gusta viajar?* **8.** *¿Por qué llegué tarde? Pues hay mil razones.*

Por is also used in a number of fixed expressions.

por Dios	for heaven's sake	**por lo general**	generally, in general
por ejemplo	for example	**por lo menos**	at least
por eso	that's why	**por primera/última vez**	for the first/last time
por favor	please	**por si acaso**	just in case
por fin	finally		

Para

The preposition **para** has many English equivalents, including *for*. Underlying most of them is reference to a goal or a destination.

- *in order to* + infinitive

  Se quedaron en Andorra **para esquiar**. — *They stayed in Andorra to (in order to) ski.*
  Sólo regresaron **para cenar**. — *They only came back to have dinner.*

  Ramón estudia **para (ser) abogado**. — *Ramon is studying to be a lawyer.*

- *for*, when *for* means the following:

  a. *destined for, to be given to*

  Le regalé un libro **para su hijo**. — *I gave him a book for his son.*
  Todo esto es **para ti**. — *All of this is for you.*

  b. *for (by) a specified future time*

  Para mañana estudien Uds. la página 72. — *For tomorrow, study page 72.*
  Lo tengo que terminar **para la semana que viene**. — *I have to finish it by next week.*

  c. *toward, in the direction of*

  Salieron **para Acapulco** ayer. — *They left for Acapulco yesterday.*

Emphasis: ***Para*** = "for" with concept of destination. **A.** Destined for whom? → *para su hijo* **B.** Destined for what point in time? → *para mañana* **C.** Geographical destination, in space? → *Salieron para Lima.* **D.** Destined for what use? → *un vaso para agua*

¿Cómo se dice? (Coordinated with uses of *para*): **1.** They came back to eat lunch/to rest. **2. a.** It's for her/me. **b.** The exercise is for Monday/Friday. **c.** They left for Bolivia/Costa Rica. **ch.** It's a wine/beer glass. **d.** For an American/German, he speaks French well. **e.** She works for Ramón/Mr. Jiménez. (***¡OJO! el*** *señor Jiménez*) ch. *to be used for*

Es un vaso **para agua**. — *It's a water glass (a glass for water).*

¡OJO! Compare the preceding sentence with this one:

Es un vaso **de agua**. — *It's a glass (full)* of water.

d. *compared with others, in relation to others*

Para mí el español es fácil. — *For me Spanish is easy.*
Para (ser) extranjera habla muy bien el inglés. — *She speaks English very well for a foreigner.*

e. *in the employ of*

Trabajan **para ese hotel**. — *They work for that hotel.*

[Práctica A–C]

Para versus *por*

Sometimes either **por** or **para** can be used in a given sentence, but there will always be a difference in meaning, depending on which one is used. Compare the following pairs of sentences.

Emphasis: Contrast meaning of pairs of sentences.

Vamos **para** las montañas. — *Let's head toward the mountains.*
Vamos **por** las montañas. — *Let's go through the mountains.*

Déle el dinero **para** el carro. — *Give her the money for (so that she can buy) the car.*

Déle el dinero **por** el carro. — *Give her the money (in exchange) for the car. (Buy the car from her.)*

Es alto **para** su edad. — *He's tall for his age (compared to others of the same age).*

Es alto **por** su edad. — *He's tall because of his age. (He's no longer a child.)*

[Práctica CH–E]

Preliminary Exercise: *¿Por o para?* **1.** This money is for you. **2.** This money is for your education. **3.** I'll trade you this for that. **4.** Spanish is very easy for me. **5.** They left the party around 9:30. **6.** I think they traveled by bus. **7.** Do this exercise for tomorrow. **8.** They gave him a medal for his heroic act. **9.** He worked for me when I was sick. **10.** For an American, you speak Spanish very well! **11.** They did not hire her on account of her age. **12.** We traveled through the city for hours.

Práctica

A. **Preguntas.** Conteste con oraciones completas, usando **por** y las expresiones entre paréntesis u otras, si quiere. Toda la clase debe llegar a un acuerdo sobre la respuesta más adecuada para cada pregunta.

1. Supongamos que Uds. son muy ricos. ¿Cómo preferirían viajar? ¿En qué tipo de hotel preferirían quedarse? ¿Y si tuvieran que ahorrar? (barco, avión, autobús, ...)

Follow-up A: ***Preguntas:*** **1.** *¿Cómo prefiere Ud. viajar, por barco o por avión? ¿por avión o por tren? ¿por tren o por autobús?* **2.** *¿Habla Ud. mucho por teléfono? ¿con quién? ¿Por qué?* **3.** *¿Le gusta caminar por el parque? ¿por la playa? ¿por el zoo? ¿por la carretera?* **4.** *¿Prefiere Ud. estudiar/bañarse/jugar al tenis por la mañana, por la tarde o por la noche?* **5.** *¿Está Ud. nervioso/a hoy? ¿por un examen? ¿por una cita con el dentista/médico?* **6.** *¿Cuánto me da por este libro/bolígrafo? ¿por mi coche?* **7.** *¿Se han sacrificado sus padres por Ud.? ¿Ud. se ha sacrificado por ellos?*

Follow-up A: Students give reason for use of *por* in each case (in preparation for *por* vs. *para* contrast).

2. ¿Cómo se enteran Uds. de lo que pasa en otros países? ¿Cómo se enteran de las noticias de su universidad (o su barrio)? ¿y de lo que les pasa a sus amigos? ¿Cuál es la mejor manera de enterarse en cada caso? (televisión, radio, teléfono, ...)
3. ¿A qué hora y por qué lugares les gusta a muchos hispanos dar paseos? ¿Por qué cree que pasean tanto? (las plazas, el centro, la noche, la tarde, ...)
4. ¿Cuándo es mejor estudiar? ¿ver la tele? ¿Es demasiado estudiar (por) 10 horas todos los días? ¿Es bueno ver la tele (por) media hora todos los días? (la mañana, la tarde, la noche, ...)
5. _____, un(a) estudiante en esta clase, está muy nervioso/a hoy. ¿Por qué será? (un examen, una cita con el dentista, su primera cita con alguien que le gusta de una manera especial, ...)
6. ¿Cuánto hay que pagar por una comida estupenda en esta ciudad? ¿por un almuerzo regular en esta universidad? ¿Cuál es el mejor sitio para cenar? ¿para almorzar? ¿y el peor? (más de 20 dólares, más de cinco dólares, ...)
7. De todos los profesionales, ¿cuáles cree Ud. que se sacrifican más por sus clientes? (médicos, enfermeros, bomberos [*firefighters*], ...)

B. Escoja una respuesta para cada pregunta o situación. Luego invente un contexto para cada diálogo. ¿Dónde están las personas que hablan? ¿Quiénes son? ¿Por qué dicen lo que dicen?

1. ¡Huy! Acabo de jugar al básquetbol por dos horas.
2. ¿Por qué quieres que llame a Pili y Adolfo? Nunca están en casa por la noche, sobre todo a estas horas.
3. ¿No vas a comer nada? ¿por lo menos un sándwich?
4. ¡Cuánto lo siento, don Javier! Sé que he llegado con una hora de retraso. No fue mi intención hacerle esperar.
5. Es imposible que tome el examen hoy, por muchas razones.
6. ¿No has oído? Juana acaba de tener un accidente horrible.
7. ¡Pero, papá, quiero ir!
8. Ay, Mariana, pensaba que sabías lo del terremoto. Murieron más de cien personas.

a. ¡Por Dios! ¡Qué desgracia!
b. Te digo que no, por última vez.
c. No se preocupe, joven. Lo importante es que por fin está aquí.
ch. ¡Por Dios! ¿Qué le pasó?
d. No, gracias. No tengo mucha hambre y además tengo que salir en seguida.
e. ¿Por ejemplo? Dígame...
f. Ah, por eso estás tan cansado.
g. Llámalos de todas formas, por si acaso...

Preliminary Exercises:
- *En el restaurante. Dé oraciones nuevas según las indicaciones:* **1.** *Estamos aquí para _____. (comer, cenar, almorzar, desayunar)* **2.** *Para mi padre, traiga la paella, por favor. (madre/pescado, hermanito/bistec, abuela/paella también, mí/pollo)*

C. Imagine que Uds. están en los siguientes lugares. ¿Para qué están allí? Trabajando todos juntos, den todas las respuestas que puedan.

MODELO: en una playa de Acapulco → Estamos aquí para nadar... para tomar el sol... para descansar...

1. en un banco, en Buenos Aires
2. en la Dirección de Personal de una empresa internacional

• *¿Para dónde salieron estas personas? Haga oraciones según las indicaciones.* **Modelo:** *Ponce de León salió para la Florida.* **1.** *Colón / la India* **2.** *los astronautas / la luna* **3.** *Lewis y Clark / el oeste* **4.** *Hernán Cortés / México*

3. en la Ciudad de México
4. en un taller de automóviles

Suggestion CH: Encourage students to use *por* and *para* in their descriptions of the vacations these people should take: *por* (duration of the vacation), *salir para*, *para* + infinitive (purpose of going there), and so on.

Follow-up CH: *¿Va Ud. a hacer un viaje este año? ¿adónde? ¿Cuándo sale para (lugar)?*

CH. ¿Para dónde deben salir de vacaciones durante el siguiente verano estas personas? Compare sus respuestas con las de sus compañeros. ¿Quién ha sugerido el lugar más interesante?

1. Una abogada cubanoamericana, de Los Ángeles, tiene mucho interés en llegar a conocer las raíces (*roots*) de su familia.
2. Un estudiante de esta universidad no tiene mucho dinero, pero le gustan mucho todos los deportes acuáticos.
3. Su profesor(a) de español se interesa mucho, claro, en las culturas hispánicas. Quiere visitar un sitio que no conozca todavía.
4. Un matrimonio con cuatro hijos quiere que éstos conozcan la diversidad y grandeza de la naturaleza de este país.
5. Un joven profesor chicano que vive en Kansas quiere llegar a conocer la herencia cultural mexicana en este país.

D. **Entrevista.** Hágale preguntas a su profesor(a) para saber la siguiente información.

1. la tarea para mañana y para la semana que viene
2. lo que hay que estudiar para el examen final
3. si para él/ella son interesantes o aburridas las ciencias
4. la opinión que tiene de la pronunciación de Uds., para ser principiantes
5. cuál es el mejor curso de español para Ud. para el semestre (trimestre) que viene

Variation E: Students give reason for each use of *por* or *para*. Expand items with further personalization.

Follow-up E: ***Preguntas:*** **1.** *¿Para qué (profesión) estudia Ud.?* **2.** *¿Para qué compañía trabaja Ud. (su padre/madre/esposo/a)?* **3.** *Para Ud. ¿son más difíciles los exámenes escritos o los orales? ¿los exámenes de matemáticas o los de historia?* **4.** *¿Tiene Ud. mucho que hacer para mañana? ¿mucho que leer? ¿mucho que escribir?* **5.** *¿Tiene Ud. que comprar algo esta noche? ¿algo para su casa/apartamento/cuarto? ¿algo para un amigo? ¿algo para la familia?*

E. Complete los siguientes diálogos y oraciones con **por** o **para.**

1. Los Pastor Rosco salieron _____ el Perú ayer. Van _____ avión, claro, pero luego piensan viajar en coche _____ todo el país. Van a estar allí _____ dos meses. Va a ser una experiencia extraordinaria _____ toda la familia.
2. —Buscamos un regalo de boda _____ nuestra nieta. ¿No tienen Uds. unos vasos elegantes de cristal _____ vino?
   —Claro que sí, señor. Tenemos éstos _____ quince dólares cada uno y también éstas _____ veinte.
3. Mi prima Graciela quiere estudiar _____ (ser) doctora. _____ eso trabaja _____ un médico _____ la mañana; tiene clases _____ la tarde.
4. —No dejes la tarea _____ mañana, ¿eh?
   —No te preocupes, mamá. Hoy _____ la noche voy a estudiar _____ el examen.
5. —¿_____ qué están Uds. aquí todavía? Yo pensaba que iban a dar un paseo _____ el parque.
   —Íbamos a hacerlo, pero _____ fin no fuimos _____ la nieve.

Conversación

A. **Preguntas**

1. En esta ciudad, ¿es agradable caminar por los parques públicos? ¿por el centro? ¿Hay mucha gente que corra por los parques? ¿por las calles? ¿Por dónde le gusta a Ud. caminar cuando quiere pensar y estar solo/a? ¿cuando quiere ver vistas bonitas?
2. Explíquele a un amigo hispano que no conoce muy bien los Estados Unidos cómo se llega del estado de Washington a California por coche. (Hay que pasar por ______.) ¿de Maine a la Florida? ¿de Nueva York a Chicago?
3. ¿Quién se sacrificó por Ud. durante su niñez? ¿Hay alguien que se esté sacrificando ahora para que Ud. asista a la universidad? ¿Por quién se sacrifican los padres, por lo general? ¿Los hijos se sacrifican por los padres en esta sociedad?

B. **Situaciones.** Invente todas las preguntas que pueda sobre los siguientes dibujos. Luego use las preguntas para entrevistar a dos compañeros. ¿Están de acuerdo todos en lo que dijeron sobre los dibujos?

MODELO: ¿Cómo se llama la niña?
¿Para quién canta?
Para ser una niña pequeña, ¿canta bien o mal?
¿Cuántos años tendrá?
¿Es muy alta para su edad?
¿Para qué se han reunido todas estas personas?
¿Por qué está sentada la gente?

1. 

2. 

3. 

4. 

Notas comunicativas: Explaining Your Reasons

Here is a handy phrase to use when you are trying to explain your reasons for doing—or *not* doing—something.

La razón por la cual no pude asistir es que tuve que prepararme para un examen.	*The reason why (for which) I couldn't attend is that I had to prepare for an exam.*

Note the use of a similar structure to express *which* or *whom* in phrases like the following:

Una persona **por la cual...**	*A person for whom . . .*
Un derecho **por el cual...**	*A right for which . . .*

C. **Entrevista.** Con un compañero (una compañera), haga y conteste preguntas para ponerse de acuerdo sobre los siguientes temas. Luego dígale a la clase lo que Uds. han acordado.

1. un lugar en esta ciudad por donde es peligroso (muy agradable) caminar
2. una persona con quien, por lo general, es difícil (fácil) comunicarse
3. un derecho por el cual Uds. (no) se sacrificarían
4. la forma más económica y a la vez más agradable de viajar
5. una cosa que—para los dos—es muy fácil (difícil) de hacer
6. la edad más apropiada para salir con un chico (una chica) por primera vez (para casarse)
7. una razón por la cual se disculpa (*it's O.K.*) faltar a clase (a un examen)
8. una cantidad de dinero que se considera excesiva cuando se trata de comprar un coche (una entrada para un partido importante)
9. la mejor manera de informarse de las noticias internacionales (del tiempo)
10. una razón por la cual (no) sería buena idea emigrar a otro país (inmigrar a este país)

Guadalajara, México

En la recepción

—¿Cuál es la tarifa de una habitación con pensión completa?
—¿Con o sin baño?
—Con baño privado, si es posible.
—Mil trescientos pesos la noche, señor.
—Está bien. Quisiéramos quedarnos dos noches.
—Muy bien, señor.

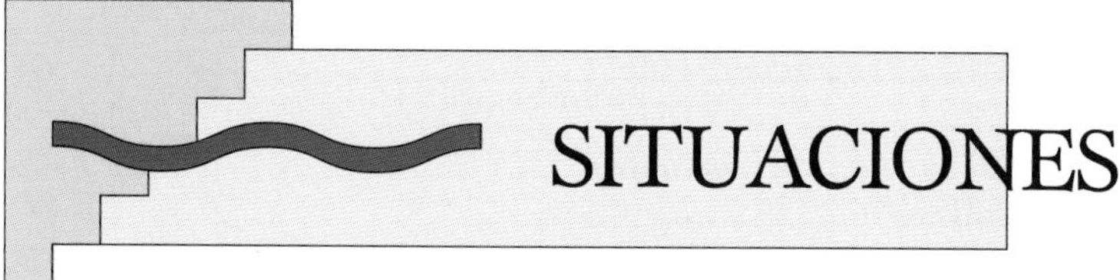

SITUACIONES

Situaciones: See IM for suggestions, additional exercises, and supplementary dialogues and exercises.

Optional: *Situaciones. Con su profesor(a) o con otro/a estudiante, haga Ud. uno de los siguientes papeles.*
1. Ud. va a hacer un viaje al Perú y quiere que un(a) agente de viajes le haga las reservaciones. Pero cuando Ud. habla con él/

Viajando en el extranjero

En la aduana argentina

—¿Su nacionalidad, por favor?
—Soy colombiana. Aquí tiene Ud. mi pasaporte.

ENTRADA ARRIVAL ARRIVEE	USO OFICIAL OFFICIAL USE RESERVE A L'ADMINISTRATION	SALIDA DEPARTURE DEPART
Empresa y N° de vuelo o viaje Company and N° of flight or voyage Compagnie et N° de vol		**Empresa y N° de vuelo o viaje** Company and N° of flight or voyage Compagnie et N° de vol

Tarjeta internacional de entrada-salida - International card of arrival/departure - Carte internationale d'arrivée depart

Para ser completado con letra de imprenta - Complete in block letters - Completer en lettres capitales

REPUBLICA ARGENTINA

Apellidos
Family Name
Nom

Nombres
Name
Prénom

Fecha de Nacimiento Día / Day / Jour — Mes / Month / Mois — Año / Year / Année — **Sexo** / Sex / Sex M F — **Uso oficial** / Official use / Reservé a l'Administ.
Date of Birth
Date de Naissance

Nacionalidad
Nationality
Nationalité

Ocupación
Occupation
Profession

País de residencia habitual
Usual residence country
Domicile

Dirección en Argentina
Address in Argentina
Adresse en Argentina ______

Tipo y N° de documento
Type and number of document
Clase et N° de document ______

Expedido por - Issued by - Delivré par ______

—Muchas gracias. Y esa maleta... ¿es suya?

—Sí, señor, es mía, pero contiene solamente objetos de uso personal. No tengo nada que declarar.

—Aunque sea así, ábrala, por favor. Es necesario que la registremos.

—Muy bien, señor.

—A ver, ropa... libros... nada de alcohol ni de cigarrillos... pues todo está bien. Puede salir ahora, señorita.

En la fila° de inmigraciones, Uruguay cola

—Pasaporte, por favor.

—Aquí lo tiene.

—¿Cuánto tiempo piensa quedarse?

—Dos semanas.

—Está bien. Le doy treinta días. Puede pasar.

—Gracias.

Entrando en un país extranjero

—Pasaporte. ¿En qué vuelo llegó? ¿Cuánto tiempo piensa permanecer° en el país? ¿ ?

—El número de vuelo está aquí, en el billete. Voy a quedarme cinco semanas.

—¿Tiene una dirección aquí en la que se le pueda localizar°? ¿ ?

—En casa de mis primos. Aquí tengo las señas.° dirección

—¿Cuenta con dinero suficiente para cubrir sus gastos durante el tiempo que permanezca en el país?

—Sí, señor. Aquí tiene los recibos° de los cheques de viajero que traigo conmigo. *receipts*

—Está bien. Eso es todo.

ella, descubre que ha planeado un viaje imposible para Ud. Él/Ella le sugiere que se quede en hoteles de lujo y que alquile un coche por todo un mes. Explíquele que Ud. no tiene tanto dinero y que es preciso que le arregle algo más barato. **2.** *Después de pasar seis horas buscando alojamiento en la capital de Costa Rica, Ud. entra en el Hotel La Paz con sus tres perros. El/La recepcionista le explica que sí tienen habitaciones pero que no permiten que los animales se queden en el hotel. ¿Qué le dice Ud.?* **3.** *Ud. pasó una mala noche en un cuarto de la Pensión Fuentes. Por la mañana baja a la recepción para explicarles por qué Ud. está tan descontento/a con la habitación.*

Conversación

Con un compañero (una compañera), haga los papeles de inspector(a) de aduanas y de viajero/a. A continuación se dan las preguntas del inspector (de la inspectora). Hay muchas maneras de contestar cada pregunta.

MODELO: INSPECTOR: Su pasaporte, por favor. →
VIAJERO/A:
- Sí, cómo no.
- Claro.
- Aquí tiene mi pasaporte.
- Un momento, por favor. Está en esta maleta.

1. ¿Ciudadanía?
2. ¿Algo que declarar?
3. Hmm. Ud. trae muchos cigarrillos americanos.
4. ¿Son suyas todas estas maletas?
5. ¿Qué lleva en la pequeña?
6. ¿Cuánto tiempo va Ud. a estar en nuestro país?
7. Doscientos pesos, por favor.

UN POCO DE TODO

A. Complete las siguientes oraciones con el tiempo del verbo que sea apropiado.

1. ¡Ay, Tomás está saliendo para el aeropuerto! Dígale que (*volviera/vuelva/haya vuelto*) en seguida. Tiene una llamada urgente.
2. Teníamos que encontrar la dirección de Luisa en Bogotá. Preguntamos por todas partes, pero no había nadie que (*sepa/haya sabido/supiera*) dónde vivía.
3. ¿Su habitación? La están preparando ahora mismo para que Uds. la (*puedan/hayan podido/pudieran*) ocupar en media hora.
4. Es lástima que uno tarde tanto tiempo en pasar por la aduana. Ojalá que tus amigos no (*tienen/tenían/hayan tenido*) problemas.
5. ¿No sabes el precio de la habitación? ¡Es imposible que no te lo (*digan/hayan dicho/dicen*) todavía!
6. Déjame explicarte lo que va a pasar cuando (*pasas/pases/pasaste*) por la aduana.

B. **Entre abuelo y nieta.** Complete el siguiente diálogo con **por** o **para**.

NIETA: Abuelito, ¿_____ qué vivimos aquí en Nueva York?
ABUELO: Porque perdí mi finca (*farm*), hija, y entre la falta de trabajo en Puerto Rico y la oportunidad de trabajar _____ el negocio de la familia de un amigo aquí, tu abuela y yo decidimos emigrar.

NIETA: Entonces, ¿_____ qué dices a veces que preferirías vivir allí todavía?
ABUELO: Mira, es que somos de otra cultura, de otra lengua... Pero tú has nacido aquí; _____ ti todo es diferente. _____ nosotros la Isla es nuestra patria. No salimos _____ gusto sino (*but rather*) _____ necesidad.
NIETA: ¿Es _____ eso que les gusta regresar todos los años?
ABUELO: Claro, _____ estar con los nuestros, en nuestro ambiente...

Ahora complete las oraciones según el diálogo.

1. La razón por la cual los abuelos salieron fue _____.
2. La razón por la cual regresan todos los años es _____.
3. La razón por la cual la nieta está a gusto en los Estados Unidos es _____.

C. **¡Qué mala suerte!** Describa Ud. lo que está pasando—y lo que va a pasar—en este dibujo. Use las preguntas como guía.

1. ¿Quién será el viajero? ¿Cómo es?
2. ¿Quiénes lo esperan?
3. ¿Cómo es el inspector?
4. ¿Qué problema va a haber?
5. ¿Cómo se resolverá el problema?

Ahora cuente Ud. la historia de otra manera, completando estas oraciones lógicamente.

1. El viajero cree que tan pronto como _____, (él) _____.
2. Lleva los artículos de contrabando para (que) _____.
3. No cree que el inspector _____.
4. Se porta como si _____.
5. En cuanto el inspector vea _____, (él) _____.
6. Aunque el viajero _____, va a tener que _____.
7. Después de que el viajero _____, el inspector _____.

CH. **El primer viaje a Guadalajara.** Complete the following story with the correct form of the words in parentheses, as suggested by the context. When two possibilities are given in parentheses, select the correct word.

El día que salí para México, (*ser/estar*[1]) nublado. Iba a la Universidad de Guadalajara (*por/para*[2]) presentarme a un examen oral (*por/para*[3]) entrar en la Facultad de Medicina. Yo me (*haber preparar*[4]) con cuidado y (*esperar*[5]) saber todas las respuestas. Aunque en el pasado siempre (*haber sacar*[6]) buenas notas en ciencias, (*saber/conocer*[7]) que los profesores mexicanos (*ser/estar*[8]) muy exigentes. (*Tener:* yo[9]) miedo (*a/de*[10]) que me (*hacer:* ellos[11]) alguna pregunta imposible. —Si yo (*poder*[12]), me dije al despertarme (*por/para*[13]) la mañana, me (*quedar*[14]) en cama. Pero no (*ser/estar*[15]) así, y a las diez (*por/de*[16]) la mañana (*subir:* yo[17]) (*en el/al*[18]) avión.

Cuando (*llegar:* yo[19]) a Guadalajara, (*llover*[20]) ligeramente. (*Ir:* yo[21]) al hotel y (*empezar*[22]) a repasar mis apuntes.° (*Leer*[23]) hasta las tres, cuando (*por/para*[24]) fin (*acostarse*[25]). (*Ser/Estar*[26]) tan cansada que (*dormirse*[27]) casi inmediatamente.

°*notes*

Al día siguiente, después (*de/que*[28]) vestirme con cuidado, (*tomar*[29]) un taxi (*por/para*[30]) la Facultad. Los examinadores ya (*ser/estar*[31]) allí esperándome.

—(*Sentarse*[32]) Ud. aquí y no (*tener*[33]) miedo— me (*decir*[34]) ellos. —Aquí todos (*ser/estar:* nosotros[35]) amigos. Y con esas palabras todos me (*sonreír*[36]).

Fue como si (yo: *tomar*[37]) un tranquilizante. (*Empezar*[38]) el examen y (*contestar:* yo[39]) como si (*tener*[40]) los libros (*abrir*[41]) en la mesa. Después, ellos me (*decir*[42]) que yo (*haber/salir*[43]) muy bien y que todos (*esperar*[44]) verme allí el año siguiente. (*Regresar:* yo[45]) al hotel como si (*volar*[46]), casi sin (*tocar*[47]) el suelo. ¡Qué felicidad! ¡Y cómo (*brillar*[48]) el sol!

¿Cierto, falso o no lo dice? Si no lo dice, ¿qué cree Ud.? Explique.

1. La persona que habla es un hombre.
2. Es de los Estados Unidos.
3. Se ha preparado muy bien para el examen.
4. Creía que el examen iba a ser fácil.
5. Los examinadores lo/la trataron con cortesía y respeto.
6. Ya se ha graduado en la Facultad de Medicina.

VOCABULARIO

Theme vocabulary previously listed as active: *el cheque, ir, la multa, pagar, quedarse, viajar*

CRUZANDO LA FRONTERA

declarar to declare
registrar to search, examine

la aduana customs
los derechos (de aduana) (customs) duty
el extranjero abroad
la inmigración immigration
el/la inspector(a) (de aduanas) (customs) inspector
la nacionalidad nationality
el pasaporte passport
la planilla form (*to fill out*)
el uso (personal) (personal) use
el/la viajero/a traveler

EL ALOJAMIENTO

confirmar to confirm
reservar to reserve

el botones/mozo bellhop
la comodidad comfort
el/la gerente manager
la habitación room (*in a hotel*)
para una persona single
con/sin baño/ducha with(out) bath/shower
el hotel (de lujo) (luxury) hotel
el/la huésped(a) guest
la pensión boardinghouse
pensión completa room and full board
media pensión room and breakfast plus one other meal
la propina tip (*to a bellhop, etc.*)
la recepción front desk
la reservación reservation

con (_____ días de) anticipación (_____ days) in advance
desocupado/a unoccupied, vacant, free

VERBOS

aterrizar to land
compartir to share
entregar to hand in, over

PALABRAS ADICIONALES

por lo menos at least
por si acaso just in case
tener algo que (decir, hacer...) to have something to (say, do . . .)

Frases útiles para la comunicación	
la razón por la cual	the reason why, for which

UN PASO MÁS 19

OPTIONAL SECTION

Actividad A. ¿Sabe Ud. usar un horario de tren?

Preliminary Activity A: *Diga la hora usando el sistema de 24 horas:* 1. *la una de la tarde* 2. *las diez de la noche* 3. *las ocho y media de la noche* 4. *las once y diez de la noche* 5. *las cuatro menos veinte de la tarde* 6. *las doce menos cuarto de la noche*

Para usar un horario de tren, hay que saber que se emplea el mismo sistema que usan los militares, es decir, que usan un sistema de veinticuatro horas. Así no hay necesidad de decir «de la mañana (tarde/noche)». Ponen 2.20 si el tren sale a las 2.20 de la mañana y ponen 14.20 si sale a las 2.20 de la tarde; ponen 10.30 si sale a las 10.30 de la mañana y 22.30 si sale a las 10.30 de la noche.

MADRID-Chamartín

ASTURIAS SANTANDER

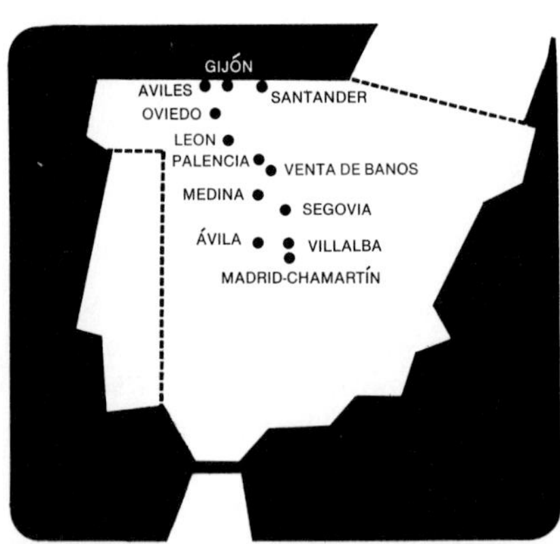

MADRID ⟷ SANTANDER ⟷ MADRID

955 Electro-tren 1-2	923 Exp. 1-2 A	925 Exp. 1-2 B		ESTACIONES		956 Electro-tren 1-2	924 Exp. 1-2 A	926 Exp. 1-2 C
15.20	23.10	23.40	S.	**MADRID-Ch.**	L l.	21.55	7.45	8.03
	23.48	0.27	L l.	Villalba de G.	S.		7.01	7.11
	23.49	0.28	S.	Villalba de G.	L l.		7. –	7.10
	0.59	1.38	S.	**SEGOVIA**	S.		5.59	6.15
	2.34	3.12	L l.	Medina del C.	S.		4.08	4.27
16.47			L l.	**ÁVILA**	S.	20.21		
16.48			S.		L l.	20.20		
17.36			L l.	Medina del C.	S.	19.32	4.08	4.27
17.37	2.39	3.16	S.		L l.	19.31	4.04	4.23
18.02	3.12	3.48	L l.	**VALLADOLID**	S.	19.07	3.34	3.53
18.04	3.17	3.53	S.		L l.	19.05	3.29	3.49
18.25	3.47	4.23	L l.	Venta de Baños	S.	18.44	3. –	3.21
18.25	3.57	4.27	S.		L l.	18.44	2.56	3.17
18.33	4.08	4.38	L l.	**PALENCIA**	S.	18.36	2.45	3.06
18.35	4.14	4.44	S.		L l.	18.32	2.42	3.03
	4.40	5.10		Fromista			2.15	2.36
	4.55	5.25		Osorno			1.59	2.20
	5.16	5.46		Herrera del P.			1.39	2. –
	5.28	5.55		Alar del Rey S.Q.			1.31	1.52
19.36	5.52	6.18		Aguilar de C.		17.30	1.12	1.32
	6.06	6.32		Mataporquera			0.58	1.18
20.04	6.30	6.56		Reinosa		17.02	0.36	0.56
	7.03	7.29		Barcena			23.58	0.18
	7.23	7.49		Los Corralas de B.			23.38	23.58
	7.31	7.58		Las Caldas de B.			23.29	23.49
20.56	7.37	8.04	L l.	Torrelavega	S.	16.07	23.23	23.42
20.59	7.42	8.09	S.		L l.	16.06	23.19	23.39
	7.56	8.22		Renedo			23.06	23.26
21.24	8.20	8.46	L l.	**SANTANDER**	S.	15.40	22.45	23.05

A Auto-expreso.

ELECTROTREN. Servicio de buffet frío y bar.

LITERAS

Con billete de 2ª clase se puede ocupar una plaza de litera, abonando un suplemento.

EQUIPAJES

El transporte de equipaje facturado es gratuito hasta 30 kilogramos por billete y hasta 15 kilogramos para los niños con medio billete.

AUTO-EXPRESO

Madrid-Gijón-Madrid y Madrid-Santander-Madrid.

Esto servicio permite al viajero transportar su automóvil de origen a destino del tren mediante la adquisición de un boletín complementario.

VENTA DE BILLETES HASTA CON SESENTA DÍAS

Ahora conteste las preguntas según el horario.

1. Si Ud. quisiera ir de Madrid a Santander de la manera más rápida posible, ¿qué tren debería tomar?
2. Si Ud. vive en Ávila y tiene ganas de visitar a unos parientes que viven en Reinosa, ¿puede tomar cualquier tren?

3. Si Ud. viajara de Madrid a Santander y quisiera dormir en el tren, ¿cuál debería tomar?
4. Si Ud. quiere ir de Madrid a Ávila, ¿qué trenes *no* puede tomar?
5. ¿Qué es el servicio auto-expreso? ¿Qué tren debe Ud. tomar si desea transportar su coche desde Madrid a Santander?
6. ¿A qué hora sale el electrotrén de Madrid (estación de Chamartín) para Santander? ¿A qué hora llega a Santander? ¿El electrotrén para en Segovia? ¿A qué hora pasa por Reinosa?
7. Si Ud. desea viajar de Santander a Madrid de noche y con litera, ¿qué tren debe tomar? ¿A qué hora sale de Santander? ¿A qué hora llega a Madrid?
8. ¿A qué hora llega el tren-exprés 926 a Valladolid? ¿A qué hora sale?
9. ¿Cuál es el último tren de noche que sale de Segovia? ¿Este tren para en Ávila?
10. ¿Se ofrecen comidas en los electrotrenes? ¿Se ofrecen literas? ¿Por qué sí o por qué no? Si se toma el electrotrén 956 en Santander, ¿cuánto tiempo se tarda en llegar a Madrid? ¿Cuánto se tarda si se toma el exprés 926? ¿Cuál es más rápido, el electrotrén o el exprés? ¿Cuál de los dos preferiría Ud.? ¿Por qué?

A propósito... Getting a Place to Stay

The following phrases will be useful to you in arranging for lodging in a Spanish-speaking country.

Frases útiles para el hotel/la pensión

un hotel de lujo	*a deluxe hotel*
un hotel de primera (segunda) clase	*a first-class (second-class) hotel*
para una noche (dos noches)	*for one night (two nights)*
¿Necesita Ud. mi pasaporte?	*Do you need my passport?*
¿Aceptan Uds. cheques de viajero (tarjetas de crédito)?	*Do you accept traveler's checks (credit cards)?*

While you are staying in a hotel or pension, you may need to make a phone call or answer one. Here are some typical expressions that are part of phone courtesy.

Contestando

¿Diga? ¿Aló? ¿Sí?	*Hello?*
¿De parte de quién?	*Who's calling?*
¿Quiere dejar un recado?	*Would you like to leave a message?*

Llamando

Habla Juan Ordás.	*This is Juan Ordás.*
¿Está Cecilia Hernández, por favor?	*Is Cecilia Hernández there (at home), please?*
Sí, quisiera saber...	*Yes, I would like to know...*
Perdón. Marqué mal el número.	*Pardon me. I dialed the wrong number.*

KRYSTAL LE OFRECE 3 DESTINOS

HOTEL KRYSTAL IXTAPA

260 habitaciones y suites con vista al mar y terraza privada, aire acondicionado y televisión a colores • Café • Restaurant Gourmet • Lobby Bar con música viva y pista para bailar • Grill y Bar Musical • Alberca con cascada • Canchas de tenis • Facilidades para golf • Actividades en la playa • 8 Salones para banquetes y convenciones (el más grande para 1300 personas).

HOTEL KRYSTAL CANCUN

• En la mejor playa de Cancún • 260 habitaciones y suites con TV a color, aire acondicionado y terraza privada • Café • Restaurant de Especialidades • Restaurant en la playa • 3 bares • Alberca con cascada • Canchas de tenis • Facilidades para golf • Actividades en la playa • Facilidades para convenciones para hasta 300 personas **(El Hotel Krystal se encuentra frente al Centro de Convenciones de Cancún)**

HOTEL KRYSTAL ZONA ROSA

• 335 habitaciones y suites con TV a color, teléfono y aire acondicionado • Alberca • Estacionamiento • Café • Restaurante de Especialidades • Centro Nocturno • Lobby Bar con música viva • Facilidades para convenciones (5 salones de juntas).

MEXICO,D.F. IXTAPA CANCUN
ZONA ROSA

RESERVACIONES:
Liverpool 155, Tels.: 511-8779 y 525-2650
06600 México, D.F.
Telex: 017-72349

Galeana 940 Sur, 2° Piso
Monterrey, N.L.
Tel.: 44-6416

Av. Américas 24-6 Guadalajara, Jal.
Tel.: 16-80-60
Telex:068-3237

OFICINAS GENERALES: Av. Cuauhtémoc 1236-PB Tel.:575-5837 • 575-5877 • 575-6373

▲ Actividad B. Problemas del viajero

Con un compañero (una compañera) o con el profesor (la profesora), haga los papeles de viajero y recepcionista en la siguiente situación. El viajero debe contestar sin leer primero las preguntas. Haga el diálogo dos veces: primero en un hotel de lujo, luego en una pensión u hotel de tercera categoría.

En la recepción. El viajero busca una habitación y quiere pagar con cheque.

RECEPCIONISTA: Sí, señor(a). ¿En qué puedo servirlo/la?
VIAJERO/A: ______________________.
RECEPCIONISTA: ¿La prefiere Ud. con ducha o con baño?
VIAJERO/A: ______________________.
RECEPCIONISTA: Muy bien. Tenemos una habitación en el tercer piso. ¿Necesita ayuda con el equipaje?
VIAJERO/A: ______________________.
RECEPCIONISTA: ¿En qué forma piensa Ud. pagar, por favor?
VIAJERO/A: ______________________.
RECEPCIONISTA: Lo siento, pero no los aceptamos. Pero sí aceptamos cheques de viajero, si Ud. tiene documentación.

Una conversación telefónica. ¿Cómo responde Ud. en estas situaciones?

1. Ud. llama a su amigo Pepe a su casa. La mamá de él contesta, diciendo «¿Diga?»
2. Cuando Ud. llama a su jefe, su secretaria le pregunta «¿De parte de quién?»
3. Ud. pregunta por Consuelo y la persona que contesta dice «Perdón, pero aquí no vive ninguna Consuelo.»

Ahora, con otro/a estudiante o con el profesor (la profesora), invente una conversación telefónica. Imagine que Ud. es un(a) turista en la Ciudad de México. Busca habitación y llama al Hotel Fénix para pedir información sobre las tarifas y las habitaciones disponibles. Quiere reservar una habitación para dos personas si puede pagar ese precio. Sea cortés y trate de conseguir toda la información que necesita.

LECTURA CULTURAL

Lectura: See IM for suggestions and additional exercises and activities.

Los hispanos vistos por sí mismos

La persona de Maine que hace un viaje a Texas puede quedar maravillada al darse cuenta° de que los dos estados, tan diferentes en su geografía, herencia cultural y estilo de vida, forman parte del mismo país. Efectivamente, los Estados Unidos *son* estados, no una cultura monocromática sino un rico mosaico.

al... *upon realizing*

Lo mismo ocurre con nuestros vecinos al sur del Río Grande. Los países hispánicos de Norteamérica, Centroamérica y Sudamérica sorprenden por la variedad de culturas, paisajes,° gentes... Inclusive sorprenden a los mismos hispanos. A continuación algunos hispanos de este hemisferio nos ofrecen algunas de las impresiones que se formaron de los países del mundo hispánico que visitaron durante sus viajes.

landscapes

Impresiones de Costa Rica: La belleza del campo, con sus casitas bien cuidadas, pintadas, encortinadas. Su gente amable, muy amanerada. La ausencia de mujeres vendiendo en los puestos del mercado. (Quienes venden son los hombres, en su mayoría.)

Impresiones de Guatemala: La belleza de las diferentes tribus de indios, su frescura, sus trajes multicolores.

Una salvadoreña, hablando de otros países de Centroamérica

Recuerdo que la manera de hablar de los cubanos me llamaba mucho la atención por lo aprisa,° lo que causaba que no pronunciaran las palabras completas. «Pescado» era «pecao»... También me fascinaba su gran sentido del humor. Hacían chistes de todo lo que pasaba, de cosas como las canciones, los anuncios de radio, los políticos y la vida en general.

rápido

Una mexicana, comentando un viaje a Cuba

Cuando fui a la Argentina, viajé por el interior y por la primera vez, vi y escuché a indios reales, de carne y hueso, hablar su lengua (guaraní). Hasta ese momento, los indios eran, para mí, un concepto abstracto y distante, pero en ese momento, por la primera vez, me sentí parte de una cultura que se impuso por la fuerza sobre esta otra cultura, tan válida como la mía. ... Me encantó la experiencia y me quedé bastante más tiempo que lo anticipado.

Al contrario, cuando fui al Paraguay, el contacto con la población en general y con los indios en particular, me deprimió,° ya que viven en un estado de miseria generalizada...

depressed

En Perú es impresionante el entrar en contacto con una civilización milenaria e imponente. El gran tamaño° de las ruinas, la originalidad de la cultura nativa, dejan en evidencia lo relativo de la presencia europea y más que nada estimulan a cuestionar el eurocentrismo del cono sur.

size

Un uruguayo, hablando de aspectos de la Argentina, del Paraguay y del Perú

Me llamó la atención la naturaleza salvaje... el idioma que habla mucha gente allí (el Paraguay es bilingüe y el guaraní se habla tanto como el castellano)... la cantidad de gente pobre durmiendo en las calles... los ricos-ricos y los pobres-pobres... el acceso a tantos productos norteamericanos... las noticias sociales que ocupan una buena parte del periódico (las fiestas de quince años, los bautismos), entre las que se ve hasta el presidente a veces... los lugares para visitar que todavía no se han convertido en lugares turísticos y que son muchos...
Una argentina, hablando de un viaje al Paraguay

Comprensión

A. De los siguientes temas, ¿cuál(es) no se mencionó (mencionaron) en los comentarios anteriores?

_____ la lengua del país
_____ el contraste entre la pobreza y la riqueza
_____ la comida
_____ la población indígena
_____ los medios de transporte
_____ la ropa

B. Busque en la lectura un ejemplo de los siguientes conceptos.

1. Un ejemplo de la influencia de los Estados Unidos:
2. Algo de interés arqueológico:
3. Un paisaje interesante:
4. Un comentario sobre la vivienda:

Para escribir

Escriba una breve descripción de aspectos de un viaje que Ud. haya hecho a otra parte de los Estados Unidos. Trate de comentar algunos de los mismos temas que se han mencionado en la lectura y otros aspectos interesantes de su viaje.

CAPÍTULO VEINTE

EN EL EXTRANJERO

Madrid, España

▲ De compras

—Necesito comprar jabón y champú. ¿Quieres acompañarme?

—Cómo no. ¿Adónde vas?

—Hay una farmacia cerca, ¿no?

—Es cierto. Queda muy cerca de aquí, en la esquina.

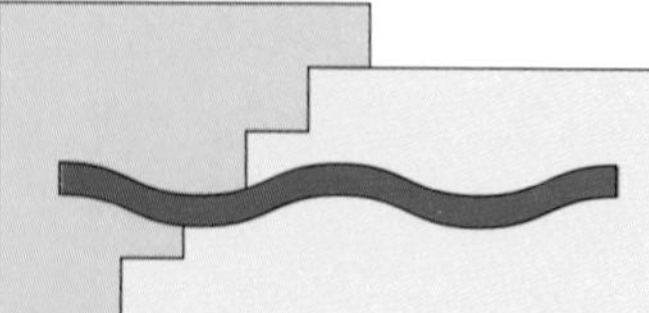

EN EL EXTRANJERO: PALABRAS ÚTILES

• See also

• See model for vocabulary presentation and other materials in Supplementary *Vocabulario: Preparación* Materials, chapter by chapter, IM.

En el extranjero: Palabras útiles:
• See detailed supplementary materials and exercises for this section bound into the back of this Annotated Instructor's Edition.

Las cosas		Los lugares	
el champú	shampoo	**el café**	café
el jabón	soap	**el correo**	post office
la pasta dental	toothpaste	**la estación del metro**	subway stop
la tarjeta postal	postcard	**el estanco**	tobacco stand/shop
los fósforos	matches	**la farmacia**	pharmacy, drugstore
el papel para cartas	stationery	**la papelería**	stationery store
el paquete	package	**la parada del autobús**	bus stop
la revista	magazine	**la pastelería**	pastry shop
el sello	stamp	**el quiosco**	kiosk (*small outdoor stand where a variety of items is sold*)
el sobre	envelope		
el batido	drink similar to a milkshake		
una copa / un trago	(*alcoholic*) drink		
el pastelito	small pastry		

Notas culturales: De compras en el extranjero

Madrid, España

Aunque los nombres de muchos lugares y tiendas del mundo hispánico se parecen a los de los Estados Unidos, no siempre son iguales los productos que en ellos se venden. Tomen en cuenta sobre todo las siguientes diferencias.

- En las farmacias no venden la variedad de cosas—dulces, tarjetas postales, etcétera—que se venden en las farmacias de los EE.UU.* Sólo se venden, por lo general, medicinas y productos para la higiene personal como jabón, pasta dental, champú...
- En los estancos, además de productos tabacaleros, se venden sellos, así que (*so*) uno no tiene que ir a los correos para comprarlos. También se venden sobres y tarjetas postales en los estancos.
- En los quioscos se vende una gran variedad de cosas: periódicos, revistas, libros, etcétera, pero también lápices, papel para cartas...

*EE.UU. is one way to abbreviate **Estados Unidos. E.U.** and **USA** are also used.

A. Conteste en oraciones completas.

1. ¿Dónde se compra el champú? ¿el jabón?
2. ¿Cuál es la diferencia entre una farmacia de los Estados Unidos y una farmacia de España?
3. ¿Dónde se puede comprar sellos en España? (dos lugares)
4. Si se necesitan cigarrillos o fósforos, ¿adónde se va?
5. ¿Qué es un quiosco? ¿Qué cosas se venden allí?
6. ¿Qué venden en una papelería?

B. ¿Cierto o falso? Corrija las oraciones falsas.

1. Se puede comprar batidos y pastelitos en una pastelería.
2. Si yo quisiera tomar una copa, iría a un quiosco.
3. Se va a un quiosco para mandar paquetes.
4. Es más rápido ir a pie que tomar el metro.
5. Se va a un café a comprar champú.
6. Si yo necesitara pasta dental, iría al correo.
7. Se pueden comprar fósforos en un estanco.
8. Un batido se hace con vino.

Preparaciones para un año en el extranjero

Ud. está considerando la posibilidad de pasar un año fuera de los EE.UU. Piensa que lo mejor para dominar una lengua es vivir en alguno de los países en que se habla. Y tiene razón. Pero... ¿en que país? El español se habla en muchos lugares. México y Centroamérica están fácilmente al alcance (*within reach*). ¿Y Sudamérica? Allí podría aprender español y conocer también la rica cultura precolombina. ¿Y España? ¿No le gustaría llegar a conocer la cultura y la tierra en donde nació el español? ¿No le atrae conocer cómo se mezclan lo hispano y lo europeo? En 1992 se conmemorará el quinto centenario del descubrimiento de América. ¡Venga a descubrir el Viejo Mundo!

Joe, un estudiante norteamericano, piensa pasar un año en España, pero tiene algunas dudas y quiere hacer muchas preguntas. Para tantear (*to feel out*) el terreno, le ha escrito a Maripepa, una amiga española que conoció en los EE.UU. cuando ésta estudiaba inglés en su universidad. Maripepa, que ahora vive en España, le contesta con entusiasmo, dándole también las señas de un amigo suyo norteamericano que está pasando un año en Madrid. A continuación se presentan las cartas que le fueron escritas a Joe por estas dos personas.

Madrid, 7 de marzo

Querido Joe,

¡Cuánto me alegro de que por fin te hayas animado a escribirme y más todavía por eso que me cuentas de que tal vez te decidas a pasar un año en España! ¡Me parece genial! Has mejorado mucho tu español en estos últimos meses y, desde luego,° un año en mi país sería perfecto.

Comprendo perfectamente todos tus temores. Alejarte° de tu familia, de tus amigos, de tu país es siempre difícil, pero estoy segura de que te alegrarás mucho de haber venido. Puede que al principio te cueste acostumbrarte a nuestra manera de vivir y de ver la vida, pero verás qué bien lo vas a pasar. Y no te preocupes tanto por la alimentación y la atención médica... ¡que° aquí ya sabemos lo que es una vacuna°!

Si vienes, tendrás ocasión de saborear la comida española, que por cierto no tiene nada que ver con esas deliciosas enchiladas que tomábamos allí. Y sinceramente España va a ser una cita obligatoria muy pronto. ¿No recuerdas que en el 92 habrá una Feria Mundial en Sevilla con motivo del quinto centenario del descubrimiento de América? La Feria permanecerá abierta varios meses, y ya se están celebrando numerosas actividades conmemorativas. Además, los Juegos Olímpicos de 1992 tendrán lugar en Barcelona. ¡Qué más se puede pedir! Tienes que venir pronto... ¡antes de que venga medio mundo!

Me resulta muy difícil decirte cuál es la mejor ciudad española para pasar un año. Para mí, Madrid sería la mejor, pero probablemente no estoy siendo imparcial. Vivo y estudio en Madrid, como sabes, y estoy encantada. Además, como hace tan poco que regresé después de pasar un año en los EE.UU., la nostalgia que tenía me hace verlo todo maravilloso por aquí.

Madrid tiene unos 4 millones de habitantes. Es una gran ciudad pero no agobiante,° bueno, si dejamos el tráfico de lado.° En los últimos años las actividades culturales se han multiplicado por toda la ciudad. Está llena de galerías de arte, de cafés-concierto, de salas especiales de cine... Lo mismo puedes ir a una actuación de Tina Turner como a un recital de Plácido Domingo. De verdad que Madrid tiene un ambiente muy alegre y divertido, y eso que al principio los españoles te van a parecer más serios que los mexicanos y los sudamericanos. El acento castellano siempre resulta más seco.° (¿Recuerdas lo melodioso que te parecía el acento de mi compañera colombiana y el de Carmen, la puertorriqueña?) Pero por otro lado Madrid sería la ciudad «crisol»° española por excelencia y creo que me entiendes. Aquí es muy difícil sentirse extranjero. Hay gente procedente de todas las partes del país y tal vez por eso es una ciudad muy acogedora.°

Otra ventaja es que está en el centro del país, es decir que te puede resultar mucho más fácil moverte desde aquí. Además hay un montón de lugares interesantes en un radio de cien kilómetros: Toledo, Ávila, Segovia, El Escorial, Aranjuez, ...*

desde... *of course*
To distance yourself
for / *shot, injection*
overwhelming / de... *out*
terse
melting pot
appealing

Toledo... "monument cities" close to Madrid where many historical buildings have been preserved. Among sights to be seen are: Toledo, paintings by El Greco and Moorish and Jewish architecture from the Middle Ages; Ávila, home of Santa Teresa de Jesús, the mystic poet and saint; Segovia, where a famous Roman aqueduct still brings water into the city from the sierra; El Escorial, site of the famous monastery of the same name; Aranjuez, site of the summer palace of the Bourbon kings.

Estoy de acuerdo contigo en que lo mejor es que asistas a la universidad. Por cierto conozco a un chico que estudia en las «Reunidas», una asociación de varias instituciones norteamericanas que dan cursos para estudiantes estadounidenses en español y con profesores españoles. Las clases son en la Universidad Complutense de Madrid,* donde yo voy. Aquí te mando sus señas para que le escribas con toda confianza. Él puede darte otras impresiones sobre la vida madrileña.

Y otra cosa. Quedas invitado a pasar una temporadita° en mi casa. Así que decídete y vente unos días antes de que empiece el curso. Será un placer volverte a ver. Hasta pronto. Recibe un abrazo de tu amiga.

short while

Maripepa

Madrid, 28 de abril

Hola, Joe:

Ya me había dicho nuestra amiga que me escribirías y trataré de contestar a todas tus preguntas lo mejor que pueda. Antes que nada quiero decirte que has hecho una buena elección. Pasar un año en España va a ser una gran experiencia.

Empecemos con tus preguntas sobre la universidad. El centro de estudios está en la Ciudad Universitaria, un gran *campus* al noroeste de la ciudad. Aunque queda algo lejos del centro, está muy bien comunicado por metro y autobús. Las clases son generalmente por la mañana, pero no es raro que se tenga clases por la tarde. Lo normal es que los norteamericanos que estudiamos con las Reunidas llevemos varios cursos aquí, y como mínimo uno en la universidad regular como un estudiante español más.

Lo primero que te va a llamar la atención es el compañerismo que hay entre los estudiantes. Hay un espíritu entre los estudiantes de un mismo curso y especialidad muy distinto a lo que yo conocía. Pero dejemos esto.° Supongo que ya habrás recibido un buen sobre lleno de folletos sobre el funcionamiento de las cuestiones académicas, ¿no?

Pero... *But enough about that.*

Creo que la siguiente cuestión importante es el alojamiento. Yo no he tenido particularmente más suerte que otros compañeros. Por eso puedo decir que no es muy complicado encontrar sitio. Al principio me quedé en una pensión muy simpática en el centro. La llevaba una familia acostumbrada a los estudiantes, el precio era bastante razonable y además incluía la comida. Al cabo de un mes aproximadamente, conocí a dos estudiantes españoles que acababan de alquilar un piso° y

apartamento

*La Universidad Complutense de Madrid, o Central, es la universidad más grande de España, con un total aproximado de ciento treinta mil estudiantes. Madrid tiene dos universidades más: la Politécnica y la Universidad Autónoma.

buscaban a alguien más. Y aquí estoy. Encantado. El piso está por la zona de Chamberí, no muy lejos de la universidad pero al menos fuera del ambiente puramente universitario. No sé, son preferencias personales pero no quería vivir por Moncloa o Argüelles.° Quería conocer otros ambientes además del universitario. Lo bueno que tiene Madrid es que la gente sale mucho y todos los barrios tienen su gracia o como se dice por aquí, «su rollo».

Moncloa... barrios estudiantiles

Me preguntas sobre las cosas que no debes olvidar traer. De ropa, tienes que traer de todo. Madrid tiene un clima continental bastante seco, y verdaderamente tiene cuatro estaciones. ¡Cuidado con los aparatos eléctricos! Trae cosas que se puedan adaptar al sistema europeo, y es más, te recomendaría que no cargases° demasiado. Con lo que vas a pagar de exceso de equipaje puedes comprarte lo que necesites aquí.

bring

Y pasemos a la comida. Lo normal es hacer la comida fuerte del día entre las dos y las tres y media de la tarde, y cenar muy tarde, entre las nueve y las once de la noche. Al principio todo me parecía que tenía mucho aceite y también me llamaba la atención la cantidad de pescado que se toma... ¡y con lo poco que a mí me gustaba! Sin embargo, ahora no sé qué va a ser de mí cuando regrese a casa sin bocadillos° de calamares fritos° ni la paella de los domingos, ni el jamón serrano°.

snacks

calamares... *fried squid* / jamón . . . *cured ham*

No sé qué más cosas podría decirte. Recuerdo que entre las cosas que más me llamaron la atención cuando llegué están las lavanderías. Sí, aquí se usan mucho menos que en los EE.UU. Por lo general todo el mundo tiene lavadora en su casa, incluso en los sitios de alquiler, y no en el sótano° del edificio sino dentro de cada apartamento. ¡Ah! También, aquí se fuma mucho, o al menos se fuma mucho en los lugares públicos.

basement

También hay que acostumbrarse a los horarios comerciales. Las tiendas abren de 10 a 1:30–2 y de 4:40–5 a 8 de lunes a sábado. Los grandes almacenes no cierran al mediodía y la oficina central de Correos está abierta hasta las diez de la noche. Por otro lado, el domingo es el último día de la semana, es decir, es el día de descanso. Prácticamente no hay ninguna actividad comercial. Es el día perfecto para echarse la siesta después de comer.

Y te podría seguir llenando hojas° y hojas sobre esta ciudad, pero creo que es mejor que tú la vayas descubriendo, ¿no? De todas formas, no dejes de escribirme si deseas saber algo más. ¿Estarías interesado en quedarte con mi habitación cuando la deje? Pienso quedarme hasta septiembre y creo que tú querías venir antes de que comience el curso, ¿no? Puedes verla y si te interesa, es para ti.

pages

Hasta pronto. Recibe un cordial saludo de

David

Follow-up:
- What kind of letter would an Hispanic student write to folks back home if he/she came to study at your campus?
- What kinds of culture shock did you experience when you moved from home to campus? Write a letter (in Spanish) to your parents describing experience.

Una guía de Madrid

La Plaza Mayor

¿Qué haría Ud. si tuviera la oportunidad de pasar un año como estudiante en Madrid? Seguramente no pasaría todo su tiempo en las clases. Una parte importante de su educación consistiría en conocer España y, en especial, Madrid. En la siguiente guía encontrará algunos lugares y actividades de interés.

Tienda de antigüedades en El Rastro

El centro comercial La Vaguada

Compras. El mercado más grande y curioso de Madrid es el Rastro. Este mercado al aire libre abre sus cientos de tiendas y puestos los domingos por la mañana. Todo lo nuevo, lo viejo, lo artesanal° y las antigüedades están aquí a su alcance.° No se lo pierda.

La zona de Goya y Serrano es la zona elegante tradicional, y no sólo por la ropa. Los diseños más modernos los encontrará en la calle Almirante y alrededores.° Si busca objetos de alta artesanía vaya a las tiendas de Artespaña. Madrid cuenta con varias cadenas de grandes almacenes en donde encontrará cualquier cosa que necesite, y si busca un centro comercial «a la americana» no se olvide de La Vaguada. Su interesante arquitectura ya merece una visita.

lo... *crafts*
a... *within reach*
surrounding areas

Restaurantes y vida nocturna. En Madrid hay muchos y excelentes restaurantes en los que podrá saborear lo mejor de la comida castellana° y española: paella valenciana, bacalao a la vizcaína,° fabada asturiana,° cochinillo° a la segoviana, gazpacho andaluz... Y para la persona de gustos internacionales, Madrid cuenta con numerosos restaurantes que le ofrecen sus especialidades procedentes de todos los rincones° del mundo. Y sin olvidarnos de la Nueva Cocina.

Si le gusta tomar un aperitivo antes de almorzar o cenar, dése una vuelta° por los alrededores de la Plaza Mayor y por las calles próximas a la Puerta del Sol. ¡No deje de probar las tapas° que le ofrezcan!

of Castille
bacalao... *cod in a tomato-based sauce* / fabada... *stew of ham, beans, pigs' ears, black sausage, bacon* / *roast suckling pig*
corners
dése... *take a stroll*
hors d'œuvres

Hacer vida nocturna en Madrid no significa únicamente salir a ver un espectáculo, que los hay y muy variados. Los madrileños salen «a dar una vuelta por el centro» después de cenar, a tomar un café tranquilamente o a sentarse en una terraza al aire libre si hace buen tiempo. Las zonas más frecuentadas por los jóvenes son Argüelles, Malasaña, Huertas. En Azca se mezclan los bares tranquilos y elegantes para adultos con los disco-bares y discotecas que están de moda.

Tapas en un bar madrileño

Parques. Madrid cuenta con grandes parques como El Retiro, el Jardín Botánico, Rosales y el parque del Oeste o la Casa de Campo. También se puede pasear por calles ajardinadas o bulevares, como el Prado, Recoletos y la Castellana. En el Zoo de Madrid, situado en la Casa de Campo, está Chulín,* uno de los pocos osos panda nacidos en cautiverio. Madrid cuenta desde hace poco con un gran planetario en el parque de Tierno Galván.

Deportes. Si Ud. es aficionado a los deportes podrá practicar su deporte favorito. Hay estadios, campos deportivos, gimnasios y varios campos de golf. Para los amantes de la hípica° Madrid cuenta con numerosos picaderos° y el famoso hipódromo de La Zarzuela. Si le emociona la velocidad, vaya a ver las carreras de motos y de automóviles en el circuito del Jarama. La Pinilla y Navacerrada son dos estaciones de esquí a menos de dos horas de la ciudad.

horseback riding / riding schools

Cine, teatro, música. El cine es una de las actividades favoritas de los madrileños y en los numerosos teatros de la ciudad se representan obras clásicas y modernas, tanto españolas como extranjeras. El Festival Internacional de Teatro cada año atrae a más participantes. Hay temporada de ópera y de conciertos, y no faltan las representaciones de ballet y de danza. ¿Ha visto o escuchado alguna zarzuela española? Las zarzuelas son parecidas a las óperas pero con partes no cantadas y, por supuesto, todo en español. Durante el verano hay representaciones de todo esto al aire libre.

Con tanta actividad es evidente que uno puede pasar muchas horas agradables en Madrid. Pero ¡cuidado! No se olvide de los estudios en la universidad.

El Retiro

Ejercicio escrito final

Which of the preceding activities appeals to you the most? What parts of the Spanish-speaking world are you most interested in visiting? Express your preferences by writing paragraphs to complete the following statements.

1. Si yo estuviera en (Madrid, Buenos Aires, Cuernavaca, ¿ ?), ...
2. Si yo pudiera viajar a cualquier lugar del mundo, ...

*Derived from the slang word **chulo** (*attractive, cute*).

APPENDIX 1

USING ADJECTIVES AS NOUNS

Nominalization means using an adjective as a noun. Adjectives used as nouns are often called pronouns because they can take the place of a noun.

In Spanish, adjectives can be nominalized in a number of ways, all of which involve dropping the noun that accompanies the adjective, then using the adjective in combination with an article or other word. One kind of adjective, the demonstrative, can simply be used alone. In most cases, these usages parallel those of English, although the English equivalent may be phrased differently from the Spanish.

Article + adjective
Simply omit the noun from an *article* + *noun* + *adjective* phrase.

el **libro** azul → **el azul** (*the blue one*)
la **hermana** casada → **la casada** (*the married one*)
el **señor** mexicano → **el mexicano** (*the Mexican*)
los **pantalones** baratos → **los baratos** (*the inexpensive ones*)

Using the article with a **de** + *noun* phrase is a similar construction. Like the *article* + *adjective* phrase, it permits you to drop the noun.

la **casa** de Julio → **la de Julio** (*Julio's*)
los **coches** del Sr. Martínez → **los del Sr. Martínez** (*Mr. Martinez's*)

In both cases, the construction is used to refer to a noun that has already been mentioned. The English equivalent uses *one* or *ones*, or a possessive without the noun.

—¿Necesitas el libro grande?
—No. Necesito **el pequeño**.
—*Do you need the big book?*
—*No. I need the small one.*

—¿Quién es la mujer morena?
—¿**La morena**? Es mi hermana.
—*Who's the brunette woman?*
—*The brunette? She's my sister.*

—¿Usamos el coche de Ernesto?
—No. Usemos **el de Ana**.
—*Shall we use Ernesto's car?*
—*No. Let's use Ana's.*

Note that in the preceding examples the noun is mentioned in the first part of the exchange (**libro, mujer, coche**) but not in the response or rejoinder.

Note also that a demonstrative can also be used to nominalize an adjective: **este rojo** (*this red one*), **esos azules** (*those blue ones*).

Lo + adjective
As seen in **Capítulo 12**, **lo** combines with the masculine singular form of an adjective to describe general qualities or characteristics. The English equivalent is expressed with words like *part* or *thing*.

lo mejor	*the best thing (part), what's best*
lo mismo	*the same thing*
lo comico	*the funny thing (part), what's funny*

Article + stressed possessive adjective
The stressed possessive adjectives—but not the unstressed possessive—can be used as possessive pronouns: **la maleta suya** → **la suya**. The article and the possessive form agree in gender and number with the noun to which they refer.

Éste es mi **banco**. (¿Dónde está **el suyo**?
This is my bank. Where is yours?
Sus **bebidas** están preparadas; **las nuestras**, no.
Their drinks are ready; ours aren't.
No es la **maleta** de Juan; es **la mía**.
It isn't Juan's suitcase; it's mine.

Note that the definite article is frequently omitted after forms of **ser: ¿Esa maleta? Es suya.**

Demonstrative pronouns
The demonstrative adjective can be used alone, without a noun. In general, an accent mark is added to the demonstrative pronoun to distinguish it from the demonstrative adjectives (**este, ese, aquel**).

Necesito este diccionario y **ése**.
I need this dictionary and that one.
Estas senoras y **aquéllas** son las hermanas de Sara, ¿no?
These women and those (over there) are Sara's sisters, aren't they?

It is acceptable (though not yet the norm) in modern Spanish, per the **Real Academia Española de la Lengua**, to omit the accent on demonstrative pronouns when context makes the meaning clear and no ambiguity is possible.

APPENDIX 2

ADDITIONAL PERFECT FORMS (INDICATIVE AND SUBJUNCTIVE)

Some indicative verb tenses have corresponding perfect forms in the indicative and subjunctive moods. Here is the present system.

el presente:	yo hablo, como, pongo
el presente perfecto:	yo he hablado/comido/puesto
el presente perfecto del subjuntivo:	yo haya hablado/comido/puesto

Other indicative forms that you have learned also have corresponding perfect indicative and subjunctive forms. Here are the most important ones, along with examples of their use. In each case, the tense or mood is formed with the appropriate form of **haber**.

El pluscuamperfecto del subjuntivo

yo hubiera hablado, comido, vivido, *etc.*
tú hubieras hablado, comido, vivido, *etc.*
Ud., él, ella hubiera hablado, comido, vivido, *etc.*
nosotros hubiéramos hablado, comido, vivido, *etc.*
vosotros hubierais hablado, comido, vivido, *etc.*
Uds., ellos, ellas hubieran hablado, comido, vivido, *etc.*

These forms correspond to **el pluscuamperfecto del indicativo (Capítulo 14)**. These forms are most frequently used in **si** clause sentences, along with the conditional perfect. See examples below.

El futuro perfecto

yo habré hablado, comido, vivido, *etc.*
tú habrás hablado, comido, vivido, *etc.*
Ud., él, ella habrá hablado, comido, vivido, *etc.*
nosotros habremos hablado, comido, vivido, *etc.*
vosotros habréis hablado, comido, vivido, *etc.*

Uds., ellos, ellas habrán hablado, comido, vivido, *etc.*

These forms correspond to **el futuro (Capítulo 17)**. These forms are most frequently used to tell what *will have already happened* at some point in the future. (In contrast, the future tells what *will happen.*)

Mañana **hablaré** con Miguel.	*I'll speak to Miguel tomorrow.*
Para las tres, ya **habré hablado** con Miguel.	*By three, I'll already have spoken to Miguel.*
El año que viene **visitaremos** a los nietos.	*We'll visit our grandchildren next year.*
Para las Navidades, ya **habremos visitado** a los nietos.	*We'll already have visited our grandchildren by Christmas.*

El condicional perfecto

yo habría hablado, comido, vivido, *etc.*
tú habrías hablado, comido, vivido, *etc.*
Ud., él, ella habría hablado, comido, vivido, *etc.*
nosotros habríamos hablado, comido, vivido, *etc.*
vosotros habríais hablado, comido, vivido, *etc.*
Uds., ellos, ellas habrían hablado, comido, vivido, *etc.*

These forms correspond to **el condicional (Capítulo 18)**. These forms are frequently used to tell what *would have happened* at some point in the past. (In contrast, the conditional tells what one *would do.*)

Yo **hablaría** con Miguel.	*I would speak with Miguel (if I were you, at some point in the future).*
Yo **habría hablado** con Miguel.	*I would have spoken with Miguel (if I were you, at some point in the past).*

Note the use of the conditional to make suggestions about the present or future, the conditional perfect to make suggestions about the past.

***Si* clause: Sentences about the past**

You have learned (**Capítulo 18**) to use the past subjunctive and conditional to speculate about the present in **si** clause sentences: what *would happen* if a particular event *were* to (or *were not* to) occur.

Si **tuviera** el tiempo, **aprendería** francés.	*If I had the time, I would learn French (in the present or at some point in the future).*

The perfect forms of the past subjunctive and the conditional are used to speculate about the past: what *would have happened* if a particular event *would have* (or *would not have* occurred).

En la escuela superior, si **hubiera tenido** el tiempo, **habría aprendido** francés.	*In high school, if I had had the time, I would have learned French.*

Dependent Clause: *Si* Clause	**Independent Clause**
si + imperfect subjunctive	conditional
si + past perfect subjunctive	conditional perf.

APPENDIX 3

VERBS

A. Regular Verbs: Simple Tenses

INFINITIVE PRESENT PARTICIPLE PAST PARTICIPLE	INDICATIVE					SUBJUNCTIVE		IMPERATIVE
	PRESENT	IMPERFECT	PRETERITE	FUTURE	CONDITIONAL	PRESENT	IMPERFECT	
hablar hablando hablado	hablo hablas habla hablamos habláis hablan	hablaba hablabas hablaba hablábamos hablabais hablaban	hablé hablaste habló hablamos hablasteis hablaron	hablaré hablarás hablará hablaremos hablaréis hablarán	hablaría hablarías hablaría hablaríamos hablaríais hablarían	hable hables hable hablemos habléis hablen	hablara hablaras hablara habláramos hablarais hablaran	habla tú, no hables hable Ud. hablemos hablen
comer comiendo comido	como comes come comemos coméis comen	comía comías comía comíamos comíais comían	comí comiste comió comimos comisteis comieron	comeré comerás comerá comeremos comeréis comerán	comería comerías comería comeríamos comeríais comerían	coma comas coma comamos comáis coman	comiera comieras comiera comiéramos comierais comieran	come tú, no comas coma Ud. comamos coman
vivir viviendo vivido	vivo vives vive vivimos vivís viven	vivía vivías vivía vivíamos vivíais vivían	viví viviste vivió vivimos vivisteis vivieron	viviré vivirás vivirá viviremos viviréis vivirán	viviría vivirías viviría viviríamos viviríais vivirían	viva vivas viva vivamos viváis vivan	viviera vivieras viviera viviéramos vivierais vivieran	vive tú, no vivas viva Ud. vivamos vivan

B. Regular Verbs: Perfect Tenses

INDICATIVE					SUBJUNCTIVE	
PRESENT PERFECT	PAST PERFECT	PRETERITE PERFECT	FUTURE PERFECT	CONDITIONAL PERFECT	PRESENT PERFECT	PAST PERFECT
he has ha hemos habéis han } hablado, comido, vivido	había habías había habíamos habíais habían } hablado, comido, vivido	hube hubiste hubo hubimos hubisteis hubieron } hablado, comido, vivido	habré habrás habrá habremos habréis habrán } hablado, comido, vivido	habría habrías habría habríamos habríais habrían } hablado, comido, vivido	haya hayas haya hayamos hayáis hayan } hablado, comido, vivido	hubiera hubieras hubiera hubiéramos hubierais hubieran } hablado, comido, vivido

C. Irregular Verbs

INFINITIVE PRESENT PARTICIPLE PAST PARTICIPLE	INDICATIVE					SUBJUNCTIVE		IMPERATIVE
	PRESENT	IMPERFECT	PRETERITE	FUTURE	CONDITIONAL	PRESENT	IMPERFECT	
andar andando andado	ando andas anda andamos andáis andan	andaba andabas andaba andábamos andabais andaban	anduve anduviste anduvo anduvimos anduvisteis anduvieron	andaré andarás andará andaremos andaréis andarán	andaría andarías andaría andaríamos andaríais andarían	ande andes ande andemos andéis anden	anduviera anduvieras anduviera anduviéramos anduvierais anduvieran	anda tú, no andes ande Ud. andemos anden
caer cayendo caído	caigo caes cae caemos caéis caen	caía caías caía caíamos caíais caían	caí caíste cayó caímos caísteis cayeron	caeré caerás caerá caeremos caeréis caerán	caería caerías caería caeríamos caeríais caerían	caiga caigas caiga caigamos caigáis caigan	cayera cayeras cayera cayéramos cayerais cayeran	cae tú, no caigas caiga Ud. caigamos caigan
dar dando dado	doy das da damos dais dan	daba dabas daba dábamos dabais daban	di diste dio dimos disteis dieron	daré darás dará daremos daréis darán	daría darías daría daríamos daríais darían	dé des dé demos deis den	diera dieras diera diéramos dierais dieran	da tú, no des dé Ud. demos den
decir diciendo dicho	digo dices dice decimos decís dicen	decía decías decía decíamos decíais decían	dije dijiste dijo dijimos dijisteis dijeron	diré dirás dirá diremos diréis dirán	diría dirías diría diríamos diríais dirían	diga digas diga digamos digáis digan	dijera dijeras dijera dijéramos dijerais dijeran	di tú, no digas diga Ud. digamos digan
estar estando estado	estoy estás está estamos estáis están	estaba estabas estaba estábamos estabais estaban	estuve estuviste estuvo estuvimos estuvisteis estuvieron	estaré estarás estará estaremos estaréis estarán	estaría estarías estaría estaríamos estaríais estarían	esté estés esté estemos estéis estén	estuviera estuvieras estuviera estuviéramos estuvierais estuviera	está tú, no estés esté Ud. estemos estén
haber habiendo habido	he has ha hemos habéis han	había habías había habíamos habíais habían	hube hubiste hubo hubimos hubisteis hubieron	habré habrás habrá habremos habréis habrán	habría habrías habría habríamos habríais habrían	haya hayas haya hayamos hayáis hayan	hubiera hubieras hubiera hubiéramos hubierais hubieran	
hacer haciendo hecho	hago haces hace hacemos hacéis hacen	hacía hacías hacía hacíamos hacíais hacían	hice hiciste hizo hicimos hicisteis hicieron	haré harás hará haremos haréis harán	haría harías haría haríamos haríais harían	haga hagas haga hagamos hagáis hagan	hiciera hicieras hiciera hiciéramos hicierais hicieran	haz tú, no hagas haga Ud. hagamos hagan

C. Irregular Verbs (continued)

INFINITIVE PRESENT PARTICIPLE PAST PARTICIPLE	INDICATIVE PRESENT	 IMPERFECT	 PRETERITE	 FUTURE	 CONDITIONAL	SUBJUNCTIVE PRESENT	 IMPERFECT	IMPERATIVE
ir yendo ido	voy vas va vamos vais van	iba ibas iba íbamos ibais iban	fui fuiste fue fuimos fuisteis fueron	iré irás irá iremos iréis irán	iría irías iría iríamos iríais irían	vaya vayas vaya vayamos vayáis vayan	fuera fueras fuera fuéramos fuerais fueran	ve tú, no vayas vaya Ud. vayamos vayan
oír oyendo oído	oigo oyes oye oímos oís oyen	oía oías oía oíamos oíais oían	oí oíste oyó oímos oísteis oyeron	oiré oirás oirá oiremos oiréis oirán	oiría oirías oiría oiríamos oiríais oirían	oiga oigas oiga oigamos oigáis oigan	oyera oyeras oyera oyéramos oyerais oyeran	oye tú, no oigas oiga Ud. oigamos oigan
poder pudiendo podido	puedo puedes puede podemos podéis pueden	podía podías podía podíamos podíais podían	pude pudiste pudo pudimos pudisteis pudieron	podré podrás podrá podremos podréis podrán	podría podrías podría podríamos podríais podrían	pueda puedas pueda podamos podáis puedan	pudiera pudieras pudiera pudiéramos pudierais pudieran	
poner poniendo puesto	pongo pones pone ponemos ponéis ponen	ponía ponías ponía poníamos poníais ponían	puse pusiste puso pusimos pusisteis pusieron	pondré pondrás pondrá pondremos pondréis pondrán	pondría pondrías pondría pondríamos pondríais pondrían	ponga pongas ponga pongamos pongáis pongan	pusiera pusieras pusiera pusiéramos pusierais pusieran	pon tú, no pongas ponga Ud. pongamos pongan
querer queriendo querido	quiero quieres quiere queremos queréis quieren	quería querías quería queríamos queríais querían	quise quisiste quiso quisimos quisisteis quisieron	querré querrás querrá querremos querréis querrán	querría querrías querría querríamos querríais querrían	quiera quieras quiera queramos queráis quieran	quisiera quisieras quisiera quisiéramos quisierais quisieran	quiere tú, no quieras quiera Ud. queramos quieran
saber sabiendo sabido	sé sabes sabe sabemos sabéis saben	sabía sabías sabía sabíamos sabíais sabían	supe supiste supo supimos supisteis supieron	sabré sabrás sabrá sabremos sabréis sabrán	sabría sabrías sabría sabríamos sabríais sabrían	sepa sepas sepa sepamos sepáis sepan	supiera supieras supiera supiéramos supierais supieran	sabe tú, no sepas sepa Ud. sepamos sepan
salir saliendo salido	salgo sales sale salimos salís salen	salía salías salía salíamos salíais salían	salí saliste salió salimos salisteis salieron	saldré saldrás saldrá saldremos saldréis saldrán	saldría saldrías saldría saldríamos saldríais saldrían	salga salgas salga salgamos salgáis salgan	saliera salieras saliera saliéramos salierais salieran	sal tú, no salgas salga Ud. salgamos salgan

ser siendo sido	soy eres es somos sois son	era eras era éramos erais eran	fui fuiste fue fuimos fuisteis fueron	seré serás será seremos seréis serán	sería serías sería seríamos seríais serían	sea seas sea seamos seáis sean	fuera fueras fuera fuéramos fuerais fueran	sé tú, no seas sea Ud. seamos sean
tener teniendo tenido	tengo tienes tiene tenemos tenéis tienen	tenía tenías tenía teníamos teníais tenían	tuve tuviste tuvo tuvimos tuvisteis tuvieron	tendré tendrás tendrá tendremos tendréis tendrán	tendría tendrías tendría tendríamos tendríais tendrían	tenga tengas tenga tengamos tengáis tengan	tuviera tuvieras tuviera tuviéramos tuvierais tuvieran	ten tú, no tengas tenga Ud. tengamos tengan
traer trayendo traído	traigo traes trae traemos traéis traen	traía traías traía traíamos traíais traían	traje trajiste trajo trajimos trajisteis trajeron	traeré traerás traerá traeremos traeréis traerán	traería traerías traería traeríamos traeríais traerían	traiga traigas traiga traigamos traigáis traigan	trajera trajeras trajera trajéramos trajerais trajeran	trae tú, no traigas traiga Ud. traigamos traigan
venir viniendo venido	vengo vienes viene venimos venís vienen	venía venías venía veníamos veníais venían	vine viniste vino vinimos vinisteis vinieron	vendré vendrás vendrá vendremos vendréis vendrán	vendría vendrías vendría vendríamos vendríais vendrían	venga vengas venga vengamos vengáis vengan	viniera vinieras viniera viniéramos vinierais vinieran	ven tú, no vengas venga Ud. vengamos vengan
ver viendo visto	veo ves ve vemos veis ven	veía veías veía veíamos veíais veían	vi viste vio vimos visteis vieron	veré verás verá veremos veréis verán	vería verías vería veríamos veríais verían	vea veas vea veamos veáis vean	viera vieras viera viéramos vierais vieran	ve tú, no veas vea Ud. veamos vean

D. Stem-changing and Spelling Change Verbs

INFINITIVE PRESENT PARTICIPLE PAST PARTICIPLE	INDICATIVE					SUBJUNCTIVE		IMPERATIVE
	PRESENT	IMPERFECT	PRETERITE	FUTURE	CONDITIONAL	PRESENT	IMPERFECT	
pensar (ie) pensando pensado	pienso piensas piensa pensamos pensáis piensan	pensaba pensabas pensaba pensábamos pensabais pensaban	pensé pensaste pensó pensamos pensasteis pensaron	pensaré pensarás pensará pensaremos pensaréis pensarán	pensaría pensarías pensaría pensaríamos pensaríais pensarían	piense pienses piense pensemos penséis piensen	pensara pensaras pensara pensáramos pensarais pensaran	piensa tú, no pienses piense Ud. pensemos piensen
volver (ue) volviendo vuelto	vuelvo vuelves vuelve volvemos volvéis vuelven	volvía volvías volvía volvíamos volvíais volvían	volví volviste volvió volvimos volvisteis volvieron	volveré volverás volverá volveremos volveréis volverán	volvería volverías volvería volveríamos volveríais volverían	vuelva vuelvas vuelva volvamos volváis vuelvan	volviera volvieras volviera volviéramos volvierais volvieran	vuelve tú, no vuelvas vuelva Ud. volvamos vuelvan

D. Stem-changing and Spelling Change Verbs (continued)

INFINITIVE PRESENT PARTICIPLE PAST PARTICIPLE	INDICATIVE					SUBJUNCTIVE		IMPERATIVE
	PRESENT	IMPERFECT	PRETERITE	FUTURE	CONDITIONAL	PRESENT	IMPERFECT	
dormir (ue, u) durmiendo dormido	duermo duermes duerme dormimos dormís duermen	dormía dormías dormía dormíamos dormíais dormían	dormí dormiste durmió dormimos dormisteis durmieron	dormiré dormirás dormirá dormiremos dormiréis dormirán	dormiría dormirías dormiría dormiríamos dormiríais dormirían	duerma duermas duerma durmamos durmáis duerman	durmiera durmieras durmiera durmiéramos durmierais durmieran	duerme tú, no duermas duerma Ud. durmamos duerman
sentir (ie, i) sintiendo sentido	siento sientes siente sentimos sentís sienten	sentía sentías sentía sentíamos sentíais sentían	sentí sentiste sintió sentimos sentisteis sintieron	sentiré sentirás sentirá sentiremos sentiréis sentirán	sentiría sentirías sentiría sentiríamos sentiríais sentirían	sienta sientas sienta sintamos sintáis sientan	sintiera sintieras sintiera sintiéramos sintierais sintieran	siente tú, no sientas sienta Ud. sintamos sientan
pedir (i, i) pidiendo pedido	pido pides pide pedimos pedís piden	pedía pedías pedía pedíamos pedíais pedían	pedí pediste pidió pedimos pedisteis pidieron	pediré pedirás pedirá pediremos pediréis pedirán	pediría pedirías pediría pediríamos pediríais pedirían	pida pidas pida pidamos pidáis pidan	pidiera pidieras pidiera pidiéramos pidierais pidieran	pide tú, no pidas pida Ud. pidamos pidan
reír (i, i) riendo reído	río ríes ríe reímos reís rien	reía reías reía reíamos reíais reían	reí reíste rió reímos reísteis rieron	reiré reirás reirá reiremos reiréis reirán	reiría reirías reiría reiríamos reiríais reirían	ría rías ría riamos riáis rían	riera rieras riera riéramos rierais rieran	ríe tú, no rías ría Ud. riamos rían
seguir (i, i) (ga) siguiendo seguido	sigo sigues sigue seguimos seguís siguen	seguía seguías seguía seguíamos seguíais seguían	seguí seguiste siguió seguimos seguisteis siguieron	seguiré seguirás seguirá seguiremos seguiréis seguirán	seguiría seguirías seguiría seguiríamos seguiríais seguirían	siga sigas siga sigamos sigáis sigan	siguiera siguieras siguiera siguiéramos siguierais siguieran	sigue tú, no sigas siga Ud. sigamos sigan
construir (y) construyendo construido	construyo construyes construye construimos construís construyen	construía construías construía construíamos construíais construían	construí construiste construyó construimos construisteis construyeron	construiré construirás construirá construiremos construiréis construirán	construiría construirías construiría construiríamos construiríais construirían	construya construyas construya construyamos construyáis construyan	construyera construyeras construyera construyéramos construyerais construyeran	construye tú, no construyas construya Ud. construyamos construyan
producir (zc) produciendo producido	produzco produces produce producimos producís producen	producía producías producía producíamos producíais producían	produje produjiste produjo produjimos produjisteis produjeron	produciré producirás producirá produciremos produciréis producirán	produciría producirías produciría produciríamos produciríais producirían	produzca produzcas produzca produzcamos produzcáis produzcan	produjera produjeras produjera produjéramos produjerais produjeran	produce tú, no produzcas produzca Ud. produzcamos produzcan

APPENDIX 4

ANSWERS TO ¿RECUERDA UD.? EXERCISES

GRAMMAR SECTION 8 1. nosotros/as 2. tú 3. vosotros/as 4. yo 5. Ud., él, ella

GRAMMAR SECTION 14 1. ¿De quién son estos regalos? 2. Son de Carmen. 3. ¡¿La boda de Carmen es hoy?! 4. Sí, y todos los parientes de Miguel vienen.

GRAMMAR SECTION 16 querer: qu**ie**ro, qu**ie**res, qu**ie**re, qu**ie**ren; poder: p**ue**do, p**ue**des, p**ue**de, p**ue**den

GRAMMAR SECTION 23 1. Sí, me gusta... (No, no me gusta...) ¿Le gusta... ? 2. Sí, me gusta jugar... (No, no me gusta jugar...) ¿Le gusta jugar... ? 3. Sí, me gusta viajar... (No, no me gusta viajar...) ¿Le gusta viajar... ? 4. Me gusta más ir a fiestas (descansar, comer). ¿Qué le gusta más ?

GRAMMAR SECTION 27 1. Directo: los libros; Indirecto: nos 2. Directo: los 3. Directo: el menú; Indirecto: me 4. Directo: lo 5. Directo: el dinero; Indirecto: te 6. Directo: lo 7. Directo: te 8. Directo: me

GRAMMAR SECTION 33 1. La Navidad es más interesante que el Día de Gracias. 2. Nuestro árbol de Navidad es más alto que el árbol fuera de la casa. 3. ¡Esta fiesta es mejor que un regalo! 4. Mis hermanos son mayores que yo.

GRAMMAR SECTION 43 1. Tráiganme el libro. 2. No se lo den a ella. 3. Siéntese aquí, por favor. 4. ¡No se siente en esa silla! 5. Díganles la verdad. 6. ¡Díganselа ahora! 7. Nunca se la digan a ella. (No se la digan nunca a ella.) 8. Cuídese. 9. Lleve una vida sana. 10. Escúcheme.

GRAMMAR SECTION 46
EJERCICIO A 1. hablaron 2. comieron 3. vivieron 4. jugaron 5. perdieron 6. durmieron 7. rieron 8. leyeron 9. estuvieron 10. tuvieron 11. fueron 12. vistieron 13. trajeron 14. dieron 15. supieron 16. pudieron 17. dijeron 18. destruyeron 19. creyeron 20. mantuvieron
EJERCICIO B daba, dábamos; iba, íbamos; era, éramos

GRAMMAR SECTION 47 1. Es su derecho. 2. ¿Y mis derechos? 3. Es nuestra obligación. 4. ¡Es su gobierno también! 5. Su prensa no los informa bien. 6. Nuestros delitos no eran serios. 7. Su bienestar es importante. 8. ¡Es nuestro país también!

APPENDIX 5

ANSWERS TO EXERCISES

ANTE TODO: PRIMERA PARTE

SALUDOS Y EXPRESIONES DE CORTESÍA PRÁCTICA B 1. Muy buenas. (Buenas tardes.) (Muy buenas tardes.) 2. Hasta luego. (Hasta mañana.) (Adiós.) 3. Así así. (Bien, gracias.) (Muy bien, gracias.) (¡Muy bien!) ¿Y tú? 4. ¿Qué tal? (¿Cómo estás?) 5. Bien, gracias. (Muy bien, gracias.) ¿Y usted? 6. Buenas noches. (Muy buenas.) (Adiós). (Hasta mañana.) 7. De nada. 8. Hasta mañana. (Hasta luego.) (Adiós.) 9. ______. (Me llamo ______.) 10. Igualmente. (Encantado/a.)
CONVERSACIÓN B 1. Con permiso. 2. Perdón. 3. Por favor. (Perdón.) 4. Con permiso. 5. Perdón. 6. Con permiso.

EL ALFABETO ESPAÑOL
PRÁCTICA A 1. c 2. d 3. h 4. a 5. e 6. g 7. b 8. f 9. ch

ANTE TODO: SEGUNDA PARTE

MÁS COGNADOS PRÁCTICA B 1. Es una cosa. 2. Es un animal. 3. Es una comida. 4. Es un deporte. 5. Es una nación. 6. Es una persona. 7. Es un lugar (una cosa). 8. Es una bebida. 9. Es un animal. 10. Es una cosa. 11. Es un lugar. 12. Es un concepto. 13. Es una persona. 14. Es una nación. 15. Es una persona. 16. Es un lugar. 17. Es un animal. 18. Es una bebida (una comida). 19. Es un deporte. 20. Es un instrumento musical. 21. Es un concepto.
CONVERSACIÓN A 1. —¿Qué es un saxofón? —Es un instrumento musical. 2. —¿Qué es un autobús? —Es una cosa. 3. —¿Qué es una estación? —Es un lugar. 4. —¿Qué es un doctor? —Es una persona. 5. —¿Qué es Bolivia? — Es una nación. 6. —¿Qué es una Coca-Cola? —Es una bebida. 7. —¿Qué es una enchilada? —Es una comida. 8. —¿Qué es una jirafa? —Es un animal.
CONVERSACIÓN B *Partial answers:* Diego Rivera: muralista, México; Fernando Valenzuela: jugador de béisbol, México; Geraldo Rivera: reportero, los Estados Unidos; Fidel Castro: primer ministro, Cuba; Rita Moreno: actriz, Puerto Rico/los Estados Unidos; Ricardo Montalbán: actor, México; Lee Treviño: jugador de golf, los Estados Unidos; Julio Iglesias: cantante, España; Severiano Ballesteros: jugador de golf, España

LOS NÚMEROS 0–30 PRÁCTICA A 1. cuatro señoras 2. doce noches 3. un café 4. veintiún (veinte y un) cafés 5. catorce días 6. una clase 7. veintiuna (veinte y una) ideas 8. once tardes 9. quince estudiantes 10. trece teléfonos 11. veintiocho (veinte y ocho) bebidas 12. cinco guitarras 13. un león 14. treinta señores 15. veinte oficinas

PRÁCTICA B 1. Dos y cuatro son seis. 2. Ocho y diecisiete (diez y siete) son veinticinco (veinte y cinco). 3. Once y uno son doce. 4. Tres y dieciocho (diez y ocho) son veintiuno (veinte y uno). 5. Nueve y seis son quince. 6. Cinco y cuatro son nueve. 7. Uno y trece son catorce. 8. Quince menos dos son trece. 9. Nueve menos nueve son cero. 10. Trece menos ocho son cinco. 11. Catorce y doce son veintiséis (veinte y seis). 12. Veintitrés (Veinte y tres) menos trece son diez.

CONVERSACIÓN B 1. tres pesos 2. ocho dólares 3. doce pesos 4. catorce pesetas 5. veintiún (viente y un) dólares 6. once pesetas

ANTE TODO: TERCERA PARTE

¿QUÉ HORA ES? PRÁCTICA A 1. Es la una. 2. Son las seis. 3. Son las once. 4. Es la una y media. 5. Son las tres y cuarto (quince). 6. Son las siete menos cuarto (quince). 7. Son las cuatro y cuarto (quince). 8. Son las doce menos cuarto (quince) en punto. 9. Son las nueve y diez en punto. 10. Son las diez menos diez en punto.

PRÁCTICA B 1. Son las dos y diecinueve (diez y nueve) (veinte) de la mañana. 2. Son las cinco y cuarto (quince) de la mañana. 3. Son las nueve y media de la mañana. 4. Son las doce menos veinte de la noche. 5. Son las dos menos uno de la tarde. 6. Son las diez y veintidós (veinte y dos) de la noche. 7. Es la una y siete de la mañana. 8. Son las seis y dieciséis (diez y seis) de la tarde.

CONVERSACIÓN A 1. —¿Cuándo llegamos a Sevilla? —A las once de la mañana. 2. —¿Cuándo llegamos a Buenos Aires? —A las doce menos seis de la noche. 3. —¿Cuándo llegamos a Los Ángeles? —A la una y cuarto (quince) de la tarde. 4. —¿Cuándo llegamos a Miami? —A las nueve menos veintinueve (veinte y nueve) de la noche. 5. —¿Cuándo llegamos a Málaga? —A las seis menos veinticinco (veinte y cinco) de la mañana. 6. —¿Cuándo llegamos a Cali? —A las dos y media en punto de la mañana.

CONVERSACIÓN B 1. —¿A qué hora es la clase de francés? —A las dos menos cuarto (quince) de la tarde... ¡en punto! 2. —¿A qué hora es la sesión de laboratorio? —A las tres y diez de la tarde... ¡en punto! 3. —¿A qué hora es la excursión? —A las nueve menos diez de la mañana... ¡en punto! 4. —¿A qué hora es el concierto? —A las siete y media de la noche... ¡en punto!

LAS PALABRAS INTERROGATIVAS: UN RESUMEN

PRÁCTICA A 1. ¿A qué hora... ? ¿Cuándo... ? 2. ¿Dónde... ? 3. ¿Qué... ? ¿Quién... ? 4. ¿Cómo... ? 5. ¿Cómo... ? 6. ¿Cuántos... ? 7. ¿Cuánto... ? ¿Cuántos... ? 8. ¿Cuál... ? 9. ¿Qué... ? 10. ¿Cuándo... ? ¿A qué hora... ? 11. ¿Qué hora es? 12. ¿Quién... ? ¿Cómo... ?

CONVERSACIÓN *Possible answers:* 1. ¿A qué hora es la película? 2. ¿Dónde está el libro? 3. ¿Qué es el regalo? (¿Qué es esto?) 4. ¿Cuál es la capital de España? 5. ¿Cuánto es el libro? 6. ¿Quién es el fantasma?

CAPÍTULO 1 VOCABULARIO: PREPARACIÓN

¿DÓNDE? LA UNIVERSIDAD

EJERCICIO A 1. Están en la clase. C la profesora D la estudiante A el papel CH el lápiz E el bolígrafo B la mesa F la silla G la calculadora 2. Están en la biblioteca. CH el libro E el diccionario B el cuaderno D el bolígrafo C la mesa A el estudiante F la silla 3. Están en la librería. B la estudiante CH el lápiz D el cuaderno A el bolígrafo C el dinero E la mochila 4. Están en la oficina. CH (*or* A) la secretaria A (*or* CH) la consejera C el profesor D el escritorio B el diccionario

EJERCICIO B 1. Es hombre. 2. Es mujer. 3. Es hombre. 4. Es hombre.

LAS MATERIAS EJERCICIO A 1. Es para una clase de matemáticas. 2. Es para una clase de inglés. 3. Es para una clase de historia. 4. Es para una clase de computación. 5. Es para una clase de sicología. 6. Es para una clase de español. 7. Es para una clase de historia. 8. Es para una clase de historia.

GRAMMAR SECTION 1 PRÁCTICA A 1. el 2. la 3. el 4. la 5. el 6. el 7. la 8. el 9. la 10. la 11. el 12. la 13. un 14. una 15. un 16. un 17. una 18. una 19. un 20. una 21. un

PRÁCTICA B 1. Hay un consejero en la oficina. 2. Hay una profesora en la clase. 3. Hay un lápiz en la mesa. 4. Hay un cuaderno en el escritorio. 5. Hay un libro en la mochila. 6. Hay un bolígrafo en la silla. 7. Hay una palabra en el papel. 8. Hay una oficina en la biblioteca.

CONVERSACIÓN A 1. Conchita es estudiante también. 2. Carlos Ortega es profesor también. 3. Juanita es dependienta también. 4. José es mi amigo también.

CONVERSACIÓN B 1. —¿El cliente? —Es una persona. 2. —¿El inglés? —Es una materia. 3. —¿La residencia? —Es un edificio. 4. —¿El dependiente? —Es una persona. 5. —¿El hotel? —Es un edificio. 6. —¿El comercio? —Es una materia.

GRAMMAR SECTION 2 PRÁCTICA A 1. las mesas 2. los libros 3. los amigos 4. las oficinas 5. unos cuadernos 6. unos lápices 7. unas extranjeras 8. unos bolígrafos 9. unos edificios 10. el profesor 11. la calculadora 12. la niña 13. el lápiz 14. un papel 15. una tarde 16. una residencia 17. una silla 18. un escritorio

PRÁCTICA B 1. mujer, estudiante 2. niño, profesor 3. extranjeros, amigos, estudiantes

PRÁCTICA C 1. los estudiantes 2. unas residencias 3. una dependienta en la librería 4. los extranjeros 5. los secretarios 6. unas profesoras

GRAMMAR SECTION 3 PRÁCTICA A *Possible answers:* 1. (No) Necesito dinero. 2. No cantamos en francés. 3. (No) Deseamos practicar el español. 4. No trabajo en la biblioteca. 5. Ud., profesor(a), (no) enseña muy bien. 6. No tomamos cerveza en clase. 7. No tomo ocho clases este semestre. 8. Ud., profesor(a), (no) habla muy bien el alemán.

PRÁCTICA B 1. cantan 2. bailan 3. busca 4. habla 5. desea 6. bailar 7. baila 8. necesitan // 1. falso 2. falso 3. cierto 4. cierto

GRAMMAR SECTION 4 PRÁCTICA A Possible answers. 1. —¿Miguel habla con el dependiente? (¿Habla Miguel con el dependiente?) —No. Irma habla con el dependiente. 2. —¿Irma desea pagar la mochila? (¿Desea Irma pagar la mochila?) —No. Miguel paga la mochila. 3. —¿Hildebrando busca un libro de historia? (¿Busca Hildebrando un libro de historia?) —Sí. Hildebrando busca un libro de historia. 4. —¿Irma también busca un libro de historia? (¿También busca Irma un libro de historia?) —No. Alicia busca un libro de historia. 5. —¿Alicia estudia historia? (¿Estudia Alicia historia?) —Sí. Alicia estudia historia. 6. —¿Ramón es una persona impaciente? (¿Es Ramón una persona impaciente?) —No. Ramón es una persona paciente. 7. —¿Hay tres dependientes en la librería hoy? (En la librería, ¿hay tres dependientes hoy?) —No. Hay sólo un dependiente en la librería hoy.

PRÁCTICA B *Possible answers:* 1. ¿Trabaja Ud. en la librería? ¿Trabajas (tú) en la librería todos los días? 2. ¿Habla Alicia español muy bien? ¿Alicia habla español muy bien? 3. ¿Regresa Ud. a casa hoy? ¿Regresas (tú) a casa hoy? 4. ¿Estudian Uds. (¿Estudiáis) mucho para la clase de matemáticas? ¿Uds. estudian (¿Estudiáis) mucho para la clase de matemáticas? 5. ¿Busca Jaime un diccionario? ¿Jaime busca un diccionario? 6. ¿Necesitan Uds. (un) lápiz? ¿Uds. necesitan (un) lápiz? (¿Necesitáis lápiz?)

UN POCO DE TODO EJERCICIO B 1. ¿Buscas un diccionario? 2. ¿No trabaja Paco aquí en la cafetería? 3. ¿Necesitan Uds. una calculadora para la clase de cálculo? 4. ¿Que tal si tomamos una Coca-Cola? 5. ¿No deseas estudiar unos minutos más? // 1. No, busco mi mochila. 2. No, él trabaja en la biblioteca. 3. No, necesitamos una calculadora para la clase de química. 4. No, no

quiero tomar una Coca-Cola. Prefiero tomar ______. 5. No, quiero regresar a casa.
EJERCICIO CH. 1. me 2. el 3. los 4. Practicamos 5. la 6. una 7. habla 8. cantamos 9. canto 10. cantan 11. las 12. la 13. buscar 14. la 15. comprar 16. una 17. la 18. Los // 1. No. Unos amigos de Tomás hablan español. 2. Sí. 3. No. Tomás estudia mucho.

CAPÍTULO 2 VOCABULARIO: PREPARACIÓN

LA FAMILIA . . . EJERCICIO B 1. Falso. Juan es el esposo de Elena. 2. Cierto. 3. Falso. Carmencita es la nieta de Joaquín. 4. Cierto. 5. Cierto. 6. Falso. Juanito es el hijo de Juan. 7. Falso. Elena es la hermana de Luis.
EJERCICIO C 1. el abuelo y la abuela 2. el padre y la madre 3. el hermano y la hermana 4. el nieto y la nieta 5. el tío y la tía 6. el sobrino y la sobrina
EJERCICIO CH 1. abuela 2. primo 3. tía 4. abuelo 5. La hija de mis tíos es mi prima. *Possible answers:* 6. El hijo de mi hermano o de mi hermana es mi sobrino. 7. El hermano de mi padre o de mi madre es mi tío. 8. El padre de mi padre o de mi madre es mi abuelo.
ADJETIVOS. EJERCICIO A 1. (El chimpancé) Es tonto. 2. (José) Es perezoso. 3. (Pablo) Es alto. 4. (El demonio) Es malo, antipático y feo. 5. (Paco Pereda) Es soltero y joven. 6. (El lápiz) Es nuevo y largo. 7. (Marta) Es delgada y rubia. 8. (La familia Gómez) Es pequeña y pobre.
LOS NÚMEROS 31–100 EJERCICIO A 1. Treinta y cincuenta son ochenta. 2. Cuarenta y cinco y cuarenta y cinco son noventa. 3. Treinta y dos y cincuenta y ocho son noventa. 4. Setenta y siete y veintitrés (veinte y tres) son cien. 5. Cien menos cuarenta son sesenta. 6. Noventa y nueve menos treinta y nueve son sesenta. 7. Ochenta y cuatro menos treinta y cuatro son cincuenta. 8. Setenta y ocho menos treinta y seis son cuarenta y dos. 9. Ochenta y ocho menos veintiocho (veinte y ocho) son sesenta.
PRONUNCIACIÓN B 1. examen (*ends in* -n) 2. lápiz (*written accent mark*) 3. necesitar (*ends in consonant*) 4. perezoso (*ends in vowel*) 5. actitud (*ends in consonant*) 6. acción (*written accent mark*) 7. hermana (*ends in vowel*) 8. compran (*ends in* -n) 9. compramos (*ends in consonant*) 10. hombre (*ends in vowel*) 11. peso (*ends in vowel*) 12. mujer (*ends in consonant*) 13. lugar (*ends in consonant*) 14. natural (*ends in consonant*) 15. plástico (*written accent mark*) 16. sobrinos (*ends in consonant*)
GRAMMAR SECTION 5 PRÁCTICA B *Possible answers:* 1. Es de los Estados Unidos. 2. Es de Alemania. 3. Es de Italia. 4. Es de México. 5. Es de Francia. 6. Es de Inglaterra.
PRÁCTICA C 1. Carlos Miguel es médico. Es de Cuba. Ahora trabaja en Milwaukee. 2. Maripili es extranjera. Es de Burgos. Ahora trabaja en Miami. 3. Mariela es dependienta. Es de Buenos Aires. Ahora trabaja en Nueva York. 4. Juan es dentista. Es de Lima. Ahora trabaja en Los Ángeles.
GRAMMAR SECTION 6 PRÁCTICA A 1. morena, lista, trabajadora 2. viejo, alto, grande, interesante 3. inteligentes, viejos, religiosos 4. buenas
PRÁCTICA C Juana tiene veinte años. Es casada. Es baja y rubia y también muy fea. Es muy trabajadora—¡le gusta estudiar! También es muy delgada—¡le gusta hacer ejercicio! No es como su hermano Juan, pero es muy simpática de todos modos.
PRÁCTICA CH 1. francesa, Francia 2. español, España 3. alemanes, Alemania 4. portugués, Portugal 5. italianas, Italia 6. inglés, Inglaterra
PRÁCTICA D 1. Esta mujer es la esposa de Manolo. 2. Estos primos son de San Francisco. 3. Estas nietas son de California también. 4. Esta joven morena es mi hermana Cecilia. 5. Este hombre guapo es el tío Julián.
PRÁCTICA E 1. un cliente: Busco un coche pequeño. Busco un coche francés. Busco un coche grande. 2. un cliente: Por favor, quiero comprar un diccionario completo. Por favor, quiero comprar un diccionario barato. Por favor, quiero comprar un diccionario nuevo. 3. un empleado: Estas novelas son alemanas. Estas novelas son nuevas. Estas novelas son mexicanas. 4. un empleado: ¿Buscan una excursión fascinante? ¿Buscan una excursión larga? ¿Buscan una excursión barata?
PRÁCTICA F María es una buena estudiante. Es lista y trabajadora y estudia mucho. Es argentina, de la gran ciudad de Buenos Aires; por eso habla español. Quiere ser profesora de español; por eso estudia en esta universidad. // María es alta y guapa; también es muy delgada, pues hace mucho ejercicio. Le gustan las fiestas grandes de la universidad y tiene buenos amigos aquí, pero también tiene buenos recuerdos de sus amigos y parientes argentinos.
GRAMMAR SECTION 7 PRÁCTICA A Mariana es la abuela de Luisa. Arturo es el tío de Luisa. Isabel es la tía de Luisa. Teodoro es el padre de Luisa. Benita es la madre de Luisa. Miguel es el primo de Luisa. María es la prima de Luisa. Anita es la hermana de Luisa. Antonio es el hermano de Luisa.
PRÁCTICA B 1. —¿De quién es la casa en Beverly Hills? —Es de... 2. —¿De quién es la casa en Viena? —Es de... 3. —¿De quién es la camioneta? —Es de... 4. —¿De quién es el perro? —Es de... 5. —¿De quién son las fotos de la Argentina? —Son de... 6. —¿De quién son las mochilas con todos los libros? —Son de...
PRÁCTICA C *Possible answers:* 1. El médico regresa al hospital. 2. El dependiente regresa a la librería. 3. La profesora regresa a la biblioteca. 4. El estudiante regresa al cuarto en la residencia. 5. El decano regresa a la oficina.
UN POCO DE TODO EJERCICIO A 1. Yo soy la abuela panameña. 2. El nuevo nieto es de los Estados Unidos. 3. Juan José es el padre del nieto. 4. Juan José también es el hijo del abuelo panameño. 5. Una de las tías del nieto es médica. 6. Otra tía es una profesora famosa. 7. La madre del niño es norteamericana. 8. La hermana del niño se llama Concepción. // 1. Son de Panamá. 2. Es de los Estados Unidos.
EJERCICIO B 1. abuelo 2. prima 3. hermano 4. padre 5. tía
EJERCICIO C 1. —¿De dónde eres tú? —Soy de Guadalajara. —Ah, eres mexicano/a. —Sí, por eso hablo español. 2. —¿De dónde eres tú? —Soy de París. —Ah, eres francés (francesa). —Sí, por eso hablo francés. 3. —¿De dónde eres tú? —Soy de Roma. —Ah, eres italiano/a. —Sí, por eso hablo italiano. 4. —¿De dónde eres tú? —Soy de San Francisco. —Ah, eres norteamericano/a. —Sí, por eso hablo inglés. 5. —¿De dónde eres tú? —Soy de Madrid. —Ah, eres español(a). —Sí, por eso hablo español. 6. —¿De dónde eres tú? —Soy de Londres. —Ah, eres inglés (inglesa). —Sí, por eso hablo inglés. 7. —¿De dónde eres tú? —Soy de Berlín. —Ah, eres alemán (alemana). —Sí, por eso hablo alemán. 8. —¿De dónde eres tú? —Soy de Lima. —Ah, eres peruano/a. —Sí, por eso hablo español.
EJERCICIO CH 1. todas 2. hispánicas 3. grandes 4. del 5. de la 6. grandes 7. típica 8. todas 9. trabajan 10. necesario 11. urbanos 12. son 13. muchos 14. industrializada 15. trabaja 16. media 17. alta 18. hablar 19. hispánica 20. norteamericana // 1. Falso. Todas las familias hispánicas no son iguales. 2. Cierto. 3. Cierto. 4. Cierto.

CAPÍTULO 3 VOCABULARIO: PREPARACIÓN

DE COMPRAS, LA ROPA EJERCICIO A *Possible answers:* 1. El Sr. Rivera lleva un traje, zapatos, calcetines, una camisa, una corbata y un cinturón. También tiene un impermeable. 2. La Srta. Alonso lleva una blusa, una falda (un vestido), una chaqueta, medias y zapatos. El perro lleva un suéter. 3. Sara lleva una blusa, una falda y botas. 4. Alfredo lleva una camisa (una chaqueta), una camiseta, pantalones y sandalias. Necesita comprar una camisa nueva, pantalones nuevos y zapatos.
EJERCICIO B *Possible answers:* 1. almacén 2. regatear 3. comprar, pre-

cio 4. venden 5. un vestido corto/una camisa elegante 6. traje/un vestido 7. traje de baño 8. traje 9. traje 10. traje de baño 11. sandalias 12. seda, algodón 13. El centro 14. centros comerciales
EJERCICIO C 1. En un almacén hay precios fijos, ¿no? (¿verdad?) 2. Regateamos mucho en los Estados Unidos, ¿no? (¿verdad?) 3. En México no hay muchos mercados, ¿verdad? 4. Los *bluejeans* Calvin Klein son muy baratos, ¿no? (¿verdad?) 5. Es necesario llevar traje y corbata a clase, ¿no? (¿verdad?) 6. Estudias en la biblioteca por la noche, ¿no? (¿verdad?) 7. Buscas un perro o un gato, ¿no? (¿verdad?) 8. Eres una persona muy independiente, ¿no? (¿verdad?) 9. Tienes una familia muy grande, ¿no? (¿verdad?) 10. No hay examen mañana, ¿verdad?
LOS NÚMEROS 100 Y MÁS EJERCICIO A 1. siete mil trescientas cuarenta y cinco pesetas 2. cien dólares 3. cinco mil setecientos diez quetzales 4. seiscientos setenta bolívares 5. dos mil cuatrocientas ochenta y seis pesetas 6. un millón de dólares 7. quinientos veintiocho (veinte y ocho) pesos 8. ochocientos treinta y seis bolívares 9. ciento una pesetas 10. cuatro millones de dólares 11. seis millones quinientos mil pesos 12. veinticinco (veinte y cinco) millones de pesetas
GRAMMAR SECTION 8 PRÁCTICA A 1. Leo el periódico por la mañana. 2. Hay grandes rebajas en el almacén Celso García. 3. Mi amiga Anita insiste en ir conmigo al centro. 4. Cree que debemos llegar temprano. 5. Abren el almacén a las diez. 6. Las rebajas son estupendas: ¡Venden de todo! 7. Todos compran algo. 8. Anita cree que yo no debo comprar mucho... 9. ...pero compro una camiseta y dos pares de sandalias. 10. Más tarde Anita y yo comemos juntas en un café. // 1. Mi amiga lee... 3. Insisto en ir con ella al centro. 4. Creo que... 7. Todos compran algo. 8. Creo que ella (mi amiga) no debe comprar mucho... 9. ...pero compra... 10. Más tarde ella (mi amiga) y yo comemos juntas en un café.
PRÁCTICA B 1. deben 2. cree 3. debemos 4. insiste 5. leer 6. come 7. lee 8. Abro 9. leo 10. creo // 1. su padre 2. Paquita 3. Paquita 4. su padre
PRÁCTICA C 1. No debemos comer durante la clase. 2. Debemos asistir a clase todos los días. 3. No debemos llevar traje de baño a clase. 4. Debemos aprender las palabras nuevas. 5. (No) Insiste en hablar español en clase. 6. (No) Insiste en explicar toda la gramática. 7. (No) Insiste en dar exámenes con frecuencia. 8. (No) Insiste en llevar traje y corbata/un vestido elegante a clase.
PRÁCTICA CH 1. —¿Él comprende (¿Comprende él) español? —Creo que no, y ella no comprende inglés. —¿Qué lengua debemos hablar entonces? 2. Anita tiene dos hijos, Pablo y Teresa. Él no cree en Santa Claus, pero ella todavía cree en él.
GRAMMAR SECTION 9 PRÁCTICA A 1. (Sara) Tiene muchos exámenes. 2. Por eso viene a la universidad todos los días. 3. Prefiere estudiar en la biblioteca porque allí no hay mucho ruido. 4. Hoy trabaja hasta las ocho de la noche. 5. Quiere leer más pero no puede. 6. Por eso regresa a la residencia. 7. Tiene ganas de descansar un poco... 8. ...pero es imposible porque unos amigos vienen a mirar la tele. // 1. Tengo (Tenemos) muchos exámenes. 2. Por eso vengo (venimos)... 3. Prefiero (Preferimos)... 4. Hoy trabajo (trabajamos)... 5. Quiero (Queremos) leer más pero no puedo (podemos). 6. Por eso regreso (regresamos)... 7. Tengo (Tenemos)...
PRÁCTICA B 1. tengo ______ años. 2. tengo miedo. 3. tengo ganas de regresar a casa. 4. Tengo prisa. 5. No tienes razón.
PRÁCTICA C *Possible answers:* 1. miedo 2. prisa 3. años, tienen ganas 4. que 5. razón, tiene razón, tiene que 6. miedo (de ellos) (que estudiar)
GRAMMAR SECTION 10 PRÁCTICA A 1. (Yo) Voy a la residencia. 2. Francisca va al almacén para trabajar. 3. (Tú) Vas a otra clase. 4. Jorge y Carlos van al bar. 5. (Nosotros) Vamos a la biblioteca. 6. El profesor (La profesora) va ______.
PRÁCTICA B 1. Vamos a llegar al centro a las diez de la mañana. 2. Los niños van a querer comer algo. 3. Voy a comprar unos chocolates para Lupita. 4. Raúl va a buscar una blusa de seda. 5. No vas a comprar esta blusa de rayas, ¿verdad? 6. Vamos a tener que buscar algo más barato. 7. ¿Vas a poder ir de compras mañana también?
PRÁCTICA C 1. Voy a ir al mercado con Uds., ¡pero no voy a regatear! 2. Vamos a vender el carro viejo, pero no vamos a comprar otro, ¿verdad? 3. Vas a buscar gangas, pero las cosas no van a ser baratas.
UN POCO DE TODO EJERCICIO A 1. ¿Tiene Ud. experiencia trabajando en una tienda de ropa? 2. ¿Cuántos años tiene Ud.? 3. Ud. asiste a clases en la universidad todas las mañanas, ¿no? 4. ¿Puedo trabajar siempre por la noche? 5. ¿A qué hora abren Uds. el almacén? 6. No tengo que llegar a las ocho, ¿verdad? // *Possible answers:* 1. Sí, (No, no) tengo experiencia trabajando en una tienda de ropa. 2. Tengo ______ años. 3. Sí, (No, no) asisto a clases todas las mañanas. 4. Sí, (No, no) puede trabajar siempre por la noche. 5. Abrimos el almacén a las ______ de la mañana. 6. Sí, (No, no) tiene que llegar a las ocho.
EJERCICIO CH 1. de 2. una 3. va 4. gran 5. elegantes 6. los 7. son 8. fijos 9. pequeñas 10. una 11. El 12. de la 13. cree 14. otros 15. va 16. puede 17. debe 18. los 19. tiene 20. regatear 21. que 22. ir 23. pequeñas 24. informal 25. grandes 26. debe 27. pagar 28. el 29. a // 1. Falso. Hay una gran variedad de tiendas. 2. Falso. En los almacenes los precios son fijos. 3. Falso. Es posible comprar limones en una frutería. 4. Falso. El primer precio que menciona el vendedor es casi siempre muy alto.
REPASO 1 México—0; Honduras—0; Costa Rica—0; Guatemala—0; Nicaragua—0; Panamá—0; El Salvador—0. Managua—Nicaragua; San José—Costa Rica; la Ciudad de Panamá—Panamá; la Ciudad de México—México; la Ciudad de Guatemala—Guatemala; San Salvador—El Salvador; Tegucigalpa—Honduras.

CAPÍTULO 4 VOCABULARIO: PREPARACIÓN
¿QUÉ DÍA ES HOY? EJERCICIO A *Possible answers:* 1. Hoy es ______. Mañana es ______. Si hoy es sábado, mañana es domingo. Si hoy es jueves, mañana es viernes. Ayer fue ______. 2. Tenemos clase todos los días (los lunes, los martes, los miércoles, los jueves y los viernes). 3. Sí, (No, no) estudio mucho durante el fin de semana. Y los domingos por la noche también. (No estudio los domingos por la noche.) 4. Me gusta (ir de compras). Sí, (No, no) me gusta salir con los amigos los sábados por la noche.
LAS RELACIONES SENTIMENTALES EJERCICO A 1. d 2. c 3. b 4. ch 5. a
EJERCICIO B 1. esposo 2. noviazgo 3. una cita 4. boda 5. cita 6. amistad 7. matrimonio 8. amor
¿DÓNDE ESTÁ?: LAS PREPOSICIONES EJERCICIO A *Possible answers:* 1. El bar está a la izquierda de la iglesia. 2. La ambulancia está delante del hospital. 3. El cine está a la izquierda del hospital y a la derecha de la iglesia. 4. La iglesia está detrás del parque. 5. El cura está delante de la iglesia. 6. Los novios están delante de la iglesia también. 7. El niño está en el parque. 8. Los árboles están en el parque también. 9. La mamá está a la derecha del niño. 10. El parque está delante del cine y la iglesia.
EJERCICIO C 1. ella 2. ti, contigo 3. él 4. tú, yo, contigo, ella 5. contigo, ti
GRAMMAR SECTION 12 PRÁCTICA A 1. Estoy en la residencia por la tarde. 2. Leo en el periódico que hay una película española en el cine Ave-

nida. 3. La película está doblada en inglés. 4. No quiero estar en mi cuarto toda la tarde. 5. Por eso invito a Gloria. 6. Ella está enferma; no puede ir conmigo. 7. Luego hablo por teléfono con Carlos. 8. Él está libre esta tarde. 9. ¡Estamos en el cine a las seis! 10. A las nueve estamos en un café hablando de la película.
Carlos: 1. Mi amigo está... 2. Lee... 4. No quiere estar... 5. Por eso invita... 6. Ella está enferma; no puede ir con él. 7. Luego habla por teléfono conmigo. 8. Yo estoy libre...
PRÁCTICA B 1. ...estoy leyendo un libro. 2. ...están comiendo en un restaurante. 3. ...están descansando. 4. ...estamos comiendo a las cinco. 5. ...está escribiendo cartas. 6. ...están visitando a los tíos.
GRAMMAR SECTION 13 PRÁCTICA A 1. mal (enferma) 2. sucio 3. cerrada 4. preocupado 5. nervioso
PRÁCTICA B 1. El florero es un regalo de boda. Es para Alicia y Jorge. Es del Almacén Carrillo. Es de cristal. Es grande y verde. Está en una caja bonita. Es un regalo caro pero... ¡Alicia y Jorge son buenos amigos!
2. Los jóvenes son mis primos argentinos. Son de Buenos Aires. Están visitando a los parientes norteamericanos este mes. Están a la derecha de los abuelos en la foto. Son muy simpáticos. Están en San Francisco esta semana.
PRÁCTICA C 1. son 2. estar 3. está 4. están 5. son 6. es 7. es 8. son // 1. Sí. 2. No. Bailamos mucho en las fiestas. 3. No. No es necesario salir con chaperona. 4. No. Tiene mucha importancia para mí.
PRÁCTICA CH 1. Es norteamericano. 2. Está sucio. 3. Están ocupados esta noche. 4. Estoy muy bien hoy. 5. Es viejo, muy viejo. 6. Es muy difícil. 7. Es muy interesante.) 8. No está de acuerdo con nosotros. 9. Son rubios y cariñosos. 10. Está abierta esta tarde.
PRÁCTICA D 1. Estas flores son para ti. 2. Estoy un poco nervioso/a. 3. ¡Estás muy bonita esta noche! 4. Es necesario estar en casa para las doce. ¿Está claro? 5. Ah, el restaurante está cerrado. 6. ¡Estos tacos están buenos! 7. La película es excelente, ¿verdad? (¿no?) 8. Son las once, pero no estoy cansado/a todavía.
GRAMMAR SECTION 14 PRÁCTICA A 1. su problema, dinero, amor 2. tus camisetas, novias, chaquetas 3. mi cita, suéter, coche, boda, amistad 4. sus trajes, limitaciones 5. nuestras camisas 6. nuestro sombrero
PRÁCTICA B 1. Su primo Julián es cariñoso. 2. Sus hermanitos son traviesos. 3. Sus tíos son generosos. 4. Su prima es pequeña todavía. 5. Su abuela es vieja ya. 6. Su esposo es muy trabajador. // 1. Mi primo Julián es cariñoso. 2. Mis hermanitos... 3. Mis tíos... 4. Mi prima... 5. Mi abuela... 6. Mi esposo...
PRÁCTICA C 1. ¡Nuestros precios son bajos! 2. ¡Nuestra ropa es elegante! 3. ¡Nuestros dependientes son amables! 4. ¡Nuestro estacionamiento es gratis!
PRÁCTICA CH 1. ¡Nuestro amor es imposible! 2. Su noviazgo fue muy largo, ¿no? (¿verdad?) 3. Su novia es encantadora, ¿verdad? (¿no?) 4. Tu boda va a ser cara. 5. Sus parientes son muy amables. 6. Me gusta su madre especialmente.
GRAMMAR SECTION 15 PRÁCTICA A 1. Esta sala es muy bonita. 2. ¡Estos regalos deben ser de la familia de novio! 3. Esta recepción es muy elegante. 4. Esos jóvenes son amigos de la novia. 5. Esa señora no puede bailar bien. 6. Esos niños no tienen ganas de estar en la recepción. 7. ¡Este champán está delicioso! 8. Esa mujer mayor no está muy contenta.
PRÁCTICA B 1. —¡Ah, aquella ropa es barata! 2. —¡Ah, aquellos periódicos son magníficos! 3. —¡Ah, aquel hotel es fenomenal! 4. —¡Ah, aquellos dependientes son simpáticos! 5. —¡Ah, en aquellos almacenes los precios son fijos!
PRÁCTICA C 1. c 2. b 3. ch 4. a
UN POCO DE TODO EJERCICIO A 1. Esta mujer es mi madre. Es doctora. 2. Este hombre es mi padre. Es una persona muy generosa. 3. Estas mujeres son mis tías Elena y Eugenia. Están en España este año. 4. Este hombre (Esta mujer) es mi novio/a. Está estudiando en México ahora. 5. Esta mujer es mi abuela. Es muy vieja pero simpática. 6. Este perro (Este animal) es mi perro. Está contento porque está con la familia.
EJERCICIO D 1. Me 2. compras 3. ganas 4. buscar 5. del 6. trabaja 7. Mis 8. son 9. están 10. políticas 11. viene 12. nuestra 13. celebran 14. eso 15. ir 16. de 17. la 18. Quiero 19. doce 20. comenzando 21. Sus 22. llevan 23. voy 24. tienen 25. estás 26. estás 27. leyendo 28. inglesa 29. vamos 30. muchas 31. estos 32. unos 33. Encantada 34. estoy // *Possible answers:* 1. la autora de la historia 2. Margarita 3. los niños de los (señores) Suárez 4. la madre de la autora de la historia 5. Ana Suárez 6. Margarita o la autora de la historia 7. todos los niños de los Suárez

CAPÍTULO 5 VOCABULARIO: PREPARACIÓN
¿QUÉ TIEMPO HACE HOY? EJERCICIO A *Possible answers:* 1. Hace calor. 2. Hace fresco. 3. Hace frío. 4. Llueve. 5. Hace frío. (Nieva.)
EJERCICIO B *Possible answers:* 1. Joaquín, no debes vivir en Seattle, porque allí llueve mucho. 2. Joaquín, no debes vivir en Los Ángeles, porque allí hay mucha contaminación. 3. Joaquín, no debes vivir en Phoenix, porque allí hace mucho calor y nunca llueve. 4. Joaquín, no debes vivir en New Orleans, porque allí hace mucho calor y llueve mucho. 5. Joaquín, no debes vivir en Buffalo, porque hace mucho frío y mucho calor.
EJERCICIO C Possible answers. 1. Está nevando y el señor tiene frío. 2. Hace mucho sol y el hombre tiene mucho calor. 3. Hace mucho viento y las personas (los jóvenes) tienen frío. 4. Está lloviendo y las personas están tristes. 5. Hay mucha contaminación y las personas no están bien. 6. Hace muy buen tiempo y los jóvenes están contentos. 7. Hace fresco y los jóvenes están contentos.
LOS MESES Y LAS ESTACIONES DEL AÑO EJERCICIO A 1. El doce es viernes. 2. El primero es lunes. 3. El veinte es sábado. 4. El dieciséis (diez y seis) es martes. 5. El once es jueves. 6. El cuatro es jueves. 7. El veintinueve (veinte y nueve) es lunes.
EJERCICIO B 1. el siete de marzo 2. el veinticuatro (veinte y cuatro) de agosto) 3. el primero de diciembre 4. el cinco de junio 5. el diecinueve (diez y nueve) de septiembre de mil novecientos ochenta y nueve 6. El treinta de mayo de mil ochocientos cuarenta y dos 7. El treinta y uno de enero de mil seiscientos sesenta 8. El cuatro de julio de mil setecientos setenta y seis
EJERCICIO C 1. ch 2. b 3. d 4. e 5. c 6. f 7. ______
EJERCICIO CH 1. El Día de la Raza es (se celebra) el doce de octubre. 2. El Día del Año Nuevo es el primero de enero. 3. El Día de los Enamorados (de San Valentín) es el catorce de febrero. 4. El Día de la Independencia de los Estados Unidos es el cuatro de julio. 5. El Día de los Inocentes en los Estados Unidos es el primero de abril. 6. La Navidad es el veinticinco (veinte y cinco) de diciembre.
GRAMMAR SECTION 16 PRÁCTICA B 1. pensamos 2. volvemos 3. empieza 4. duerme 5. sirve 6. juega 7. cerramos 8. preferimos
PRÁCTICA C 1. Pienso 2. Entro 3. Pido 4. Prefiero 5. No sirven 6. Pido 7. Sirven 8. Como y vuelvo 9. Duermo
PRÁCTICA CH 1. Nora está mirando la televisión. 2. Papá está pidiendo la comida. 3. El perro está durmiendo en el sofá. 4. Pepito y Carlos están jugando en sus cuartos. 5. Están haciendo mucho ruido. 6. Mamá está empezando a perder la paciencia.
GRAMMAR SECTION 17 PRÁCTICA A *Possible answers:* 1. Emilia es más alta que Sancho. 2. Emilia no es tan tímida como Sancho. Emilia es más

extrovertida. 3. Sancho no es tan atlético como Emilia. 4. Sancho es más intelectual (que Emilia) porque lleva muchos libros. 5. Emilia no es tan estudiosa como Sancho. Sí, es tan trabajadora (como él). 6. Es difícil indicar quién es más listo. Una persona atlética puede ser lista y una persona estudiosa puede ser tonta.
PRÁCTICA C 1. mejor 2. peores 3. mayor 4. menor 5. más grande 6. más pequeño (menos grande)
PRÁCTICA CH 1. Alfredo tiene tanto dinero como Graciela. 2. Graciela tiene tantas cervezas como Alfredo. 3. Alfredo tiene tantos libros como Graciela. 4. Graciela tiene tantos bolígrafos como Alfredo. 5. Alfredo tiene más cuadernos que Graciela. 6. Graciela tiene más cartas que Alfredo.
PRÁCTICA E 1. más de diez dólares 2. menos de cien estudiantes 3. menos de veinte sillas 4. ¿Tiene(s) más de dieciocho (diez y ocho) años? 5. ¡Ella tiene más de noventa años! 6. Soy menor que ella.
GRAMMAR SECTION 18 PRÁCTICA A 1. Qué 2. Qué 3. Cuál 4. Qué 5. Cuáles 6. Qué 7. Qué 8. Cuál
UN POCO DE TODO EJERCICIO A 1. Empiezo a ser una estudiante ejemplar. 2. Vuelvo a casa con más libros que Elena. 3. No pierdo tanto tiempo en la cafetería como Raúl. 4. El próximo semestre pienso tomar tantos cursos difíciles como Estela. 5. Pido menos consejos que Felipe. 6. Hago mejores preguntas que Antonio. // 1. Rosario empieza a ser una estudiante ejemplar, pero ¡nosotras, no! 2. Rosario vuelve a casa con más libros que Elena, pero ¡nosotras, no! 3. Rosario no pierde tanto tiempo en la cafetería como Raúl, pero ¡nosotras, sí! 4. El próximo semestre Rosario piensa tomar tantos cursos difíciles como Estela, pero ¡nosotras, no! 5. Rosario pide menos consejos que Felipe, pero ¡nosotras, más! 6. Rosario hace mejores preguntas que Antonio, pero ¡nosotras, no!
EJERCICIO D 1. muchas 2. es 3. es 4. salgo 5. llevar 6. los 7. puede 8. a 9. cortos 10. durante 11. hace 12. nieva 13. gran 14. mucho 15. ese 16. tomando 17. va 18. hacer 19. es 20. llevan // 1. improbable 2. probable 3. improbable

CAPÍTULO 6 VOCABULARIO: PREPARACIÓN

LA COMIDA, LAS COMIDAS EJERCICIO A 1. la sopa 2. la ensalada 3. el vino 4. la zanahoria 5. el bistec 6. el arroz 7. el queso 8. la papa 9. la manzana 10. la banana 11. la leche 12. el té 13. el pan 14. el helado 15. el pastel 16. el huevo
EL INFINITIVO EJERCICIO A *Possible answers:* 1. Acabo de comprar comida. 2. Acabo de bailar con mi novio/a (amigo/a). 3. Acabo de comprar un libro (papel, un bolígrafo, un cuaderno, etc.). 4. Acabo de comprar un regalo (una blusa, una camiseta, una camisa, etc.). // *Possible answers:* 1. Estoy en el cine. 2. Estoy en la biblioteca (en casa, en la residencia, ...). 3. Estoy en mi coche (en la cafetería, en casa, en un café, ...). 4. Estoy en la residencia (en casa, en mi apartamento, ...). 5. Estoy en la clase de español (en México, en España, ...). 6. Estoy en mi coche (en el autobús).
EJERCICIO B 1. ¡Quiero volver a esquiar! 2. ¡Quiero volver a nadar! 3. ¡Quiero volver a dormir! 4. ¡Quiero volver a estudiar! 5. ¡Quiero volver a mirar la tele (el programa)! 6. ¡Quiero volver a ver la película!
GRAMMAR SECTION 19 PRÁCTICA A 1. No hay nada interesante en el menú. 2. No tienen ningún plato típico. 3. El profesor no cena allí tampoco. 4. Mis amigos no almuerzan allí nunca. 5. No preparan nada especial para grupos grandes. 6. No hacen nunca platos nuevos (ningún plato nuevo). 7. Y no sirven paella tampoco.
PRÁCTICA B 1. Sí, hay algo. Hay un periódico en la mesa. No, no hay nada en la mesa. Sí, hay algo. Hay un carro en la calle. No, no hay nada en la calle. Sí, hay algo. Hay un pueblo en la montaña. No, no hay nada en la montaña. 2. Sí, hay alguien. Hay varias familias en el restaurante. No, no hay nadie. Sí, hay alguien. Hay niños en el parque. No, no hay nadie. Sí, hay alguien. Hay muchos estudiantes en la biblioteca. No, no hay nadie.
PRÁCTICA C A la hora de la cena. 1. ¿Hay algo especial esta noche? 2. Sirven (Se sirve) la cena a las seis en su casa también. 3. Nadie cena (está cenando) en casa esta noche, ¿verdad? 4. No queremos pedir nada en este momento. 5. No hay ningún restaurante en esa calle. En la residencia, antes del examen. 1. Nadie comprende (entiende) eso. 2. Marcos no puede escribir esta oración tampoco. 3. Nunca estudia(s) con Carmen. ¿Por qué no? 4. ¡Nadie está tan cansado/a como yo! 5. ¿Nadie tiene ganas de dormir?
GRAMMAR SECTION 20 PRÁCTICA A José Feliciano sabe cantar en español. Mikhail Baryshnikov sabe bailar. Fernando Valenzuela sabe jugar al béisbol. Mary Lou Retton sabe hacer ejercicios gimnásticos. James Michener sabe escribir novelas. Chris Evert sabe jugar al tenis. Julia Child sabe cocinar bien.
PRÁCTICA B Adán conoce a Eva. Romeo conoce a Julieta. Rhett Butler conoce a Scarlett O'Hara. Antonio conoce a Cleopatra. Jorge Washington conoce a Marta.
PRÁCTICA C 1. Conozco, sé 2. Conozco, sé 3. conozco, sé 4. Sé, conozco 5. conozco, sé 6. Sé, sé, conozco
PRÁCTICA CH 1. Los martes Roberto nunca sale de su apartamento antes de las doce. 2. Espera a su amigo Samuel delante de su casa. 3. Los dos esperan juntos el autobús. 4. Cuando llegan a la universidad, buscan a su amiga Ceci en la cafetería. 5. Ella acaba de empezar sus estudios allí y no conoce a mucha gente todavía. 6. A veces ven a la profesora de historia en la cafetería y hablan un poco con ella. 7. Es una persona muy interesante que sabe mucho de esa materia. 8. A las dos todos tienen la clase de sicología. 9. Siempre oyen conferencias interesantes y hacen algunas preguntas. 10. A veces tienen la oportunidad de conocer a los conferenciantes. 11. A las cinco Roberto y Samuel vuelven a esperar el autobús. 12. Cuando entra en el (su) apartamento, Roberto siempre busca a su compañero Raúl para hablar un poco con él. 13. Los dos preparan la cena juntos y luego miran la televisión. // 1. Ceci 2. la profesora de historia 3. Roberto 4. Samuel // 1. Los martes nunca salgo de mi apartamento... 2. Espero a mi amigo Samuel... 3. (Los dos) Esperamos... 4. Cuando llegamos a la universidad, buscamos a nuestra amiga... 6. A veces vemos a la profesora de historia en la cafetería y hablamos... 8. A las dos todos tenemos... 9. Siempre oímos conferencias interesantes y hacemos... 10. A veces tenemos... 11. A las cinco Samuel y yo volvemos... 12. Cuando entro en el (mi) apartamento, siempre busco a mi compañero... 13. (Los dos) Preparamos la cena juntos y luego miramos la televisión.
GRAMMAR SECTION 21 PRÁCTICA A *Possible answers:* 1. —¿Las sandalias? —¡Claro que las necesito! —¿Las gafas de sol? —¡Claro que las necesito! —¿Los pantalones cortos? —¡Claro que los necesito! —¿Las camisetas? —¡Claro que las necesito! —¿La crema bronceadora? —¡Claro que la necesito! —¿El reloj? —No, no lo necesito. 2. —¿Los huevos? —Sí, tengo que usarlos. —¿La leche? —No, no tengo que usarla. —¿El azúcar? —Sí, tengo que usarlo. —¿El chocolate? —Sí, tengo que usarlo. —¿La vainilla? —No, no tengo que usarla. 3. —¿La sopa de espárragos? —Sí, (No, no) voy a pedirla. —¿El pan? —Sí, (No, no) voy a pedirlo. —¿Las chuletas de cerdo? —Sí, (No, no) voy a pedirlas. —¿Las patatas fritas? —Sí, (No, no) voy a pedirlas. —¿El café? —Sí, (No, no) voy a pedirlo. —¿El helado de vainilla? —Sí, (No, no) voy a pedirlo.
PRÁCTICA B 1. El camarero trae los vasos y los pone en la mesa. 2. Luego trae el menú y los señores lo leen. 3. «¿Los platos del día? Voy a explicarlos (Los voy a explicar) ahora mismo.»

4. Al señor le gusta el bistec y va a pedirlo (lo va a pedir). 5. La señora prefiere el pescado fresco pero no lo tienen hoy. 6. «Ernestito, debes comer con el tenedor. ¿Por qué no lo usas?» 7. El niño necesita tenedor y el camarero lo trae. 8. Todos prefieren vino tinto. Por eso el señor lo pide. 9. «¿La cuenta? El dueño está preparándola (la está preparando) en este momento.» 10. El señor quiere pagar con tarjeta de crédito pero no la trae. 11. Por fin, la señora toma la cuenta y la paga.
PRÁCTICA C *Possible answers:* 1. —¿Cuándo me invitas a cenar en tu casa? —Te invito a cenar (el sábado) 2. —¿Cuándo me invitas a almorzar contigo? —Te invito a almorzar (mañana). 3. —¿Cuándo me invitas a nadar en tu piscina? —Te invito a nadar (esta tarde). 4. —¿Cuándo me invitas a ver una película? —Te invito a ver una película (el viernes). 5. —¿Cuándo me invitas a ir contigo a la playa? —Te invito a ir conmigo (el domingo). // 1. —¿Cuándo nos invitas a cenar en tu casa? —Los invito... 2. —¿Cuándo nos invitas a almorzar contigo? —Los invito... 4. —¿Cuándo nos invitas a ver una película? —Los invito... 5. —¿Cuándo nos invitas a ir contigo a la playa? —Los invito...
PRÁCTICA CH 1. —¿Comiste jamón anoche? —Sí, lo comí. (No, no lo comí.) 2. —¿Comiste zanahorias anoche? —Sí, las comí. (No, no las comí.) 3. —¿Comiste papas fritas anoche? —Sí, las comí. (No, no las comí.) 4. —¿Comiste salmón anoche? —Sí, lo comí. (No, no lo comí.) 5. —¿Comiste enchiladas anoche? —Sí, las comí. (No, no las comí.) 6. —¿Comiste helado anoche? —Sí, lo comí. (No, no lo comí.)
PRÁCTICA D 1. —¡Porque acabo de estudiarla! 2. —¡Porque acabo de visitarlo! 3. —¡Porque acabo de aprenderlas! 4. —¡Porque acabo de comprarlo! 5. —¡Porque acabo de pagarlas! 6. —¡Porque acabo de prepararlas! 7. —¡Porque acabo de comprarla! 8. —¡Porque acabo de ayudarte!
PRÁCTICA E 1. ¡No, no lo preferimos! 2. ¡No, no lo comprendemos! 3. ¡No, no lo deseamos! 4. ¡No, no lo pensamos! 5. ¡No, no lo aceptamos! 6. ¡No, no lo esperamos!
UN POCO DE TODO EJERCICIO D 1. Soy 2. es 3. Llega 4. a 5. Nunca 6. que 7. abrir 8. hacer 9. cierra 10. veo 11. las 12. preparando 13. que 14. saben 15. nuestros 16. ofrecemos 17. nuestro 18. Estos 19. son 20. están 21. estamos // 1. probable 2. probable 3. probable 4. improbable 5. improbable

CAPÍTULO 7 VOCABULARIO: PREPARACIÓN
¡VAMOS DE VACACIONES! EJERCICIO A 8, 5, 3, 2, 7, 1, 9, 4, 6
EJERCICIO B 1. a 2. c 3. a 4. c 5. b
EJERCICIO CH 1. Harry 2. Harry 3. don Gregorio 4. Harry 5. Harry 6. don Gregorio 7. don Gregorio
NOTAS LINGÜÍSTICAS EJERCICIO A *Possible answers*: 1. En la clase de español se habla español. No se habla inglés. 2. En un mercado al aire libre se regatea. No se paga el primer precio. 3. En un avión se viaja. No se baila. 4. En una discoteca se baila. No se estudia. 5. En una tienda de ropa se paga un precio fijo. No se regatea. 6. En una fiesta se canta. No se lee. 7. En la calle se camina. No se duerme. 8. En la cafetería de los estudiantes se almuerza. No se regatea.
GRAMMAR SECTION 22 PRÁCTICA A 1. En el restaurante, el camarero me trae el menú. El camarero me explica los platos del día. El cocinero me prepara la comida. El camarero me sirve la comida. El dueño me da la cuenta. 2. En clase, el profesor (la profesora) me explica la gramática. Los otros estudiantes me hacen preguntas. El profesor (La profesora) me da exámenes. Un compañero me presta un lápiz o un papel.
PRÁCTICA B 1. Les llamo un taxi. 2. Les bajo las maletas. 3. Les guardo el equipaje. 4. Les facturo el equipaje. 5. Les guardo el puesto en la cola. 6. Les guardo el asiento en la sala de espera. 7. Les busco el pasaporte. 8. Por fin, les digo adiós. // 1. Le/Te llamo... 2. Le/Te bajo... 3. Le/Te guardo... 4. Le/Te facturo... 5. Le/Te guardo... 6. Le/Te guardo... 7. Le/Te busco... 8. Por fin, le/te digo...
PRÁCTICA C *Possible answers:* 1. Todos le mandan flores. Le escriben cartas (tarjetas). Las enfermeras le dan medicinas. De comer, le sirven pan tostado. 2. Los niños les prometen a sus padres ser buenos. Les piden muchos regalos. También le escriben cartas a Santa Claus. Le piden juguetes. Los padres les mandan tarjetas navideñas a sus amigos. Les regalan flores y fruta. 3. La azafata nos sirve café. El camarero nos ofrece vino. El piloto nos dice que todo está bien. 4. Mi amigo me presta su coche. Mis padres me preguntan si necesito dinero. Luego me dan un coche nuevo. 5. En la clase de computación, todos le preguntan al profesor qué debemos estudiar. El profesor les explica a los estudiantes la materia.
PRÁCTICA CH te, le, le, le, te, le, le, le
GRAMMAR SECTION 23 PRÁCTICA A 1. (No) Me gusta el vino. 2. (No) Me gustan los niños pequeños. 3. (No) Me gusta la música clásica. 4. (No) Me gustan los discos de Barbra Streisand. 5. (No) Me gusta el invierno. 6. (No) Me gusta hacer cola. 7. (No) Me gustan las clases que empiezan a las ocho. 8. (No) Me gusta el chocolate. 9. (No) Me gustan las películas de horror. 10. (No) Me gusta cocinar. 11. (No) Me gustan las clases de este semestre. 12. (No) Me gusta la gramática. 13. (No) Me gustan los vuelos con muchas escalas. 14. (No) Me gusta bailar en las discotecas.
PRÁCTICA B 1. A mi padre le gusta el océano. Le gustaría ir a la playa. 2. A mis hermanitos les gusta nadar también. Les gustaría ir a la playa. 3. A mi hermano Ernesto le gusta correr. Le gustaría ir al campo. 4. A mis abuelos les gusta descansar. Les gustaría estar en casa. 5. A mi madre le gusta la tranquilidad. Le gustaría visitar un pueblecito en la costa. 6. A mi hermana Elena le gustan las discotecas. Le gustaría pasar las vacaciones en una ciudad grande. 7. A mí me gusta... Me gustaría... // *Possible answers:* 1. A mi hermana Elena le gustaría ir a Nueva York. 2. A mi padre le gustaría estar en Acapulco. 3. Mis abuelos no quieren salir de casa. 4. A mi madre le gustaría ir a Hyannis Port. 5. Mi hermano Ernesto quiere ir a un club deportivo en las montañas.
PRÁCTICA C 1. A mi padre le gustan las anchoas, pero no le gusta el chorizo. 2. A mi madre le gusta el chorizo, pero no le gusta mucho el queso. 3. A mis hermanos les gusta el queso, pero no les gustan los champiñones. 4. ¡A mí me gusta todo y me gustaría tener una pizza ahora mismo!
PRÁCTICA CH 1. A mi madre le gusta viajar en avión, pero no le gustan los vuelos largos. No le gustaría ir a la China por avión. 2. A mi padre no le gusta hacer cola y no le gustan las demoras. 3. A mis hermanos les gusta subir en seguida al avión, pero no les gusta guardarle un puesto a nadie. 4. ¡Y a mí me gusta viajar con todos ellos!
GRAMMAR SECTION 24 PRÁCTICA A lleguemos, ayude, subas, perdamos, dé 1. a 2. a 3. a 4. a 5. b 6. a
PRÁCTICA B 1. bailes, cenes, mires esto, llegues a tiempo, busques a Anita. 2. aprenda? escriba? lea? responda? asista a clases? 3. empiece, juegue, lo piense, lo sirva, lo pida, ¿verdad? 4. pidamos eso, almorcemos ahora, los perdamos, durmamos allí, la cerremos, lo encontremos aquí. 5. lo conozcan, lo hagan, lo traigan, lo sepan, lo digan. 6. venga, salga ahora, lo ponga, lo oiga, sea su amiga. 7. lo tenga? lo vea? esté allí? dé una fiesta? vaya al cine contigo?
PRÁCTICA C 1. Mis hermanitos quieren que vayamos a la playa también. 2. Ernesto quiere que volvamos a hacer *camping* en las montañas. 3. Mis abuelos quieren que no salgamos de la ciudad en todo el verano. 4. Mamá quiere que sólo hagamos unas excursiones cortas. 5. Elena quiere que visitemos Nueva York.

PRÁCTICA CH Sr. Casiano,... no trabaje tanto. no sea tan impaciente. no critique tanto a los otros. no sea tan impulsivo. no fume tanto. no beba cerveza ni otras bebidas alcohólicas. no almuerce muy fuerte. no cene muy fuerte. no salga tanto con los amigos. no vaya a las discotecas. no vuelva tarde a casa.
PRÁCTICA D 1. Lleguen Uds. a tiempo. 2. Lean Uds. la lección. 3. Escriban Uds. una composición. 4. Abran Uds. los libros. 5. No piensen Uds. en inglés. 6. Estén en clase mañana. 7. Traigan los libros a clase. 8. No olviden los verbos nuevos.
PRÁCTICA E *Possible answers:* 1. —¿Inglés 1? —Sí, tómelo. 2. —¿Ciencias políticas? —Sí, tómelas. 3. —¿Historia de Latinoamérica? —Sí, tómela. 4. —¿Química orgánica? —No, no la tome. 5. —¿Cálculo 1? —No, no lo tome. 6. —¿Comercio? —No, no lo tome. 7. —¿Español 2? —Sí, tómelo.
PRÁCTICA F *Possible answers:* 1. —¿Alcohol? —No lo beba. 2. —¿Verduras? —Cómalas. 3. —¿Pan? —No lo coma. 4. —¿Dulces? —No los coma. 5. ¿Leche? —No la beba. 6. —¿Hamburguesas con queso? —No las coma. 7. —¿Frutas? —Cómalas. 8. —¿Carne? —Cómala. 9. —¿Pollo? —Cómalo. 10. —¿Refrescos dietéticos? —Tómelos.
UN POCO DE TODO EJERCICIO A 1. Quiero que me compres un boleto de primera clase; (yo) te espero aquí. 2. Ojalá que no haya muchos pasajeros; a mí no me gusta nada hacer cola. 3. No fumen Uds., por favor; a mi compañero no le gusta el humo. 4. Queremos que el vuelo llegue a tiempo; no nos gusta esperar. 5. No quiero que Ud. me facture el equipaje; mis maletas son nuevas y no quiero que Uds. las pierdan.
EJERCICIO B 1. Haga Ud. las maletas. Quiero que haga las maletas. 2. No olvide Ud. la cartera. No quiero que olvide la cartera. 3. Vaya al aeropuerto. Quiero que vaya al aeropuerto. 4. No llegue tarde. No quiero que llegue tarde. 5. Compre su boleto de ida y vuelta. Quiero que compre su boleto de ida y vuelta. 6. Facture las maletas. Quiero que facture las maletas. 7. Haga cola. Quiero que haga cola. 8. Dé (Déle) su boleto al camarero. Quiero que le dé su boleto al camarero. 9. Suba al avión. Quiero que suba al avión. 10. Busque su asiento. Quiero que busque su asiento.
EJERCICIO C *Possible answers:* 1. No la cante más. (No la toque. No la escuche.) 2. Cómprelo. 3. No lo compre. 4. Léala. 5. No lo lea. 6. Cómprela. 7. Visítela. 8. No lo haga.
EJERCICIO CH 1. Les 2. algo 3. la 4. la 5. conocen 6. Está 7. la 8. dice 9. es 10. más 11. incaicos 12. quiero 13. visiten 14. es 15. Vayan 16. mejores 17. compren 18. muchos 19. países 20. visitan 21. Sé 22. les gustar // 1. Falso. Machu-Picchu está en Perú. 2. Cierto. 3. Cierto. 4. Falso. Muchos turistas de todos los países del mundo visitan Machu-Picchu.

CAPÍTULO 8 VOCABULARIO: PREPARACIÓN
LOS CUARTOS... EJERCICIO A *Possible answers:* 1. el garaje/un coche 2. la sala/un televisor, un sillón, una mesita, una lámpara 3. la alcoba/una cama 4. el cuarto de baño/el esposo 5. la cocina 6. el comedor/la mesa, las sillas, los platos 7. el patio/los árboles, las flores
EJERCICIO B *Possible answers:* 1. la cocina. Una madre habla con su hija. 2. la cocina. Una madre habla con su hija. 3. la alcoba. Una madre les habla a los hijos mayores. 4. el baño. Un padre habla con su hijo. 5. la sala. Una esposa habla con su esposo. 6. la sala. Los señores de la casa hablan con las visitas. 7. la sala. Un esposo habla con su esposa. 8. la cocina. Una madre habla con su hijo.
TENGO... QUIERO... NECESITO... EJERCICIO A 1. f 2. e 3. a 4. g 5. d 6. b 7. ch 8. c
EJERCICIO CH *Possible answers:* 1. Los trofeos de tenis son de Adela porque le gusta jugar al tenis. 2. La tienda de campaña y el saco de dormir son de Geraldo porque le gusta hacer *camping* en las montañas. 3. La alarma de seguridad es de los señores de Inza porque son muy ricos y tienen una colección de pinturas de un valor incalculable. 4. Las piezas de cerámica son de Laura porque tiene una pequeña colección de figuras de animales. 5. El acuario de agua salada es de Ernesto porque le interesan los peces.
GRAMMAR SECTION 25 PRÁCTICA A Possible answers. 1. La jefa pide que yo no hable tanto por teléfono. 2. Insiste en que Alicia empiece a llegar a las ocho. 3. Recomienda que el Sr. Morales busque otro puesto. 4. Quiere que todos sean (seamos) más cuidadosos con los detalles. 5. Insiste en que tengamos el inventario listo para el miércoles. 6. Prohíbe que los empleados fumen en su oficina. 7. Pide que la Sra. Medina lleve un trabajo importante a casa este fin de semana. 8. No quiere que los empleados le pidan aumentos este año.
PRÁCTICA C 1. paguemos 2. vayan 3. tome 4. regale 5. vea 6. descanse 7. vaya
PRÁCTICA CH *Possible answers:* 1. Preferimos que el nuevo televisor esté en la sala. ¡Nos gusta ver la tele todos juntos! 2. Queremos que el televisor portátil esté en la cocina. ¡A mamá le gusta ver la tele mientras cocina! 3. Es necesario que el equipo estereofónico esté en la alcoba de Julio. ¡Le gusta escuchar música mientras estudia! 4. Es preciso que el sillón grande esté en la sala. ¡Nos gusta leer el periódico allí! 5. Preferimos que las bicicletas de los niños estén en el patio. ¡Les gusta jugar allí! 6. Es preciso que la computadora esté en la oficina. ¡Nos gusta hacer las cuentas allí! 7. Queremos que el acuario esté en la alcoba de Anita. ¡Le gusta mirar los peces!
PRÁCTICA D 1. Quiero que Ud. prepare (haga) el inventario. 2. Insisto en que esté listo para mañana. 3. Si no puede hacerlo para entonces, quiero que trabaje este fin de semana. 4. Es urgente que esté en mi escritorio a las ocho de la mañana. 5. (Le) Recomiendo que lo empiece en seguida.
GRAMMAR SECTION 26 PRÁCTICA A 1. Me gusta mucho que estén contentos mis amigos (funcione bien mi coche, vengan todos a mis fiestas, estén bien mis padres). 2. Tengo miedo de que haya mucho tráfico en la carretera mañana (no venga nadie a mi fiesta, haya una prueba mañana, ocurra una crisis internacional, el jefe no me dé un aumento).
PRÁCTICA B 1. Sara espera que le den un aumento. 2. A ti te sorprende que haya tanto trabajo. 3. Armando teme que lo vayan a despedir. 4. A nosotros no nos gusta que sean tan altos los impuestos. 5. A mí no me gusta que nos den sólo dos semanas de vacaciones. 6. Todos tienen (tenemos) miedo de que no haya aumentos este año. 7. El jefe siente que tenga que despedir a cinco empleados.
PRÁCTICA C 1. use, no funcione 2. me despida, tenga que, cambie 3. nos den, sean, no podamos 4. estén, les gusten, reciban
PRÁCTICA CH 1. Siente que su (tu) estéreo no funcione (esté funcionando). 2. ¡Es increíble que no tenga(s) un compact disc todavía! 3. ¡Qué lástima que cuesten tanto (sean tan caros)! 4. ¡Qué extraño que saquen nuevos modelos cada año (todos los años)! 5. Me alegro de que no tenga(s) que tener el equipo más moderno.
PRÁCTICA A 1. un nuevo trabajo 2. unos contratos 3. unas cuentas 4. un aumento 5. una carta 6. una computadora
GRAMMAR SECTION 27 PRÁCTICA B 1. ¿Hay más pan? Me lo pasas, por favor. 2. ¿Hay más tortillas? Me las pasas, por favor. 3. ¿Hay más tomates? Me los pasas, por favor. 4. ¿Hay más fruta? Me la pasas, por favor. 5. ¿Hay más vino? Me lo pasas, por favor. 6. ¿Hay más jamón? Me lo pasas, por favor.
PRÁCTICA C 1. Acaban de decírnosla. 2. Sí, quiero que me lo leas, por favor. 3. No, no tiene que dárselos aquí. 4. Claro que estoy guardándoselo. 5. ¿No quieres que te los compre? 6. Te lo puedo guardar. 7. Sí, se la recomiendo, señores. 8. La azafata nos la va a servir en el avión.

PRÁCTICA CH *Possible answers:* 1. —¡No te preocupes! Yo te las lavo también. 2. —¡No te preocupes! Yo te los compro. 3. —¡No te preocupes! Yo te la compro también. 4. —¡No te preocupes! Yo te la lavo. 5. —¡No te preocupes! Yo te lo arreglo. 6. —¡No te preocupes! Yo te lo arreglo.
PRÁCTICA D 1. No se lo está vendiendo (a María). No se lo está vendiendo (a los Sres. Benítez). No me lo está vendiendo. Se lo está vendiando a Esteban. 2. No se la está sirviendo (a Carlos). No se la está sirviendo (a unos señores). No nos la está sirviendo. Se la está sirviendo a Emilia. 3. No se las va a mandar (a Tomás). No se las va a mandar (a los Sres. Padilla). No me las va a mandar. Se las va a mandar a Carmen. 4. No se los recomienda (a Raúl y Celia). No se los recomiendo (a Pilar). No me los recomienda. Se los recomienda a Lucas.
UN POCO DE TODO EJERCICIO B *Possible answers:* 1. —Oye, ¿me prestas tus discos de Menudo? —Lo siento, pero no puedo. Se los di a Roberto. 2. —Oye, ¿me prestas tu bicicleta vieja? —Lo siento, pero no puedo. Se la di a mi hermanito. 3. —Oye, ¿me prestas tu libro de francés? —Lo siento, pero no puedo. Se lo di a mi madre. 4. —Oye, ¿me prestas tu máquina de escribir vieja? —Lo siento, pero no puedo. Se la di a Susana. 5. —Oye, ¿me prestas tu maleta vieja? —Lo siento, pero no puedo. Se la di a Teresa. 6. —Oye, ¿me prestas tu televisor viejo? —Lo siento, pero no puedo. Se lo di a mis padres.
EJERCICIO D 1. Sabes 2. ser 3. regrese 4. terminar 5. mis 6. puedan 7. qué 8. de 9. sabes 10. tantas 11. Sólo 12. que 13. tengas 14. Me 15. tenga 16. pocas 17. conseguir 18. algún 19. soy 20. es 21. Espere 22. Sabe 23. al 24. busca 25. puede 26. su 27. bien 28. soy 29. vaya 30. se los // 1. Carlos 2. los padres de Carlos 3. Fred 4. Carlos 5. la Sra. Carrillo 6. la Sra. Carrillo

CAPÍTULO 9 VOCABULARIO: PREPARACIÓN
LOS QUEHACERES DOMÉSTICOS... EJERCICIO A *Possible answers:* 1. la alcoba 2. el comedor 3. la cocina, el patio/garaje 4. la cocina 5. todos los cuartos 6. la alcoba 7. el baño; el baño/patio/garaje 8. la cocina 9. la sala, la alcoba 10. el garaje, la alcoba
EJERCICIO B *Possible answers:* 1. Se usa para lavar las ventanas. 2. Se usa para preparar el café. 3. Se usa para sacudir los muebles. 4. Se usan para sacar la basura. 5. Se usa para lavar los platos. 6. Se usa para lavar los platos en el lavaplatos. 7. Se usa para lavar la ropa. 8. Se usa para limpiar el baño.
EJERCICIO C 1. secar; plancharla 2. refrigerar 3. cocinar 4. lavar 5. acondicionar
MÁS VERBOS ÚTILES EJERCICIO *Possible answers:* 1. El despertador 2. Una buena película 3. El padre 4. El camarero 5. El barbero 6. La enfermera 7. Mi compañera 8. La madre 9. Un estudiante
GRAMMAR SECTION 28 PRÁCTICA A 1. Me levanto a las siete. 2. Mi esposo/a se levanta más tarde cuando puede. 3. Nos bañamos por la mañana. 4. Por costumbre, los niños se bañan por la noche. 5. Me visto antes de desayunar. 6. Mi esposo/a se viste después de tomar un café. 7. Por la noche, los niños se acuestan muy temprano. 8. (Yo) Me acuesto más tarde, a las once. 9. Por lo general, mi esposo/a se acuesta más tarde que yo. // 1. yo 2. los niños 3. los niños 4. yo
PRÁCTICA B 1. se sientan, sentarse 2. quitarme, quitarte 3. lavarme, se lava (bañarme, se baña) 4. nos despertamos, despertarte 5. poniéndome, ponerse 6. te diviertes, divirtiéndote 7. me acuesto, se acuesta
PRÁCTICA CH 1. Es necesario que se despierte más temprano. ¡Despiértese más temprano! 2. Es necesario que se levante más temprano. ¡Levántese más temprano! 3. Es necesario que se bañe más. ¡Báñese más! 4. Es necesario que se quite esa ropa sucia y se ponga ropa limpia. ¡Quítese esa ropa sucia y póngase ropa limpia! 5. Es necesario que planche su ropa y se viste mejor. ¡Planche su ropa y vístese mejor! 6. Es necesario que estudie más. ¡Estudie más! 7. Es necesario que no se divierta tanto. ¡No se divierta tanto! 8. Es necesario que vaya más a la biblioteca. ¡Vaya más a la biblioteca! 9. Es necesario que no se acueste tan tarde. ¡No se acueste tan tarde! 10. Es necesario que ayude con los quehaceres. ¡Ayude con los quehaceres! 11. Es necesario que saque la basura, por lo menos. ¡Saque la basura!
PRÁCTICA D 1. —¿Quiere Ud. que me quite el suéter ahora? —Sí, quíteselo, por favor. 2. —¿Quiere Ud. que me quite la camisa/la blusa ahora? —Sí, quítesela, por favor. 3. —¿Quiere Ud. que me quite los pantalones ahora? —Sí, quíteselos, por favor. 4. —¿Quiere Ud. que me quite la camiseta ahora? —Sí, quítesela, por favor. 5. —¿Quiere Ud. que me quite los calcetines/las medias ahora? Sí, quíteselos/las, por favor. 6. —¿Quiere Ud. que me quite toda la ropa ahora? —Sí, quítesela, por favor.
GRAMMAR SECTION 29 PRÁCTICA A 1. Salí del apartamento a las nueve. 2. Llegué a la biblioteca a las diez. 3. Estudié toda la mañana para el examen de química. 4. Escribí todos los ejercicios del libro de texto. 5. A las doce y media almorcé con unos amigos en la cafetería. 6. A la una fui al laboratorio. 7. Hice todos los experimentos del manual de laboratorio. 8. Tomé el examen a las cuatro. 9. Lo comenté con mis amigos: ¡fue horrible! 10. Regresé a casa y ayudé a Evangelina a preparar la cena. // 1. Me quedé en casa todo el día. 2. Por la mañana vi que el portero no sacó la basura. 3. Por eso llamé al dueño del edificio. 4. Tomé café con unos vecinos, que se fueron a las once y media. 5. Limpié la casa entera: sacudí los muebles, pasé la aspiradora, hice las camas, planché la ropa de las dos... 6. El electricista llegó a las dos. 7. Arregló la luz del comedor. 8. Barré el suelo otra vez después de que él salió. 9. Fui al garaje para dejar allí las cajas. 10. Empecé a preparar la cena a las cinco. // 1. Evangelina 2. Teresa 3. Evangelina 4. Teresa 5. Evangelina 6. Teresa // 1. Evangelina se quedó... 2. Por la mañana vio... 3. Por eso llamó... 4. Tomó... 5. Limpió...: sacudió los muebles, pasó la aspiradora, hizo las camas, planchó... 6. El electricista llegó... 7. Arregló... 8. Evangelina barrió... 9. Fue... 10. Empezó... // 1. Teresa salió... 2. Llegó... 3. Estudió... 4. Escribió... 5. A las doce y media almorzó... 6. A la una fue... 7. Hizo... 8. Tomó... 9. Lo comentó... 10. Regresó a casa y me ayudó a preparar la cena.
PRÁCTICA B 1. Julián hizo cola para comprar una entrada de cine. La compró por fin. Entró en el cine. Vio la película. Le gustó mucho. Encontró a unos amigos frente al cine. Fue a un café con ellos. Regresó a casa tarde. 2. Mis compañeros de cuarto fueron a la universidad por la mañana. Regresaron temprano a casa. Sacudieron los muebles de la sala. Lavaron la ropa. La sacaron de la secadora. Limpiaron la casa entera. Lo prepararon todo para la fiesta de este fin de semana. 3. Llegué a la universidad a las ______. Asistí a clases. Fui a la cafetería. Almorcé con ______. Le presté un libro a ______.
PRÁCTICA C 1. Pasé un semestre estudiando en México. 2. Mis padres me pagaron el vuelo... 3. ...pero yo trabajé para ganar el dinero para la matrícula y los otros gastos. 4. Viví con una familia mexicana encantadora. 5. Aprendí mucho sobre la vida y la cultura mexicanas. 6. Visité muchos sitios de interés turístico e histórico. 7. Mis amigos me escribieron muchas cartas. 8. Les mandé muchas tarjetas postales. 9. Les compré muchos recuerdos a todos. 10. Volví a los Estados Unidos al final de agosto.
UN POCO DE TODO EJERCICIO A 1. Orlando y Patricia se vieron en clase. 2. Se miraron. 3. Se saludaron. 4. Se hablaron mucho. 5. Empezaron a llamarse por teléfono constantemente. 6. Se mandaron regalos. 7. Se escribieron durante las vacaciones. 8. Se ayudaron con los problemas. 9. Se casaron.

10. No se llevaron bien. 11. Se separaron. 12. Se divorciaron.
EJERCICIO C *Possible answers:* 1. Son las dos de la mañana. Están en la cocina. 2. El esposo se levantó primero. La esposa se despertó después y escuchó a alguien en la cocina. 3. No, no comió mucho para la cena. No tiene sueño porque tiene hambre. Está sacando comida del refrigerador. 4. La esposa está sacando una foto. Sí, le sorprende. La esposa quiere probar que su esposo se levanta durante la noche para comer. Quiere que su esposo no coma tanto. 5. No, la esposa no va a comer nada. Van a acostarse otra vez en media hora.
EJERCICIO CH 1. Me levanté 2. hice 3. saqué 4. desperté 5. bañé 6. hice 7. me bañé 8. llevé 9. volviste 10. te acostaste 11. Hice 12. planché
EJERCICIO D 1. todas 2. del 3. todos 4. aparecieron 5. son 6. Beba 7. deliciosa 8. estás 9. nueva 10. viaja 11. puede 12. tener 13. cada 14. se afeita 15. se bañan 16. se lavan 17. demuestra 18. sin 19. del 20. algunos 21. cambiaron 22. este 23. anima 24. cambiaron 25. es 26. prometan 27. ganó 28. Es // 1. Falso. Hay muchos anuncios publicitarios internacionales. 2. Cierto. 3. Cierto. 4. Falso. En las culturas hispánicas los anuncios tienen mensajes tan materialistas como los de los Estados Unidos.

CAPÍTULO 10 VOCABULARIO: PREPARACIÓN

LOS DÍAS FESTIVOS Y LAS FIESTAS
EJERCICIO A 1. la Navidad 2. una sorpresa 3. los entremeses, los refrescos 4. el Día de los Muertos 5. sentirse feliz, sonreír, reírse 6. sentirse triste, llorar 7. la Noche Vieja 8. ¡felicitaciones!

MÁS EMOCIONES EJERCICIO A *Possible answers:* 1. Me pongo felicísimo/a. Le digo gracias. 2. Me pongo muy triste. (Lloro.) 3. Me río/sonrío. 4. Me siento aburridísimo/a, pero me porto bien. No me voy; me quedo en la fiesta. 5. Les doy más vino y entremeses. 6. Me pongo nerviosísimo/a. 7. Me siento muy feliz (triste, enojado/a). 8. Me enojo. 9. Me pongo muy triste y le pido perdón. 10. Voy a una tienda y compro queso y nachos. Le ofrezco más bebidas a la gente y pongo música para bailar.

GRAMMAR SECTION 31 PRÁCTICA A 1. Todos estuvimos en casa de los abuelos antes de las nueve. 2. Pusimos muchos regalos debajo del árbol. 3. Los tíos y primos vinieron con comida y bebidas. 4. Los niños quisieron dormir pero no pudieron. 5. Tuve que ayudar a preparar la comida. 6. Hubo una cena especial para los mayores. 7. Más tarde algunos amigos vinieron a cantar villancicos. 8. Los niños fueron a sus alcobas a las diez y se acostaron. 9. A las doce todos se desearon "¡Feliz Navidad!" 10. Al día siguiente todos dijeron que la fiesta estuvo estupenda. // 1. Falso. Hubo mucha gente en la fiesta. 2. Falso. También vinieron unos amigos. 3. Cierto. 4. No lo dice.
PRÁCTICA B estuviste, Tuve, dijiste, dije, Vinieron, tuvimos, hice // 1. la persona 2 2. la persona 1 3. la persona 2 4. la persona 1
PRÁCTICA C 1. Estuviste en el comedor. ¿Por qué no pusiste la mesa? 2. Fuiste al garaje. ¿Por qué no sacaste la ropa de la secadora? 3. Pasaste por la alcoba. ¿Por qué no hiciste las camas? 4. Estuviste en la sala. ¿Por qué no pudiste pasar la aspiradora 5. Fuiste a la cocina. ¿Por qué no pusiste los platos en el lavaplatos?
PRÁCTICA CH En 1969 los estadounidenses pusieron a un hombre en la luna. Adán y Eva supieron que las serpientes son malas. Jorge Washington estuvo en Valley Forge con sus soldados. Los europeos trajeron el caballo al Nuevo Mundo. Stanley conoció a Livingston en África. María Antonieta dijo "que coman pasteles." // *Possible answers:* 1. Los rusos pusieron a la primera mujer en el espacio. 2. John F. Kennedy dijo «Ich bin ein Berliner» cuando visitó Berlín. 3. Cleopatra conoció a Marco Antonio en Egipto. 4. Los conquistadores trajeron los caballos a América y llevaron el tabaco a Europa.

GRAMMAR SECTION 32 PRÁCTICA A 1. Los niños durmieron muy mal. 2. El bebé se despertó a las tres de la mañana. 3. No recordaste traerme el libro que (yo) te pedí. 4. Raúl perdió las llaves del coche. 5. La criada les sirvió a los niños el pastel para la fiesta. 6. Empecé a perder la paciencia con ella. 7. Raúl se rió del jefe y el jefe lo despidió. 8. Los abuelos no se despidieron hasta las once.
PRÁCTICA B 1. se sentó, vino, pidió, recordó, pidió, sirvió, quiso, dijo, pedí 2. se acostó, se durmió, Durmió, se despertó, Se vistió, salió, vio, sonrieron 3. me vestí, fui, me divertí, volví, decidió, vio, se divirtió, Perdió, sintió

GRAMMAR SECTION 33 PRÁCTICA 1. En efecto, son las empleadas más trabajadoras de todas. 2. En efecto, es la mejor secretaria de la oficina. 3. En efecto, es la oficina más eficiente de la compañía. 4. En efecto, es la plaza más pequeña de la ciudad. 5. En efecto, son las ciudades más grandes del país. 6. En efecto, es el metro más rápido del mundo. 7. En efecto, son los capítulos más importantes del texto. 8. En efecto, es la residencia más ruidosa de la universidad. 9. En efecto, ¡es la peor clase del departamento!

UN POCO DE TODO EJERCICIO A *Possible answers:* Ayer, Domingo Meléndez se despertó a las ocho y se levantó inmediatamente. Se bañó, se vistió y desayunó. Tomó sólo un café con leche. Fue a la universidad y asistió a clases toda la mañana. Almorzó con unos amigos a las tres en la cafetería estudiantil y se divirtió hablando con ellos. Se despidió de ellos y fue a la biblioteca. Se quedó allí estudiando toda la tarde. Volvió a casa a las ocho. Ayudó a su madre a preparar la cena, puso la mesa y cenó con la familia. Después de cenar, puso los platos en el lavaplatos. Trató de estudiar pero no pudo. Por eso miró la televisión. Le dijo buenas noches a su madre y salió a las once a reunirse con unos amigos en un bar. Tomó unas copas con ellos y bailó un poco con una amiga. Volvió a casa a la una. Se quitó la ropa y se acostó. Leyó un poco, puso el despertador y se durmió pronto. // Ayer, me desperté... me levanté... Me bañé, me vestí y desayuné. Tomé sólo... Fui... asistí... Almorcé con... me divertí... Me despedí de ellos y fui... Me quedé allí... Volví a casa... Ayudé a... puse la mesa y cené con... Después de cenar, puse... Traté de estudiar pero no pude. Por eso miré. Le dije buenas noches a... y salí a... Tomé... bailé... Volví... Me quité la ropa y me acosté. Leí..., puse el despertador y me dormí...
EJERCICIO B E1: ¿Qué esperan tus niños que les traiga Santa Claus este año? E2: ¿Santa Claus? Mis niños no lo conocen; en nuestra casa los Reyes Magos les traen regalos a los niños. E1: ¿Ah, sí? E2: Sí, y no llegan en Nochebuena sino el seis de enero. // La persona 1 no es hispánica. Es posible que la persona 2 sea hispánica.
EJERCICIO CH 1. algunos 2. ciertos 3. son 4. conmemora 5. de 6. Muchos 7. esta 8. cree 9. apareció 10. a 11. de 12. dejó 13. ver 14. todas 15. son 16. el 17. es 18. el 19. el 20. de la 21. Llegan 22. otros 23. pasarlo 24. permite 25. corran 26. la 27. a la 28. Algunas 29. corren 30. hay 31. esta 32. es 33. la 34. describió 35. su 36. es 37. hablar 38. conocieron 39. tuvo 40. hispánicas // 1. Falso. Algunas fiestas hispánicas no son religiosas. 2. Falso. Muchos mexicanoamericanos celebran esta fiesta también. 3. Falso. Es para todos. 4. Cierto.

CAPÍTULO 11 VOCABULARIO: PREPARACIÓN

ME LEVANTÉ...
EJERCICIO A *Possible answers:* 1. f Están en una oficina. 2. d Están en casa. 3. ch Están en un autobús. 4. c Están en

la calle. 5. b Están en la puerta de una casa. 6. e Están en una oficina. 7. a Están en casa.

EJERCICIO B *Possible answers:* la llave = abrir (cerrar, perder); la pierna = doler (caminar); la mano = escribir (levantar); el brazo = romper; las aspirinas = doler (tomar); la cabeza = pensar (doler); la luz = apagar (ver); los pies = correr (tropezar, caminar); el despertador = poner

TALKING ABOUT HOW THINGS ARE DONE: ADVERBS EJERCICIO A *Possible answers:* 1. pacientemente 2. inmediatamente 3. tranquilamente 4. fácilmente 5. Posiblemente 6. totalmente 7. directamente 8. constantemente 9. puntualmente

GRAMMAR SECTION 34 PRÁCTICA A 1. Vivía en casa de sus padres. 2. Todos los días asistía a la escuela primaria. 3. Caminaba a la escuela con su mejor amigo. 4. Por la mañana aprendía a leer y escribía en la pizarra. 5. A las diez bebía leche y dormía un poco. 6. Iba a casa para almorzar y regresaba a la escuela. 7. Estudiaba geografía y hacía dibujos. 8. Jugaba al vólibol con sus compañeros en el patio de la escuela. 9. Camino de casa, compraba dulces y se los comía. 10. Frecuentemente pasaba por la casa de sus abuelos. 11. Cenaba con sus padres y (les) ayudaba a lavar los platos. 12. Veía la tele un rato y se acostaba a las ocho. // 1. No lo dice. 2. No. Caminaba a la escuela. 3. No lo dice. 4. Sí. 5. No lo dice. 6. No lo dice. // 1. Yo vivía en casa de mis padres. 2. Todos los días asistía... 3. Caminaba... mi mejor amiga. 4. Por la mañana aprendía... escribía... 5. A las diez bebía... dormía... 6. Iba... regresaba... 7. Estudiaba... hacía... 8. Jugaba... con mis compañeros... 9. Camino de casa, compraba... me los comía. 10. Frecuentemente pasaba... mis abuelos. 11. Cenaba con mis padres... ayudaba... 12. Veía... me acostaba...

PRÁCTICA B 1. Tina estaba durmiendo. 2. Su padre estaba leyendo el periódico. 3. Su hermano mayor estaba jugando con Júpiter. 4. Su madre estaba hablando por teléfono. 5. Sus abuelos estaban mirando el álbum de fotos.

PRÁCTICA CH 1. tenía 2. vivía 3. nevaba (llovía) 4. gustaba 5. estaban 6. podía 7. hacía 8. íbamos // Eran las ocho, y yo leía (estaba leyendo) mientras mi amigo escribía (estaba escribiendo) una carta. Había poco ruido, y nevaba afuera. No esperábamos a nadie y creíamos que iba a ser una noche tranquila.

GRAMMAR SECTION 35 PRÁCTICA A 1. rompieron muchos platos y vasos 2. quedó la cartera en casa 3. rompió la pierna 4. acabó el vino 5. olvidó llenar el tanque? 6. perdieron las gafas

PRÁCTICA B *Possible answers:* Pablo se levantó tarde, a las ocho, porque se le olvidó poner el despertador. Salió de casa descalzo porque se le olvidó ponerse los calcetines y zapatos. No pudo abrir la puerta del coche porque se le perdieron las llaves del coche. No tuvo dinero porque se le quedó en casa la cartera. Su jefe se ofendió porque a Pablo se le olvidó saludarlo. Pablo no tenía toda la información necesaria para su cliente porque se le quedaron todos los papeles en casa. Tenía muchísima hambre a las diez porque se le olvidó desayunar (tomar el desayuno). Pablo arruinó la chaqueta del traje del vicepresidente de la compañía porque se le cayó una taza de café.

UN POCO DE TODO EJERCICIO A *Possible answers:* 1. Anoche la señora Ochoa sirvió la cena temprano porque todos tenían mucha hambre. 2. Durante la cena los niños se rieron mucho porque estaban muy contentos. 3. Apagamos las luces a las diez porque teníamos sueño y queríamos dormir. 4. Cecilia se acostó tarde porque tenía que terminar un trabajo. 5. A Lorenzo se le olvidó poner el despertador porque estaba muy distraído. 6. A la mañana siguiente no salimos para las montañas porque nevaba mucho.

EJERCICIO CH 1. tenía 2. Diariamente 3. preguntaba 4. contestó 5. mandó 6. llevó 7. dejó 8. llevó 9. alegremente 10. vivían 11. volvieron 12. encontraron 13. volvió 14. contestó 15. planeó 16. Llegó 17. ofreció 18. la mordió 19. cayó 20. encontraron 21. se enteró 22. ocurrió 23. fue 24. besó 25. se recobró 26. inmediatamente 27. salieron 28. felizmente 29. se casaron // 1. los enanitos 2. el padre de Blancanieves 3. la madrastra 4. el príncipe 5. Blancanieves 6. el espejo mágico 7. el criado 8. la madrastra 9. la ardilla 10. los enanitos

CAPÍTULO 12 VOCABULARIO: PREPARACIÓN

MÁS PARTES..., LA SALUD... EJERCICIO A 1. el ojo 2. la nariz 3. la boca 4. la garganta 5. los pulmones 6. el corazón 7. el estómago

EJERCICIO B *Possible answers:* 1. Esto significa que es necesario dormir ocho horas cada noche. 2. Esto significa que es necesario hacer media hora de ejercicio todos los días. 3. Esto significa que no se debe ir a una fiesta todas las noches. 4. Esto significa que es necesario comer bien, dormir lo suficiente y hacer ejercicio regularmente.

EN EL CONSULTORIO DEL MÉDICO EJERCICIO A 1. resfriado 2. respira 3. enfermo, enfermero/a 4. tos 5. dolor

EJERCICIO B *Possible answers:* 1. el corazón 2. el estómago 3. la boca 4. los pulmones 5. la nariz 6. los ojos 7. la cabeza/el estómago

EJERCICIO C *Possible answers:* 1. Anamari está muy bien de salud. Nunca le duelen los pies. Nunca tiene fiebre. Siempre hace ejercicio. Es bueno que corra todos los días. 2. Martín tiene un resfriado. Le duele todo el cuerpo. Tiene fiebre. El médico le dice que beba muchos líquidos. Le va a dar un jarabe. Es mejor que se quede (guarde) en cama. 3. Inés tiene apendicitis. Le duele el estómago. Tiene fiebre. El médico y la enfermera mandan que espere la ambulancia. Es necesario que vaya al hospital.

EJERCICIO CH *Possible answers:* (...) PACIENTE: Es que me siento muy mal. Me duele la cabeza y tengo una fiebre muy alta. (...) PACIENTE: No, pero la enfermera me la tomó y tenía 38,5. DOCTOR: ¿Tiene dolor de estómago? ¿Se siente mareado/a? PACIENTE: No, respiro con dificultad; estoy muy congestionado/a. Toso tanto que me duelen también los pulmones. Es que me duele el cuerpo entero. DOCTOR: Vamos a ver. Abra Ud. la boca, por favor, y saque la lengua. Hmm... tiene la garganta bastante inflamada. Ahora la respiración... Respire Ud. profundamente... (...) DOCTOR: Bueno, aquí tiene Ud. una receta. Vaya a la farmacia y compre este jarabe para la tos. (...) Para la fiebre, tome un par de pastillas cada cuatro horas y este antibiótico para combatir la infección. (...)

GRAMMAR SECTION 36 PRÁCTICA A 1. éramos, vivíamos, íbamos, nos quedábamos 2. Eran, apagaron, Dejé, me levanté 3. trabajaba, viste 4. se resfrió, guardó 5. me enfermé, Estuve 6. tosía, hablaba, esperaba, vino, tomó, examinó, dio

PRÁCTICA B 1. ¿Por qué se fueron sin pedir nada esos clientes? Porque yo no los atendí como debía. 2. ¿Por qué se le cayeron los vasos? Porque llevaba mucho en la bandeja. 3. ¿Por qué se equivocó tanto con los pedidos? Porque no sabía bien los detalles del menú. 4. ¿Por qué te dormiste en clase hoy? Porque tenía mucho sueño. 5. ¿Por qué se te olvidó hacer la tarea para hoy? Porque estaba distraído con el nuevo perrito. 6. ¿Por qué te reíste tanto que la maestra te mandó a la oficina del director? Porque mis amigos hacían cosas cómicas.

PRÁCTICA C 1. Cuando conocí a los Sres. Quintero, ya conocía a su hijo. 2. Sabía leer cuando tenía cinco años. 3. Y podía tocar el piano antes de empezar a ir a la escuela. 4. Trataron de enseñar a su hija a tocar cuando tenía cinco años. 5. Pero ella no quiso practicar diez horas al día. 6. ¿Cómo supiste todo eso?

PRÁCTICA CH *Possible answers:* se levantó: *completed action.* hacía: *description.* Cerró: *completed action.* tenía: *description.* Parecía: *description.* funcionaba: *description.* Se preparó: *completed action.* se puso: *completed action.* llamó: *completed action.* pasaba: *action in progress.* dijo: *completed action.* sabía: *description (mental state).* iba: *action in progress.* esperaba: *action in progress.* llamó: *completed action.* vivía: *description.* estaba: *action in progress.* // We were walking: imperfect, action in progress. we caught sight of: preterite, completed action. He looked: imperfect, description. were: imperfect, description. He said: preterite, completed action. he was hungry: imperfect, description (physical state). he asked: preterite, completed action. We gave: preterite, completed action. we had: imperfect, description. he was: imperfect, description.

PRÁCTICA D estaba, entró, preguntó, quería, dijo, sentía, salieron, Vieron, se rieron, hacía, entraron, tomaron, Eran, regresaron, se acostó, estaba, empezó // 1. Rubén estudiaba cuando Soledad entró. 2. (Soledad) Le preguntó si quería ir al cine con ella. 3. Porque estaba aburrido con sus estudios. 4. Sí, la película les gustó porque era muy cómica. 5. Porque hacía frío. 6. No. Eran las dos cuando regresaron a casa. 7. Soledad se acostó y Rubén empezó a estudiar otra vez.

PRÁCTICA E conocí, hicimos, era, organizaba, venían, Había, hablaba, bailaba, llamaron, dijeron, hacíamos, Vino, dijo, era, queríamos, podíamos, despedimos, eran, aprendió, hace, invita

CONVERSACIÓN B 1. se llamaba 2. eran 3. quería 4. dijo 5. lleves 6. salió 7. preguntó 8. contestó 9. dijo 10. se fue (iba) 11. llegó 12. entró 13. tenía 14. saltó 15. corrió 16. llegó 17. encontró 18. le dijo 19. se enteró 20. corría 21. avisó 22. saltó 23. se abalanzó 24. salió 25. vio 26. ocurrió 27. le disparó 28. le hizo 29. regresó 30. la abrazó 31. le prometió

GRAMMAR SECTION 37 PRÁCTICA A 1. que 2. quien 3. Lo que 4. que 5. que 6. lo que 7. quién 8. lo que 9. lo que

PRÁCTICA B 1. —Lo que necesito es el termómetro. —¿Cuál? —El termómetro que está en el armario. 2. —Lo que necesito es el jarabe. —¿Cuál? — El jarabe que está en el consultorio. 3. —Lo que necesito es el frasco. —¿Cuál? —El frasco que está en mi bolsa. 4. —Lo que necesito es la bolsa. —¿Cuál? —La bolsa que está en el escritorio. 5. —Lo que necesito es el teléfono del especialista. —¿Cuál? —El teléfono del especialista que está en mi agenda. 6. —Lo que necesito es el nombre del hospital. —¿Cuál? —El nombre del hospital que está en ese pueblo.

UN POCO DE TODO EJERCICIO A 1. Cuando yo era niño, pensaba que lo mejor de estar enfermo era guardar cama. 2. Lo peor era que con frecuencia me resfriaba durante las vacaciones. 3. Una vez me puse muy enfermo durante la Navidad y mi madre llamó a un médico con quien tenía confianza. 4. El Dr. Matamoros vino a (la) casa y me dio un antibiótico porque yo tenía mucha fiebre. 5. Eran las cuatro de la mañana cuando por fin empecé a respirar sin dificultad. 6. Desgraciadamente el día de la Navidad tuve que tomar un jarabe y no me gustó nada el sabor. 7. Lo bueno de esta enfermedad era que mi padre tuvo que dejar de fumar mientras yo estaba enfermo. // 1. Cuando mi hijo era niño,... 2. Lo peor era que con frecuencia se resfriaba... 3. Una vez se puso muy enfermo durante la Navidad y yo llamé a un médico con quien tenía confianza. 5. Eran las cuatro de la mañana cuando por fin empezó... 6. Desgraciadamente el día de la Navidad él tuvo que tomar un jarabe y no le gustó nada el sabor. 7. Lo bueno de esta enfermedad era que su padre tuvo que dejar de fumar mientras él estaba enfermo.

EJERCICIO B 1. que 2. Estaba 3. quien 4. jugaba 5. llamaron 6. que 7. vino 8. preocupaba 9. perdía 10. era 11. llamó 12. quienes 13. conocía

EJERCICIO CH 1. tenía 2. me caí 3. montaba 4. rompió 5. que 6. vieron 7. llamaron 8. que 9. llevó 10. dolía 11. tenía 12. quería 13. vi 14. empecé 15. llamó 16. estaba 17. trabajaba 18. localizaron 19. dio 20. dejé 21. contaban 22. examinaban 23. lo más divertido 24. fue 25. se cubrieron 26. Eran 27. estaba 28. llegamos 29. tenía 30. quería 31. se sentía 32. hice 33. preparé 34. fue 35. lo bueno // 1. la recepcionista 2. yo (el niño) 3. las personas que vieron el accidente 4. yo (el niño) 5. los médicos

CAPÍTULO 13 VOCABULARIO: PREPARACIÓN

LOS COCHES EJERCICIO A 1. f 2. g 3. h 4. ch 5. b 6. e 7. c 8. a 9. i 10. d // *Possible answers:* 1. Las luces que controlan la circulación; son de color rojo, amarillo y verde. 2. Los vehículos que se ven en la carretera o en la calle forman la circulación. 3. Encontrar un lugar donde se puede dejar el coche. 4. Lo que hace el coche para poder funcionar. 5. El lugar adonde vamos cuando el coche necesita gasolina. 6. Una carretera grande que no tiene semáforos y donde se puede viajar rápidamente.

ORDINALS EJERCICIO A 1. Manuel está en el quinto grado. 2. Teresa está en el tercer grado. 3. Eduardo está en el séptimo grado. 4. Jesús está en el primer grado. 5. Pablo está en el décimo grado. 6. Evangelina está en el segundo grado.

EJERCICIO B 1. La décima es Alicia; la quinta es Raúl; la tercera es Jorge; la novena es Teodoro; la segunda es María. 2. Angela está en la cuarta posición; Cecilia está en la octava posición; Juan está en la séptima posición; Simón está en la primera posición; Linda está en la sexta posición.

GRAMMAR SECTION 38 PRÁCTICA 1. Es verdad que sólo pagué mil dólares por el coche. 2. Es cierto que el coche funcionó bien por dos meses. 3. Ahora dudo que el carro arranque otra vez. 4. ¿Cree Ud. que sea (es) la transmisión? 5. Es mejor que Ud. lo deje aquí hasta mañana. 6. No estoy seguro de que pueda arreglarlo. 7. Creo que es probable que Ud. tenga que comprar otro coche. 8. Es posible que en la agencia le den cien dólares por el coche. // 1. Cierto. 2. No, no es seguro que tenga que comprar otro coche. 3. No lo dice.

GRAMMAR SECTION 39 PRÁCTICA A Quiero que el vendedor me enseñe los últimos modelos (me explique cómo funciona cada coche, me diga cuáles son las ventajas y las desventajas de cada modelo). Me va a sorprender que cuesten tanto los coches hoy día (sean tan fáciles de manejar, haya tantos modelos distintos). Es posible que el vendedor me proponga un plan para pagar a plazos (me pida me tarjeta de crédito, me diga que espere,...)

PRÁCTICA B Le digo que me lave los platos (me haga las camas, mantenga el carro en buenas condiciones, me cambie el aceite cada tres meses, escriba todos los cheques).

UN POCO DE TODO EJERCICIO A 1. Dudo que Marcos limpie toda la casa hoy. Sé que no va a querer limpiar la mañana tampoco. 2. No creo que mi compañero/a se acueste muy temprano esta noche. ¡Y mañana es probable que se acueste a las dos de la mañana! 3. No es posible que demos una fiesta este sábado. Vamos a tratar de hacer una el fin de semana que viene. 4. Estoy seguro/a de que Enrique no hace la cama todos los días. Dudo que la haga hoy. 5. Ojalá que me despierte a tiempo mañana. Ayer no me desperté hasta las once.

EJERCICIO CH 1. una 2. acaba 3. de 4. que 5. mucho 6. que 7. marque 8. tan 9. está 10. preocupes 11. — 12. el 13. funcionan 14. quedar 15. puede 16. el 17. esa 18. hay 19. pare 20. un 21. rápido 22. llegar 23. que 24. ver 25. ver 26. calienta 27. eres 28. Primero

29. las 30. quinto 31. lleguemos 32. quiero 33. lleguemos

CAPÍTULO 14 VOCABULARIO: PREPARACIÓN

NUEVA TECNOLOGÍA... EJERCICIO B a. la pantalla b. el teclado c. las teclas ch. el disco

EJERCICIO C *Possible answers:* 1. La pantalla es donde se puede ver lo que se ha escrito. 2. Las teclas son lo que se usa para escribir en un ordenador. 3. El disco es lo que se usa para archivar la información o el programa. 4. La impresora escribe en un papel lo que uno escribió. 5. El lenguaje es la "lengua" que uno tiene que saber para usar ciertos programas en la computadora. 6. El programador es la persona que sabe usar un ordenador.

EL MEDIO AMBIENTE... EJERCICIO A *Possible answers:* 1. el campo 2. el campo 3. la ciudad 4. el campo 5. la ciudad 6. la ciudad 7. el campo 8. el campo 9. la ciudad 10. el campo

EJERCICIO B *Possible answers:* 1. La fábrica es un lugar donde se hacen las cosas, por ejemplo, los coches. 2. Un campesino es una persona que vive en el campo. 3. Un delito es algo ilegal. 4. Una finca tiene muchos animales domésticos y muchas plantas. 5. Todas estas cosas son parte de la naturaleza: los árboles, la vegetación, las rocas, las montañas, los animales, los recursos naturales. 6. Las personas que viven en un sitio forman su población. 7. La soledad es la condición de estar solo. 8. Un rascacielos es un edificio muy alto.

GRAMMAR SECTION 41 PRÁCTICA A 1. agotadas 2. limitadas 3. acostumbrados 4. cerrada 5. apagadas 6. desconectado, cerrado

PRÁCTICA B 1. La tienda no está abierta todavía. 2. No están casados todavía. 3. Las ventanas no están cerradas todavía. 4. La tierra no está cubierta de nieve todavía. 5. El equipaje no está facturado todavía. 6. La mesa no está puesta todavía. 7. El medio ambiente no está destruido todavía. 8. El error no está descubierto todavía. 9. El problema no está resuelto todavía.

GRAMMAR SECTION 42 PRÁCTICA A 1. Hemos recorrido la finca entera. 2. Hemos visto las vacas y los toros. 3. Hemos montado a caballo. 4. Hemos hablado con los campesinos. 5. Hemos respirado el aire puro. 6. Hemos visto los efectos del desarrollo industrial.

PRÁCTICA B 1. —Estás cocinando, ¿no? —No, ya he cocinado. 2. —Estás descansando, ¿no? —No, ya he descansado. 3. —Estás lavando los platos, ¿no? —No, ya los he lavado. 4. —Estás leyendo el periódico, ¿no? —No, ya lo he leído. 5. —Estás poniendo la mesa, ¿no? —No, ya la he puesto. 6. —Jorge dice que le mandes una invitación a Pablo. —Pero ya se la he mandado. 7. —Jorge dice que hables con Concepción. —Pero ya he hablado con ella. 8. —Jorge dice que vayas a su casa. —Pero ya he ido allí. 9. —Jorge dice que veas ______. —Pero ya la he visto. 10. —Jorge dice que escribas la composición esta tarde. —Pero ya la he escrito.

PRÁCTICA C 1. Es probable que Uds. ya hayan estudiado el problema. 2. No creo que hayan descubierto la solución todavía. 3. Es posible que ya hayan consultado con unos expertos. 4. Es dudoso que ya hayan arreglado la situación. 5. Espero que ya hayan reconocido la necesidad de evitar situaciones parecidas en el futuro.

PRÁCTICA CH 1. Dudo que hayan alquilado todos. 2. Es posible que ya hayan vuelto. 3. Sí, y me alegro mucho de que se hayan mudado. 4. No creo que los hayan pagado todavía. 5. Es probable que ya se haya arreglado. 6. ¡Ay, siento que se haya muerto!

UN POCO DE TODO EJERCICIO A 1. He madrugado esta mañana. Nunca me he levantado tan temprano. 2. Ellos se han preocupado mucho por los niños. Nunca se han preocupado tanto. 3. Hoy Juan ha faltado al trabajo por primera vez. Nunca ha faltado antes. 4. Nos hemos divertido mucho en aquella película. Nunca nos hemos reído tanto. 5. Has pedido vino con la comida. Antes siempre has bebido leche.

EJERCICIO B 1. —¿Ya están hechas las maletas? —No, no las he hecho. —¡Hombre! Es imposible que no las hayas hecho todavía. 2. —¿Ya están comprados los boletos? —No, no los he comprado. —¡Hombre! Es imposible que no los hayas comprado todavía. 3. —¿Ya está preparada la cena? —No, no la he preparado. —¡Hombre! Es imposible que no la hayas preparado todavía. 4. —¿Ya está facturado el equipaje? —No, no lo he facturado. —¡Hombre! Es imposible que no lo hayas facturado todavía. 5. —¿Ya están sacudidos los muebles? —No, no los he sacudido. —¡Hombre! Es imposible que no los hayas sacudido todavía. 6. —¿Ya están archivado los datos? —No, no los he archivado. —¡Hombre! Es imposible que no los hayas archivado todavía.

EJERCICIO D 1. admirado 2. fue 3. visto 4. tanta 5. tan 6. los 7. enseñando 8. floreció 9. cubierta 10. brillantes 11. Oí 12. vi 13. construyendo 14. un 15. Pasé 16. cenar 17. comer 18. descansé 19. mudarnos 20. hablábamos 21. pensábamos 22. cotidianas 23. estamos 24. tan 25. haya sido // 1. No lo dice. 2. No lo dice. 3. Cierto. Se infiere porque habla mucho de los animales. 4. Cierto. 5. No lo dice.

CAPÍTULO 15 VOCABULARIO: PREPARACIÓN

LOS PASATIEMPOS EJERCICIO A 2, 1, 5, 3, 7, 6, 8, 4, 9

LOS DEPORTES EJERCICIO A *Possible answers:* 1. la raqueta. Las otras palabras son lugares donde se puede practicar un deporte. 2. el juego. Los otros son deportes. 3. el jugador. Las otras son cosas que se usan cuando se practica un deporte. 4. el equipo. Las otras son cosas que se usan cuando se practica un deporte. 5. la pista. Las otras son personas.

GRAMMAR SECTION 43 PRÁCTICA A 1. Raúl, no gastes tanto dinero en gasolina, por favor. 2. Raúl, no manejes rápidamente, por favor. 3. Raúl, no cierres la ventana, por favor. 4. Raúl, no dobles en la esquina, por favor. 5. Raúl, no pares en la esquina, por favor. 6. Raúl, no leas el mapa, por favor. 7. Raúl, no sigas todo derecho, por favor. 8. Raúl, no digas que vamos a llegar tarde, por favor. 9. Raúl, no seas muy descortés conmigo, por favor. 10. Raúl, no arranques muy rápidamente, por favor.

PRÁCTICA B *Possible answers:* 1. No los dejes allí hoy, por favor. 2. No regreses tarde hoy, por favor. 3. No la uses hoy, por favor. 4. No entres allí hoy, por favor. 5. No corras ni juegues allí hoy, por favor. 6. No vayas allí hoy, por favor. 7. No la mires tanto hoy, por favor. Y no veas esos programas hoy, por favor. 8. No le digas mentiras hoy, por favor. 9. No te olvides de sacarla hoy, por favor. 10. No seas insolente hoy, por favor.

PRÁCTICA C 1. Llega a la escuela puntualmente. 2. Entra en la clase sin hacer tanto ruido. 3. Quítate el abrigo y siéntate. 4. Saca el libro de matemáticas y ábrelo en la página 10. 5. Escribe el problema dos en la pizarra. 6. Lee las nuevas palabras y apréndelas para mañana. 7. Ven aquí a hablar conmigo sobre esta composición. 8. Ayuda a Carlitos con su composición.

PRÁCTICA CH *Possible answers:* 1. No entres en mi cuarto y no uses mis cosas sin permiso, por favor. No toques nada aqui. 2. Ayuda con las tareas domésticas. Pon la mesa, por favor. 3. No hagas las cosas tan rápidamente. Ten paciencia y cuidado. 4. Desayuna, por favor. No salgas sin tomar algo por la mañana. 5. Escúchame, por favor, y pon atención. 6. No me contestes con ese tono de voz, por favor. Mírame cuando te hablo. 7. Dile la verdad a papá, por favor. 8. Acuéstate cuando yo te lo digo, por favor. Sé obediente, como Eufemia.

GRAMMAR SECTION 44 PRÁCTICA A 1. No, hombre, no hay nadie que conozca el camino. No, no hay nadie que pueda arreglarlo. 2. Pero, señor, aquí no tenemos ningún secretario que sepa español. Siento decírselo, pero no hay nadie que tenga tiempo de terminarlo

para mañana. 3. No hay nada que me guste. Pero sí ya tenemos dos sillones que son grandes.
PRÁCTICA B 1. ¿Hay librerías que vendan (donde vendan) libros usados? 2. ¿Hay tiendas donde se pueda comprar revistas de Latinoamérica? 3. ¿Hay cafés cerca de la universidad donde se reúnan muchos estudiantes? 4. ¿Hay discotecas donde se pueda bailar? 5. ¿Hay apartamentos cerca de la universidad que sean buenos y baratos? 6. ¿Hay cines donde pasen películas en español? 7. ¿Hay canchas de tenis donde se pueda jugar por la noche? 8. ¿Hay un gimnasio en la universidad donde se juegue al ráquetbol? 9. ¿Hay parques donde la gente corra o dé paseos? 10. ¿Hay museos donde hagan exposiciones de arte latinoamericana? // 1. Falso. Le interesa mucho. 2. Cierto. 3. Cierto. 4. Falso. Busca un apartamento.
GRAMMAR SECTION 45 PRÁCTICA A Pues, para que podamos estacionar el coche (no perdamos el principio de la función, podamos comprar entradas, consigamos buenas butacas, no tengamos que hacer cola, compremos palomitas antes de que empiece la película, hablemos con Raúl y Ceci).
PRÁCTICA B 1. No voy a menos que dejemos a los niños en casa. 2. Yo también prefiero que vayamos solos para que pasemos un rato libre sin ellos. 3. Esta vez voy a aprender a esquiar con tal que tú me lo enseñes. 4. Quiero que salgamos temprano por la mañana a menos que nieve mucho. 5. Es importante que lleguemos a la cabaña antes de que empiece a nevar en las montañas. 6. Compra leña aquí en caso de que no haya leña en la cabaña. 7. Deja un recado en caso de que tus padres nos llamen. // 1. No lo dice. 2. No lo dice. 3. Falso. 4. No lo dice.
UN POCO DE TODO EJERCICIO A 1. Trata de despertarte antes de que suene el despertador, por favor. 2. Busca a alguien que se levante a las cinco de la mañana para correr. 3. Pon la mesa y ten la comida preparada antes de que empiece el noticiero de las seis. 4. En caso de que tengas un rato libre el sábado, compra las entradas para el cine. 5. Duerme con las ventanas abiertas para que entre aire.
EJERCICIO C 1. de 2. fue 3. divertida 4. te reíste 5. nadie 6. pase 7. lo que 8. prefiero 9. profundos 10. esa 11. que 12. vimos 13. pasada 14. escojas 15. lleves 16. ninguna 17. doblada 18. sabes 19. gustan 20. es 21. inició 22. continuó 23. contraataca 24. es 25. caracterizada 26. especiales 27. que 28. vuelven 29. encabezadas 30. escrita 31. dirigida 32. basa 33. los 34. ocurrida 35. cambió 36. murieron 37. conocido 39. una 39. van
REPASO 5 La Argentina—8; el Brasil—10; Bolivia—6; Colombia—7; Chile—3; el Ecuador—5; el Paraguay—4; el Perú—9; el Uruguay—1; Venezuela—2. Brasilia—el Brasil; Buenos Aires—la Argentina; Bogotá—Colombia; Santiago—Chile; La Paz—Bolivia; Asunción—el Paraguay; Quito—el Ecuador; Caracas—Venezuela; Montevideo—el Uruguay; Lima—Perú.

CAPÍTULO 16 VOCABULARIO: PREPARACIÓN
LAS NOTICIAS EJERCICIO A 1. a 2. e 3. h 4. f 5. ch 6. c 7. g 8. d 9. b
GRAMMAR SECTION 46 PRÁCTICA A *Possible answers:* Mis padres querían que yo me portara bien (que sacara buenas notas, que me pusiera la ropa vieja para jugar, que no jugara en las calles, que no luchara con mis amigos, que no trajera animales a casa). Mis padres no querían que mirara mucho la televisión (que comiera muchos dulces). Mis maestros me pedían que estudiara mucho (que sacara buenas notas). Yo buscaba amigos que vivieran en nuestro barrio (que tuvieran muchos juguetes, que vinieran a mi casa a jugar). Yo siempre quería que los miembros de mi familia creyaran en Santa Claus (que tuvieran un árbol de Navidad muy alto, que fueran a la playa en verano, que pasaran juntos los días feriados).
PRÁCTICA B 1. Los obreros querían que les dieran un aumento de sueldo. Un hecho. 2. Fue (Era) posible que los trabajadores siguieran en huelga hasta las Navidades. Una opinión. 3. Fue (Era) necesario que las víctimas recibieran antención médica en la Clínica Sagrado Corazón. Un hecho. 4. Fue (Era) lástima que no hubiera espacio para todos allí. Una opinión. 5. Los terroristas pidieron que los oficiales no los siguieran. Un hecho. 6. Parecía imposible que el gobierno escuchara sus demandas. Una opinión. 7. Fue (Era) necesario que el gobierno informara a todos los ciudadanos del desastre. Un hecho. 8. Dudaba que la paz mundial estuviera fuera de nuestro alcance. Una opinión. 9. Lee Iacocca prefería que la nueva fábrica se construyera en México. Un hecho. 10. Temía que el número de votantes fuera muy bajo en las próximas elecciones. Una opinión.
PRÁCTICA C 1. Los indios temían que los colonos les quitaran toda la tierra. 2. A los colonos no les gustaba que tuvieran que pagarle impuestos al rey. 3. Parecía imposible que la joven república tuviera éxito. 4. A los del sur no les gustaba que los gobernaran los del norte. 5. A los abolicionistas no les gustaba que algunos no tuvieran las mismas libertades. 6. Era necesario que se declararan en huelga los obreros para obtener algunos derechos. 7. Era terrible que hubiera dos guerras mundiales. 8. Para que nosotros vivamos en paz, es cuestión de aprender a comunicarnos con las demás naciones. 9. También es necesario que haya leyes que garanticen los derechos de todos.
PRÁCTICA CH 1. El ladrón no pensaba entrar en la casa a menos que no oyera ningún ruido. 2. No iba a molestar a los dueños con tal que encontrara dinero y objetos de valor. 3. Un amigo lo acompañaba en caso de que hubiera alguna dificultad. 4. El amigo rompió la ventana para que el ladrón pudiera entrar. 5. El ladrón entró silenciosamente para que los dueños no se despertaran. 6. Salió antes de que los dueños pudieran llamar a la policía.
PRÁCTICA D 1. Debiera(s) conducir más lentamente. 2. ¿No pudiera(s) pensar en los demás esta vez? 3. Quisiéramos que considerara(s) sus (tus) obligaciones. 4. ¿Cómo (¿De qué manera) quisiera pagar, señora? 5. Debiéramos proteger el bienestar de ellos (su bienestar) primero.
GRAMMAR SECTION 47 PRÁCTICA A mía, suya, mía, mía, suya
PRÁCTICA B 1. —Esta maleta, ¿es de Juan? —No, no es suya. 2. —Esta maleta, ¿es de Uds.? —No, no es nuestra. 3. —Esta maleta, ¿es de Alicia? —No, no es suya. 4. —Esta maleta, ¿es de Ud.? —No, no es mía. 5. —Esta maleta, ¿es tuya? —No, no es mía. 6. —¿Y este despertador? —No, no es mío. El mío es más pequeño. 7. —¿Y estos zapatos? —No, no son míos. Los míos son más pequeños. 8. —¿Y esta llave? —No, no es mía. La mía es más pequeña. 9. —¿Y este televisor? —No, no es mío. El mío es más pequeño. 10. —¿Y estas pastillas? —No, no son mías. Las mías son más pequeñas. 11. —¿Y este periódico? —No, no es mío. El mío es más pequeño.
UN POCO DE TODO EJERCICIO A 1. Era increíble que hubiera tantos problemas mundiales. 2. No creía que nadie supiera todas las soluciones. 3. Sentía que no se pudiera resolver todos los problemas. 4. Las autoridades siempre negaban que la culpa fuera suya. 5. Los ciudadanos pidieron que alguien hiciera algo por ellos. 6. Era necesario que todos cumplieran con las responsabilidades suyas. 7. Había suficientes recursos para que nadie sufriera ninguna privación. 8. ¿Había un gobierno que fuera mejor que el nuestro? 9. Dudaba que se formara nunca una sociedad perfecta. 10. Sugería (Sugerí) que todos los ciudadanos trabajaran juntos para crear un mundo mejor.

EJERCICIO B *Possible answers:* 1. Yo prefería que fuéramos a la playa... ¡solos! 2. Yo quería que alquiláramos una casa nueva y con todas las comodidades. Quería que todos nuestros parientes vinieran a visitarnos. 3. Yo insistía en que gastáramos menos en comida y vivienda. Quería que gastáramos más en la educación de los niños. 4. Yo prefería que fuéramos a ver una película francesa y que usáramos mi coche. 5. Yo quería que pasáramos la última Navidad con mi familia y que pasáramos la Nochebuena con los padres de él/ella.
EJERCICIO CH 1. recibido 2. intensificar 3. cree 4. piensan (pensaban) 5. emitidas 6. mandaron 7. aumentaran 8. ocurriera 9. preguntando 10. asistir 11. por 12. organizada 13. celebrar 14. de la 15. aparece 16. esté 17. ha dicho 18. extranjeros 19. estar 20. ver

CAPÍTULO 17 VOCABULARIO: PREPARACIÓN
EJERCICIO A 1. e 2. ch 3. d 4. c 5. a 6. b
EJERCICIO B *Possible answers:* 1. Una señora compra unas peras en un supermercado; paga al contado. Regresa a casa después. 2. En un almacén una señora está comprando un sombrero. Paga con su tarjeta de crédito. Después va a una zapatería para comprar zapatos. 3. Un señor está pagando la cuenta en un restaurante con cheque. Después va a regresar a su oficina.
EJERCICIO C *Possible answers:* 1. La cantidad de dinero que uno tiene para gastar y para pagar los gastos. 2. Gastar muy cuidadosamente, pagando lo menos posible; reducir los gastos. 3. Una cantidad de dinero que uno recibe de otra persona (o de un banco). 4. La cantidad que uno tiene que pagar por algo. 5. La cantidad de dinero que uno paga, generalmente por mes, para poder vivir en una casa o en un apartamento que es de otra persona. 6. Cuando se paga una parte del precio total cada mes. // Una cuenta corriente es el dinero que uno necesita para pagar los gastos corrientes, de cada día. Una cuenta de ahorros es el dinero que uno ahorra para el futuro. Un talonario de cheques es el librito que se usa con la cuenta corriente. Una libreta de ahorros es el librito que se usa con la cuenta de ahorros. Ingresar dinero en una cuenta es cuando se deposita dinero en la cuenta. Sacar dinero de una cuenta es cuando uno quita dinero de la cuenta para gastarlo.
GRAMMAR SECTION 48 PRÁCTICA A 1. (Yo) Hablaré sólo español. Leeré mucho en español; periódicos, revistas,... Conoceré a mucha gente joven. Veré un programa del Ballet Folklórico. 2. (Tú) Te levantarás temprano todos los días. Comerás comida típica. Aprenderás mucho sobre la historia de México. Visitarás todos los museos. 3. (Nosotros) Cambiaremos mucho dinero en los bancos. Escribiremos muchas tarjetas postales. Compraremos muchos recuerdos. Regatearemos en los mercados. 4. (Uds.) No usarán demasiado las tarjetas de crédito. Querrán pagarlo todo al contado. Tratarán de adaptarse a un presupuesto. Regresarán a los Estados Unidos con algún dinero. 5. Gustavo gastará todo su dinero muy pronto. Pasará todo el tiempo con otros turistas. Tendrá que volver pronto a los Estados Unidos. Estará muy descontento con el viaje. // 1. Falso. Gustavo gastará todo su dinero muy pronto. 2. Falso. Algunos aprenderán mucho de la cultura del país. 3. Cierto.
PRÁCTICA B 1. Gregorio pagará tarde todas las cuentas. 2. Tratará de adaptarse a un presupuesto. 3. Volverá a hacer el presupuesto el próximo mes. 4. No ingresará nada en la cuenta de ahorros. 5. Se quejará porque no tiene (tendrá) suficiente dinero. 6. Seguirá usando las tarjetas de crédito. 7. Les pedirá dinero a sus padres. 8. Buscará trabajo de tiempo parcial. // 2
PRÁCTICA C 1. El señor Adams dice que pagará al contado. 2. Es posible que la señora Walsh use su tarjeta de crédito. 3. La señorita Berry cobrará un cheque en el banco. 4. Es necesario que la tienda mande la cuenta a la casa de Karen.
GRAMMAR SECTION 49 PRÁCTICA A 1. Julio empezará a ahorrar más dinero en cuanto le den un aumento de sueldo; deje de gastar tanto. 2. Pagaré todas mis cuentas tan pronto como tenga el dinero para hacerlo; sea absolutamente necesario. 3. Susana dice que dejará de usar sus tarjetas de crédito tan pronto como encuentre un buen trabajo; reciba el sueldo del primer mes. 4. Mis compañeros pagarán la matrícula después de que sus padres les manden un cheque; cobren su cheque en el banco. 5. No podré pagar el alquiler hasta que saque el dinero de mi cuenta de ahorros; ingrese el dinero en mi cuenta corriente. 6. Los García no van a retirarse hasta que su hijo termine sus estudios universitarios; se establezca y se case. 7. Vamos a volver a hablarle a Ernesto cuando nos devuelva los cien dólares que le prestamos; deje de pedirnos más dinero.
PRÁCTICA B 1. se graduó, le dieron, se gradúe, le darán 2. era, quería, tenía, decidió, termine, pueda 3. escribe, tenga, escribió, le mandaran, va, llegue 4. estudiaba, terminara, deja, haya, tenga, hayan
UN POCO DE TODO EJERCICIO A 1. Será necesario que ahorremos más. 2. Yo no usaré tanto las tarjetas de crédito. 3. Mamá buscará un trabajo donde le paguen más. 4. Pediremos un préstamo en el banco. 5. ¿Crees que nos lo den (darán)? 6. Papá estará tranquilo cuando todos empiecen a economizar. 7. Debes (Deberás) pagar siempre al contado. 8. No habrá manera de que nos vayamos de vacaciones este verano.
PRÁCTICA B 1. Miguel y Carmen se casaron antes de que los padres de Miguel volvieran a Colombia. 2. Te dije lo de la boda en cuanto lo supe. 3. Los padres se sorprendieron también cuando Miguel les dio la noticia. 4. Miguel y Carmen pensaban ir de luna de miel tan pronto como terminara el semestre. 5. Les íbamos a dar una fiesta después de que regresaran de su viaje. 6. Tuvimos que cambiar de planes cuando anunciaron que se habían separado por el momento. 7. Carmen piensa esperar a Miguel hasta que éste regrese de Colombia.
PRÁCTICA C 1. viajarán 2. vivirán 3. del 4. que 5. vivirán 6. diseñadas 7. construidas 8. construirá 9. tendrán 10. participar 11. estuvieran 12. tuvieran 13. viajaran 14. que 15. tendrá 16. una 17. vendida 18. al 19. privado 20. de 21. utilizados 22. del 23. informó 24. encabezados 25. dio 26. formalizará
PRÁCTICA CH 1. 3 2. 1 3. 6 4. 5 5. 2 6. 4

CAPÍTULO 18 VOCABULARIO: PREPARACIÓN
PROFESIONES Y OFICIOS EJERCICIO A 1. el/la plomero/a 2. el/la abogado/a 3. el/la siquiatra 4. el/la enfermero/a 5. el/la criado/a 6. el/la obrero/a 7. el/la periodista
EN BUSCA DE UN PUESTO *Possible answers:* 13, 2, 5, 7, 1, 4, 14, 9, 11, 3, 8, 10, 12, 6
GRAMMAR SECTION 50 PRÁCTICA A gustaría, trabajaría, Podría, Tomaría, Comería, Vería, sería, tendría, Podría, tendría // 1. Cierto. 2. Falso. Le gusta nadar. 3. Falso. Tendría que usar su tarjeta de crédito. 4. No lo dice.
PRÁCTICA B 1. —¿Estudiarías italiano? —No. Estudiaría chino. 2. —¿Renunciarías a un puesto sin avisar? —No. Renunciaría con dos semanas de anticipación. 3. —¿Harías un viaje a España? —No. Haría un viaje a la Argentina. 4. —¿Saldrías sin apagar el estéreo? —No. Saldría sin apagar las luces. 5. —¿Seguirías un presupuesto rígido? —No. Seguiría uno flexible. 6. —¿Gastarías menos en ropa? —No. Gastaría menos en libros. 7. —¿Pondrías el aire acondicionado en invierno? —No. Pondría el aire acondicionado en verano. 8. —¿Alquilarías un coche de lujo? —No. Alquilaría uno económico. 9. —¿Dejarías de estudiar?

10. —¿Vivirías en otra ciudad? 11. —¿Serías presidente de los Estados Unidos? 12. —¿Te gustaría conocer a una persona famosa?

GRAMMAR SECTION 51 PRÁCTICA B 1. Si encontrara un anuncio interesante, llamaría a la empresa. 2. Si la empresa me mandara una solicitud, la llenaría. 3. Si me pidieran el currículum, se lo mandaría. 4. Si me interesara el salario, pediría una entrevista. 5. Si me dieran una entrevista, trataría de caerle bien al entrevistador. 6. Si él me hiciera muchas preguntas, contestaría honestamente. 7. Si yo tuviera preguntas que hacer sobre la empresa, las haría durante la entrevista. 8. Si me ofrecieran el puesto, estaría muy contento/a.

PRÁCTICA C 1. Habla como si viviera en un palacio. 2. Habla como si lo recordara todo. 3. Habla como si fuera experta en todo. 4. Habla como si lo tuviera ya. 5. Habla como si tuviera muchos amigos.

PRÁCTICA CH 1. Si tuviéramos tiempo, compraríamos flores. 2. Si el nuevo coche no estuviera en el taller, lo usarías. 3. Si hubiera linterna, miraría el mapa. 4. Si pudiera ver el nombre de la calle, doblaría aquí. 5. Si reconociera la casa, pararía aquí. 6. Si quisiera caminar, podrías estacionar aquí. 7. Si me lo pidieras con calma, dejaría de criticar tu manera de conducir.

UN POCO DE TODO EJERCICIO A 1. Si yo fuera tú, no haría eso. 2. Si yo estuviera allí, se lo diría claramente. 3. Si yo pudiera viajar a Espana, aprendería mucho. 4. Si me darías el dinero, yo podría comprar el boleto. 5. Si yo no tuviera que trabajar, estaría contentísimo/a.

EJERCICIO B 1. —Estaré en el bar a las dos. —¿No dijiste que estarías allí a las doce? —¡Que no! Dije que estaría allí a las dos. Entendiste mal. 2. —Estudiaré con Juan. —¿No dijiste que estudiarías con Juana? —¡Que no! Dije que estudiaría con Juan. Entendiste mal. 3. —Iré de vacaciones en julio. —¿No dijiste que irías de vacaciones en junio? —¡Que no! Dije que iría en julio. Entendiste mal. 4. —Te veré en casa. —¿No dijiste que me verías en clase? —¡Que no! Dije que te vería en casa. Entendiste mal. 5. —Compraré la blusa rosada. —¿No dijeste que comprarías la blusa roja? —¡Que no! Dije que compraría la blusa rosada. Entendiste mal.

EJERCICIO CH 1. después de 2. quería 3. gustó 4. salió 5. llegó 6. trajeran 7. tampoco 8. dejó 9. experimentó 10. El 11. por 12. representó (representaba) 13. sabía 14. inglesa 15. había estudiado 16. había aprendido 17. también 18. a la 19. había sido 20. para 21. tomó 22. Por 23. consiguió 24. buen 25. se acostumbraran 26. Decidieron 27. lo que 28. la 29. han acostumbrado 30. Son 31. este 32. estuvieran 33. sería // 1. Falso. Emigró porque no le gustó el sistema. 2. Cierto. 3. No lo dice. 4. No lo dice. 5. Cierto. 6. Falso. Hay cosas que añoran.

REPASO 6 el vascuence—el País Vasco, el gallego—Galicia, el catalán—Cataluña; la capital del país—Madrid, Don Quijote—Castilla—La Mancha, las naranjas—Valencia

CAPÍTULO 19 VOCABULARIO: PREPARACIÓN

EN UN VIAJE AL EXTRANJERO EJERCICIO B *Possible answers:* ¿De dónde es Ud.? // Su pasaporte, por favor. // ¿Tiene Ud. algo que declarar? // Me abre la maleta, por favor. // Pero este abrigo de pieles... ¡Hay que declararlo! // Vale más de la cantidad permitida para compras en el extranjero. // El diez por ciento de lo que Ud. pagó.

EL ALOJAMIENTO EJERCICIO A *Possible answers:* 1. un hotel grande 2. un hotel grande 3. una pensión pequeña 4. un hotel grande 5. un hotel grande 6. un pensión pequeña 7. un hotel grande 8. una pensión pequeña 9. un hotel grande 10. un hotel grande 11. una pensión pequeña 12. una pensión pequeña 13. un hotel grande 14. una pensión pequeña

GRAMMAR SECTION 52 PRÁCTICA B 1. f 2. g 3. d 4. c 5. e 6. ch 7. b 8. a

PRÁCTICA E 1. para, por, por, por, para 2. para, para, por, por 3. para, Por, para, por, por 4. para, por, para 5. Por, por, por, por

UN POCO DE TODO EJERCICIO A 1. vuelva 2. supiera 3. puedan 4. hayan tenido 5. hayan dicho 6. pases

EJERCICIO B por, para, por, para, Para, por, por, por, para // 1. la necesidad. 2. para estar con los suyos, en su ambiente. 3. porque nació aquí.

EJERCICIO CH 1. estaba 2. para 3. para 4. había preparado 5. esperaba 6. había sacado 7. sabía 8. eran 9. Tenía 10. de 11. hicieran 12. pudiera 13. por 14. quedaría 15. era 16. de 17. subí 18. al 19. llegué 20. llovía 21. Fui 22. empecé 23. Leí 24. por 25. me acosté 26. Estaba 27. me dormí 28. de 29. tomé 30. para 31. estaban 32. Siéntese 33. tenga 34. dijeron 35. somos 36. sonrieron 37. tomara 38. Empezó 39. contesté 40. tuviera 41. abiertos 42. dijeron 43. había salido 44. esperaban 45. Regresé 46. volara 47. tocar 48. brillaba // 1. No lo dice. 2. No lo dice. 3. Cierto. 4. Falso. Tenía miedo del examen. 5. Cierto. 6. No lo dice.

CAPÍTULO 20

EJERCICIO A 1. Se compra el champú y el jabón en una farmacia. 2. En una farmacia de España no venden la variedad de cosas que se venden en las farmacias de los Estados Unidos. 3. En España se puede comprar sellos en los estancos y en el correo. 4. Se va al estanco. 5. Un quiosco es una pequeña tienda donde se venden periódicos, revistas, libros, etcétera. 6. En una papelería venden papel para cartas, sobres, lápices, etcétera.

EJERCICIO B 1. Cierto. 2. Falso. Iría a un bar. 3. Falso. Se va al correo para mandar paquetes. 4. Falso. Es más rápido tomar el metro. 5. Falso. Se va a una farmacia a comprar champú. 6. Falso. Iría a una farmacia. 7. Cierto. 8. Falso. Un batido se hace con leche.

VOCABULARIES

The **Spanish–English Vocabulary** contains all the words that appear in the text, with the following exceptions: (1) most close or identical cognates that do not appear in the chapter vocabulary lists; (2) most conjugated verb forms; (3) diminutives in **-ito/a**; (4) absolute superlatives in **-ísimo/a**; (5) most adverbs in **-mente**; (6) most vocabulary that is glossed in the text; and (7) much vocabulary from realia and authentic readings. Active vocabulary is indicated by the number of the chapter in which a word or given meaning is first listed (**A** = **Ante todo**); vocabulary that is glossed in the text is not considered to be active vocabulary and is not numbered. Only meanings that are used in the text are given. The **English–Spanish Vocabulary** is based on the chapter lists of active vocabulary. It includes all words and expressions necessary to do the translation exercises in the text and in the **Workbook** that accompanies the text.

The gender of nouns is indicated, except for masculine nouns ending in **-o** and feminine nouns ending in **-a**. Stem changes and spelling changes are indicated for verbs: **dormir (ue, u); llegar (gu).**

Words beginning with **ch, ll,** and **ñ** are found under separate headings, following the letters **c, l,** and **n,** respectively. Similarly, **ch, ll,** and **ñ** within words follow **c, l,** and **n,** respectively. For example, **coche** follows **cóctel, calle** follows **calor,** and **añadir** follows **anuncio.**

The following abbreviations are used:

adj.	adjective	*inf.*	infinitive	*poss.*	possessive
adv.	adverb	*inv.*	invariable in form	*prep.*	preposition
approx.	approximately	*irreg.*	irregular	*pron.*	pronoun
conj.	conjunction	*L.A.*	Latin America	*refl. pron.*	reflexive pronoun
d.o.	direct object	*m.*	masculine	*s.*	singular
f.	feminine	*Mex.*	Mexico	*Sp.*	Spain
fam.	familiar	*n.*	noun	*sub. pron.*	subject pronoun
form.	formal	*obj.* (*of prep.*)	object (of a preposition)	*subj.*	subjunctive
gram.	grammatical term	*p.p.*	past participle	*v.*	verb
i.o.	indirect object	*pl.*	plural		

SPANISH–ENGLISH VOCABULARY

A

a to (A); at (*with time*); **a la(s)...** at (hour) (A); **a partir de** starting from; **a qué hora...?** (at) what time. . . ? (A); **a tiempo** on time (7)
a menos que unless (15)
abajo below
abalanzarse (c) to pounce
abandonar to abandon
abandono abandonment
abarcar (qu) to cover (*a topic*)
abierto/a *p.p.* open(ed) (4)
abogado/a lawyer (18)
abolir to abolish
abono fertilizer; membership
abrazo hug
abrigarse (gu) to wrap oneself up (*with clothing*)
abrigo coat (3)
abril *m.* April (5)
abrir (*p.p.* **abierto/a**) to open (3)
absoluto/a absolute
absurdo/a absurd
abuelo/a grandfather/mother (2)
abuelos *pl.* grandparents (2)
abultamiento *n.* swelling
abundancia abundance
abundar to be plentiful

aburrido: estar aburrido/a to be bored (4); **ser aburrido/a** to be boring
acabar to finish (11); to put an end to; **acabar de** + *inf.* to have just (*done something*) (6); **acabarse** to run out of (11)
académico/a academic
acampar to camp
acariciante *adj.* caressing
acaso: por si acaso just in case (19)
acceso access
accidente *m.* accident
acción *f.* action
aceite *m.* oil (13)
aceitoso/a oily
acelerado/a fast, accelerated (14)
acelerador *m.* accelerator
acelerar to accelerate, speed up
acelga Swiss chard
acento accent
aceptable acceptable
aceptación *f.* acceptance
aceptar to accept
acera sidewalk (15)
acerca de *prep.* about, concerning
acercar (qu) to bring nearer; **acercarse** to approach, draw near
acomodar to accommodate
acompañado/a accompanied
acompañar to accompany, go with (15)
acondicionado: aire (*m.*) **acondicionado** air conditioning
acondicionador *m.* air conditioner (9)
aconsejar to advise
acontecer (zc) to happen
acontecimiento event, happening (16)
acoplar to fit, join (together)
acordarse (ue) (de) to remember (11)
acostar (ue) to put to bed (9); **acostarse** to go to bed (9)
acostumbrarse (a) to get used, accustomed (to); to be accustomed (to)
actitud *f.* attitude
activar to activate
actividad *f.* activity
activista *m., f.* activist
activo/a active
acto act, ceremony, action
actor *m.* actor
actriz *f.* (*pl.* **actrices**) actress
actual *adj.* current, present day, up-to-date (11); *n. m.* this month
actualidad *f.* actuality; right now (14); **en la actualidad** at present, at the present time
actuar to act
acuario aquarium (8)
acuerdo agreement; **de acuerdo** agreed; **no estoy de acuerdo** I don't agree (2); **ponerse** (*irreg.*) **de acuerdo** to reach an agreement
Adán Adam
adaptar to adapt
adecuado/a adequate
adelantar to pass (*a car*)
adelante ahead, forward; **de ahora en adelante** from now on; **más adelante** later on
adelanto advance
adelgazar (c) to make thin, slender; **adelgazarse** to become thin
además (de) besides, in addition (to) (11)
adentro de inside
aderezar (c) to season
adherir (ie, i) to stick
adicional additional (A)
adiós good-bye (A)
aditivo alimentario food additive
adivinar to guess
adjetivo adjective (2)
adjunto/a enclosed, attached
administración *f.* administration; **administración comercial** business administration
administrativo/a administrative
admiración *f.* admiration
admirar to admire
admitir to admit; to accept
adolescente *adj.* adolescent
¿adónde? where (to)? (3)
adoptar to adopt
adorar to adore
adosado/a affixed
adquirir (ie) to acquire
adquisición *f.* acquisition
aduana customs (19); **derechos de aduana** customs duty (19); **inspector(a) de aduanas** (customs) inspector (19)
adulto adult
adverbio adverb
aéreo/a *adj.* air, of or pertaining to air travel; **línea aérea** airline
aerolínea airline
aeropuerto airport (7)
afectar to affect
afecto affection
afeitado *n.* shave
afeitadora shaver, razor
afeitar to shave (9); **afeitarse** to shave oneself (9)
aficionado/a *n.* fan, enthusiast (15); *adj.* fond; **aficionado/a a** fond of
afiliado/a affiliated
afín similar
afirmar to affirm; to maintain firmly
afirmativo/a affirmative
afortunado/a fortunate
africano/a African
afrocubano/a Afro-Cuban
afuera outside (5)
afueras: en las afueras in, on the outskirts (9)
agencia agency; **agencia de empleos** employment agency; **agencia de viajes** travel agency
agenda diary
agente *m., f.* agent; **agente de viajes** travel agent
ágil agile
agobiante overwhelming
agosto August (5)
agotar to deplete; **agotarse** to exhaust oneself
agradable agreeable, pleasant
agradar to please
agradecer (zc) to thank
agradecido/a grateful
agradecimiento gratitude; appreciation
agregar (gu) to add
agricultura agriculture
agrio/a sour
agua *f.* (*but* **el agua**) water (5); **cama de agua** water bed (8)
aguacate *m.* avocado
aguantar to put up with, endure, tolerate
aguar to dilute; to spoil (*a party*)
aguardiente *m.* brandy
aguinaldo Christmas gift or carol
ahí there
ahora now (2); **ahora mismo** right now (4)
ahorrar to save (money) (17)
ahorros: cuenta de ahorros savings account (17); **libreta de ahorros** bank book (17)
aire *m.* air (14); **aire acondicionado** air conditioning; **aire acondicionador** *m.* air conditioner (9)
aislado/a isolated
aislamiento isolation
ajardinado/a having gardens
ajedrez *m.* chess (15); **jugar (ue) (gu) al ajedrez** to play chess (15)
ajedrezado/a checkered
ajo garlic
al (*contraction of* **a** + **el**) to the; **al** + *inf.* upon, while, when + *verb form*; **al (mes, año, etcétera)** per (month, year, etc.)
alargar (gu) to prolong
alarma alarm
alcalde *m.* mayor
alcaldía mayor's office
alcance *m.* reach
alcanzar (c) to get up to; to reach
alcoba bedroom (8)
alcohólico/a alcoholic
alegrarse (de) to be happy (about) (13)
alegre happy (4); bright (*color*)
alegría happiness, joy
alejarse to keep away
alemán *m.* German (*language*) (1)
alemán, alemana German (2)
Alemania Germany
alergia allergy
alérgico/a allergic
alfombra rug (8)
alfombrado *n.* carpeting
algo something, anything (3)
algodón *m.* cotton (3)
alguien someone, anyone (6)
algún, alguno/a some, any (6);

algún día some day; **alguna vez** once; ever
alianza alliance
alimentación *f.* food
alimentar (de) to feed, live (on)
alimentario: aditivo alimentario food additive
alimento food
alma *f.* (*but* **el alma**) soul
almacén *m.* department store (3)
almacenar to store
almorzar (ue) (c) to have lunch (5)
almuerzo lunch; noon meal (6)
aló hello (*telephone*)
alojamiento *n.* lodging (19)
alojar to accommodate; to house
alquilar to rent (9)
alquiler *m.* rent (9)
alrededor de *prep.* around
alrededores *m. pl.* environs, outskirts, surroundings
alta: dar (*irreg.*) **de alta** to discharge (*from the service*)
altar *m.* altar
alteración *f.* irregularity
alto *n.* stop, pause
alto/a tall (2); high
altura height
alumbrarse to shine, give light
alumno/a student
allá there
allí there (3)
ama *f.* (*but* **el ama**) **de casa** housekeeper; lady of the house, housewife
amable kind, nice (2)
amanecer (zc) to dawn
amanerado/a courteous
amante *m., f.* lover, sweetheart
amar to love
amarillo/a yellow (3)
Amazonas *m. s.* Amazon
ambición *f.* ambition
ambidextro/a ambidextrous, using both hands with equal ease
ambientación *f.* setting
ambiental environmental
ambientarse to adapt oneself
ambiente *m.* environment, atmosphere; **medio ambiente** environment (14)
ambos/as both
ambulancia ambulance
amenaza threat
ameno/a pleasant
americano/a American
amigdalitis *f.* tonsillitis
amigo/a friend (1)
amistad *f.* friendship (4)
amistoso/a friendly
amo master
amontonado/a piled up, crowded one on top of another
amor *m.* love (4)
amparo shelter, protection
amplio/a large, ample, spacious
amueblar to furnish (*a house, etc.*)
análisis *m.* analysis
analizar (c) to analyze
anaranjado/a *adj.* orange (3)
anciano/a elderly person
ancho/a wide; **a sus anchas** at one's ease
anchoas *f. pl.* anchovies
andar (*irreg.*) to run, function (*with machines*); to go; to walk; **andar en bicicleta** to ride a bicycle
anfitrión, anfitriona host(ess)
ángel *m.* angel
anglosajón, anglosajona Anglo-Saxon
angustia anguish
anillo ring
animación *f.* animation
animado/a animated; **dibujos** (*m. pl.*) **animados** cartoons
animal *m.* animal
animar to animate, excite
ánimo courage
anomalía anomaly
anoche last night (9)
anónimo/a anonymous
ansiedad *f.* anxiety
ante before; **ante todo** first of all
anteayer the day before yesterday (9)
antecedente *m.* antecedent (*of a pronoun*)
anteojos *m. pl.* (eye)glasses
antepasado/a *n.* ancestor
anterior previous, preceding; (at the) front; **anterior a** before, previous to
anterioridad: con anterioridad previously
antes *adv.* sooner, before; **antes de** *prep.* before (4); **antes (de) que** *conj.* before (15)
antibiótico antibiotic (12)
anticipación: con (_____ días de) anticipación (_____ days) in advance (19)
anticipar to anticipate
anticuado/a antiquated
antigüedades *f. pl.* antiques
antiguo/a old
antipático/a unpleasant (2)
antónimo antonym
antropología anthropology
anualmente annually
anunciar to announce (7)
anuncio ad (9); announcement (9)
añadir to add
año year (5); **año bisiesto** leap year; **Año Nuevo** New Year; **el año pasado** last year; **tener** (*irreg.*) _____ **años** to be _____ years old (2)
apagar (gu) to turn off (11)
aparato apparatus, appliance (9)
aparecer (zc) to appear
aparente apparent
apartado postal post office box
apartamento apartment; **casa de apartamentos** apartment house
aparte (de) aside (from)
apellido surname, family name, last name (2)
apenas scarcely
apendicitis *f. s.* appendicitis
apeticible attractive
apio celery
aplicar (qu) to apply; **aplicarse** to apply oneself; to be used for
apodo nickname
aportación *f.* contribution
aporte *m.* contribution
apoyar to support (16)
apoyo support
apreciar to appreciate, esteem, value; to notice
aprender to learn (3)
aprendizaje *m.* learning
aprisa rapidly
aprobar (ue) to pass (*an exam*)
apropiado/a appropriate
aprovechar to make good use of; **aprovecharse de** to profit by, take advantage of
aproximadamente approximately
apuntes *m. pl.* notes
aquel, aquella *adj.* that (*over there*) (4); **aquél, aquélla** *pron.* that one (*over there*); **en aquel entonces** back then, in those days (11)
aquello that, that thing, that fact (4)
aquellos/as *adj.* those (*over there*) (4); **aquéllos/as** *pron.* those (ones) (*over there*)
aquí here (1); **aquí mismo** right here; **por aquí** around here
árabe *m.* Arabic
Arabia Saudita Saudi Arabia
araña spider
árbitro arbitrator
árbol *m.* tree (10)
arco iris rainbow
archipiélago canario Canary Islands
ardilla squirrel
arena sand
arete *m.* earring
argentino/a Argentine, Argentinian
armario closet
arqueológico/a archaeological
arquitecto/a architect
arquitectura architecture
arrancar (qu) to start (*a motor*) (13)
arreglar to fix, repair (8); to arrange
arriba above; on top
arriendo *n.* leasing
arrojar to throw; toss
arrope *m.* syrup
arroyo stream
arroz *m.* rice
arruinar to ruin
arte *m., f.* art; **las artes liberales** liberal arts
artesanal related to crafts
artesanía crafts
artículo article
artista *m., f.* artist
artístico/a artistic
arveja pea (6)
ascendencia heritage
ascenso promotion
aseo cleanliness

asequible available
asesinar to murder, assassinate
asesinato murder, assassination (16)
asfixiarse to suffocate
así so, thus; that way (10)
así así so-so (A)
asiento seat (7)
asistencia assistance
asistir (a) to attend, go to (*a class, play, etc.*) (3)
asociación *f.* association
asociado/a associate; member
asociar to associate; **asociarse (con)** to be associated (with)
aspecto aspect; appearance
aspiradora vacuum cleaner (9); **pasar la aspiradora** to vacuum (9)
aspirante *m., f.* candidate (*for a job*), applicant (18)
aspirar to aspire
aspirina aspirin (11)
astigmatismo astigmatism
astrológico/a astrological
astrólogo/a astrologist
astronauta *m., f.* astronaut
astronomía astronomy
asumir to assume
asunto matter
asustado/a frightened
atacar (qu) to attack
ataque *m.* attack; **ataque al corazón** heart attack
Atenas *s.* Athens
atención *f.* attention; **prestar atención** to pay attention
atender (ie) to be attentive, heed
atentado *n.* attack
atentamente attentively, carefully
aterrizar (c) to land (19)
atleta *m., f.* athlete
atlético/a athletic
átomo atom
atracción *f.* attraction
atractivo *n.* attractiveness
atractivo/a attractive
atraer (*like* **traer**) to attract
atrasado/a late (7); slow, backward; **estar atrasado/a** to be late (7)
atraso backwardness
atravesar (ie) to pass
atrevido/a daring, bold
atribuir (y) to attribute; to credit
atún *m.* tuna (6)
aumentar to increase (17)
aumento raise, increase (8)
aun *adv.* even
aún *adv.* still, yet
aunque although (8)
auscultar to listen (*medical*)
ausentarse to be absent
auténtico/a authentic
autobús *m. s.* bus (7); **estación** (*f.*) **de autobuses** bus station (7); **parada del autobús** bus stop (20)
automático/a automatic
automóvil *m.* car, automobile (13)
autopista freeway (13)
autor(a) author, writer
autoridad *f.* authority
autorización *f.* authorization
autorizado/a authorized
autostop *m.* hitchhiking
avance *m.* advance
avanzado/a late (*hour*)
ave *f.* (*but* **el ave**) bird
avenida avenue
aventura adventure
avergonzado/a embarrassed (10)
averiguar (gü) to find out
avión *m.* plane (7)
avisar to advise, warn
aviso announcement; advertisement
¡ay! *interjection* alas!
ayer yesterday (9)
ayuda help, assistance (7)
ayudante *m., f.* assistant
ayudar to help (6)
ayuntamiento city council
azafata female flight attendant (7)
azteca *m., f.* Aztec
azúcar *m.* sugar (5)
azucena lily
azul blue (3)

B

bacalao codfish
bachillerato *course of studies equivalent to high school, junior college*
bagazo pulp
bahía bay
bailar to dance (1)
bailarina ballerina
baile *m.* dance
bajar (de) to get down (*from*); to get off (*of*) (7)
bajo *prep.* under
bajo/a short (*in height*) (2); low; *m. pl.* bottoms (*of pants*); **clase** (*f.*) **baja** lower class; **planta baja** ground floor, first floor (9)
balneario beach resort
baloncesto basketball
banana banana (6)
banca *n.* banking
bancario/a *adj.* banking
banco bank (17)
bandeja tray
bandera flag
bañadora bathing suit
bañar to bathe (9); **bañarse** to take a bath (9)
bañera bathtub (9)
baño bath; bathroom, restroom (8); **traje** (*m.*) **de baño** swim/bathing suit (3)
bar *m.* bar
barato/a inexpensive, cheap (2)
barba beard
barbacoa barbecue
barbería barber shop
barbero barber
barco boat, ship (7)
barrer el suelo to sweep the floor (9)
barrio neighborhood (16); district
basado/a based
base *f.* base, basis; **en base** basic
básquetbol *m.* basketball (15)
bastante rather, quite; enough, sufficient; a lot
bastar to be enough
basura garbage (9); **sacar (qu) la basura** to take out the garbage (9)
batería battery (13)
batido milkshake (20)
bautismo baptism
bautizar (c) to baptize
bautizo baptism
bebé *m.* baby
beber to drink (3)
bebida *n.* drink, beverage (6)
béisbol *m.* baseball (15)
Belén Bethlehem
Bélgica Belgium
belleza beauty
bello/a beautiful (14)
bendición *f.* blessing
bendito/a blessed
beneficiar to benefit
beneficio benefit
besar to kiss
beso kiss
biblioteca library (1)
bibliotecario/a librarian (18)
bicicleta bicycle (8); **andar/pasear en bicicleta** to ride a bicycle (15)
bicho insect
bien *n. m.* good; *adv.* well (A); **está bien** it's okay, fine (4); **estar** (*irreg.*) **bien** to be comfortable (*temperature*); **muy bien** very well, fine (A); **pasarlo bien** to have a good time (10); **¡qué bien!** great!
bienes *m. pl.* possessions, property (8)
bienestar *m.* well-being (12); welfare
bienvenido/a welcome (2)
bilingüe bilingual
bilingüismo bilingualism
billete *m.* ticket (7); **billete de ida** one-way ticket (7); **billete de ida y vuelta** round-trip ticket (7); **billete kilométrico** *train ticket sold in coupon form, valid for a certain distance in kilometers*
biología biology
bis *adv.* twice, repeat
bistec *m.* steak (6)
bisturí *m.* scalpel (*surgical*)
Blancanieves *f. s.* Snow White
blanco/a white (3); **vino blanco** white wine (6)
bledo: (no) me importa un bledo I don't give a darn
bluejeans *m. pl.* jeans (3)
blusa blouse (3)
boca mouth (12)
bocadillo snack
bocina horn
boda wedding (4)
bodega wine cellar
bodeguero/a owner of a wine cellar
bola ball
boletín *m.* bulletin

boleto ticket (4); **boleto de ida** one-way ticket (7); **boleto de ida y vuelta** round-trip ticket (7)
boliche *m.* bowling
bolígrafo (ballpoint) pen (1)
bolsa purse (3); bag
bolsillo pocket
bolso purse; bag
bomba bomb
bombero/a firefighter
bonito/a pretty (2)
bordillo curb
bordo: a bordo on board
borracho/a drunk
borrador *m.* rough copy, draft
borrar to erase
bosque *m.* forest
bostezar (c) to yawn
bostezo yawn
bota boot (3)
botella bottle
botones *m. s.* bellhop (19)
brasa ember, coal
Brasil *m.* Brazil
brazo arm (11)
brécol *m.* broccoli
breve short
brillante bright, brilliant
brillantez *f.* brilliance
brillo shine
brío spirit; energy
brisa breeze; **brisa marina** sea breeze
británico/a British
broma joke
bronce *m.* bronze
bronceado suntan
bronceador *m.* suntan lotion
buen, bueno/a *adj.* good (2); **buenas noches** good evening, night (A); **buenas tardes** good afternoon, evening (A); **buenos días** good morning (A); **hace buen tiempo** it's good weather (5); **muy buenas** good afternoon, evening; **bueno** *adv.* well, okay; **lo bueno** the good news (12)
buganvilla bougainvillea (*tropical American woody vines with brilliant purple or red flowers*)
buho owl
bujía spark plug
bulevar *m.* boulevard
bullicio hustle and bustle
buque *m.* boat
burla joke
busca: en busca de in search of (18)
buscador(a) searcher
buscar (qu) to look for (1)
búsqueda search
butaca armchair, easy chair; seat (*in a theater*) (15)

C

caballero gentleman
caballo horse; **montar a caballo** to ride horseback (14)
cabaña cabin
cabello hair
caber (*irreg.*) to fit
cabeza head (11)
cabina cab; cabin (*in a ship*) (7)
cabo: llevar a cabo to carry out; **al cabo de** after, in (*with time*)
cabra goat
cacharros *m. pl.* utensils
cada *inv.* each, every (8)
cadena chain; channel
caer (*irreg.*) to fall (11); **caerle bien (mal) a alguien** to make a good (bad) impression on someone (18); **caer en la trampa** to fall into the trap; **caerse** to fall down (11)
café *m.* coffee (3); café (3); coffee shop (3)
cafetera coffee pot (9)
cafetería cafeteria, café
caja box, case
cajero/a cashier (17)
cajón *m.* drawer
calabaza squash
calamares *m.pl.* squid
calcetines *m.* socks (3)
calculadora calculator (1)
cálculo calculus
calefacción *f.* heating, heat; **calefacción central** central heat
calendario calendar
calentar (ie) to heat, warm
calentura fever, temperature
calidad *f.* quality
caliente hot
calma *n.* calm
calmarse to calm down, be calm
calor *m.* heat; **hace calor** it's hot (weather) (5); **tener** (*irreg.*) **calor** to be (feel) warm (hot) (5)
calzoncillos underpants, shorts
calzones *m.* shorts
calle *f.* street (3)
calloso/a callous
cama bed (8); **cama de agua** water bed (8); **guardar cama** to stay in bed (12); **hacer** (*irreg.*) **la cama** to make the bed (9)
cámara camera
camarero/a waiter/waitress (6); flight attendant (7)
camarones *m. pl.* shrimp (6)
cambiar (de) to change (8); **cambiar de idea** to change one's mind; **cambiar de lugar** to move (*something*) (11)
cambio change; (rate of) exchange (currency) (17); **cambio de ritmo** change of pace; **en cambio** on the other hand (9); **transmisión** (*f.*) **de cambios** manual shift
caminante *m., f.* hitchhiker
caminar to walk (11)
camino street, road (13); way
camión *m.* truck
camioneta station wagon (2)
camisa shirt (3)
camiseta T-shirt (3)
campaña: tienda de campaña tent
campeón, campeona champion
campeonato championship
campesino/a *n.* farm worker, peasant (14); *adj.* country
campestre *adj.* rural, country
camping*: hacer** (*irreg.*) ***camping to go camping (15)
campo *n.* country(side) (8); (playing) field (15)
canal *m.* (T.V.) station (16)
canción *f.* song
cancha (de tenis) (tennis) court (15)
canela cinnamon
cansado/a tired (4)
cantante *adj.* singing, who sings
cantar to sing (1)
cantidad *f.* quantity, amount
canto song
caña cane
capacidad *f.* capacity
capaz (*pl.* **capaces**) capable
Caperucita Roja Little Red Riding Hood
capilla chapel
capital *f.* capital (city)
capitán *m.* pilot; captain
capítulo chapter
capó hood (*car*) (13)
captar to capture
capturar to capture
capullo cocoon
cara face; side
característica characteristic
caracterizar (c) (por) to be characterized (by)
¡caramba! goodness me!, darn it!
carbón *m.* coal
cárcel *f.* jail
carecer (zc) to lack
cargar (gu) to charge (*to an account*) (17)
cargo post, position; charge
Caribe *m.* Caribbean
caribeño/a Caribbean
cariño affection
cariñoso/a affectionate (4)
carmín *m.* crimson
carne *f.* meat (6)
carnet (*m.*) **de conducir** driver's license
carnicería butcher shop
caro/a expensive (3)
carpeta folder
carrera course of study; race; career, profession (8)
carreta cart
carretera highway (8)
carro car
carta letter (3); menu; (playing) card (15); **a la carta** a la carte; **carta de ajuste** test pattern (*television*) **jugar (ue) (gu) a las cartas** to play cards (15); **papel** (*m.*) **para cartas** stationery (20)
cartel *m.* poster (8)
cartera wallet (3)
cartero mailman
cartón *m.* cardboard

casa house, home (2); **casa de apartamentos** apartment house; **(estar) en casa** (to be) (at) home (2); **regresar a casa** to return home
casado/a married (2)
casamiento wedding
casarse (con) to marry (11)
cáscara peel
casi almost (2)
caso case; **en caso de que** in case (15)
castaño/a (chestnut) brown
castellano Spanish
castigar (gu) to punish (16)
castillo castle
casualidad: dar (*irreg.*) **la casualidad que** to just happen that
catalán *m. language of* **Cataluña**
Cataluña Catalonia (*province of Spain*)
catarro cold (*health*)
catedral *f.* cathedral
categoría category
católico/a Catholic
catorce fourteen (A)
caucho rubber
causa cause; **a causa de** because of, on account of
cautivante *adj.* captivating
cautiverio captivity
cazador(a) hunter
cebolla onion
cebra zebra
ceder to yield
celebración *f.* celebration
celebrar to celebrate (10)
cementerio cemetery
cena supper, evening meal (6)
cenar to have, eat supper, dinner (6); to eat out, dine out (6)
centenario centennial
central central; **calefacción** (*f.*) **central** central heat
centrarse (en) to focus, center (on)
céntrico/a central, focal
centro center; downtown (3); **centro comercial** shopping mall (3)
ceñido/a tight-fitting
cerámica ceramic, tile
cerca de *prep.* near, close to (4)
cercanía closeness
cercano/a close-by
cerdo: chuleta de cerdo pork chop (6)
cerebro skull; brain
ceremonia ceremony
cero zero (A)
cerrado/a closed (4)
cerrar (ie) to close (5)
cervato fawn
cervecería beer hall
cerveza beer (1)
césped *m.* lawn, grass
cesta basket; **cesta de la compra** shopping basket
cestería basketmaking
ceviche *m. spiced dish of raw fish marinated in lemon juice*
ciego/a blind
cielo sky; heaven
cien(to) one hundred (2); **cientos** hundreds; **por ciento** percent
ciencia science; **ciencia ficción** science fiction; **ciencias** sciences (1); **ciencias policiales** *pl.* police science; **ciencias políticas** *pl.* political science
científico/a scientific
cierto/a certain; true; **es cierto** it's certain (13)
ciervo deer
cifra figure, number
cigarrillo cigarette
cinco five (A)
cincuenta fifty (2)
cine *m.* movie theater; movies (4)
cinta tape
cinturón *m.* belt (3); **cinturón de seguridad** seat belt
circuito track, racing circuit
circulación *f.* traffic (13)
circular to circulate; to drive
círculo circle
circunstancia circumstance; incident
cirugía surgery; **cirugía estética** cosmetic surgery
cita date, appointment (4); quotation
citado/a booked up, committed (4)
citar to cite
ciudad *f.* city (2)
ciudadanía citizenship
ciudadano/a citizen (16)
cívico/a civic (16)
civilización *f.* civilization
clamarse to cry out
claro/a clear; **está claro** it's clear, obvious (4); **claro** of course
clase *f.* class (1); kind; **clase alta** upper class; **clase baja** lower class; **clase media** middle class; **clase turística** tourist class (7); **primera clase** first class (7)
clásico/a classic; classical
cláusula clause
clausura closing
cliente *m., f.* client
clima *m.* climate (5)
climático/a climatic
clínico/a clinical
club *m.* club
cobarde coward
cobrar to cash (*a check*) (17); to charge (*someone for an item or service*) (17)
cobre *m.* copper
cocer (ue) (z) to cook
cocina kitchen (8); cooking
cocinar to cook (6)
cocinero/a chef
coctel *m.* cocktail party; cocktail
coche *m.* car (2)
cochino pig
código code
coger (j) to pick up
cogido: estar (*irreg.*) **cogidos/as de las manos** to hold hands
cognado cognate (6)
cojín *m.* cushion
cola line; **hacer** (*irreg.*) **cola** to stand in line (7)
colaborar to collaborate
colección *f.* collection
colectivo/a collective
colega *m., f.* colleague
colegiado/a high school student
colegio elementary or secondary school
colgante *adj.* hanging
colgar (ue) (gu) to hang
colilla cigarette butt
colmena beehive
colocar (qu) to place
colombiano/a Colombian
Colón: Cristóbal Colón Christopher Columbus
colonia colony; camp
colonizar (c) to colonize, settle
coloquial colloquial
color *m.* color (3)
colorido *n. s.* colors, coloring
columna column
collar *m.* necklace
comandante *m.* commander
combatir to fight
combinación *f.* combination
combustible *m.* fuel
comedia play (*theater*), comedy (15)
comedor *m.* dining room (8)
comentar to comment (on); to discuss
comentario comment, commentary
comenzar (ie) (c) to commence, begin
comer to eat (3)
comercial *adj.* commercial, business; **administración** (*f.*) **comercial** business administration; **centro comercial** shopping mall (3)
comerciante *m., f.* merchant, shopkeeper (18)
comercio business (1)
comestibles *m.pl.* food
cometer to commit
comí, comiste, comió I ate, you ate, he/she/it ate (6)
cómico/a comic, funny, amusing
comida food (5); midday meal, meal
comienzo *n.* beginning
comité *m.* committee
como as a (1); like; since; **como si** + *past subj.* as if... (18); **como si nada** as if nothing were wrong; **tan pronto como** as soon as (17)
¿cómo? how? (A); what? I didn't catch that (4); **¿cómo es ______ ?** what is ______ like?; **¿cómo está(s)?** how are you? (A); **¡cómo no!** of course!; **¿cómo que... ?** what do you mean...?; **¿cómo se dice... ?** how do you say...?; **¿cómo se llama Ud.?, ¿cómo te llamas?** what is your name? (A)
cómoda bureau, chest of drawers (8)
comodidad *f.* comfort (19)
cómodo/a comfortable (9)
compact disc *m.* compact disc (player) (8)

compañero/a companion; friend; **compañero/a de cuarto** roommate (6)
compañía company; **compañía naviera** shipping company
comparación *f.* comparison
comparar to compare
compartir to divide into equal parts; to share (19)
compasión *f.* compassion
competencia competition
complejo/a complex
complemento object (*gram.*)
complementario/a complementary
completar to complete
completo/a complete; **pensión** (*f.*) **completa** room and full board (19)
complicado/a complicated
comportamiento behavior
comportarse to behave oneself
composición *f.* composition
compra *n.* purchase; **cesta de la compra** shopping basket; **de compras** shopping (3)
comprador(a) buyer, purchaser; shopper, customer
comprar to buy (1)
compras: de compras shopping (3)
comprender to understand (3); to comprise
comprensión *f.* comprehension
comprensivo/a comprehensive, capable of understanding
compuesto/a (por/de) composed (of)
computación *f.* computer science (1)
computador *m.* computer (*L.A.*)
computadora computer (8) (*L.A.*)
común common, usual, ordinary
comunal *adj.* community
comunicación *f.* communication (18)
comunicar (qu) to communicate, inform of; **comunicarse (qu) (con)** to communicate (with) (16)
comunicativo/a communicative
comunidad *f.* community
comunista *m., f.* communist
con with (1); **con cheque** by check (17); **con frecuencia** frequently (1); **con tal (de) que** provided that (15)
concentración *f.* concentration
concentrado/a concentrated
concentrar to concentrate
concierto concert
concilio council
conclusión *f.* conclusion
concurso contest
condado county
condición *f.* condition; **en buenas condiciones** in good condition
conducción *f.* driving
conducente *adj.* conducive, leading
conducir (*like* **producir**) to conduct; to drive (*a vehicle*) (13); **licencia/carnet** (*m.*) **de conducir** driver's license
conducta conduct, behavior
conductor(a) driver (13); conductor
confianza confidence
confiar (en) to confide (in); to trust (in)
confidencial confidential
confirmación *f.* confirmation
confirmar to confirm (19)
conformarse (con) to make to (with)
confort *m.* comfort
confundido/a confused
confundir to confuse
congelado/a frozen
congelador *m.* freezer (9)
congelar to freeze
congestionado/a congested (12)
conjugar (gu) to conjugate
conjunción *f.* conjunction (15)
conjunto totality, whole
conjunto/a jointly
conmemorar to commemorate
conmigo with me (3)
connotación *f.* connotation
conocer (zc) to know, be acquainted with (6)
conocido/a known, well-known
conocimiento knowledge
conquistador(a) conqueror
consecuencia consequence
conseguir (i, i) (g) to get, obtain (8)
consejero/a counselor, advisor (1)
consejo advice (4); counsel
conservación *f.* preservation
conservador(a) conservative
conservar to conserve, save (14)
consideración *f.* consideration
considerar to consider, think
consigna baggage check
consigo with him, with her, with you (**Ud., Uds.**)
consistir (en) to consist (of)
consolar (ue) to console
constante firm, persevering, loyal; constant
constar (de) to consist, be composed (of)
constipado/a suffering from a cold
constituir (y) to constitute; to be
construcción *f.* construction
construido/a constructed, built
construir (y) to build (14)
consulta consultation, conference
consultar to consult
consultorio (medical) office (12)
consumidor(a) consumer
consumir to consume
consumista *adj.* consumer
contabilidad *f.* accounting
contacto contact
contado: al contado (in) cash (17)
contador(a) accountant
contagioso/a contagious
contaminación *f.* pollution (5); **hay contaminación** there is pollution (5)
contaminar to pollute (14)
contar (ue) to count; to tell (about) (10); **contar con** to have; to count on
contener (*like* **tener**) to contain, hold (13)
contenido content
contento/a happy (4)
contestar to answer (4)
contexto context
contigo with you (*fam.*) (4)
continente *m.* continent
continuación: a continuación immediately after; below
continuar to continue
contra against
contrario: lo contrario the opposite
contraste *m.* contrast
contrato contract
contribuir (y) to contribute
controlar to control
controvertible controversial
convención *f.* convention
convencional conventional
convenir (*like* **venir**) to agree; to be desirable; to be worth one's while
conversación *f.* conversation
convertirse (ie, i) (en) to become
cónyuge *m., f.* spouse
coñac *m.* brandy
cooperativa *n.* cooperative
copa drink (*alcoholic*) (20)
corazón *m.* heart (12); **ataque** (*m.*) **al corazón** heart attack
corbata tie (*clothing*) (3)
cordialidad *f.* cordiality, warmth
cordillera mountain range
coro chorus
correa belt
correcto/a correct, right
corregir (i, i) (j) to correct
correo mail; post office (20); **oficina de correos** post office; **por correo** by mail
correr to run (7); to pass (*time*); **correr (el) peligro** to be in danger
correspondencia correspondence; **mantener** (*like* **tener**) **correspondencia** to correspond
corresponder to correspond
correspondiente *adj.* corresponding
corrida bullfight
corriente *adj.* common, average, ordinary; **cuenta corriente** checking account (17)
corte *f.* court (*judicial*)
cortés courteous
cortesía courtesy, politeness
corto/a short (*in length*) (2)
cosa thing (1)
cosecha harvest
cosmopolita *m., f.* cosmopolitan
costa coast
costar (ue) to cost (13); **costar trabajo** to find it difficult
costarricense Costa Rican
costumbre *f.* custom; **como de costumbre** as usual; **de costumbre** usually, generally; **por costumbre** out of habit
cotidiano/a daily, every day (15)
creación *f.* creation
creador(a) creative

crear to create
creativo/a creative
crecer (zc) to grow
creciente *adj.* increasing
crecimiento growth
crédito credit; **tarjeta de crédito** credit card (17)
creencia belief
creer (y) (en) to think, believe (in) (3); **creo que sí (no)** I think so (I don't think so) (1)
crema cream
Creta Crete
cría offspring
criado/a servant, maid (9)
criminal *m., f.* criminal
criminología criminology
crisis *f.* crisis
cristal *m.* crystal
cristiano/a Christian
crítica criticism
criticar (qu) to criticize
cruce (*m.*) **para peatones** pedestrian crossing
crucero cruise
cruciletras *m. s.* crossword puzzle
crudo/a raw
cruzar (c) to cross (19)
cuaderno notebook (1)
cuadra block (*group of houses*); stable
cuadro painting; picture; **cuadros escoceses** plaid; **de cuadros** plaid (3)
cual: la razón por la cual the reason why, for which (19)
¿cuál? what?, which? (A); **¿cuál(es)?** which one(s)?
cualquier(a) any (12)
cuando when; **de vez en cuando** from time to time (11)
¿cuándo? when? (A)
cuanto: en cuanto *conj.* as soon as (17); **en cuanto a** *prep.* with regard to, regarding
¿cuánto/a? how much? (A)
¿cuántos/as? how many? (A)
cuarenta forty (2)
cuartilla page
cuarto *n.* room (1); **compañero/a de cuarto** roommate (6); quarter; **(las dos) menos cuarto** a quarter till (two) (A); **(las dos) y cuarto** (two) fifteen, a quarter after (two) (*with time*) (A); **en cuarto menguante** on the wane
cuarto/a *adj.* fourth (13)
cuatro four (A)
cuatrocientos/as four hundred (3)
cubano/a Cuban
cubanoamericano/a Cuban American
cubierto *n.* place setting
cubierto/a (de) *p.p.* covered (with)
cubo pail, bucket
cubrir (*p.p.* **cubierto/a**) to cover (14)
cuchara spoon (6)
cucharita teaspoon (6)
cuchillo knife (6)
cuenta check, bill (6); account (17); **cuenta corriente** checking account (17); **cuenta de ahorros** savings account (17); **darse** (*irreg.*) **cuenta de** to realize; **tomar/tener** (*irreg.*) **en cuenta** to keep/have in mind (16)
cuentakilómetros *m. s.* mileage recorder (*in kilometers*)
cuento story
cuero leather
cuerpo body (11)
cuervo crow
cuestión *f.* question, matter (17)
cuestionar to ask questions about
cueva cave
cuidado care; **con cuidado** carefully; **¡cuidado!** careful!, be careful! **tener** (*irreg.*) **cuidado** to be careful (15)
cuidadoso/a careful
cuidar to take care of; **cuidarse** to take care of oneself (12)
culminar to culminate
culpa fault
cultivar to cultivate; to grow
cultivo cultivation
culto worship, cult
culto/a cultured, educated
cultura culture
cumpleaños *m. s.* birthday (5)
cumplir to accomplish; to reach (*a birthday*); **cumplir con** to fulfill (*an obligation*)
cuna cradle
cuota *n. s.* fees
cupón *m.* ticket
cupos *m. pl.* spaces available
curar to cure, heal
curiosidad *f.* curiosity
curioso/a curious; unusual
currículum *m.* résumé (18)
cursivo: letras cursivas italics
curso course (1)
cuyo/a whose

CH

chalet *m.* chalet
champán *m.* champagne
champiñón *m.* mushroom
champú *m.* shampoo (20)
chaqueta jacket (3)
charla talk, presentation
cheque *m.* check (8); **con cheque** by check (17); **talonario de cheques** checkbook (17)
chichón *m.* bump, bruise
chicle *m.* chewing gum
chico/a *n.* child; boy, girl; *adj.* small (11)
chileno/a Chilean
chimpancé *m.* chimpanzee
chino/a Chinese
Chipre Cyprus
chisme *m.* gossip, misrepresentation
chiste *m.* joke (10)
chocar (qu) (con) to run into, collide (with), hit (13)
chocolate *m.* chocolate
choque *m.* accident, collision (16)
chorro stream
choza hut
chuleta (de cerdo) (pork) chop (6)

D

dama lady, woman
danza dance
danzarín *m.* dancer
dañino/a harmful
daño harm; **hacerse** (*irreg.*) **daño** to hurt oneself (11)
dar (*irreg.*) to give (7); **dar una fiesta** to give a party (10); **dar un paseo** to take a walk (15); **darse cuenta (de)** to realize; **darse la mano** to shake hands; **(Eso) Me da igual.** (That's) It's all the same to me. (11)
dato fact
de *prep.* of, from (A); **¿de dónde es Ud.?** where are you from? (2); **de joven** as a youth (12); **de la mañana/tarde/noche** in the morning/afternoon/evening (A); **de nada** you're welcome (A); **de niño/a** as a child (11); **¿de quién?** whose? (2); **de repente** suddenly (12); **de verdad** really (11); **de vez en cuando** from time to time (11)
debajo *adv.* underneath, below; **debajo de** *prep.* under(neath), below (4)
deber *m.* responsibility, obligation (16)
deber + *inf.* should, must, ought to (*do something*) (3)
debido/a proper
debido a due to
débil weak
decano/a dean
decenio decade
decidir to decide (13)
décimo/a *adj.* tenth (13)
decir (*irreg.*) to say, tell (7); **es decir** that is to say; **eso quiere decir (que)** that means (that); **dime** tell me (*fam.*) (11)
decisión *f.* decision
declarar to declare (19)
decoración *f.* (interior) decoration, decor
decorar to decorate
decorativo/a decorative
dedicación *f.* dedication
dedicarse (qu) to dedicate oneself
dedo finger; **dedo índice** index finger
deducir (zc) to deduce, infer
defender (ie) to defend; **defenderse** to defend oneself
defensa defense
defensivo/a defensive
defenso defense
defensor(a) defender, protector
deficitario/a lacking

definición *f.* definition
definitivo/a definitive
deformado/a deformed
dejar to leave (behind) (9); to quit (18); to let, allow; **dejar de** + *inf.* to stop (*doing something*) (12)
del (contraction of **de** + **el**) of, from the
delante de *prep.* in front of (4)
delantero/a *adj.* front
delgado/a thin (2); **intestino delgado** small intestine
delicioso/a delicious
delito crime (14)
demanda demand; petition, claim, lawsuit
demandar to sue; to request
demás other, rest of; **lo demás** the rest, the remaining; **los/las demás** others, other people (16)
demasiado *adv.* too, too much (9)
demasiado/a *adj.* too much
democracia democracy
demonstración *f.* demonstration
demora delay (7)
demostrar (ue) to demonstrate
demostrativo/a demonstrative (4)
densidad *f.* density, thickness
denso/a dense (14)
dental: pasta dental toothpaste (20)
dentista *m., f.* dentist
dentro de *prep.* inside
departamento department
depender (de) to depend (on)
dependiente/a clerk (1)
deporte *m.* sport (12)
deportista *adj.* sports-minded (15)
deportivo/a *adj.* sporting, sports
depositar to deposit
depositario/a trustee
depósito storage yard
deprimir to depress
derecha: a la derecha (de) to the right (of) (*direction*) (4); **salir a derechas** to turn out right
derecho *n.* right (16); **derechos** (*pl.*) **de aduana** customs duty (19); **derecho** *adv.* (straight) ahead (7); **todo derecho** straight ahead (13)
derivar to incline, drift
derramar to spill
desacuerdo disagreement
desafinado/a out of tune
desafío challenge
desagradable disagreeable
desagüe *m.* drain
desaparecer (zc) to disappear
desaparición *f.* disappearance
desarme *m.* disarmament
desarrollar to develop (14)
desarrollo development (14)
desastre *m.* disaster (16)
desastroso/a disastrous, miserable
desayunar to eat breakfast (6)
desayuno breakfast (6)
descansado/a rested
descansar to rest (3)
descanso *n.* rest; sleep
descapotable convertible (*with cars*) (8)
descartable disposable
descendencia descent
descendente *adj.* descending, downward
descenso descent
desconectar to unplug
desconocido/a unknown
descortés discourteous
describir (*p.p.* **descrito/a**) to describe; to trace
descripción *f.* description
descubierto/a *p.p.* discovered; uncovered
descubrir (*p.p.* **descubierto/a**) to discover (14)
descuidado/a careless
descuidar to neglect
desde *prep.* from; **desde que** *conj.* since; **desde luego** of course
desear to want (1)
desempleo unemployment
deseo desire, wish
desesperadamente desperately
desesperante desperate
desfile *m.* parade
desgraciadamente unfortunately
deshacer (*like* **hacer**) to get rid of
desierto desert
desigualdad *f.* inequality (16)
desinflado: llanta desinflada flat tire (13)
deslizar (c) to glide
deslumbrante *adj.* dazzling
desocupado/a unoccupied, vacant, free (19)
desordenado/a unorganized
despacio *adv.* slowly
despechado/a peevish; indignant
despedida closing (*of a letter*); leave-taking, good-bye
despedir (i, i) to fire (8); **despedirse (de)** to say good-bye (to), take leave (of) (10)
despegar (gu) to take off (*airplane*) (7)
despejado clear (weather)
desperdicio waste
desperfecto defect
despertador *m.* alarm clock (9)
despertar (ie) to wake (*someone up*) (9); **despertarse** to awaken, wake up (9)
desprender (de) to deduce (from)
después later, afterwards (9); **después de** *prep.* after (4); **después (de) que** *conj.* after (17)
destacar (qu) to stand out
destinar to allot, earmark (*money*)
destino destination; destiny
destrucción *f.* destruction
destruir (y) to destroy (14)
desvanecido: caer desvanecido/a to fall in a faint
desventaja disadvantage (13)
desviación *f.* detour
detalle *m.* detail (6)
detención *f.* arrest
detener (*like* **tener**) to detain
deteriorarse to deteriorate
deterioro deterioration
determinado/a determined; specific
determinante *m.* determinant
determinar to determine
detrás de *prep.* behind (4)
deuda debt
devengado/a due, outstanding
devoción *f.* devotion
devolución *f.* return
devolver (ue) (*p.p.* **devuelto/a**) to return (*something*) (17); to refund, give back
día *m.* day (1); **buenos días** good morning (A); **día festivo** holiday (10); **hoy en día** nowadays; **todos los días** every day (1)
diagnosticar (qu) to diagnose
diagnóstico diagnosis
diálogo dialogue
diamante *m.* diamond
diapositiva slide
diario newspaper
diario/a daily
dibujo cartoon; sketch, drawing; **dibujos animados/cómicos** cartoons
diccionario dictionary (1)
diciembre *m.* December (5)
dictador *m.* dictator (16)
dictadura dictatorship (16)
dictar to dictate
dicho *n.* saying
dicho/a *p.p.* said
diecinueve nineteen (A)
dieciocho eighteen (A)
dieciséis sixteen (A)
diecisiete seventeen (A)
diente *m.* tooth; **pasta de dientes** toothpaste
dieta diet; **a dieta** on a diet (6)
dietético/a *adj.* diet, dietetic
diez ten (A)
diferencia difference; **a diferencia de** unlike
diferenciarse to differ
diferente different
difícil difficult, hard (4)
dificultad *f.* difficulty
difunto/a dead, deceased
digestión *f.* digestion
digestivo/a digestive
dígito digit
dignificar (qu) to dignify
dime (*fam.*) tell me (11)
Dinamarca Denmark
dinámico/a dynamic
dinero money (1)
Dios *m.* God; **por Dios** for heaven's sake
diputado deputy
dirección *f.* address (9); direction; **Dirección de Personal** personnel, employment office (18); **libreta de direcciones** address book
directamente directly
directivo: junta directiva board of directors

directo/a direct
director(a) manager, director (8); **director(a) de personal** director of personnel (18)
directorio directory
dirigir (j) to direct; **dirigirse** to make one's way (*to*)
disc: compact disc *m.* compact disc (player) (8)
disciplina discipline
disco (phonograph) record; computer disc (14); **frenos** (*m. pl.*) **de disco** disc brakes
discoteca disco(theque)
discreto/a discreet
discriminación *f.* discrimination
disculpa excuse, apology
disculparse to excuse oneself, apologize; **discúlpeme** pardon me (11)
discurrir to discuss
discurso speech
diseñar to draw, design; **diseñar programas** to design, write programs (14)
diseño design
disfrazado/a de disguised as
disfrutar (de) to enjoy
disgusto annoyance, displeasure
disparar to fire, shoot
disponer (*like* **poner**) (**de**) to have the use (of)
disponible available, on hand
dispuesto/a (a) disposed (to)
distancia distance
distinto/a different
distracción *f.* distraction
distraído/a distracted, absent-minded (11)
distribuir (y) to distribute
diversión *f.* diversion, entertainment, amusement
diverso/a diverse; various
divertido/a amusing, funny, pleasant
divertir (ie, i) to amuse, entertain (9); **divertirse** to have a good time, enjoy oneself (9); **que te diviertas** I hope you have a good time (15)
dividir to divide
divorciado/a divorced
divorciarse to get divorced
divorcio *n.* divorce (4)
doblado/a dubbed (15)
doblar to turn (7)
doble double
doce twelve (A)
docena dozen
docente *adj.* teaching, educational
doctor(a) doctor
documental *m.* documentary
documento document
dólar *m.* dollar
doler (ue) to hurt, ache (11)
dolor *m.* pain; **tener dolor de** to have a pain in (12)
doméstico/a domestic (9); **aparato doméstico** home appliance; **quehaceres domésticos** household chores (9)
domicilio residence, home; **a domicilio** at home
dominar to dominate
domingo Sunday (4)
don *title of respect used with a man's first name*
donde where
¿dónde? where? (A); **¿adónde?** where (to)? (3); **¿de dónde es Ud.?** where are you from? (2); **¿dónde estará ... ?** where can ... be? I wonder where ... is? (17); **¿dónde estaría?** where could ... have been? (18)
dondequiera wherever
doña *title of respect used with a woman's first name*
dorado/a golden
dormir (ue, u) to sleep (5); **dormirse** to fall asleep (9)
dormitorio bedroom
dos two (A); **dos veces** twice (3)
doscientos/as two hundred (3)
drama *m.* drama, play
dril *m.* duckcloth
droga drug
droguería drugstore
ducha shower (19)
duda doubt; **no hay duda** there's no doubt
dudar to doubt (13)
dudoso/a doubtful
dueño/a owner (6); landlord/lady
dulce *m.* sweet, piece of candy (7); **dulces** sweets (7)
duración *f.* duration
durante during; for (*a period of time*) (4)
durar to last (16)
duro/a hard

E

e and (*used instead of* **y** *before words beginning with* **i** *or* **hi**)
ecología ecology
economía economy
económico/a economical; economic
economizar (c) to economize (17)
ecuatoriano/a Ecuadorean
echar to throw; **echar de menos** to miss
edad *f.* age; **la mayoría de edad** adult age, full legal age
edición *f.* edition
edificio *n.* building (1)
educación *f.* education; **educación elemental** elementary education; **educación secundaria** high school education
educacional educational
educativo/a educational
efectivo/a effective
efecto effect; **en efecto** in effect
eficiente efficient
Egipto Egypt
egoísmo selfishness
egoísta *m., f.* egotistical, selfish
¿eh? *tag phrase with approximate English equivalent of* okay?
ejecutivo/a executive
ejemplar exemplary
ejemplo example; **por ejemplo** for example (3)
ejercer (z) to exercise; to practice (*a profession*) (18)
ejercicio exercise (3); **hacer** (*irreg.*) **ejercicio** to exercise, get exercise (12)
ejército army
el the (*m. definite article*)
él *sub. pron.* he; *obj. of prep.* him
elección *f.* election; choice
electricidad *f.* electricity
electricista *m., f.* electrician
eléctrico/a electric
electrodoméstico: aparatos electrodomésticos electrical home appliances
electrólisis *f.* electrolysis
electrónico/a electronic
elegante elegant
elegir (i, i) (j) to select, choose
elemental elementary; **educación** (*f.*) **elemental** elementary education
elemento element
elevar to raise up, elevate
eliminar to eliminate
ella *sub. pron.* she; *obj. of prep.* her
ello it, that; **todo ello** all that
ellos/as *sub. pron.* they; *obj. of prep.* them
embarazada pregnant
embarcación *f.* ship
embargo: sin embargo however, nevertheless
embarque: puerta de embarque loading gate
emborracharse to get drunk
emergencia: sala de emergencias emergency room (12)
emigrar to emigrate
emitir to utter, declare; to give off
emoción *f.* emotion (10)
emocional emotional
emocionante *adj.* touching, thrilling
emotivo/a emotional; exciting
empezar (ie) (c) to begin (5); **empezar a** + *inf.* to begin to (*do something*)
empleado/a employee (8)
empleo job, employment; **agencia de empleos** employment agency
empresa corporation; business (18)
empresarial *adj.* management
empresario/a *n.* manager; *adj.* business
empujar to push
en in, on, at (A)
enamorado/a *adj.* in love; *n.* sweetheart, lover; **Día** (*m.*) **de los Enamorados** Valentine's Day
enamorarse (de) to fall in love (with)
enanito/a dwarf
encabezar (c) to head
encajar to circle
encantado/a pleased to meet you (A)

encantador/a *adj.* charming
encantar to enchant (14); **me encanta(n)...** is/are exciting to me (8)
encanto *n.* charm
encargado/a charged (*with a task*)
encender (ie) to light
encendido/a fiery
encima *adv.* above, over; overhead; **encima de** *prep.* on top of (4)
encontrar (ue) to find (7)
encuentro *n.* meeting
encuesta survey
encuestado/a interviewed
enchilada *rolled tortilla filled with meat, cheese, etc., and covered with a chili sauce*
enchufar to plug in
enchufe *m.* plug
enemistad *f.* animosity
energía energy (14)
enero January (5)
enfático/a emphatic
enfermarse to get sick (12)
enfermedad *f.* illness (12)
enfermería infirmary, hospital
enfermero/a nurse (9)
enfermo/a sick (4); **ponerse enfermo/a** to get sick
enfrente *adv.* in front, opposite; **enfrente de** *prep.* in front of
engañoso/a deceptive
engordar to fatten, make fat; to gain weight
enlace *m.* marriage, union
enlatado/a *adj.* canned
enojado/a angry
enojarse to get angry (10)
enorme enormous
enrogecimiento *n.* reddening
ensalada salad (6)
ensayo essay
enseñanza *n.* teaching
enseñar to teach (1)
entender (ie) to understand (5)
enterarse (de) to find out (about) (16)
entero/a whole, entire (9); **limpiar la casa entera** to clean the whole house (9)
entonces then, in that case; **en aquel entonces** at that time, back then, in those days (11)
entrada entrée, main course; ticket (*for an event or performance*) (15); entryway, entry
entrar (en, a) to enter, go in (4)
entre *prep.* between, among (4)
entrecruzar (c) to intersect
entrega *n.* handing over
entregar (gu) to hand in, over (19)
entremeses *m. pl.* appetizers, hors d'oeuvres (10)
entrenamiento *n.* training
entresemana: días (*m. pl.*) **de entresemana** weekdays
entretención *f.* entertainment
entretenimiento entertainment
entrevista interview
entrevistador(a) interviewer (18)
entrevistar to interview (18)
entusiasmado/a enthusiastic
envasado *n.* bottling
envase *m.* container, bottle
envenenado/a poisoned
enviar to send
envidia envy
envoltorio wrapper
envuelto/a wrapped
enyesadura *n.* plastering
episodio episode
época era; time (*period*) (11)
equipado/a *adj.* equipped
equipaje *m.* baggage, luggage (7)
equipo team (5); equipment; **equipo estereofónico** stereo equipment (8); **equipo fotográfico** photographic equipment (8)
equis: rayos (*m. pl.*) **equis** X-rays
equivalente *m.* equivalent
equivaler (*like* **valer**) to be equivalent
equivocación *f.* mistake
equivocado/a mistaken
equivocarse (qu) to be wrong, make a mistake (11)
era era (11)
ermitaño hermit
error *m.* error
es la... it is . . . o'clock (A)
escala stopover; scale; **hacer** (*irreg.*) **escalas** to have, make stopovers (7)
escalera ladder (12); **escaleras** *pl.* stairs, steps
escándalo scandal
escandinavo/a Scandinavian
escaparse to escape
escasez *f.* (*pl.* **escaseces**) lack, scarcity (14)
escena scene
escoba broom
escocés: cuadros escoceses plaid
escoger (j) to choose, select
escolar *adj.* of or pertaining to school
esconderse to hide
escondido/a hidden
escribir (*p.p.* **escrito/a**) to write (3); **escribir a máquina** to type (14); **máquina de escribir** typewriter (8)
escrito/a *p.p.* written
escritor(a) writer
escritorio desk (1)
escuchar to listen (to) (5)
escuela school (11); **escuela primaria** elementary school; **escuela secundaria** high school
escultor(a) sculptor/sculptress
escultura sculpture
escurrir to drain; **escurrirse** to sneak away
ese, esa *adj.* that (4); **ése, ésa** *pron.* that one
esencial essential
esforzarse (ue) (c) to make an effort
esfuerzo *n.* effort
esmero care
eso that, that thing, that fact (4); **eso es** that's right; **por eso** therefore, that's why
esófago esophagus
esos/as *adj.* those (4); **ésos/as** *pron.* those (ones)
espacio space
espacioso/a spacious
espada sword
espantapájaros *m. s.* scarecrow
España Spain
español *m.* Spanish (*language*) (1)
español(a) Spanish (2); **de habla española** Spanish-speaking
especial *adj.* special; **en especial** especially
especialidad *f.* specialty
especialista *m., f.* specialist
especializarse (c) to major (*in an academic area*)
especialmente especially
especie *f.* species, kind, class, type
especulación *f.* speculation, venture
espejo mirror (9)
espera: sala de espera waiting room (7)
esperanza hope, wish (16)
esperar to wait (for) (6); to expect (6); to hope
espíritu *m.* spirit
esplendor *m.* splendor
esposo/a husband, wife (2)
esqueleto skeleton
esquiar to ski (15)
esquina corner (*of a street*) (13)
esquís *m. pl.* skis (15)
estable *adj.* stable
establecerse (zc) to establish oneself
estación *f.* season (5); station (7); **estación de autobuses** bus station (7); **estación de gasolina** gas station (13); **estación del metro** metro (subway) stop (20); **estación del tren** train station (7)
estacionamiento parking (lot)
estacionar(se) to park (13); **prohibido estacionarse** no parking (13)
estadía *n.* stay (*period of time at a place*)
estadio stadium (15)
estado state
Estados Unidos *pl.* United States
estadounidense *m., f.* person from the United States
estafeta branch post office
estallar to explode
estallido *n.* outbreak (*of a conflict, war, etc.*)
estancia stay, sojourn; ranch; room
estanco tobacco stand, shop (20)
estante *m.* bookshelf (8)
estar (*irreg.*) to be (14); **¿dónde estará... ?** where can . . . be? I wonder where . . . is? (17); **¿dónde estaría?** where could he or she have been? (18); **está** is (*located*) (A); **está bien** it's okay, fine (4); **está claro** it's clear (4); **está nublado** it's cloudy, overcast (5); **estar**

aburrido/a to be bored (4); **estar atrasado/a** to be late (7); **estar bien** to be comfortable (*temperature*) (5); **estar de acuerdo (con)** to be in agreement (with); **estar de vacaciones** to be on vacation (7); **estar cogido/as de las manos** to hold hands; **estar en alza** to be rising (*in popularity*); **estar listo/a (para)** to be ready, prepared (to) (8); **estar seguro/a** to be sure, certain (13); **no estoy de acuerdo** I don't agree (2); **zona estar** living area
estatal *adj.* state
estatua statue
estatuilla statuette
estatura stature, height
este *m.* east
este/a *adj.* this (2); **éste/a** *pron.* this one; **en este momento** at the moment, right now (4); **esta noche** tonight (2); **este** uh, um (*vocalized pause*)
estéreo stereo
estereofónico/a: equipo estereofónico stereo equipment (8)
estereotipo stereotype
estético esthetics
estilista *m., f.* stylist, designer
estilizar (c) to stylize
estilo style; **estilo de vida** lifestyle
estimar to estimate
estimular to stimulate
esto this, this thing, this matter (4)
estómago stomach (12); **dolor** (*m.*) **de estómago** stomach ache
estos/as *adj.* these (2); **éstos/as** *pron.* these (ones)
estrecho/a narrow; tight
estreno premier
estrella star; **estrella fugaz** shooting star
estricto/a strict
estructura structure
estudiante *m., f.* student (1)
estudiantil *adj.* of or pertaining to student(s)
estudiar to study (1)
estudio *n.* study; **estudios** studies, schoolwork
estudioso/a studious
estufa stove (9)
estupendo/a wonderful, marvelous
estúpido/a stupid
etcétera et cetera
etiqueta tag, label (*on clothing*)
eurocentrismo fixation on Europe
Europa Europe
europeo/a European
evaluación *f.* evaluation
evaluar to evaluate
evaporación *f.* evaporation
evitable avoidable
evitar to avoid (14)
exacto *adv.* exactly
exacto/a exact
exagerar to exaggerate
exaltarse to get worked up, overexcited
examen *m.* exam (2)
examinar to examine (12)
excedente *m.* surplus
exceder to exceed
excelente excellent
excepción *f.* exception
excepcional exceptional
excesivo/a excessive
exclamar to exclaim
excluir (y) to exclude
excursión *f.* excursion, trip
exhibir to exhibit, show
exigencia demand
exigente *adj.* demanding (8)
exigir (j) to demand
exilio exile
existencia existence
existente existing
existir to exist
éxito success; **tener** (*irreg.*) **éxito** to be successful
exnovio/a ex-boyfriend, ex-girlfriend
exótico/a exotic
experiencia experience; experiment
experimentar to experience; to experiment
experimento experiment
experto/a expert
explicación *f.* explanation
explicar (qu) to explain (7)
exploración *f.* exploration
explorador(a) explorer
explotación *f.* exploitation
explotar to exploit (14)
exposición *f.* show
expresar to express
expresión *f.* expression
expreso express train
expuesto/a exposed
extendido/a extended
extenso/a extensive
externo/a external
extranjero *n.* abroad (19); **en al extranjero** to travel abroad (20); **ir al extranjero** to go abroad
extranjero/a *n.* foreigner (1); *adj.* foreign
extrañar to miss (*the presence of someone or something*); to be strange; to surprise
extraño/a strange; **es (qué) extraño** it is (how) strange (8)
extraordinario/a extraordinary
extremo/a extreme
exultante *adj.* exulting

F

fa: ni fu ni fa so-so
fábrica factory (14)
fabricante *m.* manufacturer, maker
fabuloso/a fabulous
faceta facet
fácil easy (4)
facilidad *f.* ease; ability, facility (*for learning or doing something*)
facilitar to facilitate
factor *m.* factor
factura bill, invoice (17)
facturar to check (*baggage*) (7)
facultad *f.* campus; department (*of a university*)
falda skirt (3)
falso/a false
falta lack; fault; **sin falta** without fail
faltar to be absent, missing, lacking (10)
fallar to fail, falter
fama fame
familia family (2)
familiar *n. m.* relation, member of the family; *adj.* family-related, of the family (2)
famoso/a famous
fango mud
fantasía fantasy
fantasma *m.* ghost, phantom
fantástico/a fantastic
faringe *f.* pharynx
farmacéutico/a pharmacist
farmacia drugstore, pharmacy (12)
farmacología pharmacology
fascinante *adj.* fascinating
fascinar to fascinate; to enchant
fatal terrible, bad; fatal
fauna animal life
favor *m.* favor; **favor de repetir** please repeat (4); **por favor** please (A)
favorito/a favorite
febrero February (5)
fecha date (5); **¿cuál es la fecha?** what is the date? (5)
felicidad *f.* happiness; **felicidades** *pl.* congratulations
felicitaciones *f. pl.* congratulations (10)
feliz (*pl.* **felices**) happy (10); **Felices Pascuas** Merry Christmas; **Feliz Navidad** Merry Christmas
femenino/a feminine
fenomenal phenomenal
fenómeno phenomenon
feo/a ugly (2)
feriado: día (*m.*) **feriado** holiday
feroz (*pl.* **feroces**) ferocious
festivo: día (*m.*) **festivo** holiday (10)
fibra fiber
fichero (card) file; index
fiebre *f.* fever (12)
fiel honest, faithful; loyal
fiesta party (1); feast; holiday; **dar** (*irreg.*) / **hacer** (*irreg.*) **una fiesta** to give a party (10)
figura figure
figurita figurine
fijarse to imagine; **fijarse en** to take notice (of), pay attention (to)
fijo/a fixed; **precio fijo** fixed price (3)
filosofía philosophy
fin *m.* end; **a fin de** in order to, so as to; **a fines de** at the end of; **al fin** at last; in the end; **fin de semana** weekend (1); **por fin** finally, at last (7)

final *n. m.* final; end; **a finales de** at the end of (*with time*) (9); **al final de** at the end of (17); *adj.* final
finalmente finally (9)
financiero/a financial
finca farm (14); **finca raíz** real estate
fingir (j) to pretend
firma signature
firmar to sign
física *s.* physics
físico/a *adj.* physical; *n. m.* appearance
flan *m.* caramel custard (6)
flexibilidad *f.* flexibility
flor *f.* flower
flora plant life
floreado/a flowered
florecer (zc) to flower, blossom, bloom
Florida: Pascua Florida Easter (10)
flotar to float
fluir (y) to flow
flujo flow
folleto pamphlet
fondo: en el fondo in the back
forma form, manner
formación *f.* formation
formalidad *f.* formality
formalizar (c) to formalize
formar to form
formato format
forzar (ue) (c) to force
fósforo match (*for lighting things*) (20)
foto(grafía) *f.* photo(graph); **sacar (qu) fotos** to take pictures, photographs (8)
fotográfico/a photographic; **equipo fotográfico** photographic equipment (8)
fracasado/a failed
fractura fracture
francés *m.* French (*language*) (1)
francés, francesa *adj.* French (2)
Francia France
franqueo postage; **manejo y franqueo** postage and handling
frasco flask, bottle
frase *f.* phrase; sentence (1)
frazada blanket
frecuencia frequency; **con frecuencia** frequently (1); **¿con qué frecuencia?** how often? (3)
frecuente frequent
frecuentemente frequently
frenos brakes (13); **frenos de disco** disc brakes
frente a facing
fresa strawberry
fresco/a fresh; **hace fresco** it's cool (*weather*) (5)
frigorífico refrigerator (*Sp.*)
frijol *m.* bean (6)
frío *n.* cold(ness)
frío/a *adj.* cold; **hace (mucho) frío** it's (very) cold (weather) (5); **tener** (*irreg.*) **(mucho) frío** to be (feel) (very) cold (5)
frito/a fried; **papa frita** French fried potato (6)
frívolo/a frivolous
frontera border, frontier (19)
fruta fruit (6)
fu: ni fu ni fa so-so
fuego fire
fuente *f.* source
fuera *adv.* out, outside (6); **fuera de** *prep.* out of
fuerte strong; heavy, big (*meal*); **plato fuerte** main dish
fugaz: estrella fugaz shooting star
fui, fuiste, fue (*from* **ir**) I, you, he/she/it went (7)
fumador(a) smoker; **no fumador(a)** nonsmoker
fumar to smoke (7); **sección** (*f.*) **de (no) fumar** (non)smoking section (7)
función *f.* function; performance, show (15)
funcionar to function; to run, work (*with machines*) (8)
funcionario/a official
fundar to found, establish
furioso/a furious, angry (4)
fútbol *m.* soccer; **fútbol (norte)americano** football (15)
futuro *n.* future (17)
futuro/a *adj.* future

G

gabán *m.* overcoat
gafas (eye)glasses (12)
galón: millas por galón miles per gallon
gallego/a from Galicia (*area of Spain*)
galleta cookie (6)
gallo rooster; **Misa del Gallo** midnight Mass (*on Christmas Eve*)
gambas *pl.* shrimp
ganancias earnings (17)
ganar to earn (8); to win (8); **ganar terreno** to gain ground
ganas: tener ganas de + *inf.* to feel like (*doing something*) (3)
ganga bargain; **fue una ganga** it was a bargain (steal) (3)
garaje *m.* garage (8)
garantizar (c) to guarantee
garganta throat (12)
gas *m.* gas; heat (9)
gasolina gasoline (13); **estación** (*f.*) **de gasolina** gas station (13)
gasolinera gas station (13)
gastar to use, expend (13); to spend (*money*) (4)
gastos expenses (17)
gato/a cat (2)
generación *f.* generation
general general; **en general** generally, in general; **por lo general** generally, in general (2)
generalizado/a generalized
género genre, type
generoso/a generous
genial funny, pleasant
gente *f. s.* people (6)
geografía geography
gerente *m., f.* manager (19)
gerundio gerund
gestión *f.* measure, step
gesto gesture
gimnasia: hacer (*irreg.*) **gimnasia** to do gymnastics
gimnasio gymnasium (15)
girar to revolve, turn
gobernar (ie) to govern, rule (16)
gobierno government (8)
golf *m.* golf (15)
golpe *m.* blow (*injury*)
golpista *adj.* having to do with a *coup d'état*
goma rubber
gordo/a fat, plump (2)
gorro cap
gozar (c) to enjoy
grabador (*m.*) **de vídeo** video recorder, VCR (8)
grabar to record
gracia grace
gracias thanks (A); **Día** (*m.*) **de Gracias** Thanksgiving Day; **muchas gracias** thank you very much, many thanks (A)
gracioso/a funny
grado degree (*temperature; university*); grade
graduado/a graduate
graduarse (en) to graduate (from)
gramática grammar
gran, grande large, big (2); great (2)
granada grenade
granja farm
granjero farmer
grasa grease
gratis *inv.* free, gratis
grato/a pleasant
gratuito/a free
grave grave, important; serious
griego/a Greek
grillo cricket
gripe *f.* grippe, influenza
gris gray (3)
gritar to shout
grueso/a: intestino grueso large intestine
grupo group
guapo/a handsome, good-looking (2)
guardar to save (*a place*) (7); to watch over (7); **guardar cama** to stay in bed (12)
guardia *m.* guard
guerra war (16)
guía *m., f.* guide; **guía** (*f.*) **telefónica** telephone book
guisante *m.* pea
guitarra guitar
gustar to be pleasing (7); **¿le/te gusta... ?** do you like . . . ? (A); **¡me gusta muchísimo!** I like it a lot! (6); **me gustaría...** I would really like . . . (7); **no, no me gusta...** no, I don't like . . . (A); **¡no me gusta (para) nada!** I don't like it at all!

(6); **sí, me gusta...** yes, I like ... (A); **¿te/le gusta... ?** do you like ... ? (A)
gusto *n.* like, preference; taste; pleasure; **a gusto** comfortable, "at home"; **mucho gusto** pleased to meet you (A)

H

haba bean
Habana Havana
haber (*irreg.*) *infinitive form of* **hay** (13); to have (*auxiliary*); **va a haber** there's going to be; **había (habías, había,** etc.) + *p.p.* I (you, he/she/it) had (*done something*) (14); **he, has, ha viajado** I, you have traveled, he/she/it has traveled (7)
haber *n. m.* credit
había (habías, había) + *p.p.* I (you, he/she/it) had (*done something*) (14)
habitación *f.* room (19); **una habitación doble** a double room; **una habitación con/sin baño/ducha** a room with(out) a bath/shower (19); **una habitación para una persona** a single room (19)
habitante *m., f.* inhabitant
hábito habit
habla *f.* (*but* **el habla**) speech (*language*); **de habla española** Spanish-speaking
hablar to speak; to talk (1); *n. m.* dialect, speech
hace + *time* ago (10); **hace** + *period of time* + **que** + *present tense* to have been (*doing something*) for (*a period of time*) (3)
hacer (*irreg.*) to do; to make (5); **hace buen (mal) tiempo** it's good (bad) weather (5); **hace calor (fresco, frío, sol, viento)** it's hot (cool, cold, sunny, windy) (weather) (5); **hacer autostop** to hitchhike; **hacer *camping*** to go camping (15); **hacer cola** to stand in line (7); **hacer ejercicio** to exercise, get exercise (12); **hacer el papel (de)** to play the role (of); **hacer escalas** to have/make stopovers (7); **hacer la cama** to make the bed (9); **hacer las maletas** to pack one's suitcases (7); **hacer un viaje** to take a trip (5); **hacer una fiesta** to give a party (10); **hacer una pregunta** to ask a question (5); **hacerse** to become (10); **hacerse daño** to hurt oneself (11); **hacer planes para** + *inf.* to make plans to (*do something*) (15); **¿qué tiempo hace?** what's the weather like? (5)
hacia toward
hallar to find
hambre *f.* hunger; **tener** (*irreg.*) **hambre** to be hungry (6)
hamburguesa hamburger (6)
harina flour
hasta *prep.* until; **hasta luego** see you later (A); **hasta mañana** until tomorrow, see you tomorrow (A); **hasta que** *conj.* until (17)
hay there is, there are (A); **hay contaminación** there is pollution (5); **hay que** + *inf.* it's necessary to (*do something*) (13); **no hay** there is/are not (A); **no hay más remedio** nothing can be done about it (10)
hazaña deed
he, has, ha + **viajado** I, you have traveled, he/she/it has traveled (7)
hebreo/a Hebrew
hecho *n.* fact, event (10); **de hecho** in fact
hecho/a *p.p.* made, done
helado ice cream (6)
hemisferio hemisphere
heredero/a heir
herencia inheritance
herida *n.* wound; injury
herido/a wounded
hermano/a brother, sister (2)
hermoso/a beautiful
héroe *m.* hero
hervido/a boiled
hervir (ie, i) to boil
hidalgo knight
hidrógeno hydrogen
hiedra ivy
hielo ice (5)
hierba grass; herb
hierro iron; **óxido de hierro** iron oxide
hígado liver
higiene *f.* hygiene
higiénico: papel (*m.*) **higiénico** toilet paper
hijo/a child (2); son/daughter (2); **hijos** *m. pl.* children (2)
himno hymn
hipopótamo hippopotamus
hispánico/a Hispanic
hispano/a *n.* Hispanic (*person*); *adj.* Hispanic
historia history (1)
histórico/a historical
historieta amusing story
hockey *m.* hockey (15)
hogar *m.* home, house
hoguera bonfire
hoja leaf
hola hi (A)
hombre *m.* man (1); **¡hombre!** well!, man!; **hombre de negocios** businessman (18)
hondo/a deep
hondureño/a Honduran
honrado/a honest, upright
honrar to honor
hora hour; **¿a qué hora?** (at) what time? (A); **hora de** + *inf.* time to (*do something*); **por hora** per hour; **¿qué hora es?** what time is it? (A)
horario schedule, timetable
horno oven (9)
hortaliza vegetable
hospedaje *m.* housing
hospedarse to stay
hospital *m.* hospital
hotel *m.* hotel (19); **hotel de lujo** luxury, first-class hotel (19)
hoy today (A)
huelga *n.* strike (*labor*) (16)
hueso bone
huésped(a) guest (19)
huevo egg (6)
huir (y) to flee
humanidad *f.* humanity
humano human; **ser** (*m.*) **humano** human being
humilde humble
humo *n.* smoke (7)
humor *m.* humor

I

ida *n.* departure; (**billete** [*m.*] / **boleto**) **de ida** one-way (ticket) (7); **(billete/boleto) de ida y vuelta** round-trip (ticket)
idea idea; **cambiar de idea** to change one's mind
ideal ideal
identificado: no identificado/a unidentified
identificar (qu) to identify
ideología ideology
idioma *m.* language
iglesia (4) church
ignorar to be ignorant of
igual equal, same; **igual que** the same as; **por igual** equally; **(eso) me da igual** (that's) (it's) all the same to me (11)
igualdad *f.* equality (16)
igualmente likewise (A)
ilimitado/a unlimited
iluminar to illuminate, light up
ilusión *f.* illusion; dream
ilustrar to illustrate
imagen *f.* image
imaginación *f.* imagination
imaginar(se) to imagine
imaginativo/a imaginative
imitar to imitate
impaciente impatient
impedir (i, i) to impede, stop
imperfecto/a imperfect
imperio empire
impermeable *m.* raincoat (3)
imponente imposing
imponer (*like* **poner**) to impose
importado/a imported
importancia importance
importante important
importar to be important, matter; to import; **no (me) importa nada** it doesn't matter (to me) (at all) (11)
imposible impossible

imprenta: letra de imprenta print(ing)
imprescindible indispensable
impresión *f.* impression
impresionante impressive
impresora printer (18)
improbable improbable, unlikely
improvisado/a improvised
impuesto tax (8)
impulsar to launch
impulsivo/a impulsive
inauguración *f.* inauguration
inca *m.* Incan
incaico/a *adj.* Inca, Incan
incalculable incalculable
incendio fire
incidente *m.* incident
incluido/a included
incluir (y) to include
inclusive including
incluso *adv.* even, including
incluso/a *adj.* included
incómodo/a uncomfortable (10)
incompleto/a incomplete
incomprensible incomprehensible
inconveniente *m.* drawback, disadvantage
incorporar to incorporate
increíble incredible; **es increíble** it's incredible (8)
independencia independence
independiente independent
independizarse (c) to become independent
indicación *f.* indication
indicado/a indicated
indicar (qu) to indicate, point out
indicativo (*gram.*) indicative (mood)
índice: dedo índice index finger
indiferencia indifference
indio/a Indian
indiscreto/a indiscreet
individuo individual, person
industria industry
inesperadamente unexpectedly
inesperado/a unexpected
inevitable unavoidable
inexplicablemente inexplicably
inexplorado/a unexplored
infancia infancy
infantil of, or pertaining to, a child or children
infección *f.* infection
inferir (ie, i) to infer
infierno hell
infinidad *f.* infinity
infinitivo infinitive
inflación *f.* inflation
inflamado/a inflamed
influencia influence
información *f.* information; **archivar la información** to store information (14)
informar to inform (16); **informarse** to inquire, find out
informática data processing (14)
informe *m.* report
ingeniería engineering
ingeniero/a engineer
ingenio ingenuity
ingenuo/a innocent
Inglaterra England
inglés *m.* English (*language*) (1)
inglés, inglesa English (2)
ingresar to put in, deposit (17)
ingresos *pl.* earnings
iniciación *f.* initiation
inicial *n. f., adj.* initial
inmediato/a immediate
inmejorable unsurpassable, unbeatable
inmigración *f.* immigration (19)
inmigrante *n., m., f., adj.* immigrant
inocente *n.* fool; *adj.* innocent
inolvidable unforgettable
inquilino/a tenant, renter (9)
inscribir (*pp.* **inscrito/a**) to enroll
inscripción *f.* enrollment
insistir en + *inf.* to insist on (*doing something*) (3)
insólito/a unusual
insomnio insomnia
inspector(a) (de aduanas) (customs) inspector (19)
instantáneo/a instant; instantaneous
institución *f.* institution
instituto institute; secondary school
instrucción *f.* instruction
instrumento instrument
insular of an island
insulto insult
inteligente intelligent
intención *f.* intention
intensivo/a intensive
intentar to try
intercambiar to exchange
intercambio interchange, exchange
interesante *adj.* interesting
interesar to interest, be interesting; **me interesa(n)...** ...is/are interesting to me (8)
interior *n. m., adj.* interior; inside
intermedio middle
internacional international
interno/a internal
interpretación *f.* interpretation
intérprete *m., f.* interpreter; performer, artist
interrogativo/a interrogative (A)
interrumpir to interrupt
intervención *f.* intervention
intestino intestine; **intestino delgado** small intestine; **intestino grueso** large intestine
intocable untouchable
invadir to invade
invención *f.* invention
inventar to invent
inventario inventory (8)
invento invention
inversor(a) investor
investigación *f.* investigation
investigar (gu) to investigate
invierno winter (5)
invitado/a *n.* guest; *adj.* invited (4)
invitar to invite (4)
inyección *f.* shot, injection (12); **ponerle** (*irreg.*) **una inyección** to give (someone) a shot, injection(12)
ir (*irreg.*) to go (3); **ir a** + *inf.* to be going to (*do something*) (3); **ir al extranjero** to go abroad; **ir de vacaciones** to go on vacation (7); **irse** to leave, go away (9)
irrealizable unattainable
irritado/a irritated, annoyed
irrumpir to erupt
isla island
Italia Italy
italiano/a Italian
itinerario itinerary
izquierda: a la izquierda (de) to the left (*of*) (*directions*) (4)
izquierdo/a left (*direction*) (4); **levantarse con el pie izquierdo** to get up on the wrong side of the bed (11)

J

jabón *m.* soap (20)
jamás never (6)
jamón *m.* ham (6)
Japón *m.* Japan
jarabe *m.* (cough) syrup (12)
jardín *m.* garden
jarra jug, pitcher
jaspeado/a variegated
jefe/a boss (8)
jerez *m.* sherry
Jesucristo Jesus Christ
jirafa giraffe
joven *n. m., f.* young person; *adj.* young (2); **de joven** as a youth (12)
jubilarse to retire (*from work*)
judía green bean
juego game (*card, board*) (15); play (*in a game*) (15)
jueves *m. s.* Thursday (4)
juez *m.* (*pl.* **jueces**) judge
jugador(a) *n.* player (15)
jugar (ue) (gu) (a) to play (*sports, games*) (5); **jugar a las cartas/al ajedrez** to play cards/chess (15)
jugo juice (6)
juguete *m.* toy (9)
juicio judgment
julio July (5)
junio June (5)
junto a alongside of, next to
juntos/as together (6)
jurado jury
jurídico/a legal, juridical
justificar (qu) to justify
juvenil youthful
juzgar (gu) to judge; to form or give an opinion

K

kilo(gramo) *m.* kilogram (*approx. 2.2 pounds*)
kilometraje *m.* mileage (*distance in kilometers*)
kilómetro kilometer (*approx. .62 miles*)

L

la the (*f.* definite article)
la *d.o.* you (*form. s.*), her, it (*f.*)
labor *f.* work
laborable *adj.* work (*day*)
laboratorio lab, laboratory
lado side
ladrón, ladrona thief
lago lake
laguna lagoon
lamentar to be sorry, regret
lámpara lamp (8)
lana wool (3)
langosta lobster (6)
lanzar (c) to throw
lápiz *m.* (*pl.* **lápices**) pencil (1)
largo/a long (2)
las you (*form. pl.*), them (*f.*)
lástima *n.* pity, too bad; **es lástima** it's a shame (8); **¡qué lástima!** what a shame! (8)
lata (tin) can
latín *m.* Latin (*language*)
Latino América Latin America
latino/a Latin (*person*)
latinoamericano/a Latin American
lavadora washer, washing machine (9)
lavandería laundry; laundromat
lavaplatos *m. s.* dishwasher (9)
lavar to wash (8); **lavar las ventanas** to wash the windows (9); **lavar(se)** to wash (oneself) (9); to get washed (9)
le *i.o.* to/for you (*form. s.*), him, her, it
lección *f.* lesson
lectura reading
leche *f.* milk (6)
lechuga lettuce (6)
leer (y) to read (3)
lejía bleach
lejos de *prep.* far from (4)
lengua language; tongue (12)
lenguaje *m.* (computer) language (14)
lenteja lentil
lentes (*m. pl.*) (**de contacto**) contact lenses (12)
lento/a slow (11)
leña (fire)wood
les *i.o.* to/for you (*form. pl.*), them
letra letter (*of alphabet*); **letra de imprenta** print(ing); **letras** *pl.* letters; arts; **letras cursivas** italics
levantar to lift, raise (9); **levantar pesas** to lift weights; **levantarse** to get up, stand up (9); **levantarse con el pie izquierdo** to get up on the wrong side on the bed (11)
ley *f.* law (16)
liberado/a liberated
libertad *f.* liberty, freedom (16)
libra pound
libre free (4); **un rato libre** a few free minutes (15); **ratos libres** free, spare time (15)
librería bookstore (1)
libreta de ahorros bank book (17)
libro book (1); **libro de texto** textbook (1)
licencia license (13); **licencia de manejar (conducir)** driver's license
liceo high school
licor *m.* liqueur
liga league
ligero/a *adj.* light (*in weight*); slight
limitar to limit
límite *m.* limit; border; **límite de velocidad** speed limit
limón *m.* lemon
limonada lemonade
limosnas *pl.* alms
limpiaparabrisas *m. s.* windshield wiper
limpiar to clean (9)
limpio/a clean (4)
lindo/a pretty (11)
línea line; **línea aérea** airline
lingüístico/a linguistic
linterna lantern
lío mess; **lío de tráfico** traffic jam
liquidación *f.* sale
líquido liquid
liso/a smooth
lista list
listado/a striped
listo: estar listo/a to be ready, prepared (8); **ser listo/a** to be smart, clever (2)
litera berth (*on a train*)
literatura literature
lo *d.o.* you (*form. s.*), him, it (*m.*); **lo que** what, that which (7); **lo** + *adj.* (*m. s.*) the _____ thing/part/news (12); **lo bueno/malo** the good news/the bad news (12); **lo siento** I'm sorry (4); **lo suficiente** enough (12)
lobo wolf
localizar (c) to find, locate
loco/a crazy (11)
locura madness; insanity
locutor(a) *n.* radio announcer
lógico/a logical
lograr to achieve; to gain, obtain, attain
lona canvas
los *d.o.* you (*form. pl.*), them (*m.*)
lotería lottery
lubricar (qu) to lubricate
lucidez *f.* lucidity
lucir (zc) to dress to advantage; to show off; to shine
luchar to fight (16)
luego then, next (1); later; **desde luego** of course; **hasta luego** see you later (A)
lugar *m.* place (1); **cambiar de lugar** to move (*something*) (11); **tener** (*irreg.*) **lugar** to take place (15)
lujo luxury (19); **hotel** (*m.*) **de lujo** luxury hotel (19)
lujoso/a luxurious
luminoso/a bright
luna moon; **luna de miel** honeymoon (4)
lunares *m. pl.* polka dots
lunes *m. s.* Monday (4)
lustro year
luz *f.* (*pl.* **luces**) light (9); electricity (9)

LL

llamar to call (6); **¿cómo se llama Ud.?, ¿cómo te llamas?** what is your name? (A); **llamarse** to be named, called (9); **me llamo** _____ my name is _____ (A)
llano *n.* level ground, plain
llanta tire (13); **llanta desinflada** flat tire (13); **llanta radial** radial tire
llave *f.* key (11)
llegada arrival (7)
llegar (gu) to arrive (2); **llegar a ser** to become (10); **llegar a tiempo** to arrive on time
llenar to fill (up) (13); to fill out (*a form*) (18)
lleno/a full
llevar to wear (3); to carry (3); to take (*someone or something somewhere*) (3); to have been (*in a certain place for a period of time*); **llevarse bien/mal (con)** to get along well/badly (with); **llevar una vida** _____ to lead a _____ life (12)
llorar to cry (10)
llover (ue) to rain (5)
lluvia rain
lluvioso/a rainy

M

madera wood
madrastra stepmother
madre *f.* mother (2)
madrileño/a from Madrid
madrugar (gu) to get up early (14)
maduro/a mature
maestro/a grade school teacher (8)
mágico/a *adj.* magic, magical
magnífico/a magnificent, wonderful
mago: Reyes (*m. pl.*) **Magos** Magi, Three Wise Men
mal *n. m.* evil, badness
mal *adv.* badly (1); ill, not well; **pasarlo mal** to have a bad time (10)
mal, malo/a *adj.* bad (2); **hace mal tiempo** it's bad weather (5); **lo malo** the bad news (12)
maldad *f.* wickedness
maldito/a cursed, damned
maleducado/a ill-mannered, rude; poorly brought up
maleta suitcase (5); **hacer** (*irreg.*) **las maletas** to pack one's suitcases (7)
maletero porter (7)
maletín *m.* small suitcase

malévolo/a malevolent
malgastar to waste
malpensado/a wicked, malicious
malvado/a evil, wicked
mamá mom, mother (2)
mandar to send (7); to order (8)
mandato command
¿mande? what?, pardon me? (*Mex.*)
manejar to drive (8); to use, operate (*a machine*) (14); **licencia de manejar** driver's license
manejo operation, use (*of a machine*) (14); handling; **manejo y franqueo** postage and handling
manera manner, way
manga sleeve; mob
manía mania
manifestación *f.* manifestation
mano *f.* hand (9); **darse** (*irreg.*) **la mano** to shake hands; **escalera de mano** ladder; **estar** (*irreg.*) **cogidos/as de las manos** to hold hands; **hecho/a a mano** handmade; **meter mano en** to have a hand in
manteca lard; grease
mantel *m.* tablecloth
mantener (*like* **tener**) to maintain, keep up (13); to leave; **mantener correspondencia** to correspond
mantequilla butter
manzana apple (6)
mañana *n.* morning; *adv.* tomorrow (A); **de la mañana** in the morning (A); **hasta mañana** until tomorrow, see you tomorrow (A); **pasado mañana** the day after tomorrow (4); **por la mañana** in the morning (1)
mapa *m.* map
máquina machine; **escribir a máquina** to type (14); **máquina de escribir** typewriter (8)
mar *m., f.* sea
maratón *m.* marathon
maravilla wonder, marvel
maravilloso/a wonderful, marvelous
marca brand, make
marcado/a marked
marcador *m.* marker
marcar (qu) to dial; to mark
marcharse to leave
mareado/a nauseated (12)
marfil *m.* ivory
marido husband
marihuana marijuana
marino/a *adj.* sea; **brisa marina** sea breeze
mariposa butterfly
mariscos *pl.* shellfish (6)
marrón *m.* brown
martes *m. s.* Tuesday (4)
marzo March (5)
más more (1); most; **más... que** more ... than (5); **sus más y sus menos** its/his/her good and bad points
matar to kill
matemáticas mathematics (1)
materia subject (*in school*) (1)
material *m.* material (3)
materialista materialistic
matrícula *s.* registration fees (1); registration
matrimonio marriage (4); married couple
matutino morning paper
máximo/a maximum
maya *m., f.* Mayan
mayo May (5)
mayor older (5); greatest, greater
mayoría majority; **la mayoría de edad** adult age, full legal age
mazo deck (*of cards*)
me *d.o.* me; *i.o.* to, for me; *refl. pron.* myself
mecánico mechanic (13)
medalla medal
media: (las tres) y media (three) thirty, half past (three) (*with time*) (A); **media pensión** (*f.*) room and breakfast plus one other meal (19)
mediano/a middle; average
medianoche *f.* midnight
mediante by means of
medias *pl.* stockings (3)
medicina medicine (12)
médico/a (medical) doctor (2); *adj.* medical
medida measurement; measure
medio *n.* means; **medio ambiente** environment (14); **el Medio Oriente** the Middle East
medio/a *adj.* half, middle; intermediate; average; **clase** (*f.*) **media** middle class
mediodía *m.* midday
medioeste *m.* midwest
medir (i, i) to measure; to be ______ tall
meditar to meditate
mejor better (5); best (5)
mejorar to improve
melocotón *m.* peach
memoria memory (14)
mencionar to mention
menor younger (5); least
menos less; minus; least; **menos... que** less ... than (5); **a menos que** unless (15); **echar de menos** to miss (*the presence of someone or something*); **más o menos** more or less; **por lo menos** at least (19); **sus más y sus menos** its/his/her good and bad points
mensaje *m.* message
mensual monthly
mente *f.* mind
mentira lie
menú *m.* menu (6)
mercado market(place) (3)
mercantil *adj.* commercial, mercantile
merecer (zc) to deserve (16)
merendar (ie) to snack
merienda snack
mes *m. s.* month (5); **...al mes** ... a month (3)
mesa table (1); **poner** (*irreg.*) **la mesa** to set the table (9)
mesero/a waiter/waitress
meseta plain
mesita end table (8)
mesón *m.* inn; tavern
metal *m.* metal
metro subway; **estación** (*f.*) **del metro** metro (subway) stop (20)
metrópoli *f.* city, metropolis
metropolitano/a metropolitan
mexicano/a Mexican (2)
mexicanoamericano/a Mexican-American
México Mexico
mezcla mixture
mezclar to mix
mezclilla *light cloth woven with different sorts of threads*
mezquita mosque
mi(s) *poss.* my (4)
mí *obj. of prep.* me
miamense *m., f.* from Miami
microcomputadora microcomputer (14)
microonda microwave
microordenador *m.* microcomputer
miedo fear; **tener miedo (de)** to be afraid (of) (3)
miel *f.* honey; **luna de miel** honeymoon (4)
miembro member
mientras while (8)
miércoles *m. s.* Wednesday (4)
miga crumb
mil *m.* a thousand, one thousand (3)
«mili» *f.* military service
militante *adj.* militant
milla mile (13); **millas por hora** miles per hour
millón (de) *m.* million (3)
millonario/a millionaire
mimado/a spoiled (*child*)
miniatura: en miniatura in miniature
minidiálogo minidialogue
mínimo minimum
ministerio ministry
minoría minority
minoritario/a *adj.* minority
minuto *n.* minute (*time*)
mío/a(s) *poss.* my, (of) mine
miopia myopia, nearsightedness
mirar to look (at); to watch (2)
misa Mass; **Misa del Gallo** midnight Mass (*on Christmas Eve*)
mismo/a self; same (9); **ahora mismo** right now (4)
mitad *f.* half
mixto mixed
mobilidad *f.* mobility
mochila backpack (1)
moda fashion; **de última moda** the latest style (3)
modales *m. pl.* manners
modelo model
moderación *f.* moderation
moderno/a modern
modesto/a modest
modo: de todos modos anyway
molestar to bother; **molestarse** to

get upset; **no vale la pena (molestarse por eso)** it's not worth it (to get upset about that) (11)
molestia *n.* bother
momentito just a minute, second
momento moment; **de momento** right now, for the time being; **en este momento** right now, at this very moment (4)
monarquía monarchy
moneda money, currency (17)
monitor *m.* monitor, screen (14)
mono monkey
monótono/a monotonous
monstruo monster
montaña mountain (4)
montañoso/a mountainous
montar to ride; **montar a caballo** to ride horseback (14)
monte *m.* mountain
montón *m.* heap, pile
monumento monument
morado/a purple (3)
morder (ue) to bite
moreno/a brunette (2)
morir(se) (ue, u) (*p.p.* **muerto/a**) to die (10)
mosca fly
mostrador *m.* counter (*of a ticket window, store, etc.*)
mostrar (ue) to show, exhibit
moto(cicleta) *f.* (8) motorcycle
motor *m.* motor, engine
mover (ue) to move
movimiento movement
mozo bellhop (19)
muchacho/a young man/woman; boy/girl
muchachón *m.* big boy
muchísimo: ¡me gusta muchísimo! I like it a lot! (6)
mucho/a *adj.* a lot of, many (2); *adv.* much, a lot (1); **muchas gracias** thank you very much, many thanks (A); **mucho gusto** pleased to meet you (A); **muchas veces** frequently, a lot
mudanza moving (*from one residence to another*)
mudarse to move (*from one residence to another*) (14)
mueblería furniture store
muebles *m. pl.* furniture (8); **sacudir los muebles** to dust the furniture (9)
muela molar
muerte *f.* death
muerto/a *p.p.* dead, died; killed
mujer *f.* woman (1); **mujer de negocios** businesswoman (18)
multa fine, ticket (11); **poner** (*irreg.*) **una multa** to give a fine/ticket
mundial *adj.* world
mundo world
muñeca doll (8)
murmullo murmur
músculo muscle
museo museum; **visitar un museo** to visit a museum (15)
música music
muy very (1); **muy bien** very well, fine (A); **muy buenas** good afternoon/evening

N

nácar *m.* mother-of-pearl
nacer (zc) to be born
nacional national
nacionalidad *f.* nationality (19)
nada nothing, not anything (6); **como si nada** as if nothing were wrong; **de nada** you're welcome (A); **¡no me gusta (para) nada!** I don't like it at all! (6); **no (me) importa nada** it doesn't matter (to me) (at all) (11)
nadar to swim (6)
nadie no one, nobody, not anybody (6)
naranja *n.* orange (*fruit*) (6)
naranjo/a orange (*color*)
nariz *f.* nose (12)
nata cream
natación *f.* swimming (15)
natal native, of birth
natural: recursos naturales natural resources (14)
naturaleza nature (14)
Navidad *f.* Christmas (10); **Feliz Navidad** Merry Christmas
navideño/a *adj.* Christmas
necesario/a necessary (2)
necesidad *f.* necessity, need
necesitar to need (1)
negar (ie) (gu) to deny (13)
negocio business (14); **hombre** (*m.*) / **mujer** (*f.*) **de negocios** businessman/woman (18)
negro/a black (3)
nervioso/a nervous (4)
nevar (ie) to snow (5)
nevera refrigerator
ni neither; nor; **ni... ni** neither ... nor; **ni siquiera** not even
nicaragüense *n. m., f., adj.* Nicaraguan
nido nest
nieto/a grandson/daughter (2); **nietos** grandchildren
nieva (*from* **nevar**) it is snowing
nieve *f.* snow
ningún, ninguno/a no, none, not any (6)
niñez *f.* (*pl.* **niñeces**) childhood
niño/a child; boy/girl (1); **de niño/a** as a child (11)
nivel *n. m.* level
no no (A); not; **¿no?** right?, don't they (you, *etc.*)? (3); **no hay** there is not/are not
nocivo/a harmful
nocturno/a *adj.* night, nocturnal
noche *f.* night (1); **buenas noches** good evening/night (A); **de la noche** in the evening, at night (A); **de noche** at night, by night; **esta noche** tonight; **Noche Vieja** New Year's Eve (10); **por la noche** in the evening (1); **todas las noches** every night
Nochebuena Christmas Eve (10)
nombrado/a appointed, named
nombre *m.* (first) name (2)
norma norm
noroeste *m.* northwest
norte *m.* north
Norteamérica North America
norteamericano/a North American; from the United States (2); **fútbol** (*m.*) **norteamericano** football (15)
nos *d.o.* us; *i.o.* to, for us; *refl. pron.* ourselves
nosotros/as *sub. pron.* we; *obj. of prep.* us
nota grade (*in a class*) (10); note
noticia notice; piece of news (10); **noticias** news (16)
noticiero newscast (16)
novecientos/as nine hundred (3)
novedades *f.* news (16)
novela *n.* novel (3)
novelista *m., f.* novelist
noveno/a *adj.* ninth (13)
noventa ninety (2)
noviazgo courtship, engagement (4)
noviembre *m.* November (5)
novio/a boy/girlfriend (4); fiancé(e) (4); groom/bride (4)
nublado/a cloudy, overcast; **está nublado** it's cloudy, overcast (5)
nuestro/a(s) *poss.* our; (of) ours (4)
nueve nine (A)
nuevo/a new (2); **Año Nuevo** New Year
nuez *f.* (*pl.* **nueces**) nut
número number (A)
nunca never (3)

O

o or (A)
obedecer (zc) to obey (16)
objeto object
obligación *f.* obligation
obligar (gu) to oblige, compel
obra work (*of art, literature, etc.*)
obrero/a worker, laborer (16)
observar to observe; to watch
obstáculo obstacle
obstante: no obstante nevertheless, notwithstanding
obtener (*like* **tener**) to get, obtain
obvio/a obvious
ocasión *f.* occasion
ocasionar to cause
océano ocean
octavo/a *adj.* eighth (13)
octubre *m.* October (5)
oculista *m., f.* optometrist, eye specialist
ocultar to hide
ocupado/a busy, occupied (4)
ocupar to occupy; **ocuparse** to be in charge of
ocurrir to happen, occur
ochenta eighty (2)

ocho eight (A)
ochocientos/as eight hundred (3)
odiar to hate
oeste west
ofender to offend, insult
oficial *adj.* official
oficina office (1)
oficio trade (18); service
ofrecer (zc) to offer (16)
oiga(n) hey, listen (*to get someone's attention*) (*form.*)
oír (*irreg.*) to hear (6)
ojalá + *past subjunctive* I wish . . . could/would (16); **ojalá que** + *subjunctive* I wish, hope that (*something happens*) (7)
ojo eye (12); **¡ojo!** watch out!
Olimpíada *s.* Olympic Games
olvidar to forget (7); **olvidarse (de)** to forget (about) (10)
olla pot
opaco/a opaque; dull
opcional optional
ópera opera
operación *f.* operation
operar to operate
opinar to think, have an opinion
opinión *f.* opinion
oponerse (*like* **poner**) **(a)** to be opposed (to)
oportunidad *f.* opportunity
opuesto: lo opuesto the opposite
oración *f.* sentence (*gram.*)
orden *f.* order, command; *m.* order (*sequence*)
ordenador *m.* computer (*Sp.*) (8)
orgánico: química orgánica organic chemistry
organizado/a organized
organizar (c) to organize
orgulloso/a proud
oriente *m.* east; **el Medio Oriente** the Middle East
origen *m.* origin
orilla bank (*of a river*)
oro gold
orquesta orchestra
os *d.o.* you (*fam. pl. Sp.*); *i.o.* to, for you (*fam. pl. Sp.*); *refl. pron.* yourselves (*fam. pl. Sp.*)
oscuridad *f.* darkness
oscuro/a *adj.* dark
oso bear
ostentar to have, hold (*a title*)
ostra oyster
otoño fall (*season*) (5)
otro/a other, another (2); **otra vez** again
óxido: óxido de hierro iron oxide
oye hey, listen (*to get someone's attention*) (*fam.*)

P

paciencia patience
paciente *n.m., f.* patient (12); *adj.* patient
Pacífico Pacific
padecer (zc) to suffer, feel deeply
padre *m.* father (2)
padres *m.* parents (2)
padrino patron; godfather; sponsor
paella paella (*dish made with rice, shellfish, often chicken, and flavored with saffron*)
pagar (gu) to pay (for) (1)
página page
pago payment
país *m.* country, nation (4)
paisaje *m.* countryside, landscape
pájaro bird (8)
palabra word (A)
palacio palace
palma palm, palm tree
palmera palm tree
pan *m.* bread (6); **pan dulce** sweet roll
panadería bakery
panameño/a Panamanian
pandilla group of friends
pantalones *m. pl.* pants (3)
pantalla screen (14)
pantera panther
papa potato (*L.A.*); *m.* pope; **papa frita** French fried potato (6)
papá *m.* dad, father (2)
papel *m.* paper (1); role; **hacer** (*irreg.*) **un papel** to play a role; **papel higiénico** toilet paper; **papel para cartas** stationery (20)
papelería stationery store (20)
paquete *m.* package (20)
par *m.* pair (3)
para *prep.* (intended) for (1); in order to (1); **para que** *conj.* so that (15)
parabrisas *m. s.* windshield
parada stop; **parada del autobús** bus stop (20)
parado/a stopped
paraguas *m. s.* umbrella
paraguayo/a Paraguayan
paraíso paradise
paralizado/a paralyzed
parar to stop (13)
parcial: de tiempo parcial part-time (8)
pardo/a brown (3)
parecer (zc) to seem, appear (7); **¿qué te parece?** what do you think?
parecido/a similar
pared *f.* wall (8)
pareja couple; partner
paréntesis *m. s.* + *pl.* parenthesis; **entre paréntesis** in parentheses
pariente/a *n.* relative (2)
parque *m.* park (4)
párrafo paragraph
parrilla grill
párroco parish priest
parte *f.* part; **de parte de** on behalf of; **por todas partes** everywhere
participante *m., f.* participant
participar to participate
participio pasado (*gram.*) past participle
particular particular; private
partido game (*in sports*), match (15)
partir: a partir de starting from
pasado *n.* past
pasado/a past, last (*in time*) (9); **pasado mañana** the day after tomorrow (4)
pasaje *m.* passage, ticket (7); passengers
pasajero/a passenger (7)
pasaporte *m.* passport (19)
pasar to spend (*time*) (4); to pass (*someone, something*) (4); to happen; **pasar por** to come by to pick up (*someone, something*) (4); **pasar la aspiradora** to vacuum (9); **pasarlo bien (mal)** to have a good (bad) time (10); **que lo pases bien** (I hope you) have a good time (15)
pasatiempo pastime, diversion (15)
Pascua (Florida) Easter (10)
pasear en bicicleta to go for a bike ride (15)
paseo stroll, promenade; **dar** (*irreg.*) **un paseo** to take a walk (15)
pasillo hall, corridor
pasión *f.* passion
paso step; pace; **ceda el paso** yield
pasta paste; **pasta de dientes** toothpaste; **pasta dental** toothpaste (20)
pastel *m.* cake, pie (6)
pastelería pastry shop (20)
pastelito small pastry (20)
pastilla pill (12)
pasto pasture; fodder
pastor(a) pastor; shepherd; **pastor** (*m.*) **alemán** German shepherd (*dog*)
patata potato (*Sp.*)
patinaje *m.* skating
patinar to skate (15)
patio patio (8); yard (8)
pato duck
patria motherland, native land
patrón: santa patrona patron saint
pavo turkey
payaso clown
paz *f.* (*pl.* **paces**) peace (16)
peatón, peatona pedestrian; **cruce** (*m.*) **para peatones** pedestrian crossing
pedazo piece
pedir (i, i) to ask for, order (5); **pedir prestado/a** to borrow (17)
pegar (gu) to hit, strike (11); to stick (on)
pelado/a peeled
pelear to fight
película movie (4)
peligro danger
peligroso/a dangerous (10)
pelo hair
pelota ball (15)
peluquero/a hairdresser
pena: no vale la pena it's not worth it (11)
pendiente *m.* earring
penicilina penicillin
península peninsula
pensar (ie) to think (5); to intend (5); **pienso que...** I think that . . . (5); **¿qué piensas de... ?** what do you think of/about . . . ? (5)

pensión *f.* boarding house (19); **media pensión** room and breakfast plus one other meal (19); **pensión completa** room and full board (*all meals included*) (19)
peor worse (5); worst
pequeño/a small, little (2)
perder (ie) to lose (5); to miss (*a bus, plane, social function, etc.*)
perdón pardon me, excuse me (A)
perdonar to pardon, forgive
perdone pardon (11)
perejil *m.* parsley
perezoso/a lazy (2)
perfecto/a perfect, fine
perfume *m.* perfume
periódico newspaper (3)
periodismo journalism
periodista *m., f.* journalist
permanente permanent
permiso permission; **(con) permiso** pardon me, excuse me (A)
permitir to permit, allow (8)
pero *conj.* but (1)
perro/a dog (2)
persa *m., f.* Persian
persona *f.* person (1)
personaje *m.* character (*of a story, play*)
personal *n. m.* personnel; **Dirección** (*f.*) **de Personal** personnel, employment office (18); **director(a) de personal** director of personnel (18); *adj.* personal; **uso personal** personal use (19)
personalidad *f.* personality
perspectiva perspective
pertenecer (zc) to relate, belong
perteneciente *adj.* belonging
pertinente (a) related, having to do (with)
peruano/a Peruvian
pesa: levantar pesas to lift weights
pesado/a boring (10)
pesar *n. m.* worry, concern; *v.* to weigh; **a pesar de** in spite of
pesca catch (*of fish*); fishing
pescadería fish market
pescado fish (*cooked*) (6)
pesebre *m.* manger
peseta *unit of currency in Spain*
pesimista pessimistic
peso weight; *unit of currency in Mexico and several other Latin American countries*
petróleo petroleum, oil
pez *m.* (*pl.* **peces**) fish (*live*) (8)
pianista *m., f.* pianist
picadillo minced meat, hash
picante hot, spicy
picar (qu) to prick, pierce; to chop
picnic *m.* picnic
picher *m.* pitcher (*in sports*)
pie *m.* foot (11); **al pie de** at the bottom of; **levantarse con el pie izquierdo** to get up on the wrong side of the bed (11)
piedra stone
piel *f.* skin; **pieles** *pl.* furs
pierna leg (11)
pieza piece (*of music*); part
píldora pill
piloto/a pilot
pino pine (tree)
pingüino penguin
pintar to paint
pintor(a) painter
pintura painting (8)
piña pineapple
pirámide *f.* pyramid
pisar to step on
piscina swimming pool (8)
piso floor; **primer piso** second floor (first floor up) (9)
pista (de baile) (dance) floor
pizarra blackboard (6)
placer *m.* pleasure
plan *m.* plan; **hacer** (*irreg.*) **planes para** + *inf.* to make plans to (*do something*) (15)
plancha iron
planchar to iron (9)
planear to plan
planeta *m.* planet
planilla form (*to fill out*) (19)
planta plant; floor (*of a building*); **planta baja** ground floor, first floor (9)
plantear to pose (*a question*)
plasmarse to come into being
plástico plastic
plata silver (*metal*)
plátano banana
plateado silver plated
plato plate (6); dish (6)
playa beach (5)
playera T-shirt
plaza square; place, space; **plaza de toros** bullring
plazo time limit; **a plazos** in installments (17)
pleito suit (*legal*)
pleno/a full
pluriempleo moonlighting
plomero/a plumber (18)
población *f.* population (14)
pobre poor (2)
pobreza poverty
poco/a *adj.* little, few (3); **poco** *adv.* little, a little bit (1); **poco a poco** little by little
poder (*irreg.*) to be able, can (3); **¿podría Ud. ...?** could you . . . ? (13)
poema *m.* poem
poeta *m., f.* poet
policía *m., f.* police officer (13); *f.* police (force)
política *n. f. s.* politics
político/a *n.* politician; *adj.* political; **ciencias políticas** *pl.* political science
pollo chicken (6)
ponche *m.* punch
poner (*irreg.*) to put, place (5); to turn on (*appliances*); **poner el despertador** to set the alarm clock; **poner la mesa** to set the table (9); **poner una multa** to give a fine/ticket; **ponerle una inyección** to give (someone) a shot, injection (12); **ponerse** to put on (*clothing*) (9); **ponerse** to become, get (10); **ponerse de acuerdo** to reach an agreement
por *prep.* in (*the morning, evening, etc.*) (1); because of (10); for; per; by; through; during; on account of; for the sake of; **por ciento** percent; **por completo** completely; **por Dios** for heaven's sake; **por ejemplo** for example (3); **por eso** therefore, that's why (2); **por favor** please (A); **por fin** finally, at last (7); **por hora** per hour; **por igual** equally; **por lo general** generally, in general (2); **por lo menos** at least (19); **por medio de** by means of; **por parte de** on behalf of; **por primera (última) vez** for the first (last) time; **por si acaso** just in case (19); **por supuesto** of course; **por último** finally
porcelana porcelain
porcentaje *m.* percentage
porción *f.* portion
¿por qué? why? (2)
porque because (2)
portarse to behave (oneself) (10)
portátil portable; **radio** (*f.*) **portátil** portable radio (8)
portero/a building manager (9); doorman (9)
portugués, portuguesa Portuguese; *m.* (language)
posar to alight, settle
poseer (*like* **ver**) to possess
posibilidad *f.* possibility
posible possible (2)
posición *f.* position
postal: (tarjeta) postal *f.* postcard (7)
posteriormente previously
postre *m.* dessert (6)
postulante *m., f.* applicant
postura position
potencia power; **de alta potencia** high potency
práctica practice
practicante *m., f.* type of nurse or intern
practicar (qu) to practice (1); to participate in (*sports*)
práctico/a practical
precio price (3); **precio fijo** fixed price (3)
precioso/a precious; lovely
preciso/a necessary (8)
precolombino/a pre-Columbian (before Columbus)
preferencia preference
preferible preferable; **es preferible** it's preferable (8)
preferir (ie, i) to prefer (3); **prefiero** + *inf.* I prefer to (*do something*) (1)
pregunta question; **hacer** (*irreg.*) **una pregunta** to ask a question (5)
preguntar to ask, inquire (7)
premio prize; **el premio gordo** the grand prize

prensa press; news media (16)
preocupación *f.* preoccupation, worry, care, concern
preocupado/a worried (4)
preocuparse (por) to worry (about) (14); **no te preocupes** (*fam.*) don't worry (8)
preparación *f.* preparation
preparado/a prepared
preparar to prepare (9)
preparativo/a preparative, qualifying; **preparativos** *n. m. pl.* preparations
preposición *f.* (*gram.*) preposition (4)
presentar to introduce; to present
presente *n. m.* present (*time; tense*)
presidente/a president
presión *f.* pressure, tension (11); blood pressure; **sufrir muchas presiones** to be under a lot of pressure (11)
prestado: pedir prestado/a to borrow (17)
préstamo *n.* loan (17)
prestar to lend (7); **prestar atención** to pay attention
prestigio prestige
presupuesto budget (17)
pretérito (*gram.*) preterite
previo/a previous
previsión *f.* prediction
primariamente primarily
primario/a principal; primary; **escuela primaria** elementary school
primavera spring (5)
primer, primero/a *adj.* first (13); **el primer piso** second floor (first floor up) (9); **el primero de ____** the first of (*month*) (5); **por primera vez** for the first time; **primera clase** first class (7); **primero** *adv.* first (of all)
primo/a cousin (2)
princesa princess
príncipe *m.* prince
principiante *m., f.* beginner
principio beginning
prisa haste, hurry; **tener** (*irreg.*) **prisa** to be in a hurry (3)
prisión *f.* prison
prisionero/a prisoner
privación *f.* lack
privado/a private
probabilidad *f.* probability (17)
probablemente probably
probar (ue) to taste, try
problema *m.* problem
procedente de coming from
proceso process
procurar to try
producir (*irreg.*) to produce
producto product (9)
profesión *f.* profession (18)
profesional *m., f.* professional
profesionalizado/a professionalized
profesor(a) professor (1)
profundo/a profound; deep
programa *m.* program (14)
programador(a) programmer
progresivo/a progressive
progreso progress
prohibido/a prohibited, forbidden; **prohibido estacionarse** no parking (13)
prohibir to prohibit, forbid (8)
prometer to promise
pronombre *m.* pronoun; **pronombre reflexivo** reflexive pronoun; **pronombre sujeto** subject pronoun
pronóstico prognosis
pronto soon; **tan pronto como** as soon as (17)
pronunciar to pronounce
propenso/a inclined, prone
propiedad *f.* property
propina tip (*given to a waiter, etc.*) (19)
propio/a *adj.* own, one's own (11)
proponer (*like* **poner**) to propose
proporcionar to furnish, grant, supply
propósito purpose; **a propósito** by the way
próspero/a prosperous
protagonista *m., f.* protagonist, main character
proteger (j) to protect (14)
proteína protein
protestar to protest (16)
protón *m.* proton
proveer (*like* **ver**) to provide
provocar (qu) to provoke; to cause
próximo/a next (*in time*) (4); **la próxima vez** the next time
proyección *f.* projection
proyecto project
prueba quiz (5)
publicitario/a: anuncio publicitario ad(vertisement)
público/a *adj.* public (14); **Administración** (*f.*) **Pública** Public Administration
pueblo town
puerro leek, scallion
puerta door (3); **puerta de embarque** loading gate
puertorriqueño/a Puerto Rican
pues well . . . (1)
puesto *n.* position, place (*in line*) (7); job (8)
puesto/a *p.p.* put, placed
pulmón *m.* lung (12)
pulpo octopus
pulsera bracelet
punto point; dot; **en punto** exactly, on the dot (*time*) (A); **punto de partida** point of departure; **punto de vista** point of view
puntual punctual
puñal *m.* knife
puro/a pure (14)

Q

que that, who (2); **lo que** what, that which (7); **que** + *subjunctive* I hope + *verb form* (15)
¿qué? what? which? (A); **¡qué** + *noun*! what a . . .! (7); **¡qué bien!** great!; **¡qué extraño!** how strange! (8); **¡qué lástima!** what a shame! (8); **¿qué tal?** how are you (doing)? (A)
quedar to remain, be left (11); **no queda(n)** there is (are) none left; **quedarse** to stay, remain (9)
quehacer *m.* task, chore (9)
quejarse (de) to complain (about) (10)
querer (*irreg.*) to want (3); to love (*with persons*) (7); **fue sin querer** it was unintentional (11); **(no) quiero** + *inf.* I want (don't want) to (*do something*) (1)
querido/a dear (4); beloved
queso cheese (6)
quien who
¿quién(es)? who?, whom? (A); **¿de quién?** whose? (2); **¿quién será?** who can that be?, I wonder who it is (17)
química chemistry; **química orgánica** organic chemistry
quina chinchona bark
quince fifteen (A)
quinceañera *celebration in honor of a girl's fifteenth birthday*
quinientos/as five hundred (3)
quinto/a *adj.* fifth (13)
quiosco kiosk (*small outdoor stand where a variety of items are sold*) (20)
quitar to remove, take away (9); **quitarse** to take off (*clothing*) (9); to take out, withhold
quizá(s) perhaps (15)

R

rábano turnip
radiador *m.* radiator
radial: llanta radial radial tire
radical *m.* stem, radical (*gram.*)
radio *f.* radio (set) (5); **radio portátil** portable radio (8)
radiografía X-ray
radiología radiology
raíz *f.* (*pl.* **raíces**) root; stem, radical (*gram.*); **finca raíz** real estate
rallar to grate
ramo bouquet; branch
ranchero rancher (14)
rancho ranch
rápido/a *adj.* fast; **rápido** *adv.* fast, rapidly
raqueta racket (15)
raro/a rare, unusual; strange (13)
rascacielos *m. s.* skyscraper (14)
rasgo characteristic
rato short period of time; **un rato libre** a few free minutes (15); **ratos libres** *pl.* spare, free time (15)
ratón *m.* mouse
raya: de rayas striped (3)
rayo: rayos equis X-rays
raza race (*of people*)
razón *f.* reason; **la razón por la cual**

the reason why, for which (19); **no tener** (*irreg.*) **razón** to be wrong; **tener razón** to be right (3)
reacción *f.* reaction
reaccionar to react (10)
realidad *f.* reality; **en realidad** really
realizador(a) director
realizar (c) to bring about, realize
realmente really
rebajar to cut, reduce (*prices*)
rebajas sales, reductions (3)
rebelde *n. m., f.* rebel; *adj.* rebellious
rebozo shawl, cloak
recado message
recepción *f.* front desk (19); reception
recepcionista *m., f.* receptionist
receta prescription (12)
recibir to receive (3)
recibo receipt
recién + *adj.* recently
reciente recent
recíproco/a reciprocal
recitar to recite
recobrar to recover; **recobrarse** to recover, recuperate
recoger (j) to pick up
recomendación *f.* recommendation
recomendar (ie) to recommend (8)
recompensa compensation
reconocer (zc) to recognize
reconstruido/a reconstructed, rebuilt
recordar (ue) to remember (10); to bring to mind
recorrer to pass through (14); to cover (*territory, miles, etc.*) (14)
recreo recreation
recuadro box
recuerdo memory (2); souvenir
recuperar to recover, regain
recurso recourse; **recursos (naturales)** (natural) resources (14)
rechazar (c) to reject
red *f.* net (15)
redactar to write
redentor *m.* redeemer
redondo/a round
reducir (*like* **producir**) to reduce, cut down
referente a concerning, regarding
referirse (ie, i) (a) to refer (to)
reflejar to reflect
reflexivo/a reflexive; **pronombre** (*m.*) **reflexivo** (*gram.*) reflexive pronoun
reforma *n.* reform
refrán *m.* proverb
refrescante *adj.* refreshing
refresco soft drink (5); refreshment (10)
refrigerador *m.* refrigerator (9)
refugio refuge
regalar to give (*as a gift*) (7)
regalo present, gift (2)
regañar to scold
regatear to haggle, bargain (3)
régimen *m.* regime, diet
región *f.* region
registrar to search, examine (19)
regla rule
reglamento *s.* regulations
regresar to return (1); **regresar a casa** to go home (1)
regreso: boleto de regreso return ticket
regulador *m.* regulator; control (knob)
regularidad: con regularidad regularly
reina queen (16)
reírse (i, i) (de) to laugh (about) (10)
relación *f.* relation
relativo/a relative
reloj *m.* watch (3); clock
rellenar to stuff
remedio remedy; **no hay más remedio** nothing can be done about it (10)
remunerar to pay
renovado/a renovated
renta income
renunciar (a) to resign (from) (18); to deny oneself
reparación *f.* repair
reparar to repair
repartir to give out
repasar to review
repaso *n.* review
repente: de repente suddenly (12)
repetir (i, i) to repeat; **repite** (*fam.*) repeat (4); **favor de repetir** please repeat (4)
reportero/a reporter (16)
representación *f.* representation
representante *m., f.* representative
representar to represent; to present (*a play, etc.*)
reproche *m.* reproach, reproof
repuesto/a spare (*tire, etc.*)
requerir (ie, i) to require
requisito requirement (14)
reserva reservation
reservación *f.* reservation (19)
reservar to reserve (19)
resfriado cold (*illness*) (12)
resfriarse to get/catch a cold (12)
residencia residence; **residencia (estudiantil)** dormitory (1)
residencial residential
resolver (ue) (*p.p.* **resuelto/a**) to solve, resolve (14)
respetar to respect
respeto respect
respiración *f.* respiration, breathing
respirar to breathe (12)
responder to answer, respond
responsabilidad *f.* responsibility (16)
responsable responsible
respuesta *n.* answer (6)
restaurante *m.* restaurant (6)
resto rest, remainder
resuelto/a *p.p.* solved, resolved
resultado result
resultar to result, turn out
retablo carving
retirarse to retire (*from work*)
retraído/a reserved
retraso tardiness; delay
retrato portrait
reunión *f.* reunion
reunir to unite; to reunite; **reunirse (con)** to get together (with) (15)
revelar to reveal
reverso reverse
revisar to check, examine, inspect (13)
revisión *f.* inspection
revista magazine (3)
revitalizante *adj.* revitalizing
revolución *f.* revolution
rey *m.* king (16); **Reyes Magos** Wise Men
rico/a rich (2)
ridículo/a ridiculous
riesgo danger, risk
rígido/a rigid
rincón *m.* inside corner; remote place
río river
ritmo rhythm, pace (14); **cambio de ritmo** change of pace
robar to steal
robo robbery
rodilla knee
rojo/a red (3)
romántico/a romantic
romper (*p.p.* **roto/a**) to break (11)
ropa clothing (3)
rosa *n.* rose; **de color rosa** pink
rosado/a pink (3)
roto/a *p.p.* broken (13); **estar roto/a** to be exhausted, worn out (*with people*)
rubio/a blond(e) (2)
ruido noise (3)
ruidoso/a noisy
ruso/a Russian
rueda wheel (*Sp.*)
ruta route
rutina routine, habit
rutinario/a *adj.* routine

S

sábado Saturday (4)
saber (*irreg.*) to know (6); + *inf.* to know how to (*do something*)
sabor *m.* taste; flavor
saborear to taste, savor
sabotear to sabotage
sacar (qu) to take out, remove; to get, receive (*with grades*); to stick out (*one's tongue*) (12); **sacar (fotos)** to take (pictures, photographs) (8); **sacar la basura** to take out the garbage (9)
sacerdote *m.* priest; clergyman
saco de dormir sleeping bag
sacrificar (qu) to sacrifice
sacrificio sacrifice
sacudir (los muebles) to dust (the furniture) (9)
sagrado: Sagrada Familia Holy Family
sal *f.* salt
sala room; living room (8); **sala de clase** classroom; **sala de espera**

waiting room (7); **sala de emergencias (urgencia)** emergency room (12)
salado/a: agua salada salt water
salario salary, wages
salida departure (7); exit; loss
salir (*irreg.*) to leave, go out (5); to appear; to turn out to be; **salir a derechas** to turn out right
salmón *m.* salmon (6)
salón *m.* room
saltar to jump
salud *f.* health (12)
saludar to greet (9)
saludo greeting
salvadoreño/a Salvadorean
salvaje savage
salvar to save
salvo except
sandalia sandal (3)
sándwich *m.* sandwich (6)
sangre *f.* blood
sano/a healthy (12); wholesome
Sansón Samson
santo/a holy, blessed; saint; **¡Santo Dios!** my goodness!
satisfacer (*like* **hacer**) to satisfy
Saudita: Arabia Saudita Saudi Arabia
se (*impersonal*) one; *refl. pron.* yourself (*form.*), himself, herself, yourselves (*form.*), themselves
sea: o sea in other words
secadora clothes dryer (9)
secarropa clothes dryer
sección (*f.*) section; **sección de (no) fumar** (no) smoking section (7)
seco/a dry; barren, arid
secretario/a secretary (1)
secuencia sequence, series
secundaria secondary; **la (escuela) secundaria** high school; **educación** (*f.*) **secundaria** high school education
sed *f.* thirst; **tener** (*irreg.*) **sed** to be thirsty (6)
seda silk (3)
sefardí *m., f.* Sephardic Jew
segregar (gu) to secrete
seguida: en seguida immediately (12)
seguir (i, i) (g) to continue, follow (7)
según according to
segundo *n.* second (*time*)
segundo/a *adj.* second (13); **Segunda Guerra Mundial** Second World War; **segundo piso** third floor (second floor up) (9)
seguridad *f.* security, safety; certainty
seguro *n.* insurance; **seguro médico** medical insurance; **seguro social** Social Security
seguro/a sure, certain; **estar seguro/a** to be sure, certain (13); **es seguro que** it is sure, certain that (13); **seguro que** of course
seis six (A)
seiscientos/as six hundred (3)
selección *f.* team
seleccionar to choose
selva jungle
sello stamp (20)
semáforo traffic signal (13)
semana week (1); **... a la semana** ... a week (3); **fin** (*m.*) **de semana** weekend (3); **la próxima semana** next week (4)
semblanza portrait, likeness
semejante similar
semestre *m.* semester
senador(a) senator
sencillo/a simple
sendero path
sensible sensitive; lamentable
sentado/a seated, sitting
sentar (ie) to seat, lead to a seat (9); **sentarse** to sit down (9)
sentido *n.* sense; meaning
sentimiento feeling, emotion, sentiment
sentir (ie, i) to regret (8); to feel sorry (8); **sentir celos** to be jealous; **sentirse** to feel (10)
señal *f.* sign; signal; **señal de tráfico** traffic signal
señalar to point out
señas *f. pl.* direction
señor (Sr.) *m.* Mr., sir (A); gentleman
señora (Sra.) Mrs. (A); lady
señores (Sres.) *m. pl.* Mr. and Mrs.; gentlemen
señorita (Srta.) Miss (A); young lady
separar to separate
se(p)tiembre *m.* September (5)
séptimo/a *adj.* seventh (13)
ser (*irreg.*) to be (2); **es la/son las** ___ it's ______ o'clock (A); **llegar (gu) a ser** to become (10); **¿quién será?** who can that be?, I wonder who it is (17); **ser en** + *place* to take place in/at (*place*) (10); **ser listo/a** to be smart, clever (2); **serán las ocho** it must be (probably is) eight o'clock (17); **sería** it would be (13); **soy, eres, es** I am, you are, he/she/it is (A)
ser (*n. m.*) **humano** human being
serie *f.* series
serio/a serious
serpiente *f.* snake
servicio service (13); **servicios** restrooms; **servicios humanos** human services
servir (i, i) to serve (5)
sesenta sixty (2)
setecientos/as seven hundred (3)
setenta seventy (2)
sexo sex
sexto/a *adj.* sixth (13)
si if (1)
sí yes (A)
sicología psychology (1)
siempre always (3)
siesta nap, siesta; **dormir (ue, u) la siesta** to take a nap
siete seven (A)
siglo century
significado *n.* meaning
significar (qu) to mean
signo sign
siguiente following, next (5)
sílaba syllable
silencioso/a silent
silla chair (1)
sillón *m.* armchair (8)
simpático/a nice (2); likable (2)
simplemente simply
sin *prep.* without (4); **fue sin querer** it was unintentional (11); **sin embargo** however, nevertheless; **sin falta** without fail; **sin que** *conj.* without
sincero/a sincere
sindicato labor union
sinfónico/a symphonic
sino but (rather)
síntoma *m.* symptom (12)
siquiera: ni siquiera not even
sistema *m.* system
sistemático/a systematic
sitio place
situación *f.* situation
situado/a located
sobre *n.* envelope (20); *prep.* about, above, on; **sobre todo** above all, especially (17)
sobrevivir to survive
sobrino/a nephew/niece (2)
social social; **trabajador(a) social** social worker (18)
sociedad *f.* society
socio/a member
sociólogo/a sociologist
socorro *n.* help
sofá *m.* sofa (8)
soja soy bean
sol *m.* sun (5); **hace sol** it's sunny (5); **tomar el sol** to sunbathe (15)
solamente *adv.* only (11)
soldado/a soldier
soledad *f.* solitude (14)
soler (ue) + *inf.* to tend to, be in the habit of (*doing something*)
solicitar to solicit, ask for
solicitud *f.* application form (18)
sólo *adv.* only (1)
solo/a *adj.* alone (7)
soltar (ue) to free; to give off
soltero/a single (not married) (2)
solución *f.* solution
solucionar to solve
sombrero hat (3)
sombrío/a somber
someter to submit
son las ______ it is ______ o'clock (A)
sonar (ue) to ring; to sound
sonreír (i, i) to smile (10)
sonrisa smile
soñar (ue) (con) to dream (about)
sopa soup (6)
sorprender to surprise, be surprising; **me (te, le...) sorprende** it is surprising to me (you, him ...) (8)
sorpresa surprise (10)
sótano basement
soy, eres, es (*from* **ser**) I am, you are, he/she/it is (A)
su(s) *poss.* his, her, its, your (*form. s., pl.*), their (4)

suave *adj.* soft; mild, gentle
suavizar (c) to soften; to temper
subdesarrollado/a underdeveloped
subir (a) to go up (into, onto) (7); to get on, in (*a plane, car, etc.*) (7); to carry up; to raise
subjuntivo subjunctive (*gram.*)
subordinado: claúsula subordinada (*gram.*) subordinate clause
suburbio suburb
suceder to happen
sucio/a dirty (4)
sucursal *f.* branch (office) (18)
Sudamérica South America
sudamericano/a South American
sudar to sweat
sudoeste *m.* southwest
suegro/a father/mother-in-law
sueldo salary (8)
suelo floor (9)
suelto/a loose
sueño sleepiness; dream; **tener** (*irreg.*) **sueño** to be sleepy (9)
suerte *f.* luck; **buena suerte** good luck; **por suerte** luckily, fortunately; **¡qué mala suerte!** what bad luck! (11)
suéter *m.* sweater (3)
suficiente sufficient, enough; **lo suficiente** enough (12)
sufijo suffix
sufrir to suffer; **sufrir muchas presiones** to be under a lot of pressure (11)
sugerencia suggestion
Suiza Switzerland
sujeto subject (*gram.*) **estar sujeto/a** to be subject
suma: en suma in short
sumamente extremely
sumar to total
superar to exceed
superlativo *n.* superlative (*gram.*)
supermercado supermarket
superstición *f.* superstition
supervivencia survival
suponer (*like* **poner**) to suppose
suposición *f.* supposition
supuesto: por supuesto of course
sur *m.* south
suroeste *m.* southwest
surtido supply, assortment
suscribir (*p.p.* **suscrito/a**) to subscribe
suspenso F., failing grade
sustantivo noun (1)
sustituto *n.* substitute
suyo/a *poss.* your, of yours (*form. s., pl.*) his, of his; her, (of) hers; its; their, of theirs

T

tabacalero/a related to tobacco
tabaco tobacco
tabla chart, table
tacaño/a stingy
taco taco (*tortilla filled with meat, vegetables*)
tacto touch
Tailandia Thailand
tal such (a); **con tal que** provided that (15); **¿qué tal?** how are you (doing)? (A); **tal vez** perhaps, maybe (4)
talonario de cheques checkbook (17)
talla size
taller *m.* (repair) shop (13); service station; workshop
tamaño size
también also (A)
tambor *m.* drum
tampoco neither, not either (6)
tan as, so; **tan pronto como** as soon as (17); **tan... como** as . . . as (5)
tanque *m.* tank (13)
tanto/a as much; **tanto/a... como** as much . . . as (5) **tanto** *adv.* as, so much; **no es para tanto** it's not that serious; **por lo tanto** thus
tantos/as as many; so many
tapizado/a upholstered with tapestry
taquilla ticket office (15)
tardar (en + *inf.*) to take time (*to do something*)
tarde *f.* afternoon, evening; **buenas tardes** good afternoon/evening (A); **de la tarde** in the afternoon/evening (A); **por la tarde** in the afternoon/evening (1); **todas las tardes** every afternoon/evening; *adv.* late (1); **más tarde** later; **tarde o temprano** sooner or later
tarea homework (11)
tarifa tariff, rate
tarjeta card (7); **tarjeta de crédito** credit card (17); **tarjeta postal** postcard (7)
tasa tax; rate
taxi *m.* taxi
taxista *m., f.* cab driver
taza cup (11)
te *d.o.* you (*fam. s.*); *i.o.* to, for you (*fam. s.*); *ref. pron.* yourself (*fam. s.*)
té *m.* tea (6)
teatro theater (15)
teclado keyboard
teclas keys (*of computer, typewriter, etc.*) (14)
técnicamente technically
tecnología technology
technológico/a technological
telefonear to telephone
telefónico/a *adj.* telephone; **guía telefónica** telephone book
teléfono telephone (5); **(número de) teléfono** telephone number (5)
telenovela soap opera
televidente *m., f.* television viewer
tele(visión) *f.* television, TV
televisor *m.* television set (5)
tema *m.* theme, topic (15)
temblar (ie) to tremble, shake
temer to fear (8)
temeroso/a fearful
temperatura temperature (12)
tempestad *f.* storm
templado/a cool, temperate
temporada season
temporal temporary
temprano *adv.* early (1)
temprano/a early; young (*age*)
tendido/a lying down
tenedor *m.* fork (6)
tener (*irreg.*) to have (3); **no tener razón** to be wrong; **tener ______ años** to be ______ years old (2); **tener algo que (decir, hacer...)** to have something to (say, do . . .) (19); **tener calor/frío** to be (feel) warm/cold (5); **tener cuidado (de)** to be careful (about) (15); **tener dolor de ______** to have a pain in ______ (12); **tener en cuenta** to keep/have in mind, take into account (16); **tener ganas de** + *inf.* to feel like (*doing something*) (3); **tener hambre** to be hungry (6); **tener lugar** to take place (15); **tener miedo (de)** to be afraid (of) (3); **tener prisa** to be in a hurry (3); **tener que** + *inf.* to have to (*do something*) (3); **tener que ver (con)** to have to do (with); **tener razón** to be right (3); **tener sed** to be thirsty (6); **tener sueño** to be sleepy (9)
tengo, tienes, tiene I have, you have, he/she/it has (2)
tenis *m. s.* tennis (15)
tentativa attempt
teórico/a theoretical
tercer, tercero/a *adj.* third (13); **tercer piso** fourth floor (third floor up) (9)
terciopelo velvet
terminación *f.* ending
terminar to finish (4)
termómetro thermometer
termostato thermostat
terrateniente *m.* landowner
terremoto earthquake
territorio territory
tersura smoothness
testigo/a witness (16)
testimonio testimony
texto text (1); **libro de texto** textbook (1)
ti *obj. of prep.* you (*fam. s.*)
tiempo (verb) tense; time (5); weather (5); **a tiempo** on time (7); **de tiempo parcial** part-time (8); **hace buen (mal) tiempo** it's good (bad) weather (5); **¿qué tiempo hace?** what's the weather like? (5)
tienda shop, store (3)
tierra land, earth
tímido/a timid, shy
tinta ink
tinto: vino tinto red wine (6)
tintorería dry cleaner
tío/a uncle/aunt (2)
típico/a typical
tipo *n.* kind

tiro: a tiros shooting, with shots
título title; degree
tiza chalk
toalla towel
tobillo ankle
tocadiscos *m., s.* record player
tocar (qu) to play (*a musical instrument*) (5); **tocarle a uno** to be someone's turn (9)
todavía still, yet (4)
todo/a all, every (2); everything; **ante todo** first of all; **de todo** everything (3); **de todos modos** anyway; **sobre todo** above all, especially (7); **todas las tardes (noches)** every afternoon (night); **todo derecho** straight ahead (13); **todo ello** all that; **todos los días** every day (1)
tolerante tolerant
tolerar to tolerate
tomar to take (1); to drink (1); to eat; **tomar el sol** to sunbathe (15); **tomar en cuenta** to keep/have in mind, take into account (16); **tomarle la temperatura a alguien** to take someone's temperature
tomate *m.* tomato (6)
tono tone
tontería foolish, silly thing (4)
tonto/a silly, foolish (2)
torcer (ue) (z) to twist
toro bull; **plaza de toros** bullring
torpe clumsy (11)
torpeza clumsiness
tortilla omelet (*Sp.*); tortilla (*round, flat bread made of corn or wheat flour*) (*Mex., Central America*)
tos *f. s.* cough (12)
toser to cough (12)
tostado brown
tostador *m.* toaster
tostadora toaster (9)
total *m.* total; *adj.* total; **en total** in all; **total que** the result/upshot is
trabajador(a) *n.* worker; *adj.* hard-working (2); **trabajador(a) social** social worker (18)
trabajar to work (1)
trabajo job (8); written work (8); (term) paper (8); **costar (ue) trabajo** to find it difficult
tradición *f.* tradition
tradicional traditional
traducción *f.* translation
traducir (*like* **producir**) to translate
traductor(a) translator
traer (*irreg.*) to bring (6)
tráfico traffic (13); **señal** (*f.*) **de tráfico** traffic signal
tragedia tragedy
trago (alcoholic) drink (20)
traje *m.* suit (3) **traje de baño** swim/bathing suit (3)
trama plot (*of play or novel*) (15)
trámite *m.* transaction
tranquilidad *f.* peace, tranquility
tranquilizante *m.* tranquilizer
tranquilo/a calm, tranquil (7)
transbordador *m.* (space) shuttle
transformar to transform, change
tránsito traffic
translado transfer
transmisión *f.* transmission; **transmisión automática** automatic transmission; **transmisión de cambios** manual shift
transpirar to perspire
transporte *m.* (means of) transportation (14)
tras after
traslúcido/a translucent
tratamiento treatment (12)
tratar to treat (give treatment); **tratar (de)** + *inf.* to try to (*do something*) (9); **tratarse de** to be a matter of; **trato** deal, pact; treatment; **trato hecho** it's a deal
través: a través (de) through, by means of
travieso/a mischievous (4)
trayectoria development
trébol *m.* clover
trece thirteen (A)
treinta thirty (2)
tren *m.* train (7); **estación** (*f.*) **del tren** train station (7)
tres three (A)
trescientos/as three hundred (3)
tribu *f.* tribe
trigo wheat
trimestre *m.* trimester
tripulado/a manned
triste sad (4)
tristeza sadness
triturador (*m.*) **de basuras** garbage disposal
trofeo trophy (8)
tronco log
tropezar (ie) (c) to stumble, slip; to strike against; **tropezar con** to bump into (11)
trucha trout
tu(s) *poss.* your (*fam. s.*) (4)
tú *sub. pron.* you (*fam. s.*); **¿y tú?** and you? (A)
tubo digestivo alimentary canal
tumba tomb
turismo tourism
turista *m., f.* tourist
turístico/a *adj.* tourist; **clase** (*f.*) **turística** tourist class (7)
turno turn
Turquía Turkey
tuve (que)... I had (to) . . . (9)
tuyo/a(s) *poss.* your, (of) yours (*fam. s.*)

U

u or (*used instead of* **o** *before words beginning with* **o** *or* **ho**)
ubicar (qu) to locate, place
último/a last; latest; final (16); **de última moda** the latest style (3); **la última vez** the last time; **por último** finally
un, uno/a one, a, an (*indefinite article*); **cada uno/a** each one
único/a only; unique
unido/a united; **Estados Unidos** United States
unión *f.* union
unir to unite
universidad *f.* university (1)
universitario/a *n.* university student; *adj.* university, of the university
unos/as some, several, a few
uperizado/a treated, preserved
urbanización *f.* urbanization
urbano/a urban
urbe *f.* city
urgencia: sala de urgencia emergency room (12)
urgente urgent; **es urgente** it's urgent (8)
uruguayo/a Uruguayan
usado/a used
usar to use; to operate (*a machine*) (14)
uso operation, use (*of a machine*) (14); **uso personal** personal use (19)
usted (Ud., Vd.) *sub. pron.* you (*form. s.*); *obj. of prep.* you (*form. s.*); **¿y usted?** and you? (A)
ustedes (Uds., Vds.) *sub. pron.* you (*form. pl.*); *obj. of prep.* you (*form. pl.*)
utensilio utensil (6)
útil useful; helpful (1); **útiles** *n. m. pl.* (writing) materials
utilizar (c) to use, make use of

V

vaca cow
vacaciones *f. pl.* vacation (7); **estar** (*irreg.*) **de vacaciones** to be on vacation (7); **ir** (*irreg.*) **de vacaciones** to go on vacation (7)
vacilación: sin vacilación without hesitation
vacilar: sin vacilar without hesitation
vacío/a empty; unoccupied, uninhabited
vacuna shot, vaccination
vagar (gu) to wander
valer (valgo) to be worth; **no vale la pena** it's not worth it (11)
válido/a valid
valiente brave, courageous
valioso/a valuable
valor *m.* value
vamos a... (*from* **ir**) let's go . . . (3)
vanidad *f.* vanity
vanidoso/a vain, conceited
vano: en vano in vain
vapor *m.* steam
vaquero cowboy
variación *f.* variation
variar to vary
variedad *f.* variety
varón *m.* male
vasco/a Basque

vascuense *m.* Basque language
vaso (drinking) glass; **vaso sanguíneo** blood vessel
vecindad *f.* neighborhood
vecino/a neighbor (9)
vegetariano/a vegetarian
vehículo vehicle
veinte twenty (A)
velocidad *f.* speed, velocity (13)
vemos: ¡nos vemos! (*from* **ver**) see you around! (3)
venado deer
vencer (z) to overcome, conquer
vendedor(a) salesperson (18)
vender to sell (3); **venden de todo** they sell everything (3)
venezolano/a Venezuelan
venir (*irreg.*) to come (3)
venta sale
ventaja advantage (13)
ventana window; **lavar las ventanas** to wash the windows (9)
ventanilla (car) window
ventilador *m.* fan
ver (*irreg.*) to see (6); **a ver** let's see; **tener** (*irreg.*) **que ver (con)** to have to do (with); **¡nos vemos!** see you around! (3)
veraneo summer holiday(s)
veraneante *m., f.* vacationer
veraniego/a *adj.* summer
verano summer (5)
verbo verb (1)
verdad *f.* truth; **de verdad** real; really (11); **¿verdad?** right? (2)
verdadero/a true, real (13)
verde green (3)
verduras vegetables (6)
verificar (qu) to verify
versión *f.* version
verso poem, verse
verter (ie) to spill
vertido spilling
vesánico/a insane, mad
vestido dress (3)
vestimienta *s.* clothes
vestir (i, i) to dress (9); **vestirse** to get dressed (9)
vez *f.* (*pl.* **veces**) time, occasion; **a veces** at times, sometimes (3); **de vez en cuando** from time to time (11); **dos veces** twice (3); **en vez de** instead of (17); **la primera (última) vez** the first (last) time; **muchas veces** frequently, a lot; **otra vez** again; **por primera vez** for the first time; **a la vez** at the same time (13); **tal vez** perhaps, maybe (4); **una vez** once (3)
viajado: he, has, ha viajado I/you have traveled, he/she/it has traveled (7)
viajar to travel (5); **viajar al extranjero** to travel abroad
viaje *m.* trip, voyage (7); **de viaje** on a trip; **hacer** (*irreg.*) **un viaje** to take a trip (5)
viajero/a traveler (19)
viajes: agencia de viajes travel agency; **agente** (*m., f.*) **de viajes** travel agent
vibrar to vibrate
vicepresidente/a vice-president
víctima victim
vida life (4); **llevar una vida ______** to lead a ______ life (12)
vídeo: grabador (*m.*) **de vídeo** video recorder, VCR (8)
vieja: Noche (*f.*) **Vieja** New Year's Eve (10)
viejo/a *n.* old man/woman; *adj.* old (2)
viene: el año que viene next year; **la semana que viene** next week
viento wind (5); **hace viento** it's windy (5)
viernes *m. s.* Friday (4)
vietnamita *m., f.* Vietnamese
vigente in effect; viable
villancico Christmas carol
vino (blanco, tinto) (white, red) wine (6)
violencia violence
violín *m.* violin
violoncelo cello
virgen *f.* virgin
visita guest, visitor; visit
visitante *m., f.* visitor
visitar to visit (4); **visitar un museo** to visit a museum (15)
vista view (9); **punto de vista** point of view
visto/a *p.p.* seen
vitamina vitamin
viudo/a widower/widow
vivienda housing (14)
vivir to live (3)
vivo/a alive, living; alert; bright (*of colors*)
vocabulario vocabulary
volador(a) *adj.* flying
volante *m.* (steering) wheel
volar (ue) to fly
volcán *m.* volcano
vólibol *m.* volleyball (15)
volumen *m.* volume
voluntad *f.* will
volver (ue) (*p.p.* **vuelto/a**) to return (5); **volver a** (+ *inf.*) to do (*something*) again (6)
vomitar to vomit
vosotros/a *sub. pron.* you (*fam. pl. Sp.*); *obj. of prep.* you (*fam. pl. Sp.*)
votante *m., f.* voter
votar to vote (16)
voz *f.* (*pl.* **voces**) voice
vuelo flight (7)
vuelta tour
vuelto/a *p.p.* returned; **de ida y vuelta** *adj.* round-trip
vuestro/a(s) *poss.* your (*fam. pl. Sp.*) (4); (of) yours (*fam. pl. Sp.*)

Y

y and (A)
ya already, now (4); **ya no** no longer; **ya que** since, considering that (12)
yerba grass; herb
yeso plaster
yo *sub. pron.* I
yoga *m.* yoga
yogur(t) *m.* yogurt
yuca yucca

Z

zanahoria carrot (6)
zapatería shoe store
zapato shoe (3)
zona zone; **zona estar** living area
zoo zoo
zumo juice (*Sp.*)

ENGLISH–SPANISH VOCABULARY

A

able: to be able **poder** (*irreg.*)
above **sobre**
abroad **extranjero**
absent: to be absent (lacking) **faltar**
absent-minded **distraído/a**
accelerated **acelerado/a**
accompany **acompañar**
account: v. to take into account **tomar, tener** (*irreg.*) **en cuenta**; *n.* (*in a bank*) **cuenta**; checking account **cuenta corriente**; savings account **cuenta de ahorros**
acquainted: to be acquainted with **conocer (zc)**
ad **anuncio**
addition: in addition (besides) **además**
address *n.* **dirección** *f.*
advance: (______ days) in advance **con (______) días de anticipación**
advantage **ventaja**
advertisement **anuncio**
advice **consejo**
advisor **consejero/a**
affectionate **cariñoso/a**
afraid: to be afraid (of) **tener** (*irreg.*) **miedo (de)**
after *prep.* (*with time*) **después de;** *conj.* **después (de) que**
afternoon **tarde** *f.*; good afternoon **buenas tardes**; in the afternoon **de/por la tarde**
afterwards **después**
ago: (two years) ago **hace (dos años)**
agree **estar** (*irreg.*) **de acuerdo**
ahead: straight ahead **todo derecho**
air **aire** *m.*
air conditioner **(aire) acondicionador** *m.*
airplane **avión** *m.*
airport **aeropuerto**
alarm clock **despertador** *m.*
all *adj.* **todo/a**
allow **permitir**
alone *adj.* **solo/a**
almost **casi**
already **ya**
also **también**
although **aunque**
always **siempre**
among **entre**
amuse **divertirse (ie, i)**
and **y**
angry **furioso/a**; to get angry **enojarse**
announce **anunciar**
another **otro/a**
answer *v.* **contestar**; *n.* **respuesta**
antibiotic **antibiótico**
any **algún, alguno/a; cualquier(a)**; not any **ningún, ninguno/a**
anybody **alguien**; not anybody **nadie**
anyone **alguien**; not anyone **nadie**
anything: not anything **nada**
apple **manzana**
appliance **aparato**
application (form) **solicitud** *f.*
appointment **cita**
April **abril** *m.*
aquarium **acuario**
arm **brazo**; arm chair **sillón** *m.*
arrival **llegada**
arrive **llegar (gu)**
as: as if . . . **como si...** (+ *past subj.*); as soon as **en cuanto, tan pronto como**
ask **preguntar**; to ask (for) **pedir (i, i)**; to ask a question **hacer** (*irreg.*) **una pregunta**
asleep: to fall asleep **dormirse (ue, u)**
aspirin **aspirina**
assassination **asesinato**
assistance **ayuda**
at **en; a** (*with time*); at least **por lo menos**
attend **asistir (a)**
attendant: flight attendant **camarero** *m.*, **azafata/camarera**
August **agosto**
aunt **tía**
automobile **automóvil** *m.*
autumn **otoño**
avoid **evitar**

B

back then **en aquel entonces**
backpack **mochila**
bad **mal, malo/a**; it's bad weather **hace mal tiempo**
badly **mal**
baggage **equipaje** *m.*
ball **pelota**
banana **banana**
bank **banco**; bank book **libreta de ahorros**
bargain *v.* **regatear**; *n.* **ganga**
baseball **béisbol** *m.*
basketball **básquetbol** *m.*
bath **baño**; to take a bath **bañarse**
bathe **bañar**
bathroom **baño**
bathtub **bañera**
battery **batería**
be **ser** (*irreg.*); **estar** (*irreg.*); to be ______ years old **tener** (*irreg.*) ______ **años**; to be (feel) hungry, thirsty **tener hambre, sed**
beach **playa**
bean **frijol** *m.*
beautiful **bello/a**
because **porque**; because of **por**
become **hacerse** (*irreg.*) (*p.p.* **hecho/a**), **ponerse** (*irreg.*) (*p.p.* **puesto/a**); **llegar (ue) a ser**
bed **cama**; to go to bed **acostarse (ue)**; to put to bed **acostar (ue)**; to stay in bed **guardar cama**; water bed **cama de agua**
bedroom **alcoba**
beer **cerveza**
before (*with time*) *prep.* **antes de;** *conj.* **antes (de) que**
begin **empezar (ie) (c)**
behave **portarse**
behind **detrás de**
believe (in) **creer (y) (en)**
bellhop **botones** *m. s.*, **mozo**
belt **cinturón** *m.*
besides **además**
best **mejor**
better **mejor**
between **entre**
beverage **bebida**
bicycle **bicicleta**
big **gran, grande**
bike: to ride a bike **pasear en bicicleta**
bill **cuenta, factura**
bird **pájaro**
birthday **cumpleaños** *m. s.*
bit: a little bit **un poco**
black **negro/a**
blackboard **pizarra**
blond *adj.* **rubio/a**
blouse **blusa**
blue **azul**
board: room and full board **pensión** (*f.*) **completa**
boardinghouse **pensión** *f.*
boat **barco**
book **libro**
booked up (committed) **citado/a**
bookshelf **estante** *m.*
bookstore **librería**
boot **bota**
border (*political*) **frontera**
bored **aburrido/a**
boring **pesado/a**
borrow **pedir (i, i) prestado/a**
boss **jefe/a**
box office **taquilla**
boy **niño**
boyfriend **novio**
brakes **frenos**
branch (office) **sucursal** *f.*
bread **pan** *m.*
break **romper** (*p.p.* **roto/a**)
breakfast **desayuno**; to have breakfast **desayunar**
breathe **respirar**
bride **novia**
bring **traer** (*irreg.*)
broken **roto/a**
brother **hermano**
brown **pardo/a**
brunette *adj.* **moreno/a**
budget **presupuesto**
build **construir (y)**
building *n.* **edificio**

bump: to bump into **tropezar (ie) (c) con**
bureau (*furniture*) **cómoda**
bus **autobús** *m.;* bus station **estación** (*f.*) **de autobuses;** bus stop **parada del autobús**
business **comercio, negocio; empresa**
businessman/woman **hombre** (*m.*) / **mujer** (*f.*) **de negocios**
busy **ocupado/a**
but **pero**
buy **comprar**

C

cabin (*in a ship*) **cabina**
café **café** *m.*
cake **pastel** *m.*
calculator **calculadora**
call *v.* **llamar**
called: to be called **llamarse**
calm **tranquilo/a**
camping: to go camping **hacer** (*irreg.*) (*p.p.* **hecho/a)** ***camping***
can *v.* **poder** (*irreg.*)
candidate **aspirante** *m., f.*
candy: piece of candy **dulce** *m.*
car **coche** *m.,* **automóvil** *m.*
card **tarjeta;** credit card **tarjeta de crédito;** (playing) card **carta;** postcard **tarjeta postal**
care: to take care of oneself **cuidarse**
career **carrera**
careful: to be careful **tener** (*irreg.*) **cuidado**
carrot **zanahoria**
carry **llevar**
case: in case **en caso de que;** just in case **por si acaso**
cash *v.* (*a check*) **cobrar;** *adv.* **al contado**
cashier **cajero/a**
cat **gato/a**
catch a cold **resfriarse**
celebrate **celebrar**
certain: (a) certain **cierto/a;** (*to be*) certain **seguro/a**
chair **silla;** arm chair **sillón** *m.*
chalkboard **pizarra**
change *v.* **cambiar (de)**
channel (*T.V.*) **canal** *m.*
charge *v.* (*someone for an item or service*) **cobrar;** (*to an account*) **cargar (gu)**
cheap **barato/a**
check *v.* **revisar;** to check (*baggage*) **facturar;** *n.* **cheque** *m.;* (*restaurant*) **cuenta;** by check **con cheque**
checkbook **talonario de cheques**
checking account **cuenta corriente**
cheese **queso**
chess **ajedrez** *m.*
chicken **pollo**
child **niño/a; hijo/a;** as a child **de niño/a**
chop: (pork) chop **chuleta (de cerdo)**
chore **quehacer** *m.*
Christmas **Navidad** *f.;* Christmas Eve **Nochebuena**
church **iglesia**
citizen **ciudadano/a**
city **ciudad** *f.*
civic **cívico/a**
class **clase** *f.;* first class **primera clase;** tourist class **clase turística**
clean *v.* **limpiar;** *adj.* **limpio/a**
cleaner: vacuum cleaner **aspiradora**
clear: it's clear **está claro**
clerk **dependiente/a**
clever **listo/a**
climate **clima** *m.*
clock: alarm clock **despertador** *m.*
close *v.* **cerrar (ie);** close to *prep.* **cerca de**
closed **cerrado/a**
clothes dryer **secadora**
clothing *n.* **ropa**
cloudy: it's cloudy (weather) **está nublado**
clumsy **torpe**
coat *n.* **abrigo**
coffee **café** *m.;* coffee shop **café** *m.*
coffeepot **cafetera**
cold (*illness*) **resfriado;** it's cold weather **hace frío;** to be cold **tener** (*irreg.*) **frío;** to get/catch cold **resfriarse**
collide (with) **chocar (qu) (con)**
collision **choque** *m.*
color **color** *m.*
come **venir** (*irreg.*); to come by to pick up (*someone, something*) **pasar por**
comedy **comedia**
comfort **comodidad** *f.*
comfortable **cómodo/a;** to be comfortable (temperature) **estar** (*irreg.*) **bien**
committed (booked up) **citado/a**
communicate (with) **comunicarse (qu) (con)**
compact disc (player) **compact disc** *m.*
complain (about) **quejarse (de)**
computer **computadora** (*L.A.*); **ordenador** *m.* (*Sp.*); computer disc **disco;** computer language **lenguaje** *m.*
computer science **computación** *f.*
conditioner: air conditioner **(aire) acondicionador** *m.*
confirm **confirmar**
congested **congestionado/a**
congratulations **felicitaciones** *f.*
conserve **conservar**
considering that **ya que**
contact lens **lente** (*m.*) **(de contacto)**
contain **contener** (*like* **tener**)
content *adj.* **contento/a**
continue **seguir (i, i) (g)**
convertible *adj.* (*with cars*) **descapotable**
cook *v.* **cocinar**
cookie **galleta**
cool: it's cool (weather) **hace fresco**
corner (street) **esquina**
corporation **empresa**
cost **costar (ue)**
cotton **algodón** *m.*
cough *v.* **toser;** *n.* **tos** *f.;* cough syrup, **jarabe** *m.*
country **país** *m.;* country(side) **campo**
course **curso**
court: (tennis) court **cancha**
courtship **noviazgo**
cousin **primo/a**
cover *v.* **cubrir** (*p.p.* **cubierto/a**); to cover (*miles, territory*) **recorrer**
crazy **loco/a**
cream: ice cream **helado**
credit card **tarjeta de crédito**
crime **delito**
cross **cruzar (c)**
cry **llorar**
cup **taza**
currency **moneda**
current *adj.* **actual**
custard **flan** *m.*
customs **aduana;** customs duty **derechos de aduana;** customs inspector **inspector (a) de aduanas**

D

dad **papá** *m.*
daily **cotidiano/a**
dance *v.* **bailar**
dangerous **peligroso/a**
data processing **informática**
date (*appointment*) **cita;** (*calendar*) **fecha**
daughter **hija**
day **día** *m.;* day after tomorrow **pasado mañana;** day before yesterday **anteayer;** every day **todos los días**
dear (*term of affection*) **querido/a**
December **diciembre** *m.*
decide **decidir**
declare **declarar**
delay *n.* **demora**
demanding *adj.* **exigente**
dense **denso/a**
deny **negar (ie) (gu)**
department store **almacén** *m.*
departure **salida**
deposit *v.* **ingresar**
deserve **merecer (zc)**
design **diseñar**
desk **escritorio;** front desk (*hotel*) **recepción** *f.*
dessert **postre** *m.*
destroy **destruir (y)**
detail **detalle** *m.*
develop **desarrollar**
development **desarrollo**
dictator **dictador(a)**
dictatorship **dictadura**

dictionary **diccionario**
die **morirse (ue, u)** (*p.p.* **muerto/a**)
diet: to be on a diet **estar** (*irreg.*) **a dieta**
difficult **difícil**
dining room **comedor** *m.*
dinner **cena**; to have, eat dinner **cenar**
director **director(a)**
dirty **sucio/a**
disadvantage **desventaja**
disaster **desastre** *m.*
disc: compact disc (player) **compact disc** *m.*; computer disc **disco**
discover **descubrir** (*p.p.* **descubierto/a**)
dish **plato**
dishwasher **lavaplatos** *m. s.*
divorce *n.* **divorcio**
do **hacer** (*irreg.*) (*p.p.* **hecho/a**); to do (*something*) again **volver a** (+ *inf.*); to have been doing something **hace** + *period of time* + **que** + *present tense*
doctor (*medical*) **médico/a**
dog **perro/a**
doll **muñeca**
door **puerta**
doorman **portero**
dormitory **residencia**
dot: on the dot (*with time*) **en punto**
doubt **dudar**
downtown **centro**
dress *v.* **vestir (i, i)**; *n.* **vestido**
dressed: to get dressed **vestirse (i, i)**
drink *v.* **beber; tomar**; *n.* **bebida**; (*alcoholic*) **copa, trago**; soft drink **refresco**
drive **manejar; conducir** (*like* **producir**)
driver **conductor(a)**
drugstore **farmacia**
dryer: clothes dryer **secadora**
dubbed **doblado/a**
during **durante**
dust *v.* **sacudir**
duty: customs duty **derechos de aduana**

E

each **cada** (*inv.*)
early **temprano**; to get up early **madrugar (gu)**
earn **ganar**
earnings **ganancias**
Easter **Pascua (Florida)**
easy **fácil**
eat **comer**
economize **economizar (c)**
egg **huevo**
eight **ocho**
eighteen **dieciocho**
eighth **octavo/a**
eighty **ochenta**
either: not either **tampoco**
electricity **luz** *f.* (*pl.* **luces**)
eleven **once**
embarrassed **avergonzado/a**
emergency room **sala de emergencias/urgencia**
emotion **emoción** *f.*
employee **empleado/a**
employment office **Dirección** (*f.*) **de Personal**
enchant **encantar**
end: at the end of **al final de**
end table **mesita**
energy **energía**
engagement **noviazgo**
English *n., adj.* **inglés** *m.*, **inglesa** *f.*; English language **inglés** *m.*
enjoy: to enjoy oneself **divertirse (ie, i)**
enough **lo suficiente**
enter **entrar (en, a)**
entertain **divertir (ie, i)**
enthusiast **aficionado/a**
envelope **sobre** *m.*
environment **medio ambiente** *m.*
equality **igualdad** *f.*
equipment **equipo**
era **época**
especially **sobre todo**
Eve: Christmas Eve **Nochebuena**; New Year's Eve **Noche Vieja**
evening **tarde** *f.*; **noche** *f.*; in the evening **de/por la tarde, noche**
event **acontecimiento; hecho**; recent event **novedad** *f.*
every *adj.* **cada** (*inv.*); **todo/a**; every day **todos los días**
exactly (*with time*) **en punto**
exam **examen** *m.*
examine **examinar**; (*search*) **registrar**
example **ejemplo**; for example **por ejemplo**
exchange: (rate of) exchange **cambio**
exciting: to be exciting to one **encantarle a uno**
excuse me **perdón** (*to apologize*); **con permiso** (*to get through*)
exercise *v.* **hacer** (*irreg.*) (*p.p.* **hecho/a**) **ejercicio**; *n.* **ejercicio**
expect **esperar**
expend **gastar**
expense **gasto**
expensive **caro/a**
explain **explicar (qu)**
exploit **explotar**
eye **ojo**

F

factory **fábrica**
fall *v.* **caer** (*irreg.*); to fall asleep **dormirse**; to fall down **caerse**; *n.* (*season*) **otoño**
family *n.* **familia**; *adj.* **familiar**
fan **aficionado/a**
far from **lejos de**
farm **finca**
farm worker **campesino/a**
fast **acelerado/a**
fat **gordo/a**
father **padre** *m.*
fear *v.* **temer**
February **febrero**
feel **sentirse (ie, i)**; to feel cold, warm/hot **tener** (*irreg.*) **frío, calor**; to feel like (*doing something*) **tener ganas de** (+ *inf.*); to feel sorry **sentir (ie, i)**
fees: registration fees **matrícula** *s.*
fever **fiebre** *f.*
fiancé(e) **novio/a**
field: (playing) field **campo**
fifteen **quince**
fifth **quinto/a**
fifty **cincuenta**
fight *v.* **luchar**
fill (up) **llenar**; to fill out (*a form*) **llenar**
finally **finalmente, por fin**
find **encontrar (ue)**; to find out (about) **enterarse (de)**
fine *n.* **multa**; *adv.* **(muy) bien**; it's fine **está bien**
finish **terminar; acabar**
fire *v.* (dismiss) **despedir (i, i)**
first *n.* **primero**; *adj.* **primer, primero/a**
fish (*alive*) **pez** *m.* (*pl.* **peces**); (*prepared as food*) **pescado**
five **cinco**
fix **arreglar**
fixed: fixed price **precio fijo**
flat tire **llanta desinflada**
flight **vuelo**
floor **suelo**; (*building*) **piso**; ground floor **planta baja**
follow **seguir (i, i) (g)**
following *adj.* **siguiente**
food **comida**
foolish **tonto/a**
foolishness **tontería**
foot **pie** *m.*
football **fútbol** (*m.*) **norteamericano**
for **para; por**; for example **por ejemplo**
forbid **prohibir**
foreigner **extranjero/a**
forget **olvidar**; to forget (about) **olvidarse (de)**
fork **tenedor** *m.*
form (*to fill out*) **planilla**
forty **cuarenta**
four **cuatro**
fourteen **catorce**
fourth **cuarto/a**
free **libre; desocupado/a**
freedom **libertad** *f.*
freeway **autopista**
freezer **congelador** *m.*
French *n., adj.* **francés** *m.*, **francesa** *f.*; French language **francés** *m.*
frequency **frecuencia**
frequently **con frecuencia**
Friday **viernes** *m.*
fried: French fried potato **papa frita**
friend **amigo/a**

friendship **amistad** *f.*
from **de**
front: in front of **delante de**
fruit **fruta**
function *v.* **funcionar**
furniture **muebles** *m. pl.*

G

game (card, board) **juego;** (match) **partido**
garage **garaje** *m.*
garbage **basura**
gas **gasolina;** (heating) **gas** *m.;* gas station **gasolinera, estación** (*f.*) **de gasolina**
gasoline **gasolina**
general: in general **por lo general**
generally **por lo general**
German *n., adj.* **alemán** *m.,* **alemana** *f.;* German language **alemán** *n.*
get (obtain) **conseguir (i, i) (g);** (become) **ponerse** (*irreg.*) (*p.p.* **puesto/a**); to get down (from) **bajar (de);** to get off (of) **bajar (de);** to get on (a vehicle) **subir (a);** to get up **levantarse;** to get up early **madrugar (gu);** to get up on the wrong side of the bed **levantarse con el pie izquierdo**
girl **niña**
girlfriend **novia**
give **dar** (*irreg.*); to give (*as a gift*) **regalar**
glasses (prescription) **gafas**
go **ir** (*irreg.*); let's go to . . . **vamos a...** ; to be going to (*do something*) **ir a** (+ *inf.*); to go away **irse;** to go home **regresar a casa;** to go on vacation **ir** (*irreg.*) **de vacaciones;** to go out **salir** (*irreg.*); to go to (attend) **asistir (a);** to go up **subir (a);** to go with **acompañar**
golf **golf** *m.*
good *n.* **bien;** *adj.* **buen, bueno/a;** good afternoon/evening **buenas tardes;** good evening/night **buenas noches;** good morning **buenos días;** it's good weather **hace buen tiempo**
good-bye **adiós;** to say good-bye (to) **despedirse (i, i) (de)**
good-looking **guapo/a**
govern **gobernar (ie)**
government **gobierno**
grade (academic) **nota;** grade school teacher **maestro/a**
granddaughter **nieta**
grandfather **abuelo**
grandmother **abuela**
grandparents **abuelos**
grandson **nieto**
gray **gris**
great **gran, grande**
green **verde**
greet **saludar**
groom **novio**
guest **huésped(a)**
gymnasium **gimnasio**

H

haggle **regatear**
half: it's half past (two, three . . .) **son las (dos, tres...) y media**
ham **jamón** *m.*
hamburger **hamburguesa**
hand **mano** *f.;* on the other hand **en cambio;** to hand in/over **entregar (gu)**
handsome **guapo/a**
happening *n.* **acontecimiento**
happy **alegre, contento/a; feliz** (*pl.* **felices**); to be happy (about) **alegrarse (de)**
hard-working **trabajador(a)**
hat **sombrero**
have **tener** (*irreg.*); (*auxiliary v.*) **haber** (*irreg.*); to have a good time **divertirse (ie, i);** to have just (*done something*) **acabar de** (+ *inf.*); to have something to (say, do . . .) **tener algo que (decir, hacer...);** to have stopovers **hacer** (*irreg.*) **escalas;** to have to (*do something*) **tener que** (+ *inf.*)
head **cabeza**
health **salud** *f.*
healthy **sano/a**
hear **oír** (*irreg.*)
heart **corazón** *m.*
heat(ing) **gas** *m.*
help *v.* **ayudar;** *n.* **ayuda**
her *poss.* **su**
here **aquí**
hi **hola**
highway **carretera**
his *poss.* **su**
history **historia**
hit **pegar (gu)**
hockey **hockey** *m.*
hold **contener** (*like* **tener**)
home **casa;** at home **en casa**
homework **tarea**
honeymoon **luna de miel**
hood (*car*) **capó**
hope *n.* **esperanza;** I hope that . . . **ojalá que** (+ *subj.*)
hors d'oeuvres **entremeses** *m. pl.*
horse **caballo;** to ride horseback **montar a caballo**
hot: it's hot (weather) **hace calor;** to be/feel hot **tener** (*irreg.*) **calor**
hotel: (luxury) hotel **hotel** (*m.*) **(de lujo)**
house **casa**
household *adj.* **doméstico/a**
housing *n.* **vivienda**
how **¿cómo?;** how are you? **¿cómo está(s)?, ¿qué tal?;** how many? **¿cuántos/as?;** how much? **¿cuánto/a?**
hundred **cien, ciento**
hungry: to be (very) hungry **tener** (*irreg.*) **(mucha) hambre**
hurry: to be in a hurry **tener** (*irreg.*) **prisa**
hurt **doler (ue);** to hurt oneself **hacerse** (*irreg.*) **daño**
husband **esposo**

I

ice **hielo**
if **si**
illness **enfermedad** *f.*
immediately **en seguida**
immigration **inmigración** *f.*
impression: to make a good/bad impression on someone **caerle** (*irreg.*) **bien/mal a alguien**
in **en;** in (the morning, evening, etc.) **de/por (la mañana, la noche, etc.)**
increase *v.* **aumentar;** *n.* **aumento**
incredible **increíble**
inequality **desigualdad** *f.*
inexpensive **barato/a**
inform **informar**
information **información** *f.*
injection **inyección** *f.;* to give (*someone*) an injection **ponerle** (*irreg.*) **una inyección**
inquire **preguntar**
insist: to insist (*on doing something*) **insistir (en** + *inf.*)
inspector **inspector(a)**
installments: in installments **a plazos**
instead of **en vez de**
intend **pensar (ie)** (+ *inf.*)
interesting: to be interesting to (*someone*) **interesarle a uno**
interview *v.* **entrevistar**
interviewer **entrevistador(a)**
inventory **inventario**
invite **invitar**
iron *v.* **planchar**

J

jacket **chaqueta**
January **enero**
jeans ***bluejeans*** *m. pl.*
job **trabajo, puesto**
joke **chiste** *m.*
juice **jugo**
July **julio**
June **junio**
just: just in case **por si acaso;** to have just (*done something*) **acabar de** (+ *inf.*)

K

key **llave** *f.;* (*on a keyboard*) **tecla**
kind **simpático/a**
king **rey** *m.*
kiosk **quiosco**
kitchen **cocina**
knife **cuchillo**
know **saber** (*irreg.*) (*a fact; how to*); **conocer (zc)** (*someone; to be acquainted with*)

L

lack **escasez** *f.* (*pl.* **escaseces**)
lacking: to be lacking **faltar**
ladder **escalera**
lamp **lámpara**
land *v.* **aterrizar (c)**
language: (computer) language **lenguaje** *m.*
large **grande**
last *v.* **durar;** *adj.* (in time) **pasado/a;** at last **por fin;** last night **anoche**
late *adj.* **atrasado/a;** *adv.* **tarde**
later **después;** see you later **hasta luego**
latest (most recent) **último/a**
laugh (at) **reírse (i, i) (de)**
law **ley** *f.*
lawyer **abogado/a**
lazy **perezoso/a**
lead: to lead a . . . life **llevar una vida...**
learn **aprender**
least: at least **por lo menos**
leave **irse** (*irreg.*); **salir** (*irreg.*); to leave *(behind)* **dejar;** to take leave (of) **despedirse (i, i) (de)**
left: on/to the left of **a la izquierda de**
leg **pierna**
lend **prestar**
letter (*correspondence*) **carta**
lettuce **lechuga**
liberty **libertad** *f.*
librarian **bibliotecario/a**
library **biblioteca**
license **licencia**
life **vida**
lift *v.* **levantar**
light *n.* **luz** *f.* (*pl.* **luces**)
like **gustar;** do you like . . . ? **¿te (le) gusta... ?;** no, I don't like . . . **no, no me gusta... ;** yes, I like . . . **sí, me gusta... ;** like that *adv.* **así**
likeable **simpático/a**
likewise **igualmente**
line **cola;** to stand in line **hacer** (*irreg.*) **cola**
listen (to) **escuchar**
little *adj.* **poco/a;** *adv.* **poco**
live **vivir**
living room **sala**
loan *n.* **préstamo**
lobster **langosta**
lodging **alojamiento**
long **largo/a**
look (at) **mirar;** to look for **buscar (qu)**
lose **perder (ie)**
lot: a lot *adv.* **mucho;** a lot of *adj.* **mucho/a**
love *v.* **querer** (*irreg.*); *n.* **amor** *m.*
luck **suerte** *f.*
luggage **equipaje** *m.*
lunch **almuerzo;** to have, eat lunch **almorzar (ue) (c)**
lungs **pulmones** *m.*
luxury **lujo**

M

machine: washing machine **lavadora**
magazine **revista**
maid **criada**
maintain (keep up) **mantener** (*like* **tener**)
make **hacer** (*irreg.*) (*p.p.* **hecho/a**)
mall: shopping mall **centro comercial**
man **hombre** *m.*
manager **director(a), gerente** *m., f.;* building manager **portero/a**
many **muchos/as**
March **marzo**
market (place) **mercado**
marriage **matrimonio**
married **casado/a**
marry **casarse (con)**
match (game) **partido**
matches **fósforos**
material **material** *m.*
mathematics **matemáticas**
matter **cuestión** *f.;* it doesn't matter (to me) (at all) **no (me) importa (nada)**
May **mayo**
meal **comida**
meat **carne** *f.*
mechanic **mecánico/a**
media: news media **prensa**
medicine **medicina**
memory (remembrance) **recuerdo;** (*computer*) **memoria**
menu **menú** *m.*
merchant **comerciante** *m., f.*
Mexican *n., adj.* **mexicano/a**
microcomputer **microcomputadora**
mile **milla**
milk **leche** *f.*
milkshake **batido**
mind: to keep/have in mind **tomar, tener** (*irreg.*) **en cuenta**
minute: free minute **rato libre**
mirror **espejo**
mischievous **travieso/a**
miss **señorita (Srta.)**
mistake: to make a mistake **equivocarse (qu)**
mom **mamá**
moment: at this very moment **en este momento**
Monday **lunes** *m.*
money **dinero;** (*currency*) **moneda**
monitor **monitor** *m.*
month **mes** *m.;* (once) a month **(una vez) al mes**
more **más**
morning **mañana;** good morning **buenos días;** in the morning **de/por la mañana**
mother **madre** *f.*
motorcycle **motocicleta**
mountain **montaña**
mouth **boca**
move **mudarse;** to move (*something*) **cambiar de lugar**
movie **película;** movie theater **cine** *m.;* movies **cine** *m.*
Mr. **señor (Sr.)** *m.*
Mrs. **señora (Sra.)**
much *adj.* **mucho/a;** *adv.* **mucho;** too much **demasiado**
museum **museo**
must **deber** (+ *inf.*)
my *poss.* **mi**

N

name (first) **nombre** *m.*; (last) **apellido;** my name is _____ **me llamo** _____; what is your name? **¿cómo se llama Ud.?, ¿cómo te llamas?**
named: to be named **llamarse**
nation **país** *m.*
nationality **nacionalidad** *f.*
natural resources **recursos** (*m.*) **naturales**
nature **naturaleza**
nauseated **mareado/a**
near *prep.* **cerca de**
necessary **necesario/a;** it is necessary **es necesario/preciso, hay que** (+ *inf.*)
need *v.* **necesitar**
neighbor **vecino/a**
neighborhood **barrio**
neither **tampoco**
nephew **sobrino**
nervous **nervioso/a**
net **red** *f.*
never **jamás, nunca**
new **nuevo/a**
news **noticias** *f.*, **novedades** *f.;* newscast **noticiero;** news media **prensa;** piece of news **noticia;** the bad news **lo malo;** the good news **lo bueno**
next *adj.* (*in time*) **próximo/a;** (*in order*) **siguiente;** *adv.* **luego**
nice **simpático/a; amable**
niece **sobrina**
night **noche** *f.;* at night **de/por la noche;** last night **anoche**
nine **nueve**
nineteen **diecinueve**
ninety **noventa**
ninth **noveno/a**
no *adv.* **no;** *adj.* **ningún, ninguno/a;** no one *pron.* **nadie;** no parking **prohibido estacionarse**
nobody **nadie**
noise **ruido**
none **ningún, ninguno/a**
North American *n.; adj.* **norteamericano/a**
nose **nariz** *f.*
not **no;** not any **ningún, ninguno/a;** not anybody **nadie;** not anything **nada;** not . . . at all **no... nada**
notebook **cuaderno**
nothing **nada;** nothing can be done about it **no hay más remedio**
novel **novela**
November **noviembre** *m.*

now **ahora**; right now **ahora mismo, en este momento, en la actualidad**
number **número**
nurse **enfermero/a**

O

obey **obedecer (zc)**
obligation **deber** *m.*
obtain **conseguir (i, i) (g)**
October **octubre** *m.*
of **de**
offer **ofrecer (zc)**
office **oficina;** (*medical*) **consultorio**
officer: police officer **policía** *m., f.*
oil **aceite** *m.*
okay: it's okay **está bien**
old **viejo/a**
older **mayor**
once **una vez**
one **un, uno/a**
only *adv.* **sólo, solamente**
open *v.* **abrir** (*p.p.* **abierto/a**)
open(ed) *adj.* **abierto/a**
operate (*machine*) **manejar, usar**
operation (*of a machine*) **manejo, uso**
or **o**
orange *n.* **naranja;** *adj.* **anaranjado/a**
order *v.* **mandar; pedir (i, i);** *prep.* in order to **para**
other *adj.* **otro/a;** *pron.* other people, others **los demás**
ought **deber** (+ *inf.*)
our *poss.* **nuestro/a**
out: to eat out **cenar fuera**
outside *adv.* **afuera**
outskirts **afueras**
oven **horno**
overcast: it's overcast (*weather*) **está nublado**
own *adj.* **propio/a**
owner **dueño/a**

P

pace **ritmo**
pack: to pack one's suitcases **hacer** (*irreg.*) (*p.p.* **hecho/a**) **las maletas**
package **paquete** *m.*
pain: to have a pain in **tener** (*irreg.*) **dolor de**
painting **pintura**
pair **par** *m.*
pants **pantalones** *m. pl.*
paper **papel** *m.;* term paper **trabajo**
pardon **perdón** *m.;* pardon me **perdone/discúlpeme** (*form. s.*)
parents **padres** *m. pl.*
park *v.* **estacionar (se);** *n.* **parque** *m.*
parking: no parking **prohibido estacionarse**
part **parte** *f.*
part-time **de tiempo parcial**
party **fiesta;** to give a party **hacer** (*irreg.*) / **dar** (*irreg.*) **una fiesta**
pass **pasar;** to pass through **recorrer**
passage (*ticket*) **pasaje** *m.*
passenger **pasajero/a**
Passover **Pascua**
passport **pasaporte** *m.*
past *adj.* **pasado/a**
pastime **pasatiempo**
pastry **pastel** *m.;* pastry shop **pastelería**
patient **paciente** *m., f.*
patio **patio**
pay (for) **pagar (gu)**
peace **paz** *f.* (*pl.* **paces**)
peas **arvejas**
peasant **campesino/a**
pen **bolígrafo**
pencil **lápiz** *m.* (*pl.* **lápices**)
people **gente** *f.s.*
performance (*show*) **función** *f.*
perhaps **tal vez, quizá(s)**
permit *v.* **permitir**
person **persona** *f.*
personal **personal**
personnel **Dirección** (*f.*) **de Personal;** personnel director **director(a) de personal**
pharmacy **farmacia**
photo (graph) **foto** *f.;* to take photos **sacar (qu) fotos**
photographic **fotográfico/a**
pick: to come by to pick up (*someone, something*) **pasar por**
picture **foto;** to take pictures **sacar (qu) fotos**
pie **pastel** *m.*
pill **pastilla**
pink **rosado/a**
place *v.* **poner** (*irreg.*) (*p.p.* **puesto/a**); *n.* **lugar** *m.;* (*in line*) **puesto;** to take place (in/at) **tener** (*irreg.*) **lugar, ser (en)**
plaid **de cuadros**
plan **plan** *m.*
plate **plato**
play *v.* (instrument) **tocar (qu);** (sports) **jugar (ue) (gu);** *n.* **comedia;** (*in a game*) **juego**
player **jugador(a)**
please **por favor;** please (*do something*) **favor de** (+ *inf.*); pleased to meet you **mucho gusto, encantado/a**
pleasing: to be pleasing **gustar**
plot **trama**
plumber **plomero/a**
police officer **policía** *m., f.*
pollute **contaminar**
pollution **contaminación** *f.*
pool: swimming pool **piscina**
poor **pobre**
population **población** *f.*
pork **cerdo**
portable **portátil**
porter **maletero**
position (job) **puesto**
possible **posible**
post office **correo**
postcard **tarjeta postal**
poster **cartel** *m.*
potato **papa;** French fried potato **(papa) frita**
practice *v.* **practicar (qu);** (*profession*) **ejercer (z)**
prefer **preferir (ie, i)**
preferable **preferible**
preference **preferencia**
prepare **preparar**
prepared: to be prepared **estar listo/a**
prescription **receta**
present *n.* **regalo**
press *n.* **prensa**
pressure: to be under a lot of pressure **sufrir muchas presiones**
pretty **bonito/a, lindo/a**
price **precio;** fixed price **precio fijo**
printer **impresora**
processing: data processing **informática**
product **producto**
profession **profesión** *f.,* **carrera**
professor **profesor(a)**
program **programa** *m.;* to write (computer) programs **diseñar programas**
prohibit **prohibir**
protect **proteger (j)**
protest *v.* **protestar**
provided (that) **con tal que**
psychology **sicología**
public **público/a**
punish **castigar (gu)**
pure **puro/a**
purple **morado/a**
purse **bolsa**
put **poner** (*irreg.*) (*p.p.* **puesto/a**); to put on (*clothing*) **ponerse**

Q

quarter: it's a quarter after (two, three . . .) **son las (dos, tres...) y cuarto**
queen **reina**
question **pregunta;** (matter) **cuestión** *f.;* to ask a question **hacer** (*irreg.*) **una pregunta**
quit **dejar**
quiz **prueba**

R

racket **raqueta**
radio (set) **radio** *f.*
rain *v.* **llover (ue)**
raincoat **impermeable** *m.*
raise *v.* **levantar;** *n.* **aumento**
rancher **ranchero/a**
react **reaccionar**
read **leer (y)**
ready: to be ready **estar listo/a**
real **verdadero/a**
really **de verdad**
reason **razón** *f.;* the reason why, for which **la razón por la cual**
receive **recibir**
recommend **recomendar (ie)**
red **rojo/a**
reduction (sale) **rebaja**

refrigerator **refrigerador** *m.*
regret **sentir (ie, i)**
relationship **relación** *f.*
relative (*family*) **pariente** *m.*
remain **quedar**
remember **recordar (ue); acordarse (ue) de**
remove **quitar**
rent *v.* **alquilar;** *n. m.* **alquiler**
renter **inquilino/a**
repair *v.* **arreglar;** repair shop **taller** *m.*
repeat **repetir (i, i)**
reporter **reportero/a**
requirement **requisito**
reservation **reservación** *f.*
reserve **reservar**
resign: to resign (from) **renunciar (a)**
resolve **resolver (ue)** (*p.p.* **resuelto/a**)
resources: natural resources **recursos** (*m.*) **naturales**
responsibility **responsabilidad** *f.*, **deber** *m.*
rest *v.* **descansar**
restaurant **restaurante** *m.*
résumé **currículum** *m.*
return **regresar; volver (ue)** (*p.p.* **vuelto/a**); to return (*something*) **devolver** (*p.p.* **devuelto/a**)
rhythm **ritmo**
rice **arroz** *m.*
rich **rico/a**
ride: to ride a bike **pasear en bicicleta;** to ride horseback **montar a caballo**
right *n.* (*political*) **derecho;** *adj.* **derecho/a;** on/to the right of **a la derecha de;** right? **¿verdad?, ¿no?;** right now **ahora mismo, en este momento, en la actualidad;** to be right **tener** (*irreg.*) **razón**
road **camino**
room **cuarto, sala;** (*in a hotel*) **habitación** *f.*; dining room **comedor** *m.*; room and breakfast plus one other meal **media pensión** *f.*; room and full board **pensión** (*f.*) **completa;** waiting room **sala de espera**
roommate **compañero/a de cuarto**
round-trip *adj.* **de ida y vuelta**
rug **alfombra**
rule *v.* **gobernar (ie)**
run **correr;** (*operate*) **funcionar;** to run into (collide) **chocar (qu) con;** to run out of **acabar**

S

sad **triste**
salad **ensalada**
salary **sueldo**
sale **rebaja**
salesperson **vendedor(a)**
salmon **salmón** *m.*
same **mismo/a;** it's all the same to me **me da igual**
sandal **sandalia**
sandwich **sándwich** *m.*
Saturday **sábado**
save (*a place*) **guardar;** (*money*) **ahorrar**
savings account **cuenta de ahorros**
say **decir** (*irreg.*) (*p.p.* **dicho/a**)
school **escuela;** grade school teacher **maestro/a**
sciences **ciencias**
screen **monitor** *m.*; **pantalla**
search *v.* **registrar;** *n.* **busca;** in search of **en busca de**
season *n.* **estación** *f.*
seat *v.* **sentar (ie);** *n.* **asiento;** (*in a theater*) **butaca**
second **segundo/a**
secretary **secretario/a**
section **sección** *f.*; (non)smoking section **sección de (no) fumar**
see **ver** (*irreg.*) (*p.p.* **visto/a**); see you around **nos vemos**
seem **parecer (zc)**
sell **vender;** they sell everything **venden de todo**
send **mandar**
September **se(p)tiembre** *m.*
servant **criado/a**
serve **servir (i, i)**
service **servicio**
set: to set the table **poner** (*irreg.*) (*p.p.* **puesto/a**) **la mesa**
seven **siete**
seventeen **diecisiete**
seventh **séptimo/a**
seventy **setenta**
shame: it is/what a shame **es (una)/qué lástima**
shampoo **champú** *m.*
share *v.* **compartir**
shave (oneself) **afeitar(se)**
shellfish **mariscos** *m. pl.*
ship **barco**
shirt **camisa;** T-shirt **camiseta**
shoe **zapato**
shop **tienda;** (repair) shop **taller** *m.*
shopkeeper **comerciante** *m., f.*
shopping **de compras;** shopping mall **centro comercial**
short (*in height*) **bajo/a;** (*in length*) **corto/a**
shortage **escasez** *f.* (*pl.* **escaseces**)
shot **inyección** *f.*; to give (*someone*) a shot **ponerle** (*irreg.*) **una inyección**
should **deber** (+ *inf.*)
show (performance) **función** *f.*
shower **ducha**
shrimp **camarones** *m. pl.*
sick **enfermo/a;** to get sick **enfermarse**
sickness **enfermedad** *f.*
sidewalk **acera**
signal: traffic signal **semáforo**
silk **seda**
silly **tonto/a;** silly thing **tontería**
since **ya que**
sing **cantar**
single (*not married*) **soltero/a;** single room (*in a hotel*) **habitación** (*f.*) **para una persona**
sister **hermana**
sit: to sit down **sentarse (ie)**
six **seis**
sixteen **dieciséis**
sixth **sexto/a**
sixty **sesenta**
skate *v.* **patinar**
ski *v.* **esquiar;** *n.* **esquí** *m.*
skirt **falda**
skyscraper **rascacielos** *m. s.*
sleep **dormir (ue, u)**
sleepy: to be sleepy **tener** (*irreg.*) **sueño**
slender **delgado/a**
slow **lento/a**
small **pequeño; chico/a**
smart **listo/a**
smile *v.* **sonreír (i, i)**
smoke *v.* **fumar;** *n.* **humo**
smoking: (non)smoking section **sección** (*f.*) **de (no) fumar**
snow *v.* **nevar (ie)**
so *adv.* **así;** so-so **así así;** *conj.* so that **para que**
soap **jabón** *m.*
soccer **fútbol** *m.*
social: social worker **trabajador(a) social**
socks **calcetines** *m.*
sofa **sofá** *m.*
soft drink **refresco**
solitude **soledad** *f.*
solve **resolver (ue)** (*p.p.* **resuelto/a**)
some **algún, alguno/a**
someone **alguien**
something **algo**
sometimes **a veces**
son **hijo**
soon: as soon as **en cuanto, tan pronto como**
soup **sopa**
Spanish *n., adj.* **español(a);** Spanish language **español** *m.*
speak **hablar**
speed **velocidad** *f.*
spend (*money*) **gastar;** (*time*) **pasar**
spoon **cuchara**
sport **deporte** *m.*
sports-minded *n., adj.* **deportista** *m., f.*
spring **primavera**
stadium **estadio**
stamp *n.* **sello**
stand: to stand in line **hacer** (*irreg.*) (*p.p.* **hecho/a**) **cola;** to stand up **levantarse**
start (*motor*) **arrancar (qu)**
station **estación** *f.*; bus station **estación de autobuses;** gas station **gasolinera, estación de gasolina;** station wagon **camioneta;** train station **estación del tren**
stationery **papel** (*m.*) **para cartas;** stationery store **papelería**
stay *v.* **quedarse**
steak **bistec** *m.*
steal *n.* (*bargain*) **ganga**
stereo equipment **equipo estereofónico**

stick: to stick out (*tongue*) **sacar (qu)**
still *adv.* **todavía**
stockings **medias**
stomach **estómago**
stop *v.* **parar;** to stop (*doing something*) **dejar de** (+ *inf.*)
stopovers: to have stopovers **hacer** (*irreg.*) (*p.p.* **hecho/a) escalas**
store: to store information **archivar la información;** department store **almacén** *m.*
stove **estufa**
straight ahead **todo derecho**
strange **extraño/a, raro/a**
street **calle** *f.*, **camino**
strike *v.* (hit) **pegar (gu);** *n.* (*labor*) **huelga**
striped **de rayas**
student **estudiante** *m., f.*
study **estudiar**
style **moda;** in the latest style **de última moda**
subject (*school*) **materia**
suburbs **afueras**
subway **metro;** subway stop **estación** (*f.*) **del metro**
suddenly **de repente**
sugar **azúcar** *m.*
suit **traje** *m.*
suitcase **maleta;** to pack one's suitcases **hacer** (*irreg.*) **las maletas**
summer **verano**
sunbathe **tomar el sol**
Sunday **domingo**
sunny: it's sunny (weather) **hace sol**
supper **cena**
support *v.* **apoyar**
surprise *n.* **sorpresa**
surprising: to be surprising to one **sorprenderle a uno**
sweater **suéter** *m.*
sweep **barrer**
sweets **dulces** *m.*
swim **nadar**
swimming **natación** *f.;* swimming pool **piscina**
swimsuit **traje** (*m.*) **de baño**
symptom **síntoma** *m.*

T

table **mesa;** end table **mesita**
take **tomar; llevar;** to take a trip **hacer** (*irreg.*) **un viaje;** to take a walk **dar** (*irreg.*) **un paseo;** to take away **quitar;** to take off (*clothing*) **quitarse;** to take off (*flight*) **despegar (gu);** to take out **sacar (qu);** to take photos **sacar fotos**
talk **hablar**
tall **alto/a**
tank **tanque** *m.*
taste *n.* **gusto**
tax **impuesto**
tea **té** *m.*
teach **enseñar**
team **equipo**
teaspoon **cucharita**
telephone **teléfono;** telephone number **teléfono**
television set **televisor** *m.*
tell **decir** (*irreg.*) (*p.p.* **dicho/a**); to tell about **contar (ue)**
temperature **temperatura**
ten **diez**
tenant **inquilino/a**
tennis **tenis** *m. s.*
tenth **décimo/a**
test **examen** *m.*
textbook **libro de texto**
thank you **gracias;** thank you very much, many thanks **muchas gracias**
that *adj.* **ese/a;** that (over there) **aquel, aquella;** that one *pron.* **ése/a; eso;** that one (over there) **aquél, aquélla; aquello;** *conj.* **que;** that which **lo que**
theater **teatro**
theme **tema** *m.*
then **luego**
there **allí;** there is, are **hay;** there was, were **había;** there will be **habrá**
these *adj.* **estos/as;** these (ones) *pron.* **éstos/as**
thin **delgado/a**
thing **cosa**
think **pensar (ie); creer (y);** I think so **creo que sí**
third **tercer, tercero/a**
thirsty: to be (very) thirsty **tener** (*irreg.*) **(mucha) sed**
thirteen **trece**
thirty **treinta**
this *adj.* **este/a;** this one *pron.* **éste/a; esto**
those *adj.* **esos/as;** those (over there) **aquellos/as;** *pron.* **ésos/as;** those (over there) **aquéllos/as**
thousand **mil**
three **tres**
throat **garganta**
Thursday **jueves** *m.*
thus **así**
ticket **boleto, billete** *m.;* (*for a performance*) **entrada;** (*fine*) **multa;** (*passage*) **pasaje** *m.*
tie **corbata**
time **hora; tiempo; vez** *f.* (*pl.* **veces**); (*period*) **época;** at the same time **a la vez;** at times **a veces;** at what time? **¿a qué hora?;** free time **ratos libres;** from time to time **de vez en cuando;** on time **a tiempo;** part-time **de tiempo parcial;** to have a bad time **pasarlo mal;** to have a good time **divertirse (ie, i), pasarlo bien;** what time is it? **¿qué hora es?**
tip (*to a bellhop, etc.*) **propina**
tire *n.* **llanta**
tired **cansado/a**
to **a**
toaster **tostadora**
tobacco stand/shop **estanco**
today **hoy**
together **juntos/as;** to get together (with) **reunirse (con)**
tomato **tomate** *m.*
tomorrow **mañana;** day after tomorrow **pasado mañana;** until tomorrow, see you tomorrow **hasta mañana**
tongue **lengua**
tonight **esta noche**
too much **demasiado**
toothpaste **pasta dental**
top: on top of **encima de**
topic **tema** *m.*
tourist class **clase** (*f.*) **turística**
toy **juguete** *m.*
trade (job) **oficio**
traffic **tráfico, circulación** *f.;* traffic signal **semáforo**
train **tren** *m.;* train station **estación** (*f.*) **del tren**
tranquil **tranquilo/a**
transportation: (means of) transportation **transporte** *m.*
travel **viajar**
traveler **viajero/a**
treatment **tratamiento**
tree **árbol** *m.*
trip **viaje** *m.;* round-trip *adj.* **de ida y vuelta;** to take a trip **hacer** (*irreg.*) (*p.p.* **hecho/a) un viaje**
trophy **trofeo**
true **verdadero/a**
try: to try to (*do something*) **tratar de** (+ *inf.*)
T shirt **camiseta**
Tuesday **martes** *m.*
tuna **atún** *m.*
turn (*a corner*) **doblar;** to be someone's turn **tocarle (qu) a uno;** to turn off (*lights, appliances*) **apagar (gu)**
TV set **televisor** *m.*
twelve **doce**
twenty **veinte**
twice **dos veces**
two **dos**
type **escribir** (*p.p.* **escrito/a) a máquina**
typewriter **máquina de escribir**

U

ugly **feo/a**
uncle **tío**
uncomfortable **incómodo/a**
under(neath) **debajo de**
understand **comprender**
unintentional: it was unintentional **fue sin querer**
university **universidad** *f.*
unless **a menos que**
unoccupied **desocupado/a**
unpleasant **antipático/a**
until **hasta que**
upset: to get upset **molestarse**
urgent **urgente**
use *v.* (*expend*) **gastar;** *n.* (*of a machine*) **uso, manejo**
utensils: eating utensils **utensilios de comer**

V

vacant **desocupado/a**
vacation **vacaciones** *f. pl.;* to be on vacation **estar** (*irreg.*) **de vacaciones;** to go on vacation **ir** (*irreg.*) **de vacaciones**
vacuum *v.* **pasar la aspiradora;** vacuum cleaner **aspiradora**
VCR **grabador** (*m.*) **de vídeo**
vegetables **verduras**
very **muy**
view **vista**
visit *v.* **visitar**
volleyball **vólibol** *m.*
vote **votar**

W

wait (for) **esperar**
waiter **camarero**
waiting room **sala de espera**
waitress **camarera**
wake **despertar (ie);** to wake up **despertarse (ie)**
walk **caminar;** to take a walk **dar** (*irreg.*) **un paseo**
wall **pared** *f.*
wallet **cartera**
want **desear; querer** (*irreg.*)
war **guerra**
warm: to be/feel warm **tener** (*irreg.*) **calor;** it's warm (weather) **hace calor**
wash (oneself) **lavar(se)**
washing machine **lavadora**
watch: *v.* **mirar**; to watch over **guardar;** *n.* **reloj** *m.*
water **agua** *f.* (*but:* **el agua**); water bed **cama de agua**
way: in that way **así;** one-way **de ida**
wear **llevar**
weather **tiempo;** what's the weather like? **¿qué tiempo hace?**
wedding **boda**
Wednesday **miércoles** *m.*
week **semana;** (once) a week **(una vez) a la semana**
weekend **fin** (*m.*) **de semana**
welcome **bienvenido/a;** you're welcome **de nada**
well **bien;** well (now) **pues . . .**
well-being **bienestar** *m.*
what (that which) **lo que;** what? **¿qué?, ¿cómo?;** what a . . . ! **¿qué** (+ *n.*)!; what is ______ like? **¿cómo es** ______**?;** what is your name? **¿cómo se llama Ud.?, ¿cómo te llamas?;** what time is it? **¿qué hora es?**
when **cuando;** when? **¿cuándo?**
where **donde;** where? **¿dónde?;** where (to)? **¿adónde?;** where are you from? **¿de dónde es Ud.?**
which **cual;** which? **¿cuál?;** that which **lo que**
while **mientras**
white **blanco/a**
who *rel. pron.* **que**; *sub. and obj. pron.* **quien;** who? **¿quién?;** *pl.* **¿quiénes?**
whole **entero/a**
whom? **¿quién?;** *pl.* **¿quiénes?**
whose? **¿de quién?**
why **por qué;** why? **¿por qué?;** that's why **por eso**
wife **esposa**
win **ganar**
window **ventana**
windy: it's windy (*weather*) **hace viento**
wine **vino;** red (white) wine **vino tinto (blanco)**
winter **invierno**
wish *n.* **esperanza;** I wish that . . . **ojalá que** (+ *subj.*)
with **con;** with me **conmigo;** with you (*fam.*) **contigo**
without **sin**
witness *n.* **testigo/a**
woman **mujer** *f.*
wool **lana**
work *v.* **trabajar; funcionar** (*machines*); *n.* **trabajo**
worker **obrero/a**
worried **preocupado/a**
worry (about) **preocuparse (por)**
worse **peor**
worth: to be worth **valer (valgo);** to be worth the trouble **valer la pena**
wrong: to be wrong **equivocarse (qu)**

Y

yard **patio**
year **año;** to be ______ years old **tener** (*irreg.*) ______ **años;** New Year's Eve **Noche Vieja**
yellow **amarillo/a**
yes **sí**
yesterday **ayer;** day before yesterday **anteayer**
yet **todavía**
you *sub. pron.* **tú** (*fam. s.*); **usted (Ud., Vd.)** (*form. s.*); **vosotros/as** (*fam. pl., Sp.*); **ustedes (Uds., Vds.)** (*pl.*); *d.o.* **te, os, lo/la, los, las;** to, for you *i.o.* **te, os, le, les;** *obj. of prep.* **ti, Ud., Uds.**
young **joven**
younger **menor**
your *poss.* **tu** (*fam. s.*); **vuestro/a** (*fam. pl., Sp.*); **su** (*form.*)
youth **joven** *m., f.;* as a youth **de joven**

Z

zero **cero**

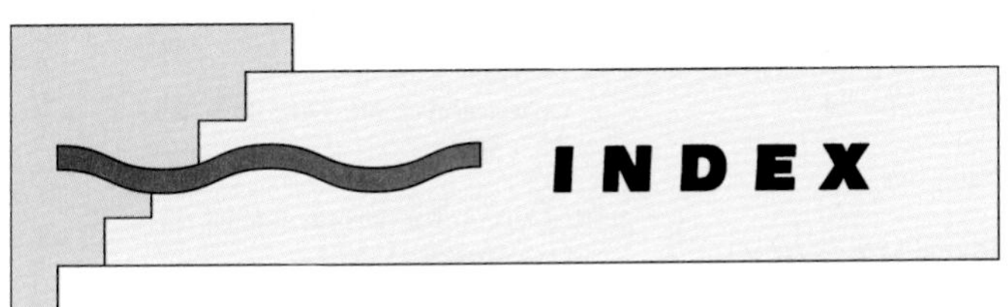

INDEX

In this index, *Study Hints* and vocabulary topic groups are listed by individual topic as well as under those headings. **A propósito...** and **Notas comunicativas sobre el diálogo** sections appear only as a group, under those headings.

(credits continued from copyright page)

88 © Stuart Cohen / Comstock; *97* © Stuart Cohen / Comstock; *117* © Peter Menzel; *118 (from top)* © Rene Burri / Magnum; © Stuart Cohen / Comstock; © Matthew Naythons / Stock, Boston; *120* © Robert Frerck / Click, Chicago; *135* © Chip & Rosa Maria de la Cueva Peterson; *152* © Peter Menzel; *167* © Abbas / Magnum; *181* © Peter Menzel; *190* © Hugh Rogers / Monkmeyer; *195* © H. Gruaert / Magnum; *205* © Owen Franken / Stock, Boston; *210 (top)* © Diana Lyn; *210 (bottom left)* © Bob Daemmrich; *210 (bottom right)* © Bob Daemmrich / Stock, Boston; *211 (top left)* © Bob Daemmrich / Stock, Boston; *211 (top right)* © Bettmann Newsphotos; *211 (center right)* © Carmen Lomas Garza, 1987; *211 (bottom left)* © Fabio Nosotti / LGI; *213* © Bill Ross / Click, Chicago; *217* © Stuart Cohen/ Comstock; *226* © Chip & Rosa Maria de la Cueva Peterson; *256* © Audrey Gottlieb / Monkmeyer Press, *259* © Peter Menzel; *272* © Robert Frerck / Click, Chicago; *288* © Stuart Cohen / Comstock; *301* © Paul Conklin / Monkmeyer Press; *302 (top right);* © Mario Ruiz / *Time* Magazine; *302 (center left)* © AP / Wide World Photos; *303 (top left)* © Arlene Collins / Monkmeyer Press; *303 (center right)* © Alan Carey / The Image Works; *305* © Harriet Gans / The Image Works; *316* © Peter Menzel; *328* © Mark Antman / The Image Works; *333* © Chip & Rosa Maria de la Cueva Peterson; *337* © Robert Frerck / Click, Chicago; *348* © Hugh Rogers / Monkmeyer; *359* © Stuart Cohen / Comstock; *371 (top left)* Courtesy of McMurtrey Gallery, Houston; *371 (bottom left)* © Larry Mangino / The Image Works; *372 (clockwise from top left)* © Jack Buxbaum / John F. Kennedy Center for Performing Arts; © Max Toro / courtesy of Casals Music Festival; © AP / Wide World Photos; © Mimi Forsyth / Monkmeyer Press; © Gail Greig / Monkmeyer Press; *373* © Katherine McGlynn / The Image Works; *375* © Robert Frerck / Click, Chicago; *386* © Peter Menzel; *397* © Peter Menzel; *405* © Peter Menzel; *418* © Ulrike Welsch; *426* © Joe Marquette / Reuters/Bettmann Newsphotos; *441 (bottom left)* © John Henebry, Jr. / Henebry Photography; *441 (bottom right)* © John Henebry, Jr. / Henebry Photography; *442 (top left)* © Owen Franken / Stock, Boston; *442 (top center)* © D. Goldberg / Sygma; *442 (bottom left)* © UPI / Bettmann Newsphotos; *443 (from top)* © Hugh Rogers / Monkmeyer Press; © Bendick Assoc. / Monkmeyer Press; © Chip & Rosa Maria de la Cueva Peterson; *444* © Ph. Ledru / Sygma, *446* © Peter Menzel; *457* © Alan Carey / The Image Works; *468* © Peter Menzel; *476* © Hugh Rogers / Monkmeyer Press; *487* © Owen Franken / Stock, Boston; *496* © Stuart Cohen / Comstock; *508 (bottom left)* © D. & J. Heaton / Click, Chicago; *508 (bottom right)* © Reuters / Bettmann Newsphotos; *509 (bottom left)* © Peter Menzel; *509 (bottom right)* © Larry Mangino / The Image Works; *510 (top right)* © Mark Antman / The Image Works; *510 (center left)* © Robert Frerck / Click, Chicago; *510 (bottom left)* © Paul L. Meredith / Click, Chicago; *511 (left)* © Peter Menzel; *511 (right)* Museum of Modern Art, New York (Mrs. Simon Guggenheim Fund); *512* © Peter Menzel; *523* © Peter Menzel; *533* © Chip & Rose Maria de la Cueva Peterson; *534* © Stuart Cohen / Comstock; *539 (top right)* © Christina Del Villar; *539 (center left)* © Robert Frerck / Click, Chicago; *539 (center right)* © Beryl Goldberg; *539 (bottom right)* © Brian Seed / Click, Chicago; *540* © Jorge Gracia

Realia *page 7, 12, 183, and 202 Los Domingos de ABC*; *13* Ansa International; *20* © *Diario 16*; *32* Cia. Papelería Escolar; *34* Courtesy of Caribbean University College; *44, 55, 147, 244, 260, 263, 269, 462, 465, 476, 483, 488, and 492* © Quino; *61 and 81 Telva*, Ediciones Conica; *70* AMA, Distribuciones Hogar; *84, 450, 456, and 505* © A. Mingote; *89* Courtesy of Thom McAn Shoe Company; Peanuts reprinted by permission of United Feature Syndicate, Inc.; *93, 124, and 206 Diez minutos*; *111 Tiempo*; *133 and 156 La Estrella*; *172 and 186 Muy interesante*; *176* © "El País Semanal"; *207* © PIB; *216 Cambio 16*; *232 Natura*; *235* RENFE; *241* Iberia Airlines of Spain; *242* Mexicana Airlines; *243* (*left*) Termas de Chillan; *243* (*right*) LanChile Airlines; *245 Nueva*; *246 Video Grama*—Holanda Comunicaciones S.A.; *249* Unique; *268* © A.L.I., Brussels; *442* (*middle*) © Revista Apsi, Santiago, Chile; *442* (*bottom*) Reuters Information Services; *447* El Fortin Diario; *473* Banco Central; *491* Tunon; *530* Hoteles Krystal.

Readings *page 211 (top)* from "Yo soy hijo de la tierra," by Mario A. Benítez, first published in *The Americas Review* (formerly *Revista Chicano–Riqueña*), Vol. 3, No. 4 (Fall, 1975); *211 (middle)* from "Voces del barrio," by Rolando Hinojosa, México-Texano, professor of English, University of Texas at Austin; *301* from "El entrepuente del sol," by Ralph Rewes, *Miami Mensual; 303* (*top*) from "El bilingüismo en Hialeah," by Ralph Rewes, *Miami Mensual; 303* (*bottom*) Courtesy of Bilingual Review/Press (Arizona State University), from Elías Miguel Muñoz, *En estas tierras*/In This Land (1989); *372* from "Down These Mean Streets," by Piri Thomas / © Alfred A. Knopf, Inc.; *373* from "This is not the place where i was born," from *La Bodega Sold Dreams,* 2nd ed., by Miguel Piñero (Arte Publico Press of the University of Houston), © 1985; *443* from *"El final de un problema,"* © *Ercilla* (Chile); *444* from an interview with Mario Vargas Llosa, *Cambio 16* (Madrid), January 4, 1988; *506* from *¿Crees en lo que haces?* © *Dunia* Magazine (Spain); *509* from "La otra cara de Euskadi," *Cambio 16* (Madrid), January 4, 1988.

INSTRUCTOR'S EDITION

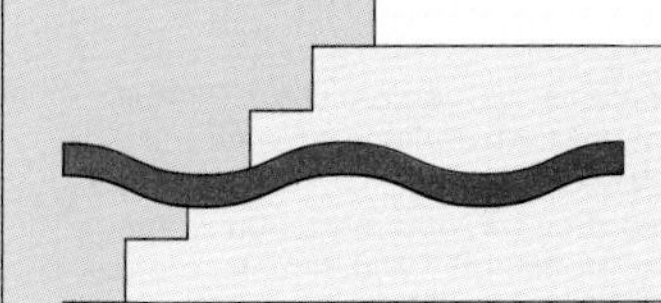

SUPPLEMENTARY MATERIALS FOR *VOCABULARIO: PREPARACIÓN* SECTIONS

NOTE:
- See also models for vocabulary presentation and other materials in Supplementary *Vocabulario: Preparación* Materials, chapter by chapter, in the Instructor's Manual.
- See also suggestions for using the Random House Spanish Video Program with the third edition of ***Puntos de partida***, in the Instructor's Manual.
- See also Listening Comprehension Activities (tapes and booklet) that accompany the third edition.
- See also exercise-specific suggestions on the pages of the Instructor's Edition.

CAPÍTULO 1

Suggestions: *¿Dónde? La universidad*, etc.

- Hold up objects or point to appropriate persons in classroom or in magazine or text pictures; model pronunciation while students listen. Use both definite and indefinite articles.
- Pronounce 7–8 vocabulary words at random. Students identify the "class" of word with the appropriate interrogative word from vocabulary list headings.
- Identify several objects or persons (point to them, show pictures, etc.), alternating correct and incorrect identifications. Students respond *sí* or *no*.
- Indicate objects or persons, offering a choice: *¿Qué es esto, una mesa o una silla?*, etc. Students give correct answer.
- Use *¿Qué es esto?* alone, indicating objects and persons but giving no prompting cue. Students answer on their own.
- **Emphasis:** Pay special attention to pronunciation of cognates.
- **Point out with things:** the/a/an is sometimes *el/un*, sometimes *la/una*. Students will learn the concept of gender later; for now, they should just listen for these words.
- **Point out for persons:** *el consejero* for male counselor, *la consejera* for female counselor. (**Note:** exact equivalent of U.S. academic counselor does not exist in most Hispanic countries.)
- **Optional:** *el borrador, la cafetería, la pizarra, la puerta, el pupitre, la tiza, la ventana*

Suggestions: *Las materias*

- Model names of academic subjects.
- Optional: *Más materias: la antropología, la biología, las comunicaciones, la contabilidad* (accounting), *la economía, la filosofía, la física, la geografía, la geología, la ingeniería, las lenguas, la literatura, la química, la sociología*. **Note:** many *-ía* cognates; *la informática = la computación.* **Suggestion:** Dictation practice with optional subjects, stressing cognate recognition.
- ***Asociaciones:*** Students give as many words as possible that they associate with these words: *las ciencias, la sicología, la biblioteca, el diccionario, el lápiz, el comercio.*

CAPÍTULO 2

Suggestions: *La familia y los parientes*

- Using the names in Exercise A as a guide, build up family tree on board (with stick figures, circles, or similar symbols). Start with recognizable cognates *padre* (*papá*) and *madre* (*mamá*); do two family members at a time, assigning first names and defining relationship as you go along; students just listen during this phase.
- After several generations are on the board, go back and check comprehension, asking questions with alternatives: *¿Quién es, el abuelo o el padre?,* etc.
- Continue procedure until all vocabulary words from *La familia y los parientes* have been presented.
- **Optional vocabulary:** *el suegro/la suegra, el cuñado/la cuñada, el yerno/la nuera.* **Suggestion:** Use optional vocabulary to extend all exercises.
- **Point out:** Use of masculine plural form—*el abuelo + la abuela = los abuelos*, etc.
- **Oral Drill:** Give feminine equivalent of *el padre, el abuelo*, etc.; give masculine equivalent of *la tía, la esposa*, etc.
- **Optional:** Students draw their own family trees and discuss them.

Optional: Expressing Affection

- **Presentation**
  Las familias hispanas usan muchos términos de cariño.
  los padres a los hijos
  mi hijo (*mi'jo*), *mi hija* (*mi'ja*)
  nené/nene, nena
  cielo (lit. heaven)
  cariño
  corazón (lit. heart)
  amor (lit. love)
  los hijos a los padres
  papá, papi, papito, papaíto
  mamá, mami, mamita, mamaíta
  Es común también el uso frecuente de los diminutivos, que conotan tamaño (size) *o cariño.*
  masculino: + –ito Juan → Juanito; Luis → Luisito; papá → papito
  femenino: + –ita Elena → Elenita; Carmen → Carmencita; mamá → mamita
- **Point out:** Role reversal in many Hispanic families re use of affection terms: parents call children *mami/papi*, spouses call each other *mi hijo/mi hija*. Use of *mi hijo/mi hija* among close friends.
- **Suggestion:** Use diminutives freely, as appropriate, as you speak Spanish in class. They will be used in exercises, dialogues, etc., in text from this point on, without glossing.

Suggestions: *Adjectivos*

- Present adjectives in pairs or semantic groups (as organized in box), using magazine drawings/photos, names of famous people, and people in class. Suggestions for negative adjectives: *feo* ("Gremlins," "The Alien," Frankenstein), *gordo* (Orson Welles, Pavarotti, John Candy, comic strip character Gordo), *malo* (Dennis the Menace, Darth Vader), *tonto* (Jerry Lewis, Steve Martin, Chevy Chase).
- Do several pairs; then go back and check comprehension, offering students alternatives: *¿Es alto o bajo Wilt Chamberlain?*, etc.
- **Point out:** *bajo* refers to height, *corto* to length; *joven* is used with people, *nuevo* with things; *guapo* refers to males/females, *bonito* usually only to females.
- **Preliminary exercise:** *¿Cuál es el antónimo de rico? ¿de bajo?*
- **Preliminary exercise:** Name famous people or people in class, using adjectives. Students verify comprehension with *sí* or *no*. Use many females so students hear adjective agreement. Example: *Miss Piggy es fea.*

Suggestions: *Los números 31–100*

- Ask, *¿Cómo se dice* twenty-one?, *¿*twenty-two? etc.
- Use the drawing exercise (*Continúe...*) to get students to produce numbers 31–39. **Emphasis:** They must be written as three words even though they sound like one.
- Model 40, 50, . . . 100. **Point out:** *-a* of *treinta, cuarenta*, etc., in contrast to the *-e* of *veinte.*
- **Counting:** whole class (40–49, 50–59); count off by students (60–69, 70–79); individual student counts (80–89, 90–99).
- Count by 10s, 0–100; by 5s, 0–100.
- Write on board: *un coche, cuarenta y un coches; una mesa, cuarenta y una mesas.* Point out similarities and emphasize use of *un* and *una*, not *unos* and *unas*, even though *coches* and *mesas* are plural.

Note: *Ciento* is used to form numbers greater than 100: *ciento uno, ciento dos*, etc. (See Ch. 3.)

Optional: If you taught 24-hour clock in *Ante todo*, review concept and add examples using numbers over 30: 3:40 *Son las tres* (*y*) *cuarenta.* 6:55 *Son las seis* (*y*) *cincuenta y cinco.*

Note: Expressing Age

- Introduction of singular forms of *tener.*
- Model age dialogue with several students, asking about the ages of some of their relatives.

Preliminary exercise (listening): Which is larger?: *¿ 30 ó 40? ¿60 ó 70? ¿50 ó 5? ¿60 ó 50? ¿100 ó 50? ¿13 ó 30? ¿40 ó 14? ¿60 ó 100?*, etc. (Note: Accent is required on word *o* when used between digits so it will not be read as part of number.)

CAPÍTULO 3

Suggestions: *De compras*

- Quickly model words and phrases.
- *Dé el antónimo: ¿comprar? ¿tienda pequeña? ¿vender muy poco? ¿pagar el precio indicado? ¿un supermercado grande? ¿caro? ¿de la época de los años 20?*
- Discuss Hispanic concept of *mercado* and *tienda.* Point out existence of large department stores as well as of small shops and open-air markets. Emphasize *el centro comercial* for student use in describing their own customs.
- Explain meaning of *regatear;* contrast with *precio fijo.* To help avoid stereotypes, point out situations in which one bargains in U.S.: buying cars, shopping in flea markets, etc.
- **Emphasis:** *de* + noun phrases to express what something is made of.

Optional exercise: *¿De qué son estos objetos?* (What are these objects made of?) *¿de metal? ¿de papel? ¿de plástico? ¿de madera?* **1.** *el dinero* **2.** *el lápiz* **3.** *el libro* **4.** *el cuaderno* **5.** *el bolígrafo* **6.** *la mesa* **7.** *la guitarra* **8.** *el refrigerador* **9.** *la fotografía* Note reentry of this topic in Ch. 8 (*Notas lingüísticas:* More About Describing Things.)

- ***Asociaciones:*** What words do you associate with *comprar, el almacén, el precio, la librería, pagar, el centro, el centro comercial*?
- ***Definiciones:*** You give definitions; students give word defined. **1.** *el antónimo de comprar* **2.** *una tienda grande donde venden de todo* **3.** *la cantidad de dinero que es necesario pagar* **4.** *el antónimo de pagar el precio fijo* **5.** *la parte céntrica de una ciudad*

Suggestions: *La ropa:*

- Model pronunciation of clothing items, pointing out items in class or in drawings/magazine photos. You may need to have drawings of *el traje, la chaqueta, la corbata, el abrigo, el impermeable, el traje de baño.* Stop after every 3–4 items to go back and review, indicating item and asking students: *¿Es una blusa o una camisa? ¿Es una camisa o un suéter?*, etc.
- **Optional:** *la gorra* (cap), *el anillo, los pendientes/los aretes, el collar.*
- **Listening exercise: *¿Sí o no?*** Make statements about what students are wearing (*Roberto lleva abrigo.*). Other students respond *sí* or *no*, as appropriate. **Variation:** Students invent similar sentences about classmates.

Suggestions: *Notas comunicativas:*

- Note reentry of *¿verdad?. ¿No?* = new material.
- **Point out:** There are many tag questions in English (e.g., Won't you?, Doesn't he?, Is she?, Will they?, etc.). English question tags correspond to subject of sentence; in Spanish they are invariable.

Preliminary exercise: *¿Sí o no?*: 1. *Ud. trabaja en la biblioteca, ¿no?* **2.** *Ud. siempre llega tarde a clase, ¿verdad?* **3.** *Ud. lleva* bluejeans *hoy, ¿verdad?* **4.** *Ud. toma café por la mañana, ¿no?* **5.** *Uds. estudian todos los días, ¿verdad?* **6.** *Uds. llegan a la universidad a las seis de la mañana, ¿no?*

Suggestions: *Los colores:*

- Model words and phrases using clothing students are wearing. Verify student comprehension periodically, with *¿sí o no?* questions.
- **Optional:** *beige* (pronounced with English *j* sound at end)
- Begin to use nominalized forms as you review colors. Example: *La camisa de Janet es roja. Y la de Susie, ¿es roja también?* (See footnote, page 92).

Suggestions: *Los números 100 y más*

- Use drawing follow-up to emphasize singular form of *mil*/plural form of *millones.*
- Model pronunciation of hundreds forms. Use hundreds forms in addition and subtraction problems, with students first verifying comprehension (*¿sí o no?*) and then giving correct answer.
- **Point out: (1)** Irregular stems of 500 (*quin-*, not *cinco*), 700, 900. **(2)** One/a thousand = *mil; un* not used. **(3)** Gender (*-cientas*) before feminine nouns. **(4)** No *y* in *ciento uno, ciento dos*, etc. *Y* occurs only between 10s and 1s digits.
- Write more complex (i.e., 154, 672) numbers on board. Students read them aloud.
- Math problems: *¿Cuántos son... ?* Again, more complex than earlier problems you did when introducing forms.
- ***¿Cómo se dice?* 1.** 500 men, 500 women; 700 male professors, 700 female professors **2.** 1,000, 2,000, 3,000 **3.** a million dollars/books (*¡OJO! un millón* ***de*** ____); 3 million Americans; 7 million *pesetas*
- **Optional:** Prepare students for learning to say years (presented in Ch. 5). Say the current year in Spanish, writing it on the board as you speak. Say a few more years, writing at the same time. Then begin to make mistakes as you write, asking students to verify with *sí o no.*

Preliminary exercise (listening): *¿Cuál es el número más grande?* 1. 100, 50, 60 **2.** 400, 600, 800 **3.** 2.000, 1.000.000, 50.000 **4.** 150, 500, 1.500 **5.** 900, 700, 500 **6.** 660, 960, 760

Preliminary exercise (speaking:) Write these numbers on the board and model them, then ask students to say them.

1. 2, 12, 20, 200
2. 3, 13, 30, 300
3. 4, 14, 40, 400
4. 5, 15, 50, 500
5. 6, 16, 60, 600
6. 7, 17, 70, 700
7. 8, 18, 80, 800
8. 9, 19, 90, 900
9. 1, 10, 100, 1.000, 1.000.000

CAPÍTULO 4

Suggestions: *¿Qué día es hoy?*

- Model pronunciation.
- Give day of the week; students say the next day.
- *¿Qué día de la semana asocia Ud. con... ? ¿las fiestas? ¿la religión? ¿el laboratorio de lenguas* (if your class has lab)? *¿la clase de español? ¿"Dallas"? ¿el fin de semana? ¿Thanksgiving? ¿las elecciones?*
- **Point out:** on Monday = *el lunes*; on Mondays = *los lunes.*
- **Point out:** Monday is first day of week on Hispanic calendars.
- *¿Cómo se dice en español?*: on Tuesday, on Wednesday, on Friday? on Fridays, on Saturdays?
- **Emphasis:** Days of week are not capitalized in Spanish.
- ***¿Sí o no?*: 1.** *Hoy es* ____. **2.** *Mañana es* ____. **3.** *No tenemos clase el miércoles.* **4.** *Los lunes tenemos examen.*

Optional: Students talk about their schedules using days of the week. ***Modelo:***

—¿Cuándo regresas a la biblioteca?
—A las dos y media. Necesito estudiar.
—¿No trabajas en la librería por la tarde?
—Sólo los martes y los jueves. Hoy no. Hoy tengo el laboratorio de química.

Suggestions: *Las relaciones sentimentales*

- Present vocabulary via definitions (see Exercise A.)
- **Optional:** *separado/a, divorciado/a. ¡OJO!*

Used with *estar*, forms of which are presented in this chapter.

- **Note:** *Un matrimonio* also means a married couple. *Amigo íntimo* means best friend.
- **Point out:** *Novio* and *novia* usually connote a more serious relationship in Hispanic cultures than boyfriend/girlfriend. (See *Notas culturales*, after B. Emphasize multiple English equivalents of *novio/a*.

Preliminary exercise:
1. *¿Qué palabras asocia Ud. con la amistad? ¿el amor? ¿una boda? ¿la luna de miel? ¿el novio? ¿la esposa?* **2.** *¿Cómo es el novio/la novia ideal? ¿Es rubio/a o moreno/a? ¿joven o viejo/a? ¿alto/a o bajo/a? ¿guapo/a o feo/a? ¿trabajador(a) o perezoso/a? ¿romántico/a o frío/a* (*cariñoso/a*)?

Suggestions: *¿Dónde está?: Las preposiciones*

- Demonstrate the meaning of the prepositions, using several classroom objects or pieces of furniture. Verify comprehension with *sí/no* questions after every few words.
- **Optional:** *junto a, al lado de*
- **Emphasis:** *antes de/después de* with time; *mi* (my) versus *mí* (me); *conmigo → contigo*; *para* = for, intended for.
- *Preguntas orales:* **1.** *¿Estoy delante de la mesa* (*clase*) *o detrás de la mesa* (*clase*)? **2.** *¿*(Student) *está lejos de* (*cerca de*) (student)? **3.** *¿Quién está a la derecha* (*izquierda*) *de ____?* **4.** *¿Quién está entre ____ y ____?*
- **Preliminary exercise:** *¡Qué confusión!* Students answer questions negatively, according to the model. ***Modelo:*** *¿Es la casa de Paco? → No, no es la casa de él.* **1.** *¿Es la blusa de Estela?* **2.** *¿Son los abrigos de los novios?* **3.** *¿Es la ropa de tus amigas?* **4.** *¿Es la chaqueta de Alfredo?* **5.** *¿Son los pantalones de los niños?*

Optional: Go back to the chapter-opener dialogue in Ch. 3, and review use of *conmigo* in context. Ask students to vary the dialogue with new information.

CAPÍTULO 5

Suggestions: *¿Qué hace hoy?*

- Model weather expressions. As you present each, ask students to tell what kind of clothing is worn for that weather.
- Review all weather expressions, asking, *¿Cómo está Ud. cuando...* (*hace sol, etc.*)? *¿Qué tiene ganas de hacer cuando... ?*

Point out:

- *Tiempo* = weather and time.
- *Hace frío/calor* (weather), *tener frío/calor* (people) (*Notas lingüísticas.* p. 154), *estar frío/caliente* (condition of things).
- **Optional:** *Hay mucha humedad/Está muy húmedo.*

Preliminary exercises:

- *¿Qué tiempo hace hoy?*
- *Imagine que hoy es un día fatal. ¿Qué tiempo hace?*
- *Ahora imagine que hoy es un día estupendo. ¿Qué tiempo hace?*
- ***Preguntas orales:*** **1.** *¿Llueve mucho en Inglaterra? ¿en el desierto Sahara?* **2.** *¿Nieva mucho en el Brasil? ¿en Minnesota?* **3.** *¿Hace mucho viento en Chicago? ¿en ____?* **4.** *¿Hace frío en Siberia? ¿en el Ecuador?* **5.** *¿Hace mucho sol en la Florida? ¿en España?* **6.** *¿Hace calor en Panamá? ¿en Alaska?*

Suggestions: *Notas lingüísticas*:

- **Note:** With these expressions, "very" is expressed with *mucho/a*.
  English I am very = adv. + adj.
  Spanish *Tengo mucha hambre* = adj. + noun.
- **Point out:** To be = to feel in these idioms.

Suggestions: *Los meses y las estaciones del año*

- Model months of year, linking them to seasons. Ask students what weather is like in each season.
- **Point out:** Many Spanish speakers do not pronounce or write *p* in *septiembre*. Months of year and seasons are not capitalized in Spanish.
- **Optional:** *¿A cuánto estamos hoy?*
- **Note:** *Mil* to express the year.

Optional: Information for presentation on the geography and climate of the Spanish-speaking world.

El hemisferio occidental se divide en dos continentes: la América del Norte y la América del Sur. La América Central no es un continente. Es parte de la América del Norte. Las Antillas, cadena de islas en el Mar Caribe, también forman parte la América Central.

En las diferentes zonas del mundo hispánico, hay muchos climas también diferentes. En los extremos geográficos (México al norte, Argentina y Chile al sur) hay cuatro estaciones: la primavera, el verano, el otoño y el invierno. En los países tropicales (desde la parte central de México hasta la parte norte de Chile) el clima alterna entre temporadas lluviosas y secas. Es común en Latinoamérica llamar a la temporada de lluvias «invierno», y a la temporada seca «verano». En este sentido, «el invierno», en Guayaquil, Ecuador, ocurre dos veces: una vez en mayo y otra vez en octubre. En el trópico la temperatura no varía con los meses del año. Depende de la altura. Hay tierras cálidas, templadas y frías.

La cordillera de los Andes bordea el Océano Pacífico a todo lo largo del continente de la América del Sur. Es una zona sísmica muy activa. Los Andes son la mayor cadena de montañas del mundo. Algunos picos son tan altos que están cubiertos de nieve todo el año, aunque algunos de ellos están muy cerca de la línea ecuatorial. El punto más alto del hemisferio occidental es el pico del Aconcagua, en la Argentina, a 6959 metros sobre el nivel del mar.

Si usted viaja a una de las ciudades más altas de Sudamérica y no está acostumbrado a vivir a estas alturas, al principio le va a ser difícil a su organismo acomodarse a la altitud. Si usted camina a paso normal por dos o tres cuadras, va a sentir que su cuerpo necesita más oxígeno y que le es difícil respirar bien. También va a notar más el efecto del alcohol sobre su cuerpo. Pero estos efectos no duran más que dos o tres semanas. Luego usted puede hacer todo: caminar, bailar y practicar los deportes.

Suggestions: Expressing Actions: *Hacer, poner,* and *salir*

Point out: irregular *yo* forms with *-g-*
Listening exercise: Give corresponding subject pronouns: *hago, hacemos, pongo, pone, pones, ponemos, sale, hacen, sales, salgo, salimos, hacéis*
Optional: *salir bien/mal en un examen*; *salir a* (*la calle, al patio, etc.*)

CAPÍTULO 6

Suggestions: *La comida, Las comidas*

- Work with half the vocabulary one day (up to and including *Las verduras*) and other half the second day.
- Use magazine pictures or other visuals to present words. Model pronunciation, then ask *sí/no* questions.
- *¿Qué comida o bebida asocia Ud. con estos colores?*: *negro, blanco, amarillo, verde, rojo, anaranjado.* (If used on first day of vocabulary presentation, allow students to have books open.)
- *¿Qué comida o bebida asocia Ud. con estos lugares?*: *Francia, Maine, la Florida, Inglaterra, México, China, Centroamérica, Colombia, San Francisco.*
- **Complete:** **1.** *Los niños beben ____.* **2.** *Se comen ____ y ____ en McDonald's.* **3.** *Con el desayuno se bebe ____.* **4.** *Los conejos* (draw ears on board) *comen ____.* **5.** *Para un almuerzo sencillo, se toma sopa y ____.* **6.** *Generalmente se comen ____ para el desayuno.* **7.** *Las Oreo son un tipo de ____.*
- ***Preguntas personales:*** **1.** *¿Toma Ud. mucho café/té? ¿Cuándo, por la mañana o por la noche? ¿Cuál contiene más cafeína, el café o el té? ¿Cuál prefiere Ud.?* **2.** *¿Bebe Ud. mucha cerveza? ¿mucho vino? ¿Qué tipo de vino prefiere, el vino tinto o el vino blanco? ¿Qué beben los estudiantes cuando estudian? ¿cuando miran la televisión? ¿cuando salen al bar?* **3.** *¿Come Ud. carne? ¿Qué tipo de carne prefiere? ¿el bistec, la hamburguesa, el jamón o las chuletas de cerdo? ¿Le gusta comer sándwiches? ¿De qué tipo? ¿de jamón? ¿de queso? ¿de jamón y queso?* **4.** *¿Come Ud. muchas ensaladas? ¿Toma la ensalada antes o después del plato principal?*
- *¿Qué comida es? Estoy tomando ____.* (Invent items for breakfast, lunch, and dinner. Students identify meal.)

Optional: *el cubierto* (*el tenedor, la cuchara, el cuchillo, la servilleta, el vaso, la copa, la taza*), *merendar, la merienda, el pavo, las uvas, la toronja, el helado de fresa* (*vainilla, chocolate*), *los caramelos*

Optional: Discuss the variety of words for names of food in the Spanish-speaking world. Examples: *papas* (L.A.) versus *patatas*

(Spain), *banana* versus *plátano*, *frijoles* versus *judías*, *camarones* versus *gambas*, *arvejas* versus *guisantes*, *tortilla* (flat pancake made of corn or flour) versus *tortilla* (*omelet*), *sándwich* (with *pan de molde*, like U.S. loaf) versus *bocadillo* (with *pan de barra*, like French bread).

Suggestions: *Oír, traer, ver*

- Model infinitives and use forms in short sentences, expanding to questions asked of students.
- Point out irregular forms. Compare *oír* to stem-changing verbs (similar pattern).
- *¡OJO!* Do not confuse *oír* (to hear) with *escuchar* (to listen); *traer* (to bring) with *llevar* (to take, carry; to wear); *ver* (to see) with *mirar* (to look at).
- **Emphasis:** *Oye/Oiga* as equivalent of English "Hey"

Preliminary exercises:

- *¡No vamos a volver a ese restaurante! Dé oraciones nuevas según las indicaciones.* **1.** *¡Hay tanto ruido! No oigo la música.* (*Juan y yo, tú, Uds., yo, Paula, vosotros*) **2.** *¡Hay poca luz* (light)*! No veo bien el menú.* (*Ud., nosotros, Andrés, los clientes, yo, tú, vosotras*) **3.** *¡Qué desgracia! ¡No traigo dinero!* (*tú, Eduardo, Uds., nosotros, vosotros*)
- ***Preguntas orales:*** ***1.*** *¿Oye Ud. bien en clase? ¿Se oye mucha música mexicana/francesa en la radio?* **2.** *¿Qué trae Ud. a clase todos los días? ¿Trae* (object)? **3.** *¿Puede Ud. ver bien sin gafas* (pantomime or draw on board)? *¿Puede ver la pizarra? ¿Ve Ud. un(a) ____ en esta clase* (*¡OJO!* not person)? **4.** *¿Qué programa de televisión ve con frecuencia? ¿Por qué? ¿Qué programa no ve nunca? ¿Por qué?* **5.** *¿Qué película nueva quiere ver? ¿Por qué?*

Suggestions: *El infinitivo:* Preposition + Infinitive

- **Emphasis:** Other preposition + infinitive structures students have already learned.
- **Preliminary exercise:**
  —*¿Quiere* (*comer*)*? —Acabo de comer.* (*ver la televisión, leer, ir al centro, desayunar, almorzar, cenar*)
  —*¿Quiere* (*estudiar más*)*? —No. Vuelvo a estudiar mañana.* (*ver la tele, jugar más, hablar con Pepe, ir de compras*)

CAPÍTULO 7

Suggestions: *¡Vamos de vacaciones!*

- Model each word, asking questions after saying each. Examples:
  El aeropuerto: *¿Es una persona o un lugar? ¿Qué tipo de transporte hay allí, un tren o un avión?*
  La azafata: *¿Es una persona o un lugar? ¿Trabaja en el aeropuerto o en el avión?* ***El camarero:*** *¿Trabaja con la azafata? ¿Hay camareros en todos los vuelos?*
  El vuelo: *¿Es una persona o una actividad? Generalmente, ¿tienen letras o números los vuelos? ¿Hay vuelos en tren?*
  El boleto: *¿Es un lugar o un objeto? ¿Se necesitan los boletos sólo para los vuelos en avión? etc.*
- **Point out:** *vacaciones* always plural; new meaning of *camarero*; *bajar* (to go down)/*subir* (to go up) versus *bajar de*/*subir a* with transport vehicles.
- ***Asociaciones:*** *¿Qué asocia Ud. con un avión/una azafata/un camarero/la sala de espera/la sección de fumar/las maletas/un boleto?*
- **Optional:** *el/la viajero/a, el cheque de viajero, la cola* (tail)

Suggestion: Use impersonal *se* in input, to prepare students for *Notas lingüísticas* in this section.

- ***¿Cierto o falso?*** (Do as *dictado* or just as listening comprehension. In either case, students correct false statements.) **1.** *Si hay una demora, el avión llega temprano.* **2.** *Los pasajeros hacen las maletas después de hacer un viaje.* **3.** *El avión está atrasado; no tenemos que esperarlo.* **4.** *Hay mucha gente en la sala de espera; no hay ningún asiento desocupado.* **5.** *La azafata nos sirve la comida durante el vuelo.* **6.** *Cuando se hace cola, generalmente es necesario esperar un poco.* **7.** *No quiero subir las maletas al avión; voy a facturarlas.* **8.** *El maletero es un objeto en que se pone la ropa.* **9.** *Los billetes sólo pueden ser de ida y vuelta.* **10.** *Al final de un vuelo, se baja del avión; no se sube.*
- ***Definiciones.*** *¿Qué palabra corresponde a las siguientes definiciones?* **1.** *La persona que nos ayuda con el equipaje en la estación de trenes.* **2.** *La cosa que se compra antes de hacer un viaje.* **3.** *El antónimo de* ***subir a***. **4.** *Se va allí cuando se hace un viaje en avión.* **5.** *Se va allí cuando se hace un viaje en tren.* **6.** *Las dos personas que nos ayudan durante un vuelo.*

Optional (*Notas comunicativas*): *Pasé... días/semanas en...*

Suggestions: *Notas lingüísticas*

Note: *Se* = English passive (*Se comen...*) has been presented for passive recognition and used frequently in listening comprehension exercises and reading passages.

Emphasis: difference between "personal you/they" (refers to definite persons) and "impersonal you/they" (does not refer to specific persons).

¿Cómo se dice en español?: **1.** You study a lot here. **2.** You don't talk in the library. **3.** You wear a suit in the office. **4.** You bargain at the market.

Preliminary exercise: Oral questions

1. *¿Qué lengua se habla en Francia? ¿en México? ¿en el Brasil? ¿en Alemania? ¿en Inglaterra? ¿en los Estados Unidos?* **2.** *¿Cuáles son las diferentes maneras de viajar? (Se viaja en...) ¿en avión? ¿en coche? ¿en tren? ¿en autobús? ¿en bicicleta?*

CAPÍTULO 8

Suggestions: *Los cuartos, los muebles y las otras partes de una casa*

- **Optional:** *el balcón, el dormitorio* (synonym for *alcoba*), *la entrada, la terraza, la cama de matrimonio/sencilla*
- Read through lists once while students listen and look at book; they need not repeat. Then, with books open, try *Definiciones* items.
  Definiciones: *¿Qué cuarto o mueble asocia Ud. con las siguientes definiciones?* **1.** *Allí se duerme.* **2.** *Allí se nada.* **3.** *Los niños nadan allí.* **4.** *Da iluminación.* **5.** *Donde se prepara la comida.* **6.** *Parte de una casa donde se pone el coche.* **7.** *Allí se pone la ropa.* **8.** *Cada cuarto tiene cuatro.* **9.** *Allí se habla con las visitas* (guests). **10.** *Allí se escriben las cartas.*
- **Point out:** *habitación* = room (in general); hotel room. Kitchen/Housekeeping vocabulary is presented in Ch. 9. Some furniture vocabulary is reentry of previously active material.
- ***Asociaciones:*** *¿Qué palabras asocia Ud. con... ? el coche, los picnics o las barbacoas, dormir, nadar, estudiar, la ropa, una cena elegante, el perro* (*el gato*), *los libros*
- ***Preguntas orales:*** ***1.*** *En su casa/apartamento, ¿tiene Ud. un cuarto favorito? ¿Cuál es? ¿Por qué lo prefiere?* **2.** *¿Tiene Ud. un mueble favorito? (un sillón especial, por ejemplo?) ¿Por qué lo prefiere?*
- **Optional:** Discuss Hispanic residences, especially as they differ from U.S. housing: interior patio; simple exterior; presence of servant's room; prevalence of condominiums. Describe Hispanic homes you have lived in or visited.

Suggestions: *Tengo... Quiero... Necesito...*

- **Note:** This section expands students' vocabulary for describing personal possessions and introduces the topic of the working world (expanded in Ch. 18, where the focus is on career choices and job interviews). The conceptual link between the two topics is working to earn money to buy the things we want or need. In addition, adult (versus typically college-aged students) should find the working-world vocabulary useful for self-expression.
- **Optional:** *la placa calentadora* (hot plate); *el/la director(a), el/la empleado/a, el puesto, la moto.*
- Read through lists once while students listen and look at the book; they need not repeat. Then, with books open, try preliminary *cierto/falso* items.
- ***¿Cierto o falso?*** ***1.*** *Martina Navratilova tiene muchos trofeos.* **2.** *Los estudiantes no pagan impuestos.* **3.** *Un cartel es una foto muy grande.* **4.** *Los peces viven en un acuario.* **5.** *Un compact disc es más barato que una radio portátil.* **6.** *Si Ud. recibe un aumento*

de sueldo, recibe más dinero. **7.** *Si a Ud. le gusta sacar fotos, necesita mucho equipo estereofónico.* **8.** *El jefe gana más que los empleados, generalmente.* **9.** *Cuando mi coche no funciona, tomo el autobús.* **10.** *Tenemos un nuevo autobús descapotable.*

- **Point out:** *el trabajo* = job, position *and* written work of many kinds, like a term paper; *conseguir* (*consigo*), like *seguir* (*sigo*); *la televisión* (the medium) versus *el televisor* (the set); *la fotografía* = *la foto* (emphasis: feminine).
- **Note:** *El computador* is also used in Latin America.
- ***Asociaciones:*** *¿Qué palabra o frase asocia Ud. con... ? diez velocidades, Picasso, la música, un jefe antipático, una película vieja, una familia grande, un compañero de cuarto antipático*
- ***Preguntas:*** **1.** *¿Qué tiene Ud. en su cuarto en la residencia (en su cuarto en casa)? Descríbalo detalladamente mientras los otros estudiantes intentan dibujarlo* (draw it). **2.** *¿Trabaja Ud. ahora o sólo estudia? ¿Es buen empleado (buena empleada) o es perezoso/a? ¿Recibe un buen sueldo? ¿Le gustaría cambiar de puesto? ¿Por qué sí o por qué no?* **3.** *¿Dónde trabaja? ¿Cómo es su jefe/a? Descríbalo/la. ¿Es muy simpático/a o es muy mandón (mandona)* (act out)? *¿Hay muchas diferencias entre un jefe y un profesor? ¿En qué son similares? ¿diferentes?*

Suggestions: *Notas lingüísticas:*

- Noun + *de* + noun; use of *ser* to express the material something is made of.
- In English a noun can be used to describe another noun; in Spanish, it cannot: a math book = *un libro de matemáticas.*

Preliminary exercises:

- Point to or hold up various classroom objects and ask *cierto/falso* questions about the material they are made of (*de metal, de madera, de plástico, de papel*).
- ***¿Dónde hay... ?*** (Students answer with the names of buildings on your campus.) *un laboratorio de química, un laboratorio de lenguas, un texto de francés, una clase de sicología, un profesor de inglés*
- ***¿Cómo se dice en español?*** **1.** my Spanish books **2.** our history exam **3.** her French class **4.** our science professor **5.** his telephone number **6.** the university cafeteria

CAPÍTULO 9

Suggestions: *Los quehaceres domésticos; Los aparatos domésticos*

- **Optional:** *la licuadora* (blender), *quitar el polvo* (synonym for *sacudir los muebles*), *limpiar toda la casa* (synonym for *limpiar la casa entera*), *barrer el piso* (synonym for *barrer el suelo*).
- **Note:** Rooms of the house and furniture vocabulary presented in Ch. 8.
- ***Asociaciones:*** *¿Qué palabras o frases asocia Ud. con... ? el aire acondicionador, la cafetera, la estufa, la secadora, el refrigerador, cocinar, limpiar la casa, el congelador, la tostadora*
- **Preguntas orales:** **1.** *¿Ud. hace la cama todos los días? ¿En qué ocasiones no la hace? Si tiene prisa por la mañana, ¿hace la cama o la deja sin hacer? Cuando visita la casa de su familia, ¿su mamá le hace la cama?* **2.** *¿Cuándo limpia Ud. la casa, durante la semana o durante el fin de semana? ¿La limpia entera o limpia sólo una parte? ¿Alguien le ayuda a limpiarla?* **3.** *¿Qué prefiere Ud., (sacudir los muebles) o (pasar la aspiradora)? Yo odio* (fill in what you dislike). *¿Quién también odia ____ ? ¿Quién lo hace en casa de Ud.?*
- *Imagine que Ud. tiene una criada. ¿Qué mandatos le va a dar en las siguientes circunstancias?* (Note: Students can use direct commands or commands with *Quiero que* + subj.) **1.** *Ud. tiene hambre.* **2.** *La comida está preparada y Ud. quiere sentarse a la mesa a comer.* **3.** *La sala está muy oscura porque entra muy poca luz* (light). **4.** *Ud. quiere que la casa esté bien arreglada porque vienen a visitarlo/la esta noche algunos amigos muy importantes de su esposo/a.*

Emphasis (Notas comunicativas): *tocar* is used like *gustar*.

Optional: *Las criadas. Muchas familias hispanas de la clase media y alta tienen una criada que vive en casa. La criada, o «la muchacha del servicio», como la llaman en algunas partes, siempre tiene su propia alcoba y también su propio baño. Ella prepara las comidas, cuida a* (takes care of) *los niños, lava la ropa y ayuda a mantener la casa limpia. Muchas veces la criada parece ser de la misma familia.*

Acuérdese (Remember) *de que la criada tiene mucho trabajo. No le cause mucho trabajo extra, y tenga cuidado de no darle órdenes bruscas. Si Ud. va a pasar una o varias noches en la casa, pregúntele a la señora de la casa qué gesto de agradecimiento* (thanks) *debe tener con la criada antes de salir. En algunas casas es costumbre dejarle una propina* (tip); *en otras, un regalito. A veces no se le deja nada* (one doesn't leave anything), *pero siempre debe darle las gracias.*

Suggestions: *¿Dónde vive Ud.?*

- **Optional:** *el ascensor* (elevator), *las escaleras* (stairs); *el piso* (floor: two meanings) versus *la planta.*
- **Emphasis:** *la planta baja* = the ground floor; see *Nota cultural.*
- ***Definiciones:*** Students give word defined. **1.** *La persona que vive al lado.* **2.** *El número y la calle donde Ud. vive.* **3.** *La cantidad de dinero que Ud. paga cada mes para vivir en su apartamento.* **4.** *La parte principal de una ciudad, donde hay muchos edificios altos.* **5.** *El antónimo de centro.* **6.** *La persona que alquila un apartamento.*
- ***¿Cierto o falso?*** Students change sentences to make them reflect their own situation. **1.** *Vivo en el centro.* **2.** *Mis vecinos son muy simpáticos.* **3.** *Tengo una vista magnífica de la ciudad.* **4.** *Alquilo un apartamento cerca de la universidad.* **5.** *El dueño de la casa de apartamentos paga la luz y el gas.* **6.** *Hay portero en mi casa de apartamentos.* **7.** *Hay portería automática* (security system).

Suggestions: *Más verbos útiles*

- Do not stress, but provide some practice with these verbs in their nonreflexive form to familiarize students with meanings. Reflexive forms will be introduced in Section 28 of this Ch.
- ***Asociaciones:*** *¿Qué acción asocia Ud. con... ?* **1.** *la cama* **2.** *la silla* **3.** *la ropa* **4.** *la mañana* **5.** *un espejo* (demonstrate) **6.** *una persona cómica*

CAPÍTULO 10

Suggestions: *Los días festivos...*

- ***Dictado:*** **Listening: *¿Cierto o falso?:*** **1.** *Hoy es el cumpleaños de ____; vamos a darle una fiesta.* **2.** *La Noche Vieja se celebra en octubre.* **3.** *Ellos sonríen cuando se sienten felices.* **4.** *No hay nada de comer ni beber, pero hay muchos refrescos y entremeses.* **5.** *La Nochebuena viene después de la Navidad.*
- **Point out:** Variations for names of holidays in Hispanic world (very little consensus); *Pascuas* frequently used in plural; *Felices Pascuas* as a general term for "Happy Holidays." Contrast Halloween (secular holiday) with the religious significance of *el Día de los muertos.*
- **Point out:** Accents on *reírse* and *sonreír.* Contrast *sentir* (*Siento que estés enfermo.*) and *sentirse* (*Me siento enfermo.*).
- **Emphasis/Contrast:** *Ser* (to take place) versus *estar* (location).
- ***Preguntas:*** **1.** *¿Se ríe Ud. con frecuencia? ¿fácilmente? ¿Sonríe fácilmente? Dé ejemplo de una situación en que Ud. sonríe. ¿Sonríe cuando está nervioso/a? ¿Cuándo* ***no*** *debe sonreír una persona? ¿Cuándo es necesario que alguien sonría?* **2.** *¿Cuándo fue la última vez que Ud. se sintió muy feliz? ¿Qué pasó ese día? ¿Alguien le dio un regalo? ¿Sacó una buena nota* (grade)? *¿Alguien le mandó dinero?* **3.** *¿Llora Ud. mucho? ¿Quiénes lloran más, los niños o los adultos? ¿las mujeres o los hombres? ¿En qué situaciones es común que lloren las personas? ¿Es bueno que los hombres no lloren con frecuencia? Cuando alguien llora, ¿qué indica?*

Suggestions: *Más emociones,* To become

- ***Preguntas:*** **1.** *¿Se enoja Ud. fácilmente? ¿Se pone contento/a fácilmente? ¿nervioso/a? ¿Cuándo se pone Ud. nervioso/a? ¿durante un examen? ¿cuando habla* *español? ¿durante una entrevista?* **2.** *¿Tiene Ud. hoy todas las cosas necesarias para la clase? ¿Se olvidó de traer algo? ¿Se olvidó alguna vez de un examen?* **3.** *¿Recuerda Ud. fácilmente los nombres? ¿los números? ¿los números de teléfono? ¿el vocabulario nuevo? ¿Qué números es muy necesario que uno recuerde?*

- **Optional:** *enojado* vs. *enojarse*
- **Point out:** Adjectives frequently used with *ponerse*: *alegre, triste, rojo, contento.* "To become" often expressed with reflexive in Spanish: *enojarse, alegrarse, enrojecerse, entristecerse*, etc. Contrast: *olvidar, olvidarse de, recordar.*
- *De los miembros de su clase de español, ¿quién... ?* **1.** *falta a clase con frecuencia?* **2.** *nunca falta?* **3.** *nunca recuerda los verbos?* **4.** *se porta de una manera cómica?* **5.** *se enoja fácilmente?* **6.** *se ríe con frecuencia?* **7.** *sonríe mucho?* **8.** *se queja con frecuencia*

Suggestions: Being emphatic

- **Communicative objectives:** how to talk about the "ultimate" in anything: the very best, worst, etc.
- **Point out:** change in stress and written accent: *fácil → facilísimo, difícil → dificilísimo*; dropped final vowel: *triste → tristísimo.*
- **Emphasis:** spelling changes: *c → qu, g → gu, z → c*: same as in subjunctive, preterite
- ***Preguntas:*** **1.** *¿Es Ud. perezosísimo/a? ¿inteligentísimo/a? ¿riquísimo/a? ¿altísimo/a?* **2.** *¿Hay una persona rica en su familia? ¿Quién es? ¿Es una persona riquísima? ¿alta? ¿altísima? ¿interesante? ¿interesantísima? ¿simpática? ¿simpatiquísima?*

CAPÍTULO 11

Suggestions: *Me levanté...*

- ***¿Qué es?:*** **1.** *Los estudiantes sufren éstas.* **2.** *Los niños hacen esto cuando se ponen furiosos.* **3.** *Dos acciones que se asocian con las personas torpes.* **4.** *Hacemos esto con las luces y con los aparatos eléctricos para conservar energía.* **5.** *Tomo esto cuando me duele la cabeza.* **6.** *El antónimo de* **tener razón.** **7.** *Una cosa que se usa para abrir y cerrar las puertas.*
- *¿Qué parte del cuerpo asocia Ud. con... ?* **1.** *el reloj?* **2.** *las medias?* **3.** *el sombrero?* **4.** *la camisa?* **5.** *los zapatos?*
- **Point out:** antonyms: *acordarse de* vs. *olvidarse de*; *doler* = like *gustar*.
- ***Preguntas:*** **1.** *¿Le duele la cabeza con frecuencia? ¿Qué toma cuando le duele? Si una persona no puede tomar aspirinas, ¿qué puede tomar? ¿En qué situaciones es común que a una persona le duela la cabeza?* **2.** *Las personas distraídas, ¿cómo son? ¿Se olvidan o se acuerdan de ciertas cosas? ¿Pierden objetos? ¿Qué tipo de objetos pierde con frecuencia una persona distraída? ¿Es Ud. distraído/a? Describa la última vez que se olvidó de las llaves. ¿Las dejó en el carro? ¿en casa? ¿En dónde las encontró?* **3.** *¿Es Ud. torpe? ¿Tropieza con frecuencia con los muebles? ¿con los pies de otras personas? ¿Qué debe Ud. decir si tropieza con otro? ¿Qué personas son típicamente torpes? ¿los jugadores de fútbol? ¿los hombres cuando bailan?* **4.** *¿Se equivoca Ud. con frecuencia en situaciones sociales (personales)? ¿Se olvida de los nombres de las personas? ¿Cuándo fue la última vez que Ud. se olvidó del nombre de alguien? ¿Qué dijo Ud.?*
- ***¿Cierto o falso?:*** **1.** *Tenemos (tres cabezas, diez piernas, etc.).* **2.** *La pierna entra en el zapato.* **3.** *Escribimos con el pie.* **4.** *Pensamos con la cabeza.*
- ***El marciano:*** Draw an imaginary creature on the board. Ask *¿Cuántas manos tiene? ¿Cuántos pies?*, etc.

Suggestions: Adverbs

Drawing 1. *Según el pianista, ¿la pieza se toca fácil o difícilmente?* **2.** *¿Cree Ud. que la tocó lenta o rápidamente?* **3.** *Para poder hacerlo, ¿qué tuvo que hacer antes el pianista, practicar mucho o poco? ¿a veces o constantemente?* **4.** *¿Toca maravillosamente este pianista?*

5. *¿Toca Ud. algún instrumento musical? ¿Cómo lo toca? ¿Cuánto tiempo hace que lo toca? ¿Cuándo empezó a tomar lecciones?*

***¡OJO!* Reminder:**
Mucho and *poco* agree with nouns when used as adjectives; when used as adverbs they are invariable: *Isabel tiene muchas amigas/estudia mucho.*

Emphasis: *-mente* added to feminine form of *-o* adjectives. If adjective does not end in *-o*, no need to add *-a* before adding *-mente*.

Point out: If adjective has accent mark, adverb derived from it will retain accent mark.

Preliminary Exercise: Rapid Response Drill: *Dé el adverbio:* **1.** *práctico* **2.** *especial* **3.** *alegre* **4.** *estupendo* **5.** *perfecto* **6.** *triste* **7.** *final* **8.** *típico* **9.** *personal* **10.** *rápido* **11.** *leal* **12.** *fácil* **13.** *cariñoso* **14.** *total* **15.** *tranquilo* **16.** *directo*

CAPÍTULO 12

Suggestions: *Más partes del cuerpo, La salud y el bienestar:*

- **Point out:** other parts of the body presented in Ch. 11; *sano* = healthy, false cognate.
- ***¿Cierto o falso?:*** **1.** *Comemos con los pulmones.* **2.** *Respiramos con la nariz.* **3.** *La comida pasa por la boca y la garganta antes de llegar al estómago.* **4.** *Se usan los ojos para ver.* **5.** *Se come bien en las cafeterías de esta universidad.* **6.** *Los estudiantes siempre se cuidan bien y duermen lo suficiente.* **7.** *Alguien que lleva una vida sana fuma mucho y toma mucho café.* **8.** *Las personas mayores no deben hacer ejercicio.* **9.** *Los cigarrillos afectan principalmente los pulmones de la persona que los fuma.* **10.** *Si una persona no ve bien, lo único que puede hacer es llevar gafas.*
- ***Preguntas:*** **1.** *¿Hace Ud. algún ejercicio físico? ¿Camina? ¿Corre? ¿Juega al ráquetbol? ¿No hace nada?* **2.** *¿Qué tipo de ejercicio es el mejor de todos? ¿Por qué?* **3.** *¿Lleva Ud. una vida sana? ¿Qué hace Ud. para cuidarse? ¿Come bien? ¿Duerme lo suficiente? ¿Practica algún deporte?*

Optional: Many Spanish proverbs and sayings have to do with health, medicine, and doctors. Here is a selection. Have students tell whether they agree or disagree.
1. *Músculos de Sansón* (Sampson) *con cerebro de mosquito.* **2.** *Si quieres vivir sano, acuéstate y levántate temprano.* **3.** *Para enfermedad de años, no hay medicina.* **4.** *De médico, poeta y loco, todos tenemos un poco.* **5.** *La salud no se compra, no tiene precio.*

Suggestions: *En el consultorio...*

- ***Preguntas:*** **1.** *¿Se necesita receta para comprar un jarabe? ¿para comprar pastillas? ¿Qué tipo de jarabe/pastillas?* **2.** *¿Qué hace Ud. cuando le duele la cabeza/la garganta? ¿Qué toma cuando está mareado/a? ¿En qué situaciones comunes se ponen mareadas las personas?* **3.** *¿Se enferma Ud. con frecuencia? De niño/a, ¿se enfermaba fácilmente? ¿Cuántas veces al año se resfría Ud.? ¿Qué puede hacer una persona para no resfriarse? ¿Qué debe hacer si está resfriada?* **4.** *¿Por qué piden los médicos que saquemos la lengua? De niño/a, ¿les sacaba la lengua a sus amigos? ¿Qué significa cuando una persona saca la lengua?*

Optional: *constipado* (synonym for *congestionado*, Spain).

- ***¿Cierto o falso?*** Students respond according to own situation. **1.** *Si la persona sentada a mi lado empieza a toser, me cambio de lugar.* **2.** *Me pongo nervioso/a en el consultorio del médico.* **3.** *Cuando tengo resfriado, nunca tomo ni pastillas ni antibióticos ni jarabes.* **4.** *Mente* (Mind) *sana en cuerpo sano.* **5.** *Me da más miedo ir al consultorio del dentista que ir al consultorio de otro médico.* **6.** *Si no corro (hago ejercicio, etc.) casi todos los días, empiezo a sentirme nervioso/a.*

Optional: Many students will have the stereotypical view that "we" get sick when traveling in Mexico or South America, but that traveling in the U.S. is perfectly safe in this regard. If you wish to discuss this topic, here is a presentation to use.

¡No beba Ud. el agua! Cuando uno viaja a cualquier parte, es muy común que se enferme un poco del estómago durante los primeros días. Con frecuencia se le echa la culpa (one blames) *a las condiciones sanitarias del nuevo lugar, a la comida, al agua o a cualquier otra circunstancia del nuevo ambiente* (environment). *La verdad, muchas veces, es que el cuerpo sencillamente está reaccionando a esos cambios, y no a ningún microbio en particular. No nos damos cuenta* (We don't realize), *por ejemplo, de que los extranjeros que vienen a visitar los Estados Unidos también se enferman al principio.*

Claro está que no todo el mundo que viaja se enferma. Pero si usted viaja a otro país es buena idea cuidarse unos días al principio del viaje hasta que su cuerpo se acostumbre al nuevo ambiente. Y recuerde que al regresar a su casa, su cuerpo va a tener que acostumbrarse de nuevo.

Suggestions (*Notas comunicativas*):

- If you have worked with nominalization, present the *lo* + adjective structure as part of that system.
- **Point out:** Students already know one expression that involves nominalization with *lo*: *lo suficiente*.
- ***¿Cómo se dice?*** the important thing/part, the bad thing/part, the interesting thing/part

Note: In Exercise D, all students need do is repeat the *lo* + adjective forms that are in the exercise items. If you wish to stress this structure, here are some additional materials to use. **Preliminary exercise:** *Cambie: lo + adjetivo:* **1.** *divertido* **2.** *peor* **3.** *interesante* **4.** *curioso* **5.** *necesario* **6.** *bueno*

Optional:

- *Exprese sus ideas sobre lo más importante de la vida. Lo más importante de la vida (no) es/son ____. (las clases, la libertad, las vacaciones, la salud, los amigos, la familia, ?)* **Note:** *Son* anticipates a plural noun.
- *¿Cómo se dice en español?* **1.** the good news **2.** the important part **3.** the worst thing **4.** what's sad is . . . **5.** the most difficult thing **6.** the easiest part **7.** the best part
- With another student, give good news and bad news for each of the following situations.

Modelo: *en el restaurante →*
Lo bueno es que la comida es excelente.
Lo malo son los precios. **1.** *en la clase de español* **2.** *en la oficina de la profesora/esta universidad* **3.** *en el aeropuerto* **4.** *en el consultorio del médico/dentista* **5.** *en casa/durante un viaje* **6.** *en el trabajo o durante una entrevista*

CAPÍTULO 13

Suggestions: *Los coches*

- ***Asociaciones.*** *¿Con qué asocia Ud.... ?* **1.** *los colores rojo, amarillo y verde* **2.** *los mecánicos* **3.** *la contaminación* **4.** *parar* **5.** *una llanta* **6.** *arrancar* **7.** *la carretera* **8.** *doblar*
- **Point out:** *gastar dinero* = to spend money
- **Optional:** *una llanta desinflada, un pinchazo*; distinction between *una llanta* and *una rueda, el chófer* (synonym for *el conductor*).
- **Listening Comprehension: *¿Cierto o falso?*** **1.** *El tanque del coche contiene aceite.* **2.** *Si el semáforo está rojo, es necesario parar.* **3.** *Un Cadillac gasta poca gasolina.* **4.** *Los frenos arrancan el coche.* **5.** *Es necesario tener una licencia para conducir.* **6.** *Si Ud. no dobla, Ud. sigue todo derecho.*
- ***Preguntas*** **1.** *En esta clase, ¿cuántos tienen coche? ¿Es viejo o nuevo su coche? ¿grande o pequeño? ¿Gasta mucha o poca gasolina? ¿mucho o poco aceite? ¿Cuánto le cuesta llenar el tanque? ¿Están en buenas condiciones los frenos?* **2.** *En general, ¿funciona bien su coche? Cuando no funciona, ¿lo arregla Ud. o se lo arregla un mecánico? ¿un amigo? ¿Es vieja o nueva la batería? ¿Le es difícil hacer arrancar el carro por la mañana? ¿Le es difícil hacerlo arrancar cuando hace frío?* **3.** *¿Tuvo Ud. alguna vez una llanta desinflada? ¿Dónde y cómo ocurrió? ¿Quién la cambió? ¿Tuvo Ud. que llamar para pedir ayuda? ¿Siempre lleva Ud. una llanta de respuesto (una quinta*—hold up five fingers—*llanta)?* **4.** *¿Maneja Ud. para venir a la facultad? ¿Es fácil estacionarse aquí? ¿Es necesario pagar para poder estacionarse en el campus? ¿Cuánto? ¿Quién encuentra un parking (estacionamiento) con más facilidad, los profesores o los estudiantes?* **5.** *¿Sabe Ud. manejar? ¿Cuántos años hace que aprendió a manejar? ¿Cuántos años tenía? ¿Quién le enseñó a manejar? ¿Tuvo Ud. algún accidente mientras aprendía? ¿Qué es lo mejor de manejar? ¿y lo peor?*

Optional: *No funciona el carro: En los Estados Unidos, cuando algo le pasa al carro, automáticamente lo llevamos a un mecánico. ¿Y qué hace el mecánico? Si tiene suerte, encuentra la parte dañada* (damaged) *y la cambia por otra nueva. En realidad no repara nada. Si no puede encontrar el problema, es muy probable que el dueño norteamericano se diga: «Bueno, este carro ya no sirve. Voy a comprarme otro.»*

En cambio, en la América Latina y en España, un coche nuevo cuesta relativamente mucho dinero y en algunos países hasta un dineral (fortune). *Además, los repuestos* (spare parts) *son costosos y los mecánicos intentan reparar verdaderamente las partes que no funcionan. Por eso es común ver coches viejos que después de quince o veinte años de uso diario todavía funcionan.*

Suggestions: Ordinals

Point out: Recall use of *el primero* with dates.
Optional: Cardinal numbers used above tenth: *Alfonso XIII (trece).*

Preliminary exercise: Listening: *¿Cierto o falso?* **1.** *El (lunes) es el (primer) día de la semana.* (Vary days, creating incorrect items.) **2.** *(Enero) es el (primer) mes del año.* (Vary months, creating incorrect items.)

CAPÍTULO 14

Suggestions: *Nueva tecnología: Las computadoras/Los ordenadores*

- **Optional:** *el computador.*
- **Point out:** *la lengua* versus *el lenguaje*; *el manejo, manejar*; *el uso, usar*; *micro-* as prefix.
- ***Asociaciones:*** *¿Qué palabra o frase asocia Ud. con... ? nueva tecnología, tecnología anticuada, un robot, una secretaria, las teclas, micro-, manejar.*
- ***Definiciones:*** **1.** *Lo que uno estudia en la universidad si le interesan las computadoras.* **2.** *El viejo método de hacer cartas o trabajos.* **3.** *Una computadora tiene una; el televisor también tiene una.* **4.** *La capacidad para recordar datos.* **5.** *Algo que una computadora y un piano tienen.* (dos cosas)
- ***Preguntas orales:*** **1.** *¿Sabe Ud. usar una computadora? ¿Cuánto tiempo hace que aprendió a usarla? ¿Lo aprendió en la escuela o en casa? ¿Quién le enseñó a usarla?* **2.** *¿Qué prefiere Ud., escribir a máquina o usar una computadora? ¿Hay algo que se haga más fácil con una máquina de escribir que con una computadora? ¿Cuál es?* **3.** *¿Cuántos ordenadores personales hay en la casa de sus padres? ¿Quién lo(s) usa más? ¿Para qué?*

Suggestions: *El medio ambiente*

- **Point out:** *el delito* = crime (for most Spanish speakers, *el crimen* = murder); *encantar* = similar to *gustar*
- **Emphasis:** forms of *destruir, construir* (footnote).
- **Optional:** *tener la culpa, echarle la culpa (a alguien).*
- **Listening comprehension:** *Dé la palabra que corresponde a la frase o definición.* **1.** *Allí se cultivan productos para comer. También hay muchos animales.* **2.** *Un edificio altísimo que se encuentra en el centro de una ciudad.* **3.** *Bonito o hermoso, no feo.* **4.** *¡Me gusta muchísimo!* **5.** *Una casa, un apartamento y una residencia estudiantil son ejemplos de esto.* **6.** *Cuando no hay suficiente cantidad de algo.* **7.** *Lo opuesto de* ***destruir***. **8.** *Una persona que trabaja en el campo.* **9.** *Un sistema político.* **10.** *Levantarse muy temprano por la mañana.* **11.** *El número de personas que vive en un lugar.* **12.** *Una carretera muy grande donde los coches corren rápidamente.*

Categorías:

- *¿Cuántos ejemplos puede Ud. dar para las siguientes categorías?* **1.** *los transportes* **2.** *la vivienda* **3.** *la naturaleza*

Optional: *Su amigo hispánico no reconoce los siguientes conceptos norteamericanos. Trate de explicárselos.* **1.** the EPA **2.** the Secretary of the Interior **3.** the welfare system **4.** the National Parks system and park rangers **5.** a parole officer **6.** the inner city

CAPÍTULO 15

Suggestions: *Los pasatiempos*

- **Listening comprehension:** *Dé la palabra que corresponde a la definición.* **Note:** Definitions are more complex than in previous chapters. **1.** *Una frase que significa* ***divertirse.*** **2.** *La acción de sentarse afuera para recibir los rayos del sol* (draw sun on board). **3.** *Una silla en el teatro o en el cine.* **4.** *El lugar donde se compran las entradas para un espectáculo.* **5.** *El período de tiempo en el que no es necesario trabajar.* **6.** *Caminar tranquilamente por el parque o por el centro.* **7.** *Un juego intelectual en el que es muy importante la habilidad de concentrarse.*

8. *Pensar en lo que uno va a hacer en el futuro. Por ejemplo, pensar en las actividades de esta noche.*

- **Point out:** *jugar a las cartas = jugar a los naipes*
- ***Preguntas:*** **1.** *¿Da Ud. paseos con frecuencia? ¿Le gusta más dar paseos por el parque o por las aceras del centro? ¿Hay lugares en este campus donde se pueda dar un buen paseo?* **2.** *¿Le gusta a Ud. ir al cine? ¿Qué tipo de películas prefiere? ¿las románticas? ¿las cómicas? ¿las de aventuras? ¿Le gustan las películas dobladas? ¿Hay una película actual que me recomiende? ¿Por qué me la recomienda?* **3.** *¿Va Ud. al teatro con frecuencia? ¿Prefiere las comedias o las tragedias? ¿las comedias contemporáneas o las antiguas? ¿Cuál fue la última comedia que Ud. vio? Explique la trama.*
- ***¿Cuál es la diferencia entre...?*** *¿una comedia y una película? ¿una butaca y un sillón? ¿jugar a las cartas y jugar al ajedrez?*

Suggestions: *Los deportes*

- **Listening comprehension:** *Dé la palabra que corresponde a la definición.* **1.** *Un deporte que dos o cuatro personas con raquetas practican al mismo tiempo.* **2.** *El lugar donde juegan partidos de fútbol.* **3.** *Antónimo de perder.* **4.** *Deporte que uno practica cuando nada.* **5.** *Lo que necesitamos para practicar un deporte.* **6.** *Lo que separa las dos mitades de una cancha de tenis.* **7.** *Una persona a quien le gustan mucho los deportes.* **8.** *Caminar muy rápidamente.* **9.** *El miembro de un equipo.*
- **Point out:** number of names of sports that are cognates with English.
- **Emphasis:** *jugar al* + name of sport; *fútbol* versus *fútbol norteamericano*.
- **Optional:** *la lucha libre* (wrestling), *levantar pesas/la halterofilia* (weightlifting), *el esquí (acuático)*, *el patinaje de ruedas/sobre hielo* (roller/ice-skating), *la gimnasia*.
- ***Preguntas:*** **1.** *¿Pasea Ud. en bicicleta con frecuencia? ¿Corre? ¿Juega al tenis? ¿Qué hace cuando quiere hacer un poquito de ejercicio? ¿Qué hace cuando quiere tomar un poco de sol?* **2.** *¿Es Ud. aficionado/a al básquetbol? ¿al béisbol? ¿A qué deportes es Ud. aficionado/a? ¿Practica Ud. estos deportes o prefiere mirarlos?*

CAPÍTULO 16

Suggestions: *Las noticias*

- ***Definiciones:*** **1.** *Cuando una persona asesina a alguien.* **2.** *Cuando un grupo de obreros o empleados deja de trabajar para protestar por inconformidad con alguna condición de su trabajo.* **3.** *Las otras personas en nuestra comunidad (en el mundo).* **4.** *La acción de conformarse con una ley, una regla o un mandato.* **5.** *Cuando se sabe algo por primera vez.* **6.** *Una responsabilidad.*
- **Point out:** *el derecho* vs. *a la derecha*; *el/la testigo* (-*o* ending remains the same).
- ***Dictado:*** **1.** *Merecemos sueldos mucho más altos, pero el jefe no quiere darnos un aumento.* **2.** *Es necesario que nos declaremos en huelga.* **3.** *Pero el jefe va a despedir a los obreros que protesten.* **4.** *No te preocupes. Él no tiene derecho a hacerlo. Lo que dice es puro egoísmo.* **5.** *La ley garantiza nuestra libertad y nuestro bienestar, ¿verdad?* **6.** *Sí, pero hay que tomar en cuenta que los ciudadanos tienen deberes y responsabilidades también.*
- ***Preguntas*** **1.** *¿Cómo se entera Ud. de los acontecimientos diarios? ¿Lee el periódico o mira las noticias en la tele? ¿Cree todo lo que lee en los periódicos? ¿Cree que la prensa y la tele informan bien al público? ¿que siempre presentan todos los aspectos de un caso o de una situación?* **2.** *En este país, ¿hay una ley que proteja la libertad de prensa? ¿Existe tal ley en otros países también? ¿Qué derechos individuales se garantizan en la constitución?* (Put on board: *la libertad de* _____.) (See *Actividad A, Un paso más 16.*) **3.** *¿Vota Ud. en todas las elecciones? ¿Votó en las últimas elecciones para presidente? ¿en las últimas elecciones municipales? ¿Cree Ud. que el votar es un deber?¿Bajo qué tipo de gobierno no es posible votar con libertad?* **4.** *¿Cree Ud. que siempre debemos obedecer la ley? ¿Hay leyes que sean más importantes que otras? ¿Siempre obedece Ud. las leyes de tránsito? ¿Qué castigos hay para los delitos menores? ¿y para los delitos más graves?*

Optional:
¿Un deber o un derecho? Having rights also means respecting others' rights and liberties. Others are entitled to the same rights that you enjoy, and their needs and priorities may be quite different from your own. With another student or in a group, list two or three rights that also imply responsibilities. Follow the models.
Modelos: *El derecho a fumar implica la responsabilidad de no fumar en ciertas circunstancias: en un restaurante, en un ascensor* (elevator)... *El derecho a llevar armas implica la responsabilidad de no abusar de ellas.*

Optional: *Explíquele a su amigo hispánico los siguientes conceptos o instituciones estadounidenses.* **1.** the Bill of Rights **2.** the Declaration of Independence **3.** civil rights **4.** "Read him his rights." **5.** to get one's just desserts **6.** to look out for #1

CAPÍTULO 17

Suggestions: *Una cuestión de dinero*

- **Listening comprehension: *¿Cierto o falso?:*** **1.** *El alquiler es un dinero que recibimos del banco.* **2.** *Si uno quiere ahorrar dinero, es necesario ponerlo en una cuenta corriente.* **3.** *El presupuesto es un sistema que organiza la manera de gastar dinero.* **4.** *Si Ud. paga con tarjeta de crédito, carga algo a su cuenta.* **5.** *Un préstamo es un lugar donde se puede recibir dinero.* **6.** *«Aquí no se cobran cheques» significa que uno puede pagar con cheque si tiene suficiente documentación.* **7.** *Visa y Mastercard son ejemplos de facturas.* **8.** *Es la persona que nos da dinero en el banco cuando cobramos un cheque.* **9.** *Sacar es el antónimo de depositar.*
- **Point out: (1)** *cobrar un cheque* = to cash a check, but *cambiar un cheque de viajero;* **(2)** *ahorrar* (to save money, time) vs. *guardar* (to save, keep) vs. *salvar* (to save, rescue); **(3)** *gastar* (to spend money) vs. *pasar* (to spend time).
- **Note** Vocabulary for financial/banking transactions varies a good deal in the Spanish-speaking world. You may wish to adjust the theme vocabulary. Examples: *ingresar = depositar; libreta* (*de ahorros*) = *cartilla.*
- **Optional:** *los ingresos* (income), *hacer una transferencia/un giro*
- ***Preguntas:*** **1.** *¿Tiene Ud. una cuenta de ahorros? ¿en qué banco? ¿Ha ahorrado mucho dinero este año? ¿Es posible que ahorre más el año que viene? ¿Tiene también una cuenta corriente? ¿Escribe muchos cheques? ¿Hay siempre suficiente dinero en su cuenta? ¿Qué ocurre si no hay suficientes fondos en su cuenta?* **2.** *En esta clase, ¿cuántos de Uds. tienen tarjetas de crédito?* (to one student) *¿Son tarjetas nacionales como Visa o son tarjetas para tiendas locales? ¿Las usa con mucha frecuencia? ¿Las usa demasiado? ¿Tiene muchas facturas que pagar ahora?* **3.** *En general, ¿tienen muchas facturas los estudiantes? ¿Cuáles son los gastos típicos de un estudiante? ¿Tiene Ud. todos estos gastos? ¿Tiene también un presupuesto? ¿Qué porcentaje de su presupuesto es para el alquiler?* **4.** *¿Cuánto paga de alquiler? ¿Lo paga siempre el primero del mes o a veces lo paga más tarde? ¿Qué pasa si lo paga tarde?* **5.** *¿Gasta Ud. mucho dinero en ropa? ¿Cómo la paga, con tarjetas de crédito, al contado o con cheque? ¿Se queja Ud. del precio de la ropa?*

CAPÍTULO 18

Suggestions: *Profesiones y oficios*

- ***Preguntas orales:*** **1.** *¿Quién gana más dinero, un plomero o un enfermero? ¿un obrero o un siquiatra?* **2.** *¿Quién tiene el trabajo más aburrido, un siquiatra o un obrero? ¿un comerciante o un abogado? ¿un plomero o un obrero?* **3.** *¿Quién tiene más responsabilidades, un enfermero o un plomero? ¿un abogado o un comerciante?* **4.** *¿Para qué profesiones es necesario asistir a la universidad? ¿Por cuántos años?* **5.** *¿Cuál de estos trabajos le gusta más/menos? Explique por qué, dando las ventajas y desventajas.*
- **Point out:** There is little consensus in the

Spanish-speaking world about words used for females practicing certain professions. Names given here should be acceptable to most Spanish speakers, but there is considerable discussion about terms such as *la pilota*, *la médica*, etc. See *Notas culturales*.

- **Emphasis:** Students should learn the vocabulary they need for communication.
- **Optional:** Spanish concept of *tener enchufe* (to have connections): literally, to have a plug (electrical).

Suggestions: *En busca de un puesto*

- ***¿Cierto o falso?*** **1.** *Una persona que busca un puesto se llama un aspirante.* **2.** *Si a Ud. no le gusta su trabajo, debe despedirlo.* **3.** *Si a Ud. le gustaría renunciar a su trabajo, debe conseguir una solicitud.* **4.** *Para llenar una solicitud, es necesario tener bolígrafo o lápiz.*
- **Point out:** *Compañía* frequently used in company names, but *empresa* = general word for corporation, company; *caerle bien/mal* used like *gustar*; *renunciar* (option: *dimitir*) means to resign from job—never *resignar* (false cognate).
- ***Preguntas:*** **1.** *¿Cómo está Ud. durante una entrevista? ¿tranquilo/a?* **2.** *¿Cuáles son algunas razones típicas para dejar un puesto? ¿Cuáles son algunas razones típicas para despedir a un empleado?* **3.** *¿Quién estudia comercio? ¿Quiere trabajar en una gran empresa algún día? ¿En qué tipo de empresa? ¿Quiere entrar como director(a) o como empleado/a? ¿Cuáles son las cualidades necesarias de un buen director (una buena directora)?*

Optional: *Con un compañero (una compañera), invente las siguientes preguntas. Tome en cuenta las características de esta empresa: es una compañía internacional de computadoras, con oficinas y sucursales en Hispanoamérica y Europa.*

- *preguntas que un entrevistador tiende a hacer*
- *preguntas que un entrevistador no debe hacerle al aspirante*
- *preguntas que el aspirante puede o debe hacer*

Luego intercambie listas con otros dos compañeros y use las preguntas para entrevistarse mutuamente. Invente los detalles necesarios.

CAPÍTULO 19

Suggestions: *En un viaje al extranjero*

- **Listening: *¿Cierto o falso?:*** **1.** *Por lo general, cuando uno cruza una frontera, tiene que pasar por la aduana también.* **2.** *En la aduana se registran los derechos.* **3.** *El pasaporte indica la nacionalidad de uno.* **4.** *Las multas son un tipo de castigo.* **5.** *En los Estados Unidos, no es necesario llevar pasaporte a menos que uno viaje al extranjero.*
- **Point out:** *derechos* (*de aduana*) = always plural
- ***Preguntas:*** **1.** *¿Ha viajado Ud. por el extranjero? ¿Qué país(es) ha visitado? ¿Cuánto tiempo estuvo en ____? ¿Tiene ganas de volver? ¿Qué hizo allí? ¿Trabajó? ¿Estudió? ¿Visitó a sus parientes o a sus amigos?* **2.** *En esta clase, ¿cuántos tienen pasaporte? ¿Les fue difícil conseguirlo? ¿Qué hizo Ud. para conseguirlo? ¿Tuvo que pagar algo?¿Salió Ud. bien en la foto o no le gusta como salió?* **3.** *¿Ha cruzado Ud. alguna vez la frontera entre el Canadá y los Estados Unidos? ¿la frontera entre México y los Estados Unidos? ¿Tuvo problemas al cruzar? ¿Qué le pidió el inspector?¿el pasaporte? ¿una visa? ¿Qué le preguntó? ¿Estaba Ud. nervioso/a? ¿Tenía algo que declarar que no declarara antes?* **4.** *¿Siempre declara la gente lo que tiene cuando pasa por la aduana?*

Optional: *Pasando por la aduana*

Cuando uno viaja a otro país, su primer encuentro cultural puede ser en la aduana, antes de salir ni siquiera del aeropuerto. Puede haber problemas en la aduana de todos los países; pero por lo general esta experiencia es muy rutinaria. Para pasar por la aduana sin problema, lo único importante es no llevar nada que esté prohibido: cierto tipo de alimentos, plantas, ciertas sustancias químicas, etcétera. Si usted tiene alguna duda, es buena idea que se entere de cuáles son las cosas prohibidas en el país que va a visitar antes de entrar en él.

Si usted va a quedarse con una familia en el extranjero, es aconsejable que lleve consigo unos regalitos. Las calculadoras electrónicas, que ahora se compran tan baratas en los Estados Unidos, son muy buenos regalos.

Suggestions: *En el hotel o en la pensión*

- **Listening: *¿Cierto o falso?¿*** **1.** *Con frecuencia, en un motel u hotel, en su cuarto hay ducha pero no hay baño.* **2.** *Si Ud. quiere confirmar una reservación, hay que llamar al huésped.* **3.** *En los hoteles de lujo hay botones que ayudan con las maletas.* **4.** ***Propina*** *es sinónimo de* **cuenta**. **5.** *Si Ud. no ha hecho una reservación, el hotel no le puede garantizar que vaya a haber un cuarto desocupado.* **6.** *Un cuarto en un hotel de lujo cuesta mucho dinero.*
- **Option:** Students use new vocabulary to describe last stay in (luxury) hotel, motel, etc. They should give as many details as possible, using new vocabulary whenever possible.

CAPÍTULO 20

Suggestions: *Los lugares, Las cosas*

- **Listening:** *Identifique el lugar donde se hacen las siguientes actividades.* **1.** *Se compran y se venden medicamentos.* **2.** *Se puede tomar algo de beber y mirar pasar a la gente.* **3.** *Aquí se esperan los autobuses.* **4.** *Se compran cigarrillos y fósforos.* **5.** *Se compran sellos y se mandan cartas y paquetes.* **6.** *Si se tiene ganas de comer un pastel, se puede ir a este sitio.*
- **Point out:** *el correo, los correos; el sello, el timbre*
- ***Preguntas:*** **1.** *¿Adónde va Ud. si quiere tomar una copa/un trago con los amigos? ¿Le gustan los batidos? ¿Dónde se toma un buen batido en esta ciudad? En general, ¿es necesario preparar los batidos con puro helado, o se puede sustituir los ingredientes artificiales?* **2.** *¿Está bien situado el lugar donde Ud. vive? ¿Hay un correo cerca? ¿una parada de autobús? ¿Adónde va Ud. para comprar artículos de uso personal (el champú, la pasta dental, etcétera)? ¿Hay una tienda de comestibles cerca de donde Ud. vive?* **3.** *¿Hay quioscos en los Estados Unidos? ¿Qué cosa espera Ud. comprar en un quiosco?* **4.** *¿Cuánto vale un sello para mandar una carta de primera clase? ¿Se puede usar un sello de primera clase para mandar una carta a México? ¿a España?*

ABOUT THE AUTHORS

Marty Knorre was formerly Associate Professor of Romance Languages and Coordinator of basic Spanish courses at the University of Cincinnati, where she taught undergraduate and graduate courses in language, linguistics, and methodology. She received her Ph.D. in foreign language education from The Ohio State University in 1975. Dr. Knorre is coauthor of *Cara a cara* and *Reflejos* and has taught at several NEH Institutes for Language Instructors. Most recently she has pursued a Masters of Divinity at McCormick Theological Seminary.

Thalia Dorwick is Executive Editor of Foreign Languages for Random House, where she is responsible for the foreign language college list in Spanish, French, Italian, and German. She has taught at Allegheny College, California State University (Sacramento), and Case Western Reserve University, where she received her Ph.D. in Spanish in 1973. Dr. Dorwick is the coauthor of several textbooks and the author of several articles on language teaching issues. She was recognized as an Outstanding Foreign Language Teacher by the California Foreign Language Teachers Association in 1978.

Bill VanPatten is Assistant Professor of Spanish at the University of Illinois, Urbana–Champaign, where he directs the Undergraduate Program in Teacher Education as well as the M.A. Program in Applied Linguistics and the Ph.D. Program in Second Language Acquisition. He teaches courses ranging from beginning Spanish to doctoral seminars in language learning and is the author of numerous articles, chapters, and books on second language acquisition and foreign language learning. In addition, he has received several awards for language teaching and curriculum development. He received his Ph.D. in Spanish from the University of Texas at Austin in 1983.

Hildebrando Villarreal is Professor of Spanish at California State University, Los Angeles, where he teaches undergraduate and graduate courses in language and linguistics. He received his Ph.D. in Spanish with an emphasis in Applied Linguistics from UCLA in 1976. Professor Villarreal is the author of several reviews and articles on language, language teaching, and Spanish for Native Speakers of Spanish. He is the author of an upcoming intermediate textbook that focuses on reading skills.

Puntos de partida

MAR CARIBE
Barranquilla
Cartagena
Lago de Maracaibo
Caracas
OCÉANO ATLÁNTICO
VENEZUELA
Río Orinoco
Río Magdalena
GUAYANA
SURINAM
GUAYANA FRANCESA
Manizales
Bogotá
COLOMBIA
Cali
Otavalo
Quito
ECUADOR
ECUADOR
Iquitos
Río Amazonas
Cajamarca
PERÚ
BRASIL
Machu Picchu
Lima
Pisac
Cuzco
Ayacucho
BOLIVIA
Lago Titicaca
La Paz
Sucre
Potosí
Brasilia
Río Paraná
PARAGUAY
Río de Janeiro
Salta
Asunción
OCÉANO PACÍFICO
Iguazú
Río Uruguay
URUGUAY
Montevideo
Santiago
Buenos Aires
Punta del Este
Río de la Plata
OCÉANO ATLÁNTICO
CHILE
ARGENTINA
Temuco
América del Sur
0 200 400 600 800 Millas
0 200 400 600 800 Kilómetros
Estrecho de Magallanes
TIERRA DEL FUEGO